I0902189

Koren Talmud Bavli

THE NOÉ EDITION

PEASAḤIM • PART TWO

Steinsaltz Center

KOREN

תלמוד בבלי

KOREN TALMUD BAVLI

THE NOÉ EDITION

פסחים

PESAḤIM

Daf 21a through Daf 50a

COMMENTARY BY

Rabbi Adin Even-Israel Steinsaltz

EDITOR-IN-CHIEF

Rabbi Dr Tzvi Hersh Weinreb

SENIOR CONTENT EDITOR

Rabbi Dr Shalom Z Berger

EXECUTIVE EDITOR

Rabbi Joshua Schreier

•

STEINSALTZ CENTER

KOREN PUBLISHERS JERUSALEM

Supported by the Matanel Foundation

Koren Talmud Bavli, The Noe Edition
Vol. 4.2: Tractate Pesaḥim, Daf 21a through Daf 50a
Paperback, ISBN, 978-965-7765-39-5

First Hebrew/English paperback edition, 2020

Koren Publishers Jerusalem Ltd.
PO Box 4044, Jerusalem 91040, ISRAEL
PO Box 8531, New Milford, CT 06776, USA
www.korenpub.com

Steinsaltz Center

Steinsaltz Center is the parent organization of institutions established by Rabbi Adin Even-Israel Steinsaltz

PO Box 45187, Jerusalem 91450 ISRAEL
Telephone: +972 2 646 0900, Fax +972 2 624 9454
www.steinsaltz-center.org

This book was published in cooperation with the Israel Institute for Talmudic Publications.

הִנֵּה יָמִים בָּאִים, נְאֻם אֲדֹנָי יֱהֹוִה, וְהִשְׁלַחְתִּי רָעָב בָּאָרֶץ,
לֹא־רָעָב לַלֶּחֶם וְלֹא־צָמָא לַמַּיִם, כִּי אִם־לִשְׁמֹעַ אֵת דִּבְרֵי יהוה.

Behold, days are coming – says the Lord God – I will send a hunger to the land, not a hunger for bread nor a thirst for water, but to hear the words of the Lord. (AMOS 8:11)

The Noé edition of the Koren Talmud Bavli
with the commentary of Rabbi Adin Even-Israel Steinsaltz
is dedicated to all those who open its covers
to quench their thirst for Jewish Knowledge,
in our generation of Torah renaissance.

This beautiful edition is for the young, the aged,
the novice and the savant alike,
as it unites the depth of Torah knowledge
with the best of academic scholarship.

Within its exquisite and vibrant pages,
words become worlds.

It will claim its place in the library of classics,
in the bookcases of the Beit Midrash,
the classrooms of our schools,
and in the offices of professionals and business people
who carve out precious time to grapple with its timeless wisdom.

For the Student and the Scholar

DEDICATED BY LEO AND SUE NOÉ

Steinsaltz Center

Executive Director, Steinsaltz Center

Rabbi Meni Even-Israel

Managing Editor

Rabbi Jason Rappoport

Editors

Rabbi Joshua Amaru, *Coordinating Editor*
Rabbi David Jay Derovan
Betzalel Philip Edwards
Rabbi Dov Karoll
Rabbi Adin Krohn
Sally Mayer
Rabbi Avishai Magence, *Content Curator*
Rabbi Jonathan Mishkin
Jay Shapiro
Shira Shmidman
Rabbi Michael Siev
Avi Steinhart
Rabbi David Strauss
Amiel Vick
Rabbi Abe Y. Weschler

Senior Content Editor

Rabbi Dr. Shalom Z. Berger

Copy Editors

Aliza Israel, *Coordinator*
Bracha Hermon
Ita Olesker
Debbie Ismailoff
Shira Finson
Ilana Sobel
Deena Nataf

Language Consultants

Dr. Stephanie E. Binder, *Greek & Latin*
Rabbi Yaakov Hoffman, *Arabic*
Dr. Shai Secunda, *Persian*
Shira Shmidman, *Aramaic*

KOREN

Design & Typesetting

Raphaël Freeman, *Design & Typography*
Dena Landowne Bailey, *Typesetting*
Tani Bayer, *Jacket Design*

Images

Eliahu Misgav, *Illustration*
Yehudit Cohen, *Image Acquisition*

Digital Edition

Raphaël Freeman, *Team Leader*
Eliyahu Skoczylas, *Senior Architect*
Tani Bayer, *User Interface Design*
Dena Landowne Bailey, *Concept*
Rabbi Hanan Benayahu, *Concept*
Laura Messinger, *Commercial Liaison*

Introduction by the Publisher

The Talmud has sustained and inspired Jews for thousands of years. Throughout Jewish history, an elite cadre of scholars has absorbed its learning and passed it on to succeeding generations. The Talmud has been the fundamental text of our people.

Beginning in the 1960s, Rabbi Adin Even-Israel Steinsaltz שליט״א created a revolution in the history of Talmud study. His translation of the Talmud, first into modern Hebrew and then into other languages, as well the practical learning aids he added to the text, have enabled millions of people around the world to access and master the complexity and context of the world of Talmud.

It is thus a privilege to present the *Koren Talmud Bavli*, an English translation of the talmudic text with the brilliant elucidation of Rabbi Steinsaltz. The depth and breadth of his knowledge are unique in our time. His rootedness in the tradition and his reach into the world beyond it are inspirational.

Working with Rabbi Steinsaltz on this remarkable project has been not only an honor, but a great pleasure. Never shy to express an opinion, with wisdom and humor, Rabbi Steinsaltz sparkles in conversation, demonstrating his knowledge (both sacred and worldly), sharing his wide-ranging interests, and, above all, radiating his passion. I am grateful for the unique opportunity to work closely with him, and I wish him many more years of writing and teaching.

Our intentions in publishing this new edition of the Talmud are threefold. First, we seek to fully clarify the talmudic page to the reader – textually, intellectually, and graphically. Second, we seek to utilize today's most sophisticated technologies, both in print and electronic formats, to provide the reader with a comprehensive set of study tools. And third, we seek to help readers advance in their process of Talmud study.

To achieve these goals, the *Koren Talmud Bavli* is unique in a number of ways:

- The classic *tzurat hadaf* of Vilna, used by scholars since the 1800s, has been reset for great clarity, and opens from the Hebrew "front" of the book. Full *nikkud* has been added to both the talmudic text and Rashi's commentary, allowing for a more fluent reading with the correct pronunciation; the commentaries of *Tosafot* have been punctuated. Upon the advice of many English-speaking teachers of Talmud, we have separated these core pages from the translation, thereby enabling the advanced student to approach the text without the distraction of the translation. This also reduces the number of volumes in the set. At the bottom of each *daf*, there is a reference to the corresponding English pages. In addition, the Vilna edition was read against other manuscripts and older print editions, so that texts which had been removed by non-Jewish censors have been restored to their rightful place.
- The English translation, which starts on the English "front" of the book, reproduces the *menukad* Talmud text alongside the English translation (in bold) and commentary and explanation (in a lighter font). The Hebrew and Aramaic text is presented in logical paragraphs. This allows for a fluent reading of the text for the non-Hebrew or non-Aramaic reader. It also allows for the Hebrew reader to refer easily to the text alongside. Where the original text features dialogue or poetry, the English text is laid out in a manner appropriate to the genre. Each page refers to the relevant *daf*.

- Critical contextual tools surround the text and translation: personality notes, providing short biographies of the Sages; language notes, explaining foreign terms borrowed from Greek, Latin, Persian, or Arabic; and background notes, giving information essential to the understanding of the text, including history, geography, botany, archaeology, zoology, astronomy, and aspects of daily life in the talmudic era.
- Halakhic summaries provide references to the authoritative legal decisions made over the centuries by the rabbis. They explain the reasons behind each halakhic decision as well as the ruling's close connection to the Talmud and its various interpreters.
- Photographs, drawings, and other illustrations have been added throughout the text – in full color in the Standard and Electronic editions, and in black and white in the Daf Yomi edition – to visually elucidate the text.

This is not an exhaustive list of features of this edition, it merely presents an overview for the English-speaking reader who may not be familiar with the "total approach" to Talmud pioneered by Rabbi Steinsaltz.

Several professionals have helped bring this vast collaborative project to fruition. My many colleagues are noted on the Acknowledgments page, and the leadership of this project has been exceptional.

RABBI MENACHEM EVEN-ISRAEL, DIRECTOR OF THE STEINSALTZ CENTER, was the driving force behind this enterprise. With enthusiasm and energy, he formed the happy alliance with Koren and established close relationships among all involved in the work.

RABBI DR. TZVI HERSH WEINREB שליט״א, EDITOR-IN-CHIEF, brought to this project his profound knowledge of Torah, intellectual literacy of Talmud, and erudition of Western literature. It is to him that the text owes its very high standard, both in form and content, and the logical manner in which the beauty of the Talmud is presented.

RABBI JOSHUA SCHREIER, EXECUTIVE EDITOR, assembled an outstanding group of scholars, translators, editors, and proofreaders, whose standards and discipline enabled this project to proceed in a timely and highly professional manner.

RABBI MEIR HANEGBI, EDITOR OF THE HEBREW EDITION OF THE STEINSALTZ TALMUD, lent his invaluable assistance throughout the work process, supervising the reproduction of the Vilna pages.

RAPHAËL FREEMAN, EXECUTIVE EDITOR OF KOREN, created this Talmud's unique typographic design which, true to the Koren approach, is both elegant and user friendly.

It has been an enriching experience for all of us at Koren Publishers Jerusalem to work with the Steinsaltz Center to develop and produce the *Koren Talmud Bavli*. We pray that this publication will be a source of great learning and, ultimately, greater *avodat Hashem* for all Jews.

Matthew Miller, Publisher
Koren Publishers Jerusalem
Jerusalem 5772

Contents

For the vocalized Vilna Shas layout, please open as a Hebrew book.

Introduction to **Perek II**

Seven days shall you eat matzot, yet on the first day you shall remove leaven from your houses; for whoever eats leavened bread from the first day until the seventh day, that soul shall be cut off from Israel.

(Exodus 12:15)

You shall eat no leavened bread with it; seven days shall you eat matzot with it, the bread of affliction; for you came out of the land of Egypt in haste; that you may remember the day when you came out of the land of Egypt all the days of your life.

(Deuteronomy 16:3)

And they shall eat the meat on that night, roast with fire, and matzot; with bitter herbs they shall eat it.

(Exodus 12:8)

Aside from the prohibition against possessing leaven on Passover, it is prohibited to eat it or derive any benefit from it. Although the prohibition against eating leaven is stated explicitly in the Torah, the prohibition against deriving benefit is not. This elicits the question of what exactly is the source for the prohibition. Also, what is the relationship between the two prohibitions? Is the prohibition against deriving benefit an independent prohibition parallel to that of eating, or is there really only one broadly defined prohibition of consuming leaven in any manner, which includes both eating and benefiting? These issues, as they relate both to leaven and to other items from which it is prohibited to derive benefit, are discussed at length in this chapter.

The prohibition against possessing leaven relates specifically to leaven owned by a Jew during the week of Passover. To what extent does this also apply to the prohibition against deriving benefit from leaven? May one eat or derive benefit from leaven owned by a gentile? What is the status of leaven that was illegally in the possession of a Jew over Passover? May one derive benefit from it after the Festival has ended?

This chapter also begins to discuss the mitzvot to consume three items: *Matzot*, bitter herbs, and the Paschal lamb, on the first night of Passover. Which kinds of grains may be used to make the *matzot*? Which liquids may be used knead them? The Gemara similarly considers which vegetables qualify for the mitzva to eat bitter herbs. May only one kind of vegetable be used, or are there different options, and if so, is there a preference? With regard to both the *matza* and bitter herbs, the question arises what the *halakha* is in cases where they are produced from foods that are prohibited for various reasons or with various halakhic statuses, such as *teruma* or tithes.

The chapter concludes with a discussion of the preparation of the Paschal lamb, the obligation to roast it, and the prohibition against cooking it.

מתני׳ כָּל שָׁעָה שֶׁמּוּתָּר לֶאֱכוֹל – מַאֲכִיל לִבְהֵמָה לְחַיָּה וְלָעוֹפוֹת, וּמוֹכֵר לַגּוֹי, וּמוּתָּר בַּהֲנָאָתוֹ, עָבַר זְמַנּוֹ – אָסוּר בַּהֲנָאָתוֹ, וְלֹא יַסִּיק בּוֹ תַּנּוּר וְכִירַיִם. רַבִּי יְהוּדָה אוֹמֵר: אֵין בִּיעוּר חָמֵץ אֶלָּא שְׂרֵיפָה, וַחֲכָמִים אוֹמְרִים: אַף מְפָרֵר וְזוֹרֶה לָרוּחַ אוֹ מַטִּיל לַיָּם.

MISHNA For the **entire time that it is permitted to eat** leavened bread, **one** may also **feed**[H] it to his **domesticated animals, to non-domesticated animals, and to birds; and one** may **sell** it **to a gentile; and it is permitted to** derive **benefit from it.** After **its time passes, it is prohibited to** derive **benefit from it, and one may not** even **light an oven or a stove with** leavened bread. With regard to the manner of removal of leavened bread, **Rabbi Yehuda says: The removal of leavened bread is** to be accomplished **only** through **burning. And the Rabbis say:** Burning is not required, as **one** may **even crumble** it **and throw** it **into the wind or cast** it **into the sea.**[H]

גמ׳ כָּל שָׁעָה שֶׁמּוּתָּר לֶאֱכוֹל – מַאֲכִיל, הָא כָּל שָׁעָה שֶׁאֵינוֹ מוּתָּר לֶאֱכוֹל – אֵינוֹ מַאֲכִיל, לֵימָא מַתְנִיתִין דְּלָא כְּרַבִּי יְהוּדָה, דְּאִי רַבִּי יְהוּדָה – הָא אִיכָּא חָמֵשׁ דְּאֵינוֹ אוֹכֵל, וּמַאֲכִיל. דִּתְנַן, רַבִּי מֵאִיר אוֹמֵר: אוֹכְלִין כָּל חָמֵשׁ, וְשׂוֹרְפִין בִּתְחִלַּת שֵׁשׁ, רַבִּי יְהוּדָה אוֹמֵר: אוֹכְלִין כָּל אַרְבַּע, וְתוֹלִין כָּל חָמֵשׁ, וְשׂוֹרְפִין בִּתְחִלַּת שֵׁשׁ!

GEMARA The Gemara reads the mishna precisely: For the **entire time that it is permitted to eat** leavened bread, **one** may **feed** it to his animals. **However,** apparently, for the **entire time that it is not permitted to eat** leavened bread, **one** may **not feed** his animals. **Let us say that the mishna is not in accordance with** the opinion of **Rabbi Yehuda. As,** if it were in accordance with the opinion of **Rabbi Yehuda, isn't there** the **fifth** hour, when **one** may **not eat** leavened bread **but one** may **feed**[N] it to his animals? **As we learned** in a mishna that **Rabbi Meir says: One** may **eat** leavened bread on the morning of the fourteenth day of Nisan for **the entire fifth** hour, **and he burns** it **at the beginning of the sixth** hour. **Rabbi Yehuda says: One** may **eat** it for **the entire fourth** hour, **he suspends** his consumption of it for **the entire fifth** hour, **and he burns it at the beginning of the sixth** hour. Apparently, there is an hour in which it is prohibited to eat leavened bread, but it is permitted to feed it to one's animals.

וְאֶלָּא מַאי – רַבִּי מֵאִיר הִיא, הַאי ״כָּל שָׁעָה שֶׁמּוּתָּר לֶאֱכוֹל מַאֲכִיל״? כָּל שָׁעָה שֶׁאוֹכֵל מַאֲכִיל מִיבְּעֵי לֵיהּ!

The Gemara asks: **Rather, what** can be said? This mishna follows the opinion of **Rabbi Meir.**[N] If so, **this** statement: For the **entire time that it is permitted to eat** leavened bread **one** may **feed,** is imprecise. **It should have** said: For the **entire time that** one **eats** leavened bread **he** may **feed.** As it stands, there is no parallel between the phrase: It is permitted to eat, and the phrase: One may feed. Therefore, it appears that the mishna is referring to two different people or cases.

אָמַר רַבָּה בַּר עוּלָּא: מַתְנִיתִין רַבָּן גַּמְלִיאֵל הִיא. דִּתְנַן, רַבָּן גַּמְלִיאֵל אוֹמֵר: חוּלִּין נֶאֱכָלִין כָּל אַרְבַּע, תְּרוּמָה כָּל חָמֵשׁ, וְשׂוֹרְפִין בִּתְחִלַּת שֵׁשׁ. וְהָכִי קָאָמַר: כָּל שָׁעָה שֶׁמּוּתָּר לֶאֱכוֹל כֹּהֵן בִּתְרוּמָה – יִשְׂרָאֵל מַאֲכִיל חוּלִּין לִבְהֵמָה לְחַיָּה וְלָעוֹפוֹת.

Rabba bar Ulla said: The mishna is in accordance with the opinion of **Rabban Gamliel. As we learned** in a mishna that **Rabban Gamliel says: Non-sacred** leavened bread may **be eaten** on the fourteenth of Nisan during **the entire fourth** hour, leavened bread that is ***teruma*** may be eaten during **the entire fifth** hour, **and one burns** the leavened bread **at the beginning of the sixth** hour. **And this is** what the mishna **is saying:** For the **entire time that it is permitted** for **a priest to partake of *teruma*,** although an Israelite may not eat leavened bread at that time, **an Israelite** may **feed non-sacred** food **to his domesticated animals, to non-domesticated animals, and to birds.**

לָמָּה לִי לְמִיתְנָא בְּהֵמָה, לָמָּה לִי לְמִיתְנָא חַיָּה? צְרִיכָא, דְּאִי תְּנָא בְּהֵמָה – דְּאִי מְשַׁיְּירָא חָזֵי לָהּ, אֲבָל חַיָּה דְּאִי מְשַׁיְּירָא קָמַצְנְעָא לָהּ – אֵימָא לָא.

The Gemara continues to read the mishna precisely. The mishna states that one may feed his leavened bread to his domesticated animals, to non-domesticated animals, and to birds. The Gemara asks: **Why do I** need the mishna **to teach** about the case of **domesticated animals, and why do I** need it **to teach** about **non-domesticated animals** as well? The *halakha* should be the same for both cases. The Gemara answers: It is **necessary** to teach us both cases, **as had it taught** only about **domesticated animals,** one would have said that it is permitted feed them **because if** the animal **leaves over** some leavened bread **one will see** what is left over and dispose of it. **However,** with regard to **a non-domesticated animal, if it leaves over** any of the leavened bread, **it hides it** to save for later. Therefore, one could **say** that it is **not** permitted to feed it so close to the time when leavened bread is prohibited.

HALAKHA

To eat and to feed – לֶאֱכוֹל וּלְהַאֲכִיל: On Passover eve one may sell his leavened bread or feed it to an animal even during the fifth hour of the day, when he may not eat it himself. However, one must watch the animal to ensure that it does not hide any leavened bread, and one must remove whatever is left over (see Rosh; *Shulḥan Arukh, Oraḥ Ḥayyim* 443:1).

How does one remove leavened bread – כֵּיצַד מְבַעֲרִים הֶחָמֵץ: One may remove leavened bread in numerous ways, e.g., burning it, crumbling it into the wind, or casting it into the sea. If the bread is hard, he should crumble it before casting it into the sea (Rambam). The common practice is to burn one's leavened bread, out of concern for those authorities who accept the opinion of Rabbi Yehuda (*Shulḥan Arukh, Oraḥ Ḥayyim* 445:1, and in the comment of the Rema).

NOTES

One may not eat but one may feed – אֵינוֹ אוֹכֵל וּמַאֲכִיל: The proof that Rabbi Yehuda permits this, although he did not say so explicitly, is based on his statement that during the fifth hour one's consumption of leavened bread is suspended. If there is nothing else he can do with it during that time, why isn't he obligated to burn it immediately (Maharam Ḥalawa).

The opinion of the mishna – שִׁיטַת הַמִּשְׁנָה: In the Jerusalem Talmud it is stated that this mishna follows the opinion of Rabbi Meir, because there no distinction is made between the formulations of: One eats, and: It is permitted to eat, while the Gemara here does distinguish between the two.

NOTES

In any case it will hide it – מִיהַת מַצְנְעָא: Some explain that since one knows that this undomesticated animal will hide what is left over, he nullifies the leavened bread before giving it to this animal; therefore, he does not transgress any prohibition involving the leavened bread afterward. This is not the case with a domesticated animal, since one assumes that he will see what is left over and he will nullify it then. However, on occasion one will not pay attention or will forget to do so, and will then transgress the prohibitions of: It shall not be seen and it shall not be found (*Mikhtam*). Alternatively, the concern is that one might find the leavened bread on the animal during Passover, and although he nullified it previously, he will consider it important again and thereby violate the prohibitions (*Nimmukei Yosef*).

One may not sell his leavened bread – לֹא יִמְכּוֹר חֲמֵצוֹ: Apparently Beit Shammai's reason for concern is that people might say that it is the Jew's leavened bread, and he will be suspected of wrongdoing (Maharam Ḥalawa).

HALAKHA

Selling of leavened bread – מְכִירַת חָמֵץ: It is permitted to sell one's leavened bread to a gentile before Passover even if he knows that it will remain in the possession of the gentile during the entire Festival, in accordance with the opinion of Beit Hillel (*Shulḥan Arukh, Oraḥ Ḥayyim* 445:2).

וְאִי תְּנָא חַיָּה – מִשּׁוּם דְּאִי מְשַׁיְּירָא מִיהַת מַצְנְעָא, אֲבָל בְּהֵמָה זִימְנִין דִּמְשַׁיְּירָא וְלָא מַסִּיק אַדַּעְתֵּיהּ, וְקָאֵי עֲלֵיהּ בְּבַל יֵרָאֶה וּבְבַל יִמָּצֵא – אֵימָא לָא, צְרִיכָא.

And had it taught only the case of **a non-domesticated animal,** one might say that it is permitted to feed leavened bread to such an animal **because if it leaves over** any food **in any case it will hide** it,[N] and the owner will not violate the prohibition: It shall not be seen. **However,** with regard to **a domesticated animal, sometimes it leaves over** food, **and it does not enter his mind** that the animal will do so. **And** in that case both prohibitions: **It shall not be seen and it shall not be found,** would **apply to him.** Consequently, one could **say** that it would **not** be permitted for him to feed a domesticated animal. Therefore, **it was necessary** to teach both cases.

עוֹפוֹת לָמָּה לִי? אַיְּידֵי דִּתְנָא בְּהֵמָה וְחַיָּה, תְּנָא נָמֵי עוֹפוֹת.

The Gemara asks: **Why do I** need the mishna to mention **birds** as well? The Gemara answers: There is no inherent need to mention birds; however, **since** the mishna **taught** the cases of **domesticated animals and non-domesticated animals, it also taught** the case of **birds,** as these are normally grouped together.

״וּמוֹכְרוֹ לְגוֹי״. פְּשִׁיטָא! לְאַפּוֹקֵי מֵהַאי תַּנָּא דְּתַנְיָא, בֵּית שַׁמַּאי אוֹמְרִים: לֹא יִמְכּוֹר אָדָם חֲמֵצוֹ לְגוֹי, אֶלָּא אִם כֵּן יוֹדֵעַ בּוֹ שֶׁיִּכְלֶה קוֹדֶם פֶּסַח. וּבֵית הִלֵּל אוֹמְרִים: כׇּל שָׁעָה שֶׁמּוּתָּר לֶאֱכוֹל – מוּתָּר לִמְכּוֹר.

It was stated in the mishna that whenever it is permitted to eat leavened bread, one may also **sell it to a gentile.** The Gemara asks: Isn't that **obvious,** as the mishna already taught that one may benefit from it? The Gemara answers: This is stated **to exclude** the opinion **of this *tanna*, as it was taught** in a *baraita* that **Beit Shammai say: A person** may **not sell his leavened bread**[N] **to a gentile unless he knows that** the leavened bread **will be consumed before Passover.** According to Beit Shammai, a person retains some responsibility for his leavened bread even when it is no longer in his possession. **And Beit Hillel say:** For the **entire time that it is permitted** for a Jew **to eat** leavened bread, **it is** also **permitted for him to sell it** to a gentile. The Jew ceases to be responsible for leavened bread sold to a gentile from the moment it is sold.[H]

Perek **II**
Daf **21** Amud **b**

NOTES

Rabbi Yehuda ben Beteira's opinion – שִׁיטַת רַבִּי יְהוּדָה בֶּן בְּתֵירָא: See *Tosafot*, who suggest that Rabbi Yehuda ben Beteira may contend that Beit Shammai and Beit Hillel agree about this issue (*Mikhtam*).

HALAKHA

Charred leavened bread – חָמֵץ שֶׁחֲרָכוֹ: If leavened bread was charred prior to the time of its prohibition to the extent that a dog would not eat it (*Tosafot*), it is permitted to derive benefit from it on Passover, in accordance with Rava's ruling (*Shulḥan Arukh Oraḥ Ḥayyim* 442:9, 445:2).

Hours by rabbinic law – שָׁעוֹת דְּרַבָּנַן: By Torah law, one may not benefit from leavened bread on Passover eve from the end of the sixth hour. By rabbinic law, one may not benefit from leavened bread from the beginning of the sixth hour (*Shulḥan Arukh, Oraḥ Ḥayyim* 442:9, 443:1).

רַבִּי יְהוּדָה בֶּן בְּתֵירָא אוֹמֵר: כּוּתָּח וְכׇל מִינֵי כוּתָּח – אָסוּר לִמְכּוֹר שְׁלֹשִׁים יוֹם קוֹדֶם לַפֶּסַח.

Rabbi Yehuda ben Beteira, who agrees in principle with Beit Shammai's opinion, **says:** With regard to *kutaḥ*, a dip that contains leavened breadcrumbs, **and all types of *kutaḥ*, it is prohibited to sell** it to a gentile **thirty days before Passover.** Because *kutaḥ* is spicy, people use only a bit at a time, so it will likely last until Passover.[N]

״וּמוּתָּר בַּהֲנָאָה״. פְּשִׁיטָא! לָא צְרִיכָא שֶׁחֲרָכוֹ קוֹדֶם זְמַנּוֹ. וְקָא מַשְׁמַע לַן כִּדְרָבָא, דְּאָמַר רָבָא: חֲרָכוֹ קוֹדֶם זְמַנּוֹ – מוּתָּר בַּהֲנָאָה, אֲפִילּוּ לְאַחַר זְמַנּוֹ.

It was stated in the mishna that as long as leavened bread may be eaten, **it is permitted to** derive **benefit** from it. The Gemara asks: Isn't that **obvious?** The Gemara answers: **No, it is necessary to teach this** in a case **where one charred** the leavened bread with fire **before its time,** i.e., before it became prohibited, rendering it inedible. **And it teaches us** that the *halakha* **is in accordance with** the opinion of **Rava. As Rava said:** If one **charred** leavened bread[H] **before its time, it is permitted to** derive **benefit from it even after its time,** since it no longer has the legal status of leavened bread.

״עָבַר זְמַנּוֹ אָסוּר בַּהֲנָאָתוֹ״. פְּשִׁיטָא! לָא צְרִיכָא, לְשָׁעוֹת דְּרַבָּנַן. דְּאָמַר רַב גִּידֵּל, אָמַר רַב חִיָּיא בַּר יוֹסֵף, אָמַר רַבִּי יוֹחָנָן: הַמְקַדֵּשׁ מִשֵּׁשׁ שָׁעוֹת וּלְמַעְלָה אֲפִילּוּ בְּחִיטֵּי קוּרְדְּנָיָתָא – אֵין חוֹשְׁשִׁין לְקִדּוּשִׁין.

It was stated in the mishna: After **its time passes, it is prohibited to benefit from it.** The Gemara asks: Isn't that **obvious?** The Gemara answers: **No, it is necessary for** the mishna to teach that it remains prohibited to benefit from leavened bread during additional **hours** that are delineated **by rabbinic law.**[H] **As Rav Giddel said** that **Rav Ḥiyya bar Yosef said** that **Rabbi Yoḥanan said:** With regard **to one who** takes wheat grains that may have come into contact with water and become leavened and **betroths** a woman with the leaven **from** the beginning of **the sixth hour,** when the leaven is prohibited by rabbinic law, **and onward** on Passover eve, **even** if he betrothed her **with wheat from the mountains,** which is especially hard and unlikely to become leavened, nonetheless, **we are not concerned that** this **betrothal** is valid. This is because when performing a betrothal with money one must give the woman an object worth as least the value of a *peruta*, and leaven from which one is prohibited to benefit is considered worthless.

״וְלֹא יַסִּיק בּוֹ תַּנּוּר וְכִירַיִם״. פְּשִׁיטָא! לָא צְרִיכָא, לְרַבִּי יְהוּדָה, דְּאָמַר: אֵין בִּיעוּר חָמֵץ אֶלָּא שְׂרֵיפָה. סָלְקָא דַּעְתָּךְ אָמִינָא: הוֹאִיל וְאָמַר רַבִּי יְהוּדָה מִצְוָתוֹ בִּשְׂרֵיפָה, בַּהֲדֵי דְּקָא שָׂרֵיף לֵיהּ לִיתְהֲנֵי מִינֵּיהּ, קָא מַשְׁמַע לַן.

It was stated in the mishna: **And one may not** even **light an oven or a stove** with leavened bread once it becomes prohibited. The Gemara asks: Isn't that **obvious**, as this is also a type of benefit? The Gemara answers: **No, it is necessary** to teach this due **to** the opinion **of Rabbi Yehuda**, who **said** that **the removal of leavened bread is** to be performed only **through burning.** Otherwise, **it could enter your mind to say: Since Rabbi Yehuda said that its mitzva is** performed through **burning, while one is burning it let him benefit from it.** Therefore, **it teaches us** that it is prohibited to benefit from leavened bread even while burning it.

אָמַר חִזְקִיָּה: מִנַּיִן לְחָמֵץ בְּפֶסַח שֶׁאָסוּר בַּהֲנָאָה – שֶׁנֶּאֱמַר: ״לֹא יֵאָכֵל חָמֵץ״ – לֹא יְהֵא בּוֹ הֶיתֵּר אֲכִילָה. טַעְמָא דִּכְתַב רַחֲמָנָא ״לֹא יֵאָכֵל חָמֵץ״ הָא לָא כְּתַב לֹא יֵאָכֵל – הֲוָה אָמִינָא אִיסּוּר אֲכִילָה – מַשְׁמַע, אִיסּוּר הֲנָאָה – לָא מַשְׁמַע.

Ḥizkiya said: From where is it derived in the mishna **that it is prohibited to** derive **benefit from leavened bread on Passover?**[H] **As it is stated: "Leavened bread shall not be eaten"** (Exodus 13:3). Since the verse uses the passive, it should be understood as follows: **There shall be no permitted consumption of it** at all, even deriving benefit, as benefit could be exchanged for money, which could be used to buy food. The Gemara reads precisely: **The reason** deriving benefit is prohibited **is that the Merciful One writes** in the Torah: **"Leavened bread shall not be eaten." Had** the Torah **not written: "Shall not be eaten,"** and instead used the active form: You shall not eat, **I would have said** that the **prohibition of eating is implied** but that **the prohibition of** deriving **benefit**[N] **is not implied.**

וּפְלִיגָא דְּרַבִּי אֲבָהוּ, דְּאָמַר רַבִּי אֲבָהוּ: כׇּל מָקוֹם שֶׁנֶּאֱמַר ״לֹא יֵאָכֵל״ ״לֹא תֹאכַל״ ״לֹא תֹאכְלוּ״ – אֶחָד אִיסּוּר אֲכִילָה וְאֶחָד אִיסּוּר הֲנָאָה (מַשְׁמַע), עַד שֶׁיְּפָרֵט לָךְ הַכָּתוּב כְּדֶרֶךְ שֶׁפֵּרַט לָךְ בִּנְבֵילָה.

The Gemara comments: **And** this conclusion **disagrees with** the opinion of **Rabbi Abbahu,** as **Rabbi Abbahu said** that **wherever it is stated: "It shall not be eaten," "You,** singular, **shall not eat,"** or **"You,** plural, **shall not eat,"** both **a prohibition of eating and a prohibition of** deriving **benefit**[H] **are implied, unless the verse specifies** that one may benefit, **in the manner that it specified with regard to an** unslaughtered **animal carcass.**[N]

דְּתַנְיָא: ״לֹא תֹאכְלוּ כׇל נְבֵלָה לַגֵּר אֲשֶׁר בִּשְׁעָרֶיךָ תִּתְּנֶנָּה וַאֲכָלָהּ אוֹ מָכֹר לְנׇכְרִי וגו׳״. אֵין לִי אֶלָּא לְגֵר בִּנְתִינָה וּלְגוֹי בִּמְכִירָה, לְגֵר בִּמְכִירָה מִנַּיִן? תַּלְמוּד לוֹמַר: ״לַגֵּר אֲשֶׁר בִּשְׁעָרֶיךָ תִּתְּנֶנָּה אוֹ מָכֹר״. לְגוֹי בִּנְתִינָה מִנַּיִן? תַּלְמוּד לוֹמַר: ״תִּתְּנֶנָּה וַאֲכָלָהּ אוֹ מָכֹר לְגוֹי״. נִמְצֵאתָ אוֹמֵר: אֶחָד גֵּר וְאֶחָד גּוֹי, בֵּין בִּמְכִירָה בֵּין בִּנְתִינָה, דִּבְרֵי רַבִּי מֵאִיר.

As it was taught in a *baraita*: **"You shall not eat of any unslaughtered animal; you may give it to the resident alien who is within your gates, that he may eat it; or you may sell it to a foreigner;** for you are a sacred people to the Lord your God" (Deuteronomy 14:21). **I have** derived **only** that it is permitted **to a resident alien through giving and to a gentile through selling. From where** do I derive that it is permitted **to a resident alien through selling? The verse states: "You may give it to the resident alien who is within your gates…or you may sell it,"** meaning that one has the option to do either of these. **From where is it derived** that it is permitted **to a gentile through giving** and one is not required to sell it to him? **The verse states: "You may give it… that he may eat it, or you may sell it to a foreigner."** Therefore, **you may say** that he may transfer it to **both a resident alien and a gentile, both through giving and through selling.** This is **the statement of Rabbi Meir.**

רַבִּי יְהוּדָה אוֹמֵר: דְּבָרִים כִּכְתָבָן, לְגֵר בִּנְתִינָה וּלְגוֹי בִּמְכִירָה. מַאי טַעְמָא דְּרַבִּי יְהוּדָה? אִי סָלְקָא דַּעְתָּךְ כִּדְאָמַר רַבִּי מֵאִיר – לִיכְתּוֹב רַחֲמָנָא ״לַגֵּר אֲשֶׁר בִּשְׁעָרֶיךָ תִּתְּנֶנָּה וַאֲכָלָהּ וּמָכֹר״ ״אוֹ״ לָמָּה לִי? שְׁמַע מִינַּהּ לִדְבָרִים כִּכְתָבָן.

The *baraita* concludes: **Rabbi Yehuda says:** These **matters are** meant to be understood **as they are written;** he may transfer an unslaughtered animal carcass **to a resident alien** only **through giving and to a gentile** only **through selling.**[H] The Gemara asks: **What is the reason for** the opinion of **Rabbi Yehuda?** The Gemara answers: **If it could enter your mind** to understand the verse **in accordance** with that which **Rabbi Meir said, then let the Merciful One write: You may give it to the resident alien who is within your gates that he may eat it and sell it** to a foreigner. **Why do I** need the word **"or"** between these two options? **Learn from it** that **the matters are** to be understood **as they are written.**

וְרַבִּי מֵאִיר: ״אוֹ״ – לְהַקְדִּים נְתִינָה דְּגֵר לִמְכִירָה דְּגוֹי. וְרַבִּי יְהוּדָה: הָא לָא צְרִיךְ קְרָא, כֵּיוָן דְּגֵר אַתָּה מְצֻוֶּה לְהַחֲיוֹתוֹ, וְגוֹי אִי אַתָּה מְצֻוֶּה לְהַחֲיוֹתוֹ – לָא צְרִיךְ קְרָא, סְבָרָא הוּא.

The Gemara asks: **And** how does **Rabbi Meir** explain the formulation of the verse? The Gemara answers that Rabbi Meir would explain that the word **"or"** teaches one **to give precedence to giving to a resident alien over selling to a gentile.**[N] The Gemara asks: **And** from where does **Rabbi Yehuda** derive this *halakha*? According to Rabbi Yehuda, **this** matter **does not need a verse, since you are commanded to sustain a resident alien,** as it is a mitzva for one to sustain a resident alien who has renounced idol worship, **and you are not commanded to sustain a gentile. There is no need for a verse** to teach this; **it is** based on a **logical inference.**[N]

HALAKHA

Prohibition of deriving benefit – אִיסּוּר הֲנָאָה: It is prohibited by Torah law to derive benefit from leavened bread during Passover (Rambam *Sefer Zemanim, Hilkhot Ḥametz UMatza* 1:2).

Prohibitions of eating and…deriving benefit – אִיסּוּר אֲכִילָה...וַהֲנָאָה: Wherever the Torah says: "You shall not eat," or uses a similar expression, it means that one may neither eat nor benefit from the prohibited item, unless the verse explicitly permits deriving benefit. This ruling is in accordance with the opinion of Rabbi Abbahu, as the discussion in the Gemara is in accordance with his opinion (Rambam *Sefer Kedusha, Hilkhot Ma'akhalot Asurot* 8:15).

What does one do with an animal carcass – מַה עוֹשִׂים בִּנְבֵילָה: One may give an animal carcass to a resident alien as a gift. However, one may only sell it to a gentile; he may not give it to him as a gift (Rambam *Sefer HaMadda, Hilkhot Avoda Zara* 10:4).

NOTES

It shall not be eaten…the prohibition of deriving benefit – לֹא יֵאָכֵל וְאִיסּוּר הֲנָאָה: Some explain that the phrase: You shall not eat, is a commandment directed to people, while the more general wording: "It shall not be eaten," is used to prohibit all types of consumption, even feeding to dogs, meaning that one may not derive any benefit from the prohibited item (Rashash).

In the manner that it specified with regard to an animal carcass – כְּדֶרֶךְ שֶׁפֵּרַט בִּנְבֵילָה: This detail, that one may derive benefit from an animal carcass, is not specifically derived from what is written here, that a gentile may eat it; rather, it is derived from other sources. In fact, the opposite is true; a principle, and not this specific detail, is derived from this verse. Had it not been stated explicitly that one may derive benefit from an animal carcass, one might have thought that it is prohibited to do so, as is the case with regard to other items that one may not eat.

To give precedence to giving to a resident alien over selling to a gentile – לְהַקְדִּים נְתִינָה דְּגֵר: Clearly, the intention is not that one is obligated to give gifts to a resident alien at his own expense, as even with regard to a fellow Jew one is required to do so only when the laws of charity dictate it. However, in this particular case the animal carcass does not have much value, since most people may not eat it, and the resident alien will benefit greatly from it. Therefore, one should give it to him as a gift rather than sell it to a gentile for a small profit (*Tosafot*).

It is based on a logical inference – סְבָרָא הוּא: Some connect this disagreement between Rabbi Meir and Rabbi Yehuda with another dispute with regard to the definition of a resident alien. Rabbi Meir understands that a resident alien is a gentile who accepts upon himself not to worship idols. According to the opinion of the Rabbis, a resident alien must accept the seven Noahide commandments upon himself. According to another opinion, he is not a resident alien until he abides by all of the commandments in the Torah except for the prohibition against eating animal carcasses. According to the opinion of Rabbi Meir, a resident alien is not much different from any other gentile; therefore, a verse is necessary to derive that one should give precedence to the resident alien. However, according to this third opinion, that seems to parallel the opinion of Rabbi Yehuda here, a resident alien has more in common with Jews, so it is logical to help him first (*Yefe Einayim*).

בִּשְׁלָמָא לְרַבִּי מֵאִיר, דְּאָמַר אֶחָד גֵּר וְאֶחָד גּוֹי, בֵּין בִּמְכִירָה בֵּין בִּנְתִינָה. מִדְּאִיצְטְרִיךְ קְרָא לְמִישְׁרָא נְבֵילָה בַּהֲנָאָה – הָא כָּל אִיסּוּרִין שֶׁבַּתּוֹרָה אֲסוּרִין בֵּין בַּאֲכִילָה בֵּין בַּהֲנָאָה.

The Gemara applies this discussion to the previously mentioned topic. **Granted,** Rabbi Abbahu's opinion is reasonable **according to Rabbi Meir, who said** that one may transfer an animal carcass **to both a convert and a gentile, both through selling and through giving. From** the fact that **a verse was necessary to permit** one to derive **benefit from an animal carcass,** one can learn that with regard to **all** other **prohibitions in the Torah** about which it states only that one may not eat an item, **it is prohibited both to eat it and to derive benefit from it.**

אֶלָּא לְרַבִּי יְהוּדָה, דְּאָמַר לִדְבָרִים כִּכְתָבָן הוּא דַּאֲתָא – הָא כָּל אִיסּוּרִים שֶׁבַּתּוֹרָה מְנָא לֵיהּ דַּאֲסוּרִין בַּהֲנָאָה? נַפְקָא לֵיהּ מִ״לַּכֶּלֶב תַּשְׁלִיכוּן אֹתוֹ״,

However, according to Rabbi Yehuda, who said that the word "or" **comes to** teach that the **matters are** to be understood **as they are written, from where does he derive** with regard to **all prohibitions** of eating **mentioned in the Torah that it is prohibited to** derive **benefit** as well? The Gemara answers: **He derives it** from another verse. It is stated with regard to an animal with a condition that will cause it to die within twelve months [*tereifa*]: "And you shall be sacred men to Me, therefore you shall not eat any flesh that is torn of beasts in the field; **you shall cast it to the dogs"** (Exodus 22:30).

Perek **II**
Daf **22** Amud **a**

אוֹתוֹ אַתָּה מַשְׁלִיךְ לַכֶּלֶב, וְאִי אַתָּה מַשְׁלִיךְ לַכֶּלֶב כָּל אִיסּוּרִין שֶׁבַּתּוֹרָה. וְרַבִּי מֵאִיר: אוֹתוֹ אַתָּה מַשְׁלִיךְ לַכֶּלֶב, וְאִי אַתָּה מַשְׁלִיךְ לַכֶּלֶב חוּלִּין שֶׁנִּשְׁחֲטוּ בָּעֲזָרָה.

The Gemara concludes: **It,** i.e., a *tereifa,* **you** may **throw to a dog, but you** may **not throw all** other items **prohibited by Torah law to a dog,** as both eating and deriving benefit are prohibited. The Gemara asks: **And** what *halakha* does **Rabbi Meir** learn from this verse? The Gemara answers that Rabbi Meir draws the following inference: **It, you** may **throw to a dog, but you** may **not throw** the meat of **a non-sacred animal that was slaughtered in the** Temple **courtyard**[NH] **to a dog,** as it is prohibited to benefit from it.

וְאִידָּךְ: חוּלִּין שֶׁנִּשְׁחֲטוּ בָּעֲזָרָה לָאו דְּאוֹרַיְיתָא הִיא.

And from where does **the other** Sage, Rabbi Yehuda, learn this *halakha* about non-sacrificial meat that was slaughtered in the Temple courtyard? The Gemara answers: He holds that the prohibition of deriving benefit from the meat of a **non-sacrificial animal that was slaughtered in the courtyard is not by Torah law;** rather, the Sages decreed that it is prohibited. Since it is not prohibited by Torah law, no verse is necessary.

מְתִיב רַבִּי יִצְחָק נַפָּחָא: וַהֲרֵי גִּיד הַנָּשֶׁה, דְּרַחֲמָנָא אָמַר: ״עַל כֵּן לֹא יֹאכְלוּ בְנֵי יִשְׂרָאֵל אֶת גִּיד הַנָּשֶׁה״, וּתְנַן: שׁוֹלֵחַ אָדָם יָרֵךְ לַגּוֹי, וְגִיד הַנָּשֶׁה בְּתוֹכוֹ, מִפְּנֵי שֶׁמְּקוֹמוֹ נִיכָּר!

Rabbi Yitzḥak Nappaḥa raised an objection: And yet there is still the prohibition of **the sciatic nerve,**[N] **as the Merciful One says: "Therefore the children of Israel may not eat the sciatic nerve"** (Genesis 32:33), **and we learned** in a mishna: **A person** may **send the thigh** of an animal **to a gentile** as a gift **with the sciatic nerve inside it,**[H] he is not required to remove it. This is **due to** the fact that **its place is clear,** and it is obvious that this nerve has not been removed. Therefore, there is no concern that another Jew will assume that the first Jew removed this portion of the animal, which might cause him to accidentally eat the sciatic nerve. Apparently, one may benefit from this prohibited portion of the animal even though the verse says that one may not eat it.

NOTES

A non-sacred animal that was slaughtered in the Temple courtyard – **חוּלִּין שֶׁנִּשְׁחֲטוּ בָּעֲזָרָה**: It is unclear whether the prohibition to slaughter non-sacred animals in the Temple, or to eat or benefit from such animals, is by Torah law or by rabbinic law (see Rashi). Either way, the prohibition is clearly based on the verse: "You shall not eat any flesh that is torn of beasts in the field." Among the various explanations is that it is prohibited to eat an animal that was slaughtered outside of its proper place. This leads to Rabbi Meir's statement that one may throw an animal carcass to a dog, but one may not do so with the meat of a non-sacrificial animal that was slaughtered in the Temple courtyard.

Sciatic nerve – **גִּיד הַנָּשֶׁה**: This nerve, known in Latin as nervus ischiadicus, runs down the back of the hind leg of an animal. The sciatic nerve is one of the parts of a kosher domestic animal and a kosher non-domestic animal that by Torah law is prohibited for consumption (Genesis 32:33). In addition to the nerve itself, it is prohibited by rabbinic law to eat any of the flesh surrounding it or the fat that encloses it.

Sciatic nerve running through a piece of meat

HALAKHA

A non-sacred animal that was slaughtered in the Temple courtyard – **חוּלִּין שֶׁנִּשְׁחֲטוּ בָּעֲזָרָה**: It is prohibited to benefit from non-sacrificial animals that were slaughtered in the Temple courtyard, as stated in the mishna in tractate *Temura* (Rambam *Sefer Kedusha, Hilkhot Sheḥita* 2:2).

The thigh…with the sciatic nerve inside it – **יָרֵךְ...וְגִיד הַנָּשֶׁה בְּתוֹכוֹ**: One may send the thigh of an animal to a gentile without removing the sciatic nerve, even in the presence of another Jew. There is no concern that this other Jew will eat the sciatic nerve, since it is apparent that it has not been removed (*Shulḥan Arukh, Yoreh De'a* 65:11).

קָסָבַר רַבִּי אַבָּהוּ: כְּשֶׁהוּתְּרָה נְבֵילָה – הִיא וְחֶלְבָּהּ וְגִידָהּ הוּתְּרָה. הָנִיחָא לְמַאן דְּאָמַר יֵשׁ בַּגִּידִין בְּנוֹתֵן טַעַם! אֶלָּא לְמַאן דְּאָמַר אֵין בַּגִּידִין בְּנוֹתֵן טַעַם, מַאי אִיכָּא לְמֵימַר?

The Gemara rejects this: **Rabbi Abbahu holds** that **when it was permitted** by the Torah to derive benefit from **an animal carcass, it, its fats, and its sinews,** such as the sciatic nerve, were all **permitted.** Therefore, the sciatic nerve is included in this exception and one may benefit from it. The Gemara challenges: **It works out well according to the one who said that sinews give flavor,** meaning that they have the taste of meat and therefore have the legal status of meat of an animal carcass. **However, according to the one who says** that **sinews do not give flavor**[HN] and are not categorized as meat, **what can be said?** If they are not considered to be meat, why are they included in the exception made for an animal carcass?

מַאן שָׁמְעַתְּ לֵיהּ דְּאָמַר "אֵין בַּגִּידִין בְּנוֹתֵן טַעַם" – רַבִּי שִׁמְעוֹן, דְּתַנְיָא: הָאוֹכֵל מִגִּיד הַנָּשֶׁה שֶׁל בְּהֵמָה טְמֵאָה, רַבִּי יְהוּדָה מְחַיֵּיב שְׁתַּיִם, וְרַבִּי שִׁמְעוֹן פּוֹטֵר.

The Gemara answers: **Whom did you hear that said** that **sinews do not give flavor?** It is **Rabbi Shimon, as it was taught** in a *baraita*: With regard to **one who eats the sciatic nerve from a non-kosher domesticated animal, Rabbi Yehuda deems** him **liable** to receive **two** sets of lashes: One for eating the sciatic nerve and one for eating the meat of a non-kosher animal. **And Rabbi Shimon exempts** him entirely, since according to his opinion the prohibition to eat the sciatic nerve applies only to a kosher animal. In addition, one violates the prohibition of eating from a non-kosher animal only when it has the flavor of meat.[H]

רַבִּי שִׁמְעוֹן הָכִי נַמִי דְּאָסַר בַּהֲנָאָה. דְּתַנְיָא: גִּיד הַנָּשֶׁה מוּתָּר בַּהֲנָאָה, דִּבְרֵי רַבִּי יְהוּדָה, וְרַבִּי שִׁמְעוֹן אוֹסֵר.

And it indeed follows logically that just as Rabbi Shimon exempts one who eats the sciatic nerve in that particular case, **so too here, Rabbi Shimon prohibits** deriving **benefit** from the sciatic nerve. **As it was taught** in a *baraita*: **It is permitted to** derive **benefit from the sciatic nerve;**[H] this is **the statement of Rabbi Yehuda, and Rabbi Shimon prohibits** it. Since Rabbi Shimon holds that the sciatic nerve does not give flavor, it cannot be included in the exception of the animal carcass. Therefore, from the verse that prohibits eating the sciatic nerve he learns that one may not benefit from it either, in accordance with the opinion of Rabbi Abbahu. Rabbi Abbahu's position fits according to both opinions. However, the mishna that indicates that it is permitted to derive benefit from the sciatic nerve is in accordance with the opinion of Rabbi Yehuda, as he holds that the sciatic nerve gives flavor and is therefore included in the exception of the animal carcass.

וַהֲרֵי דָּם, דְּרַחֲמָנָא אָמַר: "כָּל נֶפֶשׁ מִכֶּם לֹא תֹאכַל דָּם", וּתְנַן: אֵלּוּ וָאֵלּוּ מִתְעָרְבִין בָּאַמָּה וְיוֹצְאִין לְנַחַל קִדְרוֹן, וְנִמְכָּרִין לַגַּנָּנִין לְזֶבֶל, וּמוֹעֲלִין בּוֹ!

The Gemara further challenges Rabbi Abbahu's opinion: **And** yet there is the prohibition of eating **blood, as the Merciful One says:** "Therefore I said to the children of Israel: **No soul of you shall eat blood,** neither shall any convert that dwells among you eat blood" (Leviticus 17:12). According to Rabbi Abbahu's opinion, one may derive from this verse that in addition to the prohibition against eating blood, it is prohibited to benefit from it as well. **And we learned** in a mishna: Both **these and these,** the remnants of the blood from sin-offerings brought on the altar and other blood sprinkled on it, descend and **mix in the canal** from which water leaves the Temple. They then **exit to the Kidron Valley**[B] **and are sold** at a special price **to gardeners as a fertilizer. And** one who does not first purchase the blood from the Temple **misuses consecrated property.**[H] Apparently, under certain circumstances, one may benefit from blood which it is prohibited to consume.

HALAKHA

The taste of the sciatic nerve – טַעַם גִּיד הַנָּשֶׁה: The sciatic nerve has no taste, and therefore, if it fell into a stew with other meat, it is permitted to eat the other meat. This ruling is in accordance with the conclusion of the Gemara in tractate *Ḥullin* (*Shulḥan Arukh, Yoreh De'a* 65:9).

The sciatic nerve of a non-kosher animal – גִּיד הַנָּשֶׁה שֶׁל בְּהֵמָה טְמֵאָה: If one eats the sciatic nerve of a non-kosher animal, he is exempt from punishment because the prohibition only applies to kosher animals. In addition, sinews are not considered to be meat, and consequently they do not have the legal status of non-kosher meat (Rambam *Sefer Kedusha, Hilkhot Ma'akhalot Assurot* 8:5).

Benefit from the sciatic nerve – הֲנָאָה בְּגִיד הַנָּשֶׁה: Although it is prohibited to eat the sciatic nerve, it is permitted to benefit from it (*Shulḥan Arukh, Yoreh De'a* 65:10).

Misuse of consecrated property with regard to sacrificial blood – מְעִילָה בְּדַם הַקֳּדָשִׁים: If one uses sacrificial blood that drained into the canal and exited the Temple, without purchasing it from the Temple treasury, he has violated the prohibition of misuse of consecrated property. According to the Ra'avad, this is considered misuse by rabbinic law (Rambam *Sefer Avoda, Hilkhot Me'ila* 2:11).

BACKGROUND

Kidron Valley – נַחַל קִדְרוֹן: This diagram illustrates the area of the Temple Mount, the large rectange, as well as the Temple. The Kidron Valley riverbed, into which the Giḥon spring flows, passes near the walls of the Temple Mount. The Temple Mount is located just above the slope of the valley, so that liquids naturally run off from the Temple Mount into the Kidron Valley.

Temple Mount and surrounding area

NOTES

Sinews do not give flavor – אֵין בַּגִּידִין בְּנוֹתֵן טַעַם: At first glance this disagreement is puzzling, since it should be verifiable whether sinews have a taste. Rather, this dispute appears to be related to the question of whether the prohibition against eating the sciatic nerve includes the smaller and softer surrounding sinews as well. While these surrounding sinews have a distinct taste, the sciatic nerve itself is hard and does not have the taste of meat. Therefore, those who maintain that these surrounding sinews are part of the legal definition of the sciatic nerve contend that the sciatic nerve has a taste. Those who maintain that these smaller sinews are not included in the prohibition hold that the sciatic nerve does not have a taste (Maharam Ḥalawa; Rashba in tractate *Ḥullin*).

NOTES

Like water [*kamayim*], meaning, like most water – כַּמַּיִם רוֹב מַיִם: This explanation is supported by the punctuation of the word *kamayim* with a *pataḥ*, meaning: Like the water, i.e., water that is known. It stands to reason, then, that it refers to ordinary water familiar to everyone and not to some special type of water (Rav Ya'akov Emden).

Not like water that is offered as a libation – לֹא כַּמַּיִם הַנִּיסָּכִין: This answer is acceptable even to those who claim that the ritual of water libation on *Sukkot* is not required by Torah law. It is referring here to any water from which one may not benefit, such as the water from the water basin in the Temple courtyard, and water offered as a libation is only meant to serve as an example of that (Maharam Ḥalawa).

שָׁאנֵי דָּם דְּאִיתְקַשׁ לְמַיִם, דִּכְתִיב: ״לֹא תֹּאכְלֶנּוּ עַל הָאָרֶץ תִּשְׁפְּכֶנּוּ כַּמָּיִם״, מַה מַּיִם מוּתָּרִין – אַף דָּם מוּתָּר.

The Gemara answers: **Blood is different, as it is juxtaposed** in the Torah **to water. As it is written** with regard to blood: **"You shall not eat it; you shall pour it out upon the earth like water"** (Deuteronomy 12:24). From here it is derived: **Just as it is permitted** to benefit from **water, so too, it is permitted** to benefit from **blood.**

וְאֵימָא כַּמַּיִם הַמִּתְנַסְּכִים עַל גַּבֵּי הַמִּזְבֵּחַ! אָמַר רַבִּי אַבָּהוּ: ״כַּמָּיִם״ – רוֹב מַיִם. מִידֵּי ״רוֹב מַיִם״ כְּתִיב?! אֶלָּא אָמַר רַב אַשִׁי: כַּמַּיִם הַנִּשְׁפָּכִין! וְלֹא כַּמַּיִם הַנִּיסָּכִין.

The Gemara asks: **And say** instead that blood is meant to be **like water offered as a libation on the altar,** which is consecrated and from which one is prohibited to benefit. **Rabbi Abbahu said:** The comparison to permitted water can be deduced from that which the verse says: **"Like water [*kamayim*],"** meaning, like **most water;**[N] and one is permitted to benefit from most types of water. The Gemara asks: **And is it written: Most water?** The Torah wrote: "Like water," which could indicate a comparison to any type of water. **Rather, Rav Ashi said** that the verse should be understood as follows: **Like water that is poured out,** from which one may benefit, **and not like water that is offered as a libation.**[N] Water offered on the altar is described using the term libation, and not using the term poured as found in the verse.

וְאֵימָא כַּמַּיִם הַנִּשְׁפָּכִין לִפְנֵי עֲבוֹדָה זָרָה! הָתָם נַמִי נִיסּוּךְ אִיקְּרִי, דִּכְתִיב: ״יִשְׁתּוּ יֵין נְסִיכָם״.

The Gemara asks: **And say** that blood is meant to be **like water poured before idolatry,** from which one may not benefit. The Gemara rejects this: **There,** that **is also called a libation** and not pouring, **as it is written:** "Who did eat the fat of their sacrifices, **and drink the wine of their libations**" (Deuteronomy 32:38).

Perek **II**
Daf **22** Amud **b**

NOTES

A cup of wine to a nazirite – כּוֹס יַיִן לְנָזִיר: Although there is a general restriction of offering another person a prohibited item, this particular example is selected because since everyone else may drink wine, it is deemed likely that the nazirite may forget his oath and accidentally drink the wine offered to him (*Tosafot*).

Before the blind – לִפְנֵי עִוֵּר: The Sages expand upon the prohibition mentioned in the verse: "You shall not put a stumbling block before the blind," explaining that it refers to any type of situation where one may cause someone else to stumble, literally or figuratively. Practically speaking, this includes the prohibition against enabling someone to commit a sin. However, it only applies to situations where this individual would not have been able to commit the sin without the assistance of another person. A classic example of this is when one transfers a prohibited item from the opposite side of a river, as it would otherwise have been inaccessible.

HALAKHA

Before the blind – לִפְנֵי עִוֵּר: It is prohibited to offer a cup of wine to a nazirite or a limb torn from a living animal to descendants of Noah when the prohibited item is in a place that the person cannot not reach by himself (*Sefer Mitzvot Gadol*, negative mitzva 168).

וּלְחִזְקִיָּה, לְמַאי הִלְכְתָא אִיתְקַשׁ דָּם לְמַיִם? לְכִדְרַבִּי חִיָּיא בַּר אַבָּא. דְּאָמַר רַבִּי חִיָּיא בַּר אַבָּא אָמַר רַבִּי יוֹחָנָן: מִנַּיִן לְדַם קָדָשִׁים שֶׁאֵינוֹ מַכְשִׁיר, שֶׁנֶּאֱמַר ״לֹא תֹּאכְלֶנּוּ עַל הָאָרֶץ תִּשְׁפְּכֶנּוּ כַּמָּיִם״, דָּם שֶׁנִּשְׁפַּךְ כַּמַּיִם – מַכְשִׁיר, שֶׁאֵינוֹ נִשְׁפַּךְ כַּמַּיִם – אֵינוֹ מַכְשִׁיר.

The Gemara asks: **According to Ḥizkiya,** who says that: You shall not eat, indicates only that eating is prohibited but that benefit is permitted, **for what *halakha* is blood juxtaposed to water?** According to his opinion, there is no need for the verse to teach that one may benefit from blood. The Gemara answers that he needs this verse **to derive** that which was taught by **Rabbi Ḥiyya bar Abba, as Rabbi Ḥiyya bar Abba said** that **Rabbi Yoḥanan said: From where** is it derived **that the blood of sacrifices does not render** food **susceptible** to ritual impurity? **As it is stated: "You shall not eat it; you shall pour it out upon the earth like water"** (Deuteronomy 12:24). **Blood that is poured out like water,** such as that of a slaughtered, non-sacrificial animal, **renders** food **susceptible** to ritual impurity. However, sacrificial blood, **which is not poured out like water** and is instead sprinkled on the altar, **does not render** food **susceptible** to ritual impurity.

וַהֲרֵי אֵבֶר מִן הַחַי, דִּכְתִיב: ״לֹא תֹאכַל הַנֶּפֶשׁ עִם הַבָּשָׂר״, וְתַנְיָא, רַבִּי נָתָן אוֹמֵר: מִנַּיִן שֶׁלֹּא יוֹשִׁיט אָדָם כּוֹס יַיִן לְנָזִיר, וְאֵבֶר מִן הַחַי לִבְנֵי נֹחַ – תַּלְמוּד לוֹמַר: ״וְלִפְנֵי עִוֵּר לֹא תִתֵּן מִכְשֹׁל״. הָא לַכְּלָבִים – שָׁרֵי!

The Gemara further challenges Rabbi Abbahu's opinion: **And** yet there is the prohibition against eating **a limb** cut **from a living** animal, **as it is written:** "Only be steadfast in not eating the blood; for the blood is the life; **and you shall not eat the life with the flesh**" (Deuteronomy 12:23). **And it was taught** in a *baraita* that **Rabbi Natan says: From where** is it derived **that a person** may **not offer a cup of wine to a nazirite,**[N] who is prohibited from drinking wine, and that he may not offer **a limb** cut **from a living animal to a descendant of Noah,** who is prohibited by Noahide law from eating a limb from a living animal? **The verse states: "You shall not put a stumbling block before the blind"** (Leviticus 19:14).[NH] Causing another person to sin is like placing a stumbling block before a blind person; one who does so violates this prohibition. The prohibition of giving a limb from a living animal to a gentile is apparently due only to the prohibition of placing a stumbling block. **However, it is permitted** for one to throw it **to dogs.** Therefore, despite the fact that the verse says: "You shall not eat it," apparently there is no prohibition against benefiting from this prohibited item. This challenges Rabbi Abbahu's principle.

שָׁאנֵי אֵבֶר מִן הַחַי, דְּאִיתְקַשׁ לְדָם. דִּכְתִיב: ״רַק חֲזַק לְבִלְתִּי אֲכֹל הַדָּם כִּי הַדָּם הוּא הַנָּפֶשׁ״.

The Gemara answers: **A limb from a living animal is different, as it is juxtaposed** in the Torah **to blood. As it is written: "Only be steadfast in not eating the blood; for the blood is the life;** and you shall not eat the life with the flesh" (Deuteronomy 12:23). Just as it is permitted to benefit from blood, it is likewise permitted to benefit from a limb torn from a living animal.

וּלְחִזְקִיָּה, לְמַאי הִלְכְתָא אִיתְקַשׁ אֵבֶר מִן הַחַי לְדָם? אָמַר לְךָ: דָּם הוּא דְּאִיתְקַשׁ לְאֵבֶר מִן הַחַי, מָה אֵבֶר מִן הַחַי – אָסוּר, אַף דָּם מִן הַחַי אָסוּר. וְאֵי זֶה – זֶה דַּם הַקָּזָה, שֶׁהַנֶּפֶשׁ יוֹצְאָה בּוֹ.

The Gemara asks: **And according to Ḥizkiya,** in order to teach **what *halakha* is** the prohibition against eating **a limb from a living animal juxtaposed to** the prohibition against eating **blood?** The Gemara answers: **He** could have **said to you** that the juxtaposition comes to teach the opposite. **It is blood that is juxtaposed to a limb from a living animal** to teach the following: **Just as a limb from a living animal is prohibited, so too, blood of a living being is prohibited. And** to **which** blood is **this** referring? **This** is referring to **blood** spilled in the process **of bloodletting,**[H] **through which the soul departs.** That is considered to be blood from a living being, and even the descendants of Noah are prohibited from eating it (Rabbeinu Ḥananel).

וַהֲרֵי שׁוֹר הַנִּסְקָל, דְּרַחֲמָנָא אָמַר: ״לֹא יֵאָכֵל אֶת בְּשָׂרוֹ״. וְתַנְיָא: מִמַּשְׁמַע שֶׁנֶּאֱמַר ״סָקוֹל יִסָּקֵל הַשּׁוֹר״ אֵינִי יוֹדֵעַ שֶׁהִיא נְבֵלָה, וּנְבֵלָה אֲסוּרָה בַּאֲכִילָה? וּמַה תַּלְמוּד לוֹמַר ״לֹא יֵאָכֵל״ מַגִּיד לְךָ הַכָּתוּב, שֶׁאִם שְׁחָטוֹ לְאַחַר שֶׁנִּגְמַר (אֶת) דִּינוֹ – אָסוּר.

The Gemara asks: **And** yet there is the prohibition against eating the meat from **an ox that is stoned,**[H] **as the Merciful One says:** "And if an ox gores a man or a woman to death, the ox shall be surely stoned, **and of its flesh shall not be eaten;** but the owner of the ox shall be clear" (Exodus 21:28). **And it was taught** in a *baraita*: **By inference from that which is stated: "The ox shall surely be stoned,"** in which case it is not to be slaughtered properly, **don't I know that it is an animal carcass, and it is prohibited to eat an animal carcass? What** does it mean when **the verse states: "Its** flesh **shall not be eaten"? The verse is telling you that** even **if one slaughtered** the ox **after its verdict had been reached** but before it had been carried out, **it is** still **prohibited.**

אֵין לִי אֶלָּא בַּאֲכִילָה, בַּהֲנָאָה מִנַּיִן? תַּלְמוּד לוֹמַר ״וּבַעַל הַשּׁוֹר נָקִי״. מַאי מַשְׁמַע? שִׁמְעוֹן בֶּן זוֹמָא אוֹמֵר: כְּאָדָם שֶׁאוֹמֵר לַחֲבֵירוֹ ״יָצָא פְּלוֹנִי נָקִי מִנְּכָסָיו וְאֵין לוֹ בָּהֶם הֲנָאָה שֶׁל כְּלוּם״.

The *baraita* continues: **I have** derived **only** that one is prohibited **from eating** this ox; **from where** do I derive that one is prohibited **from** deriving **benefit** from it as well? **The verse states: "But the owner of the ox shall be clear [*naki*]."** The Gemara asks: **From where may it be inferred** that one may not benefit from this ox? **Shimon ben Zoma says:** This is **like a person who says to his fellow: So-and-so was left clear [*naki*] of his property, and he has no benefit from it at all.** Similarly, "But the owner of the ox shall be clear" means that he has no benefit from the ox.

טַעְמָא – דִּכְתַב ״וּבַעַל הַשּׁוֹר נָקִי״. דְּאִי מִ״לֹּא יֵאָכֵל״ – אִיסּוּר אֲכִילָה מַשְׁמַע, אִיסּוּר הֲנָאָה – לֹא מַשְׁמַע!

The Gemara infers from the verse that **the reason** that it is prohibited to derive benefit from the ox **is that** the Torah specifically **wrote: "But the owner of the ox shall be clear."** As, **if** this prohibition were derived **from: "It shall not be eaten,"** apparently the **prohibition of eating would be implied,** but **the prohibition of** deriving **benefit would not be implied.** This presents a challenge even for Ḥizkiya, who agrees that the passive formulation: "It shall not be eaten," indicates that in addition one may not benefit from the item.

לְעוֹלָם ״לֹא יֵאָכֵל״ – אִיסּוּר אֲכִילָה וְאִיסּוּר הֲנָאָה מַשְׁמַע. ״וּבַעַל הַשּׁוֹר נָקִי״ – לַהֲנָאַת עוֹרוֹ הוּא דַּאֲתָא. וְאִיצְטְרִיךְ, סָלְקָא דַּעְתָּךְ אָמִינָא: ״לֹא יֵאָכֵל אֶת בְּשָׂרוֹ״ כְּתִיב, בְּשָׂרוֹ – אִין, עוֹרוֹ – לָא, קָא מַשְׁמַע לַן.

The Gemara answers: **Actually,** the phrase: **"It shall not be eaten"** indicates both **a prohibition of eating and a prohibition of** deriving **benefit.** And the phrase: **"But the owner of the ox shall be clear," comes to** prohibit deriving **benefit from the hide** of the ox that has been stoned. **And** it is **necessary** to mention this explicitly, as **it could enter your mind to say** that since **it is written: "Its flesh shall not be eaten,"** with regard to **its flesh, yes,** it is prohibited, but with regard to **its hide, no,** it is not. Therefore, the verse **teaches us** that it is prohibited to benefit from its hide as well.

וּלְהָנָךְ תַּנָּאֵי דְּמַפְּקִי לֵיהּ לְהַאי קְרָא לִדְרָשָׁה אַחֲרִינָא, לַחֲצִי כּוֹפֶר וְלִדְמֵי וְלָדוֹת, הֲנָאַת עוֹרוֹ מְנָא לְהוּ? נָפְקָא לְהוּ מֵ״אֶת בְּשָׂרוֹ״ – אֶת הַטָּפֵל לִבְשָׂרוֹ.

The Gemara asks: **And** according **to those *tanna'im* who expound this verse:** "But the owner of the ox shall be clear," **for another interpretation,** namely, to teach that the owner of an innocuous ox, i.e., one that is not known to cause damage with the intent to injure, is exempt from the payment of **half** of the **indemnity** if that ox killed a person, or that he is exempt from **payment for offspring** if his ox gores a pregnant woman and causes her to miscarry; **from where do they derive** this prohibition against **benefiting from** the ox's **hide?** The Gemara answers: **They derive** this *halakha* from the wording: **"Of [*et*] its flesh."** The verse could have been formulated: And its flesh shall not be eaten. The addition of the word *et* comes to include **that which is secondary to the flesh,** i.e., the hide.

HALAKHA

Blood of bloodletting – דַּם הַקָּזָה: One who eats blood drawn from an animal through bloodletting, which leaves the animal in a steady stream, is liable to receive *karet*, as this is considered blood through which the soul departs (Rambam *Sefer Kedusha, Hilkhot Ma'akhalot Assurot* 6:3).

An ox that is stoned – שׁוֹר הַנִּסְקָל: One may not eat or benefit from an ox after it has been condemned to be stoned, even if it was slaughtered before the verdict was carried out, in accordance with the Gemara here (Rambam *Sefer Kedusha, Hilkhot Ma'akhalot Assurot* 4:22).

וְאִידָךְ: ״אֶת״ לָא דָּרֵישׁ.

The Gemara asks: **And the other** *tanna*, who derives the prohibition against benefiting from the hide from the verse: "But the owner of the ox shall be clear," what does he learn from the additional word *et*? The Gemara answers: This Sage **does not interpret** the word **et** as a means to derive new *halakhot*. He considers the word *et* to be an ordinary part of the sentence structure and not a source for exegetical exposition.

כִּדְתַנְיָא: שִׁמְעוֹן הָעַמְסוֹנִי, וְאָמְרִי לָהּ נְחֶמְיָה הָעַמְסוֹנִי, הָיָה דּוֹרֵשׁ כׇּל אֶתִּים שֶׁבַּתּוֹרָה. כֵּיוָן שֶׁהִגִּיעַ לְ״אֶת ה׳ אֱלֹהֶיךָ תִּירָא״ – פֵּירַשׁ. אָמְרוּ לוֹ תַּלְמִידָיו: רַבִּי, כׇּל אֶתִּים שֶׁדָּרַשְׁתָּ מָה תְּהֵא עֲלֵיהֶן? אָמַר לָהֶם: כְּשֵׁם שֶׁקִּבַּלְתִּי שָׂכָר עַל הַדְּרִישָׁה, כָּךְ אֲנִי מְקַבֵּל שָׂכָר עַל הַפְּרִישָׁה. עַד שֶׁבָּא רַבִּי עֲקִיבָא וְדָרַשׁ: ״אֶת ה׳ אֱלֹהֶיךָ תִּירָא״ – לְרַבּוֹת תַּלְמִידֵי חֲכָמִים.

As it was taught in a *baraita*: **Shimon HaAmmassoni, and some say** that it was **Neḥemya HaAmmassoni, would interpret all** occurrences of the word **et in the Torah,** deriving additional *halakhot* with regard to the particular subject matter. **Once he reached** the verse: **"You shall be in awe of [*et*] the Lord your God;**[N] you shall serve Him; and to Him you shall cleave, and by His name you shall swear" (Deuteronomy 10:20), **he withdrew** from this method of exposition, as how could one add to God Himself? **His students said to him: Rabbi, what will be with all the *etim* that you interpreted** until now? **He said to them: Just as I received reward for the interpretation, so I shall receive reward for** my **withdrawal** from using this method of exposition. The word *et* in this verse was not explained **until Rabbi Akiva came and expounded: "You shall be in awe of [*et*] the Lord your God":** The word *et* comes **to include Torah scholars,** and one is commanded to fear them just as one fears God. In any case, Shimon HaAmmassoni no longer derived additional *halakhot* from the word *et*.

וַהֲרֵי עׇרְלָה, דְּרַחֲמָנָא אָמַר: ״עֲרֵלִים לֹא יֵאָכֵל״. וְתַנְיָא: ״עֲרֵלִים לֹא יֵאָכֵל״ – אֵין לִי אֶלָּא אִיסּוּר אֲכִילָה, מִנַּיִן שֶׁלֹּא יֵהָנֶה מִמֶּנּוּ, שֶׁלֹּא יִצְבַּע בּוֹ, וְלֹא יַדְלִיק בּוֹ אֶת הַנֵּר – תַּלְמוּד לוֹמַר: ״וַעֲרַלְתֶּם עׇרְלָתוֹ. עֲרֵלִים לֹא יֵאָכֵל״ – לְרַבּוֹת אֶת כּוּלָּם.

The Gemara further challenges: **And** yet there is the prohibition of **fruit that grows on a tree during the first three years after it was planted [*orla*],**[N] **as the Merciful One says:** "And when you come into the land, and you shall plant all types of trees for food, then you shall count the fruit thereof as prohibited; three years shall it be **prohibited [*arelim*]** to you; **it shall not be eaten"** (Leviticus 19:23). **And it was taught** in a *baraita*: "Shall it be **prohibited** to you; **it shall not be eaten": I have only derived a prohibition to eat** it. **From where do I derive that one may not** even **benefit from it,** e.g., that **he may not paint with** the dye that can be extracted from the fruit, **nor may he light a lamp with** its oil?[H] **The verse states: "You shall count the fruit thereof [*orlato*] as prohibited [*araltem*];** three years shall it be **prohibited [*arelim*] to you; it shall not be eaten."** This repetition of the term *arel* comes **to include all forms** of benefit.

טַעְמָא – דִּכְתַב רַחֲמָנָא ״וַעֲרַלְתֶּם עׇרְלָתוֹ עֲרֵלִים״, הָא לָאו הָכִי – הֲוָה אָמֵינָא אִיסּוּר אֲכִילָה – מַשְׁמַע, אִיסּוּר הֲנָאָה – לָא מַשְׁמַע!

The Gemara reads precisely: **The reason** that all forms of benefit are prohibited **is that the Merciful One writes: "You shall count** the fruit thereof **as prohibited [*araltem*];** three years **shall it be prohibited [*arelim*]."** The double use of the word *arel* indicates a two-fold prohibition. **However, were that not** the case, **I would have said: The prohibition of eating is indicated** here; however, **the prohibition to** derive **benefit is not indicated.** This is a challenge even to Ḥizkiya's opinion, as the verse says: "It shall not be eaten," indicating that it is prohibited to derive benefit as well.

לְעוֹלָם ״לֹא יֵאָכֵל״ מַשְׁמַע בֵּין אִיסּוּר אֲכִילָה בֵּין אִיסּוּר הֲנָאָה, וְשָׁאנֵי הָתָם דִּכְתִיב ״לָכֶם״. וְאִיצְטְרִיךְ, סָלְקָא דַּעְתָּךְ אָמֵינָא: הוֹאִיל וּכְתַב ״לָכֶם״ – שֶׁלָּכֶם יְהֵא, קָמַשְׁמַע לַן.

The Gemara rejects this. **Actually,** in general, **"it shall not be eaten" indicates both a prohibition of eating and a prohibition to** derive **benefit. However, it is different there,** with regard to *orla*, **as it is written:** "Three years shall it be prohibited [*arelim*] **to you." And,** therefore, **it was necessary** for the verse to repeat the prohibition using several terms, as **it could enter your mind to say** that **since it wrote "to you"** it means that **it shall be yours,** namely that one is permitted to benefit from it. Therefore, **it teaches us** that it is prohibited to derive benefit.

וְאֶלָּא הַשְׁתָּא דִּכְתִיבִי הָנָךְ קְרָאֵי, ״לָכֶם״ לָמָּה לִי? לִכְדְתַנְיָא: ״לָכֶם״ – לְרַבּוֹת אֶת הַנָּטוּעַ

The Gemara asks: **However, now that these** words in the **verses are written,** indicating the prohibition to derive benefit from *orla*, **why do I** need the words **"to you,"** i.e., what does this phrase teach us here? The Gemara answers: **As it was taught** in a *baraita*: That which is stated: **"To you,"** comes **to include that which is planted**

NOTES

You shall be in awe of [*et*] the Lord your God – אֶת ה׳ אֱלֹהֶיךָ תִּירָא: Many different issues were discussed with regard to this *baraita*, from several different angles. Some ask why Shimon HaAmmassoni did not hesitate when interpreting the verse: "And you shall love the [*et*] Lord, your God" (Deuteronomy 6:5), which appears earlier in the Torah. They suggest that it is easy to explain how Torah scholars could be included in the mitzva to love; however, it is more difficult to offer such an explanation about fear and awe, which are linked to reward and punishment (Maharsha; see Rif). Alternatively, perhaps the word *et* can be expounded upon in other ways aside from adding to the meaning of a verse. For example, it can be understood as a pause, or as an indication of a distinction between two different concepts. Therefore, Shimon HaAmmassoni was not troubled by these other verses. However, because in this case the word *et* is the first word of the verse containing the mitzva, he understood that it must be used in an inclusive manner (*Iyyun Ya'akov*). A similar story is cited in the Jerusalem Talmud, although there the word *et* is interpreted to include both God and His Torah.

Fruit that grows on a tree during the first three years after it was planted [*orla*] – עׇרְלָה: It is prohibited to eat or derive benefit from the fruit that grows during the first three years after a tree has been planted; see Leviticus 19:23. This prohibition applies only to the fruit but not to the other parts of the tree. In addition, the prohibition does not apply to trees planted as a fence either for property delineation or as a wind buffer rather than for their fruit.

HALAKHA

Benefit from *orla* – הֲנָאַת עׇרְלָה: It is prohibited to eat or benefit from *orla* fruit, in accordance with the *baraita* (*Shulḥan Arukh, Yoreh De'a* 294:1).

לרבים. רבי יהודה אומר: להוציא את הנטוע לרבים.

for the public;[H] all the details of the prohibition of *orla* apply to a tree planted for public purposes. **Rabbi Yehuda says:** This verse comes **to exclude a tree planted for the public,** i.e., it is exempt from the laws of *orla*.

מאי טעמא דתנא קמא – דכתיב "ונטעתם" – ליחיד משמע לרבים לא משמע, כתב רחמנא "לכם" – להביא את הנטוע לרבים. ורבי יהודה – "ונטעתם" משמע בין לרבים בין ליחיד, ו"לכם" – בין יחיד בין רבים משמע, הוי רבוי אחר רבוי, ואין רבוי אחר רבוי אלא למעט.

The Gemara explains: **What is the reason** for the opinion **of the first *tanna*? As it is written: "And you shall plant."** That the mitzva applies **to an individual is indicated,** since planting a tree is ordinarily an individual activity; however, that the mitzva of *orla* applies to a tree planted **for the public is not indicated** by the verse. Therefore, **the Merciful One writes "for you"** in the plural, **to include** within this prohibition **that which is planted for the public. And Rabbi Yehuda** concedes that the phrase **"and you shall plant" indicates** that *orla* applies **both to** a tree planted **for the public and for an individual;** and the phrase **"for you"** also **indicates** that *orla* applies **both to** a tree planted for **an individual and for the public.** If so, then this **is one amplificatory expression after another,** and there is a principle that **one amplificatory expression after another is restrictive.** Therefore, the term: "For you" comes to exclude from this prohibition a tree planted for the public.

והרי תרומה, דרחמנא אמר: "וכל זר לא יאכל קדש" ותנן: מערבין לנזיר ביין ולישראל בתרומה!

The Gemara further challenges Rabbi Abbahu's opinion: **And** yet there is the prohibition that a non-priest shall not eat ***teruma*****, as the Merciful One says: "No stranger shall eat of the sacred food;** a tenant of a priest, or a hired servant, shall not eat of the sacred food" (Leviticus 22:10). **And we learned** in a mishna: **One** may **establish an *eiruv*,** such as a joining of Shabbat boundaries,[N] **on behalf of a nazirite**[H] **with wine,** even though he may not drink it. **And** one may establish an *eiruv* **on behalf of an Israelite with *teruma*,** although it is prohibited for him to eat it. Apparently, it is permitted for an Israelite to derive benefit from the *teruma* even though the verse says: "He shall not eat." This appears to be a challenge to the opinion of Rabbi Abbahu.

אמר רב פפא: שאני התם, דאמר קרא "תרומתכם" – שלכם תהא. ואידך: תרומתכם דכל ישראל קאמר.

Rav Pappa said: It is different there, with regard to *teruma*, **as the verse said:** "And **your *teruma*** shall be reckoned unto you, as though it were the grain of the threshing floor, and as the fullness of the winepress" (Numbers 18:27). The Sages derived from the inclusion of the possessive pronoun "your" that the *teruma* **shall be yours;**[N] therefore, it is permitted for an Israelite to benefit from *teruma*. The Gemara asks: **And** what does **the other** Sage, Ḥizkiya, derive from this phrase, as he holds that: "He shall not eat" already indicates that it is permitted to benefit from *teruma*? The Gemara answers: According to his opinion the phrase: **"Your *teruma*"** is referring to all of the *teruma* **of the entire Jewish people.** This is common biblical vernacular, and nothing may be derived from it.

HALAKHA

That which is planted for the public – הנוטע לרבים: If a person plants a tree for public use in his own field, it is bound by the restrictions of *orla*. If he did so outside of Eretz Yisrael, the tree is exempt from the *halakhot* of *orla* (*Shulḥan Arukh, Yoreh De'a* 294:25).

One may establish an *eiruv* on behalf of a nazirite – מערבין לנזיר: One may establish an *eiruv* for a nazirite with wine and for an Israelite with *teruma* (*Shulḥan Arukh, Oraḥ Ḥayyim* 386:8).

NOTES

Joining of Shabbat boundaries – עירוב תחומין: It is prohibited to walk more than 2,000 cubits from one's home on Shabbat. However, the entire city in which he lives is considered his place of residence, and the 2,000 cubits are measured from the city limits. Since this prohibition, at least its major aspects, is rabbinic in origin, the Sages also provided a method to extend the limit of 2,000 cubits. By placing, before Shabbat, enough food for a small meal somewhere within one's 2,000-cubit limit, even at its farthest edge, one establishes that location as his place of residence for Shabbat, and the 2,000 cubits are subsequently measured from there. This placing of food to extend the distance one is permitted to walk on Shabbat is called the joining of boundaries, and the *halakhot* governing the subject are detailed in tractate *Eiruvin*. A blessing is recited when placing a joining of boundaries: Concerning the commandment of joining.

The *teruma* shall be yours – תרומתכם שלכם תהא: The Gemara here seems to state that an Israelite may derive benefit from *teruma*. This presents a difficulty, as it is clear from other sources that an Israelite is prohibited not only to eat and drink *teruma*, but also to anoint himself with it. However, a distinction can be made between deriving benefit from *teruma* in a manner that diminishes or consumes the *teruma*, which is prohibited, and deriving benefit from *teruma* in a manner that neither diminishes nor consumes it, which is permitted. Therefore, as stated in the mishna, the benefit derived from using *teruma* for an *eiruv* is permitted, as is the benefit of discretion, i.e., benefit accrued from the option of giving *teruma* and tithes to the Levite that he chooses (see *Me'iri*).

וַהֲרֵי נָזִיר, דְּרַחֲמָנָא אָמַר: ״מֵחַרְצַנִּים וְעַד זָג לֹא יֹאכֵל״, וּתְנַן: מְעָרְבִין לַנָּזִיר בַּיַּיִן! אָמַר מָר זוּטְרָא: שָׁאנֵי הָתָם דְּאָמַר קְרָא ״נִזְרוֹ״ – שֶׁלּוֹ יְהֵא.

The Gemara continues to challenge Rabbi Abbahu's opinion: **And** yet there is the prohibition against **the nazirite** eating grape products, **as the Merciful One says:** "All the days of his naziriteship **he shall eat nothing** that is made of the grapevine, **from the seeds to the grape skin**" (Numbers 6:4). **And we learned** in the mishna: **One may establish an *eiruv*** on behalf of **a nazirite with wine** even though he may not drink it. Apparently, a nazirite may derive benefit from wine despite the fact that the verse says that he may not drink it. **Mar Zutra said: It is different there, as the verse said: "His naziriteship."** He derives from this verse that **it shall be his;** in other words, the nazirite may continue to own wine and to benefit from it.

רַב אַשִׁי אָמַר: ״קָדֹשׁ יִהְיֶה גַּדֵּל פֶּרַע שְׂעַר רֹאשׁוֹ״ – גִּידּוּלוֹ קָדוֹשׁ, וְאֵין דָּבָר אַחֵר קָדוֹשׁ. מִידֵּי ״וְאֵין דָּבָר אַחֵר״ כְּתִיב?! אֶלָּא, מְחַוַּורְתָּא כִּדְמָר זוּטְרָא.

Rav Ashi said: This *halakha* is derived from another source. As the verse says: **"He shall be sacred, he shall let the locks of the hair of his head grow long"** (Numbers 6:5). Rav Ashi reads the verse precisely to indicate that **the growth** of the nazirite's hair **is sacred** and must be burned, **but no other element** of his naziriteship **is sacred.** In other words, he may derive benefit from the other elements prohibited to him during his naziriteship, i.e., from grape products. The Gemara challenges: **And is it written: No other element**[N] of his naziriteship? There is no indication that this statement means that the prohibition against deriving benefit is limited to this one element. **Rather, it is clear** that the derivation of this *halakha* is **in accordance with** the explanation of **Mar Zutra.**

וַהֲרֵי חָדָשׁ, דְּרַחֲמָנָא אָמַר: ״לֶחֶם וְקָלִי וְכַרְמֶל לֹא תֹאכְלוּ עַד עֶצֶם הַיּוֹם הַזֶּה״, וּתְנַן: קוֹצֵר לַשַּׁחַת וּמַאֲכִיל לַבְּהֵמָה!

The Gemara continues to challenge Rabbi Abbahu's opinion: **And** yet there is the prohibition of **new** grain, which was harvested before the bringing of the *omer* offering, **as the Merciful One says: "And you shall eat neither bread, nor parched grain, nor fresh stalks until this day itself,** until you have brought the offering of your God; it is a statute forever throughout your generations in all your dwellings" (Leviticus 23:14). **And we learned** in a mishna: **One** may **harvest** grain before the *omer* **as fodder**[H] **and feed it**[N] **to his animal.** Apparently, one may derive benefit from this grain even though the verse says: "You shall not eat."

אָמַר רַב שְׁמַעְיָה: שָׁאנֵי הָתָם דְּאָמַר קְרָא ״קְצִירְכֶם״ – קְצִירְכֶם שֶׁלָּכֶם יְהֵא. וְאִידָּךְ: ״קְצִירְכֶם״ דְּכָל יִשְׂרָאֵל מַשְׁמַע.

Rav Shemaya said: It is different there, as the verse said: "Your harvest" (Leviticus 23:10), indicating that **your harvest will be yours.** In other words, one may benefit from it, as it is still considered to be his. The Gemara asks: **And** what does **the other** Sage, Ḥizkiya, derive from this phrase? The Gemara answers that according to his opinion, **"your harvest"** is referring to the harvest **of the entire Jewish people.** This is common biblical vernacular, and nothing may be derived from it.

וַהֲרֵי שְׁרָצִים, דְּרַחֲמָנָא אָמַר: ״שֶׁקֶץ הוּא לֹא יֵאָכֵל״, וּתְנַן: צַיָּידֵי חַיָּה וְעוֹפוֹת וְדָגִים, שֶׁנִּזְדַּמְּנוּ לָהֶם מִינִין טְמֵאִין – מוּתָּרִין לְמוֹכְרָן לַגּוֹיִם! שָׁאנֵי הָתָם, דְּאָמַר קְרָא ״לָכֶם״ – שֶׁלָּכֶם יְהֵא.

The Gemara challenges both opinions. **And** yet there is the prohibition against eating **creeping animals, as the Merciful One says:** "And every creeping thing that swarms upon the earth **is a detestable thing; it shall not be eaten"** (Leviticus 11:41). **And we learned** in a mishna: **If hunters of undomesticated animals, birds, and fish happen to catch non-kosher species** that they did not intend to trap, **it is permitted for them to sell** them **to gentiles.**[H] Apparently, one may derive benefit from non-kosher species even though the verse says: "It shall not be eaten." The Gemara answers: **It is different there, as the verse said: "For you"** (Leviticus 11:10), indicating that **they will be yours,** that one may derive benefit from them.

NOTES

And is it written, no other element – מִידֵּי וְאֵין דָּבָר אַחֵר כְּתִיב: A limitation of this type can be applied only where there is some hint to it in the verse. For example, if the verse explicitly said that the extra hair grown by the nazirite is consecrated, one could derive that this is only the case for his hair, but not for any other item. Since no such limitation is found in the verse itself, it should be understood in a straightforward manner.

One may harvest as fodder and feed it – קוֹצֵר לַשַּׁחַת וּמַאֲכִיל: Some explain that one is permitted to harvest grain at this time only because the grain is still unripe and therefore does not yet have the legal status of prohibited new grain; consequently, it would be permitted for even a person to eat it (see *Me'iri*). Others explain that one is permitted to harvest even grain that is fully ripened to feed to one's animal, but this allowance is limited to wheat; one may not harvest barley for that purpose until after the *omer* is offered (*Tzafnat Pane'aḥ*).

HALAKHA

One may harvest as fodder – קוֹצֵר לַשַּׁחַת: One may harvest grain that is less than a third of its full growth for animal feed, even before the *omer* has been offered (Rambam *Sefer Avoda, Hilkhot Temidin UMusafin* 7:15).

Commerce with non-kosher creatures – מִסְחָר בִּדְבָרִים טְמֵאִים: One may not engage in commerce with impure animals that are designated for consumption. One may sell animals that are not designated for consumption although people may sometimes eat them. If one happened to trap a non-kosher animal, or if a merchant received non-kosher animals along with other items that he purchased, he may sell them. However, one should not be involved in trading these animals at all *ab initio* (*Shulḥan Arukh, Yoreh De'a* 117).

אִי הָכִי, אֲפִילּוּ לְכַתְּחִלָּה נַמִּי! שָׁאנֵי הָכָא, דְּאָמַר קְרָא ״יִהְיוּ״ – בַּהֲוָיָיתָן יְהוּ.

The Gemara asks: **If so,** that it is permitted to derive benefit from these creeping animals, then **even** if one intends to catch them it should **also** be permitted to sell them to gentiles *ab initio*. However, the mishna indicates that this is prohibited. The Gemara answers: **It is different here,** in the case of creeping animals, **as the verse said: "They shall be"** (Leviticus 11:11). It is derived from this that **they shall be as they are.** In other words, they should remain in their detestable state, and one should stay away from them.

וּלְחִזְקִיָּה, לָמָּה לִי לְמִיכְתַּב ״לֹא יֵאָכֵל״ וּמַיְיתִי ״לָכֶם״ לְמִישְׁרְיֵיהּ? לָא לִכְתּוֹב רַחֲמָנָא ״לֹא יֵאָכֵל״ וְלָא בָּעֵי ״לָכֶם״! אָמַר לָךְ חִזְקִיָּה: טַעְמָא דִּידִי נַמִּי מֵהָכָא.

The Gemara asks: **And according to** the opinion of **Ḥizkiya, why do I** need the verse **to write: "It shall not be eaten,"** to teach that one may not derive benefit from them, **and** afterward **to say: "For you," to permit** deriving benefit from **them? Let the Merciful One not write: "It shall not be eaten," and it will not need** to say: **"For you." Ḥizkiya** could have **said to you: My reason is also** derived **from here,** as this verse is a central source for my opinion. Since the verse needed to say explicitly: "For you," it is evident that when the Torah writes only: "It shall not be eaten," it is indicating that it is prohibited to benefit from the item as well.

וַהֲרֵי חָמֵץ, דְּרַחֲמָנָא אָמַר: ״לֹא יֵאָכֵל חָמֵץ״, וְתַנְיָא, רַבִּי יוֹסֵי הַגְּלִילִי אוֹמֵר: תְּמַהּ עַל עַצְמְךָ, הֵיאַךְ חָמֵץ אָסוּר בַּהֲנָאָה כׇּל שִׁבְעָה? שָׁאנֵי הָתָם, דְּאָמַר קְרָא: ״וְלֹא יֵרָאֶה לְךָ שְׂאוֹר״ – שֶׁלְּךָ יְהֵא.

The Gemara further challenges the opinions of Ḥizkiya and Rabbi Abbahu: **And** yet there is the prohibition of **leavened bread,** as **the Merciful One says: "Leavened bread shall not be eaten,"** and **it was taught** in a *baraita* that **Rabbi Yosei HaGelili says: Be astounded with yourself;**[N] **how is it prohibited** to derive **benefit** from **leavened bread** for **all seven** days? Apparently, he holds that it is permitted for one to derive benefit from leavened bread for all seven days of Passover and certainly afterward. The Gemara answers: **It is different there, as the verse said:** "*Matzot* shall be eaten throughout the seven days; and no leavened bread shall be seen with you, **neither shall there be leaven seen with you,** in all your borders" (Exodus 13:7). The phrase "with you" indicates that **it is yours,** i.e., it is still considered to be in one's possession, and it is permitted for him to derive benefit from it.

וְרַבָּנַן: שֶׁלְּךָ אִי אַתָּה רוֹאֶה, אֲבָל אַתָּה רוֹאֶה שֶׁל אֲחֵרִים וְשֶׁל גָּבוֹהַּ. וְאִידָּךְ: תְּרֵי ״לְךָ״ כְּתִיבִי.

The Gemara asks: **And** what do **the Rabbis,** who say that it is prohibited to derive benefit from leavened bread, learn from the phrase "with you"? The Gemara answers: They derive that **you** may **not see your own** leavened bread; **however, you** may **see** that **of others and** that which is consecrated **to God** but remained in one's possession. The Gemara asks: **And** what does **the other** Sage, Rabbi Yosei HaGelili, say about this *halakha*? The Gemara answers: There are **two** occurrences of the phrase **"with you" written.** One indicates that it is permitted to see leavened bread that belongs to a gentile, and the other indicates that one may derive benefit from leavened bread.

וְאִידָּךְ: חַד בְּגוֹי שֶׁכִּיבְּשׁוֹ וְחַד בְּגוֹי שֶׁלֹּא כִּיבְּשׁוֹ. וְאִידָּךְ: תְּלָתָא לְךָ כְּתִיבִי. וְאִידָּךְ: חַד בִּשְׂאוֹר וְחַד בְּחָמֵץ, וּצְרִיכִי.

The Gemara asks: **And** according to the opinion of **the other** Sages, the Rabbis, why is the phrase "with you" written twice? They explain: **One** is written **with regard to a gentile whom he has conquered,** i.e., who is under his control. **And the other** is written **with regard to a gentile whom he has not conquered.** In either case, one is permitted to keep the gentile's leavened bread in his possession on Passover. **And** from where does **the other** Sage, Rabbi Yosei HaGelili, derive this *halakha* that one may see even the leavened bread of a gentile who is under his control? He points out that there are **three** occurrences of the phrase **"with you" written. And** what do **the other** Sages, the Rabbis, learn from the extra instance of the phrase "with you"? They learn that it is used **once** to teach about **leaven, and once** to teach about **leavened bread. And they are** both **necessary** and must be mentioned explicitly, as one cannot derive this principle with regard to leavened bread from leaven or vice versa.

NOTES

Be astounded with yourself – תְּמַהּ עַל עַצְמְךָ: This expression means: How can you make this claim without any explanation or verse to support it? Some explain that the reason Rabbi Yosei HaGelili permits one to derive benefit from leavened bread on Passover is that he adds another positive mitzva with regard to a different issue, so he cannot count this prohibition among the 613 commandments that are traditionally understood to be contained in the Torah (*Mitzpeh Eitan*).

NOTES

Ritual impurity of fat – טוּמְאַת חֵלֶב: It seems that this discussion should be understood as pertaining to a *tereifa*, an animal with a condition that will cause it to die within twelve months. An animal carcass is itself ritually impure, in which case the question would be whether the impurity takes effect upon the fat. However, with regard to a *tereifa* there is no ritual impurity at all (Maharam Ḥalawa).

לימא כתנאי: "יעשה לכל מלאכה", מה תלמוד לומר לכל מלאכה? שיכול למלאכת גבוה יהא מותר, למלאכת הדיוט יהא אסור – תלמוד לומר: "לכל מלאכה", דברי רבי יוסי הגלילי.

The Gemara suggests: **Let us say** this dispute between Ḥizkiya and Rabbi Abbahu with regard to the implication of the phrase: It shall not be eaten, **is parallel to a** dispute between ***tanna'im***. The verse states: "And the fat of the animal carcass, and the fat of that which is torn of beasts, **may be used for any other service;** but you shall surely not eat of it" (Leviticus 7:24). **What** does it mean when **the verse states: "For any other service"? I might** have thought **that** with regard **to the Temple service it should be permitted** to use this fat for the following reason: Because fats may generally be offered on the altar, it is as though it is permitted to consume them; therefore, they may be used for other sacred purposes as well. **However,** I might have thought that with regard **to common use it should be prohibited** to use them, as the verse states: "You shall surely not eat of it." Therefore, **the verse states: "For any other service,"** meaning that its use is permitted in all contexts. This is **the statement of Rabbi Yosei HaGelili.**

רבי עקיבא אומר: שיכול למלאכת הדיוט יהא טהור, למלאכת גבוה יהא טמא – תלמוד לומר: "לכל מלאכה".

Rabbi Akiva says: Although its use is clearly permitted, I **might** have thought **that** despite the fact that an animal carcass is impure, with regard **to common use** its fat **should be** ritually **pure;** however, with regard **to the Temple service it should be** ritually **impure.**[N] Therefore, **the verse states: "For any other service,"** meaning that it is considered pure in all contexts.

ורבי יוסי הגלילי: לטומאה ולטהרה לא איצטריך קרא, כי איצטריך קרא – לאיסור ולהיתר. ורבי עקיבא: איסור והיתר לא צריך קרא, כי איצטריך קרא – לטומאה ולטהרה.

The Gemara explains their dispute: **Rabbi Yosei HaGelili** holds that **with regard to purity and impurity no verse is necessary,** as there is no reason to assume that the fat of an animal carcass is impure. **The verse is necessary to** establish the **prohibited or permitted** status of this fat. **And Rabbi Akiva** holds that to teach whether this fat is **prohibited or permitted no** separate **verse is necessary; it is necessary** to establish its status with regard **to ritual purity or impurity.**

Perek **II**
Daf **23** Amud **b**

מאי לאו בהא קמיפלגי, דרבי יוסי הגלילי סבר: "לא תאכלו" משמע בין איסור אכילה בין איסור הנאה, וכי אתא קרא – למישרייה לנבילה בהנאה הוא דאתא. ורבי עקיבא סבר: איסור אכילה – משמע, איסור הנאה לא משמע. וכי אתא קרא – לטומאה וטהרה!

The Gemara asks: **What, is it not that they disagree about this,** the following issue? **Rabbi Yosei HaGelili holds: "You shall not eat" indicates both the prohibition of eating and the prohibition of** deriving **benefit;** therefore, one may not derive benefit from an animal carcass. **And when the verse came** and said: "For any other service," **it came to permit** one to derive **benefit from an animal carcass. And Rabbi Akiva holds: "You shall not eat" indicates** that there is only **a prohibition of eating; it does not indicate a prohibition of** deriving **benefit.** Therefore, no verse is necessary to learn that it is permitted to derive benefit from an animal carcass. **When the verse came** and said: "For any other service," **it came** to teach about the *halakhot* of **ritual purity and impurity.** Apparently, there is a tannaitic dispute about the meaning of the words: "You shall not eat."

לא, דכולי עלמא "לא תאכלו" – משמע בין איסור אכילה בין איסור הנאה. והכא בהא קמיפלגי; רבי יוסי הגלילי סבר: כשהותרה נבילה – היא הותרה, חלבה וגידה – לא הותרו. וכי איצטריך קרא – להיתר הנאה הוא דאתא. ורבי עקיבא סבר: כשהותרה נבילה – חלבה וגידה נמי הותרו, וכי איצטריך קרא – לטומאה וטהרה.

The Gemara rejects this assumption. **No,** it is possible to say **that everyone** holds that **"You shall not eat" indicates both a prohibition of eating and a prohibition of** deriving **benefit. And here, they disagree about this: Rabbi Yosei HaGelili holds that when it was permitted** to derive benefit from **an animal carcass,** the carcass itself **was permitted;** however, **its fat and its sinews were not permitted. And the** phrase "for any other service" in the **verse is necessary to permit** one to derive **benefit** from this fat. However, **Rabbi Akiva holds: When it was permitted** to derive benefit **from an animal carcass, it was also permitted** to derive benefit from **its fat and sinews.** Therefore, the phrase "for any other service" in **the verse is necessary for** the issue of **purity and impurity.**

וְרַבִּי יוֹסֵי הַגְּלִילִי, אַשְׁכַּחַן חֵלֶב דְּשָׁרְיֵיהּ רַחֲמָנָא בַּהֲנָאָה, אֶלָּא גִּיד נֵימָא דְּאָסוּר! אִיבָּעֵית אֵימָא: הָכִי נַמִּי דְּאָסוּר, אִיבָּעֵית אֵימָא: מַיְיתִי לָהּ בְּקַל וָחוֹמֶר; וּמַה חֵלֶב שֶׁעָנוּשׁ כָּרֵת – מוּתָּר בַּהֲנָאָה, גִּיד שֶׁאֵינוֹ עָנוּשׁ כָּרֵת – לֹא כָּל שֶׁכֵּן?!

The Gemara asks: **And** according to the opinion of **Rabbi Yosei HaGelili, we find that the Merciful One** explicitly **permits** one to derive **benefit from fat; however, let us say** that **the sinew** of the sciatic nerve **is prohibited.** The Gemara answers: **If you wish, say** that **it is indeed so that it is prohibited** to derive benefit from the sciatic nerve. And **if you wish, say** instead that one is permitted to derive benefit from the sciatic nerve, and Rabbi Yosei HaGelili **derives that** the sciatic nerve is permitted **through** an ***a fortiori*** inference: **If** with regard to forbidden **fat, for which one is punished with *karet*** if he eats it intentionally, **it is permitted** to derive **benefit,** with regard to the sciatic **nerve,** for which **the punishment** for one who eats it **is not *karet*, all the more so** is it **not** clear that it is permitted to derive benefit?

וְרַבִּי שִׁמְעוֹן דְּאָסַר; אִיכָּא לְמִיפְרַךְ: מָה לַחֵלֶב שֶׁכֵּן הוּתַּר מִכְּלָלוֹ אֵצֶל חַיָּה, תֹּאמַר בְּגִיד שֶׁלֹּא הוּתַּר מִכְּלָלוֹ אֵצֶל חַיָּה.

The Gemara asks: **And** why does **Rabbi Shimon, who prohibits** deriving benefit from the sciatic nerve, not accept this *a fortiori* inference? The Gemara answers: This inference **can be refuted,**[N] as it is possible to say: **What is** unique **to fat?** It is **that it is released from its general** prohibition **with regard to non-domesticated animals,** as the prohibition only applies to the fats of kosher domesticated animals. **Can you say** the same **with regard to the** sciatic **nerve, which is not released from its general** prohibition **with regard to non-domesticated animals** and remains prohibited? Apparently, in some ways the prohibition of the sciatic nerve is more stringent than that of fat.

וְאִידָךְ: בִּבְהֵמָה קָאָמְרִינַן, בִּבְהֵמָה מִיהַת לָא אִישְׁתְּרִי.

The Gemara asks: **And** how does **the other** Sage, Rabbi Yosei, who permits one to derive benefit from the sciatic nerve based on this *a fortiori* inference, respond? The Gemara says: When **we state** this *a fortiori* inference, it is **with regard to a domesticated animal; in any case, with regard to a domesticated animal** its fat **is not permitted.** Since with regard to a domesticated animal the prohibition of fat is more stringent than that of the sciatic nerve, the *a fortiori* inference is valid.

מִכְּדִי אוֹתְבִינְהוּ כָּל הָנֵי קְרָאֵי וְשָׁנֵינְהוּ, חִזְקִיָּה וְרַבִּי אַבָּהוּ בְּמַאי פְּלִיגִי? בְּחָמֵץ בַּפֶּסַח וְאַלִּיבָּא דְּרַבָּנַן, בְּשׁוֹר הַנִּסְקָל וְאַלִּיבָּא דְּדִבְרֵי הַכֹּל. חִזְקִיָּה נָפֵיק לֵיהּ מִ״לֹּא יֵאָכֵל״, וְרַבִּי אַבָּהוּ נָפֵיק לֵיהּ מִנְּבֵילָה.

After discussing numerous cases that involve prohibitions of eating and deriving benefit, the Gemara asks: **Since we raised objections from all of these verses and answered them,** and in every case it is apparent that despite the fact that the verse said: "You shall not eat" there was no dispute as to whether or not one may derive benefit from these items, then **with regard to what** issue **do Ḥizkiya and Rabbi Abbahu disagree?**[N] The Gemara answers: They disagree **with** regard to **leavened bread on Passover, in accordance with** the opinion of **the Rabbis,** who prohibit one to derive benefit from it; and they disagree **with** regard to **an ox that is stoned, in accordance with everyone.** The Gemara explains: **Ḥizkiya derived** that it is prohibited to derive benefit in this case **from** the words: **"It shall not be eaten," and Rabbi Abbahu derived** that it is prohibited **from** the fact that the Torah explicitly had to permit one to derive benefit in the case of **an animal carcass.**

מִכְּדִי, בֵּין לְמָר וּבֵין לְמָר אֲסוּרִין בַּהֲנָאָה – מַאי בֵּינַיְיהוּ? אִיכָּא בֵּינַיְיהוּ: חוּלִּין שֶׁנִּשְׁחֲטוּ בָּעֲזָרָה. חִזְקִיָּה סָבַר ״לֹא יֵאָכֵל״ – לְמַעוֹטֵי הָנֵי, ״אֹתוֹ״ – לְמַעוֹטֵי חוּלִּין שֶׁנִּשְׁחֲטוּ בָּעֲזָרָה.

The Gemara asks: **Now, both according to** the one **Master and according to** the other **Master, it is prohibited** to derive **benefit** from these items. The fact that they disagree about the source of this *halakha* notwithstanding, **what is** the practical difference **between them?** The Gemara answers: The practical difference **between them is** with regard to **non-sacrificial animals that were slaughtered in the** Temple **courtyard. Ḥizkiya holds: "It shall not be eaten"** comes **to exclude these** cases of leavened bread and the ox that is stoned. Although in most cases a prohibition against eating does not extend to a prohibition against deriving benefit, the language of the verse in these cases indicates that there is a prohibition against deriving benefit as well. Furthermore, **"It shall be thrown to the dog"** comes **to exclude non-sacrificial animals slaughtered in the** Temple **courtyard,** indicating that it is prohibited to derive benefit from them.

NOTES

This can be refuted – אִיכָּא לְמִיפְרַךְ: Even though an *a fortiori* inference appears to be one of the most straightforward methods for expounding upon the Torah, its application is no simple matter. One of the ways to reject an *a fortiori* inference is through the type of refutation brought here. An *a fortiori* inference is based on the assumption that one case is more stringent than another. If one can prove that the supposed lenient case has a more stringent element, or that the stringent case has a more lenient element, then the *a fortiori* inference has been undermined. Even if the refutation does not undermine the overall imbalance in stringency between the cases, it still may be enough to prove that the *a fortiori* inference cannot serve as a basis for halakhic deductions in this case.

With regard to what do they disagree – בְּמַאי פְּלִיגִי: This question is surprising in this case, as the difference in principle between the two opinions, which is the typical answer to this question, is clear. The principle underlying each opinion is clearly presented, given all the exceptions that have been cited, and it seems that the principle each one advances is actually quite limited, resulting only in each finding different sources for the same *halakhot*. The more pertinent question is the next question asked by the Gemara: What is the practical difference between the two opinions? Nonetheless, it appears that this question is asked here as a means to summarize the lengthy discussion in the Gemara.

רַבִּי אַבָּהוּ סָבַר: ״אֹתוֹ״ – לְמַעוֹטֵי הָנֵי, חוּלִּין שֶׁנִּשְׁחֲטוּ בָּעֲזָרָה – לָאו דְּאוֹרַיְיתָא נִינְהוּ.

However, **Rabbi Abbahu holds** that according to Rabbi Yehuda, who maintained that the prohibition against eating an animal carcass cannot be used to derive the prohibition against deriving benefit: **"It** shall be thrown to the dog" comes **to exclude these** two cases, leavened bread and an ox that is stoned, where deriving benefit is prohibited. And the prohibition to derive benefit from **non-sacrificial animals slaughtered in the** Temple **courtyard is not by Torah law,** as there is no source from which to derive this prohibition. Therefore, the only practical difference between them is whether the prohibition of deriving benefit from non-sacrificial animals slaughtered in the Temple courtyard is by Torah law or by rabbinic law.

יְתֵיב הַהוּא מֵרַבָּנַן קַמֵּיהּ דְּרַבִּי שְׁמוּאֵל בַּר נַחְמָנִי, וְיָתֵיב וְקָאָמַר מִשְּׁמֵיהּ דְּרַבִּי יְהוֹשֻׁעַ בֶּן לֵוִי: מִנַּיִן לְכָל אִיסּוּרִין שֶׁבַּתּוֹרָה דִּכִי הֵיכִי דַּאֲסוּרִין בַּאֲכִילָה הָכִי נַמִי אֲסוּרִין בַּהֲנָאָה, וּמַאי נִיהוּ – חָמֵץ בַּפֶּסַח וְשׁוֹר הַנִּסְקָל. ״מִנַּיִן״?! תֵּיפּוֹק לֵיהּ מִ״לֹּא יֵאָכֵל״! ״לֹא יֵאָכֵל״ – אִיסּוּר אֲכִילָה מַשְׁמַע לֵיהּ, אִיסּוּר הֲנָאָה – לֹא מַשְׁמַע לֵיהּ.

The Gemara relates: **One of the Sages sat before Rabbi Shmuel bar Naḥmani, and he sat and said in the name of Rabbi Yehoshua ben Levi: From where is it derived** with regard **to all the prohibitions in the Torah that just as it is prohibited to eat them, so too, it is prohibited to benefit from them? And what are** the prohibited objects to which this statement refers? They are **leavened bread on Passover and an ox that is stoned.** The Gemara asks: Why ask **from where? Derive** the prohibition from the phrase: **"It shall not be eaten."** The Gemara answers that **he derived a prohibition of eating** this item from: **"It shall not be eaten";** however, **he did not derive a prohibition of** deriving **benefit**[N] from this phrase.

תֵּיפּוֹק לֵיהּ מִנְּבֵילָה! סָבַר לָהּ כְּרַבִּי יְהוּדָה, דְּאָמַר: דְּבָרִים כִּכְתָבָן.

The Gemara challenges: **Derive** this general prohibition against deriving benefit **from** the fact that the Torah had to explicitly permit one to benefit from an **animal carcass.** The Gemara answers: Rabbi Yehoshua ben Levi **holds in accordance with** the opinion of **Rabbi Yehuda, who said** with regard to an animal carcass: The **matters are as they are written,** and the words in the verse do not indicate anything beyond their simple meaning.

אִי סָבַר לָהּ כְּרַבִּי יְהוּדָה – תֵּיפּוֹק לֵיהּ מֵהֵיכָא דְּנָפְקָא לֵיהּ לְרַבִּי יְהוּדָה מִ״לַּכֶּלֶב תַּשְׁלִיכוּן אֹתוֹ״!

The Gemara challenges: **If he holds in accordance with** the opinion of **Rabbi Yehuda,** then **let him derive** this *halakha* **from where Rabbi Yehuda derives it,** i.e., **from** the verse: "And you shall be sacred men unto Me; therefore you shall not eat any flesh that is torn of beasts in the field; **you shall cast it to the dog**" (Exodus 22:30). Rabbi Yehuda expounded that one may throw it to a dog, but one may not throw any of the other prohibited items mentioned in the Torah to a dog. From this he infers that it is prohibited to derive benefit from leavened bread on Passover or from other similar items.

קָסָבַר: חוּלִּין שֶׁנִּשְׁחֲטוּ בָּעֲזָרָה דְּאוֹרַיְיתָא, מִנַּיִן? דִּכְתִיב: ״כׇּל חַטָּאת אֲשֶׁר יוּבָא מִדָּמָהּ וגו׳״.

The Gemara responds: This Sage **holds** that the prohibition to derive benefit from **non-sacrificial animals that were slaughtered in the** Temple **courtyard is by Torah law,** and that it is the word "it" in the verse that indicates they are prohibited. And **from where** is it derived that this prohibition against deriving benefit applies to leavened bread and to an ox that is stoned as well? **As it is written: "And no sin-offering, of which any of the blood is brought** into the Tent of Meeting to make atonement in the sacred place, shall be eaten; it shall be burnt with fire" (Leviticus 6:23).

שֶׁאֵין תַּלְמוּד לוֹמַר ״בָּאֵשׁ תִּשָּׂרֵף״ וּמַה תַּלְמוּד לוֹמַר בָּאֵשׁ תִּשָּׂרֵף? אִם אֵינוֹ עִנְיָן לְגוּפוֹ, דִּכְתִיב ״וְהִנֵּה שֹׂרָף״ – תְּנֵהוּ עִנְיָן לְכָל אִיסּוּרִין שֶׁבַּתּוֹרָה.

As there is **no** need for **the verse to state: "It shall be burnt with fire"; And** for **what** purpose then does **the verse state: "It shall be burnt with fire"? If it does not** apply to the subject **matter itself** in its context, **as it is** already **written:** "And Moshe diligently inquired about the goat of the sin-offering, **and, behold, it was burnt"** (Leviticus 10:16), **apply it to the matter of all the prohibitions in the Torah.**

NOTES

He did not derive a prohibition of deriving benefit – אִיסּוּר הֲנָאָה לֹא מַשְׁמַע לֵיהּ: It appears that Rabbi Yehoshua ben Levi is presenting an alternate opinion of how to understand the verses. Rabbi Abbahu contends that "You shall not eat" indicates that it is prohibited both to eat and to derive benefit from the item, while according to Ḥizkiya this means that one is prohibited only to eat the item. However, Rabbi Abbahu and Ḥizkiya agree that the expression "It shall not be eaten" indicates that one is prohibited to derive benefit from a certain item as well. Rabbi Yehoshua ben Levi, on the other hand, claims that even this phrase indicates only that it is prohibited to eat the given item; however, deriving benefit from it is permitted.

וְאִם אֵינוֹ עִנְיָן לַאֲכִילָה – תְּנֵהוּ עִנְיָן לְאִיסּוּר הֲנָאָה.

And if it does not apply to **the matter of** the prohibition against **eating,** as the prohibition against eating these items has already been mentioned, **apply it to the matter of the prohibition of** deriving **benefit.**

אִי מָה כָּאן בִּשְׂרֵיפָה – אַף כׇּל אִיסּוּרִין שֶׁבַּתּוֹרָה בִּשְׂרֵיפָה! אָמַר קְרָא: ״בַּקֹּדֶשׁ בָּאֵשׁ תִּשָּׂרֵף״, בַּקֹּדֶשׁ – בִּשְׂרֵיפָה, וְאֵין כׇּל אִיסּוּרִין שֶׁבַּתּוֹרָה בִּשְׂרֵיפָה.

The Gemara continues: **Lest** one say that the verse indicates that **just as here,** the sin-offering is disposed of **with burning, so too, all the prohibited** items **in the Torah** must be disposed of **with burning,** therefore **the verse said: "In the sacred place…shall be burnt with fire"** (Leviticus 6:23).[N] This indicates that only that which is disqualified **in the sacred place** is disposed of **with burning, but all** other **prohibited** items **in the Torah** need **not** be disposed of **with burning.**

וְהַאי ״בַּקֹּדֶשׁ בָּאֵשׁ תִּשָּׂרֵף״ לְהָכִי הוּא דַּאֲתָא? הַאי מִיבְּעֵי לֵיהּ לְכִדְרַבִּי שִׁמְעוֹן! דְּתַנְיָא, רַבִּי שִׁמְעוֹן אוֹמֵר: ״בַּקֹּדֶשׁ בָּאֵשׁ תִּשָּׂרֵף״ – לִימֵּד עַל חַטָּאת שֶׁשּׂוֹרְפִין אוֹתָהּ בַּקֹּדֶשׁ, וְאֵין לִי אֶלָּא זוֹ בִּלְבַד, פְּסוּלֵי קׇדְשֵׁי קָדָשִׁים וְאֵימוּרֵי קָדָשִׁים קַלִּים מִנַּיִן – תַּלְמוּד לוֹמַר: ״(וְכׇל) בַּקֹּדֶשׁ בָּאֵשׁ תִּשָּׂרֵף״.

Rabbi Shmuel bar Naḥmani asked: **And did this** verse: **"In the sacred place…shall be burnt with fire," come to** teach **this** *halakha*? **It is needed** to teach **in accordance with** the opinion of **Rabbi Shimon, as it was taught** in a *baraita* that **Rabbi Shimon says: "In the sacred place…shall be burnt with fire"**; this **taught that one** must **burn** a disqualified **sin-offering in the sacred place,** and not outside the Temple. **And I have only** derived **this,** meaning the sin-offering. **From where do I derive that disqualified offerings of the most sacred order and portions consumed** on the altar, such as the fats **of offerings of minor sanctity** that become impure, are burned in the Temple courtyard? **The verse states: "In the sacred place…shall be burnt with fire."** This indicates that any disqualified offering must be burned in the sacred place.

אֲמַר לֵיהּ: רַבִּי יוֹנָתָן רַבָּךְ מֵהַאי קְרָא קָאָמַר לַהּ: ״וְאִם יִוָּתֵר מִבְּשַׂר הַמִּלֻּאִים וּמִן הַלֶּחֶם עַד הַבֹּקֶר וגו׳״ שֶׁאֵין תַּלְמוּד לוֹמַר ״לֹא יֵאָכֵל״, וּמָה תַּלְמוּד לוֹמַר ״לֹא יֵאָכֵל״ – אִם אֵינוֹ עִנְיָן לְגוּפֵיהּ, דְּהָא כְּתִיב: ״וְשָׂרַפְתָּ אֶת הַנּוֹתָר בָּאֵשׁ״ – תְּנֵהוּ עִנְיָן לִשְׁאָר אִיסּוּרִין שֶׁבַּתּוֹרָה. וְאִם אֵינוֹ עִנְיָן לַאֲכִילָה – תְּנֵהוּ עִנְיָן לְאִיסּוּר הֲנָאָה.

The Sage who taught this *halakha* to Rabbi Shmuel bar Naḥmani **said to him: Rabbi Yonatan, your teacher, said that** same *halakha* **from this verse: "And if the flesh of the consecration** offering, **or of the bread, remains until the morning,** then you shall burn the leftover with fire; it shall not be eaten, because it is sacred" (Exodus 29:34). **As** there is no need for **the verse to state: "It shall not be eaten," what** is the meaning when **the verse states: "It shall not be eaten"? If it does not refer to the** subject **matter itself, as it is** already **written** explicitly: **"Then you shall burn the leftover with fire,"** which indicates that one may not eat it, **refer it to the matter of the other prohibitions in the Torah. And if it does not refer to the matter of** the prohibition against **eating,** as eating these items is explicitly prohibited, **refer it to the matter of the prohibition of** deriving **benefit.** This indicates that it is prohibited for one to derive benefit from any item that it is prohibited for him to eat.

אִי מָה כָּאן בִּשְׂרֵיפָה, אַף כׇּל אִיסּוּרִין שֶׁבַּתּוֹרָה בִּשְׂרֵיפָה – אָמַר קְרָא ״וְשָׂרַפְתָּ אֶת הַנּוֹתָר״ – נוֹתָר בִּשְׂרֵיפָה, וְאֵין כׇּל אִיסּוּרִין שֶׁבַּתּוֹרָה בִּשְׂרֵיפָה.

The Gemara continues: **Lest** one say that the verse indicates that **just as here,** the sin-offering is disposed of **with burning, so too, all the prohibited** items **in the Torah,** from which one may not benefit, must be disposed of **with burning,** therefore **the verse said: "You shall burn the leftover,"** indicating that the **leftover**[N] sacrificial meat must be disposed of **with burning; however, all** other **prohibitions in the Torah** need **not** be disposed of **with burning,** despite the fact that it is prohibited to derive benefit from them.

וְהַאי ״לֹא יֵאָכֵל״ לְהָכִי הוּא דַּאֲתָא? הַאי מִיבְּעֵי לֵיהּ לְכִדְרַבִּי אֶלְעָזָר, דְּאָמַר רַבִּי אֶלְעָזָר: ״לֹא יֵאָכֵל כִּי קֹדֶשׁ הוּא״ – כֹּל שֶׁבַּקֹּדֶשׁ פָּסוּל בָּא הַכָּתוּב לִיתֵּן לֹא תַעֲשֶׂה עַל אֲכִילָתוֹ!

The Gemara challenges: **And did this** phrase: **"It shall not be eaten," come to** teach **this** prohibition against deriving benefit? **This** phrase **is needed** to teach **in accordance with** the opinion of **Rabbi Elazar, as Rabbi Elazar said** with regard to the statement in the verse: **"It shall not be eaten, because it is sacred,"** that **the verse comes to place a negative** mitzva of **eating on whatever has been** rendered **disqualified in the sacred place.** In other words, this verse teaches a general *halakha* that one who eats from offerings that have been disqualified in the Temple transgresses a negative mitzva and is liable to be flogged. It teaches nothing with regard to a prohibition against deriving benefit.

NOTES

In the sacred place…shall be burnt with fire – בַּקֹּדֶשׁ בָּאֵשׁ תִּשָּׂרֵף: It seems that the verse is expounded upon in the following manner: The verse says: "And any sin-offering, from which any of the blood is brought into the Tent of Meeting to make atonement in the sacred place, shall not be eaten; it shall be burned with fire." The Gemara singles out certain words from this phrase, creating the adapted phrase: "In the sacred place…shall be burned with fire." This new phrase indicates that any item that became impure in the sacred place in the Temple must be burned with fire (Maharam Ḥalawa).

Leftover – נוֹתָר: Part of an offering left over after the time permitted for it to be eaten. One who eats the leftover portion of an offering is subject to *karet*. The Sages decreed that the leftover portion should be considered ritually impure, so that the priests would be prompt and meticulous in its removal.

אָמַר אַבַּיֵי: לְעוֹלָם מִקְּרָא קַמָּא, וְאֵיפוּךְ. דְּלִיכְתּוֹב "בָּאֵשׁ תִּשָּׂרֵף" וְלָא בָּעֵי "לֹא תֵאָכֵל", מַה תַּלְמוּד לוֹמַר "לֹא תֵאָכֵל"? אִם אֵינוֹ עִנְיָן לְגוּפוֹ, דְּנָפְקָא לֵיהּ מִדְּרַבִּי אֶלְעָזָר – תְּנֵהוּ עִנְיָן לְכָל אִיסּוּרִין שֶׁבַּתּוֹרָה. וְאִם אֵינוֹ עִנְיָן לַאֲכִילָה – תְּנֵהוּ עִנְיָן לְאִיסּוּר הֲנָאָה.

Abaye said: Actually, derive this *halakha* **from the first verse** cited by Rabbi Yehoshua ben Levi: "And any sin-offering, of which any of the blood is brought into the tent of meeting to make atonement in the sacred place, shall not be eaten; it shall be burnt with fire" (Leviticus 6:23). **And reverse** the construct of his exposition. **Let** the verse **write: "It shall be burnt with fire," and it** will **not need** to write: **"Shall not be eaten."** For **what** purpose then does **the verse state: "It shall not be eaten"? If it does not apply to** the subject **matter itself, as that was** already **derived from** the statement of **Rabbi Elazar** that whatever has been rendered disqualified in the sacred place may not be eaten, **apply it to all** other **prohibitions in the Torah,** including leavened bread on Passover and a stoned ox. **And if it does not** apply to the prohibition against **eating,** which is written explicitly, then **apply it to the prohibition of** deriving **benefit.**

אִי מַה כָּאן בִּשְׂרֵיפָה, אַף כָּל אִיסּוּרִין שֶׁבַּתּוֹרָה בִּשְׂרֵיפָה – אָמַר קְרָא "הַנּוֹתָר" – הַנּוֹתָר בִּשְׂרֵיפָה, וְאֵין כָּל אִיסּוּרִין שֶׁבַּתּוֹרָה בִּשְׂרֵיפָה.

The Gemara asks: **Lest** one say that the verse indicates that **just as here,** the leftover sacrificial meat is disposed of **with burning, so too, all the prohibited** items **in the Torah,** from which one may not benefit, must be disposed of **with burning,** therefore **the verse said:** "You shall burn **the leftover,"** indicating that the **leftover** sacrificial meat must **be** disposed of **with burning; however, all** other **prohibited** items **in the Torah** need **not** be disposed of **with burning.**

אֲמַר לֵיהּ רַב פַּפָּא לְאַבַּיֵי: וְאֵימָא לְיִחוּדֵי לֵיהּ לָאו לְגוּפֵיהּ הוּא דַּאֲתָא? דְּאִי מִדְּרַבִּי אֶלְעָזָר – אֵין לוֹקִין עַל לָאו שֶׁבִּכְלָלוֹת!

Rav Pappa said to Abaye: And why do you hold that the phrase: "You shall not eat," describing the sin-offering that was sacrificed inside the Sanctuary, is not needed for other purposes? **Say** that this expression **comes** in order **to designate a negative** mitzva for this prohibition **itself. As, if** this prohibition were derived only **from** the source quoted by **Rabbi Elazar,** there will be a prohibition to eat the meat of the sin-offering whose blood was brought into the sanctuary; however, one would not be liable to be flogged for violating it, because **one is not flogged for** violating **a negative** mitzva **stated in general terms.**[N] One is not flogged for violating a negative mitzva that contains several different prohibitions, such as this one, which refers to all disqualified offerings. This is because the negative mitzva is formulated too broadly. Therefore, it is possible to say that when the Torah states: "You shall not eat" with regard to this issue, it is teaching that there is a particular prohibition here and that one is flogged for violating it. If so, the verse cannot indicate a general prohibition against deriving benefit.

אֶלָּא אָמַר רַב פַּפָּא: מֵהָכָא "וְהַבָּשָׂר אֲשֶׁר יִגַּע בְּכָל טָמֵא לֹא יֵאָכֵל בָּאֵשׁ יִשָּׂרֵף", שֶׁאֵין תַּלְמוּד לוֹמַר "לֹא יֵאָכֵל", מַה תַּלְמוּד לוֹמַר לֹא יֵאָכֵל?

Rather, this suggestion should be rejected, and **Rav Pappa said** that one derives this *halakha* **from here: "And the flesh that touches any impure thing shall not be eaten; it shall be burnt with fire.** And as for the flesh, every one that is pure may eat of it" (Leviticus 7:19). **As** there is **no** need for **the verse to state: "It shall not be eaten," what** does it mean when **the verse states: "It shall not be eaten"?**

אִם אֵינוֹ עִנְיָן לְגוּפוֹ, דְּהָא נָפְקָא לֵיהּ מִקַּל וָחוֹמֶר מִמַּעֲשֵׂר הַקַּל: וּמַה מַּעֲשֵׂר הַקַּל אָמְרָה תּוֹרָה "לֹא בִעַרְתִּי מִמֶּנּוּ בְּטָמֵא", בְּשַׂר קֹדֶשׁ חָמוּר לֹא כׇּל שֶׁכֵּן?!

If it does not refer to the subject **matter itself, as that** can be **derived by** means of **an *a fortiori*** inference **from** the second **tithe,** the *halakhot* of **which** are more **lenient** than those of offerings, then it must refer to something else. As it is possible to say: **If** with regard to the second **tithe, which is** more **lenient** because it does not have the status of an offering, **the Torah said** that when one recites the confession over the tithes, when destroying the tithes remaining in one's possession that had not yet been given to the appropriate recipient, he says: "I have not eaten from it in my mourning, **neither have I removed it while impure**" (Deuteronomy 26:14), indicating that it is prohibited for one to remove tithes while impure, then with regard to **consecrated meat,** which is more **stringent, all the more so** is it **not** clear that it may not be eaten while a person is impure?

NOTES

Negative mitzva stated in general terms – לָאו שֶׁבִּכְלָלוֹת: A Torah prohibition containing several particular prohibitions of different kinds. For example, the verse: "You shall not eat anything with the blood" (Leviticus 19:26) contains several prohibitions, among them the prohibition against eating an animal before it is dead, the prohibition against eating a sacrificial animal before its blood has been sprinkled on the altar, and the prohibition forbidding judges who have condemned a man to death from eating on the day of his execution. No punishment is administered by an earthly court for the violation of a prohibition of this kind, even if one violates all the individual prohibitions at once.

וְכִי תֵּימָא: אֵין מַזְהִירִין מִן הַדִּין – הֶקֵּישָׁא הוּא, דִּכְתִיב: "לֹא תוּכַל לֶאֱכֹל בִּשְׁעָרֶיךָ מַעְשַׂר דְּגָנְךָ תִּירֹשְׁךָ וְיִצְהָרֶךָ וּבְכֹרֹת בְּקָרְךָ וגו'".

And if you say that there is a general principle that **we do not warn,** i.e., we may not deduce a prohibition, **through logical derivation**[N] alone, then one could respond that his issue is not only derived through an *a fortiori* inference; rather, **it is** also derived from an analogy based on **a juxtaposition. As it is written: "You may not eat within your gates the tithe of your grain, or of your wine, or of your oil, or the firstborn of your herd** or of your flock, nor any of your vows which you have vowed, nor your voluntary offerings, nor the offering of your hand" (Deuteronomy 12:17). Since the verse itself juxtaposes tithes to offerings, it indicates that there is a prohibition with regard to offerings just as there is with regard to tithes.

מַה תַּלְמוּד לוֹמַר "לֹא יֵאָכֵל"? אִם אֵינוֹ עִנְיָן לְגוּפוֹ – תְּנֵהוּ עִנְיָן לְכׇל אִיסּוּרִין שֶׁבַּתּוֹרָה, וְאִם אֵינוֹ עִנְיָן לַאֲכִילָה – תְּנֵהוּ עִנְיָן לַהֲנָאָה.

The Gemara continues explaining Rav Pappa's opinion: For **what purpose** then does **the verse state: "It shall not be eaten"** with regard to impure consecrated meat? **If it does not** apply to **the** subject **matter** of this verse **itself,** as that prohibition is derived from the second tithe, then **apply it to the matter of all prohibited** items **in the Torah. And if it does not** apply to the prohibition against **eating,** since that is clear, **apply it to the prohibition of** deriving **benefit.**

אִי מָה כָּאן בִּשְׂרֵיפָה, אַף כׇּל אִיסּוּרִין שֶׁבַּתּוֹרָה בִּשְׂרֵיפָה – אָמַר קְרָא "הַנּוֹתָר" – הַנּוֹתָר בִּשְׂרֵיפָה וְאֵין כׇּל אִיסּוּרִין שֶׁבַּתּוֹרָה בִּשְׂרֵיפָה,

And if you say: **Lest** one say that the verse indicates that **just as here,** the meat that became impure in the Temple is disposed of **with burning, so too, all the prohibited** items **in the Torah** must be disposed of **with burning,** therefore **the verse said: "The leftover,"** indicating **that the leftover** sacrificial meat must be disposed of **with burning; however, all** other **prohibited** items **in the Torah** need **not** be disposed of **with burning.**

אֲמַר לֵיהּ רָבִינָא לְרַב אָשֵׁי: וְאֵימָא לַעֲבוֹר עָלָיו בִּשְׁנֵי לָאוִין? לָאו מִי אָמַר אַבָּיֵי: אָכַל פּוּטִיתָא – לוֹקֶה אַרְבַּע,

Ravina said to Rav Ashi: And say that this expression: "It shall not be eaten," comes to teach not the prohibition against deriving benefit, but rather that one who transgresses this negative mitzva **violates two prohibitions.** And there is precedent for such an explanation, as **didn't Abaye say** with regard to a parallel case: **If one ate a small water creature [*putita*],**[NB] **he is flogged** with **four** sets of lashes[N] because one violates four prohibitions when eating such a creature? Two of these prohibitions are found in the verse that discusses all types of creeping animals: "You shall not make yourselves detestable with any swarming thing that swarms, neither shall you make yourselves impure with them, that you should be defiled by them" (Leviticus 11:43). A third prohibition applies to creeping animals that live in the water, as the verses say: "And all that have neither fins nor scales…They shall be a detestable thing unto you; you shall not eat of their flesh" (Leviticus 11:10–11). A fourth prohibition is cited in the verse: "And whatever does not have fins and scales you shall not eat; it is impure unto you" (Deuteronomy 14:10).

נְמָלָה – לוֹקֶה חָמֵשׁ,

Similarly, if one ate **an ant, he is flogged** with **five** sets of lashes, two sets for the previously mentioned prohibitions of eating a creeping animal, a third based on the verse: "And every creeping thing that swarms upon the earth is a detestable thing; it shall not be eaten" (Leviticus 11:41), and a fourth based on the verse: "All creeping things that swarm upon the earth, them you shall not eat; for they are a detestable thing" (Leviticus 11:42). A fifth prohibition is stated in the verse: "You shall not make yourselves impure through every creeping thing that swarms upon the earth" (Leviticus 11:44).

BACKGROUND

Small water creature [*putita*] – פּוּטִיתָא: Though it is universally agreed that a *putita* is a small water creature, there is no consensus among commentators or academic scholars as to what specifically this creature is. Rabbeinu Yeruḥam translates it as caracol, the Spanish word for snail. The Rambam, on the other hand, deduces from the enumerated punishment (see note) that the *putita* must possess a set of characteristics not seen together in any animal currently known to man, eliciting from the Ra'avad the frustrated pronouncement: "This gatherer has gathered things that do not exist in the world!"

Marine snail

NOTES

We do not warn through logical derivation – אֵין מַזְהִירִין מִן הַדִּין: This is based on the fundamental principle that a court may not administer punishment if there were no witnesses who warned the perpetrator before he committed the transgression. So too, it is understood that one cannot be punished for a transgression unless the Torah issues a warning that the act is prohibited. Such warnings cannot be deduced through an *a fortiori* inference alone, although they may be deduced through a verbal analogy and other common methods of extrapolation passed down through tradition. The reason for this is that one cannot be certain of the particular reasoning behind a prohibition; therefore, although a prohibition may make logical sense, that does not guarantee that it is, in fact, prohibited.

If one ate a small water creature – אָכַל פּוּטִיתָא: One transgresses the prohibition of eating this creature even if one consumes less than an olive-bulk. This is because it is a whole creature in its original form, and its consumption is deemed significant.

He is flogged with four sets of lashes – לוֹקֶה אַרְבַּע: In his introduction to *Sefer HaMitzvot*, the Rambam lists basic principles about enumerating negative mitzvot. As a general rule, he states: Even if a prohibition is mentioned many times, one does not commit numerous violations if he transgresses it, as the multiple sources serve merely as a repetition of the same principle. He cites several proofs to support this opinion. Based on this opinion, he presents a somewhat forced explanation of the Gemara's statement here with regard to one who eats a *putita*. The Rambam claims that this is a unique creature to which several different categories of prohibition apply: It is a creeping animal that lives in the water, it is a flying insect, and it also can live on the land. However, most authorities follow the opinion of the *ge'onim*, understanding this Gemara in a straightforward way to mean that one receives several sets of lashes for violating the numerous prohibitions pertaining to the same act.

צִירְעָה – לוֹקֶה שֵׁשׁ! אֲמַר לֵיהּ: כׇּל הֵיכָא דְּאִיכָּא לְמִדְרַשׁ – דָּרְשִׁינַן, וְלָא מוֹקְמִינַן בְּלָאוֵי יְתֵירֵי.

If one ate **a hornet, he is flogged** with **six** sets of lashes. Since a hornet creeps along the ground, all of the previously mentioned prohibitions with regard to an ant apply to it as well. An additional prohibition is stated in the following verse: "And all flying insects are impure to you; they shall not be eaten" (Deuteronomy 14:19). Based on this precedent, it is possible to say that the addition of the phrase "It shall not be eaten" with regard to impure meat indicates merely an additional negative mitzva for which one would be punished; however, it does not necessarily indicate a prohibition to derive benefit. Rav Ashi **said to him: Anywhere that it is possible to expound** a new *halakha*, **we expound, and we do not establish** the verse as containing **additional negative** mitzvot with regard to that same prohibition.

״וְהַבָּשָׂר אֲשֶׁר יִגַּע בְּכׇל טָמֵא לֹא יֵאָכֵל״ דְּרֵישֵׁיהּ לָמָּה לִי – לְרַבּוֹת עֵצִים וּלְבוֹנָה. ״וְהַבָּשָׂר כׇּל טָהוֹר יֹאכַל בָּשָׂר״ דְּסֵיפֵיהּ לָמָּה לִי – לְרַבּוֹת אֵימוּרִין.

The Gemara asks: **Why do I** need **the beginning** of the verse: **"And the flesh that touches any impure thing shall not be eaten"** (Leviticus 7:19)? The Gemara explains: This comes **to include wood and incense;**[NH] although they are not eaten, they are susceptible to ritual impurity of foods. The Gemara asks: **Why do I** need **the end** of this verse: **"And as for the flesh, every one that is pure may eat of it"** (Leviticus 7:19)? The Gemara answers: This comes **to include** the **sacrificial parts** of the animal offered on the altar, such as the fats; they, too, have the legal status of meat and are susceptible to ritual impurity of foods. If these portions become ritually impure and one eats them, even if he is pure, he is liable to be flogged.

אֵימוּרִין מֵהָתָם נָפְקָא, דְּתַנְיָא: ״וְהַנֶּפֶשׁ אֲשֶׁר תֹּאכַל בָּשָׂר מִזֶּבַח הַשְּׁלָמִים אֲשֶׁר לַה׳״ – לְרַבּוֹת אֶת הָאֵימוּרִין!

The Gemara challenges: The *halakha* that these **sacrificial parts** can become impure and are then prohibited to be eaten **is derived from there,** i.e., from another source, **as it was taught** in a *baraita*: **"But the soul that eats from the flesh of the sacrifice of peace-offerings, which belong to the Lord,** having his impurity upon him, that soul shall be cut off from his people" (Leviticus 7:20). The added words "which belong to the Lord" come **to include** these **sacrificial parts,** which are meant to be offered to God and not eaten by other people, within this prohibition against eating sacrificial meat when it is impure.

הָתָם טוּמְאַת הַגּוּף – בְּכָרֵת, הָכָא טוּמְאַת בָּשָׂר – בְּלָאו.

The Gemara rejects this: **There,** it is referring to a case of **impurity of the body;**[H] if one who is ritually impure eats sacrificial parts he is punishable **with *karet*. Here,** it is referring to a case of **impurity of the flesh,**[H] where the meat is impure but the person eating it is pure; one who does so is merely in violation **of a negative** mitzva.

אָמַר רַבִּי אַבָּהוּ אָמַר רַבִּי יוֹחָנָן: כׇּל אִיסּוּרִין שֶׁבַּתּוֹרָה אֵין לוֹקִין עֲלֵיהֶן אֶלָּא דֶּרֶךְ אֲכִילָתָן. לְמַעוֹטֵי מַאי? אָמַר רַב שִׁימִי בַּר אַשִׁי: לְמַעוֹטֵי שֶׁאִם אָכַל חֵלֶב חַי, שֶׁפָּטוּר.

After discussing the prohibitions against eating and deriving benefit from certain items, the Gemara cites that which **Rabbi Abbahu said** that **Rabbi Yoḥanan said:** With regard to **all prohibitions** against eating **in the Torah, one may be flogged for** violating **them only** if he eats the prohibited item in its usual **manner of consumption.** The Gemara asks: **To exclude what** case did Rabbi Yoḥanan say this? **Rav Shimi bar Ashi said: To exclude** a case **where one eats raw fat;** he teaches **that** one who does so **is exempt,** since this is not the usual manner of eating it.

אִיכָּא דְּאָמְרִי, אָמַר רַבִּי אַבָּהוּ אָמַר רַבִּי יוֹחָנָן: כׇּל אִיסּוּרִין שֶׁבַּתּוֹרָה אֵין לוֹקִין עֲלֵיהֶן אֶלָּא דֶּרֶךְ הֲנָאָתָן. לְמַעוֹטֵי מַאי? אָמַר רַב שִׁימִי בַּר אַשִׁי: לְמַעוֹטֵי שֶׁאִם הִנִּיחַ חֵלֶב שֶׁל שׁוֹר הַנִּסְקָל עַל גַּבֵּי מַכָּתוֹ, שֶׁהוּא פָּטוּר. וְכׇל שֶׁכֵּן אוֹכֵל חֵלֶב חַי שֶׁהוּא פָּטוּר.

Some say that this is what **Rabbi Abbahu said** that **Rabbi Yoḥanan said:** With regard to **all prohibitions** against deriving benefit **in the Torah, one is flogged for** violating **them only** if he derives **benefit** from the prohibited item in the usual **manner.**[NH] The Gemara asks: **To exclude what** case did Rabbi Yoḥanan say this? **Rav Shimi bar Ashi said: To exclude** a case **where one placed the fat of an ox that is stoned on his wound** to help it heal. He teaches **that,** although one generally may not derive benefit from forbidden fats, in this case **he is exempt** because these fats are not normally used for medicinal purposes. **And all the more so one who eats raw fat is exempt,** as this is certainly not an ordinary way to benefit from fat.

NOTES

To include wood and incense – לְרַבּוֹת עֵצִים וּלְבוֹנָה: This derivation is an amplification based on the unique form used in the verse: "And the flesh [*vehabasar*]," which indicates that the verse is referring to meat as well as to something else. Although not everyone accepts that an additional *vav*, "and," can serve as the basis for an exposition, when the letters *vav* and *hey*, meaning "and the," appear before a word everyone agrees that this indicates an amplification of what is written.

Some say…derives benefit in the usual manner – אִיכָּא דְּאָמְרִי...דֶּרֶךְ הֲנָאָתָן: This second version of the statement is more lenient, as the first version indicates that the limitation of: Its usual manner, applies only to the prohibition against eating; however, with regard to the prohibition of deriving benefit, it implies that any manner of benefit renders one liable to be flogged (see Ritva).

HALAKHA

The ritual impurity of wood and incense – טוּמְאַת עֵצִים וּלְבוֹנָה: Although wood and incense are not foods, they can become impure as food does with regard to sacrifices. Therefore, they can become disqualified to be offered on the altar (Rambam *Sefer Avoda, Hilkhot Issurei Mizbe'aḥ* 6:8).

Impurity of the body – טוּמְאַת הַגּוּף: An impure person who eats the portions of an offering that are consumed on the altar is punished by *karet*, as stated in the Torah and as explained in the Gemara (Rambam *Sefer Avoda, Hilkhot Pesulei HaMukdashin* 18:18).

Impurity of the flesh – טוּמְאַת בָּשָׂר: A ritually pure person who eats impure offerings violates a prohibition and is flogged, as stated in the Gemara (Rambam *Sefer Avoda, Hilkhot Pesulei HaMukdashin* 18:12).

Deriving benefit from a prohibited item – הֲנָאָה מֵאִיסּוּר: One violates the prohibition against deriving benefit from a food only when one consumes it in an ordinary manner, with the exceptions of diverse kinds planted in a vineyard and meat in milk. This ruling is in accordance with the second version of the statement made in the name of Rabbi Yoḥanan, as the *halakha* generally follows the latter version of a statement (Rambam *Sefer Kedusha, Hilkhot Ma'akhalot Assurot* 14:10).

אִתְּמַר נַמִּי, אָמַר רַב אַחָא בַּר עַוְיָא, אָמַר רַב אַסִי, אָמַר רַבִּי יוֹחָנָן: הִנִּיחַ חֵלֶב שֶׁל שׁוֹר הַנִּסְקָל עַל גַּבֵּי מַכָּתוֹ – פָּטוּר, לְפִי שֶׁכׇּל אִיסּוּרִין שֶׁבַּתּוֹרָה אֵין לוֹקִין עֲלֵיהֶם אֶלָּא דֶּרֶךְ הֲנָאָתָן.

It was also stated that **Rav Aḥa bar Avya said** that **Rav Asi said** that **Rabbi Yoḥanan said: If one placed the fat of an ox that is stoned on his wound** for medicinal purposes, **he is exempt, because** with regard to **all prohibitions** against deriving benefit **in the Torah, one is flogged for** violating **them only** if he derives **benefit** from the prohibited item in its usual **manner.**

אָמַר רַבִּי זֵירָא, אַף אֲנַן נַמִּי תְּנֵינָא: אֵין סוֹפְגִין אֶת הָאַרְבָּעִים מִשּׁוּם עׇרְלָה, אֶלָּא עַל הַיּוֹצֵא מִן הַזֵּיתִים וּמִן הָעֲנָבִים בִּלְבָד. וְאִילּוּ מִתּוּתִים תְּאֵנִים וְרִמּוֹנִים – לֹא. מַאי טַעְמָא – לָאו מִשּׁוּם דְּלָא קָאָכֵיל לְהוּ דֶּרֶךְ הֲנָאָתָן?

Rabbi Zeira said: We, too, have also learned in a mishna that the Rabbis said: **One absorbs the forty** lashes **due to** drinking the juice squeezed from ***orla*** fruits **only for** that which **seeps from olives,** oil, **and from grapes,** wine. **In contrast,** for drinking the juice that seeps from **mulberries, figs, and pomegranates** one is **not** flogged, despite the fact that it is prohibited to consume those juices.[H] **What is the reason** for this? Is it **not because he is not eating them in their usual manner of** deriving **benefit?** Generally, these fruits are eaten and not squeezed for their juice.

אֲמַר לֵיהּ אַבָּיֵי: בִּשְׁלָמָא אִי אַשְׁמְעִינַן פְּרִי גּוּפָא דְּלָא קָאָכֵיל לֵיהּ דֶּרֶךְ הֲנָאָתוֹ – שַׁפִּיר. אֶלָּא הָכָא – מִשּׁוּם דְּזֵיעָה בְּעָלְמָא הוּא.

Abaye said to him that this mishna does not necessarily prove this same point: **Granted, had the** mishna **taught us** the case of **the fruit itself, as he is not eating it in its usual manner of** deriving **benefit, it** would work out **well. However, here,** where the case is with regard to their juice, the reason he is not flogged is **because it is merely moisture**[N] that drips from the fruit, which is not considered to be an essential part of the fruit.

אָמַר אַבָּיֵי: הַכֹּל מוֹדִים בְּכִלְאֵי הַכֶּרֶם שֶׁלּוֹקִין עֲלֵיהֶן אֲפִילּוּ שֶׁלֹּא כְּדֶרֶךְ הֲנָאָתָן. מַאי טַעְמָא – מִשּׁוּם דְּלָא כְּתִיב בְּהוּ אֲכִילָה.

Abaye said: All concede with regard to prohibited mixtures of **diverse kinds** planted **in a vineyard**[H] **that one is flogged for** deriving benefit from **them even** if he does **not** benefit from them **in their usual manner. What is the reason** for this? It is **because no** prohibition against **eating is written about them** explicitly in the Torah. Therefore, the verse is interpreted to mean that it is prohibited to benefit from them in any manner; rather, one must burn them immediately.

מֵיתִיבִי, אִיסִי בֶּן יְהוּדָה אוֹמֵר: מִנַּיִן לְבָשָׂר בְּחָלָב שֶׁהוּא אָסוּר – נֶאֱמַר כָּאן: ״כִּי עַם קָדוֹשׁ אַתָּה״, וְנֶאֱמַר לְהַלָּן: ״וְאַנְשֵׁי קֹדֶשׁ תִּהְיוּן לִי״ מָה לְהַלָּן אָסוּר – אַף כָּאן אָסוּר.

The Gemara **raises an objection. Isi ben Yehuda says: From where** is it derived **that it is prohibited** to eat **meat** that has been cooked **in milk?**[N] **It is stated here: "For you are a sacred people** unto the Lord your God. You shall not cook a kid in its mother's milk" (Deuteronomy 14:21). **And it is stated there: "And you shall be sacred men unto Me;** therefore you shall not eat any flesh that is torn of beasts in the field [*tereifa*]; you shall cast it to the dogs" (Exodus 22:30). **Just as there,** with regard to a *tereifa*, **it is prohibited** to eat it, **so too here,** with regard to meat in milk, **it is prohibited** to eat it.

וְאֵין לִי אֶלָּא בַּאֲכִילָה, בַּהֲנָאָה מִנַּיִן? אָמַרְתָּ קַל וָחוֹמֶר: וּמָה עׇרְלָה שֶׁלֹּא נֶעֶבְדָה בָּהּ עֲבֵירָה – אֲסוּרָה בַּהֲנָאָה, בָּשָׂר בְּחָלָב שֶׁנֶּעֶבְדָה בּוֹ עֲבֵירָה – אֵינוֹ דִּין שֶׁיְּהֵא אָסוּר בַּהֲנָאָה?

From the above comparison **I have derived only** that it is prohibited to **eat** it, as it is prohibited to eat a *tereifa*; **from where** do I derive that it is prohibited to derive **benefit** from it as well? **You may state an *a fortiori*** inference: **If** with regard to ***orla*, through which no sin has been committed,** as it is part of the ordinary growth process of the tree to produce fruit during the first three years, yet still **it is prohibited** to deriving **benefit** from it; then with regard to **meat in milk, through which a sin has been committed,** as the two were illicitly cooked together, **is it not right that it should be prohibited** to derive **benefit** from it?

Perek **II**
Daf **25** Amud **a**

מָה לְעׇרְלָה שֶׁכֵּן לֹא הָיְתָה לָהּ שְׁעַת הַכּוֹשֶׁר, תֹּאמַר בְּבָשָׂר בְּחָלָב שֶׁהָיְתָה לוֹ שְׁעַת הַכּוֹשֶׁר! חָמֵץ בְּפֶסַח יוֹכִיחַ, שֶׁהָיָה לוֹ שְׁעַת הַכּוֹשֶׁר וְאָסוּר בַּהֲנָאָה.

The Gemara rejects this inference: **What** comparison can be made **to *orla*,** which is more stringent than meat in milk, **as it never had a time when it was fit?** Can **you say** the same **with regard to meat in milk, which had a time when it was fit?** Unlike *orla* fruits, which were prohibited from the beginning of their existence, both meat and milk were permitted on their own before they were cooked together. Therefore, the Gemara brings other proofs: **Let leavened bread on Passover prove** that this issue is not a factor, **as it had a time when it was fit,** before Passover, **and** yet **it is prohibited** to derive **benefit** from it.

HALAKHA

Prohibition of *orla* – אִיסּוּר עׇרְלָה: It is prohibited to eat *orla*, fruit that grows in the first three years after a tree has been planted. It is likewise prohibited to drink liquids or juices that seep out from these fruits; however, with regard to drinking *orla* liquid or juice, one is flogged only for drinking olive oil and wine (Rambam *Sefer Kedusha, Hilkhot Ma'akhalot Assurot* 10:22).

Diverse kinds planted in a vineyard – כִּלְאֵי הַכֶּרֶם: It is prohibited to derive benefit from prohibited mixtures of diverse kinds planted in a vineyard. One who derives benefit from them, even in an unusual manner, is flogged (*Shulḥan Arukh, Yoreh De'a* 155:3).

NOTES

Because it is merely moisture – דְּזֵיעָה בְּעָלְמָא: Based on this source and others, it appears that liquid that seeps out of a food is not treated in the same way as the food itself; therefore, the Gemara refers to it as merely moisture. However, wine and oil are exceptions to this rule; since the Torah lists them explicitly with regard to *teruma*, they have the same legal status as other produce.

The prohibitions of meat in milk – אִיסּוּרֵי בָּשָׂר בְּחָלָב: The prohibition of meat in milk is stated in the Torah three times, although each time the verse explicitly mentions only the prohibition against cooking meat in milk. The prohibitions against eating and to deriving benefit from meat in milk are derived through various hints and expositions.

מַה לְּחָמֵץ בַּפֶּסַח – שֶׁכֵּן עָנוּשׁ כָּרֵת, תֹּאמַר בְּבָשָׂר בְּחָלָב שֶׁאֵינוֹ עָנוּשׁ כָּרֵת! כִּלְאֵי הַכֶּרֶם יוֹכִיחוּ, שֶׁאֵין עָנוּשׁ כָּרֵת – וְאָסוּר בַּהֲנָאָה.

The Gemara rejects this: **What** comparison can be made to **leavened bread on Passover,** which is a stringent prohibition, **as** one who eats it **is punished with *karet*?** Can **you say** the same **with regard to** one who eats **meat in milk, who is not punished with *karet*?** The Gemara answers: **Let** the case of **diverse kinds** planted **in the vineyard**[N] **prove** that this is not relevant, **as** one who violates that prohibition **is not punished with *karet*, and** yet **it is prohibited** to derive **benefit** from the resulting mixtures.

וְאִם אִיתָא, נִיפְרוֹךְ: מַה לְּכִלְאֵי הַכֶּרֶם – שֶׁכֵּן לוֹקִין עֲלֵיהֶן אֲפִילּוּ שֶׁלֹּא כְּדֶרֶךְ הֲנָאָתָן.

The Gemara returns to the issue of Abaye's statement with regard to the unique stringency of diverse kinds planted in a vineyard: **And if it is so** that one is flogged for deriving benefit from diverse kinds planted in a vineyard, even if one derives benefit from them in an unusual manner, **we can challenge** this last proof: How can one compare meat in milk to diverse kinds in a vineyard, **as** with regard to diverse kinds in a vineyard, **one is flogged even if he** derives **benefit from them in an unusual manner?**

וְאַבַּיֵי: תֹּאמַר בְּמַאי? תֹּאמַר בְּבָשָׂר בְּחָלָב שֶׁאֵין לוֹקִין עָלָיו אֶלָּא דֶּרֶךְ הֲנָאָתוֹ – אַטּוּ בְּבָשָׂר בְּחָלָב 'אֲכִילָה' כְּתִיבָה בֵּיהּ?

And how would **Abaye** respond to this question? When one draws this challenge to its logical conclusion with the phrase: Can **you say,** and explains in detail how the prohibition of meat in milk differs from that of diverse kinds in a vineyard, **with regard to what** difference would the challenge be raised? **You** may **say** that **with regard to meat in milk one is flogged only for** deriving **benefit in the usual manner,** as opposed to the *halakha* with regard to diverse kinds, according to which one is flogged even for deriving benefit in an unusual manner. However, **is that to say** that the term **eating is written** in the Torah **with regard to meat in milk?** The basis for this *halakha* with regard to diverse kinds in a vineyard is the lack of the term eating in the verse; however, the prohibition of meat in milk is also missing that term. Therefore, there are no grounds for this challenge: If the lack of the word eating leads to the conclusion that one is flogged even when deriving benefit in an unusual manner, logically that punishment should apply to both diverse kinds and meat in milk.

וְאִידָךְ דְּקָא מוֹתִיב לַהּ סָבַר: לְהָכִי קָא גָּמַר מִנְּבֵילָה, מַה נְּבֵילָה דֶּרֶךְ הֲנָאָתָהּ – אַף בָּשָׂר בְּחָלָב דֶּרֶךְ הֲנָאָתוֹ.

The Gemara asks: **And the other** Sage, **who raised this objection,** holds that **for this** reason Isi ben Yehuda **derives** this aspect of the prohibition **from** the case of **an animal carcass. Just as** with regard to **an animal carcass** one is flogged only **when** deriving **benefit in the usual manner,**[N] as the verse that prohibits it uses the term eating, **so too,** with regard to **meat in milk,** one is flogged only when deriving **benefit in the usual manner.** Despite what is written in the Gemara, the fact that one is flogged only for deriving benefit from the animal in the usual manner is not derived from the carcass of an unslaughtered animal but from *tereifa*, an animal with a condition that will cause it to die within twelve months. With regard to *tereifa* it is written: "And you shall be holy men unto Me; therefore you shall not eat any flesh that is torn of beasts in the field [*tereifa*]; you shall cast it to the dogs" (Exodus 22:30). From the fact that one may cast it to the dogs it can be derived that one may derive benefit in any manner other than the usual manner, i.e., eating.

וְאַבַּיֵי: לְהָכִי לֹא כָּתַב אֲכִילָה בְּגוּפוֹ – לוֹמַר שֶׁלּוֹקִין עָלָיו אֲפִילּוּ שֶׁלֹּא כְּדֶרֶךְ הֲנָאָתוֹ.

And Abaye holds that **for this** reason it **did not write** the term **eating** in the verse **itself** with regard to the prohibition of meat in milk: In order **to say that one is flogged even** when deriving **benefit in an unusual manner.**

וְלִיפְרוֹךְ מַה לְּכִלְאֵי הַכֶּרֶם – שֶׁכֵּן לֹא הָיְתָה לוֹ שְׁעַת הַכּוֹשֶׁר! אָמַר רַבִּי אַדָּא בַּר אַהֲבָה: זֹאת אוֹמֶרֶת: כִּלְאֵי הַכֶּרֶם עִיקָּרָן נֶאֱסָרִין, הוֹאִיל וְהָיְתָה לָהֶן שְׁעַת הַכּוֹשֶׁר קוֹדֶם הַשְׁרָשָׁה.

The Gemara continues. **Let** Isi ben Yehuda **challenge: What** comparison can be made **to diverse kinds in a vineyard, as** the forbidden produce **had no time that it was fit** because the prohibition came into effect as soon as the produce began to grow? **Rabbi Adda bar Ahava said:** Apparently, since this question was not asked, **that is to say that** with regard to **diverse kinds in a vineyard, their roots are forbidden** as well, including the seeds and saplings from which the mature plants grow. Therefore, no challenge can be raised, **since they had a time when they were fit, before taking root.**

NOTES

Diverse kinds planted in the vineyard – כִּלְאֵי הַכֶּרֶם: It is prohibited to plant or maintain other crops in a vineyard (Deuteronomy 22:9). In contrast to the prohibition against a mixture of diverse kinds, the prohibited crop grown in a vineyard may not be eaten or used. It renders the entire vineyard prohibited, and all the produce must be burned.

Just as with regard to an animal carcass one is flogged only when deriving benefit in the usual manner – מַה נְּבֵלָה דֶּרֶךְ הֲנָאָתָהּ: Although there is no prohibition against deriving benefit from a *tereifa*, this *halakha* is derived in the following way: Just as there is a prohibition against eating a *tereifa*, and it is prohibited only when one eats it in the usual manner, so too, with regard to the prohibition of meat in milk, which includes a prohibition against deriving benefit, it is prohibited only to derive benefit in the usual manner (Maharam Ḥalawa).

מְתִיב רַב שְׁמַעְיָה: הַמַּעֲבִיר עָצִיץ נָקוּב בַּכֶּרֶם, אִם הוֹסִיף מָאתַיִם – אָסוּר. הוֹסִיף – אִין, לֹא הוֹסִיף – לָא!

Rav Shemaya raised an objection based on what was taught in a mishna: With regard to **one who transfers a perforated pot** with seeds in it **into a vineyard, if** the size of the seeds growing in the pot **increases** by one **two-hundredth**[N] of their previous size, such that the permitted portion is not two hundred times the forbidden, newly grown portion, then the mixture **is prohibited** due to the prohibition against planting diverse kinds in a vineyard. The forbidden portion is nullified only if it comprises less than one two-hundredth of the mixture. The Gemara reads precisely: **If it increases, yes,** it is prohibited; **if it does not increase, no,** it is not prohibited. Apparently, only additional growth is prohibited, and not the seeds themselves.

אָמַר רָבָא: תְּרֵי קְרָאֵי כְּתִיבִי, כְּתִיב: ״הַזֶּרַע״, וּכְתִיב: ״הַמְּלֵאָה״, הָא כֵּיצַד? זָרוּעַ מֵעִיקָּרוֹ – בְּהַשְׁרָשָׁה, זָרוּעַ וּבָא, הוֹסִיף – אִין, לֹא הוֹסִיף – לָא.

Rava said: Two verses are written about this *halakha*, i.e., two separate terms in one verse indicate two separate prohibitions. The verse states: "You shall not sow your vineyard with two kinds of seed; lest the fullness of the seed which you have sown be forfeited together with the increase of the vineyard" (Deuteronomy 22:9). **It is written: "The seed,"** indicating that it is prohibited once it is planted and takes root, **and it is written: "The fullness,"** indicating that it is prohibited only if it has grown. **How can these** two terms be reconciled? If it were **planted initially**[H] in the vineyard, it becomes prohibited immediately **upon taking root.** If it were **planted** elsewhere **and brought**[H] into the vineyard later, such as in a perforated pot, then the following distinction applies: If **its** size **increases** in the vineyard, **yes, it** is prohibited; if **its** size **does not increase, no,** it is not prohibited.

אָמַר רַבִּי יַעֲקֹב אָמַר רַבִּי יוֹחָנָן: בַּכֹּל מִתְרַפְּאִין, חוּץ מֵעֲצֵי אֲשֵׁירָה. הֵיכִי דָמֵי? אִי נֵימָא דְּאִיכָּא סַכָּנָה – אֲפִילּוּ עֲצֵי אֲשֵׁירָה נַמִי! וְאִי דְּלֵיכָּא סַכָּנָה – אֲפִילּוּ כׇּל אִיסּוּרִין שֶׁבַּתּוֹרָה נַמִי לָא!

The Gemara discusses another matter pertaining to deriving benefit. **Rabbi Ya'akov said** that **Rabbi Yoḥanan said** with regard to objects from which it is prohibited to derive benefit: **One** may **heal oneself with any substance except for wood of a tree designated for idolatry** [*asheira*].[N] The Gemara asks: **What are the circumstances? If we say** it is a case in which **there is danger** to a person's life, then it is permitted to use **even the wood of an *asheira*. And if** it is a situation **where there is no danger,** then **all the prohibited** substances **in the Torah also** may **not** be used, as one may not derive benefit from them.

לְעוֹלָם דְּאִיכָּא סַכָּנָה, וַאֲפִילּוּ הָכִי – עֲצֵי אֲשֵׁירָה לָא. דְּתַנְיָא, רַבִּי אֱלִיעֶזֶר אוֹמֵר: אִם נֶאֱמַר ״בְּכׇל נַפְשְׁךָ״ לָמָּה נֶאֱמַר ״בְּכׇל מְאֹדֶךָ״, וְאִם נֶאֱמַר ״בְּכׇל מְאֹדֶךָ״ לָמָּה נֶאֱמַר ״בְּכׇל נַפְשְׁךָ״?

The Gemara answers: **Actually,** it is referring to a case where **there is danger, and even so,** one my **not** derive benefit from **the wood of an *asheira*. As it was taught** in a *baraita* that **Rabbi Eliezer says: If it is stated:** "And you shall love the Lord your God with all your heart, **and with all your soul,"** why **is it stated: "And with all your might"** (Deuteronomy 6:5)? **And if it is stated: "With all your might,"**[N] **why is it stated: "With all your soul"**? One of these statements appears to be superfluous.

אֶלָּא לוֹמַר לְךָ: אִם יֵשׁ אָדָם שֶׁגּוּפוֹ חָבִיב עָלָיו מִמָּמוֹנוֹ – לְכָךְ נֶאֱמַר ״בְּכׇל נַפְשְׁךָ״, וְיֵשׁ אָדָם שֶׁמָּמוֹנוֹ חָבִיב עָלָיו מִגּוּפוֹ – לְכָךְ נֶאֱמַר ״בְּכׇל מְאֹדֶךָ״.

Rather, it is **to tell you** that **if there is a person whose body is more beloved to him than his property, therefore it is stated: "With all your soul."**[N] The verse teaches that one must be willing to sacrifice his life to sanctify God's name. **And there is a person whose property is more beloved to him than his body, therefore it is stated: "With all your might."** Rabbi Eliezer understands the phrase: "With all your might," to mean: With all your possessions. Apparently, there are circumstances in which a person must be prepared to die rather than be healed with a prohibited substance.

כִּי אֲתָא רָבִין אָמַר רַבִּי יוֹחָנָן: בַּכֹּל מִתְרַפְּאִין, חוּץ מֵעֲבוֹדָה זָרָה וְגִילּוּי עֲרָיוֹת

When Ravin came from Eretz Yisrael to Babylonia, he **said** that **Rabbi Yoḥanan said: One** may **heal oneself with any substance** from which one may not derive benefit,[H] **except for idolatry or forbidden sexual relations**

NOTES

If the size increases by one two-hundredth – אִם הוֹסִיף מָאתַיִם: The forbidden portion of diverse kinds planted in a vineyard is nullified in a mixture of one part in two hundred. This is derived from the *halakhot* pertaining to *teruma*. There is no prohibition against deriving benefit from *teruma*, and it is nullified in a mixture of one part in one hundred. However, it is prohibited to derive benefit from diverse kinds planted in a vineyard; therefore, it is nullified only in a mixture of one part in two hundred.

Wood of an *asheira* – עֲצֵי אֲשֵׁירָה: Although deriving benefit from an *asheira* is not actual idolatry, it is still prohibited, as one may not derive benefit from any appurtenances of idolatry either.

And if it is stated, with all your might – וְאִם נֶאֱמַר בְּכׇל מְאֹדֶךָ: Some versions of the Gemara do not contain this statement, since this expression is normally understood to be a reference to one's property, and people are generally more concerned about their lives than their property. Furthermore, the words "with all your soul" appear in the verse before the words "with all your might" (*Mikhtam*).

With all your soul – בְּכׇל נַפְשְׁךָ: The verse does not specify the mitzvot for which one must sacrifice his life to sanctify God's name. On the contrary, there is a principle: "You shall live through them" (Leviticus 18:5), i.e., that one should not die through performing mitzvot. However, based on the context, it is clear that the verse indicates that one must be willing to sacrifice his life in order to accept the yoke of Heaven.

HALAKHA

Planted initially – זָרוּעַ מֵעִיקָּרָא: If grain or plants were sown in a vineyard, it is prohibited to derive benefit from them once they take root, as is the case with all diverse kinds planted in a vineyard (*Shulḥan Arukh, Yoreh De'a* 296:9).

If it were planted and brought – זָרוּעַ וּבָא: If one transferred a perforated pot to a vineyard and left it there, and it grew so that it increased by at least one two-hundredth of its previous size, then it is prohibited to derive benefit from it due to the prohibition of diverse kinds in a vineyard (*Shulḥan Arukh, Yoreh De'a* 296:17).

With what may one heal oneself – בַּמָּה מִתְרַפְּאִין: When a person's life is in danger, any prohibitions in the Torah may be violated for medical purposes, except for the prohibitions against idolatry, forbidden sexual relations, and bloodshed (*Shulḥan Arukh, Yoreh De'a* 155:2).

וּשְׁפִיכוּת דָּמִים.

or bloodshed.

עֲבוֹדָה זָרָה – הָא דַּאֲמַרַן. גִּילּוּי עֲרָיוֹת וּשְׁפִיכוּת דָּמִים – דְּתַנְיָא, רַבִּי אוֹמֵר: ״כִּי כַּאֲשֶׁר יָקוּם אִישׁ עַל רֵעֵהוּ וּרְצָחוֹ נֶפֶשׁ כֵּן הַדָּבָר הַזֶּה״ וְכִי מָה עִנְיַן רוֹצֵחַ אֵצֶל נַעֲרָה הַמְאוֹרָסָה?

That one may not heal oneself with **idolatry** even when his life is in danger is learned **from that** which **we** just **said,** based on the verse: "With all your soul and with all your might." From where is this *halakha* derived with regard to **forbidden sexual relations and murder? As it was taught** in a *baraita* that **Rabbi** Yehuda HaNasi **says:** The verse says about one who rapes a betrothed woman: "But you shall do nothing to the young woman; the young woman has committed no sin worthy of death; **for as when a man rises against his neighbor, and slays him, so too with this matter**" (Deuteronomy 22:26). **What does a murderer have to do with a betrothed young woman** who was raped? Why would the verse mention murder in this context?

הֲרֵי זֶה בָּא לְלַמֵּד וְנִמְצָא לָמֵד, מַקִּישׁ רוֹצֵחַ לְנַעֲרָה הַמְאוֹרָסָה. מַה נַּעֲרָה הַמְאוֹרָסָה נִיתָּן לְהַצִּילָהּ בְּנַפְשׁוֹ – אַף רוֹצֵחַ נִיתָּן לְהַצִּילוֹ בְּנַפְשׁוֹ. וְנַעֲרָה הַמְאוֹרָסָה מֵרוֹצֵחַ, מָה רוֹצֵחַ – יֵהָרֵג וְאַל יַעֲבוֹר, אַף נַעֲרָה הַמְאוֹרָסָה – תֵּהָרֵג וְאַל תַּעֲבוֹר.

Rather, the mention of murder **comes** in order **to teach**[N] a *halakha* about the betrothed young woman, **and it turns out** that, in addition, **it derives** a *halakha* from that case. The Torah **juxtaposes a murderer to a betrothed young woman** to indicate that **just as** in the case of a betrothed young woman **one may save her by** taking the rapist's **life, so too, one may save** a potential murder victim **by** taking the pursuer's **life.**[NH] Conversely, it is possible to learn about the case of **a young betrothed woman from** the case of **a murderer. Just as** with regard to a potential **murderer** the *halakha* is that if one is being forced to murder someone else, **he** should allow himself to **be killed and not transgress**[H] that prohibition, **so too,** with regard to **a betrothed young woman** the *halakha* is that **she** should allow herself to **be killed and not transgress** the prohibition of forbidden relations.

וּשְׁפִיכוּת דָּמִים גּוּפֵיהּ מְנָלַן? סְבָרָא הוּא; כִּי הַהוּא דַּאֲתָא לְקַמֵּיהּ דְּרָבָא, אֲמַר לֵיהּ: מָרִי דּוּרָאי אֲמַר לִי ״זִיל קַטְלֵיהּ לִפְלָנְיָא, וְאִי לָא – קָטְלִינָא לָךְ״. אֲמַר לֵיהּ: לִיקְטְלוּךְ וְלָא תִּיקְטוֹל. מַאי חָזֵית דִּדְמָא דִּידָךְ סוּמָּק טְפֵי? דִּילְמָא דְּמָא דְּהַהוּא גַּבְרָא סוּמָּק טְפֵי?

The Gemara asks: **And from where do we** derive **this** *halakha* with regard to **murder itself?** The Gemara answers: **It is** based on **logical reasoning** that one life is not preferable to another. The Gemara relates an incident to demonstrate this: This is **similar** to **a certain man who came before Rava** and **said to him: A local official said to me: Go kill so-and-so, and if not I will kill you. Rava said to him:** It is preferable that **he should kill you and you should not kill. What did you think, that your blood is redder**[N] and more precious than his? **Perhaps that man's blood is redder.** Apparently, one may not save his own life by taking someone else's.

מָר בַּר רַב אַשִׁי אַשְׁכְּחֵיהּ לְרָבִינָא דְּשָׁיֵיף לָהּ לִבְרַתֵּיהּ בְּגוּהַרְקֵי דְּעָרְלָה, אֲמַר לֵיהּ: אֵימוּר דַּאֲמוּר רַבָּנַן בִּשְׁעַת הַסַּכָּנָה, שֶׁלֹּא בִּשְׁעַת הַסַּכָּנָה מִי אֲמוּר?

The Gemara relates: **Mar bar Rav Ashi found Ravina rubbing his daughter with unripe** olives **[*guharkei*][L] of *orla***[N] for medicinal purposes. Mar bar Rav Ashi **said to him: Say** that **the Sages said** that one may derive benefit from such a prohibited item **at a time of danger;** however, **who says** that one is permitted to do so **when** it is **not a time of danger?**

אֲמַר לֵיהּ: הַאי אִישְׁתָּא צְמִירְתָּא נַמִי כִּשְׁעַת הַסַּכָּנָה דָּמְיָא. אִיכָּא דְּאָמְרִי, אֲמַר לֵיהּ: מִידֵּי דֶּרֶךְ הֲנָאָה קָא עָבֵידְנָא?

Ravina **said to him: A high fever**[B] **is also deemed a time of danger,** and one may derive benefit from a prohibited item in such a situation. **Some say** that Ravina **said to him** as follows: **Am I deriving benefit in a usual manner?** The usual way to derive benefit from these olives is to use them after they have become ripe, so that their oil can be drawn out. Since Ravina was not deriving benefit in the usual manner, he was permitted to do so, although his daughter's life was not in danger.[H]

אִיתְּמַר, הֲנָאָה הַבָּאָה לוֹ לָאָדָם בְּעַל כָּרְחוֹ. אַבַּיֵי אָמַר: מוּתֶּרֶת, וְרָבָא אָמַר: אֲסוּרָה.

The Gemara continues to discuss various *halakhot* that apply to prohibited items. **It was stated:** With regard to deriving **benefit** from a prohibited item **that comes to a person against his will,** i.e., one's circumstance results in his deriving benefit although he did not place himself in that circumstance in order to derive benefit, **Abaye said:** Deriving benefit in this manner is **permitted, and Rava said:** It is **prohibited.**

NOTES

Comes to teach, etc. – בָּא לְלַמֵּד וכו׳: Some explain this to mean that the juxtaposition of the murderer and the betrothed young woman indicates a leniency. Just as murder is a prohibition that one violates actively, so too, for a betrothed young woman to be liable she must violate the prohibition actively, rather than passively (*Nimmukei Yosef*).

Save him by taking the pursuer's life – לְהַצִּילוֹ בְּנַפְשׁוֹ: The precise meaning of this expression is not entirely clear. One could understand it to mean that one should save the pursued at the expense of the pursuer's life; however, this lacks grammatical consistency, as the same third-person pronoun is used to refer to two different people. Therefore, it seems that the preferable explanation is that one may save the pursuer from this stringent transgression by taking his, the pursuer's, life (*Tosafot, Sanhedrin* 73a).

That your blood is redder – דִּדְמָךְ סוּמָּק טְפֵי: Some explain this as follows: The reason one is permitted to commit a serious transgression, such as violating Shabbat, in order to save a life is that by transgressing the mitzva this one time, the person saved will be able to live and fulfill many more mitzvot. However, in this case that rationale does not apply, as one cannot know whether the potential murderer or the potential victim is to be preferred in this regard. Rava is asking: Who says that your blood is redder, i.e., purer and cleaner, than the blood of this other person, such that you will live a longer life of fulfilling mitzvot (Rabbeinu Yehonatan; *Nimmukei Yosef*)?

Unripe *orla* – גּוּהַרְקֵי עָרְלָה: Some explain that this phrase refers to grains of *orla* (Rabbeinu Ḥananel; *Arukh*).

HALAKHA

One may save him by taking the pursuer's life – נִיתָּן לְהַצִּילוֹ בְּנַפְשׁוֹ: If one person is pursuing another person to kill him, one should save the pursued in any way possible, even if one must take the assailant's life (Rambam *Sefer Nezikim, Hilkhot Rotze'aḥ UShmirat HaNefesh* 1:6).

A murderer…should be killed and not transgress – רוֹצֵחַ יֵהָרֵג וְאַל יַעֲבוֹר: If a person is threatened that he will be killed if he does not kill another person, he should be killed and not kill the other person. Similarly, if a person is forced to have sexual relations with a betrothed young woman, or anyone else with whom sexual relations would be a capital offense, then he should allow himself to be killed rather than commit this transgression (*Shulḥan Arukh, Yoreh De'a* 157:1).

Medicinal use of prohibited items – רִיפּוּי בְּאִיסּוּר: One may use prohibited items for medicinal purposes only if one's life is in danger. However, this applies only if he derives benefit from the prohibited item in its usual manner. If he does so in an unusual manner, he is permitted to use the item for medicinal purposes even if he is not in mortal danger (*Shulḥan Arukh, Yoreh De'a* 155:50).

LANGUAGE

Guharkei – גּוּהַרְקֵי: The *Arukh* has a version of the Gemara that reads *gurkei*. This word may be derived from the Middle Iranian gurak, which is related to the New Persian yoragī, meaning unripe fruit.

BACKGROUND

High fever – אִישְׁתָּא צְמִירְתָּא: This refers to a type of illness, perhaps one that causes a daily recurrence of high fever. Presumably the name of this malady, which literally means fiery illness, comes either from the high fever it causes or from the shivering attacks that accompany it.

אֶפְשָׁר וְקָא מִיכַּוֵּין, לָא אֶפְשָׁר וְקָמִיכַּוֵּין – כּוּלֵּי עָלְמָא לָא פְּלִיגִי דְּאָסוּר. לָא אֶפְשָׁר וְלָא מִיכַּוֵּין – כּוּלֵּי עָלְמָא לָא פְּלִיגִי דְּשָׁרֵי. כִּי פְּלִיגִי – דְּאֶפְשָׁר וְלָא מִיכַּוֵּין.

The Gemara explains: In a case where **it is possible** to avoid deriving benefit **and he intends** to derive benefit from the prohibited object, or where **it is not possible** to avoid it **and he intends** to derive benefit, **everyone agrees that it is prohibited,** because he intended to derive benefit that was prohibited. And when it is **not possible** to avoid it **and he does not intend** to derive benefit, **everyone agrees that it is permitted,** as one had no choice in the matter. **Where they disagree** is in a case **where it is possible** for him to avoid the prohibition, and **he does not intend**[N] to derive benefit from it.

וְאַלִּיבָּא דְּרַבִּי יְהוּדָה, דְּאָמַר "דָּבָר שֶׁאֵין מִתְכַּוֵּין – אָסוּר" – כּוּלֵּי עָלְמָא לָא פְּלִיגִי דְּאָסוּר. כִּי פְּלִיגִי – אַלִּיבָּא דְּרַבִּי שִׁמְעוֹן, דְּאָמַר "דָּבָר שֶׁאֵין מִתְכַּוֵּין מוּתָּר". אַבָּיֵי – כְּרַבִּי שִׁמְעוֹן, וְרָבָא אָמַר: עַד כָּאן לָא קָא אָמַר רַבִּי שִׁמְעוֹן – אֶלָּא הֵיכָא דְּלָא אֶפְשָׁר, אֲבָל הֵיכָא דְּאֶפְשָׁר – לָא.

The Gemara limits the dispute further: **And according to Rabbi Yehuda, who said** that **an unintentional** prohibited **act is prohibited, everyone agrees that it is prohibited,** as Rabbi Yehuda maintains that one's action is more significant than his intent. **Where they disagree** is **in accordance with** the opinion **of Rabbi Shimon,** who **said** that **an unintentional** prohibited **act is permitted.** Apparently, **Abaye** holds **in accordance with** the opinion of **Rabbi Shimon. And Rava** would **say: Rabbi Shimon stated** his opinion **only** with regard to a case **where it is not possible** to avoid the prohibition. **However,** in a case **where it is possible** to avoid the prohibition, **no,** he did not permit one to derive benefit from such a prohibition even unintentionally. This is one version of the dispute.

אִיכָּא דְּאָמְרִי: אֶפְשָׁר וְלָא מִיכַּוֵּין – הַיְינוּ פְּלוּגְתַּיְיהוּ דְּרַבִּי יְהוּדָה וְרַבִּי שִׁמְעוֹן. לָא אֶפְשָׁר וְלָא קָא מִיכַּוֵּין – כּוּלֵּי עָלְמָא לָא פְּלִיגִי דְּשָׁרֵי, כִּי פְּלִיגִי – דְּלָא אֶפְשָׁר וְקָא מִיכַּוֵּין. וְאַלִּיבָּא דְּרַבִּי שִׁמְעוֹן דְּאָזֵיל בָּתַר כַּוָּונָה – כּוּלֵּי עָלְמָא לָא פְּלִיגִי דְּאָסוּר. כִּי פְּלִיגִי – אַלִּיבָּא דְּרַבִּי יְהוּדָה, דְּאָמַר: לָא שְׁנָא מִתְכַּוֵּין וְלָא שְׁנָא שֶׁאֵין מִתְכַּוֵּין – אֶפְשָׁר אָסוּר.

Some say that the dispute should be understood as follows: In a case where **it is possible** to avoid deriving benefit **and he does not intend** to derive benefit, **this is the** case of **dispute between Rabbi Yehuda and Rabbi Shimon.** Where **it is not possible** to avoid it **and he does not intend** to derive benefit from the prohibited item, **everyone agrees that it is permitted** to do so. **Where they disagree** is in a case **where it is not possible** to avoid deriving benefit **and he intends** to derive benefit from it. The Gemara limits the dispute further: **According to** the opinion of **Rabbi Shimon, who follows** one's **intent, everyone agrees** that **it is prohibited. Where they disagree** is **in accordance with** the opinion **of Rabbi Yehuda, who said: There is no difference** whether **one intends or does not intend;** the issue is whether he can avoid it or not. Therefore, if it is **possible** to avoid deriving benefit, **it is prohibited.**

אַבָּיֵי כְּרַבִּי יְהוּדָה,

Based on this understanding of the dispute, **Abaye** holds **in accordance with** the opinion of **Rabbi Yehuda.** In other words, in a case where it is not possible to avoid the situation completely, even if one has intent it is permitted.[N]

NOTES

It is possible and he does not intend – אֶפְשָׁר וְלָא מִיכַּוֵּין: In this case the phrase: It is possible, means that it is possible for one to achieve the desired outcome in another way without much difficulty. It is not possible means that achieving the desired outcome differently would require a great deal of effort and trouble (Ritva; Maharam Ḥalawa).

NOTES

The dispute between Abaye and Rava – מַחְלוֹקֶת אַבָּיֵי וְרָבָא:

The Disputants		It is possible and he intends	It is not possible and he intends	It is possible and he does not intend	It is not possible and he does not intend
First Version	Abaye	Prohibited	Prohibited	Rabbi Yehuda: Prohibited Rabbi Shimon: Permitted	Permitted
	Rava	Prohibited	Prohibited	Rabbi Yehuda: Prohibited Rabbi Shimon: Prohibited	Permitted
Second Version	Abaye	Prohibited	Rabbi Yehuda: Permitted Rabbi Shimon: Prohibited	Rabbi Yehuda: Prohibited Rabbi Shimon: Permitted	Permitted
	Rava	Prohibited	Rabbi Yehuda: Prohibited Rabbi Shimon: Prohibited	Rabbi Yehuda: Prohibited Rabbi Shimon: Permitted	Permitted

Perek **II**
Daf **26** Amud **a**

וְרָבָא אָמַר לָךְ: עַד כָּאן לָא קָאָמַר רַבִּי יְהוּדָה שֶׁאֵין מִתְכַּוֵּין כְּמִתְכַּוֵּין – אֶלָּא לְחוּמְרָא, אֲבָל מִתְכַּוֵּין כְּשֶׁאֵין מִתְכַּוֵּין לְקוּלָּא – לָא.

And Rava could have **said to you: Rabbi Yehuda stated** that **one who lacks intent** has the same legal status **as one who has intent only with regard to a stringency.** In other words, a lack of intent does not negate the fact that the prohibited act has been performed and one is liable. **However,** to say that **one who has intent** has the same legal status **as one who lacks intent** such that it leads **to a leniency, no.** There is no evidence that Rabbi Yehuda would agree that it would ever be permitted for one who has intent to derive benefit from an otherwise prohibited object, even if he could not avoid the situation.[H]

HALAKHA

Benefit against one's will – הֲנָאָה בְּעַל כָּרְחוֹ: If one derives benefit from a prohibited item against his will, yet he intends to derive benefit from it, then it is prohibited for him to do so. However, if he does not intend to derive benefit from it, it is permitted. This is in accordance with Rava's opinion in the second version of the Gemara, as the *halakha* generally follows the second version. The *halakha* is also generally in accordance with the opinion of Rava in his disputes with Abaye (Rambam *Sefer Kedusha, Hilkhot Ma'akhalot Assurot* 14:12).

NOTES

The Sanctuary is different as it was constructed for its interior – שָׁאנֵי הֵיכָל דִּלְתוֹכוֹ עָשׂוּי: Some explain that this means that only the internal portion of the Sanctuary was consecrated, and therefore one would not be deriving benefit from consecrated property by utilizing its shade (Maharam Ḥalawa). Others say that one who stands in this shade is deriving benefit from the Sanctuary in an unusual manner, which is permitted (see *Tosafot*). Some suggest that this case is lenient because it involves the mitzva of Torah study. However, it is also possible that the preference that one should not derive benefit even in an unusual manner is only when the object is part of another prohibition, such as a prohibition to eat it. However, since the prohibition against deriving benefit from the Temple is due to the Temple's sanctity, it is permitted to benefit in an unusual manner (*Me'iri*).

Renovations of the Temple – תִּקּוּנֵי הַקֹּדֶשׁ: Artisans who enter the Temple to perform repairs must enter in containers so they do not gaze upon the Sanctuary. If this is not possible, they may enter in an ordinary manner. According to the Rambam, they must enter even the outer Sanctuary in containers (Rambam *Sefer Avoda, Hilkhot Beit HaBeḥira* 7:23).

The sight – מַרְאֶה: Some explain that the visual benefit discussed here is that which is stated in tractate *Sukka*, which tells of women who would separate superior grains of wheat from inferior ones by the light of the torches in the Celebration of Drawing Water. By doing so, they would derive benefit from light that originated in the Temple; this is the sight described here (*Arukh*, based on the Jerusalem Talmud). Others claim that this refers to enjoying the beauty of the Temple (Rashi).

Artisan in the Holy of Holies

They established a higher standard – מַעֲלָה עָשׂוּ: The prohibition against entering the Temple in an ordinary manner to perform repairs does not stem from the prohibition of misuse of consecrated property. Rather, this is a special decree to emphasize the sanctity of the Temple.

אֲמַר אַבַּיֵי: מְנָא אָמִינָא לָהּ – דְּתַנְיָא: אָמְרוּ עָלָיו עַל רַבָּן יוֹחָנָן בֶּן זַכַּאי שֶׁהָיָה יוֹשֵׁב בְּצִילּוֹ שֶׁל הֵיכָל וְדוֹרֵשׁ כָּל הַיּוֹם כּוּלּוֹ. וְהָא הָכָא, דְּלָא אֶפְשָׁר וּמִיכַּוֵּין – וְשָׁרֵי.

Abaye said: From where do I say my opinion? **As it was taught** in a *baraita*: **They said about Rabban Yoḥanan ben Zakkai that he would sit** in the street adjacent to the Temple Mount **in the shade of the Sanctuary**[H] **and expound** to a large number of people **all day long. And here, isn't it** a case where **it was not possible** to act differently, as there was no other place where so many people could congregate, **and he** certainly **intended** to derive benefit from the shade of the Sanctuary, **and yet it was permitted?** Apparently, when it is not possible to avoid the situation and one intends to derive benefit, it is permitted to do so.

וְרָבָא אָמַר: שָׁאנֵי הֵיכָל דִּלְתוֹכוֹ עָשׂוּי.

And Rava said in response: **The Sanctuary is different, as it was constructed for its interior.**[N] It is prohibited to derive benefit only from the interior of the Sanctuary walls, because it was constructed for the use of its internal space; there is no prohibition at all to benefit from its shade when on the outside.

אָמַר רָבָא: מְנָא אָמִינָא לָהּ – (דְּתַנְיָא): לוּלִין הָיוּ פְּתוּחִין בַּעֲלִיַּית בֵּית קָדְשֵׁי הַקֳּדָשִׁים, שֶׁבָּהֶן מְשַׁלְשְׁלִין אֶת הָאוּמָּנִים בְּתֵיבוֹת, כְּדֵי שֶׁלֹּא יָזוּנוּ עֵינֵיהֶם מִבֵּית קָדְשֵׁי הַקֳּדָשִׁים. וְהָא הָכָא, דְּלָא אֶפְשָׁר וְקָא מִיכַּוֵּין – וְאָסוּר.

Rava said: From where do I say this? As it was taught in a *baraita*: **There were openings in the loft of the Holy of Holies through which they would lower artisans in containers** into the Holy of Holies, **so that their eyes would not gaze** upon the Holy of Holies itself when they were renovating it.[N] **And here, isn't** it a case **where it was not possible** to act differently? It was necessary to renovate the Holy of Holies periodically, and it is impossible to do so without entering the chamber. **And** since it is plausible that the artisan **will intend** to enjoy the appearance of the Holy of Holies, **it** should be **prohibited.**

וְתִסְבְּרָא?! וְהָאָמַר רַבִּי שִׁמְעוֹן בֶּן פָּזִי אָמַר רַבִּי יְהוֹשֻׁעַ בֶּן לֵוִי מִשּׁוּם בַּר קַפָּרָא: קוֹל וּמַרְאֶה וְרֵיחַ אֵין בָּהֶן מִשּׁוּם מְעִילָה! אֶלָּא: מַעֲלָה עָשׂוּ בְּבֵית קָדְשֵׁי הַקֳּדָשִׁים.

The Gemara rejects this: **And** how **can you understand** the *baraita* as a proof? **Didn't Rabbi Shimon ben Pazi say** that **Rabbi Yehoshua ben Levi said in the name of Bar Kappara: The sound** of the musical instruments in the Temple, and **the sight**[NH] **and smell** of the incense **are not subject to** the prohibition of **misuse of consecrated property?** This is because the prohibition of deriving benefit from a consecrated object applies only to its tangible use. **Rather, they established a higher standard**[N] of stringency with regard to **the Holy of Holies** and decreed that one may not even gaze upon it. Therefore, no principle can be derived from the case.

אִיכָּא דְּאָמְרִי; אָמַר רָבָא: מְנָא אָמִינָא לָהּ – דְּתַנְיָא, אָמַר רַבִּי שִׁמְעוֹן בֶּן פָּזִי, אָמַר רַבִּי יְהוֹשֻׁעַ בֶּן לֵוִי, מִשּׁוּם בַּר קַפָּרָא: קוֹל וּמַרְאֶה וְרֵיחַ אֵין בָּהֶן מִשּׁוּם מְעִילָה. מְעִילָה הוּא דְּלֵיכָּא, הָא אִיסּוּרָא – אִיכָּא.

Some say this statement differently. **Rava said: From where do I say this? As it was taught** in a *baraita*: **Rabbi Shimon ben Pazi said** that **Rabbi Yehoshua ben Levi said in the name of Bar Kappara: The sound** of the musical instruments in the Temple and **the sight and smell** of the incense **are not subject to** the prohibition of **misuse of consecrated property.** The implication is that **there is no** violation of the prohibition of **misuse of consecrated property** by Torah law in this case. **However, there is a** violation of the **prohibition** by rabbinic law.

מַאי לָאו – לְאוֹתָן הָעוֹמְדִין בִּפְנִים, דְּלָא אֶפְשָׁר וְקָא מִיכַּוֵּין, וְאָסוּר– לֹא, לְאוֹתָן הָעוֹמְדִין בַּחוּץ.

What, is it not referring **to those standing inside** the Sanctuary, for whom **it is not possible** that they will not hear these sounds or they will not observe the sight and smell of the incense? **And** in such a case, if **they intend** to derive benefit, **it is prohibited.** The Gemara rejects this: **No,** it is referring **to those who are standing outside.** Since they are not required to be there at that time, it is a case where it is possible to avoid the situation and one intends to derive benefit, which is prohibited according to all opinions.

HALAKHA

The shade of the Sanctuary – צֵל הַקֹּדֶשׁ: One who sits in the shade of the Temple does not violate the prohibition of misuse of consecrated property, although he is deriving benefit from it, as stated in the Gemara here (Rambam *Sefer Avoda, Hilkhot Me'ila* 5:5).

The sound and the sight – קוֹל וּמַרְאֶה: One should not derive benefit from the sounds and sights of the Temple, *ab initio*. However, if one did derive benefit from the Temple in this way, he has not violated the prohibition of misuse of consecrated property (Rambam *Sefer Avoda, Hilkhot Beit HaBeḥira* 5:16).

גּוּפָא, אָמַר רַבִּי שִׁמְעוֹן בֶּן פָּזִי, אָמַר רַבִּי יְהוֹשֻׁעַ בֶּן לֵוִי, מִשּׁוּם בַּר קַפָּרָא: קוֹל וּמַרְאֶה וְרֵיחַ אֵין בָּהֶן מִשּׁוּם מְעִילָה. וְרֵיחַ אֵין בּוֹ מִשּׁוּם מְעִילָה? וְהָא תַּנְיָא: הַמְפַטֵּם אֶת הַקְּטוֹרֶת לְהִתְלַמֵּד בָּהּ אוֹ לְמוֹסְרָהּ לַצִּיבּוּר – פָּטוּר, לְהָרִיחַ בָּהּ – חַיָּיב. וְהַמֵּרִיחַ בָּהּ – פָּטוּר, אֶלָּא שֶׁמָּעַל.

Apropos this *halakha*, the Gemara discusses the matter **itself. Rabbi Shimon ben Pazi said that Rabbi Yehoshua ben Levi said in the name of Bar Kappara: The sound** of the musical instruments in the Temple and **the sight and smell** of the incense **are not subject to** the prohibition of **misuse of consecrated property.** The Gemara asks: **Isn't smell subject to** the prohibition of **misuse of consecrated property? Wasn't it taught** in a *baraita*: **One who prepares the incense**[NH] mixture in order **to teach** himself how to prepare it **or to transfer it to the community is exempt** from punishment. However, if one prepares it in order **to smell it,**[H] **he is liable** to receive punishment, as it states in the Torah: "He who makes it in order to smell it shall be cut off from his people" (Exodus 30:38). **And one who** actually **smells** the incense mixture is **exempt** from the punishment of *karet* and from bringing a sin-offering; **however, he has misused consecrated property.** Apparently, the *halakha* of misuse of consecrated property applies to smelling.

אֶלָּא אָמַר רַב פַּפָּא: קוֹל וּמַרְאֶה – אֵין בָּהֶן מִשּׁוּם מְעִילָה, לְפִי שֶׁאֵין בָּהֶן מַמָּשׁ. וְרֵיחַ, לְאַחַר שֶׁתַּעֲלֶה תִּמְרוּתוֹ – אֵין בּוֹ מִשּׁוּם מְעִילָה, הוֹאִיל וְנַעֲשֵׂית מִצְוָתוֹ.

Rather, Rav Pappa said: Sound and sight are not subject to the prohibition of **misuse of consecrated property, because they have no substance.**[B] **And** with regard to **the smell** of the spices themselves, the following distinction applies: The smell of the incense that is emitted when the spices are placed on the coals is subject to the prohibition, since this is the way the mitzva is performed; however, the smell that is emitted **after** the flame catches and **the column of smoke rises is not subject to** the prohibition of **misuse of consecrated property, since its mitzva has** already **been performed.**[H]

לְמֵימְרָא דְּכָל הֵיכָא דְּנַעֲשֵׂית מִצְוָתוֹ אֵין בּוֹ מִשּׁוּם מְעִילָה? וַהֲרֵי תְּרוּמַת הַדֶּשֶׁן, דְּנַעֲשֵׂית מִצְוָתָהּ וְיֵשׁ בָּהּ מִשּׁוּם מְעִילָה, דִּכְתִיב: "וְשָׂמוֹ אֵצֶל הַמִּזְבֵּחַ" – שֶׁלֹּא יְפַזֵּר, "וְשָׂמוֹ" – שֶׁלֹּא יֵהָנֶה!

The Gemara asks: **Is that to say that** in **any** case **where its mitzva has** already **been performed,** the object **is not subject to** the prohibition of **misuse of consecrated property? And** the daily **removal of ashes**[NH] of the offerings from the altar occurs after **its mitzva has been performed, and** the ashes are **subject to** the prohibition of **misuse of consecrated property, as it is written:** "And the priest shall put on his linen garment, and his linen breeches shall he put upon his flesh; and he shall take up the ashes of what the fire has consumed of the burnt-offering on the altar, **and he shall put them beside the altar**" (Leviticus 6:3). The Sages derive from the phrase: "And he shall put them" **that he** may **not scatter** these ashes; rather, they should be placed gently. **"And he shall put them"** also indicates **that one** may **not** derive **benefit** from these ashes.

מִשּׁוּם דְּהָווּ תְּרוּמַת הַדֶּשֶׁן וּבִגְדֵי כְּהוּנָּה שְׁנֵי כְתוּבִין הַבָּאִין כְּאֶחָד, וְכָל שְׁנֵי כְתוּבִין הַבָּאִין כְּאֶחָד אֵין מְלַמְּדִין.

The Gemara answers: This case does not prove a principle, **because the** *halakhot* of **removal of ashes** from the altar **and** of **the priestly garments** worn by the High Priest on Yom Kippur **are two verses that come as one.** The principle is that **two verses that come as one do not teach** a principle. In other words, if a *halakha* is stated twice, with regard to two individual cases in the Torah, the understanding is that this *halakha* applies only to those cases. Had this *halakha* applied to all other relevant cases as well, it would not have been necessary for the Torah to teach it twice. The fact that two cases are mentioned indicates that they are the exceptions rather than the rule.

תְּרוּמַת הַדֶּשֶׁן – הָא דַּאֲמַרַן, בִּגְדֵי כְּהוּנָּה – דִּכְתִיב: "וְהִנִּיחָם שָׁם" – מְלַמֵּד שֶׁטְּעוּנִין גְּנִיזָה.

The Gemara delineates the two cases: The *halakha* of the **removal of ashes is that which we said.** Where is this *halakha* stated with regard to **the priestly garments? As it is written:** "And Aharon shall come into the Tent of Meeting, and shall take off the linen garments, which he put on when he went into the sacred place, **and he shall leave them there**" (Leviticus 16:23). The phrase: "And he shall leave them" **teaches that they require burial.** Although their use for the mitzva has been completed, it is prohibited to derive benefit from them.

הָנִיחָא לְרַבָּנַן, דְּאָמְרִי: מְלַמֵּד שֶׁטְּעוּנִין גְּנִיזָה, אֶלָּא לְרַבִּי דוֹסָא דִּפְלִיג עֲלַיְיהוּ, דְּאָמַר: אֲבָל רְאוּיִין הֵן לְכֹהֵן הֶדְיוֹט, וּמַאי "וְהִנִּיחָם שָׁם" – שֶׁלֹּא יִשְׁתַּמֵּשׁ בָּהֶם בְּיוֹם כִּפּוּרִים אַחֵר, מַאי אִיכָּא לְמֵימַר?

The Gemara comments: **It works out well** that there are two cases **according to** the opinion of **the Rabbis, who say** that this verse **teaches that they require burial. However, according to** the opinion of **Rabbi Dosa, who disagrees with them** and **says:** These priestly clothes may no longer be used by the High Priest on Yom Kippur, **but they are fit** for use **by a common priest,** since these garments are similar to those worn by common priests every day. **And what** is the meaning of: **"And he shall leave them there"?** This indicates **that** the High Priest **may not use them on another Yom Kippur.** According to this opinion, **what can be said?** According to the opinion of Rabbi Dosa, there is only one verse that teaches about misuse of consecrated property with an item that has already been used for performing its mitzva. Therefore, it should be possible to derive a principle from the verse dealing with the removal of ashes.

NOTES

Incense – קְטֹרֶת: The incense mixture used in the Temple was made from specific spices in set proportions. One who prepares the incense mixture using these spices and proportions violates the prohibition: "And the incense which you shall make, according to its composition, you shall not make for yourselves; it shall be to you sacred for the Lord" (Exodus 30:37). This prohibition applies only to one who prepares this mixture in order to smell its aroma, and not to one who prepares it for any other reason. If one smells the incense offered in the Temple he does not violate this prohibition, although he is punished for misuse of consecrated property.

The removal of ashes – תְּרוּמַת הַדֶּשֶׁן: It is a positive mitzva to remove some of the ash from the altar each morning and bring it to the floor of the courtyard (Leviticus 6:3). This was the first of the daily services performed in the Temple. In addition, from time to time, when the ashes accumulated, they would be removed from the Temple to a place set aside outside Jerusalem called the Place of the Ashes.

HALAKHA

Preparing the incense – עֲשִׂיַּית קְטוֹרֶת: One who prepared the incense with the correct spices and in their exact proportions in order to smell it is liable to receive *karet*. If he did this unwittingly, he must bring a sin-offering. If he prepared it in order to practice mixing it properly or to transfer it to the public, i.e., to the Temple, he is exempt (Rambam *Sefer Avoda*, *Hilkhot Kelei HaMikdash* 2:9–10).

Smelling the incense – הֲרָחַת קְטוֹרֶת: One who smells the incense in the Temple is not punished in the same way as one who prepares it for himself, although he is liable to receive punishment for misuse of consecrated property (Rambam *Sefer Avoda*, *Hilkhot Temidin UMusafin* 2:6).

Misuse of consecrated property with smell – מְעִילָה בְּרֵיחַ: One who smells the incense after the pillar of smoke has risen is exempt. If he smells it before this point, he is liable to receive punishment for misuse of consecrated property (Rambam *Sefer Avoda*, *Hilkhot Me'ila* 5:16).

The removal of ashes – תְּרוּמַת הַדֶּשֶׁן: It is prohibited to derive benefit from the ash removed from the altar, even after its mitzva has been completed (Rambam *Sefer Avoda*, *Hilkhot Temidin UMusafin* 2:15).

BACKGROUND

Because they have no substance – לְפִי שֶׁאֵין בָּהֶן מַמָּשׁ: The Gemara distinguishes between sound and sight, which are lacking in substance, and taste and smell, which have substance. This distinction can be supported by scientific data. Both taste and smell are transferred by molecules that move from one place to another. Therefore, when one enjoys a prohibited taste or smell, he is deriving benefit from a miniscule portion of the object itself. On the other hand, sight and sound are created by waves, and no part of the prohibited object itself reaches the one enjoying them.

מִשּׁוּם דְּהָווּ תְּרוּמַת הַדֶּשֶׁן וְעֶגְלָה עֲרוּפָה שְׁנֵי כְּתוּבִין הַבָּאִין כְּאֶחָד, וְכָל שְׁנֵי כְּתוּבִין הַבָּאִין כְּאֶחָד אֵין מְלַמְּדִין.

The Gemara answers: A principle cannot be based on this verse, **because removal of ashes and the heifer whose neck is broken,**[N] from which one may not derive benefit after the ceremony, **are two verses that come as one. And two verses that come as one do not teach** a principle.

הָנִיחָא לְמַאן דְּאָמַר אֵין מְלַמְּדִין, אֶלָּא לְמַאן דְּאָמַר מְלַמְּדִין, מַאי אִיכָּא לְמֵימַר? תְּרֵי מִיעוּטֵי כְּתִיבִי, כְּתִיב ״וְשָׂמוֹ״, וּכְתִיב ״הָעֲרוּפָה״.

The Gemara asks: **It works out well according to the one who said** that **they do not teach** a principle, i.e., according to the Rabbis. **However, according to the one who said** that **they do teach** a principle, i.e., Rabbi Yehuda in tractate *Sanhedrin*, **what can be said?** The Gemara answers: **Two** phrases indicating **exclusions are written** with regard to these *halakhot*, limiting this rule to them. With regard to the removal of ashes **it is written: "And he shall put it."** The word "it" limits the *halakha* to this particular circumstance. With regard to the heifer whose neck is broken **it is written: "The** heifer **which had its neck broken"** (Deuteronomy 21:6). The word "the" indicates that this *halakha* applies only to this type of heifer and not to any other similar case.

תָּא שְׁמַע: הִכְנִיסָהּ לְרְבָקָה וְדָשָׁה – כְּשֵׁירָה, בִּשְׁבִיל שֶׁתִּינַק וְתָדוּשׁ – פְּסוּלָה.

After this tangential discussion of the laws of misuse of consecrated property, the Gemara returns to Abaye and Rava's dispute about the status of unintended benefit, seeking to prove one side or the other. **Come** and **hear** a proof based on what was taught: If **one brought** the heifer whose neck is to be broken or the red heifer **into a cow pen,**[N] **and it threshes** grain while walking with other cows, then **it is valid.** Under normal circumstances, had one used the heifer for work, it would be disqualified from use in its ceremony. However, in this case, the red heifer may still be burned, and the heifer is still fit to have its neck broken in the ritual. Apparently, the verses "Upon which a yoke has not been placed" (Numbers 19:2) and "Which has not been used for work" (Deuteronomy 21:3) still apply to it, because the owner did not intend for it to work. If he brought it in **so that it may nurse** from its mother **and so it will thresh** grain, then **it is disqualified** from use in these rituals.

וְהָא הָכָא, דְּלָא אֶפְשָׁר וְקָא מִיכַּוֵּין, וְקָתָנֵי פְּסוּלָה! שָׁאנֵי הָתָם דִּכְתִיב: ״אֲשֶׁר לֹא עֻבַּד בָּהּ״ – מִכָּל מָקוֹם.

And here, isn't it a case **where it was not possible** to act differently, as the heifer needs to nurse, **and he intended** that it thresh the grain? **And it is teaching that** the heifer **is disqualified** from use. This proves that when one intends to derive benefit, even if there is no other way to act, it is prohibited to derive benefit. The Gemara rejects this: **It is different there, as it is written: "Which has not been used for work" in any case.** Therefore, while the heifer is disqualified from use even if the situation was unavoidable, no general conclusion can be drawn from this case.

אִי הָכִי, אֲפִילּוּ רֵישָׁא נַמִי!

The Gemara challenges: **If so,** that this verse means that it has not performed any work at all, then it should apply **even to the first clause.** Even when it threshes the grain against the will of the owner, it has still done work and should be rendered disqualified.

NOTES

The heifer whose neck is broken – עֶגְלָה עֲרוּפָה: When a murder victim's corpse is found outside a town and it is not known who caused his death, the following procedure is followed (Deuteronomy 21:1–9): First, judges who are members of the Great Sanhedrin come to measure the distance between the corpse and the nearest town, to determine which town must perform the rite of the heifer whose neck is broken. This measurement is carried out even if it is obvious which town is closest to the corpse. Afterward, the elders of that town bring a heifer that has never been used for any labor, and they break its neck in a riverbed that is not tilled. The elders wash their hands and make a statement absolving themselves of guilt. If the murderer is discovered before the heifer has been killed, the rite is not performed.

If one brought the heifer into a cow pen – הִכְנִיסָהּ לְרְבָקָה: According to the *Arukh*, the expression means that the heifer is taken into a pen where it eats, and it threshes some grain as it eats and moves around.

Perek **II**
Daf **26** Amud **b**

הָא לָא דָּמְיָא אֶלָּא לְהָא: שָׁכַן עָלֶיהָ עוֹף – כְּשֵׁירָה, עָלָה עָלֶיהָ זָכָר – פְּסוּלָה. מַאי טַעְמָא?

The Gemara answers. **This** case **is comparable only to that** other case: If **a bird landed on** the red heifer[H] **it remains valid,** since this is not considered to be like bearing a yoke. If **a male** animal **mounted it**[N] to mate with it, **it is unfit** and may not be used for the ritual. The same applies in this case: When the owner moves the heifer into a pen and it threshes, since the owner is uninterested in this action, it is like the case of the bird and the heifer remains valid. The Gemara asks: **What is the reason** for the difference between the case where a bird lands on it and where a male animal attempts to mate with it?

אָמַר רַב פַּפָּא: אִי כְּתִיב ״עָבַד״ וְקָרֵינַן ״עָבַד״ – עַד דְּעָבֵיד בָּהּ אִיהוּ. אִי כְּתִיב ״עוּבַּד״ וְקָרֵינַן ״עוּבַּד״ – אֲפִילּוּ מִמֵּילָא נַמִי.

Rav Pappa said that the verse says: "And the elders of that city shall take a heifer of the herd, which has not been used for work, and which has not drawn in the yoke" (Deuteronomy 21:3). **If it were written: "He worked [*avad*]," and we read: "He worked [*avad*],"** this word choice would indicate that the heifer could still be used **until he,** the owner of the heifer himself, **used it** willingly for labor. **If it were written: "It was worked [*ubbad*]," and we read: "It was worked [*ubbad*],"** it would indicate that **even** if it performed labor **on its own it is also** prohibited to use it, since some form of labor had been done with it.

HALAKHA

If a bird landed on the red heifer – שָׁכַן עָלֶיהָ עוֹף: If a bird landed on a red heifer then it remains valid. However, if a male mounted it to mate then it is rendered unfit (Rambam *Sefer Tahara, Hilkhot Para Aduma* 1:7).

NOTES

If a male animal mounted it – עָלָה עָלֶיהָ זָכָר: Some say that this applies even if the male did not lean on the red heifer at all; once this action takes place, it is rendered unfit (*Me'iri*).

הָשְׁתָּא דִּכְתִיב ״עָבַד״ וְקָרֵינַן ״עוּבַּד״ – עוּבַּד דּוּמְיָא דְּעָבַד. מָה עָבַד דְּנִיחָא לֵיהּ – אַף עוּבַּד דְּנִיחָא לֵיהּ.

Now that it is written: "He worked [*avad*]," but we read this word as: "It was worked [*ubbad*],"[N] both meanings are intended: It is prohibited if **it is worked in a similar** manner to the way **he works.** In other words, **just as** the owner **works** the animal in a way **that is beneficial to him, so too,** the animal becomes prohibited only when **it is worked** in a way **that causes him to** derive **benefit** from this labor. Therefore, it still may be used if a bird lands on it, because the owner does not derive benefit from this in any way. However, if a male bull mates with this heifer it is rendered unfit, since the owner generally has an interest in this occurring.

תָּא שְׁמַע: אֲבֵידָה, לֹא יִשְׁטְחֶנָּה לֹא עַל גַּבֵּי מִטָּה וְלֹא עַל גַּבֵּי מָגוֹד לְצוֹרְכּוֹ, אֲבָל שׁוֹטְחָהּ לְצוֹרְכָּהּ עַל גַּבֵּי מִטָּה וְעַל גַּבֵּי מָגוֹד. נִזְדַּמְּנוּ לוֹ אוֹרְחִין – לֹא יִשְׁטְחֶנָּה לֹא עַל גַּבֵּי מִטָּה וְלֹא עַל גַּבֵּי מָגוֹד, בֵּין לְצוֹרְכָּהּ בֵּין לְצוֹרְכּוֹ!

The Gemara cites an additional proof. **Come** and **hear** from that which is taught: If one finds **a lost item, he** may **not spread it out over a bed or over a frame**[N] **for his** own **purposes,** since this is deriving benefit from an object that does not belong to him. **However, he** may **spread it out over a bed or a frame for its** own **sake** if it requires airing. **If guests happen** to come **to him, he may not spread it out, not over a bed and not over a frame, neither for its sake nor for his** own **purpose.** Apparently, the benefit is unavoidable and intended, as there is no other way for him to care for the lost object, and he benefits from having his guests see the item; nonetheless, it is still prohibited.[H] This seems to prove that Rava's opinion is correct.

שָׁאנֵי הָתָם דְּקָלֵי לַהּ; אִי מִשּׁוּם עֵינָא בִּישָׁא, אִי מִשּׁוּם גַּנָּבֵי.

The Gemara rejects this conclusion: **It is different there, as** he risks **damaging it, either due to the evil eye** that he casts upon it **or due to the thieves** who will now know that this valuable item is in his possession and will attempt to steal it. It is not prohibited because of the benefit; rather, it is prohibited due to the concern that he may damage the item.

תָּא שְׁמַע: מוֹכְרֵי כְסוּת מוֹכְרִין כְּדַרְכָּן, וּבִלְבַד שֶׁלֹּא יִתְכַּוִּין בַּחַמָּה מִפְּנֵי הַחַמָּה וּבַגְּשָׁמִים מִפְּנֵי הַגְּשָׁמִים. וְהַצְּנוּעִין מַפְשִׁילִין לַאֲחוֹרֵיהֶם בְּמַקֵּל.

The Gemara offers a final proof. **Come** and **hear** a proof based on the following mishna: **Clothing merchants** who sell garments made of diverse kinds,[H] a prohibited mixture of wool and linen, may **sell them as they normally would** to gentiles. A merchant may place the garments he is selling on his shoulders and need not be concerned about the prohibition against wearing diverse kinds, **provided he does not intend** to benefit from the garments **in the sun** as protection **from the sun, or in the rain** as protection **from the rain. However, the modest** people,[N] those who are meticulous in their performance of mitzvot, **suspend** the wool and linen garments **on a stick behind them.**

וְהָא הָכָא, דְּאֶפְשָׁר לְמֶעֱבַד כִּצְנוּעִין, וְכִי לָא מְכַוֵּין – שָׁרֵי! תְּיוּבְתָּא לְמַאן דְּמַתְנֵי לִישָּׁנָא קַמָּא דְּרָבָא, תְּיוּבְתָּא.

And here, isn't it a case where **it is possible** for all clothing merchants **to act like the modest** people and not derive benefit from the mixture of wool and linen? Nonetheless, the mishna states that **when one does not intend** to benefit from the prohibited item, **it is permitted** to do so. This presents **a conclusive refutation to he who taught the first version of Rava's** statement. According to this version, one is prohibited from deriving benefit when it is possible to avoid doing so and he does not intend to derive benefit. The Gemara concludes: Indeed, it is **a conclusive refutation.**

״וְלֹא יַסִּיק בּוֹ וכו׳״. תָּנוּ רַבָּנַן: תַּנּוּר שֶׁהִסִּיקוֹ בִּקְלִיפֵּי עׇרְלָה אוֹ בְּקַשִּׁין שֶׁל כִּלְאֵי הַכֶּרֶם, חָדָשׁ – יוּתַּץ, יָשָׁן – יוּצַּן.

It was taught in the mishna that **one may not** even **light** the oven with leavened bread. **The Sages taught** in a *baraita*: With regard to **an oven that one lit**[B] **with the peels of *orla*** fruit, **or with straw** of grain that was planted in a prohibited mixture **of diverse kinds in a vineyard,** if it was a **new** oven, and by lighting it he hardened the oven and made it stronger for use in the future, then **it** must **be shattered.** Since prohibited items were used in the process of forming the oven, one may not derive benefit from the use of the prohibited items. However, if it was an **old** oven, **it** may **be cooled,** and it is prohibited to use the oven only while it is still hot.[H]

אָפָה בּוֹ אֶת הַפַּת, רַבִּי אוֹמֵר: הַפַּת אֲסוּרָה, וַחֲכָמִים אוֹמְרִים: הַפַּת מוּתֶּרֶת. בִּישְּׁלָהּ עַל גַּבֵּי גֶחָלִים – דִּבְרֵי הַכֹּל מוּתָּר.

With regard to **one** who **baked bread in** the oven while it was heated or strengthened by the prohibited items,[H] **Rabbi** Yehuda HaNasi **says: It is prohibited** to eat or derive benefit from **the bread,** since prohibited items were involved in the process of preparation. **And the Rabbis say: It is permitted** to eat and derive benefit from **the bread.** If **he cooked** the bread **over the coals** that remained from prohibited wood, **everyone agrees** that **it is permitted.**

NOTES

Avad and *ubbad* – עָבַד וְעוּבַּד: This type of exposition appears in several places in the Talmud, where the Sages expound upon both the way a word is pronounced and the way it is written. Sometimes this method is employed even when the word is pronounced in a manner consistent with the way it is written, but it is written in a way that could be read differently. Although there is general agreement about the accepted way to read the word in such a case, the Sages use the way that the word is written as a basis for additional expositions and as a way to understand the meaning of the verse.

Frame – מָגוֹד: Some say that this refers to a vessel on which clothes are placed after they have been washed (*Arukh*).

Modest people – צְנוּעִים: Some explain that this is referring to upright people who seek to avoid any suspicion of improper conduct (Rashi). Others say that this is referring to people who are especially stringent with themselves (Rabbi Shimshon of Saens) or to those who sanctify themselves by refraining even from that which is permitted (*Me'iri*).

HALAKHA

Use of a lost object – שִׁמּוּשׁ בַּאֲבֵידָה: It is prohibited for one who finds a lost object to use it, even to spread it out, for his own purposes. However, if he must spread out the garment in order to preserve it, then it is permitted to do so, provided it is done when no guests are present (*Shulḥan Arukh*, *Ḥoshen Mishpat* 267:17).

Merchants who sell garments of diverse kinds – מוֹכְרֵי שַׁעַטְנֵז: Merchants who sell to gentiles garments made of a prohibited mixture of wool and linen may place these garments on their backs in the manner that garment merchants generally carry their wares, provided they do not intend to derive benefit from the garments. Those who are fastidious about performing mitzvot suspend the garments behind them on a stick (*Shulḥan Arukh*, *Yoreh De'a* 301:6).

An oven that one lit with objects from which one may not derive benefit – תַּנּוּר שֶׁהִסִּיקוֹ בְּאִיסּוּרֵי הֲנָאָה: With regard to an oven that was lit with wood from which it is prohibited to derive benefit, whether it is a new oven or an old oven, it may be cooled down, and then one may light it again and use it. This follows the lenient *baraita*, as the Gemara concludes that it is in accordance with the opinion of the Rabbis (*Shulḥan Arukh*, *Yoreh De'a* 142:4).

Bread baked in an oven lit with prohibited wood – פַּת שֶׁנֶּאֶפְתָה בְּתַנּוּר שֶׁהוּסַק בְּעֵצִים הָאֲסוּרִים: With regard to bread baked in an oven that had been lit with prohibited wood, if it was baked after the prohibited wood was consumed, it is permitted to eat the bread. However, if the bread was baked when the wood was still burning, it is prohibited to eat it (*Shulḥan Arukh*, *Yoreh De'a* 142:6).

BACKGROUND

An oven that one lit – תַּנּוּר שֶׁהִסִּיקוֹ: Many ovens in late antiquity were made of clay. Fire was kindled inside to heat the oven until the fuel turned to ash. The ash was then swept away to make room for dough that had been rolled out flat, which was pasted to the walls of the oven or to the heated base.

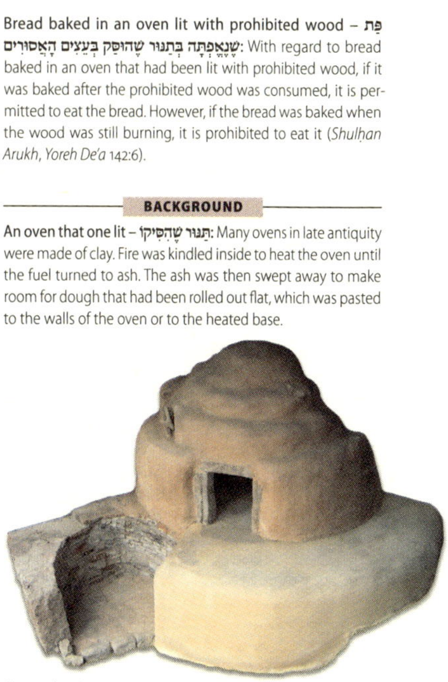

Clay oven from late antiquity

NOTES

Improvement from the wood in the bread – **שְׁבַח עֵצִים בַּפַּת:** The Gemara here makes a distinction between two similar topics: The improvement from the wood, on the one hand; and both this and that cause, on the other hand. The difference between these concepts is that improvement from the wood indicates that a small portion of the wood itself is actually present in the bread through the burning of the wood or through other processes with different prohibited items. Therefore, when the bread is improved by the wood in this way, it becomes prohibited. However, this is not the case with regard to the concept of: Both this and that cause, where the prohibited item is not present in the bread at all and instead only plays a role in achieving a certain result. Therefore, since baking bread in an oven that was strengthened using *orla* falls into this second category, there is no reason to shatter the oven.

וְהָא תַּנְיָא: בֵּין חָדָשׁ, וּבֵין יָשָׁן – יוּצַּן! לָא קַשְׁיָא, הָא – רַבִּי וְהָא רַבָּנַן.

The Gemara asks. **Wasn't it taught** in a *baraita*: **Whether** it was **an old** oven **or a new** oven **it** may **be cooled;** there is never a need to shatter the oven. The Gemara answers: This is **not difficult. This** *baraita*, which states that one is required to shatter the oven, is in accordance with the opinion of **Rabbi** Yehuda HaNasi. **And that** *baraita*, which states that it is sufficient to let the oven cool, is in accordance with the opinion of the **Rabbis.** Since the prohibited objects merely strengthen the oven, the Rabbis hold that it is enough to let the oven cool. By cooling the oven one no longer derives benefit from the prohibited items used to light it, and there is no need to shatter the oven.

אֵימוּר דְּשָׁמְעַתְּ לֵיהּ לְרַבִּי – מִשּׁוּם דְּיֵשׁ שְׁבַח עֵצִים בַּפַּת, זֶה וָזֶה גּוֹרֵם – מִי שָׁמְעַתְּ לֵיהּ?! אֶלָּא לָא קַשְׁיָא: הָא – רַבִּי אֱלִיעֶזֶר, הָא – רַבָּנַן.

The Gemara challenges this answer: **Say that you heard that Rabbi** Yehuda HaNasi prohibits one from deriving benefit from bread baked using the prohibited objects as kindling **because there is improvement from the wood** used to light the oven **in the bread,**[N] and therefore, it is prohibited. However, in a different case, namely, when **both this and that cause it,** i.e., both permitted and prohibited items contribute to the result, such as when one subsequently bakes in this oven and benefit is derived both from the prohibited wood that strengthened the oven and from permitted wood that is used in subsequent baking, **did you hear him** say that it is prohibited as well? **Rather,** reject this explanation and say: This is **not difficult. This** stringent *baraita* is in accordance with the opinion of **Rabbi Eliezer,** who says that in a case where both this and that cause it, it is prohibited. And **that** lenient *baraita* is in accordance with **the Rabbis,** who disagree with regard to that principle.

הֵי רַבִּי אֱלִיעֶזֶר? אִילֵימָא רַבִּי אֱלִיעֶזֶר דִּשְׂאוֹר, דִּתְנַן: שְׂאוֹר שֶׁל חוּלִּין וְשֶׁל תְּרוּמָה שֶׁנָּפְלוּ לְתוֹךְ עִיסָּה, וְאֵין בָּזֶה כְּדֵי לְהַחְמִיץ וְאֵין בָּזֶה כְּדֵי לְהַחְמִיץ, וְנִצְטָרְפוּ וְחִמְּצוּ, רַבִּי אֱלִיעֶזֶר אוֹמֵר: אַחַר אַחֲרוֹן אֲנִי בָּא. וַחֲכָמִים אוֹמְרִים: בֵּין שֶׁנָּפַל אִיסּוּר לְכַתְּחִלָּה, וּבֵין שֶׁנָּפַל אִיסּוּר לְבַסּוֹף – לְעוֹלָם אֵינוֹ אוֹסֵר

The Gemara asks: **Which** statement of **Rabbi Eliezer** serves as the basis for this explanation? **If you say** that it is the opinion of **Rabbi Eliezer** with regard to **leaven, as we learned** in a mishna: In a case where **non-sacred leaven and** leaven of ***teruma* fell into** non-sacred **dough, and neither one** alone **is** potent **enough to cause** the dough **to become leavened bread,** and **they** were **joined** together **and caused** the dough **to become leavened bread,** there is a dispute as to whether this dough is considered to be *teruma* or non-sacred bread. **Rabbi Eliezer says: I follow the final** element that fell into the dough. If the *teruma* fell in last, the dough is prohibited to non-priests. **And the Rabbis say: Whether the prohibited item,** i.e., the *teruma*, **fell** in **first or the prohibited item fell** in **last, it never** renders the dough **prohibited**

Perek **II**
Daf **27** Amud **a**

NOTES

Both this and that cause – **זֶה וָזֶה גּוֹרֵם:** Some explain that the principle: Both this and that cause, applies only when both items perform the same action, e.g., both provide heat. However, if the two items have different effects, then even if they both play a role in attaining a certain outcome, the resulting object is prohibited. Nonetheless, most authorities reject this distinction (Ritva).

I follow the final element – **אַחַר אַחֲרוֹן אֲנִי בָּא:** It is possible to understand Rabbi Eliezer's opinion differently. With regard to the leavening of dough, it is the last substance that completes that process, causing it to rise. Since the first amount of leaven was insufficient, it is considered as though it were not present, and the result is attributed completely to the latter amount.

עַד שֶׁיְּהֵא בּוֹ כְּדֵי לְהַחְמִיץ. וְאָמַר אַבַּיֵי: לֹא שָׁנוּ אֶלָּא שֶׁקָּדַם וְסִילֵּק אֶת הָאִיסּוּר, אֲבָל לֹא קָדַם וְסִילֵּק אֶת הָאִיסּוּר – אָסוּר. אַלְמָא: זֶה וָזֶה גּוֹרֵם אָסוּר.

until there is enough of the prohibited leaven **to cause** the dough **to become leavened bread. And Abaye said:** Rabbi Eliezer **taught** that when the permitted leaven fell in last, the mixture is permitted **only** when **he first removed the prohibited** leaven before the permitted leaven fell into the dough and made it rise. **However, if he did not first remove the prohibited leaven,** the dough **is prohibited** even if the permitted leaven fell in last. **Apparently,** when **both this and that cause**[N] the dough to become leavened bread, **it is prohibited.**

וּמְמַּאי דְּטַעֲמָא דְּרַבִּי אֱלִיעֶזֶר כְּאַבַּיֵי? דִּילְמָא טַעְמָא דְּרַבִּי אֱלִיעֶזֶר מִשּׁוּם דְּאַחַר אַחֲרוֹן אֲנִי בָּא, לָא שְׁנָא קָדַם וְסִילֵּק אֶת הָאִיסּוּר לָא שְׁנָא לֹא קָדַם וְסִילֵּק אֶת הָאִיסּוּר. אֲבָל בְּבַת אַחַת – הָכִי נַמִּי דְּשָׁרֵי!

The Gemara rejects this statement: And **from where** is it apparent **that the reason for Rabbi Eliezer's** opinion **is in accordance with Abaye's** explanation? **Perhaps the reason for Rabbi Eliezer's** opinion **is due to** the following, which Rabbi Eliezer said explicitly: **I follow the final** element.[N] **And it is no different** if **he first removed the prohibited item and it is no different** if **he did not first remove the prohibited item. However,** if they both fell in **at once it should be permitted,** because where both this and that cause the dough to become leavened bread Rabbi Eliezer rules that the mixture is permitted.

אֶלָּא: רַבִּי אֱלִיעֶזֶר דַּעֲצֵי אֲשֵׁירָה. דִּתְנַן: נָטַל הֵימֶנָּה עֵצִים – אֲסוּרִין בַּהֲנָאָה, הִסִּיק בָּהֶן אֶת הַתַּנּוּר, חָדָשׁ – יוּתַּץ, יָשָׁן – יוּצַּן.

Rather, the reference is to the opinion of **Rabbi Eliezer** with regard to **wood from an *asheira*. As we learned** in a mishna: If **one took wood from** an *asheira*, **it is prohibited to** derive **benefit from it.** With regard to one who **lit an oven with** the wood, if it was a **new** oven, **it** must **be broken.** If it was an **old** oven, **it** may **be cooled.**

אָפָה בּוֹ אֶת הַפַּת – אֲסוּרִין בַּהֲנָאָה. נִתְעָרְבָה בַּאֲחֵרוֹת וַאֲחֵרוֹת בַּאֲחֵרוֹת – כּוּלָּן אֲסוּרִין בַּהֲנָאָה. רַבִּי אֱלִיעֶזֶר אוֹמֵר: יוֹלִיךְ הֲנָאָה לְיַם הַמֶּלַח. (אָמַר) לוֹ: אֵין פִּדְיוֹן לַעֲבוֹדָה זָרָה.

If **one baked bread** with *asheira* wood as the fuel, **it is prohibited** to derive **benefit from it.**[H] If this bread **was mixed together with other** bread, **and** that **other** bread **was mixed with other** bread, **it is prohibited to derive benefit from all** of this bread. **Rabbi Eliezer says: He casts the benefit**[N] **into the Dead Sea** [***Yam HaMelaḥ***].[NB] In other words, one is not required to destroy the entire mixture when the prohibited bread is mixed with a large quantity of other bread. Instead one should designate money equal in value to the value of the original wood from the *asheira*, and he should destroy this money to offset the benefit he derived from the prohibited wood. The first *tanna* **said to him: Idolatry cannot be** monetarily **redeemed.**[N] Once the bread becomes prohibited, it cannot be redeemed by having its value cast into the Dead Sea. Apparently, the opinion of both Sages, including Rabbi Eliezer, is that when both this permitted object and that prohibited object cause a change to another item, the latter item is prohibited.

אֵימוּר דְּשָׁמְעַתְּ לֵיהּ לְרַבִּי אֱלִיעֶזֶר בַּעֲבוֹדָה זָרָה, דַּחֲמִיר אִיסּוּרָהּ – בִּשְׁאָר אִיסּוּרִין שֶׁבַּתּוֹרָה מִי שְׁמַעַתְּ לֵיהּ? אֶלָּא אִם כֵּן אַמַּאן תִּרְמְיֶיהּ? וְעוֹד, הָא תַּנְיָא בְּהֶדְיָא: וְכֵן הָיָה רַבִּי אֱלִיעֶזֶר אוֹסֵר בְּכָל אִיסּוּרִין שֶׁבַּתּוֹרָה.

The Gemara rejects this conclusion: **Say that you heard that Rabbi Eliezer** and the first *tanna* are stringent in this matter **with regard to idolatry, whose prohibition is stringent.** However, **with regard to other prohibitions in the Torah,** which are less stringent, **did you hear him** express this opinion? The Gemara responds to this question: **Rather, if** it is **so** that Rabbi Eliezer does not hold the same opinion with regard to other prohibitions, **to whom will you attribute** this *baraita*? If it is not Rabbi Eliezer who says this, then who is it? **And furthermore, wasn't it taught explicitly** in a *baraita*: **And, similarly, Rabbi Eliezer would prohibit** these types of mixtures **with regard to all prohibitions in the Torah.**

אָמַר אַבַּיֵי: אִם תִּמְצָא לוֹמַר ״זֶה וָזֶה גּוֹרֵם אָסוּר״ – רַבִּי הַיְינוּ רַבִּי אֱלִיעֶזֶר. וְאִם תִּמְצֵי לוֹמַר ״זֶה וָזֶה גּוֹרֵם מוּתָּר״ וְהָכָא מִשּׁוּם דְּיֵשׁ שְׁבָח עֵצִים בַּפַּת הוּא – הָנֵי קְעָרוֹת וְכוֹסוֹת וּצְלוֹחִיּוֹת אֲסִירִי.

Abaye said: If you say, based on the previously stated opinions, that Rabbi Yehuda HaNasi holds that when **both this and that cause, it is prohibited,** then the opinion of **Rabbi** Yehuda HaNasi **is** identical to the opinion of **Rabbi Eliezer,** as both state that it is prohibited for this same reason. **And if you say** that Rabbi Yehuda HaNasi holds that when **both this and that cause, it is permitted, and here,** where Rabbi Yehuda HaNasi rules that it is prohibited, **it is because there is improvement from the wood in the bread** itself, then in that case, deriving benefit from any of **these** earthenware **bowls, cups, and flasks**[H] that were made in such an oven should also **be prohibited,** since the improvement from the wood is in them as well. If one were to use such utensils he would be deriving benefit from a prohibited item.

כִּי פְּלִיגִי – בְּתַנּוּר וּקְדֵירָה. לְמַאן דְּאָמַר ״זֶה וָזֶה גּוֹרֵם אָסוּר״ – אָסוּר, לְמַאן דְּאָמַר ״זֶה וָזֶה גּוֹרֵם מוּתָּר״ – שָׁרֵי.

When Rabbi Yehuda HaNasi and the Sages **disagree is** in a case **where an oven and a pot** were formed using prohibited wood. **According to the one who says** that when **both this and that cause it is prohibited, it is prohibited** to derive benefit from these as well, since the prohibited item was a contributing factor in the initial formation of the object. However, **according to the one who says** that when **both this and that cause, it is permitted, it is permitted** to derive benefit from them. This is because one derives benefit from the prohibited oven and pot only once they have been subsequently heated by permitted wood. Therefore, the influence on the pot of the prohibited item is only one component in the preparation of this food.

אִיכָּא דְּאָמְרִי: אֲפִילּוּ לְמַאן דְּאָמַר ״זֶה וָזֶה גּוֹרֵם מוּתָּר״ – קְדֵירָה אֲסוּרָה, דְּהָא קִבְּלָה בִּישּׁוּלָא מִקַּמֵּי דְּנִיתָּן עֵצִים דְּהֶיתֵּירָא.

Some say that **even according to the one who says** that when **both this and that cause, it is permitted, the pot** made through the use of prohibited wood **is prohibited, since it holds the food** inside it **before the permitted wood is placed** in the oven. Therefore, one derives benefit from the prohibited vessel itself without any contribution from a permitted source.

HALAKHA

Bread baked with prohibited substances – פַּת שֶׁנֶּאֶפְתָה בְּאִיסּוּרֵי הֲנָאָה: Bread baked using *asheira* wood as fuel is prohibited. If this bread was mixed together with other bread, one should destroy money that has an equal value to that of the prohibited bread (see *Tosafot* and others). After doing so, the rest of the bread may be eaten. This ruling is in accordance with the opinion of Rabbi Yehuda HaNasi, as it is explicitly stated that the *halakha* is in accordance with his opinion (*Shulḥan Arukh, Yoreh De'a* 142:4).

Bowls, cups, and flasks – קְעָרוֹת וְכוֹסוֹת וּצְלוֹחִיּוֹת: Bowls, cups, flasks, and pots that were formed using wood from an *asheira* are prohibited, in accordance with the opinion of Rabbi Yehuda HaNasi as explained in the Gemara (*Shulḥan Arukh, Yoreh De'a* 142:5).

NOTES

He casts the benefit – יוֹלִיךְ הֲנָאָה: The benefit described here is explained in several ways. According to Rashi and the Ra'avad, this is referring to the benefit from the wood; therefore, one must cast away a sum of money that is equal in value to the wood itself. According to the Rambam, the Ra'ah, and *Tosafot*, it is referring to the benefit from the bread; therefore, one must cast away a sum of money that is equal to all the bread that was baked in a prohibited manner. Rabbeinu Tam understands that this is referring to the payment one would receive for baking the bread; according to his opinion, one must cast away this amount. The Ritva supports this opinion by explaining that if the Gemara wished to refer to the benefit from the bread or the wood, it would have said so explicitly.

He casts the benefit into the Dead Sea – יוֹלִיךְ הֲנָאָה לְיַם הַמֶּלַח: Some say that this applies only when the prohibited bread was mixed with other permitted bread, and that otherwise the benefit cannot be redeemed (Ramban; Ritva; and others). Others say that it can be redeemed even when the prohibited bread stands alone (Rashi). There is also a dispute as to whether Rabbi Eliezer permits one only to benefit from the prohibited item, e.g., by selling it (Rabbi Zeraḥya HaLevi; Ra'ah; and others), or that he holds that one may even eat it (Rabbanei Tzarfat).

Idolatry cannot be redeemed – אֵין פִּדְיוֹן לַעֲבוֹדָה זָרָה: The solution of casting away the value of the benefit of the prohibited item is offered in several different cases where a prohibited item was nullified within a mixture of permitted objects. Despite this, if one still wishes to refrain from using the prohibited object, then in these cases he takes the value of the prohibited item and destroys it. This also applies to certain cases of offerings into which a prohibited item was mixed. The Sages disagree here as to whether this principle can be applied to idolatry as well.

BACKGROUND

The Dead Sea [*Yam HaMelaḥ*] **– יָם הַמֶּלַח:** The Dead Sea mentioned by Rabbi Eliezer, literally the Sea of Salt, is also referred to in talmudic texts as the Sea of Sedom. It is common for the Gemara to suggest that a prohibited object be thrown into the Dead Sea, as there are no fish there and therefore no fishermen might chance across the object and take it for personal use. It is also possible that the high salt and mineral content of the Dead Sea were viewed by the Sages as elements that would ruin anything thrown into it.

אָמַר רַב יוֹסֵף, אָמַר רַב יְהוּדָה, אָמַר שְׁמוּאֵל: תַּנּוּר שֶׁהִסִּיקוֹ בִּקְלִיפֵּי עָרְלָה, אוֹ בְקַשִּׁין שֶׁל כִּלְאֵי הַכֶּרֶם, חָדָשׁ – יוּתַּץ, יָשָׁן – יוּצַּן. אָפָה בּוֹ אֶת הַפַּת, רַבִּי אוֹמֵר: הַפַּת מוּתֶּרֶת, וַחֲכָמִים אוֹמְרִים: הַפַּת אֲסוּרָה. וְהָתַנְיָא אִיפְּכָא! שְׁמוּאֵל אִיפְּכָא תָּנֵי.

Rav Yosef said that **Rav Yehuda said** that **Shmuel said:** With regard to **an oven that one lit with peels of *orla*** fruit, **or with straw** of grain that was planted in a prohibited mixture of **diverse kinds in a vineyard,** if it is a **new** oven, **it** must **be shattered.** If it is an **old** oven, **it** may **be cooled.** If **one baked bread in it, Rabbi** Yehuda HaNasi **says: The bread is permitted, and the Rabbis say: The bread is prohibited.** The Gemara challenges: **Wasn't the reverse taught** in the *baraita*? The Gemara answers: **Shmuel teaches the reverse,** that it is Rabbi Yehuda HaNasi who permits one to derive benefit from this bread even in the previously mentioned *baraita*.

וְאִיבָּעֵית אֵימָא: בְּעָלְמָא קָסָבַר שְׁמוּאֵל הֲלָכָה כְּרַבִּי מֵחֲבֵירוֹ, וְלֹא מֵחֲבֵירָיו, וּבְהָא – אֲפִילּוּ מֵחֲבֵירָיו. וְסָבַר: אַתְנְיֵיהּ אִיפְּכָא, כִּי הֵיכִי דְּנֵיקוּם רַבָּנַן לְאִיסּוּרָא.

And if you wish, say: Shmuel accepts the original text of the *baraita* that Rabbi Yehuda HaNasi is the one who prohibits deriving benefit from the bread. And **generally, Shmuel holds** that the ***halakha* is in accordance with** the opinion of **Rabbi** Yehuda HaNasi **over his** individual **colleague** who disagrees; however, the *halakha* does **not** follow him **over** several of **his colleagues** who disagree. **And in this** particular case, the *halakha* follows Rabbi Yehuda HaNasi **even over his colleagues. And** Shmuel **holds: I will reverse** the two sides presented here, **in order to establish the Rabbis'** opinion **as a prohibition.** Therefore, the conclusion will be to rule that it is prohibited, in accordance with the majority opinion. Although in Shmuel's version the attributions of the opinions are technically inaccurate, the benefit is that when people see that the Rabbis rule that it is prohibited in this case, they will be inclined to accept their majority opinion, which is the correct *halakha*.

בִּישְּׁלָהּ עַל גַּבֵּי גֶחָלִים – דִּבְרֵי הַכֹּל הַפַּת מוּתֶּרֶת. (אָמַר) רַב יְהוּדָה אָמַר שְׁמוּאֵל, וְרַבִּי חִיָּיא בַּר אַשִׁי אָמַר רַבִּי יוֹחָנָן; חַד אָמַר: לֹא שָׁנוּ אֶלָּא גֶּחָלִים עוֹמְמוֹת, אֲבָל גֶּחָלִים לוֹחֲשׁוֹת – אֲסוּרִין. וְחַד אָמַר: אֲפִילּוּ גֶּחָלִים לוֹחֲשׁוֹת נַמִי מוּתָּרִין.

It was taught as part of the previously stated *halakha* that if **one cooked** the bread **over coals**[N] produced from an *asheira*, **everyone agrees that the bread is permitted.** The Gemara records a dispute: **Rav Yehuda said** that **Shmuel said** one opinion, **and Rabbi Ḥiyya bar Ashi said** that **Rabbi Yoḥanan said** another opinion. **One** of them **said: They taught** this leniency **only** when one cooks with **dim coals,** whose heat is merely a remnant of the earlier lighting; **however,** when one cooks with **glowing coals,**[NH] the bread **is prohibited. And one** of them **said:** Even when **the coals are glowing,** the bread is **also permitted.**

בִּשְׁלָמָא לְמַאן דְּאָמַר לוֹחֲשׁוֹת אֲסוּרִין – מִשּׁוּם דְּיֵשׁ שֶׁבַח עֵצִים בַּפַּת. אֶלָּא לְמַאן דְּאָמַר אֲפִילּוּ לוֹחֲשׁוֹת מוּתָּרוֹת – פַּת דְּאָסַר, דְּיֵשׁ שֶׁבַח עֵצִים בַּפַּת, לְרַבִּי הֵיכִי מַשְׁכַּחַתְּ לֵיהּ? אָמַר רַב פָּפָּא: כְּשֶׁאֲבוּקָה כְּנֶגְדּוֹ.

The Gemara asks: **Granted, according to the one who said** that baking with **glowing** coals renders the bread **prohibited,** this is **because there is improvement from the** prohibited **wood in the bread. However, according to the one** who **said** that **even** when baking with **glowing** coals the bread is **permitted,** since they are no longer considered to be wood, **where do you find the case** where **Rabbi** Yehuda HaNasi **deems bread to be prohibited because there is improvement from** the prohibited **wood in it?** Why should there be a difference between glowing coals and actual burning wood? **Rav Pappa said:** The case is **when a flame is** directly **opposite** the bread. When he cooks the bread directly in front of the wood, it is improved directly by the wood. When the coals are merely glowing, there is no direct benefit from the wood.

Perek **II**
Daf **27** Amud **b**

מִכְּלָל דְּרַבָּנַן דִּפְלִיגִי עֲלֵיהּ שָׁרוּ אֲפִילּוּ כְּשֶׁאֲבוּקָה כְּנֶגְדּוֹ! אֶלָּא עֵצִים דְּאִיסּוּרָא לְרַבָּנַן הֵיכִי מַשְׁכַּחַתְּ לְהוּ? אָמַר רַב אַמִי בַּר חָמָא: בְּשַׁרְשִׁיפָא.

The Gemara asks: Does this prove **by inference that the Rabbis who disagree with** Rabbi Yehuda HaNasi **permit** one to eat this bread **even when the flame is opposite it? But** if this is the case, **where do you find the case** where **it is prohibited according to the Rabbis** to derive benefit from **wood? Rav Ami bar Ḥama said:** It is found **in** the case of **a stool** made from the wood. Although they hold that it is permitted to derive indirect benefit from the wood, even the Rabbis agree that one may not derive benefit from a stool that is made from the wood itself.

NOTES

Cooking with coals – **בִּישּׁוּל בְּגֶחָלִים**: One is permitted to cook with coals produced from prohibited wood only when there is a requirement to destroy the wood specifically through burning, as the ash of such items is permitted. However, if one is required to eliminate the object, but not necessarily through burning, as is the case with regard to leavened bread before Passover, then it is prohibited to use even the coals made from it (Rosh, citing Rabbeinu Yona).

Glowing coals – **גֶּחָלִים לוֹחֲשׁוֹת**: Coals are considered to be glowing if one can place a stick inside them and they will ignite on their own (Ritva).

HALAKHA

Glowing coals – **גֶּחָלִים לוֹחֲשׁוֹת**: One may derive benefit from coals produced from prohibited wood, even if they are still glowing. It is prohibited only if one benefits directly from the fire, in accordance with the Gemara's conclusion (*Shulḥan Arukh, Yoreh De'a* 142:7).

בְּעָא מִינֵּיהּ רָמִי בַּר חָמָא מֵרַב חִסְדָּא: תַּנּוּר שֶׁהִסִּיקוֹ בַּעֲצֵי הֶקְדֵּשׁ וְאָפָה בּוֹ הַפַּת, לְרַבָּנַן דְּשָׁרוּ בְּקַמַּיְיתָא מַאי? אֲמַר לֵיהּ: הַפַּת אֲסוּרָה. וּמַה בֵּין זוֹ לְעָרְלָה? אֲמַר רָבָא: הָכִי הָשְׁתָּא?! עָרְלָה – בְּטֵילָה בְּמָאתַיִם, הֶקְדֵּשׁ – אֲפִילּוּ בְּאֶלֶף לֹא בָּטֵיל.

Rami bar Ḥama raised a dilemma before Rav Ḥisda: With regard to **an oven that one kindled with consecrated wood and baked bread in it, according to the Rabbis, who permitted** the bread **in the first** case where it was baked with *orla* peels, **what is the *halakha*? He said to him: The bread is prohibited.** He responded: **What is the difference between this** bread **and** bread baked with ***orla*** peels? **Rava said: How can** these cases **be compared? *Orla* is nullified** in a mixture of one part in **two hundred;** it is possible that less than this amount of *orla* was absorbed by the bread. However, **consecrated** wood **is not nullified**[N] **even** in a mixture of one part in **one thousand.** Therefore, even when there is only a miniscule amount of the consecrated matter in the bread it is still prohibited.

אֶלָּא אָמַר רָבָא: אִי קַשְׁיָא לֵיהּ – הָא קַשְׁיָא: וַהֲלֹא מָעַל הַמַּסִּיק, וְכָל הֵיכָא דְּמָעַל הַמַּסִּיק – נָפְקוּ לְהוּ לְחוּלִּין!

Rather, Rava said: If it was difficult for Rami bar Ḥama, **this is** what he found **difficult: Didn't the kindler** of the fire transgress the prohibition of **misuse of consecrated property,** as anyone who unwittingly uses consecrated property for a non-sacred use violates this prohibition? **And any** case **where the kindler** of an oven **misuses consecrated property**[N] by doing so, the wood **is transferred to non-sacred** status. The wood loses its sanctity when misused, and the one who misused it must donate other wood to the Temple in its place. In that case, the wood used to heat the oven is non-sacred wood and the bread should be permitted.

אָמַר רַב פַּפָּא: הָכָא בַּעֲצֵי שְׁלָמִים עָסְקִינַן, וְאַלִּיבָּא דְּרַבִּי יְהוּדָה, דְּאָמַר: הֶקְדֵּשׁ, בְּשׁוֹגֵג – מִתְחַלֵּל, בְּמֵזִיד – אֵינוֹ מִתְחַלֵּל.

Rav Pappa said: Here, we are dealing with wood which had been set aside **for** purchasing **peace-offerings.** This wood, while sanctified, has a lesser status of sanctity and does not become fully consecrated until the blood of the offering has been sprinkled. **And** this dilemma was raised **in accordance with** the opinion of **Rabbi Yehuda, who said:** If one **unwittingly** misused **consecrated property, it becomes desecrated** and loses its elevated status. However, if one used the object **intentionally, it is not desecrated** and remains consecrated. Since the act here is intentional, the consecrated wood does not lose its status.

בְּמֵזִיד מַאי טַעְמָא לָא – כֵּיוָן דְּלָאו בַּר מְעִילָה הוּא לָא נָפֵיק לְחוּלִּין, שְׁלָמִים נַמִי, כֵּיוָן דְּלָאו בַּר מְעִילָה נִינְהוּ – לָא נָפְקָא לְחוּלִּין.

The Gemara explains: **What is the reason** that when one **intentionally** uses this object it does **not** lose its status? **Since** it is **not subject to** the *halakha* of **misuse of consecrated property,** as one is liable to bring an offering only for unwitting misuse of consecrated property, **it is not transferred to non-sacred** status. The same *halakha* applies to the wood set aside for **peace-offerings as well. Since** at that stage **it is not subject to** the *halakha* of **misuse of consecrated property,** as that applies only after the animal's blood has been sprinkled, then according to the opinion of Rabbi Yehuda, even if one unwittingly uses this wood, **it is not transferred to non-sacred** status; rather, it remains prohibited.

וְכָל הֵיכָא דְּמָעַל הַמַּסִּיק נָפְקִי לְחוּלִּין? וְהָא תַּנְיָא: כָּל הַנִּשְׂרָפִין אֶפְרָן מוּתָּר, חוּץ מֵעֲצֵי אֲשֵׁירָה. וְאֵפֶר הֶקְדֵּשׁ לְעוֹלָם אָסוּר!

The Gemara asks: **And anywhere the kindler** of an oven transgresses the prohibition of **misuse of consecrated property** by using consecrated wood, **is it transferred to non-sacred** status? **Wasn't it taught** in a *baraita*: With regard to **all** prohibited items **that must be burned, their ashes are permitted** after the burning, **except for wood from an *asheira*.**[H] **And consecrated ash**[H] **is prohibited forever.** Therefore, it is possible that when one kindles an oven with this consecrated wood, although he misuses consecrated property, the ash remains prohibited.

אָמַר רָמִי בַּר חָמָא: כְּגוֹן שֶׁנָּפְלָה דְּלֵיקָה מֵאֵילֶיהָ בַּעֲצֵי הֶקְדֵּשׁ, דְּלֵיכָּא אֱינַשׁ דְּנִמְעוֹל. רַב שְׁמַעְיָה אָמַר: בְּאוֹתָן שֶׁטְּעוּנִין גְּנִיזָה, דְּתַנְיָא: ״וְשָׂמוֹ״ – בְּנַחַת, ״וְשָׂמוֹ״ – כּוּלּוֹ, ״וְשָׂמוֹ״ – שֶׁלֹּא יְפַזֵּר.

Rami bar Ḥama said: That *baraita* is discussing a case **where a fire began on its own among consecrated wood and there is no one who misused consecrated property.** Since this is the case, even the ash that is left from this wood remains consecrated property and one may not benefit from it. **Rav Shemaya said:** This *baraita* is dealing **with those** types of consecrated ash **that require burial,** such as the ash removed from the altar. **As it was taught** in a *baraita*: "And he shall take up the ash from where the fire has consumed the burnt-offering on the altar, and he shall put it beside the altar" (Leviticus 6:3). The phrase **"And he shall put it"** indicates that he must do so **gently; "and he shall put it"** also indicates that he must place **all of it; "and he shall put it"** also indicates **that he** may **not scatter** the ashes. Apparently, even after the offering has been burned it remains sacred, and one may not derive benefit from it. However, when it was burned it was not subject to misuse of consecrated property, as its burning is a necessary step in the process of sacrificing the offerings.

NOTES

Consecrated wood is not nullified – הֶקְדֵּשׁ...לֹא בָּטֵיל: Several explanations are offered in order to explain why this is the case. Some say it is not nullified because it is an object whose prohibition is temporary, as it is possible to have one's vow consecrating the object annulled by a Sage, and any item whose prohibition can or will lapse at some future time is not subject to nullification. Others say that it will not be canceled because it is not only a question of prohibitions; rather, there is also a monetary element to its status: It is the property of the Temple, and there is no nullification with regard to ownership of property (*Me'iri*).

Misuse of consecrated property – מְעִילָה: The *halakhot* of misuse of consecrated property are stated in the Torah (Leviticus 5:14–16) and discussed in greater detail in tractate *Me'ila*. The basic principle is that anyone who derives benefit from consecrated property unwittingly, i.e., without the knowledge that it was consecrated property, transgresses this prohibition. One who does so is obligated to bring an offering and to pay to the Temple the value of the object from which he benefited. In addition, he must pay an extra one-fifth of the value as a fine. After one uses such an item it loses its consecrated status, which is transferred to the money that he pays to the Temple.

The Torah does not discuss one who derives benefit intentionally. Therefore, such a person cannot atone for deriving benefit by sacrificing an offering or by paying the additional fifth of the value as a fine.

HALAKHA

Ash from the wood of an *asheira* – אֵפֶר עֲצֵי אֲשֵׁרָה: It is prohibited to derive benefit from ash left over after an idol or an *asheira* tree has been burned (*Shulḥan Arukh, Yoreh De'a* 142:1).

Consecrated ash – אֵפֶר הֶקְדֵּשׁ: It is permitted to derive benefit from the ash left over from any consecrated item that must be burned, except for the ash removed from the outer altar, from the inner altar, and from the candelabrum. According to the Ra'avad it is prohibited to derive benefit only from the ash removed from the outer altar (Rambam *Sefer Avoda, Hilkhot Pesulei HaMukdashin* 19:13).

״רַבִּי יְהוּדָה אוֹמֵר אֵין בִּיעוּר וכו׳״. תַּנְיָא, אָמַר רַבִּי יְהוּדָה: אֵין בִּיעוּר חָמֵץ אֶלָּא שְׂרֵיפָה. וְהַדִּין נוֹתֵן: וּמָה נוֹתָר שֶׁאֵינוֹ בְּבַל יֵרָאֶה וּבַל יִמָּצֵא – טָעוּן שְׂרֵיפָה, חָמֵץ שֶׁיֶּשְׁנוֹ בְּבַל יֵרָאֶה וּבַל יִמָּצֵא – לֹא כָּל שֶׁכֵּן שֶׁטָּעוּן שְׂרֵיפָה?!

It was taught in the mishna that **Rabbi Yehuda says: The removal of leavened bread is** to be accomplished **only** through **burning. It was taught** in a *baraita* that **Rabbi Yehuda said: The removal of leavened bread is** to be accomplished **only through burning.**[N] **And a logical derivation leads** to this conclusion: **Just as** that which is **left over** from an offering after the time period in which it may be eaten, **which is not subject to** the prohibitions: **It shall not be seen, and: It shall not be found, requires burning, so too,** with regard to **leavened bread,** which is more stringent **as it is subject to** the prohibitions of: **It shall not be seen, and: It shall not be found, all the more so** is it **not** clear **that it requires burning?**

אָמְרוּ לוֹ: כָּל דִּין שֶׁאַתָּה דָּן תְּחִלָּתוֹ לְהַחְמִיר וְסוֹפוֹ לְהָקֵל – אֵינוֹ דִּין. לֹא מָצָא עֵצִים לְשׂוֹרְפוֹ – יְהֵא יוֹשֵׁב וּבָטֵל? וְהַתּוֹרָה אָמְרָה: ״תַּשְׁבִּיתוּ שְּׂאוֹר מִבָּתֵּיכֶם״ – בְּכָל דָּבָר שֶׁאַתָּה יָכוֹל לְהַשְׁבִּיתוֹ.

The Rabbis **said to him: Any logical derivation that you derive** whose **initial** teaching **is stringent but whose subsequent** consequences **are lenient**[N] **is not** a valid **logical derivation.** According to Rabbi Yehuda, if one **did not find wood to burn** his leavened bread, must **he sit idly** and not remove it? **And the Torah said: "You shall remove leaven from your houses"** (Exodus 12:15), indicating that this must be done **in any manner which you can remove it.** Apparently, Rabbi Yehuda's logical derivation leads to a leniency.

חָזַר רַבִּי יְהוּדָה וְדָנוֹ דִּין אַחֵר: נוֹתָר אָסוּר בַּאֲכִילָה וְחָמֵץ אָסוּר בַּאֲכִילָה, מַה נּוֹתָר בִּשְׂרֵיפָה – אַף חָמֵץ בִּשְׂרֵיפָה.

Then Rabbi Yehuda presented a different logical derivation based on the principle of: What do we find with regard to, rather than on an *a fortiori* inference (Rashash). **It is prohibited to eat the leftover** of offerings **and it is prohibited to eat leavened bread.** Based on this similarity, one can conclude that **just as the leftover** of offerings **requires burning, so too, leavened bread requires burning.**

אָמְרוּ לוֹ: נְבֵילָה תּוֹכִיחַ, שֶׁאֲסוּרָה בַּאֲכִילָה וְאֵינָהּ טְעוּנָה שְׂרֵיפָה. אָמַר לָהֶן: הֶפְרֵשׁ; נוֹתָר אָסוּר בַּאֲכִילָה וּבַהֲנָאָה, וְחָמֵץ אָסוּר בַּאֲכִילָה וּבַהֲנָאָה. מַה נּוֹתָר טָעוּן שְׂרֵיפָה – אַף חָמֵץ טָעוּן שְׂרֵיפָה.

They said to him: The case of **an animal carcass can prove** that eating the leftover of offerings is not a factor in determining whether or not leavened bread requires burning, **as eating** an animal carcass **is prohibited and it does not require burning.** Therefore, there is no clear connection between the prohibition to eat a particular object and a requirement to burn it. **He said to them:** There is a **difference** between these cases, as it is explicitly stated that one may benefit from an animal corpse. Therefore, the following comparison can be made: **It is prohibited to eat and** derive **benefit from the leftover** of sacrificial meat, **and it is prohibited to eat and** derive **benefit from leavened bread. Just as the leftover** of sacrificial meat **requires burning, so too, leavened bread requires burning.**

אָמְרוּ לוֹ: שׁוֹר הַנִּסְקָל יוֹכִיחַ, שֶׁאָסוּר בַּאֲכִילָה וּבַהֲנָאָה – וְאֵינוֹ טָעוּן שְׂרֵיפָה. אָמַר לָהֶן: הֶפְרֵשׁ; נוֹתָר אָסוּר בַּאֲכִילָה וּבַהֲנָאָה וְעָנוּשׁ כָּרֵת, וְחָמֵץ אָסוּר בַּאֲכִילָה וּבַהֲנָאָה וְעָנוּשׁ כָּרֵת. מַה נּוֹתָר בִּשְׂרֵיפָה – אַף חָמֵץ בִּשְׂרֵיפָה. אָמְרוּ לוֹ: חֶלְבּוֹ שֶׁל שׁוֹר הַנִּסְקָל יוֹכִיחַ, שֶׁאָסוּר בַּאֲכִילָה וּבַהֲנָאָה וְעָנוּשׁ כָּרֵת – וְאֵין טָעוּן שְׂרֵיפָה.

The Rabbis **said to him:** The case of **an ox that is stoned can prove** that this is not a clear factor, **as it is prohibited to eat and** derive **benefit** from such an ox **and it does not require burning. He said to them:** There is a **difference** between leavened bread and an ox that is stoned, as there is an additional factor that is not relevant to the ox. **It is prohibited to eat and** derive **benefit from the leftover** of sacrificial meat, and one who does so is **punished with** ***karet*****. And it is prohibited to eat and** derive **benefit from leavened bread, and** one who does so is **punished with** ***karet*****. Just as the leftover** of sacrificial meat requires **burning, so too, leavened bread** requires **burning. They said to him:** If so, **the fats of an ox that is stoned**[N] **can prove** that this too is an insignificant factor, **as it is prohibited to eat** the fats and derive **benefit** from them, and one who eats them is **punished with** ***karet*****, and they do not require burning.**

NOTES

The removal of leavened bread is to be accomplished only through burning – **אֵין בִּיעוּר חָמֵץ אֶלָּא שְׂרֵיפָה**: It seems that this dispute is only with regard to rabbinic law; by Torah law it is sufficient for one to make a declaration of nullification. However, according to Rabbi Yehuda, the ideal way to perform this mitzva is to burn one's leavened bread, while according to the Rabbis one can perform the mitzva in its ideal form by crumbling the leavened bread and throwing it to the wind (*Tosefot Rid*).

Whose initial teaching is stringent but whose subsequent consequences are lenient – **תְּחִלָּתוֹ לְהַחְמִיר וְסוֹפוֹ לְהָקֵל**: The reasoning behind this principle is that an *a fortiori* inference is used to derive a stringency by comparing a less stringent case to a more stringent one. However, if the comparison results in a leniency under certain circumstances, the *a fortiori* inference loses its logical basis. In the Jerusalem Talmud other cases are cited where a similar claim is made against Rabbi Yehuda, and it appears that Rabbi Yehuda does not agree with the idea that an *a fortiori* inference is weakened in this manner. Perhaps he abandoned this derivation in this case because he wished to prove his opinion in a manner that would also be consistent with the opinion of the Rabbis (Maharam Ḥalawa).

Fats of an ox that is stoned – **חֶלְבּוֹ שֶׁל שׁוֹר הַנִּסְקָל**: This issue is discussed in the Jerusalem Talmud and in the *Mekhilta*, where it is mentioned that according to Rabbi Yehuda there is a difference between the fats of an ox that is stoned on one hand and the removal of leavened bread and the leftover of sacrificial meat on the other. While the prohibitions of leavened bread and the leftover of sacrificial meat are both connected to time, namely, Passover and the day after the offering is sacrificed, respectively, the prohibition of the fats of an ox that is stoned is not time dependent.

חָזַר רַבִּי יְהוּדָה וְדָנוֹ דִּין אַחֵר: נוֹתָר יֶשְׁנוֹ בְּ״בַל תּוֹתִירוּ״, וְחָמֵץ בְּ״בַל תּוֹתִירוּ״. מַה נּוֹתָר בִּשְׂרֵיפָה – אַף חָמֵץ בִּשְׂרֵיפָה.

Then Rabbi Yehuda presented a different logical derivation: The prohibition against eating and deriving benefit from **leftover** sacrificial meat **is** clearly included **in the prohibition of: And you shall not leave over. And leavened bread is** also included, in a sense, **in** the prohibition of: **And you shall not leave over,** as once the time it may be eaten expires, one violates the prohibitions of: It shall not be seen, and: It shall not be found, by owning it. **Just as leftover** sacrificial meat **is subject to burning, so too, leavened bread is subject to burning.**

אָמְרוּ לוֹ: אָשָׁם תָּלוּי וְחַטַּאת הָעוֹף הַבָּא עַל הַסָּפֵק, לִדְבָרֶיךָ, יוֹכִיחוּ: שֶׁהֵן בְּ״בַל תּוֹתִירוּ״. שֶׁאָנוּ אוֹמְרִים בִּשְׂרֵיפָה – וְאַתָּה אוֹמֵר בִּקְבוּרָה! שָׁתַק רַבִּי יְהוּדָה.

They said to him: According to your opinion, an uncertain guilt-offering and a bird sacrificed **as a sin-offering in a case of doubt will prove**[N] that this comparison is not valid, **as they are** also included **in** the prohibition of: **And you shall not leave over,** since these offerings are prohibited after the time in which they may be eaten has expired. **As we say that they are subject to burning, but you say** that an uncertain guilt-offering **is subject to burial. Rabbi Yehuda was silent,** as he had no response.

אָמַר רַב יוֹסֵף: הַיְינוּ דְּאָמְרִי אֱינָשֵׁי: כַּפָּא דְּחָטָא נַגָּרָא בְּגַוָּהּ נִשְׁרוֹף חַרְדְּלָא.

Rav Yosef said: This is as people say: In the spoon that the carpenter made, the mustard will burn[N] his palate. In other words, one can be harmed by his own actions. Similarly, in this case the strongest proof against Rabbi Yehuda's opinion is the one based on Rabbi Yehuda's own statement.

(אָמַר אַבַּיֵי): סַדָּנָא בְּסַדְנֵי יָתֵיב, מִדְּוִיל יְדֵיהּ מִשְׁתַּלֵּים.

Abaye said another folk expression: **He who made the stocks** [*saddana*] **shall sit in the stocks;**[N] **he is repaid through his own handiwork.**

רָבָא אָמַר: גַּיָּרָא בְּגִירֵי מִקְטֵיל, מִדְּוִיל יְדֵיהּ מִשְׁתַּלֵּים.

Rava said another similar saying: **He who made the arrows shall be killed with his own arrows; he is repaid through his own handiwork.**

״וַחֲכָמִים אוֹמְרִים מְפָרֵר וְזוֹרֶה וכו׳״. אִיבַּעְיָא לְהוּ, הֵיכִי קָאָמַר: מְפָרֵר וְזוֹרֶה לָרוּחַ, וּמְפָרֵר וּמַטִּיל לַיָּם. אוֹ דִּילְמָא: מְפָרֵר וְזוֹרֶה לָרוּחַ, אֲבָל מַטִּיל לַיָּם בְּעֵינֵיהּ. תְּנַן נַמִי גַּבֵּי עֲבוֹדָה זָרָה כִּי הַאי גַּוְונָא: רַבִּי יוֹסֵי אוֹמֵר: שׁוֹחֵק וְזוֹרֶה לָרוּחַ, אוֹ מַטִּיל לַיָּם. וְאִיבַּעְיָא לְהוּ: הֵיכִי קָאָמַר? שׁוֹחֵק וְזוֹרֶה לָרוּחַ, וְשׁוֹחֵק וּמַטִּיל לַיָּם. אוֹ דִּילְמָא: שׁוֹחֵק וְזוֹרֶה לָרוּחַ, אֲבָל מַטִּיל לַיָּם בְּעֵינֵיהּ.

It was taught in the mishna: **And the Rabbis say** that leavened bread need not be burned; rather, **one** may even **crumble** it **and throw** it **into the wind** or the sea.[H] **A dilemma was raised before** the Sages: **With regard to what case are they speaking?** Do they mean that he must specifically **crumble** it **and throw** it **into the wind** or **crumble** it **and throw** it **into the sea? Or perhaps one** may **crumble** it **and throw** it **into the wind, but he** may **cast** it **into the sea in its pure, unadulterated form,** without crumbling it first. **We also learned** in a mishna **with regard to idolatry in a case like this** that **Rabbi Yosei says: He** may **grind** the idol **and throw** the dust **into the wind or cast it into the sea.**[H] **And a dilemma was raised before** the Sages: **With regard to what** case **are they speaking?** Must one specifically **grind** it **and throw** it **into the wind or grind** it **and throw** it **into the sea? Or** perhaps **he** may **grind** it **and throw** it **into the wind; however, he** may **throw** it **into the sea in its pure,** unadulterated form.

אָמַר רַבָּה: מִסְתַּבְּרָא, עֲבוֹדָה זָרָה דְּלַיַּם הַמֶּלַח קָא אָזְלָא – לָא בָּעֵי שְׁחִיקָה, חָמֵץ דְּלִשְׁאָר נַהֲרוֹת קָאָזֵיל בָּעֵי פֵּירוּר. אֲמַר לֵיהּ רַב יוֹסֵף: אַדְּרַבָּה, אִיפְּכָא מִסְתַּבְּרָא! עֲבוֹדָה זָרָה דְּלָא מְמִיסָה – בָּעֵי שְׁחִיקָה, חָמֵץ דְּמֵימִיס – לָא בָּעֵי פֵּירוּר.

Rabba said: It stands to reason that since idols are thrown into the Dead Sea,[N] **they do not need grinding,** as there is no concern that they will be removed and used again. However, **leavened bread that** may be **thrown into other rivers, needs crumbling** before being cast away. **Rav Yosef said to him: On the contrary, the opposite is** more **reasonable. Idols, which do not** normally **disintegrate** in the water, **need grinding.** However, **leavened bread, which disintegrates in the water** on its own, **does not need crumbling.**[H]

NOTES

According to your opinion…will prove – לִדְבָרֶיךָ יוֹכִיחוּ: Why don't the Rabbis use the *a fortiori* inference that they suggest and derive that one must burn leavened bread? Apparently they believe that one cannot derive *halakhot* of non-sacred items from *halakhot* of consecrated items (Maharam Ḥalawa; see *Tosafot*).

The mustard will burn – נִשְׁרוֹף חַרְדְּלָא: Some explain this expression to mean that the carpenter's mustard is burned in the spoon that he himself made (Rabbeinu Ḥananel).

He who made the stocks [saddana] shall sit in the stocks – סַדָּנָא בְּסַדְנֵי יָתֵיב: Some have a different version of the text, which reads *sadda'a*. This then is referring to one who builds ships and rafts and is condemned to be chained up on them (*Arukh*).

Idols…into the Dead Sea – עֲבוֹדָה זָרָה לְיַם הַמֶּלַח: This applies specifically to the Dead Sea, since it is a place devoid of people. Therefore, whatever is thrown into it is considered gone forever.

HALAKHA

Removal of leavened bread – בִּיעוּר חָמֵץ: When one removes leavened bread, he may do so by crumbling it and throwing it into the wind, by burning it, or by casting it into the sea, in accordance with the majority opinion of the Rabbis (*Shulḥan Arukh, Oraḥ Ḥayyim* 445:1).

Removal of idolatry – בִּיעוּר עֲבוֹדָה זָרָה: Idols, or any objects used for idolatry, must be ground up and then thrown into the sea or into the wind. Even Rabba seems to agree that when one does not throw them into the Dead Sea one must grind them up first (*Shulḥan Arukh, Yoreh De'a* 146:14).

Crumbling leavened bread – פֵּירוּר חָמֵץ: One may remove leavened bread by throwing it into the sea, even without crumbling it first. However, if it is hard, he should crumble it before throwing it in, in accordance with the opinion of Rav Yosef and his explanation of the *baraita* (*Shulḥan Arukh, Oraḥ Ḥayyim* 445:1).

תניא כוותיה דרבה, תניא כוותיה דרב יוסף. תניא כוותיה דרבה: היה מהלך במדבר – מפרר וזורה לרוח. היה מהלך בספינה – מפרר ומטיל לים. תניא כוותיה דרב יוסף: היה מהלך במדבר – שוחק וזורה לרוח, היה מהלך בספינה – שוחק ומטיל לים.

A *baraita* **was taught in accordance with** the opinion of **Rabba** and a *baraita* **was taught in accordance with** the opinion of **Rav Yosef.** The Gemara explains: A *baraita* **was taught in accordance with** the opinion **of Rabba: If one was walking in the desert** with leavened bread in his hand and the time came on the eve of Passover to remove it, then **he** must **crumble** the leavened bread **and throw it into the wind. If he was traveling on a ship, he** must **crumble** the leavened bread **and throw it into the sea.** And a *baraita* **was taught in accordance with** the opinion **of Rav Yosef: If one was walking in the desert** and found an idol, **he** must **grind it and throw it into the wind. If he was traveling on a ship, he** must **grind it and throw it into the sea.**

שחיקה קשיא לרבה, פירור קשיא לרב יוסף! שחיקה לרבה לא קשיא: הא – לים המלח, הא – לשאר נהרות. פירור לרב יוסף לא קשיא: הא – בחיטי, הא – בנהמא.

The Gemara comments: The requirement of **grinding** in one *baraita* **is difficult for Rabba,** since according to his opinion there is no need to grind idols before throwing them into the sea. And the requirement of **crumbling** leavened bread mentioned in the other *baraita* **is difficult for Rav Yosef,** as in his opinion leavened bread need not be crumbled before it is thrown into the sea. The Gemara answers: The requirement of **grinding is not difficult for Rabba. This** case, where one is not required to grind it, is where he throws it **into the Dead Sea. That** case, where he is required to grind it before throwing it, is where he throws it **into other rivers.** Similarly, the requirement of **crumbling is not difficult for Rav Yosef. This** case is dealing **with** a bag **of wheat** that became leavened. Since wheat does not disintegrate on its own, one must grind it up and scatter it into the water. **That** case is referring **to bread.** Since bread will disintegrate in the water on its own, there is no need to crumble it.

מתני׳ חמץ של גוי שעבר עליו הפסח – מותר בהנאה, ושל ישראל אסור בהנאה, שנאמר: ״לא יראה לך שאור״.

MISHNA It is permitted for a Jew **to derive benefit**[N] **from leavened bread of a gentile over which Passover has elapsed,**[H] i.e., leavened bread that remains after the conclusion of Passover. However, **it is prohibited to** derive **benefit from** leaven **of a Jew** over which Passover has elapsed,[H] **as it is stated:** "And no leavened bread shall be seen with you, **neither shall there be leaven seen with you,** in all your borders" (Exodus 13:7).

גמ׳ מני מתניתין? לא רבי יהודה ולא רבי שמעון ולא רבי יוסי הגלילי. מאי היא – דתניא: חמץ בין לפני זמנו בין לאחר זמנו – עובר עליו בלאו, תוך זמנו – עובר עליו בלאו וכרת, דברי רבי יהודה.

GEMARA The Gemara begins by asking: **Who is** the author of **the mishna? It is not** in accordance with the opinion of **Rabbi Yehuda, and it is not** in accordance with the opinion of **Rabbi Shimon, and it is not** in accordance with the opinion of **Rabbi Yosei HaGelili.** The Gemara clarifies this question: **What is** the case about which these Sages disagree, and what are their opinions on this issue? The Gemara explains: **As it was taught** in a *baraita*: One who eats or derives benefit from **leavened bread, whether before its time,** starting at midday on Passover eve, **or after its time,** i.e., leavened bread over which Passover has elapsed, **transgresses a negative mitzva. During its time,** on Passover itself, one who eats leavened bread **transgresses a negative mitzva and** is liable to receive ***karet.*** This is **the statement of Rabbi Yehuda.**

NOTES

It is permitted to derive benefit – מותר בהנאה: In the Jerusalem Talmud it is explained that this statement was made with regard to a place where bread baked by a gentile was considered to be prohibited. Therefore, it does not say that one may eat this leavened bread, as it was prohibited regardless. However, there are those who are lenient and permit one to eat bread baked by a gentile.

HALAKHA

Leavened bread of a gentile over which Passover has elapsed – חמץ של גוי שעבר עליו הפסח: Leavened bread of a gentile over which Passover has elapsed may be eaten by a Jew after Passover, in accordance with the mishna (*Shulḥan Arukh, Oraḥ Ḥayyim* 448:1).

Leavened bread of a Jew over which Passover has elapsed – חמץ ישראל שעבר עליו הפסח: It is prohibited to derive benefit from leavened bread of a Jew over which Passover has elapsed, in accordance with the mishna (*Shulḥan Arukh, Oraḥ Ḥayyim* 445:3).

Perek **II**
Daf **28** Amud **b**

רבי שמעון אומר: חמץ לפני זמנו ולאחר זמנו – אינו עובר עליו בלא כלום, תוך זמנו – עובר עליו בכרת ובלאו, ומשעה שאסור באכילה אסור בהנאה, אתאן לתנא קמא. רבי יוסי הגלילי אומר: תמה על עצמך, היאך חמץ אסור בהנאה כל שבעה?

Rabbi Shimon says: One who eats or derives benefit from **leavened bread,** both **before its time and after its time, does not transgress any** prohibition. **During its time one** is liable to receive ***karet*** **and transgresses a negative mitzva** for eating or deriving benefit from leavened bread. **And from the time that it is prohibited to eat** leavened bread, beginning at midday on Passover eve, **it is** also **prohibited to** derive **benefit** from it. The Gemara comments: With this last sentence **we have come to** the opinion of **the first** ***tanna,*** as this statement appears to present Rabbi Yehuda's opinion and not that of Rabbi Shimon. **Rabbi Yosei HaGelili says: Be astounded with yourself. How can it be prohibited to** derive **benefit from leavened bread for all seven** days? In other words, he disagrees with the premise that it is prohibited to derive benefit from leavened bread even during the seven days of Passover.

וּמִנַּיִן לְאוֹכֵל חָמֵץ מִשֵּׁשׁ שָׁעוֹת וּלְמַעְלָה שֶׁהוּא עוֹבֵר בְּלֹא תַעֲשֶׂה – שֶׁנֶּאֱמַר: ״לֹא תֹאכַל עָלָיו חָמֵץ״, דִּבְרֵי רַבִּי יְהוּדָה.

The *baraita* discusses a related issue: **From where** is it derived **that one who eats leavened bread** on Passover eve **from the sixth hour and onward transgresses a negative mitzva? As it is stated:** "And you shall sacrifice the Paschal lamb to the Lord your God, of the flock and the herd, in the place which the Lord shall choose to cause His name to dwell there. **You shall eat no leavened bread with it;** for seven days you shall eat *matzot*, the bread of affliction" (Deuteronomy 16:2–3). The juxtaposition of the Paschal lamb with the prohibition of leavened bread teaches that the prohibition to eat leavened bread begins from the time that the Paschal lamb is slaughtered, namely, the afternoon of the fourteenth of Nisan. **This is the statement of Rabbi Yehuda.**

אָמַר לוֹ רַבִּי שִׁמְעוֹן: וְכִי אֶפְשָׁר לוֹמַר כֵּן? וַהֲלֹא כְּבָר נֶאֱמַר: ״לֹא תֹאכַל עָלָיו חָמֵץ שִׁבְעַת יָמִים תֹּאכַל עָלָיו מַצּוֹת״. אִם כֵּן מַה תַּלְמוּד לוֹמַר ״לֹא תֹאכַל עָלָיו חָמֵץ״ – בְּשָׁעָה שֶׁיֶּשְׁנוֹ בְּקוּם אֱכוֹל מַצָּה – יֶשְׁנוֹ בְּבַל תֹּאכַל חָמֵץ, וּבְשָׁעָה שֶׁאֵינוֹ בְּקוּם אֱכוֹל מַצָּה – אֵינוֹ בְּבַל תֹּאכַל חָמֵץ.

Rabbi Shimon said to him: Is it possible to say this? Isn't it already stated: "You shall eat no leavened bread with it; for seven days you shall eat *matzot*"? Since the verse links the prohibition of leavened bread to the mitzva of eating *matza*, one should also say that one must eat *matza* on the fourteenth of Nisan. **If so, what** does it mean when **the verse states: "You shall eat no leavened bread with it"?** The verse indicates that **at a time when he is** under the obligation to **get up and eat *matza*, he is subject to** the prohibition of: **You shall eat no leavened bread. And at a time when he is** under no obligation to **get up and eat *matza*, he is not subject to** the prohibition of: **You shall eat no leavened bread.**

מַאי טַעְמָא דְּרַבִּי יְהוּדָה? תְּלָתָא קְרָאֵי כְּתִיבִי: ״לֹא יֵאָכֵל חָמֵץ״, ״וְכָל מַחְמֶצֶת לֹא תֹאכֵלוּ״, ״לֹא תֹאכַל עָלָיו חָמֵץ״. חַד לִפְנֵי זְמַנּוֹ, וְחַד לְאַחַר זְמַנּוֹ, וְחַד לְתוֹךְ זְמַנּוֹ.

The Gemara asks: **What is the reason** for the opinion **of Rabbi Yehuda?** The Gemara explains: **There are three verses** that **are written**[N] with regard to this prohibition, and in Rabbi Yehuda's opinion each one teaches that the prohibition applies at a different time. One verse states: **"Leavened bread shall not be eaten"** (Exodus 13:3). Another verse states: **"And all that which is leavened you shall not eat;** in all your habitations you shall eat *matzot*" (Exodus 12:20). And a third verse states: **"You shall eat no leavened bread with it"** (Deuteronomy 16:3). **One** verse indicates that there is a prohibition against eating leavened bread even **before its time,** on Passover eve. **One** verse indicates that there is a prohibition against eating leavened bread **after its time** as well, if a Jew owned it during Passover. **And one verse** indicates that the prohibition applies **during Passover** itself.

וְרַבִּי שִׁמְעוֹן: חַד – לְתוֹךְ זְמַנּוֹ, ״וְכָל מַחְמֶצֶת״ – מִבְּעֵי לֵיהּ, לְכִדְתַנְיָא: אֵין לִי אֶלָּא שֶׁנִּתְחַמֵּץ מֵאֵלָיו, מֵחֲמַת דָּבָר אַחֵר מִנַּיִן? תַּלְמוּד לוֹמַר: ״כָּל מַחְמֶצֶת לֹא תֹאכֵלוּ״.

The Gemara asks: **And** how does **Rabbi Shimon** interpret these three verses? The Gemara explains: **One** verse is required **to** teach about the prohibition **during its time.** The verse: **"And all that which is leavened** you shall not eat" **is required** for another *halakha*, **as it was taught** in a *baraita*: **I have** derived that leavened bread is prohibited **only if it became leavened on its own,** through its own natural process. **From where do I derive** that if it became leavened **due to another substance**[NH] it is considered to be leavened bread as well? **The verse states: "All that which is leavened you shall not eat."** This indicates that all leavened bread, no matter how it became so, is forbidden during Passover.

״לֹא יֵאָכֵל חָמֵץ״ – מִיבְּעֵי לֵיהּ לְכִדְתַנְיָא; רַבִּי יוֹסֵי הַגְּלִילִי אוֹמֵר: מִנַּיִן לְפֶסַח מִצְרַיִם שֶׁאֵין חִימּוּצוֹ נוֹהֵג אֶלָּא יוֹם אֶחָד – תַּלְמוּד לוֹמַר: ״לֹא יֵאָכֵל חָמֵץ״, וּסְמִיךְ לֵיהּ: ״הַיּוֹם אַתֶּם יֹצְאִים״.

The verse **"Leavened bread shall not be eaten" is** also **required** for another *halakha*. **As it was taught** in a *baraita* that **Rabbi Yosei HaGelili says: From where** is it derived **that the** prohibition against eating **leavened bread** during **the** first **Passover in Egypt**[N] **applied for only one day? The verse states: "Leavened bread shall not be eaten,"** and this is **juxtaposed to** the verse that states: **"This day you go forth** in the month of spring" (Exodus 13:4). This indicates that the prohibition against eating leavened bread during the first Passover in Egypt applied for only that one day.

וְרַבִּי יְהוּדָה, מֵחֲמַת דָּבָר אַחֵר מְנָא לֵיהּ? מִדְּאַפְּקֵיהּ רַחֲמָנָא בִּלְשׁוֹן מַחְמֶצֶת.

The Gemara asks: **And Rabbi Yehuda, from where does he** derive that leavened bread that became leavened **due to another substance** is prohibited? The Gemara answers: He derives it from the fact **that the Merciful One expresses** this *halakha* **with the** general **term: "That which is leavened";** no additional amplification is required.

NOTES

Three verses are written – תְּלָתָא קְרָאֵי כְּתִיבִי: Maharam Halawa explains that the verse "You shall eat no leavened bread with it" is referring to the time before Passover, the verse "All that which is leavened you shall not eat" is referring to Passover itself, and the verse "Leavened bread shall not be eaten" teaches that the prohibition applies after Passover has ended.

Became leavened on its own…if due to another substance – נִתְחַמֵּץ מֵאֵלָיו מֵחֲמַת דָּבָר אַחֵר: The conclusion reached here is that there is almost no practical difference between dough that became leavened on its own and dough that became leavened through the addition of another substance. The only difference between these two cases is with regard to the prohibition of: It shall not be found. If one actively causes the dough to become leavened or if one purchases leavened bread, he transgresses this prohibition and is flogged. However, if the dough became leavened by itself then he is not flogged, because he did not perform an action (Rambam; *Me'iri*).

The Passover in Egypt and in later generations – פֶּסַח מִצְרַיִם וְדוֹרוֹת: There are several difference between the *halakhot* of the first Passover observed by the Jewish people before they left Egypt and the *halakhot* of the festival of Passover that apply to all subsequent generations. Some of these differences, such as the requirements to designate the Paschal lamb on the tenth of Nisan and to smear its blood on the doorpost, are explicitly mentioned in the Torah. Other differences, such as the one mentioned here with regard to the prohibition against eating leavened bread beyond the first day of the Festival, are the subject of dispute among the Sages. This dispute leads to a difference in the understanding of the verses, as some verses indicate that the prohibition against eating leavened bread applied for only one day during the Passover in Egypt, while others seem to indicate that the prohibition lasted for a full seven days even during that first Passover.

HALAKHA

Became leavened due to another substance – שֶׁנִּתְחַמֵּץ...מֵחֲמַת דָּבָר אַחֵר: Leavened bread is prohibited during Passover whether it became leavened on its own or through the addition of another substance (*Sefer Mitzvot Gadol*, negative mitzva 76).

NOTES

It is written in this and it is written in that – כְּתִיב בְּהַאי וּכְתִיב בְּהַאי: Many versions of the talmudic text contain the additional term: "And they are necessary," i.e., both verses need to be mentioned. This assertion can be explained as follows: If the obligation to eat *matza* were mentioned only with regard to an uncircumcised man and a resident alien, one might say that they are obligated to eat *matza* because they are not obligated in the second *Pesaḥ*. However, this would not apply to one who was ritually impure or on a distant journey, as such a person must bring the second *Pesaḥ* at a later date. On the other hand, if the obligation to eat *matza* were mentioned only in reference to one who was ritually impure or on a distant journey, one might assume that it applies only to him, because he is also obligated to perform other mitzvot. However, with regard to an uncircumcised man or a resident alien, perhaps there would be no such obligation, since they are excluded from other mitzvot as well. Therefore, both verses are necessary (Maharam Ḥalawa).

דְּרַבִּי יוֹסֵי הַגְּלִילִי מְנָא לֵיהּ? אִי בָּעֵית אֵימָא: מִדְּסָמִיךְ לֵיהּ ״הַיּוֹם״, אִי בָּעֵית אֵימָא – סְמוּכִין לָא דָּרֵישׁ.

The Gemara asks: And this teaching **of Rabbi Yosei HaGelili** with regard to the Passover in Egypt, **from where does** Rabbi Yehuda derive it? The Gemara answers: **If you wish, say that** he derives it **from** the fact **that** the phrase **"this day" is juxtaposed to it.** In Rabbi Yehuda's opinion, the entire verse: "Leavened bread shall not be eaten" is not required to make this point; instead, this verse indicates that there is an additional time when leavened bread is prohibited. Nonetheless, the juxtaposition with the following phrase does indicate something significant, namely, that the prohibition in Egypt was limited to one day. **If you wish, say** instead that Rabbi Yehuda **does not employ** the **homiletic** method of **juxtaposition** of verses, except in limited circumstances. Accordingly, Rabbi Yehuda does not accept Rabbi Yosei HaGelili's opinion at all and holds that the prohibition against eating leavened bread during the Passover in Egypt applied for all seven days.

אָמַר מָר: וּמִנַּיִן לְאוֹכֵל חָמֵץ מִשֵּׁשׁ שָׁעוֹת וּלְמַעְלָה שֶׁהוּא עוֹבֵר בְּלֹא תַעֲשֶׂה – שֶׁנֶּאֱמַר: ״לֹא תֹאכַל עָלָיו חָמֵץ״, דִּבְרֵי רַבִּי יְהוּדָה. אָמַר לוֹ רַבִּי שִׁמְעוֹן: וְכִי אֶפְשָׁר לוֹמַר כֵּן? וַהֲלֹא כְּבָר נֶאֱמַר: ״לֹא תֹאכַל עָלָיו חָמֵץ שִׁבְעַת יָמִים תֹּאכַל עָלָיו מַצּוֹת״,

The Master said in the aforementioned *baraita*: **From where** is it derived **that one who eats leavened bread from the sixth hour and onward transgresses a negative mitzva? As it is stated: "You shall eat no leavened bread with it"; this is the statement of Rabbi Yehuda. Rabbi Shimon said to him: And is it possible to say this? Isn't it already stated: "You shall eat no leavened bread with it; for seven days you shall eat *matzot*,"** linking the time of the prohibition against eating leavened bread with the time of the mitzva to eat *matza*?

וְרַבִּי יְהוּדָה, שַׁפִּיר קָאָמַר לֵיהּ רַבִּי שִׁמְעוֹן! וְרַבִּי יְהוּדָה אָמַר לָךְ: הַהוּא לְקוֹבְעוֹ חוֹבָה אֲפִילּוּ בַּזְּמַן הַזֶּה הוּא דַּאֲתָא.

The Gemara asks: **And** indeed **Rabbi Shimon is saying well to Rabbi Yehuda,** so how does Rabbi Yehuda use this verse to support his opinion? The Gemara answers that **Rabbi Yehuda** could have **said to you:** That verse **comes to establish it as an obligation even nowadays.** One might have assumed that after the destruction of the Temple, when the Paschal lamb can no longer be brought, the obligation to eat *matza* no longer applies either. Therefore, the verse links the prohibition against eating leavened bread to the obligation to eat *matza* in order to teach that just as it is prohibited to eat leavened bread even in the absence of the Temple, so too, there remains an obligation to eat *matza* as well.

וְרַבִּי שִׁמְעוֹן לְקוֹבְעוֹ חוֹבָה מְנָא לֵיהּ? נָפְקָא לֵיהּ מִ״בָּעֶרֶב תֹּאכְלוּ״. וְרַבִּי יְהוּדָה? מִיבָּעֵי לֵיהּ לְטָמֵא וְשֶׁהָיָה בְּדֶרֶךְ רְחוֹקָה. סָלְקָא דַּעְתָּךְ אָמִינָא: הוֹאִיל וּבְפֶסַח לֹא יֹאכַל – מַצָּה וּמָרוֹר נַמִי לָא נֵיכוֹל, קָא מַשְׁמַע לָן.

The Gemara asks: **And Rabbi Shimon, from where does he** derive the need **to establish it as an obligation** even after the destruction of the Temple? The Gemara answers: **He derives it from** the following verse: "In the first month, on the fourteenth day of the month **in the evening, you shall eat** *matzot*, until the twenty-first day in the evening" (Exodus 12:18). This verse connects the obligation to eat *matza* to the date of Passover and not only to the Paschal lamb. The Gemara asks: **And Rabbi Yehuda,** what does he derive from this verse? The Gemara answers: He **requires it** to teach that there remains an obligation **for one who is** ritually **impure or on a distant journey** and cannot bring the Paschal lamb. **It could enter your mind to say that since he will not eat the Paschal lamb, he is also not** obligated **to eat *matza* and bitter herbs.** Therefore, the verse **teaches us** that he is obligated to eat them.

וְרַבִּי שִׁמְעוֹן: טָמֵא וְשֶׁהָיָה בְּדֶרֶךְ רְחוֹקָה לָא אִיצְטְרִיךְ קְרָא, דְּלָא גָּרַע מֵעָרֵל וּבֶן נֵכָר. דִּכְתִיב: ״וְכָל עָרֵל לֹא יֹאכַל בּוֹ״ – בּוֹ הוּא אֵינוֹ אוֹכֵל, אֲבָל אוֹכֵל הוּא בְּמַצָּה וּבְמָרוֹר. וְרַבִּי יְהוּדָה: כְּתִיב בְּהַאי, וּכְתִיב בְּהַאי.

And Rabbi Shimon, from where does he derive this *halakha*? In his opinion, **a verse is not necessary** to teach that **one who is** ritually **impure or on a distant journey** is obligated to eat *matza* and bitter herbs, **as he is no worse than an uncircumcised man or a resident alien. As it is written: "And no uncircumcised man shall eat of it"** (Exodus 12:48). The added emphasis in **"of it"** indicates that only **it,** the Paschal lamb, **he does not eat; however, he** must **eat *matza* and bitter herbs.** The Gemara asks: **And Rabbi Yehuda,** how would he respond? The Gemara answers: Granted, the Torah did not need to add this verse. Nonetheless, **it is written in this** context that one who is impure or on a distant journey is obligated to eat *matza* and bitter herbs. **And it is written in that**[N] context with regard to the uncircumcised man and the resident alien as well.

מַנִּי מַתְנִיתִין? אִי רַבִּי יְהוּדָה – חָמֵץ סְתָמָא קָאָמַר, אֲפִילּוּ דְּגוֹי. וְאִי רַבִּי שִׁמְעוֹן –

After clarifying the opinions of Rabbi Yehuda, Rabbi Shimon, and Rabbi Yosei HaGelili, the Gemara asks: In accordance with **whose** opinion **is the mishna** taught? **If** one suggests that it is in accordance with the opinion of **Rabbi Yehuda,** this cannot be, as Rabbi Yehuda **said leavened bread without stipulation** that the leavened bread belong to a Jew, indicating that one may not **even** benefit from leavened bread **of a gentile** over which Passover elapsed. Therefore, since this opinion contradicts the statement made in the mishna discussed here, Rabbi Yehuda can be ruled out as its author. **And if** it is in accordance with the opinion of **Rabbi Shimon,**

דְּיִשְׂרָאֵל נַמִּי מִישְׁרָא קָא שָׁרֵי. וְאִי רַבִּי יוֹסֵי הַגְּלִילִי – אֲפִילּוּ תּוֹךְ זְמַנּוֹ נַמִּי מִישְׁרָא קָא שָׁרֵי בַּהֲנָאָה!

Rabbi Shimon **also permits** one to derive benefit from leavened bread after Passover even if it was **owned by a Jew. And if** the mishna follows the opinion of **Rabbi Yosei HaGelili, he would permit** one **to** derive **benefit** from it **even during** Passover.

אָמַר רַב אַחָא בַּר יַעֲקֹב: לְעוֹלָם רַבִּי יְהוּדָה הִיא, וְיָלֵיף שְׂאוֹר דַּאֲכִילָה מִשְּׂאוֹר דִּרְאִיָּה. מָה שְׂאוֹר דִּרְאִיָּה – שֶׁלְּךָ אִי אַתָּה רוֹאֶה, אֲבָל אַתָּה רוֹאֶה שֶׁל אֲחֵרִים וְשֶׁל גָּבוֹהַּ – אַף שְׂאוֹר דַּאֲכִילָה, שֶׁלְּךָ אִי אַתָּה אוֹכֵל, אֲבָל אַתָּה אוֹכֵל שֶׁל אֲחֵרִים וְשֶׁל גָּבוֹהַּ.

Rav Aḥa bar Ya'akov said: Actually, it is possible to explain that the mishna **is** in accordance with the opinion of **Rabbi Yehuda, and** he **derives** the restrictions pertaining to **the eating of leaven from** the restrictions relating to **seeing leaven.** The prohibition against **seeing leaven** is worded: "It shall not be seen by you." It is understood to mean that **you should not see your own** or another Jew's leaven. **But you may see** leaven that belongs **to others,** i.e., gentiles, **and** leaven consecrated **to God. Similarly,** with regard to the prohibition against **eating leaven** that was owned by a Jew during Passover after Passover, **you may not eat your own** leavened bread, **but you may eat** the leavened bread **of others or** the leaven consecrated **to God** after Passover.

וּבְדִין הוּא דְּאִיבָּעֵי לֵיהּ לְמִיתְנָא דַּאֲפִילּוּ בַּאֲכִילָה נַמִּי שָׁרֵי, וְאַיְּידֵי דִּתְנָא דְּיִשְׂרָאֵל אָסוּר בַּהֲנָאָה – תְּנָא נַמִּי דְּגוֹי מוּתָּר בַּהֲנָאָה. וּבְדִין הוּא דְּאִיבָּעֵי לֵיהּ לְמִיתְנָא דַּאֲפִילּוּ בְּתוֹךְ זְמַנּוֹ מוּתָּר בַּהֲנָאָה, וְאַיְּידֵי דִּתְנָא דְּיִשְׂרָאֵל לְאַחַר זְמַנּוֹ – תְּנָא נַמִּי דְּגוֹי לְאַחַר זְמַנּוֹ.

And by right it should have **taught** that **even the eating** of leavened bread belonging to a gentile **is permitted** after the conclusion of Passover, **but since** the *tanna* **taught that it is forbidden to** derive **benefit from** leavened bread belonging to **a Jew** after Passover, **he also taught** that **it is permitted to** derive **benefit from** leavened bread belonging to **a gentile.** However, one should understand that it is permitted to eat this leavened bread as well. **And** similarly, **by right it** should have **taught that** even during Passover **it is permitted to** derive **benefit from** leavened bread that belongs to gentiles. **But since** the *tanna* **taught** about the leavened bread belonging to a **Jew after** Passover, **he also taught** about the leavened bread belonging to a gentile **after** Passover. Thus, one should not infer *halakhot* from the exact formulation of these details in the *baraita*, but rather understand that the mishna follows Rabbi Yehuda's opinion.

רָבָא אָמַר: לְעוֹלָם רַבִּי שִׁמְעוֹן הִיא, וְרַבִּי שִׁמְעוֹן קְנָסָא קָנֵיס הוֹאִיל וְעָבַר עָלֵיהּ בְּבַל יֵרָאֶה וּבַל יִמָּצֵא.

Rava said: This is not so. **Actually** our mishna **is** in accordance with the opinion of **Rabbi Shimon.** However, this is difficult, as Rabbi Shimon states that it is permitted for a Jew to derive benefit from leavened bread that had been owned by another Jew during Passover, while our mishna explicitly states that this is forbidden. This can be resolved by explaining that **Rabbi Shimon** argues that it is permitted only according to Torah law. However, one who intentionally commits such a transgression **incurs a penalty. Since he transgressed**[N] the prohibition **it shall not be seen and** the prohibition **it shall not be found,** the Sages decreed that it is forbidden for him to derive benefit from this leavened bread.[H]

NOTES

Since he transgressed – **הוֹאִיל וְעָבַר עָלֵיהּ**: This statement should not be understood as meaning that he actually violated the commandment of seeing leavened bread. Rabbi Shimon fines him even in a case where he might come to commit such a transgression, such as when the leavened bread was in a gentile's possession over Passover (see Ritva). Some claim that, as with other cases of fines, this fine applies only to one who intentionally violated this commandment, and therefore the food would be permitted to one who acted unwittingly or under duress. Similarly, it would be permitted to one who did not violate the commandment. This, however, does not appear to be the case in the Gemara (*Mikhtam*).

HALAKHA

Leavened bread over which Passover has elapsed – **חָמֵץ שֶׁעָבַר עָלָיו הַפֶּסַח**: One may not derive benefit from leavened bread that was under Jewish ownership during Passover due to a rabbinically instituted fine, in accordance with the opinion of Rabbi Shimon, as explained by Rava (Rambam *Sefer Zemanim*, *Hilkhot Ḥametz UMatza* 1:4).

בִּשְׁלָמָא לְרָבָא – הַיְינוּ דְּקָתָנֵי "שֶׁל יִשְׂרָאֵל אָסוּר", מִשּׁוּם שֶׁנֶּאֱמַר "לֹא יֵרָאֶה". אֶלָּא לְרַב אַחָא בַּר יַעֲקֹב – מִשּׁוּם "לֹא יֵאָכֵל חָמֵץ" מִיבְּעֵי לֵיהּ!

The Gemara comments: **Granted, according to** the opinion of **Rava, this** explanation **is** consistent with **that which was taught** in the mishna: Leavened bread that **belonged to a Jew is forbidden because it is stated: "It shall not be seen"** (Exodus 13:7). According to this explanation, the connection between the prohibition against deriving benefit from leavened bread that was owned by a Jew during Passover and the verse prohibiting seeing leaven during Passover is clear. The prohibition against deriving benefit from this leavened bread is a rabbinically instituted fine for transgressing the Torah prohibition of "It shall not be seen." **But according to** the opinion of **Rav Aḥa bar Ya'akov,** which states that our mishna follows the opinion of Rabbi Yehuda, and which renders forbidden by Torah law deriving benefit from leavened bread that was owned by a Jew during Passover, why is this verse cited? The mishna **should have said** that it is forbidden **due to** the verse **"Leavened bread shall not be eaten"** (Exodus 13:3), as that is the verse from which Rabbi Yehuda derives this prohibition.

מִי סָבְרַתְּ אַסֵּיפָא קָאֵי? אַרֵישָׁא קָאֵי, וְהָכִי קָאָמַר: חָמֵץ שֶׁל גּוֹי שֶׁעָבַר עָלָיו הַפֶּסַח – מוּתָּר בַּהֲנָאָה, מִשּׁוּם שֶׁנֶּאֱמַר "לֹא יֵרָאֶה לְךָ" – שֶׁלְּךָ אִי אַתָּה רוֹאֶה, אֲבָל אַתָּה רוֹאֶה שֶׁל אֲחֵרִים וְשֶׁל גָּבוֹהַּ. וְיָלֵיף שְׂאוֹר דַּאֲכִילָה מִשְּׂאוֹר דִּרְאִיָּה.

The Gemara answers: **Do you hold** that this proof **is referring to the latter clause** of the mishna, where the prohibition against deriving benefit from leavened bread owned by a Jew is discussed? **It is referring to the first clause** of the mishna, which discusses permission to derive benefit from leavened bread owned by a gentile, **and this is what it is saying: Leavened bread of a gentile, over which Passover has elapsed,** i.e., that remains after the conclusion of Passover, **it is permissible to** derive **benefit from** it, **due to** the verse where **it is stated: "It shall not be seen by you."** This indicates that **you may not see your own** leaven, **but you may see** leaven that belongs **to others and** leaven consecrated **to God. And he derives** the details **about** the prohibition **of eating leaven from** the prohibition **of seeing leaven.** The verse "It shall not be seen by you" should be understood as an explanation of what is permitted and not as an explanation of what is forbidden.

וְאָזְדוּ לְטַעְמַיְיהוּ: דְּאִיתְּמַר, הָאוֹכֵל שְׂאוֹר שֶׁל גּוֹי שֶׁעָבַר עָלָיו הַפֶּסַח, לְדִבְרֵי רַבִּי יְהוּדָה, רָבָא אָמַר: לוֹקֶה, וְרַב אַחָא בַּר יַעֲקֹב אָמַר: אֵינוֹ לוֹקֶה.

The Gemara comments that Rava and Rav Aḥa bar Ya'akov **follow their** line of **reasoning. For it was stated** that they dispute this issue: With regard to **one who eats leaven of a gentile over which Passover has elapsed,** i.e., that remains after the conclusion of Passover, **according to the statement of Rabbi Yehuda, Rava said: He is flogged,** as he has violated a Torah prohibition. **And Rav Aḥa bar Ya'akov said: He is not flogged.**

רָבָא אָמַר: לוֹקֶה, לָא יָלֵיף רַבִּי יְהוּדָה שְׂאוֹר דַּאֲכִילָה מִשְּׂאוֹר דִּרְאִיָּה. וְרַב אַחָא בַּר יַעֲקֹב אָמַר: אֵינוֹ לוֹקֶה, יָלֵיף שְׂאוֹר דַּאֲכִילָה מִשְּׂאוֹר דִּרְאִיָּה.

The Gemara explains: **Rava said** that according to Rabbi Yehuda, **he is flogged,** as **Rabbi Yehuda does not derive** the prohibition against **eating leaven from** the prohibition against **seeing leaven.** Instead, he derives the prohibition from a verse that does not use the words "to you," and therefore leavened bread owned by a gentile over Passover is forbidden in all circumstances. **Rav Aḥa bar Ya'akov said: He is not flogged,** as Rabbi Yehuda **learns** the prohibition against **eating leaven from** the prohibition against **seeing leaven,** and thus it is limited to leavened bread owned by a Jew.

וַהֲדַר בֵּיהּ רַב אַחָא בַּר יַעֲקֹב מֵהַהִיא, דְּתַנְיָא: הָאוֹכֵל חָמֵץ שֶׁל הֶקְדֵּשׁ בַּמּוֹעֵד – מָעַל, וְיֵשׁ אוֹמְרִים: לֹא מָעַל.

The Gemara notes: **Rav Aḥa bar Ya'akov retracted that** position on this matter. **As it was taught** in a *baraita*: **One who eats consecrated leavened bread during the festival** of Passover is guilty of **misuse** of consecrated items. If one performed this action unintentionally, then he must offer a guilt-offering to atone for using a consecrated item for non-sacred purposes. **And some say: He is not** guilty **of misuse** of consecrated items.

מַאן יֵשׁ אוֹמְרִים? אָמַר רַבִּי יוֹחָנָן: רַבִּי נְחוּנְיָא בֶּן הַקָּנָה הִיא. דְּתַנְיָא: רַבִּי נְחוּנְיָא בֶּן הַקָּנָה הָיָה עוֹשֶׂה אֶת יוֹם הַכִּפּוּרִים כַּשַּׁבָּת לְתַשְׁלוּמִין.

The Gemara asks: To **whom is** the phrase in the *baraita*: **Some say,** referring?[N] **Rabbi Yoḥanan said: This is Rabbi Neḥunya ben HaKana. As it was taught** in a *baraita*: **Rabbi Neḥunya ben HaKana would render** the status **of Yom Kippur the same as** that **of Shabbat with regard to payment** for damage caused by a person in violation of the prohibitions of that day.

NOTES

To whom is the phrase some say referring – מַאן יֵשׁ אוֹמְרִים: Although the Sages generally assume that the term "others" is referring to Rabbi Meir, and the term "some say" is referring to Rabbi Natan, there were cases where it was clear to the Sages of the Talmud that this principle did not apply, and consequently, in this case they asked to whom the phrase "some say" refers (*Tosafot*).

מַה שַּׁבָּת, מִתְחַיֵּיב בְּנַפְשׁוֹ וּפָטוּר מִן הַתַּשְׁלוּמִין – אַף יוֹם הַכִּפּוּרִים מִתְחַיֵּיב בְּנַפְשׁוֹ וּפָטוּר מִתַּשְׁלוּמִין.

Just as one who desecrates **Shabbat** by intentionally causing damage to his fellow's property, e.g., by lighting his stack of grain on fire, **is liable to** receive the **death** penalty, since one who intentionally desecrates Shabbat is punished by stoning **and** is therefore **exempt**[N] **from payment,** the basis for this exemption being the principle that after committing multiple transgressions, one is punished only with the most severe punishment; **so too,** one who causes damage by desecrating **Yom Kippur is liable to** receive the **death** penalty, as this violation is punished with *karet*, i.e., spiritual death at the hand of Heaven, **and is** therefore **exempt from payment.** According to this position, one who eats leavened bread during Passover and is deserving of *karet* should also be exempt from other punishments, including the penalty for misuse of consecrated items. In any case, it is clear that both Sages mentioned in the *baraita* agree that leavened bread has monetary value. This must be due to the fact that one is permitted to derive benefit from it after Passover. Therefore, it appears that they both accept Rabbi Shimon's position.

רַב יוֹסֵף אָמַר: בְּפוֹדִין אֶת הַקֳּדָשִׁים לְהַאֲכִילָן לַכְּלָבִים קָמִיפַּלְגִי.

Rav Yosef said: The dispute mentioned in this *baraita* should be understood differently. Both *tanna'im* in the *baraita* accept the opinion of Rabbi Yosei HaGelili, which states that one may derive benefit from leavened bread during Passover, and thus, in principle, one should be permitted to derive benefit from this consecrated leavened bread. Yet, unlike non-sacred leavened bread, which one may sell to gentiles or feed to dogs, it is prohibited to use consecrated leavened bread in this way. Therefore, the question whether this leavened bread has any monetary value depends on the question whether **one** may **redeem consecrated items in order to feed them to dogs,**[H] and it is about this point that the *tanna'im* **disagree.**

מַאן דְּאָמַר מָעַל, קָסָבַר: פּוֹדִין אֶת הַקֳּדָשִׁים לְהַאֲכִילָן לַכְּלָבִים. וּמַאן דְּאָמַר לֹא מָעַל – קָסָבַר: אֵין פּוֹדִין.

The one who said that **he misused** consecrated items by using this leavened bread during Passover **holds** that **one** may **redeem consecrated items in order to feed them to dogs.** Because the food may be redeemed for this purpose, the consecrated leavened bread does have some monetary value, and therefore using it is considered misuse of consecrated items. **And the one who said that he did not misuse** consecrated items **holds** that consecrated property may **not be redeemed** for this purpose, but only in order to provide food for a Jewish person. In this case, since it is forbidden to eat this leavened bread during Passover, the consecrated leavened bread has no value at all at this time. Therefore one who eats such leavened bread is not guilty of misuse of consecrated items.

רַב אַחָא בַּר רָבָא תְּנָא לַהּ

The Gemara comments: **Rav Aḥa bar Rava taught**

Perek **II**
Daf **29** Amud **b**

לְהָא שְׁמַעְתָּא מִשְּׁמֵיהּ דְּרַב יוֹסֵף בְּהָא לִישָּׁנָא: דְּכוּלֵּי עָלְמָא אֵין פּוֹדִין אֶת הַקֳּדָשִׁים לְהַאֲכִילָן לַכְּלָבִים, וְהָכָא בְּהָא קָמִיפַּלְגִי: בְּדָבָר הַגּוֹרֵם לְמָמוֹן, כְּמָמוֹן דָּמֵי.

this *halakha* in the name of Rav Yosef with the following formulation: Everyone agrees that one may **not redeem consecrated items in order to feed them to dogs. And here, they disagree** with regard to the question of whether **an item that can cause a financial** loss **is considered to be of monetary** value. The Sages disagree about the status of an object that does not have any present value but if lost or destroyed will cause the owner financial loss. In other words, they disagree as to whether such an item is considered to have inherent value. This dispute can be applied to our discussion of the opinion of Rabbi Shimon, who states that one is permitted to eat leavened bread after Passover even if it was owned by a Jew.

NOTES

Is liable to receive the death penalty and exempt – מִתְחַיֵּיב בְּנַפְשׁוֹ וּפָטוּר: This is not simply an application of the principle: He receives the greater of the two penalties, that one who committed multiple transgressions is exempt from punishment for the less severe crime. Rather, it is a Torah decree that is derived from the verses themselves, and the various Sages differ as to which verses it is derived from. The decree states that one who is liable to be punished with the death penalty for a specific offense is exempt from paying for damage that he caused through the same action. This exemption applies even when the death penalty is not implemented for lack of witnesses, a warning, or any other reason. So long as the damaging action was simultaneous with a transgression of this nature, he need not pay for damage. This concept serves as the basis for Rabbi Neḥunya ben HaKana's statement, which is an extension of this principle.

HALAKHA

Redemption of consecrated items – פִּדְיוֹן קֳדָשִׁים: One may not redeem consecrated items that are unfit for human consumption in order to feed them to dogs. Instead, such items should be left untouched and, if necessary, should be buried (Rambam *Sefer Avoda, Hilkhot Issurei Mizbe'aḥ* 2:10).

HALAKHA

An item that can cause a financial loss – דָּבָר הַגּוֹרֵם לְמָמוֹן: An item that will lead to a financial loss if destroyed, such as a promissory note, or something that will have value in the future, is treated as though it has monetary value. Therefore, if a person damages or destroys such an item he is obligated to reimburse its owner for its loss (*Shulḥan Arukh, Ḥoshen Mishpat* 386:1).

A prohibited mixture – תַּעֲרוֹבֶת אִיסוּר: Most items prohibited by the Torah, with certain notable exceptions, are nullified once they fall into a mixture, as long as they do not give flavor to it, which in practice is assessed as one part in sixty. This applies both when the mixture is the same type as the prohibited item and when it is of a different type, as the *halakha* is in accordance with the opinion of Rabbi Yoḥanan and Reish Lakish when they disagree with Rav and Shmuel (*Shulḥan Arukh, Yoreh De'a* 98:1).

NOTES

A mixture with a forbidden food – תַּעֲרוֹבֶת אִיסוּר: The many issues that arise when a portion of a prohibited food is mixed together with permitted foods are discussed at great length in tractates *Avoda Zara* and *Zevaḥim*. Numerous distinctions exist, based on the status of the prohibited food that fell in, the mixture into which it fell, and the severity of the prohibition attached to the prohibited food. However, the general principle behind these laws is that the prohibited item is nullified when it is mixed with a majority of permitted food to the extent that one considers it as though it were no longer present. However, there are several exceptions to this rule when considering an important object, such as a piece of meat fit to serve guests, a whole creature, etc. Similarly, a food might not be able to be nullified because its prohibited status can be changed to a permitted one via other means, such as a change in time or place, or a relevant action.

The principles governing mixtures are also related to the principles governing cases of uncertainty, as it is not known exactly which objects in the mixture are prohibited. However, the principle of nullification is effective to a greater extent than the principles governing cases of uncertainty, such that once an object is nullified in a mixture it is considered as though it has entirely disappeared within the majority of permitted objects, and there is no longer cause for concern with regard to its presence.

מַאן דְּאָמַר מָעַל – קָסָבַר: דָּבָר הַגּוֹרֵם לְמָמוֹן – כְּמָמוֹן דָּמֵי. וּמַאן דְּאָמַר לֹא מָעַל – קָסָבַר: דָּבָר הַגּוֹרֵם לְמָמוֹן – לָאו כְּמָמוֹן דָּמֵי.

The Gemara explains: **The one who said** that **he misused** consecrated property by using consecrated leavened bread during Passover **holds that an item that can cause a financial loss**[H] **is considered to be of monetary** value. Although the leavened bread is currently worthless, it can be eaten after Passover and will have some value at that time. It is therefore considered to have monetary value now, such that one who uses it is guilty of misuse of consecrated items. **And the one who said** that **he did not misuse** consecrated property **holds** that **an item that can cause a financial** loss **is not considered to be of monetary** value. Therefore, since the leavened bread is currently worthless, one who uses it would not be guilty of misuse of consecrated property.

רַב אַחָא בַּר יַעֲקֹב אָמַר: דְּכוּלֵּי עָלְמָא דָּבָר הַגּוֹרֵם לְמָמוֹן – כְּמָמוֹן דָּמֵי. וְהָכָא בִּפְלוּגְתָּא דְּרַבִּי יְהוּדָה וְרַבִּי שִׁמְעוֹן קָמִיפַּלְגִי. מַאן דְּאָמַר לֹא מָעַל – כְּרַבִּי יְהוּדָה, וּמַאן דְּאָמַר מָעַל – כְּרַבִּי שִׁמְעוֹן.

Rav Aḥa bar Ya'akov explains the issue as follows: **Everyone agrees that an item that can cause a financial** loss **is considered to be of monetary** value, **and here they disagree with regard to** the same point of **dispute as Rabbi Yehuda and Rabbi Shimon.** The opinion of **the one who said** that **he did not misuse** consecrated items is **in accordance with** the opinion of **Rabbi Yehuda,** who maintains that one may not derive benefit from leavened bread that was owned by a Jew during Passover. Thus, the consecrated leavened bread is worthless, since it will remain prohibited after Passover as well. **And the one who said** that **he misused** consecrated items is **in accordance with** the opinion of **Rabbi Shimon,** who maintains that one may derive benefit from leavened bread after the conclusion of Passover even if it was owned by a Jew during Passover. Therefore, the consecrated leavened bread is considered to be of monetary value, and one who uses it is guilty of misuse of consecrated items.

וְהָא רַב אַחָא בַּר יַעֲקֹב הוּא דְּאָמַר דְּרַבִּי יְהוּדָה יָלֵיף שְׂאוֹר דַּאֲכִילָה מִשְּׂאוֹר דִּרְאִיָּיה! אֶלָּא: הֲדַר בֵּיהּ רַב אַחָא בַּר יַעֲקֹב מֵהַהִיא.

The Gemara raises a challenge: **But isn't it Rav Aḥa bar Ya'akov who said** that **Rabbi Yehuda derives** the details of the prohibition against **eating leaven from** the details of the prohibition against **seeing leaven?** Just as it is permitted to see the leavened bread of a gentile or of God, so too, it is permitted to eat this type of leavened bread after Passover. Therefore, consecrated leavened bread would be permitted after Passover even according to the opinion of Rabbi Yehuda. **Rather,** it should be understood that **Rav Aḥa bar Ya'akov retracted that** explanation of Rabbi Yehuda's opinion, and agrees with Rava, who explains that Rabbi Yehuda maintains that any leavened bread in existence during Passover is forbidden afterward.

רַב אַשִׁי אָמַר: דְּכוּלֵּי עָלְמָא אֵין פּוֹדִין, וְדָבָר הַגּוֹרֵם לְמָמוֹן לָאו כְּמָמוֹן דָּמֵי, וְהָכָא בִּפְלוּגְתָּא דְּרַבִּי יוֹסֵי הַגְּלִילִי וְרַבָּנַן קָמִיפַּלְגִי. מַאן דְּאָמַר מָעַל – כְּרַבִּי יוֹסֵי, וּמַאן דְּאָמַר לֹא מָעַל – כְּרַבָּנַן.

Rav Ashi said that everyone agrees **that one does not redeem** consecrated property in order to feed it to dogs, **and** similarly, everyone agrees that **an item that can cause a financial** loss **is not considered to be of monetary** value. **And here,** in this *baraita*, **they disagree with regard to** the same point of **dispute as** do **Rabbi Yosei HaGelili and the Rabbis.** The opinion of **the one who said** that **he misused** consecrated items by eating the consecrated leavened bread is **in accordance with** the opinion of **Rabbi Yosei HaGelili,** who maintains that one may derive benefit from leavened bread that belongs to a Jew even during the seven days of Passover. Therefore, since the leavened bread has some value, one is guilty of misuse of consecrated items by using it. **And** the opinion of **the one who said** that **he did not misuse** consecrated items is **in accordance with** the opinion of **the Rabbis,** who maintain that one may not derive benefit from leavened bread during Passover, thus rendering the consecrated leavened bread worthless. Although it may have some value after Passover, an item that can cause a financial loss is not considered to be of monetary value, and therefore it is presently considered to be worthless.

אָמַר רַב: חָמֵץ בִּזְמַנּוֹ, בֵּין בְּמִינוֹ בֵּין שֶׁלֹּא בְּמִינוֹ – אָסוּר. שֶׁלֹּא בִּזְמַנּוֹ, בְּמִינוֹ – אָסוּר, שֶׁלֹּא בְּמִינוֹ – מוּתָּר.

Rav said: With regard to **leavened bread** that becomes mixed with permitted food, the following distinction applies. **During its time** of prohibition, i.e., during the seven days of Passover, **leavened bread is forbidden whether** it is mixed **with its own type,** for example, when leavened flour is mixed with *matza* flour or when unleavened *matza* is mixed with leavened *matza,* **or** it is mixed **with another type** of substance. **Not during its time** of prohibition, but rather after Passover, if it is mixed **with its own type** of substance, then **it is prohibited.** However, if it is mixed **with another type** of substance, then **it is permitted.**[HN]

בְּמַאי עָסְקִינַן? אִילֵימָא בְּנוֹתֵן טַעַם, שֶׁלֹּא בִּזְמַנּוֹ שֶׁלֹּא בְּמִינוֹ מוּתָּר?! הָא יָהֵיב טַעְמָא!

The Gemara asks: **With what are we dealing? If you say that** there is enough leavened bread such that it **gives flavor**[N] to the mixture, i.e., at least one part in sixty, then if it is **not during its time** and mixed **with another type** of substance, why **is it permitted? Doesn't it give flavor** to the mixture, and, as one who eats this mixture will distinguish the forbidden flavor, the entire mixture is forbidden?[N]

אֶלָּא בְּמַשֶּׁהוּ. חָמֵץ בִּזְמַנּוֹ בֵּין בְּמִינוֹ בֵּין שֶׁלֹּא בְּמִינוֹ אָסוּר, רַב לְטַעְמֵיהּ. דְּרַב וּשְׁמוּאֵל דְּאָמְרִי תַּרְוַיְיהוּ: כׇּל אִיסּוּרִין שֶׁבַּתּוֹרָה, בְּמִינוֹ – בְּמַשֶּׁהוּ, שֶׁלֹּא בְּמִינוֹ – בְּנוֹתֵן טַעַם.

Rather, this case is dealing **with any amount,** a minimal quantity of leavened bread[N] that has been mixed with a large quantity of matza. The *halakha* in this case is that **leavened bread during its time** of prohibition **is forbidden, whether** it is mixed **with its own type** of substance **or with another type** of substance. This statement of **Rav** conforms **to his** line **of reasoning** as follows: **As it is Rav and Shmuel who both say:** With regard to **any** foods **forbidden by the Torah** that become mixed with permitted foods, if the permitted food is of **its own type,** such that it is impossible to distinguish one from another, then even **any amount** of the prohibited substance renders the entire mixture prohibited. However, if the forbidden food was mixed **with another type** of substance, then the mixture becomes prohibited only when there is enough of the forbidden item to **give flavor** to the mixture.

רַב גְּזַר חָמֵץ בִּזְמַנּוֹ שֶׁלֹּא בְּמִינוֹ אַטּוּ מִינוֹ, וְשֶׁלֹּא בִּזְמַנּוֹ בְּמִינוֹ אָסוּר, כְּרַבִּי יְהוּדָה.

Rav rendered an additional **decree** prohibiting **leavened bread during its time** of prohibition, when that leavened bread is mixed with **another type** of food even when only a small bit of it is mixed in, **due to** the prohibition against consuming a comparable mixture **with its own type** of substance. Owing to the severity of the prohibition against consuming leavened bread during Passover, Rav thought it necessary to render this additional decree. Rav's statement that leavened bread **is forbidden not during its time,** when it is mixed **with its own type** of substance, **is in accordance with** the opinion of **Rabbi Yehuda,** who says that according to the Torah, leavened bread is forbidden even after Passover, and thus even a mixture of it is prohibited.

וְשֶׁלֹּא בְּמִינוֹ – מוּתָּר. דְּשֶׁלֹּא בִּזְמַנּוֹ וְשֶׁלֹּא בְּמִינוֹ אַטּוּ מִינוֹ – כּוּלֵּי הַאי לָא גָּזְרִינַן.

But if it is mixed with **another type** of substance **it is permitted, because** there is **no** need to go **so far** as **to render a decree with regard to** a mixture with **another type** of substance **not during its time, due to** the prohibition of a mixture with **the same type** of substance. Rav maintains that when any prohibited item falls into a mixture of a different type of substance, it is nullified, unless it gives flavor to the new mixture. Therefore, the same principle should apply to leavened bread after Passover, and a small amount should be nullified once the more serious prohibition no longer applies to it.

שְׁמוּאֵל אָמַר: חָמֵץ בִּזְמַנּוֹ, בְּמִינוֹ – אָסוּר, שֶׁלֹּא בְּמִינוֹ – מוּתָּר. שֶׁלֹּא בִּזְמַנּוֹ, בֵּין בְּמִינוֹ בֵּין שֶׁלֹּא בְּמִינוֹ – מוּתָּר. חָמֵץ בִּזְמַנּוֹ בְּמִינוֹ אָסוּר, שְׁמוּאֵל לְטַעְמֵיהּ, דְּרַב וּשְׁמוּאֵל דְּאָמְרִי תַּרְוַיְיהוּ: כׇּל אִיסּוּרִין שֶׁבַּתּוֹרָה, בְּמִינוֹ – אֲסוּרִין בְּמַשֶּׁהוּ, שֶׁלֹּא בְּמִינוֹ – בְּנוֹתֵן טַעַם.

In contrast, **Shmuel said** that if **leavened bread** becomes mixed with permitted food **during its time** of prohibition, then the following distinction applies: If it becomes mixed **with its own type** of food **it is forbidden,** but if it becomes mixed **with another type** of food **it is permitted. If it** becomes mixed together **not during its time** of prohibition, but after Passover, then regardless **of whether** it becomes mixed **with its own type or with another type** of substance, **it is permitted.** With regard to the statement that **leavened bread** mixed **with the same type** of substance **during its time** of prohibition **is forbidden, Shmuel** conforms **to his** line of **reasoning** below: **As it is Rav and Shmuel who both say:** With regard to **any** foods **prohibited by the Torah** that become mixed with permitted foods, if the permitted food is of **its own type,** such that it is impossible to distinguish one from another, then even **any amount** of the prohibited substance renders the entire mixture prohibited. However, if the prohibited food is mixed **with another type** of substance, then the mixture becomes prohibited only when there is enough of the forbidden item to **give flavor** to the mixture.

שֶׁלֹּא בְּמִינָן אַטּוּ מִינָן – לָא גָּזַר. שֶׁלֹּא בִּזְמַנּוֹ, בֵּין בְּמִינָן בֵּין שֶׁלֹּא בְּמִינָן – מוּתָּרִין, כְּרַבִּי שִׁמְעוֹן.

And Shmuel **did not render a decree** prohibiting a mixture **with another type** of substance, **due to** the prohibition against consuming a mixture with **its same type.** However, **not during its time,** but rather after Passover, the mixture **is permitted,** regardless of **whether** it was mixed **with its own type or with another type.** And this statement is **in accordance with** the opinion of **Rabbi Shimon,** who states that after Passover one may derive benefit from leavened bread that was owned by a Jew during Passover.

NOTES

Gives flavor – נוֹתֵן טַעַם: Usually, when forbidden food is mixed with permitted food, and the flavor of the forbidden food can no longer be detected, the mixture is permitted. A mixture of this kind may be given to a non-Jewish cook to determine whether or not the flavor of the non-kosher ingredients is noticeable. If this is not possible, the mixture is presumed to be kosher if it contains at least sixty times as much permitted as forbidden food, as the Sages assessed that no substance can give flavor at this ratio.

Leavened bread that gives flavor – חָמֵץ בְּנוֹתֵן טַעַם: The early commentaries ask why it is necessary for Rabbi Yoḥanan to state that a small amount of leavened bread makes the mixture forbidden, given the principle that an item that can be permitted by other means can never be nullified. As the *halakha*, which is in accordance with the opinion of Rabbi Shimon, is that leavened bread is permitted after the conclusion of Passover, it is considered an item that can be permitted by other means, and therefore any amount of leavened bread will cause the mixture to become forbidden. They answer that apparently Rabbi Yoḥanan does not render leavened bread permitted after Passover, and therefore this principle does not apply in this case (Ramban; *Milḥemet Hashem*).

Any amount of leavened bread – חָמֵץ בְּמַשֶּׁהוּ: Several different explanations are offered as the rationale behind this stringency. Some say that because the leavened bread will be permitted after Passover it is considered to be a forbidden item that can be permitted via other means, with regard to which the *halakha* is more stringent. Others say that since one is permitted to eat leavened bread during the rest of the year, it is logical that one is especially strict about it during Passover in order to prevent himself from accidentally eating it. Still others suggest that this stringency is directly connected to the punishment of *karet* and the prohibition against seeing leavened bread, neither of which applies to most other forbidden items (*Me'iri*).

וְרַבִּי יוֹחָנָן אָמַר: חָמֵץ בִּזְמַנּוֹ, בֵּין בְּמִינוֹ וּבֵין שֶׁלֹּא בְּמִינוֹ – אָסוּר בְּנוֹתֵן טַעַם. שֶׁלֹּא בִּזְמַנּוֹ, בֵּין בְּמִינָן בֵּין שֶׁלֹּא בְּמִינָן – מוּתָּר.

And Rabbi Yoḥanan said: With regard to **leavened bread** that falls into a mixture **during its time** of prohibition, **whether** it is mixed **with its own type** of substance **or another type** of substance, **it becomes prohibited only when** there is enough of the forbidden item to **give flavor** to the mixture. However, **not during its time** of prohibition, but rather after Passover, **it is** always **permitted,** regardless **of whether** it falls into a mixture **of its own type** of substance **or** whether it falls into a mixture of **another type** of substance.

חָמֵץ בִּזְמַנּוֹ בֵּין בְּמִינוֹ בֵּין שֶׁלֹּא בְּמִינוֹ בְּנוֹתֵן טַעַם – רַבִּי יוֹחָנָן לְטַעְמֵיהּ, דְּרַבִּי יוֹחָנָן וְרֵישׁ לָקִישׁ דְּאָמְרִי תַּרְוַיְיהוּ: כׇּל אִיסּוּרִין שֶׁבַּתּוֹרָה, בֵּין בְּמִינָן בֵּין שֶׁלֹּא בְּמִינָן – בְּנוֹתֵן טַעַם. שֶׁלֹּא בִּזְמַנּוֹ, בֵּין בְּמִינוֹ בֵּין שֶׁלֹּא בְּמִינוֹ – מוּתָּרִין – כְּרַבִּי שִׁמְעוֹן.

The Gemara explains this position: With regard to the statement that **leavened bread** that falls into a mixture **during its time** of prohibition, **whether with its own type** of food **or with another type** of food, then it is prohibited only **when it gives flavor** to the mixture, **Rabbi Yoḥanan** conforms **to his** line of **reasoning** below. **As** it is **Rabbi Yoḥanan and Reish Lakish who both say:** With regard to **any** foods **forbidden by the Torah** that fall into a mixture, **whether of its own type** of food **or another type** of food, the mixture **is prohibited when** there is enough of the forbidden item **to give flavor** to the mixture. If less than this amount falls into the mixture, it is nullified by the large majority of permitted food. Rabbi Yoḥanan's statement that **not during its time** of prohibition, but rather after Passover, **it is permitted,** regardless of **whether** it falls into a mixture **of its own type** of food **or** into a mixture of **another type** of food, is **in accordance with** the opinion of **Rabbi Shimon,** who maintains that leavened bread owned by a Jew during Passover is not prohibited afterward.

Perek **II**
Daf **30** Amud **a**

אָמַר רָבָא: הִלְכְתָא, חָמֵץ בִּזְמַנּוֹ, בֵּין בְּמִינוֹ בֵּין שֶׁלֹּא בְּמִינוֹ – אָסוּר בְּמַשֶּׁהוּ, כְּרַב. שֶׁלֹּא בִּזְמַנּוֹ, בֵּין בְּמִינוֹ בֵּין שֶׁלֹּא בְּמִינוֹ – מוּתָּר, כְּרַבִּי שִׁמְעוֹן.

Rava said: The *halakha* is that with regard to the prohibition against eating a mixture of **leavened bread during its time** of prohibition, i.e., during Passover, regardless of whether it is mixed **with its own type or with another type, it is forbidden,**[H] even if **any amount** becomes mixed in, **in accordance with** the opinion of **Rav. Not during its time** of prohibition, but rather after the conclusion of Passover, regardless of whether the leavened bread was mixed **with its own type or with another type, it is permitted,** even when it gives flavor to the mixture. This is **in accordance with** the opinion of **Rabbi Shimon,** who states that leavened bread owned by a Jew during Passover is permitted after Passover.[H]

וּמִי אָמַר רָבָא הָכִי? וְהָאָמַר רָבָא: רַבִּי שִׁמְעוֹן קְנָסָא קָנֵיס, הוֹאִיל וְעָבַר עָלָיו בְּ״בַל יֵרָאֶה וּבַל יִמָּצֵא״!

The Gemara asks: **Did Rava** actually **say this,** that according to Rabbi Shimon, leavened bread owned by a Jew on Passover is permitted after Passover? **But didn't Rava** himself **say** that **Rabbi Shimon imposed a penalty** forbidding one from deriving benefit from leavened bread owned by a Jew during Passover, **since he transgressed** the prohibition **it shall not be seen and** the prohibition **it shall not be found?**

הָנֵי מִילֵּי – בְּעֵינֵיהּ, אֲבָל עַל יְדֵי תַּעֲרוֹבֶת – לָא. וְאָזְדָא רָבָא לְטַעְמֵיהּ, דְּאָמַר רָבָא: כִּי הָוֵינַן בֵּי רַב נַחְמָן, כִּי הָווּ נָפְקִי שִׁבְעָה יוֹמֵי דְּפִסְחָא, אֲמַר לַן: פּוּקוּ וּזְבִינוּ חֲמִירָא דִּבְנֵי חֵילָא.

The Gemara resolves this challenge: **This** penalty **applies** only to leavened bread that is **in its pure** unadulterated form, **but** with regard to **a mixture, no,**[N] one does not impose a penalty, even though the leavened bread is still extant. The Gemara adds: **And Rava follows his** line of **reasoning,** stated elsewhere, that indicates that he rules in accordance with the opinion of Rabbi Shimon, **as Rava said: While we were** studying **in Rav Naḥman's house,** on the evening **when the seven days of Passover had passed, he said to us: Go and buy leavened bread from the gentiles**[N] who baked it on that day, the last day of Passover. Based on this story, it is clear that he maintained that one may eat leavened bread that was owned by a gentile during Passover.

HALAKHA

A mixture of leavened bread – תַּעֲרוֹבֶת חָמֵץ: During Passover, even a small bit of leavened bread that falls into a mixture renders it forbidden, whether it is mixed into the same type of substance or into a different type of substance, in accordance with Rava's ruling (*Shulḥan Arukh, Oraḥ Ḥayyim* 447:1).

Leavened bread after Passover – חָמֵץ שֶׁלֹּא בִּזְמַנּוֹ: The *halakha* with regard to a mixture containing leavened bread at a time that is not Passover, either before or after the Festival, is that the leavened bread is subject to nullification in the mixture regardless of whether it falls into the same type of substance or into a different type of substance, so long as it is less than one-sixtieth of the mixture (*Tur*). Most authorities rule that when the leavened bread fell into a mixture after Passover, the leavened bread can be nullified in a mixture so long as the permitted substance constitutes a majority of the mixture (*Be'er Heitev*; *Shulḥan Arukh, Oraḥ Ḥayyim* 447:11).

NOTES

But a mixture, no – אֲבָל עַל יְדֵי תַּעֲרוֹבֶת לָא: It is insufficient for a mixture to have a one-to-one ratio of leavened bread to permitted food in order to be permitted. Rather, the leavened bread must be nullified by the majority of the permitted food, even if it still is of sufficient quantity to impart a noticeable taste (Ritva). This principle applies only when the leavened bread fell into the mixture unintentionally. However, if one intentionally created such a mixture, Rabbi Shimon would impose a penalty, and the mixture would be forbidden (Ra'ah).

Leavened bread from the gentiles – חֲמִירָא דִּבְנֵי חֵילָא: Some explain that Rav Naḥman only instructed them to buy leaven, i.e., yeast, so that they could make their own bread, but he did not give them permission to purchase leavened bread itself. This distinction could be based on the stringency of the prohibition against leavened bread, or because Rav Naḥman himself is of the opinion that throughout the year one may not eat bread baked by gentiles (Maharam Ḥalawa).

אָמַר רַב: קְדֵירוֹת בְּפֶסַח יִשָּׁבְרוּ. וְאַמַּאי? לַשְׁהִינְהוּ אַחַר הַפֶּסַח, וְלֶיעֱבַד בְּהוּ שֶׁלֹּא בְּמִינָן! גְּזֵירָה דִּילְמָא אָתוּ לְמֶיעֱבַד בְּהוּ בְּמִינוֹ.

Rav said: Earthenware **pots** in which leavened bread was cooked **during Passover** should **be broken,** as some small quantity of the flavor of the leavened bread was absorbed into the pot. It is therefore prohibited to cook in them again, as the forbidden flavor of this leavened bread would be transmitted to the new food. The Gemara asks: **And why** was Rav so stringent with regard to these pots? **Let him retain** the pots until **after** the conclusion of **Passover and prepare** mixtures **of another type** of food **in them.** Even Rav maintains that when a small bit of leavened bread is mixed with another type of food after Passover, the mixture is permitted. The Gemara explains that he did allow this due to **a rabbinic decree that perhaps one will come to prepare a mixture of the same type in** these pots, causing their contents to become prohibited. He therefore instructed that one destroy these pots in order to avoid this pitfall.

וּשְׁמוּאֵל אָמַר: לֹא יִשָּׁבְרוּ, אֲבָל מַשְׁהֵי לְהוּ לְאַחַר זְמַנּוֹ, וְעָבֵיד בְּהוּ בֵּין בְּמִינוֹ בֵּין שֶׁלֹּא בְּמִינוֹ.

And Shmuel said: They need **not be broken. Rather, he** should **retain them**[N] **until after its time,** i.e., the conclusion of Passover, **and** then he may **prepare** food of **either the same type or another type in them.**[H]

וְאָזְדָא שְׁמוּאֵל לְטַעְמֵיהּ, דַּאֲמַר שְׁמוּאֵל לְהָנְהוּ דְּמַזְבְּנֵי כַּנְדֵּי: אַשְׁווּ זְבִינֵי אַכַּנְדַּיְכִי, וְאִי לָא – דָּרֵשְׁנָא לְכוּ כְּרַבִּי שִׁמְעוֹן.

And Shmuel follows his line of **reasoning,** stated elsewhere, **as Shmuel said to the pot merchants,** who would dramatically raise their prices after Passover: **Level the prices for your pots. And if** you do **not** bring your prices down, **I will teach you** that the *halakha* **is in accordance with** the opinion of **Rabbi Shimon,**[N] that one is permitted to derive benefit from leavened bread after Passover. This ruling would lead people to retain their vessels and desist from purchasing new vessels after Passover, and consequently the merchants would lose business.

וְלִידְרוֹשׁ לְהוּ, דְּהָא שְׁמוּאֵל כְּרַבִּי שִׁמְעוֹן סְבִירָא לֵיהּ! אַתְרֵיהּ דְּרַב הֲוָה.

The Gemara asks: **Let him** indeed **teach** this ruling **to them, for Shmuel holds** that the *halakha* is **in accordance with** the opinion of **Rabbi Shimon,** as was previously mentioned. As such, why did he not publicize his opinion on the matter? The Gemara answers: **It was Rav's locale,**[N] and therefore it would not be appropriate for Shmuel to publicly present a position with which Rav did not agree. However, when he saw the merchants raising their prices in an unfair manner, he nevertheless threatened to make his opinion on the matter public.

הַהוּא תַּנּוּרָא דְּטָחוּ בֵּיהּ טִיחַיָּא, אַסְרָהּ רָבָא בַּר אֲהִילַאי לְמֵיכְלֵיהּ לְרִיפְתָּא אֲפִילּוּ בְּמִילְחָא לְעוֹלָם, דִּילְמָא אָתֵי לְמֵיכְלֵיהּ בְּכוּתְּחָא.

The Gemara recounts: There was **a certain oven that they smeared with grease** from meat, and consequently the flavor of meat was absorbed into it, and then they used it to bake bread. **Rava bar Ahilai prohibited eating this bread even with salt,** and not just with milk. This status would apply **forever** to bread baked in this oven, even during subsequent baking, **lest one eat** such bread **with *kutaḥ*,** a dairy-based seasoning, which would be a violation of the prohibition against eating meat with milk.

מֵיתִיבִי: אֵין לָשִׁין אֶת הָעִיסָּה בְּחָלָב, וְאִם לָשׁ – כׇּל הַפַּת כּוּלָּהּ אֲסוּרָה, מִפְּנֵי הֶרְגֵּל עֲבֵירָה. כַּיּוֹצֵא בּוֹ

The Gemara **raises an objection** to this statement: It was taught that **one** may **not knead the dough with milk,**[H] **and if he** did **knead** the dough with milk, then **all of the bread is prohibited due to** concern that he will commit **a habitual transgression.** As one habitually eats bread with meat, there is a concern that one will come to eat this bread with meat as well, unwittingly transgressing the prohibition against eating meat with milk. **Similarly,**

HALAKHA

Pots on Passover – קְדֵירוֹת בְּפֶסַח: Pots used during the year for leavened bread should be cleaned from any actual particles of leavened bread and put away for the duration of Passover. However, one is permitted to use them after Passover, as stated by Shmuel and accepted by Rava (*Shulḥan Arukh, Oraḥ Ḥayyim* 451:1).

Dough with milk – עִיסָּה בְּחָלָב: It is prohibited to put milk in dough, lest one eat the bread with meat, and if he kneaded the dough with milk, the bread may not be eaten. However, one may put milk in dough if he makes small rolls that can be consumed in one sitting or if they have a unique shape that distinguishes them as dairy (*Shulḥan Arukh, Yoreh De'a* 97:1).

NOTES

He should retain them – מַשְׁהֵי לְהוּ: This appears to contradict the principle that one may not intentionally effect the neutralization of a prohibited item. As such, why was it permitted in this situation? The Ritva offers several reasons why this case is different. First, when the flavor of the leavened bread was absorbed by the walls of the pot it was still permitted, and the prohibition would apply only if it were to emerge via cooking during Passover. Second, even if the flavor of the leavened bread were transmitted by the pot, it would add a bad flavor to the food, which would not make it prohibited. Finally, it can be assumed that only a small bit of the flavor of the leavened bread will be transmitted by the pot, and consequently there is room for leniency.

I will teach you that the *halakha* is in accordance with the opinion of Rabbi Shimon – דָּרֵשְׁנָא לְכוּ כְּרַבִּי שִׁמְעוֹן: In this case Shmuel wished to prevent the pot merchants from exploiting the people's piety to turn a larger profit. Therefore, he threatened to make the lenient opinion known, which would cause many people to desist from purchasing new pots after Passover.

Rav's locale – אַתְרֵיהּ דְּרַב: Ordinarily, when a certain Sage lives in a city and the people there accept him as their leader, then he is considered the spiritual leader of that place. The residents of the city are required to accept his legal rulings so long as they were not rejected categorically by the other Sages. Therefore, even after Rav's death it was still considered unacceptable for a Sage to present a position that Rav opposed in his locale.

אֵין טָשִׁין אֶת הַתַּנּוּר בְּאַלְיָה, וְאִם טָשׁ – כׇּל הַפַּת כּוּלָּהּ אֲסוּרָה, עַד שֶׁיַּסִּיק אֶת הַתַּנּוּר, הָא הוּסַּק הַתַּנּוּר – מִיהָא שָׁרֵי. תְּיוּבְתָּא דְּרָבָא בַּר אֲהִילַאי! תְּיוּבְתָּא.

one may **not smear the** inside of an **oven with the fat tail** [*alya*] of a sheep,[N] because it is meat. **And if one** did **smear** it over the oven, then **all of the bread** baked in it **is prohibited,** lest one accidentally eat this bread with milk. However, this applies only **until one kindles the oven** and burns off this fat. The Gemara infers from this *baraita* **that if the oven was kindled** afterward then **it is permitted in any case.** This would seem to present a **conclusive refutation of** the statement of **Rava bar Ahilai** who maintains that the bread cooked in this oven is prohibited forever, even after the oven is rekindled. The Gemara concludes: Indeed, this **is a conclusive refutation** of his opinion.

אֲמַר לֵיהּ רָבִינָא לְרַב אַשִׁי: וְכִי מֵאַחַר דְּאִיתּוֹתַב רָבָא בַּר אֲהִילַאי, אַמַּאי קָאָמַר רַב קְדֵירוֹת בַּפֶּסַח יִשָּׁבְרוּ. אֲמַר לֵיהּ: הָתָם – תַּנּוּר שֶׁל מַתֶּכֶת, הָכָא בִּקְדֵירָה שֶׁל חֶרֶס.

Ravina said to Rav Ashi: Since the statement of **Rava bar Ahilai was refuted, why did Rav say** that **pots** that were used for leavened bread **on Passover** should **be broken?** Presumably, their status could be remedied in the same way as was that of this oven, by heating them on a fire until the flavor of the leavened bread absorbed in them was removed. Rav Ashi **said to him:** There is a distinction between these two cases. **There,** it is referring **to a metal oven,** which can be cleansed through an additional kindling, while **here,** it is referring **to an earthenware pot,** where additional kindling is insufficient, as the earthenware has the capacity to absorb more of the flavor of the leavened bread and it cannot be purged by fire.

וְאִיבָּעֵית אֵימָא: הָא וְהָא בְּשֶׁל חֶרֶס, זֶה – הֶסֵּיקָן מִבִּפְנִים, וְזֶה – הֶסֵּיקָן מִבַּחוּץ. וְכִי תֵּימָא הָכִי נַמִי לֶיעֱבַד לֵיהּ הַסָּקָה מִבִּפְנִים – חָיֵיס עֲלֵיהּ מִשּׁוּם דְּפָקְעָה.

If you wish, say instead that **both this,** the oven, **and that,** the pot, **are earthenware,** but that the following distinction applies. **This,** the oven, **is kindled from the inside,** and as the fire is kindled inside the oven itself, it consumes the absorbed flavor of the leavened bread. While **that,** the pot, **is kindled from the outside,** such that the flavor of the prohibited material absorbed in the pot is not purged by the fire. **And if you say, so too** here, in the case of the pot, **he should perform the kindling** procedure on the pots from the **inside** to remove that which has been absorbed, this is not reasonable. Presumably, the owner of the pot will **be concerned lest it burst** if he makes the pot too hot. Therefore, he will not use sufficient heat to ensure that the leavened bread that has been absorbed will be completely purged.[H]

הִלְכָּךְ, הַאי בּוּכְיָא – הֶסֵּיקוֹ מִבַּחוּץ הוּא, וְאָסוּר. וְאִי מָלְיֵיהּ גּוּמְרֵי – שַׁפִּיר דָּמֵי.

The Gemara concludes: **Therefore,** based on this principle, **this griddle** made from earthenware tiles that was used to bake bread is a type of oven where **the kindling is from the outside and** therefore **prohibited. But if he fills it with** burning **coals,** then **it seems well** and it can be used afterward.[H] Because this vessel is often subject to a high level of heat, the owner will not be concerned that it will break when heated.

אֲמַר לֵיהּ רָבִינָא לְרַב אַשִׁי: הָנֵי סַכִּינֵי בְּפִסְחָא הֵיכִי עָבְדִינַן לְהוּ? אֲמַר לֵיהּ: לְדִידִי חֲדַתָּא קָא עָבְדִינַן. אֲמַר לֵיהּ: תֵּינַח מָר דְּאֶפְשָׁר לֵיהּ, דְּלָא אֶפְשָׁר לֵיהּ מַאי? אֲמַר לֵיהּ: אֲנָא כְּעֵין חֲדַתָּא קָאָמִינָא; קַתַּיְיהוּ בְּטִינָא, וּפַרְזְלַיְיהוּ בְּנוּרָא, וַהֲדַר מְעַיְּילָנָא לְקַתַּיְיהוּ בְּרוֹתְחִין. וְהִלְכְתָא: אִידֵי וְאִידֵי בְּרוֹתְחִין, וּבִכְלִי רִאשׁוֹן.

Ravina said to Rav Ashi: With regard to **these knives,**[N] **how do we prepare them** for use **during Passover?** Rav Ashi **said to him: For me,** personally, **we craft new ones.** Ravina **said to him:** It works out **well for Master, as you are able** to afford new knives. However, **what** should **one who is unable** to purchase new knives do? **He said to him: I was speaking of** making them **like new** by thoroughly cleaning them in the following manner: One should cover **the** wooden **handles in mud,** so that they will not be burned, and heat **the metal with fire** until it is white-hot. **And then I place the handles** of the knives **in boiling water** in order to remove anything that had been absorbed into the wood. **And the *halakha*** is that with regard to both **this,** the blade, and **that,** the handle, it is sufficient to immerse them **in boiling water,** so long as this water is still **in a primary vessel.**[NH] The water must still be in the original pot in which it was boiled and not poured from another pot.

NOTES

Fat tail [*alya*] of a sheep – אַלְיָה: The *alya* is the long, thick, fatty tail of the genus of sheep that was common in Eretz Yisrael and the surrounding areas during the Temple era. The tail covered the entire back of the sheep, to the extent that it was difficult to ascertain the gender of the sheep, particularly in younger animals. The Torah commands that when a sheep is brought as a peace-offering, the tail is one of the parts of the animal burned on the altar. This applies only to sheep, as other animals that were sacrificed, e.g., goats, do not have this kind of tail.

These knives – הָנֵי סַכִּינֵי: Some explain that these knives require purging in boiling water and whitening by fire even though they are ordinarily used for cutting bread, because one will occasionally insert them into a pot that is cooking on the fire (*Mikhtam*).

In boiling water in a primary vessel – בְּרוֹתְחִין וּבִכְלִי רִאשׁוֹן: Most authorities explain that, in contrast to the halakhot of Shabbat, this applies only to a primary vessel that is on the fire, and not to one that has been removed from the fire.

HALAKHA

Rendering earthenware pots kosher – הַכְשָׁרַת קְדֵרוֹת לְפֶסַח: Earthenware pots that were used to cook leavened bread cannot be used during Passover, and even if one fills them with coals or places them in the oven there is still concern that he will not heat them thoroughly enough, as stated in the Gemara. The only way these vessels can be prepared for use on Passover is if they are returned to the kiln, as stated by *Tosafot* (*Shulḥan Arukh, Oraḥ Ḥayyim* 451:1).

Rendering a griddle kosher – הַכְשָׁרַת בּוּכְיָא: A griddle used for baking leavened bread cannot be used for Passover after being kindled from the outside. However, if one fills it with coals, it is permissible to use such a pan on Passover (*Shulḥan Arukh, Oraḥ Ḥayyim* 451:2).

Rendering knives kosher – הַכְשָׁרַת סַכִּינִים: In order to render a knife fit for use on Passover one must purge it in boiling water in a primary vessel, even if it is not resting on the fire (*Tur*). One must first be sure that it is entirely free of rust or other filth before this immersion (*Shulḥan Arukh, Oraḥ Ḥayyim* 451:3).

אָמַר רַב הוּנָא בְּרֵיהּ דְּרַב יְהוֹשֻׁעַ: עֵץ פָּרוּר מַגְעִילוֹ בְּרוֹתְחִין וּבִכְלִי רִאשׁוֹן. קָסָבַר: כְּבוֹלְעוֹ כָּךְ פּוֹלְטוֹ.

Rav Huna, son of Rav Yehoshua, said: A wooden ladle[N] should **be purged in boiling water in a primary vessel** in order to remove the flavor of the forbidden food that it absorbed. The Gemara states: He **holds** in accordance with the principle: **As it absorbs** the flavor of the forbidden substance, **so it emits it.** The same cooking method and level of heat that caused the flavor of the forbidden substance to be absorbed in the vessel suffices to discharge the flavor of that substance from the vessel. Therefore, a ladle that absorbed flavor of leavened bread from a pot of boiling water which was over a fire will discharge the flavor of leavened bread once it is placed in the boiling water again.

בְּעוֹ מִינֵּיהּ מֵאַמֵימַר: הָנֵי מָאנֵי דְּקוּנְיָא מַהוּ לְאִישְׁתַּמּוּשֵׁי בְּהוּ בְּפִסְחָא? יָרוֹקָא לָא תִּיבָּעֵי לָךְ – דְּוַדַּאי אֲסִירִי. כִּי תִּיבָּעֵי לָךְ – אוּכָּמֵי וְחִיוָּרֵי מַאי? וְהֵיכָא דְּאִית בְּהוּ קַרְטוֹפָנֵי – לָא תִּיבָּעֵי לָךְ, דְּוַדַּאי אֲסִירִי. כִּי תִּיבָּעֵי לָךְ – דְּשִׁיעֵי מַאי?

They raised a dilemma before Ameimar: Concerning **certain glazed** [*konya*][L] earthenware **vessels,**[HB] **what is the** ***halakha*** **with regard to using them during Passover?** The Gemara explains: With regard to **green** vessels, the dilemma need **not** even **be raised,** as **they are certainly prohibited** as their coating does not prevent them from absorbing the flavor of leavened bread. **Let the dilemma be raised** with regard to **black and white** vessels: **What is** the *halakha* here? **And** furthermore, the dilemma need **not be raised when they have cracks;** as the leavened bread will remain stuck in these cracks, **they are certainly prohibited. Let the dilemma be raised** with regard to **smooth** vessels: **What is** the *halakha* in that case?

אֲמַר לֵיהּ: חֲזֵינָא לְהוּ דְּמִידַיְיתִי, אַלְמָא בָּלְעֵי וַאֲסִירִי, וְהַתּוֹרָה הֵעִידָה עַל כְּלִי חֶרֶס שֶׁאֵינוֹ יוֹצֵא מִידֵי דוֹפְיוֹ לְעוֹלָם.

Ameimar **said to him: I saw that** some of the liquid **is expelled** [***demidayeti***]?[N] from the outside of the vessel. **Apparently they absorb and are** therefore **prohibited,** as they cannot be prepared for use on Passover through cleansing, **and the Torah testified about earthenware vessels** that when they absorb the flavor of a prohibited substance, **they will never leave their defective** status[N] and they remain permanently prohibited. The Torah states that a person may cleanse other vessels by scouring and rinsing them, whereas it states that earthenware vessels must be broken.

וּמַאי שְׁנָא לְעִנְיַן יֵין נֶסֶךְ, דְּדָרֵישׁ מָרֵימָר: מָאנֵי דְּקוּנְיָא, בֵּין אוּכָּמָא בֵּין חִיוָּרֵי וּבֵין יָרוֹקֵי – שָׁרֵי. וְכִי תֵּימָא: יֵין נֶסֶךְ – דְּרַבָּנַן, חָמֵץ – דְּאוֹרַיְיתָא. כֹּל דְּתַקּוּן רַבָּנַן – כְּעֵין דְּאוֹרַיְיתָא תַּקּוּן. אֲמַר לֵיהּ: זֶה תַּשְׁמִישׁוֹ עַל יְדֵי חַמִּין, וְזֶה תַּשְׁמִישׁוֹ עַל יְדֵי צוֹנֵן,

The Gemara asks: **What is different** about **wine** used for a **libation,** with regard to which the *halakha* of earthenware vessels is more lenient? **As Mareimar taught: A glazed** earthenware **vessel is permitted whether it is black, white, or green** if it was used to store wine belonging to gentiles.[H] Any wine that came in contact with gentiles is suspected of having been poured as a libation offering to idolatry. **And if you say** that it is possible to distinguish between the prohibition of **wine** used for a **libation,** which is a **rabbinic** prohibition, **and that of leavened bread,** which is forbidden **by Torah** law, this is difficult, as **all** ordinances **that the Sages instituted, they instituted similar to Torah** law. Once they have declared that this item is prohibited, the principles applicable to Torah prohibitions apply to it as well. Ameimar **said to him:** The distinction between the two cases is that with regard to **this** vessel, which is used for cooking during Passover, its primary **use is with hot** foods, and therefore the flavor of the leavened bread has become absorbed within its walls. **But** with regard to **this** vessel, which is used to store wine, **its** primary **use is with cool** liquids, which are not absorbed to the same degree.

LANGUAGE

Glazed [*konya*] – קוּנְיָא: From the Greek **κονία**, *konya*, meaning cement. This phrase refers to vessels plastered with lime or stucco.

HALAKHA

Glazed vessels – מָאנֵי דְּקוּנְיָא: Glazed vessels are considered the same as earthenware vessels with regard to the method of rendering them kosher for Passover (*Shulḥan Arukh, Oraḥ Ḥayyim* 451:23).

Glazed vessels and libation wine – כְּלִי קוּנְיָא בְּיֵין נֶסֶךְ: A glazed vessel, i.e., earthenware covered in glass, that has been used to store cool wine belonging to a gentile must be scoured and washed in order to be used on Passover (*Shulḥan Arukh, Yoreh De'a* 135:6).

BACKGROUND

Glazed vessels [*manei dekonya*] – מָאנֵי דְּקוּנְיָא: As described in the Talmud, *manei dekonya* are glazed vessels, where the glaze was made from different types of materials in order to give the vessel various colors. Due to the variation in material, different types of glaze also affected the degree to which the contents of the vessels were absorbed into their walls.

The image displays clay vessels coated with a red glaze from the talmudic period discovered in Dura-Europos, Babylonia, which is in modern Syria, and a clay jug with a green glaze from the same area. Note the difference between the glazed and unglazed sections of the jug.

Glazed pottery

NOTES

Wooden ladle – עֵץ פָּרוּר: Some say that this was not a ladle used for stirring but a peg placed into a cauldron full of thick stew in order to cool it down (Ritva; Maharam Ḥalawa).

Expelled [*demidayeti*] – דְּמִידַיְיתִי: Some explain that this word is related to the word for ink [*deyo*], and means that they became black as ink, for the outside of the vessel would blacken after repeated use, due to the food cooked inside it (*Me'iri*; Rabbeinu Ḥananel; Rav Yehuda ben Rav Binyamin HaRofeh).

Their defective status – מִידֵי דוֹפְיוֹ: There are variant readings for this phrase. The standard version has the word *dofyo*, meaning blemish, implying that once the forbidden substance enters an earthenware pot, the pot remains prohibited forever. However, other versions have the word *dofeno*, meaning wall. In that case, the phrase means that the forbidden substance remains absorbed within the walls of the vessel (see *Me'iri* and others).

אמר רבא בר אבא אמר רב חייא בר אשי אמר שמואל: כל הכלים שנשתמשו בהן חמץ בצונן – משתמש בהן מצה, חוץ מן בית שאור, הואיל שחימוצו קשה. אמר רב אשי: ובית חרוסת כבית שאור שחימוצו קשה דמי.

The Gemara continues discussing the ways that a vessel must be cleansed so that it can be used during Passover. **Rava bar Abba said that Rav Ḥiyya bar Ashi said that Shmuel said: Any vessel that was used for leavened bread** only **while cool can be used for *matza*,**[N] because no flavor of the leavened bread was absorbed by the vessel. The **exception** to this rule is **the leaven container** where the yeast was stored, **since its leavening is** more **potent,** and it can be assumed that the flavor from the yeast has entered the walls of the vessel even without heat. **Rav Ashi said: And the spice container,** in which potent spices that contained flour were stored, **has the same** status **as the leaven container whose leavening is potent.**[H]

אמר רבא: הני אגני דמחוזא, הואיל ותדירי למילש בהו חמירא, ומשהו בהו חמירא – כבית שאור שחימוצו קשה דמי. פשיטא! מהו דתימא: כיון דרויחא – שליט בהו אוירא ולא בלעי, קא משמע לן.

Rava said: With regard to **certain bowls of Meḥoza, since it is common to knead leavened bread in them and** then **store the leavened bread in them, they are considered to be like a leaven container whose leavening is potent.**[H] The Gemara asks: Why did Rava find it necessary to make this statement? Isn't it **obvious** that these bowls are the same as a leaven container? The Gemara answers: **Lest you say** that **since** these bowls **are spacious, the air dominates them and they do not absorb** the leavened bread in the same way as does a leaven container, therefore, **he teaches us** that no such distinction applies.

מתני׳ גוי שהלוה את ישראל על חמצו אחר הפסח – מותר בהנאה, וישראל שהלוה את גוי על חמצו אחר הפסח – אסור בהנאה.

MISHNA If **a gentile lent money to a Jew,**[H] and the Jew gave him **leavened bread as** collateral until after Passover, and **after Passover** the gentile retains this leavened bread in lieu of payment, then **one is permitted to** derive **benefit from** this leavened bread. Since the leavened bread was retained by the gentile based on the transfer that took place prior to Passover, the leavened bread is considered to have belonged to the gentile during Passover. Whereas if **a Jew lent money to a gentile,**[H] and **leavened bread** was given as collateral during Passover in the same manner as in the previous case, then **after Passover it is forbidden to** derive **benefit** from this leavened bread. Since this leavened bread was considered to be in the Jew's property during Passover, it is forbidden to derive benefit from it afterward.

גמ׳ איתמר, בעל חוב; אביי אמר: למפרע הוא גובה, ורבא אמר: מכאן ולהבא הוא גובה. כל היכא דאקדיש לוה וזבין לוה – כולי עלמא לא פליגי דאתי מלוה וטריף,

GEMARA It was stated that the *amora'im* disagree about the rights of a **creditor** with regard to collateral. **Abaye said: He retroactively collects** the property. In a case where the creditor had a lien on the property of the debtor and the debtor defaults on the loan, it is considered as if the creditor acquired rights to the collateral at the time of the loan and not at the time of collection. **And Rava said:** This is not the case, but rather, **he acquires** the collateral **from that point forward,** and has rights to the collateral only from the time that the loan was due. This dispute has ramifications for the status of the property, and actions undertaken with regard to it, during the intervening period. The Gemara sets several limitations on the scope of this dispute: **Anywhere that the debtor consecrated or sold** the field that was serving as collateral, **everyone agrees** that **the creditor can come and seize** this property and override the sale, because its status as collateral preceded its sale.

NOTES

Can be used for *matza* – מִשְׁתַּמֵּשׁ בָּהֶן מַצָּה: The early commentaries disagree about whether this statement indicates that one may use this vessel only for cold food on Passover or whether he may use it for hot food as well, as it did not absorb any flavor of leavened bread in the course of its use (see Rosh).

HALAKHA

Vessels used for cold foods – כֵּלִים שֶׁהִשְׁתַּמֵּשׁ בָּהֶן בְּצוֹנֵן: An earthenware vessel that has been used only for cold leavened bread may even be used for hot foods during Passover. The exception to this is a vessel in which leaven or a spice-flour mixture is kept, as their leavening is more potent (*Shulḥan Arukh, Oraḥ Ḥayyim* 451:22).

Vessels used for kneading – כְּלֵי לִישָׁה: Vessels used to knead leavened bread during the year require purging in boiling water if one wishes to use them on Passover, even if they were used only with cold foods. However, the common practice is not to use them at all (Rema, citing *Mordekhai*; *Shulḥan Arukh, Oraḥ Ḥayyim* 451:17).

If a gentile lent money to a Jew – גּוֹי שֶׁהִלְוָה אֶת יִשְׂרָאֵל: If a gentile lent money to a Jew, and the Jew gave him leavened bread as collateral, stating that if he does not repay the loan, the leavened bread will be transferred to the gentile from the time of the loan, then if the Jew did not pay by the set time, the leavened bread is considered to have belonged to the gentile from the time of the loan, and the Jew does not violate the prohibition: It shall not be seen (*Shulḥan Arukh, Oraḥ Ḥayyim* 441:1).

If a Jew lent money to a gentile – יִשְׂרָאֵל שֶׁהִלְוָה אֶת גּוֹי: With regard to a Jew who lent money to a gentile, and the gentile gave leavened bread as collateral, if the gentile stipulated that the leavened bread would be transferred retroactive to the time of the loan if he did not pay, and the gentile did not pay, the leavened bread is forbidden. However, if the Jew does not take responsibility for the collateral and the gentile did not stipulate that it would be acquired retroactively, the leavened bread is considered the property of the gentile and it is permitted after Passover (*Shulḥan Arukh, Oraḥ Ḥayyim* 441:2).

וְאָתֵי מַלְוֶה וּפָרֵיק. דִּתְנַן: מוֹסִיף עוֹד דִּינָר, וּפוֹדֶה אֶת הַנְּכָסִים הָאֵלּוּ. כִּי פְּלִיגִי – דְּזַבֵּין מַלְוֶה, וְקַדֵּישׁ מַלְוֶה.

Or if the debtor consecrated the property, the creditor can **come and redeem** it through a symbolic payment to the Temple. **As we learned** in a mishna: The creditor may **add an additional dinar**[NH] to the amount of the loan **and redeem**[N] **this property.** Although strictly speaking he need not redeem it, this payment was instituted so that it would not appear as though property were removed from the consecrated Temple jurisdiction without a payment. **When they disagree** is in a case **when the creditor sold or consecrated** the property in the interim between the giving of the collateral and the time the loan was due.

אַבַּיֵי אָמַר: לְמַפְרֵעַ הוּא גּוֹבֶה; כֵּיוָן דְּמְטָא זִמְנֵיהּ וְלָא פְּרַעֵיהּ – אִיגַּלַּאי מִילְּתָא לְמַפְרֵעַ דְּמֵעִיקָּרָא בִּרְשׁוּתֵיהּ הֲוָה קָאֵי, וְשַׁפִּיר אַקְדֵּישׁ, וְשַׁפִּיר זַבֵּין. וְרָבָא אָמַר: מִכָּאן וּלְהַבָּא הוּא גּוֹבֶה. כֵּיוָן דְּאִילּוּ הָווּ לֵיהּ זוּזֵי – הֲוָה מְסַלֵּיק לְהוּ בְּזוּזֵי – אִישְׁתַּכַּח דְּהָשְׁתָּא קָא קָנֵי.

Abaye said: He retroactively acquires the collateral. **Since the time arrived and he did not repay** his loan, **it has become clear retroactively that it was in** the creditor's **jurisdiction at the outset.** Therefore, **he did well to consecrate or sell** it. However, **Rava said: He collects it from that point forward, since if the** borrower **had money he would remove the** creditor's lien **with** this **money** and the lender would not acquire the property. **It is found** that the creditor **acquires** the property **now,** at the time when the loan is due, and consequently he did not have the right to consecrate or sell it before this time.

וּמִי אָמַר רָבָא הָכִי? וְהָאָמַר רָמִי בַּר חָמָא: רְאוּבֵן שֶׁמָּכַר שָׂדֶה לְשִׁמְעוֹן בְּאַחֲרָיוּת, וּזְקָפָן עָלָיו בְּמִלְוָה, וּמֵת רְאוּבֵן וַאֲתָא בַּעַל חוֹב דִּרְאוּבֵן וְטָרֵיף לֵיהּ מִשִּׁמְעוֹן, וַאֲתָא שִׁמְעוֹן וּפַיְּיסֵיהּ בְּזוּזֵי.

Before bringing proofs for either side of this dispute, the Gemara attempts to clarify Rava's position. **Did Rava** actually **say this?** A statement he makes in a different context appears to contradict the one made in his name here. **But didn't Rami bar Ḥama say: Reuven sold a field**[H] **to Shimon with a guarantee** that if the field is repossessed, Reuven will compensate Shimon for his loss.[N] Shimon did not pay for the purchase, and instead **set up** the value of the field **as a loan.** In the meantime, **Reuven died and a creditor of Reuven's came** to collect for a loan that Reuven had taken before he sold the field, as Reuven had no other land remaining, and he **seized** the land **from Shimon,** since it was mortgaged to this loan. **And Shimon went and appeased** the creditor **with money** so the creditor would allow him to keep this field.

דִּינָא הוּא דְּאָתוּ בְּנֵי רְאוּבֵן וְאָמְרִי לֵיהּ לְשִׁמְעוֹן: אֲנַן מִטַּלְטְלֵי שְׁבַק אֲבוּן גַּבָּךְ, וּמִטַּלְטְלֵי דְּיַתְמֵי לְבַעַל חוֹב לָא מִשְׁתַּעְבְּדִי.

By right, Reuven's sons can **come and say to Shimon** that he must pay them the money that he owes for the field. And they are not required to pay Shimon if he demands compensation for the repossession of his field. They can say that **our father left us movable property in your hands,** i.e., the money you owe us for the field, **and,** as a general rule, **movable property that has been left to orphans is not mortgaged to a creditor.**[N] The orphans can claim that the field belongs to Shimon, and as there is no land left for the orphans, there is no way for Shimon to recover the compensation that he is owed. The money he owes Reuven is considered movable property, and therefore he cannot recover his losses from these funds.

NOTES

Add an additional dinar – **מוֹסִיף עוֹד דִּינָר:** According to Rashi, the creditor adds a dinar to the amount of the loan and redeems the land. Others say that the debtor must pay this dinar and redeem the land, and then the lender takes the property (*Tosafot*).

Add an additional dinar and redeem – **מוֹסִיף עוֹד דִּינָר וּפוֹדֶה:** The early commentaries disagree about the reason for this addition. According to Rashi, the payment of this additional dinar is merely symbolic, so people will not think that property can lose its consecrated status without being redeemed. Others explain that although the consecrated status of this field cannot be removed without being redeemed, this redemption has no set value. As such, in this case one is permitted to redeem the consecrated property for less than its value in order to remove its consecrated status (Ra'avad).

Property guarantee – **אַחֲרָיוּת נְכָסִים:** This type of guarantee is a condition for sale of real estate. The Gemara elsewhere concludes that this condition is assumed to be part of the agreement in any sale of real estate, unless it is explicitly stipulated otherwise. As such, all property belonging to the seller would be mortgaged as collateral, guaranteeing that this sale stands. Consequently, if it turns out that this field was given as collateral for a different loan, the buyer can demand land of equal value from the other property of the seller. This clause applies only to real estate, whereas money or movable objects do not serve as guarantees for debts or sales. However, the *ge'onim* instituted other clauses with regard to these.

Responsibility of orphans – **אַחֲרָיוּתָם שֶׁל יְתוֹמִים:** Orphans, i.e., the heirs of a deceased person who were not partners in his property before his death, were granted certain rights by the Sages, specifically with regard to the proofs needed to resolve disputes regarding this property. These orphans are not required to pay their father's debt with movable property, even from the movable property that they inherited from him. Similarly, only real estate that they inherited from their father is mortgaged to his creditors.

HALAKHA

Add an additional dinar – **מוֹסִיף עוֹד דִּינָר:** If a debtor set aside property as collateral for a loan and then consecrated it, this property can be redeemed in exchange for its value and an additional dinar, so that people will not mistakenly think that consecrated property can lose its consecrated status without being redeemed. The creditor then receives his payment from this property (Rambam *Sefer Hafla'a, Hilkhot Arakhin VaḤaramim* 7:16).

Reuven sold a field, etc. – **רְאוּבֵן שֶׁמָּכַר שָׂדֶה וכו׳:** Reuven sold his field to Shimon with a guarantee, and instead of paying for the field, Shimon set up its value as a loan. Meanwhile Reuven died, and a creditor came seeking payment for a loan that Reuven had taken before he sold the field and seized the land from Shimon as payment for the loan. Shimon paid the creditor in order to keep this field. Reuven's heirs can still claim the money that he owes for the field. If Shimon is clever, he will repay them with land and reclaim this land from them based on the lien upon it, as stated in the Gemara (Rambam *Sefer Mishpatim, Hilkhot Malve VeLoveh* 11:10).

NOTES

If Shimon is clever – אי פיקח שמעון: See Rashi, who addresses the question of how a person may repay a loan with property when he has money. Others say that Shimon is not required to make additional claims in this case, but rather, as Shimon's debt is for real estate, he may pay his debt in real estate as well (Ra'avad).

HALAKHA

When orphans collect real estate – יתומים שגבו קרקע: When orphans collect land as payment for debts owed their father, this land can later be seized by creditors to whom their father owed money (*Shulḥan Arukh*, *Ḥoshen Mishpat* 107:1).

Borrower and lender – מלוה ולוה: If a person borrowed from one party and lent money to another party, the second borrower need not pay his lender and may repay his debt directly to the first creditor, in accordance with Rabbi Natan's ruling (*Shulḥan Arukh*, *Ḥoshen Mishpat* 86:1).

LANGUAGE

Deposited [*hirhin*] – הרהין: This is related to the Arabic verb أرهن, *'arhana*, which means to leave as collateral.

ואמר רבא: אי פיקח שמעון – מגבי להו ארעא, והדר גבי לה מינייהו. דאמר רב נחמן: יתומים שגבו קרקע בחובת אביהם – בעל חוב חוזר וגובה אותה מהן.

And Rava said with regard to this case: **If Shimon is clever**[N] **he will pay them** what he owes with **real estate** and not with money. Since they now have real estate received from their father's estate, Shimon **can then collect** the field **from them** as compensation for the original field that Reuven sold to Shimon. **As Rav Naḥman said:** When **orphans collect real estate**[H] **for a debt owed to their father** from one person, another **creditor can come and seize this** land **from them** in order to repay the father's debt.

אי אמרת בשלמא "למפרע הוא גובה" – אמטו להכי חוזר וגובה אותה מהן, דכמאן דגבו מחיים דאבוהון דמי. אלא אי אמרת "מכאן ולהבא הוא גובה" אמאי חוזר וגובה אותה מהן? הא הוי כמאן דזבין יתמי נכסי דמי, ואילו קני יתמי נכסי, מי קא משתעבדי לבעל חוב?

The Gemara applies this discussion to our original case. **Granted, if you say** that a creditor **collects retroactively,** and the field is considered as though it belonged to the creditor from the time of the loan, **due to this** reason, **he can then collect** the money **from them, because it is considered as though he collected it during their father's lifetime.** Because the field given by Shimon to repay his debt retroactively belonged to Reuven from the time that Shimon agreed to pay for the field, therefore Shimon can now claim this land from Reuven's heirs. **However, if you say** that **he collects** it **from this point forward, why can he then collect** this land **from them? It is as though the orphans purchased this property. And if orphans buy property, does** it become **indebted to a creditor** of their father? Only property that belonged to the father can be seized in order to pay back his debt, and therefore Rava's statement in the case appears to contradict his statement with regard to the transfer of ownership of collateral.

שאני התם, דאמר להו: כי היכי דמשתעבדנא ליה לאבוכון – משתעבדנא נמי לבעל חוב דאבוכון, מדרבי נתן. דתניא, רבי נתן אומר: מנין לנושה בחבירו מנה, וחבירו בחבירו, שמוציאין מזה ונותנין לזה – תלמוד לומר: "ונתן לאשר אשם לו".

The Gemara resolves this contradiction: **It is different there,** in this case, **as** Shimon could have **said to** Reuven's children that **just as I am indebted to your father, so too, I am indebted to your father's creditor.** And this principle can be learned **from** the statement **of Rabbi Natan** that one who lends to one person and borrows from another can be considered as a middleman between his creditor and his borrower. **As it was taught** in a *baraita*, **Rabbi Natan says: From where** is it derived **that when one lends one hundred** dinar [*maneh*] **to his fellow, and that fellow** lends a similar sum **to** a third **fellow, that we take** the money **from this one,** the second debtor, **and give it to that one,** the first creditor, without going through the middleman, who is both the first debtor and the second creditor?[H] **The verse states: "And he shall give it to him whom he has wronged"** (Numbers 5:7), which indicates that the loan should be repaid to the creditor to whom the money is ultimately owed. Therefore, payment is made to the original creditor regardless of the issue of retroactive acquisition of the collateral.

תנן: גוי שהלוה את ישראל על חמצו – אחר הפסח מותר בהנאה. אי אמרת בשלמא "למפרע הוא גובה" – אמטו להכי מותר בהנאה.

The Gemara proceeds to bring proofs for the two sides of the question of retroactive acquisition. **We learned** in the mishna: If **a gentile lent money to a Jew,** and the Jew gave him **leavened bread as** collateral during Passover, and **after Passover** the gentile attained this leavened bread in lieu of payment, then **one is permitted to** derive **benefit from** the leavened bread. The Gemara attempts to clarify this position: **Granted, if you say** that **he retroactively collects** this property, and the leavened bread was acquired retroactively by the gentile, **it is due to this** that **one is permitted to** derive **benefit from it** after Passover.

אלא אי אמרת "מכאן ולהבא הוא גובה" אמאי מותר בהנאה? ברשותא דישראל הוה קאי! הכא במאי עסקינן – כשהרהינו אצלו.

But if you say that **he collects it from this point forward,** then **why should one be permitted to** derive **benefit from** this leavened bread? The leavened bread **was in the possession of a Jew** during Passover, and therefore it should be forbidden. The Gemara answers: **With what are we dealing here?** With a case where **he deposited** [*hirhin*][L] the leavened bread **with** the gentile in his home, and since the leavened bread was in the gentile's possession during Passover, it is considered as if it belonged to the gentile, provided the gentile ultimately retains ownership of the leavened bread when the Jew defaults on the loan.

לֵימָא כְּתַנָּאֵי: יִשְׂרָאֵל שֶׁהִלְוָה לְגוֹי עַל חֲמֵצוֹ – לְאַחַר הַפֶּסַח אֵינוֹ עוֹבֵר. מִשּׁוּם רַבִּי מֵאִיר אָמְרוּ: עוֹבֵר. מַאי לָאו בְּהָא קָמִיפַּלְגִי; דְּמָר סָבַר: לְמַפְרֵעַ הוּא גּוֹבֶה, וּמָר סָבַר: מִכָּאן וּלְהַבָּא הוּא גּוֹבֶה?

The Gemara suggests: **Let us say** that this dispute is **parallel to** a dispute between *tanna'im*. As it was taught: If **a Jew lends money to a gentile** and the gentile gives him **leavened bread as** collateral, **then** the Jew **does not commit any transgression after Passover. They said in the name of Rabbi Meir that he commits a transgression.**[N] **What, isn't it that they disagree about this, that one Sage,** Rabbi Meir, **holds** that the Jew transgresses by owning leavened bread **because he retroactively collects** the leavened bread and has therefore owned it during Passover, **and one Sage,** who states that the Jew does not commit a transgression, **holds** that **he collects it from this point forward,** and therefore it was not considered to be in his possession during Passover?

וְתִסְבְּרָא?! אֵימָא סֵיפָא: אֲבָל גּוֹי שֶׁהִלְוָה לְיִשְׂרָאֵל עַל חֲמֵצוֹ – לְאַחַר הַפֶּסַח דִּבְרֵי הַכֹּל עוֹבֵר. וְהָא אִיפְּכָא מִיבְּעֵי לֵיהּ! לְמַאן דְּאָמַר הָתָם "אֵינוֹ עוֹבֵר" – הָכָא עוֹבֵר, לְמַאן דְּאָמַר הָתָם "עוֹבֵר" – הָכָא אֵינוֹ עוֹבֵר!

The Gemara rejects this explanation: **And** how can **you understand** it that way? **Say the latter clause** of that *baraita*: **However, if a gentile lends** money **to a Jew with leavened bread** as collateral, then **after Passover everyone agrees that he commits a transgression. However,** if the preceding explanation is correct, **it needed** to state **the opposite** of what it said in the first clause, as the case in the latter clause is the reverse of that in the first clause. Namely, **according to the one who said there,** in the first clause of the *baraita,* that **he does not commit a transgression,** he should say that **here,** in this case, **he does commit a transgression. And according to the one who said there,** in the first clause of the *baraita,* that **he does commit a transgression,** he should say that **here,** in the latter clause, **he does not commit a transgression.** For if the creditor retroactively acquires the collateral, then it is as though it belonged to a gentile during Passover, and therefore the Jew would not have committed a transgression by owning it.

NOTES

He commits a transgression – עוֹבֵר: The early commentaries explain that he does not transgress the prohibition: It shall not be seen, since the forbidden status of the leavened bread was established only after the fact. Instead, this means that he is obligated to eliminate it and may not use it now (*Me'iri*).

Perek **II**
Daf **31** Amud **b**

אֶלָּא הָכָא בְּמַאי עָסְקִינַן – כְּגוֹן שֶׁהִרְהִינוֹ אֶצְלוֹ, וְקָמִיפַּלְגִי בִּדְרַבִּי יִצְחָק. דְּאָמַר רַבִּי יִצְחָק: מִנַּיִן לְבַעַל חוֹב שֶׁקּוֹנֶה מַשְׁכּוֹן – שֶׁנֶּאֱמַר: "וּלְךָ תִּהְיֶה צְדָקָה", אִם אֵינוֹ קוֹנֶה מַשְׁכּוֹן – צְדָקָה מִנַּיִן? מִכָּאן לְבַעַל חוֹב שֶׁקּוֹנֶה מַשְׁכּוֹן.

Rather, with what are we dealing here? With a situation **where he,** the gentile debtor, **deposited** the leavened bread that was serving as collateral **with him,** the Jewish creditor, **and they disagree with regard to** the statement **of Rabbi Yitzḥak. As Rabbi Yitzḥak said: From where** is it derived **that a creditor acquires collateral**[H] given to him, and is considered its owner so long as the item is in his possession? **As it is stated:** "You shall surely return the pledge to him when the sun goes down, that he may sleep in his garment, and bless you; **and it shall be a righteousness for you** before the Lord your God" (Deuteronomy 24:13). Rabbi Yitzḥak infers: **If** the creditor **does not acquire the collateral,** then **from where is the righteousness** involved in returning it? In this case, the creditor would not be giving up anything of his own. **From here** it is learned **that a creditor acquires the collateral.**

תַּנָּא קַמָּא סָבַר: הָנֵי מִילֵּי – יִשְׂרָאֵל מִיִּשְׂרָאֵל – הוּא, דְּקָרֵינָא בֵּיהּ "וּלְךָ תִּהְיֶה צְדָקָה" אֲבָל יִשְׂרָאֵל מִגּוֹי – לָא קָנֵי.

The Gemara applies this principle to the explanation of the *baraita*: **The first *tanna* holds** that **this applies only when a Jew** takes collateral **from a** fellow **Jew, such that I would read** and apply the verse **"It shall be righteousness for you"** and establish that the collateral becomes the property of the lender. **However,** the verse does not speak about the case where **a Jew** takes collateral **from a gentile,** and therefore **he does not acquire** the collateral; it still belongs to the gentile. Therefore, when a Jew has leavened bread as collateral from a gentile to whom he lent money on Passover, he does not violate any prohibition, as the collateral still belongs to the gentile.

וְרַבִּי מֵאִיר סָבַר, קַל וָחוֹמֶר: יִשְׂרָאֵל מִיִּשְׂרָאֵל קָנֵי – יִשְׂרָאֵל מִגּוֹי לֹא כׇּל שֶׁכֵּן?! אֲבָל גּוֹי שֶׁהִלְוָה אֶת יִשְׂרָאֵל עַל חֲמֵצוֹ אַחַר הַפֶּסַח – דִּבְרֵי הַכֹּל עוֹבֵר. הָתָם וַדַּאי גּוֹי מִיִּשְׂרָאֵל לָא קָנֵי.

However, **Rabbi Meir holds** that one can derive **an *a fortiori* inference: If a Jew acquires** collateral **from** another **Jew, all the more so** is it **not** clear that he will he acquire collateral **from a gentile? However,** with regard to **a gentile who lends money to a Jew with leavened bread as** collateral,[H] **everyone agrees** that **he transgresses** this prohibition **after** Passover. **There,** in that case, **the gentile certainly does not acquire** collateral **from the Jew,** and such a transaction could be completed only via the usual modes of acquisition.[N]

HALAKHA

A creditor acquires collateral – בַּעַל חוֹב קוֹנֶה מַשְׁכּוֹן: When a creditor receives collateral he is considered to be a paid bailee and is therefore responsible only if it is stolen or lost (see *Tosafot*). This follows the ruling of most of the *ge'onim* (*Shulḥan Arukh, Ḥoshen Mishpat* 72:2).

Leavened bread as collateral – מַשְׁכּוֹן חָמֵץ: If a gentile lent money to a Jew with leavened bread as collateral and the Jew said to him: If I do not pay back my loan by such-and-such a time the collateral will become your property from now, i.e., retroactively, then a Jew may derive benefit from this leavened bread after Passover. Similarly, if a Jew lent money to a gentile and the gentile made a similar statement, then it is forbidden for a Jew to derive benefit from this leavened bread after Passover (*Shulḥan Arukh, Oraḥ Ḥayyim* 451:1).

NOTES

Modes of acquisition of a Jew and a gentile – קִנְיַן יִשְׂרָאֵל וְגוֹי: The effectiveness of different methods of acquisition are discussed in numerous places throughout the Talmud. In general, there are several ways through which one can acquire property, including pulling, lifting, and exchanging articles. It is unclear if these methods were established by the Sages in addition to the Torah method of acquisition through money and would therefore apply only to Jews, or if these methods are fundamentally effective and acquisition through money merely constitutes a nonbinding agreement. Due to this, there are important distinctions in the efficacy of various modes of acquisition, depending on whether they are conducted between fellow Jews or between a Jew and a gentile.

LANGUAGE

Oven [*purni*] – פּוּרְנִי: From the Latin furnus, meaning oven.

NOTES

A Jewish-owned shop and gentile workers – חֲנוּת יִשְׂרָאֵל וּפוֹעֲלִים גּוֹיִם: There are two variant readings of the text of this statement. One version, cited by Rashi and Rav Hai Gaon, is the text that appears here in the Gemara. Another version, cited by Rabbeinu Ḥananel and the Ramban, states the exact opposite ruling. According to this latter version, the explanation of the ruling is that those who are using the location are more likely to have left leavened bread there. It is therefore assumed that the leavened bread belongs to the workers rather than the store owner.

One is required to nullify the leavened bread in his heart – צָרִיךְ שֶׁיְּבַטֵּל בְּלִבּוֹ: One must entirely nullify his ownership over this leavened bread and commit never to use it again (*Mikhtam*).

HALAKHA

A Jewish-owned shop and gentile workers – חֲנוּת יִשְׂרָאֵל וּפוֹעֲלִים גּוֹיִם: If a shop and its contents are owned by a Jew and the workers who enter and exit the store are gentiles, then it is forbidden to derive benefit from leavened bread found there after Passover. Conversely, if the store and its contents are owned by a gentile and the workers are Jews, then it is permitted even to eat the leavened bread found there after Passover. Although certain versions of the talmudic text make the opposite statement (see note), most authorities rule in accordance with our version of the text (*Taz*; *Mishna Berura*; *Shulḥan Arukh, Oraḥ Ḥayyim* 449).

Leavened bread upon which a rockslide has fallen – חָמֵץ שֶׁנָּפְלָה עָלָיו מַפּוֹלֶת: When a rockslide falls on leavened bread and buries it three handbreadths deep, there is no need to dig it up, and it is sufficient to nullify one's ownership of it, as stated in the mishna in accordance with the interpretation of the Gemara (*Shulḥan Arukh, Oraḥ Ḥayyim* 333:8).

תְּנַן: גּוֹי שֶׁהִלְוָה יִשְׂרָאֵל עַל חֲמֵצוֹ – אַחַר הַפֶּסַח מוּתָּר בַּהֲנָאָה. נְהִי נַמִי דְּהִרְהִינוֹ אֶצְלוֹ, הָא אָמְרַתְּ גּוֹי מִיִּשְׂרָאֵל לָא קָנֵי! לָא קַשְׁיָא: הָא – דְּאָמַר לֵיהּ ״מֵעַכְשָׁיו״, הָא – דְּלָא אָמַר לֵיהּ ״מֵעַכְשָׁיו״.

We learned in the mishna: If **a gentile lent money to a Jew,** and the Jew gave him **leavened bread as** collateral until after Passover, and **after Passover** he retains this leavened bread in lieu of payment, then **one is permitted to** derive **benefit from** this leavened bread. **Even granted** that this is referring to a case where **he deposited** the leavened bread **with him,** the gentile, **didn't you say** that **a gentile does not acquire** collateral **from a Jew,** and if this is the case, then why is it permissible to derive benefit from this leavened bread? According to the previously stated principle, this leavened bread remains Jewish property. The Gemara resolves this question: **This is not difficult,** for **this** case, where the gentile acquires the leavened bread and therefore it is permitted to derive benefit from it, is **when** the gentile **said to him** that if he does not repay his loan, then the collateral will be acquired **from now,** i.e., from the time of the loan. **And that** case, where it is forbidden to derive benefit from the leavened bread, is **when he did not say** that it would be acquired **from now** by the gentile.

וּמְנָא תֵּימְרָא דְּשָׁנֵי לֵיהּ בֵּין הֵיכָא דְּאָמַר ״מֵעַכְשָׁיו״ וּבֵין הֵיכָא דְּלָא אָמַר ״מֵעַכְשָׁיו״ – דְּתַנְיָא: גּוֹי שֶׁהִרְהִין פַּת פּוּרְנִי אֵצֶל יִשְׂרָאֵל – אֵינוֹ עוֹבֵר. וְאִם אָמַר לוֹ ״הִגַּעְתִּיךָ״ – עוֹבֵר. מַאי שְׁנָא רֵישָׁא וּמַאי שְׁנָא סֵיפָא? אֶלָּא לָאו שְׁמַע מִינָּהּ: שָׁאנֵי הֵיכָא דְּאָמַר לֵיהּ ״מֵעַכְשָׁיו״ לְהֵיכָא דְּלָא אָמַר לֵיהּ ״מֵעַכְשָׁיו״ – שְׁמַע מִינָּהּ.

From where do you say that he distinguishes between a case **where he said** that the collateral would be acquired **from now and** a case **where he did not say** that it would be acquired **from now? As it was taught** in a *baraita*: If **a gentile deposited with a Jew bread baked in an oven** [*purni*][L] as collateral for a loan, then **he,** the Jew, **does not transgress** the prohibition it shall not be seen and the prohibition it shall not be found. **However, if he said to him: I have made them yours** from now if I do not repay my loan, then it is considered as though the bread belonged to the Jew, and **he transgresses** this prohibition. If one assumes that there is no difference between a case where the debtor says: From now, and a case where he doesn't say: From now, then **what is different in the first clause** of the *baraita* **and what is different in the latter clause? Rather,** must **one not conclude from it that there is a difference between** a case **where he says to him** that it he will acquire it **from now and** a case **where he does not say to him** that he will acquire it **from now?** The Gemara concurs: Indeed, **conclude from it** that this is the case.

תָּנוּ רַבָּנַן: חֲנוּת שֶׁל יִשְׂרָאֵל וּמְלַאי שֶׁל יִשְׂרָאֵל, וּפוֹעֲלֵי גּוֹיִם נִכְנָסִין לְשָׁם – חָמֵץ שֶׁנִּמְצָא שָׁם אַחַר הַפֶּסַח אָסוּר בַּהֲנָאָה, וְאֵין צָרִיךְ לוֹמַר בַּאֲכִילָה. חֲנוּת שֶׁל גּוֹי, וּמְלַאי שֶׁל גּוֹי, וּפוֹעֲלֵי יִשְׂרָאֵל נִכְנָסִין וְיוֹצְאִין לְשָׁם – חָמֵץ שֶׁנִּמְצָא שָׁם אַחַר הַפֶּסַח מוּתָּר בַּאֲכִילָה, וְאֵין צָרִיךְ לוֹמַר בַּהֲנָאָה.

The Sages taught in the *Tosefta*: With regard to the case of **a store** owned by **a Jew and** whose **contents belong to the Jew, and gentile workers would enter there** periodically, then **it is forbidden to** derive **benefit from the leavened bread that is found there after Passover, and needless to say,** it is forbidden **to eat** this leavened bread, for it is presumed to belong to the Jewish owner.[NH] Conversely, if **a store** is owned by **a gentile and its contents belong to the gentile, and Jewish workers enter and exit** the store, then it can be presumed that **the leavened bread that is found there after Passover** belonged to the gentile, and therefore one is **permitted to eat it** after Passover. And **needless to say,** it is permitted **to** derive **benefit from** this leavened bread.

מתני׳ חָמֵץ שֶׁנָּפְלָה עָלָיו מַפּוֹלֶת – הֲרֵי הוּא כִּמְבוֹעָר. רַבָּן שִׁמְעוֹן בֶּן גַּמְלִיאֵל אוֹמֵר: כֹּל שֶׁאֵין הַכֶּלֶב יָכוֹל לְחַפֵּשׂ אַחֲרָיו.

MISHNA **Leavened bread upon which a rockslide has fallen**[H] **is considered as though it has been eliminated,** and it is not necessary to dig it up in order to burn it. **Rabban Shimon ben Gamliel says: Any** leavened bread that has been covered to such an extent **that a dog cannot search after it** is considered to have been eliminated.

גמ׳ אָמַר רַב חִסְדָּא: וְצָרִיךְ שֶׁיְּבַטֵּל בְּלִבּוֹ. תָּנָא: כַּמָּה חֲפִישַׂת הַכֶּלֶב – שְׁלֹשָׁה טְפָחִים.

GEMARA **Rav Ḥisda said:** Although it is not necessary to dig up the leavened bread, one is nevertheless **required to nullify** the leavened bread **in his heart**[N] lest it become exposed during Passover. Although it may not be visible at the moment, this leavened bread may be uncovered during Passover, and he will transgress a prohibition by its being seen. It was **taught** in the *Tosefta*: **How much,** how deep, **will a dog search?** It will search **three handbreadths** deep.

אָמַר לֵיהּ רַב אַחָא בְּרֵיהּ דְּרַב יוֹסֵף לְרַב אָשֵׁי: הָא דְּאָמַר שְׁמוּאֵל כְּסָפִים אֵין לָהֶם שְׁמִירָה אֶלָּא בַּקַּרְקַע – מִי בָּעֵינַן שְׁלֹשָׁה טְפָחִים אוֹ לָא? אֲמַר לֵיהּ: הָכָא מִשּׁוּם רֵיחָא – בָּעֵינַן שְׁלֹשָׁה טְפָחִים, הָתָם מִשּׁוּם אִיכַּסּוּיֵי מֵעֵינָא הוּא, וְלָא בָּעֵי שְׁלֹשָׁה. וְכַמָּה? אָמַר רַפְרָם בַּר פַּפָּא מִסִּיכְרָא: טֶפַח.

Rav Aḥa, son of Rav Yosef, said to Rav Ashi: With regard to that which Shmuel said, that deposited **money is considered to be guarded** securely by an unpaid bailee, who would nonetheless not be responsible if it were stolen, **only** when it is buried **in the ground, is it necessary** to bury this deposited money **three handbreadths deep,** comparable to leavened bread, **or not? He said to him: Here,** with regard to Passover, the concern is that the dog will find the food **due to** its **smell,** and therefore **three handbreadths are required. There,** in the case of money, **it is** necessary to bury the money **in order to conceal it from view.** Therefore **it is not required** to bury it **three** handbreadths deep, as animals will not search for it and people will not see it. The Gemara asks: If this is the case, then **how** deep is one required to bury it? **Rafram bar Pappa** from the city of **Sikhra said: One handbreadth** is sufficient for the money to be considered concealed.[H]

HALAKHA

Guarding money – שְׁמִירַת כְּסָפִים: The only acceptable way to guard money, i.e., in order for an unpaid bailee not to be responsible if it is stolen, is to bury it in the ground one handbreadth deep (*Shulḥan Arukh, Ḥoshen Mishpat* 291:15).

One who unwittingly eats *teruma* – הָאוֹכֵל תְּרוּמָה בְּשׁוֹגֵג: One who unwittingly eats *teruma* must pay the original value of the *teruma* and an additional fifth, as stated in the Torah (*Rambam Sefer Zera'im, Hilkhot Terumot* 10:1).

מתני׳ הָאוֹכֵל תְּרוּמַת חָמֵץ בַּפֶּסַח, בְּשׁוֹגֵג – מְשַׁלֵּם קֶרֶן וָחוֹמֶשׁ, בְּמֵזִיד – פָּטוּר מִתַּשְׁלוּמִין וּמִדְּמֵי עֵצִים.

MISHNA **If one unwittingly eats *teruma* of leavened bread on Passover,** not realizing that the food was *teruma*, then **he must pay**[N] **the principal and an additional fifth.**[N] This is because one who unwittingly eats *teruma*[H] must compensate the priest for the value of the *teruma* and add a fifth of the value, even though the *teruma* is considered to be valueless on Passover. If he **intentionally** ate the *teruma* then **he is exempt from payment;** as he is liable to receive the severe punishment of *karet*, he is therefore exempt from the lesser punishment of payment. If he ate impure *teruma* in this manner then he is not even required to pay **its monetary** value **in wood,** for one who derives benefit from impure *teruma* calculates its value by treating it as though it were fuel for burning. While impure *teruma* can be used in this manner during the rest of the year, one may not derive any benefit from leavened bread on Passover, and therefore such *teruma* is worthless.

NOTES

If one unwittingly eats…he must pay – הָאוֹכֵל...בְּשׁוֹגֵג מְשַׁלֵּם: This payment is an opportunity for atonement provided by the Torah to the unwitting transgressor. It therefore does not belong to the priest, and the transgressor is obligated to pay even if the priest is willing to forgo the payment. For this reason, one is required to reimburse the priest for leavened bread eaten during Passover, despite the fact that it is valueless. This is not the case with regard to one who intentionally eats *teruma*, as such a person is punished in the same way as any other thief, and one who steals a worthless item is exempt from payment (*Tosefot Rid*).

In the Jerusalem Talmud, a dispute is recorded with regard to who receives payment for this *teruma*, as on Passover leavened bread is considered to be ownerless. Some say that he must repay the priest whose *teruma* he ate, while others suggest that he should repay the priestly tribe in general.

Additional fifth – חוֹמֶשׁ: An additional fifth of the value of an article added to its price as a penalty or fine, or to emphasize its importance. For example, when a person redeems his own second tithe, he must add an extra fifth of its value (Leviticus 27:31).

גמ׳ תְּנַן הָתָם: הָאוֹכֵל תְּרוּמָה בְּשׁוֹגֵג – מְשַׁלֵּם קֶרֶן וָחוֹמֶשׁ, אֶחָד הָאוֹכֵל, וְאֶחָד הַשּׁוֹתֶה,

GEMARA **We learned** in a mishna **there,** in *Terumot*: **One who unwittingly eats *teruma* pays the principal and an** additional **fifth, both one who eats** it, **and one who drinks** it.

Perek **II**
Daf **32** Amud **a**

וְאֶחָד הַסָּךְ, אֶחָד תְּרוּמָה טְמֵאָה וְאֶחָד תְּרוּמָה טְהוֹרָה – מְשַׁלֵּם חוֹמֶשׁ וְחוּמְשָׁא דְּחוּמְשָׁא.

And even with regard to **one who anoints** himself with the *teruma* oil, **both** in a case of **ritually impure *teruma* as well as** in a case of **ritually pure *teruma*, he must pay** an additional **fifth** if he unwittingly consumes this *teruma*. If he unwittingly consumes this fifth then he must pay **an** additional **fifth of the fifth.** The original fifth has a status comparable to *teruma* itself, and therefore one is required to pay an additional fifth for consuming it.[H]

אִיבַּעְיָא לְהוּ: כְּשֶׁהוּא מְשַׁלֵּם, לְפִי מִדָּה מְשַׁלֵּם אוֹ לְפִי דָּמִים מְשַׁלֵּם? כָּל הֵיכָא דְּמֵעִיקָּרָא שָׁוְיָא אַרְבְּעָה זוּזֵי וּלְבַסּוֹף שָׁוְיָא זוּזָא – לָא תִּיבְּעֵי לָךְ דְּוַדַּאי כִּדְמֵעִיקָּרָא מְשַׁלֵּם לְפִי דָּמִים, דְּלָא גָּרַע מִגַּזְלָן. דִּתְנַן: כָּל הַגַּזְלָנִין מְשַׁלְּמִין כְּשָׁעַת הַגְּזֵלָה.

A dilemma was raised before the Sages with regard to the laws of *teruma*: **When he pays** for this *teruma*, **does he pay according to the measure** of the *teruma* **or according to its monetary** value? The Gemara explains the question in greater detail: **Anywhere that** the *teruma* **is worth four *zuz* at the outset,** i.e., at the time he consumed the *teruma*, **and is worth** only **one *zuz* at the end,** at the time of payment, **do not raise a dilemma,** for in that case **he is certainly** required **to pay according to the monetary** value **at the outset.** The rationale behind this ruling is **that he is no worse than a thief,** and therefore the law in this case is the same as if he had stolen property from another person. **As we learned** in a mishna: **All thieves must repay** what they have stolen according to the value of the stolen object **at the time it was stolen,**[H] even if its value subsequently goes down.

HALAKHA

Deriving benefit from *teruma* – הֲנָאָה מִתְּרוּמָה: Anyone who unwittingly derives benefit from *teruma*, whether through eating, drinking, or anointing himself, both with ritually pure and ritually impure *teruma*, must repay the principal and an additional fifth. This fifth has the same status as *teruma*, and one who derives improper benefit from it must pay an additional fifth of this fifth (Rambam *Sefer Zera'im, Hilkhot Terumot* 10:2).

Thieves must repay according to the value at the time it was stolen – גַּזְלָנִין מְשַׁלְּמִין כְּשָׁעַת הַגְּזֵלָה: A thief must repay the owner according to the value of the stolen property at the time of the theft (*Shulḥan Arukh, Ḥoshen Mishpat* 362:2).

NOTES

An item that buyers jump at – דְּקָפֵיץ עֲלֵיהּ זְבִינֵיהּ: With regard to repayment of debt, objects that can be more readily resold by their recipients are generally considered preferred modes of payment. In this case as well, produce that the priest can more readily resell to another priest as *teruma* is deemed preferable.

כִּי תִּיבָּעֵי לָךְ – דְּמֵעִיקָּרָא שָׁוְיָא זוּזָא וּלְבַסּוֹף שָׁוְיָא אַרְבְּעָה. מַאי, לְפִי מִדָּה מְשַׁלֵּם, דְּאָמַר לֵיהּ: גְּרִיוָא אֲכַל – גְּרִיוָא מְשַׁלֵּם. אוֹ דִּילְמָא: לְפִי דָּמִים מְשַׁלֵּם, בְּזוּזָא אָכַל – בְּזוּזָא מְשַׁלֵּם?

You can raise the dilemma, however, with regard to a case **where it was worth one *zuz* at the outset,** when it was consumed, **and at the end,** at the time of the payment, **it was worth four *zuz*. What** is the ruling in that case? Does **he pay according to the measure** of *teruma*, **as the** treasurer of the consecrated property can **say to him: You ate a *se'a* and you must pay a *se'a*,** even if the value of the *teruma* has increased, **or perhaps he** must repay **according to the monetary** value, and if **he ate a *zuz*** worth of *teruma* then **he** must **pay a *zuz*?**

אָמַר רַב יוֹסֵף, תָּא שְׁמַע: אָכַל גְּרוֹגְרוֹת וְשִׁילֵּם לוֹ תְּמָרִים – תָּבֹא עָלָיו בְּרָכָה, אִי אָמְרַתְּ בִּשְׁלָמָא לְפִי מִדָּה מְשַׁלֵּם – אַמְטוּ לְהָכִי תָּבֹא עָלָיו בְּרָכָה, דַּאֲכַיל גְּרִיוָא דִּגְרוֹגְרוֹת דְּשָׁוְיָא זוּזָא, וְקָא יָהֵיב גְּרִיוָא דִּתְמָרִים דְּשָׁוְיָא אַרְבְּעָה. אֶלָּא אִי אָמְרַתְּ לְפִי דָּמִים מְשַׁלֵּם – אַמַּאי תָּבֹא עָלָיו בְּרָכָה? בְּזוּזָא אָכַל בְּזוּזָא קָא מְשַׁלֵּם!

Rav Yosef said: Come and **hear** an answer to this question from what was taught in a *baraita*: **One who ate dried figs** that were *teruma* **and paid** the priest **with dates,** may **a blessing rest upon him,** as dates are worth more than dried figs. **Granted, if you say that** one must **repay according to the measure** of *teruma* he ate, it is **due to this** that **a blessing** should **rest upon him, as he ate a *se'a* of dried figs that are worth one *zuz* and gave** in return **a *se'a* of dates worth four *zuz*. However, if you say that** he must **repay according to the monetary** value of the *teruma*, then why **should a blessing rest upon him? He ate a *zuz* worth** of *teruma* **and he paid a *zuz* worth** as compensation; what is laudatory about his payment?

אָמַר אַבָּיֵי: לְעוֹלָם לְפִי דָּמִים מְשַׁלֵּם, וְאַמַּאי תָּבֹא עָלָיו בְּרָכָה – דַּאֲכַל מִידֵּי דְּלָא קָפֵיץ עֲלֵיהּ זְבִינֵיהּ, וְקָא מְשַׁלֵּם מִידֵּי דְּקָפֵיץ עֲלֵיהּ זְבִינֵיהּ.

Abaye said: Actually one can explain that **he** must **repay according to the monetary** value of the *teruma*, **and why** is it stated that **a blessing** should **rest upon him?** This is **because he ate an item that buyers don't jump at,** i.e., it is undesirable to buyers, **but paid with an item that buyers jump at.**[N] Consequently, although the produce he gives is worth no more than the produce he ate, the priest still prefers this type of payment, as he can more easily resell this produce.

תְּנַן: הָאוֹכֵל תְּרוּמַת חָמֵץ בַּפֶּסַח, בְּשׁוֹגֵג – מְשַׁלֵּם קֶרֶן וְחוֹמֶשׁ. אִי אָמְרַתְּ בִּשְׁלָמָא לְפִי מִדָּה מְשַׁלֵּם – שַׁפִּיר. אֶלָּא אִי אָמְרַתְּ לְפִי דָּמִים מְשַׁלֵּם – חָמֵץ בַּפֶּסַח בַּר דָּמִים הוּא?! אִין, הָא מַנִּי – רַבִּי יוֹסֵי הַגְּלִילִי הִיא, דְּאָמַר: חָמֵץ בַּפֶּסַח מוּתָּר בַּהֲנָאָה

The Gemara seeks proof with regard to this dispute: **We learned** in the mishna: **One who unwittingly eats *teruma* of leavened bread on Passover** must **pay the principal and an** additional **fifth. Granted, if you say that he** must **pay according to the measure** of *teruma* that he ate, **it is well.** As he ate a *se'a* of *teruma* he must also repay a *se'a*. **However, if you say** that **he** must **pay according to the monetary** value of the *teruma*, this is difficult, for **is leavened bread on Passover of** any **monetary** value? Certainly it is not worth anything, given that it is forbidden to benefit from this food. The Gemara answers: **Yes,** this leavened bread does indeed have monetary value. In accordance with **whose** opinion **is this** mishna? **It is** in accordance with the opinion of **Rabbi Yosei HaGelili, who said** that **it is permissible to** derive **benefit from leavened bread on Passover.**

אִי הָכִי, אֵימָא סֵיפָא: בְּמֵזִיד פָּטוּר מִן הַתַּשְׁלוּמִין וּמִדְּמֵי עֵצִים. אִי רַבִּי יוֹסֵי הַגְּלִילִי, אַמַּאי פָּטוּר מִן הַתַּשְׁלוּמִין וּמִדְּמֵי עֵצִים?!

The Gemara challenges this suggestion: **If that is so,** then **say the latter clause** of the mishna, where it is stated: **If** he consumes the *teruma* **intentionally, then he is exempt from payment and from** paying the priest **for its monetary** value as **wood.** But **if** this follows the opinion of **Rabbi Yosei HaGelili,** then **why** is he **exempt from payment** to the priest for the value of the *teruma* **and for its monetary** value **in wood?** Although he is exempt from paying the additional fifth as he acted intentionally, he nonetheless should be required to compensate the priest for the financial loss he caused him, as in any other case of theft.

סָבַר לַהּ כְּרַבִּי נְחוּנְיָא בֶּן הַקָּנָה. דְּתַנְיָא: רַבִּי נְחוּנְיָא בֶּן הַקָּנָה הָיָה עוֹשֶׂה אֶת יוֹם הַכִּפּוּרִים כְּשַׁבָּת לְתַשְׁלוּמִין וכו׳.

The Gemara answers: **He holds in accordance with** the opinion of **Rabbi Neḥunya ben HaKana, as it was taught** in a *baraita*: **Rabbi Neḥunya ben HaKana rendered** the status of **Yom Kippur the same as** that of **Shabbat with regard to payment.** In his opinion, not only a person who committed a transgression punishable by a court-administered capital punishment, like one who desecrated Shabbat, is exempt from monetary payment incurred at the time of the transgression. Even one who is deserving of a divinely administered capital punishment, such as one who desecrates Yom Kippur and is punished with *karet*, is exempt from monetary payment for property he damaged in the course of such an act. Therefore, since one who consumes another person's leavened bread during Passover is deserving of *karet*, he is exempt from monetary payment incurred by this act.

כְּתַנָּאֵי: הָאוֹכֵל תְּרוּמַת חָמֵץ בַּפֶּסַח – פָּטוּר מִן הַתַּשְׁלוּמִין וּמִדְּמֵי עֵצִים, דִּבְרֵי רַבִּי עֲקִיבָא. רַבִּי יוֹחָנָן בֶּן נוּרִי מְחַיֵּיב. אָמַר לוֹ רַבִּי עֲקִיבָא לְרַבִּי יוֹחָנָן בֶּן נוּרִי: וְכִי מָה הֲנָאָה יֵשׁ לוֹ בָּהּ? אָמַר לוֹ רַבִּי יוֹחָנָן בֶּן נוּרִי לְרַבִּי עֲקִיבָא: וּמָה הֲנָאָה יֵשׁ לְאוֹכֵל תְּרוּמָה טְמֵאָה בִּשְׁאָר כָּל יְמוֹת הַשָּׁנָה, שֶׁמְּשַׁלֵּם?

The Gemara comments: The question of whether one must repay according to the measurement or the monetary value of the *teruma* is **like** a dispute between ***tanna'im*****,** as it was taught in the *Tosefta*: **If one eats *teruma* of leavened bread on Passover,**[NH] whether intentionally or unwittingly, then **he is exempt from payment and** for **its monetary** value **in wood;** this is **the statement of Rabbi Akiva.** Whereas **Rabbi Yoḥanan ben Nuri deems** him **liable** to pay. **Rabbi Akiva said to Rabbi Yoḥanan ben Nuri: What benefit can he derive from this?** What benefit could the priest have derived from this *teruma* as it is prohibited to benefit from this *teruma* and the *teruma* is therefore worthless? **Rabbi Yoḥanan ben Nuri said to Rabbi Akiva: What benefit** can one **derive from eating ritually impure *teruma* on the rest of the days of the year,** and yet nevertheless the non-priest is still obligated to **pay** for what he has taken. Despite the fact that a priest may not eat impure *teruma*, a non-priest must reimburse the priest for the principal of the *teruma* and add an additional fifth if he eats it.

אָמַר לוֹ: לֹא אִם אָמַרְתָּ בִּתְרוּמָה טְמֵאָה בִּשְׁאָר יְמוֹת הַשָּׁנָה, שֶׁאַף עַל פִּי שֶׁאֵין לוֹ בָּהּ הֶיתֵּר אֲכִילָה – יֵשׁ לוֹ בָּהּ הֶיתֵּר הַסָּקָה, תֹּאמַר בְּזֶה – שֶׁאֵין לוֹ בָּהּ לֹא הֶיתֵּר אֲכִילָה וְלֹא הֶיתֵּר הַסָּקָה. הָא לְמָה זֶה דּוֹמֶה – לִתְרוּמַת תּוּתִים וַעֲנָבִים שֶׁנִּטְמְאָה, שֶׁאֵין לוֹ בָּהּ לֹא הֶיתֵּר אֲכִילָה וְלֹא הֶיתֵּר הַסָּקָה.

Rabbi Akiva **said to him: No,** a distinction can be made between these two cases: **If you say** that he is obligated to pay **in** a case of **ritually impure *teruma* on the rest of the days of the year, that although it is not permissible to eat it,** the priest **is** nevertheless **permitted to burn it** and derive benefit from the heat generated as a result of this burning, **shall you** also **say** the same **with regard to this,** *teruma* of leavened bread during Passover, **that is not permitted to be eaten or burned?**[H] **Rather, to what may this be compared?** It is similar **to *teruma* of berries and grapes that became ritually impure, which is not permitted to be eaten or burned,** as berries and grapes are unfit for firewood.

בַּמֶּה דְּבָרִים אֲמוּרִים – בְּמַפְרִישׁ תְּרוּמָה וְהֶחְמִיצָה, אֲבָל מַפְרִישׁ תְּרוּמַת חָמֵץ – דִּבְרֵי הַכֹּל אֵינָהּ קְדוֹשָׁה.

The *Tosefta* adds: **In what** case **is this statement said,** that these *tanna'im* disagree about the reimbursement for *teruma*? It was said with regard to a case where **he separated *teruma*** in a permitted manner **and it became leavened** during Passover. **However, if he separated the *teruma* from leavened bread during Passover,** then **everyone agrees that it is not consecrated,** as it is worthless.

תַּנְיָא אִידָךְ: ״וְנָתַן לַכֹּהֵן אֶת הַקֹּדֶשׁ״ – דָּבָר הָרָאוּי לִהְיוֹת קֹדֶשׁ, פְּרָט לְאוֹכֵל תְּרוּמַת חָמֵץ בַּפֶּסַח, שֶׁפָּטוּר מִן הַתַּשְׁלוּמִים וּמִדְּמֵי עֵצִים, דִּבְרֵי רַבִּי אֱלִיעֶזֶר בֶּן יַעֲקֹב. וְרַבִּי אֶלְעָזָר חִסְמָא מְחַיֵּיב. אָמַר לוֹ רַבִּי אֱלִיעֶזֶר בֶּן יַעֲקֹב לְרַבִּי אֶלְעָזָר חִסְמָא: וְכִי מָה הֲנָאָה יֵשׁ לוֹ בָּהּ? אָמַר לוֹ רַבִּי אֶלְעָזָר חִסְמָא לְרַבִּי אֱלִיעֶזֶר בֶּן יַעֲקֹב: וְכִי מָה הֲנָאָה יֵשׁ לוֹ לְאוֹכֵל תְּרוּמָה טְמֵאָה בִּשְׁאָר יְמוֹת הַשָּׁנָה, שֶׁמְּשַׁלֵּם?

It was taught in **another** *baraita*: With regard to the verse "And if a man eats a sacred thing in error, then he shall add a fifth part in addition to it, **and shall give to the priest the sacred item"** (Leviticus 22:14), the Sages expound as follows: He must give the priest **an item that is fit to be consecrated, to the exclusion of one who eats *teruma* of leavened bread on Passover, who is exempt from payment** of the *teruma* and even from paying **its monetary** value **as wood;** this is the statement of **Rabbi Eliezer ben Ya'akov. Rabbi Elazar Ḥisma deems** him **liable** to reimburse the priest for these items. **Rabbi Eliezer ben Ya'akov said to Rabbi Elazar Ḥisma: What benefit can** the priest **derive from this** *teruma* of leavened bread, as it is prohibited to benefit from it? **Rabbi Elazar Ḥisma said to Rabbi Eliezer ben Ya'akov: What benefit can one derive from eating ritually impure *teruma* on the rest of the days of the year,** and yet a non-priest who eats it must **pay** the priest.

אָמַר לוֹ: לֹא אִם אָמַרְתָּ בִּתְרוּמָה טְמֵאָה בִּשְׁאָר יְמוֹת הַשָּׁנָה – שֶׁאַף עַל פִּי שֶׁאֵין לוֹ בָּהּ הֶיתֵּר אֲכִילָה יֵשׁ לוֹ בָּהּ הֶיתֵּר הַסָּקָה, תֹּאמַר בָּזוֹ – שֶׁאֵין לוֹ בָּהּ לֹא הֶיתֵּר אֲכִילָה וְלֹא הֶיתֵּר הַסָּקָה! אָמַר לוֹ: אַף בָּזוֹ יֵשׁ לוֹ בָּהּ הֶיתֵּר הַסָּקָה, שֶׁאִם רָצָה הַכֹּהֵן מְרִיצָהּ לִפְנֵי כַּלְבּוֹ אוֹ מַסִּיקָהּ תַּחַת תַּבְשִׁילוֹ.

Rabbi Eliezer ben Ya'akov **said to him: No,** a distinction can be made between these two cases: **If you say** he is obligated to pay **in** a case of **ritually impure *teruma* on the rest of the days of year, that although it is not permissible to eat it,** the priest **is** nonetheless **permitted to burn it** and derive benefit from the heat generated as a result of this burning, **shall you say** the same **with regard to this,** *teruma* of leavened bread during Passover, **that is not permitted to be eaten or burned?** Rabbi Elazar Ḥisma **said to him: Even** *teruma* of leavened bread on Passover **is permitted to be burned, for if the priest wishes, he may throw it before his dog or burn it under his food,** for Rabbi Elazar Ḥisma agrees with the opinion of Rabbi Yosei HaGelili that one may derive benefit from leavened bread during Passover.

NOTES

***Teruma* of leavened bread on Passover – תְּרוּמַת חָמֵץ בַּפֶּסַח:** A non-priest who eats *teruma* of leavened bread on Passover violates two transgressions, the prohibition against a non-priest eating *teruma* and the prohibition against eating leavened bread on Passover. Both prohibitions involve a severe punishment when violated intentionally, i.e., *karet* for eating leavened bread on Passover and death at the hand of Heaven in the case of eating *teruma*. There is some dispute between the authorities as to whether it is necessary to make a distinction between the nature of his intentions when violating these prohibitions, i.e., is it necessary for him to have intention with regard to the leavened bread, the *teruma*, or both?

HALAKHA

***Teruma* of leavened bread on Passover – תְּרוּמַת חָמֵץ בַּפֶּסַח:** A non-priest who eats *teruma* of leavened bread during Passover is exempt from payment, regardless of whether he did so intentionally or unwittingly, and whether it was ritually pure or ritually impure. This follows the opinion of Rabbi Akiva and Rabbi Eliezer ben Ya'akov, for the *halakha* is in accordance with their opinions in disputes with their contemporaries (*Kesef Mishne*; Radbaz; Rambam *Sefer Zera'im*, *Hilkhot Terumot* 10:6).

One who eats impure *teruma* – הָאוֹכֵל תְּרוּמָה טְמֵאָה: One who intentionally eats impure *teruma* must repay its value as firewood to the priest. However, if he ate impure *teruma* that could not be used for fuel, he is exempt from payment (Rambam *Sefer Zera'im*, *Hilkhot Terumot* 10:5).

אָמַר אַבָּיֵי: רַבִּי אֱלִיעֶזֶר בֶּן יַעֲקֹב, וְרַבִּי עֲקִיבָא, וְרַבִּי יוֹחָנָן בֶּן נוּרִי, כּוּלְּהוּ סְבִירָא לְהוּ: חָמֵץ בַּפֶּסַח אָסוּר בַּהֲנָאָה. וּבְהָא פְּלִיגִי: דְּרַבִּי עֲקִיבָא סָבַר: לְפִי דָמִים מְשַׁלֵּם, וְרַבִּי יוֹחָנָן בֶּן נוּרִי סָבַר: לְפִי מִדָּה מְשַׁלֵּם.

Abaye said: Rabbi Eliezer ben Ya'akov, Rabbi Akiva, and Rabbi Yoḥanan ben Nuri all hold[N] that **it is forbidden to** derive **benefit from leavened bread during Passover. And they disagree with regard to the following** issue: **Rabbi Akiva holds** that **one pays according to the monetary** value,[H] and therefore he need not pay anything for consuming *teruma* of leavened bread during Passover. **And Rabbi Yoḥanan ben Nuri holds** that **one pays according to the measure** of *teruma* that he consumed, such that even if he ate *teruma* of leavened bread on Passover he must repay this amount.

פְּשִׁיטָא! מַהוּ דְּתֵימָא: רַבִּי יוֹחָנָן בֶּן נוּרִי נַמִי כְּרַבִּי עֲקִיבָא סְבִירָא לֵיהּ, דְּאָמַר לְפִי דָמִים מְשַׁלֵּם. וְהָתָם הַיְינוּ טַעְמָא דְּקָא מְחַיֵּיב – מִשּׁוּם דִּסְבַר לַהּ כְּרַבִּי יוֹסֵי הַגְּלִילִי, דְּאָמַר: חָמֵץ בַּפֶּסַח מוּתָּר בַּהֲנָאָה, קָא מַשְׁמַע לַן.

The Gemara asks: Isn't this **obvious?** There does not seem to be another way to explain these opinions. The Gemara rejects this question: This statement is necessary **lest you say** that **Rabbi Yoḥanan ben Nuri also holds in accordance with** the opinion of **Rabbi Akiva** that states that **one** must **pay according to the monetary** value of the *teruma*. **And there,** in the case of leavened bread, **this is the reason that** Rabbi Yoḥanan ben Nuri **deems him liable** to pay for the *teruma* **because he holds in accordance with** the opinion of **Rabbi Yosei HaGelili, who said: It is permissible to** derive **benefit from leavened bread during Passover.** Therefore, **he teaches us** that Rabbi Yoḥanan ben Nuri agrees that one may not derive benefit from leavened bread during Passover.

וְאֵימָא הָכִי נַמִי! אִם כֵּן נֶהְדַּר לֵיהּ רַבִּי יוֹחָנָן בֶּן נוּרִי לְרַבִּי עֲקִיבָא כִּי הֵיכִי דְּמַהְדַּר לֵיהּ רַבִּי אֶלְעָזָר חִסְמָא לְרַבִּי אֱלִיעֶזֶר בֶּן יַעֲקֹב.

The Gemara suggests: **And say it is indeed so,** that Rabbi Yoḥanan ben Nuri accepts Rabbi Yosei HaGelili's position. The Gemara rejects this possibility: **If this was** the case, then **Rabbi Yoḥanan ben Nuri should have responded to Rabbi Akiva in the same way** that **Rabbi Elazar Ḥisma responded to Rabbi Eliezer ben Ya'akov,** by saying that this leavened bread may be fed to a dog thus deriving benefit from it. Since he did not offer this answer, it is clear that he agrees that deriving benefit from leavened bread during Passover is forbidden.

תָּנוּ רַבָּנַן: הָאוֹכֵל כְּזַיִת תְּרוּמָה – מְשַׁלֵּם קֶרֶן וָחוֹמֶשׁ, אַבָּא שָׁאוּל אוֹמֵר: עַד שֶׁיְּהֵא בּוֹ שָׁוֶה פְּרוּטָה. מַאי טַעְמָא דְּתַנָּא קַמָּא? אָמַר קְרָא: ״וְאִישׁ כִּי יֹאכַל קֹדֶשׁ בִּשְׁגָגָה״ – וַאֲכִילָה בִּכְזַיִת.

After mentioning cases where a person damages *teruma*, the Gemara continues with a discussion of this topic. **The Rabbis taught:** A non-priest **who eats an olive-bulk of** ***teruma***[H] must **pay the principal** value of the *teruma* itself **and an additional fifth.**[N] **Abba Shaul**[N] **says:** He is not required to pay **unless** the *teruma* he ate is **worth a** ***peruta.***[N] The Gemara explains: **What is the reason for** the opinion of **the first** ***tanna***? It is because **the verse states: "And if a man eats a sacred item in error,** then he shall add a fifth part in addition to it, and he shall give to the priest the sacred item" (Leviticus 22:14). The minimal amount that is halakhically considered **eating is an olive-bulk.**

וְאַבָּא שָׁאוּל מַאי טַעְמָא? אָמַר קְרָא: ״וְנָתַן״ – וְאֵין נְתִינָה פְּחוּתָה מִשָּׁוֶה פְּרוּטָה. וְאִידָּךְ נַמִי, הָא כְּתִיב ״יֹאכַל״? הַהוּא – פְּרָט לְמַזִּיק הוּא דַּאֲתָא.

And what is the reason for the opinion of **Abba Shaul? The verse states: "And he shall give,"** and giving **less than the value of a** ***peruta*** **is not** legally considered to be **giving.** The Gemara asks: **And** according to **the other** one, Abba Shaul, **too, isn't it written: "Eats,"** implying that there must be at least an olive-bulk portion? The Gemara answers: **That** verse **comes to exclude one who damages** ***teruma***[N] without deriving benefit from it, such that he is exempt from the requirement to add an additional fifth. This is derived from the fact that the verse specifies that only one who eats is required to add a fifth.

וְתַנָּא קַמָּא, הָכְתִיב ״וְנָתַן״? הַהוּא מִיבְּעֵי לֵיהּ לְדָבָר הָרָאוּי לִהְיוֹת קֹדֶשׁ (פְּרָט לְאוֹכֵל תְּרוּמַת חָמֵץ בַּפֶּסַח).

And according to **the first** ***tanna***, one can ask: **Isn't it written "And he shall give"?** The Gemara answers: **That** phrase **is necessary** to teach the requirement that *teruma* must be **an item that is fit to be consecrated,** as an item cannot become *teruma* unless it is has some value. This is meant **to exclude one who eats** ***teruma*** **of leavened bread on Passover,** since it is worthless and therefore cannot be designated as *teruma*.

NOTES

All hold – **כּוּלְּהוּ סְבִירָא לְהוּ:** Generally, when the Gemara cites a series of Sages who share the same line of reasoning and uses the phrase: They all hold, this line of reasoning is called a *shita*, and there is an ancient tradition that the *halakha* does not follow the line of reasoning presented in this form. However, that principle cannot be applied in this case because not all of the *tanna'im* who hold by this principle are mentioned; for example, Rabbi Yehuda and Rabbi Shimon are omitted. Rather, this statement is cited here in order to clarify the points of agreement and dispute between the *tanna'im* listed (Maharam Ḥalawa).

Must pay…an additional fifth – **מְשַׁלֵּם חוֹמֶשׁ:** Some say that the dispute between Abba Shaul and the Rabbis is related to another dispute that is recorded in the Jerusalem Talmud with regard to the nature of this additional fifth. According to one view, the obligation to pay an additional fifth stems from the sanctity of the *teruma* and therefore applies immediately when it is set aside. According to the other opinion, this payment is because one has stolen from a priest, in which case one would be obligated to make this payment only if the *teruma* came into the possession of the priest. This serves as the basis for the dispute as to whether the phrase: "And he shall give" refers to the original giving of the *teruma* to the priest and the establishment of the minimal amount of that gift, or if it refers to the paying of the fine (*Tov Re'iya*).

The opinion of Abba Shaul and the Rabbis – **דַּעַת אַבָּא שָׁאוּל וַחֲכָמִים:** Some say that according to the conclusion of the Gemara, it is the opinion of the Rabbis that requires that two criteria be fulfilled in order to demand the payment of the additional fifth: One must have eaten an olive-sized amount of the *teruma*, so that his action is actually considered to be eating, and the amount he ate must be worth at least a *peruta*, as less than this amount does not require payment (Maharam Ḥalawa).

Peruta – **פְּרוּטָה:** A copper coin, which was the smallest unit of currency. For halakhic purposes, the *peruta* is defined as the value of half a barleycorn's weight of pure silver. Traditionally this is about 24 mg of silver. The halakhic value of all coins is linked to the price of silver.

To exclude one who damages ***teruma*** – **פְּרָט לְמַזִּיק:** The early commentaries disagree with regard to the interpretation of this phrase. According to Rashi and *Tosafot*, this refers to one who damages a priest's property without deriving benefit from it. However, others say that this refers to one who harms himself by eating the *teruma*, e.g., by excessive eating (*Me'iri*; see also Rambam).

HALAKHA

One pays according to the monetary value – **לְפִי דָמִים מְשַׁלֵּם:** If a non-priest eats *teruma*, he must reimburse the priest according to the value of the *teruma* at the time when he ate it, regardless of whether its value subsequently increased or decreased. This ruling is based on the Gemara's understanding of the opinion of Rabbi Akiva, as the *halakha* follows his opinion (Rambam *Sefer Zera'im, Hilkhot Terumot* 10:26).

A non-priest who eats an olive-bulk of ***teruma*** – **הָאוֹכֵל כְּזַיִת תְּרוּמָה:** If a non-priest eats an olive-bulk of *teruma*, he is required to pay the priest the principal value of the *teruma* he ate and an additional fifth of this amount, whether or not the *teruma* is worth a *peruta*. If he ate less than an olive-bulk of *teruma*, he is required to pay the principal value of what he ate but he is not required to pay an additional fifth, in accordance with the unattributed mishna (Rambam *Sefer Zera'im, Hilkhot Terumot* 10:2).

תָּנוּ רַבָּנַן: הָאוֹכֵל תְּרוּמָה פָּחוֹת מִכַּזַּיִת – מְשַׁלֵּם אֶת הַקֶּרֶן וְאֵינוֹ מְשַׁלֵּם אֶת הַחוֹמֶשׁ. הֵיכִי דָּמֵי? אִי דְּלֵית בֵּיהּ שָׁוֶה פְּרוּטָה – קֶרֶן נַמִּי לָא לִישַׁלֵּם, וְאִי דְּאִית בָּהּ שָׁוֶה פְּרוּטָה – חוֹמֶשׁ נַמִּי לִישַׁלֵּם! לְעוֹלָם דְּאִית בָּהּ שָׁוֶה פְּרוּטָה. וַאֲפִילּוּ הָכִי, כֵּיוָן דְּלֵית בֵּיהּ כַּזַּיִת – מְשַׁלֵּם אֶת הַקֶּרֶן וְאֵינוֹ מְשַׁלֵּם אֶת הַחוֹמֶשׁ.

The Sages taught in a *baraita*: **One who eats less than an olive-bulk of *teruma* must pay the principal, but is not** required **to pay the** additional **fifth.** The Gemara asks: **What are the circumstances** of this case? **If there was not the value of a *peruta*** of *teruma*, then **he should also not** be required to **pay for the principal** either, because that is less than the amount for which one is obligated to pay. **But if there was the value of a *peruta*** of *teruma*, then **he should** be required to **pay the** additional **fifth as well.** The Gemara explains the case: **Actually,** it should be understood **that there was the value of a *peruta*** of *teruma*, **and nonetheless, since** the food **was not** at least **an olive-bulk, he is** required **to pay** only **the principal, but he does not pay the** additional **fifth.**

אֲמַרוּהָ רַבָּנַן קַמֵּיהּ דְּרַב פַּפָּא: הָא דְּלָא כְּאַבָּא שָׁאוּל, דְּאִי כְּאַבָּא שָׁאוּל – הָאָמַר: כֵּיוָן שֶׁיֵּשׁ בָּהּ שָׁוֶה פְּרוּטָה, אַף עַל גַּב דְּלֵית בֵּיהּ כַּזַּיִת! אֲמַר לְהוּ רַב פַּפָּא: אֲפִילּוּ תֵּימָא אַבָּא שָׁאוּל, אַבָּא שָׁאוּל תַּרְתֵּי בָּעֵי.

The Sages said before Rav Pappa that **this** *halakha* **is not in accordance with** the opinion of **Abba Shaul. As, if it were in accordance with** the opinion of **Abba Shaul, didn't he say:** One is obligated to pay **because there is the value of a *peruta*, even if it is not** at least **an olive-bulk? Rav Pappa said to them:** This is no proof, as **even** if **you say** that this *halakha* is in accordance with the opinion of **Abba Shaul, Abba Shaul requires two** conditions: That the *teruma* be at least an olive-bulk in volume, and that it be worth at least a *peruta*.

וּמִי בָּעֵי אַבָּא שָׁאוּל תַּרְתֵּי?! וְהָא תְּנַן, אַבָּא שָׁאוּל אוֹמֵר: אֵת שֶׁיֵּשׁ בּוֹ שָׁוֶה פְּרוּטָה – חַיָּיב בְּתַשְׁלוּמִין, אֵת שֶׁאֵין בּוֹ שָׁוֶה פְּרוּטָה – אֵינוֹ חַיָּיב בְּתַשְׁלוּמִין. אָמְרוּ לוֹ: לֹא אָמְרוּ שָׁוֶה פְּרוּטָה אֶלָּא לְעִנְיַן מְעִילָה בִּלְבַד, אֲבָל לִתְרוּמָה – אֵינוֹ חַיָּיב עַד שֶׁיְּהֵא בּוֹ כַּזַּיִת. וְאִם אִיתָא, כֵּיוָן שֶׁיֵּשׁ בּוֹ כַּזַּיִת מִיבָּעֵי לֵיהּ! תְּיוּבְתָּא.

The Gemara asks: **Does Abba Shaul** actually **require two** conditions? **Didn't we learn** in the mishna that **Abba Shaul says:** For **that** food **which is** at least **the value of a *peruta*** of *teruma*, **one is liable to** pay **compensation** to the priest, but for **that** food **which does not contain the value of a *peruta*** of *teruma*, **he is not liable to** pay **compensation** to the priest? The Rabbis **said to** Abba Shaul: **They said** that the item must be **worth a *peruta* only with regard to misuse** of consecrated items; **however, with regard to *teruma*, one is liable** to reimburse the priest **only when he eats an olive-bulk** or more. **And if it is so,** that Abba Shaul requires both conditions, and this is a case where there is an olive-bulk, then the Rabbis should have worded their objection differently. **They should** have said: **Since it is** at least **an olive-bulk,** he is liable to pay, even though it is not worth a *peruta*. The Gemara concludes: Indeed, this is **a conclusive refutation,** and Rav Pappa's position is rejected.

וְאַף רַב פַּפָּא הֲדַר בֵּיהּ, דְּתַנְיָא: "וְחָטְאָה בִּשְׁגָגָה" – פְּרָט לְמֵזִיד. וַהֲלֹא דִּין הוּא, וּמָה שְׁאָר מִצְוֹת שֶׁחַיָּיב בָּהֶן כָּרֵת – פּוֹטֵר בָּהֶן אֶת הַמֵּזִיד, מְעִילָה שֶׁאֵין בָּהּ כָּרֵת אֵינוֹ דִּין שֶׁפָּטַר אֶת הַמֵּזִיד?

The Gemara notes that **Rav Pappa** himself **also retracted** this explanation. **As it was taught** in a *baraita* with regard to the verse: "If any one commits a trespass, and sins through error, in the sacred items of the Lord, then he shall bring his guilt-offering to the Lord, a ram without blemish from the flock, according to your valuation in silver shekels, after the shekel of the sanctuary, for a guilt-offering" (Leviticus 5:15), the *baraita* explains: The phrase **"and sins through error" excludes one who** sins **intentionally** through misuse of consecrated property. Could this **not** be derived through **an *a fortiori* inference,** as follows: **Just as** with regard to **other mitzvot for which one is liable** to receive ***karet*** the verse **exempts one** from bringing an offering when the transgression was committed **intentionally, is it not right that** with regard to **misuse** of consecrated property, **which does not** incur the punishment of ***karet*,** it should **exempt one who acts intentionally?**

לֹא, אִם אֲמַרְתָּ בִּשְׁאָר מִצְוֹת – שֶׁכֵּן לֹא חַיָּיב בָּהֶן מִיתָה, תֹּאמַר בִּמְעִילָה שֶׁחַיָּיב בָּהּ מִיתָה, תַּלְמוּד לוֹמַר: "בִּשְׁגָגָה" – פְּרָט לְמֵזִיד.

The *baraita* rejects this claim: **No, if you say that** this is true with regard to **the rest of the mitzvot,** even those for which one is liable to receive *karet*, for which **one is not liable** to receive the **death** penalty if he violates them, **shall you** also **say that** this is the case with regard to **misuse** of consecrated items, for which **one is liable** to receive the **death** penalty, as this offense is punishable by death at the hand of Heaven?[N] Since one cannot logically deduce this principle, **the verse states "through error"** to **exclude one** who acted **intentionally.**

NOTES

Misuse of consecrated items, for which one is liable to receive the death penalty at the hand of Heaven – מְעִילָה שֶׁחַיָּיב בָּהּ מִיתָה: It is generally accepted that *karet* is considered more stringent than a divinely enacted penalty. As such, how is it possible to derive such an *a fortiori* argument? Some explain, based on the Jerusalem Talmud, that when one is punished with death at the hand of Heaven his property is also destroyed, unlike one who is punished with *karet*. Therefore, in this regard, death at the hand of Heaven is indeed more stringent than *karet* (*Tosefot Rabbeinu Peretz*).

וְאָמַר לֵיהּ רַב נַחְמָן בַּר יִצְחָק לְרַב חִיָּיא בַּר אָבִין: הַאי תַּנָּא, מֵעִיקָּרָא אַלִּימָא לֵיהּ כָּרֵת, וּלְבַסּוֹף אַלִּימָא לֵיהּ מִיתָה?!

And Rav Naḥman bar Yitzḥak said to Rav Ḥiyya bar Avin in wonderment with regard to this *baraita*: **This** ***tanna*** **initially** considers the punishment of ***karet*** **to be stronger** by assuming that misuse of consecrated property was less severe because it was not punished by *karet*, **and subsequently** he considers the punishment of **death** at the hand of Heaven **to be stronger** by stating that one cannot deduce this principle from other sins whose punishment is not death at the hand of Heaven.

וְאָמַר לֵיהּ; הָכִי קָאָמַר: לֹא, אִם אָמַרְתָּ בִּשְׁאָר מִצְוֹת – שֶׁכֵּן לֹא חַיָּיב בָּהֶן מִיתָה בְּפָחוֹת מִכַּזַּיִת, תֹּאמַר בִּמְעִילָה – שֶׁחַיָּיב בָּהּ מִיתָה בְּפָחוֹת מִכַּזַּיִת. וְאָמַר לֵיהּ: תָּנוּחַ דַּעְתְּךָ שֶׁהֵנַחְתָּ אֶת דַּעְתִּי וְאָמַר לֵיהּ: מַאי נִיחוּתָא? דְּרַבָּה וְרַב שֵׁשֶׁת שָׁדוּ בֵּיהּ נַרְגָּא: מַאן שָׁמְעַתְּ לֵיהּ דְּאָמַר

And Rav Ḥiyya bar Avin **said to him** that it is possible to maintain the accepted position that *karet* is more stringent by explaining **that this is what he is saying: No,** these are incomparable for the following reason: **If you say** that one is exempt from an offering when he violates **the rest of the mitzvot, for** which **one is not liable to** receive **death** at the hand of Heaven if he eats **less than an olive-bulk** of a forbidden substance, **shall you** also **say** that this is the case **with regard to misuse** of consecrated property, **for** which **one is liable to** receive **death** at the hand of Heaven if he eats **less than an olive-bulk?** Rav Naḥman bar Yitzḥak **said to him: May your mind be settled, as you have settled my mind** and put it at ease by answering this question that was troubling me. Rav Ḥiyya bar Avin **said to him: What is settling** about this explanation? **Rabba and Rav Sheshet threw an axe at** my answer; i.e., they reject my explanation, as follows: **Who did you hear that said**

Perek **II**
Daf **33** Amud **a**

HALAKHA

One who intentionally misuses consecrated items – הַזֵּיד בִּמְעִילָה: One who intentionally misuses consecrated property violates a negative commandment and is flogged (Rambam *Sefer Avoda*, *Hilkhot Me'ila* 1:3).

NOTES

Sin with regard to misuse of consecrated items and sin with regard to *teruma* – חֵטְא חֵטְא מִתְּרוּמָה: The Rabbis accept this verbal analogy and use it to derive other laws. However, they also have other derivations that teach that one who intentionally misuses consecrated property is not punished with the death penalty (*Tosefot Rabbeinu Peretz*).

הַזֵּיד בִּמְעִילָה בְּמִיתָה – רַבִּי הִיא. דְּתַנְיָא: הַזֵּיד בִּמְעִילָה, רַבִּי אוֹמֵר: בְּמִיתָה, וַחֲכָמִים אוֹמְרִים: בְּאַזְהָרָה.

that **one who intentionally misuses** consecrated items[H] is liable **to** receive **death** at the hand of Heaven? It is **Rabbi** Yehuda HaNasi. **As it was taught** in a *baraita*: With regard to **one who intentionally misuses** consecrated items, **Rabbi** Yehuda HaNasi **says** that he is liable to receive **death** at the hand of Heaven. **The Rabbis say:** he violates **a warning,** a standard prohibition, and is flogged.

מַאי טַעְמָא דְּרַבִּי? אָמַר רַבִּי אַבָּהוּ: גָּמַר חֵטְא חֵטְא מִתְּרוּמָה, מָה תְּרוּמָה בְּמִיתָה – אַף מְעִילָה בְּמִיתָה.

The Gemara asks: **What is the reason for** the opinion of **Rabbi** Yehuda HaNasi? From where does he derive his opinion? **Rabbi Abbahu said: He derives** it by means of a verbal analogy between the word **sin** stated with regard to misuse of consecrated items and the word **sin** stated **with regard to** ***teruma***.[N] With regard to misuse of consecrated items, the verse states: "If any one commits a trespass, and sins through error, in the sacred items of the Lord" (Leviticus 5:15); with regard to *teruma*, the verse states: "Lest they bear sin for it, and die due to it, if they profane it" (Leviticus 22:9). Rabbi Yehuda HaNasi makes the following comparison: **Just as** eating ***teruma*** is punishable by the **death** penalty, **so too, misusing** consecrated items is punishable by the **death** penalty.

וּמִינָהּ, מָה תְּרוּמָה בְּכַזַּיִת – אַף מְעִילָה בְּכַזַּיִת.

From this verbal analogy, the comparison between *teruma* and misuse of consecrated property can be extended to other issues as well: **Just as one** is punished only for eating at least **an olive-bulk of** ***teruma,*** **so too,** one is punished for **misusing** consecrated items only if there is at least **an olive-bulk** of consecrated items. This indicates that the *baraita* cannot be explained in accordance with the opinion of Abba Shaul, who requires that the item be worth at least a *peruta*.

וּמַתְקִיף לַהּ רַב פָּפָּא: מִמַּאי דְּרַבִּי כְּרַבָּנַן סְבִירָא לֵיהּ? דִּילְמָא כְּאַבָּא שָׁאוּל סְבִירָא לֵיהּ, דְּאָמַר: יֵשׁ בָּהּ שָׁוֶה פְּרוּטָה – אַף עַל גַּב דְּלֵית בָּהּ כַּזַּיִת.

Rav Pappa strongly objects to Rav Sheshet and Rabba's rejection of the explanation of the *baraita*: **From where** do you know that **Rabbi** Yehuda HaNasi **holds in accordance with** the opinion of **the Rabbis** that one is only punished after eating an olive-bulk of *teruma*? **Perhaps he holds in accordance with** the opinion of **Abba Shaul, who said** one is liable for eating *teruma* provided the food **contains the value of a** ***peruta*** **of** ***teruma,*** **even if it is less than an olive-bulk.** As the *halakhot* of misuse of consecrated items are derived from *teruma*, one is liable for eating both *teruma* and consecrated items only if the object is worth at least a *peruta*. As such, Rav Ḥiyya bar Avin's explanation of the *baraita* should not be rejected.

וְהָא רַב פַּפָּא הוּא דְּאָמַר דְּאַבָּא שָׁאוּל תַּרְתֵּי בָּעֵי! אֶלָּא שְׁמַע מִינָּהּ: הֲדַר בֵּיהּ.

With regard to the issue mentioned previously, the Gemara asks: **But isn't Rav Pappa the one who said** that **Abba Shaul said** that it **requires two** conditions, that the object be worth a *peruta* and that it be an olive-bulk in volume? **Rather, learn from this** that Rav Pappa **retracted** his statement with regard to Abba Shaul's opinion.

מָר בְּרֵיהּ דְּרַבָּנָא אָמַר, הָכִי קָאָמַר: לֹא, אִם אָמַרְתָּ בִּשְׁאָר מִצְוֹת, שֶׁלֹּא עָשָׂה בָּהֶן שֶׁאֵין מִתְכַּוֵּין כְּמִתְכַּוֵּין, שֶׁאִם נִתְכַּוֵּין לַחְתּוֹךְ אֶת הַתָּלוּשׁ וְחָתַךְ אֶת הַמְחוּבָּר – שֶׁפָּטוּר. תֹּאמַר בִּמְעִילָה, שֶׁאִם נִתְכַּוֵּין לְהִתְחַמֵּם בְּגִיזֵּי חוּלִּין וְנִתְחַמֵּם בְּגִיזֵּי עוֹלָה – שֶׁמָּעַל.

Mar, son of Rabbana, said the following to resolve the difficulty in the *baraita*: **This is what it is saying: No, if you say** that one is exempt from an offering **with regard to the rest of the mitzvot, where acting without intent is not treated** as though one acted **with intent,**[N] i.e., **if one intended to cut** something that is **detached** from the ground on Shabbat, which is not prohibited by Torah law, **and** mistakenly **cut** something that is **attached** to the ground, then **he is exempt** because he acted without intent; **shall you** also **say** the same **with regard to misuse** of consecrated items, about which the *halakha* is stringent, such **that if one intended to warm himself with non-sacred** wool **shearings,** and owing to an error or lack of information **he warmed himself with shearings from a burnt-offering,** then **he has misused** consecrated property? Thus misuse of consecrated property is more stringent than other commandments, in that one violates it even when acting without intent, and one cannot deduce the *halakha* in the case of misuse of consecrated property from the *halakha* in the case of the rest of the mitzvot.

רַב נַחְמָן בַּר יִצְחָק אָמַר, הָכִי קָאָמַר: לֹא, אִם אָמַרְתָּ בִּשְׁאָר מִצְוֹת, שֶׁכֵּן לֹא מִתְחַיֵּיב בָּהֶן שֶׁאֵין מִתְעַסֵּק כְּמִתְעַסֵּק, שֶׁאִם נִתְכַּוֵּין לְהַגְבִּיהַּ אֶת הַתָּלוּשׁ וְחָתַךְ אֶת הַמְחוּבָּר – שֶׁפָּטוּר. תֹּאמַר בִּמְעִילָה, שֶׁאִם הוֹשִׁיט יָדוֹ לִכְלִי לִיטּוֹל חֵפֶץ, וְסָךְ יָדוֹ בְּשֶׁמֶן שֶׁל קוֹדֶשׁ – שֶׁמָּעַל.

Rav Naḥman bar Yitzḥak said that the *baraita* should be understood differently, and **this is what it is saying: No, if you say** this leniency **with regard to rest of the mitzvot, where one who is acting unawares is not liable** in the same way **as** one who **is acting aware** of his actions, such as in a case where one intended to perform a permitted act and mistakenly performed a prohibited one, i.e., **if one intended to lift** something that is **detached** from the ground, but his knife happened to **cut** something that is **attached** to the ground, in violation of the act of harvesting on Shabbat, then **he is exempt; shall you** also **say** the same **with regard to misuse** of consecrated items, **where if one places his hand in a vessel to take an object** and unknowingly **places his hand in consecrated oil** then **he is has misused** consecrated items? Therefore, misuse of consecrated items is more stringent than other commandments, as one commits the sin of misusing consecrated property even if he uses the consecrated object while attempting to perform a different action and is unaware that he is performing a prohibited act.

אָמַר מָר: בַּמֶּה דְּבָרִים אֲמוּרִים – בְּמַפְרִישׁ תְּרוּמָה וְהֶחְמִיצָה, אֲבָל הִפְרִישׁ חָמֵץ תְּרוּמָה – דִּבְרֵי הַכֹּל אֵינָהּ קְדוֹשָׁה.

The Master said above in the *baraita*: **In what** case **is this statement said** that the *tanna'im* disagree with regard to the obligation to pay for *teruma* of leavened bread? It is said with regard to a case where **one separated *teruma*** in a permitted manner **and it became leavened** during Passover. **However, if he separated *teruma* from leavened bread** during Passover, **everyone agrees that it is not consecrated** since it is worthless.

מְנָא הָנֵי מִילֵּי? אָמַר רַב נַחְמָן בַּר יִצְחָק, אָמַר קְרָא: ״תִּתֶּן לוֹ״ – וְלֹא לְאוּרוֹ.

The Gemara asks: **From where are these matters** derived, that a worthless item cannot be designated as *teruma*? **Rav Naḥman bar Yitzḥak said** that **the verse states:** "The first fruits of your grain, your wine, your oil, and the first of the fleece of your sheep, **shall you give to him**" (Deuteronomy 18:4), **and not to his fire.** One must give the priest something that he can use for any purpose, and not something that the priest will be forced to burn as fuel. Even those who permit one to derive benefit from leavened bread during Passover agree that it may not be eaten, and therefore leavened bread cannot be consecrated as *teruma* in this case.

NOTES

With and without intent – **נִתְכַּוֵּין וְלֹא נִתְכַּוֵּין**: With regard to the significance of intent in *halakha*, there is a three-tiered hierarchy: The *halakhot* of Shabbat, the rest of the mitzvot, and the *halakhot* of the misuse of consecrated items. One is liable to be punished for misusing consecrated items even if he does so unknowingly, without intent, and even unawares, i.e., while attempting to perform a different action. With regard to other sins, one is punished only when he derives benefit from the sin, e.g., consuming forbidden foods or engaging in forbidden relations, despite the fact that it was performed without intent to commit the sinful act. However, with regard to the *halakhot* of Shabbat, since the Torah prohibited only planned, thoughtful, or creative labor, one whose actions did not accomplish his intentions is exempt.

מתיב רב הונא בריה דרב יהושע: אין תורמין מן הטמאה לטהורה, ואם תרם בשוגג – תרומתו תרומה. ואמאי? לימא "לו" ולא לאורו! לא קשיא, התם – היתה לו שעת הכושר, הכא – לא היתה לו שעת הכושר.

Rav Huna, son of Rav Yehoshua, raised an objection based on that which was taught in a mishna: **One may not separate** ***teruma*** **from ritually impure** produce **for ritually pure** produce,[NH] **but if one unwittingly separated** it in this manner then **his** ***teruma*** **is** valid ***teruma*****. And why** should this be valid *teruma*? **Let** the priest **say:** The verse requires that the *teruma* be given **"to him" and not to his fire,** and this ritually impure *teruma* must be burned. In that case, why should this produce actually become *teruma*? The Gemara answers: This is **not difficult. There,** in the case of impure *teruma*, **it had a period of fitness,** and it could have been given as *teruma* before it became impure. **Here,** in the case of leavened bread, **it did not** ever **have a period of fitness,** and therefore it cannot be consecrated as *teruma*.

ודלא היתה לו שעת הכושר היכי דמי – כגון דאחמיץ במחובר, אבל אחמיץ בתלוש – הכי נמי דקדשה? אמר ליה: אין "בגזירת עירין פתגמא ובמאמר קדישין שאילתא" וכן מורין בבי מדרשא כוותי.

The Gemara asks: **What are the circumstances** in **which** this leavened bread **did not have a period of fitness** even on Passover? This could have happened only in a case **where it** became **leavened** while it was still **attached** to the ground[N] and could not yet become *teruma*. **However,** if **it** became **leavened** after being **detached** from the ground, then can this leavened bread **indeed become consecrated** as *teruma*, even though the *baraita* indicates that no leavened bread can be designated as *teruma* during Passover? Rav Naḥman bar Yitzhak **said to** Rav Huna, son of Rav Yehoshua: **Yes,** this is indeed the case despite this puzzling limitation, and the biblical expression can be applied homiletically: **"The matter is by the decree of the watchers, and the sentence by the word of the sacred ones"** (Daniel 4:14). The Sages, who are compared to celestial beings, agree with my statement. **And so too, in the study hall, they teach in accordance with my** opinion,[N] despite the puzzling nature of this ruling.

כי אתא רב הונא בריה דרב יהושע

When Rav Huna, son of Rav Yehoshua, came,

NOTES

Separating *teruma* from ritually impure produce for ritually pure produce – תרומה מן הטמא על הטהור: If one separated *teruma* from impure produce for pure produce, this is considered *teruma* according to Torah law. However, the Sages penalized a person who does so, because he gives the priest something unusable (Rabbi Shimshon of Saens).

It became leavened while attached to the ground – דאחמיץ במחובר: The same must be said with regard to ritually impure *teruma*. If such produce was never acceptable as *teruma* and one separates *teruma* from it, this does not become *teruma* at all (*Tosefot Rabbeinu Peretz*).

In the study hall they teach in accordance with my opinion – מורין בבי מדרשא כוותי: This statement is puzzling, as there would not appear to be any practical ruling that could be derived from this discussion given that the *halakha* states that it is forbidden to derive benefit from leavened bread on Passover. However, despite the fact that in this case there are no practical ramifications to the ruling, the principle of impure *teruma* that was never fit is relevant in other contexts (Rabbi Elazar Moshe Horowitz).

HALAKHA

One may not separate *teruma* from ritually impure produce for ritually pure produce – אין תורמין מן הטמאה לטהורה: One may not separate *teruma* from ritually impure produce for ritually pure produce. However, if one did this unwittingly then the produce he separated becomes *teruma* (Rambam *Sefer Zera'im, Hilkhot Teruma* 5:8).

Perek **II**
Daf **33** Amud **b**

אמר: אמר קרא "ראשית" – ששיריה ניכרין לישראל, יצתה זו שאין שיריה ניכרין.

he said that **the verse states:** "The **first fruits** of your grain, your wine, your oil, and the first of the fleece of your sheep, shall you give him" (Deuteronomy 18:4), implying **that its remnants are recognizable**[N] **for an Israelite,** as the notion of a first part indicates that there is another portion remaining which is fit to be consumed by the Israelite. **This** ***teruma*** **is excluded as there is no recognizable remnant** left that may be consumed by the Israelite, because it is leavened bread. Since even after this portion has been separated the remainder of the produce may not be eaten, that which was separated does not become *teruma*.

יתיב רב אחא בר רב עויא קמיה דרב חסדא, ויתיב ואמר משמיה דרבי יוחנן: ענבים שנטמאו – דורכן פחות פחות מכביצה, ויינן כשר לנסכין. אלמא קסבר: משקין מיפקד פקידי, לאימת קא מיטמאי – לכי סחיט להו, לכי סחיט להו ליתיה לשיעוריה.

Rav Aḥa bar Rav Avya sat before Rav Ḥisda, and he sat and said in the name of Rabbi Yoḥanan: With regard to **grapes that became ritually impure,**[H] one should **tread on them less than an egg-bulk at a time, and the wine** that comes from them is **kosher** even **for libations** because it is ritually pure. **Apparently** Rabbi Yoḥanan **holds: The liquid is stored**[N] inside the grape, as the juice is not considered to be part of the grape itself but rather stored in the grape as though contained in a receptacle. According to Rabbi Yoḥanan's opinion, **when do** these liquids **become ritually impure?** This occurs only **when one squeezes them,** and prior to this the juice remains pure even if the grape was impure. And **when one squeezes them, there is less than the** minimum **measure** of grape flesh that would transfer ritual impurity, as food can impart ritual impurity only if it is at least an egg-bulk in size.

HALAKHA

Grapes that became ritually impure – ענבים שנטמאו: Grapes or olives that are ritually impure should be pressed less than an egg-bulk at a time, and the wine that comes from them may be used even for libations, in accordance with the statement of Rabbi Yoḥanan (Rambam *Sefer Avoda, Hilkhot Issurei Mizbe'aḥ* 6:7).

NOTES

Its remnants are recognizable – שיריה ניכרין: This explanation is challenged because it assumes that there is no significance to whether the *teruma* itself was of leavened bread or *matza*, but rather that the determining factor is the status of the remaining produce. Accordingly, it is possible that if the *teruma* taken is leavened bread but the remaining produce is *matza* then this would be acceptable *teruma*, while the reverse would not be acceptable *teruma*. This issue is raised in the Jerusalem Talmud. The resolution suggested there is that separating *teruma* in such a manner is prohibited because it involves separating *teruma* from a food that is obligated in *teruma* for a food that is exempt from *teruma*, which is unacceptable (see *Gilyon HaShas*; *Tziyyun LeNefesh Ḥayya*; Rashash).

The liquid is stored – משקין מיפקד פקידי: This dispute about the way liquid is stored within various fruits, and the way blood is stored in the body in certain circumstances, is not a factual dispute but a conceptual one. The question revolves around the status of the juice before it is pressed. Is the juice considered to be a separate entity even before it is pressed, or is it considered to be part of the fruit itself so long as it is inside the fruit, in which case it undergoes a significant change in state when it is pressed from the fruit? Alternatively, the dispute may center on the question of whether the miniscule places where the liquid is stored can be considered independent containers, or whether the liquid is merely part of the larger entity, i.e., the fruit. There is no empirical way to resolve this issue.

אִי הָכִי כְּבֵיצָה נַמִּי, דְּהָתְנַן: טְמֵא מֵת שֶׁסָּחַט זֵיתִים וַעֲנָבִים כְּבֵיצָה מְכוּוֶּנֶת – טְהוֹרִין! הָתָם – דְּאִי עֲבַד, הָכָא – לְכַתְּחִלָּה, גְּזֵירָה דִּילְמָא אָתֵי לְמֶיעְבַּד יוֹתֵר מִכְּבֵיצָה.

The Gemara challenges this statement: **If that is so, then even** if he squeezes **an egg-bulk** of grapes, the juice will still not become impure. **Didn't we learn** in a mishna: In the case of **one who is ritually impure** with impurity imparted by **a corpse** and **who squeezed olives or grapes** in the **exact** amount of **an egg-bulk,**[H] the liquid **is** ritually **pure.** Once the first drop of liquid is squeezed out, less than an egg-bulk of food remains, and it cannot render the liquid impure. In that case, why did Rabbi Yoḥanan permit squeezing only less than an egg-bulk? The Gemara answers: **There,** it was speaking of a case where the ruling was **after the fact;** however, **here,** it is discussing the ruling ***ab initio***, and the mishna states that one may press juice only from less than an egg-bulk of grapes due to a rabbinic **decree lest one come to perform** the act of squeezing on **more than an egg-bulk,** causing the liquid to become impure.

אֲמַר לֵיהּ רַב חִסְדָּא: מַאן צַיֵּית לָךְ וּלְרַבִּי יוֹחָנָן רַבָּךְ! וְכִי טוּמְאָה שֶׁבָּהֶן לְהֵיכָן הָלְכָה? אַלְמָא קָא סָבַר: מַשְׁקִין מִיבְלַע בְּלִיעִי, וְכֵיוָן דְּאִיטַּמּוּ לֵיהּ אוֹכְלָא – אִיטַּמּוּ לֵיהּ מַשְׁקִין.

Rav Ḥisda said to Rav Aḥa bar Rav Avya: **Who will listen to you and to Rabbi Yoḥanan your teacher** with regard to this issue? **As, where did the impurity that was in** the grape juice **go?** The Gemara notes that **apparently** Rav Ḥisda **holds: Liquids are absorbed** within the fruit and are therefore considered to be part of the grape itself. **And since the flesh of the grape became ritually impure, the liquid became ritually impure** as well.

אֲמַר לֵיהּ: וְאַתְּ לָא תִּיסְבְּרָא דְּמַשְׁקִין מִיפְקָד פְּקִידִי? וְהָתְנַן: טְמֵא מֵת שֶׁסָּחַט זֵיתִים וַעֲנָבִים מְכוּוֶּנֶת כְּבֵיצָה – טְהוֹרִין. אִי אָמְרַתְּ בִּשְׁלָמָא מִיפְקָד פְּקִידִי – מִשּׁוּם הָכִי טְהוֹרִין, אֶלָּא אִי אָמְרַתְּ מִיבְלַע בְּלִיעִי אַמַּאי טְהוֹרִין?

Rav Aḥa **said to him: Do you not hold** that **liquids are stored** inside the grape? **Didn't we learn** in the mishna: In the case of **one who is ritually impure** with impurity imparted by **a corpse** and **who squeezed olives or grapes** in the **exact** amount of **an egg-bulk,** using a flat wooden utensil without touching the liquid itself, the liquid is ritually **pure. Granted, if you say** that the juice is **stored** inside the grapes, then it is **due to that** reason that the liquid **is pure. But if you say** that the liquid is **absorbed** within the grapes, **why** is the juice **pure?** According to this opinion, once the grape itself becomes impure, the juice, which is attached to it and absorbed in it, becomes impure as well.

אֲמַר לֵיהּ: הָכָא בְּמַאי עָסְקִינַן – בַּעֲנָבִים שֶׁלֹּא הוּכְשְׁרוּ. לְאֵימַת מִתַּכְשְׁרִי – לְכִי סָחֵיט לְהוּ, כִּי סָחֵיט לְהוּ בְּצִיר לְהוּ שִׁיעוּרָא. דְּאִי לָא תֵּימָא הָכִי, הָא דְּתַנְיָא: הָא לְמָה זֶה דּוֹמֶה – לִתְרוּמַת תּוּתִין (זֵיתִים) וַעֲנָבִים שֶׁנִּטְמְאָה, שֶׁאֵין לוֹ בָּהּ לֹא הֶיתֵּר אֲכִילָה וְלֹא הֶיתֵּר הַסָּקָה. הָא הֶיתֵּר אֲכִילָה נַמִּי אִית בֵּיהּ, דְּאִי בָּעֵי דָּרֵיךְ לְהוּ פָּחוֹת פָּחוֹת מִכְּבֵיצָה!

Rav Ḥisda **said to him: With what are we dealing here?** We are dealing with a case where **the grapes have not been rendered susceptible** to ritual impurity, since they have not come in contact with liquids. **When do they become susceptible** to ritual impurity? This is only **once one presses them** and they become wet with their own juice. However, **when he presses them,** they decrease in volume **and are lacking the measure** of volume required to become impure. This must be the explanation, **for if you do not say so,** it is difficult to reconcile this mishna with **that which was taught** in the *baraita* cited above: **To what** may **this** case of *teruma* of leavened bread **be compared?** It may be compared **to *teruma* of berries, olives, and grapes**[N] **that became impure, which can neither be eaten nor burned.** However, according to Rabbi Yoḥanan's statement **they may even be eaten, as if one wishes he may tread less than an egg-bulk** at a time.

אָמַר רָבָא: גְּזֵירָה דִּילְמָא אָתֵי בְּהוּ לִידֵי תַּקָּלָה. אֲמַר לֵיהּ אַבָּיֵי: וּמִי חָיְישִׁינַן לְתַקָּלָה? וְהָא תַּנְיָא: מַדְלִיקִין בְּפַת וּבְשֶׁמֶן שֶׁל תְּרוּמָה שֶׁנִּטְמֵאת! אֲמַר לֵיהּ: פַּת – זָרֵיק לֵיהּ בֵּין הָעֵצִים, שֶׁמֶן שֶׁל תְּרוּמָה – רָמֵי לֵיהּ בִּכְלִי מָאוּס.

Rava said: It is possible to reject this proof, as even if this action is permitted in principle, there is **a rabbinic decree** prohibiting it **lest he encounter a stumbling block.** If one keeps ritually impure fruit of *teruma* in order to press it for its juice, it is possible that he will forget its status and accidentally eat it. **Abaye said to him: Are we concerned about** this type of **stumbling block? Wasn't it taught** in a *baraita*: **One** may **light** a fire **with bread and oil of *teruma* that became ritually impure?**[H] It can be deduced from this *baraita* that there is no concern that a person will forget and eat these foods. Rava **said to him: Bread** is only permitted when **one throws it among the wood** used for fuel so that it is ruined and no longer considered edible. ***Teruma* oil** is permitted only **when one puts it into a repulsive vessel** so that no one will drink it.

גּוּפָא, מַדְלִיקִין בְּפַת וּבְשֶׁמֶן שֶׁל תְּרוּמָה שֶׁנִּטְמֵאת. אַבָּיֵי אָמַר מִשְּׁמֵיהּ דְּחִזְקִיָּה, וְרָבָא אָמַר דְּבֵי רַבִּי יִצְחָק בַּר מָרְתָא, אָמַר רַב הוּנָא: לֹא שָׁנוּ אֶלָּא פַּת, אֲבָל חִיטֵּי – לֹא, שֶׁמָּא יָבֹא בָּהֶן לִידֵי תַּקָּלָה. וְרַבִּי יוֹחָנָן אָמַר: אֲפִילּוּ חִיטֵּי. וְאַמַּאי? נֵיחוּשׁ דִּילְמָא אָתֵי בָּהֶן לִידֵי תַּקָּלָה! כִּדְאָמַר רַב אַשִׁי:

With regard to **the** matter **itself,** it was taught: **One** may **light with bread and oil of *teruma* that became ritually impure.** The Sages limited the application of this *halakha*, as **Abaye said in the name of Ḥizkiya and Rava said** in the name of the Sages from **the school of Rabbi Yitzḥak bar Marta** that **Rav Huna said: They taught** that one may use impure *teruma* as firewood **only** with regard to **bread; however,** with regard to **wheat, no,** one may not light a fire **with it, lest one encounter a stumbling block** and eat it, because wheat will not become inedible by being placed among the firewood. **And Rabbi Yoḥanan said: Even wheat** may be used as fuel. The Gemara asks: **And why** does he permit this? **Let us be concerned lest he encounter a stumbling block.** The Gemara answers based on what **Rav Ashi said** with regard to a different issue:

HALAKHA

Olives or grapes in the exact amount of an egg-bulk – זֵיתִים וַעֲנָבִים כְּבֵיצָה מְכוּוֶּנֶת: If one who is ritually impure with impurity imparted by a corpse pressed precisely an egg-bulk of olives or grapes that had become susceptible to impurity, the liquid itself is pure provided the person did not touch the liquid (Rambam *Sefer Tahara*, *Hilkhot Tumat Okhalin* 9:2).

***Teruma* that became ritually impure – תְּרוּמָה שֶׁנִּטְמֵאת:** *Teruma* bread that becomes impure should be placed with firewood until it is burned, and oil that becomes impure must be stored in a filthy vessel until it is used for lighting. If wheat becomes impure, it must be boiled and then stored in a filthy vessel until it is used for kindling (Rambam *Sefer Zera'im*, *Hilkhot Terumot* 12:12).

NOTES

Berries, olives, and grapes – תּוּתִין זֵיתִים וַעֲנָבִים: Many versions of the text do not contain the word olives because what is squeezed from olives, i.e., olive oil, is fit for lighting even if it is ritually impure. However, it appears that some accept the version that mentions olives and distinguish between oil, which is ready for use, and olives, where there is a greater risk that one will forget their status and eat them or treat the oil squeezed from them improperly (see *Yefe Einayim*).

בשליקתא ומאיסתא. הכי נמי – בשליקתא ומאיסתא. והיכא איתמר דרב אשי? אהא, דאמר רבי אבין בר רב אחא אמר רבי יצחק: אבא שאול גבל של בית רבי היה, והיו מחמין לו חמין בחיטין של תרומה טמאה ללוש בהן עיסה בטהרה. אמאי? ניחוש דילמא אתי בהו לידי תקלה! אמר רב אשי: בשליקתא ומאיסתא.

This is referring **to boiled and repulsive** wheat,[N] i.e., wheat that one boiled and then placed in a repulsive area, in which case he need not be concerned that this wheat will accidentally be eaten; **so too** here, it is referring **to boiled and repulsive** wheat. The Gemara asks: **Where was Rav Ashi's** explanation **stated?** It was stated **with regard to this: As Rabbi Avin bar Rav Aḥa said** that **Rabbi Yitzḥak said: Abba Shaul was the** dough **kneader of Rabbi** Yehuda HaNasi's **house,**[N] **and they would heat water for him,** to make dough, **with wheat of ritually impure *teruma*,** which was purchased from priests at a low price, **in order to knead dough in ritual purity.** The Gemara asks: **Why** did they do this? **Let us be concerned lest they encounter a stumbling block** by accidentally eating this wheat. With regard to this **Rav Ashi said** that it was only done when the wheat was **boiled and repulsive** and could only be used for lighting a fire.

אביי בר אבין ורב חנניא בר אבין תנו תרומות בי רבה, פגע בהו רבא בר מתנה, אמר להו: מאי אמריתו בתרומות דבי מר? אמרו ליה: ומאי קשיא לך? אמר להו: תנן, שתילי תרומות שנטמאו ושתלן – טהורים מלטמא ואסורין מלאכול (בתרומה). וכי מאחר דטהורין מלטמא אמאי אסורין מלאכול?

After mentioning ways in which impure *teruma* was used, the Gemara mentions other *halakhot* pertaining to this issue. **Abaye bar Avin and Rav Ḥananya bar Avin taught** the tractate of ***Terumot* in the school of Rabba. Rava bar Mattana met them** and **said to them: What** novel idea can **you say** has been taught with regard to ***Terumot* in the school of** our **Master,** Rabba? **They said to him: What** is **difficult for you?** There must be some issue troubling you that has caused you to ask this question. **He said to them:** The following statement that **we learned** in the mishna in *Terumot* is unclear: **Saplings of *teruma* that became ritually impure and were planted are pure** such that they **do not impart ritual impurity** once they have been planted, **but they are prohibited to be eaten as *teruma*.**[H] The question arises: **If they do not impart ritual impurity, why is it prohibited to eat them?** If their impurity has been eliminated then it should be permitted to eat them, like other ritually pure *teruma*.

אמרו ליה, הכי אמר רבה: מאי אסורין – אסורין לזרים. ומאי קא משמע לן – גידולי תרומה תרומה, תנינא: גידולי תרומה תרומה!

Abaye bar Avin and Rav Ḥananya bar Avin **said to** Rava bar Mattana: **This is what Rabba said** in explaining this mishna: **What** does it mean that **they are prohibited** to be eaten? It means that **they are prohibited** to be eaten **by non-priests,** but a priest may eat them. Once these saplings are planted, they lose their ritual impurity but retain their status as *teruma*. Rava bar Mattana challenged this answer: If this is the case, **what is** the mishna **teaching us** with this statement? Is it teaching us that **growths of *teruma*** are considered ***teruma*?** It is unnecessary to teach this principle, as **we** already **learned: Growths of *teruma*,** i.e., produce that grows from *teruma*[H] that was planted in the ground, are considered ***teruma*.**[N] Why, then, is it necessary to teach this principle again?

וכי תימא: גידולי גידולין ומאי קא משמע לן – בדבר שאין זרעו כלה, הא נמי תנינא: הטבל גידוליו מותרין בדבר שזרעו כלה, אבל בדבר שאין זרעו כלה – אפילו גידולי גידולין אסורין באכילה! אישתיקו.

And if you say as follows: This case is referring to **the growths of growths** of *teruma*, i.e., plants that grew from the original growths of *teruma*, and **what is it teaching us?** It is teaching that **an item whose seed does not disintegrate** when planted in the ground maintains its *teruma* status. While most seeds will disintegrate, other plants, such as onions and garlic, merely continue growing when planted. In that case, this mishna would be informing us that even the growths of growths of such plants retain their *teruma* status. However, **we** already **learned** that **as well.** As the mishna states: With regard to **untithed produce** [***tevel***], **its growths,** the produce that grows from it, **are permitted in** the case of **items whose seed disintegrates; however, in** the case of **items where the seed does not disintegrate, it is prohibited to eat even the growths of growths** unless they are tithed.[H] There would be no need for the mishna to teach us this *halakha* a second time. **They were silent** and did not have an answer to this question.

NOTES

Boiled and repulsive wheat – שליקתא ומאיסתא: *Tosafot* explain that this refers to wheat that was boiled and placed in a filthy area before it became impure. Others say that the wheat was boiled before it became impure but was left in a filthy place afterward (*Tosefot Rid*). Others explain Rashi's opinion, that one is permitted to boil the wheat and let it become filthy even after it has become impure, in the following manner: The reason this is allowed is due to a principle derived from the *halakhot* of leavened bread that states that one who is acting to remove a prohibited item is not likely to sin by improperly using the item at that time.

The dough kneader of Rabbi Yehuda HaNasi's house – גבל של בית רבי: The early commentaries (see *Tosafot*) wonder: How it was permitted for Rabbi Yehuda HaNasi, who was not a priest, to use *teruma*? Some explain that it was permitted to do this because there were priests who lived in Rabbi Yehuda HaNasi's house, and it was permitted to use their *teruma* to prepare food for everyone. Others explain that deriving benefit from impure *teruma* is a rabbinic prohibition, and the Sages permit the use of such *teruma* for communal purposes even if there are no priests among those who will benefit from *teruma*. Therefore, this *teruma* could in used in the household of Rabbi Yehuda, the leader of the community, since food prepared there would be for the entire community (*Tosefot Rid*).

The prohibition of growths of *teruma* – איסור גידולי תרומה: Some explain that the Sages declared produce that grew from *teruma* to be *teruma* because they did not want priests to be retain impure *teruma* while waiting to plant it. If a priest knows that whatever grows from the *teruma* will still be *teruma*, he will be disinclined to put effort into planting it when he knows that he will soon be given more *teruma* as a gift or will be able to purchase it at a low price from another priest. Therefore, it is not worth the effort for him to plant it, and he will burn it immediately (*Tosefot Rid*).

HALAKHA

Impure *teruma* that was planted – תרומה טמאה שנזרעה: Even though produce that grows from impure *teruma* is pure, it is still prohibited to eat this *teruma*. This ruling is in accordance with the mishna and the statements of Rav Sheshet and Rav Oshaya (see *Kesef Mishne*; Rambam *Sefer Zera'im*, *Hilkhot Terumot* 11:23).

Produce that grows from *teruma* – גידולי תרומה: The Sages decreed that produce that grows from *teruma* must be treated as though it were *teruma*, and it is prohibited to non-priests (Rambam *Sefer Zera'im*, *Hilkhot Terumot* 11:21).

Produce that grows from untithed produce – גידולי טבל: If one plants untithed produce whose seed disintegrates when planted, the produce is permitted. However, if one plants a species whose seed does not disintegrate when planted, e.g., onions, its produce remains prohibited. In the latter case the third generation of plants is likewise prohibited, and only the fourth generation is permitted (Rambam *Sefer Zera'im*, *Hilkhot Ma'aserot* 6:6).

אָמְרוּ לֵיהּ: מִידֵּי שְׁמִיעַ לָךְ בְּהָא? אֲמַר לְהוּ: הָכִי אָמַר רַב שֵׁשֶׁת: מַאי אֲסוּרִין – אֲסוּרִין לַכֹּהֲנִים, הוֹאִיל וְאִיפְּסִילוּ לְהוּ בְּהֶיסַּח הַדַּעַת.

They said to Rava bar Mattana: **Have you heard something in this** regard? **He said to them: This is what Rav Sheshet said: What** is the meaning of the word **prohibited** in this context? It means that it is **prohibited for priests, since it has been disqualified for them due to the diversion of attention.**[H] *Teruma* and other consecrated property must be guarded, and when one fails to do so, it is treated as though it were impure. Therefore, these *teruma* saplings are treated as though they have become impure once the priest diverts attention from them, and they remain prohibited to him even after another generation grows from them.

הָנִיחָא לְמַאן דְּאָמַר: ״הֶיסַּח הַדַּעַת פְּסוּל הַגּוּף הָוֵי״ – שַׁפִּיר, אֶלָּא לְמַאן דְּאָמַר: ״הֶיסַּח הַדַּעַת פְּסוּל טוּמְאָה הָוֵי״ מַאי אִיכָּא לְמֵימַר?

The Gemara asks: **Granted, according to the one who says** that a **diversion of attention constitutes an inherent disqualification,**[N] **it works out well.** According to this opinion, a diversion of attention does not disqualify *teruma* due to a concern that it became impure. Instead, there is an independent rabbinic decree rendering *teruma* that has not been watched impure even when this *teruma* could not possibly have become impure. According to this opinion, one can understand why this growth may not be eaten by a priest. **But according to the one who says** that a **diversion of attention is a disqualification due to** a concern about **ritual impurity, what is there to say?** It is stated in the mishna that by planting these saplings they become pure, even if they were certainly ritually impure prior to being planted. If this is the case with regard to *teruma* that is certainly impure, all the more so should it apply to a case where there is only a chance that the *teruma* is ritually impure.

דְּאִתְּמַר: הֶיסַּח הַדַּעַת, רַבִּי יוֹחָנָן אָמַר: פְּסוּל טוּמְאָה הָוֵי, וְרַבִּי שִׁמְעוֹן בֶּן לָקִישׁ אָמַר: פְּסוּל הַגּוּף הָוֵי.

Apropos the discussion of diversion of attention, the Gemara cites a dispute between *amora'im* with regard to this issue, **as it was stated:** What is the nature of the disqualification of **diversion of attention? Rabbi Yoḥanan said: It is a disqualification** due to a concern about **ritual impurity** that may have been contracted while one's attention was diverted. And **Rabbi Shimon ben Lakish said: It is an inherent disqualification.**

רַבִּי יוֹחָנָן אָמַר: פְּסוּל טוּמְאָה הָוֵי, שֶׁאִם יָבֹא אֵלִיָּהוּ וִיטַהֲרֶנָּה – שׁוֹמְעִין לוֹ. רַבִּי שִׁמְעוֹן בֶּן לָקִישׁ אוֹמֵר: פְּסוּל הַגּוּף הָוֵי, שֶׁאִם יָבֹא אֵלִיָּהוּ וִיטַהֲרֶנָּה – אֵין שׁוֹמְעִין לוֹ.

The Gemara discusses the ramifications of this dispute: According to **Rabbi Yoḥanan,** who **said it is a disqualification** due to a concern about **ritual impurity, if Elijah comes and renders it ritually pure** then **we will listen to him,** because it was treated as impure only due to a doubt with regard to its actual status. However, according to **Rabbi Shimon ben Lakish,** who **said** that **it is an inherent disqualification,** even **if Elijah comes and renders it pure we will not listen to him.** The reason for this is that Rabbi Shimon ben Lakish believes that this decree is unrelated to the question of whether the object actually became impure.

אֵיתִיבֵיהּ רַבִּי יוֹחָנָן לְרַבִּי שִׁמְעוֹן בֶּן לָקִישׁ: רַבִּי יִשְׁמָעֵאל בְּנוֹ שֶׁל רַבִּי יוֹחָנָן בֶּן בְּרוֹקָא אוֹמֵר: לוּל קָטָן הָיָה בֵּין כֶּבֶשׁ לַמִּזְבֵּחַ בְּמַעֲרָבוֹ שֶׁל כֶּבֶשׁ, שֶׁשָּׁם הָיוּ זוֹרְקִין פְּסוּלֵי חַטַּאת הָעוֹף, וְתִעוּבַּר צוּרָתָן וְיוֹצְאִין לְבֵית הַשְּׂרֵיפָה. אִי אָמְרַתְּ בִּשְׁלָמָא פְּסוּל טוּמְאָה הָוֵי – מִשּׁוּם הָכִי בָּעֵי עִיבּוּר צוּרָה, שֶׁמָּא יָבֹא אֵלִיָּהוּ וִיטַהֲרֶנָּה, אֶלָּא אִי אָמְרַתְּ פְּסוּל הַגּוּף, לָמָּה לִי עִיבּוּר צוּרָה? וְהָתְנַן, זֶה הַכְּלָל:

Rabbi Yoḥanan raised an objection to the opinion of **Rabbi Shimon ben Lakish** based on what is taught in the *Tosefta*: **Rabbi Yishmael, son of Rabbi Yoḥanan ben Beroka, says: There was a small gap**[BH] **between the ramp and the altar on the western** side **of the ramp, where they would throw disqualified birds** that had been designated as **sin-offerings.** If birds became disqualified for any reason, such as a diversion of attention, they were left there **until their form decayed,** i.e., until the next morning, at which point they would be definitively disqualified due to remaining in the Temple overnight and could be **taken out to the place** designated for **burning. Granted, if you say** that a diversion of attention **is a disqualification** due to a concern for **ritual impurity, for this reason it requires decay of form**[N] to ensure that the bird is certainly disqualified. Currently the bird is disqualified only due to uncertainty, **and Elijah may come and render it ritually pure. However, if you say** that **it is an inherent disqualification,** then **why do I** need to leave it until **it has decay of form?** It should be definitively disqualified once there has been a diversion of attention. **But didn't we learn** in the mishna that **this is the principle:**

NOTES

Inherent disqualification – פְּסוּל הַגּוּף: In this context, this phrase means that the object has an inherent, independent prohibition associated with it, like other objects prohibited by Torah law. It appears that a similar *halakha* applies to consecrated items as well, and there is a mitzva to guard them and avoid diverting one's attention from them. If one diverts his attention from either *teruma* or an offering, it is invalidated.

Decay of form – עִיבּוּר צוּרָה: This refers to the process in which the meat loses its original form and is no longer fit to be considered meat. This requirement was implemented so as not to treat sacrificial meat with disrespect by burning it in its original form (Rashi).

BACKGROUND

The ramp, the altar, and the gap – כֶּבֶשׁ מִזְבֵּחַ וְלוּל: This schematic diagram displays the altar (on the right), the ramp, and the gap between the ramp and the altar.

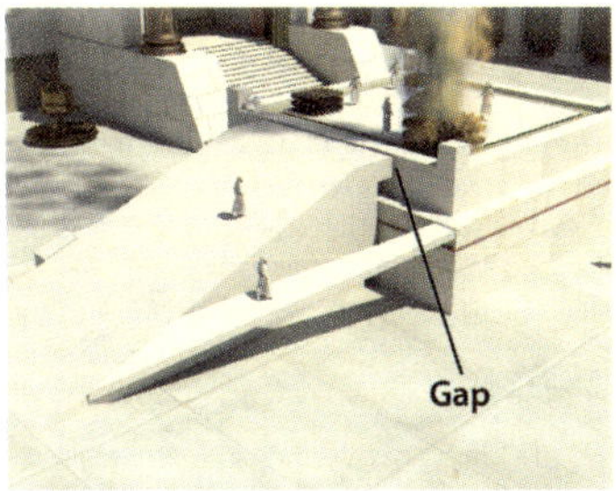

Altar, ramp, and gap between them

HALAKHA

It has been disqualified for them due to the diversion of attention – אִיפְּסִילוּ לְהוּ הֶיסַּח הַדַּעַת: If one diverted his attention from an offering, it is disqualified due to the concern that it became impure, as stated by Rabbi Yoḥanan (Rambam *Sefer Avoda, Hilkhot Pesulei HaMukdashin* 19:4).

Small gap – לוּל קָטָן: There was a space near the ramp of the altar. Birds that had been designated for sin-offerings and subsequently disqualified were placed there until their forms decayed and then taken out to the place designated for burning (Rambam *Sefer Avoda, Hilkhot Beit HaBeḥira* 2:14).

כׇּל שֶׁפְּסוּלוֹ בְּגוּפוֹ – יִשָּׂרֵף מִיָּד, בְּדָם וּבִבְעָלִים – תְּעוּבַּר צוּרָתָן וְיוֹצְאִין לְבֵית הַשְּׂרֵיפָה! אֲמַר לֵיהּ: הַאי תַּנָּא – תַּנָּא דְּבֵי רַבָּה בַּר אֲבוּהּ הוּא, דְּאָמַר: אֲפִילּוּ פִּיגּוּל טָעוּן עִיבּוּר צוּרָה.

Any offering **that has a disqualification in the body** of the animal, i.e., it has a definite disqualification with regard to the meat itself, **should be burned immediately.** If it is has a disqualification **in the blood** of the animal, e.g., if the blood was spilled, or a disqualification of **its owner,**[H] e.g., if the owner became impure, then it should be left until **its form is decayed and taken out to the place** designated for **burning.** Rabbi Shimon ben Lakish **said to him: This *tanna*,** Rabbi Yishmael, son of Rabbi Yoḥanan ben Beroka, **is** of the same opinion as the ***tanna*** who taught in **the school of Rabba bar Avuh, who said: Even *piggul*,** an offering that was invalidated due to inappropriate intent while being offered, **requires decay of form.** Even with regard to an inherent disqualification in the meat of the offering, where the Torah says explicitly that the offering should be burned, as is the case with regard to *piggul*, the animal should be set aside until the next day, when its form has decayed.

אֵיתִיבֵיהּ: נִטְמָא אוֹ שֶׁנִּפְסַל הַבָּשָׂר, אוֹ שֶׁיָּצָא חוּץ לַקְּלָעִים, רַבִּי אֱלִיעֶזֶר אוֹמֵר: יִזְרוֹק, רַבִּי יְהוֹשֻׁעַ אוֹמֵר: לֹא יִזְרוֹק. וּמוֹדֶה רַבִּי יְהוֹשֻׁעַ שֶׁאִם זָרַק – הוּרְצָה.

Rabbi Yoḥanan **raised** a further **objection to** the opinion of Rabbi Shimon ben Lakish based on another *baraita*, where it is taught: **If the meat became impure or disqualified, or if it was taken out of the walls** that delineate its permitted area, **Rabbi Eliezer says: He sprinkles** the blood of these offerings nonetheless, as in his opinion the blood may be sprinkled regardless of the status of the meat of the offering. **Rabbi Yehoshua says: He does not sprinkle** the blood unless the meat is fit to be brought as an offering. **And Rabbi Yehoshua concedes that if** the blood **was sprinkled,** the offering **is accepted.**[H]

מַאי נִפְסַל – לָאו בְּהֶיסַּח הַדַּעַת? אִי אָמְרַתְּ בִּשְׁלָמָא פְּסוּלֵי טוּמְאָה הָוֵי – הַיְינוּ דְּמַשְׁכַּחַתְּ לַהּ דִּמְרַצֵּי צִיץ. אֶלָּא אִי אָמְרַתְּ פְּסוּל הַגּוּף הָוֵי – אַמַּאי הוּרְצָה (צִיץ)?

The Gemara clarifies: To **what** type of **disqualification** is the *baraita* referring? **Is it not** disqualification on account of **a diversion of attention?** It cannot be a case where it was disqualified due to impurity or being taken outside of the walls, since these are mentioned explicitly. **Granted, if you say** that a diversion of attention is **a disqualification** based on a concern about **ritual impurity, this is** how **you** can **find** a case that the offering is accepted **because the frontplate atones** for cases where there is a disqualification related to ritual impurity.[N] **But if you say that it is an inherent disqualification, why** is the offering **accepted** according to Rabbi Yehoshua, given that it is a disqualified offering?

מַאי נִפְסַל – נִפְסַל בִּטְבוּל יוֹם. אִי הָכִי הַיְינוּ טָמֵא! תְּרֵי גַּוְונֵי טָמֵא.

Rabbi Shimon ben Lakish rejects this interpretation of the *baraita*: No, this is not a case where the offering was disqualified due to a diversion of attention. In **what** way **was** the offering **disqualified?** It was **disqualified due to** contact with **one who immersed himself during the day.** One who immersed himself during the day invalidates items due to ritual impurity. Although these items themselves are invalidated, they cannot in turn render other items ritually impure. The Gemara asks: **If that is so, this is** the same as the disqualification of **ritual impurity.** What, then, is the difference between this disqualification and that of ritual impurity previously mentioned by the *baraita*? The Gemara answers that **two types of ritual impurity** are mentioned here: One type of impurity can also impart impurity to other objects, and a second type can invalidate another object but will not impart impurity.

כִּי סְלֵיק רָבִין אַמְרַהּ לִשְׁמַעְתֵּיהּ קַמֵּיהּ דְּרַבִּי יִרְמְיָה, וַאֲמַר: בַּבְלָאֵי טִפְּשָׁאֵי, מִשּׁוּם דְּיָתְבִי בְּאַרְעָא דַּחֲשׁוֹכָא אָמְרִיתוּן שְׁמַעְתָּתָא דְּמַחְשְׁכוּ! לָא שְׁמִיעַ לְכוּ הָא דְּרַבִּי שִׁמְעוֹן בֶּן לָקִישׁ מִשְּׁמֵיהּ דְּרַבִּי אוֹשַׁעְיָא:

When Ravin ascended to Eretz Yisrael, **he stated** this ***halakha*** of Rav Sheshet **before Rabbi Yirmeya.**[P] **And** Rabbi Yirmeya **said: Foolish Babylonians! Because you dwell in a dark land, you state *halakhot* that are dim. Have you not heard this** statement of **Rabbi Shimon ben Lakish in the name of Rabbi Oshaya?**

HALAKHA

A disqualification in the body of the animal…or its owner – פְּסוּלוֹ בְּגוּפוֹ...וּבִבְעָלִים: Any offering that has a disqualification in the body of the offering must be burned immediately. However, if its disqualification is in its blood or due to its owner, it must be left overnight for its form to decay before being burned (Rambam *Sefer Korbanot*, *Hilkhot Korban Pesaḥ* 4:3).

Meat that was disqualified before the blood was sprinkled – בָּשָׂר שֶׁנִּפְסַל קוֹדֶם זְרִיקָה: If sacrificial meat became disqualified or ritually impure, or if it was removed from its proper domain, the blood may not be sprinkled. If the blood was sprinkled, the offering is accepted. This ruling is in accordance with the opinion of Rabbi Yehoshua, as his opinion is accepted in disputes with Rabbi Eliezer (Rambam *Sefer Avoda*, *Hilkhot Pesulei HaMukdashin* 1:31).

PERSONALITIES

Rabbi Yirmeya – רַבִּי יִרְמְיָה: Rabbi Yirmeya was an *amora* who was born in Babylonia and studied there in his youth, and then moved to Eretz Yisrael. It was only upon his immigration to Eretz Yisrael that he became a prominent scholar. He studied there under the disciples of Rabbi Yoḥanan, particularly Rabbi Zeira and Rabbi Abbahu.

Rabbi Yirmeya was especially sharp and would often question the boundaries of halakhic principles. Due to this he was penalized and even removed from the study hall for a time. His sharp tongue was especially evident when he referred to the *amora'im* of Babylonia as foolish Babylonians, as he did on several occasions. It should be noted that this criticism was humbly accepted by the Babylonian scholars in question.

Rabbi Yirmeya became one of the greatest Sages in Eretz Yisrael, and his statements are cited in many places in both the Jerusalem Talmud and the Babylonian Talmud. In Babylonia, his statements were often preceded by the general phrase for the teachings of scholars from Eretz Yisrael: They say in the West.

NOTES

The atonement of the frontplate – רִיצּוּי צִיץ: The Torah states that by wearing the frontplate on his forehead, "Aaron shall bear the iniquity committed in the holy things which the children of Israel shall sanctify" (Exodus 28:38). The Sages explain that the frontplate does not atone for all sins committed with the offerings in the Temple service; indeed, with regard to some offerings, the Torah states explicitly that they are not accepted. Rather, they explain that this statement applies to specific cases of ritual impurity.

מֵי הֶחָג שֶׁנִּטְמְאוּ, הִשִּׁיקָן וְאַחַר כָּךְ הִקְדִּישָׁן – טְהוֹרִין, הִקְדִּישָׁן וְאַחַר כָּךְ הִשִּׁיקָן – טְמֵאִים.

Rabbi Shimon ben Lakish said in the name of Rabbi Oshaya: With regard to **the water** used for the water libation during the **festival** of Sukkot which was drawn over the course of the day in order to be poured the next day and consequently **became impure,**[N][H] the following distinction applies: If it **was brought into contact**[N] with a ritual bath of pure water and **was then consecrated, it is ritually pure.** However, **if it was consecrated and was then** brought into **contact** with the ritual bath, **it is ritually impure.**

מִכְּדִי, זְרִיעָה נִינְהוּ – מַה לִּי הִשִּׁיקָן וְאַחַר כָּךְ הִקְדִּישָׁן, מַה לִּי הִקְדִּישָׁן וְאַחַר כָּךְ הִשִּׁיקָן? אַלְמָא: אֵין זְרִיעָה לְהֶקְדֵּשׁ. הָכָא נַמִּי: אֵין זְרִיעָה לִתְרוּמָה.

The question arises: **Since** this type of purification **is** similar **to planting,** as when the impure water came in contact with the water of the ritual bath, it is considered as though the water was planted in the ground and thereby purified,[N] **what does it matter if it was** brought into **contact and then consecrated or consecrated and then** brought into **contact? Apparently planting is not** effective with regard **to consecrated items,**[H] i.e., such items are not purified through this process. Therefore, **here too, planting is not** effective with regard **to *teruma*.** Despite the fact that planting is generally effective in removing the impure status of the water, the Sages imposed higher standards with regard to consecrated items. Similarly, the Sages imposed higher standards for removing the *teruma* status of the plants. One can explain that the produce grown from *teruma* mentioned in the *baraita* remains prohibited for non-priests because it is still considered *teruma*.

יְתֵיב רַב דִּימִי וְקָאָמַר לַהּ לְהָא שְׁמַעְתָּא. אֲמַר לֵיהּ אַבָּיֵי: הִקְדִּישָׁן בִּכְלִי קָאָמַר, אֲבָל בְּפֶה לָא עֲבוּד רַבָּנַן מַעֲלָה, אוֹ דִּילְמָא בְּפֶה נַמִּי עֲבוּד רַבָּנַן מַעֲלָה?

Rav Dimi sat and said this *halakha* that was stated by Rav Oshaya with regard to principle of bringing liquid into contact with a ritual bath. **Abaye said to him: Did** Rav Oshaya state his ruling that bringing a liquid into contact with a ritual bath is not effective for consecrated items with regard to a case where **he consecrated** the water by placing it **in a sacred vessel, but** if he consecrated it **through speech then the Sages did not impose a higher** standard, in which case the water can be purified by being brought into contact with a ritual bath? **Or perhaps the Sages imposed a higher** standard in a case **where** one consecrates it **through speech as well?**

אֲמַר לֵיהּ: זוֹ לֹא שָׁמַעְתִּי, כַּיּוֹצֵא בָּהּ שָׁמַעְתִּי. דְּאָמַר רַבִּי אַבָּהוּ אָמַר רַבִּי יוֹחָנָן: עֲנָבִים שֶׁנִּטְמְאוּ, דְּרָכָן וְאַחַר כָּךְ הִקְדִּישָׁן – טְהוֹרִים, הִקְדִּישָׁן וְאַחַר כָּךְ דְּרָכָן – טְמֵאִין. וְהָא עֲנָבִים, דִּקְדוּשַּׁת פֶּה נִינְהוּ – וַאֲפִילּוּ הָכִי עֲבוּד רַבָּנַן מַעֲלָה.

Rav Dimi **said to him: I did not hear** the *halakha* with regard to **this** case; however, **I heard** the *halakha* with regard to **a similar case. As Rabbi Abbahu said that Rabbi Yoḥanan said:** With regard to **grapes that became ritually impure, if one trod on them and afterward consecrated them, they are pure.**[H] According to this opinion, the wine inside the grape does not become impure from the grape itself. However, if **he consecrated** the grapes **and afterward pressed them, they are impure,** because the *halakha* is especially stringent with regard consecrated items. **And yet** with regard to **grapes which are** only **consecrated through speech,** as the wine/grapes offered on the altar are not brought in a sacred vessel, **even so, the Sages imposed a higher** standard such that these grapes become impure after they have been consecrated.

אֲמַר רַב יוֹסֵף: עֲנָבִים קָאָמְרַתְּ – הָכָא בַּעֲנָבִים שֶׁל תְּרוּמָה עָסְקִינַן, דִּקְדוּשַּׁת פֶּה דִּידְהוּ כִּקְדוּשַּׁת כְּלִי דָּמְיָא. אֲבָל הָנֵי דִּבְעֵי כְּלִי – בְּפֶה לָא עֲבוּד רַבָּנַן מַעֲלָה

Rav Yosef said: This case does not serve as a proof since **you spoke of grapes, and here we are dealing with grapes of *teruma*, whose consecration through speech is comparable to consecration in a** sacred **vessel,** as *teruma* cannot be consecrated by being placed in a sacred vessel. **However,** with regard to **those** items **that require a** sacred **vessel** in order to be fully consecrated, such as water used for a libation, **the Sages did not impose a higher** standard in a case where one consecrated it **through speech.** Therefore, this case cannot be used to resolve Abaye's question.

״דְּרָכָן״ – וַאֲפִילּוּ טוּבָא. וּמִי אָמַר רַבִּי יוֹחָנָן הָכִי? וְהָאָמַר רַבִּי יוֹחָנָן: עֲנָבִים שֶׁנִּטְמְאוּ – דּוֹרְכָן פָּחוֹת פָּחוֹת מִכְּבֵיצָה!

The Gemara asks about Rabbi Yoḥanan's statement with regard to wine pressed from impure grapes: The phrase **if one tread upon them** is stated without qualification, indicating that the wine is ritually pure **even** if he pressed **many** grapes at once. **And did Rabbi Yoḥanan** actually **say this? Didn't Rabbi Yoḥanan say:** With regard to **grapes that became ritually impure grapes, one** should **tread on them less than an egg-bulk at a time.** When there is less than an egg-bulk of grapes, they do not impart ritual impurity.

NOTES

The water libation during the festival became impure – מֵי הֶחָג שֶׁנִּטְמְאוּ: Rashi explains that this would come about on the Shabbat that occurs during Sukkot, when there was no possibility of refilling the vessel with water from the Shilo'aḥ spring. Others explain that this scenario could occur any time during the Festival, as the drawing of this water was performed with great ceremony and involved significant toil. Consequently it was preferable, if possible, to purify the water rather than repeat the process of drawing the water.

Bringing into contact – הַשָּׁקָה: Purifying water by bringing it into contact with a ritual bath is performed in the following manner: The water is placed in vessels that are not susceptible to ritual impurity, e.g., stone vessels, and the vessels are placed within the ritual bath so that the water of the ritual bath will come into contact with the water inside the vessel. This procedure was performed to purify water for drinking or cooking when the water in the ritual bath itself was unfit for drinking, such as is the case with seawater.

Bringing into contact with a ritual bath and planting – הַשָּׁקָה וּזְרִיעָה: The equation between these concepts is not straightforward. Based on Rabbeinu Ḥananel's explanation, it appears that the similarity between these two concepts is external, in that planting a seed in the ground resembles immersing a vessel in water. However, it seems that the basic concept that applies in both cases is not purification through immersion but purification through nullification. Just as a seed planted in the ground loses its previous form, so too, the water in the vessel becomes nullified by the water in the ritual bath.

HALAKHA

The water libation during the festival became impure – מֵי הֶחָג שֶׁנִּטְמְאוּ: If water collected for use in the water libation on the altar becomes ritually impure and is brought into contact with a ritual bath, the following distinction applies: If it is purified before it is consecrated, it may be poured out for the libation; however, if it is purified after it was consecrated, it may not be poured out for the libation, in accordance with the opinion of Rabbi Oshaya (Rambam *Sefer Avoda*, *Hilkhot Issurei Mizbe'aḥ* 6:6).

Planting…consecrated items – זְרִיעָה...הֶקְדֵּשׁ: That which grows from consecrated seeds that became impure may not be brought as an offering, as the Sages imposed higher standards for consecrated items in this regard (Rambam *Sefer Avoda*, *Hilkhot Issurei Mizbe'aḥ* 6:8).

Treading on ritually impure grapes – דְּרִיכַת עֲנָבִים שֶׁנִּטְמְאוּ: If ritually impure grapes were pressed before *teruma* was separated, it is permitted to separate *teruma* from the wine afterward. However, if *teruma* was taken first, the grapes should be pressed in quantities of less than an egg-bulk at a time so that the priests will be permitted to drink the wine (Rambam *Sefer Zera'im*, *Hilkhot Terumot* 12:11).

NOTES

Third degree ritual impurity – שְׁלִישִׁי: The further removed an object is from contact with the initial source of ritual impurity, the lower its own level of ritual impurity. An object that comes in contact with the source will have first-degree ritual impurity, any food that object touches will in turn have second-degree ritual impurity, and so on.

Degree of ritual impurity based on contact with ritually impure items

אִיבָּעֵית אֵימָא: הָכָא נַמִּי – פָּחוֹת פָּחוֹת מִכַּבֵּיצָה. וְאִיבָּעֵית אֵימָא: הָתָם – דְּנָגְעוּ לְהוּ בְּרִאשׁוֹן, דְּהָווּ לְהוּ אִינְהוּ שֵׁנִי, הָכָא – דְּנָגְעוּ בְּשֵׁנִי, דְּהָווּ לְהוּ שְׁלִישִׁי.

The Gemara answers: **If you wish, say** this answer: **Here, too,** it is to be understood that one must tread on **less than an egg-bulk at a time. And if you wish, say** this answer instead: **There,** where the Gemara requires less than an egg-bulk, it is a case where the grapes **came into contact** with an item that was impure with **first**-degree ritual impurity, such **that they became** impure with **second**-degree ritual impurity. When a liquid touches an object that is impure with second-degree ritual impurity, it becomes impure by rabbinic decree with first-degree ritual impurity. Therefore, in that case one must be careful to tread only on less than an egg-bulk at a time. **Here,** it is speaking of a case where **they came into contact** with an item that was impure with **second**-degree ritual impurity, such **that they became** impure with **third**-degree ritual impurity.[N] In that case, the liquid that comes out of the grapes would not become ritually impure at all.

אָמַר רָבָא: אַף אֲנַן נַמִּי תָּנֵינָא ״וְנָתַן עָלָיו מַיִם חַיִּים אֶל כֶּלִי״ – שֶׁתְּהֵא חִיּוּתָן בַּכְּלִי. ״וְנָתַן״ – אַלְמָא תְּלוּשִׁין נִינְהוּ, וְהָא מְחוּבָּרִין נִינְהוּ!

Rava said: We, too, have learned that the Sages created higher standards with regard to consecrated items. As it was taught that the verse says with regard to the red heifer: "And for the impure they shall take the ashes of the burning of the sin-offering, **and he shall put flowing water into a vessel**" (Numbers 19:17), which teaches that the flowing water from the spring **should flow** directly **into the vessel** in which it will be sanctified. On the other hand, the verse says **"and he shall put,"** meaning that the water should be poured into the vessel. **Apparently** the water **is detached,**[N] **but it is** clearly **attached** to the spring, as it was previously stated that the water must flow directly into the vessel.

NOTES

Apparently the water is detached – אַלְמָא תְּלוּשִׁין: See *Tosafot*, who mention another explanation of this statement, suggested by Rabbeinu Ḥananel: This statement means that despite the fact that the waters of the purification offering are physically connected to the spring, they should be considered detached for the purposes of the *halakhot* of ritual impurity. In his commentary on tractate *Para*, Rabbi Shimshon of Saens notes at least one difficulty with this explanation. If one accepts this explanation, then the stringent ruling is not based on a higher standard imposed by the Sages but dictated by the Torah itself. Although Rashi's position is difficult for other reasons, it appears to fit better within the context of the discussion here.

Perek **II**
Daf **35** Amud **a**

HALAKHA

Eating tithes in a state of purity – אֲכִילַת מַעֲשֵׂר בְּטׇהֳרָה: This is referring to the second tithe. One who eats second tithe while he is in a state of ritual impurity is flogged for violating a Torah prohibition. Once he has immersed, he may eat second tithe immediately, without waiting for the sun to set (Rambam *Sefer Zera'im, Hilkhot Ma'aser Sheni* 3:1–4).

One who immersed himself during the day with regard to *teruma* – טְבוּל יוֹם בִּתְרוּמָה: One who immersed himself during the day may not eat *teruma* until the sun has set (Rambam *Sefer Zera'im, Hilkhot Terumot* 7:2).

אֶלָּא מַעֲלָה, הָכִי נַמִּי – מַעֲלָה.

Rather, this is merely **a higher standard,** as by Torah law the water may be drawn with one vessel and sanctified in another vessel. The Sages added that this water must be sanctified in the same vessel in which it was drawn from the spring, and they found support for their opinion in the Torah. **Here too,** the Sages established **a higher standard** for a consecrated object that became ritually impure, as they decreed that it cannot be ritually purified through insertion in the ground.

אֲמַר רַב שִׁימִי בַּר אַשִׁי, אַף אֲנַן נַמִּי תָּנֵינָא: טָבַל וְעָלָה – אוֹכֵל בְּמַעֲשֵׂר. הֶעֱרִיב שִׁמְשׁוֹ – אוֹכֵל בִּתְרוּמָה. בִּתְרוּמָה – אִין, בְּקֳדָשִׁים – לָא. אַמַּאי? טָהוֹר הוּא! אֶלָּא: מַעֲלָה, הָכִי נַמִּי – מַעֲלָה.

Rav Shimi bar Ashi said: We, too, learned a similar statement in a *baraita*: When the period of ritual impurity of a *zav* or leper has been completed, and he **immersed** during the day **and emerged,** he may **eat tithes** immediately.[H] Once **the sun set for him, he** may **eat *teruma*.**[H] Rav Shimi bar Ashi infers from this statement: **With regard to *teruma*, yes,** he may eat it; however, **with regard to consecrated** food, **no,** he may not. Given that conclusion, Rav Shimi bar Ashi asks: **Why** is there a difference between *teruma* and consecrated foods? After all, **he is ritually pure. Rather,** the Sages established a **higher standard** for consecrated food, and permitted one to eat them only after sacrificing the requisite purification offering. **Here too,** the Sages established **a higher standard** for the ritual purity of consecrated liquids.

אֲמַר רַב אַשִׁי, אַף אֲנַן נַמִי תָּנֵינָא: ״וְהַבָּשָׂר״ – לְרַבּוֹת אֶת הָעֵצִים וּלְבוֹנָה. עֵצִים וּלְבוֹנָה בְּנֵי אִיטַּמּוּיֵי נִינְהוּ? אֶלָּא מַעֲלָה, הָכָא נַמִי – מַעֲלָה.

Rav Ashi said: We, too, learned another case where the Sages established a higher standard. The verse says: "And the flesh that touches any ritually impure thing shall not be eaten; it shall be burnt with fire. And as for the flesh, anyone who is ritually pure may eat from it" (Leviticus 7:19). **And the flesh** comes **to include the wood** in the Temple **and the frankincense.**[H] The Gemara asks: **Do wood and frankincense** have the **capacity to become ritually impure,** given that they are neither food nor drink? **Rather,** the Sages established **a higher standard** for these objects due to their sanctity; **here too,** the Sages established **a higher standard** for the ritual purity of consecrated liquids.

מתני׳ אֵלּוּ דְּבָרִים שֶׁאָדָם יוֹצֵא בָּהֶן יְדֵי חוֹבָתוֹ בְּפֶסַח: בַּחִטִּים, בַּשְּׂעוֹרִים, בַּכּוּסְּמִין, וּבַשִּׁיפוֹן, וּבְשִׁיבּוֹלֶת שׁוּעָל. וְיוֹצְאִין בִּדְמַאי וּבְמַעֲשֵׂר רִאשׁוֹן שֶׁנִּטְּלָה תְּרוּמָתוֹ, וּבְמַעֲשֵׂר שֵׁנִי וְהֶקְדֵּשׁ שֶׁנִּפְדּוּ, וְהַכֹּהֲנִים בְּחַלָּה וּבִתְרוּמָה,

MISHNA These are the types of grain **with which a person fulfills his obligation** to eat *matza* **on the** first night of **Passover: With wheat, with barley, with spelt** [*kusmin*],[B] **with rye** [*shifon*],[B] **and with oats** [*shibbolet shu'al*].[HNB] **And one fulfills** his obligation by eating not only *matza* made from properly tithed grains, but even **with** *matza* made from **doubtfully tithed produce, and** *matza* made **with first tithe from which its** *teruma* **was** already **taken,** or **second tithe and consecrated food that were redeemed. And priests** may eat *matza* prepared **from** *ḥalla,* the portion of dough that is given to priests, **or with** *teruma,* as priests are permitted to eat these portions.

אֲבָל לֹא בְּטֶבֶל, וְלֹא בְּמַעֲשֵׂר רִאשׁוֹן שֶׁלֹּא נִטְּלָה תְּרוּמָתוֹ, וְלֹא בְּמַעֲשֵׂר שֵׁנִי וְהֶקְדֵּשׁ שֶׁלֹּא נִפְדּוּ. חַלּוֹת הַתּוֹדָה וּרְקִיקֵי נָזִיר, עֲשָׂאָן לְעַצְמוֹ – אֵין יוֹצֵא בָּהֶן, עֲשָׂאָן לִמְכּוֹר בַּשּׁוּק – יוֹצְאִין בָּהֶן.

However, one may **not** fulfill one's obligation to eat *matza* made **with untithed produce, nor with** *matza* made from the **first tithe from which its** *teruma* **was not separated, nor with** *matza* made either from the **second tithe, nor** from **consecrated** grain **that was not redeemed.** With regard to one who prepared **loaves of** *matza* that are brought with **a thanks-offering,** or to the **wafers** brought **by a nazirite,**[N] the Sages drew the following distinction: If **he prepared them for himself,** then he **does not fulfill** his obligation to eat *matza* **with them.** However, if **he prepared them to sell them in the market** to those who require these loaves or wafers, **one fulfills** the obligation to eat *matza* **with them.**

HALAKHA

Impurity of wood and frankincense – טוּמְאַת עֵצִים וּלְבוֹנָה: Although the wood and frankincense of the Temple are not foods and therefore cannot become ritually impure by Torah law, the Sages instituted a higher standard with regard to them. Consequently, if a ritually impure object touches them they are disqualified for sacrificial use (Rambam *Sefer Avoda, Hilkhot Issurei Mizbe'aḥ* 6:8).

Grains that can be used for *matza* – דְּגָנִים לְמַצָּה: One can fulfill his obligation to eat *matza* with *matza* prepared from one of the following types of grain: Wheat, spelt, barley, rye, and oats, as stated in the mishna. The practice is to use *matza* prepared from wheat flour, *ab initio* (Rema, based on the Maharil; Rav Ya'akov HaLevi Molin; *Shulḥan Arukh, Oraḥ Ḥayyim* 453:1).

NOTES

Five types of grain – חֲמֵשֶׁת מִינֵי דָּגָן: In the Jerusalem Talmud, it is stated that the five types of grain are derived from the *halakhot* of *ḥalla*. The Gemara there adds that the verse: "And put in wheat, *sora*, barley, *nisman*, and spelt as its border" (Isaiah 28:25) is a homiletic allusion to this list. *Sora* is interpreted as oats, *nisman* is rye, while the phrase "its border" means the limit of what is considered bread.

Loaves of a thanks-offering or wafers brought by a nazirite – חַלּוֹת הַתּוֹדָה וּרְקִיקֵי נָזִיר: Four types of bread are brought with a thanks-offering, three of which are types of *matza*, namely, wafers, loaves, and flour mixed with water and oil. The fourth type consists of loaves of leavened bread. Since the loaves contain very little oil, they are not considered rich, enhanced *matza*. Likewise, the wafers of a nazirite contain only a small amount of oil (Rabbeinu Yehonatan).

BACKGROUND

Spelt [*kusmin*] – כּוּסְּמִין: Spelt, called *kusemet* in the Bible, is identified as the species *Triticum spelta* L. This grain was cultivated in Israel and the surrounding region.

Spelt is similar to wheat both in the manner of its growth and in its appearance; nevertheless, it can be distinguished by its two rows in every stalk, which contain seeds tightly connected to the chaff. The cultivation of this species is fairly uncommon both due to the difficulty involved in separating the chaff from the grain and because its stalk can easily crumble into small pieces.

Stalks of spelt

Rye [*shifon*] – שִׁיפוֹן: The identification of the species *shifon* is the subject of considerable debate. According to Rashi, it is a species of grain that is neither wheat nor barley, but *Secale cereale*, rye, a type of grain cultivated in Europe. Other commentaries suggest that it is a kind of wild wheat, while yet others claim it is actually the grain known nowadays as oats, *Avena sativa*, a tall winter grain that grows up to 1–2 m in height, whose flowers are arranged in clusters.

In Israel, this grain was used primarily as animal fodder. It was only in northern Europe that people began to consume it on a large scale, either as porridge or ground into flour and mixed with other grains in the production of bread.

Stalks of rye

Oats [*shibbolet shu'al*] – שִׁבּוֹלֶת שׁוּעָל: The identification of *shibbolet shu'al* is a matter of debate among the commentaries and the scholars, and many different suggestions have been put forward. Rashi and many other commentaries identify this grain as *Avenu sterilis*, oats, which is the meaning of *shibbolet shu'al* in modern Hebrew. However, others maintain that this plant is more likely a type of domesticated barley, perhaps *Hordeum sativum*. Although it is infrequently cultivated today, *Hordeum sativum* is sometimes used in the production of beer due to its high sugar content. Yet others suggest that *shibbolet shu'al* may actually be a type of wild barley, perhaps *Hordeum spontaneum*, a small plant found in Israel whose grain can be used to produce flour.

Oats

גמ׳ תנא: כוסמין מין חיטין, שיבולת שועל ושיפון – מין שעורין, כוסמין – גולבא, שיפון – דישרא, שיבולת שועל – שבילי תעלא. הני – אין, אורז ודוחן – לא.

GEMARA

The Gemara identifies the species mentioned in the mishna. One of the Sages **taught** in the *Tosefta*: **Spelt is a type of wheat, while oats** [*shibbolet shu'al*] **and rye** [*shifon*] **are a type of barley.** The Gemara translates the lesser-known species into the vernacular Aramaic: **Spelt** is called ***gulba***; **rye is *dishra***; and **oats are *shevilei ta'ala*.** The Gemara infers: **These** species, **yes,** they may be used for *matza*; however, **rice** [*orez*][B] **and millet** [*doḥan*],[BH] **no,** they may not be used.

מנהני מילי? אמר רבי שמעון בן לקיש, וכן תנא דבי רבי ישמעאל, וכן תנא דבי רבי אליעזר בן יעקב: אמר קרא ״לא תאכל עליו חמץ שבעת ימים תאכל עליו מצות״ דברים הבאים לידי חימוץ – אדם יוצא בהן ידי חובתו במצה, יצאו אלו שאין באין לידי חימוץ אלא לידי סירחון.

The Gemara asks: **From where are these matters,** that *matza* cannot be prepared from rice or millet, **derived? Rabbi Shimon ben Lakish said, and likewise** a Sage **of the school of Rabbi Yishmael taught, and likewise** a Sage **of the school of Rabbi Eliezer ben Ya'akov taught** that **the verse states: "You shall eat no leavened bread with it; seven days you shall eat with it *matza*,** the bread of affliction" (Deuteronomy 16:3). This verse indicates that only with **substances which will come to** a state of **leavening, a person fulfills his obligation to** eat ***matza* with them,** provided he prevents them from becoming leavened. This **excludes these** foods, i.e., rice, millet, and similar grains, **which,** even if flour is prepared from them and water is added to their flour, **do not come to** a state of **leavening but to** a state of **decay** [*siraḥon*].[N]

מתניתין דלא כרבי יוחנן בן נורי, דאמר: אורז מין דגן הוא, וחייבין על חימוצו כרת. דתניא: רבי יוחנן בן נורי אוסר באורז ודוחן, מפני שקרוב להחמיץ.

The Gemara notes: **The mishna is not in accordance with** the opinion of **Rabbi Yoḥanan ben Nuri, who said: Rice is** a full-fledged **type of grain, and one is liable** to receive ***karet* for** eating it in **its leavened** state, like other types of grain.[N] **As it was taught** in a *baraita*: **Rabbi Yoḥanan ben Nuri prohibits** eating cooked **rice and millet** on Passover, **due to** the fact **that they are close to being leavened.**

איבעיא להו: ״שקרוב להחמיץ״ – דקדים ומחמיץ, או דילמא ״קרוב להחמיץ״ הוי, חמץ גמור – לא הוי.

A dilemma was raised before the scholars who were studying this issue. What is the meaning of the expression: **That it is close to becoming leavened?** Does this mean **that it will be leavened** even **quicker** than wheat or barley? **Or** does it **perhaps** mean that **it is** only **close to being leavened,** i.e., it resembles leavened bread, but **it is not full-fledged leavened bread.** In other words, perhaps Rabbi Yoḥanan ben Nuri maintains that these grains cannot in fact become full-fledged leavened bread, and one is not punished with *karet* for eating them on Passover. However, he rules that one should nevertheless avoid eating them, due to their similarity to leavened bread.

BACKGROUND

Rice [*orez*] – אורז: Rice, *Oryza sativa*, is an annual plant from the grain family. It can grow as high as 1 m and is cultivated mostly in swamps or irrigated summer ponds. When inside their shells, rice grains are ordinarily yellow, although some strains are red.

Rice originated in the Far East, but by the mishnaic period it had been imported to Israel and was cultivated there as well.

Rice was used primarily in porridge, as its lack of gluten renders it virtually impossible to be formed into bread. Numerous attempts have been made to develop strains of rice from which bread can be prepared. Apparently, although rice does rise somewhat, it does not become leavened like wheat or barley.

Like millet, rice is classified as grain by botanical definitions; however, it is not a bread grain, in contrast to the species of grain mentioned in the mishna.

Rice plant

Millet [*doḥan*] – דוחן: The identification of *doḥan* is also debated by the commentaries and the scholars. The most commonly accepted opinion identifies it as the grain *Panicum miliaceum*. This plant grows to a height of 1–1.5 m, and its flowers are contained within long panicles. Its small seeds, 2–3 mm in diameter, are yellow or gold. Nowadays this grain is mainly used as animal fodder or as porridge. Although flour prepared from this grain cannot be used to form bread, it is sometimes added to bread made from other types of grain.

Millet stalks

HALAKHA

Rice and millet – אורז ודוחן: Rice, millet, and other grains similar to the five types are all considered *kitniyot*, legumes, with which one may not fulfill the obligation to eat *matza*. This ruling is in accordance with the majority opinion of the Rabbis, contrary to Rabbi Yoḥanan ben Nuri. Since we accept the Gemara's assertion that these other species do not become leavened, it is even permitted to cook them during Passover. However, some authorities prohibit doing so out of concern that one might mistakenly mingle one of the forbidden five types of grain with them (*Tur*; *Hagahot Maimoniyot*; *Mordekhai*). The common practice in Ashkenazi communities is not to eat any type of *kitniyot* during Passover. However, other communities maintain different customs. Some are not concerned about these stringencies at all. Others have a tradition to refrain from eating rice and millet, but they eat other types of *kitniyot*. Various other customs and traditions are observed in different locales (*Shulḥan Arukh*, *Oraḥ Ḥayyim* 453:1).

NOTES

To a state of decay [*siraḥon*] – לידי סירחון: Some commentaries explain that the word *siraḥon* in this context is related to the phrase "the overlapping excess [*seraḥ ha'odef*]" (Exodus 26:12). That is, the bread will not rise but there will be some excess matter due to the fermentation (Rav Yehuda ben Rav Binyamin HaRofeh).

The opinions of Rabbi Yoḥanan ben Nuri and the Rabbis – שיטות רבי יוחנן בן נורי וחכמים: In the Jerusalem Talmud, it is stated that the identification of certain species of grain that are fit for *matza* was based on an examination performed by the Sages to determine whether or not the flour produced from these grains will be leavened. Accordingly, the dispute between Rabbi Yoḥanan ben Nuri and the Rabbis is about whether or not the fermentation process of certain grains can be defined as leavening.

תָּא שְׁמַע, דְּתַנְיָא, אָמַר רַבִּי יוֹחָנָן בֶּן נוּרִי: אוֹרֶז מִין דָּגָן הוּא, וְחַיָּיבִין עַל חִימּוּצוֹ כָּרֵת, וְאָדָם יוֹצֵא בּוֹ יְדֵי חוֹבָתוֹ בַּפֶּסַח.

The Gemara responds: **Come and hear** a resolution to this question, **as it was taught** in a *baraita* that **Rabbi Yoḥanan ben Nuri said: Rice is** a full-fledged **type of grain.** Therefore, **one is liable** to receive ***karet*** **for** eating it in **its leavened** state, **and a person** can **fulfill his obligation** to eat *matza* **with it on Passover.** This *baraita* clearly indicates that, according to the opinion of Rabbi Yoḥanan ben Nuri, rice becomes leavened like other grains, and the expression: It is close to becoming leavened, means that it becomes leavened quicker than other grains.

וְכֵן הָיָה רַבִּי יוֹחָנָן בֶּן נוּרִי אוֹמֵר: קְרָמִית חַיֶּיבֶת בַּחַלָּה. מַאי קְרָמִית? אָמַר אַבַּיֵי: שִׁיצָנִיתָא. מַאי שִׁיצָנִיתָא? אָמַר רַב פָּפָּא: שִׁיצָנִיתָא דְּמִשְׁתַּכְחָא בֵּינֵי כַּלָּנִיתָא.

And so too, Rabbi Yoḥanan ben Nuri would say: One who has prepared bread from ***keramit***, a type of wild wheat, is **obligated to** separate ***ḥalla***, just as he must separate *ḥalla* from dough prepared of other types of grain. The Gemara asks: **What is *keramit*? Abaye said:** It is a plant called ***shitzanita***. Since this name was not widely known either, the Gemara asks: **What is *shitzanita*?**[BN] **Rav Pappa said: This is the wild grain that is found between papyrus reeds.**[B]

אָמַר רַבָּה בַּר בַּר חָנָה אָמַר רֵישׁ לָקִישׁ: עִיסָּה שֶׁנִּילּוֹשָׁה בְּיַיִן וְשֶׁמֶן וּדְבַשׁ – אֵין חַיָּיבִין עַל חִימּוּצָהּ כָּרֵת. יְתֵיב רַב פָּפָּא וְרַב הוּנָא בְּרֵיהּ דְּרַב יְהוֹשֻׁעַ קַמֵּיהּ דְּרַב אִידִי בַּר אָבִין, וִיתֵיב רַב אִידִי בַּר אָבִין וְקָא מְנַמְנֵם. אָמַר לֵיהּ רַב הוּנָא בְּרֵיהּ דְּרַב יְהוֹשֻׁעַ לְרַב פָּפָּא: מַאי טַעְמָא דְּרֵישׁ לָקִישׁ?

Rabba bar bar Ḥana said that **Reish Lakish said:** With regard to **dough that was kneaded with wine, oil, or honey, one is not liable** to receive ***karet*** **for** eating it in **its leavened** state, since these liquids will not cause the dough to be leavened. **Rav Pappa and Rav Huna, son of Rav Yehoshua, were sitting before Rav Idi bar Avin, and Rav Idi bar Avin was sitting and dozing** as his students conversed. **Rav Huna, son of Rav Yehoshua, said to Rav Pappa: What is the reason of Reish Lakish,** who maintains that one is not liable to receive *karet* for this type of leavening?

אָמַר לֵיהּ: דְּאָמַר קְרָא ״לֹא תֹאכַל עָלָיו חָמֵץ [וגו׳]״ דְּבָרִים שֶׁאָדָם יוֹצֵא בָּהֶן יְדֵי חוֹבָתוֹ בְּמַצָּה – חַיָּיבִין עַל חִימּוּצוֹ כָּרֵת. וְהָא, הוֹאִיל וְאֵין אָדָם יוֹצֵא בָּהּ יְדֵי חוֹבָתוֹ, דְּהָוְיָא לֵיהּ מַצָּה עֲשִׁירָה – אֵין חַיָּיבִין עַל חִימּוּצָהּ כָּרֵת.

Rav Pappa **said to him: The verse states: "You shall eat no leavened bread with it; seven days you shall eat with it *matza*"** (Deuteronomy 16:3). In light of the juxtaposition of leavened bread and *matza*, Reish Lakish compares these two types of bread: With regard to those **substances** through **which a person fulfills his obligation to** eat ***matza***, **one is liable** to receive ***karet*** **for** eating them in their **leavened** state. **And** with regard to **this** dough, which was kneaded with wine, oil, or honey, **since a person does not fulfill his obligation** to eat *matza* **with it,** as **it is** called **rich,** i.e., enhanced, ***matza***,[H] **one is not liable** to receive ***karet*** **for** eating it in **its leavened** state on Passover. *Matza* is called the bread of affliction, or the poor man's bread, a description that does not apply to dough prepared with wine, oil, or honey.

אֵיתִיבֵיהּ רַב הוּנָא בְּרֵיהּ דְּרַב יְהוֹשֻׁעַ לְרַב פָּפָּא: הִמְחָהוּ וּגְמָעוֹ, אִם חָמֵץ הוּא – עָנוּשׁ כָּרֵת, וְאִם מַצָּה הוּא – אֵין אָדָם יוֹצֵא יְדֵי חוֹבָתוֹ בַּפֶּסַח. וְהָא הָכָא, דְּאֵין אָדָם יוֹצֵא יְדֵי חוֹבָתוֹ בְּמַצָּה, וְחַיָּיבִין עַל חִימּוּצוֹ כָּרֵת!

Rav Huna, son of Rav Yehoshua, raised an objection to Rav Pappa: We learned with regard to one who took a baked item, **dissolved it in water, and swallowed** this mixture on Passover: **If** the baked item **is leavened bread,** he is **punished with *karet*; and if it is *matza*, a person does not fulfill his obligation** to eat *matza* **on Passover** with this food. The reason one does not fulfill the obligation to eat *matza* is because swallowing in this manner is not considered an act of eating. **But here** this is a case **where a person does not fulfill his obligation to** eat ***matza*** with this dissolved food, **and** nevertheless **he is liable** to receive ***karet*** **for** eating it in **its leavened** state. This ruling conflicts with Rav Pappa's general principle.

אִיתְּעַר בְּהוּ רַב אִידִי בַּר אָבִין, אֲמַר לְהוּ: דַּרְדְּקֵי, הַיְינוּ טַעְמָא דְּרֵישׁ לָקִישׁ: מִשּׁוּם דְּהָווּ לְהוּ מֵי פֵירוֹת,

At this point **Rav Idi bar Avin woke up,** due to their discussion, **and said to them: Children, this is the reasoning of Reish Lakish:** One is not liable to receive *karet* for eating dough kneaded with oil or honey, **because** oil and honey **are** considered **fruit juices,**

BACKGROUND

Shitzanita **– שִׁיצָנִיתָא:** The *ge'onim* call this produce *kormei de'agma*, an Aramaic name that is apparently a reference to *Glyceria fluitans*, water mannagrass, from the grain family. This perennial plant grows in areas that are covered in water. It can grow up to 1 m in height, while its leaves can be as wide as 10 cm. Although its stalks are moist and edible, water mannagrass is normally used as a high-quality animal fodder.

The grains of this plant are also edible, especially as a porridge that was known for its pleasant taste. In some places, there was a significant demand for this grain. The fact that this species is from the grain family is probably the reason for the discussion as to whether or not it is considered like other bread grains, as Rabbi Yoḥanan ben Nuri maintains that it is considered a bread grain with regard to the halakhot of leavened bread and *ḥalla*.

Water mannagrass

Papyrus reeds – כַּלָּנִיתָא: This is apparently the *Cyperus papyrus*, from the reed family. This grass-like perennial plant grows stems 2–5 m tall, with web-like clusters of small shoots sprouting from its edge. This plant can be found in swamps throughout Israel and the surrounding region. Its roots descend deep into the water, with new stems sprouting every year. These reeds were used in the construction of rafts and in forming papyrus paper. Although the root stems are also edible, nowadays they are mostly used in the production of mats.

Papyrus reeds

HALAKHA

Rich *matza* – מַצָּה עֲשִׁירָה: Dough kneaded with any liquid other than water is not considered leavened bread and may be eaten on Passover. However, one cannot fulfill his obligation to eat *matza* by consuming this so-called rich *matza* (*Shulḥan Arukh*, *Oraḥ Ḥayyim* 462:1).

NOTES

What is *shitzanita* – מַאי שִׁיצָנִיתָא: Some commentaries explain this discussion as follows: The Sages first noted that *keramit* is *shitzanita*, a species of wild grain. They then inquired what particular type of wild grain it is, to which Rav Pappa replied that it is the wild grain that grows between the papyrus reeds (Rav Ya'akov Emden).

Rashi brings two alternative definitions of *shitzanita*: *Nigella sativa*, an annual flowering plant indigenous to the Near East, which produces black seeds that can be used as a spice; and darnel, *Lolium temulentum*, a weed that grows in wheat fields and is similar in appearance to wheat.

וּמֵי פֵירוֹת אֵין מַחְמִיצִין.

and fruit juice[H] **does not** cause dough to be **leavened.** Therefore, dough prepared with these liquids is not considered full-fledged leavened bread.

"יוֹצֵא בִּדְמַאי וּבְמַעֲשֵׂר וכו'". דְּמַאי?! הָא לָא חֲזֵי לֵיהּ! כֵּיוָן דְּאִי בָּעֵי מַפְקַר לְנִכְסֵיהּ הָוֵי עָנִי וְאוֹכֵל דְּמַאי – הַשְׁתָּא נַמִי חֲזֵי לֵיהּ.

The Gemara turns to the cases of the mishna. The mishna taught that one can **fulfill** his obligation to eat *matza* **with doubtfully tithed produce**[H] **and** with produce **of the first tithe,** from which *teruma* has been separated. The Gemara asks: Can one really fulfill his obligation with **doubtfully tithed produce?** It is **not suitable for him** to eat. The Sages prohibited the eating of doubtfully tithed produce that has not been tithed. The Gemara answers: **Since, if one** so **desires** he may **renounce** all **his property,** thereby becoming a poor person who is permitted to eat doubtfully tithed produce, **now too it is suitable for him,** even though he did not declare his property ownerless. Consequently, if he used doubtfully tithed produce as *matza,* he has fulfilled the mitzva after the fact.

דִּתְנַן: מַאֲכִילִין אֶת הָעֲנִיִּים דְּמַאי וְאֶת אַכְסַנְיָא דְּמַאי. וְאָמַר רַב הוּנָא: תָּנָא, בֵּית שַׁמַּאי אוֹמְרִים: אֵין מַאֲכִילִין אֶת הָעֲנִיִּים דְּמַאי וְאֶת הָאַכְסַנְיָא דְּמַאי, וּבֵית הִלֵּל אוֹמְרִים: מַאֲכִילִין.

As we learned in a mishna: One may **feed the poor doubtfully tithed produce, and** he may also feed Jewish **soldiers** [***akhsanya***][NL] who lodge with him **doubtfully tithed produce.**[H] **And Rav Huna said** that it **was taught** that **Beit Shammai say:** One may **neither feed the poor doubtfully tithed produce, nor** feed **soldiers doubtfully tithed produce. And Beit Hillel say:** One may **feed** these groups doubtfully tithed produce. This mishna indicates that doubtfully tithed produce is not prohibited to the same extent as entirely untithed produce, as in certain situations the prohibition pertaining to doubtfully tithed produce does not take effect.

"מַעֲשֵׂר רִאשׁוֹן שֶׁנִּטְּלָה תְּרוּמָתוֹ וכו'". פְּשִׁיטָא, דְּכֵיוָן שֶׁנִּטְּלָה תְּרוּמָתוֹ חוּלִּין הָוֵי!

The mishna taught that one can fulfill the obligation to eat *matza* with produce of the **first tithe from which its *teruma*,** the *teruma* of the tithe, **was taken** and given to a priest. The Gemara asks: Isn't that **obvious,** as, **since its *teruma*** has been **taken, it is non-sacred** food? What novel element is taught by this statement?

לָא צְרִיכָא, שֶׁהִקְדִּימוֹ בְּשִׁבֳּלִים, וְנִטְּלָה הֵימֶנּוּ תְּרוּמַת מַעֲשֵׂר, וְלֹא נִטְּלָה הֵימֶנּוּ תְּרוּמָה גְּדוֹלָה, וְכִדְרַבִּי אַבָּהוּ.

The Gemara answers: **No,** it is **necessary** to teach the *halakha* in a case where a Levite **preceded** the priest while the grain was still **on its stalks.**[H] Ordinarily, the Levite would be given his first tithe only after the priest had taken the *teruma gedola*; however, in this case the Levite took his portion before the priest. **And the *teruma* of the tithe was taken** by the Levite from his tithe so that he would be permitted to eat the tithe; however, **the *teruma gedola* was not taken from** the produce at all. **And** the novel element of the mishna is **in accordance with** the opinion of **Rabbi Abbahu.**

דְּאָמַר רַבִּי אַבָּהוּ אָמַר רַבִּי שִׁמְעוֹן בֶּן לָקִישׁ: מַעֲשֵׂר רִאשׁוֹן שֶׁהִקְדִּימוֹ בְּשִׁבֳּלִים – פָּטוּר מִתְּרוּמָה גְּדוֹלָה, שֶׁנֶּאֱמַר: "וַהֲרֵמֹתֶם מִמֶּנּוּ תְּרוּמַת ה' מַעֲשֵׂר מִן הַמַּעֲשֵׂר". מַעֲשֵׂר מִן הַמַּעֲשֵׂר אָמַרְתִּי לָךְ, וְלֹא תְּרוּמָה גְּדוֹלָה וּתְרוּמַת מַעֲשֵׂר מִן הַמַּעֲשֵׂר.

As Rabbi Abbahu said that **Rabbi Shimon ben Lakish said: First tithe** in which the Levite **preceded** the priest while the grain was still **on the stalks is exempt from *teruma gedola*,** even though the Levite thereby reduces the amount of grain the priest receives. **As it is stated:** "Moreover you shall speak to the Levites and say to them: When you take from the children of Israel the tithe which I have given you from them as your inheritance, **and you shall set apart from it a gift for the Lord, a tithe from the tithe**" (Numbers 18:26). This verse teaches that the Levite is obligated to set apart a **tithe from the tithe,** i.e., the *teruma* of the tithe, **and not *teruma gedola* and the *teruma* of the tithe from the tithe.**

אָמַר לֵיהּ רַב פָּפָּא לְאַבָּיֵי: אֶלָּא מֵעַתָּה, אֲפִילּוּ הִקְדִּימוֹ בְּכְרִי נַמִי לִיפְטַר! אָמַר לֵיהּ: עָלֶיךָ אָמַר קְרָא "מִכֹּל מַתְּנֹתֵיכֶם תָּרִימוּ אֵת כָּל תְּרוּמַת ה'".

Rav Pappa said to Abaye: However, if that **is so, even** if the Levite **preceded** the priest after the kernels of grain were removed from the stalks and placed **in a pile,** the Levite should not have to separate *teruma gedola* in this case either. Abaye **said to him: With regard to your** claim, **the verse states: "From all that is given to you, you shall set apart all of that which is the Lord's *teruma*,"** of all the best of it, even its consecrated portion" (Numbers 18:29). This verse teaches that the Levites must designate a portion of the gifts they receive and give it to the priests.

HALAKHA

Fruit juice – מֵי פֵּירוֹת: Fruit juice, as well as any liquid other than water that has not been mixed with water, is not considered to cause dough to leaven at all (*Shulḥan Arukh, Oraḥ Ḥayyim* 462:1).

***Matzot* from doubtfully tithed produce** – מַצּוֹת דְּמַאי: One who eats *matza* made from doubtfully tithed produce has fulfilled his obligation (Rambam *Sefer Zemanim, Hilkhot Ḥametz UMatza* 6:7 and *Sefer Ahava, Hilkhot Berakhot* 1:20).

Eating doubtfully tithed produce – אֲכִילַת דְּמַאי: One may feed doubtfully tithed produce to the poor and to guests; however, he should inform them that they are being served doubtfully tithed produce, so that they can tithe it if they want (Rambam *Sefer Zera'im, Hilkhot Ma'aserot* 10:11).

First tithe from grain on the stalks – מַעֲשֵׂר מִן הַשִּׁבֳּלִים: A Levite who separated the first tithe from grain when it is still on its stalks is not required to separate *teruma gedola* from this tithe. However, if he separates the tithe after the grain has been placed in a pile, he must set aside *teruma gedola* (*Shulḥan Arukh, Yoreh De'a* 331).

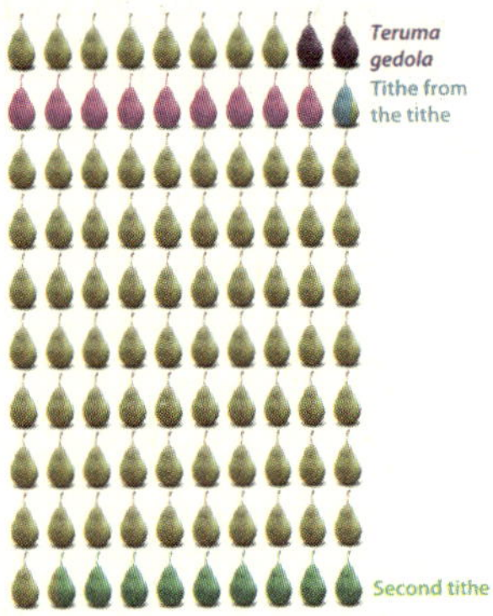

Normal tithing procedure for one hundred units of produce

NOTES

Soldiers [*akhsanya*] – אַכְסַנְיָא: Some commentaries explain that the term *akhsanya* refers to an inn whose guests are mostly poor, and that even any wealthy people staying there are without food. Under these circumstances, they are permitted to eat doubtfully tithed produce (*Me'iri*).

LANGUAGE

Soldiers [*akhsanya*] – אַכְסַנְיָא: From the Greek **ξενία**, *xenia*, meaning hospitality offered to a foreigner. Some versions of the text read *afasnia*, from the Greek **ὀψωνία**, *opsonia*, meaning provisions of food for soldiers.

וּמָה רָאִיתָ? הַאי – אִידְּגַן, וְהַאי – לָא אִידְּגַן.

The Gemara asks: **And what did you see** to lead you to require the separation of *teruma gedola* from first tithe that was taken from grain in piles and not from first tithe that was taken from grain on stalks? Abaye answers: **This** produce, after being threshed and placed into piles, is completely processed and **has become grain;**[N] **and that** produce on the stalk **did not** yet **become grain,** and the Levite is therefore exempt from separating *teruma gedola* from it. Produce that has been arranged in a pile is called grain by the Torah and is given to the priest. Once it is classified as grain, the right of the priest takes effect and the Levite is required to separate *teruma gedola* from it.

"מַעֲשֵׂר שֵׁנִי וְהֶקְדֵּשׁ שֶׁנִּפְדּוּ וכו׳". פְּשִׁיטָא! הָכָא בְּמַאי עָסְקִינַן – שֶׁנָּתַן אֶת הַקֶּרֶן וְלֹא נָתַן אֶת הַחוֹמֶשׁ, וְקָא מַשְׁמַע לַן דְּאֵין חוֹמֶשׁ מְעַכֵּב.

The mishna taught that one can fulfill his obligation to eat *matza* with **second-tithe** grain **and** with **consecrated** grain **that was redeemed.** The Gemara asks: It is **obvious** that this is the case, as consecrated grain that has been redeemed is non-sacred produce. The Gemara answers: **With what are we dealing here?** We are dealing with a case where the consecrated property was not completely redeemed, i.e., **where one gave** payment for **the principal,** the value of the tithe, **but he did not give** payment for the additional **fifth** due when redeeming consecrated items. **And** the mishna **teaches us** that failure to add **the fifth does not invalidate** the redemption. Although there is an obligation to pay this additional fifth, the neglect of this duty does not prevent the grain from becoming non-sacred.

"וְהַכֹּהֲנִים בַּחַלָּה וּבִתְרוּמָה וכו׳". פְּשִׁיטָא! מַהוּ דְּתֵימָא: מַצָּה שָׁוָה לְכׇל אָדָם בָּעֵינַן, קָא מַשְׁמַע לַן: "מַצּוֹת" "מַצּוֹת" רִיבָּה.

And the mishna further taught that **priests** can fulfill their obligation **with** *matza* of ***ḥalla*** **and with** ***teruma.***[H] The Gemara again asks: It is **obvious** that this is the case. Since a priest is permitted to eat *ḥalla* and *teruma*, he can fulfill his obligation to eat *matza* with them. The Gemara responds: This ruling is nevertheless necessary, **lest you say** that **we require** ***matza*** that may be eaten **equally by anyone,** which would mean that *matza* that may not be eaten by regular Israelites is prohibited to priests as well. The mishna therefore **teaches us** that the repetition of the words ***"matzot," "matzot"*** (Deuteronomy 16:3, 8) comes to **amplify,** i.e., one can fulfill one's obligation to eat *matza* even with foods that may be eaten only by specific people.

"אֲבָל לֹא בְּטֶבֶל וכו׳". פְּשִׁיטָא! לָא צְרִיכָא, בְּטֶבֶל טָבוּל מִדְּרַבָּנַן, שֶׁזְּרָעוֹ בְּעָצִיץ שֶׁאֵינוֹ נָקוּב.

We learned in the mishna: **However,** one may **not** fulfill this obligation **with untithed produce.**[NH] The Gemara asks: It is **obvious** that this is the case, as it is always prohibited to eat *tevel*. The Gemara explains: **No, it is necessary** to teach this *halakha* in a case **where** it is considered **untithed produce by rabbinic** law, and by Torah law the produce is permitted. For instance, this is the case with regard to grain **that one sowed in an unperforated flowerpot.** Anything grown disconnected from the ground is not defined as produce of the ground, and its owner is exempt by Torah law from tithing it. However, by rabbinic law, grain sowed in **an unperforated flowerpot** is considered untithed.

"וְלֹא בְּמַעֲשֵׂר רִאשׁוֹן שֶׁלֹּא נִטְּלָה תְּרוּמָתוֹ". פְּשִׁיטָא! לָא צְרִיכָא, שֶׁהִקְדִּימוֹ בְּכְרִי.

It was also taught in the mishna: **And** one does **not** fulfill his obligation **with** *matza* from produce **of the first tithe, whose** ***teruma,*** *teruma* of the tithe, **was not taken.** The Gemara asks: It is **obvious** that this is the case, as this produce may not be eaten. The Gemara answers: **No,** it is **necessary** for the mishna to teach this with regard to a case **where** the Levite **preceded** the priest after the kernels of grain were placed **in a pile** but before *teruma gedola* was separated from the produce.

מַהוּ דְּתֵימָא כִּדְאָמַר לֵיהּ רַב פָּפָּא לְאַבָּיֵי, קָא מַשְׁמַע לַן כִּדְשַׁנִּי לֵיהּ.

The Gemara elaborates: **Lest you say, as Rav Pappa said to Abaye,** that in that case too, the Levite should be exempt from the requirement to separate *teruma gedola* from this produce, the *tanna* of the mishna **teaches us, as Abaye responded** to Rav Pappa, that there is a difference between a case when the grain was on the stalks and when it was collected in a pile. Therefore, one may not eat this produce before separating *teruma gedola* from it.

NOTES

This has become grain – הַאי אִידְּגַן: Produce that has been arranged into a pile and smoothed over is considered to have reached the stage of the completion of its work, and it is classified as grain. The proof is the verse that is referring to "grain from the threshing floor" (Numbers 18:27). The definition of grain is important with regard to *teruma*, which is called "the first of your grain" (Deuteronomy 18:4; see *Arukh*).

***Matza* of untithed produce – מַצּוֹת טֶבֶל:** There are many difficulties concerning the meaning of this passage and its practical ramifications. Apparently, the Rabbis maintain that *matza* of untithed produce may be eaten after the fact. Some commentaries claim that *matza* of untithed produce is entirely prohibited to be eaten, even according to the Rabbis, due to the fact that eating it would be considered a mitzva that comes by means of a transgression. However, others reject this explanation, contending that this principle applies only to a commandment that involves praise of God, e.g., the sacrifice of an offering or taking the four species on *Sukkot*. By contrast, the fulfillment of other mitzvot is not nullified if they come by means of transgression (*Tosefot Rabbeinu Peretz*). Others explain that to perform a mitzva in this manner is prohibited by rabbinic law (Ramban). Yet others suggest that the Rabbis indeed prohibit this *matza* because it is a mitzva that comes by means of a transgression, and the reason why this principle is in effect is that there is no mitzva to eat a second olive-bulk of *matza*. Consequently, with regard to any consumption beyond a single olive-bulk, the mitzva no longer applies while the prohibition remains in force (*Hashlama*).

HALAKHA

***Matza* of *ḥalla* and *teruma* – מַצַּת חַלָּה וּתְרוּמָה:** Priests can fulfill their obligation to eat *matza* with *teruma* or *ḥalla*, despite the fact that this food may not be eaten by non-priests (Rambam *Sefer Zemanim, Hilkhot Ḥametz UMatza* 6:8).

***Matza* of untithed produce – מַצַּת טֶבֶל:** One cannot fulfill the obligation to eat *matza* with untithed produce, even if it is untithed by rabbinic law (Rambam *Sefer Zemanim, Hilkhot Ḥametz UMatza* 6:7).

LANGUAGE

Unminted coin [*asimon*] – אֲסִימוֹן: From the Greek ἄσημον, *asèmon*, meaning without a mark or sign, or a coin without an official imprint.

״וְלֹא בְּמַעֲשֵׂר שֵׁנִי וְהֶקְדֵּשׁ שֶׁלֹּא נִפְדּוּ וכו׳״. פְּשִׁיטָא!

It was further taught in the mishna: **And** one does **not** fulfill his obligation to eat *matza* **with second-tithe** produce **or consecrated** grain **that was not redeemed.** The Gemara asks: Isn't that, too, **obvious,** as it is prohibited to eat these foods?

לְעוֹלָם דְּנִפְדּוּ, וּמַאי ״לֹא נִפְדּוּ״ – שֶׁלֹּא נִפְדּוּ כְּהִלְכָתָן. מַעֲשֵׂר שֵׁנִי שֶׁפְּדָאוֹ עַל גַּב אֲסִימוֹן, דְּרַחֲמָנָא אָמַר ״וְצַרְתָּ הַכֶּסֶף״ – דָּבָר שֶׁיֵּשׁ לוֹ צוּרָה.

The Gemara answers: **Actually,** this is speaking of a case **where they were redeemed, and what** is the meaning of the expression: **They were not redeemed?** It means **that they were not redeemed properly,** e.g., **second-tithe** grain that **was redeemed with an unminted coin [*asimon*].**[L] **As the Merciful One says** with regard to the redemption of the second tithe: "And you shall turn it into money, and bind up the money in your hand, and go to the place which the Lord your God shall choose" (Deuteronomy 14:25). The phrase **"and bind up [*ve'tzarta*] the money"** indicates that the produce must be exchanged for **an object that has a form [*tzura*],** not unminted metal.

וְהֶקְדֵּשׁ – שֶׁחִילְּלוֹ עַל גַּבֵּי קַרְקַע, דְּרַחֲמָנָא אָמַר: ״וְנָתַן הַכֶּסֶף וְקָם לוֹ״.

And with regard to **consecrated** property, we are dealing with a case **where he redeemed it** by exchanging it **for land instead of money, as the Merciful One says: "And he will give** the fifth part of **the money** of your valuation unto it **and it shall be assured to him"** (see Leviticus 27:19). If one redeemed consecrated property with land rather than money, the consecrated status is not transferred to the land.

תָּנוּ רַבָּנַן: יָכוֹל יוֹצֵא אָדָם יְדֵי חוֹבָתוֹ בְּטֶבֶל שֶׁלֹּא נִתְקַן. כׇּל טֶבֶל נַמִי, הָא לֹא נִתְקַן!

The Sages taught: I **might** have thought that **a person fulfills his obligation** to eat *matza* **with untithed produce that was not amended** with regard to tithes. The Gemara analyzes the apparently redundant phrase **untithed produce that was not amended.** But isn't **all untithed produce also not amended,** by definition?

אֶלָּא: בְּטֶבֶל שֶׁלֹּא נִתְקַן כׇּל צוֹרְכּוֹ, שֶׁנִּטְּלָה מִמֶּנּוּ תְּרוּמָה גְּדוֹלָה וְלֹא נִטְּלָה מִמֶּנּוּ תְּרוּמַת מַעֲשֵׂר, [מַעֲשֵׂר] רִאשׁוֹן וְלֹא מַעֲשֵׂר שֵׁנִי, וַאֲפִילּוּ מַעֲשֵׂר עָנִי, מִנַּיִן?

Rather, this *baraita* is referring to **untithed produce that was incompletely amended.** How so? For example, produce **from which *teruma gedola* was taken, but** the ***teruma* of the tithe was not taken from** it. Alternatively, the **first tithe** was separated from the produce, **but not** the **second tithe; or,** it is referring **even** to grain from which all the tithes were separated, apart from the **poor man's tithe.** Although no sanctity applies to the poor man's tithe, which is simply a monetary gift to the poor, until this tithe has not been separated the grain remains untithed. **From where** is it derived that these types of grain cannot be used for *matza*?

תַּלְמוּד לוֹמַר: ״לֹא תֹאכַל עָלָיו חָמֵץ״, מִי שֶׁאִיסּוּרוֹ מִשּׁוּם בַּל תֹּאכַל עָלָיו חָמֵץ, יָצָא זֶה שֶׁאֵין אִיסּוּרוֹ מִשּׁוּם בַּל תֹּאכַל חָמֵץ, אֶלָּא מִשּׁוּם בַּל תֹּאכַל טֶבֶל.

The verse states: "You shall not eat leavened bread with it; seven days you shall eat with it *matza*" (Deuteronomy 16:3). One fulfills his obligation to eat *matza* **with** food **whose prohibition** is solely **due to** the prohibition: **Do not eat leavened bread with it,** if it was not preserved in an unleavened state. This command **excludes this** grain, **which is not prohibited due to** the prohibition: **Do not eat leavened bread, but** rather **due to** the prohibition: **Do not eat untithed produce.**

וְאִיסּוּרָא דְּחָמֵץ לְהֵיכָן אָזְלָא? אָמַר רַב שֵׁשֶׁת: הָא מַנִּי – רַבִּי שִׁמְעוֹן הִיא, דְּאָמַר: אֵין אִיסּוּר חָל עַל אִיסּוּר. דְּתַנְיָא, רַבִּי שִׁמְעוֹן אוֹמֵר:

The Gemara expresses surprise at this *baraita*. **And the prohibition of leavened bread, where did it go?** In other words, doesn't the prohibition: "You shall not eat leavened bread" apply to untithed produce as well? **Rav Sheshet said:** In accordance with **whose** opinion **is this** *baraita*? **It is** in accordance with the opinion of **Rabbi Shimon, who said: One prohibition does not take effect where another prohibition** already exists.[H] No additional prohibitions can apply to an object that is already prohibited, e.g., untithed grain. Consequently, the prohibition of leavened bread does not take effect on untithed produce. **As it was taught** in a *baraita* that **Rabbi Shimon says:**

HALAKHA

One prohibition does not take effect where another prohibition already exists – אֵין אִיסּוּר חָל עַל אִיסּוּר: There is a general principle that no additional prohibitions can apply to an action or object that is already prohibited by Torah law. There are certain exceptions to this principle, for example: Simultaneous prohibitions; a prohibition that adds a significant element to the first prohibition, such as a stricter punishment; or a more inclusive prohibition, e.g., if the second prohibition is more comprehensive than the first one. These exceptions are in accordance with the accepted opinion in the mishna and the Gemara in tractate *Keritot*, and they are contrary to Rabbi Shimon's minority opinion (Rambam *Sefer Kedusha, Hilkhot Issurei Bia* 17:8; *Hilkhot Ma'akhalot Assurot* 14:18).

הָאוֹכֵל נְבֵלָה בְּיוֹם הַכִּפּוּרִים פָּטוּר.

One who unwittingly **eats** an unslaughtered **animal** carcass **on Yom Kippur**[N] **is exempt** from bringing a sin-offering to atone for this consumption. The prohibition against eating on Yom Kippur does not apply to the already prohibited meat of an animal carcass, which means only the prohibition against eating an unslaughtered animal carcass is violated by this act.

רָבִינָא אָמַר: אֲפִילּוּ תֵּימָא רַבָּנַן; מִי שֶׁאִיסּוּרוֹ מִשּׁוּם בַּל תֹּאכַל חָמֵץ בִּלְבַד, יָצָא זֶה שֶׁאֵין אִיסּוּרוֹ מִשּׁוּם בַּל תֹּאכַל חָמֵץ בִּלְבַד, אֶלָּא אַף מִשּׁוּם בַּל תֹּאכַל טֶבֶל.

Ravina said: Even if you say that this *baraita* is in accordance with **the Rabbis,** who maintain that a prohibition can take effect where another prohibition already exists, it can be explained as follows: One fulfills his obligation to eat *matza* **with** food **whose prohibition** is **solely due to** the commandment: **Do not eat leavened bread,** which **excludes this** grain, **which is forbidden not only due to** the prohibition: **Do not eat leavened bread, but also due to** the prohibition: **Do not eat untithed produce.**

מִידֵּי ״בִּלְבַד״ כְּתִיב?! אֶלָּא מְחַוַּורְתָּא כִּדְרַב שֵׁשֶׁת.

The Gemara raises a difficulty against this explanation: **Is** the word: **Only, written** in the *baraita*? This word, which is critical for Ravina's explanation, does not appear in the *baraita* at all. **Rather, it is clear** that this must be explained **in accordance with** the explanation of **Rav Sheshet,** who maintains that the *baraita* should be attributed to Rabbi Shimon.

תָּנוּ רַבָּנַן: יָכוֹל יוֹצֵא אָדָם יְדֵי חוֹבָתוֹ בְּמַעֲשֵׂר שֵׁנִי בִּירוּשָׁלַיִם – תַּלְמוּד לוֹמַר: ״לֶחֶם עוֹנִי״ – מָה שֶׁנֶּאֱכָל בַּאֲנִינוּת, יָצָא זֶה שֶׁאֵינוֹ נֶאֱכָל בַּאֲנִינוּת אֶלָּא בְּשִׂמְחָה, דִּבְרֵי רַבִּי יוֹסֵי הַגְּלִילִי.

The Sages taught: I **might** have thought that **a person can fulfill his obligation** to eat *matza* on Passover **with** *matza* of **second tithe**[H] **in Jerusalem.** Therefore, **the verse states:** "You shall eat no leavened bread with it; seven days you shall eat with it *matza,* **the bread of affliction** [***leḥem oni***]"[N] (Deuteronomy 16:3), *oni* with the letter *ayin,* i.e., poor man's bread. As this is similar to the phrase: Bread of acute mourning [*leḥem oni*], *oni* with an *alef,* it can be inferred that this mitzva must be fulfilled with *matza* **that** can **be eaten** during a period of **acute mourning,** on the day one's close relative has died. This **excludes this** second tithe, **which cannot be eaten during** a period of **acute mourning but only** in a state **of joy,** as the Torah states: "I have not eaten from it in my acute mourning" (Deuteronomy 26:14). This is **the statement of Rabbi Yosei HaGelili.**

רַבִּי עֲקִיבָא אוֹמֵר: ״מַצּוֹת״, ״מַצּוֹת״ רִיבָּה, אִם כֵּן מָה תַּלְמוּד לוֹמַר: ״לֶחֶם עוֹנִי״ – פְּרָט לְעִיסָּה שֶׁנִּילּוֹשָׁה בְּיַיִן וְשֶׁמֶן וּדְבַשׁ.

Rabbi Akiva says: The repetition of ***matzot matzot*** serves to **amplify,** and teaches that all types of *matza* may be eaten on Passover. The *baraita* asks: **If so, what** is the meaning when **the verse states *leḥem oni,*** poor man's bread? The *baraita* answers: This phrase **excludes dough that was kneaded with wine, oil, or honey,** which is not classified as poor man's bread and therefore cannot be used for this mitzva.

מַאי טַעְמָא דְּרַבִּי עֲקִיבָא? מִי כְּתִיב ״לֶחֶם עוֹנִי״ ״עֹנִי״ כְּתִיב.

The Gemara asks: **What is the reason of Rabbi Akiva?** The Gemara explains: **Is it written** in the consonantal text ***leḥem oni*** with a *vav*? That would allude to the comparison of *matza* to food eaten by an *onen,* an acute mourner, as *onen* is also spelled with a *vav*. Actually, **it is written *leḥem oni*** without a *vav*, meaning poor man's bread.

וְרַבִּי יוֹסֵי הַגְּלִילִי: מִי קָרֵינַן ״עָנִי״? עוֹנִי קָרֵינַן. וְרַבִּי עֲקִיבָא: הַאי דְּקָרֵינַן בֵּיהּ עוֹנִי – כִּדְשְׁמוּאֵל, דְּאָמַר שְׁמוּאֵל: ״לֶחֶם עוֹנִי״ – לֶחֶם שֶׁעוֹנִין עָלָיו דְּבָרִים הַרְבֵּה.

And Rabbi Yosei HaGelili could respond: **Do we vocalize** the word as ***ani,*** as would be appropriate for a phrase meaning a poor man's bread? In fact, **we vocalize** it ***oni,*** which means oppression, affliction, or mourning. **And Rabbi Akiva** could retort: The fact **that we vocalize** the word **as *oni*** is **in accordance with** a statement of **Shmuel. As Shmuel said:** The expression ***leḥem oni*** means **bread over which many matters are recited** [***onin***], an allusion to the Passover Seder, at which one recites the Haggadah and eats *matza*.

HALAKHA

Matza of second tithe – מַצַּת מַעֲשֵׂר שֵׁנִי: *Matza* of second tithe may be used by anyone to fulfill the mitzva to eat *matza* (Rambam *Sefer Zemanim, Hilkhot Ḥametz UMatza* 6:8).

NOTES

An animal carcass on Yom Kippur – נְבֵלָה בְּיוֹם הַכִּפּוּרִים: The accepted ruling is that one who eats from an unslaughtered animal carcass on Yom Kippur is liable to bring a sin-offering, as the prohibition against eating on Yom Kippur applies even to an animal carcass. This is because the prohibition to eat on Yom Kippur is more inclusive than the prohibition against eating an animal carcass, as it adds to the scope of the earlier prohibition, and the accepted view is that a prohibition of this kind applies in addition to another prohibition. The prohibition against eating on Yom Kippur is inclusive because it applies to all types of food. Some commentaries say that it also adds to the scope of the prohibition against eating an animal carcass, as the prohibition of Yom Kippur is more severe (see the *Halakha* notes on 35b for a more detailed explanation).

Leḥem oni – לֶחֶם עוֹנִי: The dispute between Rabbi Yosei HaGelili and Rabbi Akiva with regard to the explanation of the term *leḥem oni* can be explained as follows: Rabbi Yosei claims that *oni* is a broad term that refers to pain and suffering in general, so that *leḥem oni* means the bread of affliction; whereas Rabbi Akiva contends that *oni* refers solely to poverty, in accordance with the plain meaning of the term, poor man's bread.

וְסָבַר רַבִּי עֲקִיבָא עִיסָּה שֶׁנִּילוֹשָׁה בְּיַיִן וְשֶׁמֶן וּדְבַשׁ לֹא? וְהָתַנְיָא: אֵין לָשִׁין עִיסָּה בְּפֶסַח בְּיַיִן וְשֶׁמֶן וּדְבַשׁ. וְאִם לָשׁ, רַבָּן גַּמְלִיאֵל אוֹמֵר: תִּשָּׂרֵף מִיָּד, וַחֲכָמִים אוֹמְרִים: יֵאָכֵל. וְאָמַר רַבִּי עֲקִיבָא: שַׁבַּתִּי הָיְתָה אֵצֶל רַבִּי אֱלִיעֶזֶר וְרַבִּי יְהוֹשֻׁעַ, וְלַשְׁתִּי לָהֶם עִיסָּה בְּיַיִן וְשֶׁמֶן וּדְבַשׁ, וְלֹא אָמְרוּ לִי דָּבָר.

The Gemara asks: **And does Rabbi Akiva maintain** with regard to **dough that was kneaded with wine, oil, or honey,** that it may **not** be used for *matza*? **But wasn't it taught** in a *baraita*: **One** may **not knead dough on Passover with wine, oil, or honey? And if one kneaded** dough in this manner, **Rabban Gamliel says:** The dough must **be burned immediately,**[N] as it is leavened faster than other types of dough. **And the Rabbis say** that although it is leavened quickly, one can still prevent it from being leavened, and if he does so it may **be eaten.**[H] **And Rabbi Akiva said: It was my Shabbat** to serve **before Rabbi Eliezer and Rabbi Yehoshua** during Passover (Rav Yehuda ben Rav Binyamin HaRofeh), **and I kneaded for them dough with wine, oil, and honey, and they said nothing to me** by way of objection.

וְאַף עַל פִּי שֶׁאֵין לָשִׁין – מְקַטְּפִין בּוֹ. אֲתָאן לְתַנָּא קַמָּא. וַחֲכָמִים אוֹמְרִים: אֶת שֶׁלָּשִׁין בּוֹ – מְקַטְּפִין בּוֹ, וְאֵת שֶׁאֵין לָשִׁין בּוֹ – אֵין מְקַטְּפִין בּוֹ. וְשָׁוִין שֶׁאֵין לָשִׁין אֶת הָעִיסָּה בְּפוֹשְׁרִין.

The *baraita* continues: **And although one** may **not knead** dough with these ingredients, **one** may **spread** these substances on the surface of the dough. The Gemara comments: With regard to this latter statement, **we have come** back **to** the opinion of **the first *tanna*,** who said that one may not knead bread with wine, oil, or honey. **And the Rabbis say:** With regard to dough **into which one** may **knead** wine, oil, or honey, **one** may likewise **spread** them on the dough, whereas concerning dough **into which one** may **not knead** these ingredients, **one** may **not spread**[NH] them on the dough either. **And everyone agrees that one** may **not knead the dough with warm** water, as this will cause it to be leavened quickly. In any case, it is evident from here that Rabbi Akiva himself prepared *matza* with wine, oil, and honey.

לָא קַשְׁיָא, הָא – בְּיוֹם טוֹב רִאשׁוֹן, הָא – בְּיוֹם טוֹב שֵׁנִי.

The Gemara answers: This is **not difficult,** as **this** statement of Rabbi Akiva's, which maintains that one does not fulfill his obligation with *matza* prepared with wine, oil, and honey, is referring to **the first day of the Festival,** during which there is a special commandment to eat *matza*. However, **that** second *baraita*, in which Rabbi Akiva states that he prepared this type of dough himself, pertains to **the second day** of Passover, when no special requirement to eat *matza* is in effect. On the second day, there is no mitzva to eat *matza*. It is only forbidden to own or eat leavened bread; consequently so-called rich, or enhanced *matza*, prepared from fruit juices, is permitted.

כִּדְאָמַר לְהוּ רַבִּי יְהוֹשֻׁעַ לִבְנֵיהּ: יוֹמָא קַמָּא לָא תִּלּוֹשׁוּ לִי בְּחַלְבָּא, מִכָּאן וְאֵילָךְ – לוּשׁוּ לִי בְּחַלְבָּא. וְהָתַנְיָא: אֵין לָשִׁין אֶת הָעִיסָּה בְּחָלָב, וְאִם לָשׁ – כׇּל הַפַּת אֲסוּרָה, מִפְּנֵי הֶרְגֵּל עֲבֵירָה! אֶלָּא הָכִי קָאָמַר: יוֹמָא קַמָּא לָא תִּלּוֹשׁוּ לִי בְּדוּבְשָׁא, מִכָּאן וְאֵילָךְ – לוּשׁוּ לִי בְּדוּבְשָׁא.

The Gemara adds that this is **as Rabbi Yehoshua said to his sons:** On **the first night** of Passover, **do not knead for me** dough **with milk,** but **from** the first night **onward, knead** my dough for **me with milk.** The Gemara raises a difficulty: **But wasn't it taught** in a *baraita*: Throughout the whole year **one** may **not knead dough with milk, and if he kneaded** dough with milk, **the entire bread is prohibited, due to** the fact that one will become **accustomed to sin,** by unwittingly eating it with meat? **Rather, this is what he is saying:** On **the first** night of Passover **do not knead me** dough **with honey;** however, **from then onward, knead me** dough **with honey.**

וְאִיבָּעֵית אֵימָא: לְעוֹלָם בְּחַלְבָּא, כִּדְאָמַר רָבִינָא: כְּעֵין תּוֹרָא שָׁרֵי, הָכָא נָמֵי: כְּעֵין תּוֹרָא.

And if you wish, say instead that **actually,** Rabbi Yehoshua said: **With milk, as Ravina said:** If this bread, kneaded with milk, is prepared in the shape **of an ox's eye, it is permitted.** In other words, if one forms this dough in a unique shape, e.g., the eye of an ox, one may eat it, as it is clearly distinguishable from ordinary bread. Therefore, there is no concern that it will be eaten with meat. **Here too,** the *baraita* is speaking about a case where he told them to prepare this *matza* in the shape **of an ox's eye.**

״וְשָׁוִין שֶׁאֵין לָשִׁין אֶת הָעִיסָּה בְּפוֹשְׁרִין״. מַאי שְׁנָא מִמְּנָחוֹת? דִּתְנַן: כׇּל הַמְּנָחוֹת נִילוֹשׁוֹת בְּפוֹשְׁרִין, (וּמִשְׁתַּמְּרִין) שֶׁלֹּא יֶחְמְצוּ! אִם אָמְרוּ בִּזְרִיזִין – יֹאמְרוּ בְּשֶׁאֵין זְרִיזִין?

It was incidentally mentioned in the previous *baraita*: **And everyone agrees that one** may **not knead dough with warm** water. The Gemara asks: In **what** way **is** this case **different from** that of **meal-offerings?**[N] **As we learned** in a mishna: **All meal-offerings are kneaded with warm water and are watched so that they will not be leavened.** The Gemara explains that there is a distinction between these two cases: **If they say** it is permitted **for diligent** priests to bake with warm water,[H] **shall they** also **say** the same with regard **to those who are not diligent?** The priests are diligent and expert in the Temple service and are able to take extreme care, but not everyone can be relied upon to guard the dough unfailingly.

NOTES

The dough must be burned immediately – תִּשָּׂרֵף מִיָּד: Although the Sages provide signs to identify whether dough has leavened, these apply only to ordinary dough. Since dough kneaded with wine, oil, and honey can become leavened before the appearance of these visible signs of leavening, the signs are irrelevant in this case (*Tosefot Rid*).

Knead and spread – לָשִׁים וּמְקַטְּפִים: The first *tanna* claims that one may not knead these substances into dough, but that one may spread them on top of dough. Although one may not prepare dough with a mixture of water and these substances, it is permitted to spread them on the surface of the dough. By contrast, the Rabbis claim that it is entirely prohibited to mix water and juice when preparing dough during Passover (Rabbeinu Ḥananel).

Meal-offerings – מְנָחוֹת: These include all offerings of flour or bread brought in the Temple. Among the meal-offerings are the two loaves of bread brought on *Shavuot*, the Temple shewbread, the various kinds of voluntary meal-offerings, the sinner's meal-offering, the loaves of bread accompanying a thanks-offering, the meal-offerings that accompany libations, the meal-offering of a suspected adulteress [*sota*], and the *omer* offering. Numerous complex laws apply to these meal-offerings, and most of tractate *Menaḥot* is devoted to a detailed discussion of them. Most of the meal-offerings are brought from unleavened wheat flour. Likewise, most of these offerings require taking a handful of the offering, an essential element in the sacrificial ceremony. Many types of meal-offerings have oil mixed with them or incense added to them at some stage of their preparation. The *halakhot* of meal-offerings parallel the *halakhot* of animal sacrifices in numerous respects, and many of the acts that render animal sacrifices unfit also render meal-offerings unfit.

HALAKHA

Dough that was kneaded with fruit juice – עִיסָּה שֶׁנִּילוֹשָׁה בְּמֵי פֵּירוֹת: One should not knead dough with fruit juice and water on Passover. If one did prepare a mixture of this kind, he must bake it before it is leavened, in accordance with the opinion of the Rabbis (*Shulḥan Arukh, Oraḥ Ḥayyim* 462:2).

Kneading and spreading – לִישָׁה וְקִיטּוּף: Since it is permitted to knead dough with fruit juice, it is also permitted to spread these juices on dough. The accepted practice in Ashkenazi communities is to be stringent in this regard, in light of the opinion that fruit juice leavens dough quickly. There is also a concern that water may have been mixed with the fruit juice. The custom is not to spread fruit juice on *matza* until after it has been baked (Rema). Furthermore, *matza* of this kind should not be used for the mitzva on the first night of Passover (*Shulḥan Arukh, Oraḥ Ḥayyim* 462:4).

Baking meal-offerings – אֲפִיַּית מְנָחוֹת: The dough for all baked meal-offerings can be prepared with warm water, as the attending priests would certainly be careful to prevent the dough from becoming leavened (Rambam *Sefer Avoda, Hilkhot Ma'aseh HaKorbanot* 12:21).

אִי הָכִי מִילְתַּת נַמִּי לָתֵית! אַלְמָּה אָמַר רַבִּי זֵירָא אָמַר רַבָּה בַּר יִרְמְיָה אָמַר שְׁמוּאֵל: חִיטִּין שֶׁל מְנָחוֹת – אֵין לוֹתְתִין אוֹתָהּ! לִישָׁה – בִּזְרִיזִין אִיתָא, לְתִיתָה – לֵיתָא בִּזְרִיזִין.

The Gemara raises a difficulty: **If so,** if we rely on the diligence of the priests, **let them also soak** the grains in water to help them remove the husks. **Why did Rabbi Zeira say** that **Rabba bar Yirmeya said** that **Shmuel said:** With regard to the **wheat** used **in the meal-offerings, one** may **not soak it?**[H] The Gemara answers: The **kneading** of the dough **is** performed **by diligent** priests; however, the act of **soaking is not** performed **by diligent** priests. Instead, this soaking is performed outside of the Temple confines by less reliable non-priests.

וְלִישָׁה מִי אִיתָא בִּזְרִיזִין? וְהָכְתִיב: "וְיָצַק עָלֶיהָ שֶׁמֶן וגו׳ וֶהֱבִיאָהּ אֶל הַכֹּהֵן" – מִקְּמִיצָה וְאֵילָךְ מִצְוַת כְּהוּנָּה, לִימֵּד עַל יְצִיקָה וּבְלִילָה שֶׁכְּשֵׁירָה בְּכָל אָדָם!

The Gemara asks: **And** with regard to **kneading, is it** performed only **by diligent** priests?[H] **But isn't it written:** "And when any one brings a meal-offering to the Lord, his offering shall be of fine flour; **and he shall pour oil upon it,** and place frankincense upon it. **And he shall bring it to** Aaron's sons **the priests;** and he shall take from it his handful of its fine flour, and of its oil, together with all its frankincense" (Leviticus 2:1–2). These verses indicate that **from the** scooping of a **handful**[N] **and onward,** the **mitzva** must be performed by members of **the priesthood. This teaches about the pouring** of the oil **and the stirring** of the mixture **that** they **are valid** even if they are performed **by any person,** even a non-priest.

לִישָׁה, נְהִי דִּבִזְרִיזִין לֵיתָא – בִּמְקוֹם זְרִיזִין אִיתָא. דְּאָמַר מָר: בְּלִילָה כְּשֵׁירָה בְּזָר, חוּץ לְחוֹמַת עֲזָרָה – פְּסוּלָה. לְאַפּוֹקֵי לְתִיתָה, דְּאֵינָהּ בִּזְרִיזִין, וְלֹא בִּמְקוֹם זְרִיזִין.

The Gemara answers: With regard to **kneading, although** it **is not** performed **by diligent** priests, **it is** nevertheless performed **in the place of the diligent.** Kneading may be carried out by a non-priest, but it must still be performed in the Temple courtyard. **As the Master said: Mixing is valid** if performed **by a non-priest;** however, if it is conducted **outside the walls of the courtyard,**[H] **it,** the meal offering, **is disqualified.** This serves **to exclude soaking, which is neither** performed **by** the **diligent nor** performed **in the place of the diligent.**

וּמַאי שְׁנָא מִמִּנְחַת הָעוֹמֶר? דְּתַנְיָא: מִנְחַת הָעוֹמֶר לוֹתְתִין אוֹתָהּ, וְצוֹבְרִין אוֹתָהּ! צִיבּוּר שָׁאנֵי.

The Gemara asks: **And** in **what** way **is** this case **different from** that of **the *omer* meal-offering,**[N] which must also be guarded from leavening? **As it was taught** in a *baraita*: With regard to the ***omer* offering, one soaks it**[H] **and gathers it,** without concern that it will become leavened. The Gemara answers: An act performed by the **community is different,**[N] as the Great Sanhedrin supervises these operations, and those executing them no doubt proceed with great caution.

תָּנוּ רַבָּנַן: יָכוֹל יוֹצֵא אָדָם יְדֵי חוֹבָתוֹ בְּבִכּוּרִים – תַּלְמוּד לוֹמַר: "בְּכֹל מוֹשְׁבוֹתֵיכֶם תֹּאכְלוּ מַצּוֹת" – מַצָּה הַנֶּאֱכֶלֶת בְּכָל מוֹשְׁבוֹתֵיכֶם, יָצְאוּ בִּכּוּרִים שֶׁאֵין נֶאֱכָלִין בְּכָל מוֹשְׁבוֹתֵיכֶם אֶלָּא בִּירוּשָׁלַיִם, דִּבְרֵי רַבִּי יוֹסֵי הַגְּלִילִי.

The Sages taught in another *baraita*: **I might** have thought that **one** can **fulfill his obligation by** eating *matza* prepared from the wheat **of first fruits;**[H] therefore, **the verse states: "In all of your habitations you shall eat *matzot*"** (Exodus 12:20). This verse indicates that one fulfills his obligation only with ***matza* that** may **be eaten "in all of your habitations."** This expression **excludes first fruits, which** may **not be eaten in all of your habitations, but** only **in Jerusalem.** This is **the statement of Rabbi Yosei HaGelili.**

רַבִּי עֲקִיבָא אוֹמֵר: מַצָּה וּמָרוֹר, מָה מָרוֹר שֶׁאֵינוֹ בִּכּוּרִים – אַף מַצָּה שֶׁאֵינָהּ בִּכּוּרִים. אִי מַה מָּרוֹר שֶׁאֵין בְּמִינוֹ בִּכּוּרִים – אַף מַצָּה שֶׁאֵין בְּמִינָהּ בִּכּוּרִים,

Rabbi Akiva says: That verse is not the source for this *halakha*; rather, the fact that one cannot fulfill his obligation with *matza* of first fruits is derived from the juxtaposition of ***matza* and bitter herbs: Just as bitter herbs are not first fruits,** as they are not included in the seven species to which the mitzva of first fruits applies, **so too *matza*** may **not be** from **first fruits. If** you will claim: **Just as bitter herbs** are **from a species** that are **not** brought as **first fruits, so too *matza*** must be prepared **from a species** that are **not** brought as **first fruits,** e.g., spelt,

NOTES

Handful – קְמִיצָה: Most meal-offerings require a handful to be taken by a priest and burnt on the altar; e.g., see Leviticus 2:2. This service, which parallels the slaughtering of an animal sacrifice, could be performed only by a priest. According to many authorities, the priest would scoop the flour out with the three middle fingers of his right hand, using his thumb and little finger to remove any surplus flour. He would then place the flour in a sacred vessel used in the Temple service to consecrate it. Since the priest had to scoop out an exact handful of flour, no more and no less, scooping of the handful was one of the more difficult services in the Temple.

The *omer* meal-offering – מִנְחַת הָעוֹמֶר: The Gemara assumes that equal stringency should apply to the *omer* and to leavened bread, despite the fact that the *omer* is prepared from barley and, as the Gemara will later note, barley is less likely to become leavened because it is smooth. However, given that the Sages do not apply this distinction between wheat and barley with regard to non-sacred food, it is certainly not accepted with regard to consecrated food (Rashash).

An act performed by the community is different – צִיבּוּר שָׁאנֵי: The principle that an action performed by or on behalf of the entire Jewish people will be done with great care is applicable to other situations as well. This is not because there are many people involved in the mitzva. In fact, the opposite is true, as people are more likely to be lax if they know they can rely on many other participants. Rather, a communal offering is overseen by the Great Sanhedrin, which ensures that the entire process is performed properly.

HALAKHA

Soaking the wheat for meal-offerings – לְתִיתַת מְנָחוֹת: One may not soak the wheat used for meal-offerings, lest he fail to guard it carefully from becoming leavened, as stated by Shmuel (Rambam *Sefer Avoda*, *Hilkhot Ma'aseh HaKorbanot* 12:20).

The role of the priests in the bringing of the meal-offering – תַּפְקִיד הַכֹּהֲנִים בְּהַקְרָבַת הַמִּנְחָה: All actions performed in the process of preparing a meal-offering, i.e., grinding, kneading, and baking, may be performed by non-priests. From the scooping of a handful of this offering and onward, the rite must be performed by priests (Rambam *Sefer Avoda*, *Hilkhot Ma'aseh HaKorbanot* 12:23).

Mixing outside the Temple courtyard – בְּלִילָה מִחוּץ לָעֲזָרָה: A meal-offering that is mixed outside the Temple courtyard is disqualified (Rambam *Sefer Avoda*, *Hilkhot Pesulei HaMukdashin* 11:6).

Soaking the *omer* – לְתִיתַת הָעוֹמֶר: The grain offered in the *omer* sacrifice may be soaked, as the court carefully supervises the entire process (Rambam *Sefer Avoda*, *Hilkhot Ma'aseh HaKorbanot* 12:20).

***Matza* from first fruits** – מַצַּת בִּכּוּרִים: Priests cannot fulfill the mitzva to eat *matza* with first fruits, even in Jerusalem, as this *matza* cannot be eaten outside the capital (Rambam *Sefer Zemanim*, *Hilkhot Ḥametz UMatza* 6:8).

אוֹצִיא חִיטִּין וּשְׂעוֹרִין שֶׁיֵּשׁ בְּמִינָן בִּיכּוּרִים! תַּלְמוּד לוֹמַר: ״מַצּוֹת מַצּוֹת״ – רִיבָּה. אִי מַצּוֹת מַצּוֹת רִיבָּה אֲפִילּוּ בִּיכּוּרִים נַמִי! הֲדַר בֵּיהּ רַבִּי עֲקִיבָא.

I would then think this comparison **excludes wheat and barley, which are from a species** that are brought as **first fruits**[N] and should therefore not be used for the mitzva of *matza*. Therefore, **the verse states: "*Matzot*," "*matzot*"** (Deuteronomy 16:3, 8) to **amplify** and teach that any *matza* is acceptable for this mitzva. The Gemara asks: **If** the repetition of ***matzot matzot*** comes to **amplify** this *halakha* that any *matza* is fit for Passover use, it should **also** include *matza* prepared from **first-fruit** wheat. The Gemara answers: This is indeed true, and **Rabbi Akiva retracted** his statement. He too derives the *halakha* from the verse: "In all of your habitations."

דְּתַנְיָא: יָכוֹל יֵצֵא אָדָם יְדֵי חוֹבָתוֹ בְּבִיכּוּרִים – תַּלְמוּד לוֹמַר: ״בְּכֹל מוֹשְׁבֹתֵיכֶם תֹּאכְלוּ מַצּוֹת״ – מַצָּה הַנֶּאֱכֶלֶת בְּכָל מוֹשָׁבוֹת, יָצְאוּ בִּיכּוּרִים שֶׁאֵינָן נֶאֱכָלִין בְּכָל מוֹשָׁבוֹת, אֶלָּא בִּירוּשָׁלַיִם. יָכוֹל שֶׁאֲנִי מוֹצִיא אַף מַעֲשֵׂר שֵׁנִי – תַּלְמוּד לוֹמַר: ״מַצּוֹת מַצּוֹת״ רִיבָּה.

As it was taught in a *baraita*: **I might** have thought that **a person** can **fulfill his obligation with** *matza* from **first fruit**; therefore **the verse states: "In all of your habitations you shall eat *matzot*"** (Exodus 12:20). The verse indicates that one can fulfill his obligation with ***matza* that** may **be eaten in all habitations.** It **excludes first fruits, which** may **not be eaten in all habitations, but only in Jerusalem.** I **might** have thought that I should **also exclude second-tithe** produce as fit for *matza*; therefore **the verse states: "*Matzot*," "*matzot*."** As stated above, this repetition serves to **amplify,** and it includes second tithe in the materials that may be used in the preparation of *matza*.

וּמָה רָאִיתָ לְרַבּוֹת מַעֲשֵׂר שֵׁנִי וּלְהוֹצִיא בִּיכּוּרִים – מְרַבֶּה אֲנִי מַעֲשֵׂר שֵׁנִי שֶׁיֵּשׁ לוֹ הֶיתֵּר בְּכָל מוֹשָׁבוֹת כְּדְרַבִּי (אֱלִיעֶזֶר), וּמוֹצִיא אֲנִי בִּיכּוּרִים שֶׁאֵין לָהֶן הֶיתֵּר בְּכָל מוֹשָׁבוֹת.

The Gemara asks: **And what did you see** that led you **to include second-tithe** produce due to the words *matzot matzot* **but to exclude first fruits?** The Gemara explains: **I include** the **second tithe, which has** a means by which it may be **permitted** to be eaten **in all habitations,** in accordance with the opinion of **Rabbi Eliezer,** as will be explained. **And I exclude first fruits, which do not have,** under any circumstances, a manner by which it is **permitted** to eat them **in all habitations.**

דְּאָמַר רַבִּי (אֱלִיעֶזֶר): מִנַּיִן לְמַעֲשֵׂר שֵׁנִי שֶׁנִּטְמָא שֶׁפּוֹדִין אוֹתוֹ אֲפִילּוּ בִּירוּשָׁלַיִם – תַּלְמוּד לוֹמַר: ״כִּי לֹא תוּכַל שְׂאֵתוֹ״

The Gemara explains: **As Rabbi Eliezer said: From where** is it derived **with regard to second-tithe** produce **that became ritually impure,**[H] **that one** may **redeem it even in Jerusalem?** Second-tithe produce that has been redeemed may be removed from the city. **The verse states:** "And if the way is too long for you, **so that you are not able to carry it** [*se'eto*], because the place is too far from you, which the Lord your God shall choose to set His name there, when the Lord your God shall bless you" (Deuteronomy 14:24).

וְאֵין שְׂאֵת אֶלָּא אֲכִילָה – שֶׁנֶּאֱמַר: ״וַיִּשָּׂא מַשְׂאֹת מֵאֵת פָּנָיו״.

And it is derived by means of a verbal analogy that this **carrying** [*se'et*] **is nothing other** than **eating,**[N] **as it is stated: "And portions** [*masot*] **were taken to them from before him"** (Genesis 43:34). In light of this parallel language, the Gemara understands the phrase "so that you are not able *se'eto*" to mean: So that you are not able to eat it. Like second-tithe produce that has not yet been taken into Jerusalem, second-tithe produce in the capital that cannot be eaten due to ritual impurity can be redeemed and taken out of the city. Consequently, second tithe can indeed be considered food that may be eaten "in all of your habitations."

מַאן שָׁמְעַתְּ לֵיהּ דְּאָמַר: בְּמַעֲשֵׂר שֵׁנִי נָפֵיק בֵּיהּ – רַבִּי עֲקִיבָא, וְקָמְמַעֵיט לְהוּ לְבִיכּוּרִים מִ״בְּכֹל מוֹשְׁבֹתֵיכֶם״. שְׁמַע מִינָּהּ: הֲדַר בֵּיהּ.

The Gemara applies this discussion to the issue at hand: **Who did you hear that said:** One can **fulfill his obligation** to eat *matza* **with second tithe?** It is the opinion of **Rabbi Akiva, and yet he excludes first fruits** due **to** the expression: **"In all of your habitations." Learn from this that** Rabbi Akiva **retracted** his opinion and accepted Rabbi Yosei HaGelili's derivation.

וְרַבִּי יוֹסֵי הַגְּלִילִי, תֵּיפּוֹק לֵיהּ מִ״לֶּחֶם עֹנִי״ – מִי שֶׁנֶּאֱכָל בְּאוֹנִי, יָצָא זֶה שֶׁאֵין נֶאֱכָל אֶלָּא בְּשִׂמְחָה!

The Gemara asks: **And Rabbi Yosei HaGelili,** why does he learn this *halakha* from the phrase: "In all of your habitations"? **Let him derive it from** the phrase: ***Leḥem oni*** (Deuteronomy 16:3). Rabbi Yosei HaGelili derives from this expression that *matza* must be prepared from produce **that** can **be eaten in** a state of **acute mourning;** that **excludes this** second tithe, **which** may **be eaten only in** a state of **joy.** This exposition should apply to first fruits as well, as they must also be eaten in a state of joy.

NOTES

First fruits – בִּכּוּרִים: The obligation to bring first fruits to the Temple is stated in the Torah (Deuteronomy 26:1–11) and is discussed in great detail in tractate *Bikkurim*, in the mishna and in the Jerusalem Talmud. This mitzva involves the bringing of a small amount of first fruits, one-sixtieth of the harvest, before *teruma* is separated from the crop. The first fruits must be brought from the seven types of fruit for which Israel is praised all the way to the Temple in Jerusalem. A large, festive ceremony accompanied the procession of the first fruits to the city. The owner of the fruit would bring his basket up to the altar, where he would wave it and recite the prayers of praise and thanksgiving that appear in the Torah. At this stage of the ritual, the status of the first fruits becomes like that of *teruma*, and the fruits belong to the priest.

Carrying is nothing other than eating – אֵין שְׂאֵת אֶלָּא אֲכִילָה: The verse is interpreted as follows: Second tithe can be exchanged either because "the way is too long for you," if one lives far from Jerusalem, even if the tithe is pure; or due to the fact "that you are not able to carry it," i.e., it has been brought into Jerusalem but cannot be used (Rashi).

HALAKHA

Second-tithe produce that became ritually impure – מַעֲשֵׂר שֵׁנִי שֶׁנִּטְמָא: Ritually impure second-tithe produce may be redeemed, even in Jerusalem. The fruits purchased with its redemption money must be eaten in a state of ritual purity, like second-tithe produce itself (Rambam *Sefer Zera'im*, *Hilkhot Ma'aser Sheni* 3:3).

סָבַר לֵיהּ כְּרַבִּי שִׁמְעוֹן, דְּתַנְיָא: בִּיכּוּרִים אֲסוּרִין לָאוֹנֵן, וְרַבִּי שִׁמְעוֹן מַתִּיר.

The Gemara explains: Rabbi Yosei HaGelili **maintains in accordance with** the opinion of **Rabbi Shimon,** who says that an acute mourner may eat first fruits. **As it was taught** in a *baraita*: **First fruits are prohibited to an acute mourner,**[H] **and Rabbi Shimon permits** an acute mourner to eat first fruits.

מַאי טַעְמָא דְּרַבָּנַן – דִּכְתִיב: ״לֹא תוּכַל לֶאֱכֹל בִּשְׁעָרֶיךָ״ וְאָמַר מָר: ״תְּרוּמַת יָדֶךָ״ – אֵלּוּ בִּיכּוּרִים, דְּאִיתְקַשׁ בִּיכּוּרִים לְמַעֲשֵׂר, מַה מַּעֲשֵׂר אָסוּר לָאוֹנֵן – אַף בִּיכּוּרִים אָסוּר לָאוֹנֵן.

The Gemara explains this dispute: **What is the reason for the Rabbis'** opinion, which maintains that an acute mourner may not eat first fruits? **As it is written: "You may not eat within your gates** the tithe of your corn, or of your wine, or of your oil, or the firstlings of your herd or of your flock, nor any of your vows which you vow, nor your free-will offerings, nor the offering of your hand" (Deuteronomy 12:17). **And the Master said: "The offering of your hand," these are first fruits,** as this verse **compares first fruits to** the second **tithe: Just as** the second **tithe is prohibited to an acute mourner,**[H] as stated explicitly in the Torah, **so too** are **first fruits prohibited to an acute mourner.**

וְרַבִּי שִׁמְעוֹן: תְּרוּמָה קָרֵינְהוּ רַחֲמָנָא, כִּתְרוּמָה; מַה תְּרוּמָה מוּתֶּרֶת לָאוֹנֵן – אַף בִּיכּוּרִים מוּתָּר לָאוֹנֵן.

And Rabbi Shimon says in response to this contention: First fruits **are called** *teruma* **by the Merciful One** and therefore their status is **like** that of *teruma*: **Just as** *teruma* **is permitted to an acute mourner, so too first fruits** are **permitted to an acute mourner.**

וְרַבִּי שִׁמְעוֹן, נְהִי דְּהֶיקֵּישׁ לֵית לֵיהּ שִׂמְחָה מִיהָא מִיכְתַּב כְּתִיבָא בְּהוּ, דִּכְתִיב ״וְשָׂמַחְתָּ בְכָל הַטּוֹב״!

The Gemara asks: **And Rabbi Shimon, although he does not** accept this **juxtaposition** of first fruits and second tithe, **in any case** the word **joy is written with regard to** first fruits, **as it is written: "And you shall rejoice in all the good** that the Lord has given you and your household" (Deuteronomy 26:11). In light of this, how can Rabbi Shimon permit an acute mourner to eat first fruits?

הַהוּא לִזְמַן שִׂמְחָה הוּא דַּאֲתָא, דִּתְנַן: מֵעֲצֶרֶת וְעַד הֶחָג – מֵבִיא וְקוֹרֵא, מֵהֶחָג וְעַד חֲנוּכָּה – מֵבִיא וְאֵינוֹ קוֹרֵא.

The Gemara answers: Rabbi Shimon does not learn from **that** verse that one must eat first fruits while he is personally happy; rather, **it comes** to teach us **that** first fruits should be eaten during the **period of rejoicing. As we learned** in a mishna: **From** *Shevuot* **until** *Sukkot*, **one brings** first fruits **and recites** the prayers of thanks to God that appear in the Torah. **From** *Sukkot* **until Hanukkah one** may **bring** first fruits, **but he does not recite** the portion from the Torah.[H] This mishna states that the ideal time for bringing first fruits to the Temple is during the joyous harvest season, from which it may be inferred that this verse is not referring to personal joy of the one bringing the first fruits, but rather to the period of communal joy.

תָּנוּ רַבָּנַן: ״לֶחֶם עֹנִי״ – פְּרָט לְחָלוּט וְלַאֲשִׁישָׁה. יָכוֹל לֹא יֵצֵא אָדָם יְדֵי חוֹבָתוֹ אֶלָּא בְּפַת הַדְרָאָה – תַּלְמוּד לוֹמַר: ״מַצּוֹת מַצּוֹת״ – רִיבָּה, וַאֲפִילּוּ כְּמַצּוֹת שֶׁל שְׁלֹמֹה. אִם כֵּן מַה תַּלְמוּד לוֹמַר: ״לֶחֶם עוֹנִי״ – פְּרָט לְחָלוּט וְלַאֲשִׁישָׁה.

The Sages taught that the phrase **poor man's bread** [***leḥem oni***] **excludes** *matza* that **was boiled** [***ḥalut***][N] in hot water after it was baked, which is considered to be a relative delicacy; **and** this expression also excludes *matza* that was baked as a **large cake** [***ashisha***].[N] **I might** have thought that **a person fulfills his obligation** to eat *matza* **only with coarse** [***hadra'a***][L] **bread;**[N] therefore, **the verse states: "*Matzot*," "*matzot*,"** which serves to **amplify** and include *matza* prepared with fine-grade flour. **And** in fact, one could fulfill his obligation **even with *matzot* like those of** King **Solomon,** which were prepared from the finest sifted flour.[H] **If so, what is** the meaning when **the verse states: "Poor man's bread"?** This phrase comes **to exclude boiled** *matza* **and large cakes,**[H] but it does not exclude *matza* prepared from refined flour.

HALAKHA

First fruits for an acute mourner – בִּכּוּרִים לָאוֹנֵן: It is prohibited for an acute mourner to eat first fruits, and one who does so is punished with lashes for rebelliousness, as he has violated a rabbinic prohibition (Rambam *Sefer Zera'im*, *Hilkhot Bikkurim* 3:6).

Second tithe for an acute mourner – מַעֲשֵׂר לָאוֹנֵן: As stated in the Torah, an acute mourner may not eat second-tithe produce (Rambam *Sefer Zera'im*, *Hilkhot Ma'aser Sheni* 3:5).

The time for bringing first fruits – זְמַן בִּכּוּרִים: One who brings first fruits to the Temple between *Shavuot* and *Sukkot* recites the prayers of thanks to God stated in the Torah. If he brings his first fruits between *Sukkot* and Hanukkah, they are still accepted but he does not recite these prayers (Rambam *Sefer Zera'im*, *Hilkhot Bikkurim* 4:13).

Matza prepared from fine sifted flour – מַצַּת סוֹלֶת: One may bake *matza* with even the finest of sifted flour, as *matza* made with this type of flour is still called poor man's bread (*Shulḥan Arukh*, *Oraḥ Ḥayyim* 454:3).

Boiled *matza* [*ḥalut*] and large cakes – חָלוּט וַאֲשִׁישָׁה: *Matza* that was prepared via a process of *ḥalita*, by mixing boiling water and flour before kneading, may not be used to fulfill one's obligation to eat *matza* on Passover. Nowadays, we are unfamiliar with the different types of *ḥalita*, and therefore this method is avoided altogether, even for *matza* that will not be used to fulfill the mitzva (*Shulḥan Arukh*, *Oraḥ Ḥayyim* 454:3).

LANGUAGE

Coarse [*hadra'a*] – הַדְרָאָה: According to the *Arukh*'s version of the text, this word is derived from the Latin horedeum, barley. In other words, this bread was considered low quality because it consisted of barley, as opposed to fine bread, which was prepared from wheat.

NOTES

Boiled [*ḥalut*] – חָלוּט: The commentaries provide several explanations of the term *ḥalut*, as well as for the reason this process invalidates *matza* for the mitzva. Some say that it refers to *matza* placed in boiling honey or oil, which is disqualified as *matza ashira*, enhanced *matza* (Rav Hai Gaon; Rav Yehuda ben Rav Binyamin HaRofeh; Rabbeinu Efrayim; Ramban; *Mikhtam*). Others claim that even placing *matza* in boiling water invalidates it, as this renders it a kind of delicacy (Rabbi Zeraḥya HaLevi in the *Ba'al HaMaor*; Ra'avad; Rashi possibly agrees as well). Yet others suggest that *ḥalut* refers to dough boiled in water. It cannot be used as *matza* as it was not baked, and is therefore not classified as bread (Rabbeinu Yehonatan; see the *Ba'al HaMaor*).

Ashisha – אֲשִׁישָׁה: Some commentaries say that this is dough prepared with oil and honey (*Ba'al HaMaor*; Rabbeinu Yehonatan), while others claim it is a very large *matza* that has the appearance of a significant dish, i.e., one that would not be eaten by paupers (Rav Yehuda ben Rav Binyamin HaRofeh).

Coarse [*hadra'a*] bread – הַדְרָאָה: Everyone agrees that this refers to bread prepared from poor-quality flour. Some commentaries claim that *hadra'a* is derived from *dara*, which means worm, and refers to bread prepared from wheat that has been destroyed by worms (Maharam Ḥalawa, citing Rambam; others). Other suggest that the root is *hadar*, meaning beautiful, a euphemism for inferior bread (*Mikhtam*).

וּמַאי מַשְׁמַע דְּהַאי אֲשִׁישָׁה לִישָּׁנָא דַּחֲשִׁיבוּתָא – דִּכְתִיב: ״וַיְחַלֵּק לְכָל הָעָם לְכָל הֲמוֹן יִשְׂרָאֵל לְמֵאִישׁ וְעַד אִשָּׁה לְאִישׁ חַלַּת לֶחֶם אַחַת וְאֶשְׁפָּר אֶחָד וַאֲשִׁישָׁה אַחַת וגו׳״.

The Gemara asks: **From where** may it be **inferred** that *ashisha* **is an expression** that indicates **importance? As it is written** with regard to King David's celebration after he brought the Ark of the Covenant to Jerusalem: **"And he dealt among all the people, among the whole multitude of Israel, both to men and women, to every one a cake of bread, and an** *eshpar*, **and an** *ashisha*, and all the people departed, every one to his house" (II Samuel 6:19).

וְאָמַר רַב חָנָן בַּר אַבָּא: ״אֶשְׁפָּר״ – אֶחָד מִשִּׁשָּׁה בַּפָּר, ״אֲשִׁישָׁה״ – אֶחָד מִשִּׁשָּׁה בָּאֵיפָה. וּפְלִיגָא דִּשְׁמוּאֵל, דְּאָמַר שְׁמוּאֵל: אֲשִׁישָׁה – גַּרְבָּא דְּחַמְרָא, דִּכְתִיב: ״וְאֹהֲבֵי אֲשִׁישֵׁי עֲנָבִים״.

And Rav Ḥanan bar Abba said: The word *eshpar* refers to a portion of meat equivalent to **one-sixth of an ox,** and the word *ashisha* refers to a cake prepared from **one-sixth of an** *eipha* of flour. **And** this interpretation **disputes** the opinion **of Shmuel, as Shmuel said:** *Ashisha* means **a jug of wine, as it is written: "And those who love the jug [*ashishei*] of grapes"** (Hosea 3:1).

תָּנוּ רַבָּנַן: אֵין אוֹפִין פַּת עָבָה (בְּיוֹם טוֹב) בְּפֶסַח, דִּבְרֵי בֵּית שַׁמַּאי,

The Sages taught: One may **not bake thick bread on the Festival, on Passover,** as it might be leavened before it has a chance to bake; this is **the statement of Beit Shammai.**

Perek **II**
Daf **37** Amud **a**

וּבֵית הִלֵּל מַתִּירִין. וְכַמָּה פַּת עָבָה? אָמַר רַב הוּנָא: טֶפַח, שֶׁכֵּן מָצִינוּ בְּלֶחֶם הַפָּנִים טֶפַח.

And Beit Hillel permit one to bake bread in this manner. The Gemara asks: **And how much** thickness is required for the *matza* to be considered **thick bread?**[H] **Rav Huna said:** This category includes *matza* that is **a handbreadth** thick. The proof is **as we found by the shewbread,**[N] which could not be leavened and which was **a handbreadth** thick.

מַתְקִיף לָהּ רַב יוֹסֵף: אִם אָמְרוּ בִּזְרִיזִין – יֹאמְרוּ בְּשֶׁאֵינָן זְרִיזִין? אִם אָמְרוּ בְּפַת עֲמִילָה – יֹאמְרוּ בְּפַת שֶׁאֵינוֹ עֲמִילָה?

Rav Yosef strongly objects to this explanation: **If** the Sages **said** that it is permitted to bake bread a handbreadth thick for the shewbread, which was prepared **by diligent** priests who ensured that the dough did not become leavened, will **they say** the same **with regard to** other people **who are not** as **diligent?** Furthermore, **if they said** this **with regard to well-kneaded bread,** will **they say** the same **with regard to bread that is not well kneaded?**

אִם אָמְרוּ בְּעֵצִים יְבֵשִׁין – יֹאמְרוּ בְּעֵצִים לַחִים? אִם אָמְרוּ בְּתַנּוּר חַם – יֹאמְרוּ בְּתַנּוּר צוֹנֵן? אִם אָמְרוּ בְּתַנּוּר שֶׁל מַתֶּכֶת – יֹאמְרוּ בְּתַנּוּר שֶׁל חֶרֶס?

Rav Yosef continues: **If they said** that bread a handbreadth thick is permitted in a case where the bread was cooked **with dry wood,** which was brought to the Temple during the dry summer months, as the heat generated from this type of wood would cause the bread to cook quickly before it leavened, will **they say** the same with regard to ordinary people who cook **with moist wood? If they said** this **with regard to a hot oven** in the Temple, will **they** also **say** it is permitted **with regard to a cool oven?** Finally, **if they said** so **with regard to** the shewbread, which was baked **in a metal oven** that could be heated quickly, will **they say** the same **with regard to a clay oven?** Clearly, these two cases are different, and no comparison can be drawn between the shewbread and ordinary *matza*.

אָמַר רַב יִרְמְיָה בַּר אַבָּא: שְׁאִילִית אֶת רַבִּי בְּיִחוּד, וּמַנּוּ – רַב. אִיכָּא דְּאָמְרִי: רַב יִרְמְיָה בַּר אַבָּא אָמַר רַב: שְׁאִילִית אֶת רַבִּי בְּיִחוּד, וּמַנּוּ – רַבֵּינוּ הַקָּדוֹשׁ. מַאי פַּת עָבָה? פַּת מְרוּבָּה. וְאַמַּאי קָרוּ לֵיהּ פַּת עָבָה? מִשּׁוּם דִּנְפִישָׁא בְּלִישָׁה. וְאִי בָּעֵית אֵימָא: בְּאַתְרֵיהּ דְּהַאי תַּנָּא לְפַת מְרוּבָּה פַּת עָבָה קָרוּ לֵיהּ.

Rabbi Yirmeya bar Abba said: I asked my special Rabbi, and who is this? Rav. Some say that **Rabbi Yirmeya bar Abba said** that **Rav said: I asked my special Rabbi, and who is this? Our holy Rabbi,** Rabbi Yehuda HaNasi: **What is** the meaning of the expression: *Pat ava*? He explained that it means: **A large** quantity **of bread,**[HN] a large batch of dough prepared in one session. **And why did they call it:** *Pat ava*, thick bread? It is referred to by this name **due to** the fact **that** it requires **a large** amount of **kneading. And if you wish, say** instead that **in the place where this** *tanna* **lived, a large quantity of bread was** simply **called** *pat ava*, thick bread.

HALAKHA

Thick bread – פַּת עָבָה: One should not bake *matza* a handbreadth thick during Passover *ab initio* (Rabbeinu Yeruḥam, based on the Gemara here). However, if one did so it is permitted to eat this *matza* after the fact (*Magen Avraham*; *Shulḥan Arukh*, *Oraḥ Ḥayyim* 460:5).

A large quantity of bread on a Festival – פַּת מְרוּבָּה בֶּחָג: One may bake an ovenful of bread on a Festival, even if he does not need it all on the Festival itself. However, this leniency applies only to small ovens, where the bread was pasted against the inner walls and baked, not to larger ovens. With regard to larger ovens, one may prepare only as much bread as he plans to eat during the Festival itself (*Beit Yosef*; *Shulḥan Arukh*, *Oraḥ Ḥayyim* 507:6).

NOTES

Shewbread – לֶחֶם הַפָּנִים: The Torah (Leviticus 24:5–9) describes the offering of the twelve loaves of shewbread that were placed on the sacred table in the Sanctuary each Shabbat. The bread of the previous week was divided among the priests and consumed by them. The shewbread was unleavened and placed on the table in two arrangements of six loaves each. Two bowls of frankincense were placed between them, or on top of them, according to some opinions.

A large quantity of bread – פַּת מְרוּבָּה: Some commentaries explain that Beit Shammai are concerned that some of the bread will be left over after the Festival, and it will therefore be considered as though one baked bread on a Festival for later use. Conversely, Beit Hillel claim that although one does not need all the bread, it will bake better if the oven is full (Rabbi Yehonatan; Rav Yehuda ben Rav Binyamin HaRofeh; *Nimmukei Yosef*).

מַאי טַעְמָא? אִי מִשּׁוּם דְּקָא טָרַח טִירְחָא דְּלָא צָרִיךְ – מַאי אִירְיָא בְּפֶסַח? אֲפִילּוּ בְּיוֹם טוֹב נָמֵי!

The Gemara asks: **What is the reason** for this prohibition against preparing a large batch? **If** the reason **is due to the unnecessary exertion** that is required to knead a large amount of dough, which is an improper activity on a Festival, **why** discuss **particularly** the application of this *halakha* **to Passover?** The same *halakha* **should** apply **also to other Festivals.**

אִין הָכִי נָמֵי, וְהַאי תַּנָּא בְּיוֹם טוֹב שֶׁל פֶּסַח קָאֵי. תַּנְיָא נָמֵי הָכִי, בֵּית שַׁמַּאי אוֹמְרִים: אֵין אוֹפִין פַּת עָבָה בְּיוֹם טוֹב, וּבֵית הִלֵּל מַתִּירִין.

The Gemara answers: **Yes, it is indeed so;** it is prohibited to prepare a large quantity of dough during any Festival. **And** while **this *tanna* was referring to the festival of Passover,** he incidentally mentioned a *halakha* that actually applies to other Festivals as well. The Gemara comments: **That** opinion **was also taught** in a *baraita*, which states that **Beit Shammai say: One** may **not bake *pat ava* on a Festival, and Beit Hillel permit** baking bread in this manner on a Festival.

תָּנוּ רַבָּנַן: יוֹצְאִין בְּפַת נְקִיָּה וּבְהַדְרָאָה, וּבִסְרִיקִין הַמְצוּיָּירִין בְּפֶסַח, אַף עַל פִּי שֶׁאָמְרוּ: אֵין עוֹשִׂין סְרִיקִין הַמְצוּיָּירִין בְּפֶסַח. אָמַר רַב יְהוּדָה: דָּבָר זֶה שָׁאַל בַּיְיתוֹס בֶּן זוֹנִין לַחֲכָמִים: מִפְּנֵי מָה אָמְרוּ אֵין עוֹשִׂין סְרִיקִין הַמְצוּיָּירִין בְּפֶסַח? אָמְרוּ לוֹ: מִפְּנֵי שֶׁהָאִשָּׁה שׁוֹהָה עָלֶיהָ, וּמַחְמִיצְתָּהּ.

The Sages taught: One fulfills the obligation to eat *matza* **on Passover with fine bread, with coarse bread, and** after the fact **with** *matza* **shaped in figures, although they said** that **one should not bake** *matza* **shaped in figures**[H] **on Passover** *ab initio*. **Rav Yehuda said** that **Baitos ben Zonin**[L] **asked the Sages** about **this matter: Why did** the Sages **say** that **one** may **not prepare** *matza* **shaped in figures on Passover** *ab initio*? **They said to him:** The reason is **because a woman will tarry over it** as she prepares the bread, so that she can form the figure before it is baked, **and she will** thereby **cause it to become leavened.**

אָמַר לָהֶם: אֶפְשָׁר יַעֲשֶׂנָּה בִּדְפוּס, וְיִקְבָּעֶנָּה כֵּיוָן! אָמְרוּ לוֹ: יֹאמְרוּ כׇּל הַסְּרִיקִין – אֲסוּרִין, וּסְרִיקֵי בַּיְיתוֹס – מוּתָּרִין.

He said to them: It is possible for a woman **to prepare** this *matza* **with a mold, and** she could **set it immediately,** without delaying the baking process. **They said to him:** People would fail to understand the distinction, and **they would say** that **all shaped** *matza* **is prohibited, and** yet **Baitos' shaped** *matza*[N] **is permitted.** Consequently, the Sages rejected this distinction, and prohibited all forms of *matza* shaped in figures on Passover.

אָמַר רַבִּי אֶלְעָזָר בַּר צָדוֹק: פַּעַם אַחַת נִכְנַסְתִּי אַחַר אַבָּא לְבֵית רַבָּן גַּמְלִיאֵל, וְהֵבִיאוּ לְפָנָיו סְרִיקִין הַמְצוּיָּירִין בְּפֶסַח. אָמַרְתִּי: אַבָּא, לֹא כָּךְ אָמְרוּ חֲכָמִים ״אֵין עוֹשִׂין סְרִיקִין הַמְצוּיָּירִין בְּפֶסַח״? אָמַר לִי: בְּנִי, לֹא שֶׁל כׇּל אָדָם אָמְרוּ, אֶלָּא שֶׁל נַחְתּוֹמִין אָמְרוּ.

Rabbi Elazar bar Tzadok said: Once I followed my father, Rabbi Tzadok, **into Rabban Gamliel's home, and they brought before him** *matza* **shaped in figures on Passover. I said: Father, didn't the Sages say** that **one** may **not prepare** *matza* **shaped in figures on Passover? He said to me: My son, they did not say this** prohibition **for the** *matza* of **all** ordinary **people; rather, they said so** in regard to the *matza* **of bakers,** who are under pressure to enhance the appearance of their products to in order to increase sales. The dough could leaven, since bakers might take too much time to ensure that the shape of their *matza* is exactly right.

אִיכָּא דְּאָמְרִי, הָכִי קָאָמַר לֵיהּ: לֹא שֶׁל נַחְתּוֹמִין אָמְרוּ, אֶלָּא שֶׁל כׇּל אָדָם. אָמַר רַבִּי יוֹסֵי: עוֹשִׂין סְרִיקִין כְּמִין רְקִיקִין, וְאֵין עוֹשִׂין סְרִיקִין כְּמִין גְּלוּסְקָאוֹת.

Some say that **this is** what Rabbi Tzadok **said to** his son: The Sages **did not say** that this practice is prohibited with regard to the *matza* **of bakers,** who are expert and efficient in their work and will do it quickly, but **rather** this prohibition applies to the *matza* **of all** ordinary **people.** According to both version of this exchange, it is permitted to eat this *matza* after the fact. **Rabbi Yosei said: One** may **prepare** *matzot* **shaped as thin wafers, but one** may **not prepare** *matzot* **shaped as thick loaves,** as the latter is more likely to be leavened.

תָּנוּ רַבָּנַן: הַסּוּפְגָּנִין, וְהַדּוּבְשָׁנִין, וְאִיסְקְרִיטִין, וְחַלַּת הַמַּסְרֵת, וְהַמְדוּמָּע – פְּטוּרִים מִן הַחַלָּה. מַאי חַלַּת הַמַּסְרֵת? אָמַר רַבִּי יְהוֹשֻׁעַ בֶּן לֵוִי: זֶה חָלוּט שֶׁל בַּעֲלֵי בָתִּים.

The Sages taught: Sponge-like cakes, honey cakes, spiced cakes [***eskeritin***],[L] **pan-fried bread** [***ḥallat hamasret***],[N] **and** bread prepared from **a mixture** of permitted grain and *teruma*,[N] their owners **are** all **exempt from *ḥalla*.** The Gemara clarifies these obscure terms. **What is pan-fried bread? Rabbi Yehoshua ben Levi said: This is boiled bread** baked **by** ordinary **homeowners** in a deep frying pan.

HALAKHA

Matza shaped in figures – סְרִיקִין הַמְצוּיָּירִין: One may not prepare *matza* shaped in figures on Passover. This *halakha* applies whether the shapes are formed by a mold or prepared by bakers, as we do not rely on the leniencies stated in the Gemara, in accordance with the statement of the Sages. The custom is to poke small holes in the *matzot*, which are not added to create a form, but rather to prevent the *matza* from becoming leavened. After the fact, if one shaped *matza* into a figure and it was not leavened in the process, it may even be used to fulfill one's obligation to eat *matza* (*Shulḥan Arukh*, *Oraḥ Ḥayyim* 460:4).

LANGUAGE

Baitos ben Zonin – בַּיְיתוֹס בֶּן זוֹנִין: Baitos is the Greek name Βοηθός, Boëthus, meaning helper or aide, and may be a translation of the Hebrew name Ezra. Zonin is the Greek name Ζήνων, Zeno.

Spiced cakes [*eskeritin*] – אִיסְקְרִיטִין: Apparently from the Greek ἐσχαρίτης, *escharitès*, a type of bread baked over the fire.

NOTES

Baitos' shaped *matza* – סְרִיקֵי בַּיְיתוֹס: This *halakha* is based on the well-known principle that the Sages did not distinguish between particular cases in the application of their decrees. The Sages regularly included in their decrees activities that could be reasonably viewed as exceptions, in order to maintain the overall effectiveness of the decree.

Pan-fried bread [*ḥallat hamasret*] – חַלַּת הַמַּסְרֵת: Some commentaries associate *masret*, which is written with the letter *samekh*, with the term *masret*, which is written with a *sin*. *Masret* with the letter *sin* means a frying pan, as in II Samuel 13:9. Consequently, *ḥallat masret* means bread prepared in a frying pan (*Mikhtam*). However, others claim that this bread was prepared by being boiled before it was baked (*Arukh*).

Mixture of permitted grain and *teruma* – הַמְדוּמָּע: According to most commentaries, this refers to dough prepared from non-sacred grain into which *teruma* fell. However, it is unclear who is eating this bread. It is presumably prohibited for an Israelite to eat it, due to the *teruma* it contains, while priests would not be required to separate *ḥalla* from this mixture, as they are permitted to eat *ḥalla*. Consequently, some commentaries explain that this phrase refers to a case where an Israelite unwittingly ate most of this mixture of *teruma*, or a case where a small quantity of *teruma* fell into the dough and was nullified by the far larger amount of non-consecrated dough. Yet others suggest that the dough actually belongs to a priest and claim that priests are also required to separate *ḥalla*, despite the fact that they may eat it afterward. This is similar to the *halakha* that even a priest may not eat untithed produce until he has separated its *teruma* and tithes (*Me'iri*).

LANGUAGE

Pot-boiled stew [*ilpas*] – אִילְפָּס: From the Greek λοπάς, *lopas*, referring to a large vessel used for cooking, eating, and drinking.

Greek *lopas*

אָמַר רֵישׁ לָקִישׁ: הַלָּלוּ מַעֲשֵׂה אִילְפָּס הֵן. וְרַבִּי יוֹחָנָן אָמַר: מַעֲשֵׂה אִילְפָּס חַיָּיבִין, וְהַלָּלוּ שֶׁעֲשָׂאָן בַּחַמָּה.

Reish Lakish said: These dishes **are pot-boiled stew** [*ilpas*],[L] not bread. Since this food is prepared in a pot and not in an oven, it has been boiled rather than baked, and its owner is therefore exempt from *ḥalla*. **And Rabbi Yoḥanan said:** Even the owner of bread prepared like **a pot-boiled stew**[H] **is obligated** in *ḥalla*, but the owners of **these** pan-fried breads and the other baked goods listed are exempt, **as** these breads **were baked in the sun.** Since they were not baked over a fire, they are not classified as bread with regard to the mitzva of *ḥalla*.

מֵיתִיבִי: הַסּוּפְגָּנִין וְהַדּוּבְשָׁנִין וְהָאֶיסְקְרִיטִין, עֲשָׂאָן בָּאִילְפָּס – חַיָּיבִין, בַּחַמָּה – פְּטוּרִין. תְּיוּבְתֵּיה דְּרַבִּי שִׁמְעוֹן בֶּן לָקִישׁ! אָמַר עוּלָּא, אָמַר לָךְ רַבִּי שִׁמְעוֹן בֶּן לָקִישׁ: הָכָא בְּמַאי עָסְקִינַן – שֶׁהִרְתִּיחַ וּלְבַסּוֹף הִדְבִּיק –

The Gemara **raises an objection** to the statement of Rabbi Shimon ben Lakish statement from a *baraita*: With regard to **sponge-cakes, honey cakes, or spiced cakes,** if one **prepared them in a pot,** he is **obligated** to separate *ḥalla*. However, if he prepared them **in the sun,** he is **exempt** from this mitzva. This is **a conclusive refutation** of the opinion of **Rabbi Shimon ben Lakish. Ulla said: Rabbi Shimon ben Lakish** could have **said to you: With what are we dealing here?** We are dealing with a case **where one heated** the pot over the fire **and afterward pasted** the dough to the sides of the hot pot. This is considered like baking in an oven, and one is therefore obligated to separate *ḥalla* from the dough.

אֲבָל הִדְבִּיק וּלְבַסּוֹף הִרְתִּיחַ מַאי – הָכִי נַמִי דִּפְטוּרִין, אַדְּתָנֵי סֵיפָא ״עֲשָׂאָן בַּחַמָּה פְּטוּרִין״ לִיפְלוֹג וְלִיתְנֵי בְּדִידָהּ: בַּמֶּה דְּבָרִים אֲמוּרִים – כְּגוֹן שֶׁהִרְתִּיחַ וּלְבַסּוֹף הִדְבִּיק, אֲבָל הִדְבִּיק וּלְבַסּוֹף הִרְתִּיחַ – פְּטוּרִין!

The Gemara asks: **However,** if one **pasted** the dough to the sides of the pot **and afterward heated** it, **what** is the *halakha*? **So too,** you will say **that** is he is **exempt** from the mitzva of *ḥalla*? If so, **rather than teach** in **the latter clause** of that *baraita* that the owner of the bread is **exempt if it was baked in the sun, let** the *tanna* **distinguish and teach** this *halakha* **within** the presentation of this case **itself: In what** case **is this statement,** that one who prepares this bread in a pot is obligated to separate *ḥalla*, **said? For example, when one heated the pot and afterward pasted** the bread to its sides; **but if he placed the bread** in the pot **and** then **boiled** it, he is **exempt.** Why didn't the *baraita* formulate the *halakha* in this manner?

חַסּוּרֵי מִחַסְּרָא וְהָכִי קָתָנֵי: בַּמֶּה דְּבָרִים אֲמוּרִים – שֶׁהִרְתִּיחַ וּלְבַסּוֹף הִדְבִּיק, אֲבָל הִדְבִּיק וּלְבַסּוֹף הִרְתִּיחַ – נַעֲשֶׂה כְּמִי שֶׁעֲשָׂאָן בַּחַמָּה וּפְטוּרִין.

The Gemara answers: The text of the *baraita* **is incomplete and is teaching the following: In what** case **is this statement said?** In a case **where one heated** the pot **and afterward pasted** the bread to its sides. **However,** if **one placed** the bread inside the pot **and afterward boiled** it, **it is** considered **as though it had been cooked in the sun, and** he is **exempt** from separating *ḥalla*.

תָּא שְׁמַע: יוֹצְאִין בְּמַצָּה הִינָא וּבְמַצָּה הָעֲשׂוּיָה בָּאִילְפָּס! הָכָא נַמִי: שֶׁהִרְתִּיחַ וּלְבַסּוֹף הִדְבִּיק.

Come and **hear** a difficulty from a *baraita*: One can **fulfill** the obligation to eat *matza* **with half-baked** ***matza***[H] **and pot-boiled** ***matza***.[H] Apparently, dough baked in a pot is classified as bread. The Gemara answers: **Here too,** the *baraita* is referring to a case **where one heated** the pot like an oven, **and afterward he pasted** the dough to the sides of the pot.

מַאי מַצָּה הִינָא? אָמַר רַב יְהוּדָה אָמַר שְׁמוּאֵל: כֹּל שֶׁפּוֹרְסָהּ וְאֵין חוּטִין נִמְשָׁכִין הֵימֶנָּה. אָמַר רָבָא: וְכֵן לַחֲמֵי תוֹדָה. פְּשִׁיטָא, הָכָא ״לֶחֶם״ כְּתִיב, וְהָכָא ״לֶחֶם״ כְּתִיב!

The Gemara asks: **What is half-baked** ***matza***? **Rav Yehuda said** that **Shmuel said:** This refers to **any** *matza* **that** is sufficiently baked so that **when** it is **broken no strands** of dough **emerge from its sides. Rava said: And likewise the loaves of the thanks-offering** may be used if they have been baked to this extent. The Gemara asks: It is **obvious** that this is the case, as **here,** with regard to *matza*, **"bread" is written, and there,** with regard to the loaves of the thanks-offering, **"bread"** is also **written** (Leviticus 7:13). Since both loaves are called bread, it is obvious that the same criteria should apply to both cases.

מַהוּ דְּתֵימָא: הוֹאִיל וּכְתִיב: ״וְהִקְרִיב מִמֶּנּוּ

The Gemara rejects this assertion: This statement is necessary, **lest you say** the following: **Since it is written** with regard to a thanks-offering: **"And he shall present from it**

HALAKHA

Ḥalla from pot-boiled bread – מַעֲשֵׂי אִילְפָּס בְּחַלָּה: Dough baked in a pot is subject to the obligation of *ḥalla*, even though the bread has not been prepared in an oven (*Shulḥan Arukh, Yoreh De'a* 329:8).

Half-baked *matza* – מַצָּה הִינָא: One can fulfill his obligation to eat *matza* with *matza* that has been baked to the extent that no strands of dough emerge from it when it is broken, as stated in the *baraita* and explained by the Gemara (*Shulḥan Arukh, Oraḥ Ḥayyim* 461:3).

Pot-boiled *matza* – מַצָּה הָעֲשׂוּיָה בָּאִילְפָּס: One can fulfill the obligation to eat *matza* with *matza* that was prepared by heating a pot and pasting dough to its sides. Some authorities say it is forbidden to use this *matza* if one first pasted the dough and afterward heated the pot (Rav Amram Gaon). One should therefore avoid preparing *matza* in this manner *ab initio* (*Shulḥan Arukh, Oraḥ Ḥayyim* 461:2).

אֶחָד מִכָּל קׇרְבָּן", "אֶחָד" – שֶׁלֹּא יִטּוֹל פָּרוּס, וְהָכָא כְּמַאן דִּפְרִיסָא דָּמְיָא, קָא מַשְׁמַע לַן.

one out of each offering for a gift to the Lord; it shall belong to the priest who sprinkles the blood of the peace-offerings" (Leviticus 7:14), and the word **"one"** indicates that it must be a whole loaf, i.e., **that** one should **not take a broken** piece,[H] **and here** the bread has not been properly baked, it might therefore have been thought that **it is considered as though it were broken.** Consequently, the *baraita* **teaches us** that this is nevertheless classified as bread.

מֵיתִיבִי: הַמְּעִיסָּה, בֵּית שַׁמַּאי פּוֹטְרִין, וּבֵית הִלֵּל מְחַיְּיבִין. הַחֲלִיטָה, בֵּית שַׁמַּאי מְחַיְּיבִין, וּבֵית הִלֵּל פּוֹטְרִין. אֵיזֶהוּ הַמְּעִיסָּה וְאֵיזֶהוּ הַחֲלִיטָה? הַמְּעִיסָּה – קֶמַח שֶׁעַל גַּבֵּי מוּגְלָשִׁין, הַחֲלִיטָה – מוּגְלָשִׁין שֶׁעַל גַּבֵּי קֶמַח.

The Gemara **raises an objection:** With regard to *me'isa*, dough that was boiled in water, **Beit Shammai exempt** one from separating *ḥalla*, **and Beit Hillel obligate one** to do so. As for dough that has undergone the process of ***ḥalita*, Beit Shammai obligate** one to separate *ḥalla* from it, **and Beit Hillel exempt.** The Gemara asks: **What is *me'isa* and what is *ḥalita*?**[N] The Gemara explains: ***Me'isa*** is dough prepared by pouring **flour on boiling water** [***muglashin***],[N] whereas ***ḥalita*** is formed by pouring **boiling water on flour.**[H]

רַבִּי יִשְׁמָעֵאל בְּרַבִּי יוֹסֵי אוֹמֵר מִשּׁוּם אָבִיו: זֶה וָזֶה לִפְטוּר, וְאָמְרִי לָהּ: זֶה וָזֶה לְחִיּוּב, וַחֲכָמִים אוֹמְרִים: אֶחָד זֶה וְאֶחָד זֶה, עֲשָׂאָן בְּאִילְפָּס – פָּטוּר, בַּתַּנּוּר – חַיָּיב.

Rabbi Yishmael, son of Rabbi Yosei, said in the name of his father: From both this, *me'isa*, **and that,** *ḥalita*, one **is exempt** from separating *ḥalla*. **And some say** that he said: With regard to both **this and that,** one **is obligated** to separate *ḥalla*. **And the Rabbis say:** With regard to both **this and that,** if one **prepared them in a pot, he is exempt** from the mitzva of *ḥalla*; however, if he prepared the bread **in an oven, he is obligated** to separate *ḥalla*.

וְתַנָּא קַמָּא, מַאי שְׁנָא הַמְּעִיסָּה וּמַאי שְׁנָא חֲלִיטָה? אָמַר רַב יְהוּדָה אָמַר שְׁמוּאֵל, וְכֵן אָמַר רַבִּי יְהוּדָה וְאִיתֵּימָא רַבִּי יְהוֹשֻׁעַ בֶּן לֵוִי: כְּמַחֲלוֹקֶת בָּזוֹ כָּךְ מַחֲלוֹקֶת בָּזוֹ. וְתַבְרָא, מִי שֶׁשָּׁנָה זוֹ לֹא שָׁנָה זוֹ.

The Gemara asks: And according to **the first *tanna***, who taught that Beit Shammai and Beit Hillel disagree with regard to these two cases, **what is different** about ***me'isa* and what is different** about ***ḥalita*?** Why do Beit Shammai and Beit Hillel reverse their opinions with regard to these types of bread? **Rav Yehuda said** that **Shmuel said, and likewise Rabbi Yehuda said, and some say** it was **Rabbi Yehoshua ben Levi** who **said: As is the dispute with regard to this** type of bread, **so is the dispute with regard to that** one; i.e., Beit Hillel are either lenient or stringent in both cases. **And** the variation in the *baraita* is due to **a break**[N] in its text, which is actually a combination of two sources, because **he who taught this** *baraita* **did not teach that** one, as the two statements were taught by different Sages.

קָתָנֵי מִיהַת: וַחֲכָמִים אוֹמְרִים אֶחָד זֶה וְאֶחָד זֶה, שֶׁעֲשָׂאָן בְּאִילְפָּס – פָּטוּר, בַּתַּנּוּר – חַיָּיב. תְּיוּבְתָּא דְּרַבִּי יוֹחָנָן! אָמַר לָךְ רַבִּי יוֹחָנָן: תַּנָּאֵי הִיא. דְּתַנְיָא: יָכוֹל יְהֵא מְעִיסָּה וַחֲלוּטָה חַיָּיבִין בַּחַלָּה – תַּלְמוּד לוֹמַר: "לֶחֶם",

The Gemara now states the objection: **In any event,** the *baraita* **is teaching** that **the Rabbis say:** With regard to both **this and that,** *me'isa* and *ḥalita*, **if one prepared them in a pot** he is **exempt** from the mitzva of *ḥalla*, but if he prepared them **in an oven** he is **obligated** to separate *ḥalla*. This is apparently **a conclusive refutation of Rabbi Yoḥanan,** who claims that one is obligated to separate *ḥalla* from bread cooked in a pot. The Gemara answers: **Rabbi Yoḥanan** could have **said to you: It is** a dispute between ***tanna'im***, **as it was taught** in a *baraita*: I **might** have thought that one is **obligated** to separate ***ḥalla*** from ***me'isa* and *ḥaluta***; therefore **the verse states "bread"** to inform us that this is not the case.

רַבִּי יְהוּדָה אוֹמֵר: אֵין לֶחֶם אֶלָּא הָאָפוּי בַּתַּנּוּר. רַבִּי יְהוּדָה הַיְינוּ תַּנָּא קַמָּא! אֶלָּא לָאו – מַעֲשֵׂה אִילְפָּס אִיכָּא בֵּינַיְיהוּ. תַּנָּא קַמָּא סָבַר: מַעֲשֵׂה אִילְפָּס חַיָּיבִין, וְרַבִּי יְהוּדָה סָבַר: מַעֲשֵׂה אִילְפָּס פְּטוּרִין,

Rabbi Yehuda says: Bread is nothing other than that which is **baked in an oven.** The Gemara asks: The opinion of **Rabbi Yehuda is the same as** that of **the first *tanna*. Rather, is it not** the case that **the** practical **difference between them is** in the case of bread prepared as **pot-boiled stew? The first *tanna* maintains** that one is **obligated** to separate *ḥalla* from bread prepared as **pot-boiled stew,** unlike bread prepared by *me'isa* and *ḥalita*. **And Rabbi Yehuda maintains:** Similar to *me'isa* and *ḥalita*, one is **exempt** from separating *ḥalla* from bread prepared as **pot-boiled stew,** as it was not baked in an oven.

HALAKHA

Loaves of a thanks-offering to a priest – לֶחֶם תּוֹדָה לַכֹּהֵן: A thanks-offering includes forty loaves, ten loaves of four different types. Since the priests take a tenth of each type, each receives a full loaf without breaking the loaves. However, if one brought only four loaves, one of each type, the priest's portion must be separated before the bread is baked, while it is still dough, as one may not break apart a portion of a loaf (Rambam *Sefer Avoda, Hilkhot Ma'aseh HaKorbanot* 9:22).

Boiled dough – עִיסָּה חֲלוּטָה: One must separate *ḥalla* from dough whether the flour was poured on the water or the water was poured on the flour. This ruling is in accordance with the opinion of Rabbi Yoḥanan and with the second version of Rabbi Yosei's opinion cited in the *baraita* (*Shulḥan Arukh, Yoreh De'a* 329:8).

NOTES

***Me'isa* and *ḥalita* – מְעִיסָּה וַחֲלִיטָה:** See *Tosafot*. Other commentaries note that one might have thought there is a difference between flour poured on water, in which case the water is in a primary vessel straight from the pot on the fire, and between hot water poured on flour, as this water is no longer in a primary vessel but has begun to cool (*Tosefot Rid*).

Boiling water [*muglashin*] – מוּגְלָשִׁין: The *Arukh* cites a version of the text that reads: *Mei gelashim*, i.e., *gelashim* water. *Gelashim* means boiling, presumably so called because it bubbles over [*golesh*] the edge of the pot. Other commentaries suggest that *muglashin* is derived from the Aramaic root *gelosh*, meaning bald, as scalding water will cause hair to fall off the skin. A proof for this interpretation is the Aramaic translation of the word *gibbe'ah*, bald, in the Torah (Leviticus 13:41) as *gelosh* (Ra'avad).

Break – תַּבְרָא: This word indicates that the quoted *baraita* is not a single unit. Instead it should be divided, as it contains statements taught by different Sages. Rabbeinu Ḥananel explains that this is an expression of an oath, and it serves to emphasize that the two statements are unrelated.

NOTES

If one pasted bread inside a pot and lit a torch opposite it – הדביק מבפנים ואבוקה כנגדו: Some commentaries explain that this question is referring to a pot (see *Tosafot*). The statement that this is performed by most poor people does not mean that paupers bake bread in a pot in this fashion, but rather that they heat ovens in this manner, and therefore the same *halakha* should apply if one heats a pot in this way (*Tosefot Rid*).

HALAKHA

***Halla* from dough of second-tithe produce – חלה מעיסת מעשר:** One is obligated to separate *halla* from dough of the second tithe in Jerusalem (Rambam *Sefer Zera'im, Hilkhot Bikkurim* 6:4).

לא, דכולי עלמא – מעשה אילפס פטורין, והכא – כגון שחזר ואפאו בתנור קא מיפלגי. דתנא קמא סבר: כיון שחזר ואפאו בתנור – לחם קרינן ביה, ורבי יהודה סבר: אין לחם אלא האפוי בתנור מעיקרא, וכיון דמעיקרא לאו בתנור אפייה – לאו לחם הוא.

The Gemara rejects this suggestion: **No,** it is possible to say that **everyone agrees** that the owner of bread prepared as **pot-boiled stew is exempt** from *ḥalla*, **and here they disagree** with regard to a case **where one subsequently baked it in the oven. The first *tanna* maintains that since one subsequently baked it in the oven, it is called bread,** and one must separate *ḥalla* from it. **And Rabbi Yehuda maintains** that **bread is nothing other** than that which **is initially baked in an oven, and since** this food **was not initially baked in an oven, it is not** classified as **bread.**

אמר רבא: מאי טעמא דרבי יהודה – דכתיב: "ואפו עשר נשים לחמכם בתנור אחד" לחם האפוי בתנור אחד – קרוי לחם, ושאין אפוי בתנור אחד – אין קרוי לחם,

Rava said: What is the reason of Rabbi Yehuda? As it is written: "And ten women shall bake your bread in one oven" (Leviticus 26:26). Rava learns from this verse that **bread baked in one oven is called bread, and that** which **is not baked in one oven,** but rather in several different vessels, **is not called bread.**

יתיב רבה ורב יוסף אחוריה דרבי זירא, ויתיב רבי זירא קמיה דעולא. אמר ליה רבה לרבי זירא: בעי מיניה מעולא: הדביק מבפנים והרתיח מבחוץ מהו? אמר ליה: מאי אימא ליה? דאי אמינא ליה, אמר לי: הי ניהו מעשה אילפס?

Rabba and Rav Yosef sat behind Rabbi Zeira and Rabbi Zeira sat before Ulla to hear him teach Torah. **Rabba said to Rabbi Zeira: Raise** the following **dilemma of Ulla: If one pasted** bread **inside** a pot **and heated it from the outside, what is the** *halakha*? Is one obligated to separate *ḥalla* from this bread? **He said to him: Why should I say** this question to Ulla? **For if I say** this **to him, he will say to me: What is the** *halakha* with regard to bread prepared as **pot-boiled stew?** In other words, he will reply that my question is effectively the same as that well-known case.

אמר ליה רב יוסף לרבי זירא: בעו מיניה מעולא, הדביק מבפנים ואבוקה כנגדו מהו. אמר ליה: מאי אימא ליה? דאי אמינא ליה, אמר לי: רוב עניים עושין כן.

Rav Yosef further **said to Rabbi Zeira: Raise the** following **dilemma of Ulla: If one pasted** bread **inside** a pot and lit **a torch opposite it,**[N] **what is the** *halakha*? He again **said to him: Why should I say** this question to Ulla? **As if I say** this **to him, he will say to me:** The **majority** of **poor people do this** when they use a pot for cooking, and therefore this too should be considered the same as bread prepared like pot-boiled stew.

אמר רב אסי: עיסה של מעשר שני, לדברי רבי מאיר – פטורה מן החלה, לדברי חכמים – חייבת בחלה,

Rav Asi said: With regard to **dough of second-tithe** produce, **in accordance with the statement of Rabbi Meir,** one is **exempt from** separating *ḥalla* from it. The reason is that Rabbi Meir considers second tithe to be consecrated property, which means that although its owner is entitled to use this produce, it does not in fact belong to him. By contrast, **in accordance with the statement of the Rabbis,** who maintain that second-tithe produce is the property of its owner, one is **obligated** to separate *ḥalla* from it.[H]

Perek **II**
Daf **38** Amud **a**

HALAKHA

***Matzot* of second-tithe produce – מצות של מעשר שני:** One can fulfill his obligation to eat *matza* on the first night of Passover with second-tithe produce if he is in Jerusalem, in accordance with the opinion of the Rabbis (Rambam *Sefer Zemanim, Hilkhot Ḥametz UMatza* 6:8).

A citron of second-tithe produce – אתרוג של מעשר שני: One should avoid using a second-tithe citron to fulfill his obligation to take the four species *ab initio*, as he may render it susceptible to ritual impurity. However, one who did so has fulfilled his obligation after the fact, in accordance with the opinion of the Rabbis (Rambam *Sefer Zemanim, Hilkhot Shofar VeSukka VeLulav* 8:2).

מצות של מעשר שני, לדברי רבי מאיר – אין אדם יוצא בה ידי חובתו בפסח, לדברי חכמים – יוצא בה ידי חובתו בפסח.

With regard to ***matzot* of second-tithe** produce:[H] **In accordance with the statement of Rabbi Meir, a person cannot fulfill his obligation** to eat *matza* **on** the first night of **Passover with this** *matza*. Rabbi Meir considers it consecrated property, and one must eat *matza* that belongs to him, not consecrated property. **In accordance with the statement of the Rabbis, one can fulfill his obligation with** this type of *matza* **on** the first night of **Passover.**

אתרוג של מעשר שני, לדברי רבי מאיר – אין יוצא בו ידי חובתו ביום טוב, לדברי חכמים – אדם יוצא בו ידי חובתו ביום טוב.

The same dispute applies to **a citron of second-tithe** produce:[H] **In accordance with the statement of Rabbi Meir,**[N] **one cannot fulfill his obligation** to take the four species **on the first day** of the **festival** of *Sukkot* **with this citron. In accordance with the statement of the Rabbis, a person can use this** citron **to fulfill his obligation on the** first day of the **festival** of *Sukkot*.

NOTES

Second-tithe produce, in accordance with the statement of Rabbi Meir – מעשר שני לדברי רבי מאיר: Both the Rabbis and Rabbi Meir agree that one is required to bring second-tithe produce to Jerusalem, or if this is difficult, he should redeem it for money and take this money to Jerusalem. After reaching Jerusalem, the owner must eat the second-tithe produce or food purchased with the second-tithe money. Nevertheless, the Rabbis and Rabbi Meir disagree as to whether this second-tithe produce is considered the property of its owner. According to the Rabbis, despite the fact that the Torah imposed certain limitations with regard to the place where it may be eaten, second-tithe produce is in the legal possession of its owner. Conversely, Rabbi Meir maintains that the status of second-tithe produce is that of consecrated property, and the Torah permits the owner to consume this offering only in Jerusalem. This dispute is the basis for the different opinions with regard to using second tithe for purposes other than ordinary consumption.

מַתְקִיף לָהּ רַב פַּפָּא: בִּשְׁלָמָא עִיסָּה – דִּכְתִיב: ״עֲרִיסֹתֵיכֶם״ – מִשֶּׁלָּכֶם.

Rav Pappa strongly objects to this statement: **Granted,** one must separate *ḥalla* from this **dough, as it is written:** "Of the first of your dough you shall give to the Lord a portion [*ḥalla*] for a gift throughout your generations" (Numbers 15:21). This verse can be read in a very precise manner, so that the expression **"your dough"** indicates that *ḥalla* is separated only **from** dough **that belongs to you.**

אֶתְרוֹג נַמִּי – דִּכְתִיב: ״וּלְקַחְתֶּם לָכֶם״, ״לָכֶם״ – מִשֶּׁלָּכֶם יְהֵא. אֶלָּא מַצָּה, מִי כְּתִיב ״מַצַּתְכֶם״?

With regard to **a citron too,** a similar conclusion can be drawn, **as it is written: "And you shall take for yourselves** on the first day a fruit of goodly trees, branches of palm trees, and boughs of thick trees and willows of the brook" (Leviticus 23:40). Here too, the expression **"for yourselves"** indicates that what you take **must belong to you. However,** with regard to ***matza*, is it written** that you must use **your** own ***matza*?** Since there is no such requirement, it stands to reason that even consecrated *matza* is valid for this mitzva.

אָמַר רָבָא וְאִיתֵּימָא רַב יֵימָר בַּר שְׁלָמְיָא: אָתְיָא לֶחֶם לֶחֶם, כְּתִיב הָכָא: ״לֶחֶם עֹנִי״, וּכְתִיב הָתָם: ״וְהָיָה בַּאֲכָלְכֶם מִלֶּחֶם הָאָרֶץ״. מַה לְּהַלָּן מִשֶּׁלָּכֶם – אַף כָּאן מִשֶּׁלָּכֶם.

Rava said, and some say Rav Yeimar bar Shelamya said: This principle can be **derived** by means of a verbal analogy between **"bread"** and **"bread." It is written here,** with regard to *matza*: **"Poor man's bread"** (Deuteronomy 16:3), **and it is written there,** with regard to *ḥalla*: **"And it shall be that when you eat of the bread of the land,** you shall set apart a portion for a gift to the Lord" (Numbers 15:19). **Just as there,** in the case of *ḥalla*, it must be separated only **from** food **that belongs to you, so too here,** with regard to *matza*, it must be prepared only **from** produce **that belongs to you.**

לֵימָא מְסַיַּיע לֵיהּ: עִיסָּה שֶׁל מַעֲשֵׂר שֵׁנִי פְּטוּרָה מִן הַחַלָּה, דִּבְרֵי רַבִּי מֵאִיר. וַחֲכָמִים אוֹמְרִים: חַיֶּיבֶת. לֵימָא מְסַיַּיע?! הַיְינוּ הַךְ!

The Gemara suggests: **Let us say** that the following *baraita* **supports** Rav Asi: With regard to **dough of second-tithe** produce, one is **exempt from** separating ***ḥalla*** from it; this is **the statement of Rabbi Meir. And the Rabbis say:** One is **obligated** in this mitzva. Since this is a conclusive proof, the Gemara expresses surprise at the formulation: **Let us say that it supports him. This** statement **is** identical **to that** one; i.e., the ruling of the *baraita* is identical to Rav Asi's opinion.

הָכִי קָאָמַר (לֵיהּ): לֵימָא מִדִּפְלִיגִי בְּעִיסָּה, בְּהָנָךְ נַמִּי פְּלִיגִי, אוֹ דִילְמָא: שָׁאנֵי הָתָם, דִּכְתִיב ״עֲרִיסֹתֵיכֶם עֲרִיסֹתֵיכֶם״ תְּרֵי זִימְנֵי.

The Gemara explains: **This is what** the statement: Let us say, **is saying: Let us say from** the fact that **they disagree with regard to dough, so too, they disagree with regard to these** other issues. **Or perhaps it is different there,** with regard to *ḥalla*, **as it is written: "Your dough," "your dough," twice.** This repetition might indicate that the mitzva of *ḥalla* applies only to one who maintains full ownership of the dough. Although Rabbi Meir contends that one need not separate *ḥalla* from second-tithe produce, he does not necessarily issue a similar ruling with regard to *matza* or a citron, as there is no explicit proof to this effect.

בָּעֵי רַבִּי שִׁמְעוֹן בֶּן לָקִישׁ: מַהוּ שֶׁיֵּצֵא אָדָם יְדֵי חוֹבָתוֹ בְּחַלָּה שֶׁל מַעֲשֵׂר שֵׁנִי בִּירוּשָׁלַיִם? אַלִּיבָּא דְּרַבִּי יוֹסֵי הַגְּלִילִי – לָא תִּיבָּעֵי לָךְ, הָשְׁתָּא בְּחוּלִּין לָא נָפֵיק, בְּחַלָּתוֹ מִיבַּעְיָא? כִּי תִּיבָּעֵי לָךְ – אַלִּיבָּא דְּרַבִּי עֲקִיבָא,

Rabbi Shimon ben Lakish raised a dilemma: What is the *halakha* with regard to the possibility **that a person** can **fulfill his obligation** to eat *matza* **with *ḥalla*** separated from **second-tithe** dough **in Jerusalem?** The Gemara clarifies this dilemma: **In accordance with** the opinion of **Rabbi Yosei HaGelili, do not raise** this **dilemma.** Rabbi Yosei HaGelili maintains that one can fulfill his obligation to eat *matza* only with food that may be eaten in a state of acute mourning. The Gemara explains why the dilemma does not arise according to the opinion of Rabbi Yosei HaGelili: **Now** that it has been mentioned that one **cannot fulfill** his obligation **with the non-sacred** portion of second-tithe produce, i.e., with that which was not sanctified as *ḥalla*, **is it necessary** to mention that one cannot fulfill his obligation **with its *ḥalla*? When you raise the dilemma,** it is **in accordance with** the opinion of **Rabbi Akiva.**

בְּחוּלִּין הוּא דְּנָפֵיק – דְּאִי מִיטַּמּוּ יֵשׁ לָהֶן הֶיתֵּר בַּמּוֹשָׁבוֹת, אֲבָל חַלָּה דְּאִי מִטַּמְיָא לֵית לָהּ הֶיתֵּר בַּמּוֹשָׁבוֹת, וְלִשְׂרֵיפָה אָזְלָא – לָא נָפֵיק.

The Gemara explains: Unlike Rabbi Yosei, Rabbi Akiva does not interpret the phrase "poor man's bread [*leḥem oni*]" as though it were written with an *alef*, which indicates that it is referring to the bread of acute mourning [*aninut*], i.e., the period of mourning on the day of the death of a close relative. Consequently, the following dilemma arises: It can be suggested that **it is with** the **non-sacred** portion of the second-tithe produce **that one** can **fulfill** his obligation, **for if** the produce **becomes ritually impure** it **can be permitted** to be eaten **in** any **habitation** in Israel after it has been redeemed. Rabbi Akiva agrees that any food that can be eaten in an unrestricted manner in certain circumstances can also be used for the obligation to eat *matza*. **However,** with regard to ***ḥalla*, which, if becomes ritually impure, cannot be permitted** to be eaten **in** any **habitation, but goes,** i.e., it is slated **for burning,** this *ḥalla* **cannot** be used to **fulfill** one's obligation.

NOTES

Since – הוֹאִיל: This term, since, is used as an abbreviated heading for a halakhic rationale. Certain Sages apply this type of reasoning broadly, whereas others limit or reject its application. The idea is that since a given prohibition does not apply absolutely, as there are potential situations in which it does not take effect, the prohibition can be considered limited even when the prohibition would otherwise pertain. The question of two such claims, i.e., two since arguments, mentioned subsequently in the Gemara, addresses the extent of this reasoning, as it can be claimed the rationale of since is limited to a single hypothetical scenario.

אוֹ דִּילְמָא, אָמְרִינַן: הוֹאִיל וְאִילּוּ לֹא קָרָא עָלֶיהָ שֵׁם וְאִיטַּמֵּי – אִית לָהּ הֶיתֵּר בַּמּוֹשָׁבוֹת וְנָפֵיק בָּהּ, הָשְׁתָּא נַמִי נָפֵיק.

Or perhaps we say: Since,[N] **if one had not designated** the produce as *ḥalla* **and it had become ritually impure,** it could be redeemed and **be permitted** to be eaten **in** any **habitation,** and one could **fulfill** the obligation of *matza* **with it, now too,** one can **fulfill** his obligation **with it,** despite the fact that it has been designated as *ḥalla*. Since the sanctity is not inherent in the dough itself, it does not undermine its status as fit for *matza*.

אִיכָּא דְּאָמְרִי: הָא וַדַּאי לָא תִּיבָּעֵי לָךְ, דְּוַדַּאי אָמְרִינַן "הוֹאִיל". כִּי תִּיבָּעֵי לָךְ: חַלָּה הַלָּקוּחַ בְּכֶסֶף מַעֲשֵׂר שֵׁנִי.

Some say a different version of this analysis: With regard to **this** case, **certainly do not raise the dilemma, as here we certainly** apply the principle of: **Since,** as stated above. In other words, there is no doubt that *ḥalla* taken from second-tithe produce can be used for *matza*, as its sanctity is not inherent. Rather, **when you raise the dilemma,** it is with regard to ***ḥalla* that was purchased with second-tithe money,** as this type of food can be ritually purified if it becomes ritually impure.

וְאַלִּיבָּא דְּרַבָּנַן לָא תִּיבָּעֵי לָךְ, כֵּיוָן דְּאָמְרִי יִפָּדֶה – הַיְינוּ מַעֲשֵׂר. כִּי תִּיבָּעֵי לָךְ – אַלִּיבָּא דְּרַבִּי יְהוּדָה, דְּאָמַר יִקָּבֵר.

And furthermore, **in accordance with** the opinion of **the Rabbis, do not raise** this **dilemma, since they say** that it **can be redeemed** for a second time; **this** case **is** identical to the case of second-**tithe** produce itself. In this regard, the Rabbis do not distinguish between the money with which the second tithe was redeemed and the second-tithe produce itself. **Rather, when you raise the dilemma,** it is **in accordance with** the opinion of **Rabbi Yehuda, who said** that an object that was purchased with second-tithe money and that became ritually impure must **be buried.**

דִּתְנַן: הַלָּקוּחַ בְּכֶסֶף מַעֲשֵׂר שֵׁנִי שֶׁנִּטְמָא – יִפָּדֶה, רַבִּי יְהוּדָה אוֹמֵר: יִקָּבֵר.

As we learned in a mishna with regard to food **that was purchased with second-tithe money that became ritually impure,**[H] this ritually impure food should **be redeemed** for money, with which one must purchase other food. **Rabbi Yehuda says:** It should **be buried.** Since this food was merely purchased with second-tithe money, it does not have the same degree of sanctity as the tithe itself. Therefore, its status as a second-tithe object cannot be transferred to yet a third object. Consequently, if it becomes impure, it cannot be redeemed for money but must be buried as an item for which there is no use.

מִי אָמְרִינַן: הוֹאִיל וְאִי לֹא לָקוּחַ הָוֵי, וְהוֹאִיל וְלֹא קָרָא עָלֶיהָ שֵׁם וְאִיטַּמֵּי – יֵשׁ לוֹ הֶיתֵּר בַּמּוֹשָׁבוֹת וְנָפֵיק בֵּיהּ – הָשְׁתָּא נַמִי נָפֵיק בֵּיהּ.

The Gemara clarifies the aforementioned dilemma: **Do we say** the following: **Since, if it were not purchased** with second-tithe money, **and** furthermore, **since, if one had not designated it** as *ḥalla* **and it became ritually impure,** this produce would be **permitted** to be eaten **in** any **habitation,** one can therefore **fulfill** his obligation **with it** even after its status has changed by being purchased with second-tithe money and designated as *ḥalla*?

אוֹ דִּילְמָא: חַד הוֹאִיל – אָמְרִינַן, תְּרֵי הוֹאִיל – לָא אָמְרִינַן? אָמַר רָבָא: מִסְתַּבְּרָא, שֵׁם מַעֲשֵׂר חַד הוּא.

Or perhaps we say one of these logical arguments starting with: **Since, but we do not say two** arguments of: **Since.** If so, one cannot fulfill his obligation with *matza* of *ḥalla* separated from second tithe. **Rava said: It stands to reason** that **the category of tithe is a single** designation. In other words, provided that the food is included in the general framework of second tithe, it can be used for *matza*, and this applies even to the *ḥalla* separated from second tithe.

"חַלַּת תּוֹדָה וּרְקִיקֵי נָזִיר וכו'". מְנָא הָנֵי מִילֵּי? אָמַר רַבָּה: דְּאָמַר קְרָא

We learned in the mishna that if one prepared the **loaves of a thanks-offering or a nazirite's wafers** for himself, he cannot use them to fulfill his obligation to eat *matza* on Passover.[H] The Gemara asks: **From where are these matters** derived? **Rabba said: As the verse states:**

HALAKHA

Food that was purchased with second-tithe money that became ritually impure – הַלָּקוּחַ בְּכֶסֶף מַעֲשֵׂר שֵׁנִי שֶׁנִּטְמָא: Fruit that was purchased with second-tithe money and that became ritually impure should be redeemed for money. With this money, one should purchase food that must be eaten in Jerusalem, in accordance with the opinion of the Rabbis (Rambam *Sefer Zera'im, Hilkhot Ma'aser Sheni* 7:1–2).

Matza prepared from the loaves of a thanks-offering – מַצָּה מֵחַלַּת תּוֹדָה: If one prepared loaves for a thanks-offering or a nazirite's wafers to bring with his own offering, he cannot use them to fulfill his obligation to eat *matza*. However, if one baked these loaves to sell in the market, he may use them to fulfill the obligation to eat *matza* (Rambam *Sefer Zemanim, Hilkhot Ḥametz UMatza* 6:9).

״וּשְׁמַרְתֶּם אֶת הַמַּצּוֹת״ – מַצָּה הַמִּשְׁתַּמֶּרֶת לְשֵׁם מַצָּה, יָצְתָה זוֹ שֶׁאֵין מִשְׁתַּמֶּרֶת לְשֵׁם מַצָּה אֶלָּא לְשׁוּם זֶבַח.

"And you shall guard the *matzot*" (Exodus 12:17). This verse teaches that one may use only ***matza* that has been guarded** from becoming leavened **for the purpose of** matza, i.e., with the intention of fulfilling one's obligation of *matza* with it. This explanation **excludes this** *matza*, which was prepared for a nazirite or a thanks-offering and **which was not guarded for the purpose of *matza* but for the purpose of a sacrifice.**

רַב יוֹסֵף אָמַר, אָמַר קְרָא: ״שִׁבְעַת יָמִים מַצּוֹת תֹּאכֵלוּ״ – מַצָּה הַנֶּאֱכֶלֶת לְשִׁבְעַת יָמִים, יָצְתָה זוֹ שֶׁאֵינָהּ נֶאֱכֶלֶת לְשִׁבְעַת יָמִים אֶלָּא לְיוֹם וָלַיְלָה.

Rav Yosef said a different reason: One may not use *matza* prepared for a nazirite or a thanks-offering because **the verse states: "Seven days you shall eat *matzot*"** (Exodus 12:15), which indicates that one can fulfill his obligation only with ***matza* that** can **be eaten for** all **seven days.** This requirement **excludes this** *matza*, which is of nazirite's wafers or the loaves of a thanks-offering and **which cannot be eaten for seven days,**[N] **but** only **for** one **day and** one **night.**

תַּנְיָא כְּוָותֵיהּ דְּרַבָּה, וְתַנְיָא כְּוָותֵיהּ דְּרַב יוֹסֵף. תַּנְיָא כְּוָותֵיהּ דְּרַבָּה: יָכוֹל יֵצֵא יְדֵי חוֹבָתוֹ בְּחַלּוֹת תּוֹדָה וּרְקִיקֵי נָזִיר – תַּלְמוּד לוֹמַר: ״וּשְׁמַרְתֶּם אֶת הַמַּצּוֹת״ – מַצָּה הַמִּשְׁתַּמֶּרֶת לְשֵׁם מַצָּה, יָצְתָה זוֹ שֶׁאֵינָהּ מִשְׁתַּמֶּרֶת לְשֵׁם מַצָּה אֶלָּא לְשׁוּם זֶבַח.

The Gemara comments: **It was taught** in a *baraita* **in accordance with** the opinion of **Rabba, and it was taught** in a *baraita* **in accordance with** the opinion of **Rav Yosef.** The Gemara elaborates: **It was taught** in a *baraita* **in accordance with** the opinion of **Rabba:** I **might** have thought **that one can fulfill his obligation** to eat *matza* **with the loaves of a thanks-offering or a nazirite's wafers;** therefore, **the verse states: "And you shall guard the *matzot*,"** indicating that one must use ***matza* that has been guarded** from becoming leavened **for the purpose of *matza*** on Passover. This requirement **excludes this** *matza*, **which was not guarded for the purpose of *matza* but for the purpose of a sacrifice.**

תַּנְיָא כְּוָותֵיהּ דְּרַב יוֹסֵף: יָכוֹל יֵצֵא אָדָם יְדֵי חוֹבָתוֹ בְּחַלּוֹת תּוֹדָה וּרְקִיקֵי נָזִיר, תַּלְמוּד לוֹמַר: ״שִׁבְעַת יָמִים מַצּוֹת תֹּאכֵלוּ״ – מַצָּה הַנֶּאֱכֶלֶת לְשִׁבְעָה, יָצְתָה זוֹ שֶׁאֵינָהּ נֶאֱכֶלֶת לְשִׁבְעָה אֶלָּא לְיוֹם וָלַיְלָה.

It was taught in a *baraita* **in accordance with** the opinion of **Rav Yosef:** I **might** have thought **that a person can fulfill his obligation** to eat *matza* **with the loaves of a thanks-offering or a nazirite's wafers;** therefore, **the verse states: "Seven days you shall eat *matzot*,"** from which it is inferred that one must fulfill this obligation with ***matza* that** can **be eaten for** all **seven** days. This requirement **excludes this** *matza*, **as it cannot be eaten for seven days but** only **for a day and a night.**

וְתֵיפּוֹק לֵיהּ מִ״לֶּחֶם עֹנִי״ – מִי שֶׁנֶּאֱכָל בַּאֲנִינוּת, יָצָא זֶה שֶׁאֵינוֹ נֶאֱכָל בַּאֲנִינוּת אֶלָּא בְּשִׂמְחָה!

The Gemara asks a question of both opinions: And **let him derive** this *halakha*, that one cannot fulfill his obligation to eat *matza* with the loaves of a thanks-offering or a nazirite's wafers, from the phrase **"bread of affliction [*leḥem oni*]"** (Deuteronomy 16:3). According to Rabbi Yosei HaGelili, this phrase means: One can fulfill his obligation to eat *matza* only **with** food that may **be eaten in** a state of **acute mourning.** This requirement **excludes this** *matza*, i.e., the loaves of the thanks-offering and the nazirite wafers, **which is not eaten in** a state of **acute mourning but in** a state **of joy,** as an acute mourner is prohibited from eating sacrificial foods.

סָבַר לָהּ כְּרַבִּי עֲקִיבָא, דְּאָמַר ״עֹנִי״ כְּתִיב.

The Gemara answers: Rabba and Rav Yosef both **maintain in accordance with** the opinion of **Rabbi Akiva, who said** that since ***oni***, meaning poverty, **is written,** the *matza* must be bread of poverty. According to Rabbi Akiva, this phrase does not teach the *halakha* pertaining to consumption by acute mourners.

וְתֵיפּוֹק לֵיהּ דַּהֲוָה לֵיהּ מַצָּה עֲשִׁירָה!

The Gemara asks another question: **And let him derive** this *halakha*, that one cannot fulfill his obligation to eat *matza* with the loaves of a thanks-offering or a nazirite's wafers, from the fact **that it is *matza ashira*,** enhanced *matza*, as both the loaves of the thanks-offering and the nazirite's wafers contain oil. *Matza* that contains ingredients besides flour and water is classified as *matza ashira* and cannot be used for the mitzva of eating *matza* on the first night of Passover.

אָמַר שְׁמוּאֵל בַּר רַב יִצְחָק: רְבִיעִית הִיא, וּמִתְחַלֶּקֶת הִיא לְכַמָּה חַלּוֹת.

Shmuel bar Rav Yitzḥak said: This is an incorrect definition, as the total amount of oil in these loaves or wafers **is** only **a quarter-*log*, and** as this small amount of oil **is divided between several loaves,** it is nullified in the mixture. Consequently, the loaves of the thanks-offering and the nazirite's wafers are not *matza ashira*.

NOTES

Matza **that cannot be eaten for seven days** – **מַצָּה שֶׁאֵינָהּ נֶאֱכֶלֶת לְשִׁבְעָה**: Some commentaries explain that this *matza* of a thanks-offering accompanied an offering that was actually sacrificed. Once this animal was slaughtered, the *matza* could be eaten only for the remainder of that day and the following night. However, others contend that if the mishna were speaking about this type of *matza*, it would have drawn a distinction between *matza* for which an offering had been slaughtered, which cannot be used on Passover, and *matza* that had not been designated for an offering that was slaughtered, which may be used on the Festival. For this reason, it is more logical to explain the Gemara in accordance with Rashi's explanation, that the offering was not yet slaughtered (*Tosefot Rabbeinu Peretz*).

וְתֵיפוֹק לֵיהּ דְּאֵינָן נֶאֱכָלוֹת בְּכָל מוֹשָׁבוֹת!

The Gemara again asks: **And let him derive** this *halakha*, that one cannot fulfill his obligation to eat *matza* with the loaves of a thanks-offering or a nazirite's wafers from that fact **that** these types of bread **cannot be eaten in every habitation.** It was previously stated that the obligation to eat *matza* can be fulfilled only with food that can be eaten anywhere in Israel, whereas offerings may be eaten only in Jerusalem.

אָמַר רֵישׁ לָקִישׁ: זֹאת אוֹמֶרֶת חַלּוֹת תּוֹדָה וּרְקִיקֵי נָזִיר נֶאֱכָלִין בְּנוֹב וְגִבְעוֹן.

Reish Lakish said: That is to say, the loaves of the thanks-offering and the nazirite's wafers may **be eaten in Nov and Givon.**[N] In other words, the omission of this reason indicates that offerings could have been sacrificed on the communal altars during the period when improvised altars were permitted, before the Temple was built. These offerings are not among those that can be sacrificed only: "In the place that the Lord shall choose" (Deuteronomy 12:5). This means that during that period the loaves of the thanks-offering and the nazirite's wafers could indeed have been eaten anywhere, as improvised altars were built in any place. Consequently, even after the Temple was built, the loaves of the thanks-offering and the nazirite's wafers are still considered fit to be eaten anywhere in Israel.

תַּנְיָא: אָמַר רַבִּי אֶילְעַאי, שָׁאַלְתִּי אֶת רַבִּי אֱלִיעֶזֶר: מַהוּ שֶׁיֵּצֵא אָדָם בְּחַלּוֹת תּוֹדָה וּרְקִיקֵי נָזִיר? אָמַר לִי: לֹא שָׁמַעְתִּי. בָּאתִי וְשָׁאַלְתִּי לִפְנֵי רַבִּי יְהוֹשֻׁעַ, אָמַר לִי: הֲרֵי אָמְרוּ חַלּוֹת תּוֹדָה וּרְקִיקֵי נָזִיר שֶׁעֲשָׂאָן לְעַצְמוֹ – אֵין אָדָם יוֹצֵא בָּהֶן, לִמְכּוֹר בַּשּׁוּק – יוֹצֵא בָּהֶן.

It was taught in a *baraita* that **Rabbi Ilai said: I asked Rabbi Eliezer** ben Hyrcanus: **What is** the *halakha* with regard to the possibility **that a person** can **fulfill** the obligation to eat *matza* **with the loaves of a thanks-offering or a nazirite's wafers? He said to me: I did not hear** anything about this issue. **I went and asked Rabbi Yehoshua,** who **said to me: They said,** concerning **loaves for a thanks-offering or a nazirite's wafers that** one **prepared for his own** offering, that **a person cannot fulfill his obligation with them.** However, if one baked them **to sell in the market, he** can **fulfill** his obligation **with them.**

כְּשֶׁבָּאתִי וְהִרְצֵיתִי דְּבָרִים לִפְנֵי רַבִּי אֱלִיעֶזֶר, אָמַר לִי: בְּרִית, הֵן הֵן הַדְּבָרִים שֶׁנֶּאֶמְרוּ לוֹ לְמֹשֶׁה בְּסִינַי. אִיכָּא דְּאָמְרִי: בְּרִית, הֵן הֵן הַדְּבָרִים שֶׁנֶּאֶמְרוּ לוֹ לְמֹשֶׁה בְּסִינַי?! וְלָא טַעְמָא בָּעֲיָא?

When I returned and recited these **matters to Rabbi Eliezer, he said to me** in excitement: By the **covenant, these are the** very **matters**[N] **that were stated to Moses on Mount Sinai.** Rabbi Eliezer swore that this *halakha* had been transmitted over the generations going back to Moses on Mount Sinai. **Some say** he spoke in astonishment: By the **covenant!** Are **these** in fact **the matters that were stated to Moses on Mount Sinai? And doesn't** this *halakha* **require a reason?** Since there is no explicit tradition in this regard, it is necessary to provide a reason for this distinction.

וְטַעְמָא מַאי? אָמַר רַבָּה: כֹּל לַשּׁוּק אִימְּלוֹכֵי מִימְלַךְ, אָמַר: אִי מִזְּדַבַּן – מִזְּדַבַּן, אִי לָא מִזְּדַבַּן – אֵיפּוֹק בְּהוּ אֲנָא.

The Gemara asks: **And** indeed, **what is the reason** for this distinction between these loaves one prepared for himself and those he intended to sell in the market? **Rabba said:** With regard to **anything** sold **in the market,** the merchant may **change his mind** about it. **He** might **say: If it is sold, it is sold;** but **if it is not sold** for an offering, **I will fulfill** my obligation to eat *matza* **with it.** Since the merchant had in mind from the outset that these *matzot* might be used for the mitzva on Passover, he is permitted to use them to fulfill his obligation.

NOTES

Nov and Givon – נוֹב וְגִבְעוֹן: Different *halakhot* apply to the three places where offerings were permitted at some stage to be sacrificed, namely, a small improvised altar, a great altar, and the Temple. A small altar was a private altar built by an individual for his own personal use. When it was permitted to do so, even non-priests sacrificed offerings on an improvised altar of this kind, although only a limited group of animal offerings could be sacrificed. These types of improvised altars were primarily used during the period of the Judges. A great altar was built for communal use, e.g., in Nov and Givon, and all of Israel brought their offerings to these places before the Temple was built. However, as the Ark of the Covenant was not present in these places and no permanent structure was built, they were never fully functional as a temple.

The Sages disagree with regard to which types of offerings were permitted to be sacrificed in these places. However, in places such as Shiloh, where a temporary temple was constructed, all offerings could be brought during that period, and there were only minor differences between its status and that of the eventual Temple in Jerusalem.

By the covenant, these are the matters – בְּרִית, הֵן הֵן הַדְּבָרִים: Some commentaries maintain that, according to the first version of his statement, Rabbi Eliezer is expressing astonishment: Is this what was stated to Moses on Mount Sinai? According to the second version, it is Rabbi Yehoshua who states that this is indeed a tradition going back to Moses on Mount Sinai, but he adds that a reason is nonetheless required to justify this distinction, as even *halakhot* based on ancient traditions must be based on logical grounds (*Arukh*).

מתני׳ וְאֵלּוּ יְרָקוֹת שֶׁאָדָם יוֹצֵא בָּהֶן יְדֵי חוֹבָתוֹ בַּפֶּסַח: בַּחֲזֶרֶת, בַּתַּמְכָא, וּבַחַרְחֲבִינָא, וּבְעוּלָשִׁין, וּבַמָּרוֹר. יוֹצְאִין בָּהֶן בֵּין לַחִין בֵּין יְבֵשִׁין. אֲבָל לֹא כְּבוּשִׁין וְלֹא שְׁלוּקִין וְלֹא מְבוּשָּׁלִין.

MISHNA **And these are the vegetables with which a person can fulfill his obligation** to eat bitter herbs **on Passover:**[H] One can fulfill his obligation **with** ***ḥazeret*****,**[B] **with chervil** [***tamkha***]**, and with field eryngo** [***ḥarḥavina***]**,**[B] **and with endives** [***olashin***]**,**[B] **and with** ***maror*****.**[NB] **One fulfills** his **obligation with them whether** they are **fresh** or **whether** they are **dry. However,** one does **not** fulfill his obligation if they are **pickled** in water or vinegar, **nor** if they are **over-boiled** [***shaluk***] in hot water, **nor if they are boiled** [***mevushal***]**.**[N]

וּמִצְטָרְפִין לְכַזַּיִת, וְיוֹצְאִין בְּקֶלַח שֶׁלָּהֶן. וּבַדְּמַאי, וּבְמַעֲשֵׂר רִאשׁוֹן שֶׁנִּטְּלָה תְּרוּמָתוֹ, וּמַעֲשֵׂר שֵׁנִי וְהֶקְדֵּשׁ שֶׁנִּפְדּוּ.

The mishna adds: **And all these** different types of vegetables **join together to** the measure of **an olive-bulk,** i.e., it is not necessary to eat this amount from one specific type of vegetable. **And one fulfills** his obligation by eating **their stalk,** as it is not necessary to eat the leaves. **And one fulfills** the obligation **with doubtfully tithed** produce, **with first-tithe** produce **whose** ***teruma*** **has been taken** and given to a priest, **and with** both **second-tithe** produce **and consecrated property that were redeemed.**

HALAKHA

Vegetables that may be used as bitter herbs – יָרָק לְמָרוֹר: One can fulfill the obligation to eat bitter herbs with *ḥazeret*, chervil, or any of the other species listed in the mishna. If none of these is available, he should use some other type of bitter herb. However, the later authorities agree that in this case he should not recite the blessing (*Shiltei HaGibborim*; *Magen Avraham*). It is preferable to use a species listed earlier in the mishna. One can eat the leaves or the stems but not the roots. Furthermore, one may eat either fresh leaves or dry stems, but the herbs may not be pickled or boiled (*Shulḥan Arukh*, *Oraḥ Ḥayyim* 473:5).

NOTES

And with *maror* – וּבַמָּרוֹר: Some commentaries claim that this does not refer to a specific plant but is a general term for all types of bitter herbs (Rabbi Eliyahu Mizraḥi; *Me'iri*).

Over-boiled [*shaluk*] and boiled [*mevushal*] – שָׁלוּק וּמְבוּשָּׁל: According to most commentaries, *shaluk* means very thoroughly boiled, although others explain that it refers to pouring boiling water over a vegetable, thereby cooking it slightly. By contrast, everyone agrees that *mevushal* means boiling in a normal manner (Rav Yehuda ben Rav Binyamin HaRofeh and others).

BACKGROUND

***Ḥazeret* – חֲזֶרֶת:** *Ḥazeret* is lettuce, *Lactuca sativa*, and is often identified with the romaine variety (var. *romana*), a leafy winter vegetable cultivated for human consumption. Its leaves grow up to 35 cm in height and 15 cm in width and form an edible stalk. During the first stage of growth, the leaves and stem contain a bitter milky fluid. If they are allowed to grow uninterrupted, the leaves will expand upward and may even reach a height of 1 m. Eventually this plant will harden and sprout flowers and small bitter leaves, which is why it is described by the Gemara as soft at first and harsh in the end. The identification of *ḥazeret* with horseradish is erroneous.

Romaine lettuce

Field eryngo [*ḥarḥavina*] – חַרְחֲבִינָא: This plant is apparently a shrub known as *Eryngium creticum*, a perennial plant found throughout Israel. In the winter, the plant grows several soft leaves close to the ground. Although these leaves are very bitter, they are nevertheless edible.

In the summer, these leaves fall off and a blue or purple bud up to 40 cm in size appears. This bud is surrounded by thorns from which yellow flower petals emerge. At the end of the summer, the plant is typically broken by the winds. In the following year, the roots of the plant grow once more, with the formation of green leaves in the winter.

Field eryngo

Endives [*olashin*] – עוּלָשִׁין: Apparently, this domesticated winter plant is the popular endive, *Cichorium endivia*. It grows green leaves that are eaten in a manner similar to those of lettuce. The young leaves form tightly packed clusters near the base of the plant that grow outward. The plant's flowers are often blue, although they are sometimes red or white.

Certain varieties of the endive have wider, curly leaves. Nowadays, the thick root of the plant is most commonly used in the production of a coffee substitute. Endive leaves are initially soft and tasty, but they turn very bitter when the plant grows older and produces flowers.

Endive plants

***Maror* – מָרוֹר:** Most commentaries maintain that *maror* is the common sowthistle, *Sonchus oleraceus*, from the Asteraceae family. It is an annual wild plant that grows in fields and garbage heaps in most areas of Israel. The common sowthistle reaches 30–100 cm in height and is pale green. It contains a milky fluid, or sap, that flows from the plant when its stem is broken. Its yellow flowers are arranged in the form of capitula on the end of the stalks. Most of its leaves are sharp edged and are divided into irregular lobes. The soft leaves were once used as vegetables and are still eaten in certain Mediterranean countries. During talmudic times, the common sowthistle was considered a healthy food.

Common sowthistle

גמ׳ חֲזֶרֶת – חַסָּא. עוֹלְשִׁין – הִינְדְּבֵי. תַּמְכָא, אָמַר רַבָּה בַּר בַּר חָנָה: תַּמְכְתָּא שְׁמָהּ. חַרְחֲבִינָא, אָמַר רַבִּי שִׁמְעוֹן בֶּן לָקִישׁ: אַצְוָותָא דְּדִיקְלָא. וּבְמָרוֹר – מְרִירְתָא.

GEMARA The Gemara identifies the plants mentioned by the mishna by their Aramaic names. *Ḥazeret* is **lettuce.** *Olashin* is called ***hindevi.*** With regard to ***tamkha*, Rabba bar bar Ḥana said: It is called *temakhta*** in Aramaic. As for ***harḥavina*, Rabbi Shimon ben Lakish said:** This is the plant **that** grows **around the palm tree.** The mishna taught: **And with *maror*.** The Gemara explains: This is a plant called ***merirata*.**

תָּנֵי בַּר קַפָּרָא: אֵלּוּ יְרָקוֹת שֶׁאָדָם יוֹצֵא בָּהֶן יְדֵי חוֹבָתוֹ בְּפֶסַח: בְּעוֹלְשִׁין, וּבְתַמְכָא, בְּחַרְחָלִין, בְּחַרְחֲבִינִין, וּבַחֲזָרִין. רַב יְהוּדָה אוֹמֵר: אַף עוֹלְשֵׁי שָׂדֶה, וְעוֹלְשֵׁי גִינָּה, וַחֲזֶרֶת.

Bar Kappara teaches: These are the vegetables[N] **with which a person** can **fulfill his obligation** to eat bitter herbs **on Passover: With endives, chervil, *harḥallin*, field eryngo, and *ḥazeret*. Rav Yehuda says: Also wild endives,**[B] **garden endives, and *ḥazeret*.**

עוֹלְשֵׁי גִינָּה וַחֲזֶרֶת?! הָא תָּנָא לַהּ רֵישָׁא! הָכִי קָאָמַר: אַף עוֹלְשֵׁי שָׂדֶה כְּעוֹלְשֵׁי גִינָּה וַחֲזֶרֶת. רַבִּי מֵאִיר אוֹמֵר: אַף עַסְווֹס, וְטוֹרָא, וּמַר יְרוֹאָר. אָמַר לֵיהּ רַבִּי יוֹסֵי: עַסְווֹס וְטוֹרָא – אֶחָד הוּא, וּמַר – זֶה הוּא יְרוֹאָר.

The Gemara asks: Why does Rav Yehuda mention **garden endives and *ḥazeret*? These were** already **taught in the first clause.** The Gemara explains that **this is** what Rav Yehuda **is saying: Even wild endives are** equivalent to **garden endives and *ḥazeret*** and may be used as bitter herbs on Passover. **Rabbi Meir says:** The plants ***asvas*, and *tura*, and sweet myrrh** [*mar yero'ar*][B] can **also** be used to fulfill this obligation. **Rabbi Yosei said to him: *Asvas* and *tura*** are two names for **one** plant, **and *mar*** is the same plant as ***yero'ar*.**

תָּנֵי דְּבֵי (רַבִּי) שְׁמוּאֵל, אֵלּוּ יְרָקוֹת שֶׁאָדָם יוֹצֵא בָּהֶן יְדֵי חוֹבָתוֹ בְּפֶסַח: בַּחֲזֶרֶת, בְּעוֹלְשִׁין, וּבְתַמְכָא, וּבְחַרְחֲבִינִין, וּבְחַרְגִּינִין, וּבְהַרְדּוֹפְנִין. רַבִּי יְהוּדָה אוֹמֵר: אַף חֲזֶרֶת יוֹלִין וַחֲזֶרֶת גַּלִּין כַּיּוֹצֵא בָּהֶן.

A Sage of **the school of Rabbi Samuel teaches: These are the vegetables with which a person** can **fulfill his obligation** to eat bitter herbs **on Passover: With *ḥazeret*, endives, chervil, field eryngo, *harginnin*, and *hardofannin*. Rabbi Yehuda says:** One can **also** fulfill his obligation with ***ḥazeret yolin*** and ***ḥazeret gallin*,**[B] as they are **similar to** the aforementioned vegetables.

רַבִּי אִילְעָא אוֹמֵר מִשּׁוּם רַבִּי אֱלִיעֶזֶר: אַף עַרְקַבְלִים. וְחָזַרְתִּי עַל כָּל תַּלְמִידָיו וּבִקַּשְׁתִּי לִי חָבֵר, וְלֹא מָצָאתִי. וּכְשֶׁבָּאתִי לִפְנֵי רַבִּי אֱלִיעֶזֶר בֶּן יַעֲקֹב הוֹדָה לִדְבָרַי.

Rabbi Ile'a said in the name of Rabbi Eliezer: One can **also** fulfill his obligation with ***arkablim*. And I went around all of** Rabbi Eliezer's **students looking for a colleague** who agreed with me that Rabbi Eliezer said this, **but I did not find** anyone who remembered this ruling. **But when I came before Rabbi Eliezer ben Ya'akov, he conceded to my statement.**

רַבִּי יְהוּדָה אוֹמֵר: כֹּל שֶׁיֵּשׁ לוֹ שְׂרָף. רַבִּי יוֹחָנָן בֶּן בְּרוֹקָה אוֹמֵר: כֹּל שֶׁפָּנָיו מַכְסִיפִין. אֲחֵרִים אוֹמְרִים: [כָּל] יָרָק מַר יֵשׁ לוֹ שְׂרָף וּפָנָיו מַכְסִיפִין. אָמַר רַבִּי יוֹחָנָן: מִדִּבְרֵי כּוּלָּן נִלְמַד: יָרָק מַר יֵשׁ לוֹ שְׂרָף וּפָנָיו מַכְסִיפִין. אָמַר רַב הוּנָא: הֲלָכָה כַּאֲחֵרִים.

Rabbi Yehuda says: Any plant **that has** white **sap** when it is cut may be used as bitter herbs. **Rabbi Yoḥanan ben Beroka says: Anything whose surface is light** green may be used as bitter herbs. ***Aḥerim* say: Any bitter herb** that **has sap and whose surface is light** green is fit for this mitzva. **Rabbi Yoḥanan said: From the statements of all these** Sages, **we can learn** that **a bitter green herb has sap and its surface is light** green. **Rav Huna said: The *halakha* is in accordance with** the opinion of ***Aḥerim*.**

רָבִינָא אַשְׁכְּחֵיהּ לְרַב אַחָא בְּרֵיהּ דְּרָבָא דַּהֲוָה מְהַדַּר אַמְּרִירְתָא. אָמַר לֵיהּ: מַאי דַּעְתִּיךְ – דִּמְרִירָן טְפֵי, וְהָא חֲזֶרֶת תְּנַן, וְתָנָא דְּבֵי שְׁמוּאֵל חֲזֶרֶת, וְאָמַר רַבִּי אוֹשַׁעְיָא: מִצְוָה בַּחֲזֶרֶת, וְאָמַר רָבָא: מַאי חֲזֶרֶת – חַסָּא.

Ravina found Rav Aḥa, son of Rava, searching for *merirata*[N] to use as bitter herbs. **He said to him: What is your opinion,** that you seek this particular herb? If you are looking for **that** which **is most bitter, but we learned *ḥazeret***[N] first in the mishna, which indicates that this is the preferred choice. **And** likewise, a Sage of **the school of Shmuel taught *ḥazeret*** first, before the other types of bitter herbs. **And Rabbi Oshaya said:** The optimal fulfillment of the **mitzva** is with ***ḥazeret*,**[H] **and Rava said: What is *ḥazeret*?** It is **lettuce** [*ḥassa*].

NOTES

These are the vegetables, etc. – אֵלּוּ יְרָקוֹת וכו׳: Some commentaries infer from this list that it is preferable to use vegetables that are only somewhat bitter, rather than those that are very bitter. The reason is that the Torah speaks of eating bitter herbs, indicating that one should use an herb that is normally eaten (*Nimmukei Yosef*).

Searching for *merirata* – מְהַדַּר אַמְּרִירְתָא: Some commentaries explain that Rav Aḥa, son of Rava, was searching for the bitterest of the herbs listed in the mishna (*Mikhtam*).

But we learned *ḥazeret* – וְהָא חֲזֶרֶת תְּנַן: See Rashi's explanation. Other commentaries maintain that this is a reference to a subsequent mishna that describes the Passover seder. That mishna states: They bring before him *matza* and *ḥazeret*, from which it can be inferred that it is preferable to use *ḥazeret* for this purpose (Maharam Ḥalawa; *Mikhtam*).

BACKGROUND

Wild endives – עוֹלְשֵׁי שָׂדֶה: This is apparently the common wild endive, *Cichorium pumilum*, a wild annual plant that grows in fields across Israel and at the sides of roads. It can reach 1 m in height, while the young leaves at its base form a rose-like shape. Although the leaves are edible, they are very bitter. A light blue flower grows at the end of the wild endive's stalk.

Wild endive flower

Sweet myrrh [*mar yero'ar*] – מַר יְרוֹאָר: This is apparently *Opoponax chironium*, a perennial plant from the shrub family, which grows wild in Lebanon and northern Israel. The plant can grow as high as 1.5–2 m, and its lower leaves can reach 60 cm in length and width. The upper leaves are smaller, and clusters of small yellow flowers grow atop the stalks. The thick root, which can grow up to a length of 60 cm, was used during the mishnaic period to produce an acrid resin that was utilized for medicinal purposes.

Ḥazeret gallin – חֲזֶרֶת גַּלִּין: *Ḥazeret gallin* is a type of wild lettuce, perhaps the prickly lettuce, *Lactuca serriola*. This plant grows wild in most areas of Israel, on roadsides, abandoned fields, and garbage heaps. The leaves of this lettuce are bitter and contain a milky fluid, or sap. In modern Hebrew, this plant is called *ḥassat hamatzpen*, which literally means the compass lettuce, because the edges of its leaves invariably face north or south.

Prickly lettuce leaves

HALAKHA

The optimal fulfillment of the mitzva is with *ḥazeret* – מִצְוָה בַּחֲזֶרֶת: One should preferably use *ḥazeret* for bitter herbs. In many European communities, lettuce was uncommon and was infested with worms, and therefore it became customary to use horseradish. Based on *kabbala*, some people use both horseradish and lettuce (*Shulḥan Arukh*, *Oraḥ Ḥayyim* 473:5).

מַאי חַסָּא – דְּחָס רַחֲמָנָא עִילָּוָון. וְאָמַר רַבִּי שְׁמוּאֵל בַּר נַחֲמָנִי אָמַר רַבִּי יוֹנָתָן: לָמָּה נִמְשְׁלוּ מִצְרִיִּים כְּמָרוֹר – לוֹמַר לָךְ: מַה מָּרוֹר זֶה שֶׁתְּחִילָּתוֹ רַךְ וְסוֹפוֹ קָשֶׁה, אַף מִצְרִיִּים – תְּחִילָּתָן רַכָּה וְסוֹפָן קָשֶׁה. אָמַר לֵיהּ: הָדְרִי בִּי.

The Gemara explains: **What is** the meaning of **lettuce** [*ḥassa*]? It refers to the fact **that God has mercy** [*ḥas*] **on us. And Rabbi Samuel bar Naḥmani said** that **Rabbi Yoḥanan said: Why are the Egyptians likened to bitter herbs** in the verse: "And they embittered their lives" (Exodus 1:14)? This comparison serves **to tell you** that **just as these bitter herbs are soft at first**[N] **and harsh in the end, so too, the Egyptians were soft at first,**[N] when they paid the Jews for their work, **but were harsh in the end,** as they enslaved them. This idea applies solely to *ḥazeret,* which has a bitter aftertaste, but not to other types of bitter herbs, which are bitter from the beginning. Rav Aḥa, son of Rava, **said to** Ravina: **I retract** my position and concede that it is preferable to use *ḥazeret* for bitter herbs.

אָמַר לֵיהּ רַב רְחוּמִי לְאַבַּיֵי: מִמַּאי דְּהַאי מָרוֹר מִין יָרָק הוּא? אֵימָא מְרִירְתָּא דְּכוּפְיָא! דּוּמְיָא דְּמַצָּה, מַה מַּצָּה גִּידּוּלֵי קַרְקַע – אַף מָרוֹר גִּידּוּלֵי קַרְקַע. וְאֵימָא הִירְדּוּף! דּוּמְיָא דְּמַצָּה, מַה מַּצָּה מִין זְרָעִים – אַף מָרוֹר מִין זְרָעִים,

Rav Reḥumi said to Abaye: From where is it known **that this bitter herb** that must be eaten on Passover night **is a type of vegetable?** Perhaps one could **say** that the mitzva should be performed with **the bile of a** ***kufya***[B] fish, which is very bitter, but not necessarily with a type of plant? He answered: Bitter herbs are **similar to** ***matza***; **just as** ***matza*** must be prepared only from food **that grows from the ground, so too, bitter herbs** must be from food **that grows from the ground.** The Gemara asks: How do we know that a bitter herb is specifically a vegetable rather than the bitter **oleander**[B] bush? The Gemara answers: Bitter herbs are **similar to** ***matza***; **just as** ***matza*** is prepared from **a type of plant,** but not including a tree, **so too, bitter herbs** must be from **a type of plant** that is not a tree.

וְאֵימָא הַרְזִיפוּ! דּוּמְיָא דְּמַצָּה, מַה מַּצָּה שֶׁנִּיקַּחַת בְּכֶסֶף מַעֲשֵׂר – אַף מָרוֹר שֶׁנִּיקַּח בְּכֶסֶף מַעֲשֵׂר.

The Gemara asks a similar question: Perhaps I can **say** that one may use *harzipu,* a vegetable that poisons animals, as the bitter herb. The Gemara answers: It must be **similar to** ***matza***; **just as** ***matza*** is prepared from plants **that** are fit for human consumption and **can be purchased with** second-**tithe money, so too, bitter herbs** must be from a species **that can be purchased with** second-**tithe money.**

אָמַר לֵיהּ רַבָּה בַּר רַב חָנִין לְאַבַּיֵי: אֵימָא מָרוֹר חַד! מְרוֹרִים כְּתִיב – וְאֵימָא מְרוֹרִים תְּרֵי! דּוּמְיָא דְּמַצָּה, מַה מַּצָּה מִמִּינִין הַרְבֵּה – אַף מָרוֹר מִמִּינִין הַרְבֵּה.

Rabba bar Rav Ḥanin said to Abaye: I can **say that** the **bitter herb** mentioned in the Torah includes merely **one** species, i.e., only the bitterest plant can be used for this obligation. Abaye responded: For this reason **it is written: "Bitter herbs"** (Exodus 12:8) in the plural, indicating that many types of bitter herbs are fit for this purpose. Rabba retorted: **But** one can **say that "bitter herbs"** refers to **two** different species, but no more. Abaye explained: Bitter herbs are **similar to** ***matza***; **just as** ***matza*** can be prepared from **many types** of grain, **so too, bitter herbs** can be taken from **many** different **types** of vegetables.

אָמַר רַבָּה בַּר רַב הוּנָא אָמַר רַב: יְרָקוֹת שֶׁאָמְרוּ חֲכָמִים שֶׁאָדָם יוֹצֵא בָּהֶן יְדֵי חוֹבָתוֹ בְּפֶסַח – כּוּלָּן נִזְרָעִין בַּעֲרוּגָה אַחַת. לְמֵימְרָא דְּלֵית בְּהוּ מִשּׁוּם כִּלְאַיִם.

Rabba bar Rav Huna said that **Rav said:** With regard to the **vegetables that the Sages said a person can fulfill with them his obligation** to eat bitter herbs **on Passover, they** may **all be planted in one** garden **bed.** The Gemara concludes: **That is to say that** the prohibition against planting **diverse kinds** of seeds **does not apply to them?** Rav's statement indicates that all these species are so similar that they may be planted together without violating the prohibition against planting different species of crops in one area of a field.

מְתִיב רָבָא: חֲזֶרֶת וַחֲזֶרֶת גַּלִּין, עוֹלְשִׁין וְעוֹלְשֵׁי שָׂדֶה, כְּרֵישִׁין וּכְרֵישֵׁי שָׂדֶה, כּוּסְבָּר וְכוּסְבַּר שָׂדֶה, חַרְדָּל וְחַרְדָּל מִצְרִי, וּדְלַעַת הַמִּצְרִי וְהָרְמוּצָה – אֵינָם כִּלְאַיִם זֶה בָּזֶה. חֲזֶרֶת וַחֲזֶרֶת גַּלִּין – אִין, חֲזֶרֶת וְעוֹלְשִׁין – לָא!

Rava raised an objection from a mishna: ***Ḥazeret*** **and** ***ḥazeret gallin***; **endive and wild endive; leek and wild leek; coriander and wild coriander; mustard and Egyptian mustard; and Egyptian gourd and** ***harmutza,*** a type of gourd, **are not** considered a mixture of **diverse kinds**[H] when planted **together.** This indicates that ***ḥazeret*** **and** ***ḥazeret gallin,***[N] **yes,** they may be planted together; however, ***ḥazeret*** **and endives, no,** they may not be planted together.

וְכִי תֵּימָא כּוּלְּהוּ בַּהֲדָדֵי קָתָנֵי לְהוּ – וְהָא אָמַר רַב: זוּגוֹת זוּגוֹת קָתָנֵי!

And lest you say that all these species **are taught together,** and the mishna is actually saying that any of these species may be planted together, **but didn't Rav** himself **say** that these plants **were taught in pairs,** i.e., one may plant each plant only with its pair that is listed in the mishna, due to their similarity; however, one may not, e.g., plant lettuce and endive together. It therefore remains unclear what Rav meant when he said that vegetables fit for use as bitter herbs may be planted in a single garden bed.

NOTES

Soft at first – תְּחִילָּתוֹ רַךְ: Not only at the beginning of its growth, but even when it is fully grown, *ḥazeret* is soft and sweet, although it eventually turns very bitter (*Mikhtam*).

The Egyptians were soft at first – מִצְרִיִּים תְּחִילָּתָן רַכָּה: In this context, many commentaries cite an exposition in the Jerusalem Talmud on the verse that the Egyptians enslaved the Israelites "with rigor [*befarekh*]" (Exodus 1:14). In the Jerusalem Talmud, it is explained that initially the Egyptians controlled the Israelites *befeh rakh,* with a soft mouth, but eventually they enslaved them with rigorous labor. In terms of the progression of the exile itself, this can be explained as a reference to the fact that initially, when Jacob and his family came to Egypt, Pharaoh said to Joseph: "Let your brothers dwell in the best of the land" (Genesis 47:6), but ultimately the Egyptians enslaved them.

Ḥazeret and *ḥazeret gallin*, etc. – חֲזֶרֶת וַחֲזֶרֶת גַּלִּין וכו׳: The prohibition against diverse kinds of seeds applies to two different species planted together. However, diverse strains of a single species may be planted together. This is the case even if they have different names and differ in appearance. See the Rambam's Commentary on the Mishna.

BACKGROUND

Kufya – כּוּפְיָא: Some scholars identify this fish as *Scomber colias*, the Atlantic chub mackerel.

Atlantic chub mackerel

Oleander – הִירְדּוּף: This plant, *Nerium oleander*, is an evergreen bush that can grow to a height of 4 m and has long and hard yellow-green leaves and pink flowers. The plant's sap and fruits are extremely bitter and are often poisonous for animals and even for people.

Oleander flowers

HALAKHA

Mixture of diverse kinds – כִּלְאַיִם: Lettuce and *ḥazeret gallin*; endive and wild endive; leek and wild leek; and coriander and wild coriander are all pairs of plants that are not considered prohibited diverse kinds when planted with each other. Each pair is considered a single species, notwithstanding the slight differences between the respective plants (*Shulḥan Arukh, Yoreh De'a* 297:14).

מַאי נִזְרָעִין דְּאָמַר רַב – נִזְרָעִין כְּהִלְכָתָן – כְּהִלְכָתָן תְּנֵינָא!

The Gemara explains: **What** is the meaning of the term **planted, which Rav said?** It means that these plants may **be properly planted.** In other words, they may be planted together provided that there is an appropriate amount of space between them, so that there is no violation of the prohibition against planting diverse kinds of seeds. The Gemara asks: If he wishes to inform us about planting them **properly, we** already **learned** this in a mishna:

Perek **II**
Daf **39** Amud **b**

עֲרוּגָה שֶׁהִיא שִׁשָּׁה עַל שִׁשָּׁה טְפָחִים – זוֹרְעִין בְּתוֹכָהּ חֲמִשָּׁה זֵרְעוֹנִין, אַרְבַּע עַל אַרְבַּע רוּחוֹת הָעֲרוּגָה וְאַחַת בָּאֶמְצַע. מַהוּ דְּתֵימָא: הָנֵי מִילֵּי – בִּזְרָעִין, אֲבָל בִּירָקוֹת לֹא, קָא מַשְׁמַע לַן.

With regard to a garden **bed**[HB] **that is six by six handbreadths** in area, **one** may **plant in it five** different types of **seeds, four** types **on the four sides of the bed and one** type **in the middle.** This mishna teaches that it is permitted to plant different types of seeds in one garden bed, provided that one maintains the appropriate distance between them. The Gemara explains: Rav's statement is nevertheless necessary. **Lest you say** that **that applies only to seeds, but with regard to vegetables, no,** it is prohibited to plant them in a single garden bed even if this separation is maintained, Rava **teaches us** that it is permitted to plant in this manner with vegetables as well.

לְמֵימְרָא דִּירָקוֹת אַלִּימָא מִזְּרָעִים? וְהָתְנַן: כׇּל מִינֵי זְרָעִים אֵין זוֹרְעִין בַּעֲרוּגָה אַחַת, כׇּל מִינֵי יְרָקוֹת זוֹרְעִין בַּעֲרוּגָה אַחַת! מַהוּ דְּתֵימָא: הָנֵי מָרוֹר מִין זְרָעִים נִינְהוּ, קָא מַשְׁמַע לַן.

The Gemara asks: **Is that to say that vegetables are stronger** in the level of their prohibition **than seeds?**[N] **But didn't we learn** in a mishna in *Kilayim*: With regard to **multiple types of seeds, one** may **not plant** them together **in one** garden **bed,**[H] even if there is space between them; **however,** with regard to **multiple types of vegetables, one** may **plant** them together **in one bed?** This mishna apparently indicates that the *halakha* is stricter concerning seeds. The Gemara answers: Rav's statement is necessary. **Lest you say** that **these bitter herbs are a type of seed,** not a vegetable, and therefore it is prohibited to plant them in a bed with other seeds, Rav **teaches us** that all the various bitter herbs are classified as types of vegetables.

זְרָעִים סָלְקָא דַּעְתָּךְ?! וְהָא תְּנַן "יְרָקוֹת" וְתָנֵי בַּר קַפָּרָא יְרָקוֹת, וְתָנֵי דְּבֵי שְׁמוּאֵל יְרָקוֹת! חֲזֶרֶת אִיצְטְרִיכָא לֵיהּ, סָלְקָא דַּעְתָּךְ אָמִינָא: הוֹאִיל וְסוֹפָהּ לְהַקְשׁוֹת – נֵיתִיב לָהּ רַוְוחָא טְפֵי.

The Gemara asks: **Could it** even **enter your mind** that bitter herbs are types of **seeds? But didn't we learn** the word **vegetables** in a mishna? **And bar Kappara** likewise **taught: Vegetables. And** furthermore, the Sage of **the school of Shmuel taught: Vegetables.** The Gemara explains: It was **necessary for** Rav to mention the status of ***ḥazeret. It could enter your mind to say*** that **since *ḥazeret* ultimately hardens** into a type of seed, **one** must therefore **give it more space** in a garden bed than other vegetables. Rav's statement indicates that this is not the case.

לָאו אָמַר רַבִּי יוֹסֵי בְּרַבִּי חֲנִינָא: קֶלַח שֶׁל כְּרוּב שֶׁהוּקְשָׁה – מַרְחִיבִין לוֹ בֵּית רוֹבַע. אַלְמָא: כֵּיוָן דְּסוֹפוֹ לְהַקְשׁוֹת – יָהֲבִינַן לֵיהּ רַוְוחָא טְפֵי. הָכָא נָמֵי – נֵיתִיב לָהּ רַוְוחָא טְפֵי, קָא מַשְׁמַע לַן.

The Gemara offers support for this contention: **Didn't Rabbi Yosei, son of Rabbi Ḥanina, say:** With regard to **a stalk of cabbage that has hardened, one** must **allow a *beit rova*** of space **for it,** in which no other seeds may be planted. **Apparently, since it will ultimately harden, one** must **give it more space. Here too,** in the case of the *ḥazeret*, it might have been thought that **one** is required to **give it more space.** Therefore, Rava **teaches us** that all types of bitter herbs, even lettuce, may be planted together in one bed without leaving additional space between each species.

"יוֹצְאִין בָּהֶן בֵּין לַחִין בֵּין יְבֵשִׁין כו'". אָמַר רַב חִסְדָּא: לֹא שָׁנוּ אֶלָּא בְּקֶלַח, אֲבָל בְּעָלִין, לַחִין – אִין, יְבֵשִׁין – לָא.

The mishna taught that one can **fulfill** his **obligation** to eat bitter herbs **with** these types of vegetables, **whether** they are **fresh** or **whether** they are **dried. Rav Ḥisda said: They taught** this *halakha* **only** with regard **to the stem. However,** with regard **to the leaves,** if they are **moist, yes,** they may be used as bitter herbs, but if they are **dry, no,** they may not serve as bitter herbs.[H]

וְהָא מִדְּקָתָנֵי סֵיפָא "בְּקֶלַח שֶׁלָּהֶן" מִכְּלָל דְּרֵישָׁא עָלִין! פֵּרוּשֵׁי קָא מְפָרֵשׁ, כִּי קָתָנֵי "בֵּין לַחִין בֵּין יְבֵשִׁין" – אַקֶּלַח.

The Gemara asks: **But from** the fact **that it is taught** in **the last clause** of the mishna: **In their stems,** it may **be inferred that the first clause** of the mishna refers to the **leaves.** The Gemara answers: The *tanna* **is explaining** his statement in the first clause of the mishna: **When** he **taught** that one may eat herbs **whether** they are **fresh** or **whether dried,** the *tanna* was referring **to the stem,** not the leaves.

HALAKHA

Garden bed – עֲרוּגָה: With regard to plants that are grown only in small quantities, five different species may be planted in a single garden bed that is six-by-six handbreadths in area. Four species are planted along the four sides, while the fifth is planted in the center of the bed (*Shulḥan Arukh, Yoreh De'a* 297:34).

Multiple types of seeds…in one garden bed – מִינֵי זְרָעִים...בַּעֲרוּגָה: One may not plant multiple types of seed plants in a single garden bed (*Shulḥan Arukh, Yoreh De'a* 497:37).

Stems and leaves of *maror* – קֶלַח וְעָלִים שֶׁל מָרוֹר: One may use the leaves of bitter herbs only when they are fresh, but the stems may be used even if they are dry, as stated by Rav Ḥisda (*Shulḥan Arukh, Oraḥ Ḥayyim* 473:5).

BACKGROUND

Garden bed – עֲרוּגָה: This drawing demonstrates one way to plant five different species inside a garden bed that is six-by-six handbreadths in area.

Five different species in a garden bed

NOTES

Vegetables and seeds – יְרָקוֹת וּזְרָעִים: The difference between vegetables and seeds is that the leaves of vegetables are edible, whereas the term seeds refers to plants whose seed is eaten, e.g., grains. Rabbi Shimshon of Saens explains that the reason for this distinction is that seed plants are larger than vegetables. The Rambam maintains that this difference is based on the fact that seed plants are planted in far larger quantities than vegetables.

מיתיבי: יוצאין בהן ובקלח שלהן, בין לחין בין יבשין, דברי רבי מאיר. וחכמים אומרים: לחין – יוצאין בהן, יבשין – אין יוצאין בהן. ושוין שיוצאין בהן כמושין, אבל לא כבושין ולא שלוקין ולא מבושלין.

The Gemara **raises an objection** from a *baraita*: One can **fulfill** the obligation **with** the bitter herbs themselves **or with their stems, whether** they are **fresh** or **whether** they are **dried;** this is **the statement of Rabbi Meir. And the Rabbis say:** With regard to **fresh** bitter herbs, one can **fulfill** his obligation **with them;** however, with regard to **dry** bitter herbs, one **cannot fulfill** the obligation **with them. And everyone agrees that** one can **fulfill** his obligation **with them** if they are **withered** and are no longer fresh. **However,** one may **neither** use bitter herbs that have been **pickled, nor over-boiled, nor boiled.**

כללו של דבר: כל שיש בו טעם מרור – יוצאין בו, וכל שאין בו טעם מרור – אין יוצאין בו. תרגומא אקלח. תנו רבנן: אין יוצאין בהן כמושין, משום רבי אליעזר ברבי צדוק אמרו: יוצאין בהן כמושין.

The *baraita* continues: **The principle is: Anything that has the taste of bitter herbs,** one can **fulfill** his obligation **with it; but anything that does not have the taste of bitter herbs, one cannot fulfill** his obligation **with it.** This *baraita* indicates that neither Rabbi Meir nor the Rabbis distinguish between the leaves of these herbs and their stems. The Gemara answers: **Interpret** Rabbi Meir's statement, that one can fulfill the obligation with both fresh and dried bitter herbs, as referring **to the stem** but not to the leaves. **The Sages taught:** One **cannot fulfill** the obligation **with them** when they are **withered. They said in the name of Rabbi Eliezer, son of Rabbi Tzadok:** One can **fulfill** his obligation **with them** even when they are **withered.**

בעי רמי בר חמא: מהו שיצא אדם ידי חובתו במרור של מעשר שני בירושלים? אליבא דרבי עקיבא לא תיבעי לך – השתא במצה דאורייתא נפיק – במרור דרבנן מיבעיא?!

Rami bar Ḥama raised a dilemma: What is the *halakha* with regard to the possibility **that a person** can **fulfill his obligation with bitter herbs of second-tithe** produce **in Jerusalem? In accordance with** the opinion of **Rabbi Akiva,** who permits one to fulfill the obligation to eat *matza* with second-tithe produce because it can be eaten anywhere if it becomes ritually impure, **do not raise this dilemma. Now** that it has been mentioned that in the case **of** ***matza***, where the obligation applies **by Torah** law, one can **fulfill** his **obligation** with second tithe in this manner, **is it necessary** to mention that one can use second tithe for **bitter herbs, which** nowadays applies **by rabbinic** law, as there is no Paschal lamb?

כי תיבעי לך – אליבא דרבי יוסי הגלילי מאי? במצה דאורייתא הוא דלא נפיק – אבל מרור דרבנן נפיק –

When you raise the dilemma, it is **in accordance with** the opinion of **Rabbi Yosei HaGelili,** who maintains that one cannot fulfill his obligation with *matza* of second-tithe produce. **What is** the *halakha* with regard to bitter herbs? The Gemara explains the two sides of this dilemma: Does Rabbi Yosei HaGelili say **it is** only **with regard to** ***matza*** of second-tithe produce, where the obligation applies **by Torah** law, that one does **not fulfill** the mitzva; **however,** with **bitter herbs,** a mitzva that applies **by rabbinic** law, one can **fulfill** his obligation with this second-tithe produce?

או דילמא כל דתקינו רבנן – כעין דאורייתא תקון. אמר רבא: מסתברא, מצה ומרור.

Or perhaps, everything that the Sages instituted, they instituted in a manner **similar** to the model provided **by Torah** law. If this principle is accepted, it would mean the following: Just as one may not use second-tithe produce for *matza*, so too, one may not use second tithe as bitter herbs, despite the fact that the obligation to eat them is rabbinic. **Rava said: It stands to reason** that since the verse juxtaposes ***matza*** **and bitter herbs,** similar restrictions apply to both mitzvot. Consequently, just as according to Rabbi Yosei HaGelili one cannot use second-tithe produce for *matza*, so too, one cannot use this produce for bitter herbs.

מתני׳ אין שורין את המורסן לתרנגולים, אבל חולטין. האשה לא תשרה את המורסן שתוליך בידה למרחץ, אבל שפה היא בבשרה יבש. לא ילעוס אדם חיטין ויניח על מכתו, מפני שהן מחמיצות.

MISHNA One may **not soak coarse bran**[H] **for** feeding **chickens,** lest it be leavened. **However, one** may **pour boiling water** onto the bran before feeding it to the chickens, as it will not become leavened from this brief exposure to water. **A woman** may **not soak coarse bran to bring by hand to the bathhouse** for use as a cleanser; **however, she** may **rub** coarse bran **on her dry skin.**[HN] Likewise, the Sages said: **A person** may **not chew wheat and place it on his wound,**[H] **due to** the fact **that** the wheat **will be leavened** from the saliva and his chewing.

HALAKHA

Soaking coarse bran – שרית מורסן: It is prohibited to soak coarse bran or to pour boiling water over it. Although the mishna states that it is permitted to pour boiling water over coarse bran, the *ge'onim* state that we lack the expertise to do this properly. This practice is therefore prohibited, as there is concern that it will cause the mixture to be leavened quickly (*Tur* 465; *Shulḥan Arukh, Oraḥ Ḥayyim* 465:1).

Rubbing coarse bran – שיפה במורסן: It is prohibited to rub coarse bran onto one's skin, even if the skin is dry. Although the mishna rules that this action is permitted, there is concern that people will neglect to remove all the coarse bran before coming into contact with water, and the bran will become leavened (Rosh; *Shulḥan Arukh, Oraḥ Ḥayyim* 465:2).

Chewing wheat – לעיסת חיטין: One may not chew wheat on Passover with the intention of placing it on a wound (*Shulḥan Arukh, Oraḥ Ḥayyim* 466:1).

NOTES

She may rub on her…skin – שפה היא בבשרה: Some commentaries say that a woman may rub even dry coarse bran onto her skin when it is wet from washing (*Me'iri* and others). Others claim that this refers to skin that is dry of water but moist from perspiration. The mishna is teaching that we are not concerned that her perspiration might leaven the grain (*Mikhtam*; Rosh; and others).

גמ׳ תָּנוּ רַבָּנַן, אֵלּוּ דְּבָרִים שֶׁאֵין בָּאִין לִידֵי חִימּוּץ: הָאָפוּי, וְהַמְבוּשָּׁל, וְחָלוּט שֶׁחֲלָטוֹ בְּרוֹתְחִין. מְבוּשָּׁל?! אַדְּמִבַּשֵּׁל לֵיהּ מַחְמַע! אָמַר רַב פַּפָּא: הָאָפוּי שֶׁבִּישְּׁלוֹ קָאָמַר.

GEMARA The Sages taught: The following foods **do not come to** a state of **leavening:** Foods that have already been **baked, or boiled, or over-boiled in hot water.** With regard to the statement that **boiled** food will not become leavened, the Gemara asks: Why not? **When it is boiled it will become leavened.** The Gemara answers that **Rav Pappa said:** The *tanna* merely **said** that if it was first **baked and** afterward **boiled,** it will not be leavened; however, if it was initially boiled it will become leavened.

תַּנְיָא, רַבִּי יוֹסֵי בְּרַבִּי יְהוּדָה אוֹמֵר: קֶמַח שֶׁנָּפַל לְתוֹכוֹ דֶּלֶף – אֲפִילּוּ כָּל הַיּוֹם כּוּלּוֹ – אֵינוֹ בָּא לִידֵי חִימּוּץ. אָמַר רַב פַּפָּא: וְהוּא דְּעָבֵיד טִיף לַהֲדֵי טִיף.

It was taught in a *baraita* that **Rabbi Yosei, son of Rabbi Yehuda, says:** In the case of **flour into which** water is **dripping,**[H] **even** if the water drips **the entire day** the flour **will not come to** a state of **leavening,** as the ceaseless dripping prevents fermentation. **Rav Pappa said: And that is** the case only **if one drop drips into the other,**[N] i.e., the dripping is continuous, preventing the mixture from settling.

אָמְרֵי דְּבֵי רַבִּי שֵׁילָא: וַתִּיקָא שְׁרֵי. וְהָתַנְיָא: וַתִּיקָא אָסוּר! לָא קַשְׁיָא: הָא – דַּעֲבַדְיֵהּ בְּמִשְׁחָא וּמִילְחָא, הָא – דַּעֲבַדְיֵהּ בְּמַיָּא וּמִילְחָא.

The school of Rabbi Sheila say: ***Vatika,***[H] a pastry prepared from a mixture of different liquids, is **permitted** on Passover. The Gemara raises a difficulty: **But wasn't it taught** in a *baraita* that ***vatika* is forbidden?** The Gemara answers: This is **not difficult. This** *baraita*, which states that *vatika* is permitted, is referring to a case **in which it was prepared with oil and salt,** whereas **that** *baraita* forbade *vatika* **prepared with water and salt,** as that dish will become leavened.

אָמַר מָר זוּטְרָא: לָא לִימְחֵי אִינִישׁ קִדְרָא בְּקִמְחָא דַּאֲבִישְׁנָא, דִּילְמָא לָא בָּשֵׁיל שַׁפִּיר, וְאָתֵי לִידֵי חִימּוּץ. אָמַר רַב יוֹסֵף: לָא לִיחְלוֹט אִינִישׁ

Mar Zutra said: A person should not line the edge **of a pot**[N] **with roasted flour,**[H] **lest** some of the flour **was not properly roasted and it will come to** a state of **leavening** in the pot. **Rav Yosef said: A person should not scald**

HALAKHA

Flour into which water is dripping – קֶמַח שֶׁנָּפַל לְתוֹכוֹ דֶּלֶף: A constant dripping of water into flour will not leaven the flour, provided that the dripping is continuous and one bakes the mixture immediately afterward. However, if the dripping might have been intermittent, the flour is prohibited (*Shulḥan Arukh, Oraḥ Ḥayyim* 466:6).

Vatika – וַתִּיקָא: This food, prepared from flour, oil, and salt, but not water, may be eaten during Passover. The Ashkenazic custom is to avoid foods of this kind unless they are required for one who is ill (*Shulḥan Arukh, Oraḥ Ḥayyim* 463:2, and in the comment of the Rema).

Lining a pot – לִימְחוֹת קִדְרָא: During Passover, one may not put flour into a pot to remove impurities, with the exception of *matza* meal (*Shulḥan Arukh, Oraḥ Ḥayyim* 463:3).

NOTES

If one drop drips into the other – דְּעָבֵיד טִיף לַהֲדֵי טִיף: Just as dough will not be leavened while it is being kneaded, so too, this mixture will not begin to be leavened as long as the dripping continues.

Line the edge of a pot – לִימְחֵי...קִדְרָא: Several different explanations of this case have been suggested. Some commentaries maintain that it involves the placement of flour into a dish to thicken it (*Me'iri*). Others claim that the flour is used for filling small holes in the pot (*Nimmukei Yosef*). Yet others suggest that the flour serves to reinforce the pot (*Beit Yosef*, based on the Rambam).

Perek **II**
Daf **40** Amud **a**

תְּרֵי חִיטֵּי בַּהֲדֵי הֲדָדֵי – דִּילְמָא אָזְלָא חֲדָא וְיָתְבָה בְּצִירְיָא דַּחֲבֶרְתַּהּ, וְלָא סָלֵיק לְהוּ דִּיקוּלָא דְּמַיָּא מֵאַרְבַּע רוּחָתָא, וְאָתֵי לִידֵי חִימּוּץ.

two wheat grains in boiling water at the same time, **lest one move and rest in the slit** [*tzirya*][B] **of the other,** thereby preventing **the column** [*dikkula*] **of** boiling **water**[N] **from entering all four sides** of the grain, **and** the grain **will come to** a state of **leavening.**

וְאָמַר אַבָּיֵי: לָא לִיחְרוֹךְ אִינִישׁ תְּרֵי שִׁבּוֹלֵי בַּהֲדֵי הֲדָדֵי, דִּילְמָא נָפְקֵי מַיָּא מֵהַאי וּבָלַע אִידָּךְ, וְאָתְיָא לִידֵי חִימּוּץ. אָמַר לֵיהּ רָבָא: אִי הָכִי – אֲפִילּוּ חֲדָא נָמֵי, דִּילְמָא נָפֵיק מֵהַאי רֵישָׁא וּבָלַע אִידָּךְ רֵישָׁא! אֶלָּא אָמַר רָבָא: מֵי פֵירוֹת נִינְהוּ, וּמֵי פֵירוֹת אֵינָן מַחְמִיצִין.

And Abaye said: A person may **not roast two stalks**[H] **together, lest water leave one and be absorbed by the other, and it come to be leavened. Rava said to him: If so,** one should not **even** roast **one** stalk, **lest the** liquid **leave one end** of the stalk **and be absorbed by** its **other end. Rather, Rava said:** One need not be concerned about this possibility, as **it** is considered **fruit juice, and fruit juice does not leaven** grain.

וַהֲדַר בֵּיהּ אַבָּיֵי מֵהַהִיא, דְּכֹל אַגַּב מִדְלְיֵיהּוּ לָא מַחְמְצִי. דְּאָמַר אַבָּיֵי: הַאי חַצְבָּא דַּאֲבִישְׁנָא, סְחִיפָא – שְׁרֵי, זְקִיפָא – אָסוּר. רָבָא אָמַר: אֲפִילּוּ זְקִיפָא נָמֵי שְׁרֵי, מֵי פֵירוֹת נִינְהוּ, וּמֵי פֵירוֹת אֵינָן מַחְמִיצִין.

The Gemara adds: **And Abaye retracted** his opinion with regard to **that** *halakha* of stalks, as he maintains **that anything that is absorbing** liquid **will not become leavened** unless it is fully soaked in water. **As Abaye said:** With regard to **this jug used for** drying the stalks by means of **roasting,** if it is **inverted it is permitted,** as the liquid that is discharged from one stalk will not be absorbed by the other stalks. However, if the vessel is **upright it is prohibited,** as the liquid retained in the vessel might be absorbed by the other stalks and leaven them. **Rava said: Even** if the jug is **upright, it is also permitted. This** liquid is considered **fruit juice, and fruit juice does not leaven** grain.

BACKGROUND

Slit [*tzirya*] – צִירְיָא: The visible slit on the lower portion of the wheat is the *tzirya* mentioned here. In contrast, a barley grain has several grooves that do not affect the surface area of the barley.

Kernel of wheat (left) and kernel of barley (right)

NOTES

The column [*dikkula*] of water – דִּיקוּלָא דְּמַיָּא: The *ge'onim* explain that the term *dikkula*, literally, palm tree, is used to describe a column of water that ascends in the form of palm leaves.

HALAKHA

Roast two stalks – חֲרִיכַת שְׁתֵּי שִׁיבֳּלִים: It is permitted to roast two stalks of grain together, as there is no concern that liquid will leave one stalk and be absorbed by the other. In addition, this liquid is classified as fruit juice, and therefore it does not leaven the other stalk (*Shulḥan Arukh, Oraḥ Ḥayyim* 463:1).

תָּנוּ רַבָּנַן: אֵין לוֹתְתִין שְׂעוֹרִין בְּפֶסַח, וְאִם לָתַת, נִתְבַּקְּעוּ – אֲסוּרוֹת, לֹא נִתְבַּקְּעוּ – מוּתָּרוֹת.

The Sages taught: One may **not soak barley** in water **on Passover** to make it easier to remove the chaff from the grain.[NH] **And if one did soak** barley grain **and it split, it is prohibited. If it did not split, it is permitted.**

רַבִּי יוֹסֵי אוֹמֵר: שׁוֹרֶן בְּחוֹמֶץ וְחוֹמֶץ צוֹמְתָן. אָמַר שְׁמוּאֵל: אֵין הֲלָכָה כְּרַבִּי יוֹסֵי.

Rabbi Yosei says: If one sees that the grain is expanding, **he** should **soak it in vinegar, and the vinegar will cause** the grain **to contract,** thereby preventing leavening. However, **Shmuel said: The *halakha* in not in accordance with** the opinion **of Rabbi Yosei.**

אָמַר רַב חִסְדָּא אָמַר מָר עוּקְבָא: לֹא נִתְבַּקְּעוּ מַמָּשׁ, אֶלָּא כֹּל שֶׁאִילּוּ מַנִּיחָן עַל פִּי חָבִית וְהֵן נִתְבַּקְּעוֹת מֵאֵילֵיהֶן. וּשְׁמוּאֵל אָמַר: נִתְבַּקְּעוּ מַמָּשׁ. עֲבַד שְׁמוּאֵל עוּבְדָּא בְּדוּרָא דְּבֵי בַּר חָשׁוּ נִתְבַּקְּעוּ מַמָּשׁ.

Rav Ḥisda said that **Mar Ukva said:** When the Sages were referring to a case where the barley grain split, the prohibition does **not** apply only if **it actually split** and a crack is visible. **Rather,** this is referring even to a case where **if** the barley grains **were placed on a barrel**[N] of wine **they** would **split by themselves,** due to the effect of the wine. **And** by contrast, **Shmuel said:** This *halakha* applies only if **it actually split.** The Gemara relates: **Shmuel took action** in accordance with his ruling, when he was **in the village of bar Ḥashu's house.** He prohibited only wheat grains that had **actually split,** but permitted those that were about to split.

אָמַר רַבָּה: בַּעַל נֶפֶשׁ לֹא יִלְתּוֹת. מַאי אִירְיָא בַּעַל נֶפֶשׁ? אֲפִילּוּ כּוּלֵּי עָלְמָא נָמֵי, דְּהָא תַּנְיָא: אֵין לוֹתְתִין שְׂעוֹרִין בְּפֶסַח! הָכִי קָאָמַר: בַּעַל נֶפֶשׁ – אֲפִילּוּ חִיטִּין דִּשְׁרִירִי לֹא יִלְתּוֹת.

Rabba said: A pious person will not soak wheat at all during Passover. The Gemara asks: **Why discuss particularly a pious person?** This *halakha* should apply to **everyone as well, as it was** expressly **taught** in a *baraita*: **One** may **not soak barley on Passover.** The Gemara answers that **this is** what Rabba **is saying: A pious person** will **not even soak wheat, which is firmer** than barley and less likely to split, due to the concern that it might become leavened.

אָמַר לֵיהּ רַב נַחְמָן: מַאן דְּצָיֵית לֵיהּ לְאַבָּא אָכֵיל נַהֲמָא דְּעִיפּוּשָׁא. דְּהָא בֵּי רַב הוּנָא לָתְתִי, וּבֵי רָבָא בַּר אָבִין לָתְתִי. וְרָבָא אָמַר: אָסוּר לִלְתּוֹת.

Rav Naḥman said to Rabba: **Anyone who listens to Abba,** Rabba's first name, **will eat moldy bread** during Passover, as flour cannot be properly prepared without soaking, and therefore *matza* should not be prepared from this flour. **As in Rav Huna's house they would soak** the grain, **and in Rava bar Avin's house they would** likewise **soak** their grain. **But Rava said:** Soaking grain should not be avoided merely for reasons of piety; rather, it is absolutely **prohibited to soak** grain.

אֶלָּא הָא דְּתַנְיָא "אֵין לוֹתְתִין שְׂעוֹרִין בְּפֶסַח" שְׂעוֹרִין הוּא – דְּלָא, הָא חִיטֵּי – שָׁרֵי?! לָא מִיבַּעְיָא קָאָמַר, לָא מִיבַּעְיָא חִיטִּין, כֵּיוָן דְּאִית בֵּיהּ צִירְיָא – עָיְילִי בְּהוּ מַיָּא, אֲבָל שַׂעֲרֵי דְּשִׁיעֵי – אֵימָא שַׁפִּיר דָּמֵי, קָא מַשְׁמַע לַן.

The Gemara asks: **Rather, that which is taught** in a *baraita*: **One** may **not soak barley on Passover,** indicates that **it is barley that** one may **not** soak; however, it is **permitted** to soak **wheat,** how will Rava explain this *baraita*? The Gemara explains: The *baraita* is **speaking** employing the didactic style of: **Needless to say.** It should be understood as follows: **Needless to say, wheat** may not be soaked, **since** wheat grains **have a slit through which water will enter,** and the wheat will therefore expand quickly when left to soak. **However,** in the case of **barley, which is smooth** and no water will enter the grain, one might **say** that this **seems well,** i.e., it is permitted, to soak barley. Therefore, the *baraita* **teaches us** that it is prohibited to soak even barley.

הֲדַר אָמַר רָבָא: מוּתָּר לִלְתּוֹת, דְּתַנְיָא: יוֹצְאִין בְּפַת נְקִיָּה וְהַדְרָאָה, וְאִי אֶפְשָׁר נְקִיָּה בְּלֹא לְתִיתָה.

Rava reconsidered and **then said:** This is not the case. Rather, **it is permitted to soak** grain, **as it was taught** in a *baraita*: **One** can **fulfill** his obligation **with a** *matza* **loaf** prepared from **refined** flour **and with** *matza* baked from **coarse** flour. **And it is impossible** to produce **refined** *matza* **without soaking** the grain, as this is the only way to remove the chaff completely from the grain.

אֵיתִיבֵיהּ רַב פַּפָּא לְרָבָא: הַקְּמָחִין וְהַסְּלָתוֹת שֶׁל גּוֹיִם, שֶׁל כְּפָרִים – טְהוֹרִים, וְשֶׁל כְּרַכִּין – טְמֵאִין.

Rav Pappa raised an objection to the opinion of **Rava** from a *baraita*: With regard to **flour and refined flour** that belong **to gentiles, in villages** they **are ritually pure, and in cities** they **are ritually impure.** It is assumed that grain in cities is soaked before it is ground into flour. Once water comes in contact with this grain, it becomes susceptible to ritual impurity, and it subsequently becomes impure when touched by gentiles.

דִּכְפָרִים מַאי טַעְמָא? לָאו מִשּׁוּם דְּלָא לָתְתִי, וְקָא קָרֵי לֵיהּ סוֹלֶת!

As for flour **in villages, what is the reason** that it is ritually pure? Is it **not due to** the fact **that they do not soak** the flour, and therefore it does not become liable to ritual impurity? **And** yet their flour **is** nonetheless **called refined flour.** It can be inferred from this that it is possible to prepare refined flour without soaking the grain.

NOTES

Soaking – לְתִיתָה: The process of soaking consisted of rinsing grain both to remove the straw and dirt that had become stuck to it and to allow for easier separation of the chaff before grinding. Although most Sages permit this action, and some even maintain that it is obligatory, the *ge'onim* forbade it on the basis of an ancient tradition not to soak grain that will be used on Passover at all.

Placed on a barrel [*al pi ḥavit*] – מַנִּיחָן עַל פִּי חָבִית: There are several textual versions of this phrase. One version reads: *Al pi habiv*, meaning on a clay pan in which foods are roasted. Others suggest that the correct phrase is: *Al pi aviv*, which refers to a vessel on top of which the grains are roasted (see *Tosafot*; *Mikhtam*; Ritva; and others).

HALAKHA

Soaking grain on Passover – לְתִיתָה בְּפֶסַח: One may not soak wheat or barley for use during Passover. Although the Gemara appears to permit this activity, the *ge'onim* forbade it due to concern that the grain might become leavened (*Shulḥan Arukh*, *Oraḥ Ḥayyim* 453:5).

HALAKHA

Soaking grain on Passover – לְתִיתָה בְּפֶסַח: One may not soak wheat or barley for use during Passover. Although the Gemara appears to permit this activity, the *ge'onim* forbade it due to concern that the grain might become leavened (*Shulḥan Arukh, Oraḥ Ḥayyim* 453:5).

Guarded *matzot* – מַצּוֹת שְׁמוּרוֹת: The wheat for the *matza* that a person will use to fulfill his obligation should be kept from water from the time it is harvested, or at least from when it is ground into flour, in accordance with Rava's statement. Some people are strict and use only this type of *matza* throughout the entire Festival (*Shulḥan Arukh, Oraḥ Ḥayyim* 453:4).

NOTES

***Matza* in the end – מַצָּה בָּאַחֲרוֹנָה:** According to Rashi and others, there is a specific obligation to eat at the end of the seder meal an olive-bulk of *matza* hat has been guarded with the highest level of supervision. Nowadays, this *matza* is called *afikoman*. Others claim that there is no requirement to eat this type of *matza* specifically at the end of the meal. Rather, one must consume an olive-bulk of this type of *matza* at some point during the evening; otherwise, one might eat only *matza* that had not been guarded (Ritva).

Those who cut the stalks [*kifei*] – דִּמְהַפְּכִי כִּיפֵי: The *Arukh* explains that *kifei* are bowls, and this phrase describes those who overturned bowls, using them to cover grain in sacks, to prevent the grain from coming into contact with moisture. One who grinds wheat for use during Passover must keep it from coming into contact with water from the beginning of the harvest until the end of the process (*Mikhtam*).

תַּרְגּוּמָא אַקִּמְחָא. בָּתַר דִּנְפַק אֲמַר: מַאי טַעְמָא לָא אֵימָא לֵיהּ מֵהָא; דְּאָמַר רַבִּי זֵירָא אָמַר רַב יִרְמְיָה אָמַר שְׁמוּאֵל: חִיטִּין שֶׁל מְנָחוֹת – אֵין לוֹתְתִין אוֹתָם, וְקָא קָרֵי לְהוּ סוֹלֶת!

Rava answered: You should **interpret** the distinction of the *baraita* as referring only **to** ordinary **flour,** not refined flour, which is invariably susceptible to ritual impurity due to the soaking. **After** Rava **left,** Rav Pappa **said: What is the reason** that **he did not say** a proof **from this** statement **that Rabbi Zeira said** that **Rav Yirmeya said** that **Shmuel said:** With regard to **wheat** that will be used **for meal-offerings, one** may **not soak it,** and yet it **is** nonetheless **called refined flour?** The Torah insists that the flour used for meal-offerings be prepared from refined flour.

הֲדַר אָמַר רָבָא: מִצְוָה לְלַתּוֹת, שֶׁנֶּאֱמַר ״וּשְׁמַרְתֶּם אֶת הַמַּצּוֹת״ אִי לָא דִּבְעֵי לְתִיתָה – שִׁימּוּר לְמַאי? אִי שִׁימּוּר דְּלִישָׁה – שִׁימּוּר דְּלִישָׁה לָאו שִׁימּוּר הוּא.

Rava reconsidered and **then said:** It is not only permitted to soak the grains; it is actually **a mitzva to soak** them,[H] **as it is stated: "And you shall guard the *matzot*"** (Exodus 12:17). The Gemara explains this statement: **If** it is **not** the case **that** grain **requires soaking, for what** purpose is **guarding** necessary? **If** you claim that this verse is referring to **guarding when kneading,** that cannot be the case, as **guarding** grain **while kneading is not** considered **guarding.** If one failed to protect the wheat from becoming leavened up to that point, it is of no use to be careful while kneading it. Consequently, this mitzva to guard the dough cannot be referring to the kneading stage.

דְּאָמַר רַב הוּנָא: בְּצֵקוֹת שֶׁל גּוֹיִם אָדָם מְמַלֵּא כְּרֵיסוֹ מֵהֶן, וּבִלְבַד שֶׁיֹּאכַל כְּזַיִת מַצָּה בָּאַחֲרוֹנָה. בָּאַחֲרוֹנָה – אִין, בָּרִאשׁוֹנָה – לָא.

As Rav Huna said: In the case of **dough** prepared **by gentiles,** if one knows that it has not become leavened, **a person** may **fill his stomach with them** on Passover night, **provided that he eats an olive-bulk of *matza* in the end,**[N] to fulfill the obligation to eat *matza*. The Gemara infers from this statement: With regard to the *matza* that he eats **in the end, yes,** he fulfills his obligation with this *matza*. But with regard to the *matza* he ate **in the beginning, no,** he does not fulfill the mitzva with dough prepared by gentiles.

מַאי טַעְמָא – מִשּׁוּם דְּלָא עָבֵד בְּהוּ שִׁימּוּר. וְלַעֲבֵיד לֵיהּ שִׁימּוּר מֵאֲפִיָּה וְאֵילָךְ! אֶלָּא לָאו שְׁמַע מִינַּהּ – שִׁימּוּר מֵעִיקָּרָא בָּעֵינַן.

What is the reason that one cannot fulfill his obligation to eat *matza* with dough prepared by gentiles? It is **because** he **did not perform** his duty to **guard** this dough. **But** one can **perform** his duty to **guard it from** the time of **baking and onward. Rather, isn't it** correct to **conclude from** this *baraita* **that** the grain **must** be guarded **from the beginning,** i.e., from the time it is soaked, which proves that soaking the grain is part of the process of preparing *matza*?

וּמִמַּאי? דִּילְמָא שָׁאנֵי הָתָם, דִּבְעִידָּנָא דְּנָחֵית לְשִׁימּוּר – לָא עֲבַד לַהּ שִׁימּוּר. אֲבָל הֵיכָא דִּבְעִידָּנָא דְּנָחֵית לְשִׁימּוּר עָבֵיד לַהּ שִׁימּוּר – הָכִי נַמִי דְּשִׁימּוּר דְּלִישָׁה הָוֵי שִׁימּוּר.

The Gemara rejects this: **And from where** do we know that this conclusion is correct? **Perhaps it is different there, as at the time when guarding is required,** i.e., when water was added to the flour, **he did not perform** his duty to **guard it** properly. **However,** in a case **where at the time when guarding is required,** when water is added the flour, **he** properly **performed** his duty to **guard it, so too,** it is possible that **guarding** flour at the time **of kneading is** considered proper **guarding.** Therefore, this question cannot be resolved based on the case of dough prepared by gentiles.

וַאֲפִילּוּ הָכִי לָא הֲדַר בֵּיהּ רָבָא, דַּאֲמַר לְהוּ לְהָנְהוּ דִּמְהַפְּכִי כִּיפֵי: כִּי מְהַפְּכִיתוּ – הַפִּיכוּ לְשׁוּם מִצְוָה. אַלְמָא קָסָבַר: שִׁימּוּר מֵעִיקָּרָא – מִתְּחִלָּתוֹ וְעַד סוֹפוֹ בָּעֵינַן.

And although this proof was rejected, **Rava did not retract** his statement that guarding grain must begin before kneading. **For he** would **say to those who cut** and tied **the stalks** [*kifei*][N] of grain in the field: **When you cut** the grain, **cut it for the purpose of the mitzva. Apparently,** Rava **maintains** that **it is necessary to guard** the grain **from the outset,** i.e., **from the beginning** of its preparation **until its end.**[H]

מָר בְּרֵיהּ דְּרָבִינָא

The Gemara relates with regard to **Mar, son of Ravina,**

Perek **II**
Daf **40** Amud **b**

NOTES

Bring him wheat in a trough – מַנְקְטָא לֵיהּ...בְּאַרְבֵי: Apparently, the *Arukh* has a different version of the text, according to which the mother of Mar, son of Ravina, brought him the wheat with its roots. She was careful to protect the wheat from the start of its growth through its harvest.

מַנְקְטָא לֵיהּ אִימֵּיהּ בְּאַרְבֵי.

that **his mother** would **bring him** wheat **in a trough.**[N] In other words, she would guard the wheat grains from when they were harvested by placing them in vessels and guarding them until Passover.

הַהוּא אַרְבָּא דְּחִיטֵּי דְּטָבְעָא בְּחִישְׁתָּא, שַׁרְיָא רָבָא לְזַבּוֹנֵי לַגּוֹיִם.

The Gemara relates that there was **a certain boat** carrying **wheat, which capsized** before Passover **in the Ḥishta River.**[N] **Rava permitted** its owners **to sell** the recovered grain **to gentiles** during Passover.

אֵיתִיבֵיהּ רַבָּה בַּר לֵיוָאי לְרָבָא: בֶּגֶד שֶׁאָבַד בּוֹ כִּלְאַיִם – הֲרֵי זֶה לֹא יִמְכְּרֶנּוּ לַגּוֹי, וְלֹא יַעֲשֶׂה בּוֹ מַרְדַּעַת לַחֲמוֹר, אֲבָל עוֹשִׂין אוֹתוֹ תַּכְרִיכִין לַמֵּת.

Rabba bar Levai raised an objection to the opinion of Rava from a *baraita*: With regard to **a garment in which diverse kinds,** a prohibited mixture of wool and linen, **has been lost,**[H] i.e., a wool garment into which a linen thread was sewn or vice versa, **one may not sell it to a gentile; and one** may not even **fashion it** into **a saddlecloth for a donkey.** It is prohibited to do so lest one remove a piece of this garment and sew it onto his own clothing. **However, one** may **fashion it** into **a shroud for a dead body,** as there is no concern that he will remove it from the dead

לַגּוֹי מַאי טַעְמָא לָא – לָאו מִשּׁוּם דַּהֲדַר מְזַבֵּין לְיִשְׂרָאֵל?

The Gemara clarifies this issue: **What is the reason** that one may **not** sell it **to a gentile?** Is it **not due to** the concern **that** the gentile **will resell it to a Jew?** Since the mixture of wool and linen is not visible, it is possible for a Jew to use this cloth unawares. The same concern applies to grain: It is not apparent that the grain that capsized in the river is prohibited. It should therefore be prohibited to sell this wheat to gentiles, lest they resell it to Jews.

הֲדַר אֲמַר רָבָא: לְזַבִּינְהוּ קַבָּא קַבָּא לְיִשְׂרָאֵל, כִּי הֵיכִי דְּכָלְיָא קַמֵּי פִּיסְחָא.

Rava reconsidered and **then said: He should sell** this wheat **one** *kav* **at a time,** i.e., in small measures, each **to a** different **Jew,**[N] but not to any one Jew in large quantities, **so that** all of this wheat **will be used before Passover.**[H] By selling it in this manner, all the grain will be used quickly and no one will unwittingly eat these leavened grains on Passover.

תָּנוּ רַבָּנַן: אֵין מוֹלְלִין אֶת הַקְּדֵירָה בַּפֶּסַח, וְהָרוֹצֶה שֶׁיִּמְלוֹל – נוֹתֵן אֶת הַקֶּמַח וְאַחַר כָּךְ נוֹתֵן אֶת הַחוֹמֶץ. וְיֵשׁ אוֹמְרִים: אַף נוֹתֵן אֶת הַחוֹמֶץ וְאַחַר כָּךְ נוֹתֵן אֶת הַקֶּמַח.

The Sages taught: One may **not stir** flour into **a pot** of food **on Passover**[H] to absorb the foam that has accumulated during the cooking process. **And one who wishes to stir** flour **should add the flour and afterward add vinegar,** which will prevent the flour from becoming leavened. **And some say:** One may **even add vinegar and afterward add the flour,** as vinegar prevents flour from becoming leavened even after the flour is diluted in water.

מַאן יֵשׁ אוֹמְרִים?

The Gemara asks: **Who is** the *tanna* whose opinion is introduced by the phrase **some say?**

אָמַר רַב חִסְדָּא: רַבִּי יְהוּדָה הִיא, דִּתְנַן: הָאִילְפָּס וְהַקְּדֵירָה שֶׁהֶעֱבִירָן מְרוּתָּחִין – לֹא יִתֵּן לְתוֹכָן תַּבְלִין, אֲבָל נוֹתֵן לְתוֹךְ הַקְּעָרָה אוֹ לְתוֹךְ הַתַּמְחוּי. רַבִּי יְהוּדָה אוֹמֵר: לַכֹּל הוּא נוֹתֵן, חוּץ מִדָּבָר שֶׁיֵּשׁ בּוֹ חוֹמֶץ וָצִיר.

Rav Ḥisda said: It is the opinion of **Rabbi Yehuda, as we learned** in a mishna: With regard to **a stew pot or a pot** of food **that one removed** from the fire when it was **seething,** one may **not add spices to them on Shabbat.**[H] **However, one** may **add** spices **to a dish or to** the large **plate** into which the food is poured from the pot. **Rabbi Yehuda says: One** may **add** spices **to any** food that has been removed from the fire, **except to** a dish **that contains vinegar or brine,** as this food is considered as though it were still seething, due to the pungency of the vinegar or brine. Since Rabbi Yehuda maintains that vinegar has the same effect as boiling, he would agree that vinegar, like boiling water, prevents flour from becoming leavened.

וְנוֹקְמָהּ כְּרַבִּי יוֹסֵי, (דִּתְנַן), רַבִּי יוֹסֵי אוֹמֵר: שׁוֹרָן בַּחוֹמֶץ, וְחוֹמֶץ צוֹמְתָן!

The Gemara asks: **And let us establish** the opinion of: Some say, **in accordance with** the opinion of **Rabbi Yosei. As we learned** in a mishna: **Rabbi Yosei says,** with regard to wheat grains that were soaked in water: **One** should **soak them in vinegar, and** this **vinegar will cause** the wheat **to contract** and prevent it from becoming leavened.

כִּי אַשְׁמְעִינַן לֵיהּ לְרַבִּי יוֹסֵי – הָנֵי מִילֵּי דְּאִיתֵיהּ בְּעֵינֵיהּ, אֲבָל עַל יְדֵי תַּעֲרוֹבֶת – לֹא.

The Gemara answers: **When we learn** the opinion of **Rabbi Yosei,** this **applies** only to a situation **where** the vinegar is **in its pure,** unadulterated form, in which case its pungency prevents the wheat from becoming leavened. **However,** if the vinegar is added **by means of a mixture, no,** Rabbi Yosei's statement does not apply to a case of this kind.

עוּלָּא אָמַר: אֶחָד זֶה וְאֶחָד זֶה אָסוּר, מִשּׁוּם "לֵךְ לֵךְ אָמְרִינַן נְזִירָא, סְחוֹר סְחוֹר, לְכַרְמָא לָא תִּקְרַב".

Ulla said: In **both of these** cases, whether the vinegar is added first or afterward, its use is **prohibited,** as one must avoid scenarios that might lead to a prohibition, **as per** the well-known adage: **Go around, go around,** and **do not approach the vineyard, they say to the nazirite.** Since a nazirite is prohibited from drinking wine and eating grapes, it is preferable for him to avoid a vineyard entirely. A similar principle applies to other prohibitions.

NOTES

Which capsized in the Ḥishta River – דְּטָבְעָא בְּחִישְׁתָּא: Some commentaries explain that *ḥishta* is not the name of a place, but refers to an area that contains water and reeds (*Arukh*).

He should sell this one ***kav*** **at a time, each to a different Jew** – לְזַבִּינְהוּ קַבָּא קַבָּא לְיִשְׂרָאֵל: Apparently, the Rambam had a different version of the text, according to which one may sell a *kav* at a time only to a gentile. However, with regard to a Jewish buyer, if the seller informs him of the status of the wheat, he may sell even all the grain to him (*Mikhtam*). Some commentaries say that one is not obligated to inform a Jew about the nature of this grain if he sells him a small quantity (*Ittur*); however, others disagree and maintain that he is required to inform a Jewish buyer in all cases (see *Me'iri*).

HALAKHA

A garment in which diverse kinds has been lost – בֶּגֶד שֶׁאָבַד בּוֹ כִּלְאַיִם: If a linen string was lost in a wool garment or vice versa, one may neither sell this garment to a gentile nor use it as a saddlecloth for a donkey (*Shulḥan Arukh, Yoreh De'a*, 301:8).

Wheat that became wet before Passover – חִטִּים שֶׁנִּרְטְבוּ קוֹדֶם פֶּסַח: Grain that became wet before Passover should not be retained over the Festival. Instead, one should sell the grain to a Jew well in advance of Passover, while informing the buyer before the sale that the grain must be treated as leavened. Alternatively, one should sell it in small quantities to gentiles, as the Rambam maintains (*Shulḥan Arukh, Oraḥ Ḥayyim* 467:1).

Stirring flour into a pot – מְלִילַת קְדֵרוֹת: One may not stir flour into a pot of food, even if he adds vinegar afterward. However, it is permitted to add baked *matza* to a pot of food, as stated by Ulla and Rava (*Shulḥan Arukh, Oraḥ Ḥayyim* 463:3).

A large, seething stew pot or pot – אִילְפָּס וּקְדֵירָה מְרוּתָּחִין: One may not add spices to a stew pot or pot that was cooking directly on the fire on Shabbat. This prohibition applies even if the pot has been removed from the fire, when it is classified as a primary vessel, as it will still cook the spices. However, it permitted to add spices to a secondary vessel, i.e., a vessel into which food from the pot has been poured, in accordance with the opinion of the Rabbis (*Shulḥan Arukh, Oraḥ Ḥayyim* 318:9).

LANGUAGE

Cooks [*burdikei*] – בּוּרְדִיקֵי: Possibly from the Greek βρωτικός, *brotikos*, meaning voracious, or inclined to eat. Scholars have suggested that this word should read *korduki*, which probably derives from the Middle Persian xwardīkār, an amalgam of the words xwardīg, meaning food, and kār, a suffix that functions as the agent.

BACKGROUND

Exilarch – רֵישׁ גָּלוּתָא: The Exilarch, who descended from the house of David, was recognized by the Jews as the heir to the scepter of Judah and entrusted with broad official powers. He was the leader of the Jews of the Persian Empire and their representative to the authorities, who regarded him as a member of a royal dynasty. Consequently, he enjoyed a lofty position within the Persian court. During various periods, he was even considered third in the royal hierarchy. The Exilarch was responsible for the collection of a major portion of the government taxes from the Jewish community, and could appoint leaders and judges whose powers included the imposition of corporal, and sometimes capital, punishment.

Adjacent to the Exilarch's home was a special rabbinical court appointed by him to deal with cases involving money and property in particular. He also seems to have had the authority to make certain appointments within the Jewish community throughout the country, although most of them were made in consultation with the heads of the great academies. The Exilarchs were referred to in the Talmud by the honorific title Mar before or after their name, and were devoted to the Torah. Some of them were indeed significant scholars in their own right.

רַב פַּפִּי שָׁרֵי לֵיהּ לְבוּרְדִיקֵי דְּבֵי רֵישׁ גָּלוּתָא לְמִמְחָה קְדֵירָה בַּחֲסִיסֵי. אֲמַר רָבָא: אִיכָּא דְּשָׁרֵי כִּי הַאי מִילְּתָא בְּדוּכְתָּא דִּשְׁכִיחִי עַבְדֵי?! אִיכָּא דְּאָמְרִי: רָבָא גּוּפָא מָחֵי לָהּ קִידְרָא בַּחֲסִיסֵי.

The Gemara relates: **Rav Pappi permitted the cooks [*burdikei*]**[L] **of the household of the Exilarch**[B] **to mash roasted grains**[N] **into** a **pot** of food, to dissolve the accumulated foam. **Rava said: Is there** anyone **who permits this matter in a place where servants are found?** Servants are unlikely to be careful with regard to these prohibitions. They will use raw flour for this purpose, which will lead to a violation of the prohibition against leavened bread on Passover. **Some say** that **Rava himself** would **add roasted grains into** his own **pot.**

מתני׳ אֵין נוֹתְנִין קֶמַח לְתוֹךְ חֲרוֹסֶת אוֹ לְתוֹךְ הַחַרְדָּל, וְאִם נָתַן – יֵאָכֵל מִיָּד, וְרַבִּי מֵאִיר אוֹסֵר.

MISHNA One may **not add flour to *ḥaroset*,** a seasoned, pungent food, **or to mustard,** to dull the sharp taste. In both cases, the pungency of these foods might accelerate the leavening of the flour. **And if one added** flour to either of these, the mixture may **be eaten immediately** before it is leavened; **and Rabbi Meir prohibits** this, lest the food be leavened immediately.

אֵין מְבַשְּׁלִין אֶת הַפֶּסַח לֹא בְּמַשְׁקִין וְלֹא בְּמֵי פֵירוֹת, אֲבָל סָכִין וּמַטְבִּילִין אוֹתוֹ בָּהֶן.

The mishna continues: **One** may **not boil the Paschal** lamb[N] **in** ordinary **liquids**[H] **or in fruit juices,** as the Torah explicitly states that it must be roasted. **However,** one may **baste** it while it is roasting **and dip**[N] **it into** liquid while eating it.

מֵי תַשְׁמִישׁוֹ שֶׁל נַחְתּוֹם יִשָּׁפְכוּ, מִפְּנֵי שֶׁהֵן מַחְמִיצִין.

The *tanna* further states: **Water that has been used by a baker** for cooling his hands or washing dishes should **be poured out, because** this water **leavens** the dough, as the water probably contains a small quantity of flour and dough.

גמ׳ אָמַר רַב כָּהֲנָא: מַחְלוֹקֶת – לְתוֹךְ הַחַרְדָּל, אֲבָל לְתוֹךְ חֲרוֹסֶת – דִּבְרֵי הַכֹּל יִשָּׂרֵף מִיָּד.

GEMARA **Rav Kahana said:** The **dispute** between Rabbi Meir and the Rabbis concerns a case where one adds flour **to mustard,** which is extremely pungent and will not leaven the flour immediately. **But** in a case where flour is added **to** the less pungent ***ḥaroset*,** which will leaven the flour quickly, **everyone agrees** that the mixture must **be burned immediately.**[NH]

וְתַנְיָא נַמִי הָכִי: אֵין נוֹתְנִין קֶמַח לְתוֹךְ הַחֲרוֹסֶת, וְאִם נָתַן – יִשָּׂרֵף מִיָּד. לְתוֹךְ הַחַרְדָּל, רַבִּי מֵאִיר אוֹמֵר: יִשָּׂרֵף מִיָּד, וַחֲכָמִים אוֹמְרִים: יֵאָכֵל מִיָּד. אָמַר רַב הוּנָא בְּרֵיהּ דְּרַב יְהוּדָה אָמַר רַב נַחְמָן אָמַר שְׁמוּאֵל: הֲלָכָה כְּדִבְרֵי חֲכָמִים. אָמַר לֵיהּ רַב נַחְמָן בַּר יִצְחָק לְרַב הוּנָא בְּרֵיהּ דְּרַב יְהוּדָה:

And that opinion **was also taught** in a *baraita*: **One** may **not add flour to *ḥaroset*, and if one did add** flour it should **be burned immediately.** With regard to flour that was added **to mustard, Rabbi Meir says:** It should **be burned immediately, and the Rabbis say:** It should **be eaten immediately,** before it is leavened. **Rav Huna, son of Rav Yehuda, said** that **Rav Naḥman said** that **Shmuel said: The *halakha* is in accordance with** the opinion of **the Rabbis** concerning this issue. **Rav Naḥman bar Yitzḥak said to Rav Huna, son of Rav Yehuda:**

NOTES

Roasted grains – בַּחֲסִיסֵי: See Rashi and *Tosafot*. Some commentaries explain that this term refers to flour prepared from ground *matza*, i.e., *matza* meal (*Mikhtam*; Ritva).

One may not boil the Paschal lamb – אֵין מְבַשְּׁלִין אֶת הַפֶּסַח: It is not immediately apparent why this *halakha* is mentioned in the context of the *halakhot* of leavened bread. Some commentaries explain that after discussing the case of adding flour to fruit juice, the *tanna* incidentally adds the *halakha* of fruit juice in the preparation of the Paschal lamb (*Melekhet Shlomo*; see *Tosefot Yom Tov*).

Baste and dip – סָכִין וּמַטְבִּילִין: Some commentaries explain that basting is permitted only after roasting, but it is entirely prohibited before this stage (Rabbeinu Yehonatan; *Nimmukei Yosef*).

Flour that is added to mustard or *ḥaroset* – קֶמַח לְחַרְדָּל וַחֲרוֹסֶת: Some commentaries explain the difference between these two cases as follows: Since the flavor of mustard fades quickly, it is usually eaten immediately, and there is therefore no concern that this mustard will be preserved for a significant period of time. However, other spices were generally kept for a long time. Therefore, they should be burned immediately after they become mingled with flour, lest they be retained after having become leavened (Maharam Ḥalawa).

HALAKHA

Boiling the Paschal lamb in liquids – בִּשּׁוּל הַפֶּסַח בְּמַשְׁקִין: Although it is prohibited to boil the Paschal lamb in any type of liquid before it is roasted, one may baste the meat with liquids other than water (Rambam *Sefer Korbanot*, *Hilkhot Korban Pesaḥ* 8:7–8).

Flour that fell into pungent spices – קֶמַח שֶׁנָּפַל לְתַבְלִינִים חֲרִיפִים: If flour falls into mustard that contains water, it should be eaten immediately. However if flour falls into other, less pungent spices, it must be burned as leavened bread. This ruling is in accordance with Rav Kahana's explanation of the opinion of the Rabbis in the mishna. It is the custom in Ashkenazic communities not to eat mustard at all, as it belongs in the category of *kitniyot*, legumes (*Shulḥan Arukh*, *Oraḥ Ḥayyim* 464, and in the comment of the Rema).

אַחֲרוֹסֶת קָאָמַר מָר, אוֹ אַחַרְדָּל קָאָמַר מָר? אָמַר לֵיהּ: לְמַאי נָפְקָא מִינָּהּ?

Did **the Master say** this statement **with regard to *haroset*, or did the Master say** it **with regard to mustard? He said to him: What** is the **practical difference** whether he was referring to *haroset* or mustard? Both of these are mentioned together, and the same *halakha* applies to both.

לִדְרַב כָּהֲנָא, דְּאָמַר רַב כָּהֲנָא: מַחְלוֹקֶת – לְתוֹךְ הַחַרְדָּל, אֲבָל לְתוֹךְ הַחֲרוֹסֶת – דִּבְרֵי הַכֹּל יִשָּׂרֵף מִיָּד,

He said to him: There is a difference with regard **to that** which was stated by **Rav Kahana, as Rav Kahana said:** The **dispute** between Rabbi Meir and the Rabbis concerns a case in which flour was added **to mustard. However,** if flour was added **to *haroset*, everyone agrees** that it must **be burned immediately.** Rav Nahman bar Yitzhak was asking Rav Huna, son of Rav Yehuda, whether he disagrees with Rav Kahana and maintains that the Rabbis dispute the *halakha* in the case of *haroset* as well.

אָמַר לֵיהּ: לָא שְׁמִיעַ לִי, כְּלוֹמַר לָא סְבִירָא לִי.

He said to him: I did not hear about this statement; **that is to say, I do not hold** in accordance with it. I do not distinguish between these two cases, as in my opinion the Rabbis permit one to eat even this *haroset*.

אָמַר רַב אַשִׁי: כְּוָותֵיהּ דְּרַב כָּהֲנָא מִסְתַּבְּרָא, מִדְּאָמַר שְׁמוּאֵל: אֵין הֲלָכָה כְּרַבִּי יוֹסֵי. מַאי לָאו – צְמוֹתֵי הוּא דְּלָא צָמֵית הָא חַמּוּעֵי – מְחַמְּעָא.

Rav Ashi said: It is reasonable to rule **in accordance with** the opinion of **Rav Kahana, from** the fact **that Shmuel said** that **the *halakha* is not in accordance with** the opinion of **Rabbi Yosei,** who maintains that vinegar will prevent grain from becoming leavened. **What, isn't it** correct to infer from here that vinegar added to flour **does not shrink** the grain and will **even leaven** it? According to this explanation, food that contains vinegar, e.g., *haroset*, is likely to be leavened immediately, as claimed by Rav Kahana.

לָא, דִּילְמָא לָא מְצַמֵּת צָמֵית וְלָא חַמּוּעַ מְחַמַּע.

The Gemara rejects this interpretation: **No,** this is no proof, as **perhaps** Shmuel meant that, according to the opinion of the Rabbis, vinegar will **neither cause** the wheat **to shrink nor leaven** it. Consequently, this statement cannot serve as a proof of the opinion of the Rabbis with regard to *haroset*.

״אֵין מְבַשְּׁלִין וכו׳״. תָּנוּ רַבָּנַן: ״בַּמָּיִם״ – אֵין לִי אֶלָּא בַּמַּיִם, שְׁאָר מַשְׁקִין מִנַּיִין?

The mishna taught that **one** may **not boil** the Paschal lamb in liquid. To explain this issue, the Gemara cites a *baraita* that interprets the verse: "You shall not eat it partially roasted, nor boiled in any way in water, but roasted with fire; its head with its legs, and with the innards in it" (Exodus 12:9). **The Sages taught: "In water"; I have** derived **nothing other** than the prohibition against boiling the Paschal lamb **in water. From where** do I know that it is likewise prohibited to boil it in **other liquids?**

אָמַרְתָּ: קַל וָחוֹמֶר, וּמָה מַּיִם שֶׁאֵין מְפִיגִין טַעְמָן – אֲסוּרִין, שְׁאָר מַשְׁקִין שֶׁמְּפִיגִין טַעְמָן – לֹא כׇּל שֶׁכֵּן?!

You said that this can be derived by means of **an *a fortiori* inference:**[N] **And just as water, which does not temper the taste** of the food boiled in it, **is prohibited** for boiling the Paschal lamb, with regard to **other liquids, which do temper the taste** of the food boiled in them, is it **not all the more so** that it is prohibited to boil the Paschal lamb in them?[H]

רַבִּי אוֹמֵר: בַּמַּיִם – אֵין לִי אֶלָּא מַיִם, שְׁאָר מַשְׁקִין מִנַּיִין – תַּלְמוּד לוֹמַר: ״וּבָשֵׁל מְבֻשָּׁל״ – מִכׇּל מָקוֹם.

Rabbi Yehuda HaNasi provides a different derivation and **says:** From the phrase **"In water," I have** derived **nothing other** than the prohibition against boiling the Paschal lamb **in water. From where** do I learn that it is likewise prohibited to boil it in **other liquids? The verse states: "Nor boiled in any way,"** which means: **In any case,** i.e., boiling the Paschal lamb in any type of liquid is prohibited.

מַאי בֵּינַיְיהוּ? אִיכָּא בֵּינַיְיהוּ: צְלִי קֶדֶר.

The Gemara asks: **What is** the practical difference **between** these two derivations? The Gemara answers: The practical difference **between them is** with regard to meat **that is roasted in a pot**[H] without the addition of any liquid, but is cooked in its own juices. According to Rabbi Yehuda HaNasi, it is prohibited to prepare the Paschal lamb in this manner, as this is considered boiling, whereas the Rabbis maintain that an action is classified as boiling only if one adds liquid to the meat.

NOTES

You said an *a fortiori* inference – אָמַרְתָּ קַל וָחוֹמֶר: Assuming that both of these *tanna'im* accept the principle that we do not punish on the basis of *a fortiori* argumentation, the practical difference between them is as follows: According to the first *tanna*, one who cooks in liquids other than water is not punished with lashes by Torah law, whereas Rabbi Yehuda HaNasi maintains that he is liable to receive lashes for this offense.

HALAKHA

Boiling the Paschal lamb – בִּשּׁוּל קׇרְבַּן פֶּסַח: It is prohibited to boil the Paschal lamb, and one who does so, whether in water or in other liquids, is liable to receive lashes (Rambam *Sefer Korbanot, Hilkhot Korban Pesah* 8:7).

That is roasted in a pot – צְלִי קֶדֶר: One who roasts the Paschal lamb in a pot and eats it is liable. The early commentaries ask why the Rambam rules in accordance with Rabbi Yehuda HaNasi here, contrary to the majority opinion of the Rabbis. Some say that the Rabbis actually agree with Rabbi Yehuda HaNasi's opinion, and they dispute only his derivation of this *halakha* (*Kesef Mishne*). Others suggest that the opinion of the Rabbis is not in fact the majority opinion in this particular case, as they merely accept the ruling of Rabbi Meir (Rambam *Sefer Korbanot, Hilkhot Korban Pesah* 8:8).

וְרַבָּנַן הַאי "בָּשֵׁל מְבֻשָּׁל" מַאי עָבְדִי לְהוּ? מִבָּעֵי לֵיהּ לְכִדְתַנְיָא: בִּשְּׁלוֹ וְאַחַר כָּךְ צְלָאוֹ, אוֹ שֶׁצְּלָאוֹ וְאַחַר כָּךְ בִּשְּׁלוֹ – חַיָּיב.

The Gemara asks: **And the Rabbis,** with regard to **that** phrase, **"boiled in any way," what do they do with it?** The Gemara answers: It is **required for that which was taught** in a *baraita*: **If one boiled** the Paschal lamb **and afterward roasted it, or roasted it and afterward boiled it,**[H] **he is liable** to receive lashes for boiling the Paschal lamb.

בִּשְׁלָמָא בִּשְּׁלוֹ וְאַחַר כָּךְ צְלָאוֹ חַיָּיב – דְּהָא בַּשְּׁלֵיהּ, אֶלָּא צְלָאוֹ וְאַחַר כָּךְ בִּשְּׁלוֹ הָא צְלִי אֵשׁ הוּא, אַמַּאי?

The Gemara asks: **Granted,** if one **boiled** the Paschal lamb **and afterward roasted it, he is liable, as he boiled it** first and is punished for this act. **However,** if **he roasted it and afterward boiled it,** and **it is** a food that has been **roasted by fire, why** is he liable?

אָמַר רַב כָּהֲנָא: הָא מַנִּי – רַבִּי יוֹסֵי הִיא, דְּתַנְיָא: יוֹצְאִין בְּרָקִיק הַשָּׁרוּי, וּבִמְבוּשָּׁל שֶׁלֹּא נִימּוֹחַ, דִּבְרֵי רַבִּי מֵאִיר. רַבִּי יוֹסֵי אוֹמֵר: יוֹצְאִין בְּרָקִיק הַשָּׁרוּי, אֲבָל לֹא בִּמְבוּשָּׁל, אַף עַל פִּי שֶׁלֹּא נִימּוֹחַ.

Rav Kahana said: In accordance with **whose** opinion **is this** *baraita*? It is in accordance with the opinion of **Rabbi Yosei,** who maintains that boiling after roasting nullifies the previous act of roasting. **As it was taught** in a *baraita*: One can **fulfill** his obligation to eat *matza* **with a wafer that has been soaked**[N] in water **or with a boiled** wafer **that has not** yet **dissolved;** this is **the statement of Rabbi Meir. Rabbi Yosei says: One** can **fulfill** his obligation **with a wafer that has been soaked** in a cooked dish **but not with a boiled** wafer, **even if it has not dissolved.**[H] Evidently, Rabbi Yosei maintains that food that was initially baked and subsequently boiled is no longer categorized as baked,[N] and the same presumably applies to meat that was roasted and then boiled.

עוּלָּא אָמַר: אֲפִילּוּ תֵּימָא רַבִּי מֵאִיר, שָׁאנֵי הָכָא דְּאָמַר קְרָא: "וּבָשֵׁל מְבֻשָּׁל" – מִכָּל מָקוֹם.

Ulla said: Even if **you say** that the *halakha* with regard to boiled *matza* is in accordance with the opinion of **Rabbi Meir,** there is no difficulty, as the cases of *matza* and the Paschal lamb are dissimilar in this regard. **Here,** with regard to the Paschal lamb, **it is different, as the verse states: "Nor boiled in any way,"** which indicates that it is prohibited to boil it **in any case.** No restriction of this kind is stated with regard to *matza*.

תָּנוּ רַבָּנַן: יָכוֹל צְלָאוֹ כָּל צוֹרְכּוֹ יְהֵא חַיָּיב – תַּלְמוּד לוֹמַר: "אַל תֹּאכְלוּ מִמֶּנּוּ נָא וּבָשֵׁל מְבֻשָּׁל בַּמָּיִם" נָא וּבָשֵׁל מְבֻשָּׁל אֲמַרְתִּי לְךָ, וְלֹא שֶׁצְּלָאוֹ כָּל צוֹרְכּוֹ.

The Sages taught: I **might** have thought **that** if **one roasted** the Paschal lamb **fully, he** should **be liable.** Therefore, **the verse states: "You shall not eat it partially roasted, nor boiled in any way in water"** (Exodus 12:9). This verse teaches that **I,** God, **said to you** that the Paschal lamb is prohibited if it is **partially roasted or boiled in any way, but not** if **it is fully roasted.** One who roasts the Paschal lamb fully has not violated a prohibition.

הֵיכִי דָּמֵי? אָמַר רַב אַשִׁי: דְּשַׁוְיָא חֲרוּכָא.

The Gemara asks: **What are the circumstances** of this case that render it necessary for a verse to teach that roasting the Paschal lamb fully is not a violation of a prohibition? **Rav Ashi said:** This is referring to a situation **where one burned it.**[H] The verse indicates that even one who entirely burns the Paschal lamb does not violate this prohibition.

תָּנוּ רַבָּנַן: יָכוֹל אָכַל כַּזַּיִת חַי יְהֵא חַיָּיב – תַּלְמוּד לוֹמַר: "אַל תֹּאכְלוּ מִמֶּנּוּ נָא וּבָשֵׁל מְבֻשָּׁל" נָא וּבָשֵׁל אֲמַרְתִּי לְךָ, וְלֹא חַי.

The Sages taught: I **might** have thought that **one who ate an olive-bulk** portion of the Paschal sacrifice **raw** should **be liable** for violating a prohibition. Therefore, **the verse states: "You shall not eat it partially roasted** [*na*], **nor boiled in any way in water."** This verse **teaches** that **I,** God, **said to you** that it is prohibited to eat the Paschal lamb **partially roasted or boiled, but** there is **no** prohibition against eating **it raw.**

NOTES

One can fulfill his obligation with a wafer that has been soaked – יוֹצְאִין בְּרָקִיק הַשָּׁרוּי: This evidently refers to a wafer that has been soaked in water; indeed, one version of the text of the Gemara is explicit in this regard. This wafer is considered poor man's bread, as it was common for paupers to dip their bread in water before consumption (Maharshal).

The dispute between *tanna'im* with regard to a boiled wafer – מַחְלוֹקֶת הַתַּנָּאִים בְּרָקִיק מְבוּשָּׁל: This dispute does not depend only on whether a boiled wafer retains the taste of *matza* or bread, as this could be determined by an expert taster. Instead, the dispute concerns the definition of this wafer. According to Rabbi Yosei, bread that has been boiled is no longer classified as bread, whereas Rabbi Meir maintains that it is still called bread (Maharam Ḥalawa).

HALAKHA

Roasted it and afterward boiled it – צְלָאוֹ וְאַחַר כָּךְ בִּשְּׁלוֹ: If one roasted the Paschal lamb and afterward boiled it, or boiled it and then roasted it, he is liable for violating a prohibition, as stated in the *baraita* (Rambam *Sefer Korbanot*, *Hilkhot Korban Pesaḥ* 8:8).

A wafer that was soaked for *matza* – רָקִיק הַשָּׁרוּי לְמַצָּה: One may use a soaked wafer as *matza*, but not a boiled wafer, even if it has not dissolved. The later commentaries suggest that the use of a soaked wafer is permitted only for the elderly or the sick (*Magen Avraham*), and it is the custom in many communities to be especially stringent with regard to soaked *matza*. Since there are several reasons for being careful not to eat any *matza* that has come into contact with water, it is customary in these communities to be lenient about this issue only on the eighth day of Passover, which is observed solely outside of Israel (*Shulḥan Arukh*, *Oraḥ Ḥayyim* 461:4).

Roasted it until it burned – צְלָאוֹ עַד שֶׁנִּתְחָרֵךְ: One who roasted the Paschal lamb until it burned is exempt, as stated in the *baraita* (Rambam *Sefer Korbanot*, *Hilkhot Korban Pesaḥ* 8:6).

יָכוֹל יְהֵא מוּתָּר – תַּלְמוּד לוֹמַר: "כִּי אִם צְלִי אֵשׁ". הֵיכִי דָּמֵי נָא? אָמַר רַב: כִּדְאָמְרִי פָּרְסָאֵי אֲבַרְנִים.

I might have thought that it is permitted to eat it raw *ab initio*. Therefore, the verse states: "But roasted with fire" (Exodus 12:9).[N] This teaches that the mitzva is to roast the Paschal lamb with fire, *ab initio*.[H] The Gemara asks: What are the circumstances of cooking that are defined as *na*, partially roasted? Rav said: As the Persians say: *Avarnim*,[L] half roasted.

אָמַר רַב חִסְדָּא: הַמְבַשֵּׁל בְּחַמֵּי טְבֶרְיָא בַּשַּׁבָּת – פָּטוּר. פֶּסַח שֶׁבִּשְּׁלוֹ בְּחַמֵּי טְבֶרְיָא – חַיָּיב.

Rav Ḥisda said: One who cooks food **in the hot springs of Tiberias**[HB] **on Shabbat is exempt.** One violates the Shabbat prohibition of cooking only if he uses a fire. In the case of **a Paschal** lamb **that was cooked,** i.e., boiled, **in the hot springs of Tiberias,**[NH] one is **liable** for boiling the offering.

מַאי שְׁנָא בַּשַּׁבָּת דְּלָא – דְּתוֹלְדוֹת אֵשׁ בָּעֵינַן, וְלֵיכָּא. פֶּסַח נַמִי – לָאו תּוֹלְדוֹת אֵשׁ הוּא.

The Gemara asks: **What is different with regard to Shabbat, that** one is **not** punished for cooking in this manner? The reason is **that** a fire, or **a fire derivative, is required** for an act to be defined as cooking on Shabbat, **but there is no** fire here, as the hot springs are not generated by fire. If so, **with regard to** the **Paschal** lamb **as well, it is not a fire derivative,** and it should not be considered boiling with regard to this prohibition either.

אָמַר רָבָא: מַאי חַיָּיב דְּקָתָנֵי – דְּקָא עָבַר מִשּׁוּם "צְלִי אֵשׁ".

Rava said: What is the meaning of the word **liable that** Rav Ḥisda **taught?** It means **that** in doing so **one violated** the positive mitzva, **due to** that which is written: **"Roasted with fire."** In other words, one who boils the Paschal lamb in the hot springs of Tiberias did not in fact violate the prohibition of boiling the Paschal lamb, but he has also not fulfilled the positive mitzva to roast the offering.

רַב חִיָּיא בְּרֵיהּ דְּרַב נָתָן מַתְנֵי לָהּ לְהָא דְּרַב חִסְדָּא בְּהֶדְיָא, אָמַר רַב חִסְדָּא: הַמְבַשֵּׁל בְּחַמֵּי טְבֶרְיָא בַּשַּׁבָּת – פָּטוּר, וּפֶסַח שֶׁבִּשְּׁלוֹ בְּחַמֵּי טְבֶרְיָא – חַיָּיב, שֶׁעָבַר מִשּׁוּם "צְלִי אֵשׁ".

Rav Ḥiyya, son of Rav Natan, teaches this interpretation **of Rav Ḥisda's** statement **explicitly,** i.e., that **Rav Ḥisda** himself **said: One who cooks in the hot springs of Tiberias on Shabbat is exempt, and** with regard to **a Paschal** lamb **that was cooked in the hot springs of Tiberias,** one **is liable** to receive punishment for this act. In doing so, **he violated** a positive mitzva, **due to** that which is written: **"Roasted with fire."**

אָמַר רָבָא: אֲכָלוֹ נָא –

Rava said: One who **ate** the Paschal lamb **partially roasted,**

NOTES

But roasted with fire [*tzeli esh*] – כִּי אִם צְלִי אֵשׁ: Some commentaries cite a version of the Gemara that includes only the words *tzeli esh*, roasted with fire, from the verse: "And you shall eat the meat on this night roasted with fire" (Exodus 12:8). Other versions state *ki im tzeli esh*, but roasted with fire, which refers to the next verse: "You shall not eat it partially roasted, nor boiled in any way in water, but roasted with fire" (Exodus 12:9). The difference between these two verses is that the first contains a positive mitzva to roast the Paschal lamb with fire, while the second consists of a negative prohibition not to prepare it any other way (*Me'iri*).

A Paschal lamb that was cooked in the hot springs of Tiberias – פֶּסַח שֶׁבִּשְּׁלוֹ בְּחַמֵּי טְבֶרְיָא: How is it possible to cook the Paschal lamb in the hot springs of Tiberias when this offering may be eaten only in Jerusalem and is disqualified if taken outside the city? If water from the hot springs were brought to Jerusalem, it would certainly have cooled down in the meantime and could no longer be used for cooking. Some commentaries say that this statement refers to the time before the Temple was built in Jerusalem, when it was permitted to offer the Paschal lamb in other places (Rabbi Shlomo HaKohen). However, the simplest answer is that this is not a practical question but an inquiry into the precise definition of cooking.

HALAKHA

Ate it raw – אֲכָלוֹ חַי: If one eats an olive-bulk portion of the Paschal lamb raw he is not liable to lashes for transgressing the prohibition "You shall not eat it partially roasted." However, he has violated the positive commandment to roast it "with fire" (Rambam *Sefer Korbanot, Hilkhot Korban Pesaḥ* 8:6).

One who cooks in the hot springs of Tiberias – הַמְבַשֵּׁל בְּחַמֵּי טְבֶרְיָא: Although it is prohibited to cook in the hot springs of Tiberias on Shabbat, one who does so is exempt from punishment, as this type of cooking is permitted by Torah law (Rambam *Sefer Zemanim, Hilkhot Shabbat* 9:3).

A Paschal lamb that was cooked in the hot springs of Tiberias – פֶּסַח שֶׁבִּשְּׁלוֹ בְּחַמֵּי טְבֶרְיָא: One is not liable to receive lashes for cooking the Paschal lamb in the hot springs of Tiberias, although he has not fulfilled the mitzva to eat it "roasted with fire" (Rambam *Sefer Korbanot, Hilkhot Korban Pesaḥ* 8:10).

BACKGROUND

Hot springs of Tiberias – חַמֵּי טְבֶרְיָה: The Tiberias hot springs, near the Sea of Galilee, contain geothermally heated groundwater at a constant temperature of 60° C, or 140° F. In general, the temperature of rocks within the earth increases with depth. When water percolates deeply enough into the crust, it will be heated as it comes into contact with hot rocks. Much of the earth's internal heat is produced by the decay of naturally radioactive elements, which is not fire in the normal sense of the term.

LANGUAGE

Avarnim – אֲבַרְנִים: Apparently from an amalgam of the Middle Persian abar and nēm, meaning halfway. In this context, the word means half roasted.

לוֹקֶה שְׁתַּיִם, מְבוּשָּׁל – לוֹקֶה שְׁתַּיִם, נָא וּמְבוּשָּׁל – לוֹקֶה שָׁלֹשׁ.

he **receives two** sets of **lashes,** for violating the prohibitions: "You shall not eat it partially roasted" (Exodus 12:9) and: "You shall only eat it…roasted with fire" (Exodus 12:9). One who ate it **boiled receives two** sets of **lashes,** for the prohibitions: "Nor shall it be boiled in any way in water" (Exodus 12:9), and "You shall only eat it…roasted with fire." One who ate the Paschal lamb after it had been **partially roasted and** then **boiled receives three** sets of **lashes,**[N] for eating the Paschal lamb partially roasted, for eating it boiled, and for failing to eat it roasted.

אַבָּיֵי אָמַר: אֵין לוֹקִין עַל לָאו שֶׁבִּכְלָלוֹת.

Abaye said: One does not receive lashes for a prohibition stated in general terms.[N] The prohibition inferred from the verse "You shall only eat it…roasted in fire" includes many types of cooking, and one is not punished with lashes for violating this mitzva, as it is a general prohibition that includes meat cooked in several different ways.

אִיכָּא דְּאָמְרִי: תַּרְתֵּי הוּא דְּלָא לָקֵי – חֲדָא מִיהַת לָקֵי.

Some say that Abaye said: **It is two** sets of **lashes that he does not receive,** as the mitzva that the Paschal lamb be roasted with fire does not add to the specific prohibitions against eating it partially roasted or cooked. However, **at any rate one set of lashes he does receive.**[H] Therefore, one who prepared a Paschal lamb without properly cooking it but without roasting it is punished with lashes for failing to roast it "with fire."

אִיכָּא דְּאָמְרִי: חֲדָא נַמִי לָא לָקֵי, דְּלָא מְיַיחֵד לָאוֵיהּ כְּלָאו דַּחֲסִימָה.

Some say that **one does not receive even one** set of **lashes**[N] for violating this prohibition, **as the prohibition** he transgressed **is not specific** to one matter, **like the prohibition against muzzling.** The principle that one is liable to receive lashes for violating a prohibition is derived from the juxtaposition of the mitzva: "You shall not muzzle an ox while it treads out the corn" (Deuteronomy 25:4) with the verses that deal with lashes. It is inferred from this juxtaposition that one is not liable to receive lashes for violating prohibitions that are dissimilar to that of muzzling, e.g., a prohibition that is not specific to one matter.

רָבָא אָמַר: אָכַל זָג – לוֹקֶה שְׁתַּיִם, חַרְצָן – לוֹקֶה שְׁתַּיִם, זָג וְחַרְצָן – לוֹקֶה שָׁלֹשׁ.

The Gemara cites a parallel dispute with regard to a different *halakha*. **Rava said:** If a nazirite **ate** a grape **skin he receives two** sets of **lashes,** as the verse states: "All the days that he is a nazirite he shall he eat nothing that is made of the grapevine; from pressed grapes to a grape pit he shall not eat" (Numbers 6:4). He receives two sets of lashes, one for eating food that grew on a grapevine and one for consuming the skin of a grape. Likewise, if he ate a grape **pit he receives two** sets of **lashes,** one for eating a grape pit and the other for eating a grape product. If he ate a grape **skin and** a grape **pit**[H] **he receives three** sets of **lashes,** one for eating the grape skin, one for eating the grape pit, and the third for eating a grape product.

אַבָּיֵי אָמַר: אֵין לוֹקִין עַל לָאו שֶׁבִּכְלָלוֹת. אִיכָּא דְּאָמְרִי: תַּרְתֵּי הוּא דְּלָא לָקֵי – חֲדָא מִיהַת לָקֵי. אִיכָּא דְּאָמְרִי: חֲדָא נַמִי לָא לָקֵי, דְּלָא מְיַיחֵד לָאוֵיהּ כְּלָאו דַּחֲסִימָה.

Abaye said: As with regard to the Paschal lamb, **one does not receive lashes for a prohibition stated in general terms. Some say** that according to Abaye, **it is two** sets of **lashes that he does not receive;** however, **at any rate one set of lashes he does receive.** And **some say: One does not receive even one** set of **lashes for** transgressing this prohibition, **as the prohibition** he transgressed **is not specific** to one matter, **like the prohibition against muzzling.**

NOTES

Receives three sets of lashes – לוֹקֶה שָׁלֹשׁ: Some commentaries offer a different explanation of this statement. They say that according to Rava, one actually receives four sets of lashes, and the Gemara is referring to three categories of prohibitions for which he receives them. He receives two sets of lashes for the fact that the Paschal lamb was boiled, one because it was not roasted and the second because it was cooked; a third set because it was partially roasted; and a fourth set because it was not roasted properly (*Tosefot Rid*).

A prohibition stated in general terms – לָאו שֶׁבִּכְלָלוֹת: There are different types of prohibitions stated in general terms. Sometimes a single negative statement includes multiple prohibitions. For example, the verse with regard to priests: "They shall not take a woman that is a harlot or profaned" (Leviticus 21:7), by virtue of a single negative statement prohibits priests from marrying two different categories of women. Another type of prohibition stated in general terms is exemplified here with regard to the Paschal lamb and a nazirite, where there is a particular prohibition as well as a general prohibition. Yet another type of prohibition stated in general terms occurs when the biblical text does not delineate the details of the prohibition, which are supplied by the Sages. For example, the verse: "You shall not eat over the blood" (Leviticus 19:26), is explained as referring to many types of prohibitions (see *Me'iri*).

One set of lashes he does receive…one does not receive even one set of lashes – חֲדָא לָקֵי...חֲדָא לָא לָקֵי: The meaning of this passage is subject to debate. Some commentaries explain that Rava agrees that one does not receive an additional set of lashes for a prohibition stated in general terms. However, he maintains that the verse "It shall be roasted with fire" is not in fact a prohibition stated in general terms. Instead this verse includes an additional prohibition, for which one is liable to another set of lashes. The same applies to the discussion with regard to a nazirite, as Rava contends that the phrase "nothing that is made of the grapevine" (Numbers 6:4) is referring to an additional aspect of the prohibition (Maharam Ḥalawa).

HALAKHA

Eaten partially roasted and then boiled – אָכַל נָא וּמְבוּשָּׁל: With regard to one who ate meat from a Paschal lamb that was partially roasted and then boiled, he is liable to receive only one set of lashes, as both prohibitions are included in the same general category. Apparently, the Rambam understands this dispute between Abaye and Rava in a manner similar to Rashi's understanding of it (*Leḥem Mishne*; Rambam *Sefer Korbanot, Hilkhot Korban Pesaḥ* 8:4).

Ate a grape skin and a grape pit – אָכַל זָג וְחַרְצָן: A nazirite who ate a grape skin and a grape pit is liable to receive two sets of lashes for violating the two prohibitions specified in the verse. However, he does not receive a third set of lashes for the prohibition stated in general terms in the verse (Numbers 6:4): "Nothing that is made of the grapevine" (Rambam *Sefer Hafla'a, Hilkhot Nezirut* 5:8).

תָּנוּ רַבָּנַן: אָכַל כַּזַּיִת נָא מִבְּעוֹד יוֹם – פָּטוּר, כַּזַּיִת נָא מִשֶּׁחָשֵׁיכָה – חַיָּיב. אָכַל כַּזַּיִת צָלִי מִבְּעוֹד יוֹם – לֹא פָּסַל עַצְמוֹ מִבְּנֵי חֲבוּרָה, כַּזַּיִת צָלִי מִשֶּׁחָשֵׁיכָה – פָּסַל עַצְמוֹ מִבְּנֵי הַחֲבוּרָה.

The Sages taught: If **one ate a partially roasted olive-bulk** of the Paschal lamb **while it was still day** on the fourteenth of Nisan, **he is exempt.**[H] If he ate **a partially roasted olive-bulk after dark, he is liable** to receive lashes. If **he ate a roasted olive-bulk** of the Paschal lamb **while it was still day**[H] on the fourteenth of Nisan, **he has not disqualified himself from** his **group.** Once he has started eating the offering, he may not leave the group he joined that arranged to partake together of a single Paschal lamb. Nevertheless, this case is different, as he began eating before the obligation to eat the Paschal lamb went into effect, and therefore he has not disqualified himself from his group by eating the Paschal lamb of another group. However, if he ate **a roasted olive-bulk after dark,** when he is obligated to eat the Paschal lamb, **he disqualifies himself from the group** he had joined.

תַּנְיָא אִידָךְ: יָכוֹל אָכַל כַּזַּיִת נָא מִבְּעוֹד יוֹם יְהֵא חַיָּיב, וְדִין הוּא: וּמַה בְּשָׁעָה שֶׁיֶּשְׁנוֹ בְּקוּם אֱכוֹל צָלִי – יֶשְׁנוֹ בְּבַל תֹּאכַל נָא, בְּשָׁעָה שֶׁאֵינוֹ בְּקוּם אֱכוֹל צָלִי – אֵינוֹ דִּין שֶׁיֶּשְׁנוֹ בְּבַל תֹּאכַל נָא?

It was taught in **another** *baraita*: I **might** have thought that one who **eats a partially roasted olive-bulk** of the Paschal lamb **while it was still day is liable** to receive lashes. **And this is a logical derivation** by means of an *a fortiori* inference: **If at the time when one is included in** the mitzva **to arise** and eat the **roasted** Paschal lamb, **he is** also **included in** the prohibition **not to eat** it **partially roasted,** then **at a time when one is not included in** the mitzva **to arise** and **eat** the **roasted** Paschal lamb, **isn't it right that he** should be **included in** the prohibition **not to eat** it **partially roasted?**

אוֹ לֹא: בְּשָׁעָה שֶׁאֵינוֹ בְּקוּם אֱכוֹל צָלִי – יֶשְׁנוֹ בְּבַל תֹּאכַל נָא, בְּשָׁעָה שֶׁיֶּשְׁנוֹ בְּקוּם אֱכוֹל צָלִי – אֵינוֹ בְּבַל תֹּאכַל נָא.

Or perhaps this is **not** the case, as the opposite can be stated: **At** the **time when one is not included in** the mitzva **to arise** and **eat** the **roasted** Paschal lamb, **he is included in** the prohibition **not to eat** it **partially roasted.** However, **at a time when one is included in** the mitzva **to arise** and **eat** the **roasted** Paschal lamb, **he is not included in** the prohibition **not to eat** it **partially roasted,** as the prohibition applies only before one is permitted to eat the Paschal lamb.

וְאַל תִּתְמַהּ, שֶׁהֲרֵי הוּתַּר מִכְּלָלוֹ אֵצֶל צָלִי

The Gemara adds: **And do not be confounded** by this suggestion, **as** the prohibition against eating from the Paschal lamb **is relaxed** because of special circumstances **with regard to roasted** meat. Before nightfall of the fifteenth of Nisan it is prohibited to eat the Paschal lamb regardless of how it was prepared, but once it grows dark it is permitted to eat it roasted. Perhaps the relaxation of this prohibition indicates that one who eats a partially roasted Paschal lamb after nightfall also does not violate a transgression.

תַּלְמוּד לוֹמַר: ״אַל תֹּאכְלוּ מִמֶּנּוּ נָא וּבָשֵׁל מְבֻשָּׁל בַּמָּיִם כִּי אִם צְלִי אֵשׁ״, שֶׁאֵין תַּלְמוּד לוֹמַר ״כִּי אִם צְלִי אֵשׁ״ וּמַה תַּלְמוּד לוֹמַר ״כִּי אִם צְלִי אֵשׁ״ – לוֹמַר לְךָ: בְּשָׁעָה שֶׁיֶּשְׁנוֹ בְּקוּם אֱכוֹל צָלִי – יֶשְׁנוֹ בְּבַל תֹּאכַל נָא, בְּשָׁעָה שֶׁאֵינוֹ בְּקוּם אֱכוֹל צָלִי – אֵינוֹ בְּבַל תֹּאכַל נָא

Therefore, **the verse states: "You shall not eat it partially roasted, nor boiled in any way** [*bashel mevushal*] **in water, but roasted with fire"** (Exodus 12:9). **As** there is **no** need for **the verse to state: "Roasted with fire,"** since the previous verse already said: "On this night you shall eat the meat roasted with fire" (Exodus 12:8), **what** then is the meaning when **the** second **verse states: "Roasted with fire"?** This verse comes **to tell you** that at the **time when one is included in** the mitzva **to arise** and **eat** the **roasted** Paschal lamb, **he is** also **included in** the prohibition **not to eat** it **partially roasted,** whereas **at a time when one is not included in** the mitzva **to arise** and **eat** the **roasted** Paschal lamb, **he is not included in** the prohibition **not to eat** it **partially roasted** either.

רַבִּי אוֹמֵר: אֶקְרָא אֲנִי ״בָּשֵׁל״ מַה תַּלְמוּד לוֹמַר ״מְבֻשָּׁל״ – שֶׁיָּכוֹל אֵין לִי אֶלָּא שֶׁבִּישְּׁלוֹ מִשֶּׁחָשֵׁיכָה, בִּשְּׁלוֹ מִבְּעוֹד יוֹם מִנַּיִן – תַּלְמוּד לוֹמַר: ״בָּשֵׁל מְבֻשָּׁל״ – מִכָּל מָקוֹם.

Rabbi Yehuda HaNasi **says:** I could have simply **read "boiled** [*bashel*]," as this word suffices to teach that eating a boiled Paschal lamb is prohibited after dark. **What** is the meaning when **the verse states** the seemingly superfluous word ***mevushal***, which also means boiled? These two words together are translated as "boiled in any way." **As** I **might** have thought that **I have only** derived that this prohibition applies **when it was boiled after dark,** when the obligation to eat the Paschal lamb is in effect. **From where** do I derive that one is liable **if he boils it while it was still day? The verse states** the inclusive phrase ***bashel mevushal***, which teaches that this prohibition applies **in any case.**

HALAKHA

Partially roasted meat eaten before the proper time – נָא שֶׁאֲכָלוֹ לִפְנֵי זְמַנּוֹ: If one ate from a Paschal lamb that was partially roasted or boiled while it was still day, he is not liable to receive lashes. The reason is that he does not receive lashes for violating this prohibition before the time of the eating of the Paschal lamb, as stated in the *baraita* (Rambam *Sefer Korbanot, Hilkhot Korban Pesaḥ* 8:4).

Roasted…Paschal lamb while it was still day – צָלִי מִבְּעוֹד יוֹם: One who ate an olive-bulk of roasted meat from the Paschal lamb during the day has violated the mitzva (Exodus 12:8): "And you shall eat the meat on this night" (Rambam *Sefer Korbanot, Hilkhot Korban Pesaḥ* 8:5).

NOTES

Bashel mevushal – בָּשֵׁל מְבֻשָּׁל: See *Tosafot*, who discuss this type of formulation. There is an opinion among the *tanna'im* that no *halakhot* can be derived from extraneous language of this kind. This is considered merely the Torah speaking in the language of men, even if the Torah does not usually repeat a word in this manner. Nevertheless, according to the opinion that *halakhot* can indeed be learned from this wording, all possible meanings should be derived, including those that extend beyond the ordinary implication of the term.

וְהַאי "בָּשֵׁל מְבֻשָּׁל" אַפְּקֵיהּ רַבִּי לִצְלִי קֶדֶר וְלִשְׁאָר מַשְׁקִין!

The Gemara asks: **But Rabbi** Yehuda HaNasi himself **derived** from the expression ***"bashel mevushal"***[N] the prohibition **against roasting** the meat of the Paschal lamb **in a pot,** i.e., cooking the meat in a pot without the addition of liquids, **and** the prohibition against boiling it **with other liquids.** How can he derive another *halakha* from this same phrase?

אִם כֵּן לֵימָא קְרָא אוֹ "בָּשֵׁל בָּשֵׁל" אוֹ "מְבֻשָּׁל מְבֻשָּׁל", מַאי בָּשֵׁל מְבֻשָּׁל – שְׁמַעַתְּ מִינָּהּ תַּרְתֵּי.

The Gemara answers: **If so,** i.e., if this verse is referring only to the matter of cooking meat with other liquids or without any liquids, **let the verse say either "*bashel bashel*" or "*mevushal mevushal*,"** and one *halakha* would be derived from the extraneous word. **What** is derived from the varied wording ***"bashel mevushal"*? Learn from this** verse **two** *halakhot*, one with regard to the manner of the cooking of the Paschal lamb, and the other concerning the time of its cooking.

תָּנוּ רַבָּנַן: אָכַל צָלִי מִבְּעוֹד יוֹם – חַיָּיב, וְכַזַּיִת נָא מִשֶּׁחָשֵׁיכָה – חַיָּיב.

The Sages taught: If one **ate** from **a roasted** Paschal lamb **when it was still day, he is liable** to receive lashes, and likewise if one ate **after dark an olive-bulk that was partially roasted, he is liable** to receive lashes.

קָתָנֵי צָלִי דּוּמְיָא דְּנָא, מַה נָּא בְּלָאו – אַף צָלִי בְּלָאו.

This *baraita* **taught** that the case of **roasted** meat is **similar to** the case of **partially roasted** meat: **Just as** one who consumes **partially roasted** meat is in violation **of a prohibition, so too,** one who consumes this **roasted** meat while it is still day is in violation **of a prohibition.**

בִּשְׁלָמָא נָא – כְּתִיב: "אַל תֹּאכְלוּ מִמֶּנּוּ נָא" אֶלָּא צָלִי מְנָלַן?

The Gemara asks: **Granted,** with regard to **partially roasted** meat, **it is written: "You shall not eat it partially roasted"** (Exodus 12:9). **However,** with regard to meat that has been **roasted, from where do we** derive that one who eats it before the proper time has committed a transgression?

דִּכְתִיב: "וְאָכְלוּ אֶת הַבָּשָׂר בַּלַּיְלָה הַזֶּה". בַּלַּיְלָה – אִין, בַּיּוֹם – לָא.

The Gemara answers: **As it is written: "And they shall eat the meat on that night,** roasted with fire, and *matzot*; with bitter herbs they shall eat it" (Exodus 12:8). The Gemara derives from this verse: **At night, yes,** the Paschal lamb may be eaten; however, **by day, no,** it may not be eaten in any manner.

הַאי לָאו הַבָּא מִכְּלָל עֲשֵׂה הוּא, וְכׇל לָאו הַבָּא מִכְּלָל עֲשֵׂה – עֲשֵׂה!

The Gemara asks: **This is a prohibition that comes by inference from a positive mitzva,** i.e., it is not stated in the Torah in the form of a prohibition. There is a principle that **every prohibition that comes by inference from a positive mitzva** is classified as **a positive mitzva.** One who transgresses a mitzva of this kind is considered to have transgressed a positive mitzva, not a prohibition.

אָמַר רַב חִסְדָּא: הָא מַנִּי –

The Gemara answers that **Rav Ḥisda said:** In accordance with **whose** opinion **is this** *baraita*?

Perek **II**
Daf **42** Amud **a**

HALAKHA

Unblemished animals for maintaining the Temple – תְּמִימִים לְבֶדֶק הַבַּיִת: One may not consecrate an unblemished animal for its value to be used for maintaining the Temple, as animals of this kind may be consecrated only as offerings. One who consecrates an unblemished animal for maintaining the Temple transgresses a positive mitzva (Rambam *Sefer Hafla'a*, *Hilkhot Arakhin VaHaramim* 5:6).

רַבִּי יְהוּדָה הִיא, דְּתַנְיָא: "שׁוֹר וָשֶׂה שָׂרוּעַ וְקָלוּט נְדָבָה תַּעֲשֶׂה אוֹתוֹ" – אוֹתוֹ אַתָּה מַתְפִּיס לְבֶדֶק הַבַּיִת, וְאִי אַתָּה מַתְפִּיס תְּמִימִים לְבֶדֶק הַבַּיִת. מִכָּאן אָמְרוּ: כׇּל הַמַּתְפִּיס תְּמִימִים לְבֶדֶק הַבַּיִת – עוֹבֵר בַּעֲשֵׂה.

It is in accordance with the opinion of **Rabbi Yehuda, as it was taught** in a *baraita*: "Either **a bull or a lamb that has anything too long or too short, you may offer it as a free-will offering** [to the Temple treasury]; but for a vow [as a sacrifice] it shall not be accepted" (Leviticus 22:23). From here we learn that **it,** i.e., a blemished animal, **you may consecrate for maintaining the Temple, but you may not consecrate unblemished** animals **for maintaining the Temple.** In other words, any animal fit to be sacrificed as an offering may not be consecrated for maintaining the Temple but only as an offering. **From here** the Sages **stated: Whoever consecrates unblemished** animals **for maintaining the Temple**[H] **transgresses a positive mitzva.**

אֵין לִי אֶלָּא בַּעֲשֵׂה, בְּלֹא תַעֲשֶׂה מִנַּיִן – תַּלְמוּד לוֹמַר: ״וַיְדַבֵּר ה׳ אֶל מֹשֶׁה לֵּאמֹר״ – לִימֵּד עַל כָּל הַפָּרָשָׁה כּוּלָּהּ שֶׁיְּהֵא בְּלֹא תַעֲשֶׂה, דִּבְרֵי רַבִּי יְהוּדָה

From here I have only derived that he violates a positive mitzva; from where do I derive that he also transgresses a prohibition? The verse states at the beginning of that passage: "And the Lord spoke to Moses saying" (Leviticus 22:17). This introductory statement teaches with regard to the entire portion that a prohibition applies to it. This is the statement of Rabbi Yehuda.

אָמַר לוֹ רַבִּי לְבַר קַפָּרָא: מַאי מַשְׁמַע?

The *baraita* adds that Rabbi Yehuda HaNasi said to Bar Kappara: From where may it be inferred that this is the case? How does Rabbi Yehuda derive his statement that a prohibition applies to the entire portion from the phrase "And the Lord spoke to Moses saying"?

אָמַר לוֹ: דִּכְתִיב ״לֵאמֹר״ – ״לֹא״ נֶאֱמַר בִּדְבָרִים.

He said to him: As it is written: "Saying [*leimor*]." Rabbi Yehuda expounds this term as though it read: Say no [*lo emor*]. In other words, the word **no,** an expression of prohibition, **is stated**[N] **with regard to** the subsequent **matters,**[N] which means that these mitzvot are categorized as prohibitions.

בֵּי רַב אָמְרִי: לֵאמֹר – לָאו אֱמוֹר.

In **the school** of **Rav they say** a slightly different explanation: The term: Saying, can be expounded as if it were written ***lav emor,*** meaning: **Say a prohibition.** In other words, the verse indicates that Moses was instructed to inform the Jewish people of a prohibition. This teaches that any mitzva introduced by the word *leimor* should be treated as a prohibition. Since the *halakhot* of the Paschal lamb are preceded by the phrase: "And the Lord spoke to Moses and to Aaron in the Land of Egypt saying" (Exodus 12:1), it can be inferred that the subsequent mitzvot are also prohibitions.

״מֵי תַשְׁמִישׁוֹ שֶׁל נַחְתּוֹם וכו׳״. תָּנֵי חֲדָא: שׁוֹפְכִין בִּמְקוֹם מִדְרוֹן, וְאֵין שׁוֹפְכִין בִּמְקוֹם הָאֶשְׁבּוֹרֶן. וְתַנְיָא אִידָךְ: שׁוֹפְכִין בִּמְקוֹם הָאֶשְׁבּוֹרֶן!

We learned in the mishna: **Water that has been used by a baker** for cooling his hands or washing dishes must be poured out, as it contains a small, undefined quantity of leavened dough. **It was taught** in **one** *baraita*: **One** may **pour out** this water **in a place with an incline, and he** may **not pour** it **out in a** level **place where** the water **collects. And it was taught** in **another** *baraita*: **One** may even **pour out** this water **in a** level **place where** the water **collects.**[H]

לָא קַשְׁיָא; הָא – דִּנְפִישִׁי, דְּקָווּ. הָא – דְּלָא נְפִישִׁי, דְּלָא קָווּ.

The Gemara resolves this contradiction: This is **not difficult. This** *baraita,* which states that it is prohibited to pour out this water in a level place, is referring **to a large** amount of water **that will collect** in one place. Since there is a large amount of water, the flour in the water will not be absorbed into the ground but will leaven. Conversely, **that** *baraita,* which states that it is permitted to pour out the water in a level place, is referring to a situation **where** there was **not a large amount** of water, so that it **will not collect.** Instead, this water will be absorbed into the ground before the dough leavens.

אָמַר רַב יְהוּדָה: אִשָּׁה לֹא תָלוּשׁ אֶלָּא בְּמַיִם שֶׁלָּנוּ.

Rav Yehuda said: A woman may **knead** *matza* dough **only with water that rested,**[H] i.e., water that was left indoors overnight to cool. If water is added to dough immediately after it was drawn, when it is still lukewarm, the dough will leaven at a faster rate.

דְּרָשָׁהּ רַב מַתָּנָה בְּפָפוּנְיָא. לְמָחָר אַיְיתוּ כּוּלֵּי עָלְמָא חַצְבַיְיהוּ וַאֲתוּ לְגַבֵּיהּ, וַאֲמַרוּ לֵיהּ: הַב לָן מַיָּא! אֲמַר לְהוּ: אֲנָא בְּמַיָּא דְּבִיתוּ אָמְרִי.

The Gemara relates: **Rav Mattana taught** this *halakha* **in Paphunya. On the next day,** the eve of Passover, **everyone brought their jugs to him and said to him: Give us water.** They misunderstood his expression *mayim shelanu,* water that rested, as the near homonym *mayim shelanu,* our water, i.e., water that belongs to the Sage, and they therefore came to take water from his house. **He said to them: I say** and meant: **Water that rested** [*devitu*] in the house overnight.

NOTES

No is stated – **לֹא נֶאֱמַר**: Rabbeinu Ḥananel and other early commentaries cite a version of the text that reads: *Lo yumar*, it shall not be substituted. In other words, do not exchange, i.e., violate, these matters, and anyone who does so transgresses a prohibition.

No is stated with regard to the subsequent matters – **לֹא נֶאֱמַר בִּדְבָרִים**: See *Tosafot*, who explain that this derivation applies only to a prohibition that stems from a positive mitzva. However, Rabbeinu Ḥananel apparently maintains that if the first verse of a chapter includes the word: Saying, the violation of any of its positive mitzvot constitutes the transgression of a prohibition.

HALAKHA

Pouring out water used by a baker – **שְׁפִיכַת מֵי נַחְתּוֹם**: With regard to water used by a baker to wash his hands or his vessels, after the time that leaven is forbidden, it should be poured out onto a place with an incline so it will not gather together and become leavened. Although the Gemara cites a *baraita* that permits one to pour this water onto a flat area where it will be collected, it is proper to be stringent in this regard, as the Gemara does not provide the precise parameters of the necessary circumstances for this to be permitted (*Me'iri*; *Shulḥan Arukh, Oraḥ Ḥayyim* 459:4).

Water that rested – **מַיִם שֶׁלָּנוּ**: *Matza* for Passover must be prepared with water that was left overnight, whether the water comes from cisterns, springs, or rivers (Rosh). The water should be drawn at twilight. It should be kept overnight in a house if it is warm outdoors, and it should be kept outside if it is cold, although in the latter case it should be brought into the house before sunrise. When the water is carried outside it must be covered. Since the drawing of water is part of the *matza*-baking process, it should be performed by a Jew. The water used for the *matza* that will be eaten on the first night of Passover should be drawn with specially designated vessels (*Shulḥan Arukh, Oraḥ Ḥayyim* 455:1).

דָּרַשׁ רָבָא: אִשָּׁה לֹא תָּלוּשׁ בַּחַמָּה, וְלֹא בְּחַמֵּי חַמָּה, וְלֹא בְּמַיִם הַגְּרוּפִין מִן הַמּוּלְיָיר, וְלֹא תַּגְבִּיהַּ יָדָהּ מִן הַתַּנּוּר עַד שֶׁתִּגְמוֹר אֶת כׇּל הַפַּת. (וְצָרִיךְ שְׁנֵי כֵלִים, אֶחָד שֶׁמְּקַטֶּפֶת בּוֹ וְאֶחָד שֶׁמְּצַנֶּנֶת בּוֹ אֶת יָדֶיהָ.

Rava taught: A woman may **not knead** dough for *matza* **in the sun,**[H] **nor with** water that has been **heated by the sun, nor with water collected** [***hagerufin***] **in an urn heated** by coals [***mulyar***][NL] **And** in addition, **she** may **not remove her hand**[HN] **from the oven,** i.e., interrupt her baking, **until she finishes** forming **all the loaves** from the dough, so that it should not become leavened in the interim. **And** she **requires two vessels, one in which she mixes** the water into the dough **and one in which she cools her hands** so that the heat from her hands does not cause the dough to leaven.[H]

אִיבַּעְיָא לְהוּ: עָבְרָה וְלָשָׁה מַהוּ? מָר זוּטְרָא אָמַר: מוּתָּר, רַב אַשִׁי אָמַר: אָסוּר.

A dilemma was raised before the Sages: If **she transgressed and kneaded** the dough with warm water,[H] **what is the** *halakha*? **Mar Zutra said: It is permitted** after the fact. **Rav Ashi said: It is forbidden.**

אָמַר מָר זוּטְרָא: מְנָא אָמִינָא לַהּ – דְּתַנְיָא: אֵין לוֹתְתִין הַשְּׂעוֹרִין בְּפֶסַח. וְאִם לָתַת, נִתְבַּקְעוּ – אֲסוּרִים, לֹא נִתְבַּקְעוּ – מוּתָּרִין.

Mar Zutra said: From where do I say my opinion on this issue? **As it was taught** in a *baraita*: **One** may **not soak barley on Passover, and if one soaked** barley and it **split,** the barley **is forbidden.** If it did **not split,** the barley **is permitted.** This case indicates that even if one violates the principles established by the Sages with regard to adding water to flour on Passover, the product is forbidden only after the fact if it actually leavened.

וְרַב אַשִׁי אָמַר: אַטּוּ כּוּלְּהוּ חֲדָא מְחִיתָא מְחִיתִינְהוּ? הֵיכָא דְּאִיתְּמַר – אִיתְּמַר, וְהֵיכָא דְּלָא אִיתְּמַר – לָא אִיתְּמַר.

And Rav Ashi said in response: **Is that to say** that **all of them are woven in the same** act of **weaving?** In other words, is the *halakha* identical in all cases? **Where it was stated** that the Sages did not punish the violator by rendering his food prohibited, **it was stated; and where it was not stated** that they refrained from punishing the violator, **it was not stated.** It is therefore possible that the Sages rendered dough kneaded with warm water forbidden, to punish the woman who prepared it in this manner.

הדרן עלך כל שעה

HALAKHA

May not knead in the sun – לֹא תָּלוּשׁ בַּחַמָּה: It is prohibited to knead the dough for *matza* in a place where the sun shines. On a cloudy day it is prohibited to knead this dough anywhere outdoors, based on the principle that the effect of the sun is widespread on a cloudy day. Likewise, one should not knead the dough for *matza* near a heated oven (*Shulḥan Arukh, Oraḥ Ḥayyim* 459:1).

She may not remove her hand – לֹא תַּגְבִּיהַּ יָדָהּ: Dough that is being used in the preparation of *matza* should not be left idle even momentarily, for as long as it is being worked it will not become leavened (*Shulḥan Arukh, Oraḥ Ḥayyim* 459:2).

Vessels for kneading and mixing – כֵּלִים לְלִישָׁה וּלְקִיטוּף: A woman kneading dough for *matza* should not mix the dough with the same water she uses to cool her hands. Instead, she must prepare a different vessel for this purpose (*Shulḥan Arukh, Oraḥ Ḥayyim* 459:3).

She transgressed and kneaded dough improperly – עָבְרָה וְלָשָׁה שֶׁלֹּא כַּדִּין: If a woman prepared *matza* dough in the sun or neglected to cool her hands, this *matza* is permitted after the fact, in accordance with the opinion of Mar Zutra, provided that the dough was not actually heated by the sun, as stated by the *Baḥ*, *Ḥavvot Ya'ir*, and others (*Shulḥan Arukh, Oraḥ Ḥayyim* 459:5).

NOTES

Water collected [*hagerufin*] in an urn heated by coals [*mulyar*] – מַיִם הַגְּרוּפִין מִן הַמּוּלְיָיר: Many early commentaries cite a version of the Gemara that omits the word *mulyar*, an urn heated by coals. They explain that this statement is referring to water that flows in rivers (*Arukh*; Rabbeinu Yehonatan; Rif; *Nimmukei Yosef*). This interpretation is based on the verse: "The brook Kishon swept them away [*gerafam*]" (Judges 5:21). Others suggest that this phrase is referring to water that moves a flour mill (Maharam Ḥalawa). According to this explanation, with regard to water from cisterns or wells, there is no need to keep it overnight before it can be used for *matza*, as it does not require cooling.

And she may not remove her hand – וְלֹא תַּגְבִּיהַּ יָדָהּ: Some commentaries explain that this means she should not stop working with the dough until she has baked everything. Others say that she must constantly work with the dough until it is placed in the oven. Yet others maintain that she must be careful that the oven remains lit until the last *matza* has been baked (Ritva).

LANGUAGE

An urn heated by coals [*mulyar*] – מוּלְיָיר: From the Greek μιλιάριον, *miliarion*, or the Latin miliarium, a tall, pointed copper vessel containing pipes that heat the water inside.

Summary of **Perek II**

This chapter focused on two main issues: The prohibition against deriving benefit from leaven and the delineation of which foods may be used for the mitzvot of eating *matza* and bitter herbs.

With regard to the prohibition against eating leaven, the Gemara established that there is a biblical prohibition against deriving benefit from leaven throughout the Festival. This prohibition applies to any leaven owned by a Jew, whether in his possession or under the control of a gentile. According to Torah law, leaven that remained in a Jew's possession during the Festival is permissible afterward. However, in order to discourage any laxity in this regard, the Sages forbade one to gain any benefit from such leaven.

The commandment to eat *matza* is integrally connected to the prohibition concerning leaven. Therefore, only those grains that can become leavened when left unattended may be used to produce *matza*. The Gemara limits them to the classic five grains: Wheat, barley, spelt, rye, and oats.

The vegetables that may be used for the bitter herbs are limited to those with a bitter taste, that come from plants with a sap, and that are eaten by people within a meal.

With regard to both *matza* and bitter herbs, the Gemara concluded that if prohibited produce is used in their preparation, whether the produce is prohibited by biblical or rabbinic force, one does not fulfill the mitzva of eating *matza* or bitter herbs with them. However, if the only issue is that a mitzva should have been performed with the produce before eating it, and it wasn't performed, i.e., if tithes for the priesthood were not separated, then despite the neglect, one still fulfills his obligation of eating *matza*. However, one should ensure that the mitzva is fulfilled before eating it *ab initio*.

This chapter addresses only the basic definitions of *matza* and bitter herbs. Other issues pertaining to their actual consumption at the seder on the evening of Passover are addressed in the final chapter of tractate *Pesaḥim*, Chapter Ten.

Introduction to **Perek III**

Seven days shall there be no leaven found in your houses; for whoever eats that which is leavened, that soul shall be cut off from the congregation of Israel, whether he is a stranger or born in the land. You shall eat nothing leavened; in all your habitations shall you eat matzot.

(Exodus 12:19–20)

Matzot shall be eaten seven days; and no leavened bread shall be seen with you, neither shall there be leaven seen with you, in all your borders.

(Exodus 13:7)

While the previous chapters dealt with the various prohibitions concerning leaven, the precise definition of the types of foods that are included in the prohibitions was not discussed. This issue forms the central theme of this chapter. The Torah states explicitly only that leaven and leavened bread are prohibited. However, it remains unclear whether other foods that contain leavened ingredients should also be covered by this prohibition. Is one permitted to retain possession of a mixture of leaven and other foods? Does its consumption entail the same punishment of *karet* as one who eats leavened bread? What proportion of the mixture needs to be leaven in order to entail the various prohibitions? Furthermore, what are the *halakhot* pertaining to leavened material that is not meant for consumption? Is there nevertheless a prohibition to eat it, or to be in possession of it?

Another issue discussed here is at what point in the leavening process is a food considered to have become fully leavened and therefore included in the prohibitions? This immediately gives rise to other questions: When does one need to be concerned that a food might have become leavened, and what is the status of foods that were only partially leavened?

The discussion surrounding these issues also serves to highlight the relationship between the two prohibitions concerning leaven. Is the prohibition against possessing leaven merely a biblical safeguard to ensure that one does not come to eat it, or is it an independent prohibition that exists parallel to the prohibition against eating it?

In short, this chapter serves to complete the discussions concerning the prohibitions of leaven by defining what precisely is included in the various prohibitions.

מתני׳ וְאֵלּוּ עוֹבְרִין בְּפֶסַח: כּוּתָּח הַבַּבְלִי, וְשֵׁכָר הַמָּדִי, וְחוֹמֶץ הָאֲדוֹמִי, וְזִיתוֹם הַמִּצְרִי, וְזוֹמַן שֶׁל צַבָּעִים, וַעֲמִילָן שֶׁל טַבָּחִים, וְקוֹלָן שֶׁל סוֹפְרִים.

MISHNA And for possessing **these**[N] **one transgresses** [*overin*][NH] the prohibitions of: It shall not be seen, and: It shall not be found, **on Passover,** although not all of them are considered food: **Babylonian *kutaḥ*,**[N] a dip with a sharp flavor that contains flour; **Median beer; Edomite vinegar; Egyptian *zitom*,**[L] a type of beer; **dyers' broth** [*zoman*];[L] **bakers' well-worked dough;** and ***kolan of soferim*.**

רַבִּי אֱלִיעֶזֶר אוֹמֵר: אַף תַּכְשִׁיטֵי נָשִׁים.

Rabbi Eliezer says: The same prohibition **also** applies to **women's adornments,** i.e., cosmetics, that contain leaven.

זֶה הַכְּלָל: כֹּל שֶׁהוּא מִמִּין דָּגָן – הֲרֵי זֶה עוֹבֵר בְּפֶסַח. הֲרֵי אֵלּוּ בְּאַזְהָרָה, וְאֵין בָּהֶן מִשּׁוּם כָּרֵת.

This is the principle: If one possesses **any** substance **that is** derived **from a type of grain** that became leavened, although it is not actually bread, **one transgresses** the prohibitions of: It shall not be seen, and: It shall not be found, **on Passover. These** substances are included **in the warning,**[H] i.e., the biblical prohibition of possessing leaven, **but there is no element of *karet*** if one eats them.

גמ׳ תָּנוּ רַבָּנַן, שְׁלֹשָׁה דְּבָרִים נֶאֶמְרוּ בְּכוּתָּח הַבַּבְלִי: מְטַמְטֵם אֶת הַלֵּב, וּמְסַמֵּא אֶת הָעֵינַיִם, וּמַכְחִישׁ אֶת הַגּוּף.

GEMARA Since the mishna mentions *kutaḥ*, the Gemara cites a *baraita* where *kutaḥ* is discussed. **The Sages taught** that **three things were said with regard to *kutaḥ*: It blocks the heart, it blinds the eyes, and it weakens the body.**

מְטַמְטֵם אֶת הַלֵּב – מִשּׁוּם נְסִיוּבֵי דְּחַלְבָּא, וּמְסַמֵּא אֶת הָעֵינַיִם – מִשּׁוּם מִילְחָא, וּמַכְחִישׁ אֶת הַגּוּף – מִשּׁוּם קוּמְנִיתָא דְּאוּמָּא.

The Gemara explains each statement: **It blocks the heart due to the whey.** Whey was added to *kutaḥ* and was considered to be an inferior type of food. **It blinds the eyes due to the salt** in it, which can be dangerous if it enters the eyes. **And it weakens the body due to the mold in the bread,** as one of the ingredients of *kutaḥ* was crumbs from dough that had become leavened to the point that they were nearly spoiled.

תָּנוּ רַבָּנַן: שְׁלֹשָׁה דְּבָרִים מַרְבִּין הַזֶּבֶל, וְכוֹפְפִין אֶת הַקּוֹמָה וְנוֹטְלִין אֶחָד מֵחֲמֵשׁ מֵאוֹת מִמְּאוֹר עֵינָיו שֶׁל אָדָם. אֵלּוּ הֵן: פַּת קִיבָּר, וְשֵׁכָר חָדָשׁ, וְיָרָק חַי.

After mentioning this *baraita*, the Gemara continues to discuss the nutritional effects of other foods. **The Sages taught: Three things increase** one's **waste, lower** one's **stature, and take one five-hundredth of a person's vision** if he eats them regularly. And **they are: Bread** from **coarse** flour, **new beer, and raw vegetables.**

תָּנוּ רַבָּנַן: שְׁלֹשָׁה דְּבָרִים מְמַעֲטִין אֶת הַזֶּבֶל, וְזוֹקְפִין אֶת הַקּוֹמָה, וּמְאִירִין אֶת הָעֵינַיִם. אֵלּוּ הֵן: פַּת נְקִיָּיה, בָּשָׂר שָׁמֵן, וְיַיִן יָשָׁן. פַּת נְקִיָּיה –

Similarly, **the Sages taught** in another *baraita*: **Three things decrease** one's **waste, straighten** one's **stature, and improve** one's **vision,** and **they are: Bread** from **fine** flour, **fatty meat, and aged wine.** The Gemara explains: **Fine bread**

NOTES

And for possessing these – וְאֵלּוּ: A different version of the Gemara does not include the connecting prefix *vav*, meaning: And. This omission indicates that there is no connection between this mishna and the previous one; conversely, those who accept the version with a *vav* maintain that there is a connection between the two *mishnayot*. The previous mishna explains that the water used by a baker may not be kept in one's possession on Passover, although it is not actually leavened bread. Similarly, this mishna discusses other items that are not in themselves leavened bread but contain only a small amount of leavened matter (*Melekhet Shlomo*).

Transgresses [*overin*] – עוֹבְרִין: There are different opinions with regard to the meaning of the word *overin*. Some explain that it is referring to the transgression of the prohibitions: It shall not be seen, and: It shall not be found (Rashi; *ge'onim*; Rav Yehuda ben Rav Binyamin HaRofeh; and others). Others maintain, based on the alternative translation of *over* as pass, that the word means that the items listed must be removed from the table since they contain leaven, and it is prohibited to eat them (Rabbeinu Ḥananel; *Me'iri*; Ritva). Yet others interpret this word to mean that these items must be removed from one's possession before Passover (Rabbi Zeraḥya HaLevi; Rabbeinu Gershom; Rabbeinu Yehonatan).

***Kutaḥ* – כּוּתָּח:** *Kutaḥ* was a typical Babylonian dip made from whey, salt, and bread that fermented to the point of moldiness. This dip was so sharp that it could be eaten only by the Babylonians, who were accustomed to eating it. In the Mishna, it is referred to as Babylonian *kutaḥ*.

HALAKHA

For possessing these one transgresses – אֵלּוּ עוֹבְרִין: If on Passover one possesses an item containing leaven mixed with other ingredients that is fit for consumption, he has transgressed the commandments of: It shall not be seen, and: It shall not be found. Any such items must be removed from one's possession before Passover (*Shulḥan Arukh*, *Oraḥ Ḥayyim* 442:1).

These are included in the warning – הֲרֵי אֵלּוּ בְּאַזְהָרָה: One who eats food containing a mixture of leaven on Passover is not liable to be punished with *karet*. If one eats an olive-bulk of the mixture in the time it takes to eat half a loaf of bread, then he is liable to receive lashes, in accordance with the mishna (Rambam *Sefer Zemanim*, *Hilkhot Ḥametz UMatza* 1:6).

LANGUAGE

***Zitom* – זִיתוֹם:** From the Greek ζῦθος, *zuthos*, or Latin zythum, meaning beer made from barley, especially in Egypt.

Broth [*zoman*] – זוֹמַן: From the Greek ζωμός, *zomos*, meaning broth that contains bran.

דִּסְמִידָא, בָּשָׂר שָׁמֵן – דִּצְפִירְתָּא דְּלָא אִפְּתַח. יַיִן יָשָׁן – עַתִּיק עַתִּיקֵי.

is made **from refined flour; fatty meat** refers to meat **from a goat that has not** yet **given birth;**[N] **and aged wine** refers to wine that has been **aged significantly,** for at least three years.

NOTES

A goat that has not yet given birth – צְפִירְתָּא דְּלָא אִפְּתַח: Others explain that this phrase may also refer to young birds that have not yet laid eggs (Rabbeinu Ḥananel; *Arukh*).

כָּל מִילֵּי דִּמְעַלֵּי לְהַאי – קָשֶׁה לְהַאי, וּדְקָשֶׁה לְהַאי – מְעַלֵּי לְהַאי, בַּר מִזַּנְגְּבִילָא רְטִיבָא, וּפִילְפְּלֵי אֲרִיכָתָא, וּפַת נְקִיָּיה, וּבָשָׂר שָׁמֵן, וְיַיִן יָשָׁן – דִּמְעַלֵּי לְכוּלֵּי גּוּפֵיהּ.

The Gemara states a general principle: **Any** food or medical treatment **that is effective** in healing **this** sickness or this limb **is deleterious for that** one. **And** any food or treatment **that is deleterious for this** one **is effective** in healing **that** one, **except for moist ginger,**[B] **long peppers, and bread** made of **refined** flour, **and fatty meat, and aged wine, which are effective to heal all** limbs **of the body.**

״שֵׁכָר הַמָּדִי״ – דְּרָמוּ בֵּיהּ מֵי שַׂעֲרֵי.

The Gemara returns to its discussion of the details mentioned in the mishna. Why is **Median beer** prohibited during Passover? It is because the Medians **place barley water into it.**

״וְחוֹמֶץ הָאֲדוֹמִי״. דְּשָׁדוּ בֵּיהּ שַׂעֲרֵי.

And Edomite vinegar is prohibited because the Edomites **place barley into it.**

אָמַר רַב נַחְמָן (בַּר יִצְחָק): בַּתְּחִלָּה, כְּשֶׁהָיוּ מְבִיאִין נְסָכִים מִיהוּדָה – לֹא הָיָה יֵינָם שֶׁל יְהוּדָה מַחְמִיץ עַד שֶׁנּוֹתְנִין לְתוֹכָן שְׂעוֹרִין, וְהָיוּ קוֹרִין אוֹתוֹ חוֹמֶץ סְתָם. ––

Rav Naḥman bar Yitzḥak said: Initially, when the Temple stood **and they would bring** wine **libations from Judea,** the wine would be blessed and would be preserved without any additives. **The wine of Judea would not turn to vinegar unless they placed barley into it** to achieve this effect. **And they would call** this vinegar to which barley had been added **ordinary vinegar,** since wine would not become vinegar without this additive.

וְעַכְשָׁיו אֵין יֵינָם שֶׁל אֲדוֹמִיִּים מַחְמִיץ עַד שֶׁנּוֹתְנִין לְתוֹכָן שְׂעוֹרִין, וְקוֹרִין אוֹתוֹ חוֹמֶץ הָאֲדוֹמִי, לְקַיֵּים מַה שֶּׁנֶּאֱמַר: ״אִמָּלְאָה הָחֳרָבָה״ אִם מְלֵאָה זוֹ – חֲרֵבָה זוֹ, וְאִם מְלֵאָה זוֹ – חֲרֵבָה זוֹ. רַב נַחְמָן בַּר יִצְחָק אָמַר, מֵהָכָא: ״וּלְאֹם מִלְאֹם יֶאֱמָץ.״

And now, after the destruction of the Temple, **Edomite wine does not turn to vinegar unless one places barley into it. This is called Edomite vinegar,**[N] **to fulfill that which is stated** with regard to Tyre, and the same applies to other enemies of the Jewish people: "Because Tyre has said against Jerusalem: Aha, she is broken that was the gate of the peoples; she is turned unto me; **I shall be filled with her that is laid waste**" (Ezekiel 26:2). The Sages expound: **If this one,** Jerusalem, **is full,** then **that one,** her enemy, **is laid waste; and if this** enemy **is full,** then **she,** Jerusalem, **is laid waste.** Therefore, when the Jewish people fall, their enemies can achieve the success that was once attained by the Jews. **Rav Naḥman bar Yitzḥak said:** This notion can be derived **from here,** where the verse states regarding Esau and Jacob: **"The one people shall be stronger than the other people"** (Genesis 25:23), meaning that when one nation gains power, the other is weakened, because they cannot both be strong at the same time.

תַּנְיָא, אָמַר רַבִּי יְהוּדָה: בִּיהוּדָה, בָּרִאשׁוֹנָה, הַלּוֹקֵחַ חוֹמֶץ מֵעַם הָאָרֶץ – אֵינוֹ צָרִיךְ לְעַשֵּׂר, מִפְּנֵי שֶׁחֲזָקָה אֵינוֹ בָּא אֶלָּא מִן הַתֶּמֶד. וְעַכְשָׁיו, הַלּוֹקֵחַ חוֹמֶץ מֵעַם הָאָרֶץ – צָרִיךְ לְעַשֵּׂר, שֶׁחֶזְקָתוֹ אֵינוֹ בָּא אֶלָּא מִן הַיַּיִן.

It was taught in a *baraita* that **Rabbi Yehuda said: In Judea, initially, one who would purchase vinegar from an *am ha'aretz*,** i.e., one who is not scrupulous in matters of ritual purity and tithes and is therefore suspect of not having tithed his fruit properly, would **not need to tithe it due to** the fact that **it can be assumed** that ordinary vinegar **was made only from *temed*,** a liquid produced from grape remnants. After filtering the wine from the stems, seeds, and skins, water was poured over these remnants. The liquid was then drained off and allowed to ferment until it became vinegar. This liquid was called *temed,* and it is not necessary to tithe it. Vinegar was produced in this way because the wine of that time was so strong that it did not turn to vinegar on its own. **But now, one who purchases vinegar from an *am ha'aretz* must tithe it,** as the wine nowadays turns to vinegar quickly, **and the presumption is** that vinegar **comes only from wine.**

וְסָבַר רַבִּי יְהוּדָה תֶּמֶד לָאו בַּר עַשּׂוּרֵי הוּא? וְהָא (תְּנַן): הַמְתַמֵּד וְנָתַן מַיִם בְּמִדָּה, וּמָצָא כְּדֵי מִדָּתוֹ – פָּטוּר, וְרַבִּי יְהוּדָה מְחַיֵּיב!

The Gemara asks: **But does Rabbi Yehuda hold that *temed* is not subject to tithing? Wasn't it taught** in a mishna: With regard to **one who produces *temed***[H] **and adds a measured** amount **of water and** afterward **finds a corresponding** amount of liquid to that which **he measured, he is exempt** from tithing this *temed* because it is clear that the grape produce added only flavor and did not add to the volume of the *temed.* And **Rabbi Yehuda obligates** one to tithe the *temed* even in that case. If this is so, how can Rabbi Yehuda permit a person to purchase *temed* from an *am ha'aretz*? According to his opinion in this *baraita, temed* must be tithed.

BACKGROUND

Moist ginger – זַנְגְּבִילָא רְטִיבָא: Ginger is obtained from the root of *Zingiber officinale*. Extracts of ginger are used in foods, condiments, baked confections, candies, beverages, cosmetics and perfumes. Overall, ginger products vary considerably in taste, pungency and smell, while the root varies in consistency, depending on the country of origin and the variety of the crop. Traditionally, the warming and aromatic properties of ginger have led to its use for numerous indications, including as an expectorant or to treat colds, often in teas or soups.

Ginger plant

Fresh ginger roots

NOTES

This is called Edomite vinegar – קוֹרִין אוֹתוֹ חוֹמֶץ הָאֲדוֹמִי: As indicated in the blessings given to Jacob by Isaac (Genesis 27:40), the fact that these blessings are granted to the Jewish people, rather than the descendants of Esau, is dependent upon the merits of the Jews. While the Temple stood, the libations that were poured on the altar served as a source of blessing for the wine of Jews, assuring that it would not spoil. After the destruction of the Temple and the cessation of the libations, that blessing was transferred to the Edomites, who are descendants of Esau, as stated in tractate *Megilla* 6a (Maharsha).

HALAKHA

One who produces *temed* – הַמְתַמֵּד: If one adds water to wine dregs and filters it, and he finds that there are four parts of liquid for every three parts with which he started, then he must assume that the additional portion is wine, and he is obligated to separate tithes from this mixture for the additional portion. If he finds less than four parts for every three parts he added, and certainly if he finds the same amount that he initially added, then he is not required to tithe the mixture. This ruling is in accordance with the opinion of the Rabbis who dispute Rabbi Yehuda's position, as Rabbi Yehuda is an individual Sage in dispute with many Sages, and the *halakha* accords with the majority opinion (Rambam *Sefer Zera'im*, *Hilkhot Ma'aserot* 2:7).

הָכִי קָאָמַר: לֹא נֶחְשְׁדוּ עַמֵּי הָאָרֶץ עַל הַתֶּמֶד. אִי בָּעֵית אֵימָא: נֶחְשְׁדוּ. וְלָא קַשְׁיָא: הָא – בִּדְרָווֹקָא, הָא – בִּדְפוּרְצְנֵי.

The Gemara answers: **This is** what Rabbi Yehuda **is saying:** One is required to tithe *temed*; however, ***amei ha'aretz* are not suspected** of failing to tithe ***temed.*** Because *temed* is so inexpensive, the assumption is that *amei ha'aretz* are not sparing with it and are willing to tithe it. **If you wish, say** instead that even if *amei ha'aretz* **are suspected** of failing to tithe *temed*, **and** this is **not difficult** for the following reason: **This** mishna is referring to a case where the *temed* was produced **with dregs** that contain some amount of wine, and therefore Rabbi Yehuda says that a person is required to tithe it. **That** *baraita* is referring to a case where the *temed* was produced **with grape pits; because** it is assumed that no wine is mixed into the *temed*, Rabbi Yehuda states that one is exempt from tithing it.

״וְזִיתוֹם הַמִּצְרִי וכו׳״. מַאי זִיתוֹם הַמִּצְרִי?

It is stated in the mishna that **Egyptian *zitom*** is considered leavened food. The Gemara asks: **What is Egyptian *zitom*?**

תָּנָא רַב יוֹסֵף: תִּלְתָּא שַׂעֲרֵי, תִּלְתָּא קוּרְטְמֵי, וְתִלְתָּא מִלְחָא.

Rav Yosef taught from a *baraita*: It is **one-third barley, one-third safflower, and one-third salt.**

רַב פַּפָּא מַפֵּיק שַׂעֲרֵי וּמְעַיֵּיל חִיטֵּי, וְסִימָנָיךְ סִיסָנֵי.

Rav Pappa removes barley from the list of ingredients **and includes wheat;** he maintains that Egyptian *zitom* was made with wheat rather than barley. The Gemara comments: **Your mnemonic** to remember which Sage expressed which version is the word ***sisanei***, meaning a twig basket. *Sisanei* contains the letter *samekh* twice, which can help one remember that Rav Yosef, whose name contains a *samekh*, says that Egyptian *zitom* is made from *se'orim*, barley, a word that contains the letter *sin*, which makes the same sound as *samekh*.

תָּרוּ לְהוּ, וְקָלוּ לְהוּ, וְטָחֲנֵי לְהוּ, וְשָׁתוּ לְהוּ מִדִּיבְחָא וְעַד עַצַרְתָּא. דְּקָמֵיט – מְרַפֵּי לֵיהּ, וּדְרָפֵי – מַקְמִיט לֵיהּ. לְחוֹלֶה וּלְאִשָּׁה עוּבָּרָה – סַכַּנְתָּא.

The Gemara describes how Egyptian *zitom* is prepared: Those who prepare it **soak** the ingredients together, **and** then they **roast them and grind them** together. **They drink** the mixture **from Passover to *Shavuot*.** This drink **relaxes** the bowels of one who is **constipated, and it constipates** one whose bowel movements are **loose.** However, **it is dangerous for a sick person or a pregnant woman** to drink this mixture.

״וְזוֹמָן שֶׁל צְבָעִים וכו׳״. הָכָא תַּרְגִּימוּ מַיָּא דְּחִיוְרֵי דְּצָבְעִי בְּהוּ לַבָּא.

It was taught in the mishna that **dyers' broth** is considered leavened. The Gemara explains: **Here,** in Babylonia, **they interpreted** that this is **bran water [*maya deḥivri*][N] that** people **use to dye leather.**

״וַעֲמִילָן שֶׁל טַבָּחִים וכו׳״ – פַּת תְּבוּאָה שֶׁלֹּא הֵבִיאָה שְׁלִישׁ, שֶׁמַּנִּיחָהּ עַל פִּי קְדֵירָה וְשׁוֹאֶבֶת הַזּוּהֲמָא.

It was further stated in the mishna that **bakers' well-worked dough** is also considered leavened. The Gemara explains the nature of this substance: It is **bread made from grain that was** harvested before it was **one-third** ripe and then made into a loaf. This loaf was placed **on top of a pot to draw out the filth** from the broth.

״וְקוֹלָן שֶׁל סוֹפְרִים וכו׳״ הָכָא תַּרְגּוּמָא: פֵּירוּרָא דְּאוּשְׁכָּפֵי.

It was further taught in the mishna that the ***kolan of soferim***, is considered leavened. The Gemara explains: **Here,** in Babylonia, **they interpreted that** this expression is referring to **shoemakers' glue** that is made from flour.

רַב שִׁימִי מֵחוֹזְנָאָה אָמַר: זֶה טִיפּוּלָן שֶׁל בְּנוֹת עֲשִׁירִים שֶׁמְּשַׁיְּירוֹת אוֹתוֹ לִבְנוֹת עֲנִיִּים.

Rav Shimi from Ḥozna'a said: This is the depilatory **paste of the daughters of the wealthy,[N] of which they would leave a remnant for the daughters of the poor.** It was the common practice for women to remove hair from different parts of their bodies by applying various pastes, some of which contained flour. The *kolan* of *soferim* mentioned in the mishna was such a substance. It was given this name because wealthy young women would give the paste [*kolan*] to poor young women whose fathers were schoolteachers [*soferim*], so that the poor women could utilize it as well.

אִינִי?! וְהָא תָּנָא רַבִּי חִיָּיא: אַרְבָּעָה מִינֵי מְדִינָה, וּשְׁלֹשָׁה מִינֵי אוּמָּנוּת. וְאִי אָמְרַתְּ טִיפּוּלָן שֶׁל בְּנוֹת עֲשִׁירִים – מַאי מִינֵי אוּמָּנוּת אִיכָּא?

The Gemara asks: **Is that so? But didn't Rabbi Ḥiyya teach** a mnemonic by noting that the mishna lists **four items** that are used by the ordinary people **of the state,[N]** i.e., *kutaḥ*, beer, vinegar, and *zitom*, **and three items of artisans,[N]** i.e., dyers' broth, *kolan of soferim*, and bakers' well-worked dough? **And if you say** that *kolan of soferim* **is the** depilatory **paste of the daughters of the wealthy,** then **what artisanship is there in that?** According to this interpretation, that substance does not belong on the list of artisans' items.

NOTES

Bran water [*maya deḥivri*] – מַיָּא דְּחִיוְרֵי: In the present version of the Gemara, this phrase reads *maya deḥivri*, which Rashi interprets to mean bran water. However, most early commentaries had a different version of the Gemara, which read *maya deḥizra*, meaning water that is extracted from different types of plants. It seems that flour was added to this liquid to enhance the dye.

The depilatory paste of the daughters of the wealthy – טִיפּוּלָן שֶׁל בְּנוֹת עֲשִׁירִים: According to the Ra'avad, the correct version of the Gemara should be: The sons of the wealthy would leave over these products for the sons of the poor. Otherwise, the mishna should have used the feminine form *soferot*, rather than the masculine form *soferim*. See *Tosafot*, who point out that according to Rav Shimi's explanation, it is difficult to understand Rabbi Eliezer's statement at the end of the mishna, as the latter adds nothing novel.

Some explain that in fact Rabbi Eliezer agrees with the first *tanna*, and he is merely adding that all types of cosmetics contain hardened leaven (Ra'avad). Others state that the first *tanna* prohibited cosmetics used by poor young women because their cosmetics contained a majority of flour and only a minority of other substances, while those of the wealthier women contained mostly other ingredients and only a small portion of flour (see *Ba'al HaMaor*).

Some say that the first *tanna* prohibits only hardened leaven itself, or a mixture containing true leaven, while Rabbi Eliezer prohibits a mixture containing hardened leaven as well (see *Ba'al HaMaor*; Rabbeinu Gershom). Others explain that according to Rav Shimi, the paste referred to here is specifically that which was left over for the poor young women, which became leavened in the meantime, whereas the wealthy women used their paste immediately, before it became leavened (Maharam Ḥalawa).

Four items used by the ordinary people of the state – אַרְבָּעָה מִינֵי מְדִינָה: Some explain Rabbi Ḥiyya's statement to mean simply that each of the first four items on the list is associated with a *medina*, a state, as its country of origin is contained in its name: Babylonian *kutaḥ*, Median beer, Edomite vinegar, and Egyptian *zitom*. The other three items are associated with a specific artisan, namely dyers' broth, bakers' well-worked dough, and bookmakers' glue (*Me'iri*).

Three items of artisans – שְׁלֹשָׁה מִינֵי אוּמָּנוּת: Rabbeinu Ḥananel's version of the Gemara reads: Three items of the state and four items of artisans. In his opinion, Egyptian *zitom* belongs in the latter category, as it was used primarily for medicinal purposes, and doctors are considered artisans.

וְאֶלָּא מַאי – פֵּרוּרָא דְּאוּשְׁכָּפֵי, אַמַּאי קָרֵי לֵיהּ הַאי קוֹלָן שֶׁל סוֹפְרִים? קוֹלָן שֶׁל רַצְעָנִין מִיבְּעָיָא לֵיהּ! אָמַר רַב אוֹשַׁעְיָא: לְעוֹלָם פֵּרוּרָא דְּאוּשְׁכָּפֵי, וּמַאי קָרֵי לֵיהּ קוֹלָן שֶׁל סוֹפְרִים – דְּסוֹפְרִים נַמִּי מְדַבְּקִין בְּהוּ נְיָירוֹתֵיהֶן.

The Gemara answers with another question: **Rather what,** will you say that this is referring to **shoemakers' glue?** If so, **why did** the authors of the mishna **call it bookmakers' glue** [*kolan shel soferim*]? **It should** have been called **shoemakers' glue** [*kolan shel ratzanin*]. **Rav Oshaya said: Actually,** one should explain that *kolan* is referring to **shoemakers' glue; and why is it called bookmakers' glue?** The reason is that **bookmakers also use it to attach their pages.** During the time of the mishna, this paste was referred to as bookmakers' glue.

״רַבִּי אֱלִיעֶזֶר אוֹמֵר אַף תַּכְשִׁיטֵי נָשִׁים וכו׳״. תַּכְשִׁיטֵי נָשִׁים סָלְקָא דַּעְתָּךְ?! אֶלָּא אֵימָא: אַף טִיפּוּלֵי נָשִׁים, דְּאָמַר רַב יְהוּדָה אָמַר רַב: בְּנוֹת יִשְׂרָאֵל

It is stated in the mishna: **Rabbi Eliezer says** that **women's adornments are also** prohibited as leavened food. The Gemara asks: **Could it enter your mind** to say **that adornments** made from silver, gold, or woven materials contain leaven? **Rather, say** instead that this means: **Even women's cosmetics** or other items used by women to enhance their skin are prohibited if they contain leavened ingredients. **As Rav Yehuda said that Rav said:** with regard to **the Jewish women**

Perek **III**
Daf **43** Amud **a**

שֶׁהִגִּיעוּ לְפִרְקָן וְלֹא הִגִּיעוּ לְשָׁנִים, בְּנוֹת עֲנִיִּים טוֹפְלוֹת אוֹתָן בְּסִיד, בְּנוֹת עֲשִׁירִים טוֹפְלוֹת אוֹתָן בְּסוֹלֶת, בְּנוֹת מְלָכִים בְּשֶׁמֶן הַמּוֹר, שֶׁנֶּאֱמַר: ״שִׁשָּׁה חֳדָשִׁים בְּשֶׁמֶן הַמּוֹר״.

who reached physical **maturity, but had not** yet **reached the** age of majority,[N] and women who sought to remove hair for cosmetic purposes. **They would smear daughters of the poor with lime; they would smear daughters of the wealthy with fine flour; they would smear daughters of kings with *shemen hamor*, as it was stated:** "For so were the days of their anointing filled, **six months with *shemen hamor*"** (Esther 2:12).

מַאי שֶׁמֶן הַמּוֹר? רַב הוּנָא בַּר יִרְמְיָה אוֹמֵר: סְטַכְּת, רַב יִרְמְיָה בַּר אַבָּא אָמַר: שֶׁמֶן זַיִת שֶׁלֹּא הֵבִיא שְׁלִישׁ.

The Gemara asks: **What is *shemen hamor*? Rav Huna bar Ḥiyya said: *Setaket*.**[L] **Rav Yirmeya bar Abba said:** It is **olive oil** extracted from an olive **that** has not yet **reached a third** of its growth;[N] the acidic oil is effective as a depilatory.

תַּנְיָא, רַבִּי יְהוּדָה אוֹמֵר: אַנְפִּיקְנִין – שֶׁמֶן זַיִת שֶׁלֹּא הֵבִיא שְׁלִישׁ. וְלָמָּה סָכִין אוֹתוֹ – מִפְּנֵי שֶׁמַּשִּׁיר אֶת הַשֵּׂיעָר וּמְעַדֵּן אֶת הַבָּשָׂר.

It was taught in a *baraita*: **Rabbi Yehuda says** that ***anpiknin***[L] is **olive oil** from an olive **that has not reached a third** of its growth. **And why is it spread** on the body? It is **due to** the fact **that it removes** [*mashir*] **the hair**[N] **and pampers the skin.**

״זֶה הַכְּלָל כֹּל שֶׁהוּא מִמִּין דָּגָן״. תַּנְיָא, אָמַר רַבִּי יְהוֹשֻׁעַ: וְכִי מֵאַחַר שֶׁשָּׁנִינוּ כֹּל שֶׁהוּא מִין דָּגָן הֲרֵי זֶה עוֹבֵר בְּפֶסַח – לָמָּה מָנוּ חֲכָמִים אֶת אֵלּוּ – כְּדֵי שֶׁיְּהֵא רָגִיל בָּהֶן וּבִשְׁמוֹתֵיהֶן.

The mishna states: **This is the principle:** One violates these prohibitions on Passover with **anything that is** prepared **from a type of grain. It was taught** in a *baraita* that **Rabbi Yehoshua said: Now that we learned** that by possessing **anything that is a type of grain one violates** the prohibition against leaven **during Passover, why did the Sages list these** items individually? They could have simply stated the principle. The *baraita* explains that the Sages provided a list of prohibited foods **so that** one **would become familiar with these** items **and with their names,** so that it would become widely known that these foods contain a small quantity of grain.

כִּי הָא, דְּהַהוּא בַּר מַעְרְבָא אִיקְלַע לְבָבֶל, הֲוָה בִּישְׂרָא בַּהֲדֵיהּ. אֲמַר לְהוּ: קְרִיבוּ לִי מִתְּכִילְתָּא. שְׁמַע דְּקָאָמְרִי: קְרִיבוּ לֵיהּ כּוּתָּח. כֵּיוָן דִּשְׁמַע כּוּתָּח – פֵּירַשׁ.

The Gemara cites an incident that underscores the significance of familiarity with the names of foods: **As in this** case **of that** man **from the West,** Eretz Yisrael, who **visited Babylonia,** and **had meat with him, he said to** his hosts: **Bring me a dip** with which to eat my bread. **He heard them saying: Bring him *kutaḥ*. Since he heard** the word ***kutaḥ*, he stopped** eating, as he knew that *kutaḥ* contains milk and may not be eaten with meat. This incident underscores that it is advantageous for one to familiarize himself with the names and ingredients of different foods, so that he will be aware of the nature of the food even if he does not recognize it.

״הֲרֵי אֵלּוּ בְּאַזְהָרָה״.

It is stated in the mishna: **These** substances **are included in the prohibition** but are not punishable by *karet*.[N]

NOTES

Who reached physical maturity but had not reached the age of majority – שֶׁהִגִּיעוּ לְפִרְקָן וְלֹא הִגִּיעוּ לְשָׁנִים: Some commentaries explain that this is referring to girls who have reached the age of majority but whose bodies do not yet show the signs of physical maturity. To expedite puberty, they would spread ointments on their skin to accelerate the growth of body hair (*Arukh*).

Olive oil from an olive that has not reached a third of its growth – שֶׁמֶן זַיִת שֶׁלֹּא הֵבִיא שְׁלִישׁ: Some commentaries explain that myrrh was added to the olive oil, and that it was this combination that was called myrrh oil (Rambam's Commentary on the Torah).

It removes [*mashir*] the hair – מַשִּׁיר אֶת הַשֵּׂיעָר: Some commentaries cite an alternative version of the text: It blackens [*mashḥir*] the hair. According to this explanation, it was designed to beautify rather than to serve as a depilatory (*Arukh*).

Karet – כָּרֵת: A divine punishment for serious transgressions. The precise definition of the term is a matter of debate among the commentaries, with opinions including premature or sudden death, barrenness and the death of the sinner's children, and excision of the soul from the World-to-Come. Tractate *Keritot* mentions thirty-six transgressions punishable by *karet*, all of which are violations of prohibitions, with two exceptions: Neglecting to sacrifice the Paschal lamb and failure to perform circumcision. *Karet* applies only to a person who intentionally commits a transgression. In certain instances, if the transgression was committed in the presence of witnesses, the transgressor is subject to execution by an earthly court or to the penalty of lashes. Anyone who inadvertently transgresses one of the prohibitions punishable by *karet* must bring a sin-offering as atonement.

LANGUAGE

Setaket – סְטַכְּת: From the Greek στακτή, *stakté*, meaning oil of myrrh.

Anpiknin – אַנְפִּיקְנִין: From the Greek ὀμφάκιον, *omfakiyon*, meaning oil prepared from unripe olives.

מַאן תַּנָּא דְּחָמֵץ דָּגָן גָּמוּר עַל יְדֵי תַעֲרוֹבוֹת, וְנוּקְשֶׁה בְּעֵינֵיהּ בְּלָאו?

The Gemara asks: **Who is the *tanna* who** maintains that both **full-fledged, leavened grain bread in a mixture, and hardened** leaven,[N] **in its pure,** unadulterated form,[H] which is not suitable for consumption, are both included **in a prohibition?**

אָמַר רַב יְהוּדָה אָמַר רַב: רַבִּי מֵאִיר הִיא. דְּתַנְיָא: שִׂיאוּר יִשָּׂרֵף, וְנוֹתְנוֹ לְכַלְבּוֹ. וְהָאוֹכְלוֹ – בְּאַרְבָּעִים.

The Gemara answers that **Rav Yehuda said** that **Rav said: It is** the opinion of **Rabbi Meir, as it was taught** in a *baraita*: **Leavening** dough, i.e., dough that is at the beginning of the leavening process and is presently hardened leaven, must **be burned, or** one **gives it to his dog. And one who eats it** is flogged **with forty** lashes.

הָא גּוּפָא קַשְׁיָא! אָמְרַתְּ "שִׂיאוּר יִשָּׂרֵף" – אַלְמָא: אָסוּר בַּהֲנָאָה. וַהֲדַר תָּנֵי: וְנוֹתְנוֹ לִפְנֵי כַלְבּוֹ – אַלְמָא מוּתָּר בַּהֲנָאָה!

Before analyzing the contents of the *baraita*, the Gemara addresses an apparent contradiction within the *baraita*. **This** *baraita* **itself is difficult. You said** that **leavening** dough must **be burned; apparently it is prohibited to** derive **benefit** from hardened leaven. **And then it teaches: Or** one **gives it to his dog; apparently, it is permitted to** derive **benefit** from the leaven.

הָכִי קָאָמַר: שִׂיאוּר יִשָּׂרֵף – דְּרַבִּי מֵאִיר לְרַבִּי מֵאִיר, דְּרַבִּי יְהוּדָה לְרַבִּי יְהוּדָה. וְנוֹתְנוֹ לִפְנֵי כַלְבּוֹ – דְּרַבִּי מֵאִיר לְרַבִּי יְהוּדָה.

The Gemara answers that **this is** what the *baraita* **is saying: Leavening** dough must **be burned,** i.e., leavening dough as defined **by Rabbi Meir** must be burned **in accordance with** the opinion of **Rabbi Meir,** who maintains that leavening dough is full-fledged leaven. Alternatively, the *baraita* may be explained as referring to leavening dough as defined **by Rabbi Yehuda, in accordance with** the opinion of **Rabbi Yehuda** that it is prohibited to derive benefit from leavening dough. Each *tanna* maintains that it is prohibited to derive benefit from any dough classified as leavening dough by his definition. When the *baraita* says **that one gives it to his dog,** it means: Leavening dough as defined **by Rabbi Meir,** is only hardened leaven **according to Rabbi Yehuda,** and therefore one may feed it to his dog. Rabbi Yehuda maintains that it is permitted to derive benefit from this type of leaven.

וְהָאוֹכְלוֹ בְּאַרְבָּעִים – אֲתָאן לְרַבִּי מֵאִיר.

With regard to the final statement of the *baraita*, that **one who eats** leavening dough is flogged **with forty** lashes, **we have** once again **arrived at** the opinion of **Rabbi Meir.** Rabbi Meir holds that one who eats this leavening dough, from which it is permitted to derive benefit according to Rabbi Yehuda, is flogged with forty lashes.

שָׁמְעִינַן לֵיהּ לְרַבִּי מֵאִיר: נוּקְשֶׁה בְּעֵינֵיהּ – בְּלָאו, וְכׇל שֶׁכֵּן חָמֵץ דָּגָן גָּמוּר עַל יְדֵי תַעֲרוֹבֶת.

According to this explanation of the *baraita*, **we** have **learned** that **Rabbi Meir** maintains that **hardened** leaven **in its pure,** unadulterated form, is included **in a prohibition,** and one who eats this leaven is flogged. **And all the more so,** one who eats **full-fledged, leavened grain bread in a mixture** is flogged but does not receive *karet*, as he is not eating the leaven in and of itself. Nevertheless, the prohibition against eating leavened bread on Passover applies in that case.

רַב נַחְמָן אָמַר: רַבִּי אֱלִיעֶזֶר הִיא, דְּתַנְיָא: עַל חָמֵץ דָּגָן גָּמוּר – עָנוּשׁ כָּרֵת, עַל עֵירוּבוֹ – בְּלָאו, דִּבְרֵי רַבִּי אֱלִיעֶזֶר. וַחֲכָמִים אוֹמְרִים: עַל חָמֵץ דָּגָן גָּמוּר – עָנוּשׁ כָּרֵת, עַל עֵירוּבוֹ – בְּלֹא כְלוּם. וְשָׁמְעִינַן לֵיהּ לְרַבִּי אֱלִיעֶזֶר דְּאָמַר חָמֵץ דָּגָן גָּמוּר עַל יְדֵי תַעֲרוֹבֶת בְּלָאו – וְכׇל שֶׁכֵּן נוּקְשֶׁה בְּעֵינֵיהּ.

Rav Naḥman said: The mishna **is** in accordance with the opinion of **Rabbi Eliezer, as it was taught** in a *baraita*: **For** eating **full-fledged, leavened grain bread** one is **punishable** by ***karet***, whereas **for** eating **a mixture** that contains leaven one is punished merely **for** violating **a prohibition.** This is **the statement of Rabbi Eliezer. And the Rabbis say: For** eating **full-fledged, leavened grain bread** one is **punishable by** ***karet***; however, **for** eating leaven in **its mixture** one is **not** punished **at all.**[N] **And we learned according to Rabbi Eliezer, who said** that **full-fledged, leavened grain bread in a mixture** is included **in a prohibition, and** that is true **all the more so** with regard to **hardened leaven in its pure,** unadulterated form.

וְרַב נַחְמָן, מַאי טַעְמָא לָא אָמַר כְּרַב יְהוּדָה?

The Gemara asks: **And what is the reason** that **Rav Naḥman did not state** his opinion **in accordance with** the explanation of **Rav Yehuda,** that the mishna is in accordance with Rabbi Meir's ruling?

אָמַר לָךְ: דִּילְמָא עַד כָּאן לָא קָאָמַר רַבִּי מֵאִיר הָתָם – אֶלָּא נוּקְשֶׁה בְּעֵינֵיהּ, אֲבָל חָמֵץ דָּגָן גָּמוּר עַל יְדֵי תַעֲרוֹבֶת – לָא.

The Gemara answers that Rav Naḥman could have **said to you** that the following distinction applies: **Perhaps Rabbi Meir stated** his opinion **only there,** with regard to **hardened** leaven **in its pure,** unadulterated form; **however,** with regard to **full-fledged, leavened grain bread in a mixture, no,** one is punished not with mere lashes but with *karet*.

NOTES

Hardened leaven – חָמֵץ נוּקְשֶׁה: This expression refers to inedible leaven or leavened dough that did not rise properly. Neither is considered full-fledged leaven and therefore they are not prohibited to the same degree (Ritva).

For eating leaven in its mixture one is not punished at all – עַל עֵירוּבוֹ בְּלֹא כְלוּם: Most authorities agree that this means only that one is not punished for consuming this mixture, not that eating it is actually permitted. The reason is that an olive-bulk of the mixture does not contain an olive-bulk of leaven, and therefore one is not liable for consuming this amount. However, if one eats a larger amount of the mixture, and he eats an olive-bulk of leaven in less than the amount of time it takes to eat a half-loaf of bread, he is punished with lashes, even according to the opinion of the Rabbis (Rif; Rosh).

HALAKHA

Leavend bread and leavened bread in a mixture – חָמֵץ וְתַעֲרוֹבֶת חָמֵץ: One who eats leaven in its pure, unadulterated form is punishable by *karet*. If one eats an olive-bulk of leaven in a mixture, within the amount of time it takes to consume a half-loaf of bread, he is punishable by lashes. The rationale for this *halakha* is a matter of dispute. Some commentaries claim that the *halakha* is in accordance with the opinion of the Rabbis in this case, as even they agree that one is liable to receive lashes for eating a mixture that contains this proportion of leaven (see Ra'avad and *Maggid Mishne*). Others say that the *halakha* is in accordance with the opinion of Rabbi Eliezer (*Kesef Mishne*, *Leḥem Mishne*).

וְרַב יְהוּדָה, מַאי טַעְמָא לֹא אָמַר כְּרַב נַחְמָן?

The Gemara asks: **And what is the reason** that **Rav Yehuda did not state** his opinion **in accordance with** the explanation of **Rav Naḥman,** that the mishna is in accordance with Rabbi Eliezer's ruling?

אָמַר לָךְ: עַד כָּאן לָא קָאָמַר רַבִּי אֱלִיעֶזֶר הָתָם – אֶלָּא חָמֵץ דָּגָן גָּמוּר עַל יְדֵי תַּעֲרוֹבֶת, אֲבָל נוּקְשֶׁה בְּעֵינֵיהּ – לָא אָמַר.

The Gemara answers that Rav Yehuda could have **said to you: Rabbi Eliezer stated** his opinion **only there,** with regard to **full-fledged, leavened grain bread in a mixture** that it is included in the prohibition. **However,** with regard to **hardened** leaven **in its pure,** unadulterated form, **he did not state** his ruling and perhaps Rabbi Eliezer maintains that it is permitted to eat hardened leaven.

תַּנְיָא כְּוָותֵיהּ דְּרַב יְהוּדָה: ״כָּל מַחְמֶצֶת לֹא תֹאכֵלוּ״ – לְרַבּוֹת כּוּתָּח הַבַּבְלִי, וְשֵׁכָר הַמָּדִי, וְחוֹמֶץ הָאֲדוֹמִי, וְזִיתוֹם הַמִּצְרִי. יָכוֹל יְהֵא עָנוּשׁ כָּרֵת – תַּלְמוּד לוֹמַר: ״כִּי כָּל אֹכֵל חָמֵץ וְנִכְרְתָה״ עַל חָמֵץ דָּגָן גָּמוּר – עָנוּשׁ כָּרֵת, וְעַל עֵירוּבוֹ – בְּלָאו.

The Gemara notes that **it was taught** in a *baraita* **in accordance with** the opinion of **Rav Yehuda,** who said that the *halakha* is in accordance with Rabbi Meir's opinion: **"You shall eat nothing leavened;** in all your dwellings you shall eat unleavened bread" (Exodus 12:20). The Sages taught in a *baraita*: This verse serves **to include Babylonian *kutaḥ*, Median beer, Edomite vinegar, and Egyptian *zitom*.** One **might** have thought that eating any of these items **will be punishable** by ***karet*.** Therefore, **the verse states: "For whoever eats leavened bread,** that soul **shall be cut off** from Israel" (Exodus 12:15), from which it can be derived: **For** eating **full-fledged, leavened bread** one is **punished** with ***karet*, but for** eating **its mixture** one is only in violation **of a prohibition.**

מַאן שָׁמְעַתְּ לֵיהּ דְּאָמַר עַל עֵירוּבוֹ בְּלָאו – רַבִּי אֱלִיעֶזֶר הִיא, וְאִילּוּ נוּקְשֶׁה בְּעֵינֵיהּ – לָא קָאָמַר. שְׁמַע מִינַּהּ: נוּקְשֶׁה לְרַבִּי אֱלִיעֶזֶר לֵית לֵיהּ.

The Gemara analyzes the above statement: **Whom did you hear that for** eating **a mixture** which contains leavened bread is in violation **of a prohibition? It is Rabbi Eliezer. But** the *baraita* **does not state** the *halakha* of **hardened** leaven **in its unadulterated form**. This *baraita* lists only items that contain leaven in a mixture, but not other substances whose halakhic status is that of hardened leaven, e.g., broth, worked dough, and glue. **Learn from this that Rabbi Eliezer is not of** the opinion that **hardened** leaven is prohibited.

וְרַבִּי אֱלִיעֶזֶר, עֵירוּבוֹ בְּלָאו מְנָא לֵיהּ? דִּכְתִיב: ״כָּל מַחְמֶצֶת לֹא תֹאכֵלוּ״ –

The Gemara asks: **And Rabbi Eliezer, from where does he** derive the *halakha* that leaven in **its mixture** is included **in a prohibition?** The Gemara answers that he derives it from a verse, **as it is written: "You shall eat nothing leavened."**

אִי הָכִי – כָּרֵת נַמִי לִחַיֵּיב, דְּהָא כְּתִיב: ״כִּי כָּל אֹכֵל מַחְמֶצֶת וְנִכְרְתָה״.

The Gemara challenges this derivation: **If so,** if the term includes leaven in a mixture, **let one also be liable to** receive ***karet*** for eating leaven in a mixture. **As it is written:** "Seven days no leaven shall be found in your houses; **for whosoever eats anything leavened,** that soul **shall be cut off** from the people of Israel, whether he is a sojourner or one born in the land" (Exodus 12:19). Accordingly, one should be punished with *karet* for eating anything that contains leaven.

הַהוּא מִיבָּעֵי לֵיהּ לְכִדְתַנְיָא: (מַחְמֶצֶת) – אֵין לִי אֶלָּא שֶׁנִּתְחַמֵּץ מֵאֵלָיו, מֵחֲמַת דָּבָר אַחֵר מִנַּיִין – תַּלְמוּד לוֹמַר: ״כָּל מַחְמֶצֶת וְנִכְרְתָה״.

The Gemara answers that Rabbi Eliezer **needs that** phrase: Anything leavened, in order to derive **for that which was taught** in a *baraita*: From the phrase: Anything **leavened, I have** derived **only** that an item **that became leavened on its own** is prohibited. However, **from where** do I derive that one is punished with *karet* for eating an item that became leavened **due to a different factor? The verse states:** "Whosoever eats **anything leavened… shall be cut off,"** indicating that food that became leavened due to a different factor is considered leavened bread.

אִי הָכִי – דְּלָאו נַמִי לְהָכִי הוּא דַּאֲתָא.

The Gemara asks: **If so,** if the phrase: Anything leavened, is referring to food that became leavened by means of something else, then when this same phrase appears with regard **to the prohibition,** I should explain that it **comes for that** purpose **as well.** Consequently, there should be no violation for eating a mixture that contains leaven, as apparently, the phrase: Anything leavened, does not refer to that case at all.

אֶלָּא טַעְמָא דְּרַבִּי אֱלִיעֶזֶר מִ״כָּל״

Rather, the reason for the opinion of **Rabbi Eliezer** is that he derives this *halakha* **from** the term **anything** [*kol*]. He does not derive his opinion from the term leavened; he bases his ruling on the inclusive term anything.

הָתָם נַמִי, הָכְתִיב ״כָּל״. הַהוּא מִיבָּעֵי לֵיהּ לְרַבּוֹת אֶת הַנָּשִׁים.

The Gemara raises a difficulty: **There, too,** in the verse that mentions the punishment of *karet*, **isn't it written:** "For whosoever [*kol*] eats anything leavened, that soul shall be cut off"? The Gemara answers: Rabbi Eliezer **requires that** term **to include women** who are also punishable by *karet* for eating leavened bread.

נָשִׁים, מִדְּרַב יְהוּדָה אָמַר רַב נָפְקָא. דְּאָמַר רַב יְהוּדָה אָמַר רַב, וְכֵן תָּנָא דְּבֵי רַבִּי יִשְׁמָעֵאל, אָמַר קְרָא: ״אִישׁ אוֹ אִשָּׁה כִּי יַעֲשׂוּ מִכָּל חַטֹּאת הָאָדָם״ – הִשְׁוָה הַכָּתוּב אִישׁ לְאִשָּׁה לְכָל עוֹנָשִׁין שֶׁבַּתּוֹרָה!

The Gemara asks: Is this source necessary to derive this *halakha*? The fact that **women** may not eat leavened bread is **derived from** the statement that **Rav Yehuda** said that **Rav said. As Rav Yehuda said** that **Rav said, and similarly,** the Sage in **the school of Rabbi Yishmael taught: The verse said:** "Speak to the children of Israel: **A man or woman, when they commit any of the sins of men,** to commit a trespass against the Lord, and that soul shall be guilty" (Numbers 5:6). **The Torah rendered a man equal to a woman**[N] **for all punishments of the Torah.** Since the punishment of *karet* for eating leavened bread on Passover is included in this general principle, there is no need for a separate source to include women.

אִיצְטְרִיךְ,

The Gemara answers: Nonetheless, it is **necessary** to cite a source that men and women are equal specifically with regard to the punishment of *karet* for eating leavened bread,

NOTES

The Torah rendered a man equal to a woman – הִשְׁוָה הַכָּתוּב אִישׁ לְאִשָּׁה: This comparison is referring to those places where the Torah formulates the mitzva in the masculine form. In those cases, the Torah prohibition is incumbent upon all the Jewish people, including women. However, this derivation is unnecessary in cases where the verse speaks in the plural form, which applies equally to males and females. Furthermore, this principle does not apply if the verse specifically uses the term man (*Tosafot*).

Perek **III**
Daf **43** Amud **b**

סָלְקָא דַּעְתָּךְ אָמֵינָא: הוֹאִיל וּכְתִיב ״לֹא תֹאכַל עָלָיו חָמֵץ שִׁבְעַת יָמִים תֹּאכַל עָלָיו מַצּוֹת״ כֹּל שֶׁיֶּשְׁנוֹ בְּקוּם אֱכוֹל מַצָּה – יֶשְׁנוֹ בְּבַל תֹּאכַל חָמֵץ, וְהָנֵי נָשֵׁי הוֹאִיל וְלֵיתַנְהוּ בְּקוּם אֱכוֹל מַצָּה, דְּהָוְיָא לֵיהּ מִצְוַת עֲשֵׂה שֶׁהַזְּמַן גְּרָמָא (הִיא) – אֵימָא בְּבַל תֹּאכַל חָמֵץ נַמִי לֵיתַנְהוּ, קָא מַשְׁמַע לַן.

as **it could enter your mind to say** that **since it is written: "You shall eat no leavened bread with it; seven days you shall eat with it** *matzot*" (Deuteronomy 16:3), one might have thought that **anyone included** in the obligation **to eat** ***matza*** **is also included** in the **prohibition against eating leavened bread. And these women, since they are excluded** from the obligation **to eat** ***matza*****, as it is a time-bound, positive mitzva**[N] from which they are exempt as a rule, I might **say they are also excluded from the prohibition against eating leavened bread.** Therefore, the verse **teaches us** that women are also prohibited from eating leavened bread.

וְהַשְׁתָּא דְּאִתְרַבּוּ לְהוּ בְּבַל תֹּאכַל חָמֵץ – אִיתְרַבִּי נַמִי לַאֲכִילַת מַצָּה, כְּרַבִּי (אֱלִיעֶזֶר). דְּאָמַר רַבִּי אֱלִיעֶזֶר: נָשִׁים חַיָּיבוֹת בַּאֲכִילַת מַצָּה דְּבַר תּוֹרָה, שֶׁנֶּאֱמַר: ״לֹא תֹאכַל עָלָיו חָמֵץ וגו׳״ כֹּל שֶׁיֶּשְׁנוֹ בְּבַל תֹּאכַל חָמֵץ – יֶשְׁנוֹ בַּאֲכִילַת מַצָּה. וְהָנֵי נָשֵׁי נַמִי, הוֹאִיל וְיֶשְׁנָן בְּבַל תֹּאכַל חָמֵץ – יֶשְׁנָן בְּקוּם אֱכוֹל מַצָּה.

The Gemara comments: **And now** that women **have been included in the prohibition against eating leavened bread, they** should **also be included** in the obligation **to eat** ***matza***, even though it is a time-bound, positive mitzva, **in accordance with** the opinion of **Rabbi Eliezer. As Rabbi Eliezer said: Women are obligated to eat** ***matza*** **by Torah** law, **as it is stated: "You shall eat no leavened bread with it;** seven days you shall eat with it *matzot*" (Deuteronomy 16:3). These two commandments are juxtaposed to teach that **anyone included** in **the prohibition against eating leavened bread is** also **included in** the obligation **to eat** ***matza*****. And these women too, since they** are **included** in **the prohibition against eating leavened bread, they are** also **included in** the obligation **to eat** ***matza*****.**[H]

וּמַאי חָזֵית דְּהַאי ״כָּל״ לְרַבּוּיֵי נָשִׁים וּמַפֵּקְתְּ עֵירוּבוֹ, אֵימָא לְרַבּוּיֵי עֵירוּבוֹ!

The Gemara questions this derivation: **What did you see** that led you to understand **that** the term **anything** [*kol*] comes to **include women and to exclude** leaven in **its mixture?** On the contrary, **say** that it comes **to include** in the punishment of *karet* one who eats **its mixture.**

מִסְתַּבְּרָא, קָאֵי בְּאוֹכְלִין – מְרַבֶּה אוֹכְלִין, קָאֵי בְּאוֹכְלִין מְרַבֶּה נֶאֱכָלִין?!

The Gemara answers: **It is reasonable** to explain that the verse comes to include women since the verse is **dealing with those who** are obligated in the mitzva not to **eat** leavened bread, **it includes those who eat,** as the verse says: "For anyone who eats leavened bread… shall be cut off." It stands to reason that the expression: Anyone [*kol*] includes additional people who are punishable by *karet*, not additional types of leaven. Would a verse that **is dealing with those who** may not **eat** leaven come to **include** additional types of foods that may not **be eaten?**

NOTES

A time-bound, positive mitzva – מִצְוַת עֲשֵׂה שֶׁהַזְּמַן גְּרָמָא: This refers to a positive mitzva that can be performed only at a certain time of day, or during the day rather than at night, or on certain days of the year. Generally, women and slaves are exempt from mitzvot of this kind, although there are some time-bound mitzvot that women are required to perform, e.g., *kiddush* on Shabbat and prayer. Women and slaves are required to perform only mitzvot that are not restricted to a particular time for their performance, e.g., contributing to charity, affixing a *mezuza*, etc. However, there are certain exceptions, such as Torah study, from which women and slaves are exempt.

HALAKHA

Women are obligated to eat ***matza*** **– נָשִׁים חַיָּיבוֹת בְּמַצָּה:** Women are obligated by Torah law to eat *matza* just as men are, as stated in the Gemara. The same rule applies to all other mitzvot on the first night of Passover (Rambam *Sefer Zemanim, Hilkhot Ḥametz UMatza* 6:10; *Shulḥan Arukh, Oraḥ Ḥayyim* 472:14).

מַתְקִיף לָהּ רַב נָתָן אֲבוּהּ דְּרַב הוּנָא (בְּרֵיהּ דְּרַב נָתָן): וְכָל הֵיכָא דְּקָאֵי בְּאוֹכְלִין לֹא מַרְבֶּה נֶאֱכָלִין? וְהָא תַּנְיָא: "כִּי כָּל אֹכֵל חֵלֶב מִן הַבְּהֵמָה אֲשֶׁר יַקְרִיב", אֵין לִי אֶלָּא חֵלֶב תְּמִימִין שֶׁרְאוּיִ לִיקָּרֵב, חֵלֶב בַּעֲלֵי מוּמִין מִנַּיִן – תַּלְמוּד לוֹמַר: "מִן הַבְּהֵמָה". חֵלֶב חוּלִּין מִנַּיִן – תַּלְמוּד לוֹמַר: "כִּי כָּל". וְהָא הָכָא, דְּקָאֵי בְּאוֹכְלִין וְקָא מַרְבֶּה נֶאֱכָלִין!

Rav Natan, father of Rav Huna, son of Rav Natan,[N] **strongly objects to this: And anywhere that** a verse **is dealing with those who eat, does** it necessarily **not** come to **include** additional **types of food** in the prohibition? **Wasn't it taught** in a *baraita*: **"For anyone who eats the fat of the domesticated animal, of which men present** an offering of fire to God, the soul that eats it shall be cut off from its people" (Leviticus 7:25)? The Sages interpreted this verse: **I have** derived from this verse that the prohibition applies **only** to the **fats of unblemished** animals **that are fit to be sacrificed. From where** is it derived that it is also prohibited to eat the **fats of blemished animals,** which may not be offered as sacrifices? **The verse states: "Of the domesticated animal." From where** is it derived that it is prohibited to eat the **fats of non-sacred** animals? **The verse states: "For anyone** who eats the fat." Rav Natan explains his objection: **Here, isn't** the verse **dealing with those who eat** fats, and nevertheless, its superfluous phrases come to **include** types of foods that may not **be eaten.**

הָתָם דְּלֵיכָּא אוֹכְלִין – מַרְבֶּה נֶאֱכָלִין, הָכָא דְּאִיכָּא אוֹכְלִין – לָא שָׁבֵיק לְהוּ לְאוֹכְלִין וּמַרְבֶּה נֶאֱכָלִין.

The Gemara answers: **There,** in the verse concerning prohibited fats, **where there are no** additional people **who eat** of it to include, as the prohibition already applies to everyone, the superfluous expression comes **to include** additional **foods. Here,** in the verse that deals with leavened bread, **where there are** people **who eat** of it who can be included, namely women, the verse does **not exclude** people **who eat and include** foods that are **eaten.**[N] Generally, there should be a connection between the content of a verse and that which is derived from it. Only when no other derivation is possible is a less related matter derived.

וְרַבָּנַן דְּלֵית לְהוּ עֵירוּב – "כָּל" לָא דָּרְשִׁי. אֶלָּא, נָשִׁים מְנָא לְהוּ?

The Gemara explains: **And the Rabbis, who are not of** the opinion that leaven in a **mixture** is included in the prohibition, **do not interpret** that the term: **Anything** [*kol*], comes to include other matters;[N] neither with regard to leaven in a mixture nor with regard to *karet*. The Gemara asks: **However,** in that case, **from where do they** derive that it is prohibited for **women** to eat leavened bread?

"כָּל" – לָא דָּרְשִׁי, "כִּי כָּל" דָּרְשִׁי.

The Gemara answers: Although **they do not derive** a *halakha* from the term: **Anything, they derive** a *halakha* from the expression: **For anyone** [*ki kol*], in the verse: "For anyone who eats leaven."

וְרַבִּי אֱלִיעֶזֶר, אֵימָא: "כָּל" – לְרַבּוֹת אֶת הַנָּשִׁים, "כִּי כָּל" – לְרַבּוֹת אֶת עֵירוּבוֹ!

The Gemara asks: **And** if indeed the phrase: For anyone, is a more inclusive expression than the simple word anything, then according **to Rabbi Eliezer,** another *halakha* could also be derived from here. **Say** that the phrase: **Anyone** who eats leaven, comes **to include the women,** and the phrase: **For anyone** who eats, comes **to include** leaven in **its mixture.** According to Rabbi Eliezer, then, one would be punishable by *karet* for eating leaven in a mixture.

וְכִי תֵּימָא: "כִּי כָּל" – רַבִּי אֱלִיעֶזֶר לָא דָּרֵישׁ – וְהָתַנְיָא: "שְׂאֹר בַּל תַּקְטִירוּ" אֵין לִי אֶלָּא כּוּלּוֹ, מִקְצָתוֹ מִנַּיִן – תַּלְמוּד לוֹמַר: "כָּל". עֵירוּבוֹ מִנַּיִן – תַּלְמוּד לוֹמַר: "כִּי כָּל". מַאן שָׁמְעַתְּ לֵיהּ דְּדָרֵישׁ "כָּל" – רַבִּי אֱלִיעֶזֶר, וְקָא דָּרֵישׁ "כִּי כָּל".

And lest you say that Rabbi Eliezer does not derive a *halakha* from the phrase: **For anyone** [*ki kol*], as he does not consider this an inclusive expression, the result would be another contradiction. **Wasn't** it **taught** in another *baraita*: "For no [*ki kol*] leaven nor any honey shall be offered as a burnt-offering before God" (Leviticus 2:11)? Had the verse stated only: **You shall not offer leaven, I would have** derived **nothing other** than the *halakha* that it is prohibited to sacrifice **an entire** piece of leaven. **From where** is it derived that it is also prohibited to sacrifice **part of it? The verse states: "No** [*kol*] leaven," indicating that it is prohibited to sacrifice even part of it. **From where** is it derived that it is prohibited to sacrifice leaven in **a mixture?**[NH] **The verse states: "For no** [*ki kol*] leaven." The Gemara analyzes this statement: **Whom did you hear who derives** *halakhot* from the term: *Kol*? It is **Rabbi Eliezer,**[N] **and** nevertheless, **he derives** additional details from the expression: ***Ki kol.***

קַשְׁיָא.

The Gemara concludes: This matter remains **difficult,** as no satisfactory explanation has been found for why Rabbi Eliezer does not derive from the expression *ki kol* that leaven in a mixture is also prohibited.

NOTES

Rav Natan, father of Rav Huna, son of Rav Natan – רַב נָתָן אֲבוּהּ דְּרַב הוּנָא בְּרֵיהּ דְּרַב נָתָן: Some versions of the text read only: Rav Natan, father of Rav Huna. However, it is likely that the version cited here is correct. The Gemara first identifies Rav Natan by means of his son Rav Huna. As this Rav Huna is not the Rav Huna whose opinions are typically cited, the Gemara indicates that this is another Rav Huna by repeating his father's name.

Include foods that are eaten – מַרְבֶּה נֶאֱכָלִין: Apparently, Rabbi Eliezer derives the prohibition against eating additional foods from a verse that mentions those who may eat. The reason is that he interprets the verses: "For anyone who eats leaven" and "For anyone who eats fat" in a similar manner to the verse: "All forgive iniquity" (Hosea 14:3). This verse is interpreted as though the words were reversed: God will forgive all iniquity. Here too, the verse can be read: "As one who eats any type of fat" (Rashash).

The Rabbis…do not interpret the term: Anything [*kol*], to include other matters – רַבָּנַן...כָּל לָא דָּרְשִׁי: Although a derivation of this kind is common and logical, it is possible that the Gemara means that the Rabbis, unlike Rabbi Eliezer, do not interpret the term: Anything, to include matters beyond the clear meaning of the verse (See *Tosafot*; Maharam Ḥalawa).

From where is it derived that it is prohibited to sacrifice leaven in a mixture – עֵירוּבוֹ מִנַּיִן: Some commentaries accept Rashi's explanation that this *halakha* applies to half an olive-bulk of leaven in a mixture. However, others maintain that this prohibition applies even when there is any amount of leaven present; as long as the leaven contributes taste to the mixture, it may not be burned on the altar (Maharam Ḥalawa).

Rabbi Eliezer derives *halakhot* from the term *kol* – רַבִּי אֱלִיעֶזֶר דּוֹרֵשׁ כָּל: This statement is surprising, as there is no evidence that Rabbi Eliezer derives *halakhot* from other instances of the word *kol*, e.g., "Any [*kol*] blood" (Leviticus 7:26); "Any [*kol*] fish that does not have fins and scales" (Deuteronomy 14:10); et al. Apparently Rabbi Eliezer derives *halakhot* from the word *kol* only with regard to prohibitions in which there are not many different categories, as in those prohibitions *kol* merely refers to the existing categories and does not come to include anything beyond them (see the Ra'avad's critique of the commentary of *Ba'al HaMaor*).

HALAKHA

Burning leaven in a mixture – הַקְטָרַת תַּעֲרוֹבֶת שְׂאוֹר: One who offers leaven on the altar is punished with lashes, even if the leaven is only part of a mixture (Rambam *Sefer Avoda*, *Hilkhot Issurei Mizbe'aḥ* 5:1).

אָמַר רַבִּי אַבָּהוּ אָמַר רַבִּי יוֹחָנָן: כׇּל אִיסּוּרִין שֶׁבַּתּוֹרָה אֵין הֶיתֵּר מִצְטָרֵף לְאִיסּוּר, חוּץ מֵאִיסּוּרֵי נָזִיר, שֶׁהֲרֵי אָמְרָה תּוֹרָה ״מִשְׁרַת״.

After discussing leaven in a mixture, the Gemara states a more general principle. **Rabbi Abbahu said** that **Rabbi Yoḥanan said: With regard to all prohibitions of the Torah, a permitted** substance **does not join together with a prohibited** substance. If one eats a permitted food with a prohibited food, and together they constitute the minimum prohibited measure, he is exempt from punishment for this act of consumption. This principle applies to all *halakhot* **except for the prohibitions of a nazirite,** who is liable for eating a mixture of that kind, **as the Torah said** with regard to a nazirite: "He shall abstain from wine and strong drink; he shall drink no vinegar of wine, or vinegar of strong drink, nor shall he drink anything **soaked** in grapes" (Numbers 6:3). This verse indicates that a nazirite is prohibited from consuming not only wine and vinegar, but also any food that was soaked in these liquids.

וּזְעֵירִי אָמַר: אַף שְׂאוֹר בַּל תַּקְטִירוּ.

And Ze'eiri said: Permitted and prohibited substances **also** combine with regard to **the prohibition against offering leaven** on the altar, as it states: "For no [*kol*] leaven and no [*kol*] honey shall be offered as a burnt-offering before the Lord" (Leviticus 2:11). This indicates that one is also liable for sacrificing leaven in a mixture (*Tosafot*) in addition to the liability for sacrificing pure leaven.

כְּמַאן – כְּרַבִּי אֱלִיעֶזֶר, דְּדָרֵישׁ ״כׇּל״.

The Gemara asks: **In accordance with whose** opinion did Ze'eiri issue his ruling? It is **in accordance with** the opinion of **Rabbi Eliezer, who derives** from the term ***kol*** that any mixture that contains any amount of a prohibited substance is not nullified.

אִי הָכִי –

The Gemara raises a difficulty: **If so,**

Perek **III**
Daf **44** Amud **a**

לְעִנְיַן חָמֵץ בְּפֶסַח נָמֵי.

with regard **to the matter of leavened bread on Passover** one should **also** be liable[N] for eating a prohibited substance joined together with a permitted substance.

אִין הָכִי נָמֵי, וּלְאַפּוֹקֵי מִדְּאַבָּיֵי, דְּאָמַר: יֵשׁ הַקְטָרָה לְפָחוֹת מִכְּזַיִת, קָמַשְׁמַע לַן: דְּהַקְטָרָה לָאו לְפָחוֹת מִכְּזַיִת.

The Gemara answers: **Yes, indeed it is so, and** the prohibition mentioned by Ze'eiri against sacrificing leaven in offerings was only **to exclude** the statement **of Abaye, who said: There is** significance to **offering less than an olive-bulk** of leaven on the altar,[H] and one is flogged for sacrificing an offering of that kind. By noting that one is liable because permitted substances combine with prohibited substances, the *baraita* **teaches us that an offering** of **less than an olive-bulk** is **not** considered an offering, and therefore sacrificing it is not punishable by lashes.

יָתֵיב רַב דִּימִי וְקָאָמַר לַהּ לְהָא שְׁמַעְתָּא. אֲמַר לֵיהּ אַבָּיֵי לְרַב דִּימִי: וְכׇל אִיסּוּרִין שֶׁבַּתּוֹרָה אֵין הֶיתֵּר מִצְטָרֵף לְאִיסּוּר?

Rav Dimi sat and stated this *halakha* that a permitted substance does not join together with a prohibited substance to constitute the requisite measure, except in the case of a nazirite. **Abaye said to Rav Dimi: And** is it true that with regard to **all** other **prohibitions in the Torah, a permitted** substance **does not join together with a prohibited** substance?

וְהָתְנַן: הַמִּקְפָּה שֶׁל תְּרוּמָה, וְהַשּׁוּם וְהַשֶּׁמֶן שֶׁל חוּלִּין, וְנָגַע טְבוּל יוֹם בְּמִקְצָתָן – פָּסַל אֶת כּוּלָּן. הַמִּקְפָּה שֶׁל חוּלִּין וְהַשּׁוּם וְהַשֶּׁמֶן שֶׁל תְּרוּמָה וְנָגַע טְבוּל יוֹם בְּמִקְצָתָן – לֹא פָּסַל אֶלָּא מְקוֹם מַגָּעוֹ בִּלְבַד.

But didn't we learn in a mishna: With regard to thick **soup**[N] prepared **with *teruma***[H] produce whose **garlic and oil** are **of non-sacred** produce, **and one who immersed himself during that day touched some of** the ingredients, **he disqualified all** the contents of the pot, as they are subsumed within the *teruma* soup. However, if the thick **soup** was prepared **with non-sacred** produce[H] **and the garlic and the oil were of *teruma*, and one who immersed himself during that day touched some of them, he disqualifies only** the ingredients in the **place that he touched.**

NOTES

For eating leavened bread on Passover one should also be liable – חָמֵץ בְּפֶסַח נָמֵי: Some commentaries interpret this statement as referring to all prohibited items in the Torah, not just leaven; however, as the Gemara was discussing Passover and leaven it cited this example (Maharam Ḥalawa).

Thick soup – מִקְפָּה: Elsewhere Rashi explains that this soup was prepared from a mixture of wine, spices, and pounded wheat or barley.

HALAKHA

The measure of leaven that it is prohibited to offer – שִׁיעוּר הַקְטָרַת שְׂאוֹר: It is prohibited to offer any amount of leaven on the altar, and one who offers an olive-bulk is flogged. The punishment is administered only for this quantity because less than an olive-bulk is not considered an actual offering. This ruling is in accordance with the opinion of Rava, as the *halakha* is ruled in accordance with his opinion in disputes with Abaye (Rambam *Sefer Avoda, Hilkhot Issurei Mizbe'aḥ* 5:2).

Thick soup with *teruma* – מִקְפָּה וּתְרוּמָה: If one who immersed himself during that day touches a mixture of thick soup made with *teruma* produce and non-sacred garlic and oil, the entire mixture is disqualified (Rambam *Sefer Tahara, Hilkhot Tumat Okhalin* 8:12).

Thick soup with non-sacred produce – מִקְפַּת חוּלִּין: If one who immersed himself during that day touches a thick soup of non-sacred produce and *teruma* garlic and oil, he disqualifies only that portion of the soup with which he came into contact (Rambam *Sefer Tahara, Hilkhot Tumat Okhalin* 8:13).

וְהָוֵינַן בָּהּ: מְקוֹם מַגָּעוֹ אַמַּאי פְּסוּלָה? הָא בָּטְלִי לְהוּ תַּבְלִין בְּרוֹב! וְאָמַר רַבָּה בַּר בַּר חָנָה: מַה טַּעַם – הוֹאִיל וְזָר לוֹקֶה עֲלֵיהֶן בִּכְזַיִת. הֵיכִי דָּמֵי – לָאו מִשּׁוּם דְּהֶיתֵּר מִצְטָרֵף לְאִיסּוּר?

Abaye continues. **And we discussed this** issue: **Why are the** ingredients in the **place that he touched disqualified?** The **spices,** i.e., the garlic or oil, **are nullified by the majority.** Since the major portion of the dish is composed of non-sacred produce, it should not be disqualified by contact with one who immersed himself during that day. **And Rabba bar bar Ḥana said** in reply: **What is the reason** that it becomes disqualified? It is **since a non-priest is flogged for** eating **an olive-bulk** of the soup, as anything into which *teruma* is mixed is considered *teruma* by Torah law. **What are the circumstances** of this ruling that a non-priest is flogged? Is it **not due to** the fact **that the permitted** substance **joins together with the prohibited** substance?

לֹא, מַאי כַּזַּיִת – דְּאִיכָּא כַּזַּיִת בִּכְדֵי אֲכִילַת פְּרָס.

Rav Dimi rejects this contention: **No; what is** the meaning of **an olive-bulk** in this mishna? It means **that there is** sufficient *teruma* in the mixture that when one eats from the mixture he will consume **an olive-bulk** of *teruma* **in the time it takes to eat a half-loaf**[H] of bread.[N] In that case one is liable for punishment for eating this olive-bulk, as if he ate the *teruma* alone.

וְכַזַּיִת בִּכְדֵי אֲכִילַת פְּרָס דְּאוֹרַיְיתָא הִיא? אָמַר לֵיהּ: אִין.

Abaye asked him: **Is** eating **an olive-bulk in the time it takes to eat a half-loaf** of bread prohibited **by Torah** law, and one is punished for it? He **said to him: Yes.**

אִי הָכִי, אַמַּאי פְּלִיגִי רַבָּנַן עֲלֵיהּ דְּרַבִּי אֱלִיעֶזֶר בְּכוּתָּח הַבַּבְלִי?

Abaye asked in response: **If so, why do the Rabbis disagree with Rabbi Eliezer**[N] **with regard to** eating **Babylonian *kutaḥ*,** a dip that contains flour, on Passover? The Rabbis maintain that one is not punished by Torah law for eating a mixture containing leaven. Although the Rabbis do not derive from the word: Anything [*kol*], that leaven in a mixture is prohibited, they should nonetheless hold one liable for eating an olive-bulk of a prohibited substance in the time it takes to eat a half-loaf of bread.

אֶלָּא מַאי – מִשּׁוּם דְּהֶיתֵּר מִצְטָרֵף לְאִיסּוּר, סוֹף סוֹף אַמַּאי פְּלִיגִי רַבָּנַן עֲלֵיהּ דְּרַבִּי אֱלִיעֶזֶר בְּכוּתָּח הַבַּבְלִי? אֶלָּא: הַנַּח לְכוּתָּח הַבַּבְלִי, דְּלֵית בֵּיהּ כַּזַּיִת בִּכְדֵי אֲכִילַת פְּרָס. אִי בְּעֵינֵיהּ דְּקָשָׂרֵיף וְקָאָכֵיל לֵיהּ – בָּטְלָה דַּעְתֵּיהּ אֵצֶל כׇּל אָדָם, וְאִי מִשְׁטַר קָשָׁטַר וְאָכֵיל – לֵית בֵּיהּ כַּזַּיִת בִּכְדֵי אֲכִילַת פְּרָס.

Rav Dimi said: **Rather, what** conclusion must be drawn; the reason that a non-priest is flogged for eating the *teruma* soup is **due to** the fact that a **permitted** substance **joins together with a prohibited** substance? If so, **ultimately, why do the Rabbis disagree with Rabbi Eliezer with regard to** eating **Babylonian *kutaḥ*? Rather, leave Babylonian *kutaḥ*, as** in eating that mixture **there is no** possibility that one will consume **an olive-bulk** of the leaven **in the time it takes to eat a half-loaf** of bread. **If he eats *kutaḥ* in its pure,** unadulterated form, **by swallowing it** as food, not as a dip, **his intention is** rendered **irrelevant**[N] by the opinions of **all** other **people.** It is unusual for a person to eat a pungent dip by itself, all the more so, for him to eat it so quickly. One receives no punishment for conduct that anomalous. **And if he dips** other food into the *kutaḥ* **and eats** it, he will **not** consume **an olive-bulk in the time it takes to eat a half-loaf** of bread. Due to the pungency of the dip, one needs to add only a small portion to his food.

אֵיתִיבֵיהּ: שְׁתֵּי קְדֵירוֹת, אַחַת שֶׁל חוּלִּין וְאַחַת שֶׁל תְּרוּמָה, וְלִפְנֵיהֶן שְׁתֵּי מְדוֹכוֹת, אַחַת שֶׁל חוּלִּין וְאַחַת שֶׁל תְּרוּמָה, וְנָפְלוּ אֵלּוּ לְתוֹךְ אֵלּוּ – מוּתָּרִין. שֶׁאֲנִי אוֹמֵר: תְּרוּמָה לְתוֹךְ הַתְּרוּמָה נָפְלָה, וְחוּלִּין לְתוֹךְ חוּלִּין נָפְלוּ.

Abaye **raised an objection to** Rav Dimi from a *baraita*: With regard to **two pots, one of non-sacred** produce **and the other one of *teruma*, before which** were **two mortars,** one in **which non-sacred** produce was pounded, **and one** in which ***teruma*** produce was pounded, **and** the contents of **these** mortars **fell into these** pots, but it is unknown which produce fell into which pot, **it is** all **permitted.** The reason for this ruling is **as I say,** since there is no definitive proof to the contrary, that the ***teruma* fell into the *teruma*** and the **non-sacred produce fell into** the **non-sacred produce.**

וְאִי אָמְרַתְּ כַּזַּיִת בִּכְדֵי אֲכִילַת פְּרָס דְּאוֹרַיְיתָא – אַמַּאי אָמְרִינַן ״שֶׁאֲנִי אוֹמֵר תְּרוּמָה לְתוֹךְ כו׳״? אָמַר לֵיהּ: הַנַּח לִתְרוּמַת תַּבְלִין דְּרַבָּנַן.

Abaye explains his objection: **And if you say** that eating **an olive-bulk** of a prohibited substance **in the time it takes to eat a half-loaf** of bread is prohibited **by Torah** law, **why do we say** this principle: **As I say**[N] **that the *teruma*** fell **into the** *teruma*, **etc.?** If the *teruma* produce fell into the pot containing non-sacred produce, one who eats from the mixture will consume an olive-bulk of *teruma* within the time it takes to eat a half-loaf of bread, and he will thereby violate a Torah prohibition. Rav Dimi **said to him: Leave *teruma*** separated from **spices,** which is *teruma* **by rabbinic** law. By Torah law one is required to separate *teruma* only from grain, wine and oil. The Sages are lenient with regard to *teruma* by rabbinic law.

HALAKHA

An olive-bulk in the time it takes to eat a half-loaf – כַּזַּיִת בִּכְדֵי אֲכִילַת פְּרָס: One who eats an olive-bulk of a prohibited substance in the time it takes to eat a half-loaf of bread is liable for punishment by Torah law as though he ate the entire olive-bulk all at once (Rambam *Sefer Kedusha, Hilkhot Ma'akhalot Assurot* 14:8).

NOTES

In the time it takes to eat a half-loaf of bread – בִּכְדֵי אֲכִילַת פְּרָס: Loaves of bread in *halakha* are assumed to have the fixed measure of six egg-bulks. The duration of this time period is the subject of considerable controversy. Opinions with regard to its length vary between two and nine minutes. This unit of time plays an important role in many *halakhot* related to food consumption.

Why do the Rabbis disagree with Rabbi Eliezer – אַמַּאי פְּלִיגִי רַבָּנַן עֲלֵיהּ דְּרַבִּי אֱלִיעֶזֶר: How did Abaye understand this issue? Rav Dimi demonstrated that this case is difficult regardless of how it is interpreted. Some commentaries explain that according to Abaye, the leaven in *kutaḥ* does not contribute flavor and is therefore nullified (Maharam Ḥalawa).

His intention is rendered irrelevant – בָּטְלָה דַּעְתּוֹ: There are two explanations of the relevance of this concept to the current discussion: According to Rashi, eating in this manner is not considered a form of eating at all, as this action deviates greatly from the societal norm. Therefore, one is entirely exempt for eating *kutaḥ* in that manner. Indeed, one is exempt for any consumption of this kind. According to *Tosafot*, although one who eats *kutaḥ* in this manner is in fact liable, the mishna did not address that case, as it is so unusual (Rabbi Shimon HaKohen).

As I say, and Torah law – שֶׁאֲנִי אוֹמֵר וּדְאוֹרַיְיתָא: The ruling that the *teruma* fell into the *teruma* must be a rabbinic leniency, based on the following rationale: Since it cannot be proven that the mixture is prohibited, and it might in fact be permitted, one may rely on that possibility. However, this applies only to an item that is not prohibited by Torah law, in accordance with the principle that the Sages were not lenient with regard to Torah prohibitions. It is only with regard to their own stringencies and decrees that they were lenient.

אֵיתִיבֵיהּ: שְׁתֵּי קוּפּוֹת, אַחַת שֶׁל חוּלִּין וְאַחַת שֶׁל תְּרוּמָה, וְלִפְנֵיהֶם שְׁנֵי סְאִין אַחַת שֶׁל חוּלִּין וְאַחַת שֶׁל תְּרוּמָה, וְנָפְלוּ אֵלּוּ לְתוֹךְ אֵלּוּ – מוּתָּרִין, שֶׁאֲנִי אוֹמֵר: חוּלִּין לְתוֹךְ חוּלִּין נָפְלוּ, תְּרוּמָה לְתוֹךְ תְּרוּמָה נָפְלָה. וְאִי אָמְרַתְּ כַּזַּיִת בִּכְדֵי אֲכִילַת פְּרָס דְּאוֹרַיְיתָא – אַמַּאי אָמְרִינַן ״שֶׁאֲנִי אוֹמֵר״?

Abaye **raised** another **objection** from a similar *baraita*: In a case where there are **two baskets, one** filled with **non-sacred** produce **and the other** filled with *teruma*, **and before them** were **two** vessels each containing a *se'a* of produce, **one** filled with **non-sacred** produce **and** the other **one** filled **with** *teruma*, **and these,** the contents of each of the baskets, **fell into those,** each of the *se'a* vessels. It is possible that the *teruma* fell into the non-sacred produce, and it is prohibited for non-priests to eat a mixture of *teruma* and non-sacred produce. Nevertheless, the contents of the *se'a* vessel containing the non-sacred produce are **permitted, as I say** that **the non-sacred produce fell into the non-sacred produce and the** ***teruma*** **fell into the** ***teruma***. The obligation to separate *teruma* from grain is by Torah law, **and if you say** that eating **an olive-bulk** of forbidden food **in the time it takes to eat a half-loaf** of bread is prohibited **by Torah** law, **why do we say** the principle: **As I say** the non-sacred grain fell into the non-sacred grain? Why aren't the Sages concerned that one might eat an olive-bulk of *teruma* in the time it takes to eat a half-loaf, which is prohibited by Torah law?

אָמַר לֵיהּ: הַנַּח לִתְרוּמָה בַּזְּמַן הַזֶּה, דְּרַבָּנַן.

He said to him: Leave ***teruma*** **in modern times,**[NH] as it is in effect **by rabbinic** law. Once the Jewish people were exiled from their land, the *halakhot* of *teruma* and tithes apply by rabbinic law, not Torah law. This is the basis for the lenient ruling in the case of this mixture.

וְהַאי ״מִשְׁרַת״ לְהָכִי הוּא דַּאֲתָא? הַאי מִיבָּעֵי לֵיהּ לְכִדְתַנְיָא: ״מִשְׁרַת״ –

The Gemara returns to its discussion of Rabbi Abbahu's statement with regard to the meaning of the word soaked in the verse: "He shall abstain from wine and strong drink; he shall drink no vinegar of wine, or vinegar of strong drink, nor shall he drink anything soaked in grapes," and whether or not a permitted substance combines with a prohibited one. The Gemara asks: **And does this** word: **Soaked, come to** teach **that** mixtures are prohibited in this case? That verse **is required to** derive **that which was taught** in a *baraita* elsewhere: **Soaked,**

NOTES

Teruma in modern times – תְּרוּמָה בַּזְּמַן הַזֶּה: The *Me'iri* explains that this statement is referring to the areas of Eretz Yisrael that were not consecrated upon the return of the Babylonian exiles led by Ezra at the beginning of the Second Temple era. Even those authorities who maintain that the mitzva to separate *teruma* in modern times is by Torah law, agree that in those areas of Eretz Yisrael, the obligation is by rabbinic law.

HALAKHA

Teruma in modern times – תְּרוּמָה בַּזְּמַן הַזֶּה: The *halakhot* of *teruma* apply nowadays by rabbinic decree only. By Torah law, these *halakhot* are in effect only in Eretz Yisrael and only when the entire Jewish people dwells there (*Shulḥan Arukh, Yoreh De'a* 331:2).

Perek **III**
Daf **44** Amud **b**

לִיתֵּן טַעַם כְּעִיקָּר שֶׁאִם שָׁרָה עֲנָבִים בְּמַיִם וְיֵשׁ בָּהֶן טַעַם יַיִן – חַיָּיב.

comes **to establish** the principle that the legal status of the **taste** of a forbidden food is **like** that of its **substance.** This term teaches that any food that absorbs the taste of a prohibited item assumes the status of this prohibited item itself. **As,** in a case **where one soaked grapes in water and** the water **has the taste of wine,** a nazirite **is liable** for drinking this mixture, as it assumes the status of wine.

מִכָּאן אַתָּה דָּן לְכָל הַתּוֹרָה כּוּלָּהּ: וּמָה נָזִיר שֶׁאֵין אִיסּוּרוֹ אִיסּוּר עוֹלָם, וְאֵין אִיסּוּרוֹ אִיסּוּר הֲנָאָה, וְיֵשׁ הֶיתֵּר לְאִיסּוּרוֹ – עָשָׂה בּוֹ טַעַם כְּעִיקָּר. כִּלְאַיִם, שֶׁאִיסּוּרוֹ אִיסּוּר עוֹלָם, וְאִיסּוּרוֹ אִיסּוּר הֲנָאָה, וְאֵין הֶיתֵּר לְאִיסּוּרוֹ – אֵינוֹ דִּין שֶׁיַּעֲשֶׂה טַעַם כְּעִיקָּר.

From here you derive the *halakha* with regard **to the entire Torah;** in all cases, the legal status of the taste of a forbidden food is like that of its substance. The Gemara elaborates. **Just as** with regard to **a nazirite, whose prohibition** against eating grapes **is not an eternal prohibition,** as he will be permitted to eat grapes once his period of naziriteship is over, **and** furthermore, **his prohibition is not a prohibition** against deriving **benefit** from wine, **and there is dissolution for his prohibition** against eating grape products by requesting a Sage to release him from his vow, nevertheless, in **his** case, the Torah **rendered** the legal status of the **taste** of food forbidden to him **like** that of its **substance;**[H] with regard to a forbidden mixture of **diverse kinds, whose prohibition is an eternal prohibition** [***issuro issur olam***][N] **and whose prohibition is a prohibition** against deriving **benefit, and there is no dissolution for its prohibition, is it not right that** the Torah **should render** the legal status of the **taste** of its forbidden food **like** that of its **substance?**

HALAKHA

The legal status of the taste like that of its substance – טַעַם כְּעִיקָּר: If a mixture of wine and another substance has the taste of wine, this substance is prohibited to a nazirite as though it were wine. The same principle applies to other foods that absorb the taste of a prohibited item (Rambam *Sefer Hafla'a, Hilkhot Nezirut* 5:5).

NOTES

Whose prohibition is an eternal prohibition [*issuro issur olam*], etc. – אִיסּוּרוֹ אִיסּוּר עוֹלָם וכו׳: The commentaries disagree about the precise meaning of this statement. Many commentaries reject Rashi's explanation, that the length of the term of naziriteship is determined by the vow taken by the nazirite (see *Tosafot*). The major objection to Rashi's interpretation is that it is not completely consistent with regard to the phrase: *Issuro issur olam*, as well to as the phrase: *Ein hetter le'issuro* and the opposite: *Yesh hetter le'issuro*.

Some explain these terms in the following manner: *Yesh hetter le'issuro* means: Effecting its prohibition is permitted, i.e., it is permitted to take action to cause this prohibition to take effect. This is true of the nazirite, as one may take a vow to become a nazirite, thereby rendering himself prohibited to consume grape products. Likewise, it is permitted to plant a tree and thereby cause the prohibition of *orla* to come into effect. By contrast, it is prohibited to plant forbidden mixtures, and therefore: *Ein hetter le'issuro*, effecting that prohibition is prohibited (*Tosefot Rabbeinu Peretz*; *Tosefot Rabbi Shimshon of Saens*; *Me'iri*).

Yet others explain that the term: *Issuro issur olam*, means that this prohibition applies universally, even to all descendants of Noah, as it was in effect even before the revelation at Sinai. The prohibitions of a nazirite and *orla* do not fall into this category, as they apply only to the Jewish people. However, the prohibition of diverse kinds was in effect for Adam as well, and consequently their prohibition is eternal (Maharam Ḥalawa).

וְהוּא הַדִּין לְעׇרְלָה בִּשְׁתַּיִם.

And the same is true of fruit that grows on a tree during the first three years after it was planted [*orla*], on two of three counts: Although the prohibition of *orla* is not an eternal prohibition, as one may eat the fruit of this tree after three years have passed, it is prohibited to derive benefit from *orla*, and this prohibition cannot be dissolved, as the fruits that grow during the first three years remain prohibited. Therefore, based on the same *a fortiori* inference, the principle: The legal status of its taste is like that of its substance, should apply in this case as well. Similarly, all other prohibitions in the Torah are more severe than the case of a nazirite in one of these aspects, and therefore this principle is universal. In any case, this entire derivation presents a difficulty for Rabbi Yoḥanan, who derives a different *halakha* from the term: Soaked.

הָא מַנִּי – רַבָּנַן הִיא, וְרַבִּי יוֹחָנָן דְּאָמַר כְּרַבִּי עֲקִיבָא.

The Gemara answers: In accordance with **whose opinion** is the previously cited derivation? **It is** in accordance with the opinion of **the Rabbis,** who derive this *halakha* from the term: Soaked. However, **Rabbi Yoḥanan, who said** that a permitted substance joins together with a prohibited substance, holds **in accordance with** the opinion of **Rabbi Akiva.**

הֵי רַבִּי עֲקִיבָא? אִילֵימָא רַבִּי עֲקִיבָא דְּמַתְנִיתִין, דִּתְנַן: רַבִּי עֲקִיבָא אוֹמֵר, נָזִיר שֶׁשָּׁרָה פִּתּוֹ בְּיַיִן, וְיֵשׁ בּוֹ לְצָרֵף כְּדֵי כַּזַּיִת – חַיָּיב. וּמִמַּאי דְּמִפַּת וּמִיַּיִן? דִּילְמָא מִיַּיִן לְחוּדֵיהּ.

The Gemara asks: To **which** statement of **Rabbi Akiva** is the Gemara referring? **If you say** it is referring to the opinion of **Rabbi Akiva** in the following **mishna, as we learned: Rabbi Akiva says,** with regard to **a nazirite who soaked his bread in wine,**[H] **and** the bread and the wine **contain** enough **to join together to** constitute **an olive-bulk,**[N] that **he is liable; from where do we** know **that** Rabbi Akiva means an amount of an olive-bulk taken **from the bread and the wine** together? **Perhaps** he meant that the measure is calculated **from the wine alone?**

וְכִי תֵּימָא: מִיַּיִן לְחוּדֵיהּ מַאי לְמֵימְרָא – הָא קָא מַשְׁמַע לָן: דְּאַף עַל גַּב דְּתַעֲרוֹבֶת.

The Gemara asks: **And lest you say** that if this amount is **from** the **wine alone, what** purpose is there **to state** this *halakha*, **this** statement comes to **teach us that even though** the prohibited item is **in a mixture,** one is nonetheless liable for consuming it. Since this mishna can be explained as referring to an olive-bulk from wine alone, it cannot be cited as proof for Rabbi Akiva's opinion with regard to the combination of a permitted substance with a prohibited substance.

אֶלָּא רַבִּי עֲקִיבָא דְּבָרַיְיתָא. דְּתַנְיָא, רַבִּי עֲקִיבָא אוֹמֵר: נָזִיר שֶׁשָּׁרָה פִּתּוֹ בְּיַיִן, וְאָכַל כַּזַּיִת מִפַּת וּמִיַּיִן – חַיָּיב.

The Gemara states: **Rather,** Rabbi Yoḥanan holds in accordance with the opinion of **Rabbi Akiva in the *baraita*, as it was taught** in a *baraita* that **Rabbi Akiva says: A nazirite who soaked his bread in wine and ate an olive-bulk** of the mixture **from the bread and** the **wine is liable.** This *baraita* indicates that according to Rabbi Akiva, a permitted substance joins together with a prohibited substance.

וְרַבִּי עֲקִיבָא, טַעַם כְּעִיקָּר מְנָא לֵיהּ? יָלֵיף מִבָּשָׂר בְּחָלָב. לָאו טַעְמָא בְּעָלְמָא הוּא וְאָסוּר – הָכָא נַמִי, לָא שְׁנָא.

The Gemara asks: **And Rabbi Akiva, from where** does he derive the principle: The legal status of the **taste** is **like** that of the **substance**[N] itself? The Gemara answers: **He derives** this principle from the prohibition of **meat** cooked **in milk.** In that case, there is **merely** the **taste** of the milk absorbed by the meat, **and** the mixture **is** nonetheless **forbidden. Here, too,** in the case of other prohibitions, it is **no different,** and the same principle applies.

וְרַבָּנַן: מִבָּשָׂר בְּחָלָב לָא גָּמְרִינַן, דְּחִידּוּשׁ הוּא.

The Gemara asks: **And the Rabbis,** why don't they derive this principle from meat cooked in milk? The Gemara answers: The Rabbis claim that **from meat in milk we do not derive** other prohibitions, **as** that prohibition **is a novelty.**[N]

וּמַאי חִידּוּשׁ? אִילֵימָא דְּהַאי לְחוּדֵיהּ וְהַאי לְחוּדֵיהּ שָׁרֵי, וּבַהֲדֵי הֲדָדֵי אָסוּר – כִּלְאַיִם נַמִי, הַאי לְחוּדֵיהּ וְהַאי לְחוּדֵיהּ שָׁרֵי, וּבַהֲדָדֵי אָסוּר!

The Gemara asks: **And what is** the **novelty** in that prohibition? **If you say that** it is unique in that **this** meat **alone and that** milk **alone** are each **permitted, and** yet **together they are forbidden,** that characteristic is not unique to meat cooked in milk. In the case of prohibited mixtures of **diverse kinds too, this** element **alone and that** element **alone** are each **permitted, and** yet **together they are prohibited.**

אֶלָּא: דְּאִי תָּרוּ לֵיהּ כּוּלֵּי יוֹמָא בְּחַלְבָּא – שָׁרֵי, בַּשֵּׁיל לֵיהּ בְּשׁוּלֵי – אָסוּר.

The Gemara answers: **Rather,** the novelty is **that if one soaks** meat **in milk all day, it is permitted** by Torah law, despite the fact that the meat certainly absorbed some taste of the milk, whereas **if one cooked** the meat in milk even for a short time, the mixture **is prohibited** by Torah law.

HALAKHA

Soaked his bread in wine – שָׁרָה פִּתּוֹ בְּיַיִן: If a nazirite soaks his bread in wine, and a quarter-*log* of wine, which has the same volume as an olive-bulk in liquid measurements, is absorbed in bread. If that quarter-*log* of wine can be eaten in less than the time it takes to eat a half-loaf of bread, he is liable for its consumption (Rambam *Sefer Hafla'a, Hilkhot Nezirut* 5:5).

NOTES

The joining together of prohibited substances to constitute an olive-bulk – צֵירוּף אִיסּוּר לִכְדֵי כַּזַּיִת: Although the prohibition against a nazirite drinking wine is generally determined by the liquid measure of a quarter-*log*, this wine is assessed by the dry measure of an olive-bulk because it is absorbed by the bread (Maharam Ḥalawa).

From where does he derive that the legal status of taste is like that of substance – טַעַם כְּעִיקָּר מְנָא לֵיהּ: Why doesn't the Gemara consider the possibility that Rabbi Akiva does not accept the principle that the legal status of taste is like that of substance, just as the Rabbis do not accept the principle that permitted substances join with prohibited substances? The answer given is that this principle is far more substantiated than the principle that permitted material joins with prohibited material. This is because, among other reasons, the principle concerning taste is derived by means of an *a fortiori* inference, an especially strong derivation. If Rabbi Akiva was left with no other source from which he could derive the principle that taste is like substance, he should have derived it from the term soaked (*Tosefot Rabbeinu Peretz, Tosefot Rid*).

A novelty – חִידּוּשׁ: Any *halakha* in which there is a component that is anomalous relative to all other *halakhot* is considered a novelty. A *halakha* of this kind cannot serve as the basis for deriving the parameters of other *halakhot*.

וְרַבִּי עֲקִיבָא נַמִי, בָּשָׂר בְּחָלָב וַדַּאי חִידּוּשׁ הוּא!

The Gemara asks: **And Rabbi Akiva too** certainly agrees that the *halakha* of **meat in milk is a novelty.** How can he derive a general principle from this case?

אֶלָּא: יָלֵיף מִגִּיעוּלֵי גוֹיִם, גִּיעוּלֵי גוֹיִם לָאו טַעְמָא בְּעָלְמָא הוּא – וְאָסוּר, הָכָא נַמִי – לָא שְׁנָא.

Rather, he derives the principle: The legal status of the taste is like that of the substance itself **from** the required **purging** of the vessels of **gentiles.** In the section of the Torah that deals with the spoils of Midian (Numbers 31:21–24), it states that a vessel used by a gentile to cook food must be purged through fire and purified before it may be used by a Jew. **Isn't** the **purging** of vessels of **gentiles** necessary only to cleanse them from the **mere taste** that was absorbed through the process of cooking? Even so, these vessels are **prohibited** if this cleansing was not performed. **Here, too,** it is **no different;** the same reasoning applies in all cases.

וְרַבָּנַן: גִּיעוּלֵי גוֹיִם נַמִי חִידּוּשׁ הוּא, דְּהָא כָּל נוֹתֵן טַעַם לִפְגָם מוּתָּר, דְּגָמְרִינַן מִנְּבֵילָה – וְהָכָא אָסוּר.

The Gemara comments: **And the Rabbis** do not derive this principle from this source, as they maintain that the *halakha* of **purging** vessels of **gentiles is** also **a novelty.** What is the novelty of this *halakha*? **As** in general, **anything that contributes taste** that renders the food **tainted**[N] **is permitted.** If the taste added by the prohibited food does not enhance the permitted food, then as a rule it does not render the permitted substance prohibited. **As we derive** this principle **from** the *halakha* that **an** unslaughtered **animal carcass** that is unfit for consumption is not classified as a prohibited animal carcass and is not prohibited. **However, here,** with regard to the *halakha* of purging vessels of gentiles, the Torah states that even if they contribute taste that renders the food tainted they are **prohibited.** If twenty-four hours have passed since food was cooked in a pot, the assumption is that it will contribute a negative taste to any foods cooked in the pot subsequently. Nevertheless, vessels taken from gentiles remain prohibited until they are purged, even though the taste they contribute taints the food.

וְרַבִּי עֲקִיבָא – כִּדְרַב חִיָּיא בְּרֵיהּ דְּרַב הוּנָא, דְּאָמַר: לֹא אָסְרָה תּוֹרָה אֶלָּא בִּקְדֵירָה בַּת יוֹמָא, הִלְכָּךְ לָאו נוֹתֵן טַעַם לִפְגָם הוּא.

The Gemara asks: **And** how does **Rabbi Akiva,** who derives this principle from the required purging of the vessels of gentiles, respond to the previous claim? The Gemara explains: He holds **in accordance with** the opinion subsequently cited in the name of **Rav Ḥiyya, son of Rav Huna, who said: The Torah prohibited** unpurged vessels of gentiles **only in** the case of **a pot** that was used **on that day. Therefore, it is not** a case where the pot **contributes taste** that renders the food **tainted.**

וְרַבָּנַן: קְדֵירָה בַּת יוֹמָא נַמִי לֹא אֶפְשָׁר דְּלֹא פַּגְמָה פּוּרְתָּא.

The Gemara asks: **And** what do **the Rabbis** say about deriving the *halakha* from a pot used on that day? The Gemara answers: In their opinion, **even** in the case of **a pot** used **on that day, it is impossible that** the vessel **does not slightly taint** the food absorbed in the vessel. Consequently, the *halakha* of purging vessels of gentiles is indeed a novel case from which principles cannot be derived.

אָמַר לֵיהּ רַב אַחָא בְּרֵיהּ דְּרַב אָוְיָא לְרַב אַשִׁי: מִדְּרַבָּנַן נִשְׁמַע לְרַבִּי עֲקִיבָא, מִי לָא אָמְרִי רַבָּנַן "מִשְׁרַת" לִיתֵּן טַעַם כְּעִיקָּר – מִכָּאן אַתָּה דָּן לְכָל אִיסּוּרִין שֶׁבַּתּוֹרָה. לְרַבִּי עֲקִיבָא נַמִי: מִשְׁרַת – לְהֶיתֵּר מִצְטָרֵף לְאִיסּוּר, מִכָּאן אַתָּה דָּן לְכָל אִיסּוּרִין שֶׁבַּתּוֹרָה כּוּלָּהּ!

Rav Aḥa, son of Rav Avya, said to Rav Ashi: From the opinion of **the Rabbis, let us learn** the correct interpretation of the opinion of **Rabbi Akiva. Don't the Rabbis say** that the term **soaked teaches** that the principle that the legal status of **taste is like** that of **substance** applies not only to a nazirite, but that **from here you derive** the *halakha* with regard **to all prohibitions of the Torah? According to Rabbi Akiva as well,** the term **soaked teaches** that **the permitted** substance **joins together with the prohibited** substance with regard to a nazirite, and **from here you derive** the *halakha* with regard **to all prohibitions of the Torah.** This explanation is contrary to the opinion of Rabbi Yoḥanan, who applies this principle only to a nazirite.

אָמַר לֵיהּ:

Rav Ashi **said to him:** This cannot serve as a proof,

NOTES

Contributes taste that renders the food tainted – נוֹתֵן טַעַם לִפְגָם: The principle that the legal status of taste is like that of substance applies to mixtures of different items, usually when one ingredient is permitted and the other is prohibited. The addition of taste renders a mixture prohibited only if the prohibited item improves the mixture. However, by Torah law the prohibition does not apply if the forbidden item contributes a taste that taints the mixture and renders it inedible.

NOTES

Two verses that come as one – שְׁנֵי כְתוּבִין הַבָּאִין כְּאֶחָד: This is one of the principles limiting the application of an analogy. Ordinarily, an analogy may be derived from a *halakha* stated with regard to one case in the Torah. However, if that *halakha* appears in connection with two or more cases, these cases constitute the principle of: Two verses that come for the same purpose. In this situation, the principle governing these cases is: Two verses that come for the same purpose do not teach, i.e., an analogy may not be derived from two similar cases. This is due to the fact that a *halakha* that needed to be mentioned in two different places cannot be a general principle, but must instead be an exceptional case. However, certain Sages maintain that it is impossible to derive an analogy only when a *halakha* appears in three places, i.e., the principle is: Three verses that come for the same purpose do not teach.

A permitted substance that joins together with a prohibited substance in the case of a sin-offering – חַטָּאת לְהֶיתֵּר מִצְטָרֵף לְאִיסּוּר: The early commentaries question this derivation, as the case of a sin-offering is an example of the principle that the legal status of taste is like that of substance, not the principle that permitted material joins prohibited material (see *Tosafot*). Some explain that in this case, the meat that touched the sin-offering absorbed such a large quantity of the sin-offering that it is as though part of the sin-offering itself, not only its taste, has been absorbed into the meat. Consequently, this case does in fact involve the principle that permitted substances join together with prohibited substances (see *Tosafot* in tractate *Nazir*; *Me'iri*).

Both of these cases are necessary – מִיצְרִיךְ צְרִיכִי: The reason that one cannot derive a principle from two verses that come as one is that since the principle could have been derived from one source, there was no need for the Torah to mention the *halakha* twice. However, that is true only if the *halakha* in question could have been derived from one case and applied to the other. If it can be demonstrated that it is impossible to apply the *halakhot* of each case to the other case, they can no longer be viewed as two verses that come as one. In that case, a principle may indeed be derived from them.

HALAKHA

That which touches a sin-offering – הַנּוֹגֵעַ בְּחַטָּאת: Food or a vessel that touches a sin-offering and absorbs its taste assumes the legal status of the sin-offering itself. This means that the restrictions that apply to a sin-offering with regard to when and where it may be eaten apply to this food or vessel as well. If the sin-offering is disqualified, these objects are disqualified as well (Rambam *Sefer Avoda*, *Hilkhot Ma'aseh HaKorbanot* 8:15–16).

מִשּׁוּם דַּהֲוָה נָזִיר וְחַטָּאת שְׁנֵי כְתוּבִין הַבָּאִין כְּאֶחָד, וְאֵין מְלַמְּדִין.

due to the fact that the *halakhot* of **a nazirite** and those of **a sin-offering** are **two verses that come as one**,[N] i.e., to teach the same principle, and two verses that teach the same principle **do not teach** that principle by analogy.

נָזִיר – הָא דַּאֲמַרַן, חַטָּאת מַאי הִיא? דְּתַנְיָא: ״כֹּל אֲשֶׁר יִגַּע בִּבְשָׂרָהּ יִקְדָּשׁ וגו׳״ – יָכוֹל אֲפִילּוּ לֹא בָּלְעָה, תַּלְמוּד לוֹמַר: ״בִּבְשָׂרָהּ״ – (יִקְדָּשׁ) – עַד שֶׁיִּבָּלַע בַּבָּשָׂר.

The Gemara elaborates: The derivation that a permitted substance joins together with a prohibited substance in the case of **a nazirite** is **that which we stated** above. With regard to **a sin-offering, what is** the derivation that permitted material combines with prohibited material? **As it was taught** in a *baraita* with regard to the verse: **"Anything that touches in its flesh shall become consecrated"** (Leviticus 6:20). I **might** have thought that non-sacred meat that touched any part of a sin-offering is rendered prohibited **even if it did not absorb** the taste of the sin-offering it touched. Therefore, **the verse states: In its flesh shall become consecrated,** to teach that this meat is not consecrated **until** the taste of the sin-offering **is absorbed within its flesh.**[H]

״יִקְדָּשׁ״ – לִהְיוֹת כָּמוֹהָ, שֶׁאִם פְּסוּלָה הִיא – תִּיפָּסֵל, וְאִם כְּשֵׁירָה הִיא – תֵּאָכֵל כְּחָמוּר שֶׁבָּהּ.

The *baraita* continues: **Shall become consecrated** means that **its** legal status **becomes like** that of the sin-offering itself; **that** is, **if** the sin-offering **is disqualified,** this meat **will** also **be disqualified. And if** the sin-offering **is valid,** the meat that touched it may **be eaten in accordance with the more stringent** standards **of** a sin-offering as far as when and where it may be eaten. The principle that a permitted substance joins together with a prohibited substance applies in the case of a sin-offering[N] as well. Therefore, the principle cannot be extended to the entire Torah, as a *halakha* stated in two cases is not applied elsewhere.

וְרַבָּנַן נַמִי, נֶיהֱוֵי נָזִיר וְחַטָּאת שְׁנֵי כְתוּבִין הַבָּאִין כְּאֶחָד, וְאֵין מְלַמְּדִין!

The Gemara asks: **And** according to **the Rabbis as well, let** the cases of **a nazirite and a sin-offering** be considered **two verses that come as one and they do not teach** the principle that the legal status of taste is like that of the substance with regard to the entire Torah.

אָמְרִי: הָנְהוּ מִיצְרִיךְ צְרִיכִי.

The Gemara answers that the Rabbis **say:** Both of **these** cases **are necessary**[N] as they could not have been derived from each other. Therefore, they are not two verses that come as one and it is possible to derive a principle from these two *halakhot*.

וְרַבִּי עֲקִיבָא: מַאי צְרִיכִי? בִּשְׁלָמָא אִי כָּתַב רַחֲמָנָא בְּחַטָּאת – לָא גָּמַר נָזִיר מִינָּהּ, דְּחוּלִּין מִקֳּדָשִׁים לָא גָּמְרִינַן. אֶלָּא לִכְתּוֹב רַחֲמָנָא בְּנָזִיר, וְתֵיתֵי חַטָּאת וְתִגְמוֹר מִינֵּיהּ, דְּהָא כָּל אִיסּוּרִין שֶׁבַּתּוֹרָה קָא גָּמַר מִנָּזִיר.

The Gemara asks: **And Rabbi Akiva,** who does not derive a general principle from these verses, would respond by asking: In **what** way are they **necessary? Granted, if the Merciful One had written** this principle only with regard **to a sin-offering,** one would **not derive** the *halakha* of **a nazirite from it,** as **we do not derive** *halakhot* of **non-sacred** objects **from** those of **consecrated** objects. Certain stringencies and strictures apply only to consecrated property. **However, let the Merciful One write** this principle **with regard to a nazirite, and you** could **bring** the case of the **sin-offering and derive** it from the case of a nazirite, just **as** the application of this principle to **all prohibitions in the Torah is derived from** the *halakha* of **a nazirite.** Since this principle is stated in both cases unnecessarily, these are two verses that come as one, and one cannot derive a principle from them.

וְרַבָּנַן אָמְרִי לָךְ: מִיצְרַךְ צְרִיכִי; חַטָּאת – לְהֶיתֵּר מִצְטָרֵף לְאִיסּוּר, וְחוּלִּין מִקֳּדָשִׁים לָא גָּמַר. וּמִשְׁרַת – לִיתֵּן טַעַם כְּעִיקָּר, וּמִכָּאן אַתָּה דָּן לְכָל הַתּוֹרָה כּוּלָּהּ.

The Gemara asks: **And the Rabbis,** as they maintain that the principle that the legal status of the taste of a prohibited substance is like that of the substance itself is not limited to these two cases, they would **say to you** that both sources **are necessary.** The case of the **sin-offering** is necessary **to** derive the principle **that a permitted** substance **joins together with a prohibited** substance, as **one cannot derive** the *halakhot* of **non-sacred** food **from consecrated** property. **And** the term **soaked,** which appears in the context of the *halakhot* of a nazirite, **teaches** the principle that the legal status of **taste is like** that of the **substance.** Since both examples are necessary, they are not considered two verses that come as one, and it is therefore possible to derive a principle from them. **And** consequently, **from here you derive** the *halakha* with regard **to all of the Torah in its entirety.**

וְרַבִּי עֲקִיבָא – תַּרְוַיְיהוּ לְהֶיתֵּר מִצְטָרֵף לְאִיסּוּר, וְהָווּ לְהוּ שְׁנֵי כְתוּבִין הַבָּאִין כְּאֶחָד, וְכָל שְׁנֵי כְתוּבִין הַבָּאִין כְּאֶחָד אֵין מְלַמְּדִין.

The Gemara asks: **And** how could **Rabbi Akiva** respond to this claim? The Gemara answers: Rabbi Akiva would say that **both** cases teach the principle that **a permitted** substance **joins together with a prohibited** substance, **and they are** indeed **two verses that come as one,** to teach about the same issue. **And** the rule is that **any two verses that come as one do not teach** overarching principles.

אָמַר לֵיהּ רַב אַשִׁי לְרַב כָּהֲנָא: אֶלָּא הָא דְּתַנְיָא: ״מִכֹּל אֲשֶׁר יֵעָשֶׂה מִגֶּפֶן הַיַּיִן מֵחַרְצַנִּים וְעַד זָג״ – לִימֵּד עַל אִיסּוּרֵי נָזִיר שֶׁמִּצְטָרְפִים זֶה עִם זֶה. הַשְׁתָּא לְרַבִּי עֲקִיבָא אִיסּוּר וְהֶיתֵּר מִצְטָרְפִין, אִיסּוּר וְאִיסּוּר מִיבַּעְיָא?!

Rav Ashi said to Rav Kahana: But with regard to **that which is taught** in a *baraita*: The verse: "He shall eat **nothing that is made of the grapevine, from the grape skins to the grape seed"** (Numbers 6:4), **taught with regard to prohibitions of a nazirite that** these substances **join together.**[H] If the nazirite ate only a small amount of each substance that when joined together constitute the measure that determines liability, he is liable. **Now** the following question arises: **According to Rabbi Akiva,** who maintains that **prohibited and permitted** substances **join together, is it necessary** to teach that one **prohibited** substance **joins together with** another **prohibited** substance?[N] Apparently, according to Rabbi Akiva's opinion, this derivation is unnecessary.

אָמַר לֵיהּ: אִיסּוּר וְהֶיתֵּר – בְּבַת אַחַת, אִיסּוּר וְאִיסּוּר – בָּזֶה אַחַר זֶה.

Rav Kahana **said to him** that this derivation is necessary because the two cases are not identical: Whereas **prohibited and permitted** substances combine only when they are eaten **simultaneously, prohibited and** other **prohibited** substances join together even when eaten **one after the other.** In other words, if a nazirite eats half an olive-bulk of grape skins and then eats half an olive-bulk of grape seeds, he is liable according to Rabbi Akiva.

מתני׳ בָּצֵק שֶׁבְּסִידְקֵי עֲרֵיבָה, אִם יֵשׁ כַּזַּיִת בְּמָקוֹם אֶחָד – חַיָּיב לְבָעֵר, וְאִם (לֹא) – בָּטֵל בְּמִיעוּטוֹ.

MISHNA With regard to **dough that is in the cracks of a** kneading **bowl,**[H] **if there is an olive-bulk** of dough **in one place,** one **is obligated to remove** it. **And if** the dough does **not** add up to this amount, **it is nullified due to its insignificance.**

וְכֵן לְעִנְיַן הַטּוּמְאָה, אִם מַקְפִּיד עָלָיו – חוֹצֵץ, וְאִם רוֹצֶה בְּקִיּוּמוֹ – הֲרֵי הוּא כַּעֲרֵיבָה.

And similarly, with regard to the *halakhot* of immersion to purify the bowl from **ritual impurity, if one is particular about** the dough[N] that is stuck in the cracks and he plans to remove it and use it, **it** is a foreign substance that **interposes** between the kneading bowl and the water of the ritual bath, and invalidates the immersion of the bowl, leaving it ritually impure. **And if he wants** the dough **to remain** in place, **its** status **is like** that **of the** kneading **bowl** itself and is not an interposition.

HALAKHA

The joining together of items prohibited to a nazirite – צֵירוּף אִיסּוּרֵי נָזִיר: The foods that are prohibited to a nazirite join together. This means that if a nazirite eats an olive-bulk of a mixture of grapes, grape seeds, grape skins and unripe grapes, he is flogged. Similarly, he is punished for eating a measure of an olive-bulk of these items one after another, if he does so within the time it takes to eat a half-loaf of bread (Rambam *Sefer Hafla'a, Hilkhot Nezirut* 5:3).

Dough that is in the cracks of a kneading bowl – בָּצֵק שֶׁבְּסִידְקֵי עֲרֵיבָה: If an olive-bulk of dough is stuck in one area of a kneading bowl, one is obligated to remove it. However, it is nullified if it serves to reinforce the bowl, provided there is not an olive-bulk in one place, in accordance with the second version of Rav Yehuda's statement (*Shulḥan Arukh, Oraḥ Ḥayyim* 442:7).

NOTES

Is it necessary to teach that one prohibited substance joins together with another prohibited substance – אִיסּוּר וְאִיסּוּר מִיבַּעְיָא: Actually, there is a principle that one prohibited item does not combine with another. One is not punished for eating a mixture that contains half an olive-bulk of one prohibited item and half an olive-bulk of another prohibited item. Consequently, it is not at all obvious that one prohibited substance joins together with another prohibited substance. However, since the various foods prohibited to a nazirite are all included in the same prohibition, in this particular case it is possible to derive the concept that prohibited substances join together by means of an *a fortiori* argument from the *halakha* of a mixture of permitted and prohibited substances (*Me'iri*).

If one is particular about the dough – אִם מַקְפִּיד עָלָיו: One's intention is of great significance with regard to matters of ritual purity and impurity. For example, the manner in which a person relates to an object can determine whether it is considered a vessel or an incomplete vessel, whether it is a broken or intact, or, as in this case, whether or not a substance is deemed an interposition for the purposes of ritual immersion.

NOTES

In a case where they serve to reinforce the bowl – בְּמָקוֹם שֶׁעֲשׂוּיִין לְחַזֵּק: Rashi explains that the term: Serve to reinforce, refers to dough that is placed in a crack on the base of the bowl, whereas dough that is placed in a crack on the side of the bowl does not serve to reinforce. According to the *ge'onim*, dough serves to reinforce the bowl if it is in a crack or a hole in a bowl, whereas any dough that is not in a crack does not serve to reinforce the bowl. Rav Yitzḥak ibn Giat explains that dough placed in a crack that goes all the way through the bowl serves to reinforce the bowl, while dough does not serve to reinforce the bowl if it is in a crack that does not go all the way through the bowl. The *Me'iri* suggests a similar explanation.

Dough that serves to reinforce the base of a bowl, according to Rashi

Dough on the side of a bowl that does not serve to reinforce it, according to Rashi

גמ׳ אָמַר רַב יְהוּדָה אָמַר שְׁמוּאֵל: לֹא שָׁנוּ אֶלָּא בְּמָקוֹם שֶׁאֵין עֲשׂוּיִין לְחַזֵּק, אֲבָל בְּמָקוֹם שֶׁעֲשׂוּיִין לְחַזֵּק – אֵינוֹ חַיָּיב לְבָעֵר.

GEMARA **Rav Yehuda said** that **Shmuel said: They taught** that one is obligated to remove a combined olive-bulk of leaven **only in a case where the** pieces of dough **are not** in a position where they **serve to reinforce** the kneading bowl. **However, in a case where they serve to reinforce** the bowl[N] and they will remain there for this purpose, **he is not obligated to remove** them; he may simply render them null and void.

מִכְּלָל דְּפָחוֹת מִכַּזַּיִת, אֲפִילּוּ בְּמָקוֹם שֶׁאֵין עָשׂוּי לְחַזֵּק – אֵינוֹ חַיָּיב לְבָעֵר.

The Gemara concludes: This proves **by inference** that with regard to **less than an olive-bulk, even in a place where it does not serve to reinforce** the bowl, **one is not obligated to remove** it.

אִיכָּא דְּמַתְנֵי לַהּ אַסֵּיפָא: ״וְאִם לָאו בָּטֵל בְּמִיעוּטוֹ״. אָמַר רַב יְהוּדָה אָמַר שְׁמוּאֵל: לֹא שָׁנוּ אֶלָּא בְּמָקוֹם הֶעָשׂוּי לְחַזֵּק, אֲבָל בְּמָקוֹם שֶׁאֵין עָשׂוּי לְחַזֵּק – חַיָּיב לְבָעֵר. מִכְּלָל דְּכַזַּיִת, אֲפִילּוּ בְּמָקוֹם הֶעָשׂוּי לְחַזֵּק – חַיָּיב לְבָעֵר.

Some teach the statement of Rav Yehuda with regard **to the latter clause** of the mishna: **And if** the dough is **not** an olive-bulk, **it is nullified due to its insignificance. Rav Yehuda said** that **Shmuel said: They taught** that one is obligated to remove less than an olive-bulk of dough in one place **only in a place where it serves to reinforce** the bowl; **however, in a place where it does not serve to reinforce** the bowl, **one is obligated to remove it.** This proves **by inference that** if there is **an olive-bulk** of dough in one place, **even in a place where it serves to reinforce** the bowl, **one is obligated to remove it.**

תַּנְיָא כִּלִישָּׁנָא קַמָּא, תַּנְיָא כִּלִישָּׁנָא בָּתְרָא. תַּנְיָא כִּלִישָּׁנָא קַמָּא: בָּצֵק שֶׁבְּסִידְקֵי עֲרֵיבָה, בְּמָקוֹם הֶעָשׂוּי לְחַזֵּק – אֵינוֹ חוֹצֵץ, וְאֵינוֹ עוֹבֵר. וּבְמָקוֹם שֶׁאֵין עָשׂוּי לְחַזֵּק – חוֹצֵץ וְעוֹבֵר. בַּמֶּה דְּבָרִים אֲמוּרִים – בְּכַזַּיִת, אֲבָל בְּפָחוֹת מִכַּזַּיִת, אֲפִילּוּ בְּמָקוֹם שֶׁאֵין עָשׂוּי לְחַזֵּק – אֵינוֹ חוֹצֵץ וְאֵינוֹ עוֹבֵר.

The Gemara comments: It **was taught** in a *baraita* **in accordance with the first version** of Rav Yehuda's statement, and it **was taught** in a different *baraita* **in accordance with the latter version** of his statement. The Gemara elaborates: It **was taught** in a *baraita* **in accordance with the first version** of Rav Yehuda's statement: With regard to **dough that is in the cracks of a** kneading **bowl in a place where it is serves to reinforce** the bowl, it **does not interpose** and invalidate the immersion for ritual impurity, **and one does not violate** the prohibition against having leaven in his possession during Passover. **And in a case where it does not serve to reinforce** the bowl, **it interposes, and one violates** the prohibition against having leaven in his possession on Passover. **In what** case **is this statement said?** It is **in** the case of **an olive-bulk** of dough; **however,** in a case where there is **less than olive-bulk, even in a case where it does not serve to reinforce** the bowl, **it does not interpose and** one **does not violate** a prohibition by having it in his possession.

וְתַנְיָא כִּלִישָּׁנָא בָּתְרָא: בָּצֵק שֶׁבְּסִידְקֵי עֲרֵיבָה, בְּמָקוֹם הֶעָשׂוּי לְחַזֵּק –

And it **was taught** in a different *baraita* **in accordance with the latter version** of Rav Yehuda's statement: With regard to **dough that is in the cracks of a** kneading **bowl, in a place where it serves to reinforce** the bowl,

NOTES

Delete the lenient *baraita* – סְמִי קִילְּתָא: In other words, Rav Huna maintains that this version of the *baraita* was flawed. As the *baraitot* were transmitted orally, sometimes the *tanna'im* who taught them would err in reciting them.

אֵינוֹ חוֹצֵץ וְאֵינוֹ עוֹבֵר. בְּמָקוֹם שֶׁאֵין עָשׂוּי לְחַזֵּק – חוֹצֵץ וְעוֹבֵר. בַּמֶּה דְּבָרִים אֲמוּרִים – בְּפָחוֹת מִכַּזַּיִת, אֲבָל בְּכַזַּיִת – אֲפִילּוּ בְּמָקוֹם הֶעָשׂוּי לְחַזֵּק – חוֹצֵץ וְעוֹבֵר.

it does not interpose in the immersion **and one does not violate** the prohibition against having leaven in his possession during Passover. **In a case where** the dough **does not serve to reinforce** the bowl, **it interposes** in the immersion **and one violates** the prohibition against owning leaven on Passover. **In what case is this statement said?** It is **in** a case where the dough is **less than an olive-bulk. However, if it is an olive-bulk, even in a case where it serves to reinforce** the bowl **it interposes** in the immersion **and one violates** a prohibition by having it in his possession during the Festival.

קַשְׁיָין אַהֲדָדֵי! אָמַר רַב הוּנָא: סְמִי קִילְּתָא מִקַּמֵּי חֲמִירְתָּא.

The Gemara asks: In any case, these *baraitot* **contradict each other. Rav Huna said: Delete the** first, **lenient** *baraita*[N] **from before the stringent one.**

רַב יוֹסֵף אָמַר: תַּנָּאֵי שְׁקַלְתְּ מֵעָלְמָא?! תַּנָּאֵי הִיא. דְּתַנְיָא: הַפַּת שֶׁעִיפְּשָׁה – חַיָּיב לְבָעֵר, מִפְּנֵי שֶׁרָאוּי לְשׁוֹחֲקָהּ וּלְחַמֵּעַ בָּהּ כַּמָּה עִיסּוֹת אֲחֵרוֹת.

Rav Yosef said: Have you removed the *tanna'im* from the world?[N] **It is a dispute between *tanna'im*.** The *baraita* is in accordance with the ruling of another Sage and is not the result of a flawed *baraita*, **as it was taught** in a *baraita*: With regard to **bread that grew moldy** and is no longer edible, **one is obligated to remove** it, **due to** the fact that **it is suitable to be ground and to leaven other dough.** Apparently, one is obligated to remove even inedible leaven.

רַבִּי שִׁמְעוֹן בֶּן אֶלְעָזָר אוֹמֵר: בַּמֶּה דְּבָרִים אֲמוּרִים – בִּמְקוּיֶּימֶת לַאֲכִילָה, אֲבָל כּוֹפֶת שְׂאוֹר שֶׁיִּיחֲדָהּ לִישִׁיבָה – בָּטְלָה. מִדְּאָמַר רַבִּי שִׁמְעוֹן בֶּן אֶלְעָזָר בָּטְלָה – מִכְּלָל דְּתַנָּא קַמָּא סָבַר לֹא בָּטְלָה, אַלְמָא קָסָבַר: כָּל כַּזַּיִת, אַף עַל גַּב דִּמְבַטֵּל – לָא בָּטֵיל.

Rabbi Shimon ben Elazar says: In what case **is this statement said?** In a case **where** the bread was **maintained for consumption; however, a mass of** hardened **leaven**[N] **that one designated for** the purpose **of sitting** upon it, not for consumption, **is nullified.** Rav Yosef infers from the *baraita*: **From the fact that Rabbi Shimon ben Elazar said** that this leaven **is nullified,** this proves **by inference** that **the first *tanna* maintains** that in that case, the leaven **is not nullified. Apparently,** the first *tanna* **maintains** that with regard to **any olive-bulk** of leaven, **even though one renders** it **null and void, it is not nullified.** The respective opinions of these two Sages are presented in the two conflicting *baraitot* with regard to dough in a bowl.

אָמַר לֵיהּ אַבָּיֵי: תָּרַצְתְּ בְּכַזַּיִת, פָּחוֹת מִכַּזַּיִת מִי תָּרַצְתְּ? אֶלָּא: הָא וְהָא רַבִּי שִׁמְעוֹן בֶּן אֶלְעָזָר הִיא, וְלָא קַשְׁיָא: הָא – בִּמְקוֹם לִישָׁה, הָא – שֶׁלֹּא בִּמְקוֹם לִישָׁה.

Abaye said to him: You resolved the contradiction between the *baraitot* **with regard to an olive-bulk** of leaven by establishing it as a tannaitic dispute. According to the first *tanna*, an olive-bulk of leaven cannot be nullified at all, whereas Rabbi Shimon ben Elazar maintains that it can be nullified. However, **did you resolve** the contradiction with regard to **less than an olive-bulk** of leaven? **Rather,** both **this** *baraita* **and that** *baraita* are in accordance with the opinion of **Rabbi Shimon ben Elazar, and** nevertheless it is **not difficult. This** *baraita*, where he prohibits the dough in a crack of the bowl, refers to a situation where the dough **is in** the **place** in the bowl where **kneading** takes place, as any dough he later inserts into the bowl will come into contact with the dough in the crack. However, in **that** case, Rabbi Shimon ben Elazar rules leniently, as the dough **is not in** the **place** in the bowl where **kneading** takes place.

אָמַר רַב אַשִׁי: לָא תֵּימָא שֶׁלֹּא בִּמְקוֹם לִישָׁה אַגַּבָּהּ דְּאַגָּנָא, אֶלָּא אַשִּׂיפְתָּא דְּאַגָּנָא.

Rav Ashi said: Do not say that dough **not in** the **place** in the bowl where **kneading** takes place, refers only to the area **on** the **back of,** i.e., outside **the basin; rather,** it also refers to the area **on the edge of the basin,** as dough does not come into contact with that part of the bowl.

פְּשִׁיטָא! מַהוּ דְּתֵימָא: זִמְנָא דְּאַטֵּיף וּמָטֵי לְהָתָם, קָא מַשְׁמַע לַן.

The Gemara asks: This is **obvious;** why was it necessary to make that statement? The Gemara answers: Rav Ashi's statement is necessary **lest you say** that dough **sometimes drips there** and it should therefore be considered the place in the bowl where kneading takes place. Therefore, the *baraita* **teaches us** that this is not the case, and one is not obligated to remove leavened dough from that part of the bowl.

אָמַר רַב נַחְמָן אָמַר רַב: הֲלָכָה כְּרַבִּי שִׁמְעוֹן בֶּן אֶלְעָזָר.

Rav Naḥman said that **Rav said:** The ***halakha* is in accordance with** the opinion of **Rabbi Shimon ben Elazar** that a mass of leaven designated for the purpose of sitting upon is nullified.

אִינִי? וְהָאָמַר רַב יִצְחָק בַּר אַשִׁי אָמַר רַב: אִם טָח פָּנֶיהָ בְּטִיט – בְּטֵלָה. טָח – אִין, לֹא טָח – לָא.

The Gemara asks: **Is that so? Didn't Rav Yitzḥak bar Ashi say** that **Rav said: If one covered the surface** of a mass of leaven **with mortar,**[H] the leaven **is nullified?** The Gemara infers: If **he covered** it with mortar, **yes,** it is nullified; however, if he did **not cover** it with mortar, **no,** it is **not** nullified. In this statement, Rav states that a mass of leaven is nullified only if it is covered with mortar.

מַאן דְּמַתְנֵי הָא לָא מַתְנֵי הָא.

The Gemara answers: **He who teaches this** statement **does not teach that** statement, as there is a dispute between *amora'im* with regard to Rav's opinion.

אִיכָּא דְּאָמְרִי, אָמַר רַב נַחְמָן אָמַר רַב: אֵין הֲלָכָה כְּרַבִּי שִׁמְעוֹן בֶּן אֶלְעָזָר, דְּאָמַר רַב יִצְחָק בַּר אַשִׁי אָמַר רַב: אִם טָח פָּנֶיהָ בְּטִיט – בְּטֵלָה וכו׳.

Some say an alternative version of the above statement. **Rav Naḥman said** that **Rav said:** The ***halakha* is not in accordance with** the opinion of **Rabbi Shimon ben Elazar, as Rav Yitzḥak bar Ashi said** that **Rav said: If one covered the surface** of a mass of leaven **with mortar, it is nullified.** This ruling indicates that if one did not cover the surface with mortar, the leavened dough is not nullified, in accordance with the opinion of the first *tanna*.

NOTES

Have you removed the *tanna'im* from the world – **תַּנָּאֵי שְׁקַלְתְּ מֵעָלְמָא**: Even when better answers are available, this response, which indicates that this issue is subject to a dispute of *tanna'im*, is preferable to the complete dismissal of a *baraita*. Furthermore, the *amora'im* would prefer to say that two conflicting *baraitot* represent two different opinions, rather than forcing a resolution between the two sources. Of course, that cannot resolve a contradiction within a single source.

A mass of leaven – **כּוֹפֶת שְׂאוֹר**: Some commentaries explain that this refers to balls of dough prepared from barley that was dried for use in Babylonian *kutaḥ* (*Arukh*).

HALAKHA

If one covered the surface with mortar – **טָח פָּנֶיהָ בְּטִיט**: If one uses mortar to cover a mass of hardened leavened dough, he may keep it during Passover (*Shulḥan Arukh*, *Oraḥ Ḥayyim* 442:11).

אָמַר רַב נַחְמָן אָמַר שְׁמוּאֵל: שְׁנֵי חֲצָאֵי זֵיתִים וְחוּט שֶׁל בָּצֵק בֵּינֵיהֶן, רוֹאִין: כֹּל שֶׁאִילּוּ יִנָּטֵל הַחוּט וְנִיטָּלִין עִמּוֹ – חַיָּיב לְבַעֵר, וְאִם לָאו – אֵינוֹ חַיָּיב לְבַעֵר.

Rav Naḥman said that **Shmuel said:** With regard to **two half-olive-bulk** portions of leavened dough **with a string of dough**[H] connecting **between them, one observes:** In any case **that were the string taken and** the portions are **taken with it, one is obligated to remove** the dough, as the string unites them into an olive-bulk of leaven. **And if** the portions are **not** taken with it, **one is not obligated to remove** them.

אָמַר עוּלָּא: לָא אֲמַרַן אֶלָּא בַּעֲרֵיבָה, אֲבָל בַּבַּיִת – חַיָּיב לְבַעֵר.

Ulla said: We stated this leniency that it is not necessary to remove half-olive-bulk portions of leavened dough **only** when the segments are **in a kneading bowl,** stuck separately to the sides of the bowl. **However,** if they are located **in a house,**[H] **one is obligated to remove**[N] them even in the absence of a string of dough connecting the two pieces.

מַאי טַעְמָא – דְּזִימְנִין דְּכָנֵישׁ לְהוּ, וְנָפְלִי גַּבֵּי הֲדָדֵי.

What is the reason for this? It is **because** a person **will sometimes gather them** when cleaning his house **and they will fall** adjacent **to each other.** If this occurs, the two portions will form an olive-bulk of leavened dough.

אָמַר עוּלָּא, בָּעוּ בְּמַעְרְבָא: בַּיִת וַעֲלִיָּיה מַהוּ, בַּיִת וְאַכְסַדְרָא מַהוּ, שְׁנֵי בָתִּים זֶה לִפְנִים מִזֶּה מַהוּ?

Ulla said: The Sages **raise a dilemma in the West,** Eretz Yisrael: If one piece of leavened bread was in the main area of a **house and** the other piece was **in the upper** story, **what is** the *halakha*? If one piece is in **the house** and the other is in **a portico, what is** the *halakha*? Similarly, if the two segments are in **two houses, one inside the other, what is** the *halakha*?

תֵּיקוּ.

The Gemara states: **Let** these dilemmas **stand** unresolved.

תָּנוּ רַבָּנַן: הַפַּת שֶׁעִיפְּשָׁה וְנִפְסְלָה מִלֶּאֱכוֹל לָאָדָם, וְהַכֶּלֶב יָכוֹל לְאוֹכְלָהּ – מְטַמְּאָה טוּמְאַת אוֹכָלִין בִּכְבֵיצָה, וְנִשְׂרֶפֶת עִם הַטְּמֵאָה בְּפֶסַח. מִשּׁוּם רַבִּי נָתָן אָמְרוּ: אֵינָהּ מִטַּמְּאָה.

The Sages taught: With regard to **bread that grew moldy**[H] **and was rendered inedible for consumption by a person, but a dog can eat it,** it **can become impure** with the **ritual impurity of foods in** the measure **of an egg-bulk** in size, as it is still considered food. If the moldy bread was ritually pure *teruma*, **it** may **be burned with ritually impure** *teruma*[N] **on Passover.** Once the bread is no longer fit for human consumption, the prohibition against actively rendering it impure no longer applies. **They said in the name of Rabbi Natan: It cannot become ritually impure.**

כְּמַאן אָזְלָא הָא דִּתְנַן, כְּלָל אָמְרוּ בְּטָהֳרוֹת: כֹּל הַמְיוּחָד לְאוֹכֶל אָדָם – טָמֵא עַד שֶׁיִּפָּסֵל מִלֶּאֱכוֹל לַכֶּלֶב. כְּמַאן – דְּלָא כְּרַבִּי נָתָן.

The Gemara asks: **In accordance with whose opinion is that which we learned** in a mishna: The Sages **stated** a **principle with regard to ritual purity: Any** food **that is designated as food for a person** that becomes impure remains **ritually impure until it is rendered unfit to be consumed by a dog.**[H] The Gemara reiterates: **In accordance with whose** opinion is that statement? The Gemara answers: It is **not in accordance with** the opinion of **Rabbi Natan,** as his statement indicates that food designated as food for a person is rendered ritually pure as soon as it becomes unfit to be eaten by a person.

תָּנוּ רַבָּנַן: עֲרֵיבַת הָעַבְּדָנִין שֶׁנָּתַן לְתוֹכָהּ קֶמַח, תּוֹךְ שְׁלֹשָׁה יָמִים – חַיָּיב לְבַעֵר, קוֹדֶם שְׁלֹשָׁה – יָמִים אֵינוֹ חַיָּיב לְבַעֵר. אָמַר רַבִּי נָתָן: בַּמֶּה דְּבָרִים אֲמוּרִים – שֶׁלֹּא נָתַן לְתוֹכָהּ עוֹרוֹת, אֲבָל נָתַן לְתוֹכָהּ עוֹרוֹת – אֲפִילּוּ תּוֹךְ שְׁלֹשָׁה אֵין חַיָּיב לְבַעֵר.

The Sages taught: With regard to **tanners' bowls**[H] **into which** one **placed flour** in the production process of leather,[B] if the flour was placed **within three days** of the start of Passover, **one is obligated to remove** it, as it is still considered edible leaven. However, if one added the flour **prior to three days** before Passover, **one is not obligated to remove** the contents of the bowl, as the flour will have already been rendered inedible by the odor of the vessel before the beginning of Passover, and is no longer considered edible. **Rabbi Natan said: In what** case **is this statement said?** In a case **where one did not place** animal **hides into** the bowl; **however, if one placed hides into** the bowl, **even** if Passover is **within three** days of when he placed the flour in the bowl, **he is not obligated to remove** the flour. Once the foul-smelling hides are placed in the bowl, the flour is certainly no longer edible.

אָמַר רָבָא: הֲלָכָה כְּרַבִּי נָתָן, אֲפִילּוּ יוֹם אֶחָד וַאֲפִילּוּ שָׁעָה אַחַת.

Rava said: The *halakha* **is in accordance with** the opinion of **Rabbi Natan** with regard to this issue. Consequently, there is no set time at which the flour is considered spoiled, as it is considered inedible **even one day or even one hour** after hides were added to the bowl.

HALAKHA

Two half-olive-bulk portions with a string of dough – שְׁנֵי חֲצָאֵי זֵיתִים וְחוּט: If two portions of dough, each half an olive-bulk in size, are separated in a kneading bowl, but are connected by a string of dough so that if the string of dough is lifted both pieces of leavened dough are lifted with it, one is obligated to remove them (*Shulḥan Arukh, Oraḥ Ḥayyim* 442:8).

Two half-olive-bulk portions in a house – שְׁנֵי חֲצָאֵי זֵיתִים בַּבַּיִת: If two segments of leavened dough, each half an olive-bulk in size, are located in one area of a house, the owner is obligated to remove them, as they might combine when they are gathered. If they are in two different areas of the house, one is not obligated to remove them, as it is unlikely that the two pieces will come together. Although the Gemara does not resolve this question, the *halakha* is lenient in this regard, as it is a case of uncertainty involving a rabbinic decree (*Shulḥan Arukh, Oraḥ Ḥayyim* 442:8).

Bread that grew moldy – פַּת שֶׁעִיפְּשָׁה: If bread grows so moldy before Passover that it is unfit for consumption by a dog, there is no obligation to eliminate it. If moldy bread is still fit to be eaten by a dog, it must be eliminated (*Shulḥan Arukh, Oraḥ Ḥayyim* 442:9).

Nullifying ritual impurity – ביטול טומאה: If ritually impure food is ruined to the extent that it is no longer fit for consumption by a dog, it becomes ritually pure (Rambam *Sefer Tahara, Hilkhot Tumat Okhalin* 2:18).

Tanners' bowls – עֲרֵיבַת הָעַבְּדָנִים: One is not obligated to eliminate the contents of a tanner's bowl into which flour was placed if someone places animal hides in the bowl even one hour prior to the time for removing leaven. If no one places hides in the bowl but the flour mixture sat for three days, one is similarly not obligated to remove the contents of the bowl. However, if three days have not passed since the flour was added, one is obligated to remove the bowl's contents, in accordance with the ruling of Rabbi Natan in the *Tosefta* (*Shulḥan Arukh, Oraḥ Ḥayyim* 442:1).

NOTES

In a house one is obligated to remove – בַּבַּיִת חַיָּיב לְבַעֵר: Some commentaries maintain that this statement refers to two pieces of leavened dough attached by a string of dough (*Korban Netanel*). In the Jerusalem Talmud the opposite is stated: Two half-olive-bulk pieces of leavened dough in a single kneading bowl must be eliminated, as the bowl combines them. This is not the case if the two pieces are merely in the same house, as presence in a common building does not render them a single entity. Another explanation for why the *halakha* should be more lenient with regard to dough in a house than in bowl is that dough in a kneading bowl remains clean and can be eaten afterward, which is not true of dough left elsewhere in the house (Maharam Ḥalawa).

Burned with ritually impure *teruma* – נִשְׂרֶפֶת עִם הַטְּמֵאָה: The Rif infers from here that not only is it permitted to confer impurity on ritually pure leavened *teruma*, one is even obligated to eliminate and burn it. Rabbi Aharon HaLevi maintains that although this statement does indicate that a person may burn leavened *teruma*, there is no obligation to do so.

BACKGROUND

Tanning hides – עיבוד עורות: Tanning was performed in several different manners in the mishnaic and talmudic periods, depending on the type of hide and the quality of the leather one sought to produce. Flour was added for certain types of production, e.g., for parchments and similar products, as the leavening process facilitates their production.

Leather to which flour has been added is still considered unfinished, as additional steps are required to complete the tanning process.

"וְכֵן לְעִנְיַן טוּמְאָה אִם מַקְפִּיד עָלָיו חוֹצֵץ וְאִם רוֹצֶה בְקִיּוּמוֹ הֲרֵי הוּא כַּעֲרֵיבָה".

We learned in the mishna: **And similarly, with regard to** the *halakhot* of immersion to purify the bowl from **ritual impurity, if one is particular about** the dough that is stuck in the cracks and he plans to remove it and use it, **it** is a foreign substance that **interposes**[H] between the kneading bowl and the water of the ritual bath, and invalidates the immersion of the bowl, leaving it ritually impure. **And if he wants** the dough **to remain** in place, **its** status **is like** that **of the** kneading **bowl** itself and is not an interposition.

מִי דָּמֵי? הָתָם – בְּשִׁיעוּרָא תַּלְיָא מִילְּתָא, הָכָא – בְּקְפֵידָא תַּלְיָא מִילְּתָא.

The Gemara asks: **Is it comparable?** How can the mishna compare the *halakhot* of leaven on Passover to the *halakhot* of interpositions that invalidate an immersion to purify from ritual impurity? **There,** with regard to leaven, **the matter is contingent upon the measure** of the dough, as an olive-bulk of leaven is prohibited. **Here,** with regard to interpositions that invalidate an immersion, **the matter is contingent upon** whether or not one is **particular** about the presence of the dough. In other words, with regard to interpositions it is the attitude of the owner of the bowl that is the decisive factor, not the quantity of the dough.

אָמַר רַב יְהוּדָה: אֵימָא וּלְעִנְיַן הַטּוּמְאָה אֵינוֹ כֵּן.

The Gemara answers that **Rav Yehuda said: Say** that the mishna should be read: **And with regard to** interpositions that invalidate an immersion to purify from **ritual impurity, it is not so,** as it is not the quantity of the dough but the particularity of the owner that is the decisive factor.

אָמַר לֵיהּ אַבַּיֵי: הָא "וְכֵן לְעִנְיַן טוּמְאָה" קָתָנֵי! אֶלָּא אָמַר אַבַּיֵי: הָכִי קָאָמַר: וְכֵן

Abaye said to him: Doesn't the mishna **teach: And similarly**[N] **with regard to ritual impurity.** The text of the mishna cannot be so drastically emended merely to resolve a difficulty. **Rather, Abaye said: This is** what the mishna **is saying: And similarly,**

HALAKHA

If one is particular about it, it interposes – אִם מַקְפִּיד עָלָיו חוֹצֵץ: For an impure vessel to be purified through immersion, it must be cleaned from any substance that interposes between it and the water. If the owner of the vessel does not object to the substance remaining on the surface, the immersion is effective, provided that the majority of the vessel is not covered. However, if the owner objects to the presence of the substance, the immersion of the vessel is ineffective (Rambam *Sefer Tahara, Hilkhot Mikvaot* 1:12).

NOTES

Doesn't the mishna teach: And similarly – הָא וְכֵן...קָתָנֵי: Some commentaries have noted that a difficulty of this kind, based on the phrasing of the mishna, is generally raised only when there is an alternative explanation available that would not require a deviation from the accepted text of the mishna. When there is no acceptable alternative, the emended reading of the mishna is accepted (Rashash).

Perek **III**
Daf **46** Amud **a**

לְעִנְיַן צֵירוּף טוּמְאָה בְּפֶסַח. וּבִשְׁאָר יְמוֹת הַשָּׁנָה אִיכָּא פְּלוּגְתָּא.

with regard to the combination of two pieces vis-à-vis **ritual impurity**[N] **during Passover,** when it depends upon their volume. However, **during the rest of the year there is a distinction** based upon whether the owner is particular about it or not.

הֵיכִי דָּמֵי? כְּגוֹן דְּאִיכָּא פָּחוֹת מִכְּבֵיצָה אוֹכָלִין, וְנָגְעוּ בְּהַאי בָּצֵק. בְּפֶסַח דְּאִיסּוּרוֹ חָשׁוּב – מִצְטָרֵף, בִּשְׁאָר יְמוֹת הַשָּׁנָה, דִּבְקְפֵידָא תַּלְיָא מִילְּתָא, אִם מַקְפִּיד עָלָיו – מִצְטָרֵף, אִם רוֹצֶה בְּקִיּוּמוֹ – הֲרֵי הוּא כַּעֲרֵיבָה.

The Gemara explains: **What are the circumstances** of the mishna's case? It is a case **where there is less than an egg-bulk of** ritually impure **food, and it touched this dough** in the bowl, and then it came into contact with ritually pure food. **During Passover,** when **the prohibition** that applies to the dough causes it to be considered **significant** although it is a very small quantity, **it combines** with the first piece of food. Together they are the size of an egg-bulk, which is able to transmit the ritual impurity of foods. However, **during the rest of the year, when** there is no prohibition that imparts this significance to the dough, **the matter is dependent on** the owner's **particularity; if he is particular about it,** i.e., he does not want the dough to be there, it is considered food rather than part of the bowl, and **it combines** with the other piece of food. However, **if one prefers its** continued **presence** in its current location, **it is** considered **like** part of **the kneading bowl** itself, rather than food.

מַתְקִיף לַהּ רָבָא: מִי קָתָנֵי מִצְטָרֵף? וְהָא חוֹצֵץ קָתָנֵי! אֶלָּא אָמַר רָבָא: וְכֵן לְהַעֲלוֹת טָהֳרָה לַעֲרֵיבָה.

Rava strongly objects to this: Was the language **taught** in the mishna: **Combines? Didn't** the mishna **teach** that **it interposes?** Abaye's explanation does not account for this term. **Rather, Rava said** that the mishna should be understood as saying: **And so too** with regard to **purifying the kneading bowl** via immersion.

NOTES

With regard to the combination of two pieces vis-à-vis ritual impurity – לְעִנְיַן צֵירוּף טוּמְאָה: Seemingly, it would have been simpler to say that the mishna is referring to contracting ritual impurity: On Passover, the prohibition causes an olive-bulk of dough to be considered significant and thus susceptible to contracting ritual impurity. During the rest of the year, this small amount of dough is considered to be part of the kneading bowl, in which case it is not susceptible to the ritual impurity of foods, provided the owner does not object to its presence. If the owner is particular about its presence, it is treated as dough. This explanation is not presented because the dough is prohibited during Passover in any case, and therefore its susceptibility to the ritual impurity of foods is irrelevant (*Tosafot*).

הֵיכִי דָּמֵי – כְּגוֹן דְּאִיטַּמִּי הָךְ עֲרֵיבָה, וּבָעֵי לְאַטְבּוּלֵי. בְּפֶסַח דְּאִיסּוּרוֹ חָשׁוּב – חוֹצֵץ, וְלָא סָלְקָא לַהּ טְבִילָה. בִּשְׁאָר יְמוֹת הַשָּׁנָה בִּקְפֵידָא תַּלְיָא מִילְּתָא, אִי מַקְפִּיד עָלָיו – חוֹצֵץ, וְאִם רוֹצֶה בְּקִיּוּמוֹ – הֲרֵי הוּא כָּעֲרֵיבָה.

The Gemara explains: **What are the circumstances** of the mishna's case? It is a case **where the kneading bowl became ritually impure, and** one **wishes to immerse it. During Passover, when the prohibition** of an olive-bulk of leaven causes it to be considered **significant, it interposes** between the water and the kneading bowl, **and the immersion is ineffective.** However, **during the rest of the year, the matter depends upon** whether or not the owner is **particular** about it. **If he is particular about** the dough and wishes to remove it, **it interposes** between the water and the bowl. However, **if** the owner **desires it to be present, it is** considered **like** part of the **kneading bowl** itself, and it does not interpose between the water and the bowl.

מַתְקִיף לַהּ רַב פָּפָּא: מִי קָתָנֵי "וְכֵן לְעִנְיַן טׇהֳרָה"? הָא לְעִנְיַן טוּמְאָה קָתָנֵי! אֶלָּא אָמַר רַב פָּפָּא: וְכֵן לְעִנְיַן לְהוֹרִיד טוּמְאָה לָעֲרֵיבָה.

Rav Pappa strongly objects to this: Was the language **taught** in the mishna: **And similarly with regard to ritual purity? Didn't** the mishna **teach: And similarly with regard to ritual impurity? Rather, Rav Pappa said** the mishna should be understood as saying: **And similarly with regard to the transfer of ritual impurity to the kneading bowl** via this dough.

הֵיכִי דָּמֵי – כְּגוֹן דְּנָגַע שֶׁרֶץ בְּהַאי בָּצֵק. בְּפֶסַח, דְּאִיסּוּרוֹ חָשׁוּב – חוֹצֵץ, וְלָא נָחְתָה לַהּ טוּמְאָה. בִּשְׁאָר יְמוֹת הַשָּׁנָה, דְּבִקְפֵידָא תַּלְיָא, אִם מַקְפִּיד עָלָיו – חוֹצֵץ, אִם רוֹצֶה בְּקִיּוּמוֹ – הֲרֵי הוּא כָּעֲרֵיבָה.

The Gemara explains: **What are the circumstances** of the mishna's case? It is a case **where** the carcass of **a creeping animal**[N] **touched this dough.**[H] **During Passover, when its prohibition** causes the dough to be considered **significant, it interposes** between the bowl and the creeping animal, and **ritual impurity does not descend to the kneading bowl,** i.e., the kneading bowl does not become impure. **During the rest of the year, when it depends** upon whether one is **particular** about the presence of the dough, **if he is particular about it, it interposes** between the bowl and the creeping animal and prevents the bowl from becoming impure. However, **if he desires it to be present, it is** considered **like** it is part of **the kneading bowl** itself. Therefore, the entire bowl becomes ritually impure when the carcass of the creeping animal touches the dough.

מתני׳ בְּצֵק הַחֵרֵשׁ, אִם יֵשׁ כַּיּוֹצֵא בּוֹ שֶׁהֶחְמִיץ – הֲרֵי זֶה אָסוּר.

MISHNA **Deaf dough**[NH] is dough for which it is difficult to determine if it has been leavened. It is comparable to a deaf-mute, who cannot communicate. **If there is** dough **similar to it** in that water was added to both at the same time, **which became leavened,** the deaf dough **is prohibited.** Although it has not shown external signs of becoming leavened, it can be presumed that the deaf dough has also become leavened.

NOTES

A creeping animal – שֶׁרֶץ: In broad terms, this term refers to rodents, lizards, insects, or any other small creature that crawls. In this particular case, the reference is to the *halakha* that ritual impurity is imparted by the carcasses of eight specific creeping animals (Leviticus 11:29–37). The Sages extensively debated the identification of these eight creatures. Though not definitive, the popularly accepted identifications are: weasel, mouse, toad, hedgehog, chameleon, lizard, snail, and mole. In the Talmud these eight creatures are often referred to by the term creeping animal, without any further description.

Deaf dough – בְּצֵק הַחֵרֵשׁ: See Rashi's explanation of this expression. Another explanation is that the mishna is referring to a difference that can be discerned audibly between dough that has become leavened and dough that has not become leavened. While leavened dough makes a sound when tapped, dough that has not become leavened makes no such sound. The dough described here does not make a sound when tapped and is therefore called deaf dough (Rambam). Another interpretation is that leavened dough produces a low sound, like a deaf person, as opposed to *matza*, which produces a clear sound (Ra'avad). Alternatively, just as a person who is hard of hearing processes sound slowly, so too, this dough becomes leavened slowly (Ramban). Yet another explanation is that this dough does not become leavened in the typical manner, comparable to a deaf person, who does not process information in the typical manner (*ge'onim*).

HALAKHA

The carcass of a creeping animal touched this dough – נָגַע שֶׁרֶץ בְּהַאי בָּצֵק: If the carcass of a creeping animal touched dough stuck to the side of a kneading bowl during Passover, the kneading bowl does not become ritually impure. This is because the prohibition of leaven renders the dough significant, and it is considered an independent entity from the bowl. During the rest of the year, if the owner is particular about this dough, then the kneading bowl is ritually pure; if not, it is impure. This ruling is in accordance with Rav Pappa's explanation of the mishna (Rambam *Sefer Tahara*, *Hilkhot Kelim* 20:9).

Deaf dough – בְּצֵק הַחֵרֵשׁ: With regard to dough that does not show signs of becoming leavened, if other dough prepared at the same time became leavened, this dough is also presumed to have become leavened, as stated in the mishna. If no other dough was prepared at the same time, it should be assumed that the time it would take the dough to become leavened is equal to the time it takes to walk one *mil*, which is two thousand cubits (*Shulḥan Arukh*, *Oraḥ Ḥayyim* 459:2).

גמ׳ אִם אֵין שָׁם כַּיּוֹצֵא בּוֹ מַהוּ? אָמַר רַבִּי אַבָּהוּ אָמַר רַבִּי שִׁמְעוֹן בֶּן לָקִישׁ: כְּדֵי שֶׁיֵּלֵךְ אָדָם מִמִּגְדַּל נוּנַיָא לִטְבֶרְיָא, מִיל.

GEMARA The Gemara seeks to clarify the ruling of the mishna: **If there is no dough similar to it, what is the** *halakha*? **Rabbi Abbahu said** that **Rabbi Shimon ben Lakish said:** According to the Sages, leavening occurs in the time it takes **a person** to **walk** the distance **from Migdal Nunaya**[B] to **Tiberias,**[B] which is **a** ***mil,***[HB] two thousand cubits.

וְנֵימָא מִיל! הָא קָא מַשְׁמַע לַן דְּשִׁיעוּרָא דְּמִיל כְּמִמִּגְדַּל נוּנַיָא וְעַד טְבֶרְיָא.

The Gemara asks about this formulation: Why is it necessary to mention the distance between these two places? **Let us say** that leavening begins after the time it takes a person to walk a ***mil.*** The Gemara answers: **This** statement incidentally **teaches us that the length of a** ***mil*** is the distance **from Migdal Nunaya to Tiberias.**[B]

HALAKHA

The time it takes to walk a *mil* – הִילּוּךְ מִיל: There are several different opinions with regard to this length of time. Some say that it is eighteen minutes, others suggest that it is twenty-four minutes, while others rule that it is twenty-two minutes (Vilna Gaon). With regard to the prohibitions against leaven on Passover, the universally accepted practice is to be stringent; therefore, the *halakha* is based on the shortest of these rulings. In addition to determining whether dough has become leaven, this unit of time also plays a role regarding certain *halakhot* of prayer (see Maharil; *Ḥavot Ya'ir*; *Peri Ḥadash*; *Magen Avraham*; and others; *Shulḥan Arukh*, *Oraḥ Ḥayyim* 459:2).

BACKGROUND

Migdal Nunaya – מִגְדַּל נוּנַיָא: Migdal Nunaya is also referred to in some sources as Migdala or Taricheae, which means in Greek "the place of salting fish." Today the town of Migdal is situated in the near proximity of the ancient Migdala.

In September 2009, a salvage dig of the Israel Antiquities Authority prior to the construction of a hotel revealed an ancient synagogue believed to be from approximately two thousand years ago. In the center of the main hall, which measures 120 sq m, archaeologists discovered an unusual stone carved with a seven-branched candelabrum. It is the first of its kind to be discovered from the early Roman period.

Archaeological site at Migdala

Rock with engraving of a candelabrum found in the synagogue at Migdala

Tiberias – טְבֶרְיָא: Tiberias is a city on the shore of the Sea of Galilee, founded by Herod Antipas (c. 18 CE). It was apparently constructed on the site of earlier settlements, and according to some opinions in the Talmud (*Megilla* 6a), it was the site of the biblical city of Rakkat. At the outset, Tiberias was a town with a mixed Jewish and gentile population, and the Jewish population was not distinguished for its Torah scholarship. However, after the destruction of the Temple, several prominent Torah scholars lived there, such as Ben Azzai and Rabbi Meir. Tiberias reached its apex when the Sanhedrin moved there (c. 235 CE) and it became the seat of the Great Council, presided over by Rabbi Yehuda Nesia. After him, Rabbi Yoḥanan became its leading spiritual figure and headed the yeshiva there, at which point Tiberias became the Torah center of Eretz Yisrael for many years.

Most of the disciples of Rabbi Yoḥanan, particularly those who emigrated from Babylonia, lived and continued their studies in Tiberias. Reish Lakish lived there, as did Rabbi Elazar ben Pedat, Rabbi Ami, Rabbi Yirmeya, and Rabbi Yona, and it is likely that most of the Jerusalem Talmud was redacted there. After the talmudic period, Tiberias remained a significant creative religious and spiritual center. Many of the works of aggadic midrash and numerous liturgical poems were composed there.

During the post-talmudic era, the inhabitants of Tiberias were renowned as experts in Hebrew grammar. The system of Hebrew vocalization still used today is called Tiberian vocalization, as it was formulated and established there.

Mil – מִיל: The talmudic *mil* is a unit of distance related to, but not identical to, the Roman mile, from which it received its name. One *mil* equals two thousand cubits. This is equivalent to 960 m according to Rav Ḥayyim Na'e, and 1,150 m according to the Ḥazon Ish.

Tiberias and Migdal Nunaya – טְבֶרְיָא וּמִגְדַּל נוּנַיָא:

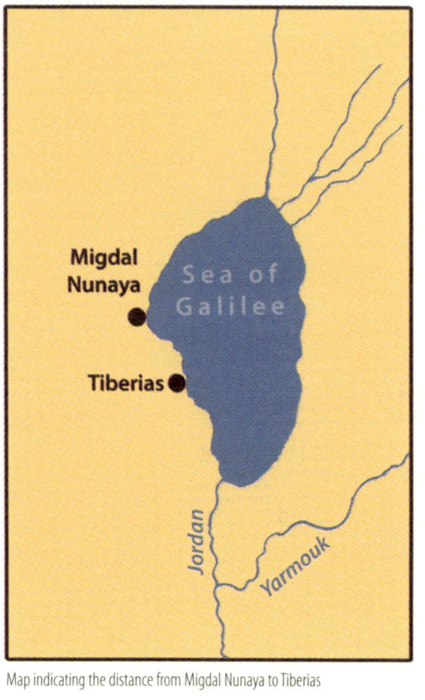

Map indicating the distance from Migdal Nunaya to Tiberias

אָמַר רַבִּי אַבָּהוּ אָמַר רַבִּי שִׁמְעוֹן בֶּן לָקִישׁ: לַגַּבָּל וְלַתְּפִלָּה וְלִנְטִילַת יָדַיִם – אַרְבָּעָה מִילִין.

Rabbi Abbahu said that **Rabbi Shimon ben Lakish said: With regard to a kneader,**[NH] i.e., one who kneads dough for others and should maintain the ritual purity of the dough; **and** similarly, **with regard to** washing one's hands for **prayer** (*Arukh*),[NH] **and with regard to washing hands**[N] before eating, one must search either for a ritual bath to immerse the vessel he is using to knead the dough, or for water to purify his hands, provided that water is accessible within the time it takes to walk **four *mil*,** eight thousand cubits.

אָמַר רַב נַחְמָן בַּר יִצְחָק: אַיְיבוּ אֲמָרָהּ, וְאַרְבָּעָה אָמַר בָּהּ, וְחָדָא מִינַּיְיהוּ עִבּוּד. דִּתְנַן: וְכוּלָּן שֶׁעִיבְּדָן אוֹ שֶׁהִילֵּךְ בָּהֶן כְּדֵי עֲבוֹדָה – טְהוֹרִין, חוּץ מֵעוֹר הָאָדָם. וְכַמָּה כְּדֵי עֲבוֹדָה? אָמַר רַבִּי (אִינְיָיא) אָמַר רַבִּי יַנַּאי: כְּדֵי הִילּוּךְ אַרְבָּעָה מִילִין.

Rav Naḥman bar Yitzḥak said: Ayvu said this *halakha*, **and he said it** about **four** cases, as opposed to the three cases mentioned previously. **And one of them** pertained to the **tanning** of hides,[H] which lasts for the time that it takes a person to walk four *mil*. **As we learned** in a mishna: **And all** types of thin, soft hides, which have the status of flesh with regard to ritual impurity because their texture is similar to flesh, **that were tanned** in order to be made into leather, **or that one trod upon** for as long as necessary **for the leatherworking** process, **are ritually pure.** They are considered to be leather and are no longer considered like the flesh of the animal, **except for** the **skin of a human** corpse, which always remains ritually impure. The Gemara asks: **How much** time must one tread upon **a hide for the leatherworking** process? **Rabbi Ayvu**[N] **said that Rabbi Yannai said:** It is the amount of time it takes to **walk four *mil*.**

אָמַר רַבִּי יוֹסֵי בְּרַבִּי חֲנִינָא: לֹא שָׁנוּ אֶלָּא לְפָנָיו, אֲבָל לְאַחֲרָיו – אֲפִילּוּ מִיל אֵינוֹ חוֹזֵר. אָמַר רַב אַחָא: וּמִינָּהּ, מִיל הוּא דְּאֵינוֹ חוֹזֵר, הָא פָּחוֹת מִמִּיל – חוֹזֵר.

Rabbi Yosei, son of Rabbi Ḥanina, said: They taught that one must search for water to wash one's hands before eating or prayer for the amount of time it takes to walk four *mil* **only** when the water **is before him,** in the direction that he is traveling. **However,** when it is **behind him, he need not return even a *mil*. Rav Aḥa said: From this** statement one may infer that **he** need **not return a *mil*, but he must return less than one *mil*** in order to obtain water.

מתני׳ כֵּיצַד מַפְרִישִׁין חַלָּה בְּטוּמְאָה בְּיוֹם טוֹב?

MISHNA **How does one separate *ḥalla*[N] in ritual impurity[N] during the Festival** day of Passover? Ordinarily, one may separate ritually pure *ḥalla* from dough and give it to a priest immediately so that he may eat it. Ritually impure *ḥalla* is unfit for a priest and must be burned, yet it is prohibited to bake or burn anything that is not fit to be eaten during the Festival day. However, it is also prohibited to wait and burn it after the Festival day, since it will become leavened in the meantime.

NOTES

With regard to a kneader – לַגַּבָּל: See the explanations of Rashi and *Tosafot*. Others explain that this teaches that the preferable time within which one may knead dough before it becomes leavened is the time it takes for an average person to walk four *mil*. This longer duration applies as long as the dough is being kneaded, as opposed to the case of the deaf dough, with regard to which the Gemara stated that it becomes leavened in the amount of time it takes to walk one *mil*. In that case, the dough was kneaded and then left alone (*ge'onim*).

With regard to prayer – לַתְּפִלָּה: Some explain that this is referring to one who experienced a seminal emission and must immerse in a ritual bath before prayer. This statement clarifies that such a person is required to walk up to four *mil* in order to immerse (Rav Sherira Gaon). Others explain that it means that one who walks this distance must recite the traveler's prayer (*ge'onim*). Others understand the expression differently and say that it informs us that one may pray despite the fact that he feels the need to relieve himself, provided he is able to wait the time it takes to walk four *mil* (Ritva).

With regard to washing hands – לִנְטִילַת יָדַיִם: Some say that this is referring to washing one's hands before prayer (*ge'onim*). Others understand that this is referring to a person who has relieved himself but has no water with which to wash. If he can find water to wash his hands within the next four *mil*, he should wait until he can wash his hands to recite the blessing: Who formed man in wisdom [*asher yatzar*], which is recited after performing one's bodily functions. However, if one cannot find water within this distance, he should clean his hands in a different way. Others suggest that this is referring to washing one's hands before eating in the following case: If one washed his hands in the morning on the condition that he would not need to do so again, he may rely on this first washing if there is no water within four *mil* (Ritva).

Rabbi Ayvu – רַבִּי (אִינְיָיא): The standard text of the Vilna Talmud makes reference to Rabbi Inya and includes a note in the margin of the text indicating that the correct version should read: Rabbi Ayvu. In context, it is clear that this alternate version is accurate.

Ḥalla – חַלָּה: The Torah commands the separation of a portion of dough, which is given to the priests (Numbers 15:20). This portion is called *ḥalla* and is governed by all the *halakhot* pertaining to *teruma*, the priests' portion of the crop. The Torah does not specify a measure for *ḥalla*. When baking for personal use, the Sages required an individual to give one twenty-fourth of his dough, while a commercial baker must give one forty-eighth. *Ḥalla* must be taken from all dough made from any one of the five types of grain, provided that the quantity of flour is at least a tenth of an *epha* in volume. If *ḥalla* is not taken, the dough is considered *tevel* and may not be eaten.

Nowadays, as all Jews have the status of being ritually impure, *ḥalla* is governed by the same *halakhot* as is ritually impure *teruma* and must be burned. Accordingly, the measures mentioned above no longer apply; only a small portion is separated from the dough and burned, and the rest of the dough may then be used. A blessing is recited for the separation of *ḥalla*, which is considered one of the mitzvot practiced particularly by women. The *halakhot* of this mitzva are discussed comprehensively in tractate *Ḥalla*.

Ḥalla in ritual impurity – חַלָּה בְּטוּמְאָה: According to the Ra'avad, this is referring to a case where enough dough was kneaded to require one to separate *ḥalla*, and only then did the dough become ritually impure. However, if the dough became impure before the obligation to separate *ḥalla* took effect, the dough should be divided into smaller pieces and baked separately, so that the obligation to separate *ḥalla* will not apply. After the pieces are baked, one may place them in a single basket (Rashba; Rabbeinu Gershom).

HALAKHA

With regard to a kneader – לַגַּבָּל: It is preferable to prepare dough in a state of ritual purity. If it is possible for one to find water to purify himself within a distance of four *mil*, he should do so. This *halakha* is in accordance with Rashi's explanation of the opinion of Rabbi Abbahu (Rambam *Sefer Zera'im*, *Hilkhot Bikkurim* 8:11).

With regard to prayer – לַתְּפִלָּה: One who needs to pray but has no water with which to wash his hands should continue on his journey for up to an additional four *mil* in order to wash them, provided the proper time for prayer will not elapse in the interim, as explained in the *Arukh*. If one has already passed a source of water, he should return to it, if it is within a distance of one *mil* (*Shulḥan Arukh*, *Oraḥ Ḥayyim* 92:4).

Tanning hides – עִיבּוּד עוֹרוֹת: If thin, soft hides, which initially have the same status as the flesh of the animal, are tanned or trodden upon, they are no longer considered flesh. They do not contract ritual impurity, as stated in the Gemara (Rambam *Sefer Tahara*, *Hilkhot She'ar Avot HaTumot* 1:9).

רבי אליעזר אומר: לא תקרא לה שם עד שתאפה. בן בתירא אומר: תטיל בצונן. אמר רבי יהושע:

Rabbi Eliezer says: A woman **should not designate it** as *ḥalla* prior to baking; rather, she should refrain from doing so **until it is baked.**[H] In other words, she should wait until she has baked all of the dough, and there is no risk of it becoming leavened. Only then should she separate *ḥalla* from it. The portion of *ḥalla* may then be kept until after the Festival day, when it may be burned. **Ben Beteira says: She should** separate the *ḥalla* before it is baked, and **place** the dough **in cold** water[N] so that it will not become leavened.[N] **Rabbi Yehoshua said:**

HALAKHA

Ritually impure *ḥalla* on Passover – חלה טמאה בפסח: One who kneads dough on a Festival day of Passover should not designate it as *ḥalla*; rather, one should bake it all together and then separate *ḥalla*. If one forgot and designated the *ḥalla*, he should place the *ḥalla* in cold water so it does not become leavened. The preferred method is in accordance with the opinion of Rabbi Eliezer, as the Gemara rules in accordance with his view. If one forgot, he may follow the opinion of ben Beteira, as the authorities state that Rabbi Eliezer did not dispute him after the fact (*Shulḥan Arukh, Oraḥ Ḥayyim* 457:2).

NOTES

She should place it in cold water – תטיל בצונן: According to this opinion, the water must be cold and must be continuously dripping into the container (*Nimukei Yosef*; Ritva).

The dispute between Rabbi Eliezer and ben Beteira – מחלוקת רבי אליעזר ובן בתירא: Several explanations are suggested for this dispute. Rabbeinu Gershom explains it as follows: According to Rabbi Eliezer it is prohibited to allow this dough to become leavened because, since one can decide to which priest to give one's *ḥalla* and thereby earn the priest's appreciation, one is considered to have a financial stake in the dough, which is a form of ownership. Therefore, allowing this dough to become leavened violates the prohibition against owning leavened bread on Passover. However, it is permissible to bake the dough because one may separate *ḥalla* after it has been baked.

Ben Beteira agrees that one may not allow the *ḥalla* to become leavened due to the prohibition against owning leavened bread, but he holds that baking the portion that will become *ḥalla* is prohibited, as it is considered unnecessary baking on the Festival. The Rosh explains that, according to Rabbi Eliezer, placing the dough in cold water is prohibited, since one might do this in an improper way (see Maharam Ḥalawa). On the other hand, according to ben Beteira, baking the dough before separating *ḥalla* is prohibited because it appears to be an unnecessary circumvention of the *halakha* (*Mikhtam*).

Perek **III**
Daf **46** Amud **b**

לא זה הוא חמץ שמוזהרין עליו בבל יראה ובבל ימצא. אלא, מפרישתה ומניחתה עד הערב, ואם החמיצה – החמיצה.

This is not the leavened bread about which we are warned with the prohibitions: **It shall not be seen, and: It shall not be found.** These prohibitions do not apply because the *ḥalla* does not actually belong to the owner of the dough; it is instead considered to be consecrated property. **Rather, she should separate** the *ḥalla* **and leave it until the evening; and if it becomes leavened,** then **it will become leavened,** but this is of no concern.

גמ׳ לימא בטובת הנאה קמיפלגי, דרבי אליעזר סבר: טובת הנאה ממון, ורבי יהושע סבר: טובת הנאה אינה ממון.

GEMARA The Gemara suggests: **Let us say** that the *tanna'im* **disagree with regard to benefit** of **discretion,**[N] i.e., benefit accrued from the option of giving *ḥalla*, *teruma* and tithes to whichever priest or Levite one chooses. The Sages debated whether this benefit has monetary value and would constitute a form of ownership. **Rabbi Eliezer holds: Benefit** of **discretion is** considered to have **monetary** value. Therefore, one owns the *ḥalla* he separates, and he must be careful to prevent it from becoming leavened. However, **Rabbi Yehoshua holds: Benefit of discretion is not** considered to have **monetary** value. One does not own the *ḥalla*, and therefore he may allow it to become leavened.

לא, דכולי עלמא סברי "טובת הנאה אינה ממון" והכא ב"הואיל" קמיפלגי. דרבי אליעזר סבר: אמרינן הואיל ואי בעי איתשיל עלה – ממוניה הוא. ורבי יהושע סבר: לא אמרינן הואיל.

The Gemara rejects this suggestion: **No, everyone holds** that **benefit of discretion is not** considered to have **monetary** value, **and here they disagree** with regard to the principle of: **Since, etc. As Rabbi Eliezer holds:**[N] **We say** that **since, if he wants, he can ask**[N] to have his separation of the *ḥalla* voided when he regrets having done so, **it is his property.** Even if one does not actually revoke the status of the *ḥalla*, the fact that the potential for such an action exists indicates that he still maintains a form of ownership of this dough. **And Rabbi Yehoshua holds: We do not say** that **since** he could theoretically revoke the status of the *ḥalla*, the dough is considered his. Consequently, he may leave it until the end of the Festival day without being concerned that it will become leavened.

איתמר, האופה מיום טוב לחול, רב חסדא אמר: לוקה, רבה אמר: אינו לוקה.

Apropos the principle: Since, etc., the Gemara cites a related dispute. **It was stated** that the *amora'im* disagree with regard to **one who bakes** bread **on a Festival** day **for** use during **the week.**[H] **Rav Ḥisda said: He is flogged** because he has desecrated the Festival. **Rabba said: He is not flogged.**

NOTES

Benefit of discretion – טובת הנאה: This term refers to one's right to distribute obligatory dues to a priest of his own choosing; a priest himself may not purchase the rights to *teruma* or *ḥalla*. Since one may not receive remuneration for the dues, there is no set value for the benefit one gains as a result of his ability to distribute the dues. Therefore, the Sages debate whether or not benefit of discretion has real monetary value.

Rabbi Eliezer holds – רבי אליעזר סבר: The early commentaries ask how it is possible to attribute this position to Rabbi Eliezer when Rabbi Eliezer is quoted elsewhere as having said that one cannot revoke the status of consecrated items (*Tosefot Yom Tov*). Some answer by claiming that *ḥalla* is different from other types of consecrated property in that it remains the property of its owner, and therefore Rabbi Eliezer agrees that it is possible to revoke its status (Rav Menaḥem Azarya de Fano). Others suggest that Rabbi Eliezer holds that one cannot revoke the status of consecrated property only when it results in leniency, but Rabbi Eliezer would not apply such a rule when it results in stringency, as in this case.

If he wants he can ask – אי בעי איתשיל: Some claim that it is possible to revoke only the status of objects that were unintentionally consecrated. Based on this explanation, the entire mishna is discussing a case where the items were accidentally consecrated (Rabbeinu Efrayim). Although there is a general rule that, *ab initio*, one may not dissolve vows to do a mitzva, this is applied only when one seeks to avoid fulfilling the mitzva. However, in this case, where the nullification is only temporary and is performed to avoid the violation of a prohibition, the request to void would be granted and the dough's status as *ḥalla* would be revoked (Ritva).

HALAKHA

One who bakes on a Festival day for use during the week – האופה מיום טוב לחול: It is prohibited to bake on a Festival day for a weekday. However, one who does so is not flogged, due to the possibility that guests might visit and one would then need the food, as stated by Rabba. Rabba's opinion is based upon the opinion of Rabbi Eliezer, whose ruling is accepted in this case (*Hagahot Maimoniyot*; *Shulḥan Arukh, Oraḥ Ḥayyim* 503:1).

רַב חִסְדָּא אָמַר: לוֹקֶה, לָא אָמְרִינַן "הוֹאִיל וּמִיקְלְעִי לֵיהּ אוֹרְחִים חֲזִי לֵיהּ". רַבָּה אָמַר: אֵינוֹ לוֹקֶה, אָמְרִינַן הוֹאִיל.

The Gemara explains the two opinions: **Rav Ḥisda said** that **he is flogged** because **we do not say** that **since guests** may happen to visit **him**,[N] the bread is **fit for him** on the Festival day itself. **Rabba said** that **he is not flogged** because **we say** that **since** guests may visit him, the bread is considered to have been baked for use on the Festival day itself. Even if guests do not actually come, he has not desecrated the Festival.

אָמַר לֵיהּ רַבָּה לְרַב חִסְדָּא: לְדִידָךְ, דְּאָמְרַתְּ לָא אָמְרִינַן הוֹאִיל – הֵיאַךְ אוֹפִין מִיּוֹם טוֹב לְשַׁבָּת? אָמַר לֵיהּ: מִשּׁוּם עֵירוּבֵי תַבְשִׁילִין.

Rabba said to Rav Ḥisda: According to you, who said that we do not say the principle: **Since, etc., how** is it permitted to **bake** on **a Festival for Shabbat? He said to him:** One is permitted to bake on a Festival for Shabbat **due to the joining of cooked foods** [*eiruv tavshilin*][N] instituted by the Sages.

וּמִשּׁוּם עֵירוּבֵי תַבְשִׁילִין שָׁרֵינַן אִיסּוּרָא דְּאוֹרַיְיתָא? אָמַר לֵיהּ: מִדְּאוֹרַיְיתָא צוֹרְכֵי שַׁבָּת נַעֲשִׂין בְּיוֹם טוֹב, וְרַבָּנַן הוּא דִּגְזַרוּ בֵּיהּ, גְּזֵירָה שֶׁמָּא יֹאמְרוּ אוֹפִין מִיּוֹם טוֹב אַף לַחוֹל. וְכֵיוָן דְּאַצְרְכוּהַ רַבָּנַן עֵירוּבֵי תַבְשִׁילִין – אִית לֵיהּ הֶיכֵּירָא.

Rabba responded: **Due to** the practice of **the joining of cooked foods,** which was instituted by the Sages, **may one permit a Torah prohibition?** Rav Ḥisda **said to him: By Torah** law, whatever one **needs** for **Shabbat** may **be done on a Festival,** and the prohibition against performing labor during the Festival does not apply to preparations for Shabbat. **It was the Sages who decreed** that one may not bake on a Festival for Shabbat, as **a decree lest** people **say** that **one may bake on the Festival even for** use during **the week. And since the Sages required a joining of cooked foods, one has a conspicuous marker** reminding him that baking on the Festival for Shabbat is permitted but baking on the Festival for a weekday is prohibited.[H]

אֵיתִיבֵיהּ: בְּהֵמָה הַמְסוּכֶּנֶת לֹא יִשְׁחוֹט אֶלָּא כְּדֵי שֶׁיָּכוֹל לֶאֱכוֹל הֵימֶנָּה כַּזַּיִת צָלִי מִבְּעוֹד יוֹם. יָכוֹל לֶאֱכוֹל – אַף עַל גַּב דְּלָא בָּעֵי לְמֵיכַל. בִּשְׁלָמָא לְדִידִי, דְּאָמְרִי "הוֹאִיל" – הוֹאִיל וְאִי בָּעֵי לְמֵיכַל מָצֵי אָכֵיל – מִשּׁוּם הָכִי יִשְׁחוֹט. אֶלָּא לְדִידָךְ, דְּאָמְרַתְּ לָא אָמְרִינַן "הוֹאִיל" – אַמַּאי יִשְׁחוֹט?

Rabba **raised an objection to** Rav Ḥisda's opinion from a *baraita*: If one wishes to slaughter **a dangerously** ill **animal**[H] before it dies on its own and becomes prohibited for consumption, **he may not slaughter** it on a Festival day **unless** there is enough time so that **he can eat an olive-bulk of it roasted while it is still day.** Rabba reads this statement precisely: The *baraita* stipulates that the slaughter is permitted if **one can eat** the meat while it is still day, **although he is not required to** actually **eat** the meat. **Granted, according to my** position, **that I said** that one may rely on the principle: **Since, etc.,** this ruling is reasonable. **Since if one wants to eat he may eat, due to that** reason alone **he may slaughter** the animal. **But** according to **you, who said that we do not say** the principle of: **Since, etc., why may he slaughter** such an animal?

אָמַר לֵיהּ: מִשּׁוּם הֶפְסֵד מָמוֹנוֹ. וּמִשּׁוּם הֶפְסֵד מָמוֹנוֹ שָׁרֵינַן אִיסּוּרָא דְּאוֹרַיְיתָא?!

Rav Ḥisda **said to him:** He is permitted to slaughter the animal **due to the monetary loss** that would be incurred by not slaughtering it, and not due to the principle of: Since, etc. Rabba asked rhetorically: **Will we permit a Torah prohibition due to monetary loss?**

אֲמַר לֵיהּ: אִין, מִשּׁוּם הֶפְסֵד מָמוֹנוֹ גָּמַר בְּלִבּוֹ לֶאֱכוֹל כַּזַּיִת, וְאִי אֶפְשָׁר לְכַזַּיִת בָּשָׂר בְּלֹא שְׁחִיטָה.

Rav Ḥisda **said to him: Yes,** although this factor on its own does not mitigate the prohibition. Rather, **due to the monetary loss** that would otherwise be incurred, **one decided to eat an olive-bulk** of the meat, although he does not need to. **And since it is impossible** to eat even **an olive-bulk of meat without slaughtering** the animal, one is permitted to slaughter the animal.

אֵיתִיבֵיהּ: לֶחֶם הַפָּנִים

Rabba **raised** another **objection to him: The shewbread** in the Temple

HALAKHA

Baking and cooking on a Festival for Shabbat – אֲפִיָּה וּבִישּׁוּל בְּיוֹם טוֹב לְצוֹרֶךְ שַׁבָּת: When a Festival occurs on a Friday, one may not bake or cook on the Festival for Shabbat without a joining of cooked foods [*eiruv tavshilin*]. This prohibition is rabbinic and was enacted so that people would not cook on a Festival for a weekday, in accordance with the opinion of Rabba (Rambam *Sefer Zemanim*, *Hilkhot Yom Tov* 6:1).

A dangerously ill animal – בְּהֵמָה הַמְסוּכֶּנֶת: One may not slaughter a dangerously ill animal during a Festival unless there is enough time left in the day to roast and eat an olive-bulk of its meat (*Shulḥan Arukh*, *Oraḥ Ḥayyim* 498:6).

NOTES

Since guests may happen to visit him – הוֹאִיל וּמִיקְלְעִי לֵיהּ אוֹרְחִים: The Maharam Ḥalawa explains that the fact that guests might visit cannot be used to permit an activity that would otherwise be prohibited. The discussion is about whether one is exempt from lashes because the certainty of the violation has been undermined; however, the action is still prohibited.

Joining of cooked foods [*eiruv tavshilin*] – עֵרוּב תַּבְשִׁילִין: *Eiruv tavshilin*, or the joining of cooked foods, is a ritual that permits one to cook and prepare food on a Festival that occurs on a Friday, for use on Shabbat. A fundamental difference between a Festival and Shabbat is that certain activities in the preparation of food are permitted on Festivals. However, the Sages decreed that food may not be prepared for use after the Festival, or even from one day of a Festival to the next. This prohibition creates a difficulty if Shabbat follows directly after a Festival. In those circumstances, the Sages permitted an individual to prepare food for Shabbat on the Festival, provided that prior to the beginning of the Festival he puts aside specifically for Shabbat a dish of bread and a cooked item. This dish is called the *eiruv tavshilin*. One who put aside a joining of cooked foods may cook on the Festival for Shabbat, as the preparation of these foods is considered the continuation of the preparation of the joining of cooked foods.

נֶאֱכָל לְתִשְׁעָה, לַעֲשָׂרָה, וּלְאַחַד עָשָׂר – לֹא פָּחוֹת וְלֹא יוֹתֵר. כֵּיצַד? כְּדַרְכּוֹ – לְתִשְׁעָה, נֶאֱפָה בְּעֶרֶב שַׁבָּת – נֶאֱכָל בַּשַּׁבָּת לְתִשְׁעָה. חָל יוֹם טוֹב לִהְיוֹת בְּעֶרֶב שַׁבָּת – נֶאֱכָל לַשַּׁבָּת לַעֲשָׂרָה. שְׁנֵי יָמִים טוֹבִים שֶׁל רֹאשׁ הַשָּׁנָה – נֶאֱכָל לַשַּׁבָּת לְאַחַד עָשָׂר, לְפִי שֶׁאֵינוֹ דּוֹחֶה לֹא אֶת הַשַּׁבָּת וְלֹא אֶת הַיּוֹם טוֹב. וְאִי אָמְרַתְּ צוֹרְכֵי שַׁבָּת נַעֲשִׂין בְּיוֹם טוֹב אַמַּאי לָא דָּחֵי יוֹם טוֹב?

may be **eaten on the ninth, tenth,** or **eleventh** days from when it is baked, **no less and no more. How so? In its usual manner** it is eaten **on the ninth** day after it was baked, as **it is baked on Shabbat eve** and **it is eaten on** the next **Shabbat, on the ninth** day from when it was baked. If **a Festival occurs on Shabbat eve,** the shewbread is not baked on the Festival day but rather on Thursday, the eve of the Festival. Consequently, **it is eaten on Shabbat** of the next week, **on the tenth** day from when it was baked. If the **two Festival days of Rosh HaShana** preceded Shabbat, the shewbread is baked on Wednesday, Rosh HaShana eve, and **it is eaten on** the next **Shabbat, on the eleventh** day from when it was baked, **because** baking the shewbread[H] **does not override Shabbat or a Festival.**[N] Rabba asks: **If you say** that whatever one **needs** for **Shabbat may be done on a Festival, why doesn't** the baking of this bread **override the Festival?** Since the shewbread is eaten on Shabbat, it should be considered food that one is permitted to prepare during the Festival.

אֲמַר לֵיהּ: שְׁבוּת קְרוֹבָה – הִתִּירוּ, שְׁבוּת רְחוֹקָה – לֹא הִתִּירוּ.

Rav Ḥisda **said to him: They permitted** one to override **the rabbinic decree** in the Temple only with regard to baking on a Festival for the **proximate** Shabbat, i.e., Shabbat that immediately follows the Festival. However, **they did not permit** one to override **the rabbinic decree** to prepare for **a distant** Shabbat,[N] namely Shabbat of the next week.

וּלְרַבָּן שִׁמְעוֹן בֶּן גַּמְלִיאֵל, דְּאָמַר מִשּׁוּם רַבִּי שִׁמְעוֹן בֶּן הַסְּגָן: דּוֹחֶה אֶת יוֹם טוֹב, וְאֵינוֹ דּוֹחֶה אֶת יוֹם צוֹם, מַאי אִיכָּא לְמֵימַר?

The Gemara asks: **And according to Rabban Shimon ben Gamliel,** who **said in the name of Rabbi Shimon, son of the deputy** High Priest, that the baking of the shewbread **overrides a Festival but does not override the fast day** of Yom Kippur, **what can be said?** Apparently, the issue is the subject of a tannaitic dispute between Rabbi Shimon, son of the deputy High Priest, who contends that it is permissible to prepare the shewbread during a Festival, and the Rabbis, who prohibit it.

בְּהָא פְּלִיגִי; מָר סָבַר: שְׁבוּת קְרוֹבָה הִתִּירוּ, שְׁבוּת רְחוֹקָה לֹא הִתִּירוּ. וּמָר סָבַר: שְׁבוּת רְחוֹקָה נַמִּי הִתִּירוּ.

The Gemara explains that they do not dispute the basic principle. Rather, **this is** the point over which **they disagree: One Sage,** i.e., the Rabbis, **holds** that **they permitted** one to override **the rabbinic decree** only to prepare for the **proximate** Shabbat, but **they did not permit** one to override **the rabbinic decree** to prepare for a **distant** Shabbat. Therefore, the baking of the shewbread does not override the Festival. **And one Sage,** Rabbi Shimon, **holds** that **they also permitted** one to override **the rabbinic decree** in order to prepare for **a distant** Shabbat.

מְתִיב רַב מָרִי: שְׁתֵּי הַלֶּחֶם אֵינָן נֶאֱכָלוֹת לֹא פָּחוֹת מִשְּׁנַיִם, וְלֹא יוֹתֵר עַל שְׁלֹשָׁה. כֵּיצַד? נֶאֱפוֹת עֶרֶב יוֹם טוֹב – נֶאֱכָלוֹת לְיוֹם טוֹב לִשְׁנַיִם, חָל יוֹם טוֹב לִהְיוֹת אַחַר הַשַּׁבָּת – נֶאֱכָלוֹת לְיוֹם טוֹב לִשְׁלֹשָׁה, לְפִי שֶׁאֵינָהּ דּוֹחָה לֹא אֶת הַשַּׁבָּת וְלֹא אֶת הַיּוֹם טוֹב. וְאִי אָמְרַתְּ צוֹרְכֵי שַׁבָּת נַעֲשִׂין בְּיוֹם טוֹב, הָשְׁתָּא דְּשַׁבָּת בְּיוֹם טוֹב שָׁרֵי – דְּיוֹם טוֹב בְּיוֹם טוֹב מִיבַּעְיָא?!

Rav Mari raised an objection: The two loaves[N] of bread that are brought as a communal offering on *Shavuot* **are eaten** by the priests **no sooner than the second** day **and no later than the third** day from when they are baked. **How so? They are** generally **baked** on **the eve of the Festival and eaten on the Festival, the second** day from their baking. If **the Festival occurs after Shabbat,** they are baked on Friday and **they are eaten on the third** day from the baking, **because** the baking of the two loaves[H] **does not override Shabbat or the Festival.** Rav Mari asks: **If you say** that whatever one **needs** for **Shabbat may be done on a Festival, now that it is permitted** to engage in the necessary preparations for **Shabbat on a Festival, is it necessary** to mention that it is permitted to bake **for the Festival** itself **on the Festival?** As such, why doesn't the baking of the two loaves override the Festival?

שָׁאנֵי הָתָם, דְּאָמַר קְרָא ״לָכֶם״ ״לָכֶם״ וְלֹא לַגָּבוֹהַּ.

The Gemara answers: **It is different there,** in the case of the two loaves, **as the verse says:** "No kind of labor shall be done on them, save that which every man must eat, that only may be done **for you**" (Exodus 12:16). This indicates that it is permitted to cook and bake only **"for you,"** i.e., for human consumption, **and not for the** One **above,** namely for the Temple service.

HALAKHA

Baking the shewbread – אֲפִיַּית לֶחֶם הַפָּנִים: Baking the shewbread does not override either Shabbat or a Festival. Therefore, when the two days of Rosh HaShana occur on Thursday and Friday, the shewbread must be baked on Wednesday. The shewbread is always eaten on the following Shabbat. In the case when Rosh HaShana occurs on Thursday and Friday, it is eaten on the eleventh day from when it was baked (Rambam *Sefer Avoda, Hilkhot Temidin* 5:10).

Baking of the two loaves – אֲפִיַּית שְׁתֵּי הַלֶּחֶם: The baking of the two loaves offered on *Shavuot* does not override Shabbat or a Festival, and consequently they must be baked before the Festival begins. If the day before the Festival occurs on Shabbat, the loaves must be baked on Friday. Therefore, there are times when the two loaves are eaten on the third day after they have been baked (Rambam *Sefer Avoda, Hilkhot Temidin* 8:8).

Preparation of the flour for the two loaves

NOTES

Laws of the shewbread – הִלְכוֹת לֶחֶם הַפָּנִים: The laws of the shewbread are stated in the Torah (Leviticus 24:6–9) and explained in tractate *Menahot*. The twelve loaves of shewbread were placed on the sacred golden table inside the Sanctuary every Shabbat. On the following Shabbat, the loaves were removed and distributed for consumption by the priests. New loaves were then placed on the table.

They did not permit one to override the rabbinic decree for a distant Shabbat – שְׁבוּת רְחוֹקָה לֹא הִתִּירוּ: At first glance, it is difficult to understand the suggestion that one may bake on a Festival for Shabbat a week later. It seems that this was the rationale: Although the loaves are eaten only on the Shabbat of the next week, the baking could be considered a necessary preparation for the proximate Shabbat, as the mitzva to place the shewbread on the sacred table pertains to Shabbat immediately following the Festival (*Tosefot Rabbeinu Peretz*).

The two loaves – שְׁתֵּי הַלֶּחֶם: Two loaves were brought as a communal offering on the festival of *Shavuot* (Leviticus 23:17). In contrast to most of the other meal-offerings, these loaves were leavened. Two lambs, the communal peace-offerings, were brought together with these two loaves. Both the loaves and the lambs were ceremonially waved. Afterward, they were divided up among the priests and eaten in the Temple courtyard.

וּלְרַבָּן שִׁמְעוֹן בֶּן גַּמְלִיאֵל, דְּאָמַר מִשּׁוּם רַבִּי שִׁמְעוֹן בֶּן הַסְּגָן: דּוֹחֶה אֶת יוֹם טוֹב, מַאי אִיכָּא לְמֵימַר? סָבַר לָהּ כְּאַבָּא שָׁאוּל, דְּאָמַר: ״לָכֶם״ – לָכֶם וְלֹא לַגּוֹיִם.

The Gemara asks: **And according to Rabban Shimon ben Gamliel, who said in the name of Rabbi Shimon, son of the deputy** High Priest, that baking the shewbread **overrides the Festival, what can be said?** How does he understand the term: For you? The Gemara answers: **He holds in accordance with** the opinion of **Abba Shaul, who said** that this verse should be understood in the following manner: Cooking and baking are permitted **for you, and not for gentiles;** for the sake of the Temple service, however, they are permitted.

שְׁלַח לֵיהּ רַב חִסְדָּא לְרַבָּה בְּיַד רַב אַחָא בַּר רַב הוּנָא: מִי אָמְרִינַן ״הוֹאִיל״, וְהָא תְּנַן: יֵשׁ חוֹרֵשׁ תֶּלֶם אֶחָד וְחַיָּיבִין עָלֶיהָ מִשּׁוּם שְׁמוֹנָה לָאוִין: הַחוֹרֵשׁ בְּשׁוֹר וַחֲמוֹר, וְהֵן מוּקְדָּשִׁים, וְכִלְאַיִם בַּכֶּרֶם,

Rav Ḥisda sent a question **to Rabba with Rav Aḥa bar Rav Huna: Do we say** the principle: **Since, etc.? Didn't we learn** in a mishna: **There is** a case in which one **plows one furrow and is liable for** violating **eight prohibitions**[N] with this single act? The mishna explains that this applies to **one who plows with an ox and a donkey,** thereby violating the prohibition: "You shall not plow with an ox and a donkey together" (Deuteronomy 22:10), **and they were consecrated,** in which case plowing with them constitutes misuse of consecrated property. If his plowing aids the growth of **food crops in a vineyard,** he has transgressed a third prohibition.

NOTES

Liable for violating eight prohibitions – וְחַיָּיבִין עָלֶיהָ מִשּׁוּם שְׁמוֹנָה לָאוִין: It is possible to add more negative commandments to this list by stating that one was plowing with several pairs of oxen and donkeys. However, this list includes only different prohibitions that one can transgress through a single action, not multiple violations of the same prohibition.

The exact way in which these eight prohibitions are enumerated is a subject of debate. According to Rashi, there are separate prohibitions to plow with a consecrated ox, which is set aside as a sacrifice, and to plow with a consecrated donkey, which is donated to the Temple treasury. According to *Tosafot*, these are counted as one negative commandment, whereas there are two commandments with regard to forbidden mixtures of diverse kinds, one for food crops in a vineyard and one for a forbidden mixture of seeds. Others note that there are two negative commandments that pertain to a nazirite: When one violates the terms of being a nazirite, he also violates the general prohibition of violating an oath derived from the verse: "He shall not violate his word" (Numbers 30:3; see *Avnei Nezer*; *Turei Even*).

Perek **III**
Daf **47** Amud **b**

וּשְׁבִיעִית בְּיוֹם טוֹב, כֹּהֵן וְנָזִיר אַבֵּית הַטּוּמְאָה. וְאִי אָמְרִינַן הוֹאִיל – אֲחֲרִישָׁה לָא לִיחַיֵּיב הוֹאִיל וַחֲזִי לְכִיסּוּי דַּם צִיפּוֹר!

And he is plowing during the **Sabbatical** year, when agricultural labor is prohibited, **on a Festival.** Additionally, the person plowing is **a priest and a nazirite,** and he is plowing **a place of ritual impurity,** i.e., a burial site. It is prohibited for a priest and a nazirite to become impure by walking over the burial spot of a corpse. Therefore, the one plowing commits two transgressions simply by traversing the field. **And if we say** the principle: **Since, etc., he should not be liable for plowing**[N] on a Festival, **since** the dirt he loosens **is fit for covering the blood**[N] **of a bird.** One who slaughters a bird or a non-domesticated animal is required by Torah law to cover the blood. Since it is possible that one will need to slaughter many such animals or birds and will not have enough dirt to cover their blood, his plowing may end up facilitating covering the blood. Therefore, it should not be considered a prohibited labor on the Festival.

אֲמַר רַב פַּפָּא בַּר שְׁמוּאֵל: בַּאֲבָנִים מְקוּרְזָלוֹת.

The Gemara answers that **Rav Pappa bar Shmuel said:** The case is one in which a person plowed **sharp stones,** i.e., clods of dirt that have hardened and are unfit to be used to cover blood.

רְאוּיוֹת לְכוֹתְשָׁן! וּכְתִישָׁה בְּיוֹם טוֹב מִי שָׁרֵי? רְאוּיוֹת לְכוֹתְשָׁן כִּלְאַחַר יָד. בְּצוּנְמָא!

The Gemara asks: Aren't these clods of dirt **fit to be crushed**[N] and used to cover blood? The Gemara responds: **Is crushing permitted on a Festival?** The Gemara counters: But they are **fit to be crushed in an unusual manner,** which is not prohibited by Torah law. The Gemara answers: The case is one in which a person plowed **hard,** rocky **soil,** which cannot be crushed.

צוּנְמָא בַּר זְרִיעָה?! צוּנְמָא מִלְּמַעְלָה, וְעָפָר תִּיחוּחַ מִלְּמַטָּה. וְתֵיפּוֹק לֵיהּ מִשּׁוּם עָפָר תִּיחוּחַ!

The Gemara asks: **Is hard soil fit for planting?** The case under discussion is one in which a person was preparing the ground in order to plant food crops in a vineyard. The Gemara answers: In this case, **there was hard soil above and** fertile, **loose soil underneath,** into which seeds could be planted. The Gemara rejects this answer: **Derive** that the act of plowing would be permitted in that case **due to the** loose **soil,** which is suitable for covering blood.

אֶלָּא אָמַר מָר בַּר רַב אַשִׁי: בְּטִינָא. וְטִינָא בַּר זְרִיעָה הוּא? בְּמְתוּנְתָּא.

Rather, Mar bar Rav Ashi said: The case is one in which a person plowed **mud,** which is not fit for covering blood. The Gemara asks rhetorically: **Is mud fit for planting?** The Gemara answers: The case is one in which a person plowed **moist earth,** which is suitable for planting but which cannot be used to cover blood.

NOTES

He should not be liable for plowing – אֲחֲרִישָׁה לָא לִיחַיֵּיב: Generally, this statement is understood to mean that since covering the blood of a slaughtered bird or non-domesticated animal is a positive commandment, it overrides the prohibition of labor on a Festival. However, several early commentaries point out that there are positive and negative commandments associated with labor on a Festival, and the general rule is that a positive commandment does not override both a positive and negative commandment. Some say that in this case the positive commandment to cover the blood does in fact override the negative commandment not to perform labor during the Festival. While the positive commandment to refrain from labor remains, one is not flogged for violating this positive commandment. However, other sources do not accept this explanation. Some explain that the question is not referring to the violation of plowing during the Festival, but instead is referring to the prohibition of plowing diverse kinds. According to this interpretation, the positive commandment of covering blood overrides the prohibition of diverse kinds, reducing the number of prohibitions for which one is flogged (*Tosefot Rabbeinu Peretz*).

Covering the blood – כִּסּוּי הַדָּם: The commandment to cover the blood of slaughtered birds and non-domesticated animals is mentioned in the Torah (Leviticus 17:13) and is described in greater detail in the sixth chapter of tractate *Ḥullin*. The essential principles of this commandment are as follows: When one slaughters a non-domesticated animal or a bird, the blood that emerges upon slaughtering must be covered with earth. This earth must be fine enough to scatter on the surface of the blood; therefore, one may not use clumps of dirt or mud for this purpose. The commandment does not apply to the blood of a domesticated animal.

Fit to be crushed – רְאוּיוֹת לְכוֹתְשָׁן: See *Tosafot*. Some explain this to mean that the clods of dirt could have been crushed before plowing, such that by plowing one could move the dirt and thereby cover the bird's blood. Otherwise, the positive commandment to cover the blood would not be fulfilled through the act of plowing itself, and therefore it could not override the negative commandment of plowing on a Festival (Rashash).

אֵיתִיבֵיהּ אַבָּיֵי: הַמְבַשֵּׁל גִּיד הַנָּשֶׁה בְּחָלָב בְּיוֹם טוֹב וְאוֹכְלוֹ, לוֹקֶה חָמֵשׁ: לוֹקֶה מִשּׁוּם מְבַשֵּׁל גִּיד בְּיוֹם טוֹב, וְלוֹקֶה מִשּׁוּם אוֹכֵל גִּיד, וְלוֹקֶה מִשּׁוּם מְבַשֵּׁל בָּשָׂר בְּחָלָב, וְלוֹקֶה מִשּׁוּם אוֹכֵל בָּשָׂר בְּחָלָב, וְלוֹקֶה מִשּׁוּם הַבְעָרָה. וְאִי אָמְרִינַן "הוֹאִיל" – אַהַבְעָרָה לָא לִיחַיַּיב, הוֹאִיל דַּחֲזֵי לֵיהּ לְצָרְכּוֹ!

Abaye raised an objection to Rabba's acceptance of the principle: Since, etc. **One who cooks the sciatic nerve**[B] **in milk on a Festival and eats it is flogged** for five distinct prohibitions.[N] How so? **He is flogged due to** the prohibition of **cooking the** sciatic **nerve on a Festival,** which is prohibited because the sciatic nerve is unfit for consumption; **and he is flogged due to** the prohibition of **eating** the sciatic **nerve,** which is explicitly prohibited by the Torah; **and he is flogged due to** the prohibition of **cooking meat in milk; and he is flogged due to** the prohibition of **eating meat** cooked **in milk;** and lastly, **he is flogged due to** the prohibition of **kindling** a fire unnecessarily on a Festival. **And if we say** the principle: **Since, etc., he should not be liable for kindling** a fire unnecessarily, **since** the fire **is fit for** use in attending to his legitimate Festival needs, e.g., cooking permitted foods.

אֲמַר לֵיהּ: אַפֵּיק הַבְעָרָה וְעַיֵּיל גִּיד הַנָּשֶׁה שֶׁל נְבֵילָה.

Rabba **said to him: Remove** the prohibition of **kindling** a fire from this list **and add** the prohibition of eating **a sciatic nerve from an animal carcass** that was not properly slaughtered.

וְהָתָנֵי רַבִּי חִיָּיא: לוֹקִין שְׁתַּיִם עַל אֲכִילָתוֹ וְשָׁלֹשׁ עַל בִּישּׁוּלוֹ, וְאִי אִיתָא: שָׁלֹשׁ עַל אֲכִילָתוֹ מִיבָּעֵי לֵיהּ!

Abaye responded: **Didn't Rabbi Ḥiyya teach** with regard to this mishna: He **is flogged twice for his eating,** as he violated the prohibitions of eating the sciatic nerve and eating meat cooked in milk, **and three** times **for his cooking,** as he violated the prohibitions of kindling a fire, cooking on a Festival, and cooking meat in milk? **And if it is** so, that the case is one in which the sciatic nerve was taken from an animal carcass, Rabbi Ḥiyya **should have** stated that he is flogged **three** times **for his eating,** as he violated the prohibitions of eating a sciatic nerve, eating meat cooked in milk, and eating an animal carcass.

אֶלָּא: אַפֵּיק הַבְעָרָה וְעַיֵּיל עֲצֵי מוּקְצֶה.

Rather, Rabba said: **Remove** the prohibition of **kindling** a fire **and add** in its place the prohibition of using **wood** that has been **set aside** from use on the Festival.

וּמוּקְצֶה דְּאוֹרַיְיתָא הוּא? אֲמַר לֵיהּ: אִין, דִּכְתִיב: "וְהָיָה בַּיּוֹם הַשִּׁשִּׁי וְהֵכִינוּ אֵת אֲשֶׁר יָבִיאוּ", וְאַזְהָרְתָהּ מֵהָכָא – מִ"לֹּא תַעֲשֶׂה כָל מְלָאכָה".

The Gemara asks: Is the prohibition against utilizing **set-aside** material prohibited **by Torah** law, such that a person is flogged for violating this prohibition? **He said to him: Yes, as it is written: "And it shall come to pass on the sixth day that they shall prepare that which they bring in"** (Exodus 16:5). This verse teaches that anything that has not been prepared before the Festival is considered to be set-aside, and it is prohibited to utilize it. This verse indicates that utilizing set-aside objects is prohibited; however, it does not formulate this prohibition as a negative commandment. Therefore, the Gemara adds that **the warning** indicating that it is a negative commandment **is from here: "You shall not perform any labor"** (Exodus 20:9). This general statement pertaining to Shabbat includes utilizing objects that were not set aside for use before Shabbat.

אֲמַר לֵיהּ: וְהָא אַתְּ הוּא דְּאָמְרַתְּ; בְּעַאי מִינֵּיהּ מֵרַב חִסְדָּא, וְאָמְרִי לָהּ בְּעַאי מִינֵּיהּ מֵרַב הוּנָא: הֵבִיא שֶׂה מֵאֲפָר וּשְׁחָטוֹ תָּמִיד בְּיוֹם טוֹב מַהוּ?

Abaye **said to him: Wasn't it you who said: I raised a dilemma before Rav Ḥisda, and some say** the correct version is: **I raised a dilemma before Rav Huna: If one brought a lamb from the meadow,** and the lamb is therefore set-aside because it was not designated for use before the Festival, **and he slaughtered it** as the **daily** offering **on a Festival, what is** the *halakha*? Is it permissible to offer this sacrifice?

וְאַתְּ אָמְרַתְּ לָן, (אֲמַר לִי) עֲלָהּ: "שֶׂה" – וְלֹא הַבְּכוֹר,

And you said to us: He said to me about this issue that the answer can be derived from a verse in Ezekiel pertaining to communal offerings. The verse states: "And one lamb of the flock, out of two hundred, from the well-watered pastures of Israel" (Ezekiel 45:15). This verse is expounded in the following manner: The word **lamb** is referring to either a male or female lamb, **but not to a firstborn,** as that status applies only to male sheep.

"אַחַת" – וְלֹא מַעֲשֵׂר,

The word **one** indicates that a sacrifice may **not** be brought from the animal **tithe.** The lamb must be one that can stand alone. An animal designated as tithe is always part of a group, as it is the tenth animal to leave the pen; therefore, it cannot be offered as a communal offering.

"מִן הַצֹּאן" – וְלֹא הַפַּלְגֵּס,

The expression: **Of the flock** indicates that only some animals of the flock may be offered, whereas one may **not** offer **a** ***palges,***[NHL] which is no longer a lamb but is not yet considered a ram.

BACKGROUND

Sciatic nerve – גִּיד הַנָּשֶׁה:

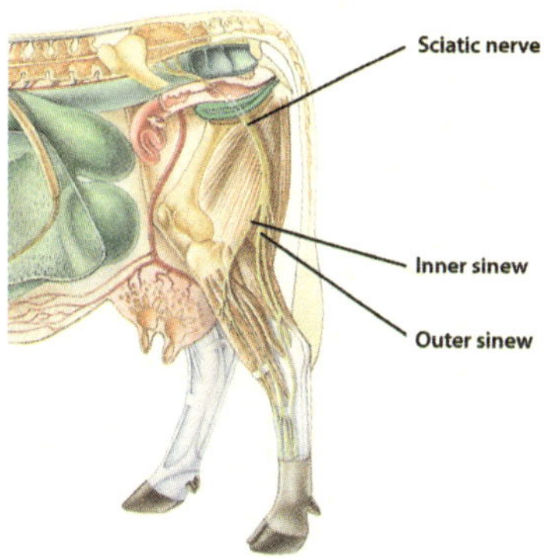

Cow's sciatic nerve

NOTES

Flogged for five distinct prohibitions – לוֹקֶה חָמֵשׁ: This *baraita* is not accepted as the *halakha*. It is ruled elsewhere that nerves and tendons do not have flavor and therefore the prohibition of cooking meat in milk does not apply to them, as they are not considered meat. Similarly, many authorities conclude that one is not flogged for eating the sciatic nerve from an animal carcass that was not properly slaughtered (*Me'iri*).

***Palges* – פַּלְגֵּס:** The Torah describes two types of male sheep that are brought as sacrifices: A lamb and a ram. A sheep is considered a lamb from when it is eight days old until it is one year old, and it becomes a ram when it is in its second year. According to the Sages, it is valid for offerings that require a ram only once a month has passed in its second year. During the first month of its second year, it is referred to as a *palges* and may not be offered as a lamb or a ram.

HALAKHA

***Palges* – פַּלְגֵּס:** A sheep between the age of one year and one year and thirty days may not be offered as either a lamb or a ram (Rambam *Sefer Avoda, Hilkhot Ma'aseh HaKorbanot* 1:14).

LANGUAGE

***Palges* – פַּלְגֵּס:** From the Greek πάλλαξ, *pallax*, meaning an intermediate age between childhood and adulthood.

״מִן הַמָּאתַיִם״ – מִמּוֹתַר שְׁתֵּי מֵאוֹת שֶׁנִּשְׁתַּיְּירוּ בַּבּוֹר. מִכָּאן לְעָרְלָה שֶׁבְּטֵילָה בְּמָאתַיִם.

The phrase: **Out of two hundred,** is expounded with regard to wine brought as a libation:[N] **From the remaining two hundred** portions **that remain in the vat.** This is referring to a case where wine prohibited as produce grown during a tree or vine's first three years [*orla*] is mixed with permitted wine. The *halakha* is that this wine mixture may be brought as a libation only if there is two hundred times more permitted wine than prohibited wine. **From here** it is derived **that *orla* is nullified in** a mixture of **two hundred.**[H]

״מִמַּשְׁקֵה יִשְׂרָאֵל״ – מִן הַמּוּתָּר לְיִשְׂרָאֵל. מִכָּאן אָמְרוּ: אֵין מְבִיאִין נְסָכִין מִן הַטֶּבֶל.

The phrase: **From the well-watered pastures of Israel,**[N] means that sacrifices may be offered only **from that which is permitted to Israel. From here,** the Sages **stated: One** may **not offer libations from untithed produce** [*tevel*],[H] since Jews are prohibited from eating *tevel.*

יָכוֹל לֹא יָבִיא מִן הַמּוּקְצֶה, אָמַרְתָּ: מַה טֶּבֶל מְיוּחָד שֶׁאִיסּוּר גּוּפוֹ גָּרַם לוֹ, אַף כֹּל שֶׁאִיסּוּר גּוּפוֹ גָּרַם לוֹ, יָצָא מוּקְצֶה שֶׁאֵין אִיסּוּר גּוּפוֹ גָּרַם לוֹ אֶלָּא אִיסּוּר דָּבָר אַחֵר גָּרַם לוֹ. וְאִי אָמְרַתְּ אִיסּוּר מוּקְצֶה דְּאוֹרַיְיתָא – מַה לִּי אִיסּוּר גּוּפוֹ מַה לִּי אִיסּוּר דָּבָר אַחֵר?

I **might** have thought that **one** may **not offer** an animal that is **set-aside** on Shabbat or during a Festival; therefore, **you** have **said: Just as *tevel* is unique in that its inherent prohibition caused it** to be prohibited for Jews to eat, **so too, anything whose inherent prohibition caused it** to be prohibited for Jews to eat is invalid as an offering. This **excludes** an animal that has been **set aside,**[H] **which** does not have **an inherent prohibition** that **caused it** to be prohibited for eating; **rather, a different prohibition,** i.e., the prohibition of utilizing set-aside objects on Shabbat, **caused it** to be prohibited for eating. **And if you say the prohibition of** utilizing **set-aside** material **is by Torah** law, **what** difference is there **to me** if a food is **inherently prohibited; and what** difference is there **to me** if it is prohibited due to **a different prohibition?**[N] If there is a distinction between these prohibitions, it must be that the prohibition of utilizing set-aside material is by rabbinic law, and therefore, like many other rabbinic decrees, it does not apply in the Temple.

וְעוֹד: הָא אַתְּ הוּא דְּאָמְרַתְּ: חִילּוּק מְלָאכוֹת לַשַּׁבָּת וְאֵין חִילּוּק מְלָאכוֹת לְיוֹם טוֹב.

And furthermore, Abaye said to Rabba: It is possible to challenge your interpretation of the *baraita* from a different angle. **Wasn't it you who said,** as cited in tractate *Makkot,* that there is **division of labors** with regard **to Shabbat,** and therefore one is required to bring two sin-offerings if he performed two prohibited labors of different primary categories in one lapse of awareness, or if he performed a prohibited labor twice, during separate lapses of awareness; however, there is **no division of labors**[H] with regard **to a Festival,**[N] and therefore one is not punished with multiple floggings for performing multiple prohibited labors? Consequently, how could one be liable for multiple floggings for the prohibition of utilizing set-aside materials and for cooking the sciatic nerve on a Festival?

אֶלָּא: אַפֵּיק הַבְעָרָה וְעַיֵּיל עֲצֵי אֲשֵׁירָה. וְאַזְהָרָה מֵהָכָא: ״וְלֹא יִדְבַּק בְּיָדְךָ מְאוּמָה מִן הַחֵרֶם״.

Rather, in order to make this *baraita* consistent with Rabba's opinion, **remove** the prohibition of **kindling** a fire **and add** in its place the prohibition of using **the wood of a tree designated for idolatry** [*asheira*]. **And the warning,** i.e., the source of the negative commandment associated with using this wood, **is** derived **from here,** a verse that relates to an idolatrous city that is burned: **"Nothing from the spoil shall cling to your hand"** (Deuteronomy 13:18).

אֲמַר לֵיהּ רַב אַחָא בְּרֵיהּ דְּרָבָא לְאַבַּיֵי: וְנִלְקֵי נַמִי מִשּׁוּם ״וְלֹא תָבִיא תוֹעֵבָה אֶל בֵּיתֶךָ״!

Rav Aḥa, son of Rava, said to Abaye: If this case is referring to using wood from an *asheira,* **one should also be flogged due to** having transgressed the prohibition of: **"You shall not bring an abominable thing into your home"** (Deuteronomy 7:26). However, this would add an extra negative commandment to the list enumerated in the *baraita.*

NOTES

Libations – נְסָכִים: This refers to the wine offered on the altar. Wine libations were offered together with burnt-offerings of animals and peace-offerings, as well as with the leper's sin-offering and guilt-offering. Different quantities of wine were offered, depending on the animal that was sacrificed: One-fourth of a *hin,* i.e., three *log,* was offered for any sheep other than a ram; one-third of a *hin,* four *log,* was offered for a ram; and half a *hin,* six *log,* was offered for a bullock. Libations of wine could also be brought as independent, voluntary offerings.

From the well-watered pastures of Israel – מִמַּשְׁקֵה יִשְׂרָאֵל: It is not immediately obvious that only foods permitted for consumption by Jews may be offered on the altar, as blood and forbidden fats, which may not be consumed, are in fact offered on the altar. As such, it must be noted that only specific forbidden foods may be offered on the altar; aside from these, only permitted foods may be offered.

What difference is there to me if it is prohibited due to a different prohibition – מַה לִּי אִיסּוּר דָּבָר אַחֵר: This question seems difficult to understand: If the prohibition against utilizing set-aside items is by rabbinic law, it would seem that this is the reason for the distinction between untithed produce and animals that are set aside; and the distinction is not that one is inherently prohibited and one is prohibited due to an external factor. Apparently, since there is no case where an object is prohibited as an offering by Torah law due to an external factor, the Sages also did not prohibit items from being brought as offerings for external reasons, as all ordinances that the Sages instituted parallel Torah law (Rabbi Elazar Moshe Horowitz).

Division of labors with regard to a Festival – חִילּוּק מְלָאכוֹת לְיוֹם טוֹב: The prohibitions of Shabbat differ from those of a Festival for the following reason: The very notion of division of labors, namely that one is liable separately for violating each of the primary categories of labor, is a novel one, and it is derived from verses in the Torah that pertain to Shabbat. Therefore, it is applied only to Shabbat and not to the Festivals.

HALAKHA

Orla is nullified in a mixture of two hundred – עָרְלָה בְּטֵילָה בְּמָאתַיִם: If produce from the first three years of a tree's growth becomes mixed with two hundred times as much permitted produce, the *orla* is nullified within the mixture. A grapevine is considered a tree in this regard. However, if it fell into a smaller amount of permitted produce, the mixture is forbidden (Rambam *Sefer Kedusha, Hilkhot Ma'akhalot Assurot* 15:14).

Libations from untithed produce [*tevel*] – נְסָכִין מִן הַטֶּבֶל: It is prohibited to bring meal-offerings or libations from *tevel* (Rambam *Sefer Avoda, Hilkhot Issurei Mizbe'aḥ* 5:9).

Offerings from animals that are set-aside – קָרְבָּנוֹת מִן הַמּוּקְצֶה: One may bring offerings of animals and wine that are set-aside during a Festival, as stated in the *baraita* (Rambam *Sefer Avoda, Hilkhot Issurei Mizbe'aḥ* 5:10).

Division of labors – חִילּוּק מְלָאכוֹת: If one performs several primary categories of labor on Shabbat during one lapse of awareness, he must bring a sin-offering for each category of labor he unwittingly performs. However, if one performs many types of labor during a Festival, he is flogged only once (Rambam *Sefer Zemanim, Hilkhot Yom Tov* 1:3).

אֶלָּא אַפֵּיק הַבְעָרָה, וְעַיֵּיל עֲצֵי הֶקְדֵּשׁ, וְאַזְהָרָה מֵהָכָא: ״וַאֲשֵׁרֵיהֶם תִּשְׂרְפוּן בָּאֵשׁ; לֹא תַעֲשׂוּן כֵּן לַה׳ אֱלֹהֵיכֶם״.

Rather, remove the prohibition of **kindling** a fire **and add** in its place the prohibition of burning **consecrated wood.**[N] **And the warning,** i.e., the source of this negative command, **is from here: "And you shall burn their *asheira* trees with fire...you shall not do this to the Lord your God"** (Deuteronomy 12:3–4). Therefore, one who burns a consecrated item in a destructive manner is punished with lashes. In conclusion, no adequate proof can be adduced from the *baraita* to reject Rabba's opinion.

אָמַר רָמִי בַּר חָמָא: הָא דְּרַב חִסְדָּא וְרַבָּה – מַחֲלוֹקֶת דְּרַבִּי אֱלִיעֶזֶר וְרַבִּי יְהוֹשֻׁעַ הִיא. דְּרַבִּי אֱלִיעֶזֶר סָבַר: אָמְרִינַן ״הוֹאִיל״, וְרַבִּי יְהוֹשֻׁעַ סָבַר: לָא אָמְרִינַן ״הוֹאִיל״.

Rami bar Ḥama said: This dispute between **Rav Ḥisda and Rabba** with regard to the principle: Since, etc., **is** a matter of **dispute** between **Rabbi Eliezer and Rabbi Yehoshua** in the mishna. **As, Rabbi Eliezer,** who says that *ḥalla* should be separated only after the bread has been baked, **holds** that **we say** the principle: **Since, etc.**[N] Since any portion of the dough could potentially be eaten if another part of the dough is designated as *ḥalla*, therefore, one is permitted to bake bread without separating *ḥalla* from it *ab initio*. **And Rabbi Yehoshua holds: We do not say** the principle: **Since, etc.**

אֲמַר רַב פַּפָּא: וְדִילְמָא, עַד כָּאן לָא קָאָמַר רַבִּי אֱלִיעֶזֶר הָתָם דְּאָמְרִינַן הוֹאִיל – אֶלָּא דִּבְעִידָּנָא דְּקָא עָיְילֵי לְתַנּוּרָא כָּל חֲדָא וַחֲדָא חַזְיָא לֵיהּ לְדִידֵיהּ, אֲבָל הָכָא דִּלְאוֹרְחִין הוּא דַּחֲזֵי, לְדִידֵיהּ לָא חֲזֵי – אֵימָא הָכִי נַמִי דְּלָא אָמְרִינַן ״הוֹאִיל״.

Rav Pappa said that this claim can be rejected in the following manner: **Perhaps Rabbi Eliezer only stated that we say** the principle: **Since, etc., there,** in the case of the separation of *ḥalla*, **because at the time that it was placed into the oven, each and every** loaf **was fit for him,** and there was no indication as to which loaf he would designate as *ḥalla*. **However, here,** in a case **where** the bread one is baking on the Festival **is fit for guests** but **is not fit for him, say that so too,** even according to the opinion of Rabbi Eliezer **we do not say** the principle: **Since, etc.**

אֲמַר רַב שֵׁישָׁא בְּרֵיהּ דְּרַב אִידִי: וְדִילְמָא לֹא הִיא. עַד כָּאן לָא קָאָמַר רַבִּי יְהוֹשֻׁעַ הָתָם דְּלָא אָמְרִינַן ״הוֹאִיל״ – אֶלָּא דְּאִיכָּא חֲדָא דְּלָא חַזְיָא, לֹא לְדִידֵיהּ וְלֹא לְאוֹרְחִין. אֲבָל הָכָא, דַּחֲזֵי מִיהַת לְאוֹרְחִין – אֵימָא הָכִי נַמִי אָמְרִינַן ״הוֹאִיל״.

Rav Sheisha, son of Rav Idi, rejected Rami bar Ḥama's statement for a different reason and **said: Perhaps that is not so. Rabbi Yehoshua only stated that we do not say** the principle: **Since, etc., there, where there is one** portion of the bread **that is not fit for him or for guests,** because the piece that is designated as *ḥalla* cannot be eaten by anyone due to the fact that it is ritually impure. **However, here,** in the case of one who is baking bread during the Festival so that it can be eaten on a weekday, **when it is at least fit for guests, say that so too,** even according to the opinion of Rabbi Yehoshua, **we say** the principle: **Since, etc.**

אֲמָרוּהָ [רַבָּנַן] קַמֵּיהּ דְּרַבִּי יִרְמְיָה וְרַבִּי זֵירָא. רַבִּי יִרְמְיָה קִיבְּלָהּ, רַבִּי זֵירָא לֹא קִיבְּלָהּ. אֲמַר לֵיהּ רַבִּי יִרְמְיָה לְרַבִּי זֵירָא: מִילְּתָא דְּקַשְׁיָא לָן וְאַתְיָא כַּמָּה שְׁנֵי, בְּמַאי פְּלִיגִי רַבִּי אֱלִיעֶזֶר וְרַבִּי יְהוֹשֻׁעַ, הַשְׁתָּא אֲמָרוּהָ מִשְּׁמֵיהּ דְּגַבְרָא רַבָּה – וְלָא נִיקַבְּלָהּ?

The Gemara recounts: **The Sages said** Rami bar Ḥama's statement **before Rabbi Yirmeya and Rabbi Zeira. Rabbi Yirmeya accepted it** and **Rabbi Zeira did not accept it. Rabbi Yirmeya said to Rabbi Zeira:** The following **matter has been difficult for us** to explain **for several years: With regard to what** principle **did Rabbi Eliezer and Rabbi Yehoshua disagree? Now** an explanation **has been stated in the name of a great man. Shall we not accept it?**

אֲמַר לֵיהּ: הֵיכִי אֲקַבְּלָהּ? דְּתַנְיָא, אָמַר לֵיהּ רַבִּי יְהוֹשֻׁעַ: לִדְבָרֶיךָ, הֲרֵי הוּא עוֹבֵר מִשּׁוּם ״לֹא תַעֲשֶׂה כָל מְלָאכָה״ וְשָׁתֵיק לֵיהּ. וְאִי אִיתָא – לֵימָא לֵיהּ: טַעְמָא דִּידִי מִשּׁוּם הוֹאִיל.

He said to him: How can I accept it? We already **learned** in a *baraita* with regard to their dispute: **Rabbi Yehoshua said to** Rabbi Eliezer: **According to your statement, one violates** the prohibition: **"You shall not perform any labor"** (Exodus 20:9). Rabbi Eliezer could not respond to this claim **and was silent.** But **if it is** as Rami bar Ḥama explained, Rabbi Eliezer **should have said to him: The reason** for **my** opinion is **due to** the principle: **Since, etc.,** on the basis of which no prohibited labor has been performed.

אֲמַר לֵיהּ: וְלִיטַעְמִיךְ, הָא דְּתַנְיָא בְּבָרַיְיתָא, אָמַר לוֹ רַבִּי אֱלִיעֶזֶר: לִדְבָרֶיךָ הֲרֵי הוּא עוֹבֵר מִשּׁוּם ״בַּל יֵרָאֶה וּבַל יִמָּצֵא״ וְשָׁתֵיק לֵיהּ. הָכִי נַמִי דְּלָא אַהֲדַר לֵיהּ? הָא קָא מַהֲדַר לֵיהּ בְּמַתְנִיתִין, דִּתְנַן: לֹא זֶהוּ חָמֵץ שֶׁמּוּזְהָרִין עָלָיו מִשּׁוּם בַּל יֵרָאֶה וּבַל יִמָּצֵא. אֶלָּא: שָׁתֵיק לֵיהּ בְּבָרַיְיתָא, וּמַהֲדַר לֵיהּ בְּמַתְנִיתִין. הָכִי נַמִי אֵימוּר: שָׁתֵיק לֵיהּ בְּמַתְנִיתִין, וְאַהֲדַר לֵיהּ בִּמְכִילְתָּא אַחֲרִיתִי.

Rabbi Yirmeya **said to him: According to your reasoning,** with regard to **that which we** already **learned in a *baraita*,** that **Rabbi Eliezer said to him: According to your statement, he transgresses** the prohibitions: **It shall not be seen, and: It shall not be found, and** in response to this challenge Rabbi Yehoshua **was silent, did he too not respond** to Rabbi Eliezer? **He responded to him in the mishna, as we learned** in the mishna that Rabbi Yehoshua said: **This is not the leavened bread about which we are warned** with the prohibitions: **It shall not be seen, and: It shall not be found. Rather,** it must be explained in the following manner: **He** appeared to be **silent in the *baraita*** simply because his response was not recorded, **but he responded in the mishna. So too,** here it is possible to **say that he** appeared **silent in the mishna, but he responded in a different tractate.**

NOTES

And add the prohibition of burning consecrated wood – **וְעַיֵּיל עֲצֵי הֶקְדֵּשׁ**: Presumably, there should be an additional prohibition for using such wood, as by doing so one is misusing consecrated property. However, since one is liable for misuse of consecrated property only if he derives benefit worth at least a small coin [*peruta*], this prohibition was not included with the other prohibitions, which one transgresses even at less than this amount (*Tosefot Rid*; *Tosefot Rabbeinu Peretz*; Maharam Ḥalawa).

Rabbi Eliezer holds that we say the principle: Since, etc. – **רַבִּי אֱלִיעֶזֶר אוֹמֵר אָמְרִינַן הוֹאִיל**: The early commentaries disagree with regard to the application of the principle: Since, etc., in this context. The explanation cited by Rashi and accepted by the Rif is that according to Rabbi Eliezer, one may bake all of the dough based upon the following application of this principle: Since one can request to have the *ḥalla* status revoked such that it would revert to being his property, he would violate the prohibitions against seeing and owning leavened dough. Therefore, according to Rabbi Eliezer, the principle: Since, etc., applies only as a stringency and not as a leniency. However, according to Rabbi Yehoshua, the principle: Since, etc., does not apply in this case and one may separate the *ḥalla* immediately without being concerned that he will violate any prohibition. This is because the potential to revoke the *ḥalla* status is dependent upon him and it is in his power to maintain the designation, in which case no problem will arise (see *Sefer HaMa'or*; *Milḥamot Hashem*; Maharam Ḥalawa).

תַּנְיָא, רַבִּי אוֹמֵר: הֲלָכָה כְּרַבִּי אֱלִיעֶזֶר, וְרַבִּי יִצְחָק אָמַר: הֲלָכָה כְּבֶן בְּתֵירָא.

It was taught in a *baraita* that **Rabbi** Yehuda HaNasi **says:** The ***halakha*** with regard to the separation of *ḥalla* from impure dough during Passover **is in accordance with** the opinion of **Rabbi Eliezer. And Rabbi Yitzḥak said:** The ***halakha*** **is in accordance with** the opinion of **ben Beteira.**

וְכַמָּה שִׁיעוּר עִיסָּה? רַבִּי יִשְׁמָעֵאל בְּנוֹ שֶׁל רַבִּי יוֹחָנָן בֶּן בְּרוֹקָה אוֹמֵר: בְּחִיטִּין – קַבַּיִן, וּבִשְׂעוֹרִין – שְׁלֹשֶׁת קַבִּין. רַבִּי נָתָן אוֹמֵר מִשּׁוּם רַבִּי אֱלִיעֶזֶר: חִילּוּף הַדְּבָרִים.

The Gemara asks: **How much dough** may be kneaded at once on Passover without concern that the dough will become leavened in the process? **Rabbi Yishmael, son of Rabbi Yoḥanan ben Beroka, says: With regard to wheat,** one may use the amount of flour that comes from **two *kav*** of grain; **and with regard to barley,** one may use the amount of flour that comes from **three *kav*. Rabbi Natan says in the name of Rabbi Eliezer: The matters are reversed.** One may knead the flour produced from three *kav* of wheat or two *kav* of barley without concern that it will become leavened.

וְהָתַנְיָא, רַבִּי יִשְׁמָעֵאל בְּנוֹ שֶׁל רַבִּי יוֹחָנָן בֶּן בְּרוֹקָה אוֹמֵר: בְּחִטִּין – שְׁלֹשֶׁת קַבִּין, וּבִשְׂעוֹרִין – אַרְבָּעָה קַבִּין! לָא קַשְׁיָא; הָא – בַּחֲסִיכְתָא, הָא – בִּמְעַלְיָיתָא.

The Gemara asks: **Wasn't it taught** in a different *baraita* that **Rabbi Yishmael, son of Rabbi Yoḥanan ben Beroka, says: With regard to wheat,** one may use the amount of flour that comes from **three *kav*** of grain, **and with regard to barley,** one may use the amount of flour that comes from **four *kav*?** The Gemara answers: This is **not difficult,** as **this** latter *baraita* is referring **to low-quality** grain, and **that** *baraita* is referring **to high-quality** grain. One can obtain a higher proportion of flour from high-quality grain than from low-quality grain, which contains a greater amount of chaff.

אָמַר רַב פַּפָּא: שְׁמַע מִינָּהּ גְּרִיעִין חִיטֵּי חֲסִיכְתָא מֵחִיטֵּי מְעַלְיָיתָא, טְפֵי מִדְּגְרִיעָן שַׂעֲרֵי חֲסִיכְתָא מִשַּׂעֲרֵי מְעַלְיָיתָא. דְּאִילּוּ הָתָם תִּילְתָּא, וְהָכָא רִיבְעָא.

Rav Pappa said: Learn from this that the extent to which **low-quality wheat is worse than high-quality wheat is greater than** the extent to which **low-quality barley is worse than high-quality barley,** i.e., the discrepancy between the different levels of quality is more significant with regard to wheat, **as there,** in the case of wheat, they differ by **one-third; and here,** in the case of barley, they differ by only **one-fourth.**

אָמַר רַב: קַבָּא מְלוֹגְנָאָה לְפִיסְחָא, וְכֵן לְחַלָּה. (וְהָתַנְיָא)

Rav said: A *kav* from the place **Melogna**[L] is the amount that can be used to prepare dough **for Passover.**[H] **And similarly, with regard to *ḥalla*,** that is the minimum amount of dough from which *ḥalla* must be separated. The Gemara asks: **Wasn't it taught** in a *baraita*:

LANGUAGE

Melogna – מְלוֹגְנָא: The *ge'onim* recorded a version of the Gemara that reads *Maglona* and indicates that this unit of measurement was from the city of Maglo, home of Ḥoni HaMe'agel. According to this explanation, Ḥoni's name should be understood as a reference to his city, i.e., Ḥoni HaMaglo'i. It is possible that it was Ḥoni himself who established this unit of measurement (Rashbatz). Others suggest that the word refers to a large unit of measurement and is related to the Greek μεγάλος, *megalos*, meaning large.

HALAKHA

A *kav* from Melogna for Passover – קַבָּא מְלוֹגְנָאָה לְפִיסְחָא: One may not knead more than an *issaron*, 43.2 egg-bulks, of dough at one time during Passover. This ruling is in accordance with the statement of Rav (*Shulḥan Arukh, Oraḥ Ḥayyim* 456:1).

Perek **III**
Daf **48** Amud **b**

חֲמֵשֶׁת רְבָעִים קֶמַח וְעוֹד חַיָּיבִין בְּחַלָּה! הָכִי קָאָמַר: קַבָּא מְלוֹגְנָאֵי נָמֵי אַהַאי שִׁיעוּרָא קָאֵי.

Dough made from **five-quarters** of a *log* of **flour and** a bit **more obligates** one to separate ***ḥalla*?**[H] The Gemara answers that **this is** what **Rav is saying: A *kav* from Melogna is the same measure as this,** as it is not a regular *kav* but a larger measure, identical to the amount from which one is required to separate *ḥalla*.

אָמַר רַב יוֹסֵף: הָנֵי נָשֵׁי דִּידַן נְהוֹג לְמֵיפָא קְפִיזָא קְפִיזָא לְפִיסְחָא. אֲמַר לֵיהּ אַבָּיֵי: מַאי דַּעְתִּיךְ – לְחוּמְרָא, חוּמְרָא דְּאָתֵי לִידֵי קוּלָּא הוּא, דְּקָא מַפְקַע לָהּ מֵחַלָּה!

Rav Yosef said: These women of our family **ordinarily bake *kefiza***[L] **by *kefiza*,**[N] i.e., three-quarters of a *log* at a time, **on Passover,** since it is easier to prevent small quantities of dough from becoming leavened. **Abaye said to him: What is your opinion?** Do you tell them to do this in order to be **stringent? That is a stringency that leads to a leniency,** as by working with small quantities **one removes** the dough **from** the obligation to separate ***ḥalla*.**

HALAKHA

The measure of flour for the obligation to separate *ḥalla* – שִׁיעוּר חַלָּה: One is required to separate *ḥalla* from bread made from 43.2 egg-bulks of flour. That is the measurement required by the Torah, as stated in the mishna (*Shulḥan Arukh, Yoreh De'a* 324:1).

LANGUAGE

***Kefiza* – קְפִיזָא:** Related to the Middle Iranian word kabiz, which refers to a measurement of volume.

NOTES

***Kefiza* by *kefiza* – קְפִיזָא קְפִיזָא:** Some have a version that reads *kefitza*, which means a small amount, i.e., less than the large amount mentioned above (Rav Yehuda ben Rav Binyamin HaRofeh).

אֲמַר לֵיהּ: דְּעָבְדַן כְּרַבִּי אֱלִיעֶזֶר, (דְּתַנְיָא), רַבִּי אֱלִיעֶזֶר אוֹמֵר: הָרוֹדֶה וְנוֹתֵן לַסַּל – הַסַּל מְצָרְפָן לְחַלָּה. וְאָמַר רַב יְהוּדָה אָמַר שְׁמוּאֵל: הֲלָכָה כְּרַבִּי אֱלִיעֶזֶר.

Rav Yosef **said to him: They do** separate *ḥalla* from the dough, **in accordance with** the opinion of **Rabbi Eliezer.**[H] **As it was taught** in a *baraita* that **Rabbi Eliezer says: One who removes** loaves of bread from an oven **and places them in a basket, the basket combines them**[N] **to** reach the quantity from which one is required to separate ***ḥalla***,[H] even if each of the loaves would not attain the necessary measure for separating *ḥalla* on their own. **And Rav Yehuda said** that **Shmuel said:** The ***halakha*** **is in accordance with** the opinion of **Rabbi Eliezer.** Therefore, the women of Rav Yosef's household would put all the finished *matzot* into a basket and separate *ḥalla* from them.

אֲמַר לֵיהּ: וְהָא אִיתְּמַר עֲלָהּ, אָמַר רַבִּי יְהוֹשֻׁעַ בֶּן לֵוִי: לֹא שָׁנוּ אֶלָּא כִּכָּרוֹת שֶׁל בָּבֶל, שֶׁנּוֹשְׁכוֹת זוֹ מִזּוֹ, אֲבָל כְּעָכִין – לֹא! הָא אִיתְּמַר עֲלָהּ, אָמַר רַבִּי חֲנִינָא: אֲפִילּוּ כְּעָכִין.

Abaye **said to him: But wasn't it stated with regard to** that *baraita* that **Rabbi Yehoshua ben Levi said: They taught** that a basket combines the loaves **only** with regard to **Babylonian loaves that bite from one another.** In other words, the loaves are slightly attached, and when one separates them, a bit from one loaf comes off with the other loaf. **However,** it does **not** apply **to** long, **rod-like loaves** [***ke'akhin***][LN] that were baked separately. Therefore, that principle cannot be applied to the case discussed here, in which each batch of *matza* was baked on its own. Rav Yosef answered: **Wasn't it stated with regard to** that *baraita* that **Rabbi Ḥanina said:** The *halakha* is in accordance with the opinion of Rabbi Eliezer **even with regard to** long, **rod-like loaves?** This indicates that Rav Yosef accepted the view of Rabbi Ḥanina.

בָּעֵי רַבִּי יִרְמְיָה: טַבְלָא שֶׁאֵין לָהּ לְבִזְבְּזִין מַהוּ? תּוֹךְ כְּלִי בָּעֵינַן – וְהָא לֵיכָּא, אוֹ דִּילְמָא: אֲוִיר כְּלִי בָּעֵינַן – וְהָא אִיכָּא? תֵּיקוּ.

In light of this discussion, **Rabbi Yirmeya raised a dilemma:** With regard to **a board without a rim** [***levizbezin***],[L] **what is the** *halakha*? Is it considered to be a vessel that combines loaves baked separately into one unit with regard to *ḥalla*? **Do we require the inside of the vessel** in order to combine the loaves, **and that is lacking,** since the board is flat rather than concave? **Or perhaps we require the airspace of the vessel, and that is** present in this case? The Gemara concludes: **Let it stand** unresolved.

תַּנְיָא, רַבִּי אֱלִיעֶזֶר אוֹמֵר: הַסַּל מְצָרְפָן, רַבִּי יְהוֹשֻׁעַ אוֹמֵר: תַּנּוּר מְצָרְפָן. רַבָּן שִׁמְעוֹן בֶּן גַּמְלִיאֵל אוֹמֵר: כִּכָּרוֹת שֶׁל בָּבֶל שֶׁנּוֹשְׁכוֹת זוֹ מִזּוֹ – מִצְטָרְפוֹת.

It was taught in a *baraita* that **Rabbi Eliezer says: A basket combines** different loaves placed in it with regard to the obligation to separate *ḥalla*. **Rabbi Yehoshua says: An oven combines them.**[N] **Rabban Shimon ben Gamliel says: Babylonian loaves that bite from one another are combined;** however, if the loaves are connected to any lesser degree, e.g., if they are together in an oven or basket, they are not considered combined for the purpose of separating *ḥalla*.

מתני׳ רַבָּן גַּמְלִיאֵל אוֹמֵר: שָׁלֹשׁ נָשִׁים לָשׁוֹת כְּאַחַת, וְאוֹפוֹת בְּתַנּוּר אֶחָד, זוֹ אַחַר זוֹ.

MISHNA **Rabban Gamliel says: Three women may knead** their dough **as one,**[N] meaning at one time, **and bake** the batches of dough **in one oven, one after the other,** and they need not be concerned that their dough will become leavened while they are waiting to use the oven.

וַחֲכָמִים אוֹמְרִים: שָׁלֹשׁ נָשִׁים עוֹסְקוֹת בְּבָצֵק כְּאַחַת, אַחַת לָשָׁה, וְאַחַת עוֹרֶכֶת, וְאַחַת אוֹפָה.

And the Rabbis say: Three women may be **engaged** in preparing **dough as one,** in the following manner: **One kneads** her dough as another **one arranges** her own dough so it takes the form of *matza*, while another **one bakes** her dough.

NOTES

The basket combines them – הַסַּל מְצָרְפָן: Some say that this applies only when the bread is moved directly from the oven to a basket, but not when it is moved somewhere else in between (*Tosefot Rid*), while others disagree (*Or Zarua*).

Long rod-like loaves – כְּעָכִים: See Rashi. According to the *ge'onim*, this phrase actually refers to dome-shaped loaves that were baked separately. Others explain that it refers to small rolls, which, due to their size, do not become pressed together and stuck to each other (Rabbeinu Yehonatan).

An oven combines them – תַּנּוּר מְצָרְפָן: According to Rashi and others, Rabbi Yehoshua contends that just as an oven combines the different rolls for the purposes of *ḥalla*, a basket certainly combines them. However, others claim that according to Rabbi Yehoshua only an oven combines them, whereas a basket does not (Ritva).

According to some, there are three opinions with regard to the obligation of separating *ḥalla*. According to one opinion, *ḥalla* is taken only from a single batch of dough, based on the verse: "The first of your dough" (Numbers 15:20). According to Rabbi Yehoshua, an oven combines discrete pieces of dough to attain the required measurement. According to Rabbi Eliezer, the loaves of bread are combined only when they are placed in one vessel (Maharam Ḥalawa).

Three women may knead their dough as one – שָׁלֹשׁ נָשִׁים לָשׁוֹת כְּאַחַת: Rabban Gamliel is presumably setting a maximum time limit with his statement, asserting that if dough sits idle for the time it takes to bake two sets of *matza* it will not become leavened, but if it remains for longer, it will become leavened. Others explain that he permits this procedure only when each batch of dough is handled the entire time; however, if more than three women join the rotation, the dough may become leavened despite being handled. According to the Rambam, the dough will not become leavened as long as it is being handled, and there is no particular significance to the fact that the case cited here discusses three women (see Rabbeinu Gershom and the Ritva). According to Rav Sa'adia Gaon and other early *ge'onim*, the case is one in which three women are preparing one batch of dough.

HALAKHA

Separating *ḥalla* on Passover – הַפְרָשַׁת חַלָּה בְּפֶסַח: On Passover, it is preferable to prepare dough in a small quantity, less than the amount from which one is required to separate *ḥalla*, in order to reduce the likelihood that the dough will become leavened. One may then bring multiple portions of dough close to each other, so that *ḥalla* can be separated from them collectively. However, it is preferable to place all of the fully baked *matzot* into one basket and to separate *ḥalla* at that point, in accordance with the statement of Rabbi Eliezer (*Shulḥan Arukh, Oraḥ Ḥayyim* 457:1).

Combining to reach the amount required for *ḥalla* – צֵירוּף לְחַלָּה: If several loaves or portions of dough are not large enough for the commandment of *ḥalla* to apply to each of them separately, the basket into which they are placed after they have been baked combines them into one batch, and *ḥalla* is separated at that point. However, baking the loaves together in one oven does not combine them to add up to the minimum quantity required for separating *ḥalla*. Placing the loaves together on a utensil that is not concave also does not combine these loaves, and there is no requirement to separate *ḥalla* in this case. Although the issue of loaves on a utensil that is not concave is unresolved in the Gemara, in practice one is not required to separate *ḥalla*, as the commandment of *ḥalla* nowadays is by rabbinic law (*Shulḥan Arukh, Yoreh De'a* 325:1).

LANGUAGE

Rod-like loaves [*ke'akhin*] – כְּעָכִין: Some explain that this means snakelike, i.e., long narrow strips that resemble a snake (*Ma'adanei Melekh*). Others explain that it is related to the Arabic كعك, *ka'k*, or the Persian kāk, meaning a loaf of bread, particularly one that is spiced.

Rim [*levizbezin*] – לְבִזְבְּזִין: Apparently from the Greek λαβίς, *labis*, meaning handle, holder, or clamp. It refers to an edge or a small frame added to the edge of a window, table or shelf.

NOTES

If the dough begins to rise she should spread cold water – תָּפַח תִּלְטוֹשׁ בְּצוֹנֵן: Some understand this expression differently, explaining that if the dough begins to rise in the oven, then one must strike it with one's hand so that it will not become leavened (*Arukh*).

Moist wood – עֵצִים לַחִים: From this statement it can be understood that at the time, dough was kneaded and arranged into loaves or *matzot* before the oven was lit, as otherwise there would be no difference between a hot or cold oven or between moist or dry wood (*Me'iri*).

HALAKHA

As long as they are engaged in the dough – כָּל זְמַן שֶׁעוֹסְקוֹת בְּבָצֵק: Dough being used to prepare *matza* should not be left idle, even for one moment. This is because as long as someone is handling the dough it will not become leavened, even if a great deal of time passes, as stated in the *baraita* (*Shulḥan Arukh, Oraḥ Ḥayyim* 459:2).

Cracked dough and dough at the beginning of the leavening process [*siur*] – סִידּוּק וְשִׁיאוּר: Dough is considered to be leavened once it has begun to rise and cracks appear on its surface. A person is liable to receive *karet* for eating such dough on Passover, even if the cracks are not intermingled. However, if the dough's surface has merely become pale, one is exempt for eating it. This ruling is in accordance with the opinion of the Rabbis in the mishna, rather than the opinion of Rabbi Yehuda (*Shulḥan Arukh, Oraḥ Ḥayyim* 459:2).

Dough rising and forming cracks

BACKGROUND

Antennae of locusts – קַרְנֵי חֲגָבִים: This expression is used to describe both the shape of the cracks as well as their size. The antennae of locusts have a distinct shape and are 12–15 mm.

Locust with antennae

רַבִּי עֲקִיבָא אוֹמֵר: לֹא כׇּל הַנָּשִׁים וְלֹא כׇּל הָעֵצִים וְלֹא כׇּל הַתַּנּוּרִים שָׁוִין. זֶה הַכְּלָל: תָּפַח – תִּלְטוֹשׁ בְּצוֹנֵן.

Rabbi Akiva says: Not all women, not all wood, and not all ovens are the same, and therefore no set rules should be established. Rather, **this is the principle:** If the dough begins to **rise, she should spread cold** water[N] in which she immersed her hands, onto the dough, in order to stop the leavening process.

גמ׳ תָּנוּ רַבָּנַן: לָשָׁה, הִיא מְקַטֶּפֶת וַחֲבֶירְתָּהּ לָשָׁה תַּחְתֶּיהָ. מְקַטֶּפֶת – הִיא אוֹפָה וַחֲבֶירְתָּהּ מְקַטֶּפֶת תַּחְתֶּיהָ, וְהַשְּׁלִישִׁית לָשָׁה. אוֹפָה – הִיא לָשָׁה, וַחֲבֶירְתָּהּ אוֹפָה תַּחְתֶּיהָ, וְהַשְּׁלִישִׁית מְקַטֶּפֶת, וְחוֹזֶרֶת חֲלִילָה. כׇּל זְמַן שֶׁעוֹסְקוֹת בְּבָצֵק אֵינוֹ בָּא לִידֵי חִימּוּץ.

GEMARA **The Sages taught** in a *baraita*: When the woman who **kneads** first completes her kneading, **she arranges** her dough **and another** woman **kneads in her place.** When the first woman finishes **arranging** her dough, **she bakes and another** woman **arranges** her dough **in her place, and the third** woman **kneads** her dough. When the first woman finishes **baking, she kneads** the dough for her next batch, **and another** woman **bakes in her place, and the third** woman **arranges** her dough, **and they continue in turn. As long as they are engaged** in handling **the dough,**[H] **it will not become leavened.**

״רַבִּי עֲקִיבָא אוֹמֵר לֹא כׇּל הַנָּשִׁים וכו׳״. תַּנְיָא, אָמַר רַבִּי עֲקִיבָא: דַּנְתִּי לִפְנֵי רַבָּן גַּמְלִיאֵל, יְלַמְּדֵינוּ רַבֵּינוּ בְּנָשִׁים זְרִיזוֹת אוֹ בְּנָשִׁים שֶׁאֵין זְרִיזוֹת? בְּעֵצִים לַחִים אוֹ בְּעֵצִים יְבֵשִׁים? בְּתַנּוּר חַם אוֹ בְּתַנּוּר צוֹנֵן? אָמַר לִי: אֵין לְךָ אֶלָּא מַה שֶּׁשָּׁנוּ חֲכָמִים, זֶה הַכְּלָל: תָּפַח תִּלְטוֹשׁ בְּצוֹנֵן.

It was taught in the mishna that **Rabbi Akiva says** that **not all women,** not all wood, and not all ovens are the same. **It was taught** in a *baraita* that **Rabbi Akiva said: I deliberated** this matter **before Rabban Gamliel,** asking: **May our master teach us** if your statement, cited in the mishna, was said **with regard to diligent women or women who are not diligent?** Was it said **with regard to** an oven fueled with **moist wood**[N] **or dry wood?** Was it said **with regard to a hot oven or a cold oven?** Rabban Gamliel himself **said to me: You have only what the Sages taught,** which is that **this is the principle:** If the dough begins to **rise** such that there is a concern that it may become leavened, **she should spread cold** water **onto** the dough to prevent it from becoming leavened.

מתני׳ שִׂיאוּר יִשָּׂרֵף, וְהָאוֹכְלוֹ פָּטוּר, סִידּוּק – יִשָּׂרֵף, וְהָאוֹכְלוֹ חַיָּיב כָּרֵת.

MISHNA Dough at the beginning of the leavening process [*siur*], must **be burned, but one who eats it is exempt** from the punishment of *karet* because the dough had not become fully leavened. Dough that has reached the stage of **cracking** must **be burned, and one who eats it** intentionally **is liable to** receive ***karet,*** as he has intentionally eaten leavened bread during Passover.

אֵיזֶהוּ שִׂיאוּר – כְּקַרְנֵי חֲגָבִים, סִידּוּק – שֶׁנִּתְעָרְבוּ סְדָקִין זֶה בָּזֶה, דִּבְרֵי רַבִּי יְהוּדָה. וַחֲכָמִים אוֹמְרִים: זֶה וָזֶה הָאוֹכְלוֹ חַיָּיב כָּרֵת. וְאֵיזֶהוּ שִׂיאוּר – כׇּל שֶׁהִכְסִיפוּ פָּנָיו, כְּאָדָם שֶׁעָמְדוּ שַׂעֲרוֹתָיו.

What is considered ***siur*?** Dough that has been leavened to the point that it has cracks that look **like the antennae of locusts.**[B] The stage of **cracking** occurs later in the leavening process, **when the cracks intermingle.** This is **the statement of Rabbi Yehuda. And the Rabbis say: One who** intentionally **eats** either **this or that,** dough with cracks like locust antennae or with cracks that have become intermingled, **is liable** to receive ***karet,*** as once dough begins to crack it has certainly become leavened. **And what is *siur*?** It is any dough **whose surface has becomes pale** like the face of **a person whose hair stands** on end due to fear.[H]

גמ׳ תָּנוּ רַבָּנַן: אֵיזֶהוּ שִׂיאוּר – כׇּל שֶׁהִכְסִיפוּ פָּנָיו כְּאָדָם שֶׁעָמְדוּ שַׂעֲרוֹתָיו. סִידּוּק – כְּקַרְנֵי חֲגָבִים, דִּבְרֵי רַבִּי מֵאִיר. וַחֲכָמִים אוֹמְרִים: אֵיזֶהוּ שִׂיאוּר – כְּקַרְנֵי חֲגָבִים, סִידּוּק – שֶׁנִּתְעָרְבוּ סְדָקִין זֶה בָּזֶה. וְזֶה וָזֶה הָאוֹכְלוֹ חַיָּיב כָּרֵת.

GEMARA **The Sages taught: What is *siur*?** It is **any** dough **whose surface has become pale** like the face of **a person whose hair stands** on end due to fear. **Cracking** is considered to have occurred when cracks **like the antennae of locusts** appear. This is **the statement of Rabbi Meir. And the Rabbis say: What is *siur*?** It is when the dough forms cracks **like the antennae of locusts,** and **cracking** is **when the cracks intermingle. And one who** intentionally **eats** either **this or that is liable** to receive ***karet.***

וְהָאֲנַן תְּנַן: שִׂיאוּר יִשָּׂרֵף, וְהָאוֹכְלוֹ פָּטוּר, דִּבְרֵי רַבִּי יְהוּדָה! אֵימָא: לְרַבִּי מֵאִיר זֶה וָזֶה הָאוֹכְלוֹ חַיָּיב כָּרֵת.

The Gemara asks: **But didn't we learn** in the mishna that ***siur* must be burned** but that **one who eats it is exempt** from *karet*; this is **the statement of Rabbi Yehuda.** The opinion attributed to the Rabbis in the *baraita* appears to be the same as that which is attributed to Rabbi Yehuda in the mishna, but according to Rabbi Yehuda, one who eats *siur* is exempt from *karet.* The Gemara answers: **Say** that the *baraita* should be understood in the following manner: **According to** the opinion of **Rabbi Meir,** whose opinion was mentioned previously, **one who** intentionally **eats** either **this or that is liable** to receive ***karet,*** whereas according to the Rabbis he is exempt.

אָמַר רָבָא: מַאי טַעְמָא דְּרַבִּי מֵאִיר – אֵין לְךָ כׇּל סֶדֶק וָסֶדֶק מִלְּמַעְלָה שֶׁאֵין לוֹ כַּמָּה סְדָקִים מִלְּמַטָּה.

Rava said: What is the reason for the opinion **of Rabbi Meir?** It is that **there is no crack above that does not have several cracks below.** Therefore, even if only one small crack appears on the surface, it is a sign that the inside of the dough is filled with cracks and has become leavened.

מתני׳ אַרְבָּעָה עָשָׂר שֶׁחָל לִהְיוֹת בְּשַׁבָּת – מְבַעֲרִין אֶת הַכֹּל מִלִּפְנֵי הַשַּׁבָּת, דִּבְרֵי רַבִּי מֵאִיר. וַחֲכָמִים אוֹמְרִים: בִּזְמַנּוֹ. רַבִּי אֱלִיעֶזֶר בַּר צָדוֹק אוֹמֵר: תְּרוּמָה – מִלִּפְנֵי הַשַּׁבָּת, וְחוּלִּין – בִּזְמַנָּן.

MISHNA With regard to **the fourteenth** of Nisan **that occurs on Shabbat,**[H] **one removes all** leaven from his possession, whether it is *teruma* or non-sacred food, **before Shabbat,**[N] except for that which will be eaten during the first part of Shabbat. In that case, one cannot remove leaven from his possession on the fourteenth of Nisan itself as he does in other years. This is **the statement of Rabbi Meir. And the Rabbis say:**[N] One may remove the leaven **at its usual time**[N] on the fourteenth of Nisan by throwing it away or declaring it ownerless. **Rabbi Eliezer bar Tzadok says:** ***Teruma*** should be removed **before Shabbat,** as only a few people are permitted to eat it and therefore one can presume that it will remain uneaten during Shabbat. However, **non-sacred** foods should be removed **at their** usual **time,** on the fourteenth of Nisan itself.

גמ׳ תַּנְיָא, רַבִּי אֱלִיעֶזֶר בַּר צָדוֹק אוֹמֵר: פַּעַם אַחַת שָׁבַת אַבָּא בְּיַבְנֶה, וְחָל אַרְבָּעָה עָשָׂר לִהְיוֹת בְּשַׁבָּת, וּבָא זוֹנִין מְמוּנֶּה שֶׁל רַבָּן גַּמְלִיאֵל, וְאָמַר: הִגִּיעַ עֵת לְבַעֵר אֶת הֶחָמֵץ. וְהָלַכְתִּי אַחַר אַבָּא, וּבִיעַרְנוּ אֶת הֶחָמֵץ.

GEMARA It was taught in the *Tosefta* that **Rabbi Eliezer bar Tzadok says: One time my father,** Rabbi Tzadok, **spent Shabbat in Yavne,**[B] **and the fourteenth** of Nisan **occurred on** that **Shabbat. Zonin,**[P] who was **the appointee of Rabban Gamliel, came and said: The time has come to remove leavened bread; and I went with my father and we removed the leavened bread.** This story serves as anecdotal evidence that leaven is removed at the usual time on the fourteenth of Nisan, even on Shabbat.

מתני׳ הַהוֹלֵךְ לִשְׁחוֹט אֶת פִּסְחוֹ וְלָמוּל אֶת בְּנוֹ, וְלֶאֱכוֹל סְעוּדַּת אֵירוּסִין בְּבֵית חָמִיו, וְנִזְכַּר שֶׁיֵּשׁ לוֹ חָמֵץ בְּתוֹךְ בֵּיתוֹ. אִם יָכוֹל לַחֲזוֹר וּלְבַעֵר וְלַחֲזוֹר לְמִצְוָתוֹ – יַחֲזוֹר וִיבַעֵר, וְאִם לָאו – מְבַטְּלוֹ בְּלִבּוֹ.

MISHNA One who is traveling on the eve of Passover **to slaughter his Paschal lamb, to circumcise his son, or to eat a betrothal feast**[HN] **in his father-in-law's house, and he remembers that he has leavened bread in his house, if he is able to return** to his house **and remove** the leaven and afterward **return to the mitzva** toward which he was traveling, **he should return** home **and remove** his leaven. **But if** there is not enough time for him to go home and remove the leaven, and still complete the mitzva that he already began, **he should nullify it in his heart,** as by Torah law this is sufficient.

לְהַצִּיל מִן הַגּוֹיִם, וּמִן הַנָּהָר, וּמִן הַלִּסְטִים, וּמִן הַדְּלֵיקָה, וּמִן הַמַּפּוֹלֶת – יְבַטֵּל בְּלִבּוֹ. וְלִשְׁבּוֹת שְׁבִיתַת הָרְשׁוּת – יַחֲזוֹר מִיָּד.

If one was traveling **to save** Jews from an attack by **gentiles,**[N] **from a flooding river, from bandits, from a fire, or from a collapsed** building, he should not even attempt to return, and instead **he should nullify** the leaven **in his heart.** This applies even if he could remove his leaven and still return to his previous activity. If he went **to establish his Shabbat** residence in order to adjust his Shabbat limit for an **optional** purpose,[N] rather than in order to fulfill a commandment, **he should return immediately** to remove his leaven.

NOTES

One removes all leaven before Shabbat – מְבַעֲרִין אֶת הַכֹּל מִלִּפְנֵי הַשַּׁבָּת: Some interpret this phrase literally, meaning that one should remove all leaven from his possession before Shabbat and not leave any for consumption on Shabbat. According to this interpretation, one would be required to eat *matza* for Shabbat meals, with the added assumption that the prohibition against eating *matza* on Passover eve applies only after midday (Rabbi Zeraḥya HaLevi; *ge'onim*).

The dispute between Rabbi Meir and the Rabbis – מַחְלוֹקֶת רַבִּי מֵאִיר וַחֲכָמִים: Some explain the basis for this dispute as follows: Rabbi Meir contends that the only acceptable method for removing leaven from one's possession is through burning, which is a prohibited labor on Shabbat. The Rabbis contend that other methods of removing leaven are acceptable, and therefore one may eliminate it on Shabbat itself (Rabbi Zeraḥya HaLevi).

Before Shabbat…at its usual time – לִפְנֵי הַשַּׁבָּת...בִּזְמַנּוֹ: Some suggest a completely different explanation of this dispute: Rabbi Meir states that one must eliminate leaven before nightfall on Friday, whereas the Rabbis disagree and state that a person must eliminate leaven on Friday before midday, as one would be required to do on Passover eve during an ordinary year. According to this explanation, Rabbi Eliezer bar Tzadok claims that one should eliminate non-sacred leaven on Friday before midday; however, *teruma* should be eliminated just prior to nightfall (*Tzafnat Pane'aḥ*).

Betrothal feast – סְעוּדַּת אֵירוּסִין: The Sages of the Jerusalem Talmud note the significance attributed here to peace and harmony between people, as the mishna compares a betrothal feast to commandments such as the Paschal lamb and circumcision, the violation of which carries the punishment of *karet*.

To save Jews from an attack by gentiles – לְהַצִּיל מִן הַגּוֹיִם: Even if one is traveling to save only Jewish property, rather than Jewish lives, he is not required to return (*Me'iri*). Even if he has enough time to accomplish both tasks, he should not return, lest he be delayed and prevented from performing the mitzva (Rabbeinu Yehonatan).

To establish his Shabbat residence for an optional purpose – לִשְׁבּוֹת שְׁבִיתַת הָרְשׁוּת: In the Jerusalem Talmud it is explained that in this case, the person is planning to travel in order to study with his master. Although this is a mitzva, it is considered optional relative to fulfilling the requirement to eliminate leaven.

HALAKHA

The fourteenth of Nisan that occurs on Shabbat – אַרְבָּעָה עָשָׂר שֶׁחָל לִהְיוֹת בְּשַׁבָּת: When Passover eve occurs on Shabbat, one must remove leaven from his possession before Shabbat, leaving only enough food for the first two Shabbat meals. This is the ruling of the Rambam and some of the *ge'onim*, in accordance with the opinions of Rabbi Eliezer bar Tzadok in the mishna and Rabbi Elazar of Bartota in the *baraita* on daf 13a (*Shulḥan Arukh, Oraḥ Ḥayyim* 444:1).

One who is traveling to perform a mitzva on Passover eve – הַהוֹלֵךְ לְמִצְוָה בְּעֶרֶב פֶּסַח: If one is traveling on Passover eve to perform a mitzva, such as circumcising his son or participating in a feast that constitutes or celebrates a mitzva, and he remembers that he has some leaven in his house, he should return home to remove it, provided he will have enough time afterward to fulfill the mitzva he had already begun. However, if he will not have time to do so, he should nullify the leaven to himself. If the time for removing leaven has already passed, he is required to return home in any case, as he can no longer nullify it to himself (*Be'er Heitev*). If one is traveling to save people from a dangerous situation, such as a flood, he should not go back for the leaven even if he will have enough time to remove the leaven and save the people. If he is traveling for his own optional needs, he should return home (*Shulḥan Arukh, Oraḥ Ḥayyim* 444:7).

BACKGROUND

Yavne – יַבְנֶה: Yavne, a town in Judea, was a center of Torah study during the Second Temple period. After the destruction of the Temple, Rabban Yoḥanan ben Zakkai reestablished the Sanhedrin there and the town attained great prominence as an important Torah center. As the seat of the Sanhedrin, Yavne was the spiritual center of the entire Jewish population in Eretz Yisrael. The Yavne Yeshiva, initially headed by Rabban Yoḥanan ben Zakkai and later by Rabban Gamliel II of Yavne, attracted many of the greatest Torah scholars of that era. At Yavne, many ordinances were enacted to restore Jewish religious and spiritual life after the destruction of the Temple. It remained an important center until the time of the bar Kokheva rebellion.

PERSONALITIES

Zonin – זוֹנִין: Zonin, from the Greek name Ζήνων, Zeno, apparently ran the internal affairs of the household of the *Nasi*. Baitos ben Zonin (see above, 37a) was apparently his son, and he also had strong ties to the household of the *Nasi*. Zonin was wealthy and very scrupulous in his observance of mitzvot, as is evident from several incidents the Talmud relates about him.

וְכֵן מִי שֶׁיָּצָא מִירוּשָׁלַיִם וְנִזְכַּר שֶׁיֵּשׁ בְּיָדוֹ בְּשַׂר קֹדֶשׁ, אִם עָבַר צוֹפִים – שׂוֹרְפוֹ בִּמְקוֹמוֹ, וְאִם לָאו – חוֹזֵר וְשׂוֹרְפוֹ לִפְנֵי הַבִּירָה מֵעֲצֵי הַמַּעֲרָכָה.

And so too, the same *halakha* applies to **one who left Jerusalem and remembered that there was consecrated meat in his hand.**[H] Meat that is taken out of Jerusalem becomes disqualified, and one is required to burn it in proximity to the Temple. **If he passed** the area of Mount **Scopus** [*Tzofim*],[B] beyond which one cannot see Jerusalem, **he burns** the meat **at the site** where **he** is located; **and if** he has **not** traveled that far, **he must return and burn it before the Temple with wood from the arrangement** on the altar, which was designated for burning consecrated items that were disqualified.

וְעַד כַּמָּה הֵן חוֹזְרִין? רַבִּי מֵאִיר אוֹמֵר: זֶה וָזֶה בִּכְבֵיצָה, רַבִּי יְהוּדָה אוֹמֵר: זֶה וָזֶה בִּכְזַיִת. וַחֲכָמִים אוֹמְרִים: בְּשַׂר קֹדֶשׁ – בִּכְזַיִת, וְחָמֵץ – בִּכְבֵיצָה.

The mishna asks: For **how much** leaven or consecrated meat is one required **to return?**[H] **Rabbi Meir says:** In both **this** case **and that** case, one must return for **an egg-bulk. Rabbi Yehuda says:** In both **this** case **and that** case, one must return for **an olive-bulk. And the Rabbis say** that the amount depends on the case: With regard to **consecrated meat,** he is required to return if he has **an olive-bulk, but** in a case where he remembers that he has **leavened bread,** he required to return only **for an egg-bulk.**

גמ׳ וּרְמִינְהוּ: הַהוֹלֵךְ לֶאֱכוֹל סְעוּדַת אֵירוּסִין בְּבֵית חָמִיו וְלִשְׁבּוֹת שְׁבִיתַת הָרְשׁוּת – יַחֲזוֹר מִיָּד.

GEMARA The Gemara **raises a contradiction** between this mishna and another source. It was taught in a *baraita*: **One who is traveling to eat a betrothal feast in his father-in-law's house or to establish his Shabbat** residence for an **optional** purpose, **must return immediately** to remove his leaven. This contradicts the mishna, which states that one who is going to a betrothal feast may nullify the leaven without returning for it, because the meal is considered a mitzva.

אָמַר רַבִּי יוֹחָנָן: לָא קַשְׁיָא; הָא – רַבִּי יְהוּדָה, הָא – רַבִּי יוֹסֵי, דְּתַנְיָא: סְעוּדַת אֵירוּסִין – רְשׁוּת, דִּבְרֵי רַבִּי יְהוּדָה. רַבִּי יוֹסֵי אוֹמֵר: מִצְוָה.

Rabbi Yoḥanan said: This is **not difficult,** as there is a tannaitic dispute with regard to the issue. **This** source, the *baraita*, is in accordance with the opinion of **Rabbi Yehuda,** while **that** source, the mishna, is in accordance with the opinion of **Rabbi Yosei. As it was taught** in a *baraita*: **A betrothal feast is optional;** this is **the statement of Rabbi Yehuda. Rabbi Yosei says:** It is a **mitzva.**

וְהָשְׁתָּא, דְּאָמַר רַב חִסְדָּא: מַחֲלוֹקֶת – בִּסְעוּדָה שְׁנִיָּה, אֲבָל בִּסְעוּדָה רִאשׁוֹנָה – דִּבְרֵי הַכֹּל מִצְוָה. אֲפִילּוּ תֵּימָא הָא וְהָא רַבִּי יְהוּדָה, וְלָא קַשְׁיָא; הָא – בִּסְעוּדָה רִאשׁוֹנָה, הָא – בִּסְעוּדָה שְׁנִיָּה.

And now that Rav Ḥisda said: The dispute between Rabbi Yehuda and Rabbi Yosei applies to **the second** betrothal feast, where the groom takes part in an additional meal with the bride's family, **but everyone agrees that the first** betrothal **feast is a mitzva,** the contradiction between the mishna and the *baraita* can be resolved differently. **Even if you say that this** mishna and **that** *baraita* are both in accordance with the opinion of **Rabbi Yehuda,** it is **not difficult. This** mishna, which relates to the meal as a mitzva, is referring to **the first meal. That** *baraita*, which assumes that the meal is not a mitzva, is referring to **the second meal.**

תַּנְיָא, אָמַר רַבִּי יְהוּדָה: אֲנִי לֹא שָׁמַעְתִּי אֶלָּא סְעוּדַת אֵירוּסִין, אֲבָל לֹא סִבְלוֹנוֹת. אָמַר לוֹ רַבִּי יוֹסֵי: אֲנִי שָׁמַעְתִּי סְעוּדַת אֵירוּסִין וְסִבְלוֹנוֹת.

It was taught in a *baraita* that **Rabbi Yehuda said: I heard only** that there is a mitzva with regard to a **betrothal feast** itself, **but not** with regard to the feast of the **gifts** [*sivlonot*],[L] when the groom would present gifts to the bride. While a festive meal was eaten on this occasion, it was not considered to be a mitzva. **Rabbi Yosei said to him: I heard** that both **a betrothal feast and** the feast of the **gifts** are considered mitzvot.

תַּנְיָא, רַבִּי שִׁמְעוֹן אוֹמֵר: כׇּל סְעוּדָה שֶׁאֵינָהּ שֶׁל מִצְוָה – אֵין תַּלְמִיד חָכָם רַשַּׁאי לֵהָנוֹת מִמֶּנָּה.

Having discussed whether a betrothal feast is a mitzva, the Gemara addresses a related issue. **It was taught** in a *baraita* that **Rabbi Shimon says: A Torah scholar may not** derive **benefit** from partaking in **any feast that is not a mitzva.**[H]

כְּגוֹן מַאי? אָמַר רַבִּי יוֹחָנָן: כְּגוֹן בַּת כֹּהֵן לְיִשְׂרָאֵל, וּבַת תַּלְמִיד חָכָם לְעַם הָאָרֶץ. דְּאָמַר רַבִּי יוֹחָנָן: בַּת כֹּהֵן לְיִשְׂרָאֵל – אֵין זִוּוּגָן עוֹלֶה יָפֶה.

The Gemara asks: **In what case** does this statement apply? **Rabbi Yoḥanan said: In a case** where **the daughter of a priest** marries **an Israelite,** or where **the daughter of a Torah scholar** marries **an ignoramus.** Although a wedding feast is generally a mitzva, it is not in this case, **as Rabbi Yoḥanan said:** When **the daughter of a priest** marries **an Israelite their union will not be auspicious,** as it is disgraceful for the priesthood when the daughter of a priest marries an Israelite.

HALAKHA

And remembered that there was consecrated meat in his hand – וְנִזְכַּר שֶׁיֵּשׁ בְּיָדוֹ בְּשַׂר קֹדֶשׁ: If one leaves Jerusalem with sacrificial meat and remembers only after he passes the area of Tzofim that he has it, he must burn it in the place where he remembers. However, if he has not yet reached that point, he must return and burn it in Jerusalem (Rambam *Sefer Avoda, Hilkhot Pesulei HaMukdashin* 19:8).

For how much is one required to return – עַד כַּמָּה הֵן חוֹזְרִין: If one leaves Jerusalem with an olive-bulk of sacrificial meat, he is required to return and burn it in Jerusalem. With regard to leaven, one must return to his house to destroy an egg-bulk, in accordance with the opinion of the Rabbis (Rambam *Sefer Avoda, Hilkhot Pesulei HaMukdashin* 19:8; *Shulḥan Arukh, Oraḥ Ḥayyim* 444:7).

A Torah scholar and an optional feast – תַּלְמִיד חָכָם בִּסְעוּדַת רְשׁוּת: It is fitting for a Torah scholar to eat optional meals only in his home and to avoid eating in the company of ignoramuses. He should not eat excessively, even in the company of scholars. It is proper for him to participate in public feasts only when they constitute a mitzva, such as at the wedding of a Torah scholar and the daughter of a Torah scholar (Rambam *Sefer HaMadda, Hilkhot Deot* 5:2).

BACKGROUND

Mount Scopus [*Tzofim*] – צוֹפִים: Authorities disagree as to whether this refers to a specific location near Jerusalem or more generally to any place from which it is possible to see [*litzpot*] the city. Some say *Tzofim* refers to Mount Scopus [*Har HaTzofim*]. Others claim that it refers to what is today known as Shuafat, located near the northern neighborhoods of modern-day Jerusalem.

View of the Old City of Jerusalem from Mount Scopus

View of Mount Scopus and Old City of Jerusalem from Sherover Promenade in southern Jerusalem

LANGUAGE

Gifts [*sivlonot*] – סִבְלוֹנוֹת: Possibly from the Greek σύμβολον, *symbolon*, meaning collateral, gift, marriage agreement, covenant, treaty, or contract.

מַאי הִיא? אָמַר רַב חִסְדָּא: אוֹ אַלְמָנָה אוֹ גְרוּשָׁה אוֹ זֶרַע אֵין לָהּ. בְּמַתְנִיתָא תָּנָא: קוֹבְרָהּ אוֹ קוֹבַרְתּוֹ, אוֹ מְבִיאָתוֹ לִידֵי עֲנִיּוּת.

The Gemara asks: **What is** meant by **this** statement that their union will be inauspicious? **Rav Ḥisda said:** The inauspicious nature of such a marriage can be identified based on the verse describing the return of a daughter of a priest to her father's house after marrying a non-priest. The verse is understood as mentioning that the marriage will result in one of three possibilities: she will **either be a widow, a divorcee, or without children** (see Leviticus 22:13). **It was taught in a *baraita*:** Either her husband **will bury her or she will bury him,** because one of them will die young, **or she will cause him to become poor.**

אִינִי? וְהָא אָמַר רַבִּי יוֹחָנָן: הָרוֹצֶה שֶׁיִּתְעַשֵּׁר – יִדָּבֵק בְּזַרְעוֹ שֶׁל אַהֲרֹן, כׇּל שֶׁכֵּן שֶׁתּוֹרָה וּכְהוּנָּה מַעֲשִׁירְתָן – לָא קַשְׁיָא: הָא – בְּתַלְמִיד חָכָם, הָא – בְּעַם הָאָרֶץ.

The Gemara asks: **Is that so? Didn't Rabbi Yoḥanan** himself **say: One who wishes to become wealthy should cling to the descendants of Aaron,** and **all the more so** should the merit of the **Torah** and the **priesthood cause them to become wealthy.** The Gemara answers: This is **not difficult,** as **this** case, where he becomes wealthy, **refers to a Torah scholar** who marries a woman of priestly lineage. In that case their union will be a successful one. **That** case, where their union will not be auspicious, refers to **an ignoramus** who marries a woman of priestly lineage.[H]

רַבִּי יְהוֹשֻׁעַ נְסֵיב כָּהַנְתָּא, חֲלַשׁ. אֲמַר: לָא נִיחָא לֵיהּ לְאַהֲרֹן דְּאֶדַּבַּק בְּזַרְעֵיהּ, דְּהָוֵי לֵיהּ חַתְנָא כִּי אֲנָא.

The Gemara relates that **Rabbi Yehoshua married a daughter of a priest** and **became ill. He said:** Apparently, **it is not satisfactory to Aaron** the priest **that I cling to his descendants, so that he has a son-in-law like me.**

רַב אִידִי בַּר אָבִין נְסֵיב כָּהַנְתָּא, נְפַקוּ מִינֵּיהּ תְּרֵי בְּנֵי סְמִיכֵי, רַב שֵׁשֶׁת בְּרֵיהּ דְּרַב אִידִי וְרַבִּי יְהוֹשֻׁעַ בְּרֵיהּ דְּרַב אִידִי. אָמַר רַב פָּפָּא: אִי לָא נְסֵיבְנָא כָּהַנְתָּא לָא אִיעַתְרִי.

The Gemara also relates that **Rav Idi bar Avin married a daughter of a priest. Two sons** who were **ordained**[N] to decide halakhic matters **came from him,** namely **Rav Sheshet, son of Rav Idi, and Rabbi Yehoshua, son of Rav Idi.** Similarly, **Rav Pappa said: Had I not married a daughter of a priest, I would not have become wealthy.**

אָמַר רַב כָּהֲנָא: אִי לָא נְסֵיבְנָא כָּהַנְתָּא – לָא גְּלַאי. אָמְרוּ לֵיהּ: וְהָא לִמְקוֹם תּוֹרָה גָּלִיתָ! לָא גְּלַאי כִּדְגָלֵי אֱינָשֵׁי.

On the other hand, **Rav Kahana,**[P] who was not a priest, **said: Had I not married a daughter of a priest, I would not have been exiled,** as Rav Kahana was forced to flee from Babylonia to Eretz Yisrael. **They said to him: But you were exiled to a place of Torah,** which is not a punishment at all. He answered: **I was not exiled as people are** generally **exiled,** i.e., I did not emigrate of my own free will; rather, I was forced to flee from the authorities.

אָמַר רַבִּי יִצְחָק: כׇּל הַנֶּהֱנֶה מִסְּעוּדַת הָרְשׁוּת לְסוֹף גּוֹלֶה, שֶׁנֶּאֱמַר: ״וְאֹכְלִים כָּרִים מִצֹּאן וַעֲגָלִים מִתּוֹךְ מַרְבֵּק״, וּכְתִיב: ״לָכֵן עַתָּה יִגְלוּ בְּרֹאשׁ גּוֹלִים״.

Rabbi Yitzḥak said: Anyone who benefits from partaking in **an optional feast,** which is not a mitzva, **will ultimately be exiled, as it is stated: "And eat the lambs of the flock and the calves out of the midst of the stall"** (Amos 6:4), **and it is written: "Therefore now they shall go into exile at the head of the exiles;** and the revelry of those who stretched themselves out shall pass away" (Amos 6:7).

תָּנוּ רַבָּנַן: כׇּל תַּלְמִיד חָכָם הַמַּרְבֶּה סְעוּדָתוֹ בְּכׇל מָקוֹם – סוֹף מַחֲרִיב אֶת בֵּיתוֹ, וּמְאַלְמֵן אֶת אִשְׁתּוֹ, וּמְיַיתֵּם אֶת גּוֹזָלָיו, וְתַלְמוּדוֹ מִשְׁתַּכֵּחַ מִמֶּנּוּ, וּמַחֲלוֹקוֹת רַבּוֹת בָּאוֹת עָלָיו, וּדְבָרָיו אֵינָם נִשְׁמָעִים וּמְחַלֵּל שֵׁם שָׁמַיִם וְשֵׁם רַבּוֹ וְשֵׁם אָבִיו, וְגוֹרֵם שֵׁם רַע לוֹ וּלְבָנָיו וְלִבְנֵי בָנָיו עַד סוֹף כׇּל הַדּוֹרוֹת.

The Gemara continues discussing a Torah scholar who benefits from optional feasts. **The Sages taught: Any Torah scholar who feasts excessively everywhere** degrades himself and brings suffering upon himself. He will **ultimately destroy his house,**[N] **widow his wife, orphan his chicks,** i.e., his children, **and his studies will be forgotten. Much dispute will come upon him, his words will not be heeded, and he will desecrate God's name and the name of his master and the name of his father. And he will cause a bad name for himself, his children, and his descendants throughout future generations.**

מַאי הִיא? אָמַר אַבָּיֵי: קָרוּ לֵיהּ בַּר מְחַים תַּנּוּרֵי. רָבָא אָמַר: בַּר מְרַקֵּיד בֵּי כּוּבֵי. רַב פַּפָּא אָמַר: בַּר מְלַחֵיךְ פִּינְכֵי. רַב שְׁמַעְיָה אָמַר: בַּר מָךְ רָבַע.

The Gemara asks: **What is this** bad reputation that he causes to himself and his descendants? **Abaye said:** His son **is called the son [*bar*] of the one who heats ovens,**[N] since this person continually heated ovens in order to prepare food for feasts. **Rava said:** His son will be called **the son of the one who dances** in **inns [*bei kuvei*],**[L] as he seems to be invited to every feast to entertain the guests. **Rav Pappa said:** His son will be called **the son of the one who licks bowls [*pinkhei*].**[L] **Rav Shemaya said:** His son will be called **the son of the one who folds** his garment **and crouches,** i.e., falls asleep drunk.

HALAKHA

Marriage to the daughter of a priest – נְשׂוּאִין לְבַת כֹּהֵן: The daughter of a priest should marry a Torah scholar in order for their marriage to be successful, as if she marries a man who is not a Torah scholar, the troubles the Sages warned about may come to pass (*Shulḥan Arukh, Even HaEzer* 2:8).

NOTES

Two sons who were ordained – תְּרֵי בְּנֵי סְמִיכֵי: The verse states with regard to the descendants of Aaron: "They will teach your laws to Jacob" (Deuteronomy 33:10). Through the merit of this marriage, Rav Idi bar Avin was granted sons who became Torah scholars (Maharsha).

Destroy his house, etc. – מַחֲרִיב אֶת בֵּיתוֹ וכו׳: Some explain that this expression means that such a person will spend all his money on these feasts. He will widow his wife by becoming deserving of divine punishment for his actions (Rav Yehuda ben Rav Binyamin HaRofeh). Dispute will come upon him as is common with drunkards, whose intoxication leads them to quarrel (Maharsha).

The son [*bar*] of the one who heats ovens – בַּר מְחַים תַּנּוּרֵי: Some say that the gluttonous person himself will be referred to by this title, and that the word *bar* does not mean son but rather is used in a general way to express a sense of belonging, as in the expression *bar mitzva*, one who is subject to mitzvot. The expression would indicate that the person is constantly engaged in this degrading activity (Maharal, Maharsha).

PERSONALITIES

Rav Kahana – רַב כָּהֲנָא: Many different Sages are referred to as Rav Kahana. The Rav Kahana mentioned here apparently refers to the one who was a disciple-colleague of Rav.

Rav Kahana came to study with Rav while still in his youth. Although he was a student of Rav with regard to traditions and sources, he was able to grasp halakhic reasoning independently. Nonetheless, he was a devoted student, zealously guarding Rav's honor. When someone once threatened to bring fabricated charges against Rav to the authorities, Rav Kahana thwarted this plan by causing the man's death. As a result of this incident, he was forced to flee to Eretz Yisrael. Once in Eretz Yisrael, he studied with scholars such as Rabbi Yoḥanan and Reish Lakish, who described him as the lion who ascended from Babylonia. However, it seems that the other scholars of Eretz Yisrael did not treat him with due respect, and he later returned to Babylonia. His statement here alludes to his move to Eretz Yisrael.

LANGUAGE

Inns [*bei kuvei*] – בֵּי כּוּבֵי: From the Arabic كوب, *kūb*, which literally means a jug without a handle, and can be used to refer to the place where the jugs are stored.

Bowls [*pinkhei*] – פִּינְכֵי: From the Greek πίναξ, *pinax*, meaning a trencher or a platter.

תָּנוּ רַבָּנַן: לְעוֹלָם יִמְכּוֹר אָדָם כׇּל מַה שֶּׁיֵּשׁ לוֹ וְיִשָּׂא בַּת תַּלְמִיד חָכָם. שֶׁאִם מֵת אוֹ גּוֹלֶה – מוּבְטָח לוֹ שֶׁבָּנָיו תַּלְמִידֵי חֲכָמִים, וְאַל יִשָּׂא בַּת עַם הָאָרֶץ – שֶׁאִם מֵת אוֹ גּוֹלֶה בָּנָיו עַמֵּי הָאָרֶץ.

On the topic of proper marriage partners, the Gemara cites the following discussion. **The Sages taught: One should always** be willing **to sell all he has** in order to **marry the daughter of a Torah scholar, as if he dies or** if he **is exiled** and he cannot raise his children, **he can be assured that his sons will be Torah scholars,** since their mother will ensure that they are well educated. **And one should not marry the daughter of an ignoramus, as if he dies or is exiled, his sons will be ignoramuses.**

תָּנוּ רַבָּנַן: לְעוֹלָם יִמְכּוֹר אָדָם כׇּל מַה שֶּׁיֵּשׁ לוֹ וְיִשָּׂא בַּת תַּלְמִיד חָכָם, וְיַשִּׂיא בִּתּוֹ לְתַלְמִיד חָכָם. מָשָׁל לְעִנְּבֵי הַגֶּפֶן בְּעִנְּבֵי הַגֶּפֶן, דָּבָר נָאֶה וּמִתְקַבֵּל. וְלֹא יִשָּׂא בַּת עַם הָאָרֶץ – מָשָׁל לְעִנְּבֵי הַגֶּפֶן בְּעִנְּבֵי הַסְּנֶה, דָּבָר כָּעוּר

Furthermore, **the Sages taught: One should always** be willing to **sell all he has** in order to **marry the daughter of a Torah scholar and** in order to **marry off his daughter to a Torah scholar.** This type of marriage can be **compared to grapes of a vine** that become intertwined **with grapes of a vine, something** which is **beautiful and acceptable**[N] to God and man. **And one should not marry the daughter of an ignoramus.** This type of marriage can be **compared to grapes of a vine** that have become intertwined **with berries of a bramble,**[B] which is **something unseemly**

NOTES

Acceptable and unacceptable – מִתְקַבֵּל וְאֵינוֹ מִתְקַבֵּל: Some explain that the metaphor indicates that the union will take hold and be fruitful (Maharsha).

BACKGROUND

Bramble – סְנֶה: This plant, which is also referred to as *vardina* in the Talmud, is apparently *Rubus sanctus*, a species of the rose family. Also called the holy bramble, it is a small flowering evergreen that either grows along the ground or climbs upward. It grows primarily near riverbeds or in other wet regions throughout Eretz Yisrael. Its leaves are made up of three or four small parts and many strong thorns, some of which are bent. Its flowers, which are approximately 2 cm in diameter, are pinkish-purple or white, and it produces black and red fruits, which are the berries of the bramble referred to in the Gemara. Although these fruits are edible, they are often small, hard, and dry, and they are vastly different from cultivated grapes.

Holy bramble

Perek **III**
Daf **49** Amud **b**

וְאֵינוֹ מִתְקַבֵּל.

and unacceptable.

תָּנוּ רַבָּנַן: לְעוֹלָם יִמְכּוֹר אָדָם כׇּל מַה שֶּׁיֵּשׁ לוֹ וְיִשָּׂא בַּת תַּלְמִיד חָכָם. לֹא מָצָא בַּת תַּלְמִיד חָכָם – יִשָּׂא בַּת גְּדוֹלֵי הַדּוֹר. לֹא מָצָא בַּת גְּדוֹלֵי הַדּוֹר – יִשָּׂא בַּת רָאשֵׁי כְּנֵסִיּוֹת. לֹא מָצָא בַּת רָאשֵׁי כְּנֵסִיּוֹת – יִשָּׂא בַּת גַּבָּאֵי צְדָקָה. לֹא מָצָא בַּת גַּבָּאֵי צְדָקָה – יִשָּׂא בַּת מְלַמְּדֵי תִינוֹקוֹת. וְלֹא יִשָּׂא בַּת עַמֵּי הָאָרֶץ, מִפְּנֵי שֶׁהֵן שֶׁקֶץ, וּנְשׁוֹתֵיהֶן שֶׁרֶץ, וְעַל בְּנוֹתֵיהֶן הוּא אוֹמֵר: "אָרוּר שׁוֹכֵב עִם כׇּל בְּהֵמָה".

The Sages taught: A person should always be willing to **sell all he has** in order to **marry the daughter of a Torah scholar. If he cannot find the daughter of a Torah scholar, he should marry the daughter of** one of the **great** people **of the generation,** who are pious although they are not Torah scholars. **If he cannot find the daughter of** one of the **great** people **of the generation, he should marry the daughter of** one **of the heads of the congregations.**[B] **If he cannot find the daughter of** one **of the heads of the congregations, he should marry the daughter of** one of **the charity collectors. If he cannot find the daughter of** one of **the charity collectors, he should marry the daughter of** one of **the schoolteachers. However, he should not marry the daughter of an ignoramus** [*am ha'aretz*][N] **because they are vermin and their wives are** similar to **a creeping animal,** as their lifestyle involves the violation of numerous prohibitions. **And with regard to their daughters** the verse **states: "Cursed is he who lies with an animal"** (Deuteronomy 27:21), as they are similar to animals in that they lack any knowledge or moral sense.[H]

BACKGROUND

Heads of congregations – רָאשֵׁי כְּנֵסִיּוֹת: This title referred to those who managed the affairs of the congregation. Those who filled this position were always well respected and continually engaged in mitzvot. Indeed, the priest who occupied this position in the Temple had a status just below that of the deputy High Priest. This title may be found on various tombstones from the talmudic period.

HALAKHA

Whom is it fitting to marry – אֶת מִי רָאוּי לִשָּׂאת: It is proper for a man to marry the daughter of a Torah scholar, or of a respectable family, or of people of action, or of those who are well known for their scrupulous performance of mitzvot (*Shulḥan Arukh, Even HaEzer* 2:6).

NOTES

Ignoramus [*am ha'aretz*] – עַם הָאָרֶץ: Many explanations are suggested for the various statements in the Gemara here with regard to ignoramuses; however, certain points are generally agreed upon. The term ignoramus is used to refer to several different types of people at different levels of knowledge and observance. It may refer to people at the lowest levels, and even to those who have studied the Bible and Mishna but have not been adequately trained in advanced talmudic logic. It appears that the statements made here apply to the most boorish type of ignoramus. In accordance with the Gemara's definition elsewhere, this is referring to one who has not studied Bible or Mishna or engaged in any type of productive activity. Such a person is not only ignorant of the Torah, but also degrades mitzva observance and does not contribute to society. One who falls into this category should be entirely avoided, as he is likely to intentionally or unintentionally violate *halakha*. The term *am ha'aretz* used in reference to an ignoramus originates from the fact that gentiles were originally called nations of the earth [*amei ha'aretz*]. Others say that the title is related to the word *amum*, meaning dim or weak, and that an ignoramus has a weak spirit (*Arukh*).

תַּנְיָא, רַבִּי אוֹמֵר: עַם הָאָרֶץ אָסוּר לֶאֱכוֹל בְּשַׂר (בְּהֵמָה), שֶׁנֶּאֱמַר: ״זֹאת תּוֹרַת הַבְּהֵמָה וְהָעוֹף״ כׇּל הָעוֹסֵק בַּתּוֹרָה – מוּתָּר לֶאֱכוֹל בְּשַׂר בְּהֵמָה וָעוֹף, וְכׇל שֶׁאֵינוֹ עוֹסֵק בַּתּוֹרָה – אָסוּר לֶאֱכוֹל בְּשַׂר בְּהֵמָה וָעוֹף.

The Gemara continues its discussion with regard to an ignoramus. **It was taught** in a *baraita* that **Rabbi** Yehuda HaNasi **says: It is prohibited for an ignoramus to eat meat, as it is stated: "This is the law [*torah*] of the beast and of the fowl"** (Leviticus 11:46). He expounds: **Anyone who engages in Torah** study **is permitted to eat the meat of animals and fowl, and anyone who does not engage in Torah** study **is prohibited to eat the meat of animals or fowl.**[N]

אָמַר רַבִּי אֶלְעָזָר: עַם הָאָרֶץ מוּתָּר לְנוֹחֲרוֹ בְּיוֹם הַכִּיפּוּרִים שֶׁחָל לִהְיוֹת בְּשַׁבָּת. אָמְרוּ לוֹ תַּלְמִידָיו: רַבִּי, אֱמוֹר לְשׁוֹחֲטוֹ! אָמַר לָהֶן: זֶה – טָעוּן בְּרָכָה, וְזֶה – אֵינוֹ טָעוּן בְּרָכָה.

The Gemara proceeds to mention some sharply negative statements of the Sages in which they overstated their negative sentiments with regard to ignoramuses, although these ignoramuses were wicked in addition to being boors (*ge'onim*). **Rabbi Elazar said: It is permitted to stab an ignoramus** to death **on Yom Kippur**[N] **that occurs on Shabbat. His students said to him: Master,** at least **say** that it is permitted **to slaughter him. He said to them:** I intentionally used the word stab, as **this** term, slaughtering, **requires a blessing** when one slaughters an animal, **and that** term, stabbing, **does not require a blessing** in any context.

אָמַר רַבִּי אֶלְעָזָר: עַם הָאָרֶץ אָסוּר לְהִתְלַוּוֹת עִמּוֹ בַּדֶּרֶךְ, שֶׁנֶּאֱמַר: ״כִּי הִיא חַיֶּיךָ וְאוֹרֶךְ יָמֶיךָ״ עַל חַיָּיו לֹא חָס – עַל חַיֵּי חֲבֵירוֹ לֹא כׇּל שֶׁכֵּן.

Rabbi Elazar said: It is prohibited to accompany an ignoramus while traveling **on the road** due to concern that the ignoramus might try to harm his traveling partner, **as it is stated** with regard to Torah: **"For it is your life and the length of your days"** (Deuteronomy 30:20). An ignoramus has not studied any Torah, indicating that **he is not concerned about his own life;** with regard **to another's life, all the more so.**

אָמַר רַבִּי שְׁמוּאֵל בַּר נַחְמָנִי אָמַר רַבִּי יוֹחָנָן: עַם הָאָרֶץ מוּתָּר לְקוֹרְעוֹ כַּדָּג. אָמַר רַבִּי שְׁמוּאֵל בַּר יִצְחָק: וּמִגַּבּוֹ.

Rabbi Shmuel bar Naḥmani said that **Rabbi Yoḥanan said: It is permitted to tear** open **an ignoramus like a fish. Rabbi Shmuel bar Yitzḥak said: And** one may cut him open **from his back** and thereby cause his immediate death by piercing his spinal cord rather than his stomach.

תַּנְיָא, אָמַר רַבִּי עֲקִיבָא: כְּשֶׁהָיִיתִי עַם הָאָרֶץ אָמַרְתִּי: מִי יִתֵּן לִי תַּלְמִיד חָכָם וַאֲנַשְּׁכֶנּוּ כַּחֲמוֹר. אָמְרוּ לוֹ תַּלְמִידָיו: רַבִּי, אֱמוֹר כַּכֶּלֶב! אָמַר לָהֶן: זֶה – נוֹשֵׁךְ וְשׁוֹבֵר עֶצֶם, וְזֶה – נוֹשֵׁךְ וְאֵינוֹ שׁוֹבֵר עֶצֶם.

It was taught in a *baraita* that **Rabbi Akiva said: When I was an ignoramus I said: Who will give me a Torah scholar** so that **I will bite him like a donkey? His students said to him: Master, say** that you would bite him **like a dog! He said to them:** I specifically used that wording, as **this one,** a donkey, **bites and breaks bones, and that one,** a dog, **bites but does not break bones.**

תַּנְיָא, הָיָה רַבִּי מֵאִיר אוֹמֵר: כׇּל הַמַּשִּׂיא בִּתּוֹ לְעַם הָאָרֶץ – כְּאִילּוּ כּוֹפְתָהּ וּמַנִּיחָהּ לִפְנֵי אֲרִי. מָה אֲרִי דּוֹרֵס וְאוֹכֵל וְאֵין לוֹ בּוֹשֶׁת פָּנִים – אַף עַם הָאָרֶץ מַכֶּה וּבוֹעֵל וְאֵין לוֹ בּוֹשֶׁת פָּנִים.

It was taught in a *baraita* that **Rabbi Meir would say: Anyone who marries off his daughter to an ignoramus** is considered **as though he binds her and places her before a lion.** Why is this so? **Just as a lion mauls** its prey **and eats and has no shame, so too, an ignoramus strikes** his wife **and** then **engages in sexual relations** with her without appeasing her first, **and has no shame.**

תַּנְיָא, רַבִּי אֱלִיעֶזֶר אוֹמֵר: אִילְמָלֵא אָנוּ צְרִיכִין לָהֶם לְמַשָּׂא וּמַתָּן – הָיוּ הוֹרְגִין אוֹתָנוּ.

It was taught in a *baraita* that **Rabbi Eliezer says: If we did not need**[N] the ignoramuses **for business, they would kill us.**

תָּנָא רַבִּי חִיָּיא: כׇּל הָעוֹסֵק בַּתּוֹרָה לִפְנֵי עַם הָאָרֶץ – כְּאִילּוּ בּוֹעֵל אֲרוּסָתוֹ בְּפָנָיו, שֶׁנֶּאֱמַר: ״תּוֹרָה צִוָּה לָנוּ מֹשֶׁה מוֹרָשָׁה״ אַל תִּקְרֵי ״מוֹרָשָׁה״ אֶלָּא ״מְאוֹרָסָה״.

The Gemara shifts to a discussion of an ignoramus who has some degree of sensitivity (*Me'iri*). **Rabbi Ḥiyya taught: Anyone who engages in Torah** study **in the presence of an ignoramus,** causing the ignoramus embarrassment and anguish over his inability to study Torah, **is considered as though he had sexual relations with** the ignoramus's **betrothed bride**[N] **in his presence, as it is stated: "Moses commanded us the Torah, an inheritance [*morasha*]** for the congregation of Jacob" (Deuteronomy 33:4). **Do not read it as inheritance [*morasha*]; rather,** read it as **betrothed [*me'orasa*].** The Torah is compared to the betrothed bride of the Jewish people until one studies it and thereby consummates his marriage with it.

NOTES

Is prohibited to eat the meat of animals or fowl – אָסוּר לֶאֱכוֹל בְּשַׂר בְּהֵמָה וָעוֹף: Some explain this statement in the following manner: Since an ignoramus is unable to distinguish between an animal or fowl that was slaughtered properly and one that was not, he may not eat them. Others say that in his boorishness he will cause his animals to develop conditions that will cause them to die within twelve months and thereby attain the status of *tereifa*, which would mean that they may not be consumed. For this reason, the Gemara mentioned the meat of animals and fowl, with regard to which these concerns exist, but did not mention fish, which do not need to be slaughtered and cannot attain the status of *tereifa* (*ge'onim*).

It is permitted to stab an ignoramus on Yom Kippur – מוּתָּר לְנוֹחֲרוֹ בְּיוֹם הַכִּיפּוּרִים: Some explain that this refers to an ignoramus who was attempting to murder someone or who was chasing a young betrothed woman in order to rape her. In such a case it is permitted to save the potential victim by killing the pursuer by any means necessary (Rif). Indeed, this is the case with regard to any type of pursuer who is on his way to commit these sins (see Ran). An ignoramus is specified only because he is more likely to commit such a crime (Ritva), as it is difficult to attribute this behavior to a Torah scholar (*Me'iri*). Most commentaries hold that this is an exaggeration and is stated only in order to encourage the study of Torah and to encourage people to keep their distance from ignoramuses (Rav Sherira Gaon; Ran; Ritva; and others).

If we did not need – אִילְמָלֵא אָנוּ צְרִיכִין: Some understand this statement in the following manner: If Torah scholars did not need the ignoramuses, they would create more boundaries between the two groups, engendering even greater animosity between them (*Ḥokhmat Mano'aḥ*).

As though he had sexual relations with the ignoramus's betrothed bride – כְּאִילּוּ בּוֹעֵל אֲרוּסָתוֹ: Some explain this expression in the following way: This is similar to a case where a man does not recognize the good qualities of his betrothed bride and divorces her, and she subsequently marries a superior man. When her first husband sees her new husband, he will certainly be anguished. Similarly, the ignoramus, who despised the study of Torah, will surely be anguished when he sees the Torah scholar engaged in Torah study (*Petaḥ Einayim*).

גְּדוֹלָה שִׂנְאָה שֶׁשּׂוֹנְאִין עַמֵּי הָאָרֶץ לְתַלְמִיד חָכָם, יוֹתֵר מִשִּׂנְאָה שֶׁשּׂוֹנְאִין אוּמּוֹת הָעוֹלָם אֶת יִשְׂרָאֵל, וּנְשׁוֹתֵיהֶן יוֹתֵר מֵהֶן. תָּנָא: שָׁנָה וּפֵירַשׁ – יוֹתֵר מִכּוּלָּן.

Similarly, he said: **The hatred which ignoramuses have for a Torah scholar is greater than the hatred that the nations of the world have for the Jewish people. And the wives** of the ignoramuses hate Torah scholars **more than** the ignoramuses themselves.[N] **It was taught** in the *Tosefta* that one **who studied** Torah **and left** his studies hates Torah scholars **more than all of them.**

תָּנוּ רַבָּנַן: שִׁשָּׁה דְּבָרִים נֶאֶמְרוּ בְּעַמֵּי הָאָרֶץ: אֵין מוֹסְרִין לָהֶן עֵדוּת, וְאֵין מְקַבְּלִין מִמֶּנּוּ עֵדוּת, וְאֵין מְגַלִּין לָהֶן סוֹד, וְאֵין מְמַנִּין אוֹתָן אַפּוֹטְרוֹפּוֹס עַל הַיְּתוֹמִים, וְאֵין מְמַנִּין אוֹתָן אַפּוֹטְרוֹפּוֹס עַל קוּפָּה שֶׁל צְדָקָה, וְאֵין מִתְלַוִּין עִמָּהֶן בַּדֶּרֶךְ. וְיֵשׁ אוֹמְרִים: אַף אֵין מַכְרִיזִין עַל אֲבֵידָתוֹ.

The Sages taught: Six statements were made with regard to ignoramuses:[N] **One may not entrust them with testimony,**[H] i.e., one may not appoint them as witnesses to a particular event or transaction. Additionally, **one may not accept testimony from them,** as they are not considered trustworthy, and **one should not reveal a secret to them,** as they will reveal it. **One may not appoint them as steward** [*apotropos*][L] **over** an estate belonging to **orphans,**[H] due to concern that they might make improper use of the orphans' property. Likewise, **one may not appoint them as guardian over a charity fund.** Finally, **one should not accompany them** while traveling **on the road,** due to concern for one's safety. **And there are those who say: One does not even announce their lost** items, meaning that if one finds a lost article from such a person, he is allowed to keep it without making an effort to locate the owner (*Me'iri*).

וְתַנָּא קַמָּא: זִמְנִין דְּנָפֵיק מִינֵּיהּ זַרְעָא מַעַלְיָא וְאָכֵיל לֵיהּ, שֶׁנֶּאֱמַר: "יָכִין וְצַדִּיק יִלְבָּשׁ".

The Gemara asks: What is the reasoning of **the first *tanna*,** who holds that one must announce having found the lost article of an ignoramus? The Gemara explains: **Sometimes upstanding offspring will come from him and will consume** the property, **as it is stated: "He may prepare it but the just shall put it on"** (Job 27:17). It is possible for a wicked person to prepare something for himself that will later be used by a righteous person.

"וְכֵן מִי שֶׁיָּצָא וכו׳".

The Gemara returns to explaining the mishna. It was taught: **And so too, one who left** Jerusalem with sacrificial meat in his possession must return to Jerusalem to burn it, just as one is required to return in order to remove leaven from his possession. According to Rabbi Meir, this *halakha* applies with regard to an egg-bulk of sacrificial meat or leaven, whereas Rabbi Yehuda disagrees and says the minimum amount for both is an olive-bulk.

לְמֵימְרָא דְּרַבִּי מֵאִיר סָבַר כַּבֵּיצָה הוּא דְּחָשֵׁיב, וְרַבִּי יְהוּדָה סָבַר כַּזַּיִת נָמֵי חָשֵׁיב? וּרְמִינְהִי: עַד כַּמָּה הֵן מְזַמְּנִין – עַד כַּזַּיִת, וְרַבִּי יְהוּדָה אוֹמֵר: עַד כַּבֵּיצָה!

The Gemara asks: **Is that to say that Rabbi Meir holds** that **an egg-bulk** is the minimal amount that is considered **significant, and Rabbi Yehuda holds that an olive-bulk is also** considered **significant?** The Gemara **raises a contradiction** from a mishna in *Berakhot*: **How much** food must one eat in order **to obligate** those with whom he ate **in a *zimmun*? An olive-bulk** of food[H] is sufficient according to the unattributed opinion in the mishna, which is generally that of Rabbi Meir. **And Rabbi Yehuda says: An egg-bulk** is the minimum measure to obligate those with whom one ate in a *zimmun*. This seems to contradict the opinions of Rabbi Meir and Rabbi Yehuda stated in the mishna here.

אָמַר רַבִּי יוֹחָנָן: מוּחְלֶפֶת הַשִּׁיטָה.

Rabbi Yoḥanan said: The opinions are reversed in one of these sources, and must be emended.

אַבָּיֵי אָמַר: לְעוֹלָם לָא תֵּיפוֹךְ; הָתָם בִּקְרָאֵי פְּלִיגִי, הָכָא בִּסְבָרָא פְּלִיגִי. הָתָם בִּקְרָאֵי פְּלִיגִי; רַבִּי מֵאִיר סָבַר: "וְאָכַלְתָּ" – זוֹ אֲכִילָה, "וְשָׂבָעְתָּ" – זוֹ שְׁתִיָּה, וַאֲכִילָה בִּכְזַיִת. וְרַבִּי יְהוּדָה סָבַר: "וְאָכַלְתָּ וְשָׂבָעְתָּ" – אֲכִילָה שֶׁיֵּשׁ בָּהּ שְׂבִיעָה, וְאֵיזוֹ זוֹ – בִּכְבֵיצָה.

Abaye said: Actually, do not reverse the opinions. **There, they disagree with regard to** the interpretation of **verses,** while **here, they disagree with regard to logical reasoning.** How so? **There,** with regard to *zimmun*, **they disagree with regard to** the interpretation of **verses. Rabbi Meir holds** that the verse: "And you shall eat and be satisfied and bless the Lord your God" (Deuteronomy 8:10) should be understood as follows: **"And you shall eat," that is eating; "and be satisfied," that is drinking.** The standard halakhic principle is that **eating** is defined as the consumption of **an olive-bulk. And Rabbi Yehuda holds: "And you shall eat and you shall be satisfied"** refers **to eating that includes satisfaction. And what is** considered eating with satisfaction? It is consumption **of an egg-bulk.**

הָכָא בִּסְבָרָא פְּלִיגִי. דְּרַבִּי מֵאִיר סָבַר: חֲזָרָתוֹ כְּטוּמְאָתוֹ, מָה טוּמְאָתוֹ בִּכְבֵיצָה – אַף חֲזָרָתוֹ בִּכְבֵיצָה, וְרַבִּי יְהוּדָה סָבַר: חֲזָרָתוֹ

However, **here,** in the cases of leaven and consecrated food, **they disagree** not with regard to the interpretation of verses but **with regard to logical reasoning, as Rabbi Meir holds:** The requirement to **return** consecrated food **is analogous to its ritual impurity. Just as its** susceptibility to **ritual impurity is** only when it is the size of **an egg-bulk, so too,** the requirement to **return it is** only when it is the size of an **egg-bulk. And Rabbi Yehuda holds:** The requirement to **return** consecrated food

NOTES

The wives hate Torah scholars more than the ignoramuses themselves – נְשׁוֹתֵיהֶן יוֹתֵר מֵהֶן: The reason for this is because the women are not involved in business and thus have less interaction with Torah scholars. The only knowledge these women have of Torah scholars is with regard to the distance the Torah scholars created between the groups. Therefore, the wives hate them to a greater degree.

Statements were made with regard to ignoramuses – דְּבָרִים נֶאֶמְרוּ בְּעַמֵּי הָאָרֶץ: They should not be selected to witness an action, since they lack the knowledge to know what to scrutinize in witnessing; their testimony is not accepted out of concern that they report imprecisely, embellish upon what they saw or heard, or testify based on that which seems to be correct without verifying that it is true; they should not be appointed as guardians over charity funds due to a concern that they will divide the money inequitably (Rabbeinu Yehonatan); and one should not accompany them when traveling, as they are unfamiliar with or unconcerned about the concept: "You shall not stand over your fellow's blood" (Leviticus 19:16), and consequently in a dangerous situation they will flee rather than save their traveling companions (*Me'iri*).

HALAKHA

The testimony of an ignoramus – עֵדוּת עַם הָאָרֶץ: One who has not studied Torah and Mishna and has no profession may serve as a witness only if he is known to be upright and to act properly. Some say, based on Rabbi Yosei's statement, that we are not particular about this today (*Shulḥan Arukh, Ḥoshen Mishpat* 34:17).

An ignoramus as a steward – אַפּוֹטְרוֹפּוֹס עַם הָאָרֶץ: When a court appoints a guardian over an estate of orphans, an ignoramus should not be appointed to this position because he is suspected of improper conduct (*Shulḥan Arukh, Ḥoshen Mishpat* 290:2).

***Zimmun* for an olive-bulk of food – זִימּוּן בִּכְזַיִת:** One who eats an olive-bulk of bread is required to join a *zimmun* and recite Grace after Meals, as stated in tractate *Berakhot* (*Shulḥan Arukh, Oraḥ Ḥayyim* 184:6, 196:4).

LANGUAGE

Steward [*apotropos*] **– אַפּוֹטְרוֹפּוֹס:** From the Greek ἐπίτροπος, *epitropos*, meaning appointee or guardian of an estate.

כְּאִיסּוּרוֹ, מָה אִיסּוּרוֹ בִּכְזַיִת – אַף חֲזָרָתוֹ בִּכְזַיִת.

is analogous to its prohibition. Just as its prohibition is only when it is the size of **an olive-bulk, so too,** the requirement to **return it is** only when it is the size of an **olive-bulk.**

תַּנְיָא, רַבִּי נָתָן אוֹמֵר: זֶה וָזֶה כִּשְׁתֵּי בֵיצִים, וְלֹא הוֹדוּ לוֹ חֲכָמִים.

Another opinion on this issue **was taught** in a *baraita*. **Rabbi Natan says:** The minimum measure for both **this and that,** leaven and sacrificial meat, is **two egg-bulks** of prohibited material, **but the Rabbis did not agree with him.**

״וְהָיָה בַּיּוֹם הַהוּא לֹא יִהְיֶה אוֹר יְקָרוֹת וְקִפָּאוֹן״. מַאי ״יְקָרוֹת וְקִפָּאוֹן״?

Incidental to the discussion of leaving Jerusalem and its surrounding area, the Gemara cites expositions of a prophetic passage, including a statement that God will eventually expand the boundaries of Jerusalem. The verse states: **"And it shall come to pass on that day that there shall not be light,** but **heavy clouds** [*yekarot*] **and thickness** [*vekippaon*]**"** (Zechariah 14:6). The Gemara asks: **What is** the meaning of the expression ***"yekarot vekippaon"*****?**[N]

אָמַר רַבִּי אֶלְעָזָר: זֶה אוֹר, שֶׁיָּקָר בָּעוֹלָם הַזֶּה, וְקָפוּי לָעוֹלָם הַבָּא.

Rabbi Elazar said: This is the **light** currently provided by the sun, **which is significant** [*yakar*] **in this world and insignificant** [*kafuy*] **in the World-to-Come,**[N] when the moon will shine as brightly as the sun does now and the sun will be seven times brighter than it is currently.

רַבִּי יוֹחָנָן אָמַר: אֵלּוּ נְגָעִים וְאֳהָלוֹת, שֶׁיְּקָרִין הֵן בָּעוֹלָם הַזֶּה וּקְפוּיִין הֵן לָעוֹלָם הַבָּא.

Rabbi Yoḥanan said: This expression refers to the tractates of ***Nega'im*** **and** ***Oholot*****, which are weighty** [*yekarim*] owing to their difficulty **in this world,** as they are among the most complex subjects, **but** will be **easy** [*kefuyin*] **in the World-to-Come,** when people will be much wiser.

וְרַבִּי יְהוֹשֻׁעַ בֶּן לֵוִי אָמַר: אֵלּוּ בְּנֵי אָדָם, שֶׁיְּקָרִין הֵן בָּעוֹלָם הַזֶּה וּקְפוּיִין הֵן לָעוֹלָם הַבָּא. כִּי הָא דְּרַב יוֹסֵף בְּרֵיהּ דְּרַבִּי יְהוֹשֻׁעַ בֶּן לֵוִי חֲלַשׁ וְאִיתְנְגִיד. כִּי הֲדַר, אֲמַר לֵיהּ אֲבוּהּ: מַאי חֲזֵית? אֲמַר לֵיהּ: עוֹלָם הָפוּךְ רָאִיתִי, עֶלְיוֹנִים לְמַטָּה וְתַחְתּוֹנִים לְמַעְלָה. אֲמַר לוֹ: בְּנִי, עוֹלָם בָּרוּר רָאִיתָ. וַאֲנַן הֵיכִי הָתָם? כִּי הֵיכִי דְּאִיתוּ אֲנַן הָכָא, הָכִי אִיתִינַן הָתָם.

And Rabbi Yehoshua ben Levi said: These are people who are considered **important** [*yekarim*] **in this world and unimportant** [*kefuyim*] **in the World-to-Come.** This is **like** the incident involving **Rav Yosef, son of Rabbi Yehoshua ben Levi,** who **became ill and** was about to **expire. When he returned** to good health, **his father said to him: What did you see** when you were about to die? **He said to him: I saw an inverted world.**[N] **Those above,** i.e., those who are considered important in this world, were **below,** insignificant, while **those below,** i.e., those who are insignificant in this world, were **above. He said to him: My son, you have seen a clear world.** The world you have seen is the true world, as in that world people's standings befit them. Rabbi Yehoshua ben Levi asked: **And where are we,** the Torah scholars, **there?** Rav Yosef responded: **Just as we are** regarded **here, so are we** regarded **there.**

וְשָׁמַעְתִּי שֶׁהָיוּ אוֹמְרִים: אַשְׁרֵי מִי שֶׁבָּא לְכָאן וְתַלְמוּדוֹ בְּיָדוֹ. וְשָׁמַעְתִּי שֶׁהָיוּ אוֹמְרִים: הֲרוּגֵי מַלְכוּת אֵין אָדָם יָכוֹל לַעֲמוֹד בִּמְחִיצָתָן.

Rav Yosef added: **And I heard that they were saying** in that world: **Praiseworthy is the one who arrives here with his studies in hand. And I** also **heard that they were saying: Those executed by the government** enjoy such an exalted status that **no one can stand in their enclosure.**

(וּמַאן) נִינְהוּ? אִילֵימָא רַבִּי עֲקִיבָא וַחֲבֵירָיו – מִשּׁוּם הֲרוּגֵי מַלְכוּת וְתוּ לָא? אֶלָּא: הֲרוּגֵי לוֹד.

The Gemara asks: **And who are these** martyrs that Rav Yosef was referring to? **If you say** that he was referring to **Rabbi Akiva and his colleagues,** who were martyred, this cannot be: Is their elevated status **due** only **to** the fact that **they were martyred by** the Roman **government and nothing more?** These men were exceptional in their piety and sanctity during their lives as well. **Rather,** it is referring to **the martyrs of Lod,**[B] Pappos and Luliyanos, who gave themselves up to be martyred for the sake of the Jewish people. They falsely admitted to killing the king's daughter in order to prevent a harsh decree from being issued against the entire community. Although they were not known for exceptional piety before that event, they are considered to be extremely holy due to their martyrdom.

״בַּיּוֹם הַהוּא יִהְיֶה עַל מְצִלּוֹת הַסּוּס קֹדֶשׁ לַה׳״. מַאי ״מְצִלּוֹת הַסּוּס״?

The Gemara continues to expound the section of the book of Zechariah cited above. The verse states: **"On that day there shall be upon the bells of the horses** [*metzillot hasus*]**: Holy unto the Lord"** (Zechariah 14:20). The Gemara asks: **What is** the meaning of the expression ***metzillot hasus*****?**

NOTES

Yekarot vekippaon – יְקָרוֹת וְקִפָּאוֹן: Some explain that these expositions are based on the discrepancy between the pronunciation and the written form of the latter word, which is written with a *yod* and pronounced as though it was written with a *vav*. With a *yod*, the word would be *yikpe'un*, meaning will be frozen. This would indicate that the expositions here describe events that will occur in the future. The *ge'onim* explain that the verse asserts that there are certain phenomena that are not constant nowadays but will be constant in the World-to-Come. For example, nowadays there is light during the day but not at night; however, in the future there will always be light.

This is light which is significant [*yakar*] in this world, and insignificant [*kafuy*] in the World-to-Come – זֶה אוֹר שֶׁיָּקָר בָּעוֹלָם הַזֶּה וְקָפוּי לָעוֹלָם הַבָּא: Aside from the simple meaning of this phrase, light is a metaphorical reference to Torah, as in the verse: "For the mitzva is a lamp, and the Torah is light" (Proverbs 6:23). According to this interpretation, the words of Torah are rare and precious in this world, similar to the verse: "And the word of the Lord was precious [*yakar*] in those days" (I Samuel 3:1). By contrast, it is stated in another verse: "And it shall come to pass afterward, that I will pour out My spirit upon all flesh" (Joel 3:1), meaning that in the World-to-Come, the word of God will be readily available to all (*Etz Yosef*).

I saw an inverted world – עוֹלָם הָפוּךְ רָאִיתִי: According to a geonic tradition, he meant that in the World-to-Come many students sit in a more elevated position than their teachers.

BACKGROUND

The martyrs of Lod – הֲרוּגֵי לוֹד: There are various traditions with regard to the meritorious act of those who were martyred in Lod and the circumstances surrounding their deaths.

According to one tradition, these martyrs were Shemaya and his brothers, who were killed on the twelfth of Adar. According to another tradition, this refers to Pappos and Luliyanos, who were killed in Lodkiya, sometimes known as Lod. They were leaders of the Jewish community and were extremely wealthy. After the daughter of the king was killed, the king blamed the Jews for her death. In order to save the community from revenge, Pappos and Luliyanos claimed responsibility for her death and were executed. Due to their willingness to sacrifice their lives for the sake of the community they were said to receive a special status in the World-to-Come, as is mentioned here and in other sources.

NOTES

In the future the Holy One, Blessed be He, will extend – עָתִיד הַקָּדוֹשׁ בָּרוּךְ הוּא לְהוֹסִיף: Some explain this exposition in the following manner: The subsequent verse states that even the pots of Judea will be consecrated for God, which raises the question of how that is possible, as it is prohibited to take sacrificial meat outside of Jerusalem. The answer is that in the future, Jerusalem will be expanded to include the entire region of Judea (Maharsha).

Is that to say that now He is not one – אַטּוּ הָאִידָּנָא לָאו אֶחָד הוּא: Only good emanates from God Himself. However, as misfortune may befall people due to their sins, God's unity is not always manifest. In the end of days, when the world will be perfected, there will no longer be evil and God's unity and inherent good will be apparent (Maharsha).

BACKGROUND

Decorative bells that one hangs between the eyes of a horse – מְצִילּוֹת שֶׁתּוֹלִין לַסּוּס בֵּין עֵינָיו:

Decorative bell between the eyes of a horse

אָמַר רַבִּי יְהוֹשֻׁעַ בֶּן לֵוִי: עָתִיד הַקָּדוֹשׁ בָּרוּךְ הוּא לְהוֹסִיף עַל יְרוּשָׁלַיִם, עַד שֶׁהַסּוּס רָץ וּמֵצִיל.

Rabbi Yehoshua ben Levi said: In the future the Holy One, Blessed be He, will extend[N] **Jerusalem** by **as much as** the distance that **a horse can run** the entire time **it casts a shadow** [*metzeil*]. Jerusalem will be so large that a horse running from one side of the city in the morning will not arrive at the other end of the city until midday, when its shadow will have disappeared.

רַבִּי אֶלְעָזָר אָמַר: כָּל מְצִילּוֹת שֶׁתּוֹלִין לַסּוּס בֵּין עֵינָיו יִהְיֶה קֹדֶשׁ לַה׳.

Rabbi Elazar said: All decorative **bells** [*metzillot*] **that one hangs between the eyes of a horse**[B] **will be sanctified to God,** i.e., they will be consecrated for the Temple treasury.

וְרַבִּי יוֹחָנָן אָמַר: כָּל בִּיזָּה שֶׁבּוֹזְזִין יִשְׂרָאֵל עַד שָׁעָה שֶׁהַסּוּס רָץ וּמֵצִיל – יִהְיֶה קֹדֶשׁ לַה׳.

And Rabbi Yoḥanan said: All spoils that the Jewish people will **take** from gentiles who wage war against them, **up to the time a horse runs and casts a shadow** [*metzeil*], i.e., half a day, **will be sanctified for God.**

בִּשְׁלָמָא לְמַאן דְּאָמַר כָּל בִּיזָּה שֶׁבָּזְזוּ יִשְׂרָאֵל – הַיְינוּ דִּכְתִיב ״וְהָיָה הַסִּירוֹת בְּבֵית ה׳ כַּמִּזְרָקִים לִפְנֵי הַמִּזְבֵּחַ״. אֶלָּא לְמַאן דְּאָמַר בְּהָנָךְ תַּרְתֵּי – מַאי ״וְהָיָה הַסִּירוֹת בְּבֵית ה׳״? מִילְּתָא אַחֲרִיתִי קָאָמַר, דְּמִתְעַתְּרִי יִשְׂרָאֵל וּמִתְנַדְּבִי וּמַיְיתִי.

The Gemara asks: **Granted, according to the one who said** that this expression refers to **all spoils that the Jewish people** will **take, this is** as **it is written** in the continuation of the verse, which mentions additional treasure donated to the Temple: **"And the pots in the Lord's house shall be like the basins before the altar." However, according to the ones who said these** other **two** explanations, **what** is the meaning of: **"And the pots in the Lord's house"?** The Gemara explains that according to these opinions the verse **is saying something else:** It is prophesying that in the future **the Jewish people will become wealthy and bring donations** to the Temple.

בִּשְׁלָמָא לְמַאן דְּאָמַר בִּיזָּה – הַיְינוּ דִּכְתִיב ״וְלֹא יִהְיֶה כְנַעֲנִי עוֹד בְּבֵית ה׳ צְבָאוֹת״. אֶלָּא לְמַאן דְּאָמַר הָנָךְ תַּרְתֵּי – מַאי ״וְלֹא יִהְיֶה כְנַעֲנִי״? אָמַר רַבִּי יִרְמְיָה: ״אֵין כָּאן עָנִי״.

The Gemara goes on to ask: **Granted, according to the one who said** that this expression refers to **spoils, this is as it is written** in the next verse: **"And** on that day **there shall no longer be a merchant** [*kena'ani*] **in the house of the Lord of hosts"** (Zechariah 14:21), as he will no longer be needed. **However, according to the ones who said these** other **two** explanations, **what** is the meaning of the expression: **"There shall no longer be a merchant"? Rabbi Yirmeya said:** The word *kena'ani* is in fact a contraction of the phrase: **There is no poor person here** [*ein kan ani*]. In other words, there will no longer be poor people, and therefore the Jews themselves will be able to donate whatever is needed in the Temple (Maharsha).

וּכְנַעֲנִי מְנָלַן דְּאִיקְּרֵי תַּגָּר – דִּכְתִיב: ״וַיַּרְא שָׁם יְהוּדָה בַּת אִישׁ כְּנַעֲנִי״. מַאי כְּנַעֲנִי? אִילֵּימָא כְּנַעֲנִי מַמָּשׁ – אֶפְשָׁר בָּא אַבְרָהָם וְהִזְהִיר אֶת יִצְחָק, בָּא יִצְחָק וְהִזְהִיר אֶת יַעֲקֹב, וִיהוּדָה אָזֵיל וְנָסֵיב?! אֶלָּא אָמַר רַבִּי שִׁמְעוֹן בֶּן לָקִישׁ: בַּת גַּבְרָא תַּגָּרָא, דִּכְתִיב: ״כְּנַעַן בְּיָדוֹ מֹאזְנֵי מִרְמָה״, וְאִיבָּעֵית אֵימָא, מֵהָכָא: ״אֲשֶׁר סוֹחֲרֶיהָ שָׂרִים כִּנְעָנֶיהָ נִכְבַּדֵּי אָרֶץ״.

And where do we derive **that a merchant is called** *kena'ani*? **As it is written: "And Judah saw there the daughter of a certain** *kena'ani*... and he took her, and went in unto her" (Genesis 38:2). **What is** the meaning of the word ***kena'ani*** in this context? **If you say** it refers to **an actual Canaanite, is it possible that Abraham warned Isaac** not to marry a Canaanite woman, **and Isaac warned Jacob** to the same effect, **and** nonetheless **Judah went and married** a Canaanite woman? **Rather, Rabbi Shimon ben Lakish said:** She was **the daughter of a merchant, as it is written: "As for the merchant** [*kena'an*], **the balances of deceit are in his hand. He loves** to oppress" (Hosea 12:8). **And if you wish, say** instead that this meaning of the word can be understood **from** the following verse, which describes Tyre: **"Whose traders are princes, whose merchants** [*kinaneha*] **are the honorable of the earth"** (Isaiah 23:8).

״וְהָיָה ה׳ לְמֶלֶךְ עַל כָּל הָאָרֶץ בַּיּוֹם הַהוּא יִהְיֶה ה׳ אֶחָד וּשְׁמוֹ אֶחָד״. אַטּוּ הָאִידָּנָא לָאו אֶחָד הוּא?!

The Gemara cites another verse from the prophecy at the end of the book of Zechariah: **"And the Lord shall be King over all the earth, on that day shall the Lord be one and His name one"** (Zechariah 14:9). The Gemara asks: **Is that to say that now He is not one?**[N]

אָמַר רַבִּי אַחָא בַּר חֲנִינָא: לֹא כָּעוֹלָם הַזֶּה הָעוֹלָם הַבָּא; הָעוֹלָם הַזֶּה, עַל בְּשׂוֹרוֹת טוֹבוֹת אוֹמֵר ״בָּרוּךְ הַטּוֹב וְהַמֵּטִיב״, וְעַל בְּשׂוֹרוֹת רָעוֹת אוֹמֵר ״בָּרוּךְ דַּיַּין הָאֱמֶת״. לָעוֹלָם הַבָּא – כּוּלּוֹ ״הַטּוֹב וְהַמֵּטִיב״.

Rabbi Aḥa bar Ḥanina said: The World-to-Come is not like this world. In this world, upon good tidings one recites: Blessed...Who is good and does good, and over bad tidings one recites: Blessed...the true Judge. In the World-to-Come one will **always** recite: **Blessed...Who is good and does good.** There will be only one mode of blessing God for tidings.

"וּשְׁמוֹ אֶחָד". מַאי "אֶחָד", אַטּוּ הָאִידָּנָא לָאו שְׁמוֹ אֶחָד הוּא?!

The verse states: "On that day shall the Lord be one **and His name one.**" The Gemara asks: **What** is the meaning of the word **one** in this context? **Is that to say that now His name is not one?**

אָמַר רַב נַחְמָן בַּר יִצְחָק: "לֹא כָּעוֹלָם הַזֶּה הָעוֹלָם הַבָּא; הָעוֹלָם הַזֶּה – נִכְתָּב בְּיוּ"ד הֵ"י וְנִקְרָא בְּאָלֶ"ף דָּלֶ"ת, אֲבָל לָעוֹלָם הַבָּא כּוּלּוֹ אֶחָד – נִקְרָא בְּיוּ"ד הֵ"י, וְנִכְתָּב בְּיוּ"ד הֵ"י.

Rav Naḥman bar Yitzḥak said: The World-to-Come is not like this world. In this world, God's name that **is written with** the letters ***yod*** and ***heh*** **is read** as *Adonai*, which begins with the letters ***alef*** and ***dalet***. God's name is not pronounced in the same way as it is written. **However, in the World-to-Come it will all be one,** as God's name will be both **read**[N] **with** the letters ***yod*** and ***heh*** **and written with** the letters ***yod*** and ***heh***.

סָבַר רָבָא לְמִדְרְשֵׁהּ בְּפִירְקָא. אֲמַר לֵיהּ הַהוּא סָבָא: "לְעֹלָם" כְּתִיב.

Rava thought to expound upon the correct punctuation and enunciation of the name of God during his public **lecture** before one of the Festivals. **A certain old man said to him:** The word **forever is written** in the verse: "This is My name forever [*le'olam*]" (Exodus 3:15) without the letter *vav*, such that it can be read *le'alem*, to conceal, meaning that the name should be concealed.

רַבִּי אָבִינָא רָמֵי: כְּתִיב, "זֶה שְּׁמִי לְעֹלָם וְזֶה זִכְרִי לְדוֹר דּוֹר". אָמַר הַקָּדוֹשׁ בָּרוּךְ הוּא: לֹא כְּשֶׁאֲנִי נִכְתָּב אֲנִי נִקְרָא, נִכְתָּב אֲנִי בְּיוּ"ד הֵ"א, וְנִקְרָא אֲנִי בְּאָלֶ"ף דָּלֶ"ת.

Rabbi Avina raised a contradiction: It is written in the verse: "**This is My name forever,**" implying a requirement to conceal the name of God, and in the very next phrase it states: "**And this is My memorial**[N] **unto all generations**" (Exodus 3:15), which indicates that the name of God is to be publicized and remembered by all. Rather, **the Holy One, Blessed be He, said: I,** i.e., My name, is **not read as I am written. I am written with** the letters ***yod*** and ***heh***, **and I am read with** the letters ***alef*** and ***dalet***.

הדרן עלך אלו עוברין

NOTES

Written...read – **נִכְתָּב וְנִקְרָא**: Some explain these names in the following way. The Tetragrammaton, the name of God that begins with *yod-heh*, refers to God's dominion over all of existence, and the name *Adonai* connotes God's dominion over the individual (Rabbi Shmuel ben Ḥofni Gaon).

My name...My memorial – **שְׁמִי...זִכְרִי**: Rashi explains that by mentioning these terms separately, the verse appears to imply that there are two separate names. "My name" refers to God's name for Himself, and "My memorial" refers to the name that is utilized by others.

Summary of **Perek III**

Although only leaven and leavened bread are explicitly prohibited in the Torah, the Gemara derived that the prohibition includes other forms of leaven as well: A mixture of leaven, even if it contains only a minute amount of actual leaven, is entirely prohibited. So too, foods that were soaked or cooked together with leaven and have absorbed its taste are prohibited even if no actual leaven is present. Furthermore, even produce that was never fully leavened is prohibited. In all these cases it is prohibited both to eat and to be in possession of them over Passover. Nevertheless, one distinction does exist; the punishment of *karet* for eating leaven applies only to eating outright leaven or leavened bread.

The Gemara further concluded that any items containing leaven that are suitable for human consumption are prohibited. Only once an item is not suitable to be eaten at all does it become permitted.

Since the prohibition of leaven applies also to partially leavened foods, the Sages were particularly stringent when it came to cases of doubt. They therefore created various safeguards to prevent any possibility that one will come to be in possession of leaven on Passover. For example, various stringent rules were put in place for one who wishes to knead dough for *matzot* on Passover, to preclude any possibility that the dough will rise.

Image Credits

p110 © Don Damerow; **p111** © HaRav Menachem Makover, courtesy of *Harenu Bevinyano*, and Koren Publishers Jerusalem Ltd.; **p123** © David Santman; **p130** © courtesy of the Temple Institute; **p133** © Michael Caviglia; **p151** © Magnus Manske; **p167** © HaRav Menachem Makover, courtesy of *Harenu Bevinyano*; **p170** lizard © Eugene Zelenko; pot © R. Loganathan; plate © Raminus Falcon; grapes © Anagoria; wine © Davide Restivo; **p173** 1st image © Piotr Panek; **p173** 2nd image © pjt56@gmx.net; **p171** left image © Friedrich Böhringer; **p171** middle image © LSDSL; **p171** right image © Rasbak; **p172** 1st image © Keith Weller; **p184** © Dan Diffendale; **p191** middle top image © Gideon Pisanty; **p191** right image © Javier Martin; **p192** 1st image © Idobi; **p193** 1st image © Francisco Marval Ugas; **p196** kernel of wheat © Photolosophy by Russ; **p214** 1st image © Ca La Jean; **p228** 1st image © Rama; **p228** 2nd image © Magnus Manske; **p233** both images © Hanay; **p237** © courtesy of the Temple Institute; **p239** © Dr. Yisrael Meir Levinger; **p244** 1st image © Chmee2; **p246** 1st image © Tamar Hayardeni; **p246** 2nd image © Deror avi; **p252** © Kuzma, www.shutterstock.com.

תלמוד בבלי

— מהדורת נאה —

פסחים חלק ב

Steinsaltz Center

KOREN

Please note that the number ranges that appear at the bottom of each daf of the Vilna pages indicate the corresponding pages of the Koren Talmud Bavli translation and commentary.

תלמוד בבלי

הוצאת קורן ירושלים

מהדורת נאה

מסכת פסחים

דף כא. עד דף נ.

COMMENTARY BY

Rabbi Adin Even-Israel Steinsaltz

EDITOR-IN-CHIEF

Rabbi Dr Tzvi Hersh Weinreb

EXECUTIVE EDITOR

Rabbi Joshua Schreier

STEINSALTZ CENTER

KOREN PUBLISHERS JERUSALEM

אין הכרעת שלישית מכרעת. דעת שלישית היא זו. שבית שמאי ובית הלל לא הזכירו לגבות דעפס דניהוי חיישינן לתקלה כלל. דאי הוו אמרו הכי: ב"ש אומרים בין בבית בין בשדה אבל תשפך(א), וב"ה אומרים בין בבית בין בשדה תיעשה זילוף, ואתה בא להכריע ולומר: בבית – כב"ה, בשדה – כבית שמאי, הויא הכרעה. אבל השתא, דלא הזכירו בית ושדה – טעמא אחרינא הוא, ולאו משום תקלה. ור' ישמעאל חייש לתקלה, והיינו תנאי: מחלוקת. ר' אליעזר ור' יהושע, שנפלה לפחות ממאה חולין טמאים. שיש בגת התחתונה פחות ממאה חולין טמאים, דאין תרומה בטילה בהן ופסדי לגמרי, דתרומה צריך אחד ומאה לבטלה. אבל היו בתחתונה מאה חולין, מאה חביות כמו זו של תרומה – דברי הכל לא יטמאנה ביד, הואיל ולא פסדי חולין, דתרומה עולה בהן, וחזו בידי טומאה כדמעיקרא לזר: מודה ר' אליעזר כו'. קס"ד אמסקנא קאי, א"אם לאו", דהא פלוגתייהו באם לאו הוא, ולהכי פריך: מודה ר' יהושע דאמר לעיל יטמאנה ביד לר' אליעזר, דאמר לא יטמאנה ביד, מיבעי ליה למיתני: בכלי שתוכו טהור וגבו טמא. והאי "מודה" לאו אסיפא קאי, אלא ארישא, דקתני: אם יכול להציל רביעית בטהרה – יציל, ואפי' כלי זה שהוא בא להציל רביעית זו בתוכו, תוכו טהור וגבו טמא. ואשמעינן ליה לר' אליעזר דאמר אל יטמאנה ביד – מודה הוא דמותר להציל בזה, ולא חיישינן דילמא נגע גבו בתרומה ומטמא לה בידים. ובכלי שנטמא במשקין דטומאתן דרבנן היא דמשכחת לה, כדתניא: כלי שנטמאו אחוריו במשקין – אחוריו טמאין; תוכו או אוגנו או אזנו או ידיו – טהורין:

הדרן עלך אור לארבעה עשר

כל שעה שמותר לאכול מאכיל. לדוקיא איצטריך, דאידוק: הא משעה שאינו מותר לאכול – אינו מותר להאכיל: ולא יסיק בו תנור וכירים. בגמרא פריך: פשיטא, הא נמי הנאה היא! גמ' כל שעה שאוכל מאכיל מבעי ליה. אבל השתא דנקט לה בתרי לישני – משמע דבתרי גברי קאי. והא ליכא למימר, דהכי קאמר: כל שעה שמותר לאכול מן התורה, מאכיל אפילו מדרבנן, ותיתוקם אליבא דר' יהודה – דהא איכא שש, דמותר לאכול מן התורה, ואסור להאכיל לדברי הכל: אלא הכי קאמר כל שעה. שיש היתר לשום אדם לאכול – מאכיל אף האסור לאכול לבהמתו כו': בהמה אי משיירא חזי ליה. שאין דרכה להצניע. אבל חיה, כגון חולדה ונמיה ואתול – דרכן להצניע: ואי תנא חיה. הוה אמינא היא עדיפא, משום דאי משיירא – מצנעא לה, *ולא עבר עליה ב"בל יראה": ולאו אדעתיה. לבטלו: קודם. שיבוא הפסח, דקסברי: מצוה עליו לבערו מן העולם, ולא שיהא קיים:

*אין הכרעת שלישית מכרעת. אמר ר' יוסי בר חנינא: אמחלוקת – שנפלה לפחות ממאה סאה חולין טמאין, אבל נפלה למאה חולין טמאין – דברי הכל תרד ותטמא ואל יטמאנה ביד. תניא נמי הכי: חבית שנשברה בגת העליונה ותחתיה מאה חולין טמאין – מודה רבי אליעזר לרבי יהושע, שאם יכול להציל ממנה רביעית בטהרה – יציל, ואם לאו – תרד ותטמא ואל יטמאנה ביד. האי מודה רבי אליעזר לרבי יהושע? מודה רבי יהושע לר' אליעזר מיבעי ליה! אמר רבא: איפוך. רב הונא בריה דרב יהושע אמר: לעולם לא תיפוך, הכא במאי עסקינן – בכלי שתוכו טהור וגבו טמא. מהו דתימא: ניגזור דילמא נגע גבו בתרומה, קמ"ל.§

הדרן עלך אור לארבעה עשר

כל שעה *בשמותר לאכול – מאכיל לבהמה לחיה ולעופות, ומוכר לגוי, ומותר בהנאתו, עבר זמנו – אסור בהנאתו, ולא יסיק בו תנור וכירים. *ר' יהודה אומר: אין ביעור חמץ אלא שריפה, [ג] וחכמים אומרים: *אף מפרר וזורה לרוח או מטיל לים.§ **גמ'** כל שעה שמותר לאכול – מאכיל, הא כל שעה שאינו מותר לאכול – אינו מאכיל, לימא מתני' דלא כר' יהודה, דאי ר' יהודה – הא איכא חמש דאינו אוכל, ומאכיל. *דתנן, ר' מאיר אומר: אוכלין כל חמש, ושורפין בתחלת שש, רבי יהודה אומר: אוכלין כל ארבע, ותולין כל חמש, ושורפין בתחלת שש! ואלא מאי – ר' מאיר היא, האי "כל שעה *שמותר לאכול מאכיל"? כל שעה שאוכל מאכיל מיבעי ליה! אמר רבה בר עולא: מתניתין רבן גמליאל היא. *דתנן, רבן גמליאל אומר: חולין נאכלין כל ארבע, תרומה כל חמש, ושורפין בתחלת שש. והכי קאמר; כל שעה שמותר לאכול כהן בתרומה – ישראל מאכיל חולין לבהמה לחיה ולעופות. למה לי למיתנא בהמה, למה לי למיתנא חיה? צריכא, דאי תנא בהמה – דאי משיירא חזי לה, אבל חיה דאי משיירא קמצנעא לה – אימא לא. ואי תנא חיה – משום דאי משיירא מיהת מצנעא, אבל בהמה זימנין דמשיירא ולא מסיק אדעתיה, וקאי עליה בבל יראה ובבל ימצא – אימא לא, צריכא. עופות ל"ל? איידי דתנא בהמה וחיה, תנא נמי עופות.§ "ומוכרו לגוי".§ פשיטא! לאפוקי מהאי תנא *דתניא, ב"ש אומרים: לא ימכור אדם חמצו לגוי, אא"כ יודע בו שיכלה קודם פסח. וב"ה אומרים: גכל שעה שמותר לאכול – מותר למכור. רבי

אין הכרעת שלישית מכרעת. פ"ה: הואיל ולא הזכירו בית שמאי ובית הלל בית ושדה, א"כ טעמא אחרינא הוא ולא משום תקלה. ולר"י נראה אע"ג דטעמא דבית שמאי משום תקלה לא חשיב הכרעה – לפי שלא גילו הראשונים דעתן לחלק בין בית לשדה, שלא הזכירו בדבריהם אחד בית ואחד שדה. וכן פ"ה לעיל *גבי ר"ג לאו מכריע הוא. והא דקולי מטלניות בין מן המוכן ובין שלא מן המוכן – טמא, דברי ר"א. ר' יהושע אומר: בין מן המוכן ובין שלא מן המוכן טהור, ר"ע אומר: מן המוכן – טמא, שלא מן המוכן – טהור, וחשיב ליה בפ' "כירה" (שבת לט: ושם) הכרעה – שהרי גילו ר' אליעזר ור' יהושע דשייך לחלק בין מן המוכן ובין שלא מן המוכן. והא דפ' "כילד מברכין" (ברכות מג:) דקאמר: ב"ש מברכים על השמן, וקאמר ר"ג: אני אכריע, שמן – זכינו לריחו וזכינו לסיכתו, הדס – לריחו זכינו, לסיכתו לא זכינו. וקאמר רבי יוחנן: הלכה כדברי המכריע. לאו משום דמכריע גמור הוא, אלא מפרש ונותן טעם לדבריו. ותדע, דאי מכריע הוא – למה הוצרך לפסוק הלכה כמותו? הא כבר א"ר יוחנן בפרק "כירה": הלכה כדברי המכריע. וק"ק לפי' זה, דהכא מאי איריא הכרעה שלישית שאין הכרעה? תיפוק ליה דהכרעת תלמיד לאו הכרעה היא, כדאמר בפ' "כירה" (שבת לט:) ארבי עקיבא! ור"ת פי': הכרעה שלישית – דור שלישי, דהיינו הכרעת תלמיד כדאמר בפ' "כירה"*:

הדרן עלך אור לארבעה עשר

כל שעה. עבר זמנו אסור בהנאה. ואסור למכור, ואם מכר – דמיו מותרין, דאין תופס את דמיו, כדתנן בפ"ב דקדושין (דף נו:): מכרן וקידש בדמיהן – מקודשת:

לימא מתניתין דלא כר' יהודה. *אף לפי המסקנא לא אתיא כר' יהודה, אלא הכי קאמר: לימא מתני' דלא כר' יהודה אלא כר' מאיר! ומסיק: דכר' מאיר נמי לא אתי:

ואי אשמעינן חיה משום דמצנעת לה. ואין עובר משום בל יטמין – דבל יטמין נפקא לן מלא ימצא, ואין זה מצוי, כיון שאין ידוע היכן הוא. וכן משמע בפ"ק (דף ו:), דפריך: וכי משכחת לה – ליבטלה. משמע: דכל כמה דלא משכחת – לא עבר בבל יראה. הק' רשב"א: היכי שרי להאכיל לחיה שדרכה להטמין? הא תנן בפ"ק (דף ט:): מה שמשייר – יניחנו בצינעא, כדי שלא תטול חולדה בפניו, ויהא צריך בדיקה אחריו. וכ"ש שאסור ליתן בפניהם! ויש לחלק בין חיה לחולדה המגדלים בבתים, דההיא לא מצנעא כולי האי כמו חולדה הטומנת בחורים ובסדקין:

וקאי עליה בבל יראה. פי': אם לא ביטלו. והוא הדין דהוה מצי למימר: דילמא אתי למיכל מיניה:

קלה א מיי' פי"ב מהל' תרומות הלכה ה:
א ב מיי' פ"א מהלכות חמץ הלכה י סמג לאוין עו טוש"ע או"ח סי' תמג סעיף א:
ב [ג] מיי' פ"ג שם הלכה יא טוש"ע א"ח סי' תמה סעיף א:
ג ג מיי' שם פ"ג הלכה יא טוש"ע או"ח סי' תמ"ג ס"א וסי' תמה סעיף ב:

רבינו חננאל

לאכרועי על ב"ה והו שאמר אין הכרעת שלישי מכרעת ושמועה זו ברגמול זומא ופרקי' בפ' ראשית הגז תנא ר' ישמעאל בר' יוסי משום אביו ארבע שנאמר וארבע צאן תחת השה תניא אמר רבי אלמלא דבריהם דברי תורה ודברי ברבי קבלה אנו דברי ברבי שומעין וכל שכן שדבריהם דברי קבלה ודברי ברבי דברי תורה והאמר מר אין הכרעת שלישית מכרע' אמר ר' יוחנן מפי שמועה אמורה מפי חגי זכריה ומלאכי: ור' האי ז"ל היה אומר בקבלה כי אינה הכרעה אלא בזמן ששנים חלוקים ואחד מכריע באחד מהן שנמצאו שנים ואחד מכריע והלכה כרבים אבל בזמן שאומר חצי דברי זה וחצי דברי זה אין זה מכריע מטעם שלישי הוא ולפיכך כשאמר ר' ישמעאל בבית תעשה זילוף כב"ה בשדה תשתפך הכל כב"ש אמרו לו הכרעה שלישית היא זו ואין הכרעה שלישי' מכרע': ועוד אמר ר' יוסי בר חנינא מחלוקת שנפלה לפחות ממאה חולין דקא פסדי חולין לגמרי אבל נפלה למאה חולין דלא פסדי להו לחולין דהא תרומה לדברי הכל עולה לאחד ומאה דברי הכל תרד ותטמא ואל יטמאנה ביד ותניא הכי דתניא חבית שנשברה בגת העליונה ותחתיה מאה חולין טמאין מודה ר' אליעזר לר' יהושע שאם יכול להציל רביעית בטהרה יציל ואם לאו תרד ותטמא ואל יטמא בידים ומקשינן והא ר' יהושע הוא דתני אף יטמא ביד והוא היה צריך עכשיו להודות לר' אליעזר שלא יטמא ביד והיכי קתני דר' אליעזר הוא שמודה לר' יהושע ואמר רב פפא אפוך ואימר מודה ר' יהושע לר' אליעזר. רב הונא בריה דרב יהושע אמר לעולם לא תפוך והכא בבא להציל רביעית בטהרה בכלי שגבו טמא ותוכו טהור מהו דתימא גזר ר' אליעזר להציל בכלי שגבו טמא כי ההיא דתנן כלי שנטמא אחוריו במשקה תוכו ואוגנו ואזנו וידיו טהורין מהו דתימא גזר ר' אליעזר דלמא אתי למנגע בהו בתרומה ויטמא קמ"ל מודה ר' אליעזר שמציל רביעית בטהרה בכלי שתוכו טהור וגבו טמא ולא חייש ר' אליעזר דלמא נגע גבו שהוא טמא ונמצא כאלו מטמא התרומה בידים: הדרן עלך אור לארבעה עשר: **כל** שעה שמותר לאכול מאכיל לבהמה ולחיה וכו' מתני' דלא כר' יהודה דאי ר' יהודה התנן ר' יהודה אומר אוכלין כל ארבע ותולין כל חמש ושורפין בתחלת שש והא איכא שעה חמשית שהוא אינו אוכל ומאכיל לבהמה ומותר בהנאתו אלא מאי ר' מאיר היא דקתני אוכלין כל חמש אי הכי כל שעה שאוכלין מאכיל מבעי ליה למתנא ולא עמדה לא זו ולא זו ואוקמינן לר"ג דתאני בפ"ק ר"ג אומר חולין נאכלין כל ארבע ותרומה כל חמש ושורפין בתחלת שש והכי קתני כל שעה שכהן מותר לאכול תרומה מאכיל ישראל חולין לבהמה ולחיה כו': **ומוכרו** לנכרי פשיטא. כלומר מאחר דקתני ומותר בהנאתו מוכרו לנכרי למאי אתא ואוקימנא לאפוקי מהני תנאי דתניא בסוף פ' יציאות השבת ב"ש אומר לא ימכור אדם חמצו לנכרי אלא אם כן יודע שכלה קודם הפסח ב"ה אומר כל שעה שמותר לאכול מותר למכור ר' יהודה בן

שבת לט. נזיר נג. חולין קלז. [ב"ק קטז.]
לעיל יג.
[לעיל יג.]
לעיל יג.
תמורה לג. [לעיל יב: לקמן כז:]
[ברב אלפס ובהרא"ש ליתא מלת אף ועיין מג"א ריש סימן תמה:]
לעיל ה: יח:
[לעיל יג.]
[לעיל יח:]
שבת יח:
ס"א נהי דעבר בבל ימצא בבל [י]ראה לא עבר

הגהות הב"ח

(א) רש"י ד"ה אין הכרעת וכו' בין בשדה תשפך הכל וכו':

גליון הש"ס

בתוס' ד"ה לימא. אף לפי המסקנא. עי' נזיר דף ב' ע"ב תד"ה לימא:

ג א מיי' פ"ג שם הלכה יא סמג שם טוש"ע או"ח סי' תמה ס"ב וסי' תמב סעיף ט:
ד ב מיי' פ"א שם הל' ט סמג שם טוש"ע או"ח סי' תמג סעיף א:
ה ג מיי' שם הלכה ב:
ו ד מיי' פ"ח מהלכות מאכלות אסורות הל' טו סמג לאוין קלט:
ז ה מיי' פ"י מהל' ע"ז הלכה ד:

ר' יהודה בן בתירא אומר: כותח וכל מיני כותח – אסור למכור שלשים יום קודם לפסח.§ "ומותר בהנאה".§ פשיטא! לא צריכא שחרכו קודם זמנו. וקמ"ל כדרבא(א), דאמר רבא: [א]חרכו קודם זמנו – מותר בהנאה, אפילו לאחר זמנו.§ "עבר זמנו אסור בהנאתו".§ פשיטא! [ב]לא צריכא, לשעות דרבנן. *דאמר רב גידל, אמר רב חייא בר יוסף, א"ר יוחנן: המקדש משש שעות ולמעלה אפילו בחיטי קורדניתא – אין חוששין לקדושין.§ "ולא יסיק בו תנור וכירים".§ פשיטא! לא צריכא(ג), לר' יהודה, דאמר; אין ביעור חמץ אלא שריפה. סלקא דעתך אמינא: הואיל ואמר ר' יהודה מצותו בשריפה, בהדי דקא שריף ליה °ליתהני מיניה, קמ"ל.§ אמר חזקיה: [ג]מנין לחמץ בפסח שאסור בהנאה – שנאמר: °"לא יאכל חמץ" – לא יהא בו היתר אכילה. (שמות יג) טעמא דכתב רחמנא "לא יאכל חמץ" הא לא כתב לא יאכל – הוה אמינא איסור אכילה – משמע, איסור הנאה – לא משמע. ופליגא דר' אבהו, *דא"ר אבהו: [ד]כל מקום שנאמר "לא יאכל" "לא תאכל" "לא תאכלו" – אחד איסור אכילה ואחד איסור הנאה (*משמע), עד שיפרט לך הכתוב כדרך שפרט לך בנבילה. *דתניא: °"לא תאכלו כל נבלה לגר אשר בשעריך תתננה ואכלה או מכר לנכרי וגו'". (דברים יד) אין לי אלא לגר בנתינה ולגוי במכירה, לגר במכירה מנין? ת"ל: "לגר אשר בשעריך תתננה או מכר". לגוי בנתינה מנין? תלמוד לומר: "תתננה ואכלה או מכר לגוי". נמצאת אומר: אחד גר ואחד גוי, בין במכירה בין בנתינה, דברי ר' מאיר. *ר' יהודה אומר: [ה]דברים ככתבן, לגר בנתינה ולגוי במכירה. מאי טעמא דרבי יהודה? אי סלקא דעתך כדאמר ר' מאיר – ליכתוב רחמנא "לגר אשר בשעריך תתננה ואכלה ומכר" "או" למה לי? שמע מינה לדברים ככתבן. ור' מאיר: "או" – להקדים נתינה דגר למכירה דגוי. ורבי יהודה: הא לא *צריך קרא, כיון דגר אתה מצווה להחיותו, וגוי אי אתה מצווה להחיותו – לא צריך קרא, סברא הוא. בשלמא לר' מאיר, דאמר אחד גר ואחד גוי, בין במכירה בין בנתינה. מדאיצטריך קרא למישרא נבילה בהנאה – הא כל איסורין שבתורה אסורין בין באכילה בין בהנאה. אלא לרבי יהודה, דאמר לדברים ככתבן הוא דאתא – הא כל איסורים שבתורה מנא ליה דאסורין בהנאה? נפקא ליה °מ"לכלב תשליכון אתו", (שמות כב)

אותו

רש"י

ר' יהודה אומר כותח. נותנין בו פירורי לחם, ואסור משום חמץ: שלשים יום. דס"ל כב"ש. וזה אינו נאכל מהר, שאין אוכלין אותו אלא מטבילין בו. והני שלשים יום – משעה שחל עליו חובת ביעור, משמשאלין בהלכות הפסח: ומותר בהנאתו. קס"ד אשעה שמותר לאכול קאי: פשיטא. דהא אמרת מאכיל ומוכר, היינו הנאה: לא צריכא כו'. והאי מותר – אלאחר זמן קאי, וכגון שחרכו באור יפה קודם זמנו, שבטל טעמו ומראיתו: עבר(ג) זמנו אסור בהנאה לשעות דרבנן ה"ג. ולא גרסי' פשיטא. דהא אפי' בפסח איצטריך לאשמועי', דהא איכא רבי יוסי הגלילי דשרי בהנאה כל שבעה, לקמן: לשעות דרבנן. כלומר: האי זמנו – זמן אכילתו משמע, ואפילו שעה ששית שאין איסורו אלא מדרבנן – הוי אסור אף בהנאה: משש שעות. על כרחך מתחלת שש משמע. דאי לאחר שש, דאסור מדאורייתא – מאי אתא לאשמעינן? פשיטא דאין מקדשין באיסורי הנאה: חיטי קורדניתא. קשות הן. ואפ"ה, אם באו לחשש חמץ, כגון שנפלו עליהן מים – אסור: פשיטא. דהא אמרת אסור בהנאתו: לא יאכל. מדקרינא לא *יאכל – משמע לא יהא בו היתר המביא לידי שום אכילה. וסתם הנאות לידי אכילה הם באות, שלוקח בדמים דבר מאכל: עד שיפרוט לך הכתוב בו. היתר הנאה, כדרך שפרט לך בנבלה. שלא היה כתוב בה אלא "לא תאכלו", והוצרך להתירה בהנאה, כדכתיב: "או מכור לנכרי". לגר בנתינה לנכרי במכירה לא גרסינן, אלא ה"ג: כדרך שפרט לך בנבלה דתניא וכו': ת"ל לגר תתננה ואכלה או מכור. דרוש ליה אגר. וכן גבי לנכרי נמי דרוש "תתננה ואכלה או מכור לנכרי": דברים ככתבן. כך מצותה: לא יתננה לנכרי, ולא ימכרנה לגר: או. לשון חילוק. ואי כר' מאיר קאמר קרא, דתרוייהו אגר ותרוייהו אנכרי – לא נכתוב "או": להקדים נתינה דגר למכירה דנכרי. אם יש גר ליתנה לו – נתינתו קודמת למכירתה לנכרי. והאי גר – בגר תושב קאמר, שקיבל עליו שלא לעבוד ע"ז, ואוכל נבלות: גר אתה מצווה להחיותו. דכתיב (ויקרא כה): "גר ותושב וחי עמך": סברא היא. מסברא אנו יודעין שנתינה לגר קודמת, דחיות הגר מצוה. אבל מכירה לנכרי, מאי מצוה איכא? ואיצטריך קרא לחלק, ולאסור ליתן במתנה לנכרי, ולמכור נבלה לגר: בשלמא. לר' אבהו אליבא דר"מ – מגי למילף, מדאיצטריך קרא למישרי נבלה, הא כל איסורין שבתורה דכתיב בהו "לא תאכל" כי הכא, אי לא הדר פריט בהו היתרא – אסורין הן באכילה ובהנאה: אלא. לר' אבהו אליבא דרבי יהודה, מנא ליה? דילמא האי פרט דנבלה – לאו למשרייה בהנאה אתא, דלא איצטריך אלא להחמיר ולומר דלנכרי במכירה ולגר בנתינה. דאי לא כתביה – הוה אמינא כל הנאות מותרות בה: נפקא ליה. לרבי אבהו ואליבא דרבי יהודה, מדכתב בטרפה "לא תאכלו", ומיעט בה "לכלב תשליכון אותו":

אותו

תוספות

רבי יהודה אומר כותח וכל מיני כותח. פור"י בשם ר"ת: דר"י אתי כב"ה, ואסר בכותח משום דשם בעליו עליו ויודעים שהוא כותח של פלוני ויסברו שמכרו בפסח ע"י גוי. אי נמי: יסברו שבפסח מכרו ישראל לגוי. ולכן אוסר ר' יהודה למכור כותח לגוי. וא"ש אף לר"ת, דמפרש בריש "אלו עוברים" (לקמן מב.) דמותר להשהות כותח בפסח:

חרכו קודם זמנו מותר בהנאה אף לאחר זמנו. וכגון שנפסל מלאכול לכלב, דבענין אחר לא הוי שרי, דומיא דפת שעיפשה בפ"ק (דף טו:): עבר זמנו אסור בהנאה פשיטא. רש"י ל"ג פשיטא. דהא רבי יוסי הגלילי פליג, ושרי חמץ בהנאה כל שבעה. ואין לפרש: 'פשיטא' דאסור בהנאה מדיוקא דרישא – °דדרך התנא בכמה מקומות לכפול את דבריו. ועוד: דלא משני שפיר. ונראה דפריך פשיטא – משום דתנא בפ"ק (דף יא:) דשורפין חמץ, אלמא אסור בהנאה. דלר' יוסי הגלילי א"צ לשורפו, אלא ירילנו לפני כלבו או ימכרנו לגוי:

בהדי דקשריף ליה ליתהני מיניה. משום דלר' יהודה, דאמר חמץ בשריפה אפרו מותר, דתניא בפ' בתרא דתמורה (ד' לד.*): כל הנשרפין אפרן מותר. וקס"ד, בהדי דקשריף ליה – ליתהני מיניה. אבל לרבנן, דאין מצותו בשריפה, והוי מן הנקברים, דאמרינן בפרק בתרא דתמורה אפרן אסור – ופשיטא לדידהו דבהדי דקשריף ליה אסור ליהנות ממנו:

כל מקום שנאמר לא יאכל. וא"ת: יהא נהנה מחמץ בפסח בכרת, דהא כתיב: "כי כל אוכל חמץ ונכרתה"! וכי תימא: אין הכי נמי – א"כ לקמן (דף כג:), דבעי: מאי איכא בין חזקיה לר' אבהו – לימא דאיכא בינייהו הא! ואור"י: דלא יאכל ולא תאכל – ילפינן מ"לא תאכלו", אבל "כי כל אוכל" לא ילפינן מ"לא תאכלו":

ליכתוב רחמנא תתננה ואכלה ומכור. משמע דאי הוי כתב הכי לא הוה דרשינן אלא כר"מ. וכן ב"איזהו נשך" (ב"מ סא.) גבי נשך ותרבית. והא דאמרי' בקדושין (ד' לג:): ורבנן, אי ס"ד כרבי יוסי הגלילי – ליכתוב רחמנא: "מפני שיבה תקום והדרת תקום והדרת פני זקן" – היינו משום דלשון והדרת לא שייך אמפני, ולשון פני לא שייך אתקום. והנך קראי דאין להן הכרעה "שאת ארור מחר משוקדים וקם" (יומא ד' נב.) – אין עניים לכאן, דהתם מלי קאי אדלעיל או אלתחת, אבל הכא תרוייהו לא מצי קיימי אגר לחודיה או אגוי לחודיה. ובפ"ב דזבחים (ד' כד.) פליגי תנאי גבי "ולקח הכהן מדם החטאת באצבעו ונתן" איכא דמוקי אצבעו אלקיחה ולא אנתינה – משום דפשטיה דקרא קאי אלקיחה דלפניו, ואיכא דמוקי לה אנתינה דלאחריו ולא אלקיחה, משום דמשכחת בדוכתא אחרינא "ולקחת מדם הפר ונתת על קרנות, המזבח באצבעך" דקאי אצבע אנתינה. ואיכא דמוקי לה אתרוייהו, משום דמשמע ליה אלקיחה כפשטא דקרא, ואנתינה נמי כדמוכח בקרא אחרינא*):

בשלמא לרבי מאיר. תימה: לר"מ נמי יקשה, דהא איצטריך לאקדומי נתינה דגר! ותי' ר"י: דודאי, אי לא הוה כתב קרא כל עיקר – הוה ידעינן מסברא לאקדומי. אבל השתא דכתב נתינה: "תתננה ואכלה ומכור", אי לא הוה כתב "או" – ה"א דאתא למידרש שאין צריך להקדים. וא"צ ליכתב נמי גר וגוי, דאי לא הוה כתב אלא גר – הוה אמינא דאתא למעוטי נתינה דגוי, ואי הוה כתוב גוי לחודיה – הוה אמינא דאתא למעוטי מכירה דגר:

*) [וע"ע תוס' יומא נח: נב: ב"מ סא. ע"ז כ. חולין קיד:]

אותו

[לקמן כז:]

קדושין נו: [ע"ש] ב"ק מח. [ע"ש] חולין קיד: [ע"ש]

[*צ"ל במשמע וכן איתא בב"ק מח.]

לעיל ז.

יאכל

ע"ז כ.

שם [לקמן כג:]

[ועי' בתוס' שבועות כג: ד"ה איבעית אימא]

רבינו חננאל

בן בתירא אומר כותח וכל מיני כותח אסור למכור שלשים יום קודם לפסח: **והלכתא** כסתמא דמתני' ואם חרכו לפני זמנו מותר בהנאתו אפי' לאחר זמן איסורו: **עבר** זמנו אסור בהנאתו אוקימנא בזמן איסורו משש שעות ולמעלה. תנן סתמא כרב המקדש משש שעות ולמעלה [בחיטין שנתן בהן מים] אפילו בחיטי קרדינתא שהן חזקות ולא מחמעי היא אין חוששין לקדושין: **אמר** חזקיה מנין לחמץ שאסור בהנאה שנאמר לא יאכל חמץ לא יהא בו היתר אכילה ומתוך דבריו שמענו דכל איסורא דלא כתיב בהו לא יאכל מותרים בהנאה ופליגא דר' אבהו דאמר כל היכא דכתיב לא יאכל לא תאכל לא תאכלו אסור בין באכילה בין בהנאה עד שיפרט לך הכתוב כדרך שפרט בנבלה לגר אשר בשעריך תתננה ואכלה וחלקו במקרא הזה ר' מאיר אומר אחד גר ואחד נכרי בין במכירה בין בנתינה ר' יהודה אומר דברים ככתבן כלומר כדכתיב קרא לגר במתנה נכרי במכירה ואמרינן לר' מאיר דאמר הנכרי והגר דינם אחד הוא התורה התירה לך אמרי' מדאצטריך קרא למישרא נבלה בהנאה מכלל דשאר איסורין שבתורה אסורין אפילו בהנאה אלא לר' יהודה דאמר דברים ככתבן כלומר לא איצטריך קרא [אלא] למיסר מתנה דנכרי ומכירה [דגר] ולגופיה הוא דאתי שאר אסורין שבתורה מנא ליה דאסירי בהנאה ואמרינן מהאי קרא נפקא ליה ובשר בשדה טרפה לא תאכלו לכלב תשליכון אותו ודייקינן אותו אתה משליך לכלב פי' זה מותר לך בהנאה שהרי אתה

הגהות הב"ח

(א) גמ' כדרבה דאמר רבה חרכו קודם זמנו: (ב) שם לא צריכא אלא לר' יהודה: (ג) רש"י ד"ה ה"ג עבר זמנו וכו' לרבנן ולא גרסינן כל"ל:

גליון הש"ס

גמ' ליתהני מיניה קמ"ל. עי' לעיל דף ה' ע"א תד"ה ואומר: תוס' עבר זמנו וכו' דדרך התנא. עי' עירובין ל' ע"ב תד"ה וליפרוק עליה. ועיין לקמן ל"ה ע"ב וצ"ע:

תורה אור

*אוֹתוֹ אַתָּה מַשְׁלִיךְ לַכֶּלֶב, וְאִי אַתָּה מַשְׁלִיךְ לַכֶּלֶב כָּל אִיסּוּרִין שֶׁבַּתּוֹרָה[א]. וְר' מֵאִיר: אוֹתוֹ אַתָּה מַשְׁלִיךְ לַכֶּלֶב, וְאִי אַתָּה מַשְׁלִיךְ לַכֶּלֶב חוּלִּין שֶׁנִּשְׁחֲטוּ בָּעֲזָרָה. וְאִידָךְ: *חוּלִּין שֶׁנִּשְׁחֲטוּ בָּעֲזָרָה לָאו דְּאוֹרַיְיתָא הִיא. מָתִיב רַבִּי יִצְחָק נַפָּחָא: וַהֲרֵי גִּיד הַנָּשֶׁה, דְּרַחֲמָנָא אָמַר: °"עַל כֵּן לֹא יֹאכְלוּ בְנֵי יִשְׂרָאֵל אֶת גִּיד הַנָּשֶׁה", *וּתְנַן: אשׁוֹלֵחַ אָדָם יָרֵךְ לַגּוֹי, וְגִיד הַנָּשֶׁה בְּתוֹכוֹ, מִפְּנֵי שֶׁמְּקוֹמוֹ נִיכָּר! קָסָבַר ר' אַבָּהוּ: *כְּשֶׁהוּתְּרָה נְבֵלָה — הִיא וְחֶלְבָּהּ וְגִידָהּ הוּתְּרָה. הָנִיחָא לְמַאן דְּאָמַר יֵשׁ בַּגִּידִין בְּנוֹתֵן טַעַם! אֶלָּא לְמַאן דְּאָמַר באֵין בַּגִּידִין בְּנוֹתֵן טַעַם, מַאי אִיכָּא לְמֵימַר? מַאן שָׁמְעַתְּ לֵיהּ דְּאָמַר "אֵין בַּגִּידִין בְּנוֹתֵן טַעַם" — רַבִּי שִׁמְעוֹן, דְּתַנְיָא: *הָאוֹכֵל מִגִּיד הַנָּשֶׁה שֶׁל בְּהֵמָה טְמֵאָה, רַבִּי יְהוּדָה מְחַיֵּיב שְׁתַּיִם, וְרַבִּי שִׁמְעוֹן גפּוֹטֵר. רַבִּי שִׁמְעוֹן הָכִי נַמִי דְּאָסַר בַּהֲנָאָה. דְּתַנְיָא: גִּיד הַנָּשֶׁה דמוּתָּר בַּהֲנָאָה, דִּבְרֵי רַבִּי יְהוּדָה, וְרַבִּי שִׁמְעוֹן אוֹסֵר. וַהֲרֵי דָּם, דְּרַחֲמָנָא אָמַר: °"כָּל נֶפֶשׁ מִכֶּם לֹא תֹאכַל דָּם", וּתְנַן: *אֵלּוּ וָאֵלּוּ מִתְעָרְבִין בָּאַמָּה הוְיוֹצְאִין לְנַחַל קִדְרוֹן, וְנִמְכָּרִין לַגַּנָּנִין לְזֶבֶל, וּמוֹעֲלִין בּוֹ! שָׁאנֵי דָּם דְּאִיתַּקַּשׁ לְמַיִם, דִּכְתִיב: °"לֹא תֹאכְלֶנּוּ עַל הָאָרֶץ תִּשְׁפְּכֶנּוּ כַּמָּיִם", מַה מַּיִם מוּתָּרִין — אַף דָּם מוּתָּר. וְאֵימָא כַּמַּיִם הַמִּתְנַסְּכִים עַל גַּבֵּי הַמִּזְבֵּחַ! אָמַר רַבִּי אַבָּהוּ: "כַּמָּיִם" — רוֹב מַיִם. מִידֵּי "רוֹב מַיִם" כְּתִיב?! אֶלָּא אָמַר רַב אַשִׁי: כַּמַּיִם הַנִּשְׁפָּכִין! וְלֹא כַּמַּיִם הַנִּיסָּכִין. וְאֵימָא כַּמַּיִם הַנִּשְׁפָּכִין לִפְנֵי ע"ז! הָתָם נַמִי נִיסּוּךְ אִיקְּרִי, דִּכְתִיב: °"יִשְׁתּוּ יֵין נְסִיכָם". וּלְחִזְקִיָּה

(בראשית לב) (ויקרא ז) (דברים יב) (שם לב) [ולקמן כז.] [ברכות מ"ב]

רש"י

אותו אתה משליך כו' כל איסורין. שֶׁנֶּאֱמַר בָּהֶן "לֹא תֹאכַל", כְּגוֹן זֶה. וּמִדְּאִיצְטְרִיךְ קְרָא לְמִשְׁרְיֵיהּ — לָא מָצֵי לְמֵילַף טַעְמָא. דְּאִי לָאו "אוֹתוֹ" הֲוָה אָמֵינָא קְרָא לְמִצְוָתֵיהּ אִיצְטְרִיךְ, שֶׁאֵין הקב"ה מְקַפֵּחַ שְׂכַר כָּל בְּרִיָּה. וְנֶאֱמַר בְּמִצְרַיִם: "לֹא יֶחֱרַץ כֶּלֶב לְשׁוֹנוֹ" (שמות יא), לְפִיכָךְ הִקְפִּידָה תּוֹרָה לִיתֵּן שְׂכָרוֹ, וְנִכְבַּד [שְׂכַר] הַכֶּלֶב מִן הַנָּכְרִי, שֶׁהַנְּבֵלָה יִמְכּוֹר לְנָכְרִי וּטְרֵפָה לַכֶּלֶב: **ור"מ.** דְּנָפְקָא לֵיהּ אִיסּוּר הֲנָאָה בִּשְׁאָר אִיסּוּרִים, מִדִּפְרַט בִּנְבֵלָה. בִּשְׁלָמָא פְּרַט הֵיתֵּר דִּטְרֵפָה — לְגוּפֵיהּ אִיצְטְרִיךְ, לְמִיפְרַט בָּהּ הֵיתֵּר. מִשּׁוּם דְּאִי לָאו דִּפְרַט בֵּיהּ — הֲוָה אָמֵינָא לִיתַּסַּר בַּהֲנָאָה. אֶלָּא "אוֹתוֹ" לָמָּה לִי? וּמְשַׁנֵּי: לְאִיסּוּר הֲנָאָה חוּלִּין שֶׁנִּשְׁחֲטוּ בָּעֲזָרָה, דְּנָפְקָא לָן *בְּהוּ אִיסּוּר אֲכִילָה, מִדִּכְתַב (דברים יב): "כִּי יִרְחַק מִמְּךָ הַמָּקוֹם וְזָבַחְתָּ וְאָכַלְתָּ" — בְּרִיחוּק מָקוֹם, דְּהַיְינוּ חוּץ לְמַחֲנֵה שְׁכִינָה אַתָּה זוֹבֵחַ וְאוֹכֵל, וְאִי אַתָּה זוֹבֵחַ וְאוֹכֵל בְּקֵרוּב מָקוֹם. וּמִשּׁוּם דְּאֵין מְפוֹרָשׁ בָּהֶן לָאו בְּהֶדְיָא בַּאֲכִילָה, אִיצְטְרִיךְ לְמֵילַף לְהוּ אִיסּוּר הֲנָאָה מֵהָכָא. וְהָכִי מַשְׁמַע: אוֹתוֹ שֶׁנֶּאֱסַר מִשּׁוּם חוּץ לִמְחִיצָה — אַתָּה מַשְׁלִיךְ לַכֶּלֶב — דְּהָא מֵהַאי קְרָא "וּבָשָׂר בַּשָּׂדֶה טְרֵפָה" נָפְקָא לָן אִיסּוּר מְחִיצָה, כְּגוֹן הוֹשִׁיט הָעוּבָּר אֶת יָדוֹ בִּשְׁעַת שְׁחִיטָה בְּפֶרֶק "בְּהֵמָה הַמַּקְשָׁה לֵילֵד" (חולין סח:). אֲבָל יֵשׁ לְךָ אַחֵר הַנֶּאֱסָר מִשּׁוּם מְחִיצָה, וְאִי אַתָּה מַשְׁלִיכוֹ לַכֶּלֶב, וְאֵיזֶה זֶה — זֶה חוּלִּין שֶׁנִּשְׁחֲטוּ בָּעֲזָרָה: **חולין שנשחטו בעזרה.** דַּאֲסִירֵי בַּהֲנָאָה — לָאו דְּאוֹרַיְיתָא, בְּפֶרֶק שֵׁנִי דְּקִדּוּשִׁין (דף נח.) אִיפְּלִיגוּ בָּהּ: **שולח אדם ירך לנכרי.** וְלָא מַצְרְכִינַן לִיטּוֹל גִּידָהּ, וְלָא גָּזְרִינַן שֶׁמָּא יִרְאֶה יִשְׂרָאֵל חֲבֵירוֹ כְּשֶׁיִּתְּנֶנָּה לוֹ וְיֵלֵךְ וְיִקְנֶה אוֹתָהּ מִן הַנָּכְרִי, וְכִסְבוּר שֶׁנִּיטַּל גִּידָהּ, הוֹאִיל וּמִתַּחַת יַד יִשְׂרָאֵל יָצְתָה, וְיֹאכְלֶנָּה בְּגִידָהּ: **מפני שמקומו ניכר.** אִם הוּא נָטוּל וְאִם לָאו. שָׁמְעִינַן מִינַּהּ מִיהָא דְּגִיד מוּתָּר בַּהֲנָאָה, וְקַשְׁיָא לְר' אַבָּהוּ: **היא** וְחֶלְבָּהּ וְגִידָהּ הוּתְּרָה. לְפִיכָךְ כָּל חֵלֶב וְכָל גִּיד מוּתָּרִין בַּהֲנָאָה, שֶׁהֵן בִּכְלַל "לַגֵּר אֲשֶׁר בִּשְׁעָרֶיךָ תִּתְּנֶנָּה וַאֲכָלָהּ", שֶׁגַּם הֵן קְרוּיִין עִמָּהּ נְבֵלָה, וַהֲרֵי לְךָ הֵיתֵּר הֲנָאָה בְּלָאו דְּגִיד, ל"ש נְבֵלָה ול"ש כְּשֵׁרָה: **הניחא** לְמ"ד יֵשׁ בַּגִּידִין. טַעַם בָּשָׂר — הֲרֵי הוּא בִּכְלַל נְבֵלָה: **אלא** לְמ"ד אֵין בַּגִּידִין. דְּאִיסּוּר נוֹתֵן טַעַם בָּשָׂר אִם נִתְבַּשְּׁלוּ עִם הַבָּשָׂר, אַלְמָא לָאו טַעַם בָּשָׂר אִית בְּהוּ, וְלָאו נְבֵלָה מִיקְּרוּ, אֶלָּא כַּעֲצָמוֹת, דְּהֵן עֵץ בְּעָלְמָא, וְלָא אִישְׁתְּרֵי בִּכְלַל נְבֵלָה. וְעֵץ הוּא וְהַתּוֹרָה חִיְּיבָה עָלָיו, מַאי אִיכָּא לְמֵימַר? וּפְלוּגְתַּיְיהוּ בְּ"גִיד הַנָּשֶׁה" (חולין צט:): **ור"ש פוטר.** לְגַמְרֵי. מִבְּהֵמָה טְמֵאָה פָּטוּר — דְּקָסָבַר: אֵין בַּגִּידִין בְּנוֹתֵן טַעַם בָּשָׂר, וּמִגִּיד נַמִי פָּטוּר — דְּכִי אַזְהַרֵיהּ רַחֲמָנָא אַגִּיד — הֵיכָא דִּבְשָׂרָהּ מוּתָּר, דְּהַיְינוּ בְּהֵמָה טְהוֹרָה. דְּהָכִי מַשְׁמַע: גִּיד לֹא תֹאכַל — הָא בָּשָׂר אֱכוֹל, אֲבָל טְמֵאָה לֹא הִזְהִיר עַל גִּידָהּ. וְהָכִי מְפָרְשִׁי' לָהּ בְּ"גִיד הַנָּשֶׁה" (שם קא.): **ולרבי שמעון**, הָכִי נַמִי דְּאָסוּר גִּיד דִּטְהוֹרָה אֲפִילּוּ בַּהֲנָאָה — אַלְמָא: "לֹא תֹאכְלוּ" — אִיסּוּר הֲנָאָה מַשְׁמַע, וּכְשֶׁהוּתְּרָה נְבֵלָה בַּהֲנָאָה — הִיא לֹא הוּתְּרָה לְר"ש, דְּלָאו בִּכְלַל נְבֵלָה הִיא. אֲבָל לְרַבִּי יְהוּדָה מוּתָּר, מִשּׁוּם דְּקָסָבַר יֵשׁ בַּגִּידִים בְּנוֹתֵן טַעַם, כִּדְקָתָנֵי: רַבִּי יְהוּדָה מְחַיֵּיב שְׁתַּיִם, הִלְכָּךְ: גִּיד בִּכְלַל בָּשָׂר, וּכְשֶׁהוּתְּרָה נְבֵלָה — הוּתְּרָה גַּם הִיא: **אלו ואלו.** שְׁיָרֵי דַּם חַטָּאוֹת הַפְּנִימִית הַנִּשְׁפָּכִין עַל יְסוֹד מַעֲרָבִי שֶׁל מִזְבֵּחַ הַחִיצוֹן, וּשְׁיָרֵי דַּם חַטָּאוֹת הַחִיצוֹנוֹת הַנִּשְׁפָּכִין עַל יְסוֹד דְּרוֹמִי — יוֹצְאִין מִן הַיְסוֹד לָרִצְפָּה דֶּרֶךְ שְׁנֵי נְקָבִים קְטַנִּים, וּמִתְעָרְבִין בָּאַמָּה — סִילּוֹן שֶׁהָיָה עוֹבֵר בָּעֲזָרָה: **ויוצאין לנחל קדרון.** כְּמוֹ "לְנַחַל אֵיתָן" (דברים כא) — עֵמֶק: **לגננים.** בַּעֲלֵי גִּנּוֹת לְזֶבֶל: **ומועלין בהן.** כְּלוֹמַר: אָסוּר לֵהָנוֹת מֵהֶן בְּלֹא דָּמִים, מִפְּנֵי שֶׁהֵן שֶׁל הֶקְדֵּשׁ. מִכָּל מָקוֹם, דָּם מוּתָּר בַּהֲנָאָה: **כמים המתנסכין.** שֶׁאֲסוּרוֹת בַּהֲנָאָה, שֶׁהֲרֵי קֹדֶשׁ הֵן, שֶׁקִּדְּשׁוּ בִּכְלֵי שָׁרֵת, וּכְתִיב (שמות ל): "כָּל הַנֹּגֵעַ בָּהֶם יִקְדָּשׁ": וּלְחִזְקִיָּה

תוספות

אותו אתה משליך. פ"ה: דבלאו "אותו" לא מצי למידרש מגופיה דקרא, דאיצטריך שאין הקב"ה מקפח שכר כל בריה. והר"י דאורלינ"ש מפרש: דאיצטריך למישרי עובר שהוציא את ידו, משום דמקרא ד"בשר בשדה טרפה" דריש נמי קדשים שיצאו חוץ למחיצתם בריש "בהמה המקשה" (חולין סח:), והוה אסרינן יד העובר בהנאה, מדאיתקש לקדשים דאסור בהנאה. כדאמר: *כל שבקודש פסול — בנא תשרף, ולכך איצטריך אותו לכל איסורים:

חולין שנשחטו בעזרה לאו דאורייתא. פ"ה: איסור הנאה. ולא משמע פשט ההלכה כן, אלא לגמרי קאמר לאו דאורייתא. וכן בסוף שמעתא, גבי הא דאמר: איכא בינייהו חולין שנשחטו בעזרה — אי אפשר לפרש בענין אחר. *ובפרק "מי שאמר הריני נזיר ושמע חבירו ואמר ואני" (נזיר כט: ושם) פריך: למ"ד כדי לחנכו במצות — הא קמייתי חולין לעזרה! ומשני: קסבר חולין שנשחטו בעזרה לאו דאורייתא. ואי לענין איסור אכילה הוו דאורייתא — אכתי תיקשי ליה היאך הקרבן נאכל, דמשמע התם שנאכל. וקשה לרשב"א, דבת"כ בפ' צו גבי נותר דרש רבי יהודה: "לא יאכל כי קודש הוא" יכול חטאת העוף הבא על הספק, ואשם תלוי וחולין שנשחטו בעזרה ישרפו — ת"ל: "הוא". מדאיצטריך למעוטי שאינם בשריפה — מכלל דאסירי בהנאה מדאורייתא: **ורבי שמעון** נמי מיסר אסר בהנאה. משמע דההיא דהשולח ירך לגוי — אתיא כר' יהודה. הק' ריב"א: דהא רבי יהודה אית ליה בפ"ק דמס' ע"ז (דף כ. ושם) דאסור ליתן להם מתנת חנם! וי"ל: דהא אמר התם* אם היה שכינו — מותר, מפני שהוא כמוכרו לו. הקשה הר"י דאורלינ"ש: היכי מצי אתי כר' יהודה? ורבי יהודה אית ליה בפ' "גיד הנשה" (חולין ק:) דגיד הנשה אסור לבני נח, וקעבר משום "לפני עור לא תתן וגו'"! ואומר ר"י דלא קשה מידי, דלא קאסר אלא לבני יעקב דוקא, דקודם מתן תורה איקרו בני נח, דהא לא ניתנה בסיני. וא"ת: תיקשי לחזקיה מרבי שמעון, דסבירא ליה דלא תאכלו איסור הנאה משמע, מדאסר גיד הנשה! וי"ל: כיון דסבר אין בגידין בנ"ט — סברא הוא, דכי אסור — בהנאה נמי אסור, דלא שייכא ביה אכילה. א"נ: חזקיה לא סבר כרבי שמעון אלא כרבי יהודה. דלכאורה נמי לא אתיא חזקיה כרבי מאיר, דלרבי מאיר פשיטא לן לעיל מדאיצטריך למישרי נבילה דכל איסורים אסורים בהנאה, וכן לקמן (דף כג:) גבי יתיב ההוא מרבנן — פשיטא ליה לגמרא דלרבי מאיר גמר מנבילה, והא דקאמר לקמן: *לימא כתנאי — היינו לרבי אבהו, דחזקיה לא מצי אתי ככ"ע: **והרי** דם דרחמנא אמר. משמע דדם לא הוי בכלל בהמה, מדלא משני: כשהותרה בהמה — דמה נמי הותרה. וקשה לר"ת, דאמר ב"המוציא יין" (שבת עו. ושם): דם נבילה, ב"ה מטמא. וקאמר התם, ר' יוסי (כרבי) יהודה דלא מטמא ב"ה אלא כשיש רביעית דם — הואיל ויכול לקרוש ולעמוד על כזית. אלמא: חשיב ליה כבשר! ותי' ר"י: דהתם לאו משום דחשיב ליה כבשר, אלא יש שום פסוק דדרשינן מיניה דדם נבילו' טמא, ומסברא משערינן ברביעי', כדאמר התם. אבל בלא ריבוי לא חשבינן דם כבשר. ובמעילה (דף יז. ושם) נמי מפיק דם השרץ מ"וזה לכם הטמא" ומשרץ גופיה לא ידעינן ליה*:

מועלין בהן. מדרבנן, ולא מדאורייתא. דבסוף "הוציאו לו" (יומא נט: ושם) אמר: אין לך דבר שנעשה מצותו ומועלים בו. ואור"י: דבמעילה, בפרק "ולד חטאת" (דף יא.) ת"ר: מועלים בדמים, דברי רבי מאיר ורבי שמעון. וחכמים אומרים: אין מועלין. ופלוגתהם אחר שיצא לנחל קדרון. דקודם זריקה קתני ר"ש התם דאין מועלין בו. והיה שם בספרים: מאי טעמא דמ"ד אין מועלין ול"ג: דמ"ד — דא"כ הוה משמע דלרבי מאיר ורבי שמעון מועלין בו מן התורה. אלא ה"ג: מאי טעמא אין מועלין. ואמתני' קאי, דקתני דם בתחלה אין מועלין בו: **מה** מים מותרים אף דם מותר. אף על גב דדם קדשים שאין נשפך כמים לא הוקש למים — מ"מ, כיון דמשמע קרא בדם חולין דשרי בהנאה, ולא תאכל דידיה היינו אכילה ולא הנאה — הוא הדין לדם קדשים. ואף על גב דאיכא תרי לאוי, חד לדם חולין וחד לקדשים — מ"מ גילוי מילתא בעלמא הוא, דכולהו לאוי דדם הוי איסור אכילה דוקא*: **ואימא** כמים הניסכים על גבי המזבח. לא פריך למילף שיהא דם אסור בהנאה, דממילא ידעינן מ"לא תאכל" אלא כלומר: מהכא לא מצי למילף דשרי בהנאה: ואבר

רבינו חננאל

אתה משליכו לכלבך ואינך משליך שאר איסורין שבתורה מיהא שמעינן לכל שאר איסורין דאסירי ואפילו בהנאה וקרא דנבלה הוא דאתי למיסר שאר אסורין אפילו בהנאה ור' יהודה אומר חולין שנשחטו בעזרה אינו מן התורה: **ומותבינן** לר' אבהו הרי גיד הנשה דכתיב ביה לא יאכל והוא מותר בהנאה דתנן שולח אדם ירך שגיד הנשה בתוכה וכו' ושנינן קסבר ר' אבהו כשהותרה הנבלה היא וחלבה וגידה הותרה כי הנבלה כמות שהיא בחלבה וגידה הותרה להמכר לנכרי ואקשי' איני שהגידים הותרו בנבלה והא תתננה ואכלה כתיב לא הותר אלא מידי דבר אכילה וגידים לאו בני אכילה נינהו דלית בהו בנותן טעם (איני) והתנן ירך שנתבשל בה גיד הנשה וכו' ואמרינן מאן אית ליה האי סברא דאין בגידין בנותן טעם ר"ש ר"ש הכי נמי דאוסר בהנאה דתניא גיד הנשה מותר בהנאה דברי ר' יהודה ור' שמעון אוסר: **הרי** דם דכתיב לא תאכל דם ומותר בהנאה [דתנן] ונמכרין לזבל ומועלין בהן ודחי' שאני דם דאיתקש למים שנאמר על הארץ תשפכנו כמים כו'

עין משפט נר מצוה

[ח א מיי' פ"ב מהלכות שחיטה הלכה כג:

ח א מיי' פ"ח מהלכות מאכלות אסורות הל' יד סמג לאוין קלד טוש"ע י"ד סי' סב סעיף יא:

ט ב מיי' פט"ו שם הל' יד סמג שם טוש"ע שם סעיף ט:

י ג מיי' פ"ב שם הלכה יח ופ"ח הלכה ה:

יא ד מיי' פ"ח שם הל' (טו) [יז] טוש"ע שם ס"י:

יב ה מיי' פ"ב מהלכות מעילה הלכה יא:

גליון הש"ס

גמ' ור"מ אותו אתה משליך לכלב. תמוה לי דלמא מה דאמ' ר"מ דאחד גר ואחד גוי בין במכירה ובין בנתינה היינו לפי האמת דכתיב אותו דאי אתה משליך לכלב כל איסורין שבתור' ממילא אצטריך קרא גבי נבילה לגר אשר בשעריך להתיר נבילה בהנאה מש"ה לא אמר לדברים ככתבן כיון דלא מייתר קרא. אבל אלו לא היה כתוב אותו אדנידוק מקרא דנבילה דלא תאכל איסור הנאה משמע היינו אומרים באמת דמיתור' דקרא אתי לדברים ככתבן וצ"ע: **רש"י** ד"ה ור"מ. ומשום דאין מפורש בהן לאו וכו'. ק"ל הא מכל מקום נילף מקרא דלא תאכל כל תועבה דגם הנאה במשמע לר"א. וכן קשה לר"י דס"ל חולין שנשחטו בעזרה לאו דאורייתא לפירוש רש"י דשחיטתו דאוריי' ליתסר בהנאה משום לא תאכל כל תועבה וצ"ע: **תוס'** ד"ה ור' שמעון וכו' שהוא כמוכרו לו. עי' עירובין סד ע"ב תוס' ד"ה ולמדנו: **באד"ה** היכי מצי אתיא כר"י. תמוה לי הא זהו ליכא קושי' כ"כ די"ל דמתני' כר"י ... : **בא"ד** א"נ חזקיה לא סבר כר"ש. עי' חולין לה ע"ב תד"ה למשרי:

קדושין נח.

[לקמן כג: קדושין נח. נזיר כט. ב"ק עב.]

[קדושין נז:]

[לקמן כג.]

חולין ק:

ע"ז מב. יומא נח:

[ולקמן כז.]

חולין נג:

גי' רש"א בפרק וע"ש

[נ"ל כר']

[וע"ע בתו' מנחות קב. ד"ה הואיל]

[וע"ע תוס' חולין נג. ד"ה דם]

תורה אור

וּלְחִזְקִיָּה, לְמַאי הִלְכְתָא אִיתְקַשׁ דָּם לְמַיִם? לְכִדְר' חִיָּיא בַּר אַבָּא. דְּאָמַר ר' חִיָּיא בַּר אַבָּא א"ר יוֹחָנָן: *מִנַּיִן לְדַם קָדָשִׁים שֶׁאֵינוֹ מַכְשִׁיר, שֶׁנֶּאֱמַר °"לֹא תֹּאכְלֶנּוּ עַל הָאָרֶץ תִּשְׁפְּכֶנּוּ כַּמָּיִם" (דברים יב), דָּם שֶׁנִּשְׁפָּךְ כַּמַּיִם — מַכְשִׁיר, שֶׁאֵינוֹ נִשְׁפָּךְ כַּמַּיִם — אֵינוֹ מַכְשִׁיר. וַהֲרֵי אֵבֶר מִן הַחַי, דִּכְתִיב: °"לֹא תֹאכַל הַנֶּפֶשׁ עִם הַבָּשָׂר" (שם), וְתַנְיָא, *רַבִּי נָתָן אוֹמֵר: אמִנַּיִן שֶׁלֹּא יוֹשִׁיט אָדָם כּוֹס יַיִן לְנָזִיר, וְאֵבֶר מִן הַחַי לִבְנֵי נֹחַ — ת"ל: °"וְלִפְנֵי עִוֵּר לֹא תִתֵּן מִכְשֹׁל" (ויקרא יט). הָא לִכְלָבִים — שָׁרֵי! שָׁאנֵי אֵבֶר מִן הַחַי, דְּאִיתְקַשׁ לְדָם. דִּכְתִיב: °"רַק חֲזַק לְבִלְתִּי אֲכֹל הַדָּם כִּי הַדָּם הוּא הַנָּפֶשׁ" (דברים יב). וּלְחִזְקִיָּה, לְמַאי הִלְכְתָא אִיתְקַשׁ אֵבֶר מִן הַחַי לְדָם? אָמַר לָךְ: דָּם הוּא דְּאִיתְקַשׁ לְאֵבֶר מִן הַחַי, מָה אֵבֶר מִן הַחַי — אָסוּר, אַף דָּם מִן הַחַי אָסוּר. וְאֵי זֶה — בזֶה דַּם הַקָּזָה, שֶׁהַנֶּפֶשׁ יוֹצְאָה בּוֹ. וַהֲרֵי שׁוֹר הַנִּסְקָל, דְּרַחֲמָנָא אָמַר: °"לֹא יֵאָכֵל אֶת בְּשָׂרוֹ" (שמות כא). *וְתַנְיָא: גמִמַּשְׁמַע שֶׁנֶּאֱמַר °"סָקוֹל יִסָּקֵל הַשּׁוֹר" (שם) אֵינִי יוֹדֵעַ שֶׁהִיא נְבֵלָה, וּנְבֵלָה אֲסוּרָה בַּאֲכִילָה? וּמָה ת"ל "לֹא יֵאָכֵל" מַגִּיד לְךָ הַכָּתוּב, שֶׁאִם שְׁחָטוֹ לְאַחַר שֶׁנִּגְמַר (אֶת) דִּינוֹ — אָסוּר. אֵין לִי אֶלָּא בַּאֲכִילָה, בַּהֲנָאָה מִנַּיִן? ת"ל °"וּבַעַל הַשּׁוֹר נָקִי" (שם). מַאי מַשְׁמַע? שִׁמְעוֹן בֶּן זוֹמָא אוֹמֵר: כְּאָדָם שֶׁאוֹמֵר לַחֲבֵירוֹ "יָצָא פְּלוֹנִי נָקִי מִנְּכָסָיו וְאֵין לוֹ בָּהֶם הֲנָאָה שֶׁל כְּלוּם". טַעְמָא — דִּכְתַב "וּבַעַל הַשּׁוֹר נָקִי". דְּאִי מִ"לֹּא יֵאָכֵל" — אִיסּוּר אֲכִילָה מַשְׁמַע, אִיסּוּר הֲנָאָה — לֹא מַשְׁמַע! לְעוֹלָם "לֹא יֵאָכֵל" — אִיסּוּר אֲכִילָה וְאִיסּוּר הֲנָאָה מַשְׁמַע. "וּבַעַל הַשּׁוֹר נָקִי" — לַהֲנָאַת עוֹרוֹ הוּא דַּאֲתָא. וְאִיצְטְרִיךְ, ס"ד אָמִינָא: "לֹא יֵאָכֵל אֶת בְּשָׂרוֹ" כְּתִיב, בְּשָׂרוֹ — אִין, עוֹרוֹ — לָא, קמ"ל. וּלְהָנָךְ תַּנָּאֵי דְּמַפְּקִי לֵיהּ לְהַאי קְרָא לִדְרָשָׁה אַחֲרִינָא, לַחֲצִי כּוֹפֶר וְלִדְמֵי וְלָדוֹת, הֲנָאַת עוֹרוֹ מְנָא לְהוּ? נָפְקָא לְהוּ מֵ"אֶת בְּשָׂרוֹ" — אֶת הַטָּפֵל לִבְשָׂרוֹ. וְאִידָךְ: *"אֶת" לָא דָּרֵישׁ. *כִּדְתַנְיָא: שִׁמְעוֹן הָעַמְסוֹנִי, (חגיגה יב.) וְאָמְרִי לַהּ נְחֶמְיָה הָעַמְסוֹנִי, *הָיָה דּוֹרֵשׁ כָּל אֶתִים שֶׁבַּתּוֹרָה. כֵּיוָן שֶׁהִגִּיעַ °לְ"אֶת ה' אֱלֹהֶיךָ תִּירָא" (דברים י) — פֵּירַשׁ. אָמְרוּ לוֹ תַּלְמִידָיו: רַבִּי, כָּל אֶתִים שֶׁדָּרַשְׁתָּ מַה תְּהֵא עֲלֵיהֶן? אָמַר לָהֶם: כְּשֵׁם שֶׁקִּבַּלְתִּי שָׂכָר עַל הַדְּרִישָׁה, כָּךְ אֲנִי מְקַבֵּל שָׂכָר עַל הַפְּרִישָׁה. עַד שֶׁבָּא ר"ע וְדָרַשׁ: "אֶת ה' אֱלֹהֶיךָ תִּירָא" — לְרַבּוֹת תַּלְמִידֵי חֲכָמִים. וַהֲרֵי עָרְלָה, דְּרַחֲמָנָא אָמַר: °"עֲרֵלִים לֹא יֵאָכֵל" (ויקרא יט). וְתַנְיָא: *"עֲרֵלִים לֹא יֵאָכֵל" — אֵין לִי אֶלָּא אִיסּוּר אֲכִילָה, דמִנַּיִן שֶׁלֹּא יֵהָנֶה מִמֶּנּוּ, שֶׁלֹּא יִצְבַּע בּוֹ, וְלֹא יַדְלִיק בּוֹ אֶת הַנֵּר — ת"ל: "וַעֲרַלְתֶּם עָרְלָתוֹ. עֲרֵלִים לֹא יֵאָכֵל" — לְרַבּוֹת אֶת כּוּלָּם. טַעְמָא — דִּכְתַב רַחֲמָנָא "וַעֲרַלְתֶּם עָרְלָתוֹ עֲרֵלִים", הָא לָאו הָכִי — הֲוָה אָמִינָא אִיסּוּר אֲכִילָה — מַשְׁמַע, אִיסּוּר הֲנָאָה — לֹא מַשְׁמַע! לְעוֹלָם "לֹא יֵאָכֵל" מַשְׁמַע בֵּין אִיסּוּר אֲכִילָה בֵּין אִיסּוּר הֲנָאָה, וְשָׁאנֵי הָתָם דִּכְתִיב "לָכֶם". וְאִיצְטְרִיךְ, סָלְקָא דַּעְתָּךְ אָמִינָא: הוֹאִיל וְכָתַב "לָכֶם" — שֶׁלָּכֶם יְהֵא, קָמַשְׁמַע לָן. וְאֶלָּא הַשְׁתָּא דִּכְתִיבִי הָנָךְ קְרָאֵי, "לָכֶם" לָמָּה לִי? לְכִדְתַנְיָא: ה"לָכֶם" — לְרַבּוֹת אֶת הַנָּטוּעַ לָרַבִּים

רש"י

וּלְחִזְקִיָּה. דְּאָמַר לְעֵיל: אִיסּוּר הֲנָאָה דְּחָמֵץ מִ"לֹּא יֵאָכֵל" — הָא "לֹא תֹאכַל" וְ"לֹא תֹאכְלוּ" לָא מַשְׁמַע לֵיהּ הֲנָאָה: לְמַאי הִלְכְתָא אִיתְקַשׁ דָּם לְמַיִם. לְמִשְׁרְיֵיהּ בַּהֲנָאָה, וּמֵהֵיכָא תֵּיתֵי לָךְ דְּנִיתַּסְרוּ? וּמִגַּבֵּילָה לָא אוֹתְבִינֵיהּ לְחִזְקִיָּה לְמַאי אִיצְטְרִיךְ קְרָא לְמִשְׁרְיֵיהּ, דְּאִי כְּר' יְהוּדָה סָבַר — לִדְבָרִים כִּכְתָבָן הוּא דַּאֲתָא, וְאִי כְּר"מ סָבַר לָהּ — אִיצְטְרִיךְ לְהַקְדִּים נְתִינָה דְּגֵר לִמְכִירָה דְּנָכְרִי: לֹא תֹאכַל הַנֶּפֶשׁ עִם הַבָּשָׂר. בְּעוֹד שֶׁהַנֶּפֶשׁ בּוֹ: בְּנֵי נֹחַ נֶאֱסַר לָהֶם אֵבֶר מִן הַחַי, דִּכְתִיב (בראשית ט): "אַךְ בָּשָׂר בְּנַפְשׁוֹ דָמוֹ לֹא תֹאכֵלוּ": לִפְנֵי עִוֵּר. אַלְמָא: לָא מִיתְּסַר אֶלָּא מִשּׁוּם "לִפְנֵי עִוֵּר לֹא תִתֵּן מִכְשׁוֹל", אֲבָל בַּהֲנָאָה אַחֲרִינִי, כְּגוֹן לְכֶלֶב — שָׁרֵי: לְבִלְתִּי אֲכוֹל הַדָּם. סֵיפֵיהּ דִּקְרָא "לֹא תֹאכַל הַנֶּפֶשׁ" וגו': מָה אֵבֶר מִן הַחַי אָסוּר. בָּאִיסּוּר הָאָמוּר בּוֹ, אַף דָּם מִן הַחַי — אָסוּר בָּאִיסּוּ' הָאָמוּר בּוֹ, כְּלוֹמַר: כָּרֵת, מִשּׁוּם דָּם גָּמוּר. מַהוּ דְּתֵימָא: "רַק חֲזַק לְבִלְתִּי אֲכוֹל הַדָּם" — אַ"וְזָבַחְתָּ מִבְּקָרְךָ וּמִצֹּאנְךָ" דִּכְתִיב לְעֵיל קָאֵי, וְדַם זְבִיחָה הוּא דְּאָסוּר, אֲבָל דַּם הַקָּזָה מוּתָּר: וְאֵיזֶה זֶה. כְּלוֹמַר: עַל אֵיזֶה דָּם מִן הַחַי אָסוּר מִשּׁוּם דָּם, הָא דַּם הַנֶּפֶשׁ כְּתִיב — עַל דַּם הַקָּזָה שֶׁל בְּהֵמָה שֶׁהַנֶּפֶשׁ יוֹצְאָה בּוֹ. יֵשׁ ד' מִינֵי דָמִים בַּהֵיקֵז, כִּדְאָמְרִינַן בִּכְרֵיתוֹת (דף כב.): בַּתְּחִלָּה שׁוֹתֵת, וּלְבַסּוֹף מְקַלֵּחַ, וְאח"כ מַשְׁחִיר, וְסוֹפוֹ שׁוֹתֵת. יֵשׁ מֵהֶן שֶׁאֵין הַנְּשָׁמָה יוֹצְאָה בּוֹ, וְיֵשׁ מֵהֶן שֶׁהַנְּשָׁמָה יוֹצְאָה בּוֹ. וְהָתָם תַּנְיָא: אֵיזֶהוּ דַּם הֵיקֵז שֶׁהַנְּשָׁמָה יוֹצְאָה בּוֹ — כָּל זְמַן שֶׁמְּקַלֵּחַ כו': שֶׁאִם שְׁחָטוֹ כו'. וְהָכִי קָאָמַר קְרָא: סָקוֹל יִסָּקֵל הַשּׁוֹר, וְאִי לֹא סְקָלוֹ — אעפ"כ לֹא יֵאָכֵל אֶת בְּשָׂרוֹ: אִיסּוּר הֲנָאָה לֹא מַשְׁמַע. וְקַשְׁיָא אֲפִילּוּ לְחִזְקִיָּה, וְכ"ש לְרַבִּי אַבָּהוּ: וּלְהָנָךְ תַּנָּאֵי. דְּבב"ק פ' "שׁוֹר שֶׁנָּגַח" (דף מא: ומב.) דְּמַפְּקֵי לֵיהּ לְהַאי "נָקִי" לִדְרָשָׁא אַחֲרִינָא, לְאַשְׁמְעִי' דְּתָם פָּטוּר מֵחֲצִי כּוֹפֶר, דְּקָאָמַר: נָקִי מֵחֲצִי כּוֹפֶר אִם הֵמִית אִישׁ. דְּאִילּוּ מוּעָד מְשַׁלֵּם כּוֹפֶר שָׁלֵם, וְהָתָם — אֲפִי' חֲצִי כּוֹפֶר לֹא מְשַׁלֵּם. וְאִיכָּא דְּמַפִּיק לֵיהּ לִדְמֵי וְלָדוֹת, אִם נָגַח אִשָּׁה הָרָה וְיָצְאוּ יְלָדֶיהָ: וְאִידָךְ. דְּנַפְקָא לֵיהּ הֲנָאַת עוֹר מִ"נָּקִי": אֶת לָא דָּרֵישׁ. לְרִיבּוּיָא, דְּסָבַר לַהּ כְּשִׁמְעוֹן הָעַמְסוֹנִי, שֶׁפֵּירֵשׁ כָּל אֶתִים שֶׁבַּתּוֹרָה לְרַבּוֹת, כֵּיוָן שֶׁהִגִּיעַ לְ"אֶת ה' אֱלֹהֶיךָ תִּירָא" אָמַר: מָה אֲרַבֶּה לִירָא עִמּוֹ? — פֵּירֵשׁ מִכּוּלָּן, וְחָזַר בּוֹ מִכָּל רִיבּוּיִין שֶׁדָּרַשׁ. דְּמִדְּהָא לָאו לְרַבּוּיֵי אָתָא — כּוּלְּהוּ נַמִי לָאו לְרַבּוּיֵי אָתוּ: לְרַבּוֹת תַּלְמִידֵי חֲכָמִים. שֶׁיְּהֵא מוֹרָא רַבָּךְ כְּמוֹרָא שָׁמַיִם: וְלֹא יִצְבַּע בּוֹ. כְּגוֹן בִּקְלִיפֵּי אֱגוֹזִים, שֶׁהַשּׁוֹמֵר אָסוּר מִשּׁוּם עָרְלָה כַּפֵּרִי עַצְמוֹ: וְלֹא יַדְלִיק בּוֹ אֶת הַנֵּר. כְּגוֹן בְּשֶׁמֶן שֶׁל עָרְלָה: וְהַשְׁתָּא דִּכְתִיבִי הָנֵי קְרָאֵי. לְאַסְרֵיהּ: לָכֶם. דְּמַשְׁמַע הֶתֵּירָא, לְמַאי אָתָא: לָרַבִּים

תוספות

ואבר מן החי לבני נח. תימה: כיון דבאבר מן החי של גוי איירי, כדאמר בפ"ק דמסכת ע"ג (דף ו:* ושם) מדקתני: לא יושיט, ולא קתני לא יתן, א"כ, היכי דייק דשרי בהנאה אי לאו לפני עור? וי"ל: דכיון דבשכר היה אסור להושיט, דאסור להשתכר באיסורי הנאה, אף על גב דדיעבד שכרו מותר, כדמשמע בפ' בתרא דמס' ע"ז (ד' סב.) — מכל מקום אסור לכתחלה. ובחנם נמי אסור, דמה שמחזיק לו הגוי טובה — חשיב כמשתכר. והא דאמר בסוף "אלו מציאות" (ב"מ לב:) גבי אם היתה טעונה יין נסך — אין זקוק לה. ואי אמרת צער בעלי חיים דאורייתא, אמאי אין זקוק לה? אע"ג דחשיב כמשתכר באיסורי הנאה, ואסור אפילו בחנם. מ"מ כיון דאינו מתכוון שיחזיק לו טובה, ומשום צער בעל חיים — חשיב כמו *לא אפשר ולא מיכוון, דשרי. א"נ: אין זקוק לה משמע ליה אפילו שלא בפני גוי, דאין מחזיק לו טובה:

סלקא דעתך אמינא בשרו אין עורו לא. וא"ת: לישתוק מעורו ומבשרו! ויש לומר: דאיצטריך בשרו, אע"ג דעבדיה כעין בשר. ומאן דלית ליה הא דרשה בפ' "שור שנגח ד' וה'" (ב"ק מא.) — אתא לדרשה אחרינא*:

מנין שלא יצבע. וא"ת: כיון דנפקא לן דאסור בהנאה, אמאי איצטריך לאסור צביעה והדלקה? ואור"י: דס"ד דצביעה לא חשיב הנאה, דלא הוי אלא חזותא בעלמא, כדאמר ב"הגוזל" (שם קא. ושם) אהך מילתא גופא. וכן הדלקה, סלקא דעתך דשריא, כיון דהוי דרך ביעורו. ולמ"ד: *אין שבח עצים בפת, דשרי עצים בהדלקה — הא דאסר קרא הכא היינו בשמן, דהוי בעין כשדולק בנר. אבל עצים — נעשה גחלים, והשלהבת באה מן הגחלים. ואם תאמר: אמאי איצטריך קרא גבי תרומה טמאה להתירה? דדרשי': *"לך" — שלך תהא להסיקה תחת תבשילך. דהכא איצטריך קרא למיסר? ויש לומר: דסלקא דעתך דנילף ממעשר הקל, דאסר ביה הבער', דכתיב: "לא בערתי ממנו" כדאמר בפ' "במה מדליקין" (שבת כה. ושם): ומה מעשר הקל אמרה תורה וכו':

לכם למ"ל לכדתניא. הקשה הר"י מקורבל: אמאי איצטריך ג' ערלים? ליכתוב תרי ערלים לצביעה והדלקה, ועל כרחך אתי' "לכם" לנטוע לרבים. דאי להיתר הדלקה אתא — לא לכתוב לכם, ולא חד מהנך ערלים, ונאסור מ"לא יאכל" הנאה, ומחד ערלים צביעה. ולהדלקה אין קרא לאסור. ואין לומר דמ"לא יאכל" משמע לאסור אפילו צביעה והדלקה, ואי הוה כתיב לא יאכל וחד ערלים — הוה אסרינן מ"לא יאכל" כל הנאה, וערלים לשום דרשה והא דמצרכי' קראי לצביעה והדלקה — היינו משום דכתב "לכם" דלכם משמע להתיר כל הנאה. ולהכי, אי הוה כתיב תרי ערלים ולכם — הוה שרינן הדלקה. אי אפשר לומר כן, דמ"לא יאכל" לא שמעינן צביעה, דהא חזותא בעלמ' הוא, כדאמר ב"הגוזל" (ב"ק קא. ושם): נטוע

עין משפט נר מצוה

יג א סמג לאוין קסח: [ע"ש בתוס' ד"ה מנין]

יד ב מיי' פ"ו מהלכות מאכלות אסורות הל' ג סמג לאוין קלז:

טו ג מיי' פ"ד שם הל' כב סמג לאוין קלה:

טז ד מיי' פ"י שם הל' ט סמג לאוין קמד טוש"ע י"ד סימן רלד סעיף א:

יז ה שם סעיף כה:

מסורת הש"ס

חולין לג. [ג:] לו: לעיל כז. [כ.] · ע"ג ו. · ב"ק מא. קדושין נו: · [לקמן כה:] · [בכ"ג לז:] · [לקמן כו:] · [שבת כה.] · ב"ק מא. קדושין נז. בכורות ו: [ע"ש] · [קדושין נז. נזיר סה: סוטה יז. ב"ק מא: מנחות יא: בכורות ו: נדה לה:] · קדושין נו: ב"ק קא.

רבינו חננאל

ולחזקיה דאמר כל איסור דלא כתיב ביה לא יאכל מותר בהנאה הרי דם דלא כתיב בהו לא יאכל למה לי למתני כמים למשריה הא שרי וקאי ושני' לא אתא למשרי לדם בהנאה דהא פשיטא ולא צריך קרא ולא אתא לאשמעי' אלא האי מנין לדם קדשים שאינו מכשיר שאין אני קורא בו תשפכנו כמים אלא על המזבח: **הרי** אבר מן החי שנא' לא תאכל הנפש עם הבשר ותניא ר' נתן אומר מנין שלא יושיט אדם כוס לנזיר ואבר מן החי לבני נח כו' ולחזקיה למאי הלכתא איתקש לדם אמר לך חזקיה הדם למד מן אבר [מן] החי שנאמר רק חזק לבלתי אכול הדם כי הדם הוא הנפש לא תאכל הנפש עם הבשר מה אבר מן החי אסור אף דם מן החי אסור להאכילו לבני נח ואיזה זה דם הקזה שהנשמה יוצא בו וענוש כרת: **הרי** שור הנסקל דכתיב ולא יאכל את בשרו וטעמא דכתיב ובעל השור נקי לאסרו אפי' בהנאה מכלל דלא יאכל איסור הנאה לא משמע וקשיא לתרוייהו ושנינן לעולם מלא יאכל נפקא ליה אפילו איסורי הנאה והאי ובעל השור נקי מבעי ליה דאסור אפי' להנאת עורו כו' והרי ערלה דכתיב ערלים לא יאכל כו' וקשיא לתרוייהו ושני' לעולם לא יאכל אחד איסור אכילה ואחד איסור הנאה במשמע ואצטריך סלקא דעתך אמינא הואיל וכתב שלש שנים יהיה לכם ערלים לא יאכל הוי אמינא שלכם הוא ומותר בהנאה קמ"ל הני קראי למיסר ואמרי' לכם מבעי ליה לכדתניא לכם להביא

לָרַבִּים. רַבִּי יְהוּדָה אוֹמֵר: לְהוֹצִיא אֶת הַנָּטוּעַ לָרַבִּים. מַאי טַעְמָא דְּתַנָּא קַמָּא – דִּכְתִיב "וּנְטַעְתֶּם" – לַיָּחִיד מַשְׁמַע לָרַבִּים לֹא מַשְׁמַע, כָּתַב רַחֲמָנָא "לָכֶם" – לְהָבִיא אֶת הַנָּטוּעַ לָרַבִּים. וְרַבִּי יְהוּדָה – "וּנְטַעְתֶּם" מַשְׁמַע בֵּין לָרַבִּים בֵּין לְיָחִיד, וְ"לָכֶם" – בֵּין יָחִיד בֵּין רַבִּים מַשְׁמַע, הָוֵי רִבּוּי *אַחַר רִבּוּי, וְאֵין רִבּוּי אַחַר רִבּוּי אֶלָּא לְמַעֵט. וַהֲרֵי תְּרוּמָה, דְּרַחֲמָנָא אָמַר: °"וְכָל זָר לֹא יֹאכַל קֹדֶשׁ" וּתְנַן: *[א]מְעָרְבִין לַנָּזִיר בְּיַיִן וּלְיִשְׂרָאֵל בִּתְרוּמָה! אָמַר רַב פָּפָּא: שָׁאנֵי הָתָם, דְּאָמַר קְרָא °"תְּרוּמַתְכֶם" – שֶׁלָּכֶם תְּהֵא. וְאִידָךְ: °תְּרוּמַתְכֶם דְּכָל יִשְׂרָאֵל קָאָמַר. וַהֲרֵי נָזִיר, דְּרַחֲמָנָא אָמַר: °"מֵחַרְצַנִּים וְעַד זָג לֹא יֹאכֵל", וּתְנַן: מְעָרְבִין לַנָּזִיר בְּיַיִן! אָמַר מָר זוּטְרָא: שָׁאנֵי הָתָם דְּאָמַר קְרָא "נִזְרוֹ" – שֶׁלּוֹ יְהֵא. רַב אַשִׁי אָמַר: °"קָדֹשׁ יִהְיֶה גַּדֵּל פֶּרַע שְׂעַר רֹאשׁוֹ" – *גִּידּוּלוֹ קָדוֹשׁ, וְאֵין דָּבָר אַחֵר קָדוֹשׁ. מִידֵּי "וְאֵין דָּבָר °אַחֵר" כְּתִיב?! אֶלָּא, מְחַוַּורְתָּא כִּדְמָר זוּטְרָא. וַהֲרֵי חָדָשׁ, דְּרַחֲמָנָא אָמַר: °"לֶחֶם וְקָלִי וְכַרְמֶל לֹא תֹאכְלוּ עַד עֶצֶם הַיּוֹם הַזֶּה", וּתְנַן: *[ב]קוֹצֵר לַשַּׁחַת וּמַאֲכִיל לַבְּהֵמָה! אָמַר רַב שְׁמַעְיָה: שָׁאנֵי הָתָם דְּאָמַר קְרָא "קְצִירְכֶם" – קְצִירְכֶם שֶׁלָּכֶם יְהֵא. וְאִידָךְ: "קְצִירְכֶם" דְּכָל יִשְׂרָאֵל מַשְׁמַע. וַהֲרֵי שְׁרָצִים, דְּרַחֲמָנָא אָמַר: °"שֶׁקֶץ הוּא° לֹא יֵאָכֵל", וּתְנַן: *[ג]צַיָּידֵי חַיָּה וְעוֹפוֹת וְדָגִים, שֶׁנִּזְדַּמְּנוּ לָהֶם מִינִין טְמֵאִין – מוּתָּרִין לְמוֹכְרָן לַגּוֹיִם! שָׁאנֵי הָתָם, דְּאָמַר קְרָא "לָכֶם" – שֶׁלָּכֶם יְהֵא. אִי הָכִי, אֲפִי' לְכַתְּחִלָּה נַמִי! שָׁאנֵי הָכָא, דְּאָמַר קְרָא "יִהְיוּ" – בַּהֲוָיָיתָן יְהוּ. וּלְחִזְקִיָּה, לָמָּה לִי לְמִיכְתַּב "לֹא יֵאָכֵל" וּמַיְיתִי "לָכֶם" לְמִישְׁרְיֵיהּ? לָא לִכְתּוֹב רַחֲמָנָא "לֹא יֵאָכֵל" וְלָא בָּעֵי "לָכֶם"! אָמַר °לָךְ חִזְקִיָּה: טַעְמָא דִּידִי נַמִי מֵהָכָא. וַהֲרֵי חָמֵץ, דְּרַחֲמָנָא אָמַר: "לֹא יֵאָכֵל חָמֵץ", וְתַנְיָא, *ר' יוֹסֵי הַגְּלִילִי אוֹמֵר: °תְּמַה עַל עַצְמְךָ, הֵיאַךְ חָמֵץ אָסוּר בַּהֲנָאָה כָּל שִׁבְעָה? שָׁאנֵי הָתָם, דְּאָמַר קְרָא: °"וְלֹא יֵרָאֶה לְךָ שְׂאוֹר" – שֶׁלְּךָ יְהֵא. וְרַבָּנַן: *שֶׁלְּךָ אִי אַתָּה רוֹאֶה, אֲבָל אַתָּה רוֹאֶה שֶׁל אֲחֵרִים וְשֶׁל גָּבוֹהַּ. וְאִידָךְ: תְּרֵי "לְךָ" כְּתִיבִי. וְאִידָךְ: חַד בְּגוֹי שֶׁכִּיבְּשׁוֹ וְחַד בְּגוֹי שֶׁלֹּא כִּיבְּשׁוֹ. וְאִידָךְ: תְּלָתָא לְךָ כְּתִיבִי. וְאִידָךְ: חַד בִּשְׂאוֹר וְחַד בְּחָמֵץ, וּצְרִיכִי. לֵימָא כְּתַנָּאֵי: *°"יֵעָשֶׂה לְכָל מְלָאכָה", מַה ת"ל לְכָל מְלָאכָה? שֶׁיָּכוֹל לִמְלֶאכֶת גָּבוֹהַּ יְהֵא מוּתָּר, לִמְלֶאכֶת הֶדְיוֹט יְהֵא אָסוּר – תַּלְמוּד לוֹמַר: "לְכָל מְלָאכָה", דִּבְרֵי רַבִּי יוֹסֵי הַגְּלִילִי. רַבִּי עֲקִיבָא אוֹמֵר: שֶׁיָּכוֹל לִמְלֶאכֶת הֶדְיוֹט יְהֵא טָהוֹר, לִמְלֶאכֶת גָּבוֹהַּ יְהֵא טָמֵא – תַּלְמוּד לוֹמַר: "לְכָל מְלָאכָה". וְרַבִּי יוֹסֵי הַגְּלִילִי: לְטוּמְאָה וּלְטָהֳרָה לָא אִיצְטְרִיךְ קְרָא, כִּי אִיצְטְרִיךְ קְרָא – לְאִיסּוּר וּלְהֶיתֵּר. וְרַבִּי עֲקִיבָא: אִיסּוּר וְהֶיתֵּר לָא צָרִיךְ קְרָא, כִּי אִיצְטְרִיךְ קְרָא – לְטוּמְאָה וּלְטָהֳרָה. מַאי

רש"י

לָרַבִּים. לְצוֹרֶךְ רַבִּים, כְּגוֹן בְּאֶמְצַע הַדֶּרֶךְ לְכָל עוֹבֵר: וּנְטַעְתֶּם לַיָּחִיד מַשְׁמַע. דְּאֵין דֶּרֶךְ רַבִּים לִנְטוֹעַ, וּלְכָל חַד וְחַד קָאָמַר וּנְטַעְתֶּם: מְעָרְבִין לַנָּזִיר. עֵירוּבֵי תְחוּמִין בְּיַיִן, אע"פ שֶׁסְּעוּדָה שֶׁאֵינָהּ רְאוּיָה לוֹ הִיא, הוֹאִיל וְאִי מִתְשִׁיל אַנְּזִירוּתֵיהּ שַׁרְיָא לֵיהּ – מְעָרְבִין. וְכֵן לְיִשְׂרָאֵל בִּתְרוּמָה, דְּאִי בָּעֵי מִיתְשִׁיל עֲלֵיהּ, דִּתְרוּמַת טָעוּת אֵינָהּ תְּרוּמָה, וְהָדְרָא לְטִיבְלָהּ, וְהָדַר מַפְרִישׁ עֲלָהּ מִינָּהּ וּבָהּ: תְּרוּמַתְכֶם. "וְנֶחְשַׁב לָכֶם תְּרוּמַתְכֶם", וּבִתְרוּמַת מַעֲשֵׂר דְּמַפְרְשִׁי לְוִיִּם כְּתִיב. וּתְרוּמָה גְּדוֹלָה אִיתְקַשׁ בְּהַהוּא קְרָא, כִּדְכְתִיב: "כַּדָּגָן מִן הַגּוֹרֶן" – דְּהַיְינוּ תְּרוּמָה גְּדוֹלָה: וְאִידָךְ. חִזְקִיָּה, דְּאָמַר "לֹא תֹאכְלוּ" לֹא מַשְׁמַע הֲנָאָה, הַאי תְּרוּמַתְכֶם לָאו לְמִישְׁרֵי הֲנָאָה אָתָא, אֶלָּא תְּרוּמַתְכֶם דְּכָל יִשְׂרָאֵל קָאָמַר, וְאוֹרְחֵיהּ דִּקְרָא לְאִישְׁתַּעוּיֵי הָכִי. יִשְׂרָאֵל לָאו דַּוְקָא, דְּהָא בַּלְוִיִּם כְּתִיב: גִּידּוּלוֹ. שֵׂיעָר שֶׁלּוֹ אָסוּר בַּהֲנָאָה, וְטָעוּן שְׂרֵיפָה, כִּדְכְתִיב: "וְנָתַן עַל הָאֵשׁ אֲשֶׁר תַּחַת זֶבַח הַשְּׁלָמִים": מִידֵּי וְאֵין דָּבָר אַחֵר כְּתִיב. דִּילְמָא גִּידּוּלוֹ, וְהוּא הַדִּין לְדָבָר אַחֵר, דְּמַאי מִיעוּט כָּתַב הָכָא? חָדָשׁ. לִפְנֵי הָעוֹמֶר: קוֹצֵר לַשַּׁחַת. אע"ג דִּכְתִיב: "עוֹמֶר רֵאשִׁית קְצִירְכֶם אֶל הַכֹּהֵן", דְּמַשְׁמַע דְּאָסוּר לִקְצוֹר לִפְנֵי הָעוֹמֶר – מוּתָּר לִקְצוֹר לַשַּׁחַת כְּשֶׁהוּא עֵשֶׂב, דְּלָאו קָצִיר הוּא: וּמַאֲכִיל לַבְּהֵמָה. אַף חִיטִּין גְּמוּרִין עַל יְדֵי קִיטּוּף, מִכָּל מָקוֹם חָדָשׁ מוּתָּר בַּהֲנָאָה: וְאִידָךְ. חִזְקִיָּה, דְּלָא נָפְקָא לֵיהּ הֲנָאָה מִ"לֹּא תֹאכְלוּ", וְלָא אִיצְטְרִיךְ קְצִירְכֶם לְמִישְׁרֵי, אָמַר לָךְ: קְצִירְכֶם דְּכָל יִשְׂרָאֵל קָאָמַר, וְאוֹרְחֵיהּ דִּקְרָא לְאִישְׁתַּעוּיֵי הָכִי: שֶׁנִּזְדַּמְּנוּ. דַּוְקָא שֶׁנִּזְדַּמְּנוּ, דְּלָא מַצְרְכִינַן לְהוּ לְהַפְקִירָן, אֲבָל לְכַתְּחִלָּה – אָסוּר לַחֲזוֹר אַחֲרֵיהֶן, כִּדְתְנַן הָתָם בְּמַסֶּ' שְׁבִיעִית (פ"ז מ"ג): אֵין עוֹשִׂין סְחוֹרָה לֹא בִּנְבֵילוֹת וּטְרֵיפוֹת, וְלֹא בִּשְׁקָצִים וּרְמָשִׂים: יִהְיוּ. "וְשֶׁקֶץ יִהְיוּ לָכֶם": וּלְחִזְקִיָּה לָמָּה לִי לְמִכְתַּב לֹא יֵאָכֵל וּמַיְיתִי לָכֶם לְמִישְׁרְיֵיהּ. בִּשְׁלָמָא לְרַבִּי אַבָּהוּ – לָא מָצֵינוּ לְאַקְשׁוּיֵי בְּכָל הָנָךְ דִּכְתִיב בְּהוּ "לֹא תֹאכַל", וַהֲדַר כְּתִיב בּוֹ הֶיתֵּר הֲנָאָה – דְּאִיצְטְרִיךְ "לֹא תֹאכְלוּ" לַאֲכִילָה, וְאִיצְטְרִיךְ הֶיתֵּירָא לַהֲנָאָה. אֶלָּא לְחִזְקִיָּה, כֵּיוָן דְּסוֹף סוֹף שָׁרֵי לֵיהּ רַחֲמָנָא בַּהֲנָאָה – לָמָּה לִי קְרָא דְּשָׁנֵי בְּדִיבּוּרָא, וְכָתַב "לֹא יֵאָכֵל" דְּמַשְׁמַע הֲנָאָה, וְאִיצְטְרִיךְ "לָכֶם" לְמִישְׁרְיֵיהּ בַּהֲנָאָה? לִיכְתּוֹב "לֹא תֹאכַל", וְתוּ לָא אִיצְטְרִיךְ לָכֶם: טַעְמָא דִּידִי. דְּאָמִינָא "לֹא יֵאָכֵל" מַשְׁמַע הֲנָאָה – מֵהָא נָפְקָא לִי (א). וְאִי לָאו הַאי קְרָא דִּכְתִיב "לֹא יֵאָכֵל" וְתוּ כָּתַב לָכֶם לְמִישְׁרְיֵיהּ – לָא הֲוָה יָדַעְנָא דְּלֹא יֵאָכֵל אִיסּוּר הֲנָאָה הוּא. וְכָל הָנָךְ קְרָאֵי דְּהֶיתֵּר הֲנָאָה, דִּכְתִיבִי גַּבֵּי "לֹא תֹאכַל" – הָא דָּרְשִׁינְהוּ חִזְקִיָּה לְמִילְּתָא אַחֲרִינָא, כִּדְאָמְרַן לְעֵיל: תְּרוּמַתְכֶם, קְצִירְכֶם, דְּכָל יִשְׂרָאֵל: תְּמַה עַל עַצְמְךָ הֵיאַךְ נֶאֱסַר חָמֵץ בַּהֲנָאָה. דְּס"ל: מוּתָּר בַּהֲנָאָה כָּל שִׁבְעָה, וְכ"ש לְאַחַר הַפֶּסַח. וּפְלִיגָא דְּרַבִּי יְהוּדָה דְּאָמַר: חָמֵץ שֶׁעָבַר עָלָיו הַפֶּסַח – אָסוּר בַּהֲנָאָה, לְקַמָּן בְּפִירְקִין (דף כח:): תְּלָתָא לְךָ כְּתִיבִי. "לֹא יֵרָאֶה לְךָ חָמֵץ", "וְלֹא יֵרָאֶה לְךָ שְׂאוֹר בְּכָל גְּבוּלֶךָ", וְעוֹד קְרָא אַחֲרִינָא: "וְלֹא יֵרָאֶה לְךָ שְׂאוֹר בְּכָל גְּבוּלְךָ שִׁבְעַת יָמִים": וּצְרִיכִי. דְּאִי כָּתַב שְׂאוֹר – מִשּׁוּם דְּחִימּוּצוֹ קָשֶׁה, אֲבָל חָמֵץ – אֵימָא מוּתָּר. וְאִי כָּתַב חָמֵץ – מִשּׁוּם דְּרָאוּי לַאֲכִילָה, אֲבָל שְׂאוֹר דְּלָא חֲזֵי לְמֵיכְלֵיהּ – אֵימָא לֹא עָבַר עָלֵיהּ. הָכִי מְפָרֵשׁ לְהוּ בְּפ"ק דְּבֵיצָה (דף ז:): לֵימָא כְּתַנָּאֵי. "לֹא תֹאכַל" דְּרַבִּי אַבָּהוּ: יֵעָשֶׂה לִמְלָאכָה. הֲוָה מָצֵי לְמִיכְתַּב גַּבֵּי חֵלֶב דִּנְבֵילָה: שֶׁיָּכוֹל. אִי לָא הֲוָה כָּתַב "לְכָל", הֲוָה אָמֵינָא: לִמְלֶאכֶת גָּבוֹהַּ יְהֵא מוּתָּר, אִם צָרִיךְ לִמְשׁוֹחַ מִמֶּנּוּ עוֹרוֹת לִמְלֶאכֶת בֶּדֶק הַבַּיִת – יְהֵא מוּתָּר, דְּהָא מִשְׁתְּרֵי חֵלֶב בַּאֲכִילָה לְגַבֵּי גָּבוֹהַּ לַמִּזְבֵּחַ. אֲבָל לִמְלֶאכֶת הֶדְיוֹט יְהֵא אָסוּר, שֶׁהֲרֵי נֶאֱמַר בּוֹ "לֹא תֹאכְלוּ", וְאִיסּוּר הֲנָאָה בְּמַשְׁמַע, ת"ל לְכָל מְלָאכָה: רַבִּי עֲקִיבָא אוֹמֵר כו'. כְּלוֹמַר, לֹא הוּצְרַךְ הַכָּתוּב לְהַתִּיר, דְּלָא הֲוָה ס"ד לְאִיסּוּר, וְלֹא בָּא אֶלָּא לְטַהֲרוֹ מִכְּלַל טוּמְאַת הַבָּשָׂר, וְלוֹמַר שֶׁאֵין חֵלֶב בִּכְלַל נְבֵילָה, וְאֵינוֹ חוֹשֵׁשׁ לְטוּמְאָה, אֶלָּא מוּתָּר לְיִשְׁתַּמֵּשׁ טָהֳרוֹת בְּעוֹר הַמָּשׁוּחַ בְּחֵלֶב נְבֵילָה. וְאִם לֹא רִיבָּה לְכָל מְלָאכָה, הָיִיתִי אוֹמֵר לִמְלֶאכֶת הֶדְיוֹט לְהִשְׁתַּמֵּשׁ בּוֹ חוּלִּין יְהֵא טָהוֹר, אֲבָל לִמְלֶאכֶת גָּבוֹהַּ לְהִשְׁתַּמֵּשׁ קָדָשִׁים יְהֵא טָמֵא: חֶלְבָּהּ

תוספות

נטוע לרבים. ברה"ר לצורך רבים, ולא כמו שפ"ה באמצע הדרך. דקתני במסכת ערלה (פ"א מ"ב): הנוטע לרבים חייב, ורבי יהודה פוטר. והדר קתני: הנוטע ברה"ר, והגוי שנטע, והגזלן כו'. מדקתני בתרי בבי – ש"מ תרי מילי נינהו:

מערבין לנזיר ביין. בפ' "בכל מערבין" (עירובין כח.) מפרש טעמא: משום דאע"ג דלא חזי להאי – חזי להאי. ולא פריך הכא אליבא דמ"ד (שם דף לא.) אין מערבין אלא לדבר מצוה, ומצות לאו ליהנות ניתנו:

נזרו שלו יהא. תימה לחזקיה "נזרו" למאי אתא? ואית ספרים דגרסינן: על נזרו מגלח, ואינו מגלח על נזירות אביו:

קוצר לשחת ומאכיל לבהמה. אף על גב דהא דקוצר לשחת – היינו דווקא לבהמה, כדמוכח במנחות, בפ' "רבי ישמעאל" (ד' עא:) – מ"מ "ומאכיל לבהמה" לא משמע ליה דקאי אקוצר לשחת, דא"כ לא פריך מידי, דחדש שאסר הכתוב היינו תבואה גמורה. אלא מאכיל לבהמה – היינו אפילו חיטין גמורין, ועל ידי קיטוף, כפ"ה. ועוד: דקתני סיפא רבי שמעון אומר יקצור ויאכל אף משהביא שליש*:

קצירכם שלכם יהא. תימה לרשב"א: מנ"ל דאתא להכי? הא איצטריך לכדדרשינן במנחות בפרק "ר' ישמעאל" (דף עב. ושם): קצירכם – ולא קציר מצוה, וחזקיה נמי לישני הכי: וי"ל: מדלא כתב ראשית קציר, והוי מצי למיכתב קצירך, וכתב קצירכם – שמע מינה תרתי:

אמר קרא יהיו בהוייתן יהו. וא"ת: א"כ סוסים וחמורים היכי זבנינן? וי"ל: דבמידי דאכילה מיירי דווקא. ובירושלמי דמסכת שביעית ספ"ח פריך: והרי חמור וגמל! ומשני: למלאכתן הן גדילים. וא"ת: דאמרי' ב"מרובה" (ב"ק פב: שם) אסור לישראל לגדל חזירים, תיפוק ליה דמדאורייתא אסור! וי"ל: דנפקא מינה למיקם בלאו, אי נמי: הא דאסור מדאורייתא – הינו להשתכר ולמכור לגוי לאכול, אבל להשתכר בשומנן או בעורן – לא. או שמגדל שלא למכור אלא למשוח ולהדליק, אפילו הכי בחזירים אסור. א"נ: בנזדמנו לו, כגון שנפלו בירושה, אין לגדלן:

שאני התם דאמר קרא לא יראה לך. תימה: דליכתב לא יאכל לחזקיה, ולא בעי לך: ומה

[שם כב: [גרסינן] לק' כח. מ"ד ליתא]

עין משפט נר מצוה

יח א מיי' פ"א מהלכות עירובין הל' יז סמג עשין דרבנן א טוש"ע או"ח סי' שפו סעיף ח:

יט ב מיי' פ"ל מהלכות תמידין הלכה טו:

כ ג מיי' פ"ח מהלכות מאכלות אסורות הל' יז סמג לאוין קלב טוש"ע י"ד סימן קיז:

מסורת הש"ס

[ב"ק מה:] | עירובין כו: [כח.] | קדושין נז: | מנחות עח. | שביעית [פ"ז מ"ד] | [לקמן כח: לב.] | [לעיל ה: וש"נ] | [עי' תוס' לעיל כב. ד"ה ור' שמעון]

תורה אור

ויקרא כב | במדבר יח | שם ו | שם | ויקרא כג | שם יא | שמות יג | ויקרא ז

רבינו חננאל

הנטוע לרבים שחייב בערלה ר' יהודה אומר לכם פרט לנטוע לרבים: **והרי** תרומה דכתיב וכל זר לא יאכל קדש ותנן מערבין לנזיר ביין ושנינן שאני התם דכתי' תרומתכם שלכם תהא: **והרי** נזיר דכתיב מחרצנים ועד זג לא יאכל ותנן מערבין לנזיר ביין ושנינן שאני התם דכתיב נזרו נזרו שלו יהא כו': **והרי** חדש דכתיב ולחם וקלי וכרמל לא תאכלו ותנן קוצר לשחת ומאכיל לבהמה (נהנה בזמן אכילתו ומותר בהנאתו) [ואף שנהנה באכילתה אלמא דמותר בהנאה] ושנינן שאני התם דכתיב קצירכם [שלכם] יהא להתיר בהנאה: **והרי** שרצים דכתיב בהו וכל השרץ השורץ על הארץ לא יאכל ותנן בשביעי' פ"ז ציידי חיה עופות ודגים (שנתמנו) [שנזדמנו] להם מינין טמאין מותר למכרן וקשיא לתרוייהו ושני' שאני התם דכתי' לכם להתיר בהנאה אי הכי אפי' לכתחלה אמאי תאני שנתמנה דאיעבד אפי' לכתחלה יהיו מותרין לצורך ודחי' אמר קרא שקץ הוא בהוייתו יהא ואקשי' לחזקיה למה לי למכתב בשרצים לא יאכל דמשמע אפילו איסור הנאה והוצרך לכתוב לכם להתיר בהנאה היה כותב ולא יאכל ולא יכתוב לכם להתיר ואנא ידענא דכל היכא דכתי' לא יאכל מותר בהנאה ואמר חזקיה אדרבה טעמא דידי מהכא מדאצטריך קרא למכתב לכם להתירו בהנאה ש"מ דכל היכא דכתיב לא יאכל אחד איסור אכילה ואחד איסור הנאה במשמע: **והרי** חמץ דכתיב לא יאכל ואמר ר' יוסי הגלילי תמה על עצמך היאך חמץ אסור בהנאה כל שבעה ודחי' שאני התם דכתיב לך שלך יהא כו': **נימא** כתנאי וחלב נבלה וחלב טרפה יעשה לכל מלאכה [מה ת"ל לכל מלאכה] ר' יוסי הגלילי אומר בין למלאכת גבוה בין למלאכת הדיוט מותר שנאמר לכל מלאכה ר' עקיבא אומר שיכול למלאכת הדיוט הוא טהור למלאכת גבוה יהא טמא ת"ל לכל מלאכה יהא טהור אם לגבוה הוא [טהור]* קל וחומר להדיוט דיקי' מדדרש ר' עקיבא לקרא בטומאה וטהרה מכלל דפשיטא ליה דמותר

הגהות הב"ח

(א) רש"י ד"ה טעמא דידי וכו' דאי לאו:

גליון הש"ס

גמ' תמה על עצמך היאך חמץ. היינו היאך אתה אומר חמץ אסור בהנאה וכן תמה על עצמך היאך תוספת בנדה סח ע"א תוס' שם ד"ה כך אמרו בסד"ה: **תוס'** ד"ה נזרו. ואינו מגלח על נזירות אביו. ק"ל הא לר"י ור"מ דס"ל בספ"ד דנזיר דבכל ענין מגלח על נזירות אביו א"כ יהא מוכח מדאיצטריך נזרו דלא יאכל איסור הנאה במשמע וא"כ איך אמרי' דא"כ חולין שנשחטו בעזרה לר"י וצ"ע:

* [נראה דחסר כאן איזה תיבות ואולי דקאי על הא דאמרינן ור"י הגלילי לטומאה ולטהרה לא איצטריך קרא וד"ק].

מַאי לָאו בְּהָא קָמִיפַּלְגִי, דְּר' יוֹסֵי הַגְּלִילִי סָבַר: "לֹא תֹאכְלוּ" מַשְׁמַע בֵּין אִיסּוּר אֲכִילָה בֵּין אִיסּוּר הֲנָאָה, וְכִי אֲתָא קְרָא — לְמִישְׁרְיֵיהּ לִנְבֵילָה בַּהֲנָאָה הוּא דַּאֲתָא. וְרַבִּי עֲקִיבָא סָבַר: אִיסּוּר אֲכִילָה — מַשְׁמַע, אִיסּוּר הֲנָאָה לֹא מַשְׁמַע. וְכִי אֲתָא קְרָא — לְטוּמְאָה וְטָהֳרָה! לֹא, דְּכ"ע "לֹא תֹאכְלוּ" — מַשְׁמַע בֵּין אִיסּוּר אֲכִילָה בֵּין אִיסּוּר הֲנָאָה. וְהָכָא בְּהָא קָמִיפַּלְגִי; רַבִּי יוֹסֵי הַגְּלִילִי סָבַר: כְּשֶׁהוּתְּרָה נְבֵילָה — הִיא הוּתְּרָה, חֶלְבָּהּ וְגִידָהּ — לֹא הוּתְּרוּ. וְכִי אִיצְטְרִיךְ קְרָא — לְהֶיתֵּר הֲנָאָה הוּא דַּאֲתָא. וְרַבִּי עֲקִיבָא סָבַר: *כְּשֶׁהוּתְּרָה נְבֵילָה — חֶלְבָּהּ וְגִידָהּ נַמִי הוּתְּרוּ, וְכִי אִיצְטְרִיךְ קְרָא — לְטוּמְאָה וְטָהֳרָה. וְר' יוֹסֵי הַגְּלִילִי, אַשְׁכַּחַן חֵלֶב דְּשָׁרְיֵיהּ רַחֲמָנָא בַּהֲנָאָה, °אֶלָּא גִּיד נֵימָא דְּאָסוּר! אִיבָּעֵית אֵימָא: הָכִי נַמִי דְּאָסוּר, אִיבָּעֵית אֵימָא: מַיְיתִי לָהּ בְּק"ו; וּמַה חֵלֶב שֶׁעָנוּשׁ כָּרֵת — מוּתָּר בַּהֲנָאָה, גִּיד שֶׁאֵינוֹ עָנוּשׁ כָּרֵת — לֹא כָּל שֶׁכֵּן?! וְר"ש דְּאָסַר; אִיכָּא לְמִיפְרַךְ: *מָה לְחֵלֶב שֶׁכֵּן הוּתַּר מִכְּלָלוֹ אֵצֶל חַיָּה, תֹּאמַר בְּגִיד שֶׁלֹּא הוּתַּר מִכְּלָלוֹ אֵצֶל חַיָּה. וְאִידָךְ: בִּבְהֵמָה קָאָמְרִינַן, בִּבְהֵמָה מִיהַת לָא אִישְׁתְּרִי. מִכְּדֵי אוֹתְבִינְהוּ כָּל הָנֵי קְרָאֵי וְשָׁנִינְהוּ, חִזְקִיָּה וְרַבִּי אַבָּהוּ בְּמַאי פְּלִיגִי? בְּחָמֵץ בַּפֶּסַח וְאַלִּיבָּא דְּרַבָּנַן, בְּשׁוֹר הַנִּסְקָל וְאַלִּיבָּא דְּדִבְרֵי הַכֹּל. חִזְקִיָּה נָפֵיק לֵיהּ מִ"לֹּא יֵאָכֵל", וְרַבִּי אַבָּהוּ נָפֵיק לֵיהּ מִנְּבֵילָה. מִכְּדִי, בֵּין לְמָר וּבֵין לְמָר אֲסוּרִין בַּהֲנָאָה — מַאי בֵּינַיְיהוּ? אִיכָּא בֵּינַיְיהוּ: חוּלִּין שֶׁנִּשְׁחֲטוּ בָּעֲזָרָה. חִזְקִיָּה סָבַר "לֹא יֵאָכֵל" — לְמַעוּטֵי הָנֵי, "אֹתוֹ" — לְמַעוּטֵי חוּלִּין שֶׁנִּשְׁחֲטוּ בָּעֲזָרָה. רַבִּי אַבָּהוּ סָבַר: "אֹתוֹ" — לְמַעוּטֵי הָנֵי, *חוּלִּין שֶׁנִּשְׁחֲטוּ בָּעֲזָרָה — לָאו דְּאוֹרַיְיתָא נִינְהוּ. יְתֵיב הַהוּא מֵרַבָּנַן קַמֵּיהּ דְּרַבִּי שְׁמוּאֵל בַּר נַחְמָנִי, וְיָתֵיב וְקָאָמַר מִשְּׁמֵיהּ דְּר' יְהוֹשֻׁעַ בֶּן לֵוִי: מִנַּיִן לְכָל אִיסּוּרִין שֶׁבַּתּוֹרָה דְּכִי הֵיכִי דַּאֲסוּרִין בַּאֲכִילָה הָכִי נַמִי אֲסוּרִין בַּהֲנָאָה, וּמַאי נִיהוּ — חָמֵץ בַּפֶּסַח וְשׁוֹר הַנִּסְקָל. "מִנַּיִן"?! תֵּיפּוֹק לֵיהּ מִ"לֹּא יֵאָכֵל"! "לֹא יֵאָכֵל" — אִיסּוּר אֲכִילָה מַשְׁמַע לֵיהּ, אִיסּוּר הֲנָאָה — לֹא מַשְׁמַע לֵיהּ. תֵּיפּוֹק לֵיהּ מִנְּבֵילָה! סָבַר לָהּ כְּר' יְהוּדָה, דְּאָמַר: *דְּבָרִים כִּכְתָבָן. אִי סָבַר לָהּ כְּר' יְהוּדָה — תֵּיפּוֹק לֵיהּ מֵהֵיכָא דְּנָפְקָא לֵיהּ לְר' יְהוּדָה °מִ"לַּכֶּלֶב תַּשְׁלִיכוּן אֹתוֹ"! קָסָבַר: חוּלִּין שֶׁנִּשְׁחֲטוּ בָּעֲזָרָה דְּאוֹרַיְיתָא, מִנַּיִן? דִּכְתִיב: °"כָּל חַטָּאת אֲשֶׁר יוּבָא מִדָּמָהּ וגו'". שֶׁאֵין ת"ל "בָּאֵשׁ תִּשָּׂרֵף" וּמַה ת"ל בָּאֵשׁ תִּשָּׂרֵף? אִם אֵינוֹ עִנְיָן לְגוּפוֹ, דִּכְתִיב °"וְהִנֵּה שֹׂרָף" — תְּנֵהוּ עִנְיָן לְכָל אִיסּוּרִין שֶׁבַּתּוֹרָה. וְאִם

(שמות כב; ויקרא ו; ויקרא י)

רש"י

חֶלְבָּהּ וְגִידָהּ לֹא הוּתְּרוּ. דְּחֵלֶב אֵינוֹ בִּכְלַל בָּשָׂר, הִלְכָּךְ לֹא הֲוָה בְּמַשְׁמַע תִּתְּנֶנָּה וַאֲכָלָהּ. וְגַבֵּי נוֹגֵעַ בְּנִבְלָתָהּ נַמִי לָאו חֵלֶב בְּמַשְׁמַע, הִלְכָּךְ "יֵעָשֶׂה לְכָל מְלָאכָה" — לֹא הוּצְרַךְ לְטַהֲרוֹ, אֶלָּא לְהַתִּירוֹ מִכְּלַל הֲנָאוֹת לֹא תֹאכַל חֵלֶב: וְרַבִּי עֲקִיבָא סָבַר. חֵלֶב בִּכְלַל נְבֵילָה, בֵּין לְהֶיתֵּר הֲנָאָה בֵּין לְטַמֵּא. הִלְכָּךְ, כִּי אִיצְטְרִיךְ קְרָא — לְטַהֲרוֹ אִיצְטְרִיךְ: וְרַבִּי שִׁמְעוֹן. דְּאָמַר לְעֵיל: גִּיד אָסוּר בַּהֲנָאָה, מִשּׁוּם דִּסְבִירָא לֵיהּ אֵין בַּגִּידִין בְּנוֹתֵן טַעַם, וְלֹא הוּתַּר בִּכְלַל נְבֵילָה, מַאי טַעְמָא לָא מַיְיתֵי לֵיהּ כְּרַבִּי יוֹסֵי לְהַתִּיר הֲנָאָה מִקַּל וָחוֹמֶר מֵחֵלֶב? מִכְּלָלוֹ. אַף בַּאֲכִילָה: וְאִידָךְ. רַבִּי יוֹסֵי אָמַר לָךְ: אֲנָא בְּחֵלֶב בְּהֵמָה קָא מַיְיתֵינָא קְרָא לְהַתִּיר בַּהֲנָאָה, דִּקְרָא בְּחֵלֶב שׁוֹר וָכֶשֶׂב קָאֵי, וְקָא שָׁרֵי לֵיהּ בַּהֲנָאָה. וּבִבְהֵמָה לֹא הוּתַּר מִכְּלָלוֹ בַּאֲכִילָה, הִלְכָּךְ אָתֵי גִּיד הַנָּשֶׁה מִינֵּיהּ: מִכְּדֵי אוֹתְבִינְהוּ כָּל הָנָךְ קְרָאֵי. דְּכָל אִיסּוּרִין שֶׁנֶּאֱמַ' בָּהֶן לֹא תֹאכַל וּמוּתָּרִין בַּהֲנָאָה: וְשָׁנִינְהוּ. רַבִּי אַבָּהוּ, וְאַשְׁכַּח בְּהוּ פְּרָטָא לְהֶיתֵּר. לֹא מָצִינוּ בְּאֶחָד מִכּוּלָּם שֶׁהֶחְמִיר בּוֹ רַבִּי אַבָּהוּ וְיֹאמַר שֶׁאָסוּר בַּהֲנָאָה, וּלְחִזְקִיָּה לִישְׁתְּרוּ. אֶלָּא דָּבָר הָאָסוּר — אָסוּר לְדִבְרֵי שְׁנֵיהֶן, וְהַמּוּתָּר — מוּתָּר לְדִבְרֵי שְׁנֵיהֶן: בְּמַאי פְּלִיגִי. דְּאֵין לָךְ אִיסּוּרֵי הֲנָאָה בְּדָבָר שֶׁנֶּאֱמַר בּוֹ לָאו בַּאֲכִילָתוֹ, שֶׁלֹּא נֶאֱמַר בּוֹ פְּרָט לְהַתִּיר, אֶלָּא הָנָךְ שְׁנֵי דְּבָרִים דִּכְתִיב בָּהֵן "לֹא יֵאָכֵל", כְּגוֹן שׁוֹר הַנִּסְקָל וְחָמֵץ בַּפֶּסַח, וּבֵין לְמָר וּבֵין לְמָר אֲסוּרִין: וְאַלִּיבָּא דְּרַבָּנַן. דִּפְלִיגִי עֲלֵיהּ דְּרַבִּי יוֹסֵי דְּאָמַר לְעֵיל: חָמֵץ בַּפֶּסַח מוּתָּר בַּהֲנָאָה: מִנְּבֵילָה. מִדְּאִיצְטְרִיךְ קְרָא לְמִישְׁרֵי נְבֵילָה, וְאִי הֲוָה כְּתִיב "לֹא תֹאכַל" נַמִי הֲוָה מִיתַּסְרִי: אִיכָּא בֵּינַיְיהוּ חוּלִּין שֶׁנִּשְׁחֲטוּ בָּעֲזָרָה. וְאַלִּיבָּא דְּר' יְהוּדָה, דְּאָמַר: מִנְּבֵילָה לָא מָצֵי לְמִיגְמַר, דִּלְדְבָרִים כִּכְתָבָן אָתָא. דְּחִזְקִיָּה סָבַר: הָנֵי תְּרֵי מִדְּשַׁנֵּי בְּדִיבּוּרֵיהּ — אִיתְּסַר. וְ"לַכֶּלֶב תַּשְׁלִיכוּן אֹתוֹ" לֹא הוּצְרַךְ לְמַעֵט אֶת אֵלּוּ וּלְאוֹסְרָן בַּהֲנָאָה, וְכִי אָתָא לְמַעוּטֵי — חוּלִּין שֶׁנִּשְׁחֲטוּ בָּעֲזָרָה אָתָא, וּכְדְפָרֵישִׁית לְעֵיל. וְר' אַבָּהוּ סָבַר: אֵין חִילּוּק בֵּין לֹא יֵאָכֵל בֵּין לֹא יֹאכַל, וְאִצְטְרִיךְ "אוֹתוֹ" לְמַעוּטֵי הָנֵי. וְהָכִי מַשְׁמַע: טְרֵיפָה, אַף עַל גַּב שֶׁכָּתַבְתִּי לָךְ לָאו בַּאֲכִילָתָהּ — אֲנִי מַתִּיר לָךְ הֲנָאָתָהּ, אֲבָל לֹא חָמֵץ וְשׁוֹר הַנִּסְקָל, שֶׁלֹּא פֵּרַטְתִּי לְךָ בָּהֵן הֶיתֵּר: חוּלִּין בָּעֲזָרָה לָאו דְּאוֹרַיְיתָא. וְכִי אָמַר רַבִּי אַבָּהוּ לֹא יֵאָכֵל אִיסּוּר הֲנָאָה מַשְׁמַע — אַלִּיבָּא דְּרַבִּי מֵאִיר אֲמָרָהּ, דְּלֵית לֵיהּ לִדְבָרִים כִּכְתָבָן. וּמִדְּאִיצְטְרִיךְ לְמִישְׁרֵי נְבֵילָה — מִכְּלָל דִּשְׁאָר אִיסּוּרִין, כְּגוֹן חָמֵץ וְשׁוֹר הַנִּסְקָל, אֲסִירֵי. וְלָאו מִשּׁוּם שִׁינּוּי הַלָּשׁוֹן, שֶׁאֵין חִילּוּק בֵּין לֹא יֹאכַל לְלֹא יֵאָכֵל לְרַבִּי אַבָּהוּ, אֶלָּא מִדְּאִיצְטְרִיךְ לְמִישְׁרֵי נְבֵילָה וְ"אוֹתוֹ" לְר"מ — לְמַעוּטֵי חוּלִּין בָּעֲזָרָה: ה"ג: וּמַאי נִינְהוּ חָמֵץ בַּפֶּסַח וְשׁוֹר הַנִּסְקָל: וְתֵיפּוֹק לֵיהּ מֵהֵיכָא דְּנָפְקָא לֵיהּ לְרַבִּי יְהוּדָה. לְעֵיל, אַלִּיבָּא דְּרַבִּי אַבָּהוּ, דְּמַיְיתֵי לֵיהּ מֵ"אוֹתוֹ" אַתָּה מַשְׁלִיךְ לַכֶּלֶב, וְאִי אַתָּה מַשְׁלִיךְ שְׁאָר אִיסּוּרִין: קָא סָבַר. הַאי תַּנָּא: חוּלִּין שֶׁנִּשְׁחֲטוּ בָּעֲזָרָה. אֲסוּרִין בַּהֲנָאָה מִדְּאוֹרַיְיתָא, וְנָפְקָא לֵיהּ מֵ"אוֹתוֹ", וּמִיבָּעֵי לֵיהּ קְרָא אַחֲרִינָא לִשְׁאָר אִיסּוּרִין: כָּל חַטָּאת אֲשֶׁר יוּבָא מִדָּמָהּ. לָאו בְּחַטָּאוֹת הַפְּנִימִיּוֹת שֶׁהוּבָא דָּמָן כְּמִצְוָתָן לִפְנִים כְּתִיב, דְּהָא בְּהֶדְיָא כְּתִיב בָּהֶן בְּפַר כֹּהֵן מָשִׁיחַ וְהֶעְלֵם דָּבָר שְׂרֵיפָתָן מִחוּץ לַמַּחֲנֶה, אֶלָּא לְלַמֵּד עַל חַטָּאת הַחִיצוֹנָה, דְּאִם הִכְנִיס דָּמָהּ לִפְנִים — פְּסוּלָה: אִם אֵינוֹ עִנְיָן לְגוּפוֹ דְּהָא כְּתִיב וְהִנֵּה שׂוֹרָף. בִּשְׂעִיר נַחְשׁוֹן, בְּ"וַיְהִי בַּיּוֹם הַשְּׁמִינִי", וְקָאָמַר לְהוּ מֹשֶׁה: לָמָּה שְׂרַפְתֶּם אוֹתוֹ, הֵן לֹא הוּבָא אֶת דָּמָהּ אֶל הַקֹּדֶשׁ פְּנִימָה. מִכְּלָל, דְּאִם הוּבָא — שַׁפִּיר עֲבֵיד דִּשְׂרָפוּהָ, אַלְמָא בַּת שְׂרֵיפָה הִיא: לְכָל אִיסּוּרִין. שֶׁנֶּאֱמַר בָּהֶן לָאו בַּאֲכִילָתָן כָּזֶה, וְעַל כָּרְחָךְ לֹא מַיְיתֵי אֶלָּא חָמֵץ בַּפֶּסַח וְשׁוֹר הַנִּסְקָל, דִּבִשְׁאָר אִיסּוּרִים כְּתִיב פְּרָטָא לְהֶיתֵּירָא:

תוספות

ומה חלב שענוש כרת מותר בהנאה. וא"ת: לימא, שור הנסקל ושאר איסורי הנאה יוכיחו, שאינן בכרת, ואפ"ה אסורין בהנאה! וי"ל: דה"פ: ומה חלב(א) שענוש כרת ואסור באכילה, ומותר בהנאה כמו נבילה עצמה. גיד, שאין ענוש כרת — לכ"ש שיהא בכלל היתר נבילה. והשתא לא שייך למימר תוכיח, ולא מצי למיעבד נמי ק"ו מדם — דדם אינו בכלל נבילה, ואפילו טומאה אין בו מטעם נבילה, כדפרישי' לעיל (דף כב.). אבל חלב הוה שפיר בכלל נבילה, דלטומאה לא הוה צריך קרא, דאדרבה לטהרו מידי נבילה מצריך קרא. והא דקאמר: היא הותרה וחלבה לא הותרה — לאו משום דלא הוי בכלל נבילה, אלא משום דלא הותרה בנבילה אלא מה שהותר בטהורה באכילה. והשתא א"ש הא דקאמר ואידך — אנן בבהמה קיימינן, דלא ילפינן אלא שיהא בכלל היתר נבילה — אבל בעלמא מודה דפריך שפיר*: **בבהמה** מיהא לא אישתרי. אין להקשות דגיד חיה מיהא ליתסר. דכיון דשל בהמה לא מיתסר בהנאה, אם כן "לא יאכל" דכתיב גבי גיד הנשה — באכילה דוקא קאמר, ומהיכא תיתי לן לאסור של חיה בהנאה? **מאי** בינייהו. תימה לרשב"א: לימא דאיכא בינייהו חמץ נוקשה, וחמץ דגן גמור ע"י תערובות, דמרבינן בריש "אלו עוברין" (לקמן מג.) מ"כל מחמצת לא תאכלו". דלחזקיה מותר בהנאה ולרבי אבהו כל מקום שנאמר לא תאכלו משמע איסור הנאה? וכי תימא כיון דמרבינן ליה לאכילה ה"ה להנאה, אם כן כרת נמי ליחייב: **דכתיב** והנה שורף. פרש"י בשעיר נחשון ובת"כ דריש בהדיא אשעיר דראש חודש, מדכתיב: "ואותה נתן לכם" וגו'. והיינו של ר"ח, דמכפר עון (ב) על טומאת מקדש וקדשיו*): **דהא** כתיב והנה שורף. פרש"י: ואמר להו משה "הן לא הובא את דמה אל הקדש פנימה". מכלל דאם הובא — שפיר עבוד דשרפוה. הקשה הרב רבינו שלמה מטרויש: הא על כרחין לאו שפיר עבוד דשרפוה דהא שרפוה בלא עיבור צורה, ואמר בפרק "כיצד צולין" (לקמן פב:): כל שפסולו בגופו — ישרף מיד, בדם ובבעלים — תעובר צורתו ויצא לשריפה, וקרא ה"ק: מדוע לא אכלתם את החטאת, הן לא הובא את דמה. הא אם הובא — שפיר עבוד דלא אכלוה. ואומר ר"י דה"פ: אם אינו ענין לגופה, דהא קיי"ל בפרק "כיצד צולין" (גם זה שם): כל שפסולו בקדש — בשריפה. וחטאת דאהרן משום מעשה שהיה, תנהו לכל איסורים: ואם

[עי' תוס' חולין קב. ד"ה חלב]

רבינו חננאל

בהנאה נמצא חזקיה כר' עקיבא ור' אבהו כר' יוסי הגלילי לא לעולם ר' עקיבא נמי לא תאכלהו איסור הנאה נמי משמע ולמה דרש הפסוק לטומאה וטהרה משום [דהיתר הנאה] כבר (למה) [למד] מנבלה קסבר כשהותרה הנבלה הבשר והחלב והגידים הותרו מ"ט שנא' ואכלה כולה משמע כמות שהיא ולא איצטריך קרא אלא לטהרה וטומאה ור' יוסי הגלילי סבר היא הותרה חלבה וגידה לא הותרו כו': **ואמרינן** מכדי אותבי' כל הני תיובתא ושני כל חד לנפשיה חזקיה ור' אבהו במאי פליגי ואמרינן פליגי בחמץ בפסח ואליבא דרבנן דאסרי אפילו בהנאה ולא כר' יוסי הגלילי דשרי ובשור הנסקל ואליבא דדברי הכל כו': **תוב** אמרי' מכדי חזקיה ור' אבהו בחמץ בפסח ובשור הנסקל מיסר אסרי בין באכילה בין בהנאה מאי בינייהו ואמרי' איכא בינייהו חולין שנשחטו [בעזרה] דקיי"ל אמרה תורה שחוט חולין [בחוץ וקדשים בפנים וזה פירש שחוט שלי כלומר שחוט חולין] במקדש בגבולך מה קדשים בחוץ אסורין אפילו בהנאה אף חולין בפנים כך אסורין חזקיה סבר איסו' חמץ בפסח ואיסו' שור הנסקל ששניהם אסורין בהנאה מלא יאכל נפקא והנבלה לדברים ככתבן הוא דאתי בא אותו למעוטי חולין שנשחטו בעזרה שיהיו אסורין בהנאה דדרשינן הכי אותו ובשר טריפה אתה משליכו לכלבך ונהנה בו ואי אתה משליך חולין שנשחטו בעזרה ור' אבהו סבר בין לא יאכל בין לא תאכל [בין לא תאכלו] כולו אחד הוא ובא לא תאכלו כל נבלה למעוטי שאר אסורין ובא אותו למעוטי חמץ בפסח ושור הנסקל אבל חולין שנשחטו בעזרה איסורן לאו דאורייתא ור' אבהו לא סבר לה כר' מאיר דאמר חולין שנשחטו בעזרה דאורייתא: **יתיב** ההוא מרבנן וקאמר מנין לחמץ ושור הנסקל שאסורין בהנאה ואמרי' ותיפוק ליה מלא יאכל כדחזקיה קסבר לא יאכל ולא תאכלו חד הוא ותיפוק ליה מנבלה כר' אבהו סבר לה כר' יהודה דאמר (ארבעה) דברים ככתבן ותיפוק ליה מאותו כר' יהודה קסבר חולין שנשחטו בעזרה מדאוריי' ואלא מנא ליה ופרשי' מדכתי' וכל חטאת אשר יובא מדמה אל אהל מועד לכפר בקדש לא תאכל באש תשרף שאין ת"ל באש תשרף דנפקא ליה מוהנה שורף דכתיב (ויקרא י יז) מדוע לא אכלתם את החטאת במקום הקודש (שם יח) הן לא הובא את דמה אל הקודש פנימה ודאי בת שריפה היא מה ת"ל באש תשרף אם אינו ענין לגופו תנהו ענין לכל איסורין

מסורת הש"ס

[לעיל כב:]

[חולין קכ.]

[לעיל כב. וש"נ]

[לעיל כח: וש"נ]

הגהות הב"ח

(א) תוס' ד"ה ומה חלב וכו' וי"ל דה"פ ומה חלב נבילה שענוש: (ב) ד"ה דכתיב וכו' דמכפר על עון טומאת כצ"ל:

גליון הש"ס

גמ' אלא גיד נימא דאסור. ק"ל לפמ"ש תוס' חולין ד"פ ג"ה דחלב הוא דחדשים גרמי דכתי' חלב שור אבל גיד חל מיד א"כ י"ל דדוקא בחלב ל"א כשהותרה דהא משכחת לה הקרא דלגר אשר בשעריך תתננה דנותן לו כולו עם החלב כגון שהפילה הבהמה דליכא איסור חלב אבל גיד דל"ש כן י"ל דאמרינן כשהותרה ועי':

*) וכן הוא להדיא בשבועות ע: וברש"י שם וכן בזבחים קה. וכן פירש"י בחומש להדיא אצל ר"ח וכן פירש"י לקמן פג: ד"ה לכך נאמר וכ"כ רש"י יומא ה: ד"ה כאשר צוה וכ"כ רש"י חולין סח: ד"ה הכל הוי

תורה אור

ואם אינו ענין לאכילה – תנהו ענין לאיסור הנאה. אי מה כאן בשריפה – אף כל איסורין שבתורה בשריפה! אמר קרא: °"בקדש באש תשרף", בקדש – בשריפה, ואין כל איסורין שבתורה בשריפה. והאי "בקדש באש תשרף" להכי הוא דאתא? האי מיבעי ליה לכדרבי שמעון! *דתניא, רבי שמעון אומר: "בקדש באש תשרף" – לימד על חטאת ששורפין אותה בקדש, ואין לי אלא זו בלבד, פסולי קדשי קדשים ואימורי קדשים קלים מנין – [א]תלמוד לומר: "(וכל) בקדש באש תשרף". אמר ליה: רבי יונתן רבך מהאי קרא קאמר לה: °"ואם יותר מבשר המלאים ומן הלחם עד הבקר וגו'" שאין תלמוד לומר "לא יאכל", ומה תלמוד לומר "לא יאכל" – אם אינו ענין לגופיה, דהא כתיב: °"ושרפת את הנותר באש" – תנהו ענין לשאר איסורין שבתורה. ואם אינו ענין לאכילה – תנהו ענין לאיסור הנאה. אי מה כאן בשריפה, אף כל איסורין שבתורה בשריפה – אמר קרא "ושרפת את הנותר" – נותר בשריפה, ואין כל איסורין שבתורה בשריפה. והאי "לא יאכל" להכי הוא דאתא? האי מיבעי ליה לכדרבי אלעזר, *דאמר ר' אלעזר: *"לא יאכל כי קדש הוא" – [ב]כל שבקדש פסול בא הכתוב ליתן לא תעשה על אכילתו! אמר אביי: לעולם מקרא קמא, ואיפוך. דליכתוב "באש תשרף" ולא בעי "לא תאכל", מה תלמוד לומר "לא תאכל"? אם אינו ענין לגופו, דנפקא ליה מדרבי אלעזר – תנהו ענין לכל איסורין שבתורה. ואם אינו ענין לאכילה – תנהו ענין לאיסור הנאה. אי מה כאן בשריפה, אף כל איסורין שבתורה בשריפה – אמר קרא "הנותר" – הנותר בשריפה, ואין כל איסורין שבתורה בשריפה. אמר ליה רב פפא לאביי: ואימא ליחודי ליה לאו לגופיה הוא דאתא? דאי מדרבי אלעזר – *אין לוקין על לאו שבכללות! אלא אמר רב פפא: מהכא °"והבשר אשר יגע בכל טמא לא יאכל באש ישרף", שאין תלמוד לומר "לא יאכל", מה תלמוד לומר לא יאכל? אם אינו ענין לגופו, דהא נפקא ליה מקל וחומר ממעשר הקל: *ומה מעשר הקל אמרה תורה °"לא בערתי ממנו בטמא", בשר קדש חמור לא כל שכן?! וכי תימא: *אין מזהירין מן הדין – היקישא הוא, דכתיב: °"לא תוכל לאכל בשעריך מעשר דגנך תירשך ויצהרך ובכרת בקרך וגו'". מה תלמוד לומר "לא יאכל"? אם אינו ענין לגופו – תנהו ענין לכל איסורין שבתורה, ואם אינו ענין לאכילה – תנהו ענין להנאה. אי מה כאן בשריפה, אף כל איסורין שבתורה בשריפה – אמר קרא "הנותר" – הנותר בשריפה ואין כל איסורין שבתורה בשריפה, אמר לי' רבינא לרב אשי: ואימא לעבור עליו בשני לאוין? לאו מי *אמר אביי: [ג]אכל פוטיתא – לוקה ארבע, נמלה – לוקה חמש, צירעה

ויקרא ו | שמות כט | שם | ויקרא ז | דברים כו | שם יב

רש"י

ואם אינו ענין. לאוסרם באכילה, דהא איסור אכילה בגופייהו כתיב. זו מדה בתורה, דבר שלא הוצרך לגופו – תנהו ענין לענין אחר, ותלמוד דבר לדבר אחר. וכל המדות הלכה למשה מסיני: לימד על חטאת. פסולה ששריפתה בקדש בעזרה. דמ"והנה שורף" לא הוה שמעינן מקום שריפתה היכן: פסולי. כל שאר קדשי קדשים, כגון מנחה ועולה ואשם שנטמאו, או שנשפך דמן, ומנחה שלא נקטר קומצה, ואימורי קדשים קלים שנטמאו. ודוקא נקט הני, שמחילתן בתוך חומת העזרה. אבל פסולי בשר קדשים קלים, שאכילתן בכל העיר – אף שריפתן, אם נפסלו, חוץ לעזרה הן. והכי נמי תנן ב"אלו עוברין" (לקמן מט.): שורפן לפני הבירה, והיינו חוץ לעזרה. ושם היה בית הדשן לכך, וכן מפורש בזבחים בפ' "טבול יום" (ד' קד:): אמר ליה. ההוא מרבנן לרבי שמואל בר נחמני, דאקשי ליה האי קושיא: רבי יונתן רבך נמי לא הוה מייתי איסור הנאה לכל איסורין מ"בקדש באש תשרף", דמבעי ליה לכדאמרת שתשרף בעזרה, אלא מהאי קרא אמר להו: דהא כתיב ושרפת. אלמא: לאו בר אכילה הוא: לכל איסורין. דוגמתן, שנאמר בהן לאו באכילתן: ואם אינו ענין לאכילה. דהא בגופייהו כתיב, תנהו ענין להנאה: אמר קרא והנותר. דהוה ליה למכתב ושרפתו באש: מיבעי ליה לכדרבי אלעזר. ליתן לא תעשה. דאי מ"ושרפת" – לא הוה ידעינן ביה איסור לאו למלקות: כל שבקודש פסול. מדכתיב: "כי קודש הוא" יתירה, לרבות על שאר פסולי קדשי קדשים בלאו, כגון פיגול ויוצא ונשפך דמו: מקרא קמא. "וכל חטאת". ולאו מ"באש תשרף", דאיצטריך לומר שישרף בעזרה, אלא מ"לא תאכל" ליכתוב באש תשרף, אלמא: לאו בר אכילה הוא, וממילא נפקא לן ביה נמי איסור לאו מהא דרבי אלעזר, דמפיק מ"לא יאכל כי קודש הוא" כל פסולי קדשים: לאו שבכללות. כגון זה, שנכלל כל הפסולין יחד: לא בערתי. אזהרה נפקא לן ביה ביבמות ב"הערל" (דף עג:): אין מזהירין. מדין קל וחומר. אף על פי שאדם דן קל וחומר מעצמו – אינה אזהרה ללאו. במסכת מכות (דף ה:) נפקא לן: היקישא הוא. ולאו קל וחומר, דאיתקש "נדריך ונדבותיך", דהיינו שלמים, למעשר דגן, דכתיב ביה: "לא בערתי ממנו בטמא". ואייתי לן מינה דאף קדשים לא יאכלו בטומאה. "ולא בערתי ממנו בטמא", אע"ג דוידוי בעלמא הוא, ואינו לאו – הא נפקא לן ביה איסור לאו ביבמות ב"הערל" מהאי קרא ד"לא תוכל לאכול בשעריך", ולהלן הוא אומר, בפסולי המוקדשים שנפדו (דברים טו): "בשעריך תאכלנו הטמא והטהור יחדיו" – טמא וטהור אוכלין בקערה אחת, יש כאן טומאת בשר לטהור, וטומאת הגוף לטמא. וקא אמר רחמנא גבי מעשר וקדשים, ההוא בשעריך דשרא לך ביה טומאה התם, בפסולי המוקדשין – הכא לא תאכל: אכל פוטיתא. לוקה ארבע. חד לאו בשרץ המים בתורת כהנים, דהוא ספר ויקרא, וחד במשנה תורה. שרץ המים: ושני לאוין כתובים בתורת כהנים בשקלים סתם (א) "לא תשקצו את נפשותיכם בכל השרץ השורץ" ו"לא תטמאו בהן". והכא לא כתיב על הארץ, ומשמע בין שרץ המים ובין שרץ הארץ – הרי ארבע: נמלה. שהוא שרץ הארץ: לוקה חמש. הני תרי דסתם שרצים, וחד "וכל השרץ השורץ על הארץ שקץ הוא לא יאכל", וחד "לכל השרץ השורץ על הארץ לא תאכלום כי שקץ הם", וחד "ולא תטמאו את נפשותיכם בכל השרץ הרומש על הארץ": לירעה

לקמן פב: | [במכו' וכמעיל' איתא אליעזר כו"ז ודע עוד דבמעילה בריתא היא דתניא ר"א אומר לא יאכל כו'] | לקמן מח: נזיר לח: ב"מ קטו: סנהדרין סג. מנחות נח: תמורה ז: כריתות ד. ה.] | מכות טז: עירובין כח.

תוספות

ואם אינו ענין לאכילה. לא אתי שפיר, דהיכי מצי לאוקמי' באיסור אכילה? דהא כתיב "באש תשרף": הא אין לוקין על לאו שבכללות. הקשה הר"ר אליעזר ממיץ ד"באלו הן הלוקין" (מכות יג.) אמר, דלאו דנותר ופיגול הוה בכלל הלוקין, ואמאי? והא לאו שבכללות הוא! ותירץ: דלגבי נותר שמפורש בהדיא, דכתיב: "ושרפת את הנותר באש לא יאכל כי קדש הוא" – לא חשיב לאו שבכללות ופיגול נמי גמרינן עון עון מנותר. אך קשה: דבפרק בתרא דמכות (דף יז: יח.) גבי זר שאכל עולה לפני זריקה לוקה חמש, פריך: ולילקי נמי מדרבי אלעזר, דאמר כל שבקודש פסול. ומאי קושיא, והא לאו שבכללות הוא*? אם אינו ענין לגופו דאתי בקל וחומר ממעשר. ואם תאמר: והא איצטריך לרביעי בקודש, כדאמרינן בפרק קמא (דף יט.)! וי"ל: דלא ליכתוב "לא יאכל" אלא ישרף: הקישא הוא. תימה: אמאי קרי ליה הקישא? תיפוק ליה דקודש כתיב בהדיא בקרא – "ובכורות בקרך וצאנך". ואזהרה למעשר נמי יליף מהאי קרא! וי"ל: דצריך הקישא משום איסור הנאה, דלא תוקי קרא ד"והבשר" לאיסור הנאה שיהא בלאו, דבפ' שני דשבת (דף כה.) לא ילפי' איסור הנאה בשמן קדש שנטמא אלא ממעשר: דכתיב לא תוכל לאכול בשעריך. האי לא חשיב לאו שבכללות, מדלא כתיב "מעשר דגנך ובכורות בקרך לא תוכל לאכלם" – ש"מ ליחודי לאו אכל חד דכתי' בקרא אתא:

לירעה

[ועי' תוס' יומא לו: ד"ה לאו ותוס' מכות יח: ד"ה כל] | מכות יח. מעילה יז: | [שבת כה.] | [יבמות כב: מכות ה:]

עין משפט נר מצוה

כא א מיי' פי"ט מהל' פסולי המוקדשין הלכה א ב:

כב ב מיי' פי"ח שם הלכה ג ד:

כג ג מיי' פ"ב מהלכות מאכלות אסורות הל' כג [רב אלפס חולין סוף פ"ג דף רפ"ב: האריך בפירושו]:

רבינו חננאל

שבתורה שיהו אסורין אפי' בהנאה ואם תאמר כל איסורין שבתורה בשרפה תלמוד לומר [בקדש] באש תשרף כל פסול שהוא בקדש בשרפה ולא שאר איסורין שבתורה: והאי בקדש מבעי ליה לכדתניא בקדש באש תשרף לימד על חטאת כו' והא דאמר ר' יונתן ואם יותר מבשר המלואים וגו' נדחו דבריו ותרצה אביי לעולם מקרא קמא והוא וכל חטאת אשר יובא מדמה אל אהל מועד וא"כ נימא קרא בקדש באש תשרף ונשתוק לא תאכל למה לי אם אינו ענין לגופיה דנפק' ליה מדר' אלעזר דאמר לא יאכל כי קדש הוא כל שבקדש פסול ליתן לא תעשה על אכילתו תנהו ענין לשאר איסורין שבתורה ודחי' תוב ואימא ליחודי ליה לאו לגופיה דאי מדר' אלעזר הוה ליה לאו שבכללות כדפירש כל שבקדש כלל כל פסולין שבקדש [וכל לאו] שבכללות אין לוקין עליו אלא א"ר פפא מהכא והבשר אשר יגע בכל טמא לא יאכל שאין ת"ל (באש ישרף) [לא יאכל] כו' עד וכי מזהירין מן הדין ודחי' הקישא הוא כלומר התורה הקישה הקדש למעשר שנאמר לא תוכל לאכול בשעריך מעשר דגנך תירושך ויצהרך ובכורות בקרך וצאנך וגו' וכל נדריך אלו קדשים: אמר ליה רבינא לרב אשי ואימא לעבור עליו בשני לאוין. כלומר לא בא מופנה שתדרוש בו ואם אינו ענין לגופו תנהו ענין לשאר איסורין אלא לגופיה בא וא"ת [והלא] כבר הוקש למעשר דכתי' ביה לאו שנאמר לא תוכל לאכול בשעריך לא יאכל עוד למה בא לחייבו בשני לאוין מי לא אמר אביי אכל פוטיתא לוקה ארבע נמלה לוקה חמש צרעה לוקה

הגהות הב"ח

(א) רש"י ד"ה לוקה ארבע וכו' בשקלים סתם אל תשקצו:

גליון הש"ס

גמרא הקישא הוא. עיין זבחים לד ע"א תד"ה והבשר:

עין משפט נר מצוה

כד א מיי' פ"ב מהלכות איסורי מזבח הלכה ח ופ"ח מהל' פסולי המוקדשין הלכה יב:
כה ב שם הלכה יח:
כו ג שם הלכה יב:
כז ד מיי' פי"ד מהל' מאכלות אסורות הל' י טוש"ע יו"ד סי' קנה סעיף ג:
כח ה מיי' פ"י שם הלכה כב:
כט ו מיי' פי"ד שם הלכה י טוש"ע יו"ד סי' קנה סעיף ג:

גמרא

צִירְעָה — לוֹקֶה שֵׁשׁ! א"ל: כָּל הֵיכָא *דְּאִיכָּא לְמִדְרַשׁ — דָּרְשִׁינַן, וְלָא מוֹקְמִינַן בְּלָאוֵי יְתֵירֵי. °"וְהַבָּשָׂר אֲשֶׁר יִגַּע בְּכָל טָמֵא לֹא יֵאָכֵל" (ויקרא ז) דְּרֵישֵׁי' (א) לָמָּה לִי — *אלְרַבּוֹת עֵצִים וּלְבוֹנָה. "וְהַבָּשָׂר כָּל טָהוֹר יֹאכַל בָּשָׂר" דְּסֵיפֵיהּ לָמָּה לִי — לְרַבּוֹת אֵימוּרִין. אֵימוּרִין מֵהָתָם נָפְקָא, *דְּתַנְיָא: °"וְהַנֶּפֶשׁ אֲשֶׁר תֹּאכַל בָּשָׂר מִזֶּבַח הַשְּׁלָמִים אֲשֶׁר לַה'" (שם) — לְרַבּוֹת אֶת הָאֵימוּרִין! בהָתָם טוּמְאַת הַגּוּף — בְּכָרֵת, גהָכָא טוּמְאַת בָּשָׂר — בְּלָאו. א"ר אַבָּהוּ א"ר יוֹחָנָן: *כָּל אִיסּוּרִין שֶׁבַּתּוֹרָה אֵין לוֹקִין עֲלֵיהֶן אֶלָּא דֶּרֶךְ אֲכִילָתָן. לְמַעוּטֵי מַאי? אָמַר רַב שִׁימִי בַּר אַשִׁי: לְמַעוּטֵי שֶׁאִם אָכַל חֵלֶב חַי, שֶׁפָּטוּר. אִיכָּא דְּאָמְרִי, א"ר אַבָּהוּ אָמַר ר' יוֹחָנָן: דכָּל אִיסּוּרִין שֶׁבַּתּוֹרָה אֵין לוֹקִין עֲלֵיהֶן אֶלָּא דֶּרֶךְ הֲנָאָתָן. לְמַעוּטֵי מַאי? אָמַר רַב שִׁימִי בַּר אַשִׁי: לְמַעוּטֵי שֶׁאִם הִנִּיחַ חֵלֶב שֶׁל שׁוֹר הַנִּסְקָל עַל גַּבֵּי מַכָּתוֹ, שֶׁהוּא פָּטוּר. וְכָל שֶׁכֵּן אוֹכֵל חֵלֶב חַי שֶׁהוּא פָּטוּר. אִתְּמַר נַמִּי, אָמַר רַב אַחָא בַּר *עַוְיָה, אָמַר רַב אַסִּי, א"ר יוֹחָנָן: הִנִּיחַ חֵלֶב שֶׁל שׁוֹר הַנִּסְקָל עַל גַּבֵּי מַכָּתוֹ — פָּטוּר, לְפִי שֶׁכָּל אִיסּוּרִין שֶׁבַּתּוֹרָה אֵין לוֹקִין עֲלֵיהֶם אֶלָּא דֶּרֶךְ הֲנָאָתָן. אָמַר ר' זֵירָא, אַף אֲנַן נַמִּי תְּנֵינָא': *האֵין סוֹפְגִין אֶת הָאַרְבָּעִים מִשּׁוּם עָרְלָה, אֶלָּא עַל הַיּוֹצֵא מִן הַזֵּיתִים וּמִן הָעֲנָבִים בִּלְבַד. וְאִילּוּ מִתּוּתִים תְּאֵנִים וְרִמּוֹנִים — לֹא. מַאי טַעְמָא — לָאו מִשּׁוּ' דְּלָא קָאָכֵיל לְהוּ דֶּרֶךְ הֲנָאָתָן? אָמַר לֵיהּ אַבָּיֵי: בִּשְׁלָמָא אִי אַשְׁמְעִינַן פְּרִי גּוּפָא דְּלָא קָאָכֵיל לֵיהּ דֶּרֶךְ הֲנָאָתוֹ — שַׁפִּיר. אֶלָּא הָכָא — מִשּׁוּם דְּזֵיעָה בְּעָלְמָא הוּא. אָמַר אַבָּיֵי: *והַכֹּל מוֹדִים בְּכִלְאֵי הַכֶּרֶם שֶׁלּוֹקִין עֲלֵיהֶן אֲפִילּוּ שֶׁלֹּא כְּדֶרֶךְ הֲנָאָתָן. מַאי טַעְמָא — מִשּׁוּם דְּלָא כְּתִיב בְּהוּ אֲכִילָה. מֵיתִיבִי, אִיסִי בֶּן יְהוּדָה אוֹמֵר (חולין קטו:): *מִנַּיִן לְבָשָׂר בְּחָלָב שֶׁהוּא אָסוּר — נֶאֱמַר כָּאן: °"כִּי עַם קָדוֹשׁ אַתָּה" (דברים יד), וְנֶאֱמַר לְהַלָּן: °"וְאַנְשֵׁי קֹדֶשׁ תִּהְיוּן לִי" (שמות כב) מַה לְּהַלָּן אָסוּר — אַף כָּאן אָסוּר. וְאֵין לִי אֶלָּא בַּאֲכִילָה, בַּהֲנָאָה מִנַּיִן? אָמַרְתָּ ק"ו: וּמָה עָרְלָה שֶׁלֹּא נֶעֶבְדָה בָּהּ עֲבֵירָה — אֲסוּרָה בַּהֲנָאָה, בָּשָׂר בְּחָלָב שֶׁנֶּעֶבְדָה בּוֹ עֲבֵירָה — אֵינוֹ דִּין שֶׁיְּהֵא אָסוּר בַּהֲנָאָה?
מַה

רש"י

צִירְעָה. שֶׁרֶץ הָעוֹף הִיא, וְגַם שׁוֹרֶצֶת עַל הָאָרֶץ, וְיֵשׁ בָּהּ אֵלּוּ חָמֵשׁ לָאוִין, וּמוֹסִיף עָלֶיהָ לָאו דְּשֶׁרֶץ הָעוֹף בְּמִשְׁנֵה תוֹרָה (יד) – "וְכֹל שֶׁרֶץ הָעוֹף טָמֵא הוּא לָכֶם לֹא יֵאָכֵלוּ". שֶׁרֶץ – לְשׁוֹן רְחוּשׁ וְנִעְנוּעַ, וְאֵינוֹ נִרְאֶה. וְאֵין בְּהֵמָה וְחַיָּה הַגְּבוֹהִין מִן הָאָרֶץ בִּכְלַל שֶׁרֶץ, הִלְכָּךְ "לֹא תְשַׁקְּצוּ אֶת נַפְשׁוֹתֵיכֶם בַּבְּהֵמָה וּבָעוֹף" וגו' דִּכְתִיב בִּקְדוֹשִׁים תִּהְיוּ – אֵינוֹ מִן הַמִּנְיָן, דְּלָאו בִּשְׁרָצִים כְּתִיב: וְהַבָּשָׂר לָמָּה לִי. הַשְׁתָּא דְּאָמְרַ' קְרָא לָאו לְגוּפֵיהּ אָתָא, אֶלָּא לְאִם אֵינוֹ עִנְיָן, תֵּינַח "וַאֲשֶׁר יִגַּע בְּכָל טָמֵא לֹא יֵאָכֵל", "וְהַבָּשָׂר" לָמָּה לִי? וּמְשַׁנֵּי: לְרַבּוֹת עֵצִים וּלְבוֹנָה לְקַבֵּל טוּמְאָה, וְאַע"ג דְּלָאו אוּכְלָא הוּא: וְהַבָּשָׂר כָּל טָהוֹר יֹאכַל לָמָּה לִי. "וְהַבָּשָׂר" יְתֵירָה מִבָּעֲיָא לֵיהּ. דְּאִילּוּ "כָּל טָהוֹר יֹאכַל בָּשָׂר" דָּרֵישׁ לֵיהּ בִּמְנָחוֹת (ד' כה:): "כָּל טָהוֹר יֹאכַל בָּשָׂר, וְהַנֶּפֶשׁ אֲשֶׁר תֹּאכַל בָּשָׂר" וגו' – הַנִּיתָּר לִטְהוֹרִין חַיָּיבִין עָלָיו מִשּׁוּם טוּמְאָה, יָצָא בָּשָׂר שֶׁנִּטְמָא לִפְנֵי זְרִיקַת דָּם. לָשׁוֹן אַחֵר: בֵּין בְּרֵישָׁא בֵּין בְּסֵיפָא, ו' יְתֵירָא מִיבַּעְיָ' לֵיהּ: לְרַבּוֹת אֶת הָאֵימוּרִין. שֶׁאִם נִטְמְאוּ, וַאֲכָלָן טָהוֹר – שֶׁיַּעֲבוֹר עֲלֵיהֶן מִשּׁוּם שְׁנֵי לָאוִין: לָאו דְּזָרוּת – שֶׁאַף הַכֹּהֵן זָר אֶצְלָם – וְלָאו דְּטוּמְאַת בָּשָׂר. וְאַדִּלְעֵיל קָאֵי, וְהָכִי קָאָמַר: לֹא יֵאָכֵל, וְהַבָּשָׂר נַמִּי שֶׁנִּטְמָא – לֹא יֵאָכֵל: אֲשֶׁר לַה'. קְרָא יְתֵירָה הוּא, דַּהֲוָה לֵיהּ לְמִכְתַּב "מִזֶּבַח הַשְּׁלָמִים וְטוּמְאָתוֹ עָלָיו", וּכְתִיב "אֲשֶׁר לַה'" – לְרַבּוֹת אַף בָּשָׂר הַקָּרֵב לַה', שֶׁאִם אֲכָלוֹ בְּטוּמְאָה – עָנוּשׁ כָּרֵת. וּמְשַׁנֵּי: הָתָם בְּטוּמְאַת הַגּוּף אַיְירֵי(ב), וְהַאי "וְטוּמְאָתוֹ עָלָיו" מוֹקְמִינַן לָהּ בִּזְבָחִים בְּפֶרֶק ב"ש (דף מג:) בְּטוּמְאַת הַגּוּף הַכָּתוּב מְדַבֵּר. וְהָכָא רַבִּינְהוּ לְאַזְהָרַת טוּמְאַת בָּשָׂר, כְּשֶׁנִּטְמְאוּ הֵם וְהוּא טָהוֹר שֶׁיְּהֵא מוּזְהָר עֲלֵיהֶן. וְהָכָא לֵיכָּא כָּרֵת אֶלָּא לָאו, דְּאִימְעַט מִכָּרֵת בִּזְבָחִים בְּפֶרֶק ב"ש: אֶלָּא דֶּרֶךְ אֲכִילָתָן. אֶלָּא אִם כֵּן אֲכָלָן דֶּרֶךְ אֲכִילָתָן: אִיכָּא דְּאָמְרִי. הָא דְּרַבִּי אַבָּהוּ – אַהֲנָאָה אִיתְּמַר, וְאַהָנָךְ דַּאֲסִירֵי בַּהֲנָאָה: חֵלֶב. אֵין דֶּרֶךְ הֲנָאָתוֹ אֶלָּא בְּהַבְעָרָה וְלִמְשׁוֹחַ עוֹרוֹת, וְלֹא לִרְפוּאָה, וְכָל שֶׁכֵּן אוֹכֵל חֵלֶב חַי: אֵין סוֹפְגִין אֶת הָאַרְבָּעִים כו'. גַּבֵּי מַשְׁקִין קָאֵי, בְּמַסֶּכֶת תְּרוּמוֹת. וְקָאָמַר, דְּאֵין כָּל מֵי פֵּירוֹת קְרוּיִין מַשְׁקִין, אֶלָּא אֵלּוּ בִּלְבַד. אֵין סוֹפְגִין אֶת הָאַרְבָּעִים עַל שׁוּם מֵי פֵּירוֹת שֶׁל עָרְלָה, מִשּׁוּם דְּכוּלְּהוּ שֶׁלֹּא כְּדֶרֶךְ הֲנָאָתָן הוּא אֶלָּא אֵלּוּ: בִּשְׁלָמָא אִי אַשְׁמְעִינַן בִּפְרִי גּוּפָא. דְּאִי אָכֵיל שֶׁלֹּא כְּדַרְכּוֹ, כְּגוֹן שֶׁבִּישֵּׁל אֱגוֹזִים אוֹ אֲפַרְסְקִין וַאֲכָלָן, וְאַשְׁמְעִינַן דְּלֹא מִחַיֵּיב: שַׁפִּיר. שָׁמְעִינַן מִינָּהּ דְּאֵין לוֹקִין אֶלָּא כְּדֶרֶךְ אֲכִילָתָן. אֲבָל הַשְׁתָּא, טַעְמָא דְּפָטוּר – מִשּׁוּם דְּלָאו פְּרִי אָכַל: בְּכִלְאֵי הַכֶּרֶם. כְּתִיב (דברים כב): "פֶּן תִּקְדַּשׁ הַמְלֵאָה", דְּמַשְׁמַע: לֹא תֵהָנֶה מִמֶּנּוּ אֶלָּא תִּשְׂרְפֶנּוּ. וּפֶן – לָאו הוּא: שֶׁהוּא אָסוּר. בַּאֲכִילָה: עָרְלָה שֶׁלֹּא נֶעֶבְדָה בָּהּ עֲבֵירָה. בִּנְטִיעוּתָהּ: בָּשָׂר בְּחָלָב שֶׁנֶּעֶבְדָה בּוֹ עֲבֵירָה. כְּשֶׁבִּישְּׁלוֹ, וְעָבַר עָלָיו עַל לָאו "לֹא תְבַשֵּׁל":
עָרְלָה

תוספות

צירעה לוקה שש. פ"ה: דהא(ג) דכתיב בקדושים: "אל תשקצו את נפשותיכם בבהמה ובעוף אשר תרמוש האדמה" וגו' – לא חשיב ליה, דבגדולים איירי דלא כתיב(ד) שרץ, ולשון שרץ דבר שהוא נד בארץ, ואינו נראה אלא ע"י שירוצו מפני קטנו. וקשה: דבפ' "ד' מיתות" (סנהדרין נט:) דרשינן: "וכל חיה הרומשת" – זה הנחש. משמע דרמישה הוה נמי בדבר הרוחש כמו נחש, שהולך על גחונו. ותי' הר"י דאורלינ"ש: דהוא קא איירי בח' שרצים, דאמרינן במעילה בפרק "קדשי מזבח" (דף טז: ושם): במובדלים ממך דיבר הכתוב, דכתיב בסיפא דקרא "אשר הבדלתי לכם לטמא" – והיינו ח' שרצים, שהן טמאים: **לרבות** את האימורים. דסד"א אין חייבין עליהם משום טומאה הואיל ואין ניתרים, ודרשינן במנחות בפרק "הקומץ את המנחה" (דף כה:) הניתר לטהורי' חייבים עליהם משום טומאה. להכי איצטריך לרבויינהו. מיהו קשה: דבמעילה בפ' "חטאת העוף" (דף י:) דריש התם מ"אשר יקרב" בכל הקדשים הכתוב מדבר, ויליף התם אימורים *וכל שאין ניתר לטהורים. ורבינו שמשון תירץ: דאיצטריך לרבויי, דסד"א דלא יבא איסור טומאה ויחול על איסור חלב: **פרט** לאוכל חלב חי. והא דאמר ב"גיד הנשה" (חולין קב:): אכל לפור טהורה, בחיה – בכל שהוא, במיתתה – בכזית! שאני עוף שהוא רך, וחזי לאומלא, וחשיב כדרך הנאתו. והא דאמר ב"הקומץ רבה" (מנחות כא.): דם שבשלו אינו עובר עליו. ופריך אביי מהא דתניא: הקפה את הדם ואכלו, או שהמחה את החלב וגמעו – חייב. ומשני: כאן שהקפה באור, וכאן שהקפה בחמה. ולפי הך דהכא נ"ל שהברייתא לגרדים קתני. הקפה את הדם בחמה ואת החלב באור. דאי בחמה – חי הוא, ופטור: **אלא** הכא משום דזיעה בעלמא הוא. תימה לר"י: דב"העור והרוטב" (חולין קכא. ושם) יליף מקרא דאין חייב משום ערלה אלא על היוצא מזיתים וענבים, דגמר ערלה פרי פרי מבכורים, ובכורי מתרומה, ובתרומה כתיב תירוש ויצהר. אם כן, אמאי איצטריך למימר הכא זיעה בעלמא הוא? וי"ל: דהא דאיצטריך למילף התם פרי פרי מבכורים – לאו למעוטי שאר משקין איצטריך, דמן הדין אפילו תירוש ויצהר לא היה(ה) ליחשב למשקין פרי דזיעה בעלמא הוא, כדאמרינן הכא. והתם איצטריך למילף שנחשוב משקה של תירוש ויצהר כמו הפרי. והשתא א"ש הא דאמר בשמעתין דזיעה בעלמא הוא, דמהאי טעמא הוא דשמעינן דמשקה אינו כפרי. מיהו, תימה: אמאי אמר דזיעה בעלמא הוא? והא טעם כעיקר דאורייתא! **אמרת** קל וחומר. תימה: היכי אלים ק"ו לאפוקי מג"ש? דניליף מנבילה בג"ש שלא תאסר בהנאה כמו נבילה, ובפרק "כל הבשר" (חולין קטז.) איכא תנא דיליף הכי, וסבר דבשר בחלב לא אסור בהנאה. ואור"ת: דההוא קרא ד"אנשי קדש" כתיב ביה נמי איסורי הנאה, דמ"בשר בשדה" דרשינן *קדשים שיצאו חוץ למחיצה. וגלי לן ק"ו דגמרינן מקדשים, ולא (*מנבילה). וא"ת: בלא ק"ו נמי מקשינן לחומרא! וי"ל דהכא ס"ד לאקשויי לקולא, משום דמפורש בהדיא בקרא היתר הנאה, דכתיב: "לכלב תשליכון אותו". הקשה הר"י דאורלינ"ש: אמאי לא ילפינן מנותר איסור אכילה, ואיסור הנאה מקדש קדש, דמההוא קדש דנותר דריש ג"ש בפ' "לולב וערבה" (סוכה מח.) ובפרק "כל הזבחים" (זבחים כח:). וי"ל: דהכא "עם קדוש" מ"אנשי קדש" דרשי' שהן ענין אחד, דקיימא קדושה אגברי. אי נמי: דנין חולין מחולין, ואין דנין חולין מקדשים*: **הכל** מודים בכלאי הכרם (לעיל). הא דלא קאמר: הכל מודים בחולין שנשחטו בעזרה – משום דכתיב בהו אכילה דמ"וזבחת ואכלת" נפקא לן. ועוד, דאיכא מאן דאמר לאו דאורייתא. והא דלא קאמר: הכל מודים בבשר וחלב – שמא משום דאין מזהירין מן הדין: **אמרת** ק"ו. איסור אכילה לא מצי למילף בק"ו מערלה, כדאמר ב"כל הבשר" (חולין קטו:) משום דאיכא למימר: חורש בשור וחמור וחוסם פי פרה יוכיח, דנעבדה בהו עבירה ושרו באכילה, אבל השתא, דיליף מקרא איסור אכילה – ליכא למימר תוכיח, דהנהו שרו באכילה:
מה

[עי' תוס' ע"ז יב: ד"ה אלא] · וכל שאין לו מתירין כצ"ל רש"ל · [בר רב עויא וכ"א לקמן לג:]

רבינו חננאל

לוקה שש הכא נמי לוקה על שני לאוין והא דאביי מפורש בפ' אלו הן חלוקין פוטיתא הוא דג טמא וכתיב בדגים (ויקרא יא יא) ושקץ יהיו לכם מבשרם לא תאכלו *וכתיב (עוד לכל השרץ השורץ לא יאכל כי שקץ הם) ועוד כתיב (שם מג) אל תשקצו את נפשותיכם בכל השרץ השורץ ולא תטמאו בהם נמצאו ארבעה לאוין באוכל שרץ סתם ולא פירש באחד מהם בארץ ודרשי' הלאוין בכל שרץ בין שרץ של ים ובין שרץ של יבשה לפיכך אמר אביי אכל פוטיתא שהיא שרץ הים לוקה עליה הללו ארבעה לאוין כלם. אבל נמלה שהיא שקץ היבשה עובר** בארבעה לאוין הללו והוסיפה התורה על שקץ של יבשה לאו חמישי שנא' (שם מד) ולא תטמאו את נפשותיכם בכל השרץ השורץ על הארץ הלכך לוקה חמש אבל צרעה שהיא שרץ העוף עובר על חמשה לאוין הללו הוסיפה עליו התור' לאו אחד שנא' (דברים יד יט) וכל שרץ העוף טמא הוא לכם לא (יאכלו) [יאכל] הלכך לוקה שש מלקיות ופרקי' הני מילי דמוקמי' ליה בלאו יתירי היכא דליכא מידי למדרש [אבל אי איכא למדרש] כי האי גונא דרשי': **מכדי** כתיב ואם האכל יאכל מבשר זבח השלמים וגו' והבשר אשר יגע בכל טמא למה לי לרבות עצים ולבונה שאם נטמאו ישרפו והבשר כל טהור יאכל בשר תו(ב) למה לי לרבות אימורין שנטמאו סד"א כל טהור יאכל בשר כתיב מידי דכהן טהור מצי למיכליה אם אכלו בטומאה חייב אבל חלבים דלא יכול למיכלינהו אפי' הוא טהור אימא לית להו חיוב משום טומאה קמ"ל. שנינו בתוספתא פ' הזורע והלחיים והקבה נוהגין בכלאים כו' ואסיקנא מהאי קרא דכתיב והנפש אשר תאכל בשר מזבח השלמים אשר לה' ונכרתה ואמרי' לה' לרבות האוכל אימורין בטומאת הגוף שהוא בכרת ובא הבשר אשר יגע בכל טמא לא יאכל לרבות בשר קדש שנטמא אכלו כהן טהור בלאו: **אמר** רבי אבהו אמר רבי יוחנן כל איסורין שבתורה אין לוקין עליהן אלא דרך הנאתן וכל שכן דרך אכילתן למעוטי אכל חלב חי ודרך הנאתן למעוטי [אם הניח] חלב של שור הנסקל על מכתו שפטור: **אמר** ר' זירא אף אנן נמי תנינא אין סופגין ארבעים משום ערלה אלא על היוצא מן הזיתים ומן הענבים הא מן התותים ומן הענבים לא משום דאינו דרך הנאתן. ושני אביי שאני התם דזיעה בעלמא הוא: **אמר** אביי הכל מודים בכלאי הכרם כיון דלא כתיב בהו אכילה לוקה עליהן אפי' שלא כדרך הנאתן ומותיב עליהן איסי בן יהודה
מהא

* דברי רבינו תמוהים דהא בהאי קרא כתיב בהדיא לכל השרץ השורץ על הארץ וגו' ובאמת הרי"ף סו"פ אלו טרפות וברמב"ם כאן ובמכות ט"ז הביאו ללאו ד' הך קרא דמשנה תורה וכל אשר אין לו וגו'.
** גם זה צ"ע דקרא דושקץ יהיו לכם מבשרם לא תאכלו כתיב רק בשרץ המים ושרץ הארץ לא נכלל כלל בהך קרא ועי' ברי"ף וברמב"ם ודברי רבינו [illegible].

מסורת הש"ס

[בכורות ו:]
[לקמן לה. וש"נ ע"ש בפירש"י]
[זבחים לו: כריתות כג: לקמן לג:]
חולין קכ: תרומות פי"א [מ"ג]
[עי' תוס' ע"ז יב: ד"ה אלא וכו' דאפשר דה"ה בע"ז לוקין אפי' שלא כדרך הנאתן ע"ש]
[מכות יח.]
[מטרפה כצ"ל]
[וע"ע תוס' בכורות י. ד"ה מה להלן]

הגהות הב"ח

(א) גמרא לא יאכל דרישיה קרא למה לי: (ב) רש"י ד"ה ומשני וכו' איירי הכא. (ג) תום' ד"ה צירעה וכו' פ"ה דהא. נ"ב עי' פ' בכל מערבין ד' כח: (ד) בא"ד דלא כתיב בהו שרץ ולשון שרץ וכו' ואינו נראה מפני קוטנו אלא על ידי שירוצו וקשה כצ"ל: (ה) ד"ה אלא וכו' לא הוי ליה ליחשב:

גליון הש"ס

גמ' שאם הניח חלב של שור הנסקל. עיין נדה לב ע"א תד"ה והכתוב: תוס' ד"ה אלא וי"ל כו' דהא דאיצטריך למילף. עי' בספר כתנות אור להגאון בעל פנים מאירות סוף פ' ברכות: תוס' ד"ה הכל מודים. והא דלא קאמר וכו' משום דאין מזהירין מן הדין. עי' ע"ז יב ע"ב תד"ה אלא ונע"ק:

מה לְעָרְלָה שֶׁכֵּן לֹא הָיְתָה לָהּ שְׁעַת הַכּוֹשֶׁר, תֹּאמַר בְּבָשָׂר בְּחָלָב שֶׁהָיְתָה לוֹ שְׁעַת הַכּוֹשֶׁר! חָמֵץ בַּפֶּסַח יוֹכִיחַ, שֶׁהָיָה לוֹ שְׁעַת הַכּוֹשֶׁר וְאָסוּר בַּהֲנָאָה. מַה לְּחָמֵץ בַּפֶּסַח – שֶׁכֵּן עָנוּשׁ כָּרֵת, תֹּאמַר בְּבָשָׂר בְּחָלָב שֶׁאֵינוֹ עָנוּשׁ כָּרֵת! כִּלְאֵי הַכֶּרֶם יוֹכִיחוּ, שֶׁאֵין עָנוּשׁ כָּרֵת – וְאָסוּר בַּהֲנָאָה. וְאִם אִיתָא, נִיפְרוֹךְ: מַה לְּכִלְאֵי הַכֶּרֶם – שֶׁכֵּן לוֹקִין עֲלֵיהֶן אֲפִילּוּ שֶׁלֹּא כְּדֶרֶךְ הֲנָאָתָן. וְאַבָּיֵי: תֹּאמַר בְּמַאי? תֹּאמַר בְּבָשָׂר בְּחָלָב שֶׁאֵין לוֹקִין עָלָיו אֶלָּא דֶּרֶךְ הֲנָאָתוֹ – [א]אַטּוּ בְּבָשָׂר בְּחָלָב 'אֲכִילָה' כְּתִיבָה בֵּיהּ? וְאִידָךְ דְּקָא מוֹתִיב לָהּ סָבַר: לְהָכִי קָא גָּמַר מִנְּבֵילָה, מַה נְּבֵילָה דֶּרֶךְ הֲנָאָתָהּ – אַף בָּשָׂר בְּחָלָב דֶּרֶךְ הֲנָאָתוֹ. וְאַבָּיֵי: לְהָכִי לֹא כָּתַב אֲכִילָה בְּגוּפוֹ – לוֹמַר שֶׁלּוֹקִין עָלָיו אֲפִי' שֶׁלֹּא כְּדֶרֶךְ הֲנָאָתוֹ. וְלִיפְרוֹךְ מַה לְּכִלְאֵי הַכֶּרֶם – שֶׁכֵּן לֹא הָיְתָה לוֹ שְׁעַת הַכּוֹשֶׁר! א"ר אַדָּא בַּר אַהֲבָה: זֹאת אוֹמֶרֶת: כִּלְאֵי הַכֶּרֶם עִיקָּרָן נֶאֱסָרִין, הוֹאִיל וְהָיְתָה לָהֶן שְׁעַת הַכּוֹשֶׁר קוֹדֶם הַשְׁרָשָׁה. מְתִיב רַב שְׁמַעְיָה: *הַמַּעֲבִיר עָצִיץ נָקוּב בַּכֶּרֶם, אִם הוֹסִיף מָאתַיִם – אָסוּר. הוֹסִיף – אִין, לֹא הוֹסִיף – לָא! אָמַר רָבָא: תְּרֵי קְרָאֵי כְּתִיבִי, כְּתִיב: *°"הַזֶּרַע", וּכְתִיב: "הַמְּלֵאָה" (דברים כב), הָא כֵּיצַד? [ב]זָרוּעַ מֵעִיקָּרוֹ – בְּהַשְׁרָשָׁה, [ג]זָרוּעַ וּבָא, הוֹסִיף – אִין, לֹא הוֹסִיף – לָא. א"ר יַעֲקֹב א"ר יוֹחָנָן: בַּכֹּל מִתְרַפְּאִין, חוּץ מֵעֲצֵי אֲשֵׁירָה. הֵיכִי דָּמֵי? אִי נֵימָא דְּאִיכָּא סַכָּנָה – אֲפִילּוּ עֲצֵי אֲשֵׁירָה נַמִּי! וְאִי דְּלֵיכָּא סַכָּנָה – אֲפִילּוּ כָּל אִיסּוּרִין שֶׁבַּתּוֹרָה נַמִּי לָא! לְעוֹלָם דְּאִיכָּא סַכָּנָה, וַאֲפִי' הָכִי – עֲצֵי אֲשֵׁירָה לָא. *דְּתַנְיָא, ר' אֱלִיעֶזֶר אוֹמֵר: אִם נֶאֱמַר °"בְּכָל נַפְשְׁךָ" (קס ו) לָמָּה נֶאֱמַר "בְּכָל מְאֹדֶךָ", וְאִם נֶאֱמַר "בְּכָל מְאֹדֶךָ" לָמָּה נֶאֱמַר "בְּכָל נַפְשְׁךָ"? אֶלָּא לוֹמַר לְךָ: אִם יֵשׁ אָדָם שֶׁגּוּפוֹ חָבִיב עָלָיו מִמָּמוֹנוֹ – לְכָךְ נֶאֱמַר "בְּכָל נַפְשְׁךָ"(א), וְיֵשׁ אָדָם שֶׁמָּמוֹנוֹ חָבִיב עָלָיו מִגּוּפוֹ – לְכָךְ נֶאֱמַר "בְּכָל מְאֹדֶךָ". כִּי אֲתָא רָבִין אָמַר רַבִּי יוֹחָנָן: [ד]בַּכֹּל מִתְרַפְּאִין, *חוּץ מֵעַ"ז וְגִילּוּי עֲרָיוֹת וּשְׁפִיכוּת

רש"י

עָרְלָה לֹא הָיְתָה לָהּ שְׁעַת הַכּוֹשֶׁר. שֶׁהַפְּרִי הַזֶּה חָנַט בְּאִיסּוּר, תֹּאמַר בְּבָשָׂר בְּחָלָב שֶׁיֵּשׁ לוֹ שְׁעַת הַכּוֹשֶׁר קוֹדֶם שֶׁנִּיתַּן בְּחָלָב: כִּלְאֵי הַכֶּרֶם יוֹכִיחוּ. וּבִשְׁחִיטַת חוּלִּין פָּרֵיךְ: וְנֵימָא עָרְלָה תּוֹכִיחַ, וְחָזַר הַדִּין. וְהָתָם מְתָרֵץ לָהּ בְּ"כָל הַבָּשָׂר". וּלְקַמָּן פָּרֵיךְ: וְנֵימָא מַה לְּכִלְאֵי הַכֶּרֶם שֶׁכֵּן לֹא הָיְתָה לָהֶם שְׁעַת הַכּוֹשֶׁר: וְאִם אִיתָא. דְּכִלְאֵי הַכֶּרֶם חֲלוּקִין לְהַחְמִיר מִשְּׁאָר אִיסּוּרִין, לִיפְרוֹךְ הַאי: וְאַבָּיֵי. אָמַר לָךְ: הֵיכִי נִיפְרוֹךְ? הֵיכִי נְסַיְּימֵהּ לְמִילְּתֵיהּ, דְּלָא נֵילַף בָּשָׂר בְּחָלָב מִינֵּיהּ? נֵימָא: תֹּאמַר בְּבָשָׂר בְּחָלָב כו' – אַטּוּ בָּשָׂר בְּחָלָב אֲכִילָה כְּתִיבָה בֵּיהּ?! הָתָם נַמִּי לוֹקִין עָלָיו אֲפִי' שֶׁלֹּא כְּדֶרֶךְ הֲנָאָתוֹ: מִנְּבֵילָה. וּנְבֵילָה אֲכִילָה כְּתִיבָא בֵּיהּ. נְבֵילָה לָאו דַּוְקָא קָאָמַר, דְּהָא מִטְּרֵיפָה גָּמְרִינַן לָהּ. וְיֵשׁ מְפָרְשִׁים דְּמִשּׁוּם דְּהַאי טְרֵיפָה דִּקְרָא אַיְירֵי בְּאֵבֶר וּבָשָׂר הַמְדוּלְדָּל בָּהּ וּשְׁחָטָהּ, כִּדְאָמְרִינַן בִּ"בְהֵמָה הַמַּקְשָׁה לֵילֵד" (חולין עג:) קָרֵי לֵיהּ נְבֵילָה, דְּדָמֵי לִנְבֵילָה דְּלָא מִשְׁתְּרוּ בִּשְׁחִיטָה. וְאֵין נִרְאֶה לִי, דִּטְרֵיפָה נַמִּי לָא מִשְׁתַּרְיָא בִּשְׁחִיטָה. וְאִי מִשּׁוּם דְּלָא מִיטַּמְּיָא – הָנָךְ נַמִּי לָא מִיטַּמְּאוּ: וְאִידָךְ. אַבָּיֵי אָמַר לָךְ: לְהָכִי לָא כְּתִיב אֲכִילָה בְּגוּפוֹ – לְלַמֶּדְךָ שֶׁלּוֹקִין כו'. הִלְכָּךְ לָא מָצֵי פָּרֵיךְ: תֹּאמַר בְּבָשָׂר בְּחָלָב כו': וְלִיפְרוֹךְ מַה לְּכִלְאֵי הַכֶּרֶם שֶׁכֵּן לֹא הָיְתָה לָהֶם שְׁעַת הַכּוֹשֶׁר. וְקָא סָלְקָא דַּעְתָּךְ שֶׁאֵין נֶאֱסָרִין אֶלָּא גִּידּוּלֵיהֶן, וְלָכֵן לֹא הָיְתָה לָהֶן שְׁעַת הַכּוֹשֶׁר: זֹאת אוֹמֶרֶת. מִדְּלָא פָּרֵיךְ הָכִי – שְׁמַע מִינָּהּ כִּלְאֵי הַכֶּרֶם עִיקָּרָן נֶאֱסָר, אַף עִיקַּר הַזְּרִיעָה עַצְמָהּ נֶאֱסְרָה. וּזְרִיעָה הָיְתָה לָהּ שְׁעַת הַכּוֹשֶׁר כָּל יָמֶיהָ עַד שֶׁנִּשְׁרְשָׁה. י"מ דְּהַאי מַקְשֶׁה נַמִּי יָדַע שֶׁאַף הַזְּרִיעָה נֶאֱסֶרֶת, אֶלָּא סָבוּר שֶׁמִּשְּׁעַת זְרִיעָה נֶאֱסֶרֶת, וְכָךְ שָׁמַעְתִּי. אֲבָל א"א לְהַעֲמִידָהּ, דְּמִיבָּעֵי לָן לְפָרוֹשֵׁי הָכִי: מַה לְּכִלְאֵי הַכֶּרֶם – שֶׁכֵּן לֹא הָיְתָה לָהֶן שְׁעַת הַכּוֹשֶׁר מִשָּׁעָה שֶׁבָּאוּ לִכְלַל כִּלְאַיִם, תֹּאמַר בְּבָשָׂר בְּחָלָב שֶׁהָיְתָה לוֹ שְׁעַת הַכּוֹשֶׁר מִשָּׁעָה שֶׁבָּא לִכְלַל זֶה, דְּאִם שׁוֹרֵהוּ כָּל הַיּוֹם בְּחָלָב – אֵינוֹ נֶאֱסָר בְּכָךְ. וּמְשַׁנֵּי: עִיקָּרָן נֶאֶסְרוּ מִשֶּׁנִּשְׁרְשׁוּ, וְלֹא מִשֶּׁנִּזְרְעוּ. וְכַמָּה גִּמְגּוּמִים יֵשׁ בָּהּ. חֲדָא: דְּטַעְמָא דְּלָא מִיתַּסַּר – ° מִשּׁוּם דַּאֲכַתִּי לָא בָּשָׂר בְּחָלָב חָשֵׁיב לֵיהּ, וַהֲרֵי הוּא כְּאִילּוּ זֶה לְבַד וְזֶה לְבַד. וְכֵן בְּכִלְאַיִם, כ"ז שֶׁלֹּא נִשְׁרְשׁוּ – הֲרֵי הֵן כְּמוּנָּחִין בְּכַדָּא. וְעוֹד: כִּי אֲמַר לְעֵיל חָמֵץ בַּפֶּסַח יוֹכִיחַ – מִיבָּעֵי לֵיהּ לְמֵימַר שֶׁהָיְתָה לוֹ שְׁעַת הַכּוֹשֶׁר מִשֶּׁנִּקְרָא חָמֵץ בַּפֶּסַח, וְהָא לֵיתָא. וְעוֹד: מִדְּמוֹתִיב רַב שְׁמַעְיָה, הוֹסִיף – אִין, לֹא הוֹסִיף – לָא, מִכְּלָל דְּלֵיכָּא מַאן דְּסָלֵיק אַדַּעְתֵּיהּ מִשְּׁעַת זְרִיעָה. אֶלָּא הֲוָה סָלְקָא דַּעְתֵּיהּ תּוֹסֶפֶת אִין, עִיקָּר לָא. וּלְשׁוֹן עִיקָּרָן מַשְׁמַע כִּדְפָרֵישִׁית, דְּלִלִישָּׁנָא בַּתְרָא הָכִי הֲוָה לֵיהּ לְמֵימַר: זֹאת אוֹמֶרֶת כִּלְאֵי הַכֶּרֶם בְּהַשְׁרָשָׁה נֶאֶסְרוּ: הַמַּעֲבִיר עָצִיץ נָקוּב בַּכֶּרֶם. וּזְרָעִים בְּתוֹכוֹ, שֶׁכְּבָר צָמְחוּ. הוֹסִיף הַצֶּמַח בַּכֶּרֶם מָאתַיִם – אֶחָד מִן הַמָּאתַיִם שֶׁיֵּשׁ בּוֹ עַכְשָׁיו, שֶׁמִּתְּחִלָּה הָיוּ בּוֹ קנ"ט שִׁיעוּרִים כְּתוֹסֶפֶת זוֹ, וְעַכְשָׁיו יֵשׁ בּוֹ מָאתַיִם – אֲסוּרִין, לְפִי שֶׁאֵין בַּהֶיתֵּר הָרִאשׁוֹן כְּדֵי לְבַטֵּל הַתּוֹסֶפֶת הָאִסּוּר. שֶׁהָעָרְלָה וְכִלְאַיִם אֵין בְּטֵלִין אֶלָּא בְּמָאתַיִם שֶׁל הֶיתֵּר לְבַד הָאִיסּוּר. לֹא הוֹסִיף מָאתַיִם, אֶלָּא פָּחוֹת כָּל שֶׁהוּא – מוּתָּר, דְּיֵשׁ בּוֹ כְּדֵי לְהַעֲלוֹת בְּאֶחָד וּמָאתַיִם. וּבְסִפְרֵי יָלֵיף לֵיהּ מִתְּרוּמָה שֶׁעוֹלָה בְּאֶחָד וּמֵאָה, וְכִלְאַיִם שֶׁכָּפַל אֶת אִסּוּרָיו שֶׁאֲסוּרִין בַּהֲנָאָה – כָּפַל אֶת עֲלִיָּיתָן. וְדַוְקָא נָקַט נָקוּב, דְּיוֹנֵק מִקַּרְקַע דֶּרֶךְ אֲוִיר: לֹא הוֹסִיף לָא. אַלְמָא: אֵין הַזְּרִיעָה נֶאֱסֶרֶת: מְלֵיאָה. גִּידּוּלִין: הַזֶּרַע. הָרִאשׁוֹן: זָרוּעַ מֵעִיקָּרוֹ. בַּכֶּרֶם בְּהַשְׁרָשָׁה, כִּדְכְתִיב: "הַזֶּרַע" מַשְׁמַע שֶׁאַף הַזְּרִיעָה נֶאֱסֶרֶת מִיהוּ קוֹדֶם הַשְׁרָשָׁה כְּמַאן דְּמַנְחָא בְּכַדָּא דָּמֵי: זָרוּעַ וּבָא. קוֹדֶם לָכֵן. הוֹסִיף – אִין, לֹא הוֹסִיף – לָא, דִּכְתִיב "מְלֵאָה": בַּכֹּל מִתְרַפְּאִין. אֲפִילּוּ בְּאִיסּוּרֵי הֲנָאָה: לָמָּה נֶאֱמַר בְּכָל מְאוֹדֶךָ. יֹאמַר הֶחָבִיב מִשְּׁנֵיהֶן, וְדַיּוֹ. וּמְפָרֵשׁ: לְפִי שֶׁפְּעָמִים שֶׁזֶּה חָבִיב וּפְעָמִים שֶׁזֶּה חָבִיב – לְכָךְ הוּצְרְכוּ שְׁנֵיהֶן, לוֹמַר: אֱהוֹב אֶת בּוֹרַאֲךָ יוֹתֵר מִן הֶחָבִיב עָלֶיךָ. וְהַמִּתְרַפֵּא בַּעֲצֵי אֲשֵׁירָה נִרְאֶה כְּמוֹדֶה בָּהּ:

תוספות

מה לערלה שכן לא היתה לה שעת הכושר. הקשה ריב"א: נילף מערלה שהיתה לה שעת הכושר, כגון נטל ענף מאילן של היתר שלא נגמרו פירותיו, והרכיבו או נטעו! ואומר ר"י: דאינו אוסר אלא מה שגדל אחר שהרכיבו או נטעו, וזה לא היה לו שעת הכושר, והענף עצמו אינו נאסר אלא מפני תערובת האיסור. ואם היה יכול להבדיל אותו הענף ממה שגדל אחרי כן – היה מותר. וכן כלאי הכרם, אי לא היה עיקרו נאסר, או מעביר עציץ נקוב חשוב לא היה לו שעת הכושר, שהאיסור הגדל אחרי כן לא היה לו מעולם שעת הכושר: מה לחמץ בפסח שכן ענוש כרת. ומשור הנסקל לא מצי למימר יוכיח, דמה לערלה ולשור הנסקל – שכן לא היה שעת הכושר לאכילה:

כלאי הכרם יוכיחו. בפ' "כל הבשר" (חולין קטו:) פריך: ונימא ערלה תוכיח, ומשני. ונראה לר"י: דהוה מצי למילף במה מצינו מכלאי הכרם לחודייהו: דמה כלאי הכרם – שכן נעבדה בו עבירה ואסורה באכילה ובהנאה – אף אני אביא בשר בחלב וכו'. אלא ניחא ליה למילף מכל הני בק"ו, דאלים טפי: מה לכלאי הכרם שכן לוקים עליו שלא כדרך כו'. תימה לרשב"א: היא גופא נילף במה מצינו מכלאי הכרם, שילקו על בשר בחלב שלא כדרך הנאה! ואומר ר"י: דליכא למילף, דאיכא למימר דשור הנסקל וחמץ שעבר עליו ב"בל יראה" יוכיח, שנעבד בו עבירה ואסור באכילה, ואינו אסור אלא כדרך הנאתו – דאכילה כתיב בהו:

עיקרן נאסרין. אומר ר"י שגם הגבעולים והקש שגדל ממנו נאסר, כדאמרינן לקמן (ד' כו:): תנור שהסיקו בקליפי ערלה או בקשין של כלאי הכרם, חדש – יותץ. וקשה לר"י: דבפרק "האשה שנפלו" (כתובות דף פ. ושם) גבי מוציא הוצאות על נכסי אשתו וכו', מפרש רב יהודה אפי' לא אכל אלא חבילי זמורות. רב יהודה לטעמיה, דאמר: אכלה ערלה וכלאים ושביעית – הוי חזקה. פי': אע"פ שבכל אלו אין יכול לאכול רק העצים, שהפירות אסורין. אלמא: עצי כלאים שרו! ואומר ר"ת: דהתם מיירי באותן עצים שהיו קודם זריעת כלאים, וקודם שהוסיף מאתים. אבל אותן שגדילין אחרי כן – אסורין מאחר שהוסיף מאתים:

הואיל והיתה לו שעת הכושר קודם השרשה. והא דאמרינן בפ"ק דמנחות (דף ו. ושם) גבי טריפה, דכלאים לא היה להם שעת הכושר – התם קאי על משקה ישראל, ומשקה לא היה לו לעולם שעת הכושר:

חוץ מעצי אשירה. נראה לר"י: דמיירי כגון שאין יכול להתרפא משאר עצים אלא בזה, כגון על ידי שדים או שום דבר אחר, משום דאתי למיטעי בתר ע"ז. וגבי בן דמא בע"ז פרק שני (דף כז: ושם) שנשכו נחש ובא יעקב איש כפר סכניא לרפאותו ולא הניחו ר' ישמעאל, משום דאפיקורסות משכא, ומפרש בירושלמי בפ' "שמנה שרצים" שהיה רוצה ללחוש לו בשם זר. אבל ע"י תחבושת – שרי, כדאמרי' התם (דף כח.) דר' אבהו רמא ליה יעקב אפיקורסא סמא אשקיה: אף

עין משפט נר מצוה

ל א מיי' פי"ד מהלכות מאכלות אסורות סי' ד ה ו טוש"ע שם:

לא ב מיי' פ"ה מהל' כלאים הל' יג טוש"ע י"ד סי' רצו סעיף ט:

לב ג מיי' שם הל' כג טוש"ע שם סעיף יז:

לג ד מיי' פ"ה מהלכות יסודי התורה הל' ו סמג עשין ה טוש"ע י"ד סי' קנה סעיף ב [רב אלפס כאן ובע"ז פ"ב ס' שלח]:

רבינו חננאל

מהא ברייתא דמייתי איסור בשר בחלב בק"ו מערלה ודחי' מה לערל' שכן וכו' חמץ בפסח יוכיח ופרכי' מה לחמץ שכן ענוש כרת כלאי הכרם יוכיחו ואם איתה נפרוך מה לכלאי הכרם שכן לוקין עליהן אפי' שלא כדרך הנאתן ופריק אביי הכי בשר בחלב נמי לוקה עליו אפי' שלא כדרך אכילתו דהא לא כתיבא ביה אכילה. (ואיסי) [ואידך] אמר לך כיון דבשר בחלב איתקש לנבלה שנאמר כי עם קדוש אתה לה' אלהיך לא תבשל גדי בחלב אמו וכתי' ואנשי קדש תהיון לי [ובשר בשדה טרפה לא תאכלו] הנה נאמר בכאן כי עם קדוש ונאמ' להלן ואנשי קדש תהיון לי וכתיב בטרפה לא תאכלו הרי אכילה כתיבא ביה בשר בחלב [נמי כאלו] אכילה כתיב' ביה ואביי אדרבה נימא להכי לא כתיב ביה אכילה בגופו לומר שלוקה שלא כדרך הנאתו ונפרוך מה לכלאי הכרם שכן לא היתה להם שעת הכושר תאמר בבשר בחלב שאם שרה בשר בחלב היום כולו מותר ואינו אסור אלא בישולו ודחי' כלאי הכרם נמי מדלא פריך הכי שמע' מינה דהיתה להם שעת הכושר משעת זריעה עד שעת השרשה *כי לא נאסר אלא עיקרן ומהאי [טעמא] דייק רב אדא בר אהבה ואמ' זאת אומר' כלאי הכרם עיקרן נאסרו: **איני** דכלאי הכרם בהשרשה נאסרין והתניא המעביר עציץ נקוב בכרם אם הוסיף מאתים אסור כלומר אם הוסיף עציץ זה בכרם כשיעור שיש בו חלק אחד במאתים חלקים כמה שיש בו נאסר דייקי' מינה מדקתני הוסיף נאסר מכלל שאם לא הוסיף אפי' השריש לא נאסר ופריק רבא כתיב המלאה וכתיב הזרע הא כיצד אם היה זרוע עד שימלא כדכתי' המלאה לא היה זרוע אלא עכשיו נזרע בהשרשה בעת שנזרע הזרע בהשרשה נאסר שנאמר הזרע:

אמר רבי יוחנן בכל מתרפאין חוץ מע"ז וגלוי עריות

* דברי רבינו הוא כפי' הרי"ף שהובא ברש"י כאן ד"ה זאת אומרת ואולי דברש"י ... בזה על דברי הר"ח ז"ל ...

מסורת הש"ס

חולין קטז. כלאים פ"ז מ"ח

[המלאה וכתיב הזרע וכן איתא בחולין קטו. וכ"כ בפירש"י דהכא]

ברכות סא: יומא פב. סנהדרין עד.

[עי' תוס' סוטה י: ד"ה טוח]

הגהות הב"ח

(א) גמ' ואם יש אדם שממונו חביב:

גליון הש"ס

ברש"י זאת אומרת. משום דאכתי לאו בשר בחלב. עי' מנחות קא: ברש"י ד"ה הואיל ובתוספות שם ד"ה פיגול:

ושפיכות דמים. ע"ז — הא דאמרן. גילוי עריות ושפיכות דמים — דתניא, *ר' אומר: °"כי כאשר יקום איש על רעהו ורצחו נפש כן הדבר הזה" (דברים כב) וכי מה ענין רוצח אצל נערה המאורסה? *הרי זה בא ללמד ונמצא למד, מקיש רוצח לנערה המאורסה. מה נערה המאורסה ניתן להצילה בנפשו — [א]אף רוצח ניתן להצילו בנפשו. ונערה המאורסה מרוצח, [ב]מה רוצח — יהרג ואל יעבור, אף נערה המאורסה — תהרג ואל תעבור. ושפיכות דמים גופיה מנלן? סברא הוא; *כי ההוא דאתא לקמיה דרבא, א"ל: מרי דוראי אמר לי "זיל קטליה לפלני', ואי לא — קטלינא לך". א"ל: ליקטלוך ולא תיקטול. מאי חזית דדמא דידך סומק טפי? דילמא דמא דההוא גברא סומק טפי? מר בר רב אשי אשכחיה לרבינא דשייף לה לברתיה בגוהרקי דערלה, אמר ליה: [ג]אימור דאמור רבנן בשעת הסכנה, שלא בשעת הסכנה מי אמור? א"ל: האי אישתא צמירתא נמי כשעת הסכנה דמיא. איכא דאמרי, א"ל: °[ד]מידי דרך הנאה קא עבידנא? איתמר, הנאה הבאה לו לאדם בעל כרחו. אביי אמר: מותרת, ורבא אמר: אסורה. אפשר וקא מיכוין, לא אפשר וקמיכוין — כולי עלמא לא פליגי דאסור. לא אפשר ולא מיכוין — כולי עלמא לא פליגי דשרי. °כי פליגי — דאפשר ולא מיכוין. ואליבא דר' יהודה, דאמר *"דבר שאין מתכוין — אסור" — כולי עלמא לא פליגי דאסור. כי פליגי — אליבא דר"ש, דאמר "דבר שאין מתכוין מותר". אביי — כרבי שמעון, ורבא אמר: עד כאן לא קא א"ר שמעון — אלא היכא דלא אפשר, אבל היכא דאפשר — לא. איכא דאמרי: אפשר ולא מיכוין — היינו פלוגתייהו דר' יהודה ור' שמעון. לא אפשר ולא קא מיכוין — כולי עלמא לא פליגי דשרי, כי פליגי — דלא אפשר וקא מיכוין. ואליבא דר' שמעון דאזיל בתר כוונה — כולי עלמא לא פליגי דאסור. כי פליגי — אליבא דר' יהודה, דאמר: לא שנא מתכוין ולא שנא שאין מתכוין — אפשר אסור. אביי כרבי יהודה, ורבא

רש"י

ושפיכות דמים. כגון אמרו לו: הרוג ישראל חבירך, ואם לאו — תיהרג: מה למדנו מרוצח לנערה המאורסה. והלא פירש בה אונס פטור, כדכתיב: "ולנערה לא תעשה דבר", אלא נראה כמי שרוצה בא ללמד כאן, ונמצא שהוקש כאן להיות למד מכאן. והכי קאמר: כרוצח כנערה, שניהן שוין. כמו "והיה כעם ככהן" (ישעיהו כד), ולא נאמר "והיה העם ככהן": ניתן להצילה. ניתן רשות לרואה שהוא רודף אחריה שיצילנה ממנו בנפשו של רודף, כדכתיב (דברים כב): "ואין מושיע לה", הא אם יש מושיע — צריך להושיעה בכל אשר יכול, אפילו בהריגתו אם אין יכול להציל באחד מאבריו — יהרגנו: יהרג. אם אמר לו נכרי: הרוג או תיהרג — יהרג ואל יעבור עבירה זו: מרי דוראי. מושל עירי: מאי חזית דדמא דידך סומק. כלומר: כלום באתה לישאל על כך, אלא מפני שאתה יודע שאין מצוה עומדת בפני פיקוח נפש, וסבור אתה שאף זו תדחה מפני פיקוח נפשך, אין זו דומה לשאר עבירות, דמ"מ יש כאן אבוד נפש, והתורה לא התירה לדחות את המצוה אלא מפני חיבת נפשו של ישראל. וכאן עבירה נעשית, ונפש אבודה. מי יאמר שנפשך חביבה לפני המקום יותר משל זה? דילמא של זה חביבה טפי עליו, ונמצא עבירה נעשית ונפש אבודה: שייף. מושח: גוהרקי דערלה. בוסר זיתים קטנים, משום רפואה. דקסבר: מותר להתרפאות באיסורי הנאה: אישתא צמירתא. חולי שקורין מלוי"י. צמירתא = חם, כמו "דצמרה צמורי" בבבא קמא (דף ס.): דרך הנאתו. לאחר שיתבשלו, ויוצא שמנן בבית הבד: מותרת. אין צריך לפרוש הימנה, כדמפרש: הכי גרסינן: אפשר וקא מיכוין לא אפשר וקא מיכוין — כולי עלמא לא פליגי דאסיר. אפשר לו ליבדל, וקא מיכוין להתקרב כדי ליהנות, כגון ריח של ע"ז. או אפילו אי אפשר לו ליבדל, ומיהו מתכוין הוא, וחביב הוא לו ליהנות: לא אפשר. לו ליבדל, ולא קא מיכוין ליהנות, דאיכא תרתי להיתר — לכ"ע שרי: כי פליגי דאפשר. לו ליבדל, ולא נבדל. ומיהו, לא קא מיכוין: פלוגתא דרבי יהודה ורבי שמעון במסכת שבת (דף כב.) בגרירת מטה וכסא וספסל, ובמסכת ביצה (דף כג:): דלא אפשר. כגון שצריך לאותן כלים, ואין יכול להגביהן על כתיפו. ואביי סבר: בקטנים נמי שרי רבי שמעון, אע"פ שאפשר להגביהן על כתיפו. והכי אמרינן במס' שבת*. ולרבא לא שרי ר' שמעון אלא בגדולים: איכא דאמרי. מודה רבא היכא דלא קא מיכוין, אע"ג שאפשר — שרי ר' שמעון, דבהכי פלוגתייהו דר' יהודה ור' שמעון. ובין לאביי ובין לרבא, לר' יהודה — אסור, לרבי שמעון — שרי: כולי עלמא. אביי ורבא לא פליגי דשרי, ואפי' לרבי יהודה: כי פליגי דלא אפשר וקא מיכוין. ומיהו, אליבא דר' שמעון דחשיבא ליה כוונה, דמתיר אפי' בדאפשר, הואיל ולא קא מיכוין, אלמא: אכוונה קפיד, היכא דקא מכוין, אע"ג דלא אפשר — אסור: ה"ג: כי פליגי אליבא דר' יהודה, דאמר: לא שנא מתכוין ולא שנא אין מתכוין, אפשר אסור. ולא גרסינן ולא אפשר שרי. דהא לא שמעינן ליה דאמר הכי. דאי שמעינן ליה הכי — היכי פליג רבא למיסר? אביי כר' יהודה. דקסבר: כיון דאסר ר' יהודה בדאפשר, אע"ג דלא קא מיכוין — שמע מינה: לא חשבינן ליה כוונה, אלא בדאפשר ולא אפשר תליא טעמא. הלכך, היכא דלא אפשר, אע"ג דקא מיכוין — לא איכפת ליה לרבי יהודה: ורבא

תוספות

אף נערה המאורסה יהרג ואל יעבור. — פי': הבועל. אבל היא — תיבעל ולא תיהרג, דקרקע עולם היא, כדאמר ב"בן סורר ומורה" (סנהדרין עד:). ובריש כתובות (דף ג:) נמי פריך: ולידרוש להו דאונס שרי. ור"י אומר: דשפיר גר' תיהרג, דהא דמשמע ב"בן סורר ומורה" ובריש כתובות דאונס שרי — היינו היכא שהיא קרקע עולם, ולא עבדה מעשה. אבל לעשות מעשה, כגון שאומר לה שתביא הערוה עליה — תיהרג ואל תעשה מעשה, דמרוצח ילפינן ורוצח לא מיחייב למימסר נפשיה — אלא כשאומר לו להרוג בידים, אבל אם אומר הנח לזרוק עצמך על התינוק או תיהרג — אינו חייב למסור עצמו כדי להציל חבירו. דאדרבה, איכא למימר: מאי חזית דדמיה דחבריה סומק טפי? דילמא דמא דידי סומק טפי. ומיהו, לדידיה אם אומרים לו הנח לתקוע אותך בערוה — יהרג ואל יעבור, דלא מצי למימר לא עבידנא מעשה. דכיון שתוקעין אותו, ואין קישוי אלא לדעת, כדאמרי' בריש "הבא על יבמתו" (יבמות נג.) ומה שהוא מתקשה — הוי מעשה*:

לא אפשר ולא מיכוין כולי עלמא לא פליגי. ללישנא קמא נראה לפרש דכ"ע קאי אאביי ורבא, ולא פליגי דשרי — היינו לרבי שמעון. דרבי יהודה אסר. דהא רבא מוקי פלוגתא דרבי יהודה ור' שמעון בלא אפשר ולא מיכוון. דבאפשר קאמר דמודה רבי שמעון לאסור. ולאיכא דאמרי לא אפשר ולא מיכוין, לכולי עלמא דשרי — האי כולי עלמא היינו ר' יהודה ור' שמעון. וא"ש דבאיכא דאמרי לא הדר ונקיט אלא מה ששנה מלשון ראשון, ולהכי לא נקט בדאיכא דאמרי "אפשר ומיכוין לכ"ע אסור". ומיירי כגון דלא הוי פסיק רישיה דבפסיק רישיה מודה רבי שמעון, וליכא למימר דאפילו בפסיק רישיה שרי הכא ר' שמעון, משום דהכא מיירי בגרירה דכלים דליכא אלא איסורא דרבנן, שהוא חופר כלאחר יד, כדאמר *ב"במה מדליקין" (שבת כט). [נפ' כירה מו: בל"ל] דהא בשמעתא מייתי עלה מידי דאורייתא, כגון מעילה וכלאים ופסול פרה. וצ"ל דכל הנהו דמייתי לא הוי פסיק רישיה. ו"לא אפשר" דכולי שמעתא, נראה לר"י דלא אפשר כדרכו אלא בטורח גדול, דהא שילשול האומנין בקופות חשיב לא אפשר. והא דאמרינן בכתובות (דף ה:) גבי מהו לבעול בתחלה בשבת, דקאמר לר' יהודה לאסור משום דבר שאין מתכוון, אע"ג דהוי לא אפשר ולא מיכוין. וצריך לומר דההיא סוגיא כרבי ירמיה, ד"במה מדליקין" *דאסר [דף כט:] לר' יהודה לא אפשר ולא מיכוון. אע"ג דאיתותב במאי דאמר קטנים אסורים אפילו לר"ש (איתותב), מ"מ במאי דאסר אפילו בגדולים לר' יהודה — לא איתותב: **אביי** כרבי יהודה. נראה דסבר אביי: הואיל ואפשר ולא מיכוין אסור, ובלא אפשר ולא מיכוין שרי. אלמא: דאיסור משום דאפשר הוא. ומה שהיה בספרים ב"במה מדליקין" (שבת כט:) ופליגא דעולא, דאמר עולא: מחלוקת בקטנים אבל בגדולים ד"ה אסור — שיבוש הוא, דבכולי שמעתא שרי טפי לא אפשר מהיכא דאפשר. וגדולים — היינו לא אפשר. אלא גרס: ד"ה מותר, והיינו כלישנא בתרא דהכא, דבלא אפשר ולא מיכוין כ"ע ל"פ דשרי:

רבינו חננאל

ושפיכות דמים ע"ז הא דאמרן עריות ושפיכות דמי' מנא לן כדתניא רבי אומר [כתיב] אין לנערה חטא מות כי כאשר יקום איש על רעהו ורצחו נפש וכי מה למדנו לרוצח מעתה וכי יש לומר אם יקום על ורצחו אין לו דין מות כמו זו הנערה שכתוב בה אין לנערה חטא מות אלא הרי זו הנערה באת ללמד לאחרים ונמצאת היא למדה הוקשה זו הנערה לרוצח מה רוצח יהרג ואל יעבור כך נערה המאורסה אם יאמר לה הישמעאלי השמעי לי ואם לאו הנני הורגך תהרג ואל תשמע לו ואם תפסה ונתחזק עליה אין לה חטא מות ורוצח גופיה שלמדה ממנו הנערה מנא לן דדינו ליהרג ואל יהרוג סברא [הוא] כההוא דאתא קמי' דרבא א"ל אמר לי מרי דוראי זיל קטליה לפניא ואי לא קטלינא לך וכו': **מר** בר רב אשי הוה שאיף גרקי דערלה. פי' גרגרים של ערלה לברתיה דהוה בה אישתא צמירתא ואמר ליה האי אישתא צמירתא סכנה היא ובמקום סכנה שרי. איכא דאמרי מידי דרך הנאתן קא עבידנא ושלא כדרך הנאתן שרי: **איתמר** הנאה הבאה לו בעל כרחו כגון שהיה עובר והריח ריח בשמים של ע"ז אביי אמר מותר רבא אמר אסור. כל היכא דאפשר פי' יש דרך אחרת ואפשר לו שלא יעבור דרך שם ומתכוין לעבור שם כדי ליהנות מן הריח של ע"ז כולי עלמא לא פליגי דאפשר לו שלא יעבור שם וכשעובר שם אינו מתכוין ליהנות ועלתה זו בתיובתא דרבא אבל אי לא אפשר ומתכוין קיימא לן דאסור כרבא

עין משפט נר מצוה

לד א מיי' פ"ה מהל' רוצח הל' ו ז סמג לאוין קסד:
לה ב מיי' פ"ה מהלכות יסודי התורה הל' ז סמג עשין ה טוש"ע יו"ד סימן קנז סעיף א:
לו ג ד מיי' שם הלכה ח סמג שם טוש"ע יו"ד סי' קנה סעיף ג [ורב אלפס כאן ובמסכת ע"ג פ"ב דף שלח:]

[וביומא פב. הלריכו תוס' טובא. ועי' תוס' יבמות נג: ד"ה אין אונס]

מסורת הש"ס

[יומא פב. סנהדרין עג. עד.]
[שם חולין כח. קיז. ערכין כט.]
סנהדרין עד. יומא פב:
שבת מח: [נ. פח: קלג. ביצה כג. יומא לד: כתובות ה: ב"ק קיג. כריתות כ:]
[דף כט:]

גליון הש"ס

גמ' מידי לדרך הנאה קעבידנא. עי' בב"ק קא. תוס' ד"ה ולא יצבע: שם כי פליגי דאפשר ולא מיכוין. עי' הרמב"ן ע"ג ד' יג ע"א אהא דאמרינן שם דמיתהני מריח ע"ז:

וְרָבָא אָמַר לָךְ עַד כָּאן. לָא שָׁמְעַתְּ לֵיהּ לְרַבִּי יְהוּדָה דְּלָא אָזֵיל בָּתַר כַּוָּונָה, אֶלָּא דְּלָא פָּטַר לֵיהּ מִשּׁוּם אֵין מִתְכַּוֵּין בִּדְאֶפְשָׁר, דְּמִתְכַּוֵּין אָסוּר לְדִבְרֵי הַכֹּל, וּמְשַׁוֵּי שֶׁאֵין מִיכַּוֵּין כְּמִתְכַּוֵּין לְחוּמְרָא לֶאֱסוֹר. אֲבָל דְּלָא חֲשִׁיבָא לֵיהּ כַּוָּונָה, דִּמְשַׁוֵּי מְכַוֵּין כְּשֶׁאֵין מִתְכַּוֵּין לְקוּלָּא, כְּגוֹן דְּלָא אֶפְשָׁר בְּשֶׁאֵין מִתְכַּוֵּין שָׁרֵי, וְנִישְׁרֵי נַמִי רַבִּי יְהוּדָה בְּמִתְכַּוֵּין דְּלָא חָשִׁיב כַּוָּונָה כְּלָל — הָא לָא שָׁמְעַתְּ לֵיהּ: הַהֵיכָל גּוֹבְהוֹ מֵאָה אַמָּה, וְאִילּוּ הוֹלֵךְ לְמֵרָחוֹק מְאֹד בָּרְחוֹב שֶׁלִּפְנֵי הַר הַבַּיִת. וּמִתּוֹךְ שֶׁרְחוֹב גָּדוֹל הָיָה, וּמַחֲזִיק בְּנֵי אָדָם הַרְבֵּה — הָיָה דּוֹרֵשׁ שָׁם מִפְּנֵי הַחַמָּה, שֶׁאֵין לְךָ בֵּית הַמִּדְרָשׁ מַחְזִיקָן: דְּלָא אֶפְשָׁר. מִלִּדְרוֹשׁ לְרַבִּים הִלְכוֹת הֶחָג: וְקָא מִיכַּוֵּין. לֵיהָנוֹת מִצֵּל הַקּוֹדֶשׁ: דִּלְתוֹכוֹ עָשׂוּי. וְאֵין הֲנָאַת צִילּוֹ נֶאֱסָרָה, דְּאֵין זֶה דֶּרֶךְ הֲנָאָתוֹ: לוּל. אֲרוּבָּה שֶׁבָּעֲלִיָּיה הַיּוֹרֶדֶת לַבַּיִת קָרֵי לוּל: הָאוּמָּנִין. כְּשֶׁיֵּשׁ בֶּדֶק בְּחוֹמַת בֵּית קָדְשֵׁי הַקֳּדָשִׁים: יָזוּנוּ. לְשׁוֹן הֲנָאָה, כִּמְזוֹנוֹת, שֶׁמַּשְׂבִּיעַ עַצְמוֹ מִמַּרְאִית נוֹי הַמְּלָאכָה וְנֶהֱנֶה: וְהָא הָכָא דְּלָא אֶפְשָׁר. שֶׁלֹּא יֵרְדוּ לְתַקֵּן, וַאֲפִילּוּ הָכִי צָרִיךְ לָתֵת אוֹתָן בְּתֵיבוֹת שֶׁלֹּא יוּכְלוּ לְהִסְתַּכֵּל אָנֶה וָאָנָה, דִּילְמָא מִיכַּוְּונֵי לֵיהָנוֹת, וְאָסוּר: קוֹל. שֶׁל כְּלֵי שִׁיר שֶׁהֵן הֶקְדֵּשׁ: וְרֵיחַ. הַקְּטוֹרֶת: אֵין בָּהֶן מִשּׁוּם מְעִילָה. דְּאוֹרָיְיתָא, הוֹאִיל וְאֵין בָּהֶם מַמָּשׁ, וְכֵיוָן דְּמִדְּאוֹרָיְיתָא שָׁרוּ, כִּי לָא אֶפְשָׁר כְּגוֹן הָכָא — אַמַּאי אַטְרְחִינְהוּ רַבָּנַן? אֶלָּא מַעֲלָה בְּעָלְמָא הֲוַאי: הָעוֹמְדִים בִּפְנִים. לְשַׁמֵּשׁ, דְּלָא אֶפְשָׁר מִלַּעֲמוֹד שָׁם, וְאָסוּר לְהוּ לִהְיוֹת מִתְכַּוְּונִים: לְאוֹתָן הָעוֹמְדִים בַּחוּץ. קָאָמַר, אֵין מְעִילָה הָא אִיסּוּרָא אִיכָּא. אֲבָל לָעוֹמְדִין בִּפְנִים — אֲפִילּוּ אִיסּוּרָא לֵיכָּא: הַמְפַטֵּם אֶת הַקְּטוֹרֶת. קְטוֹרֶת זָרָה שֶׁאֵינָהּ שֶׁל צִיבּוּר: אִם לְהִתְלַמֵּד בָּהּ אוֹ לְמוֹסְרָהּ. אַחַר פִּיטּוּמָהּ לַצִּיבּוּר פָּטוּר מִכָּרֵת. אֲבָל אִם דַּעְתּוֹ לְהַנְגִּיעַ לְצוֹרְכּוֹ לְהָרִיחַ בָּהּ, וַעֲשָׂאָהּ בַּסַּמְמָנִין הַכְּתוּבִים — חַיָּיב כָּרֵת, דִּכְתִיב (שמות ל): "אִישׁ אֲשֶׁר יַעֲשֶׂה כָמוֹהָ לְהָרִיחַ בָּהּ וְנִכְרַת": וְהַמֵּרִיחַ בָּהּ. בִּקְטוֹרֶת שֶׁל צִיבּוּר — פָּטוּר מִכָּרֵת וּמֵחַטָּאת, דְּלָא חִיְּיבָה תּוֹרָה אֶלָּא מְפַטֵּם לְהָרִיחַ: אֶלָּא שֶׁמָּעַל. שֶׁנֶּהֱנָה מִן הַקּוֹדֶשׁ, וּמֵבִיא אָשָׁם מְעִילוֹת: קוֹל וּמַרְאֶה. אֵין בָּהֶם מַמָּשׁ, וּפָטוּר לְעוֹלָם: וְרֵיחַ. יֵשׁ בּוֹ מַמָּשׁ בַּסַּמְמָנִין, לְפִיכָךְ חַיָּיב. וּדְקָא אָמַר רַבִּי יְהוֹשֻׁעַ פָּטוּר — לְאַחַר שֶׁתַּעֲלֶה תִּמְרָתוֹ בַּמִּקְדָּשׁ קָאָמַר, דְּמִשּׁוּם דְּנַעֲשֵׂית מִצְוָתוֹ וְאֵין לוֹרֶךְ גָּבוֹהַּ עוֹד בָּהּ — יָצְתָה מִכְּלַל קָדְשֵׁי ה'. וּבָרַיְיתָא בְּמֵרִיחַ בָּהּ בְּבֵיתוֹ, שֶׁנּוֹתֵן מִמֶּנָּה עַל הַגֶּחָלִים: תִּמְרָתוֹ. עַמּוּד עֲשָׁנוֹ: תְּרוּמַת הַדֶּשֶׁן. בְּכָל יוֹם הָיָה נוֹטֵל מְלֹא מַחְתָּה וְנוֹתְנָהּ אֵצֶל הַמִּזְבֵּחַ, וְהִיא נִבְלַעַת בִּמְקוֹמָהּ, כִּדְכְתִיב: "וְהֵרִים אֶת הַדֶּשֶׁן" וגו', וַאֲסוּרָה בַּהֲנָאָה, וּמוֹעֲלִין בָּהּ. כִּדְכְתִיב: "וְשָׂמוֹ אֵצֶל הַמִּזְבֵּחַ" — אַלְמָא טְעוּנָה גְּנִיזָה: וּבִגְדֵי כְהוּנָּה. אַרְבָּעָה בִּגְדֵי לָבָן שֶׁכֹּהֵן גָּדוֹל נִכְנָס בָּהֶם לִפְנַי וְלִפְנִים בְּיוֹם הַכִּפּוּרִים, דַּאֲסוּרִין שׁוּב לְהִשְׁתַּמֵּשׁ בָּהֶן, כִּדְכְתִיב: "וְהִנִּיחָם שָׁם": הָא נִיחָא לְרַבָּנַן. פְּלוּגְתַּיְיהוּ בְּמַסֶּכֶת יוֹמָא (דף כד.): כְּשֵׁרִין הֵם לְכֹהֵן הֶדְיוֹט. כָּל הַשָּׁנָה, שֶׁהֵן הֵן הַבְּגָדִים הָרְאוּיִין לְשִׁימּוּשׁ הֶדְיוֹט: כְּתוֹנֶת וּמִכְנָסַיִם וּמִצְנֶפֶת וְאַבְנֵט: עֶגְלָה עֲרוּפָה. כְּתִיב "שָׁם", דְּמַשְׁמַע שָׁם תְּהֵא קְבוּרָתָהּ: אֶלָּא לְמ"ד מְלַמְּדִין. ר' יְהוּדָה, בְּמַסֶּכֶת סַנְהֶדְרִין בִּשְׁלֹהֵי "אַרְבַּע מִיתוֹת" (סז:): הָכָא מִיעוּטֵי כְּתִיבֵי. בְּהָנֵי, לְמֵימְרָא דְּלָא תִּיגְמַר מִינַּיְיהוּ. "וְשָׂמוֹ" — לָזֶה וְלֹא לְאַחֵר, "הָעֲרוּפָה" — וְלֹא דָּבָר אַחֵר: הַכְּנִיסָהּ לִרְבָקָה. עֶגְלָה עֲרוּפָה. רְבָקָה = קופל"א בְּלַעַ"ז, שֶׁקּוֹשְׁרִין אַרְבַּע פָּרוֹת בְּיַחַד: וְדָשָׁה. תְּבוּאָה עִם חַבְרוֹתֶיהָ: כְּשֵׁירָה. שֶׁלֹּא נִתְכַּוֵּין לְכָךְ, וְלָאו עֲבוֹדָה הִיא: וְאִם נִתְכַּוֵּין שֶׁתִּינַק וְתָדוּשׁ פְּסוּלָה. וְהָכָא לָא אֶפְשָׁר שֶׁלֹּא יַכְנִיסֶנָּה שֶׁתִּינַק, וְכִי מִתְכַּוֵּין שֶׁתִּינַק וְתָדוּשׁ — פְּסוּלָה: אֲשֶׁר לֹא עוּבַּד בָּהּ מִכָּל מָקוֹם. דְּאַף עַל גַּב דִּבְעָלְמָא לָא מִיתַּסַּר — הָכָא אָסוּר: הָא

וְרָבָא [א]אָמַר לָךְ: עַד כָּאן לָא קָאָמַר ר' יְהוּדָה שֶׁאֵין מִתְכַּוֵּין כְּמִתְכַּוֵּין — אֶלָּא לְחוּמְרָא, אֲבָל מִתְכַּוֵּין כְּשֶׁאֵין מִתְכַּוֵּין לְקוּלָּא — לָא. אָמַר אַבָּיֵי: מְנָא אָמֵינָא לַהּ — דְּתַנְיָא: אָמְרוּ עָלָיו עַל רַבָּן יוֹחָנָן בֶּן זַכַּאי שֶׁהָיָה [ב]יוֹשֵׁב בְּצִילּוֹ שֶׁל הֵיכָל וְדוֹרֵשׁ כָּל הַיּוֹם כּוּלּוֹ. וְהָא הָכָא, דְּלָא אֶפְשָׁר וּמִיכַּוֵּין — וְשָׁרֵי. וְרָבָא אָמַר: שָׁאנֵי הֵיכָל דִּלְתוֹכוֹ עָשׂוּי. אָמַר רָבָא: מְנָא אָמֵינָא לַהּ — (דְּתַנְיָא): *[ג]לוּלִין הָיוּ פְּתוּחִין בַּעֲלִיַּית בֵּית קָדְשֵׁי הַקֳּדָשִׁים, שֶׁבָּהֶן מְשַׁלְשְׁלִין אֶת הָאוּמָּנִים בְּתֵיבוֹת, כְּדֵי שֶׁלֹּא יָזוּנוּ עֵינֵיהֶם מִבֵּית קָדְשֵׁי הַקֳּדָשִׁים. וְהָא הָכָא, דְּלָא אֶפְשָׁר וְקָא מִיכַּוֵּין — וְאָסוּר. וְתִסְבְּרָא?! *וְהָאָמַר ר' שִׁמְעוֹן בֶּן פָּזִי א"ר יְהוֹשֻׁעַ בֶּן לֵוִי מִשּׁוּם בַּר קַפָּרָא: [ד]קוֹל וּמַרְאֶה וְרֵיחַ אֵין בָּהֶן מִשּׁוּם מְעִילָה! אֶלָּא: מַעֲלָה עָשׂוּ בְּבֵית קָדְשֵׁי הַקֳּדָשִׁים. אִיכָּא דְּאָמְרִי; אָמַר רָבָא: מְנָא אָמֵינָא לַהּ — דְּתַנְיָא, אָמַר ר' שִׁמְעוֹן בֶּן פָּזִי, אָמַר ר' יְהוֹשֻׁעַ בֶּן לֵוִי, מִשּׁוּם בַּר קַפָּרָא: קוֹל וּמַרְאֶה וְרֵיחַ אֵין בָּהֶן מִשּׁוּם מְעִילָה. מְעִילָה הוּא דְּלֵיכָּא, הָא אִיסּוּרָא — אִיכָּא. מַאי לָאו — לְאוֹתָן הָעוֹמְדִין בִּפְנִים, דְּלָא אֶפְשָׁר וְקָא מִיכַּוֵּין, וְאָסוּר — לֹא, לְאוֹתָן הָעוֹמְדִין בַּחוּץ. גּוּפָא, א"ר שִׁמְעוֹן בֶּן פָּזִי, אָמַר ריב"ל, מִשּׁוּם בַּר קַפָּרָא: קוֹל וּמַרְאֶה וְרֵיחַ אֵין בָּהֶן מִשּׁוּם מְעִילָה. וְרֵיחַ אֵין בּוֹ מִשּׁוּם מְעִילָה? וְהָא תַּנְיָא: [ה]הַמְפַטֵּם אֶת הַקְּטוֹרֶת לְהִתְלַמֵּד בָּהּ אוֹ לְמוֹסְרָהּ לַצִּיבּוּר — פָּטוּר, [ו]לְהָרִיחַ בָּהּ — חַיָּיב. וְהַמֵּרִיחַ בָּהּ — פָּטוּר, אֶלָּא שֶׁמָּעַל. אֶלָּא אָמַר רַב פַּפָּא: קוֹל וּמַרְאֶה — אֵין בָּהֶן מִשּׁוּם מְעִילָה, לְפִי שֶׁאֵין בָּהֶן מַמָּשׁ. [ז]וְרֵיחַ, לְאַחַר שֶׁתַּעֲלֶה תִּמְרוּתוֹ — אֵין בּוֹ מִשּׁוּם מְעִילָה, הוֹאִיל וְנַעֲשֵׂית מִצְוָתוֹ. לְמֵימְרָא דְּכָל הֵיכָא דְּנַעֲשֵׂית מִצְוָתוֹ אֵין בּוֹ מִשּׁוּם מְעִילָה? וַהֲרֵי תְּרוּמַת הַדֶּשֶׁן, דְּנַעֲשֵׂית מִצְוָתָהּ [ח]וְיֵשׁ בָּהּ מִשּׁוּם מְעִילָה, דִּכְתִיב: °"וְשָׂמוֹ אֵצֶל הַמִּזְבֵּחַ" — *שֶׁלֹּא יְפַזֵּר, "וְשָׂמוֹ" — שֶׁלֹּא יֵהָנֶה! מִשּׁוּם דְּהָווּ תְּרוּמַת הַדֶּשֶׁן וּבִגְדֵי כְהוּנָּה שְׁנֵי כְתוּבִין הַבָּאִין כְּאֶחָד, וְכָל שְׁנֵי כְתוּבִין הַבָּאִין כְּאֶחָד אֵין מְלַמְּדִין. תְּרוּמַת הַדֶּשֶׁן — הָא דַּאֲמַרַן, בִּגְדֵי כְהוּנָּה — דִּכְתִיב: °"וְהִנִּיחָם שָׁם" — [ט]מְלַמֵּד *שֶׁטְּעוּנִין גְּנִיזָה. הָנִיחָא לְרַבָּנַן, דְּאָמְרִי: מְלַמֵּד שֶׁטְּעוּנִין גְּנִיזָה, אֶלָּא לְר' דּוֹסָא(א) דְּפָלֵיג עֲלַיְיהוּ, דְּאָמַר: אֲבָל רְאוּיִין הֵן לְכֹהֵן הֶדְיוֹט, וּמַאי "וְהִנִּיחָם שָׁם" — שֶׁלֹּא יִשְׁתַּמֵּשׁ בָּהֶם בְּיוֹם כִּפּוּרִים אַחֵר, מַאי אִיכָּא לְמֵימַר? מִשּׁוּם דְּהָווּ תְּרוּמַת הַדֶּשֶׁן וְעֶגְלָה עֲרוּפָה שְׁנֵי כְתוּבִין הַבָּאִין כְּאֶחָד, *וְכָל שְׁנֵי כְתוּבִין הַבָּאִין כְּאֶחָד אֵין מְלַמְּדִין. הָנִיחָא לְמ"ד אֵין מְלַמְּדִין, אֶלָּא לְמַאן דְּאָמַר מְלַמְּדִין, מַאי אִיכָּא לְמֵימַר? תְּרֵי מִיעוּטֵי כְּתִיבֵי, כְּתִיב "וְשָׂמוֹ", וּכְתִיב °"הָעֲרוּפָה". ת"ש: [י]*הִכְנִיסָהּ לִרְבָקָה וְדָשָׁה — כְּשֵׁירָה, בִּשְׁבִיל שֶׁתִּינַק וְתָדוּשׁ — פְּסוּלָה. וְהָא הָכָא, דְּלָא אֶפְשָׁר וְקָא מִיכַּוֵּין, וְקָתָנֵי פְּסוּלָה! שָׁאנֵי הָתָם דִּכְתִיב: "אֲשֶׁר לֹא עֻבַּד בָּהּ" — מִכָּל מָקוֹם. אִי הָכִי, אֲפִילּוּ רֵישָׁא נַמִי! הָא

[מסורת הש"ס: תורה אור — ויקרא ו — שם טז — דברים כא — ב"מ ל.]

שאני היכל דלתוכו עשוי. פ"ה: ואין הנאת צילו נאסרת, שאין זה דרך הנאתו. וא"ת: והא לא כתיב אכילה, ואפילו שלא כדרך הנאה יהא אסור! וי"ל: דמעילה ילפינן חטא חטא מתרומה, ובתרומה כתיב אכילה, והא דאסר בפ' "כל הצלמים" (ע"ז מח:) ליטב תחת אשירה — משום דאשירה לצל עשויה, והיא דרך הנאה. ועוד: דגבי ע"ז לא כתיב אכילה*: **והא** הכא דלא אפשר וקמיכוין ואסור. ה"מ אביי לאוקמא כרבי שמעון, דאליבא דרבי יהודה פליגי:

ותסברא והאמר רבי שמעון בן פזי קול ומראה וריח אין בהן משום מעילה. פ"ה: וכיון דמדאורייתא שרי, כי לא אפשר — אמאי אטרחוה רבנן? וקשה לר"י: הא בגרירה, דליכא איסורא דאורייתא, ופליג רבא ואסר בלא אפשר ומיכוון, ומאי קא מוכיח אביי לרבא? וי"ל דה"פ: כיון דלא אסירי אלא מדרבנן, א"כ כשהוא לצורך כגון לתקן בית קדשי הקדשים — סברא הוא דאפילו איסורא דרבנן ליכא:

מעילה הוא דליכא הא איסורא איכא. תימה: דבפרק "החליל" (סוכה נג. ושם) תניא: אשה בוררת חטים לאור של בית השואבה, והשמן והפתילה היו של קודש, כדתנן התם. ובירושלמי דייק מינה דקול ומראה וריח אין בהן משום מעילה:

לאותן העומדים בחוץ. ליכא איסורא אלא שלא יקרבו עצמן לעזרה כדי להריח יותר, דהא אמרינן (יומא דף לט:): לא היתה כלה צריכה להתבשם בירושלים מפני ריח הקטורת:

כתיב הכא ושמו וכתיב התם הערופה. תימה לר"י: אמאי איצטריך תרי מיעוטי? בחד סגי, דלהכי כתביה דלא למילף מינייהו!* וי"ל: דאי לא כתיב אלא חד מיעוטא — לא הוה מצי למעוטי אלא מילתא דלא דמי כל כך למיסר, אבל מילתא דדמי למיסר — לא. להכי איצטריך תרווייהו:

הכניסה לרבקה. בתוספתא תני ליה גבי פרה:

הא

[עין משפט נר מצוה: לז א מיי' פי"ד מהל' מאכלות אסורות הל' יב [רב אלפס כאן וכעי"ז פ"ב ד' שלח:] — לח ב מיי' פ"ה מהלכות מעילה הלכה ה: — לט ג מיי' פ"ז מהלכות בית הבחירה הל' כב: — מ ד מיי' פ"ה מהלכות מעילה הל' יו סמג עשין ריו: — מא ה מיי' פ"ב מהל' כלי המקדש הל' י: — מב ו שם הלכה טו: — מג ז מיי' פ"ה מהלכות מעילה הלכה טו: — מד ח מיי' פ"ב מהל' תמידין ומוספין הלכה טו: — מה ט מיי' פ"ח מהל' כלי המקדש הל' ה: — מו י מיי' פ"א מהלכות פרה הלכה ז:]

[ועי' תוס' ע"ז מח: ד"ה לא ישב] [ובתוספות חולין קיז: ד"ה עזין כו' עוד שם קיז: וכן בזבחים מו. הגיהו דבר זה בתיבה אחנס במעילה יח. תירלנו בשם ה"ר פרץ ע"ש וכן ביומא ס. האריכו בביאור זה]

[מסורת הש"ס: [נ"ל דתנן] — מדות ל. [פ"ד מ"ה] — כריתות ו. — תמורה לד. לקמן כז: [ע"ש וגי' רש"י ושמו אצל המזבח שלא ימעל בה אחרים אלא שיהא כולו אצל המזבח משום דהוי] — כריתות ו. חולין קיז. מעילה יא: זבחים מו. יומא יב. כד. ס. — [לקמן מה. יומא ס. קדושין כד. לד: לה. לז: מב: מג. נת. גיטין עו. נזיר לז: ע"ז נב: סנהדרין מה: סז: שבועות כו: זבחים כד. מו. נ. כתובות מט. ערכין יד: חולין סח: קיב: קיז. כריתות ו. מעילה יח:]]

הגהות הב"ח

(א) גמ' דפליג עלייהו ואמר אבל:

גליון הש"ס

תוס' ד"ה שאני. חטא חטא מתרומה. עי' שאגת אריה סי' עו ובתוס' ר"פ כל הצלמים ד"ה ימותו:

רבינו חננאל

וסמיך אביי אהא דרבן יוחנן בן זכאי שהיה יושב ודורש כל היום בצלו של היכל ודחי' רבא שאני התם דהיכל לתוכו עשוי ואין קדושה בצלו רבא אמר מהא דתנן לולין היו פתוחין בעליית קדשי קדשים שבהן היו משלשלין האומנין בתיבות כדי שלא יזונו עיניהם מבית קדשי הקדשים ש"מ דהנאה הבאה לו לאדם בעל כרחו אסור. ודחי אביי מעלה עשו דהא קול ומראה וריח אין בהן משום מעילה. איכא דאמרי רבא הוה מסתייע מזה דהוה דאיק אין בהן משום מעילה הא איסורא איכא מאי לאו באותם העומדים בפנים דלא אפשר וכיון דמכוני אסיר ודחינן לא באותן העומדים בחוץ דאפשר שלא יעמדו ולפיכך מעילה (איכא) [ליכא] איסורא איכא. ואיני דריח אין בו מעילה [והא תנן] המפטם קטרת להתלמד בה [או] למוסרה לצבור [פטור] להריח בה חייב פטור אלא שמעל ושני' הא דתני ריח אין בו מעילה לאחר שתעלה תמרתו היא שנויה מאי טעמא דהא אתעבידא מצותה והא דתני המריח פטור אלא שמעל בשלא עלתה תמרתו: **איני** והרי תרומ' הדשן דאתעבידא מצותה ומועלין בה ושני' משום דכתיב בתרומת הדשן ושמו אצל המזבח ובבגדי כהונה נמי אחר שנעשה מצוותן [יש בהם מעילה] כדכתיב והניחם שם לאו משום דטעונין גניזה הוא [ולמ"ד דראוים הם לכהן הדיוט] מפיק בגדי כהונה ומעייל עגלה ערופה כתיב וערפו שם את העגלה בנחל ולמאן דאמר מלמדין מיעט רחמנא בגדי כהונה ושמו אצל המזבח זה טעון גניזה ולא זולתו ובעגלה ערופה כתיב וערפו שם את העגלה הני אין מידי אחרינא לא:

מז א מיי' פ"א מהל' פרה הלכה ז:

מח ב מיי' פי"ג מהל' אבידה הל' יד סמג עשין עד טוש"ע חו"מ סי' רסז סעיף יז:

מט ג מיי' פ"י מהל' כלאים הל' טז סמג לאוין רעג טוש"ע י"ד סי' שא סעיף ו:

נ ד מיי' פט"ז מהלכות מאכלות אסורות הלכה כב טוש"ע י"ד סי' קמב סעיף ז:

נא ה מיי' שם הל' כד טוש"ע שם סעיף ו:

[פרה פ"ב מ"א]

נב ו ז מיי' שם הל' כב ופ"ז מהלכות ע"ז הל' יב טוש"ע שם ס"ד:

תורה אור

הָא לָא דָּמְיָא אֶלָּא לְהָא: *א שָׁכַן עָלֶיהָ עוֹף — כְּשֵׁירָה, עָלָה עָלֶיהָ זָכָר — פְּסוּלָה. מ"ט? אָמַר רַב פַּפָּא: אִי כְּתִיב °"עָבַד" וְקָרֵינַן "עָבַד" — עַד דְּעָבֵיד בָּהּ אִיהוּ. אִי כְּתִיב "עוֹבַד" וְקָרֵינַן "עוֹבַד" — אֲפִילּוּ מִמֵּילָא נַמִי. הָשְׁתָּא דִּכְתִיב "עָבַד" וְקָרֵינַן "עוֹבַד" — עוֹבַד דּוּמְיָא דְּעָבַד. מָה עָבַד דְּנִיחָא לֵיהּ — אַף עוֹבַד דְּנִיחָא לֵיהּ. ת"ש: *ב אֲבֵידָה, לֹא יִשְׁטְחֶנָּה לֹא עַל גַּבֵּי מִטָּה וְלֹא עַל גַּבֵּי מָגוֹד לְצוֹרְכּוֹ, אֲבָל שׁוֹטְחָהּ לְצוֹרְכָּהּ עַל גַּבֵּי מִטָּה וְעַל גַּבֵּי מָגוֹד. נִזְדַּמְּנוּ לוֹ אוֹרְחִין — לֹא יִשְׁטְחֶנָּה לֹא עַל גַּבֵּי מִטָּה וְלֹא עַל גַּבֵּי מָגוֹד, בֵּין לְצוֹרְכָּהּ בֵּין לְצוֹרְכּוֹ! שָׁאנֵי הָתָם דְּקָלֵי לָהּ; אִי מִשּׁוּם עֵינָא בִּישָׁא, אִי מִשּׁוּם גַּנָּבֵי. ת"ש: *ג מוֹכְרֵי כְסוּת מוֹכְרִין כְּדַרְכָּן, וּבִלְבַד שֶׁלֹּא יִתְכַּוֵּין בַּחַמָּה מִפְּנֵי הַחַמָּה וּבַגְּשָׁמִים מִפְּנֵי הַגְּשָׁמִים. וְהַצְּנוּעִין מַפְשִׁילִין לַאֲחוֹרֵיהֶם בְּמַקֵּל. וְהָא הָכָא, דְּאֶפְשָׁר לְמֶעֱבַד כִּצְנוּעִין, וְכִי לָא מְכַוֵּין — שָׁרֵי! תְּיוּבְתָּא לְמַאן דְּמַתְנֵי לִישָּׁנָא קַמָּא דְּרָבָא, תְּיוּבְתָּא.§ "וְלֹא יַסִּיק בּוֹ וכו'".§ *ת"ר: תַּנּוּר שֶׁהִסִּיקוֹ בִּקְלִיפֵּי עָרְלָה אוֹ בְּקַשִּׁין שֶׁל כִּלְאֵי הַכֶּרֶם, חָדָשׁ — יוּתַּץ, יָשָׁן — יוּצַּן. אָפָה בּוֹ אֶת הַפַּת, רַבִּי אוֹמֵר: ד הַפַּת אֲסוּרָה, וַחֲכָמִים אוֹמְרִים: הַפַּת מוּתֶּרֶת. ה בִּישְּׁלָהּ עַל גַּבֵּי גֶחָלִים — דִּבְרֵי הַכֹּל מוּתָּר. וְהָא תַּנְיָא: ו בֵּין חָדָשׁ, וּבֵין יָשָׁן — יוּצַּן! לָא קַשְׁיָא, הָא — רַבִּי וְהָא רַבָּנַן. אֵימוּר דְּשָׁמְעַתְּ לֵיהּ לְרַבִּי — ז מִשּׁוּם דְּיֵשׁ שֶׁבַח עֵצִים בַּפַּת, זֶה וָזֶה גּוֹרֵם — מִי שָׁמְעַתְּ לֵיהּ?! אֶלָּא לָא קַשְׁיָא: הָא — ר' אֱלִיעֶזֶר, הָא — רַבָּנַן. הֵי רַבִּי אֱלִיעֶזֶר? אִילֵימָא רַבִּי אֱלִיעֶזֶר דִּשְׂאוֹר, *דִּתְנַן: שְׂאוֹר שֶׁל חוּלִּין וְשֶׁל תְּרוּמָה שֶׁנָּפְלוּ לְתוֹךְ עִיסָּה, וְאֵין בָּזֶה כְּדֵי לְהַחְמִיץ וְאֵין בָּזֶה כְּדֵי לְהַחְמִיץ, וְנִצְטָרְפוּ וְחִימְּצוּ, רַבִּי אֱלִיעֶזֶר אוֹמֵר: אַחַר אַחֲרוֹן אֲנִי בָּא. וַחֲכָמִים אוֹמְרִים: בֵּין שֶׁנָּפַל אִיסּוּר *לְכַתְּחִלָּה, וּבֵין שֶׁנָּפַל אִיסּוּר לְבַסּוֹף — לְעוֹלָם אֵינוֹ אוֹסֵר.

עַד

דברים כא

רש"י

הָא לָא דָּמְיָא. תֵּירוּצָא הוּא: שָׁכַן עָלֶיהָ עוֹף. בְּפָרָה אֲדוּמָּה קָאֵי, שֶׁפָּרַח וְנָח עַל גַּבָּהּ. אע"ג דִּכְתִיב: "לֹא עָלָה עָלֶיהָ עוֹל", דְּמַשְׁמַע עָלֶיהָ אֲפִילּוּ עָלֶיהָ בְּעָלְמָא, וְאִי מִשּׁוּם דִּכְתִיב "עוֹל" — הָא מְרַבִּינַן בֵּיהּ שְׁאָר עֲבוֹדוֹת בְּמַסֶּכֶת סוֹטָה (דף מו.). אפ"ה, בְּהָא עֲלִיָּיה כְּשֵׁרָה, דְּלָא נִיחָא לֵיהּ. וְהוּא הַדִּין לְהַכְנִיסָהּ לְרַבָּקָה וְדָשָׁה: עָלָה עָלֶיהָ זָכָר פְּסוּלָה. דְּנִיחָא לֵיהּ. וְהוּא הַדִּין לְתִינַק וְתִידוֹשׁ: עוֹבַד. מַשְׁמַע מִמֵּילָא, עָבַד — מַשְׁמַע בְּיָדַיִם. וְאַף עַל גַּב דְּהַאי בְּעֶגְלָה כְּתִיב — תַּרְוַויְיהוּ יָלְפִינַן מֵהֲדָדֵי בִּגְזֵרָה שָׁוָה דְּ"עוֹל" "עוֹל", בְּמַסֶּכֶת סוֹטָה (דף מו.): לֹא יִשְׁטְחֶנָּה. בְּמוֹצֵא בֶּגֶד אֲבוּדָה קָאֵי: מָגוֹד. קבילי"א: לְצוֹרְכָּהּ. כְּדֵי שֶׁלֹּא יֹאכְלֶנּוּ עָשׁ: נִזְדַּמְּנוּ לוֹ אוֹרְחִין וכו'. אַלְמָא: אַף עַל גַּב דִּלְצוֹרְכָּהּ הוּא. וְהַיְינוּ לֹא אֶפְשָׁר, הוֹאִיל וּמִתְכַּוֵּין לְהִתְכַּבֵּד בְּשֶׁל חֲבֵירוֹ בָּאוֹרְחִין — חָשֵׁיב לֵיהּ גָּזֵל, וַאֲסִיר. וּמְשַׁנֵּי: לָאו מִשּׁוּם כַּוָּונָה הוּא, אֶלָּא מִשּׁוּם דִּבְשְׁטִיחָה זוֹ קָלֵי לָהּ. כְּלוֹמַר: מְאַבְּדָהּ בְּיָדַיִם. אִי מִשּׁוּם עֵינָא בִּישָׁא, אִי מִשּׁוּם דִּלְמָא אוֹרְחִין גַּנָּבֵי נִינְהוּ, וְגָנְבֵי לָהּ: מוֹכְרִין כְּדַרְכָּן. מְעוּטָּפִין בִּכְסוּת כִּלְאַיִם, דְּאֵין מִתְכַּוֵּין לַהֲנָאַת לְבִישָׁה: וְהַצְּנוּעִים. פְּרוּשִׁים, שֶׁמִּתְרַחֲקִין מִן הַכִּיעוּר וּמִן הַדּוֹמֶה לוֹ: לִישָּׁנָא קַמָּא דְּרָבָא. אֶפְשָׁר וְלָא מִתְכַּוֵּין אָסוּר אֲפִילּוּ לְרַבִּי שִׁמְעוֹן, דְּאִ"כ הָא מַנִּי? יֵשׁ שֶׁטּוֹעִין שֶׁמַּקְשִׁין עַל מִשְׁנָה זוֹ, אוֹתָהּ שֶׁשָּׁנִינוּ בֶּגֶד שֶׁאָבַד בּוֹ כִּלְאַיִם לֹא יִמְכְּרֶנּוּ לְגוֹי. אַלְמָא: כִּלְאַיִם אָסוּר לִמְכּוֹר. וְטָעוּת בְּיָדָם, דְּהָתָם אָבַד דַּוְקָא — שֶׁמָּא יַחֲזוֹר גּוֹי וְיִמְכְּרֶנּוּ לְיִשְׂרָאֵל, וְלֹא יַכִּיר שֶׁיֵּשׁ בּוֹ כִּלְאַיִם וְיִלְבָּשֶׁנּוּ. אֲבָל כִּלְאַיִם הַנִּיכָּר — מוּתָּר בְּכָל הֲנָאוֹת מְכִירָה: בִּקְלִיפֵּי עָרְלָה. קְלִיפֵּי אֱגוֹזִים וְרִמּוֹנִים, שֶׁאַף הֵם בִּכְלַל פְּרִי, וַאֲסוּרִין מִשּׁוּם עָרְלָה. וְכֵן קַשִּׁין שֶׁל כִּלְאֵי הַכֶּרֶם — הַכֹּל אָסוּר, דְּבְכִלְאַיִם לָא כְּתִיב פְּרִי: חָדָשׁ יוּתַּץ. שֶׁהֲרֵי עַל יְדֵי הֶיסֵּק זֶה שֶׁל עָרְלָה נִגְמַר וּמִתְקַיֵּים כּוּלּוֹ: יָשָׁן. שֶׁאֵין הֶיסֵּק זֶה מוֹעִיל לוֹ, אֶלָּא שֶׁאוֹפֶה בּוֹ פַּת: יוּצַּן. שֶׁלֹּא יֹאפֶה בּוֹ פַּת בְּהֶיסֵּק זֶה: אָפָה בּוֹ פַּת. בְּהֶיסֵּק זֶה. לְקַמָּן מוֹקֵי לָהּ כְּשֶׁאֲבוּקָה כְּנֶגְדּוֹ, שֶׁכָּל שָׁעָה שֶׁהָיְתָה פַּת בַּתַּנּוּר הָיָה דּוֹלֵק הָאוּר וְאוֹפֵהוּ, שֶׁהָיָה נֶהֱנֶה מִן הָאִיסּוּר בְּשָׁעָה שֶׁהָאִיסּוּר בָּעַיִן: רַבִּי אוֹמֵר הַפַּת אֲסוּרָה. דְּיֵשׁ שֶׁבַח עֲצֵי אִיסּוּר בַּפַּת: וַחֲכָמִים אוֹמְרִים הַפַּת מוּתֶּרֶת. (דְּהָא) סָבְרִי אֵין שֶׁבַח עֵצִים בַּפַּת מַמָּשׁ, וְהוּא הַדִּין דְּלֵית לְהוּ נַמִי חָדָשׁ יוּתַּץ אֶלָּא יוּצַּן, וְהָכִי אָמְרִי' בִּשְׁמַעְתִּין: בִּישְּׁלָהּ עַל גַּבֵּי גֶחָלִים. דִּבְרֵי הַכֹּל הַפַּת מוּתֶּרֶת, וַאֲפִילּוּ לְרַבִּי. דְּכִי אִיתְהַנֵּי פַּת מֵאִיסּוּר — כְּבָר כָּלָה וּבָטֵל, וְגֶחָלִים אִיצְטְרִיכָא לֵיהּ, דְּלָא תֵּימָא אַכַּתִּי אִיסּוּרָא בְּעֵינֵיהּ. וְכָל שֶׁכֵּן בְּתַנּוּר גָּרוּף וְאֵין אֲבוּקָה כְּנֶגְדּוֹ: הָא רַבִּי. דְּקָתָנֵי: חָדָשׁ יוּתַּץ — רַבִּי הִיא, דְּאָמַר: הַפַּת אֲסוּרָה, מִשּׁוּם דְּנִגְמְרָה בְּאִיסּוּר. וְהוּא הַדִּין לְתַנּוּר חָדָשׁ, שֶׁנִּגְמַר נַמִי ע"י הָאִיסּוּר: אֵימוּר דְּשָׁמְעַתְּ לֵיהּ לְרַבִּי דְּיֵשׁ שֶׁבַח עֵצִים בַּפַּת. כִּי שָׁמְעַתְּ לֵיהּ דְּפָלֵיג רַבִּי אַדְּרַבָּנַן — בְּיֵשׁ שֶׁבַח עֵצִים בַּפַּת לְחוּדָהּ הוּא דְּשָׁמְעַתְּ לֵיהּ, דְּרַבָּנַן הָווּ מְקִילֵי טְפֵי, וְשָׁרוּ אֲפִי' פַּת לֶאֱכוֹל. דְּאָמְרִי: אֵין שֶׁבַח עֵצִים בָּהּ, אֶלָּא שֶׁבַח הֶיסֵּק, וְאִיסּוּר(א) שֶׁבָּהּ כְּבָר כָּלָה הוּא. וְרַבִּי סָבַר: הוֹאִיל וַאֲבוּקָה כְּנֶגְדּוֹ — יֵשׁ שֶׁבַח עֵצִים, וְאִיסּוּר גָּמוּר בָּהּ. וְגַבֵּי תַּנּוּר חָדָשׁ, נְהִי דְּיֵשׁ שֶׁבַח עֵצִים בּוֹ — מִיהוּ הוּא עַצְמוֹ אֵין נֶאֱכָל, וְיֹאפוּ בּוֹ, אֶלָּא לְהֶיסֵּק אַחֵר עוֹמֵד, וְנִמְלֵאת פַּת הַנֶּאֱפֵית בּוֹ נִגְמֶרֶת ע"י אִיסּוּר וְהֶיתֵּר, עֲצֵי אִיסּוּר שֶׁגָּמְרוּ (בּוֹ) אֶת הַתַּנּוּר, וַעֲצֵי הֶיתֵּר שֶׁגָּמְרוּ אֶת הַפַּת. וְהָא הֵיכָא שֶׁמְּעִינַן לֵיהּ דְּאָסַר רַבִּי? הָא ר' אֱלִיעֶזֶר. דִּשְׁמְעִינַן לֵיהּ זֶה וָזֶה גּוֹרֵם אָסוּר. דָּבָר שֶׁאִיסּוּר וְהֶיתֵּר גָּרְמוּ לוֹ שֶׁיָּבֹא אָסוּר בַּהֲנָאָה: לְתוֹךְ עִיסָּה. שֶׁל חוּלִּין: אַחַר אַחֲרוֹן אֲנִי בָּא. אִם סִילֵּק אֶת הָרִאשׁוֹן, כִּדְמִתָּרֵץ לֵיהּ אַבַּיֵי:

לָא

תוספות

הא לא דמיא אלא להא שכן עליה עוף. מייתי לה משום דרב פפא אמר מילתיה עלה לפי שהיא משנה:

עלה עליה זכר פסולה. וא"ת: אמאי פסולה, הא ודאי לא ניחא ליה להפסיד פרה, שדמיה יקרים בשביל דבר מועט? וי"ל: דאם נאמר כשירה — הוה ניחא ליה, ולכך אין להכשירה. וא"ת: הכניסה לרבקה ודשה, אמאי כשירה? מ"ש מעלה עליה זכר דפסולה! וי"ל: דהתם לא ניחא ליה בדישתה, שאין מרויח כלום בדישתה, דבלאו הכי נידושה התבואה. וה"ר יהודה פירש: דסתם פרה בחורה היא, ומסתמא אין אדם רוצה להטריחה. וא"ת, והא דתנן:* פרה מעוברת, ר' אליעזר מכשיר וחכמים פוסלין. והכא אמר: עלה עליה זכר פסולה! וי"ל: דהלכה כחכמים דפוסלין. דה"נ ר' יהודה פליג, ואמר דוקא העלה עליה זכר, אבל עלה מעצמו — כשירה. אי נמי, הא דאמר הכא פסולה — היינו כשרואה בשעת עלייה וניחא ליה. כדאמר גבי הכשר (בפ"ק דחולין) (*דף יג.): עודהו הטל עליהן ושמח — הרי זה בכי יותן, נגבו — אינן בכי יותן. דבעינן יותן דומיא דיתן. אף על פי שאם היה יודע בעוד הטל עליהן היה שמח. והא דאמרינן בפרק "עגלה ערופה" (סוטה מו.): עול פוסל בין בשעת עבודה ובין שלא בשעת עבודה, שאר דברים אינן פוסלין אלא בשעת עבודה, מה שהזכר משמש בה — חשוב עבודה:

מגוד פירש ר"ת: כמו נגוד ליה גלימא (*עירובין ד' לד):

חדש יותץ. קסבר: יש שבח עצים בפת, וה"נ יש שבח עצים בתנור, וזה וזה גורם אסור. ויש שבח עצים בפת — היינו העצים שהן גורמים אפיית הפת, כשאבוקה כנגדו. ורבנן סברי: אין שבח עצים בפת, אף על פי שהאבוקה כנגדו, דשלהבת אינה באה מן העצים אלא מחמת מעשהו הנשרף, וא"כ היא כמו גחלת דאין האיסור בעין, וכן פירש"י. הקשה ה"ר אהרן *לרבי, הא דאמר (תרומות פ"ב מ"ג): המבשל בשבת בשוגג יאכל, ואפילו בשבת, ואמאי? נימא יש שבח מוקצה בפת, דגחלים מוקצין הן! ואומר ר"י: דלא שייך אלא באיסורי הנאה דווקא, וכן פי' הקונטרס בפרק בתרא דע"ז (דף סו. ושם) גבי תנור שהסיקו בכמון של תרומה:

בישלה על גבי גחלים. בישלה דווקא בדיעבד, אף על גב דכל הנשרפין אפרן מותר* אפילו לכתחלה — יש לחלק בין אפרן לגחלים:

בין חדש בין ישן יוצן. דזה וזה גורם מותר. אף על גב דזה וזה גורם דוקא בדיעבד מותר, כדמוכח בסוף פרק "כל הצלמים" (ע"ז מח:) דאמר רבי יוסי: אין נוטעין אגוז של ערלה. ומודה ר' יוסי שאם נטע — שהוא מותר. ותשיב ליה זה וזה גורם, דהכא הוי כדיעבד, דאם נאמר חדש יותץ — יפסיד התנור:

בין חדש ובין ישן יוצן. ואף על גב דזה וגם גורם מותר — מ"מ ישן, כיון דסגי ליה בצינון ולא מפסיד מידי אלא איסור הנאה לחודה — לכך צריך ציון:

עד

רבינו חננאל

ת"ש כסות המופקדת אצלו לא ישטחנה לא על גבי מטה ולא על גבי מגוד לצורכו אבל שטח' לצרכה נזדמנו לו אורחין בין לצורכו בין לצרכה לא ישטחנה הנה אפי' לצרכה אסור ושנינן שאני התם דקא קלא ליה כלומר כיון שרואין אותה האורחין באין בלילה וגונבין אותה נמצא כששוטחה כאלו שורפה באש: ת"ש הכניסה לפרה אדומה בגורן לרבקה. פ' לפטומ' מלשון (ירמיה מו כא) עגלי מרבק ודשה כשרה בשביל שתינק ותדוש פסולה הנה כיון שנתכוין לדוש פסלה ואוקימ' מה עבד דניחא ליה [אף עובד דניחא ליה] אע"פ שעובד בה מלאכה שלא על ידיו אלא ניחא ליה עבודה היא ונפסלת בה ת"ש מהא דתנן בסוף כלאים מוכרי כסות מוכרין כדרכן כלומר נושאין בגדי כלאים על כתפיהן ומהנין מהן ובלבד שלא יתכוין בחמה מפני החמה ובגשמים מפני הגשמים והצנועין מפשילין לאחוריהן במקל והא הכא דאפשר למעבד כצנועין ואע"ג דלא עביד כצנועין כי לא מיכוין שרי ותיובתא למאן דתאני לישנא קמא דרבא תיובתא וקיימא לן אפי' אפשר ולא קא מיכוין שרי: ולא יסיק בו תנור וכירים. ת"ר תנור שהסיקו בקליפי ערלה או בקשין של כלאי הכרם חדש יותץ ישן יוצן אפה בו את הפת ר' אומר הפת אסורה וחכמים אומרים הפת מותרת בשלה על גבי גחלים דברי הכל מותרת (*פי' יוצאי מותר עצים) איני והתניא אחד ישן ואחד חדש יוצן ושניה הא דתני [אפילו חדש] יוצן רבנן והא דתני [חדש] יותץ רבי. ואקשי' אימור דשמעת ליה לר' דיש שבח עצים בפת כלומר שבח עצי האיסור והוא אפיית הפת היה הוא ידוע בפת לפיכך שנה הפת אסורה אבל עצי היתר והתנור [של] איסור [שטעון] נתיצה גורמין אפיית הפת [מי] שמעת לרבי שאוסר בזה ואתינן לאוקמינהו לר' אליעזר ורבנן דפליגי בשאור של חולין ושל תרומה שנפלו בעיסה ואין באחד מהן שיעור לחמץ הוא לבדו העיסה ונצטרפו וחימצו ר' אליעזר אומר אחר אחרון אני בא וחכמים אומרים

* דברי רבינו אלו מקוללי הכנה הם ואולי איזה ע"ס נפל בדבריו.

מסורת הש"ס

פרה פ"ב מ"ד

ב"מ ל. [ע"ש]

שבת קכט: מו: כלאים פ"ט משנה ה

לקמן עה.

ע"ז מט. עג: תמורה יב. ערלה פ"ב מי"ח

נ"ל בתחלה וכ"א במשנה

[כפ"ב דב"מ כב.]

[וע"ע מפורש בכורות מז:]

רש"ל גרס לר"י ועי' רש"א

[נ"ל דהכא]

[תמורה לד. ולקמן כו:]

הגהות הב"ח

(א) רש"י ד"ה אימור וכו' היסק לאיסור שכבר.

גליון הש"ס

גמ' בישלה על גבי גחלים. עי' לקמן קף עה ע"א תוס' ד"ה וגרפו ובתשובת פני יהושע סי' י"ח.

עד שיהא בו כדי להחמיץ. ואמר אביי: לא שנו אלא שקדם וסילק את האיסור, אבל לא קדם וסילק את האיסור – אסור. אלמא: *זה וזה גורם אסור. וממאי דטעמא דר' אליעזר כאביי? דילמא טעמא דר' אליעזר משום דאחר אחרון אני בא, לא שנא קדם וסילק את האיסור לא שנא לא קדם וסילק את האיסור. אבל בבת אחת – ה"נ דשרי! אלא: ר' אליעזר דעצי אשירה. *דתנן: נטל הימנה עצים – אסורין בהנאה, הסיק בהן את התנור, חדש – יותץ, ישן – יוצן. אפה בו את הפת – אסורין בהנאה. נתערבה באחרות ואחרות באחרות – כולן אסורין בהנאה. רבי אליעזר אומר: [א]יוליך הנאה לים המלח. (אמר) לו: אין פדיון לע"ז. איסור דשמעת ליה לר' אליעזר בע"ז, דחמיר איסורה – בשאר איסורין שבתורה מי שמעת ליה? אלא אם כן אמאן תרמייה? ועוד, הא תניא בהדיא: וכן היה ר' אליעזר אוסר בכל איסורין שבתורה. אמר אביי: אם תמצא לומר "זה וזה גורם אסור" – רבי היינו ר' אליעזר. ואם תמצי לומר "זה וזה גורם מותר" והכא משום דיש שבח עצים בפת הוא – [ב]הני קערות וכוסות וצלוחיות אסירי. כי פליגי – בתנור וקדירה. למ"ד "זה וזה גורם אסור" – אסור, למאן דאמר *"זה וזה גורם מותר" – שרי. איכא דאמרי: אפי' למ"ד "זה וזה גורם מותר" – [ג]קדירה אסורה, דהא קבלה בישולא מקמי דניתן עצים דהיתירא. א"ר יוסף, א"ר יהודה, אמר שמואל: תנור שהסיקו בקליפי ערלה, או בקשין של כלאי הכרם, חדש – יותץ, ישן – יוצן. אפה בו את הפת, רבי אומר: הפת מותרת, וחכמים אומרים: הפת אסורה. והתניא איפכא! שמואל איפכא תני. ואב"א: בעלמא קסבר שמואל *הלכה כרבי מחבירו, ולא מחביריו, ובהא – אפי' מחביריו. וסבר: אתנייה איפכא, כי היכי דניקום רבנן לאיסורא.§ בישלה על גבי גחלים – דברי הכל הפת מותרת.§ (אמר) רב יהודה אמר שמואל, ור' חייא בר אשי א"ר יוחנן; חד אמר: לא שנו אלא גחלים עוממות, אבל גחלים לוחשות – אסורין. וחד אמר: [ד]אפילו גחלים לוחשות נמי מותרין. בשלמא למ"ד לוחשות אסורין – משום דיש שבח עצים בפת. אלא למ"ד אפילו לוחשות מותרות – פת דאסר, דיש שבח עצים בפת, לרבי היכי משכחת ליה? א"ר פפא: כשאבוקה כנגדו. מכלל

רש"י

לא שנו. דאחר אחרון אני בא, ואם נפל היתר בסוף מותר – אלא שקידם את האיסור וסילקו, מכיון שנפל בו היתר מיד, דהואיל וסילקו ועדיין לא החמיץ – בטל והלך לו. ואע"ג דהועיל בה קצת, שיכול זה האחרון לגמור חימוץ על ידו – אעפ"כ כבר בטל לו, ושוב אין חוזר וניעור בו. אבל לא קדם וסילק, ונגמר על ידי שניהם, ואינו יכול ליבטל – אסור. אלמא: זה וזה גורם אסור: דאחר אחרון אני בא. וטעמא משום דאזל בתר גמר מעשה. גמרו בהיתר – מותר, ואפי' לא קדם וסילק, דאיכא זה וזה גורם. גמרו באיסור – אסור (ואפילו קדם וסילק את האיסור): אבל בבת אחת. אם נפלו כאחת, דליכא גמרו באיסור – הכי נמי דשרי, דזה וזה גורם מותר: הימנה. מן האשירה: יוליך הנאה לים המלח. דמי עצים. מכל מקום שמעינן ליה, כל כמה דלא ממטי הנאה לים המלח – מודה הוא לת"ק בין אחדש יותץ בין אישן יוצן, בין איסור פת. אלמא: כיון דקתני חדש יותץ – אית ליה זה וזה גורם אסור. והא דתניא לעיל חדש יוצן – רבנן היא, דפליגי עליה דר', ואמרי הפת מותרת משום דלא חשיבא להו הנאת היסק ואפילו בגורם אחד לבדו, משום דליתיה לאיסורא בעיניה. וכל שכן בתנור, שאינו נאכל הוא בעצמו, ואין הנאתו בגורם אחד לבדו אלא בשני גורמים – שלו ושל היתר. ואם תאמר: לרבנן יוצן למה ליד הא שרו לפת האפויה בהיסק איסור! הני מילי דיעבד, אבל לכתחלה לא קא שרו לאפות בהיסק איסור. ולקמן פריך: עצים דאיסור לרבנן היכי משכחת לה דאסירי מדאורייתא? והוא הדין דמצי לאוקמא להא דחדש יותץ דלעיל כתנא קמא דר' אליעזר, אלא משום דלא ידעינן מנו, וניחא ליה למינקט ר' אליעזר, והוא ומחלוקתו קאמר: א"כ. דפרכת דילמא שאני ליה, אמאן תרמייה להא דתניא לעיל גבי ערלה יותץ? על כרחיך, כיון דלא משכחת תנא דקאמר זה וזה גורם אסור אלא רבי אליעזר ומחלוקתו, במסכת ע"ז, וחזינא סתמא דתני בשאר איסורי נמי הכי – רבי אליעזר קאמר לה, ולא שני ליה: אמר אביי אם תמצי לומר. ברייתא מפורשת הכי, דכי היכי דאסר רבי בפת – הכי נמי אסר בתנור, ואע"פ שאין עצמו נאכל. דאית ליה זה וזה גורם אסור. ורישא דברייתא דלעיל דערלה – רבי קאמר לה כולה: היינו ר' אליעזר. בניחותא. וליכא למיבעי מידי: ואם תמצי לומר. דסבירא ליה זה וזה גורם מותר, ורישא דההוא לאו רבי הוא אלא ר' אליעזר הוא, והתם בפת הוא דאסר רבי – משום דיש שבח עצים בגופה, ונמצא כשאוכלה – גופו הוא הנהנה מן האיסור בגורם אחד. אבל בתנור חדש וליננו – שרי: הני קערות כוסות וצלוחיות. של חרס, שצרפן בעצי אשירה – אסירי, אפילו לרבי, דהא יש שבח עצים בהן, והנאתן בלא גורם שני הוא, ועל ידי גורם ראשון הוא משתמש בהן הנאת גופו. ולא דמו לתנור, דלא מטיא הנאה לגוף מיניה עד דאיכא גורם שני: כי פליגי. רבי, דלא אסר אלא בפת, ור' אליעזר אית ליה זה וזה גורם אסור – בתנור וקדירה, שאין הגוף נהנה מהן עד שיבא גורם שני, והוא של היתר: קדירה. שצרפה כשהיא חדשה בעצי איסור: דהא מקבלה בישולה. והיכא הנאת תשמיש שמשתמש בה בלא גורם אחר. אבל תנור אין נותנין בו פת אלא לאחר הסיקה של גורם היתר: איפכא תני לה. להא ברייתא דלעיל, והיפכא מתנייה: ואי בעית אימא. שמואל נמי הכי מתנייה, ואית ליה דר' אסר ורבנן שרו. ואיהו הפך לה כדי שלא ילכו בני אדם אחרי רבים להתיר. דבעלמא, במחלוקות אחרות שנחלקו רבים על רבי – סבירא ליה לשמואל דאע"ג דהלכה כרבי מחבירו במקום יחיד, אין הלכה כמותו מחביריו, כלומר במקום רבים. ובהא סבירא ליה דהלכה כמותו, ואע"ג דרבים פליגי עליה: אפכה ואתנייה. הפכה ושנאה, כי היכי דתיקו הא מילתא דאיסורא בשם רבנן, ויעשו בני אדם כמותן, שהכל הולכין אחרי רבים, שאם אני אומר הלכה כרבי שהוא יחיד – לא יאמינו לי: גחלים עוממות. כבויות, כדכתיב (יחזקאל לא): "ארזים לא עממוהו". ומתרגמינן: "כהה" – עמיא: לוחשות. גחלים בוערות, נראות כמתנענעות ולוחשות זו לזו: אסורין. לרבי: כנגדו. כנגד הפת מבעיר העצים בפי התנור: עצים

תוספות

עד שיהא בו כדי להחמיץ. פי': באיסור. דאי יש באיסור וגם בהיתר כדי להחמיץ – נראה לרשב"א דשרי, דהא בפ' בתרא דמסכת ע"ז (דף סח.) תניא: שאור של חולין ושל תרומה שנפלו לעיסה, ובזה כדי להחמיץ ובזה כדי להחמיץ, וחימצו – אסור. ור' שמעון מתיר. והשתא הוי ר' שמעון כרבנן *דהכא. והא דתנן בסוף פ"ק דתמורה (דף יב.): אין מחמץ אחר מחמץ [אוסר], אלא לפי חשבון שבה. שאם נפל שאור של תרומה בעיסה וחימצה, וחזרה ונפלה לעיסה אחרת גדולה מזאת, אם יש בשאור כדי להחמיץ השניה – אסורה, אע"פ שנתחמצה על ידי שאור של איסור, ועל ידי עיסה ראשונה שהיה של היתר. ומוקמינן לה התם כרבנן דהכא, אור"י: מצי למימר דהתם מיירי כגון שאין בעיסה כדי להחמיץ, ובשאור של תרומה יש כדי להחמיץ:

נתערבו באחרות. אור"ת: דלא גרסי' ואחרות באחרות דבסדר המשנה לא גרס ליה, לא במסכת ע"ז ולא בסדר זרעים*:

וכן היה רבי אליעזר אוסר בכל איסורין שבתורה. השתא משמע דבכל מקום אית ליה לרבי אליעזר דזה וגם גורם אסור. ותימה לרשב"א: דתיקשי מהכא לרב הונא בר חיננא, דתניא בתמורה בפרק "כל האסורין" (דף ל: ושם): כל האסורין לגבי מזבח – ולדותיהן מותרין. ותניא עלה: ר"א אוסר. וקאמר רב הונא בר חיננא: מחלוקת כשעיברו ולבסוף נרבעו, דרבי אליעזר סבר עובר ירך אמו הוא, אבל נרבעו ולבסוף עיברו – ד"ה מותרין. אלמא לרבי אליעזר זה וזה גורם מותר*:

ובהא אפילו מחביריו. וטעמא דרבי משום דיש שבח עצים בפת, ולא מטעם דזה וזה גורם. דשמואל פסיק בהדיא בפרק "כל הצלמים" (ע"ז מט.) הלכה כר' יוסי, דזה וזה גורם מותר:

רבינו חננאל

אומרים בין שנפל בתחלה בין שנפל בסוף לעולם אין אסור עד שיהא בשאור של תרומ' כדי לחמץ ואמר אביי לא שנו שאם יהיה האחרון שאור של חולין שהעיסה מותרת אלא שקדם וסלק את האיסור שיחמיץ אבל לא קדם וסלק את האיסור אע"ג שהאחרון חולין אסור ש"מ לר' אליעזר זה וזה גורם אסור ודחי' וממאי דכדאביי היא דלמא טעמא דר' אליעזר דסבר הכל אחר גמרו אי גמר באיסורא אסור אי גמר בהיתרא מותר בין סלקו בין לא סלקו לא שנא לפיכך שנה אחר אחרון אני בא אבל הכא שנתערבו שבח עצים ושבח תנור ובבת אחת הן באין על הפת דברי הכל שרי אלא הא ר' אליעזר דתנן בע"ז פ"ג נטל הימנה מן האשרה עצים והסיק בה התנור (כו') עד ר' אליעזר אומר יוליך הנאה לים המלח כו' פי' כשיעור שכר אפיית הפת יפדה הפת

יוליך דמיה לים המלח קתני מיהת הפת אסורה ש"מ לר' אליעזר זה וזה גורם אסור ודחי' שאני התם משום חומרא דע"ז. אם כן הערלה וכלאי הכרם לאיזה איסור נדמה אותם ועוד תניא בהדיא וכן היה ר' אליעזר אומר בכל איסורין שבתורה אליבא דמאן דאמר דלרבי זה וזה [גורם] מותר והכא בפת אמאי אסר משום דיש שבח עצים בפת סבירא ליה ומש"ה קתני הפת אסורה. קערות וכוסות וקיתונות וצלוחיות שנתבשלו בעצים של איסור דברי הכל אסורות דחד גורם הוא בתנור וקדרה פליגי כי התנור אינו אופה אלא ע"י הדלקת עצים וכן הקדרה אינה מבשלת אלא בעצים שנמצאו התנור והקדרה איסור והעצים שמדליקין בהן תוך התנור ותחת הקדרה של היתר והרי שניהם גורמין לאפיית הפת ולבישול מאן דאמר זה וזה גורם מותר גם אלו מותרות ומאן דאמר אסור גם אלו אסורות: **איכא** דאמרי בקדרה דברי הכל אסור מאי טעמא דהא קדים עייל בישולא מכח הקדרה מקמי דניתי כח עצים: **שמואל** הוה מהפיך דברי רבי לרבנן ואמר וחכמים אומרים הפת אסורה וגם הברייתא דתניא וחכמים אומרים הפת מותרת הוה מהפיך לה ותאני וחכמים אומרים הפת אסורה כי היכי דתיקום דרבנן לאיסורא וקיימא לן הכי: **בשלה** על גבי גחלים דברי הכל הפת מותרת יש מי שאומר לא שנו אלא גחלים עוממות קרובות לכבוי מלשון (יחזקאל ל"א ח') ארזים לא עממוהו וכמוהו (איכה ד' א') איכה יועם זהב דהא קלי ליה איסורא אבל גחלים לוחשות הפת אסורה ויש מי שאומר אפי' לוחשות הפת מותרת אי הכי לרבי דקסבר יש שבח עצים בפת היכי משכחת

עין משפט נר מצוה

נג א מיי' שם טוש"ע שם:

נד ב מיי' פט"ז מהל' מאכלות אסורות הל' כג טוש"ע שם סעיף ה:

[ועי' תוס' ע"ז סח: ד"ה רבי שמעון]

נה ג ד מיי' שם הלכה כג טוש"ע שם סעיף ו ז:

[ועי' תוס' ע"ז מט. ד"ה נתערבו]

[ועי' תמורה ל: מה שתירצו תוס' ד"ה אבל]

מסורת הש"ס

[סנהדרין פ. וש"נ]

רש"ל מוחק זה

ע"ז מט:

[נ"ל אמרו]

[ע"ז מט. סנהדרין פ. חולין נח. תמורה לא.]

[עירובין מו: כתובות כא. נח. ב"ב קכד:]

[נראה שהוא טעות הדפוס]

מִכְּלָל דְּרַבָּנַן דִּפְלִיגִי עֲלֵיהּ שָׁרוּ אֲפִי' כְּשֶׁאֲבוּקָה כְּנֶגְדּוֹ! אֶלָּא עֵצִים דְּאִיסּוּרָא לְרַבָּנַן הֵיכִי מַשְׁכַּחַתְּ לְהוּ? א"ר אַמִּי בַּר חָמָא: בְּשַׁרְשִׁיפָא. בְּעָא מִינֵּיהּ רָמִי בַּר חָמָא מֵרַב חִסְדָּא: תַּנּוּר שֶׁהִסִּיקוֹ בַּעֲצֵי הֶקְדֵּשׁ וְאָפָה בּוֹ הַפַּת, לְרַבָּנַן דְּשָׁרוּ בְּקַמַּיְיתָא מַאי? א"ל: הַפַּת אֲסוּרָה. וּמַה בֵּין זוֹ לְעָרְלָה? אֲמַר רָבָא: הָכִי הַשְׁתָּא?! עָרְלָה — בְּטֵילָה בְּמָאתַיִם, הֶקְדֵּשׁ — אֲפִילּוּ בְּאֶלֶף לֹא בָּטֵיל. אֶלָּא אָמַר רָבָא: אִי קַשְׁיָא לֵיהּ — הָא קַשְׁיָא: וַהֲלֹא מָעַל הַמַּסִּיק, וְכָל הֵיכָא *דְּמָעַל הַמַּסִּיק — נָפְקוּ לְהוּ לְחוּלִּין! אָמַר רַב פָּפָּא: הָכָא בַּעֲצֵי שְׁלָמִים עָסְקִינַן, וְאַלִּיבָּא דְּר' יְהוּדָ', דְּאָמַר: הֶקְדֵּשׁ, בְּשׁוֹגֵג — מִתְחַלֵּל, בְּמֵזִיד — אֵינוֹ מִתְחַלֵּל. בְּמֵזִיד מַאי טַעְמָא לָא — כֵּיוָן דְּלָאו בַּר מְעִילָה הוּא לָא נָפֵיק לְחוּלִּין, שְׁלָמִים נַמִי, כֵּיוָן דְּלָאו בַּר מְעִילָה נִינְהוּ — לָא נָפְקָא לְחוּלִּין. וְכָל הֵיכָא דְּמָעַל הַמַּסִּיק נָפְקִי לְחוּלִּין? וְהָא *תַּנְיָא: כָּל הַנִּשְׂרָפִין אֶפְרָן מוּתָּר, [א]חוּץ מֵעֲצֵי אֲשֵׁירָה. [ב]וְאֵפֶר הֶקְדֵּשׁ לְעוֹלָם אָסוּר! אָמַר רָמִי בַּר חָמָא: כְּגוֹן שֶׁנָּפְלָה דְּלֵיקָה מֵאֵילֶיהָ בַּעֲצֵי הֶקְדֵּשׁ, דְּלֵיכָּא אֱינַשׁ דְּנִמְעוֹל. רַב שְׁמַעְיָ' אָמַר: [ג]בְּאוֹתָן שֶׁטְּעוּנִין גְּנִיזָה, *דְּתַנְיָא: °"וְשָׂמוֹ" — בְּנַחַת, "וְשָׂמוֹ" — כּוּלּוֹ, "וְשָׂמוֹ" — שֶׁלֹּא יְפַזֵּר. § "ר' יְהוּדָה אוֹמֵר אֵין בִּיעוּר וכו'". § תַּנְיָא, *א"ר יְהוּדָה: אֵין בִּיעוּר חָמֵץ אֶלָּא שְׂרֵיפָה. וְהַדִּין נוֹתֵן: וּמַה נּוֹתָר שֶׁאֵינוֹ בְּבַל יֵרָאֶה וּבַל יִמָּצֵא — טָעוּן שְׂרֵיפָה, חָמֵץ שֶׁיֶּשְׁנוֹ בְּבַל יֵרָאֶה וּבַל יִמָּצֵא — לֹא כָּל שֶׁכֵּן שֶׁטָּעוּן שְׂרֵיפָה?! אָמְרוּ לוֹ: כָּל דִּין שֶׁאַתָּה דָּן תְּחִלָּתוֹ לְהַחְמִיר וְסוֹפוֹ לְהָקֵל — אֵינוֹ דִּין. לֹא מָצָא עֵצִים לְשׂוֹרְפוֹ — יְהֵא יוֹשֵׁב וּבָטֵל? וְהַתּוֹרָה אָמְרָה: °"תַּשְׁבִּיתוּ שְּׂאוֹר מִבָּתֵּיכֶם" — בְּכָל דָּבָר שֶׁאַתָּה יָכוֹל לְהַשְׁבִּיתוֹ. חָזַר ר' יְהוּדָה וְדָנוֹ דִּין אַחֵר: נוֹתָר אָסוּר בַּאֲכִילָה וְחָמֵץ אָסוּר בַּאֲכִילָה, מַה נּוֹתָר בִּשְׂרֵיפָה — אַף חָמֵץ בִּשְׂרֵיפָה. אָמְרוּ לוֹ: נְבֵילָה תּוֹכִיחַ, שֶׁאֲסוּרָה בַּאֲכִילָה וְאֵינָהּ טְעוּנָה שְׂרֵיפָה. אָמַר לָהֶן: הֶפְרֵשׁ; נוֹתָר אָסוּר בַּאֲכִילָה וּבַהֲנָאָה, וְחָמֵץ אָסוּר בַּאֲכִילָה וּבַהֲנָאָה. מַה נּוֹתָר טָעוּן שְׂרֵיפָה — אַף חָמֵץ טָעוּן שְׂרֵיפָה. אָמְרוּ לוֹ: שׁוֹר הַנִּסְקָל יוֹכִיחַ, שֶׁאָסוּר בַּאֲכִילָה וּבַהֲנָאָה — וְאֵינוֹ טָעוּן שְׂרֵיפָה. אָמַר לָהֶן: הֶפְרֵשׁ; נוֹתָר אָסוּר בַּאֲכִילָה וּבַהֲנָאָה וְעָנוּשׁ כָּרֵת, וְחָמֵץ אָסוּר בַּאֲכִילָה וּבַהֲנָאָה וְעָנוּשׁ כָּרֵת. מַה נּוֹתָר בִּשְׂרֵיפָה — אַף חָמֵץ בִּשְׂרֵיפָה. אָמְרוּ לוֹ: חֶלְבּוֹ שֶׁל שׁוֹר הַנִּסְקָל יוֹכִיחַ, שֶׁאָסוּר בַּאֲכִילָה וּבַהֲנָאָה וְעָנוּשׁ כָּרֵת — וְאֵין טָעוּן שְׂרֵיפָה.

חָזַר

רש"י

עֵצִים דְּאִיסּוּרָא. דְּמִתַּסְרִי בַּהֲנָאָה, לְרַבָּנַן הֵיכִי מַשְׁכַּחַתְּ לְהוּ? בְּשַׁרְשִׁיפָא. כִּסֵּא לֵישֵׁב עָלָיו, אוֹ לַהֲדוֹס רַגְלָיו. דַּהֲנָאָתָן כְּשֶׁהֵן בָּעַיִן, וְעַל יְדֵי מַמָּשׁ. אֲבָל הֲנָאַת הֶיסֵּק — אֵין הֲנָאָתוֹ אֶלָּא לְאַחַר בִּיעוּרוֹ אוֹ בִּשְׁעַת בִּיעוּרוֹ: בְּטֵילָה בְּמָאתַיִם. הִלְכָּךְ לָא חֲמִירָא מִשֶּׁכָּלָה וְנִבְעַר אִיסּוּרוֹ: וַהֲלֹא מָעַל הַמַּסִּיק. וְחַיָּיב קָרְבַּן מְעִילָה. וְכָל דָּבָר שֶׁאֵין בּוֹ קְדוּשַּׁת הַגּוּף, כְּגוֹן בְּהֵמָה שֶׁאֵינָהּ שֶׁל קָרְבָּן, וּכְלִי שֶׁאֵינוֹ כְּלִי שָׁרֵת — כֵּיוָן שֶׁמָּעַל בּוֹ יָצָא לְחוּלִּין, דִּתְנַן (מעילה דף יט:): אֵין מוֹעֵל אַחַר מוֹעֵל בַּמּוּקְדָּשִׁין אֶלָּא בְּהֵמָה וּכְלִי שָׁרֵת בִּלְבָד. אֲבָל כָּל מִידֵּי אַחֲרִינָא — מִמְּעִילָה רִאשׁוֹנָה נָפְקָא לְחוּלִּין, דְּקַיְ"ל: אֵין מְעִילָה בְּכ"מ אֶלָּא שִׁינּוּי, שֶׁנִּשְׁתַּנָּה מִקְּדוּשָּׁתוֹ, וְאַמַּאי פַּת אֲסוּרָה? הָא קוֹדֶם שֶׁנִּתְּנוּ הַפַּת הָיָה הַהֶיסֵּק חוּלִּין! בַּעֲצֵי שְׁלָמִים. שֶׁהִתְפִּיסָן לִדְמֵי שְׁלָמִים, לְמוֹכְרָן וְלִיקַּח בִּדְמֵיהֶן שְׁלָמִים. וְקָדָשִׁים קַלִּים אֵין לָהֶם מְעִילָה, דְּלָאו "קָדְשֵׁי ה'" קָרֵינַן בֵּיהּ, שֶׁכּוּלָּן לַבְּעָלִים, וְאֵין לַגָּבוֹהַּ בָּהֶן אֶלָּא לְאַחַר זְרִיקַת דָּמִים אֶת הָאֵימוּרִין. וְאִיסּוּרָא מִיהָא רְכִיבָה עֲלַיְיהוּ, וּמִמְּעִילָה הוּא דְּאִימְעִיטִי, בְּמַסֶּכֶת מְעִילָה: וְאַלִּיבָּא דְּרַבִּי יְהוּדָה. פָּשַׁט לֵיהּ רַב חִסְדָּא בְּקִדּוּשִׁין בְּפ"ב (דף נה.), דְּאָמַר: הֶקְדֵּשׁ בְּמֵזִיד אֵין מִתְחַלֵּל. אִם נֶהֱנָה מִמֶּנּוּ בְּמֵזִיד — לֹא יָצָא לְחוּלִּין. הִלְכָּךְ, בִּשְׁלָמִים שׁוֹגֵג דִּידְהוּ כְּמֵזִיד דְּהֶקְדֵּשׁ — דְּהָא לָאו בְּנֵי מְעִילָה נִינְהוּ. וְהָכִי נַמִי הֲוָה מָצֵי לְמֵימַר: הָכָא כְּשֶׁהִסִּיקוֹ מֵזִיד עָסְקִינַן. מִיהוּ שֶׁהִסִּיקוֹ מַשְׁמַע שׁוֹגֵג וּמֵזִיד, וְכֵיוָן דְּמָצֵי לְאוֹקְמָהּ בֵּין בְּשׁוֹגֵג בֵּין בְּמֵזִיד — אוֹקְמָהּ: כָּל הַנִּשְׂרָפִין. בִּשִׁילְהֵי פֶּרֶק בַּתְרָא דִּתְמוּרָה מְפָרֵשׁ אֵלּוּ נִשְׂרָפִין וְאֵלּוּ נִקְבָּרִין: וְאֵפֶר הֶקְדֵּשׁ לְעוֹלָם אָסוּר. לְהָכִי נָקַט גַּבֵּי הֶקְדֵּשׁ 'לְעוֹלָם', וְגַבֵּי אֲשֵׁירָה לָא נָקַט לְעוֹלָם, מִשּׁוּם דַּאֲשֵׁירָה יֵשׁ לָהּ הֶיתֵּר אִם שׂוֹרְפָהּ נָכְרִי וּבִטְּלָהּ. אֲבָל הֶקְדֵּשׁ אֵין בּוֹ בִּיטּוּל. וְהָכִי מְפוֹרָשׁ בְּשִׁילְהֵי תְּמוּרָה: רָמִי בַּר חָמָא וְרַב שְׁמַעְיָה אַאֵפֶר הֶקְדֵּשׁ לְעוֹלָם אָסוּר מְהַדְּרִי: בְּאוֹתוֹ אֵפֶר שֶׁטָּעוּן גְּנִיזָה. קָאָמַר לְעוֹלָם אָסוּר, וְזֶהוּ אֵפֶר שֶׁל תְּרוּמַת הַדֶּשֶׁן, שֶׁלֹּא הָיְתָה מְעִילָה בְּהֶסֵּיקוֹ: כָּל דִּין שֶׁאַתָּה דָּן. שֶׁמִּתְּחִלָּתוֹ אַתָּה דָּנוֹ כְּדֵי לְהַחְמִיר עָלָיו, שֶׁהֲרֵי חָמוּר הוּא. וְאַתָּה מֵבִיא לוֹ חוֹמֶר אַחֵר, כִּדְקָאָמַרְתְּ: חָמֵץ שֶׁהוּא בְּ"בַל יֵרָאֶה" אֵין דִּין שֶׁטָּעוּן שְׂרֵיפָה. וְסוֹפוֹ נִמְצָא שֶׁחוֹמֶר שֶׁאַתָּה מוֹסִיף עָלָיו גּוֹרֵם לוֹ לְהָקֵל: אֵינוֹ דִּין. שֶׁהֲרֵי הַדִּין מְלַמֵּד שֶׁיְּהֵא חָמוּר, וַהֲרֵי הוּא מְקִילּוֹ: שֶׁאִם לֹא מָצָא עֵצִים יֵשֵׁב וְיִבָּטֵל. בִּתְמִיָּה. וְאַף עַל גַּב דְּאָמְרִי' בְּפֶרֶק קַמָּא (דף יב:) לְרַבִּי יְהוּדָה: "אֲבָל בִּשְׁעַת בִּיעוּרוֹ הַשְׁבָּתָתוֹ בְּכָל דָּבָר" — גַּבֵּי פְּלוּגְתַּיְיהוּ מִיהָא קוּלָּא הִיא, בְּמִי שֶׁהוּא רוֹצֶה לְנַהֵג בְּשַׂיירָא, אוֹ בְּתוֹךְ שְׁלֹשִׁים, דְּאָמְרִינַן: *זָקוּק לְבַעֵר. וּכְשֶׁאֵין עֵצִים לְשׂוֹרְפוֹ — יְהֵא יוֹשֵׁב וּבָטֵל, וְלֹא יְבַעֲרֶנּוּ: וְדָנוֹ דִּין אַחֵר. שֶׁאֵינוֹ קַל וָחוֹמֶר, אֶלָּא גְּזֵירָה שָׁוָה, וּבֵין לְקוּלָּא וּבֵין לְחוּמְרָא — בָּתְרָהּ אָזְלִינַן, דִּגְזֵירַת הַכָּתוּב הוּא, וְאֵין לְהָשִׁיב עָלָיו "תְּחִלָּתוֹ לְהַחְמִיר וְסוֹפוֹ לְהָקֵל":

חָמֵץ

תוספות

מכלל דרבנן שרו כשאבוקה כנגדו. ואם תאמר: לרבנן, הואיל ובאבוקה כנגדו חשיב כמו שלהבת באה מן הגחלים, מאי פריך בסוף "לולב הגזול" (סוכה מ.) וב"הגוזל עצים" (ב"ק קא:): והא איכא עצים דמשחן, שהנאתן וביעורן שוה? הא בשעת הנאה מבוערין הן כבר במקום השלהבת! ויש לומר: משום(א) דשיעור כזה לא חשיב הנאה אחר ביעורן לענין שביעית, שהרי באכילה דמינה ילפינן התם ליכא לגמרי הנאה וביעורן שוה, ולא ממעטינן אלא שאר עצים שאין הנאתן אלא אחר שנעשו גחלים לגמרי. ולרבי עצים דלא משחן — נמי הוה ליה למיסר, דלדידיה כשאבוקה כנגדו הנאתן וביעורן שוה. ואיכא למימר: הואיל ורוב הנאה אחר ביעור — אית לן למימר דלא אסרה תורה בהן. אבל תימה: למאן דאמר לוחשות לרבי אסורים, אמאי לא אסר בכל עצים בשביעית, שהרי הנאתן וביעורן שוה. הואיל ולא חשיב להו מבוערות כשהן לוחשות, דבאותן הוי עיקר הנאה:

הקדש אפי' באלף לא בטיל. תימה: מה חומר היא זו? הלא הקדש דבר שיש לו מתירין הוא ע"י חילול, ומטעם זה אין דינו להיות בטל אפילו באיסור קל, אפילו מדרבנן, כדאמרינן בריש ביצה (דף ד.):

בעצי שלמים. ה"מ לאוקמי בעצי הקדש ובמזיד, ואליבא דרבי יהודה, אלא דלאו אורחא דמלתא לעבור במזיד:

ורמינהו כל הנשרפין וכו'. ה"מ לאוקמי בעצי שלמים:

חוץ מעצי אשירה. תימה לרשב"א: תיהוי כעבודת גלולים שנשתברה מאליה, דשריא, כדאמרינן בפרק "כל הצלמים" (ע"ז מא:)! ואין לומר דהכא איירי באשירה של ישראל, דאין לה ביטול עולמית. דהא בסוף תמורה (ד' לד.) מפרש דלהכי לא עריב ותני אפר הקדש ואשירה לעולם אסורין — משום דאשירה יש לה היתר אם שורפה עו"ג, דבטלה:

אין ביעור חמץ אלא שריפה. נראה דהלכה כרבי יהודה, דסתם לן תנא כותיה בפרק בתרא דתמורה (ד' לג:). וא"ת: א"כ בהא דאמר *ר' יהודה: סוכה אינה נוהגת אלא בארבע מינין שבלולב, יהא נמי הלכה כמותו — דהתם נמי לא פליגי רבנן אלא מטעם דכל דין שתחלתו להחמיר וסופו להקל (ב) אין דין. ובפ"ק דסוכה (ד' יא.) סתם לן תנא כרבנן, דקתני: הדלה עליה את הגפן ואת הדלעת, אם קצצן — כשירה! וי"ל: דהכא קיימא לן כרבי יהודה משום דין אחר, דיליף במה מצינו. אף על גב דאמרו לו חטאת העוף ואשם תלוי יוכיחו, ושתיק — מ"מ לדידן סבירא לן כרבנן. דאמרי חטאת ואשם בשריפה, וליכא תוכיח: **מה** נותר בשריפה אף חמץ בשריפה. וא"ת: למאן דדריש לעיל (ד' כד.) הנותר בשריפה ואין דבר אחר בשריפה, היכי יליף רבי יהודה חמץ בשריפה מנותר? ותירץ רשב"א: דלית לן למעוטי מנותר אלא שאר איסורין, אבל חמץ דדמי לנותר בכרת ובבל תותירו — לא ממעטינן. וא"ת: לעיל היכי יליף שאר אסורין בהם איסו ענין? נוקי קרא בחמץ בפסח דוקא, דדמי ליה טפי! וי"ל דלחמץ בפסח לא צריך [קרא], דמצי למילף במה מצינו: **חלבו** של שור הנסקל יוכיח. הקשה ריב"א: היא גופה נילף מנותר שיהא בשריפה דדמי ליה, ותירץ: דלא דמי ב"בל תותירו":

עין משפט נר מצוה

נו א מיי' פ"ז מהלכות ע"ז הל' י טוש"ע י"ד סי' קמב סעיף א:

נז ב ג מיי' פי"ט מהל' פסולי המוקדשין הלכה יג:

רבינו חננאל

משכחת לה ושני' בשאבוקה כנגדה ומכח האבוקה נאפת ורבנן דשרי אפי' כשאבוקה כנגדו עצי איסור היכי משכחת לה ושני' בשרשפא פי' כסא לשבת בו כגון זה אסרה תורה: **בעי** מיניה רמי בר חמא מרב חסדא תנור שהוסק בעצי הקדש ואפה בו פת לר' המתיר [מהו] וא"ל הפת אסורה ומה בין עצי הקדש לעצי ערלה אמר רבא משום דערלה בטלה במאתים והקדש אפי' באלף לא בטיל קשיא ליה לרבא והא קיי"ל כי המסיק בעצי הקדש מעל וכיון דמעל נפקי להו העצים לחולין [ואמאי] הפת אסורה ומשני רב פפא בעצי הקדש שאמרנו במאי עסקינן כגון שהקדישם בתורת שלמים וכר' יהודה [דתני] בקדושין פ"ב הקדש בשוגג מתחלל במזיד אין מתחלל במזיד מאי טעמא אינו מתחלל משום דלאו בר מעילה הוא הכא נמי בעצי הקדש המוקדשים בתורת שלמים כיון דשלמים לאו בני מעילה נינהו לא נפקי לחולין ומקשי' וכל היכי דמעל המסיק נפקי לחולין והתניא כל הנשרפין אפרן מותר חוץ מעצי אשרה ואפר הקדש דלעולם אסור ואי אמרת מעל המסיק ונפקי לחולין אמאי אסור ושנינה כגון שנפלה דליקה מאליה דליכא איניש דלימעול לפיכך תאני אפר הקדש לעולם אסור. רב שמעיה אמר האי דקתני אפר הקדש לעולם אסור כגון תרומת הדשן שטעון גניזה ושמועה זו תרומת הדשן שהוא טעון גניזה בסוף תמיד כדתניא ושמו אצל המזבח ושמו בנחת ושמו כלו (בנחת) ושמו שלא יפזר: ר' יהודה אומר אין ביעור חמץ אלא שריפה. תניא אמר ר' יהודה אין ביעור חמץ אלא שריפה והדין נותן ומה נותר שאינו בבל יראה ובבל ימצא וכו' עד

תורה אור: ויקרא ו | שמות יב

[ענין כזה תמו' ר"ה כח.] | תמורה לג. | שם לעיל כו. [ע"ש] | [לעיל ה: יב: כח. תמור לז.] | [סוכה לו: וש"נ] | [לעיל ו.]

הגהות הב"ח

(א) תוס' ד"ה מכלל וכו' ויש לומר דמשום שיעור כזה לא חשיב: (ב) ד"ה אין ביעור וכו' וסופו להקל אינו דין:

גליון הש"ס

גמ' כל דין שאתה תחלתו להחמיר. עי' ב"ב קלו ע"ב תוס' ד"ה דתני וזבחים יב ע"ב תד"ה בן עזאי:

חזר

גמרא

חָזַר רַבִּי יְהוּדָה וְדָנוֹ דִּין אַחֵר: נוֹתָר יֶשְׁנוֹ בְּ"בַל תּוֹתִירוּ", וְחָמֵץ בְּ"בַל תּוֹתִירוּ". מַה נּוֹתָר בִּשְׂרֵיפָה — אַף חָמֵץ בִּשְׂרֵיפָה. אָמְרוּ לוֹ: אָשָׁם תָּלוּי וְחַטַּאת הָעוֹף הַבָּא עַל הַסָּפֵק, לִדְבָרֶיךָ, יוֹכִיחוּ: שֶׁהֵן בְּ"בַל תּוֹתִירוּ". שֶׁאָנוּ אוֹמְרִים בִּשְׂרֵיפָה — וְאַתָּה אוֹמֵר בִּקְבוּרָה! שָׁתַק ר' יְהוּדָה. אָמַר רַב יוֹסֵף: הַיְינוּ דְּאָמְרִי אֱינָשֵׁי: כַּפָּא דְּחָטָא נַגָּרָא בְּגַוֵּוהּ נִשְׂרוֹף חַרְדְּלָא. (*אָמַר אַבַּיֵי): סַדָּנָא בְּסַדְנֵי יָתֵיב, מְדַוִּיל יְדֵיהּ מִשְׁתַּלֵּים. רָבָא אָמַר: גִּירָא בְּגִירֵי מְקַטֵּיל, מְדַוִּיל יְדֵיהּ מִשְׁתַּלֵּים.§ "וַחֲכ"א [א]מְפָרֵר וְזוֹרֶה וכו'".§ אִיבַּעְיָא לְהוּ, הֵיכִי קָאָמַר: מְפָרֵר וְזוֹרֶה לָרוּחַ, וּמְפָרֵר וּמַטִּיל לַיָּם. אוֹ דִּילְמָא: מְפָרֵר וְזוֹרֶה לָרוּחַ, אֲבָל מַטִּיל לַיָּם בְּעֵינֵיהּ. *וּתְנַן נַמִּי גַּבֵּי ע"ז כִּי הַאי גַּוְונָא: ר' יוֹסֵי אוֹמֵר: [ב]שׁוֹחֵק וְזוֹרֶה לָרוּחַ, אוֹ מַטִּיל לַיָּם. וְאִיבַּעְיָא לְהוּ: הֵיכִי קָאָמַר? שׁוֹחֵק וְזוֹרֶה לָרוּחַ, וְשׁוֹחֵק וּמַטִּיל לַיָּם. אוֹ דִּילְמָא: שׁוֹחֵק וְזוֹרֶה לָרוּחַ, אֲבָל מַטִּיל לַיָּם בְּעֵינֵיהּ. אָמַר רַבָּה: מִסְתַּבְּרָא, ע"ז דְּלַיָּם הַמֶּלַח קָא אָזְלָא — לָא בָּעֵי שְׁחִיקָה, חָמֵץ דְּלִשְׁאָר נְהָרוֹת קָאָזֵיל בָּעֵי פֵּירוּר. א"ל רַב יוֹסֵף: [ג]אַדְּרַבָּה, אִיפְּכָא מִסְתַּבְּרָא! ע"ז דְּלָא מְמִיסָה — בָּעֵי שְׁחִיקָה, חָמֵץ דְּמֵמִים — לָא בָּעֵי פֵּירוּר. תַּנְיָא כְּוָותֵיהּ דְּרַבָּה, תַּנְיָא כְּוָותֵיהּ דְּרַב יוֹסֵף. תַּנְיָא כְּוָותֵיהּ דְּרַבָּה: הָיָה מְהַלֵּךְ בַּמִּדְבָּר — מְפָרֵר וְזוֹרֶה לָרוּחַ. הָיָה מְהַלֵּךְ בִּסְפִינָה — מְפָרֵר וּמַטִּיל לַיָּם. תַּנְיָא כְּוָותֵיהּ דְּרַב יוֹסֵף: הָיָה מְהַלֵּךְ בַּמִּדְבָּר — שׁוֹחֵק וְזוֹרֶה לָרוּחַ, הָיָה מְהַלֵּךְ בִּסְפִינָה — שׁוֹחֵק וּמַטִּיל לַיָּם. שְׁחִיקָה קַשְׁיָא לְרַבָּה, פֵּירוּר קַשְׁיָא לְרַב יוֹסֵף! שְׁחִיקָה לְרַבָּה לָא קַשְׁיָא: הָא — לְיָם הַמֶּלַח, הָא — לִשְׁאָר נְהָרוֹת. פֵּירוּר לְרַב יוֹסֵף לָא קַשְׁיָא: הָא — בְּחִיטֵּי, הָא — בְּנַהֲמָא.§ **מתני'** *[ד]חָמֵץ שֶׁל גּוֹי שֶׁעָבַר עָלָיו הַפֶּסַח — מוּתָּר בַּהֲנָאָה, וְשֶׁל יִשְׂרָאֵל [ה]אָסוּר בַּהֲנָאָה, שֶׁנֶּאֱמַר: °"לֹא יֵרָאֶה לְךָ שְׂאוֹר".§ **גמ'** מַנִּי מַתְנִיתִין? לָא רַבִּי יְהוּדָה וְלָא רַבִּי שִׁמְעוֹן וְלָא רַבִּי יוֹסֵי הַגְּלִילִי. מַאי הִיא — דְּתַנְיָא: חָמֵץ [ו]בֵּין לִפְנֵי זְמַנּוֹ בֵּין לְאַחַר זְמַנּוֹ — עוֹבֵר עָלָיו בְּלָאו, תּוֹךְ זְמַנּוֹ — עוֹבֵר עָלָיו בְּלָאו וְכָרֵת, דִּבְרֵי רַבִּי יְהוּדָה. רַבִּי

תורה אור: שמות יג

רש"י

חָמֵץ יֶשְׁנוֹ בְּבַל תּוֹתִירוּ. לֹא יֵרָאֶה וְלֹא יִמָּצֵא: **אָשָׁם תָּלוּי.** בָּא עַל סְפֵק כָּרֵת, כְּגוֹן: חֵלֶב וְשׁוּמָּן לְפָנָיו, וְשָׁגַג בְּאֶחָד מֵהֶן, וְאֵינוֹ יוֹדֵעַ אֵיזֶה מֵהֶן אָכַל. וְאִם שְׁחָטוֹ וְאֵירַע בּוֹ פְּסוּל אוֹ נוֹתָר — פְּלִיגִי ר' יְהוּדָה וְרַבָּנַן בִּשִׁילְהֵי פֶּרֶק בַּתְרָא דִּתְמוּרָה*, לְר' יְהוּדָה בִּקְבוּרָה, לְרַבָּנַן בִּשְׂרֵיפָה: **חַטַּאת הָעוֹף הַבָּא עַל הַסָּפֵק.** כְּגוֹן הַפִּילָה, סָפֵק וָלָד סָפֵק אֵינוֹ וָלָד — אֵינָהּ אוֹכֶלֶת בַּקָּדָשִׁים, שֶׁמָּא וָלָד הוּא, עַד שֶׁתָּבִיא כַּפָּרָתָהּ. הָעוֹלָה בָּאָה עַל תְּנַאי: אִם יָלַדְתִּי — הֲרֵי הִיא לְחוֹבָתִי, וְאִם לָאו — הֲרֵי הִיא נְדָבָה. וְחַטָּאת הָעוֹף מְבִיאָתוֹ עַל הַסָּפֵק. וְאֵין כָּאן מִשּׁוּם חוּלִּין בָּעֲזָרָה, דְּמִקְּרָאֵי נָפֵיק בְּמַסֶּכֶת נָזִיר, בְּפֶרֶק "מִי שֶׁאָמַר" (דף כט.). וַאֲסוּרָה בַּאֲכִילָה שֶׁמָּא חוּלִּין הִיא, וּמְלִיקָתָהּ שַׁוְיָהּ נְבֵילָה. וּפְלִיגֵי בָּהּ רַבִּי יְהוּדָה וְרַבָּנַן בְּפֶרֶק בַּתְרָא דִּתְמוּרָה*: חַטַּאת הָעוֹף הַבָּאָה עַל הַסָּפֵק — תִּשָּׂרֵף, רַבִּי יְהוּדָה אוֹמֵר: יְטִילֶנָּה לָאַמָּה: **וְאַתָּה אוֹמֵר בִּקְבוּרָה.** אָשָׁם תָּלוּי קָאֵי, דְּקָאָמַר ר' יְהוּדָה יִקָּבֵר, וְאַע"ג שֶׁהַנּוֹתָר מִמֶּנּוּ אָסוּר בַּאֲכִילָה וּבַהֲנָאָה, וְעָנוּשׁ כָּרֵת, וְהוּא בְּבַל תּוֹתִירוּ: **כַּפָּא דְּחָטָא נַגָּרָא.** כַּף בָּזָךְ שֶׁחָקַק הָאוּמָּן — בְּתוֹכוֹ יִשְׂרוֹף אֶת לְשׁוֹנוֹ וְאֶת חִכּוֹ בְּחַרְדָּל. לִישָּׁנָא אַחֲרִינָא: יִשְׂרוֹף = הוּמִי"ר בְּלַעַ"ז, כְּמוֹ שׁוֹרְפָהּ חַיָּה, בְּ"ע"ז" (דף כט:): **סַדָּנָא.** נַגָּר עוֹשֶׂה סַד לָשׂוּם בּוֹ רַגְלֵי אֲסִירִים, כְּמוֹ: "וְתָשֵׂם בַּסַּד רַגְלַי" (איוב יג): **מְדַוִּיל יְדֵיהּ מִשְׁתַּלֵּים.** מֵהֲרָמַת יָדוֹ וּמִמְּלַאכְתּוֹ מִשְׁתַּלֵּם שְׂכָרוֹ, כְּשֶׁנִּמְלָא גַּנָּב: **גִּירָאָה.** עוֹשֶׂה חִצִּים: **אוֹ דִּילְמָא.** לָרוּחַ הוּא דְּבָעֵי פֵּירוּר, שֶׁמָּא יִזְרְקֶנּוּ שָׁלֵם וְיִמְצָאֶנּוּ אַחֵר וְיֹאכְלֶנּוּ. אֲבָל לַיָּם — מַטִּיל בְּעֵינֵיהּ, דְּמֵמִים וְנִימּוֹק מֵאֵלָיו. לְשׁוֹן שְׁחִיקָה שַׁיָּיךְ בְּמַתֶּכֶת, וּלְשׁוֹן פֵּירוּר שַׁיָּיךְ בְּפַת: **יָם הַמֶּלַח.** [הַנִּקְרָא מי"ר בטיא"ה], אֵין סְפִינָה עוֹבֶרֶת בּוֹ: **בָּעֵי פֵּירוּר.** שֶׁמָּא תִּפְגַּע בּוֹ סְפִינָה וְתִטְּלֶנּוּ, וְלָאו אַדַּעְתַּיְיהוּ: **לָא מְמִיסָה.** אֵין הַמַּיִם מְמַסּוֹת אוֹתוֹ: **תַּנְיָא כְּוָותֵיהּ דְּרַבָּה.** דְּחָמֵץ בָּעֵי פֵּירוּר: **תַּנְיָא כְּוָותֵיהּ דְּרַב יוֹסֵף.** דְּע"ז בָּעֵי שְׁחִיקָה: **בְּחִיטֵּי.** שֶׁהֶחְמִיצוּ בָּעֵי פֵּירוּר — כְּלוֹמַר: פִּיזּוּר — שֶׁלֹּא יִתֵּן בְּשַׂק וְיִזְרְקֵם, אֶלָּא יְפַזְּרֵם עַל פְּנֵי הַמַּיִם, שֶׁלֹּא יוּכַל אָדָם לְלַקְּטָן מֵעַל פְּנֵי הַמַּיִם: **מתני'** מִשּׁוּם שֶׁנֶּאֱמַר לֹא יֵרָאֶה לְךָ. בַּגְּמָרָא מְפָרֵשׁ לָהּ מִשּׁוּם קְנָסָא, דְּעָבַר עֲלֵיהּ מִשּׁוּם בַּל יֵרָאֶה: **גמ'** בֵּין לִפְנֵי זְמַנּוֹ. מִשֵּׁשׁ שָׁעוֹת עַד שֶׁתֶּחְשַׁךְ:(א) לְאַחַר זְמַנּוֹ. מִשֶּׁעָבַר הַפֶּסַח עוֹבֵר עָלָיו בְּלָאו, וְאִם אֲכָלוֹ — אֵינוֹ עָנוּשׁ כָּרֵת. וּלְקַמָּן מְפָרֵשׁ לָלָאו: תּוֹךְ זְמַנּוֹ. בַּמּוֹעֵד וּמִשָּׁעָה

תוספות

חזר ר' יהודה ודנו דין אחר. הא דקרי ליה השתא דין אחר טפי מהני דלעיל, אומר ריב"א: משום דהשתא אין צריך לאיסור אכילה והנאה וענוש כרת, אלא בלד דבל תותירו לחודיה מלינו למילף, דליתיה בכולהו: **וחמץ** הרי הוא בבל תותירו. תימה לר"י: היכי עביד לעיל קל וחומר מנותר שאינו בבל יראה ובל ימלא? והא חשיב הכא בל תותירו כמו בל יראה! ואומר ר"י: דמכל מקום נראה דעביד שפיר קל וחומר, דנותר אינו בבל יראה, דמיד שהותיר — עובר, ושוב אינו עובר. אבל חמץ, אפי' לאחר שהותיר — עובר בכל שעה בבל יראה:

אמרו לו אשם תלוי יוכיח. תימה לרשב"א: לדבריהם דרבנן, דאמרו שהם בשריפה — אמאי לא ילפינן חמץ מנותר שהוא בשריפה? ואומר ר"י: דמשמע להו* הנותר בשריפה, ולא כל איסורין שבתורה בשריפה, ואפי' חמץ: **ואתה** אומר בקבורה. טעמא דר' יהודה דריש בת"כ מ"כי קדש הוא" — הוא בשריפה ולא חטאת עוף ואשם תלוי בשריפה:

ותנן נמי גבי ע"ז. אומר ר"י: דרבנן דמתניתין היינו רבי יוסי דפרק "כל הצלמים" (ע"ז מג:). אי נמי, מתני' דהכא א"ש כרבנן דהתם, דאמרו לו: אף היא נעשה זבל ומגדל צמחים, ורחמנא אמר: "לא ידבק בידך וגו'". והא דשרו הכא — היינו משום דבחמץ כתיב לא יאכל, ואינו אסור אלא כדרך הנאה. וכי האי גוונא לאו דרך הנאה היא. אבל בע"ז לא כתיב אכילה, ואסור אפי' שלא כדרך הנאה:

חמץ דלשאר נהרות. דלא מצינו שהיה שונה בשום מקום גבי חמץ ים המלח. אבל גבי ע"ז אשכחן בכמה דוכתין, כי האי דלעיל יוליך הנאה לים המלח. הלכך: סתם ים דתני גבי ע"ז — הוי ים המלח. מיהו, לרבה מועלת שחיקה בשאר נהרות כדקאמר בסמוך: כאן בים המלח כאן בשאר נהרות: **איפכא** מסתברא. לשון איפכא אינו מיושב, דמה שייך איפכא; כיון שרבה משוה אותם: **ע"ז** דלא ממיסה בעי שחיקה. לכאורה משמע דלרב יוסף בעי שחיקה אפילו בים המלח, דמסתמא אמאי דקאמר רבה אין צריך שחיקה דהיינו בים המלח — קאמר רב יוסף דבעי שחיקה. ועוד: אי בשאר נהרות דוקא קאמר רב יוסף דבעי שחיקה, ולא בים המלח, ולא פליג ארבה בע"ז אלא בחמץ — א"כ מאי קאמר תניא כוותיה דרב יוסף? ומאי קאמר נמי שחיקה קשיא לרבה? ולפי זה לרב יוסף בשאר נהרות לא מהני שחיקה, מדקמצריך להוליך לים המלח. ואין נראה, דהא ר' יוסי מייתי ראיה מ"ויזר על פני המים" — משמע דמהניא שחיקה בשאר נהרות. ועוד: דבכל מקום דמזכיר ים המלח בע"ז ובשאר דוכתין לא מזכיר שחיקה, ובכמה דוכתין מלינו דקתני ים המלח — ואפי' הכי מהני בשאר נהרות. דבסוף "כל הצלמים" (ע"ז מט:) תנן, ר' אליעזר אומר: יוליך הנאה לים המלח. ואמרינן התם בגמרא גבי חבית: שקול ד' זוזי ושדי לנהרא. וכן בנזיר (דף כד.) ובמעילה (דף יא.) תנן גבי מפריש מעות לנזיר ומת — יוליך לים המלח. ובערכין (דף כט.) אמרינן גבי הקדש: שקול ארבעה זוזי ושדי בנהרא. לכך נראה דגם לרב יוסף לא בעי שחיקה אלא בשאר נהרות, כמו לרבה. אלא דרבה סבירא ליה דמטיל לים סתם דע"ז — היינו ים המלח, ובלא שחיקה כדתנא רישא גבי צורת לבנה וצורת חמה ובכמה דוכתי, יוליך לים המלח. ורב יוסף מוקי לה בשאר נהרות, ועל ידי שחיקה, מדלא תני בהדיא יטיל לים המלח. וליכא בין רבה לרב יוסף אלא חמץ בשאר נהרות. וא"ת: לרבנן, דלית להו בע"ז (מפרר) [שוחק] וזורה לרוח מה יעשו מע"ז? אטו כל שעה יוליך לים המלח? דלרבנן לא מהני שחיקה בשאר נהרות, דקתני התם, אמרו לו: משם ראיה הרי הוא אומר "ויזר על פני המים" — לא נתכוין משה אלא לבודקן כסוטה. ומדאיצטריך להאי טעמא — מכלל דלא מהני שחיקה בשאר נהרות. ויש לומר: דלרבנן מפרר וזורה לרוח במקום שאין מגדל צמחים(ב), וכן אמרינן התם: וטעמא: לפי שהמים מוליכים אותו על ידות הנהר. רבי

רבינו חננאל

חזר ר' יהודה ודנו דין אחר נותר הרי הוא בבל תותירו וחמץ הרי הוא בבל תותירו מה נותר טעון שריפה אף חמץ טעון שריפה אמרו לו חטאת העוף הבאה על הספק ואשם תלוי לדבריך יוכיחו שהן בבל תותירו כדכתיב (ויקרא ז טו) לא יניח ממנו עד בקר ואנו אומרים בשריפה ואתה אומר בקבורה דתנן בסוף תמורה אשם תלוי ישרף [ר"י אומר יקבר] חטאת העוף הבא על הספק ישרף ר' יהודה אומר יטילנה לאמה ותניא כיצד אמר רבי יהודה יטילנה לאמה מנתחה אבר אבר ומשליכה לפני אמה ומתגלגלת ויורדת לנחל קדרון: **ת"ר** אשם תלוי וחטאת [העוף] הבאה על הספק וחולין שנשחטו בעזרה ר' יהודה אומר יקברו ר' שמעון אומר ישרפו שתק ר' יהודה. ירושלמי אשם תלוי בשיטתך יוכיח שאסור באכילה ובהנאה וחייבין עליו ויש בו זמן ואתה אומר בקבורה ולא בשרפה פירושו אשם תלוי שנודע לו אחר שחיטה וחטאת העוף הבאה על הספק שנודע לו אחר מליקתה דתנן בכריתות פ' [המביא אשם (ד' כה)] חטאת העוף הבאה על הספק אם משנמלקה נודע לו הרי זו תקבר: **שתק** ר' יהודה היינו דאמרי אינשי כפא דחטט נגרא כו' פירוש כמו משל אומרין בני אדם הכף שחטטו בני אדם וחקקו כי חטט וחקק אחד הוא כגון החוטט בגדיש לעשות לו סוכה בתוכו שורפין חרדל שלו כלומר שאלו לא מצא הכף שחקקו לא היו שורפין החרדל שלו וכן היה ר' יהודה אומר אילולי לא השיבוהו מדבריו לא היו משתקין אותו: **פי'** סדנא כמו היה יושב בספינה או באסדא והם כבלים שנותנין ברגלי הכלואים בבית הכלא: **גיראה** האומן העושה החצים: **וחכמים** אומרים מפרר וזורה לרוח או מטיל לים ותנן נמי גבי ע"ז כי האי גוונא ר' יוסי אומר שוחק וזורה לרוח ומטיל לים [ואיבעיא לן היכי קאמר מפרר ושוחק וזורה לרוח או מפרר ושוחק ומטיל לים] או כשמטיל לים לא בעי לא פרירה ולא שחיקה ופשיט רבא כי החמץ דאזיל אפילו בשאר נהרות לעולם צריך פירור אבל ע"ז דלים המלח הוא דאזיל לא בעי פירור ואקשי' עלה והתניא היה מהלך במדבר שוחק וזורה לרוח בספינה שוחק ומטיל לים ומשני הא דתניא שוחק בשאר נהרות כי קאמינא אנא דע"ז לא צריכה שחיקה שמשליכה לים הגדול רב יוסף אמר חמץ כשמשליכין אותו לים לא בעי פירור אבל ע"ז לעולם בעי שחיקה ואקשי' עלה והתניא היה מהלך במדבר מפרר וזורה לרוח בספינה מפרר ומטיל לים ומשני' הא דתניא מפרר בחטים כי קאמינא דלא בעי פרירה בנהמא והלכתא כרבה דאמר חמץ בעי פירור: **מתני'** חמץ של נכרי שעבר עליו הפסח מותר כו' מני מתני' לא ר' יהודה ולא ר' שמעון ולא ר' יוסי הגלילי מאי היא דתניא חמץ לפני זמנו ולאחר זמנו וכו' מני

עין משפט נר מצוה

נח א מיי' פ"ג מהלכות חמץ הלכה יא סמג עשין לט טוש"ע או"ח סימן תמה סעיף א:
נט ב מיי' פ"ח מהלכות ע"ז הלכה ו טוש"ע י"ד סי' קמו סעיף יד:
ס ג מיי' שם הל' ו ופ"ג מהל' חמץ הלכה יא סמג עשין לט טוש"ע א"ח סי' תמה סעיף א:
סא ד מיי' פ"ד מהלכות חמץ הלכה א ב טוש"ע א"ח סי' תמה סעיף א:
סב ה מיי' פ"א מהל' חמץ הל' ד סמג לאוין עו טוש"ע שם סעיף ג:
סג ו מיי' שם הלכה ח:

מסורת הש"ס

[ל.]
[נ"ל אביי אמר]
[ל.]
ע"ז מג:
רש"ל
[עירובין סד:]
[לעיל כד.]

הגהות הב"ח

(א) רש"י ד"ה בין לפני וכו' שתחשך בין לאחר זמנו נ"ל והד"א: (ב) תוס' ד"ה ע"ז וכו' למחים והכי אמרינן התם.

רַבִּי שִׁמְעוֹן אוֹמֵר: חָמֵץ לִפְנֵי זְמַנּוֹ [א]וּלְאַחַר זְמַנּוֹ – אֵינוֹ עוֹבֵר עָלָיו בְּלֹא כְּלוּם, תּוֹךְ זְמַנּוֹ – עוֹבֵר עָלָיו בְּכָרֵת וּבְלָאו, וּמִשָּׁעָה שֶׁאָסוּר בַּאֲכִילָה אָסוּר בַּהֲנָאָה, אָתְאָן לְתַנָּא קַמָּא. *ר' יוֹסֵי הַגְּלִילִי אוֹמֵר: תְּמַהּ עַל עַצְמְךָ, הֵיאַךְ חָמֵץ אָסוּר בַּהֲנָאָה כָּל שִׁבְעָה? וּמִנַּיִן לְאוֹכֵל חָמֵץ מִשֵּׁשׁ שָׁעוֹת וּלְמַעְלָה שֶׁהוּא עוֹבֵר בְּלֹא תַעֲשֶׂה – שֶׁנֶּאֱמַר: °"לֹא תֹאכַל עָלָיו חָמֵץ", דִּבְרֵי רַבִּי יְהוּדָה. אָמַר לוֹ ר' שִׁמְעוֹן: וְכִי אֶפְשָׁר לוֹמַר כֵּן? וַהֲלֹא כְּבָר נֶאֱמַר: "לֹא תֹאכַל עָלָיו חָמֵץ שִׁבְעַת יָמִים תֹּאכַל עָלָיו מַצּוֹת". אִם כֵּן מַה ת"ל "לֹא תֹאכַל עָלָיו חָמֵץ" – בְּשָׁעָה שֶׁיֶּשְׁנוֹ בְּקוּם אֱכוֹל מַצָּה – יֶשְׁנוֹ בְּבַל תֹּאכַל חָמֵץ, וּבְשָׁעָה שֶׁאֵינוֹ בְּקוּם אֱכוֹל מַצָּה – אֵינוֹ בְּבַל תֹּאכַל חָמֵץ. מ"ט דְּר' יְהוּדָה? תְּלָתָא קְרָאֵי כְּתִיבִי: °"לֹא יֵאָכֵל חָמֵץ", °"וְכָל מַחְמֶצֶת לֹא תֹאכֵלוּ", °"לֹא תֹאכַל עָלָיו חָמֵץ". חַד לִפְנֵי זְמַנּוֹ, וְחַד לְאַחַר זְמַנּוֹ, וְחַד לְתוֹךְ זְמַנּוֹ. וְרַבִּי שִׁמְעוֹן: חַד – לְתוֹךְ זְמַנּוֹ, "וְכָל מַחְמֶצֶת" – מִבָּעֵי לֵיהּ, *לְכִדְתַנְיָא(א): [ב]אֵין לִי אֶלָּא שֶׁנִּתְחַמֵּץ מֵאֵלָיו, מֵחֲמַת דָּבָר אַחֵר מִנַּיִן? תַּלְמוּד לוֹמַר: "כָּל מַחְמֶצֶת לֹא תֹאכֵלוּ". "לֹא יֵאָכֵל חָמֵץ" – מִיבָּעֵי לֵיהּ *לְכִדְתַנְיָא; רַבִּי יוֹסֵי הַגְּלִילִי אוֹמֵר: מִנַּיִן לְפֶסַח מִצְרַיִם שֶׁאֵין חִימּוּצוֹ נוֹהֵג אֶלָּא יוֹם אֶחָד – תַּלְמוּד לוֹמַר: "לֹא יֵאָכֵל חָמֵץ", וּסְמִיךְ לֵיהּ: °"הַיּוֹם אַתֶּם יֹצְאִים". וְר' יְהוּדָה, מֵחֲמַת דָּבָר אַחֵר מְנָא לֵי'? מִדְּאַפְקֵיהּ רַחֲמָנָא בִּלְשׁוֹן מַחְמֶצֶת. דְּר' יוֹסֵי הַגְּלִילִי מְנָא לֵיהּ? אִי בָּעֵית אֵימָא: מִדְּסָמִיךְ לֵיהּ "הַיּוֹם", אִי בָּעֵית אֵימָא – *סְמוּכִין לָא דָּרֵישׁ. אָמַר מָר: וּמִנַּיִן לְאוֹכֵל חָמֵץ מִשֵּׁשׁ שָׁעוֹת וּלְמַעְלָה שֶׁהוּא עוֹבֵר בְּלֹא תַעֲשֶׂה – שֶׁנֶּאֱמַר: "לֹא תֹאכַל עָלָיו חָמֵץ", דִּבְרֵי רַבִּי יְהוּדָה. אָמַר לוֹ ר' שִׁמְעוֹן: וְכִי אֶפְשָׁר לוֹמַר כֵּן? וַהֲלֹא כְּבָר נֶאֱמַר: "לֹא תֹאכַל עָלָיו חָמֵץ שִׁבְעַת יָמִים תֹּאכַל עָלָיו מַצּוֹת", וְרַבִּי יְהוּדָה, שַׁפִּיר קָאָמַר לֵיהּ רַבִּי שִׁמְעוֹן! וְרַבִּי יְהוּדָה אָמַר לָךְ: הַהוּא לְקוֹבְעוֹ חוֹבָה אֲפִילּוּ בַּזְּמַן הַזֶּה הוּא דַּאֲתָא. וְר' שִׁמְעוֹן לְקוֹבְעוֹ חוֹבָה מְנָא לֵיהּ? נָפְקָא לֵיהּ °מִ"בָּעֶרֶב תֹּאכְלוּ". וְר' יְהוּדָה? *מִיבָּעֵי לֵי' לְטָמֵא וְשֶׁהָיָה בְּדֶרֶךְ רְחוֹקָה. סָלְקָא דַּעְתָּךְ אָמִינָא: הוֹאִיל וּבְפֶסַח לֹא יֹאכַל – מַצָּה וּמָרוֹר נַמִי לָא נֵיכוֹל, קמ"ל. וְר' שִׁמְעוֹן: טָמֵא וְשֶׁהָיָה בְּדֶרֶךְ רְחוֹקָה לָא אִיצְטְרִיךְ קְרָא, דְּלָא גָּרַע מֵעָרֵל וּבֶן נֵכָר. דִּכְתִיב: °"וְכָל עָרֵל לֹא יֹאכַל בּוֹ" – *בּוֹ הוּא אֵינוֹ אוֹכֵל, אֲבָל אוֹכֵל הוּא בְּמַצָּה וּבְמָרוֹר. וְרַבִּי יְהוּדָה: כְּתִיב בְּהַאי, וּכְתִיב בְּהַאי. מַנִּי מַתְנִיתִין? אִי רַבִּי יְהוּדָה – חָמֵץ סְתָמָא קָאָמַר, אֲפִילּוּ דְּגוֹי. וְאִי רַבִּי שִׁמְעוֹן – דְּיִשְׂרָאֵל

(שמות יג; שמות יב; דברים טז; שמות יג; שמות יב; שם)

רש"י

וּמִשָּׁעָה שֶׁאָסוּר בַּאֲכִילָה. הַיְינוּ מִשֵּׁשׁ שָׁעוֹת וּלְמַעְלָה, דַּאֲמַרַן לִפְנֵי זְמַנּוֹ בְּלָאו. וְהָא מִילְּתָא – רַבִּי יְהוּדָה קָאָמַר לָהּ, כִּדְמְפָרֵשׁ בַּגְּמָרָא: אָתְאָן לְתַנָּא קַמָּא: תְּמַהּ עַל עַצְמְךָ וכו'. דַּאֲפִילּוּ בְּתוֹךְ הַמּוֹעֵד קָאָמַר דְּמוּתָּר בַּהֲנָאָה, וְקָא מְתַמַּהּ אַהָנֵי דְּאָסְרִי: לֹא תֹאכַל עָלָיו. מִשְּׁעַת שְׁחִיטָה, דְּהַיְינוּ מִשֵּׁשׁ שָׁעוֹת וּלְמַעְלָה, שֶׁחַמָּה נוֹטָה לְהַעֲרִיב: הָכִי גָּרְסִינַן: חָמֵץ אֵין לִי אֶלָּא שֶׁנִּתְחַמֵּץ מֵאֵלָיו: מִנַּיִן לְפֶסַח מִצְרַיִם. שֶׁלֹּא נָהֲגוּ בּוֹ אִיסּוּר חָמֵץ אֶלָּא יוֹם אֶחָד: ת"ל לֹא יֵאָכֵל חָמֵץ וּסְמִיךְ לֵיהּ הַיּוֹם אַתֶּם יוֹצְאִים. לֹא יֵאָכֵל חָמֵץ הַיּוֹם: וְאִי בָּעֵית אֵימָא סְמוּכִין לָא דָּרֵישׁ. רַבִּי יְהוּדָה אֶלָּא בְּמִשְׁנֵה תוֹרָה לְחוּד, וְהָכִי שָׁמְעִינַן לֵיהּ בְּפֶרֶק קַמָּא דִּיבָמוֹת (ד' ד.*), הִלְכָּךְ לֵית לֵיהּ דְּרַבִּי יוֹסֵי הַגְּלִילִי: לְקוֹבְעוֹ חוֹבָה. הַאי "שִׁבְעַת יָמִים(ב) תֹּאכְלוּ מַצּוֹת" לָאו לְאַקּוּשֵׁי אִיסּוּר חָמֵץ לְמִצְוַת אֲכִילַת מַצָּה אָתָא, אֶלָּא לְאַקּוּשֵׁי אֲכִילַת מַצָּה לְאַזְהָרַת חָמֵץ – לְקְבּוֹעַ אֲכִילַ' מַצָּה חוֹבָה לְדוֹרוֹת כָּל זְמַן שֶׁהוּא מוּזְהָר עַל הֶחָמֵץ, וַאֲפִילּוּ בִּזְמַן שֶׁאֵין פֶּסַח. דְּלָא תֵּימָא: "עַל מַצּוֹת וּמְרוֹרִים יֹאכְלוּהוּ" כְּתִיב, אִי אִיכָּא פֶּסַח – מִיחַיֵּיב בַּאֲכִילַת מַצָּה, וְאִי לָא – לָא: בָּעֶרֶב תֹּאכְלוּ מַצּוֹת. קְרָא יְתֵירָה הוּא, דְּהָא כְּתִיב: "עַל מַצּוֹת וּמְרוֹרִים יֹאכְלוּהוּ": לְטָמֵא וְשֶׁהָיָה בְּדֶרֶךְ רְחוֹקָה. שֶׁאַף עַל פִּי שֶׁאֵינוֹ עוֹשֶׂה פֶּסַח – חַיָּיב בַּאֲכִילַת מַצָּה: לָא נֵיכוֹל. לֹא נִתְחַיֵּיב: עָרֵל. שֶׁמֵּתוּ אֶחָיו מֵחֲמַת מִילָה: בֶּן נֵכָר. מִי שֶׁנִּתְנַכְּרוּ מַעֲשָׂיו לְאָבִיו שֶׁבַּשָּׁמַיִם, וְלֹא לְכָל הַתּוֹרָה: כְּתִיב בְּהַאי. עָרֵל וּבֶן נֵכָר, וּכְתִיב טָמֵא וְשֶׁהָיָה בְּדֶרֶךְ רְחוֹקָה דְּלֵיכוֹל מַצּוֹת, וְאַף עַל גַּב דְּמָצֵי יָלֵיף מִינֵּיהּ. הִלְכָּךְ אִיצְטְרִיךְ הֶיקֵּישָׁא לְקוֹבְעוֹ חוֹבָה. וּמִקְּרָאֵי אַחֲרִינֵי טוּבָא, כְּגוֹן "שִׁבְעַת יָמִים מַצּוֹת תֹּאכֵלוּ", וּכְגוֹן "מַצּוֹת יֵאָכֵל אֵת שִׁבְעַת הַיָּמִים" – לָא נָפְקָא לֵיהּ קְבִיעוּת חוֹבָה, דְּהָנְהוּ לָאו חוֹבָה נִינְהוּ, אֶלָּא: מַצּוֹת יֵאָכֵל וְלֹא חָמֵץ. וְאִם רָצָה לִיזּוֹן שֶׁלֹּא מֵחָמֵץ וְשֶׁלֹּא מִמַּצָּה – הָרְשׁוּת בְּיָדוֹ. וְתֵדַע, דְּהָא בְּכוּלְּהוּ כְּתִיב: "אֵת שִׁבְעַת הַיָּמִים", וְחוֹבַת מַצָּה אֵינוֹ אֶלָּא לַיְלָה הָרִאשׁוֹן, כִּדְיָלְפִינַן בְּפֶרֶק בַּתְרָא*. אֲבָל מֵהַהוּא קְרָא נָפְקָא לָן חוֹבַת לַיְלָה הָרִאשׁוֹן, מִדִּכְתִיב לְהֶיקֵּישָׁא גַּבֵּי פֶּסַח, וּכְדִכְתִיב: "תֹּאכַל עָלָיו מַצּוֹת", כִּי פֶּסַח לַיְלָה הָרִאשׁוֹן, אַף הֶיקֵּישָׁא שֶׁלֹּא בִּזְמַן פֶּסַח – לְלַיְלָה רִאשׁוֹנָה. וְאַהָנֵי הֶיקֵּישָׁא לְקוֹבְעוֹ חוֹבָה בַּזְּמַן הַזֶּה, וְאַהָנֵי "עָלָיו" לְמֵימְרָא דִּקְבִיעַת חוֹבָה דְּהֶיקֵּישָׁא לָאו לְכָל שִׁבְעָה, אֶלָּא לְלַיְלָה הָרִאשׁוֹן: דְּיִשְׂרָאֵל

(תורה אור: דברים טז; שמות יג; דברים טז; שמות יג; שמות יב; שם)

תוספות

רבי שמעון אומר חמץ לפני זמנו ולאחר זמנו אינו עובר עליו בלא כלום. נראה דלרבי שמעון, נהי דאין עובר עליו בלאו דחמץ לפני זמנו – מודה הוא דאסור באכילה משש שעות ולמעלה, מדאמרינן בפ"ק (לעיל דף יד.): אין שורפין תרומה טהורה עם *הטמאה, משמע: הא לבדה – שורפין בשש. ואי מותרת לאכול – יאכלנה עד הלילה! ועוד: דקאמר משעה שאסור באכילה אסור בהנאה – אתאן לת"ק. מכלל דלרבי שמעון אסור באכילה, אע"פ שאינו אסור בהנאה, דהיינו אחר שש. ונראה דנפקא ליה מ"תשביתו" ומ"אך" חלק. ומשמע: תשביתו שלא כדרך הנאה, דהיינו אכילה. אבל להסיקו תחת תבשילו – מותר לרבי שמעון. וא"ת: למה שורפין בשש לרבי שמעון? יסיקנו עד הלילה מעט מעט תחת תבשילו! וי"ל: דגזרינן שמא יאכלנו. וכן לרבי יוסי הגלילי, דשרי חמץ להסיקו תחת תבשילו – היינו הכל ביחד, אבל מעט מעט – לא, שמא יאכלנו. דמסתמא אית ליה אור לארבעה עשר בודקין וכו':

אם כן מה תלמוד לומר לא תאכל עליו. הלשון דחוק, ונראה לרשב"א דהכי פירושו: והלא כבר נאמר "תאכל עליו מצות" והוא "עליו" – ע"כ אאכילת פסח קאי – הכי נמי "לא תאכל עליו חמץ" – קאי נמי אשעת אכילת פסח. וקשה: אמאי איצטריך קרא להכי, מהיכא תיתי שיהא בבל תאכל חמץ בי"ד? דהא כולהו קראי מצרכינן לקמן אליבא דרבי שמעון:

וחד לפני זמנו. וא"ת: ולחזקיה מנלן איסור הנאה לפני זמנו דליכא אלא חד "לא יאכל" והוא מסברא מוקמינן לתוך זמנו! ואור"י: כיון דחד מהנהו קראי משמע איסור הנאה – לא נחלק ביניהם:

מחמת דבר אחר. פי' ריב"א: מחמת דבר אחר דלאו מינו, דעל ידי שאור מיקרי חמץ טפי משנתחמץ מאליו, כדמוכח בפרק "כל המנחות" (מנחות נג:). אלא כגון שנתחמץ על ידי שמרי יין, שמייבשין השמרים בתנור כאשר עושין בארץ אשכנז, ול"ד לעיסה שנילושה ביין, דלית ביה כרת ויש בה לאו:

ואידך נפקא לה מבערב תאכלו מצות. תימה לר"י: דבפ' קמא דקדושין (ד' לז:) נפקא לן בזמן הזה "ממושבותיכם" דכתיב גבי מצה, והיינו דלא כחד! ועוד: תימה לרב אחא בר יעקב, דאית ליה בשילהי "ערבי פסחים" (לקמן קכ.) מצה בזמן הזה דרבנן, ודריש התם לכולהו קראי דלא ככל התנאים*:

כל ערל לא יאכל בו וכל בן נכר לא יאכל בו בו הוא אינו אוכל אבל אוכל הוא במצה ומרור. תימה: גבי בן נכר, שהוא מומר, אמאי איצטריך קרא? פשיטא שחייב לאכול מצה, דהא חייב בכל מצות האמורות בתורה! ואי קמשמע לן דמאי אכיל מצה אע"ג דאסור בפסח – הא נמי פשיטא, דאטו מצה קדושה אית בה? וי"ל: דאיצטריך להיכא דנשחט הפסח כשהיה מומר ועשה תשובה, דאף על גב דלא אכיל בפסח דאין נאכל אלא למנויו, מכל מקום חייב לאכול מצה ומרור*:

ערל. פי' הקונטרס: שמתו אחיו מחמת מילה. ולפירושו פסול נמי בתרומה, דב"הערל" (יבמות ע. ושם) יליף תרומה מפסח בגז"ש, ד"תושב ושכיר". והא דמיבעיא לן התם (דף עא): ערל קטן מהו לסוכו שמן של תרומה, ערלה שלא בזמנה פוסלת או לא? יש לחלק בין שלא בזמנה דקטן, שאין חייב למול כיולא בו, למתו אחיו מחמת מילה דכיולא בו חייבין. ותדע, דהא טומטום אינו אוכל בתרומה, בפרק "הערל" (שם עב.), אף על גב דמסברא אין חייב לקרוע, הוא הדין מתו אחיו מחמת מילה, דאינו אוכל – אף על גב דאינו חייב למול:

בדין

רבינו חננאל

מני אי ר' יהודה חמץ סתמא קתני דאסור ואפי' דנכרי אי ר' שמעון הא אמר לאחר

עין משפט נר מצוה

סד א מיי' פ"א מהל' חמץ הל' ד:
סה ב מיי' שם הלכה ו סמג לאוין עו:

[עי' בהרא"ש דאסברא טפי דמוקמינן לה כר"ש להך מתני' בדף כ:]

[וע"ע תוס' לקמן קכ. ד"ה רב אחא בר יעקב]

מסורת הש"ס

[לעיל כג. לקמן לב.]

[וכן בברכות כח:]

לקמן מג.

לקמן נו.

[ברכות כח: יבמות ד. סנהדרין פז:]

[קכ.]

לקמן קכ.

לקמן נו. וקכ. יבמות ע.

[וע"ע תוס' לקמן קכ. ד"ה כל בן נכר]

הגהות הב"ח

(א) גמרא לכדתניא חמץ אין לי: (ב) רש"י ד"ה לקובעו וכו' שבעת ימים תאכל עליו מצות לאו:

דִּיִשְׂרָאֵל נַמִּי מִישְׁרָא קָא שָׁרֵי. וְאִי ר' יוֹסֵי הַגְּלִילִי – אֲפִי' תּוֹךְ זְמַנּוֹ נַמִּי מִישְׁרָא קָא שָׁרֵי בַּהֲנָאָה! אָמַר רַב אַחָא בַּר יַעֲקֹב: לְעוֹלָם ר' יְהוּדָה הִיא, וְיָלֵיף שְׂאוֹר דַּאֲכִילָה מִשְּׂאוֹר דִּרְאִיָּה. מַה שְּׂאוֹר דִּרְאִיָּה – *שֶׁלְּךָ אִי אַתָּה רוֹאֶה, אֲבָל אַתָּה רוֹאֶה שֶׁל אֲחֵרִים וְשֶׁל גָּבוֹהַּ – אַף שְׂאוֹר דַּאֲכִילָה, שֶׁלְּךָ אִי אַתָּה אוֹכֵל, אֲבָל אַתָּה אוֹכֵל שֶׁל אֲחֵרִים וְשֶׁל גָּבוֹהַּ. וּבְדִין הוּא דְּאִיבָּעֵי לֵיהּ לְמִיתְנָא דַּאֲפִילּוּ בַּאֲכִילָה נַמִּי שָׁרֵי, וְאַיְּידֵי דִּתְנָא דְּיִשְׂרָאֵל אָסוּר בַּהֲנָאָה – תְּנָא נַמִּי דְּגוֹי מוּתָּר בַּהֲנָאָה. וּבְדִין הוּא דְּאִיבָּעֵי לֵיהּ לְמִיתְנָא דַּאֲפִילּוּ בְּתוֹךְ זְמַנּוֹ מוּתָּר בַּהֲנָאָה, וְאַיְּידֵי דִּתְנָא דְּיִשְׂרָאֵל לְאַחַר זְמַנּוֹ – תְּנָא נַמִּי דְּגוֹי לְאַחַר זְמַנּוֹ. רָבָא אָמַר: לְעוֹלָם רַבִּי שִׁמְעוֹן הִיא, *וְרַבִּי שִׁמְעוֹן [א]קְנָסָא קָנֵיס הוֹאִיל וְעָבַר עָלֵיהּ בְּבַל יֵרָאֶה וּבַל יִמָּצֵא. בִּשְׁלָמָא לְרָבָא – הַיְינוּ דְּקָתָנֵי "שֶׁל יִשְׂרָאֵל אָסוּר", מִשּׁוּם שֶׁנֶּאֱמַר "לֹא יֵרָאֶה". אֶלָּא לְרַב אַחָא בַּר יַעֲקֹב – מִשּׁוּם "לֹא יֵאָכֵל חָמֵץ" מִיבָּעֵי לֵיהּ! מִי סָבְרַתְּ אַסֵּיפָא קָאֵי? אַרֵישָׁא קָאֵי, וְהָכִי קָאָמַר: חָמֵץ שֶׁל גּוֹי שֶׁעָבַר עָלָיו הַפֶּסַח – מוּתָּר בַּהֲנָאָה, מִשּׁוּם שֶׁנֶּאֱמַר "לֹא יֵרָאֶה לְךָ" – שֶׁלְּךָ אִי אַתָּה רוֹאֶה, אֲבָל אַתָּה רוֹאֶה שֶׁל אֲחֵרִים וְשֶׁל גָּבוֹהַּ. וְיָלֵיף שְׂאוֹר דַּאֲכִילָה מִשְּׂאוֹר דִּרְאִיָּה. וְאָזְדוּ לְטַעֲמַיְיהוּ: דְּאִיתְּמַר, הָאוֹכֵל שְׂאוֹר שֶׁל גּוֹי שֶׁעָבַר עָלָיו הַפֶּסַח, לְדִבְרֵי רַבִּי יְהוּדָה, רָבָא אָמַר: לוֹקֶה, וְרַב אַחָא בַּר יַעֲקֹב אָמַר: אֵינוֹ לוֹקֶה. רָבָא אָמַר: לוֹקֶה, לָא יָלֵיף רַבִּי יְהוּדָה שְׂאוֹר דַּאֲכִילָה מִשְּׂאוֹר דִּרְאִיָּה. וְרַב אַחָא בַּר יַעֲקֹב אָמַר: אֵינוֹ לוֹקֶה, יָלֵיף שְׂאוֹר דַּאֲכִילָה מִשְּׂאוֹר דִּרְאִיָּה. וַהֲדַר בֵּיהּ רַב אַחָא בַּר יַעֲקֹב מֵהַהִיא, דְּתַנְיָא: הָאוֹכֵל חָמֵץ שֶׁל הֶקְדֵּשׁ בַּמּוֹעֵד – מָעַל, וְיֵשׁ אוֹמְרִים: לֹא מָעַל. *מַאן יֵשׁ אוֹמְרִים? אָמַר רַבִּי יוֹחָנָן: רַבִּי נְחוּנְיָא בֶּן הַקָּנָה הִיא. *דְּתַנְיָא: ר' נְחוּנְיָא בֶּן הַקָּנָה הָיָה עוֹשֶׂה אֶת יוֹם הַכִּפּוּרִים כַּשַּׁבָּת לְתַשְׁלוּמִין. מַה שַּׁבָּת, מִתְחַיֵּיב בְּנַפְשׁוֹ וּפָטוּר מִן הַתַּשְׁלוּמִין – אַף יוֹם הַכִּפּוּרִים מִתְחַיֵּיב בְּנַפְשׁוֹ וּפָטוּר מִתַּשְׁלוּמִין. רַב יוֹסֵף אָמַר: בְּפוֹדִין אֶת הַקֳּדָשִׁים לְהַאֲכִילָן לַכְּלָבִים קָמִיפַּלְגִי. מַאן דְּאָמַר מָעַל, קָסָבַר: *פּוֹדִין אֶת הַקֳּדָשִׁים לְהַאֲכִילָן לַכְּלָבִים. וּמַאן דְּאָמַר לֹא מָעַל – קָסָבַר: *אֵין פּוֹדִין. רַב אַחָא בַּר רָבָא תְּנָא לָהּ לְהָא

רש"י

דְּיִשְׂרָאֵל נַמִּי מִישְׁרָא שָׁרֵי. בַּהֲנָאָה לְאַחַר זְמַנּוֹ: **לְעוֹלָם ר' יְהוּדָה הִיא.** דְּאַע"ג דְּנָפְקָא לֵיהּ מִקְּרָאֵי דִּלְאַחַר זְמַנּוֹ אָסַר קְרָא – בִּשְׂאוֹר דְּיִשְׂרָאֵל קָאָמַר, אֲבָל דְּגוֹי – שָׁרֵי: **וְיָלֵיף שְׂאוֹר דַּאֲכִילָה.** כְּלוֹמַר: חָמֵץ דְּגַבֵּי "לֹא יֵאָכֵל" מִשְּׂאוֹר דִּרְאִיָּה. וּמוּתָּר חֲמֵצוֹ שֶׁל גּוֹי אַף בַּאֲכִילָה, וַאֲפִי' בַּפֶּסַח, מִן הַתּוֹרָה: **לְעוֹלָם ר' שִׁמְעוֹן הִיא.** דְּאָמַר מִדְּאוֹרַיְיתָא לָא מִיתְּסַר חָמֵץ אַחַר זְמַנּוֹ. הִלְכָּךְ: דְּגוֹי שָׁרֵי, וּמִיהוּ דְּיִשְׂרָאֵל אָסוּר מִקְּנָסָא דְּקָנְסוּהוּ רַבָּנַן, מִשּׁוּם דְּעָבַר בְּבַל יֵרָאֶה: **בִּשְׁלָמָא לְרָבָא.** דְּאָמַר טַעְמָא דְּאָסוּר בַּהֲנָאָה מִשּׁוּם קְנָסָא, דְּעָבַר בְּבַל יֵרָאֶה הוּא – הַיְינוּ דְּתָנָא מַתְנִי' אָסוּר מִשּׁוּם "לֹא יֵרָאֶה לְךָ": **וְאָזְדוּ לְטַעְמַיְיהוּ.** רָבָא וְרַב אַחָא בַּר יַעֲקֹב: **מָעַל.** חַיָּיב קָרְבַּן מְעִילָה, דְּקָסָבַר: חָמֵץ דְּהֶקְדֵּשׁ בַּפֶּסַח בַּר דָּמִים הוּא, וְאַפְקְעֵיהּ לְהֶקְדֵּשׁ, כְּר' שִׁמְעוֹן דְּאָמַר חָמֵץ לְאַחַר הַפֶּסַח מוּתָּר. וְאַע"ג דִּקְנָסָא קָנֵיס – ה"מ בַּחֲמֵצוֹ שֶׁל הֶדְיוֹט, הוֹאִיל וְעָבַר עָלָיו בְּבַל יֵרָאֶה. אֲבָל הַאי, דִּבְהֶיתֵּרָא שַׁהְיֵי' גַּבֵּיהּ, דְּאָמַר מָר (לעיל דף ה:): אֲבָל אַתָּה רוֹאֶה שֶׁל אֲחֵרִים וְשֶׁל גָּבוֹהַּ – אַחַר הַפֶּסַח הֲוָה מְזַבֵּין לֵיהּ גִּיזְבָּר לְיִשְׂרָאֵל, וְאָכְלִי לֵיהּ: **וְיֵשׁ אוֹמְרִים לֹא מָעַל.** כִּדְמְפָרֵשׁ, דְּהוֹאִיל וְנִתְחַיֵּיב כָּרֵת מִשּׁוּם אֲכִילָה, פָּטוּר מִן הַתַּשְׁלוּמִין כְּרַבִּי נְחוּנְיָא, וּבְמָקוֹם שֶׁאֵין קֶרֶן אֵין חוֹמֶשׁ וְאֵין מְעִילָה: **אֶת יוה"כ כַּשַּׁבָּת.** הַמַּדְלִיק גָּדִישׁ בְּיוה"כ וּמִתְחַיֵּיב כָּרֵת – פָּטוּר מִן הַתַּשְׁלוּמִין כְּאִילּוּ הִדְלִיקוֹ בְּשַׁבָּת, שֶׁהוּא מִתְחַיֵּיב בְּנַפְשׁוֹ מִיתַת ב"ד. דִּפְשִׁיטָא לָן דְּפָטוּר מִלְּשַׁלֵּם, כִּדְכְתִיב (שמות כא): "וְלֹא יִהְיֶה אָסוֹן עָנוֹשׁ יֵעָנֵשׁ", הָא אִם אָסוֹן יִהְיֶה – לֹא יֵעָנֵשׁ. שֶׁאַף יוה"כ, שֶׁמִּיתָתוֹ בִּידֵי שָׁמַיִם, שֶׁנִּכְרָתִים חַיָּיו וּבָנָיו – אָסוֹן הוּא קָרוּי, שֶׁנֶּאֱ' (בראשית מב): "וּקְרָאָהוּ אָסוֹן", הִלְכָּךְ פָּטוּר מִלְּשַׁלֵּם. וְהָכִי פָּרְשִׁינַן לָהּ בְּ"אֵלּוּ נְעָרוֹת". יֵשׁ טוֹעִים דְּקַשְׁיָא לְהוּ: כִּי פָּטַר ר' נְחוּנְיָא בְּמֵזִיד פָּטַר, דְּבַר כָּרֵת הוּא – וְהָכָא בְּשׁוֹגֵג עָסְקִינַן, מִדְּקָתָנֵי מָעַל, וְשׁוֹגֵג לָאו בַּר כָּרֵת הוּא. וְטָעוּת הוּא זֶה, דְּגַבֵּי חָמֵץ מֵזִיד הוּא, וְגַבֵּי הֶקְדֵּשׁ שׁוֹגֵג הוּא, דְּלָא יָדַע שֶׁהוּא שֶׁל הֶקְדֵּשׁ: **וְרַב יוֹסֵף אָמַר.** לֹא הֲוָה סְבִירָא לְהָנָךְ תַּנָּאֵי כְּרַבִּי שִׁמְעוֹן, דְּאָמַר: תּוֹךְ זְמַנּוֹ אָסוּר בַּהֲנָאָה – דְּכוּלֵּי עָלְמָא מוֹדוּ דְּפָטוּר, הוֹאִיל וְהַשְׁתָּא מִיהָא לָא חֲזִי, וְלָאו מָמוֹנָא הוּא. וְאַע"ג דְּסוֹפוֹ גּוֹרֵם הוּא לְמָמוֹן לְאַחַר הַפֶּסַח. אֶלָּא אַלִּיבָּא דְּר' יוֹסֵי הַגְּלִילִי פְּלִיגִי, דְּאָמַר תּוֹךְ זְמַנּוֹ נַמִּי שָׁרֵי בַּהֲנָאָה, וּבְפוֹדִין קֳדָשִׁים לְהַאֲכִילָן לִכְלָבִים קָא מִיפַּלְגִי. מַאן דְּאָמַר מָעַל – סָבַר דְּרָאוּי הָיָה בְּאוֹתָהּ שָׁעָה לִפְדּוֹת לַאֲכִילַת כְּלָבִים, וּבַר דָּמִים הוּא. וּדְר' נְחוּנְיָא לֵית לֵיהּ: וּמַאן דְּאָמַר לֹא מָעַל סָבַר אֵין פּוֹדִין. הִלְכָּךְ לָא חֲזִי. וּפְלוּגְתָּא דְּתַנָּאֵי הִיא בִּתְמוּרָה (דף לא.): "תִּזְבַּח" – וְלֹא גִּיזָּה, "בָּשָׂר" – וְלֹא חָלָב, "וְאָכַלְתָּ" – וְלֹא לִכְלָבִים – מִכָּאן שֶׁאֵין פּוֹדִין. וְאִיכָּא דְּדָרֵישׁ: "תִּזְבַּח וְאָכַלְתָּ" – אֵין לְךָ בָּהֶן הֶיתֵּר אֲכִילָה אֶלָּא לְאַחַר זְבִיחָה, לְמַעוּטֵי גִּיזָּה וְחָלָב. אֲבָל לֹא לִכְלָבֶיךָ – לָא דָּרֵישׁ: לְהָא

תוספות

בדין הוא דאפי' תוך זמנו מותר. פרש"י: מותר באכילה. וקשה: דאי אפשר אם לא יהא שלו בשעת אכילה, דאם נתן לו הגוי – הרי הוא שלו. ואם גזל מגוי – הרי חייב באחריותו, ולא גרע מחמץ שחייב באחריותו דהוי כשלו. ועוד, לקמן דקאמר ואזדו לטעמייהו, דפליגי בחמץ שעבר עליו הפסח – ליפלגו בפסח גופיה! ונראה לריב"א: דהא דקאמר אפי' תוך זמנו מותר – היינו בהנאה. והא דקאמר אבל אתה אוכל של אחרים – לאו דוקא. אי נמי: אחר זמנו קאמר. ומיהו: בשל גבוה קשה לפרש בתוך הפסח, דאם לא פדאו – אסור בהנאה, ואם פדאו – הרי הוא שלו! ושמא י"ל: אבל אתה נהנה משל גבוה, שלא יהא איסור חמץ, אבל איסור הקדש – יש:

מאן יש אומרים ר' נחוניא. תימה לר"י: דמאן דיליף אסון אסון בריש "אלו נערות" (כתובו' ל.)(א) ואית ליה מיתה בידי שמים פטור מן התשלומים לר' נחוניא, אם כן לרבי, דאמר לקמן (דף לג.): הזיד במעילה במיתה – אמאי פוטר כרת מתשלומים? והא אע"ג דבעלמא פוטר מיתה מתשלומין – הכא לא פטר, דגלי לן קרא דבשוגג חייב, וה"ה כרת, אע"ג דבכרת הוא במזיד, בשוגג – יתחייב! ואור"י: דבמיתה, דגלי לן קרא דלא פטרה הכא מתשלומים – גלי. בכרת, דלא גלי – לא גלי. וא"ת, והא אמר לקמן (דף לא:): האוכל תרומת חמץ בפסח, בשוגג – משלם קרן וחומש. ומוקמי' לה כר' נחוניא, ואפ"ה מיחייב בתשלומין. משום דכי היכי דלא מיפטר מתשלומין משום חיוב מיתה דתרומה – הכי נמי לא מיפטר משום כרת של חמץ! ואור"י: דתשלומי תרומה מחמת כפרה הם, כדמוכח במסכת תרומות (פ"ו מ"א), דתנן: אם רצה כהן למחול – אינו יכול למחול. וכיון דכפרה הוא – אין כרת פוטרו משום "קם ליה בדרבה מיניה". ותדע, דהא מאן דלא יליף אסון אסון, ולא פטר מיתה בידי שמים מתשלומין – אם כן אוכל תרומת חמץ אמאי משלם? דלא שייך למימר כיון שמיתה אינה פוטרת ה"ה כרת – דהא מיתה לא פטרה בשום מקום. אלא ע"כ מטעם כפרה הוא. ועוד אור"י: דהכא אתי אליבא דרבנן, דאמרי: הזיד במעילה באזהרה*:

רבי נחוניא היא. אע"ג דהכא בשוגג איירי, מדקתני "מעל ולא מעל" – מ"מ קיימא לן כחזקיה, דאמר*: חייבי מיתות שוגגין פטורים מן התשלומין, וה"ה כרת לר' נחוניא. הקשה ריב"א: אמאי פטורין הכא מקרבן מעילה משום דקם ליה בדרבה מיניה? הא אמר ב"המצניע" (שבת צג:): המוציא אוכלים בכלי, שגג באוכלים והזיד בכלי – חייב על האוכלים חטאת. ועל הכלי סקילה. אלמא: קם ליה בדרבה מיניה לא פטר מקרבן! ותירץ: כיון דפטר מקרן וחומש – פטר נמי מקרבן, שאין אשם מעילות בא אלא כשיש קרן וחומש: **אין** פודין את הקדשים וכו'. הקשה הר"ח: דבפ"ב דבכורות (דף יד:) משמע דלא פליגי אלא היכא שקדם הקדישן למומן, אבל קדם מומן להקדישן, הואיל ומעולם לא קדשו קדושת הגוף – כ"ע מודים דפודים. והכא משמע דפליגי, אפי' בקדושת דמים! ותי' ר"י, דה"ק: אין פודין מדרבנן. ואין לתמוה: אטו משום חששא דרבנן נפקיע מעילה דאורייתא? דכיון דאמרו רבנן אין פודין – לא שויא מידי. והא דאמר בהתערובות (זבחים עא.*): נתערבו בשור שנעבדה וכו' בכלאים וטריפה – ירעו עד שיסתאבו וימכרו. והשתא ע"כ יאכיל לכלבים, דלישראל טריפה אסורה ליה, אתי שפיר, אפילו למאן דאמר אין פודין דהא דאין פודין – היינו היכא דלא חזו לאכילה, אבל הכא – חזו לאדם אם היו ניכרים. דהא רבי עקיבא שרי בבכורות (דף לג.) לזמן גוי על הבכור. ובזבחים, בפ' "טבול יום" (דף קד.) *מוכח שר' עקיבא אוסר בכור טריפה בעל מום להאכיל לכלבים, שאפילו העור אסור כשנמצא טריפה קודם הפשט, והיכא דשרי לישראל – איתקש לצבי ולאיל: **אין** פודין. תימה לר"י: אע"ג דאין פודין – נמעול. דהא לאחר שנשרף ונעשה אפר יכול לפדותו

רבינו חננאל

זמנו דישראל נמי שרי בהנאה אי ר' יוסי הגלילי כו' ואוקמה רב אחא בר יעקב כר' יהוד' ואמר דר' יהודה יליף שאור דאכילה שנאמר (שמות יב יט) שבעת ימים שאור לא ימצא בבתיכם כי כל אוכל מחמצת וכתיב (שם טו) תשביתו שאור מבתיכם כי כל אוכל חמץ וגו' ויליף האי שאור דאכילה משאור דראיה שנאמר ולא יראה לך שאור ומפרש בשאור דראיה לך ודרשי' ביה שלך אי אתה רואה אבל אתה רואה של אחרים ושל גבוה ובדין הוא דליתני במתני' הכי חמץ של נכרי שעבר עליו הפסח מותר באכילה ובתוך זמנו נמי מותר בהנאה ואיידי דבעי מיתנא סיפא ושל ישראל אסור דאפי' בהנאה נמי חמץ ישראל שעבר עליו הפסח אסור תנא רישא נמי של נכרי שעבר עליו הפסח מותר בהנאה. רבא אמר מתני' ר' שמעון היא דסבירא ליה דלפני זמנו ולאחר זמנו אינו עובר עליו בלא כלום ומתני' דקתני ושל ישראל אסור לאחר זמנו קנסא הוא דקנים ליה משום דשהיי' גביה ועבר עליה על לא יראה ועל לא ימצא בשלמא לרבא דאוקמה למתני' לר' שמעון ומשום דעבר על לא יראה קנסוהו היינו דקתני במתני' ושל ישראל אסור משום שנאמר לא יראה לך אלא לרב אחא דמוקים כר' יהודה משום לא תאכל מבעי ליה למיתנא ומשני רב אחא בר יעקב מי סברת אסיפא דקתני ושל ישראל אסור קאי לא ארישא קאי והכי קתני חמץ של נכרי מותר שנאמר לא יראה לך אלא לרב אחא דמוקים כר' יהודה משום לא תאכל... לא יראה לך שאור ויליף שאור דאכילה משאור דראיה כדאמרן: **ואזדו** לטעמייהו דאיתמר האוכל חמץ של נכרי שעבר עליו הפסח לדברי ר' יהודה רבא אמר לוקה דהא סתמא קתני לא שנא דישראל ולא שנא דנכרי חמץ לפני זמנו ולאחר זמנו עובר בלאו ואמרי' מאי טעמיה דר' יהודה תלתא קראי כתיבי חד לפני זמנו שנאמר לא תאכל עליו חמץ והוא משעה ששית עד שחיטת הפסח וחד לאחר זמנו לא יאכל חמץ ותוך זמנו שחייב לאו וכרת שנאמר כי כל אוכל מחמצת ונכרתה וגו' ולא יליף שאור דאכילה משאור דראיה רב אחא בר יעקב אומר אינו לוקה יליף שאור כו': **והדר** ביה רב אחא בר יעקב דתניא האוכל חמץ של הקדש במועד מעל ויש אומרים לא מעל מאן יש אומרים א"ר חסדא ר' נחוניא הוא דפטר מחויב כרת מן תשלומין כמחויב מיתת ב"ד וכיון שאוכל חמץ בפסח חייב כרת הוא ופטור מלשלם קרבן מעילה: **רב** יוסף אמר בפודין קדשים להאכילם לכלבים פליגי. פי' החמץ אע"פ שהוא קדש בין בפסח בין לאחר הפסח אסור באכילה מיהו פודין אותו להאכילו לכלבים והרי ממון הוא והנהנה מממון של הקדש מעל ת"ק סבר פודין ולפיכך מעל ויש אומרים סבר אין פודין את הקדשים להאכילן לכלבים:

עין משפט נר מצוה

סו א מיי' פ"א מהלכות חמץ הל' ד סמג לאוין עו:

מסורת הש"ס

[לעיל ה: כג.]

[לקמן ל.]

[וע"פ מ"ש תוס' ב"ב נג: ד"ה מאן וכו' יתבאר נמי הכא]

[בכורות טו: תמורה יז. לא. לג:]

[בכורות טו. שבועות יא: תמורה יז. ל: לא.]

כתובות ל. שבועות לו. לקמן לב. [מגילה ז: תוספתא ב"ק פ"ז]

[וע"ע תוס' כתובות ל: ד"ה זר]

[כתובות לה.]

[וע"ש תוס' ד"ה וכטריפה]

[וע"ש תוס' ד"ה אמר ר' עקיבא]

הגהות הב"ח

(א) תוס' ד"ה מאן וכו' בריש אלו נערות. נ"ב וע"ש בדף ל תוס' בד"ה זר שאכל:

סז א מיי' פ"ז מהלכות חובל הל' ז טוש"ע ח"מ סי' שפו סעיף א:
סח ב מיי' פט"ו מהל' מאכלות אסורות הלכה ו סמג לאוין קמא טוש"ע י"ד סימן לח סעיף א:

[ועי"ע תוס' קדושין נו: ד"ה המקדש וכו']

לְהָא שְׁמַעְתָּא מִשְּׁמֵיהּ דְּרַב יוֹסֵף בְּהָא לִישָּׁנָא: דְּכוּלֵּי עָלְמָא אֵין פּוֹדִין אֶת הַקֳּדָשִׁים לְהַאֲכִילָן לַכְּלָבִים, וְהָכָא בְּהָא קָמִיפַּלְגִי: בְּדָבָר הַגּוֹרֵם לְמָמוֹן, כְּמָמוֹן דָּמֵי. מַאן דְּאָמַר מָעַל – *קָסָבַר: אדָּבָר הַגּוֹרֵם לְמָמוֹן – כְּמָמוֹן דָּמֵי. וּמַאן דְּאָמַר לֹא מָעַל – קָסָבַר: דָּבָר הַגּוֹרֵם לְמָמוֹן – לָאו כְּמָמוֹן דָּמֵי. רַב אַחָא בַּר יַעֲקֹב אָמַר: דְּכוּלֵּי עָלְמָא דָּבָר הַגּוֹרֵם לְמָמוֹן – כְּמָמוֹן דָּמֵי. וְהָכָא בִּפְלוּגְתָּא דְּרַבִּי יְהוּדָה וְרַבִּי שִׁמְעוֹן קָמִיפַּלְגִי. מַאן דְּאָמַר לֹא מָעַל – כְּרַבִּי יְהוּדָה, וּמַאן דְּאָמַר מָעַל – כְּר"ש. וְהָא רַב אַחָא בַּר יַעֲקֹב הוּא דְּאָמַר דְּר' יְהוּדָה יָלֵיף שְׂאוֹר דַּאֲכִילָה מִשְּׂאוֹר דִּרְאִיָּיה! אֶלָּא: הֲדַר בֵּיהּ רַב אַחָא בַּר יַעֲקֹב מֵהַהִיא. רַב אַשִׁי אָמַר: דְּכוּלֵּי עָלְמָא אֵין פּוֹדִין, וְדָבָר הַגּוֹרֵם לְמָמוֹן לָאו כְּמָמוֹן דָּמֵי, וְהָכָא בִּפְלוּגְתָּא דְּרַבִּי יוֹסֵי הַגְּלִילִי וְרַבָּנַן קָמִיפַּלְגִי. מַאן דְּאָמַר מָעַל – כְּרַבִּי יוֹסֵי, וּמַאן דְּאָמַר לֹא מָעַל – כְּרַבָּנַן.§ אָמַר רַב: חָמֵץ בִּזְמַנּוֹ, בֵּין בְּמִינוֹ בֵּין שֶׁלֹּא בְּמִינוֹ – אָסוּר. שֶׁלֹּא בִּזְמַנּוֹ, בְּמִינוֹ – אָסוּר, שֶׁלֹּא בְּמִינוֹ – מוּתָּר. בְּמַאי עָסְקִינַן? אִילֵימָא בְּנוֹתֵן טַעַם, שֶׁלֹּא בִּזְמַנּוֹ שֶׁלֹּא בְּמִינוֹ מוּתָּר?! הָא יָהֵיב טַעְמָא! אֶלָּא בְּמַשֶּׁהוּ. חָמֵץ בִּזְמַנּוֹ בֵּין בְּמִינוֹ בֵּין שֶׁלֹּא בְּמִינוֹ אָסוּר, רַב לְטַעְמֵיהּ. *דְּרַב וּשְׁמוּאֵל דְּאָמְרִי תַּרְוַיְיהוּ: כָּל אִיסּוּרִין שֶׁבַּתּוֹרָה, בְּמִינוֹ – בְּמַשֶּׁהוּ, שֶׁלֹּא בְּמִינוֹ – בְּנוֹתֵן טַעַם. רַב גָּזַר חָמֵץ בִּזְמַנּוֹ שֶׁלֹּא בְּמִינוֹ אַטּוּ מִינוֹ, וְשֶׁלֹּא בִּזְמַנּוֹ בְּמִינוֹ אָסוּר, כְּרַבִּי יְהוּדָה. וְשֶׁלֹּא בְּמִינוֹ – מוּתָּר. דְּשֶׁלֹּא בִּזְמַנּוֹ וְשֶׁלֹּא בְּמִינוֹ אַטּוּ מִינוֹ – כּוּלֵּי הַאי לָא גָּזְרִינַן. שְׁמוּאֵל אָמַר: חָמֵץ בִּזְמַנּוֹ, בְּמִינוֹ – אָסוּר, שֶׁלֹּא בְּמִינוֹ – מוּתָּר. שֶׁלֹּא בִּזְמַנּוֹ, בֵּין בְּמִינוֹ בֵּין שֶׁלֹּא בְּמִינוֹ – מוּתָּר. חָמֵץ בִּזְמַנּוֹ בְּמִינוֹ אָסוּר, שְׁמוּאֵל לְטַעְמֵיהּ, דְּרַב וּשְׁמוּאֵל דְּאָמְרִי תַּרְוַיְיהוּ: כָּל אִיסּוּרִין שֶׁבַּתּוֹרָה, בְּמִינוֹ – אֲסוּרִין בְּמַשֶּׁהוּ, שֶׁלֹּא בְּמִינוֹ – בְּנוֹתֵן טַעַם. שֶׁלֹּא בְּמִינָן אַטּוּ מִינָן – לֹא גָּזַר. שֶׁלֹּא בִּזְמַנּוֹ, בֵּין בְּמִינָן בֵּין שֶׁלֹּא בְּמִינָן – מוּתָּרִין, כְּר' שִׁמְעוֹן. וְרַבִּי יוֹחָנָן אָמַר: חָמֵץ בִּזְמַנּוֹ, בֵּין בְּמִינוֹ וּבֵין שֶׁלֹּא בְּמִינוֹ – אָסוּר בְּנוֹתֵן טַעַם. שֶׁלֹּא בִּזְמַנּוֹ, בֵּין בְּמִינָן בֵּין שֶׁלֹּא בְּמִינָן – מוּתָּר. חָמֵץ בִּזְמַנּוֹ בֵּין בְּמִינוֹ בֵּין שֶׁלֹּא בְּמִינוֹ בְּנוֹתֵן טַעַם – ר' יוֹחָנָן לְטַעְמֵיהּ, *דְּר' יוֹחָנָן וְרֵישׁ לָקִישׁ דְּאָמְרִי תַּרְוַיְיהוּ: בכָּל אִיסּוּרִין שֶׁבַּתּוֹרָה, בֵּין בְּמִינָן בֵּין שֶׁלֹּא בְּמִינָן – בְּנוֹתֵן טַעַם. שֶׁלֹּא בִּזְמַנּוֹ, בֵּין בְּמִינוֹ בֵּין שֶׁלֹּא בְּמִינוֹ – מוּתָּרִין – כְּר' שִׁמְעוֹן.

אָמַר

רש"י

לְהָא **שְׁמַעְתָּא.** דְּרַב יוֹסֵף: דְּכוּלֵּי עָלְמָא **אֵין פּוֹדִין.** וְאַלִּיבָּא דְּר' שִׁמְעוֹן הוּא דִּפְלִיגִי, דְּשָׁרֵי לֵיהּ לְאַחַר פֶּסַח אַף לַאֲכִילַת יִשְׂרָאֵל. וּבְהָא פְּלִיגִי: מַאן דְּאָמַר מָעַל – סָבַר אַף עַל גַּב דְּהַשְׁתָּא לָא חֲזֵי, הוֹאִיל וּלְקַמֵּיהּ גּוֹרֵם לְמָמוֹן הוּא – כְּמָמוֹן דָּמֵי: הָכִי גָּרְסִינַן: רַב אַחָא בַּר יַעֲקֹב אָמַר דְּכוּלֵּי עָלְמָא כְּמָמוֹן דָּמֵי: וּמַאן דְּאָמַר **לֹא** מָעַל. כְּרַבִּי יְהוּדָה, דְּאָמַר: אַף לְאַחַר הַפֶּסַח אָסוּר בַּהֲנָאָה, וְכָל שֶׁכֵּן בַּפֶּסַח עַצְמוֹ. הִלְכָּךְ: לָאו מָמוֹן אִיכָּא, דִּלְיִשְׂרָאֵל לָא חֲזֵי. וְלָאו גּוֹרֵם לְמָמוֹן אִיכָּא – שֶׁאִם יִפָּדֶה לֹא יֵהָנֶה מִמֶּנּוּ. וּלְגוֹי לָא מִזְדַּבַּן, דְּאֵין פּוֹדִין אֶת הַקֳּדָשִׁים לְהַאֲכִילָן לִכְלָבִים: וּמ"ד מָעַל כְּר"ש. דְּאָמַר: רָאוּי הוּא לְאַחַר הַפֶּסַח אַף (לְאָדָם) [לְיִשְׂרָאֵל], וַהֲוָה לֵיהּ גּוֹרֵם לְמָמוֹן: **מִשְּׂאוֹר** דִּרְאִיָּיה. וְשֶׁל הֶקְדֵּשׁ – אַף בַּפֶּסַח מוּתָּר, וְהָכָא אָמַר לְרַבִּי יְהוּדָה לֹא מָעַל: הָכִי גָּרְסִינַן: רַב אַשִׁי אָמַר דְּכוּלֵּי עָלְמָא אֵין פּוֹדִין וְדָבָר הַגּוֹרֵם לְמָמוֹן לָאו כְּמָמוֹן דָּמֵי. כְּלוֹמַר: דְּכוּלֵּי עָלְמָא לְגוֹי לָא מְזַבְּנִינַן לֵיהּ בַּפֶּסַח, וּמִשּׁוּם דִּלְאַחַר הַפֶּסַח דַּחֲזֵי לְיִשְׂרָאֵל – לָא מְחַיְּיבִי לֵיהּ. דְּדָבָר הַגּוֹרֵם לְמָמוֹן לָאו כְּמָמוֹן דָּמֵי. וְהָכָא טַעְמָא דִּמְעִילָה – מִשּׁוּם דְּסָבַר לָהּ כְּרַבִּי יוֹסֵי הַגְּלִילִי, דְּאָמַר אַף תּוֹךְ זְמַנּוֹ מוּתָּר בַּהֲנָאָה. הִלְכָּךְ חֲזֵי לְמִפְרְקֵיהּ וּלְהַסִּיקוֹ תַּחַת תַּבְשִׁילוֹ. וּמַאן דְּאָמַר לֹא מָעַל – כְּרַבָּנַן, דְּאָמְרִי חָמֵץ בַּפֶּסַח אָסוּר בַּהֲנָאָה. וְאִי מִשּׁוּם דְּמָצֵי לְשַׁהוּיֵי לְאַחַר זְמַן כְּר"ש – הַשְׁתָּא מִיהָא לָאו מָמוֹן הוּא: חָמֵץ בִּזְמַנּוֹ וכו'. מְפָרֵשׁ כּוּלֵּיהּ לְקַמֵּיהּ: **אִי** נֵימָא בְּנוֹתֵן טַעַם שֶׁלֹּא בִּזְמַנּוֹ שֶׁלֹּא בְּמִינוֹ מוּתָּר. בִּתְמִיָּה, הָא יָהֵיב טַעְמָא! וְרַב, מִדְּקָאָמַר שֶׁלֹּא בִּזְמַנּוֹ בְּמִינוֹ אָסוּר – גַּלֵּי דַּעְתֵּיהּ דִּכְר' יְהוּדָה סְבִירָא לֵיהּ, דְּאָמַר אַף לְאַחַר הַפֶּסַח אָסוּר: **שֶׁלֹּא** בְּמִינוֹ. נַמִי בִּזְמַנּוֹ אָסוּר. וְאַע"ג דְּאִית לֵיהּ לְרַב דְּכָל אִיסּוּרִין שֶׁלֹּא בְּמִינוֹ בְּנוֹתֵן טַעַם – רַב גָּזַר בְּחָמֵץ בִּזְמַנּוֹ, הוֹאִיל וּבְכָרֵת הוּא, שֶׁלֹּא בְּמִינוֹ אַטּוּ מִינוֹ. וְאַע"ג דְּבְחֵלֶב וָדָם לֹא גָּזַר שֶׁלֹּא בְּמִינוֹ אַטּוּ מִינוֹ – הָתָם הוּא דִּבְדִילֵי מִינַּיְיהוּ, אֲבָל חָמֵץ לָא בְּדִילֵי מִינֵּיהּ, הוֹאִיל וְאוֹכְלוֹ כָּל יְמוֹת הַשָּׁנָה: **שֶׁלֹּא** בִּזְמַנּוֹ בְּמִינוֹ **אָסוּר** כְּרַבִּי יְהוּדָה. דְּאָמַר: לְאַחַר הַפֶּסַח דְּאוֹרַיְיתָא, הִלְכָּךְ אַף תַּעֲרוֹבֶת אָסוּר: **שֶׁלֹּא** בְּמִינוֹ מוּתָּר. דְּשֶׁלֹּא בִּזְמַנּוֹ, דְּאֵינוֹ בְּכָרֵת, שֶׁלֹּא בְּמִינוֹ אַטּוּ מִינוֹ לֹא גָּזַר, כִּי הֵיכִי דְּלָא גָּזַר בְּבָשָׂר בְּחָלָב וּבִשְׁאָר אִיסּוּרִין: **וּשְׁמוּאֵל** **אָמַר** כו'. בְּמַשֶּׁהוּ עָסְקִינַן. שֶׁלֹּא בְּמִינוֹ – מוּתָּר כִּשְׁאָר אִיסּוּרִין. דְּלָא גָּזַר שְׁמוּאֵל בְּחָמֵץ שֶׁלֹּא בְּמִינוֹ אַטּוּ מִינוֹ: **כְּרַבִּי** שִׁמְעוֹן. דִּלְאַחַר זְמַנּוֹ שָׁרֵי, וַאֲפִי' בְּנוֹתֵן טַעַם נַמִי שָׁרֵי. וּלְקַמָּן פָּרֵיךְ: וְהָא אָסַר לֵיהּ ר' שִׁמְעוֹן מִשּׁוּם קְנָסָא:

אָמַר

תוספות

לפדותו, ומותר בהנאה! ויש לומר: דכיון דכמו שהוא עכשיו לא שוי מידי – לא שייכא ביה מעילה. והיינו נמי טעמא דכל איסורי הנאה אין מקדשין בהן האשה, אע"ג דכל הנשרפין אפרן מותר. ואפילו אי דבר הגורם לממון כממון דמי, ומעל – לא דמי. דהתם חזי לאחר הפסח, שהוא כמו בעין. ועוד יש לומר: הא דאין מקדשין באיסורי הנאה – היינו היכא דלית ביה שוה פרוטה לכשיהא אפר. ולתירוץ קמא קשה(א): הא חזי בעיניה שלא כדרך הנאה*: **הדר** ביה רב אחא. תימה: דבפרק קמא דחולין (דף ד:) אמר: סברוה הא מני – ר' יהודה, דאמר: חמצן של עוברי עבירה לאחר הפסח מותר מיד, מפני שמחליפים. והכא מסקינן לר' יהודה אפילו חמץ של גוי אסור אחר הפסח! ויש לומר: דהתם סברוה כס"ד דהכא לרב אחא מעיקרא. ורבינו תם מפרש: לאו דווקא מיד, דהא צריך שיהא שיעור להחליף. והוא הדין שיהא חמץ זה ראוי לעשות אחר הפסח:

רב אשי **אמר** דכולי **עלמא.** וקשה לר"י היכי גרסינן? אי גרסינן "דכולי עלמא פודין" – אם כן לרבנן אמאי לא מעל? אף על גב דלישראל אסור בהנאה – מכל מקום ימכרנו לגוי ההקדש עצמו. ואי גריס "אין פודין" אפילו לרבי יוסי הגלילי אמאי מעל? ויש לומר: דגרסי' "אין פודין" ואף על גב דאין פודין להאכיל לכלבים, מכל מקום שרי להסיק תחת תבשילו *וכדפרישית, דהכא דקדושת דמים אין פודין מדרבנן, ולא גזרו רבנן אלא שלא להאכילו לכלבים, אבל היכא דאין פודין מדאורייתא דהיינו היכא דאיכא קדושת הגוף – אין פודין אפי' להסיק, דהא תניא (*בפ"ק) דבכורות (דף טו.): אם מתו – יקברו. וקאמר התם: ממאי דהאי אם מתו יקברו, משום דבעי העמדה והערכה – דילמא משום דאין פודין הקדשים להאכילן לכלבים. והשתא, אי טעמא משום דאין פודין, אמאי יקברו? והא ראוי להסיקו תחת תבשילו! אלא ודאי מדאורייתא אין חילוק. וכן לעיל (דף כב.) דרשינן: ואי אתה משליך לכלב כל איסורין שבתורה, ואסירי אפילו להסקה. אלמא: מדאורייתא אין לחלק בהנאה. ואם תאמר: לרבנן, אמאי לא מעל? הלא הקדש יכול למכור לגוי על מנת שיסיקנו לפניו! ויש לומר: דגזרינן שמא יאכלנו הגוי. וכהאי גוונא אמר במסכת ע"ז (דף טו.): אין מוכרין בהמה לגוי על מנת לשוחטה וכו'. ומכאן מוכיח ר"י שהמשהה חמץ בפסח, ודעתו לבערו – אינו עובר באותה שהייה. דאי אמרת עובר – אכתי אמאי מעל לרבי יוסי? הא מיד כשיפדה אותו הוא שלו, ומודה רבי יוסי דשלך אי אתה רואה! אלא ודאי לא עבר, וטעמא משום דלא יראה *ניתק לעשה, ולכך אינו עובר כשמבערו לבסוף:

[ועי' תוס' כ"ק נג: ד"ה לענין כלים]
[נ"ל בפ"ב]

רבינו חננאל

פי' דבר הגורם לממון כגון מי שגזל חמץ זה של הקדש אם הוא בעינו מחזירו לו לנגזל ופטור דתנן גזל חמץ ועבר עליו הפסח אומר לו הרי שלך לפניך וכיון שאכלו נתחייב הגזלן לשלם לו ממון ואע"פ שחמץ בפסח אינו ממון השבתתו גורם ממון. רב אחא בר יעקב אומר כולי עלמא דבר הגורם לממון לאו כממון דמי והכא בפלוגתא דר' שמעון ורבנן פליגי ת"ק כר' שמעון דאמר תוך זמנו הוא דעבר עליו בלאו לאחר זמנו אינו עובר עליו בלא כלום וממון מעליא הוא לפיכך מעל ויש אומרים כר' יהודה דאמר אפי' לאחר זמנו עובר בלאו ואמרינן והא רב אחא הוא דאמר דר' יהודה יליף שאור דאכילה משאור דראיה מה שאור דראיה של גבוה מותר בראיה כך שאור דאכילה של גבוה מותר לאחר זמנו אפי' באכילה ולמה לא מעל אלא ודאי הדר ביה: רב אשי אמר כולי עלמא אין פודין קדשים להאכילן לכלבים ודבר הגורם לממון לאו כממון דמי והכא בפלוגתא דר' יוסי הגלילי ורבנן קא מיפלגי ת"ק כר' יוסי הגלילי דקתני ותמה על עצמך האיך חמץ אסור בהנאה כל שבעה ויש אומרים כרבנן. ירושלמי מתני' דקתני חמץ של נכרי שעבר עליו הפסח מותר בהנאה במקום שלא נהגו לאכול פת של גוים אבל במקום שנהגו לאכלו מותר אפי' באכילה פי' כגון שהיה ישראל רואהו ומסייעהו באפיית אותה הפת וקיי"ל בזמן שישראל רואהו כגון הבצקת של גוים דאמור רבנן אדם ממלא כרסו מהן אלו וכיוצא בהן: **אם** היה גגו של נכרי סמוך לגגו של ישראל הרי זה דוחפו בקנה היתה שבת או יום טוב כופה עליו כלי. רב אמר צריך שיאמר בשעה שיבער בא"י אמ"ה אקב"ו על בעור חמץ וצריך נמי שיאמר כל חמץ שישנו ברשותי ואיני יודע בו יהא בטל: **אמר** רב חמץ בזמנו בין במינו בין שלא במינו אסור אפי' במשהו רב לטעמיה דאמר כל איסורין שבתורה במינו במשהו וגזרה שלא במינו אטו במינו. שלא בזמנו כלומר אחר הפסח במינו אסור במשהו סבר לה כר' יהודה שלא במינו לאחר הפסח מותר דלא גזר. ושמואל אמר חמץ בפסח במינו אסור במשהו שמואל לטעמיה דאמר כל איסורין שבתורה במינן במשהו שלא במינו שרי ולא גזר שלא במינו אטו מינו שלא בזמנו בין במינו בין שלא במינו מותר כר' שמעון. ור' יוחנן אמר חמץ בפסח בין במינו בין שלא במינו אסור בנותן טעם ר' יוחנן לטעמיה דאמר כל איסורין שבתורה בין

[לעיל ה:] כתובות לד. ב"ק עא: נח: [קה.] שבועות לב. לג:
ע"ז עג:
סס
[עי' לקמן לה. תד"ה בפרטיה]

הגהות הב"ח

(א) תום' ד"ה אין פודין וכו'. ולתירוץ קמא קשה. נ"ב עיין בתוס' פ' האיש מקדש דף ט בד"ה המקדש בערלה:

אָמַר רָבָא: הִלְכְתָא, [א]חָמֵץ בִּזְמַנּוֹ, בֵּין בְּמִינוֹ בֵּין שֶׁלֹּא בְּמִינוֹ — אָסוּר בְּמַשֶּׁהוּ, כְּרַב. [ב]שֶׁלֹּא בִּזְמַנּוֹ, בֵּין בְּמִינוֹ בֵּין שֶׁלֹּא בְּמִינוֹ — מוּתָּר, כְּרַבִּי שִׁמְעוֹן. וּמִי אָמַר רָבָא הָכִי? וְהָאָמַר רָבָא: *רַבִּי שִׁמְעוֹן קְנָסָא קָנֵיס, הוֹאִיל וְעָבַר עָלָיו בְּ"בַל יֵרָאֶה וּבַל יִמָּצֵא"! הָנֵי מִילֵּי — בְּעֵינֵיהּ, אֲבָל עַל יְדֵי תַּעֲרוֹבֶת — לָא. וְאָזְדָא רָבָא לְטַעְמֵיהּ, דְּאָמַר רָבָא: כִּי הֲוֵינַן בֵּי רַב נַחְמָן, כִּי הָווּ נָפְקִי שִׁבְעָה יוֹמֵי דְּפִסְחָא, אֲמַר לָן: פּוּקוּ וּזְבִינוּ חֲמִירָא דִּבְנֵי חֵילָא.§ *אָמַר רַב: קְדֵירוֹת בַּפֶּסַח יִשָּׁבְרוּ. וְאַמַּאי? לַשְׁהִינְהוּ אַחַר הַפֶּסַח, וְלֶיעֱבַד בְּהוּ שֶׁלֹּא בְּמִינָן! גְּזֵירָה דִּילְמָא אָתוּ לְמֶיעֱבַד בְּהוּ בְּמִינוֹ. וּשְׁמוּאֵל אָמַר: [ג]לֹא יִשָּׁבְרוּ, אֲבָל מַשְׁהֵי לְהוּ לְאַחַר זְמַנּוֹ, וְעָבֵיד בְּהוּ בֵּין בְּמִינוֹ בֵּין שֶׁלֹּא בְּמִינוֹ. וְאָזְדָא שְׁמוּאֵל לְטַעְמֵיהּ, דַּאֲמַר שְׁמוּאֵל לְהָנְהוּ דִּמְזַבְּנֵי כַּנְדֵּי: אַשְׁווּ זְבִינֵי אַכַּנְדֵּיכִי, וְאִי לָא — דָּרְשִׁינָא לְכוּ כְּרַבִּי שִׁמְעוֹן. וְלִידְרוֹשׁ לְהוּ, דְּהָא שְׁמוּאֵל כְּרַבִּי שִׁמְעוֹן סְבִירָא לֵיהּ! אַתְרֵיהּ דְּרַב הֲוָה. *הַהוּא תַּנּוּרָא דְּטָחוּ בֵּיהּ טִיחַיָּא, אַסְרָהּ רָבָא בַּר אֲהִילַאי לְמֵיכְלֵי' לְרִיפְתָּא אֲפִי' בְּמִילְחָא לְעוֹלָם, דִּילְמָא אָתֵי לְמֵיכְלֵיהּ בְּכוּתָּחָא. מֵיתִיבִי: *°[ד]אֵין לָשִׁין אֶת הָעִיסָּה בְּחָלָב, וְאִם לָשׁ — כָּל הַפַּת כּוּלָּהּ אֲסוּרָה, מִפְּנֵי הֶרְגֵּל עֲבֵירָה. כַּיּוֹצֵא בּוֹ

אֵין

אָמַר רָבָא הִלְכְתָא כו'. ש"מ דְּפָסַק רָבָא הִלְכְתָא דְּכָל אִיסּוּרִין שֶׁבַּתּוֹרָה בְּמִינָן בְּמַשֶּׁהוּ, וְלָא שָׁנֵי לָן בֵּין חָמֵץ לִשְׁאָר אִיסּוּרֵי, אֶלָּא בְּהָא מִילְּתָא: דְּגָזַר שֶׁלֹּא בְּמִינָן אַטּוּ מִינָן. שָׁמְעִינַן מִינָּהּ: חָלָב שֶׁנָּפַל לִקְדֵירָה – אוֹסֵר בְּמַשֶּׁהוּ, וְכֵן הֲלָכָה. וְהָא דְּקִי"ל כָּל אִיסּוּרִין שֶׁבַּתּוֹרָה בְּשִׁשִּׁים – בְּשֶׁלֹּא בְּמִינָן הוּא: שֶׁלֹּא בִּזְמַנּוֹ בֵּין בְּמִינוֹ בֵּין שֶׁלֹּא בְּמִינוֹ מוּתָּר. אֲפִילּוּ בְּנוֹתֵן טַעַם: אֲבָל ע"י תַּעֲרוֹבֶת לֹא. וַאֲפִי' שֶׁהֶיְיתָה בְּעֵינֶיהָ וְעָבַר עָלֶיהָ – לָא קָנֵיס לְמֵיסַר תַּעֲרוֹבֶת דִּילֵיהּ: וְאָזְדָא רָבָא. דְּאָמַר הֲלָכָה כְּר' שִׁמְעוֹן, לְטַעְמֵיהּ דְּאָמַר נַמִי בְּעָלְמָא חָמֵץ שֶׁל גּוֹי שֶׁעָבַר עָלָיו הַפֶּסַח – מוּתָּר אַף בַּאֲכִילָה, הוֹאִיל וְלֵיכָּא לְמִיקְנַס בֵּיהּ מִידֵי. וְאִי רַבִּי יְהוּדָה חָמֵץ סְתָמָא קָאָמַר וַאֲפִילּוּ דְּגוֹי: בְּנֵי חֵילָא. גּוֹיִם, אַע"פ °שֶׁאֲפָאוּהוּ יוֹם זֶה שֶׁעָבַר, וְהוּא פֶּסַח: אָמַר רַב קְדֵירוֹת בַּפֶּסַח יִשָּׁבְרוּ. רַב לְטַעְמֵיהּ, דְּאָמַר: חָמֵץ אַף לְאַחַר זְמַנּוֹ אָסוּר בַּהֲנָאָה כְּר' יְהוּדָה, וְאִית לֵיהּ בְּמַשֶּׁהוּ, וְקָסָבַר: נוֹתֵן טַעַם לִפְגָם – אָסוּר. וְלֵית הִלְכְתָא כְּוָותֵיהּ מִתְּרֵי טַעֲמֵי, חֲדָא: דְּאוֹקֵי רָבָא הִלְכְתָא דְּתַעֲרוֹבֶת לְאַחַר זְמַנּוֹ מוּתָּר כְּר"שׁ, וְהַאי פָּחוֹת מִתַּעֲרוֹבֶת הוּא. וְעוֹד: דְּקִי"ל נוֹתֵן טַעַם לִפְגָם מוּתָּר, וְזֶה מִשֶּׁעָבְרוּ עָלָיו יְמֵי הַפֶּסַח – הוּפַג טַעְמוֹ בְּדוֹפְנֵי הַכְּלִי: וְלֶיעֱבַד בְּהוּ שֶׁלֹּא בְּמִינוֹ. דְּהָא מוֹדֵי רַב לְעֵיל דְּחָמֵץ שֶׁלֹּא בִּזְמַנּוֹ שֶׁלֹּא בְּמִינוֹ בְּמַשֶּׁהוּ מוּתָּר, וְהַאי מַשֶּׁהוּ חָשֵׁיב לְהוּ: כַּנְדֵּי. קְדֵרוֹת לְאַחַר הַפֶּסַח: אַשְׁווּ זְבִינַיְיכוּ. אַל תַּעֲלוּ דְּמֵיהֶן יוֹתֵר מִשָּׁוְויָ': כְּר"שׁ. דְּמוּתָּרוֹת הַקְּדֵרוֹת הַיְשָׁנוֹת לְאַחַר הַפֶּסַח: כְּר"שׁ ס"ל. כְּדַאֲמַרַן לְעֵיל: דְּטָחוּ בֵּיהּ טִיחַיָּא. שׁוּמָּן נָתְנוּ בּוֹ בְּקַרְקָעִיתוֹ, וְנוֹתֵן טַעַם בַּלֶּחֶם: לְעוֹלָם. אֲפִילּוּ חָזַר וְהוּסַּק: אֲפִילּוּ בְּמִילְחָא. לְהָכִי נָקַט אֲפִילּוּ בְּמִילְחָא, שֶׁאֵין דֶּרֶךְ לֶאֱכוֹל פַּת בְּלֹא מֶלַח אוֹ לִיפְתָּן:

טָשִׁין

[לעיל כט.]

זבחים לה:

[שם]

לקמן לו. זבחים לה: ב"מ נא.

אמר רבא הלכתא חמץ בזמנו בין במינו ובין שלא במינו אסור בכל שהוא כרב. פסק רש"י בחולין דמין במינו במשהו, כרבי יהודה, דאמר בפ' "כל הבשר" (חולין קט.) מין במינו לא בטיל. ואף רבי קאמר התם נראין דברי רבי יהודה, מכלל דהלכתא הכי. ועוד הביא ראיה מהא דפליגי אביי ורבא בפרק בתרא דע"ז (דף סו.): חלא דחמרא וחלא דשיכרא, חמירא דחיטי וחמירא דשערי, רבא אמר: במשהו, אביי אמר: בנותן טעם. משום דמר סבר: בתר שמא אזלינן, ומר סבר: בתר טעמא אזלינן. אלמא: בין לאביי בין לרבא מין במינו במשהו. ועוד פסק רבא בשמעתא: מין במינו במשהו, כרב. ור"ת אומר: דכל אלו אינם ראיות, דאין הלכה לא כר' יהודה ולא *כרבי. והיא דפ' בתרא דמס' ע"ז פלוגתא דאביי ורבא – מצי למימר דחמירא וחלא דטבל ויין נסך, דמודו ר' יוחנן ור"ל שהם במשהו. ודשמעתא, אי גר' במשהו כרב – י"ל שפוסק בחמץ כרב, ולא מטעמי' דרב. דס"ל בכל איסורין שבתורה במינו במשהו, ורבא לית ליה אלא דוקא בחמץ בפסח, משום חומרא דחמץ. וגם רב יהודאי גאון פסק כן, דדוקא בחמץ פסק רבא כרב. דשאלו מקמיה: כל איסורין שבתורה במשהו כרב, או בנותן טעם כר"י? והשיב: מדאמר רבא חמץ בזמנו בין במינו בין שלא במינו במשהו – א"כ בהא [מיהו] הלכה כרב במשהו. אבל בשאר איסורין – בנ"ט כר' יוחנן וכר"ל. ועוד אומר ר"ת: דלא גרסי' במשהו כרב, וכן משמע בה"ג דלא גרס ליה. וסבר רבא גם בחמץ כר' יוחנן, והא דלא פסק בהדיא הלכה כר' יוחנן – משום דה"א דלא פסק כוותיה אלא בזמנו, אבל שלא בזמנו לא, דלא תקשי דרבא אדרבא. דהא אמר רבא קנסא הוא דקניס ר' שמעון כדפרי', להכי איצטריך לפרש. ומביא ר"ת ראיה דבהדיא סבירא ליה לרבא בפ' "גיד הנשה" (חולין צז: ושם) מין במינו בס', דקאמר: אמרו רבנן בטעמא כו', מין במינו דליכא למיקם אטעמא, אי נמי מין שלא במינו וליכא קפילא – בס'. ואין לדחות דמיירי בחמרא חדתא ועיגבי, דהוי טעמא אחד והוי בס', משום דרבא בתר שמא אזיל ולא חשיב מינו – דא"כ אמאי קרי ליה מין במינו? וב"הקומץ רבה" (מנחות כג. ושם) משני רבא: דסבר ר' יהודה מין במינו וד"א וכו', מכלל דאיהו לית ליה, ובפ' "התערובת" (זבחים עט. ושם) קסבר ר"א בן יעקב מין במינו בטל. וסתמא דגמרא קאמר בשילהי מסכת ביצה (ד' לט: ושם): שפיר עבוד דאחיכו עליה, חיטי בחיטי, נהי דלרבי יהודה לא בטל – לרבנן מיבטל בטיל. מכלל דהכי הלכתא. ורש"י גופיה פסק בפרק בתרא דמס' ע"ז (ד' סו.) גבי פלוגתא דאביי ורבא – דהלכתא כרבי יוחנן, דסבר בנ"ט. ובה"ג של אספמיא פסק דחתיכה בחתיכות בנ"ט, ומייתי מדרבא בפ' "גיד הנשה" (חולין צז.). ויין נסך דקאמר התם במשהו – אומר ר"ת: דוקא כשנתנסך לפני ע"ז. דלמתני' קאי, דבעי תרתי: דבר שבמנין, ואיסורי הנאה. °אבל סתם יינן, דשרי בהנאה – בס'. ובתשובת הגאונים שכתב רבינו יוסף טוב עלם מצא ר"ת: יין נסך שנתנסך ממנו לפני ע"ז – אסור בהנאה, ואינו בטל אפילו באלף. כמו ששנינו: *אלו אסורין ואיסורן איסור הנאה בכל שהוא: יין נסך וכו'. מכלל דשאר איסורין, וסתם יינן, חוץ מטבל ויין נסך בין במינו ובין שלא במינו – בנ"ט. ובחמץ בפסח לא עשה ר"ת מעשה, אע"ג דבשאלתות דרב אחאי* נמי איתא דרבא אית ליה גם בחמץ בנ"ט: [וע"ע תוס' חולין צז. ד"ה אמר רבא]: **אמר** רב קדירות בפסח ישברו. בפ' בתרא דמס' ע"ז (דף סח: ושם) גבי עכברא בשיכרא מספקא ליה אי קסבר רב נותן טעם לפגם אסור, או מותר ועכבר' בשיכרא אשבוחי משבח. ואי ס"ל מותר – אפ"ה קאמר הכא שפיר ישברו. דנ"ט לפגם דוקא בדיעבד שרי אבל לכתחלה אסור, דגזרינן שאינו בת יומא אטו בת יומא. ועוד: דהתם שרי – לפי שפוגם טעמו כמו שהוא בעין, אבל הכא אינו פוגם אלא מחמת ששהה בדופני הכלי: **לשהינהו** עד אחר הפסח וליעבד בהו שלא במינן. תימה לר"י: נהי דסבירא לן דטעמא דחמץ בקדירה חשיב משהו, שאין רגילין להשתמש הרבה ביחד, מ"מ הא תנן: אין מבטלין איסור לכתחלה, ואפי' איסורא דרבנן אין מבטלין. דאם לא כן – מה הועילו חכמים בתקנתם שאסרו עד ששים? הואיל שיכול להוסיף ולבטל האיסור! ולא דמי לעצים שנשרו מן הדקל לתנור בי"ט, שמרבה עליהן עצים מוכנים ומסיקן (ביצה ד' ד:) – דהתם איסור מוקצה אין לו שורש מן התורה, אבל מידי דאית לי' שורש מן התורה – לא. ומפרש ה"ר יוסף: הואיל ואיכא תרתי לטיבותא, שהוא נותן טעם לפגם ומשהו שלא במינו – בכה"ג מבטלין. ולדבריו צ"ל דה"פ: וליעבד שלא במינו, אי ס"ל לרב נותן טעם לפגם מותר. ור"י מפרש: דכיון שהקדירות של חרס הן, אם יהיו אסורין ואין להם תקנה – זה חשוב דיעבד. ואע"ג דלענין איסור קדירה שאין בת יומא אסרינן לה. אע"פ שאין לה תקנה – משום דהתם בלע איסור הרבה. אבל הכא, ליכא אלא משהו, והואיל ושלא במינו הוא – יכול לבטל, וכדיעבד דמי: **דילמא** אתי למיעבד במינו. לעיל לא גזר שלא במינו אטו מינו – דהא לא שכיח שיתערב לו חמץ. אבל הכא, להתיר לבשל בהן – איכא למיגזר: **ואפילו** במלחא. והא דאמר ב"כיצד צולין" (לקמן עו.): פת שאפאה עם הצלי בתנור אסור לאוכלו בכותח אבל במלח שרי – התם לא אסירא אלא מטעם ריח דליכא איסור כולי האי: **דילמא** אתי למיכליה בכותח. ותימה: וליכליה בכותח, דהא נותן טעם בנ"ט הוא, כדאמר בפ' "כל הבשר" (חולין קיא: ושם): דגים שעלו בקערה – מותר לאוכלן בכותח! וי"ל: דקאמר התם נמי לגון שחתכו בסכין אסור לאוכלו בכותח, ופירש"י: משום חורפא דלגון בלע טפי מדגים רותחים שעלו בקערה. ולפי זה, דגים שנתבשלו בקדירה – אסור לאוכלן בכותח, דע"י בישול בלעי יותר מדאי. וכן נמי הכא, מחום התנור בלעי טפי. ולפי' אחר שפ"ה שם דלגון אסור, לפי שפעמים שהשמנונית קרוש על הסכין ואינו ניכר, ואיכא בלגון טעם בשר ממש – קשה הכא, כיון שנתקנח התנור יפה או הוסק פעם אחרת – אמאי אסור לאוכלו בכותח? וי"ל: דשומן שעל החרס אינו יכול °לקנח יפה:

והלכתא

[ע"ז עד. ע"ש]

[פ' נו סי' פ]

י"ג כרב

סט א מיי' פ"א מהל' חמץ הל' ה ופט"ו מהל' מאכלות אסורות הל' ט סמג לאוין עח טוש"ע א"ח תמז סעיף א:

ע ב מיי' שם טוש"ע שם סעיף יא:

עא ג מיי' פ"ה מהל' חו"מ הל' כה סמג שם טוש"ע א"ח סי' תנא סעיף א:

עב ד מיי' פ"ט מהל' מאכלות אסורות הל' כב סמג לאוין קמא טוש"ע י"ד סימן נז סעיף א:

גליון הש"ס

גמ' אין לשין את העיסה בחלב. עי' שבת עח ע"ב תד"ה תחת איספוגי: **רש"י** ד"ה בני חילא כו' שאופיהו. עי' ב"י יו"ד סי' קיב: **תום'** ד"ה אמר רבא אבל סתם יינם דשרי בהנאה. תמוה לי הא סתם יינם אסור בהנא' כדמוכח בכמה דוכתי במס' ע"ג וגם ובחולין כתבו תו' סתם אבל סתם יינם בטל בס'. וכאן נלע"ד דט"ס הוא בתוס': **תום'** ד"ה דלמא אתי כו' אינו יכול לקנח יפה. עי' מ"ק דף יז ע"א ברש"י ד"ה ומהניא כי טחיא:

רבינו חננאל

בין במינן בין שלא במינן מותר כר' שמעון: **אמר** רבא הלכתא חמץ בפסח שהוא זמן איסורו בין במינו בין שלא במינו אסור במשהו כרב לאחר הפסח שלא בזמנו בין במינו בין שלא במינו מותר כר' שמעון דהא רב ושמואל ור' יוחנן שלא בזמנו שלא במינו כולן שוין בזה שמותר. ואקשינן ומי אמר רבא הכי והא רבא הוא דאוקים למתני' כר' שמעון דאמר אע"ג דסבר ר' שמעון דחמץ לאחר הפסח שרי קנס משום דעבר עליה בבל יראה ובל ימצא ושני' אין ר' שמעון לעולם קנים לאחר הפסח מיהו לא קנים אלא היכא דאיתיה לחמץ שעבר עליו הפסח בעיניה אבל על ידי תערובות אפי' במינו לא קנים: **ואזדא** רבא לטעמיה דאמר כי הוינא בי רב נחמן כי הוו נפקו יומי דפסחא הוה אמר לן פוקו אייתו חמירא דבני חילא מראין הדברים דחמירא*) דא דבני חילא ברשות ישראל הות ואע"ג דכדידהו הות דמיא הוה שרי רב נחמן דהא על ידי תערובות היא: **אמר** רב קדרות בפסח ישברו חיישינן לשהויינהו לאחר הפסח ולבשל בהו שלא במינן גזרה דלמא אתי לבשל בהו במינן ושמואל אמר אחר זמנן מותר לבשל בהן בין במינן בין שלא במינן ואזדא שמואל לטעמיה דאמר שמואל להני דמזבני כנדי פי' כנדי כגון אגני דפחרא אשוו זבינו כלומר מכרו בזול ולא תמכרו ביוקר ואי לא דרשינא לכו כר' שמעון דשרי בישנים לאחר הפסח בין במינו בין שלא במינן והאי דלא דרש להו דמשום אתריה דרב [הוה] ולא הוה בעי לאורוי קמיה רב וקיי"ל בהא כשמואל: **ההוא** תנורא דטחיה בשומן של בשר אסריה (רבא) [רבה] בר אהילאי למיפא ביה פת לעולם אע"פ שמסיקין אותו חייש דלמא אתו למיכל הפת ההוא בחלב ומותבינן עליה אין לשין העיסה בחלב

*) עיין לעיל דף ה ע"ב א"ל רבא לבני מחוזא בעירו חמירא דבני חילא וכו' וע"ע היטב בהשגות הראב"ד בפ"ד מהל' חו"מ הלכה ג' ובכ"מ ובלח"מ שם ועי' בח"י סי' ת"מ סק"ד בשם הירושלמי ודו"ק.

עג א מיי' פ"ה מהל' חו"מ הל' כב טוש"ע א"ח סי' תנא ס"ח:
עד ב מיי' פ"ה מהל' חו"מ הל' כב סמג לאוין עח טוש"ע א"ח סי' תנא סעיף ג:
עה ג מיי' שם הל' כה טוש"ע שם סעיף כג:
עו ד מיי' פי"א מהל' מאכלות אסורות הל' יט סמג לאוין קמח טוש"ע י"ד סי' קלה סעיף ו:
עז ה ו מיי' שם הל' מהל' חמץ הל' כב סמג לאוין עח טוש"ע א"ח סי' תנא סעיף כג:
עח ז מיי' שם טוש"ע שם סעיף יז:
עט ח מיי' פ"ד מהלכות חמץ הל' ה טוש"ע א"ח סי' תמא ס"א:
פ ט שם סעיף ב:

*אין טָשִׁין אֶת הַתַּנּוּר בְּאַלְיָה, וְאִם טָשׁ – כָּל הַפַּת כּוּלָּהּ אֲסוּרָה, עַד שֶׁיַּסִּיק אֶת הַתַּנּוּר, הָא הוּסַּק הַתַּנּוּר – מִיהָא שָׁרֵי. תְּיוּבְתָּא דְּרָבָא בַּר אֲהִילַאי! תְּיוּבְתָּא. אֲמַר לֵיהּ רָבִינָא לְרַב אַשִׁי: וְכִי מֵאַחַר דְּאִיתּוֹתַב רָבָא בַּר אֲהִילַאי, אַמַּאי קָאָמַר רַב קְדֵירוֹת בַּפֶּסַח יִשָּׁבְרוּ. אֲמַר לֵיהּ: הָתָם – תַּנּוּר שֶׁל מַתֶּכֶת, הָכָא בִּקְדֵירָ' שֶׁל חֶרֶס. וְאִיבָּעֵית אֵימָא: הָא וְהָא בְּשֶׁל חֶרֶס, זֶה – הֶסֵּיקָן מִבִּפְנִים, וְזֶה – הֶסֵּיקָן מִבַּחוּץ. וְכִי תֵּימָא ה"נ לֶיעֱבַד לֵיהּ הַסָּקָה מִבִּפְנִים – [א]חָיֵיס עֲלֵיהּ מִשּׁוּם דְּפָקְעָה. הִלְכָּךְ, הַאי *בּוּכְיָא – הֶסֵּיקוֹ מִבַּחוּץ הוּא, וְאָסוּר. וְאִי מָלְיֵיהּ גּוּמְרֵי – שַׁפִּיר דָּמֵי. א"ל רָבִינָא לְרַב אַשִׁי: הָנֵי סַכִּינֵי(א) בְּפִסְחָא הֵיכִי עָבְדִינַן לְהוּ? אֲמַר לֵיהּ: לְדִידִי חֲדַתָּא קָא עָבְדִינַן. אֲמַר לֵיהּ: תֵּינַח מָר דְּאֶפְשָׁר לֵיהּ, דְּלָא אֶפְשָׁר לֵיהּ מַאי? אֲמַר לֵיהּ: אֲנָא כְּעֵין חֲדַתָּא קָאָמִינָא; קַתְיָיהוּ בְּטִינָא, וּפַרְזְלַיְיהוּ בְּנוּרָא, וַהֲדַר מְעַיְּילָנָא לְקַתְיָיהוּ בְּרוֹתְחִין. [ב]וְהִלְכְתָא: אִידִי וְאִידִי בְּרוֹתְחִין, וּבִכְלִי רִאשׁוֹן. אָמַר רַב הוּנָא בְּרֵיהּ דְּרַב יְהוֹשֻׁעַ: עֵץ פָּרוּר מַגְעִילוֹ בְּרוֹתְחִין וּבִכְלִי רִאשׁוֹן. קָסָבַר: כְּבוֹלְעוֹ כָּךְ פּוֹלְטוֹ. *בְּעוֹ מִינֵּיהּ(ב) מֵאַמֵימַר: הָנֵי מָאנֵי דְּקוּנְיָא מַהוּ לְאִישְׁתַּמּוּשֵׁי בְּהוּ בְּפִסְחָא? יָרוֹקָא לָא תִּיבָּעֵי לָךְ – דְּוַדַּאי אֲסִירִי. כִּי תִּיבָּעֵי לָךְ – אוּכָּמֵי וְחִיוָּרֵי מַאי? וְהֵיכָא דְּאִית בְּהוּ קַרְטוּפָנֵי – לָא תִּיבָּעֵי לָךְ, דְּוַדַּאי אֲסִירִי. כִּי תִּיבָּעֵי לָךְ – דְּשִׁיעֵי מַאי? א"ל: [ג]חֲזֵינָא לְהוּ דְּמִידַּיְיתִי, אַלְמָא בָּלְעִי וַאֲסִירִי,(ג) וְהַתּוֹרָה הֵעִידָה עַל כְּלִי חֶרֶס שֶׁאֵינוֹ יוֹצֵא מִידֵי דוֹפְיוֹ לְעוֹלָם. וּמַאי שְׁנָא *לְעִנְיַן יֵין נֶסֶךְ, דְּדָרֵישׁ מָרֵימָר: [ד]מָאנֵי דְּקוּנְיָא, בֵּין אוּכָּמָא בֵּין חִיוָּרֵי וּבֵין יָרוֹקֵי – שָׁרֵי. וְכִי תֵּימָא: יֵין נֶסֶךְ – דְּרַבָּנַן, חָמֵץ – דְּאוֹרַיְיתָא(ד). *כָּל דְּתַקּוּן רַבָּנַן – כְּעֵין דְּאוֹרַיְיתָא תַּקּוּן. אֲמַר לֵיהּ: זֶה תַּשְׁמִישׁוֹ עַל יְדֵי חַמִּין, וְזֶה תַּשְׁמִישׁוֹ עַל יְדֵי צוֹנֵן, אָמַר רָבָא בַּר אַבָּא אָמַר רַב חִיָּיא בַּר אַשִׁי אָמַר שְׁמוּאֵל: [ה]כָּל הַכֵּלִים שֶׁנִּשְׁתַּמְּשׁוּ בָּהֶן חָמֵץ בְּצוֹנֵן – מִשְׁתַּמֵּשׁ בָּהֶן מַצָּה, חוּץ מִן בֵּית שְׂאוֹר, הוֹאִיל שֶׁחִימּוּצוֹ קָשֶׁה. אָמַר רַב אַשִׁי: [ו]וּבֵית חֲרוֹסֶת כְּבֵית שְׂאוֹר שֶׁחִימּוּצוֹ קָשֶׁה דָּמֵי. אֲמַר רָבָא: [ז]הָנֵי אַגָּנֵי דִּמְחוֹזָא, הוֹאִיל וּתְדִירִי לְמֵילַשׁ בְּהוּ חֲמִירָא, וּמַשְׁהוּ בְּהוּ חֲמִירָא – כְּבֵית שְׂאוֹר שֶׁחִימּוּצוֹ קָשֶׁה דָּמֵי. פְּשִׁיטָא! מַהוּ דְּתֵימָא: כֵּיוָן דִּרְוִיחָא – שַׁלִּיט בְּהוּ אֲוִירָא וְלָא בָּלְעִי, קמ"ל.§

מתני' [ח]גּוֹי שֶׁהִלְוָה אֶת יִשְׂרָאֵל עַל חֲמֵצוֹ אַחַר הַפֶּסַח – מוּתָּר בַּהֲנָאָה, [ט]וְיִשְׂרָאֵל שֶׁהִלְוָה אֶת גּוֹי עַל חֲמֵצוֹ אַחַר הַפֶּסַח – אָסוּר בַּהֲנָאָה.§

גמ' אִיתְּמַר, בַּעַל חוֹב; אַבַּיֵי אָמַר: לְמַפְרֵעַ הוּא גּוֹבֶה, וְרָבָא אָמַר: מִכָּאן וּלְהַבָּא הוּא גּוֹבֶה. כָּל הֵיכָא דְּאַקְדֵּישׁ לֹוֶה וְזַבֵּין לֹוֶה – כּוּלֵּי עָלְמָא לָא פְּלִיגִי דְּאָתֵי מַלְוֶה וְטָרֵיף, וְאָתֵי

תוספות

והלכתא אידי ואידי ברותחין. תימה, דתניא בתוספתא דע"ז: הסכין והשפוד והאסכלא – מלבנן באור. ובפרק קמא דחולין (דף ח: ושם) אמר: כגון שליבנה באור. אלמא: צריך ליבון! ותירץ ר"ת: דאמר בירושלמי דמיירי בסכינים ארוכים שצולין בהם בשר, דומיא דשפוד, וכן ההוא דחולין. ועוד: יש לחלק בין התירא בלע ובין איסורא בלע, כדמחלק רב אשי בשילהי מסכת ע"ז. והא דמצריך להו רב אשי הכא ליבון – מחמיר על עצמו היה:

התורה העידה על כלי חרס שאינו יוצא מידי דופיו לעולם דכתיב ביה ישבר. וא"ת: תיפוק ליה דחזינן להו דמידייתי, והיינו אחר הגעלה, דאי לפני הגעלה – שאר כלים נמי מידייתי! וי"ל: דלעולם מיירי קודם הגעלה, וכמו שפ"ה בע"ז (דף לג.) – דמידייתי בחוץ. וכיון דמידייתי מבחוץ – בלעי טפי. וא"ת: והלא יוצא מידי דופיו ע"י כבשונות, דבזבחים בפ' "דם חטאת" (דף צו. ושם) פריך: וליהדרינהו לכבשונות, ואמאי קדירות במקדש ישברו? ומשני: לפי שאין כבשונות בירושלים. הא יש כבשונות – שרו בחזרה לכבשונות. וכן לעיל אמר: (אבל) קדירה לא – דלמא חייס עלה. הא לאו הכי – שרי קדירות בהיסק מבפנים. וכן אמר: אי מליא גומרי – שפיר דמי. ואור"ת: דזה לא חשיב יוצא מידי דופיו, דכיון שהסיקו – נעשה ככלי חדש, שכן דרך כלי חרס כשעושין אותו נותנו אותו בכבשן להסיקו. וא"ת: והיכי מייתי ראיה מדכתיב "ישבר"? דילמא גזירת הכתוב הוא, דאפי' תלאו באויר התנור בעי התם *רבא בר חמא אי קפיד רחמנא אבישול בלא בלוע, או לא. וי"ל: *דלכלי נחושת מועיל שטיפה ומריקה אפילו בבישול ובלוע. א"כ מה שהקפיד בכלי חרס אבישול בלא בלוע – היינו לפי שעשאו כבישול וכבלוע. ולר"ת יש להקשות: תנור שנטמא אמאי חולקין לשלשה? כיון דחשיב כאחד[א] [א] – ליעבד ליה היסק ותו לא! ונראה לרשב"א: *דמיירי בקדרה שאין דרכה להסיק, כשמחזירין אותה לכבשונות – אז פנים חדשות באו לכאן. אבל תנור, כל שעה ושעה מסיקו מבפנים – ולאו כפנים חדשות דמי, וצריך שבירה:
באחריות

רש"י

טשין. לשון טח: מאחר דאיתותב רבא בר אהילאי. ושמעינן דהיסק מועיל לכלי חרס, קדירות בפסח אמאי ישברו? יסיקם ויתלבנו: א"ל. רב מוקים ליה להאי דקתני עד שיוסק, דמשמע: הא הוסק שרי – בתנור של מתכת, אבל של חרס – התורה העידה עליו שאינו יוצא מידי דופיו לעולם: חיים עלייהו. ואי שרית ליה על ידי היסק פנים – מורה היתירא, וסמיך אהיסק בחוץ: בוכיא. כלי שהוא מרעפים, שקורין טייל"ש, ואופין ומטגנין בו ככר: לדידי חדתא עבדא. לצורכי עושין סכינים חדשים: למר אפשר ליה. שהרי עשיר אתה: קתייהו בטינא. להגן עליהם שלא ישרפם האור: והלכתא. לא צריך לאותבינהו בנורא, אלא פרזלייהו כי קתייהו נמי סגי להו בהגעלה ברותחין: עץ פרור. שמגיסין בו הקדרה: כבולעו כך פולטו. כבולעו מתוך כלי ראשון, כך פולטו בכלי ראשון: קוניא. פלומי"ר בלע"ז, ושל חרס הוא וטוח באבר: ירוקי. עשויין מקרקע שחופרים ממנה צריף, אלו"ם בלע"ז, והוא עז ובולע לעולם: ה"ג: ירוקי לא תיבעי לך דודאי אסירי דמצרפי ובלעי. דמצרפי צריף: קרטופני. בקעים: כי תיבעי לך דשיעי. שאין חלקים: דמידייתי. פולטין המשקין מדופנן החיצון, ובלע"ז טרשטדט"ש. וכיון דמידייתי – ודאי בלעי, והואיל ובלעי – שוב אינן פולטין. שהתורה העידה על כלי חרס, שכיון שבלע – אינו יוצא מידי דופיו לעולם, שהרי בכלי עץ ומתכות כתב לך "ישטף", "תעבירו באש", "ומורק ושוטף", אבל בכלי חרס – ישבר: חמין. תשמישו ע"י חמין כל השנה, אבל יין נסך – לא נשתמש בו אלא צונן: בית חרוסת. כלי שנותנין בו חומץ, וכל דבר שיש לו קיהוי, ורגילין ליתן בו קמח, ועשוי לטבל בו בשר כל ימות השנה. והקמח מתחמץ מחמת הקיהוי. ולשון חרוסת – קיהוי, אייגירו"ש בלע"ז: בית שאור. כלי שהאשה שורה ומנחת בו את השאור, ונותנתו בעיסה. ופעמים שהוא שוהה שם בלילה: אגני. עריבות, מיי"ן: **מתני'** גוי שהלוה את ישראל. מעות על חמצו קודם הפסח, ועבר עליו הפסח – מותר בהנאה. ולקמיה בגמרא מוקי לה כשהרהינו אצלו בביתו, ושוהה אצל הגוי כל ימות הפסח. דכיון דמטא זמניה ולא פרעיה, ומחוסר גוביינא נמי לא הוה, שהרי אצלו נתון – איגלאי מילתא למפרע דמשעה שהרהינו אצלו הוה דידיה: ישראל שהלוה את הגוי כו'. נמי, כיון דהרהינו אצלו ומטא זמניה ולא פרעי' – מההיא שעתא דאוזפיה קם ליה ברשותיה: **גמ'** בעל חוב. המלוה את חבירו, ושיעבד לו נכסיו, שאם לא אפרע לך עד יום פלוני – גבה מנכסי, והגיע זמן ולא פרע: אביי אמר למפרע הוא גובה. גבייתו שגבה עכשיו – איגלאי מילתא דמשעה שהלווהו עמדו נכסיו הללו בחזקתו: ורבא אמר. אינן בחזקתו אלא מיכן ולהבא. ולקמיה מפרש למאי נפקא מינה: כל היכא דאקדיש לוה. נכסיו בתוך הזמן: או זבין לוה. מוכרן לאחרים: כולי עלמא לא פליגי. אפילו לרבא, דקאמר: עד עכשיו היו ברשות לוה – מודה הוא דאין מכירתו לאחרים מכירה, ואין הקדישו הקדש – שהרי ממושכנין הן למלוה. ואף על גב שהן שלו – אינן ברשותו, ורחמנא אמר (ויקרא כז): "ואיש כי יקדיש את ביתו קדש", מה ביתו ברשותו – אף כל ברשותו: דאתי מלוה וטריף. מן הלקוחות בחנם: ואתי

רבינו חננאל

בחלב מפני הרגל עבירה כלומר שלא יאכל הפת ההוא בבשר ואם לש כל הפת אסורה כיוצא בו אין (שטין) [טשין] את התנור באליה מפני הרגל עבירה שלא יאכל הפת בחלב ואם (שטמ) [טש] כל הפת שתאפה באותו תנור אסורה עד שיוסק התנור ש"מ שאם הוסק מותר ועלתה בתיובת' (לרבא) [לרבה] בר אהילאי: **ואקשי'** לרב נמי נסקינהו להני קדרות מבפנים ויבשל בהו ומשני תנור היינו דרך תשמישו והסיקו מבפנים אבל קדרות דלאו היינו אורחייהו ואי אמרת לי' לאסוקינהו מבפנים חאים עלייהו חאים דלמא פקעי ולא עביד הלכך גזרי' בהו. פי' בוכיא כגון טגן של חרס שאופין עליו עוגו' אי מלייה גחלי' וארתחה שפיר דמי למיפא עליה מצה ואסקינא הסכינין ויורותיהן הלכתא ברותחין בכלי ראשון פי' ביורה מלאה מים רותחין והיא על גבי כירה וכן עץ פרור והוא התרווד שמנער בו הקדרות רותחו' דקיימ' לן כבולען כך פולטן כשם שבליעתן ברותחין כך פליטתן ברותחין ואסיקנא הני מאני דקוניא פי' כלי חרס שנשתמש בהן נכרי אפי' בשאר ימות השנה אסירי לאשתמושי בהו ישראל בין אוכמי בין חיוורי וכל שכן ירוקא ולא תימא הני דאית בהו קרטופני כגון סדקין [אלא] אע"ג דשיעי כיון דמדייתו כלומר *) נשחורים משחל שחלי וכלהו אסירי להשתמש בהן כל ימות השנה וכל שכן בפסח אבל הני מאני דקוניא דאשתמשו בהו נכרים ביין נסך שרו כדדריש מרימר ואע"ג דחמץ דאורייתא ויין נסך דרבנן וכל דתקון רבנן כעין דאורייתא תקון חמץ בפסח תשמישו בחמין הלכך לעולם אסור אבל יין נסך תשמישו בצונן**) ובהרהתחה סגי להו: **אמר** רב זביד הלכתא משמיה דשמואל כל הכלים של חרש שנשתמשו בהן בצונן משתמש בהן בפסח חוץ מבית שאור והוא כלי חרש שמצניעין בו שאור מפני שחימוצו קשה ונבלע כח החימוץ בכלי ובית חרוסת דינו כגון בית שאור דאסור: **אמר** רבא אגני דמשהו בהו חמירא אע"ג דרוויחי ושליט בהו אוירא כבית שאור דמי ואסירי ולא שרינן מאני דקוניא אלא החדשים וכל שכן כלי חרס אחרים דלא שרו אלא חדשים: **מתני'** נכרי שהלוה את ישראל על חמצו לאחר הפסח מותר בהנאה אוקימנא בשהרהינו אצלו להאי חמץ אצל הנכרי והוא אצל הנכרי וקבע לו זמן קודם הפסח דכיון דעבר הזמן קנייה הנכרי ונעשה כחמצו של נכרי: **איתמר** בעל חוב אביי אמר למפרע הוא גובה משעת ההלואה ואם מכר המלוה או הקדיש נכסיו של לוה והגיע הזמן ולא פרעו נתברר כי מאותה העת שעשה מעות העת עשוי ... אמר מכאן ולהבא הוא גובה ומה שהקדיש או מכר המלוה לא עשה כלום שלא היו שלו הלא תראה שאלו היה לו מעות ללוה היה מסלקו במעות ולא היה יכול לומר לו לקרקע הוא קנוי לו ונמצא כי עכשיו קנה הנכסים אבל אם מכר הלוה הכל מודים דאתי מלוה וטריף ואי אקדיש

*) תיבות אלו מסוגלין הכנה ואולי צ"ל פי' כמו מסחילין (כבלה ד' לה) ומשחל שחלי (ביומא ל' עת) כנ"ל.
**) נראה דמפרש דמיירי בכלים שמכניסין לקיום והוליא כן מהא דאמר רבא בע"ז ...

מסורת הש"ס

[עי' תוס' ב"ב קי. ד"ה נשוט]
[וכ"ה בערוך אמנם בזבחים אי' בוביא וכ"ה בשאלתות פ' מטות סי' קלו וכ"ה בפרישה בי"ד סי' קנ]
ע"ז לג: כתובות קז.
שם איתא רמי
כיון לדלכלי מהר"ס
[ע"ז שם]
[לקמן לט: קטו: יומא לא. יבמות יח. גיטין סה. סו. ע"ז לד. בכורות נב.]

גליון הש"ס

גמ' אין טשין. ועי' ב"ב קי ע"א תוד"ה נשוט:

הגהות הב"ח

(א) גמרא הני סכיני דפיסחא: (ב) שם בעו מיניה ממרימר הני מאני דקוניא: (ג) שם בלעי ואסירי מ"ט התורה העידה: (ד) שם חמץ דאורייתא והא כל דתקון:

הגהות מהר"ב לנדא

א] תוס' ד"ה התורה העידה וכו' כיון לחשיב כאחד. נ"ל כיון לחשיב כאחד:

הגהות מהר"ב רנשבורג

[א] תוס' ד"ה התורה העידה כו' כיון דחשיב כאחד. נמחק מלת כאחד ונ"ב נ"ל כאחר ור"ל דחשיב ע"י ההיסק ככלי אחר וכ"ה בתוס' זבחים צו ע"א יעו"ש:

ואתי מלוה ופריק. *דתנן: [א]מוסיף עוד דינר, ופודה את הנכסים האלו. כי פליגי – דזבין מלוה, וקדיש מלוה. אביי אמר: למפרע הוא גובה; כיון דמטא זמניה ולא פרעיה – איגלאי מילתא למפרע דמעיקרא ברשותיה הוה קאי, ושפיר אקדיש, ושפיר זבין. ורבא אמר: מכאן ולהבא הוא גובה. כיון דאילו הוו ליה זוזי – הוה מסליק להו בזוזי – אישתכח דהשתא קא קני. ומי אמר רבא הכי? *והאמר רמי בר חמא: [ב]ראובן שמכר שדה לשמעון באחריות, וזקפן עליו במלוה, ומת ראובן ואתא בעל חוב דראובן וטריף ליה משמעון, ואתא שמעון ופייסיה בזוזי – דינא הוא דאתו בני ראובן ואמרי ליה לשמעון: אנן מטלטלי שבק אבון גבך, ומטלטלי דיתמי לבעל חוב לא משתעבדי. ואמר רבא: אי פיקח שמעון – מגבי להו ארעא, והדר גבי לה מינייהו. *דאמר רב נחמן: [ג]יתומים שגבו קרקע בחובת אביהם – בעל חוב חוזר וגובה אותה מהן. אי אמרת בשלמא "למפרע הוא גובה" – אמטו להכי חוזר וגובה אותה מהן, דכמאן דגבו מחיים דאבוהון דמי. אלא אי אמרת "מכאן ולהבא הוא גובה" אמאי חוזר וגובה אותה מהן? הא הוי כמאן דזבין יתמי נכסי דמי, ואילו קני יתמי נכסי, מי קא משתעבדי לבעל חוב? שאני התם, דאמר להו: כי היכי דמשתעבדנא ליה לאבוכון – משתעבדנא נמי לבעל חוב דאבוכון, מדר' נתן. *דתניא, רבי נתן אומר: [ד]מנין לנושה בחבירו מנה, וחבירו בחבירו, שמוציאין מזה ונותנין לזה – ת"ל: °"ונתן לאשר אשם לו". תנן: גוי שהלוה את ישראל על חמצו – אחר הפסח מותר בהנאה. אי אמרת בשלמא "למפרע הוא גובה" – אמטו להכי מותר בהנאה. אלא אי אמרת "מכאן ולהבא הוא גובה" אמאי מותר בהנאה? ברשותא דישראל הוה קאי! הכא במאי עסקינן – כשהרהינו אצלו. לימא כתנאי: ישראל שהלוה לגוי על חמצו – לאחר הפסח אינו עובר. משום רבי מאיר אמרו: עובר. מאי לאו בהא קמיפלגי; דמר סבר: למפרע הוא גובה, ומר סבר: מכאן ולהבא הוא גובה? ותסברא?! אימא סיפא: אבל גוי שהלוה לישראל על חמצו – לאחר הפסח דברי הכל עובר. והא איפכא מיבעי ליה! למאן דאמר התם "אינו עובר" – הכא עובר, למאן דאמר התם "עובר" – הכא אינו עובר!

אלא

תורה אור: במדבר ה

רש"י

ואתי מלוה ופריק. מן ההקדש בדבר מועט – כדי שלא יאמרו: הקדש יוצא בלא פדיון – וגובה חובו, כדתנן בערכין בפרק "שום היתומים": הקדיש בתשעים מנה והיה חובו מאה מנה – מוסיף מלוה זה על הלואתו דינר, ופודה את הנכסים הללו מיד הקדש בדינר זה ונוטלן בחובו, ודינר דיהיב מפרש טעמא התם: שלא יאמרו הקדש יוצא בלא פדיון. ואף על גב דאמר רבא (כתובות דף נט:): הקדש חמץ ושיחרור מפקיעין מידי שיעבוד – דוקא קדושת הגוף קאמר רבא, כגון קונמות או בהמה לקרבן, או בגד שפירסו על המת, כי ההיא דיבמות (דף סו:) גבי אילטלא דמילתא דפירסוה יתמי אמיתנא, דהוה משתעבד לכתובת האשה, דאמר רבא: קנייה מיתנא. אבל קדושת דמים לא אמרינן: כי פליגי דאקדיש מלוה. בתוך הזמן את הקרקע המשועבד לו, ולא הקדיש את החוב אלא הקרקע. והשתא כשהגיע הזמן ולא פרעו זה, והוא בא לגבותה מן הלוה – חוזר בו מן ההקדש: כיון דאילו הוה ליה זוזי. ללוה ביום הזמן, הוה מסלק ליה למלוה מן הקרקע בזוזי – אישתכח שלא היה הקרקע קנוי לו עדיין, אלא עכשיו כשהוא גובה אותה בחובו היא נקנית לו: באחריות. שמא יטלנה בעל חוב דראובן משמעון בשביל חוב ששיעבדה לו ראובן – שישלם לו ראובן זה מעותיו לשמעון, ולא היו לו נכסים עוד על דבר אחריות זה: וזקפן עליו במלוה. שלא היו מעות לשמעון, שפסק על שדה זו, וכתב לראובן שטר עליהן, ושיעבד נכסיו לו עליהן: ומת ראובן. המוכר, ובא בעל חובו וטורפה משמעון, ועדיין לא נתן שמעון המעות לראובן ולא ליתומיו. ופייסיה שמעון לבעל חוב דראובן באותן מעות: דינא הוא. אע"ג דאבוהון קביל עליה אחריות מכירה זו – אפילו הכי יכולין בני ראובן לבא על שמעון, ולומר: אנן מטלטלי שבק אבון גבך – לא היית חייב עליו אלא מעות, ולא היה לך ליתנן לבעל חוב, ולא לעכבן בשביל אחריות מכירתך. דמטלטלי דיתמי לא שיעבדום חכמים לבעל חוב, דקרקע של יתומים הוא דאמרינן בעל חוב גובה אותה בחובת אביהן, משום דמחיים חל שיעבודא עליהן. אבל על מעות שלא היו בעין – לא חייל שיעבודו מחיים עליהן, וכשהן בעין – אין כאן לוה. ולבעלי המעות, דהיינו יתומים – לא הלוה זה כלום: ואמר רבא גרסינן: אי פיקח. זה שמעון, יטעון ויאמר להם: אין לי מעות לפרוע לכם, אלא קרקע יש לי. ונותנה להם בחובותם, וחוזר וגובה אותם מהם בשביל אחריות מכירה שקבל אביהן עליו. דהשתא כי אגבי להו הא ארעא – איגלאי מילתא דלאו מטלטלי הוא דשביק גביה, אלא קרקע: בעל חוב. אחר של אביהן, חוזר וגובה אותה מהן. אלמא, אמרינן: הנוטל קרקע בחובו, מאותה שעה שנתן לו המעות – נקנית לו: אא"ב. אמרינן איגלאי מילתא למפרע שהיתה קנויה לאביהן, קרקע זה שגבו בחוב אביהן – משום הכי בע"ח אחר של אביהן חוזר וגובה אותה מהן דכמאן דגבי לה מחיים דאבוהון דמי: אלא אי אמרת. כל הגובה קרקע בחובו אינה קנויה לו אלא מגבייה ואילך, אמאי בעל חוב אחר חוזר וגובה אותה מהן? לא יהא דבר זה אלא כמי שקנו יתומים קרקע במעות שלהן, מי הוה משתעבדא לבעל חוב?! שאני התם דאמר להו כי היכי דמשתעבדנא לאבוכון משתעבדנא נמי לבעל חוב דאבוכון מדרבי נתן. לעולם מכאן ולהבא הוא גובה, ומאי דאמר רב נחמן: בעלמא בעל חוב חוזר וגובה אותה מהן – משום דאמר להן בעל חוב ליתומים: מכח מי באתם וגביתם קרקע זו – מכח שיעבוד של אביכן. וכי היכי דמשתעבדא לאבוכון קרקע זו של לוה שלוה מאביכם, משתעבדא נמי לדידי, שהייתי מלוה של אביכן, והמחויב לו כלום – משועבד לי, מדרבי נתן. הלכך, קדם שיעבודי עליה אפי' אצל לוה שהיתה ברשותו. ושמעון נמי אמר להו לבני ראובן: כי היכי דהוי נכסיי משועבדין לאביכם בשביל חובו – היו משועבדין גם לעצמי מכח אביכן, שהיה לוה אצלי מחמת אחריות המכירה, מדר' נתן. דמה לי אני, מה לי אחר. הלכך: אע"פ שלא היתה קנויה לאביכם מחיים – חל שיעבודי עליה אצל עצמי: לאשר אשם לו. לאשר הלוהו לו לא נאמר, אלא "לאשר אשם לו" – לאשר הקרן שלו. בבבא קמא *אמרינן: אשם – זה קרן: תנן גוי שהלוה כו'. קס"ד השתא בשלא משכנו לו, אלא שיעבדו לו כשאר לווים: שאם לא אתן לך עד יום פלוני – בא לביתי וגבה מחמץ זה: כשהרהינו אצלו. בביתו של גוי נתנו. קס"ד השתא דטעמא משום דהוה ליה תורת משכון, ובעל חוב קונה משכון: ישראל שהלוה את הגוי על חמצו. קודם הפסח, לאחר הפסח אינו עובר אם נהנה ממנו: מאי לאו. בשלא הרהינו, ובהא קמיפלגי: דת"ק סבר מכאן ולהבא הוא גובה כו': אימא סיפא דברי הכל עובר. ואי טעמא משום להבא ולמפרע הוא – איפכא הוה לן לאפוכי פלוגתייהו בהא, ולא לאשויי דעתייהו, דלמאן דאמר לעיל ברישא עובר – אלמא למפרע הוא גובה, הכא הוה ליה למימר אינו עובר, משום דבשעת הלואה קם ליה ברשות גוי. ולמאן דאמר התם כו':

אלא

ערכין כג: | כתובות לב. | ב"ק מג. כתובות לב. קי. ב"ב קכה. | קדושין טו. כתובות יט. ופס. גיטין לז. ב"ק מ: | [דף קי.]

תוספות

באחריות. שלא באחריות פשיטא דיתן ליורשיו, אפילו לא זקפן עליו במלוה. אבל באחריות, קמ"ל. דה"א: יעכבם לעצמו, דה"ל כתופס מחיים. קמ"ל דלא חשיב ליה כתופס מחיים. כיון דזקפן עליו במלוה: ופייסיה בזוזי. רבותא נקט, אף על פי שנתן מעות – לא מצי למימר המעות שנתחייבתי לאביכם נתתי לו: משתעבדנא לב"ח דאבוכון מדרבי נתן. וא"ת: גבי מטלטלים נמי נימא הכי! ונראה לר"י: דדוקא גבי קרקע שייך למימר הכי, דבת שיעבוד היא. דכשהקרקע זו משועבדת לראובן – חשבינן ליה כאילו היא בידו. דהא אם מכרה או משכנה – חוזר ראובן וגובה אותה, ולכך משועבדת נמי לבע"ח. אבל מטלטלים – אין להחשיבם כאילו הם ביד ראובן. כיון שאילו מכרם או משכנם אין גובה מהן. ומכאן יש להוכיח דהלכה כרבי נתן, דהא רבא קאי כוותיה בשמעתין:

אלא

עין משפט נר מצוה

פא א מיי' פ"ז מהלכות ערכין הלכה טז:
פב ב מיי' פי"א מהל' מלוה הלכה י סמג עשין לד:
פג ג מיי' שם הלכה ט וסמג שם טוש"ע ח"מ סי' קז סעיף א:
פד ד מיי' פ"ב שם הלכה ו סמג עשין לג טוש"ע ח"מ סי' פו סעיף א:

רבינו חננאל

אקדיש לוה אתי מלוה ופריק להנהו נכסי דתנן בערכין פ"ו מוסיף עוד דינר ופודה את הנכסים האלו ומקשי' ומי אמר רבא הכי והאמרי' ראובן שמכר שדה לשמעון באחריות וזקפן עליו במלוה ומת ראובן ואתי בעל חוב למטרף משמעון ופייסיה שמעון בזוזי דינא הוא דלימרו בני ראובן אנן מטלטלי שבק אבון גבך כלומר האי מלוה דאית לאבונא גבך מטלטלי הוא ומטלטלי לבעל חוב לא משתעבדי אמר רבא ואי שמעון פקח הוא מגבי להו ליתמי קרקע בחובייהו והדר שמעון תבע להו באחריות דקבל עליה אבוהון וטרף ליה להאי ארעא מדרב נחמן דאמר יתומים שגבו קרקע בחובות אביהם בעל חוב חוזר וגובה מהן אי אמרת בשלמא רבא סבר למפרע הוא גובה שפיר דאמרינן מחיי אבוהון הות קניא הא ארעא דגבו להו בניה אלא אי אמרת מכאן ולהבא הוא גובה וכאלו זבני יתמי האידנ' ארעא [ומי] משתעבדא לבעל [חוב] דאבוהון ושני' הכא טעמא אחרינא היא דאמר להו שמעון ליתמי דראובן בההיא שעתא דזקפי עלי אבוכון מלוה כי היכי דאשתעבדי לאבוכון הכי אשתעבדי לבעל חוב דיליה כדר' נתן דתני מנין שמוציאין מן הלוה של ראובן ונותנין למלוה של ראובן שנאמר ונתן לאשר אשם לו ואקשי' לרבא ממתני' דקתני נכרי שהלוה את ישראל על חמצו כו' אי אמרת למפרע הוא גובה היינו דמותר בהנאה דאמרי' מההיא שעתא דיזיף ישראל מנכרי על חמצו [לאו] ברשו' ישראל קאי וחמץ של נכרי קרינא ביה לפיכך שרי אלא אי אמרת מכאן ולהבא וכו' ושני' בשהרהינו אצל הנכרי: נימא כתנאי ישראל שהלוה את נכרי על חמצו וקבע לו זמן לפרעו אחר הפסח אינו עובר עליו משום ר' מאיר אמרו עובר מאי לאו בהא קא מיפלגי וכו' ופשוטה

פה א מיי' פ"י מהלכות שכירות הלכה א סמג עשין לד טוש"ע ח"מ סי' עב סעיף ב:
פו ב מיי' פ"ד מהלכות חמץ הל' ה טוש"ע או"ח סי' תמא סעי' א:
פז ג טוש"ע א"ח סי' תמט:
פח ד ה מיי' פ"ג מהל' חמץ הל' יא סמג עשין לט טוש"ע או"ח סי' תלג סעיף ח:
פט ו ז מיי' פ"ד מהל' שאלה ופקדון הלכה ד סמג עשין פח טוש"ע ח"מ סי' רצא סעיף (יח) [טו]:
צ ח מיי' פ"י מהלכות תרומות הל' א:
צא ט שם הל' ב:

אֶלָּא הָכָא בְּמַאי עָסְקִינַן — כְּגוֹן שֶׁהִרְהִינוֹ אֶצְלוֹ, וְקָמִיפַּלְגִי בִּדְר' יִצְחָק. *דְּא"ר יִצְחָק: [א]מִנַּיִן לְבַעַל חוֹב שֶׁקּוֹנֶה מַשְׁכּוֹן — שֶׁנֶּאֱמַר: °"וּלְךָ תִּהְיֶה צְדָקָה", אִם אֵינוֹ קוֹנֶה מַשְׁכּוֹן — צְדָקָה מִנַּיִן? מִכָּאן לְבַעַל חוֹב שֶׁקּוֹנֶה מַשְׁכּוֹן. ת"ק סָבַר: הָנֵי מִילֵּי — יִשְׂרָאֵל מִיִּשְׂרָאֵל — הוּא, דְּקָרֵינָא בֵּיהּ "וּלְךָ תִּהְיֶה צְדָקָה" אֲבָל יִשְׂרָאֵל מִגּוֹי — לָא קָנֵי. וְר"מ סָבַר, קַל וָחוֹמֶר: יִשְׂרָאֵל מִיִּשְׂרָאֵל קָנֵי — יִשְׂרָאֵל מִגּוֹי לֹא כָּל שֶׁכֵּן?! אֲבָל גּוֹי שֶׁהִלְוָה אֶת יִשְׂרָאֵל עַל חֲמֵצוֹ אַחַר הַפֶּסַח — דִּבְרֵי הַכֹּל עוֹבֵר. הָתָם וַדַּאי גּוֹי מִיִּשְׂרָאֵל לָא קָנֵי. תְּנַן: גּוֹי שֶׁהִלְוָה (א) יִשְׂרָאֵל עַל חֲמֵצוֹ — אַחַר הַפֶּסַח מוּתָּר בַּהֲנָאָה. נְהִי נַמִי דְּהִרְהִינוֹ אֶצְלוֹ, הָא אָמְרַתְּ גּוֹי מִיִּשְׂרָאֵל לָא קָנֵי! לָא קַשְׁיָא: [ב]הָא — דְּאָמַר לֵיהּ "מֵעַכְשָׁיו", הָא — דְּלָא אָמַר לֵיהּ "מֵעַכְשָׁיו". וּמְנָא תֵּימְרָא דְּשָׁנֵי לֵיהּ בֵּין הֵיכָא דְּאָמַר "מֵעַכְשָׁיו" וּבֵין הֵיכָא דְּלָא אָמַר "מֵעַכְשָׁיו" — דְּתַנְיָא: גּוֹי שֶׁהִרְהִין פַּת פּוּרְנִי אֵצֶל יִשְׂרָאֵל — אֵינוֹ עוֹבֵר. וְאִם אָמַר לוֹ "הִגַּעְתִּיךָ" — עוֹבֵר. [דף פא:] מַאי שְׁנָא רֵישָׁא וּמַאי שְׁנָא סֵיפָא? אֶלָּא לָאו שְׁמַע מִינָּהּ: שָׁאנֵי הֵיכָא דְּא"ל "מֵעַכְשָׁיו" לְהֵיכָא דְּלָא אָמַר לֵיהּ "מֵעַכְשָׁיו" — שְׁמַע מִינָּהּ. ת"ר: *[ג]חֲנוּת שֶׁל יִשְׂרָאֵל וּמְלַאי שֶׁל יִשְׂרָאֵל, וּפוֹעֲלֵי גוֹיִם נִכְנָסִין לְשָׁם — חָמֵץ שֶׁנִּמְצָא שָׁם אַחַר הַפֶּסַח אָסוּר בַּהֲנָאָה, וְאֵין צָרִיךְ לוֹמַר בַּאֲכִילָה. חֲנוּת שֶׁל גּוֹי, וּמְלַאי שֶׁל גּוֹי, וּפוֹעֲלֵי יִשְׂרָאֵל נִכְנָסִין וְיוֹצְאִין לְשָׁם — חָמֵץ שֶׁנִּמְצָא שָׁם אַחַר הַפֶּסַח מוּתָּר בַּאֲכִילָה, וְאֵין צָרִיךְ לוֹמַר בַּהֲנָאָה.§ **מתני'** *[ד]חָמֵץ שֶׁנָּפְלָה עָלָיו מַפּוֹלֶת — הֲרֵי הוּא כִּמְבוֹעָר. רַבָּן שִׁמְעוֹן בֶּן גַּמְלִיאֵל אוֹמֵר: כֹּל שֶׁאֵין הַכֶּלֶב יָכוֹל לְחַפֵּשׂ אַחֲרָיו.§ **גמ'** אָמַר רַב חִסְדָּא: [ה]וְצָרִיךְ שֶׁיְּבַטֵּל בְּלִבּוֹ. תָּנָא: כַּמָּה חֲפִישַׂת הַכֶּלֶב — שְׁלֹשָׁה טְפָחִים. אֲמַר לֵיהּ רַב אַחָא בְּרֵיהּ דְּרַב יוֹסֵף לְרַב אַשִׁי: הָא דְּאָמַר שְׁמוּאֵל *[ו]כְּסָפִים אֵין לָהֶם שְׁמִירָה אֶלָּא בְּקַרְקַע — מִי בָּעֵינַן שְׁלֹשָׁה טְפָחִים אוֹ לֹא? אֲמַר לֵיהּ: הָכָא מִשּׁוּם רֵיחָא — בָּעֵינַן שְׁלֹשָׁה טְפָחִים, הָתָם מִשּׁוּם אִיכְסוּיֵי מֵעֵינָא הוּא, וְלָא בָּעֵי שְׁלֹשָׁה. וְכַמָּה? [ז]אָמַר רַפְרַם בַּר פָּפָּא מִסִּיכְרָא: טֶפַח.§ **מתני'** הָאוֹכֵל תְּרוּמַת חָמֵץ בְּפֶסַח, בְּשׁוֹגֵג — מְשַׁלֵּם קֶרֶן וָחוֹמֶשׁ, בְּמֵזִיד — פָּטוּר מִתַּשְׁלוּמִין וּמִדְּמֵי עֵצִים.§ **גמ'** תְּנַן הָתָם: *[ח]הָאוֹכֵל תְּרוּמָה בְּשׁוֹגֵג — מְשַׁלֵּם קֶרֶן וָחוֹמֶשׁ, [ט]אֶחָד הָאוֹכֵל, וְאֶחָד הַשּׁוֹתֶה, וְאֶחָד

תורה אור: דברים כד

אלא. רֵישָׁא וְסֵיפָא כְּשֶׁהִרְהִינוֹ, אֲבָל בְּלֹא הִרְהִינוֹ — דְּכוּלֵּי עָלְמָא: מִכָּאן וּלְהַבָּא הוּא גּוֹבֶה: **קונה משכון.** כָּל יְמֵי הַלְוָאָה הַמַּשְׁכּוֹן קָנוּי לוֹ, וְאִם נֶאֱנַס — חַיָּיב בְּאוֹנָסִין, שֶׁאֵינוֹ עָלָיו לֹא כְּשׁוֹמֵר חִנָּם וְלֹא כְּשׁוֹמֵר שָׂכָר שֶׁפְּטוּרִין בְּאוֹנָסִין, אֶלָּא כּוּלּוֹ בִּרְשׁוּתֵיהּ וּבִשְׁמִירָתוֹ עוֹמֵד: **ולך תהיה צדקה.** בַּהֲשָׁבַת הָעֲבוֹט כְּתִיב. אִי אָמְרַתְּ קוֹנֶה מַשְׁכּוֹן — אִיכָּא צְדָקָה בְּהָא שְׁכִיבָה שֶׁשָּׁכַב בְּשִׂמְלָתוֹ, שֶׁהִשְׁאִיל לוֹ זֶה דָּבָר הַקָּנוּי לוֹ. וְאִם אֵינוֹ קוֹנֶה — צְדָקָה בְּהַשְׁכָּבָה זוֹ מִנַּיִין? עַל שֶׁלּוֹ שָׁכַב! **אבל ישראל מגוי לא.** הִלְכָּךְ לֹא עָבַר עֲלֵיהּ, דְּאָמַר מָר (לעיל דף כט.): אֲבָל אַתָּה רוֹאֶה שֶׁל אֲחֵרִים: **תנן גוי שהלוה וכו'.** וְאוֹתִיבְנָא לְרָבָא לְעֵיל, וְשַׁנִּינַן: כְּשֶׁהִרְהִינוֹ אֶצְלוֹ. וְהָא אָמְרַתְּ הַשְׁתָּא דִּבְרֵי הַכֹּל גּוֹי מִיִּשְׂרָאֵל לֹא קָנֵי: **לא קשיא.** מַתְנִיתִין דְּאָמַר לֵיהּ כְּשֶׁהִרְהִינוֹ אֶצְלוֹ: אִם לֹא אֶתֵּן לְךָ עַד יוֹם פְּלוֹנִי — יְהֵא שֶׁלְּךָ מֵעַכְשָׁיו. הִלְכָּךְ: גּוֹי שֶׁהִלְוָה אֶת יִשְׂרָאֵל — קָם לֵיהּ חָמֵץ בִּרְשׁוּת גּוֹי. וְיִשְׂרָאֵל שֶׁהִלְוָה אֶת הַגּוֹי — קָם לֵיהּ בִּרְשׁוּת יִשְׂרָאֵל. בָּרַיְיתָא דְּלֹא אָמַר לֵיהּ מֵעַכְשָׁיו, אֶלָּא כִּשְׁאָר מַשְׁכּוֹן נְתָנוֹ לוֹ, וְקָבַע לוֹ זְמַן שֶׁאִם לֹא יִפְרַע לוֹ — יִגְבֶּה חוֹבוֹ מִמַּשְׁכּוֹנוֹ, וְיָשׁוּם אוֹתוֹ בְּדָמִים. הִלְכָּךְ, בְּגוֹי שֶׁהִלְוָה לְיִשְׂרָאֵל — דִּבְרֵי הַכֹּל, אֲפִילּוּ לֹא פָּרַע לֵיהּ — אָסוּר לְיִשְׂרָאֵל לֵיהָנוֹת מִמֶּנּוּ, דְּכָל יְמוֹת הַפֶּסַח שֶׁל יִשְׂרָאֵל הָיָה, דְּמִכָּאן וּלְהַבָּא הוּא גּוֹבֶה. וְאִי מִשּׁוּם דְּהִרְהִינוֹ — גּוֹי מִיִּשְׂרָאֵל לֹא קָנֵי. וְיִשְׂרָאֵל שֶׁהִלְוָה פְּלִיגֵי: מַאן דְּאָסַר סָבַר, כֵּיוָן שֶׁהִרְהִינוֹ — בַּעַל חוֹב קוֹנֶה מַשְׁכּוֹן, וְלֵיכָּא לְמֵימַר הָכָא מִכָּאן וּלְהַבָּא גּוֹבֶה. וּמַאן דְּשָׁרֵי קָסָבַר, יִשְׂרָאֵל מִגּוֹי לֵיכָּא צְדָקָה, וְלָא קָנֵי מַשְׁכּוֹן: **ומנא תימרא.** דַּאֲפִילּוּ כְּשֶׁהִרְהִינוֹ שָׁאנֵי לָן בֵּין אָמַר "מֵעַכְשָׁיו" לְלֹא אָמַר "מֵעַכְשָׁיו": **פת פורני.** פַּת גְּדוֹלָה הָאֲפוּיָה בְּתַנּוּר גָּדוֹל, כְּעֵין תַּנּוּרִים שֶׁלָּנוּ. שֶׁהַתַּנּוּרִים שֶׁלָּהֶם הָיוּ קְטַנִּים, וּמִיטַּלְטְלִין, וּפִיהֶם לְמַעְלָה, וּמַדְבִּיקִין הַפַּת בַּדְּפָנוֹת, שֶׁאֵין אוֹפִין בָּהּ אֶלָּא פִּתִּים קְטַנִּים. וְאוֹרְחָא דְּמִילְּתָא נָקַט, דְּאַיְּידֵי דַּחֲשִׁיבֵי שָׁקֵיל לֵיהּ בְּמַשְׁכּוֹן: **אינו עובר.** בַּפֶּסַח, דְּקָסָבַר: יִשְׂרָאֵל מִגּוֹי לָא קָנֵי מַשְׁכּוֹן: **הגעתיך.** מֵעַכְשָׁיו קָאָמַר, אִם לֹא אֶפְרַע לְךָ עַד יוֹם פְּלוֹנִי — עוֹבֵר. וְאַף עַל פִּי שֶׁלֹּא הִגִּיעַ הַזְּמַן — שֶׁמָּא כְּשֶׁיַּגִּיעַ לֹא יִפְרַע, וְנִמְצָא עוֹבֵר לְמַפְרֵעַ בְּ"בַל יֵרָאֶה": **מאי שנא רישא כו'.** אִי הִגַּעְתִּיךָ לָאו מֵעַכְשָׁיו הוּא, מַאי קָא מְהַנֵּי? דִּבְלָאו הִגַּעְתִּיךָ נַמִי, כִּי מָטָא זִמְנֵיהּ וְלֹא פָּרַע — שָׁקֵיל לֵיהּ בְּחוֹבוֹ: **ומלאי של ישראל.** פַּת וְיַיִן הַנִּמְכָּר בְּתוֹכָהּ: **אסור בהנאה.** דְּלָא תָּלֵינַן לֵיהּ בְּפוֹעֲלִין, אֶלָּא מִן שֶׁל מְלַאי הָיָה, וְשֶׁל יִשְׂרָאֵל הוּא: **גמ' צריך שיבטל בלבו.** שֶׁמָּא יְפַקַּח הַגַּל בַּמּוֹעֵד, וְנִמְצָא עוֹבֵר עָלָיו: **כספים.** שֶׁל פִּיקָּדוֹן, אֵין לָהֶם שְׁמִירָה אֶלָּא בַּקַּרְקַע. וְאִם לֹא נְתָנָן בַּקַּרְקַע וְאָבְדוּ — פְּשִׁיעָה הִיא אֶצְלוֹ, וְחַיָּיב. דְּשׁוֹמֵר חִנָּם חַיָּיב בִּפְשִׁיעָה: **משום ריחא.** שֶׁהַכֶּלֶב מְרִיחוֹ וּמְחַטְּטוֹ וּמוֹצִיאוֹ: **מסיכרא.** מָקוֹם: **מתני' בשוגג.** שֶׁשָּׁגַג בִּתְרוּמָה, וַאֲפִילּוּ הֵזִיד בֶּחָמֵץ — מְשַׁלֵּם קֶרֶן וָחוֹמֶשׁ. וְאַף עַל גַּב דְּלָא הֲוָה שָׁוְיָא מִידֵי, דְּחָמֵץ בְּפֶסַח אָסוּר בַּהֲנָאָה, מִיהוּ שׁוֹגֵג דִּתְרוּמָה דִּכְתִיב בֵּיהּ: "וַחֲמִישִׁיתוֹ יוֹסֵף עָלָיו וְנָתַן לַכֹּהֵן אֶת הַקֹּדֶשׁ" — דָּבָר הָרָאוּי לִהְיוֹת קוֹדֶשׁ, שֶׁאֵינוֹ יָכוֹל לְשַׁלֵּם לוֹ הַמָּעוֹת אֶלָּא הַפֵּירוֹת, וְהַתַּשְׁלוּמִין נַעֲשִׂין תְּרוּמָה כִּדְלְקַמָּן — לָאו לְפִי דָּמִים מְשַׁלֵּם, אֶלָּא לְפִי מִדָּה מְשַׁלֵּם. הִלְכָּךְ: לָאו בָּתַר דָּמִים אָזְלִינַן: **במזיד.** שֶׁהֵזִיד בִּתְרוּמָה, אֲפִילּוּ שָׁגַג בֶּחָמֵץ — פָּטוּר מִן הַתַּשְׁלוּמִין: **ומדמי עצים.** אִם תְּרוּמָה טְמֵאָה הִיא — אֵין מְשַׁלֵּם לוֹ דְּמֵי עֵצִים שֶׁהָיְתָה רְאוּיָה לְהֶיסֵּק תַּחַת תַּבְשִׁילוֹ, מִשּׁוּם דִּתְרוּמָה מֵזִיד אֵין בָּהּ חוֹמֶשׁ, וְאֵין תַּשְׁלוּמֶיהָ לְכַפָּרָה, וְאֵין נַעֲשִׂין תְּרוּמָה. דְּגַבֵּי חוֹמֶשׁ "בִּשְׁגָגָה" כְּתִיב, אֲבָל מֵזִיד — אֵינוֹ אֶלָּא כִּשְׁאָר גַּזְלָן בְּעָלְמָא, וּמְשַׁלֵּם מָעוֹת, וּלְפִי דָּמִים, וְלֹא לְפִי הַמִּדָּה. וְחָמֵץ בַּפֶּסַח לָאו בַּר דָּמִים, דְּאָסוּר בַּהֲנָאָה, וְאַף לְהֶיסֵּק לֹא הֲוֵי חֲזֵי לֵיהּ, וְלָאו מִידֵי אַפְסְדֵיהּ:

וְאֶחָד

אלא הב"ע שהרהינו **אצלו** וקמיפלגי בדרבי יצחק. תימה לריב"א: אביי היאך יתרץ הכן? דע"כ בדרבי יצחק קמיפלגי, וסיפא דקתני גוי שהלוה את ישראל על חמצו — אמאי דברי הכל עובר אע"ג דלא קנה? כיון דלמפרע הוא גובה! ורישא נמי, אמאי אינו עובר למ"ד כיון דלמפרע הוא גובה? ומפרש ריב"א: דהשתא, כי מוקי פלוגתא בדרבי יצחק — מיירי שלא בא ישראל לידי גבייה, שפדאו גוי לבסוף, דלא שייך השתא פלוגתא דאביי ורבא כלל. אלא בהא קמיפלגי: דלמאן דאמר עובר — ס"ל דקני ליה ישראל מגוי, וה"ל ברשות ישראל, ומ"ד אינו עובר — ס"ל דלא קני ליה, והרי לא היה ברשותו. ובסיפא ד"ה עובר — דלא קני ליה גוי לכ"ע, והרי היה ברשות ישראל. ומיהו, מתניתין דקתני גוי שהלוה וכו' מותר בהנאה — מיירי שלא פדאו ישראל, דאי פדאו, אע"ג דמוקי לה בסמוך בדאמר ליה מעכשיו — מכל מקום מאי מהני? **בדרבי** יצחק קמיפלגי. תימה: הא ר' יצחק לא קאמר דקני משכון אלא שלא בשעת הלואה, כדמוכח ב"האומנין" (בבא מציעא פב.). והכא ישראל שהלוה לגוי על חמצו תנן, דמשמע בשעת הלואה, כדמשמע ב"האומנין"*, דקתני: הלוהו על המשכון — שומר שכר. והתניא: שומר חנם! ומשני: הא — דמשכנו בשעת הלואתו, והא — שלא בשעת הלואתו. ופריך: והא אידי ואידי על המשכון קתני! ויש לומר: דהכי פירושו, כיון דשלא בשעת הלואה קונה לגמרי כדרבי יצחק — א"כ לענין חמץ יש לנו לחושבו כאילו הוא שלו, לעבור בלא ימצא אף בשעת הלואה, דחשבינן ליה מצוי. וכן יש לפרש ב"השולח" (גיטין לז.) גבי המלוה על המשכון אינו משמט, מדרבי יצחק. כיון דקני ליה שלא בשעת הלואה — בשעת הלואה נמי מיקרי של אחיך בידך: **שקונה** משכון. פ"ה: קונה משכון לענין חיוב אונסין. ור"י אומר: דב"האומנין" (ב"מ פב.) משמע דלא הוי אלא שומר שכר, דהלוהו על המשכון שומר שכר בעי למימר התם בגמרא דסבר לה כרבי יצחק. וכולה שמעתא חמצו של גוי ביד ישראל איירי שלא קבל עליו ישראל אחריות, דאי קבל — הרי הוא שלו, ועובר עליו, כדמוכח בפ"ק (דף ה:): **ואם** אמר הגעתיך עובר. לאביי רישא איירי כשפדאו, וסיפא — כי אמר הגעתיך, היינו שאינו רוצה לפדותו:

דבר

רבינו חננאל

היא ואוקימנה בשהרהינו אצלו ואמר לו קנה מעכשיו וכדר' יצחק דאמר בעל *)חוב קונה משכון ופליגי ת"ק לית ליה הא דר' יצחק ור' מאיר אית ליה ומתמהי' וכי דר' יצחק תנאי היא ושני' [דכ"ע] אית להו דר' יצחק והכא בהא קא מיפלגי ת"ק סבר ישראל מישראל דבר צדקה הוא קני אבל משכון דנכרי דלאו בר צדקה הוא לא קני ור' מאיר סבר ק"ו משכון דישראל קני ליה המלוה משכון דנכרי לא כל שכן אבל נכרי שהלוה את ישראל על חמצו וקבע לו זמן לפרעו אחר הפסח דברי הכל עובר דלא קני הנכרי חמצו של ישראל אלא ברשות ישראל קאי ועובר עליו ומקשי' תנן נכרי שהלוה את ישראל על חמצו אחר הפסח מותר בהנאה והאמרת נכרי מישראל לא קני ואפי' הרהינו אצלו ושני' משנתינו בשפירש לו קני מעכשיו כדתניא נכרי שהרהין פת פורני אצל ישראל אינו עובר בפסח ואם אמר לו הגעתיך כלומר קני מעכשיו עובר וכך סוגיא דשמעתא זו סלקא והוא כגון הא דתנן (בב"מ דף סה) הלוהו על שדהו ואמר לו אם איני מביא לך עד שלש שנים הרי הוא [שלך] מעכשיו**) כו': **ת"ר** חנות של נכרי ומלאי של נכרי. כלומר הסחורה שבתוך החנות לנכרי ופועלי ישראל נכנסין לשם ועושין מלאכתן חמץ שנמצא שם אחר הפסח אסור בהנאה ואין צריך לומר באכילה כלומר חמץ של ישראל הוא וכן חנות של ישראל ומלאי של ישראל ופועלי נכרים נכנסין שם חמץ שנמצא שם אחר הפסח מותר באכילה ואין צריך לומר בהנאה כללא דמילתא בתר פועלין אזלינן אם פועלין ישרא[ל]
ואסור ואם של נכרים מותר: **חמץ** שנפלה עליו מפולת ונטמן בעפר אם הוא טמון שלשה טפחים בכדי שאין הכלב יכול לחפש אחריו כלומר אינו מריח ריח החמץ הרי הוא כמבוער ואין חייב
ולשרפו אבל צריך לבטלו ולא תימא אפי' בשמירת הפקדון כך כי הא דאמר שמואל כספים אין להם שמירה אלא בקרקע ולא בעינן כולי האי אלא טפח בלבד סגי דכיון דמשום אכסויי מעינא הוא דיו
לא חיישי' הלכך אפי' הוא טמון בקרקע טפח סגי ליה: **מתני'** האוכל תרומת חמץ בפסח בשוגג משלם קרן וחומש במזיד הואיל וחייב כרת פטור מן התשלומי' ומדמי העצים פי' לא תאמר
שאכלת אתה כאלו שרפת אותה ונהנת ממנה ואתה חייב לשלם כפי הנאתך אלא אפי' כעצים העומדין לשרפה אין חייב לשלם שהחמץ בפסח איסורי הנאה הוא ולית ליה לכהן לשרפה וליהנות ממנה א
יהא פטור מן התשלומי' דהא לית דמים דאיסורא הנאה הוא ואמרי' מתני' ר' יוסי הגלילי הוא דאמר ותמה על עצמך האיך חמץ אסור בהנאה כל שבעה כדבעי' למימר קמן: **תנן** התם בתרומה פ"ו האוכל תרומה שוגג
משלם

ב"מ פב. גיטין לז. שבועות מד. [קדושין ח:]
[תוספתא פ"ב ע"ש]
ב"מ מב. לעיל ח.
ב"מ שם
תרומות פ"ו [מ"א] ב"מ נד:

הגהות הב"ח
(א) גמ' שהלוה את ישראל על חמצו:

*) משמע דרבינו הי' לו גי' אחרת בגמ' דמעיקרא ס"ד דפליגי בדר' יצחק גופא אי ב"ח קונה משכון או לא.
**) במשנה שם לא הוזכר דמיירי מעכשיו אכן בש"ס שם ד' סו ע"ב מוקמינן דאמר ליה קני מעכשיו.

מסורת הש"ס

עין משפט נר מצוה

צב א מיי' פ"ב מהל' גזילה הל' ב סמג עשין עג טוש"ע ח"מ סי' שסב סעיף ב:
צג ב מיי' פ"י מהל' תרומות הלכה ו:
צד ג שם הלכה ה:

גמ' ואחד הסך. דאמרי' בפרק בתרא דיומא (דף עו:): סיכה כשתיה. ושתיה בכלל אכילה. והכא כתיב: "כי יאכל קדש בשגגה", דאילו גזלה והשליכה לנהר, אפי' בשוגג, דלא ידע שהיא תרומה – אינו משלם חומש אלא קרן, כשאר מזיק חולין דעלמא, דאמר מר (לקמן ע"ב): "כי יאכל" – פרט למזיק: וחומש תורה אור חומשא. שהתשלומין נעשין תרומה, ואם חזר ואכל בשוגג אותו חומש ראשון – חוזר ומשלם חומשו עליו: **איבעיא** להו. כיון דגבי תרומה בשוגג קפיד רחמנא אתשלומי פירות ולא מעות, כדכתיב: "ונתן לכהן את הקודש", לפי מדה משלם או לפי דמים משלם? בגזלן דחולין שוגג או מזיד, וכן גזלן דתרומת מזיד – לא איבעיא לן, כיון דלא קפיד רחמנא אתשלומין דידהו, דאמר "ישיב" – לרבות אפילו שוה כסף, ואפילו סובין – ודאי לפי דמים משלם. אבל בתרומה שוגג איבעיא לן, הואיל והקפידה התורה לשלם פירות: **כל היכא דמעיקרא**. כשאכלה הויא שויא הך גריוא ד' זוזי, והשתא כשמשלם שויא זוזא ותו לא – לא מיבעיא לן. נהי נמי דאיכפר ליה אכילת תרומה בתשלומי מדה, מיהו ממונא דכהן [אוכל] (ממונא) הוא, ולא גרע משאר ממונא דחולין, שהדיינין גובין ממנו כשעת גזילה, כדכתיב (ויקרא ה): "אשר גזל" – כמו שגזל: **גריוא** משלם. ואע"ג דשויא השתא טפי, או דילמא לפי דמים משלם, דאע"ג דהקפידה התורה לשלם פירות – לא הקפידה אלא לפי הדמים, כשאר תשלומין. ומה שישלם – ישלם בפירות: גרוגרות. תאנים יבשים: תמרים. חשובין מתאנים, ודמיהן מרובים: **אכל** גרוגרות. דתרומה, שוגג: **זבינא**. לוקחים: **אימא סיפא במזיד פטור** מן התשלומין ואי ר' יוסי הגלילי **אמאי פטור**. אי אמרת בשלמא רבנן, וטעמא דרישא משום דלפי מדה משלם – סיפא דאינו אלא כשאר גזלן דמשלם מעות, ולפי דמים – פטור מן התשלומין. דחמץ בפסח לאו בר דמים הוא. אלא אי אמרת ר' יוסי הגלילי, ובר דמים הוא, אמאי פטור? כרבי **נחוניא** בן הקנה. דאמר: המתחייב כרת פטור מן התשלומין. ויליף טעמא מאסון אסון. והוא הדין למתחייב מיתת שמים, כגון אוכל תרומה מזיד. וסיפא דמתני' בהזיד בתרומה ולא בחמץ, ופטור משום מיתה. ובדין הוא דלישמעי' במזיד דתרומה דעלמא, דלאו חמץ בפסח, דפטור מתשלומין

ואחד הסך, אחד תרומה טמאה ואחד תרומה טהורה – משלם חומש וחומשא דחומשא. **איבעיא להו**: כשהוא משלם, לפי מדה משלם או לפי דמים משלם? כל היכא דמעיקרא שויא ארבעה זוזי ולבסוף שויא זוזא – לא תיבעי לך דודאי כדמעיקרא משלם לפי דמים, [ב]דלא גרע מגזלן. דתנן: [א]*כל הגזלנין משלמין כשעת הגזלה. כי תיבעי לך – דמעיקרא שויא זוזא ולבסוף שויא ארבעה. מאי, לפי מדה משלם, דא"ל: גריוא אכל – גריוא משלם. או דילמא: לפי דמים משלם, בזוזא אכל – בזוזא משלם? אמר רב יוסף, תא שמע: *אכל גרוגרות ושילם לו תמרים – תבא עליו ברכה, אי אמרת בשלמא לפי מדה משלם – אמטו להכי תבא עליו ברכה, דאכיל גריוא דגרוגרות דשויא זוזא, וקא יהיב גריוא דתמרים דשויא ארבעה. אלא אי אמרת לפי דמים משלם – אמאי תבא עליו ברכה? בזוזא אכל בזוזא קא משלם! אמר אביי: לעולם לפי דמים משלם, ואמאי תבא עליו ברכה – דאכל מידי דלא קפיץ עליה זביניה, וקא משלם מידי דקפיץ עליה זביניה.§ תנן: האוכל תרומת חמץ בפסח, בשוגג – משלם קרן וחומש. אי אמרת בשלמא לפי מדה משלם – שפיר. אלא אי אמרת לפי דמים משלם – חמץ בפסח בר דמים הוא?! אין, הא מני – ר' יוסי הגלילי היא, דאמר: *חמץ בפסח מותר בהנאה. אי הכי, אימא סיפא: במזיד פטור מן התשלומין ומדמי עצים. אי ר' יוסי הגלילי, אמאי פטור מן התשלומין ומדמי עצים?! סבר לה כר' נחוניא בן הקנה. דתניא: *רבי נחוניא בן הקנה היה עושה את יום הכפורים כשבת לתשלומין וכו'. כתנאי: [ב]*האוכל תרומת חמץ בפסח – פטור מן התשלומין ומדמי עצים, דברי רבי עקיבא. ר' יוחנן בן נורי מחייב. אמר לו רבי עקיבא לר' יוחנן בן נורי: וכי מה הנאה יש לו בה? אמר לו ר' יוחנן בן נורי לר"ע: ומה הנאה יש לאוכל תרומה טמאה בשאר כל ימות השנה, שמשלם? אמר לו: לא אם אמרת בתרומה טמאה בשאר ימות השנה, שאע"פ שאין לו בה היתר אכילה – [ג]יש לו בה היתר הסקה, תאמר בזה – שאין לו בה לא היתר אכילה ולא היתר הסקה. *הא למה זה דומה – לתרומת תותים וענבים שנטמאה, שאין לו בה לא היתר אכילה ולא היתר הסקה. בד"א – במפריש תרומה והחמיצה, אבל מפריש תרומת חמץ – דברי הכל אינה קדושה. תניא אידך: °"ונתן לכהן את הקדש" (ויקרא כב) – דבר הראוי להיות קדש, פרט לאוכל תרומת חמץ בפסח, שפטור מן התשלומים ומדמי עצים, דברי ר' אליעזר בן יעקב. ור"א חסמא מחייב. אמר לו ר"א בן יעקב לר"א חסמא: וכי מה הנאה יש לו בה? אמר לו ר"א חסמא לר"א בן יעקב: וכי מה הנאה יש לו לאוכל תרומה טמאה בשאר ימות השנה, שמשלם? אמר לו: לא אם אמרת בתרומה טמאה בשאר ימות השנה – שאע"פ שאין לו בה היתר אכילה יש לו בה היתר הסקה, תאמר בזו – שאין לו בה לא היתר אכילה ולא היתר הסקה! אמר לו: אף בזו יש לו בה היתר הסקה, שאם רצה הכהן *מריצה לפני כלבו או מסיקה תחת תבשילו. אמר

דבר הראוי להיות קודש פרט לאוכל תרומת חמץ. פי' הפסוק משמע שיתן לו דבר הראוי להיות קודש כמו שאכל, וא"כ מה שאכל בעינן דבר הראוי להיות קודש, וחמץ בפסח אינו ראוי להיות קודש, כדתניא לעיל. אבל מפריש (א) חמץ – ד"ה אין קדוש. ואע"ג דבכל ענין פטור הכא מתשלומין, אפי' שהיה לה שעת הכושר. ולקמן מוקמא הא דלד"ה אין קדוש – היינו שלא היה לה שעת הכושר, אור"ת: היינו לרבי יוסי הגלילי. אבל לראב"י, הואיל וסבירא ליה דחמץ בפסח אסור בהנאה – אפילו היה לה שעת הכושר אין ראוי להיות קודש, דאין כאן נתינה. והיינו דקאמר ליה ראב"י: מה הנאה יש לו בה. כלומר: הואיל ואין לו הנאה בה, אית ליה למעוטי מקרא כדפרישית: ואין

משום מיתה. ומשום רישא נקט מילתא בחמץ בפסח, דאשמועינן דהיכא דשגג בשתיהם – חייב, דחמץ בר דמים הוא. ושוגג דרישא דשגג בשתיהן, דאי שגג בחמץ והזיד בתרומה – מאי חומש איכא? ואי שגג בתרומה והזיד בחמץ – אמאי משלם? הא איחייב ליה כרת. וסיפא אשמועינן, דהזיד בתרומה, אפילו שגג בחמץ – פטור, דמיתה בידי שמים כי כרת. דאי הזיד בחמץ, והא דפטר ליה משום כרת הוא דפטר ליה – לשמעי' כולה מתני' בחמץ חולין של חבירו, וניתני: שוגג חייב, ומזיד פטור משום כרת: **כתנאי**. לפי מדה או לפי דמים: פטור מתשלומין. בין שוגג בין מזיד: מה הנאה יש לו. לכהן בה, ומה הפסידו זה? הרי אסור בהנאה: ומה הנאה יש לו. לכהן בתרומה טמאה, שאסורה באכילה לכהן. ואי אכלה זר שוגג – משלם קרן וחומש. דליכא למאן דפליג אסתמא דתנן לעיל: אחד תרומה טהורה ואחד תרומה טמאה. וטעמא, משום דלפי מדה משלם, ואע"ג דלאו בר דמים הוא: היתר הסקה. דכתיב (במדבר יח): "ואני הנה נתתי לך את משמרת תרומותי" – שתי תרומות במשמע, אחת טהורה ואחת טמאה. וכתיב "לך תהיה" – להסקה: תרומת תותים וענבים. משקה הן, ואינן ראויין להסקה. ולזלף נמי לא, כדאמרינן בפ"ק (דף כ:) משום תקלה. ובההוא נמי סבירא ליה דזר האוכלה פטור מלשלם. ור' יוחנן בן נורי מחייב, דקסבר: לפי מדה משלם: **בד"א**. דמשכחת תרומת חמץ בפסח דקדשה – בהפריש תרומה והחמיצה, והוא הדין להפרישה חמץ קודם הפסח: **אבל מפריש תרומת חמץ**. בפסח, כגון חטים שהחמיצו – דברי הכל, אפי' לרבי יוסי הגלילי דשרי חמץ בפסח בהנאה, וחזיא ליה להסקה – אינה קדושה. ולקמן מפרש טעמא, בשילהי שמעתין: **את הקדש**. משמע את הקדש שאכל. אלמא: ראוי להיות קדש היה, שכשישלם דוגמתן יהא שם קדש חל עליו: פרט לאוכל תרומת חמץ בפסח. שכשמשלם דוגמתן אין שם קדש חל עליו: **וכי מה הנאה** יש לו. לכהן בה, ומה הפסידו? נהי נמי דלית לך הא דרשה, מיהו מה ישלם, הואיל ואין לו דמים? אמר

רבינו חננאל

משלם קרן וחומש אחד האוכל ואחד השותה ואחד הסך אחד אוכל תרומה טהורה ואחד אוכל תרומה טמאה משלם חומשא וחומש חומשא והוא חומשא מלבר כדקתני בהדיא שיהא הוא וחומשו חמשה שנאמר ויסף חמישיתו עליו דברי ר' יאשיה: **איבעיא** להו לפי מדה משלם קב אכל קב וחומשו משלם או לפי דמים משלם. כלומר כפי שהיה שוה בשעה שאכלו וכל היכא דהויא שויא ארבעה זוזי בעידן אכילתה והשתא שויא זוזא לא מיבעיא לן דודאי ארבעה זוזי משלם דלא גרע מגזלה דתנן כל הגזלנין משלמין כשעת הגזלה כי תיבעי לן דמעיקרא הוית שויא זוזא והשתא שויא ארבעה מאי ואתא רב יוסף למפשט לפי מדה משלם מיהא אכל גרוגרו' ושלם לו תמרים תבוא עליו ברכה כלומר שאכל קב גרוגרות שדמיהם זוזא ושלם קב תמרים ששוים ארבעה זוזי ודחה אביי לעולם לפי דמים משלם ואמאי תבוא עליו ברכה ואי אית למימר וכי כל המשלם דבר שחייב בו מחזיקין לו טובה ומברכים אותו יש לך לומר לאו משום דקא משלם [יותר] אלא משום דמשלם דבר מעולה דקפיץ עליה זיבונא ואקשי' על אביי ממתני' דקתני האוכל תרומת חמץ בפסח בשוגג משלם כו' ואי אמרת לפי דמים משלם חמץ בפסח בר דמים הוא ומשני' מתני' ר' יוסי הגלילי היא דאמר חמץ בפסח מותר בהנאה סיפא דקתני במזיד פטור סבר לה ר' יוסי הגלילי כר' נחוניא בן הקנה דפוטר חייבי כריתות מן התשלומים: **כתנאי** יש תנא שאומ' לפי דמים משלם ויש תנא שאומר לפי מדה משלם דתניא האוכל תרומת חמץ בפסח בשוגג משלם קרן וחומש במזיד פטור מן התשלומים ומדמי העצים דברי ר' עקיבא ר' יוחנן בן נורי מחייב אמר לו ר' עקיבא לר' יוחנן בן נורי מה הנאה יש לו שמשלם כו' עוד השיבו ר' עקיבא לא אם אמרת בתרומה טמא' בשאר ימות השנה שאע"פ שאין לו בה [היתר אכילה יש לו בה] היתר הסקה תאמר בחמץ בפסח שאין לו בה היתר הנאה כלל לא באכילה ולא בהסקה חמץ בפסח למה הוא דומה לתרומת תותים וענבים שנטמאת שאין לה היתר אכילה כלל ולא היתר הסקה דלאו בני הסקה נינהו בד"א במפריש תרומה והחמיצה אבל המפריש תרומת חמץ דברי הכל אינה קדושה: **תניא** אידך ונתן לכהן את הקדש דבר הראוי להיות קדש פרט לאוכל חמץ תרומה בפסח שפטור דברי ר' אליעזר בן יעקב ר' אלעזר חסמא מחייב אמר לו ר' אליעזר בן יעקב וכי מה הנאה יש לו וכו' עד אמר לו ר' אלעזר חסמא אף חמץ בפסח יש לו היתר שאם רצה מסיקה תחת תבשילו או מריצה לפני כלבו ודאי ר' אלעזר חסמא אית ליה כי חמץ בפסח מותר בהנאה אבל ר' עקיבא

ב"ק לג: וש"נ
עירובין כט:
[לעיל כג. כח:]
לעיל כט. [וש"נ]
[תוספתא פ"א]
[לקמן לג:]
[עי' תוס' ביצה כז: ד"ה ועל]

הגהות הב"ח

(א) תום' ד"ה דבר וכו' לעיל אבל מפריש תרומת חמץ וכו' ולקמן מוקמי'. נ"ב בד' לג סוף ע"א:

גליון הש"ס

גמ' דלא גרע מגזלן. ק"ל הא מ"מ כ"מ דאם אינו חייב רק מדין גזלן יכול לשלם חד גריוא בפירות לצאת ידי כפרה והשאר משלם במעות והכהן יכול למחול וגם החומש הוא רק מן חד גריוא. אבל אם לפי דמים צריך לשלם ד' גריוא וחומש' מפרי והכהן אין יכול למחול: **תוד"ה** דבר כו' אע"ג דבכל ענין פטור הכא מתשלומין. ק"ל למאי נקטו קושייתם בדרך דמסתמא קאמ' בכל ענין הלא א"א כלל בגוונא אחרינא דהא אכל תרומת חמץ א"כ המאכל היה לה שעת הכושר דאל"כ לא משכחת שהיא תרומה וצ"ע:

צה א מיי' שם הל' כו:
צו ב ג שם הל' ב:

אָמַר אַבַּיֵי: רַבִּי אֱלִיעֶזֶר בֶּן יַעֲקֹב, וְרַבִּי עֲקִיבָא, וְר' יוֹחָנָן בֶּן נוּרִי, כּוּלְּהוּ סְבִירָא לְהוּ: חָמֵץ בְּפֶסַח אָסוּר בַּהֲנָאָה. וּבְהָא פְּלִיגִי; דְּרַבִּי עֲקִיבָא סָבַר: א לְפִי דָּמִים מְשַׁלֵּם, וְרַבִּי יוֹחָנָן בֶּן נוּרִי סָבַר: לְפִי מִדָּה מְשַׁלֵּם. פְּשִׁיטָא! מַהוּ דְּתֵימָא: רַבִּי יוֹחָנָן בֶּן נוּרִי נַמִי כְּרַבִּי עֲקִיבָא סְבִירָא לֵיהּ, דְּאָמַר לְפִי דָּמִים מְשַׁלֵּם. וְהָתָם הַיְינוּ טַעְמָא דְּקָא מְחַיֵּיב — מִשּׁוּם דְּסָבַר לָהּ כְּרַבִּי יוֹסֵי הַגְּלִילִי, דְּאָמַר: *חָמֵץ בְּפֶסַח מוּתָּר בַּהֲנָאָה, קמ"ל. וְאֵימָא הָכִי נַמִי! אִם כֵּן נֶהְדַּר לֵיהּ רַבִּי יוֹחָנָן בֶּן נוּרִי לְר' עֲקִיבָא כִּי הֵיכִי דְּמַהְדַּר לֵיהּ רַבִּי אֶלְעָזָר חִסְמָא לְר' אֱלִיעֶזֶר בֶּן יַעֲקֹב.§ ת"ר: ב הָאוֹכֵל כַּזַּיִת תְּרוּמָה — מְשַׁלֵּם קֶרֶן וָחוֹמֶשׁ, אַבָּא שָׁאוּל אוֹמֵר: עַד שֶׁיְּהֵא בּוֹ שָׁוֶה פְּרוּטָה. מ"ט דְּתַנָּא קַמָּא? אָמַר קְרָא: °"וְאִישׁ כִּי יֹאכַל קֹדֶשׁ בִּשְׁגָגָה" — וַאֲכִילָה בִּכְזַיִת. וְאַבָּא שָׁאוּל מַאי טַעְמָא? אָמַר קְרָא: "וְנָתַן" — וְאֵין נְתִינָה פָּחוֹת מִשָּׁוֶה פְּרוּטָה. וְאִידָּךְ נַמִי, הָא כְּתִיב "יֹאכַל"? הַהוּא — *פְּרָט לְמַזִּיק הוּא דַּאֲתָא. וְתַנָּא קַמָּא, הַכְתִיב "וְנָתַן"? הַהוּא מִיבְּעֵי לֵיהּ לְדָבָר הָרָאוּי לִהְיוֹת קֹדֶשׁ, (פְּרָט לָאוֹכֵל תְּרוּמַת חָמֵץ בְּפֶסַח).§ ת"ר: ג הָאוֹכֵל תְּרוּמָה פָּחוֹת מִכַּזַּיִת — מְשַׁלֵּם אֶת הַקֶּרֶן וְאֵינוֹ מְשַׁלֵּם אֶת הַחוֹמֶשׁ. הֵיכִי דָּמֵי? אִי דְּלֵית בֵּיהּ שָׁוֶה פְּרוּטָה — קֶרֶן נַמִי לָא לִישַׁלֵּם, וְאִי דְּאִית בָּהּ שָׁוֶה פְּרוּטָה — חוֹמֶשׁ נַמִי לִישַׁלֵּם! לְעוֹלָם דְּאִית בָּהּ שָׁוֶה פְּרוּטָה. וַאֲפִילּוּ הָכִי, כֵּיוָן דְּלֵית בֵּיהּ כַּזַּיִת — מְשַׁלֵּם אֶת הַקֶּרֶן וְאֵינוֹ מְשַׁלֵּם אֶת הַחוֹמֶשׁ. אַמְרוּהָ רַבָּנַן קַמֵּיהּ דְּרַב פַּפָּא: הָא דְּלָא כְּאַבָּא שָׁאוּל, דְּאִי כְּאַבָּא שָׁאוּל — הָאָמַר: כֵּיוָן שֶׁיֵּשׁ בָּהּ שָׁוֶה פְּרוּטָה, אע"ג דְּלֵית בֵּיהּ כַּזַּיִת! אֲמַר לְהוּ רַב פַּפָּא: אֲפִילּוּ תֵּימָא אַבָּא שָׁאוּל, אַבָּא שָׁאוּל תַּרְתֵּי בָּעֵי. וּמִי בָּעֵי אַבָּא שָׁאוּל תַּרְתֵּי?! וְהָא *תְּנַן, אַבָּא שָׁאוּל אוֹמֵר: אֶת שֶׁיֵּשׁ בּוֹ שָׁוֶה פְּרוּטָה — חַיָּיב בְּתַשְׁלוּמִין, אֶת שֶׁאֵין בּוֹ שָׁוֶה פְּרוּטָה — אֵינוֹ חַיָּיב בְּתַשְׁלוּמִין. אָמְרוּ לוֹ: לֹא אָמְרוּ שָׁוֶה פְּרוּטָה אֶלָּא לְעִנְיַן מְעִילָה בִּלְבַד, אֲבָל לִתְרוּמָה — אֵינוֹ חַיָּיב עַד שֶׁיְּהֵא בּוֹ כַּזַּיִת. וְאִם אִיתָא, כֵּיוָן שֶׁיֵּשׁ בּוֹ כַּזַּיִת מִיבְּעֵי לֵיהּ! תְּיוּבְתָּא. וְאַף רַב פַּפָּא הֲדַר בֵּיהּ, דְּתַנְיָא: °"וְחָטְאָה בִּשְׁגָגָה" — פְּרָט לְמֵזִיד. וַהֲלֹא דִּין הוּא, וּמָה שְּׁאָר מִצְוֹת שֶׁחַיָּיב בָּהֶן כָּרֵת — פּוֹטֵר בָּהֶן אֶת הַמֵּזִיד, מְעִילָה שֶׁאֵין בָּהּ כָּרֵת אֵינוֹ דִּין שֶׁפָּטַר אֶת הַמֵּזִיד? לֹא, אִם אָמַרְתָּ בִּשְׁאָר מִצְוֹת — שֶׁכֵּן לֹא חַיָּיב בָּהֶן מִיתָה, תֹּאמַר בִּמְעִילָה שֶׁחַיָּיב בָּהּ מִיתָה, ת"ל: "בִּשְׁגָגָה" — פְּרָט לְמֵזִיד. וַאֲמַר לֵיהּ רַב נַחְמָן בַּר יִצְחָק לְרַב חִיָּיא בַּר אָבִין: הַאי תַּנָּא, מֵעִיקָּרָא אַלִּימָא לֵיהּ כָּרֵת, וּלְבַסּוֹף אַלִּימָא לֵיהּ מִיתָה?! וַאֲמַר לֵיהּ; הָכִי קָאָמַר: לֹא, אִם אָמַרְתָּ בִּשְׁאָר מִצְוֹת — שֶׁכֵּן לֹא חַיָּיב בָּהֶן מִיתָה בְּפָחוֹת מִכַּזַּיִת, תֹּאמַר בִּמְעִילָה — שֶׁחַיָּיב בָּהּ מִיתָה בְּפָחוֹת מִכַּזַּיִת. וַאֲמַר לֵיהּ: *תָּנוּחַ דַּעְתְּךָ שֶׁהֵנַחְתָּ אֶת דַּעְתִּי וא"ל: מַאי נִיחוּתָא? דְּרַבָּה וְרַב שֵׁשֶׁת שָׁדוּ בֵּיהּ נַרְגָּא: מַאן שָׁמְעַתְּ לֵיהּ דְּאָמַר

הַזִּיד

תורה אור: ויקרא כב; שם ה

רש"י

אָמַר אַבַּיֵי ר' עֲקִיבָא וְר' יוֹחָנָן בֶּן נוּרִי. אע"ג דְּמִחַיֵּיב בְּתַשְׁלוּמִין, סְבִירָא לְהוּ דְּאֵין לוֹ דָּמִים. וּבְהָא פְּלִיגִי רַבִּי עֲקִיבָא וְר' יוֹחָנָן בֶּן נוּרִי: א"כ. דִּסְבִירָא לֵיהּ מוּתָּר, נֶיהְדַּר לֵיהּ ר' יוֹחָנָן לְרַבִּי עֲקִיבָא: אַף לָזֶה יֵשׁ לוֹ הֶיתֵּר הַסָּקָה: כַּזַּיִת תְּרוּמָה. בִּשְׁאָר יְמוֹת הַשָּׁנָה קָאֵי: פְּרָט לְמַזִּיק. תְּרוּמָה שֶׁל כֹּהֵן, אֲפִי' בְּשׁוֹגֵג, שֶׁאֵינוֹ מְשַׁלֵּם חוֹמֶשׁ אֶלָּא קֶרֶן, כִּשְׁאָר מַזִּיק חוּלִּין: הַהוּא מִיבְּעֵי לֵיהּ דָּבָר הָרָאוּי לִהְיוֹת קֹדֶשׁ. וְכוּלֵּיהּ קְרָא מִשּׁוּם סֵיפָא אִצְטְרִיךְ: דְּאִית בָּהּ שָׁוֶה פְּרוּטָה. וְלֵיכָּא כַּזַּיִת, כְּגוֹן שְׁנַת בַּצּוֹרֶת: כֵּיוָן דְּלֵית בָּהּ כַּזַּיִת כו'. דַּאֲכִילָה כְּתִיבָא בָּהּ: אַמְרוּהָ רַבָּנַן קַמֵּיהּ דְּרַב פַּפָּא. דִּקְדְּקוּ מִלִּבָּן, וְאָמְרוּ לְפָנָיו: דְּהָא מַתְנִי' דְּקָפְדָא אַכַּזַּיִת — דְּלָא כְּאַבָּא שָׁאוּל, דְּהָא שָׁמְעִינַן לֵי' דְּקָפֵיד אַפְּרוּטָ' וְלָא אַכַּזַּיִת: תַּרְתֵּי בָּעֵי. שֶׁיְּהֵא בּוֹ כַּזַּיִת, דְּהָא אֲכִילָה כְּתִיבָא בֵּיהּ, וְשֶׁיְּהֵא בְּדָמָיו פְּרוּטָה, דְּהָא כְּתִיב "וְנָתַן": חַיָּיב בְּתַשְׁלוּמִין. אַתְּרוּמַת שׁוֹגֵג קָאֵי, וְקֶרֶן וָחוֹמֶשׁ קָאָמַר: לְעִנְיַן מְעִילָה. בְּנֶהֱנֶה מֵהֶקְדֵּשׁ גָּבוֹהַּ, דְּהָתָם לָא כְּתִיב אֲכִילָה. אֲבָל לִתְרוּמָה, אֲפִי' יֵשׁ בּוֹ שָׁוֶה פְּרוּטָה — אֵין חַיָּיב חוֹמֶשׁ עַד שֶׁיְּהֵא בּוֹ כַּזַּיִת. מִכְּלָל לְאַבָּא שָׁאוּל, אע"ג דְּלֵיכָּא כַּזַּיִת. דְּאִם אִיתָא דְּתַרְתֵּי בָּעֵי, וּבְיֵשׁ בּוֹ כַּזַּיִת קָאֵי אַבָּא שָׁאוּל, וְקָאָמַר דאע"ג דְּאִית בֵּיהּ כַּזַּיִת בָּעֵינַן פְּרוּטָ' — הָכִי הֲוָה לְהוּ לְמֵימַר: "כֵּיוָן דְּיֵשׁ בּוֹ כַּזַּיִת — חַיָּיב": וְחָטְאָה בִּשְׁגָגָ'. בִּמְעִילָ' דְּהֶקְדֵּשׁ כְּתִיב: וַהֲלֹא דִּין הוּא. דְּמֵזִיד פָּטוּר מִקָּרְבָּן, וְלָמָּה לִי קְרָא? שֶׁחִיֵּיב בָּהֶן הַכָּתוּב כָּרֵת. כְּגוֹן חֵלֶב וָדָם: פָּטַר בָּהֶן אֶת הַמֵּזִיד. מִקָּרְבָּן, דְּגַבֵּי חַטָּאת "שְׁגָגָה" כְּתִיב: לֹא חַיָּיב בָּהֶן מִיתָה. בִּידֵי שָׁמַיִם. אֲבָל מְעִילָה חַיָּיב עַל זְדוֹנָהּ מִיתָה, כִּדְלְקַמָּן. וְדִילְמָא מִיתָה חֲמִירָא מִכָּרֵת: וַאֲמַר לֵיהּ רַב נַחְמָן גָּרְסִינַן. הַאי תַּנָּא אַלִּימָא לֵיהּ כָּרֵת מִמִּיתָה מֵעִיקָּרָא דְּקָתָנֵי מְעִילָה שֶׁלֹּא חַיָּיב בָּהּ כָּרֵת אֶלָּא מִיתָה כו', אַלְמָא כָּרֵת חֲמִירָא. וּלְבַסּוֹף אַלִּימָא לֵי' מִיתָה, דְּקָתָנֵי תֹּאמַר בִּמְעִילָה כו': וא"ל. רַבִּי חִיָּיא: לְעוֹלָם כָּרֵת אַלִּימָא לֵיהּ, וְהָךְ סֵיפָא דְּמַתְנִי' הָכִי קָאָמַר: לֹא, אִם אָמַרְתָּ בִּשְׁאָר מִצְוֹת — שֶׁהֲרֵי לֹא חַיָּיב בָּהֶן אֲפִילּוּ מִיתָה בְּפָחוֹת מִכַּזַּיִת; תֹּאמַר בִּמְעִילָה, שֶׁחַיָּיב בָּהּ מִיהָא מִיתָה בְּפָחוֹת מִכַּזַּיִת? בְּכוּלְּהוּ גָּרְסִינַן וַאֲמַר לֵיהּ, וּמַתְקִיף לֵיהּ רַב פַּפָּא כו' עַד הֲדַר בֵּיהּ: וּמַאי נִיחוּתָא. אִיכָּא, דְּהָא רַבָּה וְרַב שֵׁשֶׁת שָׁדוּ בֵּיהּ נַרְגָּא בְּהַאי פֵּירוּקָא דְּתָרֵיצַת, וּמַקְשׁוּ הָכִי: הֵיכִי אָמְרִי' דְּתַנָּא אַפָּחוֹת מִכַּזַּיִת מְחַיֵּיב מִיתָה: מַאן שָׁמְעַתְּ לֵיהּ דְּאָמַר מְעִילָה וּזְדוֹנָהּ מִיתָה רַבִּי. וְעַל כָּרְחָךְ מִתְּרוּמָה גָּמַר לָהּ, כִּדְמְפָרְשִׁינַן. וְכֵיוָן דְּמִתְּרוּמָה גָּמַר — לָא מַשְׁכַּח בָּהּ מִיתָה אֶלָּא בְּכַזַּיִת כִּתְרוּמָה, דִּתְרוּמָה גַּבֵּי מִיתָה כְּתִיב בָּהּ אֲכִילָה. דְּמִיתָה דִּתְרוּמָה נָפְקָא לָן מִדְּסָמִיךְ "וְכָל זָר לֹא יֹאכַל קֹדֶשׁ" גַּבֵּי "וּמֵתוּ בוֹ כִּי יְחַלְּלוּהוּ" בְּ"אֵלּוּ הֵן הַנִּשְׂרָפִין" בְּסַנְהֶדְרִין (דף פג:):

הֵזִיד

[לעיל כג. כח:]
[יומא פ: פא. ב"מ נט: מעילה יט.]
[תוספתא דתרומות פ"ז ע"ש וצ"ל והתניא]
[שבת קנב: יומא סז: סנהדרין ל: מנחות מה. ק.]

תוספות

ואין נתינה פחות משוה פרוטה. ורבנן נמי לא פליגי אלא משום דכתיב אכילה. וא"ת: והא קיימא לן (חולין דף קלז:) דחטה אחת פוטרת את הכרי, אע"ג דכתיב בה נתינה, דכתיב "תתן לו"! וב"הזהב" (ב"מ מז.) אמר: קונין בכלי, אע"פ שאין בו שוה פרוטה, אע"ג דכתיב "ונתן לרעהו"! וגבי גט נמי אמרינן (גיטין דף כ.): כתבו על איסורי הנאה — כשר, אע"ג דכתיב "ונתן בידה"! ויש לומר: דהכא ודאי בעינן שוה פרוטה, דנתינה קיימא אתשלומין, והוי כמו השבת גזילה שאין בפחות משוה פרוטה. ולהכי, משום דכתיב "ונתן" — משמע שפיר נתינה חשובה. אבל שאר מילי, אע"ג דכתיב בהן נתינה — לא בעינן שוה פרוטה. מיהו, קשה לר"י, דרבי יהודה דריש בכריתות (דף ו:): "ואשר יתן ממנו על זר" — בכזית, ויליף נתינה מתרומה. ואדיליף מתרומה בכזית, נילף מכל נתינה לחומרא, דהוו בכל שהוא כגון מתן דמים ומתן בהונות שאין בהן שיעור, והוי נמי דומי' דסיכה דהוי בכל שהוא! ולמ"ד התם נתינה בכל שהוא — א"ש*: **ההוא** מיבעיא ליה לדבר הראוי להיות קודש. ואע"ג דמ"את הקודש" דרשינן דבר הראוי להיות קודש — אצטריך נמי "ונתן". דאי כתב "את הקודש" לחודיה ה"א דלא אתא למעוטי אלא מעות, אבל כל פירות ישלם, להכי כתב "ונתן" דמשמע שהפירות של נתינה בעינן ראוי להיות קודש: **מעילה** שלא חייב בה כרת אינו דין שפטר בה את המזיד. תימה: נימא היא הנותנת, דשאר מצות שהן חמורות, שהן בכרת — אין לזדונה כפרה. אבל מעילה, שהיא קלה שאין בה כרת — יש לזדונה כפרה. וכה"ג איכא בריש מכות (דף ב:), דקאמר ק"ו, ומה הוא שעושה מעשה במזיד — אינו גולה, עדים שלא עשו מעשה — אינו דין שלא יגלו? היא הנותנת, הוא שעשה מעשה במזיד — לא יגלה, כי היכי דלא תיהוי ליה כפרה. הן שלא עשו מעשה — יגלו, דתיהוי להו כפרה. ועוד: ארבעה המביאין על הזדון כשגגה יוכיחו, דאין בהן כרת וחייבין על זדונם: הבא על שפחה חרופה, ונזיר טמא, ושבועת העדות. והפקדון *(תוספתא דכריתות פ"א). ואומר ר"י דשפיר פריך בלאו הכי: לא אם אמרת וכו'. ומיהו קשה לר"י: אמאי איצטריך בכריתות (דף ט.) בשפחה חרופה "אשר חטא" לרבות זדון, וגבי נזיר נמי דריש מ"פתאום" לרבות זדון. דאי משום דלא נילף ממעילה, דאמעיט מזדון — אדרבה, משבועת העדות והפקדון אית לן למילף, דלחומרא מקשינן:

ומינה

[ועי' תוספות גיטין כ. ד"ה דילמא כו' שיישבו קושיא זו וע"ע תוס' מנחות ס. ד"ה מי בעינן ותוס' ב"מ מז. ד"ה קונים בכלי]
רש"ל מ"ז
[וכ"ה להדיא במשנה דכריתות ח: ד' מביאין על הזדון כשוגג ומפרש שם (ט.) במשנה עצמה אלו מביאין כו']

רבינו חננאל

עקיבא ור' יוחנן בן נורי ור' אליעזר בן יעקב יש לומר כי כולהו סבירא להו חמץ בפסח אסור בהנאה ובהא פליגי מאן דפטר סבר לפי דמים משלם וחמץ בפסח אין לו דמים לפיכך פטור ומאן דמחייב סבר לפי מדה משלם ואע"פ שאין לו דמים כיון שאינו משלם אלא לפי מדה חייב לשלם ולית לן למימר ממאי (דר' יוחנן בן נורי) [דסבר לפי מדה משלם דלמא סבירא ליה כר"י הגלילי] ונמצא דחמץ בפסח מותר בהנאה סבירא ליה דאי הכי הוי ליה לרבי יוחנן בן נורי לאהדורי לר' עקיבא אף חמץ בפסח יש לו היתר שאם רצה מסיקה או מריצה לפני כלבו כי היכי דמהדר ר' אלעזר חסמא ש"מ: **ת"ר** אכל כזית תרומה משלם קרן וחומש מ"ט דכתיב ואיש כי יאכל קדש בשגגה ויסף חמישיתו עליו ואכילה בכזית אכילה היא אבא שאול אומר אינו משלם עד שיהיה בה שוה פרוטה מאי טעמא דכתיב ונתן לכהן את הקדש ואין נתינה בפחות משוה פרוטה. תנא אכל פחות מכזית תרומה משלם קרן ואינו משלם חומש ואוקימנה דלא כאבא שאול דאי אבא שאול כיון דאית ביה שוה פרוטה אע"ג דלא הוי כזית ואמר רב פפא אפי' תימא אבא שאול [אבא שאול] תרתי בעי שיהיה בו כזית ושוה פרוטה. איני דאבא שאול לא בעי אלא אם יש כזית והתניא אבא שאול אומר כל שיש בו שוה פרוטה חייב בתשלומין וכל שאין בו שוה פרוטה אינו חייב אמרו לו לא אמרו שוה פרוטה אלא לענין מעילה אבל לענין תרומה עד שיהא בה כזית מכלל דהשתא*) לאבא שאול לא מחייב ואם איתא דאבא שאול לא הוה מחייב עד דאית ביה כזית כיון שיש בה כזית חייב הוה להו למימר ועלתה בתיובתא לרב פפא: **ואף** רב פפא הדר ביה דתניא נפש כי תמעול מעל וחטאה בשגגה מקדשי ה' פרט למזיד שאינו מביא קרבן והלא דין הוא ומה שאר מצות שחייב בהן כרת פטור המזיד מקרבן מעילה שלא חייב בה כרת אינו דין שיפטור בה המזיד לא אם אמרת בשאר מצות שכן לא חייב בהן מיתה כו' וקשיא לן האי תנא מעיקרא אלימא ליה כרת ויליף מעילה שהוא במיתה מחייבי כריתות בקל וחומר והדר פריך תאמר במעילה שחייב בה מיתה מכלל שהמיתה חמורה מן הכרת ושנינן לעולם כרת חמורה כי פריך בפחות מכזית פריך דליתא בחייבי כריתות ואיתא במעילה שהיא במיתה ויליף חטא חטא מתרומה כתיב במעילה ונפש כי תמעול מעל וחטאה בשגגה

מקדשי

*) אולי צ"ל מכלל דבש"פ לבד לאבא שאול ג"כ חייב דאם איתא וכו'.

הזיד במעילה במיתה – רבי היא. דתניא: *הזיד במעילה, רבי אומר: במיתה, וחכמים אומרים: [א]באזהרה. מאי טעמא דרבי? אמר רבי אבהו: *גמר חטא חטא מתרומה, מה תרומה במיתה – אף מעילה במיתה. ומינה, מה תרומה בכזית – אף מעילה בכזית. ומתקיף לה רב פפא: ממאי דרבי כרבנן סבירא ליה? דילמא כאבא שאול סבירא ליה, דאמר: יש בה שוה פרוטה – אע"ג דלית בה כזית. והא רב פפא הוא דאמר דאבא שאול תרתי בעי! אלא ש"מ: הדר ביה. מר בריה דרבנא אמר, הכי קאמר: לא, אם אמרת בשאר מצות, שלא עשה בהן שאין מתכוין כמתכוין, שאם נתכוין לחתוך את התלוש וחתך את המחובר – שפטור. תאמר במעילה, שאם נתכוין להתחמם בגיזי חולין ונתחמם בגיזי עולה – שמעל. רב נחמן בר יצחק אמר, הכי קאמר: לא, אם אמרת בשאר מצות, שכן לא מתחייב בהן שאין מתעסק כמתעסק, שאם נתכוין להגביה את התלוש וחתך את המחובר – שפטור. תאמר במעילה, שאם הושיט ידו לכלי ליטול חפץ, וסך ידו בשמן של קודש – שמעל. אמר מר: בד"א – במפריש תרומה והחמיצה, אבל הפריש חמץ תרומה – דברי הכל אינה קדושה. מנא הני מילי? *אמר רב נחמן בר יצחק, אמר קרא: °"תתן לו" [דברים יח] – ולא לאורו. מתיב רב הונא בריה דרב יהושע: *[ב]אין תורמין מן *הטמאה לטהורה, ואם תרם בשוגג – תרומתו תרומה. ואמאי? לימא "לו" ולא לאורו! לא קשיא, התם – היתה לו שעת הכושר, הכא – לא היתה לו שעת הכושר. ודלא היתה לו שעת הכושר היכי דמי – כגון דאחמיץ במחובר, אבל אחמיץ בתלוש – הכי נמי דקדשה? א"ל: אין, °"בגזירת עירין פתגמא [דניאל ד] *ובמאמר קדישין שאילתא" וכן מורין בבי מדרשא כוותי. כי אתא רב הונא בריה דרב יהושע אמר

רש"י

הזיד. בהנאת קדש, ששגגתו מעילה: ר' אומר במיתה. כדמפרש: גמר חטא חטא, הנאת קדש מאכילת תרומה. כתיב הכא: "וחטאה בשגגה", וכתיב בתרומה: "לא ישאו עליו חטא ומתו בו" וגו' (ויקרא כב): וחכ"א באזהרה. רבנן נמי אית להו גזירה שוה דר', דהא עיקר מילתא דמעילה בהא גזירה שוה גמרי בפרק חמישי דמעילה (דף יח:) בברייתא גבי פגם ונהנה, ובדבר שפגם נהנה, ובתלוש מן הקרקע, ובשליח שעשה שליחותו – כל הני מתרומה גמרי בה, ואזהרה נמי מתרומה גמרי: מה אכילת תרומה הזהיר, דכתיב: (א) "לא יאכל קודש" – אף הנאת הקדש דמעילה הזהיר. ומיהו, מיתה לא גמרינן מינה, כדמפרשי רבנן טעמייהו בסנהדרין, דמיעט רחמנא בתרומה "ומתו בו", והאי "בו" מיעוטא: "בו" ולא במעילה. וכן עיקר: מאי טעמא דרבי גרסינן: ומינה. היינו נרגא. כלומר: וכיון דמיתה מהכא נפקא לן, על כרחיך הכי תילף: ומינה, מה תרומה מיתה הכתובה בה אכילה כתובה, דהוא כזית – אף מעילה אין מיתה עד דאיכא כזית. וליכא למימר דתנא הכי: תאמר במעילה שחייב בה מיתה בפחות מכזית: ומתקיף לה גרסינן: ומתקיף לה רב פפא. להני דשדו ביה נרגא: ממאי דרבי. בתרומה, כרבנן דפליגי אדאבא שאול סבירא ליה, דבעו כזית בתרומה? דילמא כאבא שאול סבירא ליה, ושפיר מצי למילף מינה מיתה במעילה, דהיא בשוה פרוטה מתרומה, אפילו לפחות מכזית: מר בריה דרבנא אמר. הא מתניתא דלעיל בשיבושא איתני בבי מדרשא, והכי קאמר סיפא: לא, אם אמרת בשאר מצות – שכן לא חייב בהן קרבן בשוגג (ב) שאין מתכוין לאותה מלאכה, כשוגג שמתכוין לאותה מלאכה: שאם נתכוון לחתוך את התלוש. שהוא מתכוין לדבר המותר, וחתך את המחובר, שאפילו בשבת פטור – דמלאכת מחשבת בעינן, שיתכוין לחתיכת מחובר. ומיהו, שגג בשבת, שאינו יודע שהוא שבת, או אינו יודע שהמלאכה זו אסורה: תאמר במעילה שאם נתכוון כו' שמעל. כגון: היו כאן גיזי חולין וגיזי עולה, ונתכוין ליטול של חולין והלכה ידו על של עולה, ומכיר הוא מי עולה ומי חולין, אלא שנסתכל במקום אחר, דהיינו שאין מתכוין למעשה זה. וחייב מעילה, ד"וחטאה בשגגה" כל דהו כתיב, ולא כתב בה מיעוטא כדכתיב בשבת: "מלאכת מחשבת", וכתיב בשאר מצות: "אשר חטא בה" – פרט למתעסק. והיינו מתעסק – שמתעסק בדבר אחר, ובא זה לידו: ר"נ בר יצחק אמר. הא לא הוה ליה למיתני, דהא בשאר מצות נמי, אם היה מתעסק בחתיכה ואפי' בשל היתר ועלתה בידו חתיכת איסור, ואע"ג דאין מתכוין לזו – מלאכת מחשבת היא, וחייב. אלא הכי קאמר: לא, אם אמרת בשאר מצות, שכן לא חייב בהן שאין מתעסק בדבר היתר ושגג באיסור כיוצא בו, כמתעסק בדבר היתר ועלה בידו איסור: שאם נתכוון להגביה את התלוש. דהיינו אין מתעסק בחתיכה לגמרי, ואפי' בשל היתר וחתך מחובר – שפטור, ולא עשאו כמתעסק לחתוך תלוש וחתך מחובר: תאמר במעילה שאם הושיט ידו כו'. ולא היה מתעסק בשום סיכה, ואפילו בשל היתר, וסך ידו בשמן של קודש שמעל: אמר מר במה דברים אמורים כו' דברי הכל. קאמר, ואפי' למאן דשרי הנאת חמץ בפסח קאמר: תתן לו. בתרומה כתיב, "ראשית דגנך" וגו': ולא לאורו. אפי' היא ראויה להסיק, הואיל ואינה ראויה לאכילה: אין תורמין מן הטמא על הטהור. לכתחלה, שמפסיד את הכהן: בשוגג. שלא ידע שטבל זה טמא: שהיתה לו שעת הכושר. שנראית כבר לתרומה, קודם שנטמא. והא דלעיל – בחמץ שלא היתה לו שעת הכושר לתרום ממנו, דקודם שחל הפסח היה מחובר, והחמיץ במחובר. וכל זמן חיבורו לא היה ראוי לחול שם תרומה עליו, ד"ראשית דגנך" כתיב – משנדגן, ודיגון לשון אסיפה והעמדת כרי הוא: עירין. מלאכים. כלומר: תלמידי חכמים, שהם כמלאכי השרת, אמרי בבית המדרש כמותי, דהא דקתני לעיל אינה קדושה – בשהחמיץ במחובר קאמר: ובמאמר קדישין שאילתא. מקרא הוא בדניאל: מורין. הוראה: כוותי. כמותי: רב הונא בריה דרב יהושע אמר. אפילו בשהחמיץ בתלוש נמי קאמר דאינה קדושה:

דקאמר

תוספות

ומינה מה תרומה בכזית. אע"ג דבסוף "כל התדיר" (זבחים לא:), ובפרק בתרא דמנחות (דף קז.) איכא למ"ד דרבי סבר דון מינה ואוקי באתרה – הכא אין לומר אוקי באתרה: מה מעילה דממון שוה פרוטה אף מעילה דאכילה כן. דהא אכילה דהקדש מאכילה דתרומה יליף, והיאך יהיה בו מיתה אם לא כשיעור אכילת תרומה? דבשאר נהנה ליכא מיתה אלא אאכילה, אפילו לרבי דומיא דתרומה. ואם תאמר, אמאי אין מפרש: לא אם אמרת בשאר מצות – שלא חייב מיתה עד דהוי כזית בכדי אכילת פרס, תאמר במעילה דאפי' בעינן כזית – הא תנן בפרק "הנהנה" (מעילה יח:): ליצרף את המעילה אפי' לזמן מרובה! וי"ל, דאיכא נמי למיפרך: דנילף מתרומה שלא יצטרף: **אף** מעילה בכזית. תימה לר"י: דהכא משמע דמאן דיליף חטא חטא סבירא ליה דמעילה בכזית כמו תרומה, וכולהו אית להו גזירה שוה דפרק "הנהנה" (גם זה שם) יליף מעילה מתרומה למילי טובא. ורבנן לא פליגי ארבי אלא לענין מיתה, משום דכתיב "בו" ולא במעילה. ואם כן, מ"ט דרבנן דלעיל, דאמרי לא אמר שוה פרוטה אלא לענין מעילה, אבל בתרומה – עד שיהא בו כזית: **נתכוין** לחתוך את התלוש ותלש את המחובר. ר"ת מפרש: נמצא שהוא מחובר, דאי נתכוון לחתוך תלוש זה וחתך מחובר אחר – מאי איריא נתכוון לתלוש, אפילו נתכוון לחתוך מחובר זה וחתך מחובר אחר פטור, הואיל ולא איתעבידא מחשבתו. דתניא בהדיא בפרק "ספק אכל" (כריתות כ.): היו לפניו שתי נרות, ונתכוון לכבות את זה וכבה את זה – פטור: **תתן** לו ולא לאורו. אור"י דלא איצטריך למידרש מ"לו" אלא לר' יוסי הגלילי, דאית ליה חמץ מותר בהנאה. °דלהנך תנאי דאסרי חמץ בהנאה – נפקא לן מ"ונתן לכהן את הקודש" – דבר הראוי להיות קודש. או מ"תתן" לחודיה – שאין ליתן אלא מידי דשרי בהנאה לכל הפחות, דשייכא ביה נתינה. ולכך משמע ליה למידרש מ"תתן לו" – דבר הראוי לאכילה, ולא דבר שאין ראוי אלא לאורו, והיינו תרומה טמאה, דלא חזיא אלא לאורו. דאיסור הנאה מ"תתן" נפקא. ואם תאמר: ובעל הגמרא, דבעי מנהני מילי, והא הנך תנאי דהך ברייתא דהפריש חמץ תרומה ד"ה אינה קדושה, כיון דסבירא להו דאסור בהנאה – דבר פשוט הוא דאינו קדוש, ומאי קבעי ליה? יש לומר: דפשיטא ליה לגמרא דלא איצטריך למיתני בברייתא ד"ה אלא לרבי יוסי הגלילי, דמשום דהנך דאסירי בהנאה לא איצטריך למיתני, ולהכי בעי: מנהני מילי לרבי יוסי הגלילי? אי נמי: רב נחמן גופיה, דמפרש "לו" ולא לאורו, קאמר "מה"מ" – לפי שהיה פשוט לו דאליבא דכ"ע קתני הכי, וכה"ג איכא בכמה דוכתי*:

אמר

עין משפט נר מצוה

צז א מיי' פ"א מהל' מעילה הלכה ג:

צח ב מיי' פ"ה מהל' תרומות הלכה ח:

[מן הטמא על הטהור כצ"ל]

[ומאמר קדישין כצ"ל]

[ועי' תוס' ביצה לח. ד"ה וא"ר יוחנן יומא עו. ד"ה הני ה' טעויין ב"מ כח. ד"ה וכמה ב"ב כב: ד"ה וכמה ובכורות כט. סוף ד"ה היכי ובנזיר ל. ד"ה פשיטא]

מסורת הש"ס

סנהדרין [פג.] פד.

[קדושין מב: סנהדרין פד. זבחים מה. תמורה ג. מעילה יח:]

שבת כה:

מנחות כה: תרומות פ"ב מ"ב יבמות פט.

תורה אור

הגהות הב"ח

(א) רש"י ד"ה וחכמים וכו' הזהיר דכתיב וכל זר לא יאכל: (ב) ד"ה מר בריה כו' בשוגג כשאין מתכוין:

גליון הש"ס

תוס' ד"ה תתן לו. להנך תנאי לאסרי חמץ בהנאה. יש לעיין דלכאורה לא צריך קרא כלל דהא אין יכול לקרות שם תרומ' לאיסורי הנא' דלאו דידי' הוי כדאמרינן ב' דברים עשאן הכתוב כו ועי' כריתות דף כד ע"א:

רבינו חננאל

מקדשי ה' וכתיב בתרומה ולא תשא עליו חטא בהרימכם את חלבו ונדחה ולא אשכחן מאן דאמר הזיד במעיל' במיתה אלא רבי דתניא הזיד במעילה ר' אומר במיתה וחכמים אומרים באזהרה ואמרינן מאי טעמא דרבי גמר חטא חטא מתרומה מה תרומה במיתה דכתיב ומתו בו כי יחללוהו אף מעילה במיתה ומינה מה תרומה בכזית חייב פחות מכזית פטור אף מעילה כך. ואסיקנא דודאי רב פפא דאמר אבא שאול בעי תרתי כזית ושוה פרוטה הדר ביה: **מר** בריה דרבנא אמר לא הכי קתני לא אם אמרת בשאר מצות שכן לא עשה בהן שאין מתכוין כמתכוין שאם נתכוון לחתוך את התלוש בשדה וחתך את המחובר שפטור תאמר במעילה שאם נתכוון להתחמם בגיזי חולין ונתחמם בגיזי עולה שמעל. ורב נחמן בר יצחק אמר שאם נתכוון להגביה התלוש וחתך המחובר פטור תאמר במעילה שאם נתכוון להושיט ידו לחביות ליטול חפץ וסך שמן של תרומה: **בד"א** במפריש תרומה והחמיצה אבל הפריש חמץ תרומה דברי הכל אינה קדושה דא"ק ראשית דגנך תתן לו כלומר תתן לו תרומה מה שהן ראויה לו לאכילה ולא מה שאין ראוי לו ואע"פ שראוי לאורו בעינן לו ממש ומותבינן מדתנן בתרומות פ"ב אין תורמין מן הטמא על הטהור ואם תרם בשוגג תרומתו תרומה אמאי והא אינה ראויה לו ופרקי' שאני הכא דהיתה לה שעת הכושר קודם שתטמא אבל הא דתניא הפריש חמץ תבואה בפסח דברי הכל אינה קדושה כגון שהוכשר החטים והחמיצו והן מחוברין קודם קצירתן שלא היתה להם שעת הכושר כלל. ואמרי' מכלל דאי היתה לה שעת הכושר כגון דהחמיצה אחר תלישה הכי נמי דקדשה. אמר ליה רב נחמן בר יצחק אין הכי נמי בגזירת עירין פתגמא ובמאמר קדישין שאלתא וכך מורין בבי מדרשא

צט א מיי' פ"ב מהל' תרומות הלכה יא ופ"ו מהל' איסורי מזבח הלכה ז:

ק ב מיי' פ"ט מהלכות טומאת אוכלין ה"ב: [שבת כו.]

קא ג ד מיי' פי"ב מהלכות תרומה הלכה יב:

אָמַר: אָמַר קְרָא °"רֵאשִׁית" – *שֶׁשְּׁיָרֶיהָ נִיכָּרִין לְיִשְׂרָאֵל, יָצְתָה זוֹ שֶׁאֵין שְׁיָרֶיהָ נִיכָּרִין. יְתֵיב רַב אַחָא בַּר רַב עָוְיָא קַמֵּיהּ דְּרַב חִסְדָּא, וִיתֵיב וְאָמַר מִשְּׁמֵיהּ דְּר' יוֹחָנָן: *אעֲנָבִים שֶׁנִּטְמְאוּ – דּוֹרְכָן פָּחוֹת פָּחוֹת מִכַּבֵּיצָה, וְיֵינָן כָּשֵׁר לַנְּסָכִין. אַלְמָא קָסָבַר: מַשְׁקִין מִיפְקַד פְּקִידִי, לְאֵימַת קָא מִיטַּמְּאִי – לְכִי סָחֵיט לְהוּ, לְכִי סָחֵיט לְהוּ לֵיתֵיהּ לְשִׁיעוּרֵיהּ. אִי הָכִי כַּבֵּיצָה נַמִי, *דְּהָתְנַן: בטְמֵא מֵת שֶׁסָּחַט זֵיתִים וַעֲנָבִים כְּבֵיצָה מְכוּוֶּנֶת – טְהוֹרִין! הָתָם – דְּאִי עֲבַד, הָכָא – לְכַתְּחִלָּה, גְּזֵירָה דִּילְמָא אָתֵי לְמֶיעְבַּד יוֹתֵר מִכַּבֵּיצָה. א"ל רַב חִסְדָּא: *מַאן צַיֵּית לָךְ וּלְרַבִּי יוֹחָנָן רַבָּךְ! וְכִי טוּמְאָה שֶׁבָּהֶן לְהֵיכָן הָלְכָה? אַלְמָא קָא סָבַר: מַשְׁקִין מִיבְלַע בְּלִיעִי, וְכֵיוָן דְּאִיטַּמּוּ לֵיהּ אוֹכְלָא – אִיטַּמּוּ לֵיהּ מַשְׁקִין. אֲמַר לֵיהּ: וְאַתְּ לָא תִּיסְבְּרָא דְּמַשְׁקִין מִיפְקַד פְּקִידִי? וְהָתְנַן: טְמֵא מֵת שֶׁסָּחַט זֵיתִים וַעֲנָבִים *מְכוּוֶּנֶת כַּבֵּיצָה – טְהוֹרִין. אִי אָמְרַתְּ בִּשְׁלָמָא מִיפְקַד פְּקִידִי – מִשּׁוּם הָכִי טְהוֹרִין, אֶלָּא אִי אָמְרַתְּ מִיבְלַע בְּלִיעִי אַמַּאי טְהוֹרִין? א"ל: הָכָא בְּמַאי עָסְקִינַן – בַּעֲנָבִים שֶׁלֹּא הוּכְשְׁרוּ. לְאֵימַת מִתַּכְשְׁרִי – לְכִי סָחֵיט לְהוּ, *כִּי סָחֵיט לְהוּ בְּצִיר לְהוּ שִׁיעוּרָא. דְּאִי לָא תֵּימָא הָכִי, הָא דְּתַנְיָא: *הָא לָמָה זֶה דּוֹמֶה – לִתְרוּמַת תּוּתִין (זֵיתִים) וַעֲנָבִים שֶׁנִּטְמְאָה, שֶׁאֵין לוֹ בָּהּ לֹא הֶיתֵּר אֲכִילָה וְלֹא הֶיתֵּר הַסָּקָה. הָא הֶיתֵּר אֲכִילָה נַמִי אִית בֵּיהּ, דְּאִי בָּעֵי דָּרֵיךְ לְהוּ פָּחוֹת פָּחוֹת מִכַּבֵּיצָה! אָמַר רָבָא: גְּזֵירָה *דִּילְמָא אָתֵי בְּהוּ לִידֵי תַּקָּלָה. אֲמַר לֵיהּ אַבַּיֵּי: וּמִי חָיְישִׁינַן לְתַקָּלָה? וְהָא תַּנְיָא: מַדְלִיקִין בְּפַת וּבְשֶׁמֶן שֶׁל תְּרוּמָה שֶׁנִּטְמֵאת! אֲמַר לֵיהּ: גפַּת – זָרֵיק לֵיהּ בֵּין הָעֵצִים, שֶׁמֶן שֶׁל תְּרוּמָה – רָמֵי לֵיהּ בִּכְלִי מָאוּס. גּוּפָא, מַדְלִיקִין בְּפַת וּבְשֶׁמֶן שֶׁל תְּרוּמָה שֶׁנִּטְמֵאת. אַבַּיֵּי אָמַר מִשְּׁמֵיהּ דְּחִזְקִיָּה, וְרָבָא אָמַר דְּבֵי רַבִּי יִצְחָק בַּר מָרְתָא, אָמַר רַב הוּנָא: לֹא שָׁנוּ אֶלָּא פַּת, אֲבָל חִיטֵּי – לֹא, שֶׁמָּא יָבֹא בָּהֶן לִידֵי תַּקָּלָה. וְרַבִּי יוֹחָנָן אָמַר: דאֲפִילּוּ חִיטֵּי. וְאַמַּאי? נֵיחוּשׁ דִּילְמָא אָתֵי בָּהֶן לִידֵי תַּקָּלָה! כִּדְאָמַר רַב אַשִׁי:

בִּשְׁלִיקְתָא

רש"י

דְּאָמַר קְרָא רֵאשִׁית. מַשְׁמַע שֶׁתְּהֵא הִיא רֵאשִׁית, וְאֵלּוּ שִׁירַיִים נִיכָּרִים – שֶׁתְּהֵא הִיא מַתִּירָתָן לְיִשְׂרָאֵל. וְאִי בְּמַפְרִישׁ תְּרוּמַת חָמֵץ – מַה הֶיתֵּר יֵשׁ בִּשְׁיָרֶיהָ שֶׁתְּהֵא רֵאשִׁיתָן עוֹשָׂה שִׁירַיִים? כִּי הֲווּ מֵעִיקָּרָא טֶבֶל הֲווּ שָׁרֵי בַּהֲנָאָה וַאֲסוּרִין בַּאֲכִילָה – הָשְׁתָּא נַמִי שָׁרוּ בַּהֲנָאָה וַאֲסוּרִין בַּאֲכִילָה מִשּׁוּם חָמֵץ, וּלְעִנְיַן מַאי הָווּ שִׁירַיִים?

פָּחוֹת מִכַּבֵּיצָה. אוֹכֶל טָמֵא, אֵין מְטַמֵּא אֲחֵרִים: וְיֵינָן כָּשֵׁר לִנְסָכִים. דְּאֵינוֹ מְטַמֵּא: קָסָבַר מַשְׁקִין מִיפְקַד פְּקִידִי. מוּפְקָדִין הֵן בְּתוֹךְ הַזָּג, וְאֵינָן חִיבּוּר לוֹ, אֶלָּא כְּמִי שֶׁנּוֹתְנִין בִּכְלִי. וּכְשֶׁנִּטְמָא הַזָּג – לֹא נִטְמָא מַשְׁקֶה בִּכְלַל זָג טוּמְאַת אוֹכָלִין, דְּלָאו אוֹכֶל דִּכְוָותֵיהּ חֲשִׁיבִי בַּהֲדַיְיהוּ. וְטוּמְאַת מַשְׁקִין נַמִי לֹא נִטְמְאוּ. וְאַע"פ שֶׁמַּשְׁקֶה מְקַבֵּל טוּמְאָה בְּכָל שֶׁהוּא – דְּלֹא הָיָה שָׁם מַשְׁקֶה עָלָיו מֵעוֹלָם, וְאֵין צֵירוּף חֲבֵירָיו עִמּוֹ – דְּהָא זָג זֶה לֹא נָגַע בְּמַשְׁקִין שֶׁבַּחֲבֵירוֹ: לְאֵימַת מִיטַּמּוּ. מַשְׁקִין – לְכִי סָחֵיט לְהוּ, וְהַנִּסְחָטִין נוֹגְעִין לְכָל הַזָּגִים יַחַד, וְכִי סָחֵיט לְהוּ – לֵיתֵיהּ לְשִׁיעוּרֵיהּ, דְּאֵין בַּזָּגִין כַּבֵּיצָה לִיתֵּן טוּמְאָה, דְּהָא פָּחוֹת מִכַּבֵּיצָה דָּרַךְ: בְּכַבֵּיצָה נַמִי. דְּהָא כִּי נָפֵיק מַשְׁקִין מִינַּיְיהוּ – חָסֵר לֵיהּ שִׁיעוּרֵיהּ. אוֹכֶל וּמַשְׁקֶה מְקַבֵּל טוּמְאָה בְּכָל שֶׁהֵן, אֲבָל אֵין מְטַמֵּא אֲחֵרִים אֶלָּא אוֹכֶל כַּבֵּיצָה וּמַשְׁקֶה בִּרְבִיעִית. וְהָכִי תַּנְיָא בְּתוֹרַת כֹּהֲנִים: "מִכָּל הָאוֹכֶל" – מְלַמֵּד שֶׁמִּטַּמֵּא בְּכָל שֶׁהוּא. יָכוֹל יְטַמֵּא לַאֲחֵרִים בְּכָל שֶׁהוּא – ת"ל: "אֲשֶׁר יֵאָכֵל" – אוֹכֶל הַנֶּאֱכָל בְּבַת אַחַת, וְהַיְינוּ כַּבֵּיצָה, כִּדְאָמְרִינַן בְּפֶרֶק יוה"כ (יומא פ.): אֵין בֵּית הַבְּלִיעָה מַחֲזֶקֶת יוֹתֵר מִבֵּיצַת תַּרְנְגוֹלֶת. וַאֲנִי שָׁמַעְתִּי דְּאַף לְקַבֵּל טוּמְאָה בָּעֵי כַּבֵּיצָה: טְמֵא מֵת שֶׁסָּחַט זֵיתִים וַעֲנָבִים כְּבֵיצָה מְכוּוֶּנֶת טָהוֹר. וְכִדְמַסִּיק מִילְּתָא בְּמַסֶּכֶת טְהָרוֹת: וּבִלְבַד שֶׁלֹּא יִגַּע בַּמַּשְׁקֶה. וּכְגוֹן שֶׁדְּרָכָן בִּפְשׁוּטֵי כְּלֵי עֵץ, שֶׁאֵין מִטַּמְּאִין, שֶׁאֵין כָּאן מְטַמֵּא מַשְׁקֶה אֶלָּא הַזָּגִין שֶׁנָּגַע בָּהֶן הַטָּמֵא קוֹדֶם לָכֵן בְּיָדַיִם, שֶׁהוּא לֹא נִזְהָר אֶלָּא מִשֶּׁיֵּצֵא מַשְׁקֶה, וּכְשֶׁהַמַּשְׁקִין נוֹגְעִין בַּזָּגִין – כְּבָר חָסַר שִׁיעוּר כַּבֵּיצָה. וְיוֹתֵר מִכַּבֵּיצָה כָּל דְּהוּ קָתָנֵי הָתָם בְּהֶדְיָא טָמֵא, שֶׁכֵּיוָן שֶׁיָּצְאָה טִפָּה רִאשׁוֹנָה – נִטְמֵאת הַטִּפָּה בְּכַבֵּיצָה, שֶׁעֲדַיִין הָיָה בָּאוֹכֶל כַּבֵּיצָה. אע"ג דְּאֵין מַשְׁקֶה הַנִּבְלָע בָּאוֹכֶל מְקַבֵּל טוּמְאָה עִמּוֹ – מַשְׁלִים הוּא אֶת שִׁיעוּרוֹ. דִּכְוָותָהּ תְּנַן הָתָם טוּבָא. וּבִמְנָחוֹת (דף נד:) נַמִי מַיְיתֵי לָהּ בַּגְּמָרָא: כַּבֵּיצָה אוֹכָלִין שֶׁהִנִּיחוּ בַּחַמָּה וְנִתְמַעֲטוּ – טְהוֹרִין, וְכֵן כַּזַּיִת חֵלֶב וּפִיגּוּל וְנוֹתָר. חָזַר וְהִנִּיחָן בַּגְּשָׁמִים וְתָפְחוּ – טְמֵאִין, וְחַיָּיבִין עֲלֵיהֶן מִשּׁוּם פִּיגּוּל וְנוֹתָר וְחֵלֶב. וְאע"ג דִּגְשָׁמִים הַנִּבְלָעִין בְּתוֹכוֹ לָאו חֵלֶב נִינְהוּ, דְּאִי סָחֵיט לְהוּ וְשָׁתֵי מִינַּיְיהוּ כַּזַּיִת פָּטוּר, אֲפִילּוּ הָכִי, כָּל כַּמָּה דִּבְגַוֵּיהּ נִינְהוּ – מַשְׁלְמֵי לְשִׁיעוּרֵיהּ. וּטְמֵא מֵת דַּוְקָא נָקַט, שֶׁאֵינוֹ מְטַמֵּא בְּהֶיסֵּט. וְהוּא הַדִּין לִטְמֵא שֶׁרֶץ וְכָל טוּמְאַת מַגָּע, וְרֵישָׁא דְּכוּלְּהוּ נָקַט. אֲבָל זָב, שֶׁמְּטַמֵּא בְּהֶיסֵּט, שֶׁסָּחַט אֲפִילּוּ גַּרְגִּיר יְחִידִי – תְּנַן הָתָם דִּמְטַמֵּא אֲפִילּוּ בִּפְשׁוּטֵי כְּלֵי עֵץ, דְּכֵיוָן דְּיָצְאָת טִפָּה רִאשׁוֹנָה *וְנִטַּל הָעֵץ וְהִגְבִּיהוֹ – נִטְמְאוּ מַשְׁקִין שֶׁעַל הָעֵץ בְּמַשָּׂא, דְּמַשְׁקֶה מְקַבֵּל טוּמְאָה בְּכָל שֶׁהוּא. וּכְשֶׁחָזַר וּנְתָנוֹ לְתוֹכוֹ – נִתְעָרֵב טָמֵא בַּטָּהוֹר, וְהַכֹּל טָמֵא: הָתָם דְּאִי עָבֵיד קָאָמַר. שֶׁסָּחַט. אֲבָל הָכָא, בְּבָא לִימָּלֵךְ מַה יַּעֲשֶׂה – נֵימָא לֵיהּ: דְּרוֹךְ פָּחוֹת מִכַּבֵּיצָה, אֲבָל כַּבֵּיצָה לֹא, דִּילְמָא אָתֵי לְמֶיעְבַּד יוֹתֵר מִכַּבֵּיצָה, וּכְשֶׁיּוֹצְאָה טִפָּה רִאשׁוֹנָה עֲדַיִין יֵשׁ בָּאוֹכֶל כַּבֵּיצָה, וְנִטְמֵאת הַטִּפָּה וְחוֹזֶרֶת וּמִתְעָרֶבֶת בַּמַּשְׁקִין: טוּמְאָה שֶׁבָּהֶן. שֶׁקִּיבְּלוּ תְּחִלָּה עִם הָאוֹכֶל כְּשֶׁנִּטְמְאוּ הָעֲנָבִים: מַשְׁקִין בְּלִיעִי. בָּאוֹכֶל הֵן בְּלוּעִין מִכָּל דְּפָנוֹתָיו, וְחִיבּוּר הֵן לוֹ, וְנִטְמְאוּ עִמּוֹ: אַמַּאי טְהוֹרִין. הֲרֵי נִטְמְאוּ הָעֲנָבִים בְּמַגַּע טְמֵא מֵת, וְאע"פ שֶׁלֹּא נָגַע בַּמַּשְׁקֶה – נִטְמָא: כִּי סָחֵיט לְהוּ לֵיתֵיהּ לְשִׁיעוּרֵיהּ. וּכְשֶׁנּוֹגֵעַ בָּאוֹכֶל הַנָּגוּב וְדוֹחֵהוּ אֶל תַּחַת הַמָּדוֹךְ – אֵין בָּהֶן שִׁיעוּר כְּדֵי לְקַבֵּל טוּמְאָה, וְהוּא זָהִיר מִלִּיגַּע בַּמַּשְׁקֶה, כִּדְקָתָנֵי בְּהֶדְיָא: וּבִלְבַד שֶׁלֹּא יִגַּע בִּמְקוֹם הַמַּשְׁקֶה: דְּאִי לָא תֵּימָא הָכִי. דְּמַשְׁקִין בְּלִיעִי וְאִיטַּמּוּ, אֶלָּא מִיפְקַד פְּקִידִי, וְאֵין מִטַּמְּאִין בִּנְגִיעַת טוּמְאָה בָּאוֹכֶל: הָא דְּתַנְיָא. לְעֵיל כו' לִתְרוּמַת תּוּתִים וַעֲנָבִים, דְּמַשְׁמַע שֶׁנִּטְמְאוּ תּוּתִים וַעֲנָבִים קוֹדֶם דְּרִיכָה, וְקָתָנֵי: אֵין לוֹ בָּהּ הֶיתֵּר אֲכִילָה. הָא הֶיתֵּר אֲכִילָה נַמִי אִית בָּהּ! דְּאִי בָּעֵי, דָּרֵיךְ לָהּ פָּחוֹת מִכַּבֵּיצָה: לִידֵי תַּקָּלָה. כְּשֶׁהוּא דּוֹרְכָן, שֶׁמָּא יֹאכַל מֵהֶן: מַדְלִיקִין בְּפַת וּבְשֶׁמֶן כו'. וְהָא וַדַּאי בְּחַד שַׁעְתָּא לָא מַדְלִיק שֶׁמֶן כּוּלֵּיהּ, אֶלָּא לִזְמַן מְרוּבֶּה, וְלָא חָיְישִׁינַן דִּילְמָא אָכֵיל מִינֵּיהּ: אֶלָּא פַּת. דְּכִי זָרֵיק לֵיהּ מִמְּאִיסָא, וְתוּ לָא אָתֵי לְמֵיכְלֵיהּ: אֲבָל חִיטֵּי. אִי נַמִי זָרֵיק לְהוּ – לָא מִמְּאִיסֵי:

בִּשְׁלִיקְתָא

תוספות

אמר קרא ראשית ששיריה ניכרים. ואם תאמר: והא שיריה ניכרים, דמעיקרא הוה אסירא בהנאה של כילוי, כגון הדלקה וכיוצא בו, מידי דהוה אטבל טמא דאין מדליקין בו. ומשעת הרמה ואילך – מדליקין בו! וי"ל: דדוקא בטבל טמא אין מדליקין, כדדרשינן: *"את משמרת תרומותי" – בשתי תרומות הכתוב מדבר, מה תרומה טהורה אין לך בה אלא משעת הרמה ואילך,– אף תרומה וכו'. אבל בטבל של חמץ – מדליקין, דלא איירי אלא בשתי תרומות:

לאימת מתכשרי לכי סחיט להו וכי סחיט להו בציר ליה שיעוריה. מכאן מקשה ר"ת לפ"ה, דפירש דכל שהוא מקבל טומאה מן התורה. דהא מכי נפיק מינה פורתא מתכשרי, ומיד מקבל טומאה כל הנשאר, דמשקין מיבלע בליעי! וה"ר יוסף תירץ: דאע"פ שאוכל מקבל טומאה בפחות מכביצה – אין מקבל הכשר בפחות מכביצה. ואומר ר"י: דהיינו טעמא ד"מאשר יאכל" נפקא ליה לטמא אחרים בכביצה – אוכל הנאכל בבת אחת. ועלה קאי "אשר יבא עליו מים" אלמא: לא מקבל הכשר בפחות מכביצה. ועוד מקשה ר"ת, דאמרינן בפ' "אלו עוברין" (לקמן מד.): השום והשמן של תרומה ומקפה של חולין ונגע טבול יום במקצתו – לא פסל אלא מקום מגעו. וכתב בכל הספרים: והוינן בה, מקום מגעו אמאי פסול? והא לא הוי כביצה! אלמא: לא מקבל טומאה בכל שהוא. ורש"י מוחק שם מן הספרים, ומפרש בדוחק. ועוד, ה"ר אליהו מביא ראיה מת"כ, דדרשינן גבי כלי חרס דכתיב "ואותו תשבורו": אותו אתה שובר לטהרתו, ואי אתה שובר אוכלין לטהרתן. ואי מקבל טומאה בכל שהוא – פשיטא דלא מהני להו שבירה! והיא דת"כ שהביא רש"י, שאוכל מטמא בכל שהוא – אסמכתא היא, ומילי טובא מפיק מקרא בת"כ וליתנהו אלא אסמכתא. ורש"י בעצמו חזר בו בפ' "אותו ואת בנו" (חולין דף פב.) בשמעתא דפרה מטמאה טומאת אוכלים, דהקשה: למה לה קבלת טומאה היא גופה מטמא אדם ובגדים! ותירץ רש"י: דכי האי גוונא מפרש בכריתות בפ' "דם שחיטה" (דף כא.): כגון שחיפוה בפחות מכביצה בצק. אי משוית ליה אוכל – מצטרף ליה בהדי בצק, ומקבל האי בצק טומאה אם יגע בטומאה. ומטמא שאר אוכלין. ואי לאו אוכל הוא – לא מקבל האי בצק טומאה, דלית בה שיעור, וכי נגעי ביה אוכלין אחריני – טהורין הן, שאין נוגעין בנבילה אלא בבצק. לשון רש"י: [וע"ע תוס' שבת לא. ד"ה אי לענין ותו' זבחים לא. ד"ה אמר]

בשליקתא

רבינו חננאל

מדרשא כואתי: רב הונא בריה דרב יהושע אמר בעינן ראשית ששיריה מותר לישראל יצאת תרומת חמץ בפסח ששיריה אסורה לישראל: אמרי משמיה דר' יוחנן ענבים שנטמאו דורכן פחות פחות מכביצה ויינם כשר לנסכים אלמא קסבר משקין מיפקד פקיד בזוגין ולא נגע בהו טומאה אימת איטמו לכי סחיט להו בתר דסחיט להו ליכא אוכל כביצה דלטמא להו להני משקין ואקשי' אי הכי לדרכינון אפי' כביצה נמי דהא תנן בטהרות פ"ג טמא מת שסחט זיתים וענבים כביצה מכוונת משקה הנסחט מהן טהור ובלבד שלא יגע במקום המשקה יתר מכביצה טמא שמכיון שיצאת טיפה ראשונה נמצאת מכביצה ושני' מתני' התם משום דאיעבד וסחט אבל לכתחלה לא שרינן ליה דאי שרינ' כביצה חיישי' דלמא אתי למעבד הוא ביותר מכביצה ותנן יתר מכביצה טמא שמכיון שיצאת טיפה ראשונ' נטמאת מכביצה לפיכך לא שרינן אלא פחות פחות מכביצה: אמר רב חסדא והלא ענבים הללו שנטמאו קתני מכלל דטמאין הם ואם כן טומאה שלהם להיכן הלכה דיינן כשר לנסכים ודייקי' מדבריו דאמר אנה הלכה טומאתן מכלל דקסבר הוא משק' בענבים מבלע בליעי וכיון שנטמאו הענבים הן והמשקין שבהן נטמאו ביחד וכיון שנטמאו יחד אנה הלכה טומאתן ואקשי' איני שאם נטמאו הענבים נטמאו גם המשקין והא טמא מת שנגע בענבים טמאן ותנן טמא מת שסחט ענבים כביצה מכוונת טהור אע"פ שנגע בהן וטמאן ואי אמרת נטמאו גם המשקין אמאי תנן טהור ושנינ' אליבא דרב חסדא בשלא הוכשרו ולא טמאן מגע טמא מת אימת מטמו לכי מתכשרו מן המשק' דמסחטי מינייהו בתר דסחטו מינייהו כל דהו בצר ליה שיעורו דביצה דהא כביצה מכוונת הוו וכיון דבצרו מכביצה לא מטמו אבל הני ענבים דאמר ר' יוחנן הוכשרו דהא נטמאו קאמר דאי לא תימא הכי דמשקה בענבים בליע הא דתניא הא למה זה דומה לתרומת תותים וענבים שנטמאת שאין לה היתר אכילה ולא היתר הסקה כלל אמאי לית ליה והא אי דרך להו פחות פחות מכביצה שרו בשתיה. אמר רב פפא ההיא גזירה היא משום דחיישי' דלמא אתי לידי תקלה כלומר כמות שהם או יסחטם יותר מכביצה: מותיב עליה אביי מדליקין בפת ובשמן של תרומה שנטמאת ואי חיישינן דלמא אתי לידי תקלה היכי שרינן ליה ושני' פת זורקה לבין העצים שמן נמי רמי ליה בבלי מאום וכיון דמאיסי לא אתי למיכל מינייהו וכן חיטי

[עירובין לז: חולין קטז:] [לקמן לד: ע"ש תוס' חולין קיז: ד"ה ולא שומר] שבת קמה: טהרות פ"ג [מ"ג] [נדרים נט. שבועות יז: מעילה יג:] [נ"ל כביצה מכוונת] [עי' תוס' כריתות יג. ד"ה כיון דינק] ס"א ל"ג [לעיל כ: וש"נ] [לעיל לב.] ס"א ונתנו בתוכו

גליון הש"ס

גמ' יצאתה זו שאין שיריה נכרין. תמוה לי דא"כ לא תליא כלל בתרומ' אם היא חמץ או לא ותלי הכל בשיריים דמשכחת דמפריש תרומת חמץ ביש לו סאה חמץ וט' סאין שאינן חמץ דיכול לקרות לסאה חמץ תרומה על הט' סאין דהא שיריה נכרין ובהיפוך אם הט' סאין חמץ וסאה שאינו חמץ א"י להפריש סאה זו על הט' סאין דאין שיריה נכרין: דורכן פחות. עיין חולין קי"ז ע"ב תוס' ד"ה ולא שומר: א"ל אביי ומי חיישינן לתקלה. ק"ל דאיך סבר אביי דלא חיישי' לתקלה דמשקין בלועי וטמאים מ"מ הא חזי לזילוף אע"כ דחיישי' לתקלה וכמ"ש רש"י לעיל דף לב ע"א וצ"ע: בתום' ד"ה לאימת וכו' אין מקבל הכשר. עיין כריתות יג ע"א תוס' ד"ה כיון:

בִּשְׁלִיקָתָא וּמְאִיסְתָּא. הָכִי נַמִּי – בִּשְׁלִיקָתָא וּמְאִיסְתָּא. וְהֵיכָא אִיתְּמַר דְּרַב אַשִׁי? אַהָא, דְּאָמַר רַבִּי אָבִין בַּר רַב אַחָא א"ר יִצְחָק: אַבָּא שָׁאוּל גַּבָּל שֶׁל בֵּית רַבִּי הָיָה, וְהָיוּ מְחַמְּמִין לוֹ חַמִּין בְּחִיטִּין שֶׁל תְּרוּמָה טְמֵאָה לָלוּשׁ בָּהֶן עִיסָּה בְּטָהֳרָה. אַמַּאי? נֵיחוּשׁ דִּילְמָא אָתֵי בְּהוּ לִידֵי תַּקָּלָה! א"ר אַשִׁי: בִּשְׁלִיקָתָא וּמְאִיסְתָּא. אַבַּיֵי בַּר אָבִין וְרַב חֲנַנְיָא בַּר אָבִין תָּנוּ תְּרוּמוֹת בֵּי רַבָּה, פָּגַע בְּהוּ רָבָא בַּר מַתָּנָה, אֲמַר לְהוּ: מַאי אַמְרִיתוּ בִּתְרוּמוֹת דְּבֵי מָר? אֲמַרוּ לֵיהּ: וּמַאי קַשְׁיָא לָךְ? אֲמַר לְהוּ: *תְּנַן, אשְׁתִילֵי תְרוּמוֹת שֶׁנִּטְמְאוּ וּשְׁתָלָן(א) – טְהוֹרִים מִלְּטַמֵּא וַאֲסוּרִין מִלֶּאֱכוֹל (בַּתְּרוּמָה). וְכִי מֵאַחַר דִּטְהוֹרִין מִלְּטַמֵּא אַמַּאי אֲסוּרִין מִלֶּאֱכוֹל? אֲמַרוּ לֵיהּ, הָכִי אָמַר רַבָּה: מַאי אֲסוּרִין – אֲסוּרִין לְזָרִים. וּמַאי קמ"ל – גִּידוּלֵי תְרוּמָה תְּרוּמָה, *תְּנֵינָא: בגִּידוּלֵי תְרוּמָה תְּרוּמָה! וְכִי תֵּימָא: גִּידוּלֵי גִּידוּלִין וּמַאי קמ"ל – בְּדָבָר שֶׁאֵין זַרְעוֹ כָּלֶה, *הָא נַמִּי תְּנֵינָא: גהַטֶּבֶל גִּידוּלָיו מוּתָּרִין בְּדָבָר שֶׁזַּרְעוֹ כָּלֶה, אֲבָל בְּדָבָר שֶׁאֵין זַרְעוֹ כָּלֶה – אֲפִי' גִּידוּלֵי גִּידוּלִין אֲסוּרִין בַּאֲכִילָה! אִישְׁתִּיקוּ. א"ל: מִידִי שְׁמִיעַ לָךְ בְּהָא? אֲמַר לְהוּ: הָכִי אֲמַר רַב שֵׁשֶׁת: מַאי אֲסוּרִין – דאֲסוּרִין לַכֹּהֲנִים, הוֹאִיל וְאִיפְּסִילוּ לְהוּ בְּהֶיסַּח הַדַּעַת. הָנִיחָא לְמ"ד: "הֶיסַּח הַדַּעַת פְּסוּל הַגּוּף הָוֵי" – שַׁפִּיר, אֶלָּא לְמ"ד: "הֶיסַּח הַדַּעַת פְּסוּל טוּמְאָה הָוֵי" מַאי אִיכָּא לְמֵימַר? דְּאִיתְּמַר: הֶיסַּח הַדַּעַת, רַבִּי יוֹחָנָן אָמַר: הפְּסוּל טוּמְאָה הָוֵי, וְרַבִּי שִׁמְעוֹן בֶּן לָקִישׁ אָמַר: פְּסוּל הַגּוּף הָוֵי. רַבִּי יוֹחָנָן אָמַר: פְּסוּל טוּמְאָה הָוֵי, שֶׁאִם יָבֹא אֵלִיָּהוּ וִיטַהֲרֶנָּה – שׁוֹמְעִין לוֹ. רַבִּי שִׁמְעוֹן בֶּן לָקִישׁ אוֹמֵר: פְּסוּל הַגּוּף הָוֵי, שֶׁאִם יָבֹא אֵלִיָּהוּ וִיטַהֲרֶנָּה – אֵין שׁוֹמְעִין לוֹ. אֵיתִיבֵיהּ רַבִּי יוֹחָנָן לרשב"ל: *ר' יִשְׁמָעֵאל בְּנוֹ שֶׁל רַבִּי יוֹחָנָן בֶּן בְּרוֹקָא אוֹמֵר: *ולוּל קָטָן הָיָה בֵּין כֶּבֶשׁ לַמִּזְבֵּחַ בְּמַעֲרָבוֹ שֶׁל כֶּבֶשׁ, שֶׁשָּׁם הָיוּ זוֹרְקִין פְּסוּלֵי חַטַּאת הָעוֹף, וּתְעוּבַּר צוּרָתָן וְיוֹצְאִין לְבֵית הַשְּׂרֵיפָה. אִי אָמְרַתְּ בִּשְׁלָמָא פְּסוּל טוּמְאָה הָוֵי – מִשּׁוּם הָכִי בָּעֵי עִיבּוּר צוּרָה, שֶׁמָּא יָבֹא אֵלִיָּהוּ וִיטַהֲרֶנָּה, אֶלָּא אִי אָמְרַתְּ פְּסוּל הַגּוּף, לָמָּה לִי עִיבּוּר צוּרָה? *וְהָתְנַן, *זֶה הַכְּלָל: כל

רש"י

בשליקתא ומאיסתא. לאחר שנטמאו שולקן, ואח"כ זורקן לבין העצים והן נמאסות. ורב הונא חייש דלמא אכיל להו מקמי דלשלקינהו, או בשעה ששולקן. והיו מחמין לו חמין בחיטין של תרומה טמאה. שהיו לוקחין אותם מכהנים בזול: ללוש בהן עיסה בטהרה. כלומר: אע"פ שרבי אוכל חולין בטהרה היה – לא חייש דילמא נגעו הני חטים טמאים בעיסה – דבטלו להו מתורת אוכל ולא מטמאו: תנו תרומות. מסכת תרומות: מאי אמריתו. תירוש וטעמא בתרומות שאתם שונים בבית ...

תוספות

בשליקתא ומאיסתא. קצת נראה דוקא שהן כבר מאוסות מותר להסיקן אבל למאס – אסור, דבתוך כך אתי בה לידי תקלה, כמו בדריכת ענבים דבפרק "הלוקח בהמה" (בכורות דף לג.) אמרינן: סאה תרומה טמאה שנפלה לתוך מאה חולין טהורים, ר"א אומר: תרום ותרקב. וכמס' תרומות בפ"ה גרסינן: תרום ותשרף. ואומר ר"ת: דבמאיסתא – תשרף, ויהנה ממנו בשעת שריפה: **מחמין** לו חמין בחיטין של תרומה. פי' ר"ת: לכהנים של בית רבי היו עושין. ...

עין משפט
נר מצוה

קח א מיי' פ"ד מהל' ק"פ הלכה ג:

קט ב מיי' פ"ח מהל' פסולי המוקדשין הלכה לג:

קי ג מיי' פ"ו מהלכות איסורי מזבח הל' ו:

קיא ד שם הלכה ח:

קיב [ה מיי' פי"ב מהל' תרומות הלכה יח:

*[א]כׇּל שֶׁפְּסוּלוֹ בְּגוּפוֹ – יִשָּׂרֵף מִיָּד, בְּדָם וּבִבְעָלִים – תְּעוּבַּר צוּרָתָן וְיוֹצְאִין לְבֵית הַשְּׂרֵיפָה! א"ל: הַאי תַּנָּא – תַּנָּא דְּבֵי רַבָּה בַּר אֲבוּהּ הוּא, *דְּאָמַר: אֲפִילּוּ פִּיגּוּל טָעוּן עִיבּוּר צוּרָה. *אֵיתִיבֵיהּ: נִטְמָא אוֹ שֶׁנִּפְסַל הַבָּשָׂר, אוֹ שֶׁיָּצָא חוּץ לַקְּלָעִים, רַבִּי אֱלִיעֶזֶר אוֹמֵר: יִזְרוֹק, רַבִּי יְהוֹשֻׁעַ אוֹמֵר: [ב]לֹא יִזְרוֹק. וּמוֹדֶה רַבִּי יְהוֹשֻׁעַ שֶׁאִם זָרַק – הוּרְצָה. מַאי נִפְסַל – לָאו בְּהֶיסַּח הַדַּעַת? אִי אָמְרַתְּ בִּשְׁלָמָא פְּסוּלֵי טוּמְאָה הָוֵי – הַיְינוּ דְּמַשְׁכַּחַתְּ לַהּ דִּמְרַצֵּי צִיץ. אֶלָּא אִי אָמְרַתְּ פְּסוּל הַגּוּף הָוֵי – אַמַּאי הוּרְצָה (צִיץ)? מַאי נִפְסַל – נִפְסַל בִּטְבוּל יוֹם. אִי הָכִי הַיְינוּ טָמֵא! תְּרֵי גַּוְונֵי טָמֵא. כִּי סְלֵיק רָבִין אֲמָרָהּ לִשְׁמַעְתֵּיהּ קַמֵּיהּ דְּר' יִרְמְיָה, *וַאֲמַר: בַּבְלָאֵי טִפְּשָׁאֵי, מִשּׁוּם דְּיָתְבִי בְּאַרְעָא דַּחֲשׁוֹכָא אֲמַרִיתוּן שְׁמַעְתָּתָא דִּמְחַשְׁכוּ! לָא שְׁמִיעַ לְכוּ הָא דְּרַבִּי שִׁמְעוֹן בֶּן לָקִישׁ מִשְּׁמֵיהּ דְּר' אוֹשַׁעְיָא: [ג]מֵי הֶחָג שֶׁנִּטְמְאוּ, הִשִּׁיקָן וְאַחַר כָּךְ הִקְדִּישָׁן – טְהוֹרִין, הִקְדִּישָׁן וְאַחַ"כ הִשִּׁיקָן – טְמֵאִים. מִכְּדִי, זְרִיעָה נִינְהוּ – מָה לִי הִשִּׁיקָן וְאַחַ"כ הִקְדִּישָׁן, מָה לִי הִקְדִּישָׁן וְאַחַר כָּךְ הִשִּׁיקָן? אַלְמָא: [ד]אֵין זְרִיעָה לְהֶקְדֵּשׁ. הָכָא נַמִי: אֵין זְרִיעָה לִתְרוּמָה. יְתֵיב רַב דִּימִי וְקָאָמַר לָהּ לְהָא שְׁמַעְתָּא. אֲמַר לֵיהּ אַבָּיֵי: הִקְדִּישָׁן בִּכְלִי קָאָמַר, אֲבָל בַּפֶּה לָא עֲבוּד רַבָּנַן מַעֲלָה, אוֹ דִּילְמָא בַּפֶּה נַמִי עֲבוּד רַבָּנַן מַעֲלָה? אֲמַר לֵיהּ: זוֹ לֹא שָׁמַעְתִּי, כַּיּוֹצֵא בָּהּ שָׁמַעְתִּי. דְּאָמַר ר' אַבָּהוּ אָמַר רַבִּי יוֹחָנָן: עֲנָבִים שֶׁנִּטְמְאוּ, דְּרָכָן וְאַחַ"כ הִקְדִּישָׁן – טְהוֹרִים, הִקְדִּישָׁן וְאַחַ"כ דְּרָכָן – טְמֵאִין. וְהָא עֲנָבִים, דִּקְדוּשַּׁת פֶּה נִינְהוּ – וַאֲפִילּוּ הָכִי עֲבוּד רַבָּנַן מַעֲלָה. אֲמַר רַב יוֹסֵף: עֲנָבִים קָאָמְרַתְּ – הָכָא [ה] בַּעֲנָבִים שֶׁל תְּרוּמָה עָסְקִינַן, דִּקְדוּשַּׁת פֶּה דִּידְהוּ כִּקְדוּשַּׁת כְּלִי דָּמְיָא. אֲבָל הָנֵי דְּבָעֵי כְּלִי – בַּפֶּה לָא עֲבוּד רַבָּנַן מַעֲלָה. "דְּרָכָן" – וַאֲפִילּוּ טוּבָא. וּמִי אָמַר רַבִּי יוֹחָנָן הָכִי? וְהָאָמַר רַבִּי יוֹחָנָן: *עֲנָבִים שֶׁנִּטְמְאוּ – דּוֹרְכָן פָּחוֹת פָּחוֹת מִכַּבֵּיצָה! אִיבָּעֵית אֵימָא: הָכָא נַמִי – פָּחוֹת פָּחוֹת מִכַּבֵּיצָה. וְאִבָּעֵית אֵימָא: הָתָם – דְּנָגְעוּ לְהוּ בְּרִאשׁוֹן, דַּהֲווּ לְהוּ אִינְהוּ שֵׁנִי, הָכָא – דְּנָגְעוּ בְּשֵׁנִי, דַּהֲווּ לְהוּ שְׁלִישִׁי[א]. אָמַר רָבָא: אַף אֲנַן נַמִי תְּנֵינָא °"וְנָתַן עָלָיו מַיִם חַיִּים אֶל כֶּלִי" – *שֶׁתְּהֵא חִיּוּתָן בִּכְלִי. "וְנָתַן" – אַלְמָא תְּלוּשִׁין נִינְהוּ, וְהָא מְחוּבָּרִין נִינְהוּ! אֶלָּא

תורה אור: במדבר יט

רש"י

כׇּל שֶׁפְּסוּלוֹ בְּגוּפוֹ. פְּסוּל וַדַּאי, וּבַבָּשָׂר עַצְמוֹ – יִשָּׂרֵף מִיָּד: בְּדָם. כְּגוֹן נִשְׁפַּךְ הַדָּם: וּבִבְעָלִים. כְּגוֹן נִטְמְאוּ בְּעָלִים וְהַפֶּסַח קַיָּים, וְאֵין כָּאן מִי שֶׁיֹּאכְלֶנּוּ. וְדָם, אַע"פ שֶׁפְּסוּל גָּמוּר הוּא, אֲפִילּוּ הָכִי – הוֹאִיל וְאֵינוֹ כַּבָּשָׂר עַצְמוֹ – בָּעֵי עִיבּוּר צוּרָה: תַּנָּא דְּבֵי רַבָּה בַּר אֲבוּהּ. עִיקַּר מִילְּתָא לָא יָדַעְנָא הֵיכָא, וְטַעְמָא דְּמִילְּתֵיהּ בְּ"כֵּיצַד צוֹלִין": אֲפִילּוּ פִּיגּוּל. שֶׁפְּסוּל הַגּוּף הוּא, טָעוּן עִיבּוּר צוּרָה. וְהָכָא לָא מָצֵי לְשַׁנּוּיֵי כְּדִמְשַׁנֵּי לְקַמֵּיהּ: מַאי פְּסוּלֵי חַטָּאת הָעוֹף – שֶׁנִּפְסְלוּ בִּטְבוּל יוֹם, דְּהַיְינוּ טוּמְאָה וְצוּרָה לָמָּה לִי? רַבִּי אֱלִיעֶזֶר אוֹמֵר יִזְרוֹק. אֶת הַדָּם. ר' אֱלִיעֶזֶר לְטַעְמֵיהּ, דְּאָמַר בְּ"כֵּיצַד צוֹלִין": דָּם, אַף עַל פִּי שֶׁאֵין בָּשָׂר: רַבִּי יְהוֹשֻׁעַ אוֹמֵר לֹא יִזְרוֹק. ר' יְהוֹשֻׁעַ לְטַעְמֵיהּ, דְּאָמַר: אִם אֵין בָּשָׂר – אֵין דָּם. וְיָצָא חוּץ לַקְּלָעִים – בִּבְשַׂר קׇדְשֵׁי הַקֳּדָשִׁים קָאָמַר, שֶׁמְּחִיצָה שֶׁלָּהֶן חוֹמַת עֲזָרָה, כִּדְכְתִיב בְּכוּלְּהוּ: "בַּחֲצַר אֹהֶל מוֹעֵד יֹאכְלוּהָ". וְאִם יָצָאת – נִפְסֶלֶת, כִּדְיָלְפִינַן בְּ"כֵּיצַד צוֹלִין" מֵ"אֶל הַקּוֹדֶשׁ פְּנִימָה": מַאי נִפְסַל לָאו בְּהֶיסַּח הַדַּעַת. בִּתְמִיָּה. דְּכֵיוָן דְּתָנָא נִטְמָא וְיָצָא, מַאי פְּסוּל אִיכָּא תּוּ? אִי נִפְסַל בַּעֲבוֹדַת דָּם, כְּגוֹן בְּמַחֲשֶׁבֶת חוּץ לִמְקוֹמוֹ וְחוּץ לִזְמַנּוֹ – לָא קָרֵי נִפְסַל בָּשָׂר, שֶׁהֲרֵי אַף הַדָּם נִפְסַל, וּבְהָא לָא נֵימָא ר' אֱלִיעֶזֶר יִזְרוֹק: אִי אָמְרַתְּ בִּשְׁלָמָא. פְּסוּל חֲשַׁשׁ טוּמְאָה הוּא – מִשּׁוּם הָכִי מוֹדֶה רַבִּי יְהוֹשֻׁעַ שֶׁאִם זָרַק הוּרְצָה. דַּאֲפִילּוּ נִטְמָא וַדַּאי, וְאַע"ג דְּטוּמְאָה פְּסוּל הַגּוּף הָוֵי – מְרַצֶּה צִיץ. וּלְכַתְּחִלָּה לֹא יִזְרוֹק, דְּקָא סָבַר רִיצּוּי צִיץ בְּדִיעֲבַד הוּא. וְיוֹצֵא, אַע"ג דְּלָא מְהַנֵּי לֵיהּ צִיץ – הוּרְצָה בְּדִיעֲבַד. דְּאַע"ג דְּר' יְהוֹשֻׁעַ בָּעֵי תַּרְתֵּי, דָּם וּבָשָׂר, מִיהוּ הוֹאִיל וְהַבָּשָׂר בְּעַיִן, וּפְסוּל יוֹצֵא פְּסוּל מֵחֲמַת דָּבָר אַחֵר הוּא – חָשְׁבִינַן לֵיהּ פְּסוּל חֶסְרוֹן מְחִיצוֹת בְּפֶרֶק קַמָּא דִּמְנָחוֹת בְּסוֹפוֹ, אִיכָּא לְמֵימַר בְּדִיעֲבַד הוּרְצָה: אֶלָּא אִי הֶיסַּח הַדַּעַת פְּסוּל הַגּוּף הוּא. וְלַיִן נַמִי לָא מְרַצֵּי עֲלֵיהּ, אַמַּאי הוּרְצָה? ה"ג: אֶלָּא אִי אָמְרַתְּ פְּסוּל הַגּוּף הָוֵי אַמַּאי הוּרְצָה. וְלָא גָּרְסִינַן: פְּסוּל הַגּוּף מִי קָא מְרַצֵּי צִיץ. דְּהָא פְּסוּל יוֹצֵא נַמִי לָא מְרַצֵּי צִיץ, כְּדְאָמְרִינַן בְּפֶרֶק קַמָּא (דף טז:): הָא אֵינוֹ נוֹשֵׂא אֶלָּא עֲוֹן טוּמְאָה: נִפְסַל בִּטְבוּל יוֹם. וְטַעְמָא מִשּׁוּם צִיץ: אֲמָרָהּ קַמֵּיהּ דְּר' יִרְמְיָה. הָא דְּרַב שֵׁשֶׁת לְעֵיל, דַּאֲסוּרִין מִלֶּאֱכוֹל מִשּׁוּם הֶיסַּח הַדַּעַת הוּא: שְׁמַעְתָּתָא דִּמְחַשְׁכָן. כְּשֶׁאֵין יוֹדְעִין טַעְמוֹ שֶׁל דָּבָר בּוֹדִין מִלִּבָּם טַעַם שֶׁאֵינוֹ: אַתְרָא דִּמְחַשְׁכָא. בָּבֶל עֲמוּקָּה: לָא שְׁמִיעַ לְכוּ כו'. וּמִכָּאן יְכוֹלִין לִלְמוֹד טַעְמָהּ שֶׁל מִשְׁנָה, דַּאֲסוּרִין מִלֶּאֱכוֹל – מִשּׁוּם מַעֲלָה. דְּאַף עַל גַּב דִּמְהַנְיָא זְרִיעָה לְחוּלִּין – עֲבוּד רַבָּנַן מַעֲלָה דְּלָא תְּהַנֵּי לִתְרוּמָה, לְהַעֲלוֹת לָהּ טׇהֳרָה גְּמוּרָה לְהֶיתֵּר אֲכִילָה. וּמִיהוּ, מִלְּטַמֵּא טִהֲרוּ – דִּלְהָא לָא עֲבוּד מַעֲלָה: מֵי הֶחָג. כְּגוֹן שֶׁל נִיסּוּךְ הַמַּיִם. דְּשַׁבָּת שֶׁבְּתוֹךְ הֶחָג הָיוּ מְמַלְּאִין אוֹתָן מֵעֶרֶב שַׁבָּת, וּכְשֶׁנִּטְמְאוּ אֵין יְכוֹלִין לֵילֵךְ וּלְמַלְּאוֹת מִן הַשִּׁילוֹחַ בְּשַׁבָּת, וְטוֹרַח הוּא לְמַלְּאוֹת מִבּוֹר הַגָּדוֹל בְּגַלְגַּל – וְהָלַךְ וְהִשִּׁיקָם בְּמַיִם שֶׁבָּעֲזָרָה, וּמַיִם שֶׁלְּקָחָן לְהוּ הַשָּׁקָה, דְּזוֹ הִיא זְרִיעָתָן מִשֶּׁעָבְרוּ עֲלֵיהֶן מֵי הַמִּקְוֶה, וְנַעֲשָׂה חִיבּוּר, וּבָטְלוּ: וְאַחַ"כ הִקְדִּישָׁן. שֶׁעֲדַיִין לֹא קָרָא עֲלֵיהֶן שֵׁם, אוֹ לֹא קִידְּשׁוּ בִּכְלֵי שָׁרֵת – טְהוֹרִין: אֵין זְרִיעָה לְהֶקְדֵּשׁ. לְטַהֲרוֹ בְּכָךְ, דְּמַעֲלָה עָשׂוּ בַּקֳּדָשִׁים, הָכָא נַמִי אֵין זְרִיעָה לִתְרוּמָה, דְּמַעֲלָה עָשׂוּ: לְהָא שְׁמַעְתָּא. דְּרַבִּי אוֹשַׁעְיָא: הִקְדִּישָׁן בִּכְלֵי שָׁרֵת קָאָמְרַתְּ. דְּכֵיוָן דִּקְדוּשִּׁין הֵן קְדוּשַּׁת הַגּוּף – עַבְדִינְהוּ לְהוּ רַבָּנַן מַעֲלָה. אֲבָל מִשּׁוּם קְדוּשַּׁת פֶּה, דְּמִלְּאָן בִּכְלֵי חוֹל לְשֵׁם חַג – לָא עַבְדֵי לְהוּ מַעֲלָה, וּמְהַנְיָא לְהוּ הַשָּׁקָה: זוֹ לֹא שָׁמַעְתִּי. בְּמַעֲלָה זוֹ דִּזְרִיעָה לֹא שָׁמַעְתִּי אִם בַּפֶּה אִם בִּכְלִי, אֲבָל בְּמַעֲלָה אַחֶרֶת שָׁמַעְתִּי דְּאַף בִּקְדוּשַּׁת פֶּה עַבְדוּהָ רַבָּנַן, וְאִיכָּא לְמֵילַף מִינַּהּ דְּהוּא הַדִּין לְכׇל מַעֲלוֹת שֶׁבַּקּוֹדֶשׁ: דְּרָכָן וְאַחַר כָּךְ הִקְדִּישָׁן טְהוֹרוֹת. לִנְסָכִים. וְר' יוֹחָנָן לְטַעְמֵיהּ, דְּאָמַר לְעֵיל: מַשְׁקִין מִיפְקָד פְּקִידֵי, וְלָא קַבְּלֵי טוּמְאָה עִם הָאוֹכֶל. וּלְקַמֵּיהּ מְפָרֵשׁ הֵיכִי דָּרֵיךְ לְהוּ: הִקְדִּישָׁן וְאַחַ"כ דְּרָכָן טְמֵאוֹת. קָא ס"ד הִקְדִּישׁ יֵינוֹ לִנְסָכִים: טְמֵאוֹת. דַּעֲבוּד רַבָּנַן מַעֲלָה בַּקֳּדָשִׁים, דְּמִיטַּמֵּא מַשְׁקֶה עִם הָאוֹכֶל. וְלָא אָמְרִינַן בְּהוּ מַשְׁקִין מִיפְקָד פְּקִידֵי. וְהָא עֲנָבִים קְדוּשַּׁת פֶּה הֵן, דְּאִי נַמִי נְתָנָן לִכְלִי – אֵין כְּלִי מְקַדְּשָׁן, דְּאֵין כְּלֵי שָׁרֵת מְקַדְּשִׁין אֶלָּא דָּבָר הָרָאוּי לוֹ, כִּדְיָלְפִינַן בִּ"שְׁחִיטַת קָדָשִׁים"* גַּבֵּי מִזְבֵּחַ, שֶׁנֶּאֱמַר: "כׇּל הַנּוֹגֵעַ בַּמִּזְבֵּחַ יִקְדָּשׁ" – שׁוֹמֵעַ אֲנִי בֵּין רָאוּי בֵּין שֶׁאֵינוֹ רָאוּי, תַּלְמוּד לוֹמַר: עוֹלָה. וּכְלֵי שָׁרֵת דּוּמְיָא דְּמִזְבֵּחַ נָפְקָא לַן הָתָם: בַּעֲנָבִים שֶׁל תְּרוּמָה. וְהַאי "הִקְדִּישָׁן" – קְדוּשַּׁת תְּרוּמָה קָאָמַר, דִּבְתְרוּמָה לָא שַׁיְּיכָא קְדוּשַּׁת כְּלִי, לֹא בְּיַיִן וְלֹא בַּעֲנָבִים: אֲבָל הָנֵי. מֵי הֶחָג: דְּרָכָן וַאֲפִילּוּ טוּבָא. לְעֵיל קָמְהַדַּר. אָמְרַתְּ: דְּרָכָן וְאַחַר כָּךְ הִקְדִּישָׁן – טְהוֹרוֹת. וַאֲפִילּוּ טוּבָא בְּבַת אַחַת?! בִּתְמִיָּה. וְהָא אָמְרַתְּ לְעֵיל: פָּחוֹת פָּחוֹת מִכַּבֵּיצָה. דְּאִי יוֹתֵר – הָא אִיטַּמּוּ מַשְׁקִין בְּכַבֵּיצָה מִילֵּאת טִיפָּה רִאשׁוֹנָה טוּמְאַת הָאוֹכֶל, שֶׁהֲרֵי יֵשׁ בָּהּ כְּשִׁיעוּר: הָכִי גָּרְסִינַן: אִי בָּעֵית אֵימָא הָכָא נַמִי בְּפָחוֹת מִכַּבֵּיצָה וְאִי בָּעֵית אֵימָא הָתָם דְּבָעֵינַן פָּחוֹת מִכַּבֵּיצָה שֶׁנָּגְעוּ עֲנָבִים בָּרִאשׁוֹן. כְּגוֹן טְמֵא שֶׁרֶץ אוֹ טְמֵא נְבֵילָה, וְכׇל שֶׁכֵּן טְמֵא מֵת. דְּכֵיוָן דַּהֲווּ עֲנָבִים שֵׁנִי – טִימְּאוּ אֶת הַמַּשְׁקִין בְּכַבֵּיצָה מִשֶּׁיָּצָאת טִיפָּה רִאשׁוֹנָה. וְאַף עַל פִּי שֶׁהֵן חוּלִּין – דְּכׇל הַפּוֹסֵל אֶת הַתְּרוּמָה מְטַמֵּא מַשְׁקִין לִהְיוֹת תְּחִלָּה, וְ"שֵׁנִי עוֹשֶׂה שְׁלִישִׁי בִּתְרוּמָה" לָא גָּרְסִינַן – דְּהָא בְּחוּלִּין עָסְקִינַן. דְּאִי בִּתְרוּמָה – הָא אֲמַרַן דַּעֲבוּד מַעֲלָה שֶׁמְּטַמְּאָה מַשְׁקֶה עִם הָאוֹכֶל: הָכָא דְּנָגְעוּ. עֲנָבִים בְּשֵׁנִי, דַּהֲווּ לְהוּ שְׁלִישִׁי. עֲנָבִים שֶׁנַּעֲשׂוּ עַל טׇהֳרַת תְּרוּמָה מַשְׁכַּחַתְּ בְּהוּ שְׁלִישִׁי. הִלְכָּךְ, דְּרָכָן וְאַחַר כָּךְ הִקְדִּישָׁן, שֶׁקָּרָא לָהֶן שֵׁם תְּרוּמָה – טְהוֹרִין, וַאֲפִילּוּ דָּרַךְ הַרְבֵּה יַחַד – שֶׁהָאוֹכֶל שְׁלִישִׁי לֹא עָשָׂה לַמַּשְׁקֶה כְּלוּם. וּמִתְּחִלָּה לֹא נִטְמְאוּ עִם הָאוֹכֶל – דְּקוֹדֶם קְרִיאַת שֵׁם לָא עֲבוּד מַעֲלָה. הִקְדִּישָׁן לִתְרוּמָה וְאַחַ"כ דְּרָכָן – טְמֵאִין, דְּמִקְּרִיאַת שֵׁם חָלָה הַמַּעֲלָה עֲלֵיהֶן, וְנַעֲשָׂה הַמַּשְׁקִין כְּאוֹכֶל הַכֹּל אֶחָד: אַף אֲנַן נַמִי תְּנֵינָא. דַּעֲבוּד רַבָּנַן מַעֲלָה בַּקֳּדָשִׁים, וַאֲפִילּוּ בִּקְדוּשַּׁת פֶּה: שֶׁתְּהֵא חִיּוּתָן בִּכְלִי. בְּאוֹתוֹ כְּלִי עַצְמוֹ שֶׁהוּא מְקַדֵּשׁ בּוֹ מֵי חַטָּאת בְּאֶפְרָן צָרִיךְ לְמַלְּאוֹתוֹ מִן הַמַּעְיָן, וְלֹא יְמַלְּאֵם בִּכְלִי אַחֵר וִיעָרֶה לְתוֹךְ זֶה. וְכָתַב "וְנָתַן" – דְּמַשְׁמַע תְּלוּשִׁין, דְּמוּתָּר לְמַלְּאוֹתוֹ בִּכְלִי אַחֵר וִיעָרֶה לְתוֹךְ זֶה: אֶלָּא

תוספות

שאם זרק הורצה. אף על גב דאין ציץ מרצה על היוצא, רבי יהושע סבר זריקה מועלת ליוצא, כרבי עקיבא דריש מעילה (דף ו:) דאמר: זריקה מועלת להוציא בשר מידי מעילה, וכל שכן להרצאה. דהא רבי אליעזר דאמר הכא יזרוק, קאמר התם דלהוצאה ממעילה לא מהניא:

ונתן אלמא תלושין והא מחוברין נינהו. פירוש: ד"ונתן" משמע דחשיב להו תלושין, והיינו לענין קבלת טומאה, אף על פי שהן מחוברין. והשתא מייתי ראיה דאין השקה להקדש מן התורה, וכן בתרומה נמי עבוד רבנן מעלה. ופ"ה דחוק:

כוסמין

רבינו חננאל

השרפה וכיון שנפסל הסיח דעתו ממנו הניחא לדידי דאמינא פסול טומאה הוא מש"ה בעי עיבור צורה אלא לדידך דאמרת פסול הגוף הוא למה לי עיבור צורה התנן זה הכלל כל שפסולו בגוף ישרף מיד בדם ובבעלים תעובר צורתו כלומר כל זמן שיתכן שיאכל מניחין אותו שמא יבוא אליהו ויתירנו באכילה עד שיסריח וישנה מצורת בשר שאי אפשר להאכל כלל ויצא לשרפה קתני מיהא כל שפסולו בגופו ישרף מיד ושנינ' האי תנא סבר אפילו פגול שאינו מרצה לעולם והוא ודאי פסול הגוף טעון עיבור צורה דיליף עון עון מנותר: ותוב מותיב עליה מהא [דתני'] נטמא הבשר או נפסל או יצא חוץ לקלעי' כו' קתני מיהא אם זרק הורצה וכי פסול הגוף בר הרצאה הוא ומשני' רבי שמעון בן לקיש מאי נפסל דקתני נפסל בטבול יום דלא מסח דעתיה ותרי גוני טומאה קתני: ר' ירמיה פשיט ליה לבעיא דרבה בר מתנה מהא דאמר ריש לקיש מי החג שנטמא השיקן ואחר כך הקדישן טהורין הקדישן ונטמאו ואחר כך השיקן טמאין פי' כיצד משיקן נותנן בכלי גללים או בכלי אבנים או בכלי אדמה וממלא אותו הכלי מן המים ומטבילן במי מקוה כדי שיהיו מי מקוה צפין עליו ועלתה להם טהרה והיינו השקתן וכבר פירשנוה ביום טוב. פי' הקדיש מים לנסך אותם בחג ונטמאו והשיקן פי' ששקען במי מקוה לטהרן אע"פ שנכנסו תחת המים שנמצאו כאלו זרועים הם במקוה לא עלתה להם טהרה שאין הזריעה מטהרת בהקדש כך שתילי תרומה אע"פ ששקען וזרען בקרקע לא עלתה להם (התרה) [טהרה] ומאי אסורה אסורה לכהנים: א"ל לרב דימי בקדושת כלי קאמרת כגון אלו ימי החג וכיוצא בהן שנקדשו בכלי הקדש עבדו בהן רבנן מעלה שאין זריעה מטהרת בהקדש שנקדש בכלי הקדש אבל אם הקדישה קדושה בפה שאמר זה קדש ועדיין לא בא בכלי קדש הא מיבעיא לי יש לו זו המעלה שהרי כבר נקדש או לא אמר לו זו בהדיא לא שמעתי כיוצא בה שמעתי דאמר רבה בר בר חנה אמר ר' יוחנן ענבים שנטמאו דרכן ואח"כ הקדישן טהורין הקדישן ואח"כ דרכן טמאין הרי ענבים הללו קדושת פה נינהו שעדיין לא באו בכלי ואינם יין לנסך ואפילו הכי עבוד להו מעלה ודחי רב יוסף ואמר הני ענבים דאמר רבי יוחנן ענבים דתרומה הן דקדושת הפה (נינהו) [דידהו] קדושה גמורה היא וכיון שאמר הרי אלו תרומה כקדושת כלי דמיא קדושתן אבל קדש דבעו כלי כגון ניסוך המים וכיוצא בו בפה בלא קדושת כלי לא עשו בהן מעלה ואקשי' אהא ומי אמר ר' יוחנן ענבים שנטמאו דורכן כלו וטהורים והא איהו דאמר סוחטן פחות פחות מכביצה ושני' הכי נמי מאי דרכן דקתני נמי פחות פחות מכביצה. איבעית אימא התם דאמר רבי יוחנן פחות פחות מכביצה דנגעי בשרץ והוו להו ענבים ראשון דמטמו אחריני והכא דקתני כגון שנטמאו במים שנטמא בשרץ דהוו להו ענבים שני ואין שני עושה שלישי בחולין ואי תרומה נינהו דנגעי בולד שני דהוו להו ענבים שלישי ואין שלישי עושה רביעי בתרומה: אמר רבא אף אנן נמי תנינא דבקדושת כלי עבדו בהן מעלה דכתיב ונתן עליו מים חיים אל כלי שתהא חיותן בכלי מדקאמר ונתן

מסורת הש"ס

לקמן עג: פב:

ג"ז שם

מנחות נ: לקמן עז: [זבחים קד.]

ל"ג

יומא נז. זבחים מ: מנחות נב.

[לעיל לג:]

סוטה טז:

גליון הש"ס

תוס' ד"ה ונתן וכו' ופ"ה דחוק. עיין בר"ש פ"ט מ"ג דפרה:

הגהות מהר"ב רנשבורג

[א] גמרא אמר רבא אף אנן נמי תנינא וכו'. נ"ב ל"ע דעל זה לא שייך אף אנן נמי תנינא כיון דאינו בלשון הברייתא אלא סתמא דש"ס אמרו אבל בתמורה י"ב ע"ב איתא כך וכמ"ש בס"ם שלנו יעוש"ה כי בש"ס שלנו איננו אבל מלאתי כן בילקוט רמז תשס"ב:

אֶלָּא מַעֲלָה, הָכִי נַמִי – מַעֲלָה. אֲמַר רַב שִׁימִי בַּר אַשִׁי, אַף אֲנַן נַמִי תְּנֵינָא: *טָבַל וְעָלָה – אאוֹכֵל בְּמַעֲשֵׂר. בהֶעֱרִיב שִׁמְשׁוֹ – אוֹכֵל בִּתְרוּמָה. בִּתְרוּמָה – אִין, בְּקָדָשִׁים – לָא. אַמַּאי? טָהוֹר הוּא! אֶלָּא: *מַעֲלָה, ה"נ – מַעֲלָה? אֲמַר רַב אַשִׁי, אַף אֲנַן נַמִי תְּנֵינָא: °"וְהַבָּשָׂר" – *גלְרַבּוֹת אֶת הָעֵצִים וּלְבוֹנָה. עֵצִים וּלְבוֹנָה בְּנֵי אִיטַּמּוּיֵי נִינְהוּ? אֶלָּא *מַעֲלָה, הָכָא נַמִי – מַעֲלָה.§

מתני' דאֵלּוּ דְּבָרִים שֶׁאָדָם יוֹצֵא בָּהֶן יְדֵי חוֹבָתוֹ בְּפֶסַח: בַּחִטִּים, בַּשְּׂעוֹרִים, בַּכּוּסְּמִין, וּבַשִּׁיפוֹן, וּבְשִׁיבּוֹלֶת שׁוּעָל. וְיוֹצְאִין בִּדְמַאי וּבְמַעֲשֵׂר רִאשׁוֹן שֶׁנִּטְּלָה תְרוּמָתוֹ, וּבְמַעֲשֵׂר שֵׁנִי וְהֶקְדֵּשׁ שֶׁנִּפְדּוּ, וְהַכֹּהֲנִים בַּחַלָּה וּבַתְּרוּמָה, אֲבָל לֹא בַּטֶּבֶל, וְלֹא בְּמַעֲשֵׂר רִאשׁוֹן שֶׁלֹּא נִטְּלָה תְּרוּמָתוֹ, וְלֹא בְּמַעֲשֵׂר שֵׁנִי וְהֶקְדֵּשׁ שֶׁלֹּא נִפְדּוּ. חַלּוֹת הַתּוֹדָה וּרְקִיקֵי נָזִיר, עֲשָׂאָן לְעַצְמוֹ – אֵין יוֹצֵא בָּהֶן, עֲשָׂאָן לִמְכּוֹר בַּשּׁוּק – יוֹצְאִין בָּהֶן.§

גמ' *תָּנָא: *כּוּסְּמִין מִין חִיטִּין, שִׁיבּוֹלֶת שׁוּעָל וְשִׁיפוֹן – מִין שְׂעוֹרִין, כּוּסְּמִין – גּוּלְבָּא, שִׁיפוֹן – דִּישְׁרָא, שִׁיבּוֹלֶת שׁוּעָל – שִׁבּוֹלֵי תַעֲלָא. ההָנֵי – אִין, אוֹרֶז וְדוֹחַן – לָא. מְנָהָנֵי מִילֵּי? *אָמַר רַבִּי שִׁמְעוֹן בֶּן לָקִישׁ, וְכֵן תָּנָא דְּבֵי רַבִּי יִשְׁמָעֵאל, וְכֵן תָּנָא דְּבֵי ר' אֱלִיעֶזֶר בֶּן יַעֲקֹב: אָמַר קְרָא °"לֹא תֹאכַל עָלָיו חָמֵץ שִׁבְעַת יָמִים תֹּאכַל עָלָיו מַצּוֹת" דְּבָרִים הַבָּאִים לִידֵי חִימּוּץ – אָדָם יוֹצֵא בָּהֶן יְדֵי חוֹבָתוֹ בְּמַצָּה, יָצְאוּ אֵלּוּ שֶׁאֵין בָּאִין לִידֵי חִימּוּץ אֶלָּא לִידֵי סִירָחוֹן. מַתְנִיתִין דְּלָא כְּרַבִּי יוֹחָנָן בֶּן נוּרִי, דְּאָמַר: אוֹרֶז מִין דָּגָן הוּא, וְחַיָּיבִין עַל חִימּוּצוֹ כָּרֵת. *דְּתַנְיָא: רַבִּי יוֹחָנָן בֶּן נוּרִי אוֹסֵר בְּאוֹרֶז וָדוֹחַן, מִפְּנֵי שֶׁקָּרוֹב לְהַחְמִיץ. אִיבַּעְיָא לְהוּ: "שֶׁקָּרוֹב לְהַחְמִיץ" – דְּקָדֵים וּמַחְמִיץ, אוֹ דִילְמָא "קָרוֹב לְהַחְמִיץ" הָוֵי, חָמֵץ גָּמוּר – לָא הָוֵי. תָּא שְׁמַע, דְּתַנְיָא, *אָמַר רַבִּי יוֹחָנָן בֶּן נוּרִי: אוֹרֶז מִין דָּגָן הוּא, וְחַיָּיבִין עַל חִימּוּצוֹ כָּרֵת, וְאָדָם יוֹצֵא בּוֹ יְדֵי חוֹבָתוֹ בְּפֶסַח. וְכֵן *הָיָה רַבִּי יוֹחָנָן בֶּן נוּרִי אוֹמֵר: קְרָמִית חַיֶּיבֶת בַּחַלָּה. מַאי קְרָמִית? אָמַר אַבַּיֵי: שִׁיצָנִיתָא. מַאי שִׁיצָנִיתָא? אָמַר רַב פַּפָּא: שִׁיצָנִיתָא דְּמִשְׁתַּכְחָא בֵּינֵי כַּלָּנִיתָא. אָמַר רַבָּה בַּר בַּר חָנָה אָמַר רֵישׁ לָקִישׁ: ועִיסָּה שֶׁנִּילּוֹשָׁה בְּיַיִן וְשֶׁמֶן וּדְבַשׁ – אֵין חַיָּיבִין עַל חִימּוּצָהּ כָּרֵת. יְתֵיב רַב פַּפָּא וְרַב הוּנָא בְּרֵיהּ דְּרַב יְהוֹשֻׁעַ קַמֵּיהּ דְּרַב אִידִי בַּר אָבִין, וִיתֵיב רַב אִידִי בַּר אָבִין וְקָא מְנַמְנֵם. א"ל רַב הוּנָא בְּרֵיהּ דְּרַב יְהוֹשֻׁעַ לְרַב פַּפָּא: מַאי טַעְמָא דְּרֵישׁ לָקִישׁ? א"ל: דְּאָמַר קְרָא "לֹא תֹאכַל עָלָיו חָמֵץ [וגו']" דְּבָרִים שֶׁאָדָם יוֹצֵא בָּהֶן יְדֵי חוֹבָתוֹ בְּמַצָּה – חַיָּיבִין עַל חִימּוּצוֹ כָּרֵת. וְהָא, הוֹאִיל וְאֵין אָדָם יוֹצֵא בָּהּ יְדֵי חוֹבָתוֹ, זדְּהָוְיָא לֵיהּ מַצָּה עֲשִׁירָה – אֵין חַיָּיבִין עַל חִימּוּצָהּ כָּרֵת. אֵיתִיבֵיהּ רַב הוּנָא בְּרֵיהּ דְּרַב יְהוֹשֻׁעַ לְרַב פַּפָּא: *הִמְחָהוּ וּגְמָעוֹ, אִם חָמֵץ הוּא – עָנוּשׁ כָּרֵת, וְאִם מַצָּה הוּא – אֵין אָדָם יוֹצֵא יְדֵי חוֹבָתוֹ בְּפֶסַח. וְהָא הָכָא, דְּאֵין אָדָם יוֹצֵא יְדֵי חוֹבָתוֹ בְּמַצָּה, וְחַיָּיבִין עַל חִימּוּצוֹ כָּרֵת! אִיתְּעַר בְּהוּ רַב אִידִי בַּר אָבִין, אֲמַר לְהוּ: *דַּרְדְּקֵי, הַיְינוּ טַעְמָא דְּרֵישׁ לָקִישׁ: מִשּׁוּם דְּהָווּ לְהוּ מֵי פֵּירוֹת, וּמֵי

רש"י

אֶלָּא מַעֲלָה. בְּעָלְמָא הוּא, מִדְּרַבָּנַן – שֶׁתְּהֵא חִיּוּתָן בַּכְּלִי, וְאַסְמְכוּהָ רַבָּנַן אַקְּרָא: הָכָא נַמִי מַעֲלָה. בְּעָלְמָא הוּא, דְּאֵין זְרִיעָה לִתְרוּמָה וַאֲסוּרִין מִלֶּאֱכוֹל: תְּנֵינָא. דַּעֲבוּד רַבָּנַן מַעֲלָה בְּקָדָשִׁים, אֲפִילּוּ מִדְּאוֹרַיְיתָא: בְּקָדָשִׁים לָא. אִם טוּמְאָה דְּבַת כַּפָּרָה הִיא, כְּגוֹן זָב וְזָבָה וְיוֹלֶדֶת: וְהַבָּשָׂר. "כָּל טָהוֹר יֹאכַל" וגו' – וָי"ו יְתֵירָה, לְרַבּוֹת עֵצִים וּלְבוֹנָה שֶׁל קוֹדֶשׁ לְטוּמְאָה. וְקָאֵי אַדִּלְעֵיל "וְהַבָּשָׂר אֲשֶׁר יִגַּע בְּכָל טָמֵא לֹא יֵאָכֵל, וְהַבָּשָׂר": אִיטַּמּוּיֵי נִינְהוּ. בִּתְמִיָּה, הָא לָאו אוֹכֶל נִינְהוּ! מתני' אֵלּוּ דְּבָרִים שֶׁאָדָם יוֹצֵא בָּהֶן יְדֵי חוֹבָתוֹ. מִשּׁוּם חוֹבַת מַצָּה בַּלַּיְלָה רִאשׁוֹנָה שֶׁהוּא מְחוּיָּיב לֶאֱכוֹל מַצָּה, כְּדִכְתִיב (שמות יב): "בָּעֶרֶב תֹּאכְלוּ מַצּוֹת": שִׁיבּוֹלֶת שׁוּעָל. אבייני"א, שִׁיבּוֹלֶת שֶׁלָּהּ עָשׂוּי כִּזְנַב שׁוּעָל: שִׁיפוֹן. סיגל"א: יוֹצְאִין בִּדְמַאי. תְּבוּאָה הַנִּלְקַחַת מֵעַם הָאָרֶץ, וְהִיא נִקְרֵאת דְּמַאי. סָפֵק עִישְּׂרָהּ סָפֵק לֹא עִישְּׂרָהּ, וְחִייְבוּ חֲכָמִים לְהַפְרִישׁ מַעַשְׂרוֹתֶיהָ מִסָּפֵק. וְאִם אָכַל מַצָּה מִמֶּנָּה, וְלֹא הִפְרִישׁ מַעֲשֵׂר מִמֶּנָּה – יָצָא: וּבְמַעֲשֵׂר רִאשׁוֹן. שֶׁל לְוִיִּם: שֶׁנִּטְּלָה תְּרוּמָתוֹ. תְּרוּמַת מַעֲשֵׂר לַכֹּהֵן, וּמִכָּאן וְאֵילָךְ הַמַּעֲשֵׂר מוּתָּר לְזָרִים: וְהַכֹּהֲנִים בַּחַלָּה וּבַתְּרוּמָה. אֲבָל יִשְׂרָאֵל בִּתְרוּמָה לָא, כִּדְיָלֵיף לְקַמָּן: "לֹא תֹאכַל עָלָיו חָמֵץ, שִׁבְעַת יָמִים תֹּאכַל עָלָיו מַצּוֹת" – מִי שֶׁאֵינוֹ מוּזְהָר עַל חִימּוּצוֹ אֶלָּא מִשּׁוּם חָמֵץ הַטָּה יוֹצֵא בּוֹ יְדֵי חוֹבַת מַצָּה, יָצָא זֶה שֶׁאָסוּר מֵחֲמַת אִיסּוּר אַחֵר: וְלֹא בְּמַעֲשֵׂר שֵׁנִי. חוּץ לִירוּשָׁלַיִם: עֲשָׂאָן לְעַצְמוֹ. לֶחֶם תּוֹדָה וְנָזִיר: אֵין יוֹצֵא בָּהֶן. וַאֲפִילּוּ לֹא שָׁחַט הַזֶּבַח עֲלֵיהֶן, וְלֹא קָרָא שֵׁם עֲלֵיהֶן, אֶלָּא שֶׁעֲשָׂאָן לְדַעַת כֵּן. וְטַעְמָא מְפָרֵשׁ בַּגְּמָ': לִמְכּוֹר בַּשּׁוּק. לְצוֹרְכֵי לַחְמֵי תוֹדָה וּנְזִירוּת – יוֹצֵא בָּהֶן אִם לֹא מָכַר לָהֶן, וְטַעְמָא מְפָרֵשׁ בַּגְּמָרָא: גמ' מִין חִיטִּין. לְעִנְיַן תְּרוּמָה, דְּאֵין תּוֹרְמִין מִמִּין עַל שֶׁאֵינוֹ מִינוֹ, וְתוֹרְמִין חִיטִּין עַל כּוּסְּמִין: דִּישְׁרָא. סיגל"א: גּוּלְבֵּי. אִיספילט"א בְּלַע"ז: שִׁבּוֹלֵי תַעֲלָא. אבייני"א. תַּעֲלָא – תַּרְגּוּם שֶׁל שׁוּעָל: דְּבָרִים הַבָּאִין לִידֵי חִימּוּץ אָדָם יוֹצֵא בָּהֶן. מִשּׁוּם מַצָּה, אִם עֲשָׂאָן מַצָּה: אוֹרֶז וָדוֹחַן. אֵין עוֹשִׂין חָמֵץ, וְאִם מַחְמִילִין אוֹתָן – מַסְרִיחִין: אוֹסֵר בְּאוֹרֶז וָדוֹחַן. לֶאֱכוֹל הֵימֶנּוּ תַּבְשִׁיל בְּפֶסַח. יֵשׁ מְפָרְשִׁים לִמְנָחוֹת, מִשּׁוּם דְּכָל הַמְּנָחוֹת בָּאוֹת מַצָּה. וְשִׁיבּוּשׁ הוּא, דְּאֵין מִנְחָה בָּאָה אֶלָּא חִטִּים, דִּכְתִיב (שמות כט): "סוֹלֶת חִטִּים תַּעֲשֶׂה אוֹתָם". חוּץ מִמִּנְחַת הָעוֹמֶר, שֶׁאֵינָהּ בָּאָה אֶלָּא שְׂעוֹרִין, [וְכֵן] מִנְחַת סוֹטָה. וּפְשִׁיטָא דְּדוֹחַן לָא, וּמַאן פָּלֵיג עֲלֵיהּ דְּרַבִּי יוֹחָנָן בְּהָא, וּמִי מַתִּיר: שֶׁקָּרוֹב לְחִימּוּץ. הִלְכָּךְ: בָּא לִידֵי חִימּוּץ, וּלְדִידֵיהּ יוֹצְאִין בּוֹ מִשּׁוּם מַצָּה: חָמֵץ גָּמוּר לָא הָוֵי. וְנָפְקָא מִינָּהּ דְּאֵין עָנוּשׁ כָּרֵת, וְאִם אֲכָלוֹ בְּשׁוֹגֵג – אֵין מֵבִיא קָרְבָּן: קְרָמִית. מְפָרֵשׁ לְקַמֵּיהּ: חַיֶּיבֶת בַּחַלָּה. דְּמִין דָּגָן הָוֵי. וְאַע"ג דְּחַלַּת לֶחֶם כְּתִיב בָּהּ, וְגָמַר לֶחֶם לֶחֶם מִלֶּחֶם עוֹנִי, בִּמְנָחוֹת בְּפֶרֶק "רַבִּי יִשְׁמָעֵאל" (דף ע:) – אוֹרֶז [א] נַמִי לֶחֶם הוּא: שִׁיצָנִיתָא. קֶלַח שֶׁקּוֹרִין ניי"ל בְּלַע"ז. עָגוֹל הוּא כְּעֵין דּוֹחַן, וְשָׁחוֹר. לִישָּׁנָא אַחֲרִינָא שָׁמַעְתִּי: אשדרניל"א, וְנִמְצֵאת בַּשִּׁיפוֹן: כַּלָּנִיתָא. מ"ק בְּלַע"ז: בְּיַיִן וּבְשֶׁמֶן. דְּלֹא נָתַן בָּהּ מַיִם: אֵין חַיָּיבִין עַל חִימּוּצוֹ כָּרֵת. דְּמֵי פֵּירוֹת אֵין מַחְמִילִין, כִּדְלְקַמָּן: מַצָּה עֲשִׁירָה. וְרַחֲמָנָא אָמַר: "לֶחֶם עוֹנִי": הִמְחָהוּ וּגְמָעוֹ. אַשּׁוּם לֶחֶם דְּמִין דָּגָן קָאֵי, וְאַשְׁמְעִינַן דִּגְמִיעָה כַּאֲכִילָה לְחַיְּיבוֹ: הִמְחָהוּ. דישטנפרי"ר בְּלַע"ז, שֶׁהִמְחָהוּ בַּמַּיִם: אֵין אָדָם יוֹצֵא בָּהּ יְדֵי חוֹבָתוֹ. דְּלָאו דֶּרֶךְ אֲכִילָה קָאָכֵיל לֵיהּ: דְּמַאי

תוספות

כוסמין מין חיטין שיבולת שועל ושיפון מין שעורין. רש"י פירש לענין דאין תורמין ממין על שאין מינו. ור"י אומר: דבמנחות בפרק "ר' ישמעאל" (דף ע.) מוכח בהדיא דברייתא לענין חלה מיתני'. יש מקשין, דתנן במסכת חלה (פ"ד מ"ג): החיטה אינה מצטרפת עם הכל חוץ מן הכוסמין, והשעורין מצטרפין עם הכל חוץ מן החיטין. אלמא: כוסמין בהדי שעורין שפיר דמי! ואומר ר"י: דכוסמין מין חיטין – כלומר אף מין חיטין, וכל שכן מין שעורין. שיבולת שועל ושיפון – מין שעורין ולא מין חטין. והא דתניא התם בריש המסכת, חמשה דברים חייבין בחלה: החיטין והשעורין והכוסמין ושיבולת שועל ושיפון, הרי אלו חייבין בחלה ומצטרפין זה עם זה – אומר ר"י, דמשני בירושלמי: כאן בנשוך וכאן בבלול. פי': בנשוך – שכל אחת ואחת נעשה עיסה בפני עצמה, ואחר כן נשכו ונתחברו יחד – התם ודאי אין מצטרפין כולם, אלא כמו שמפורשין. בבלול – שכל הקמחים נילושים יחד ועשו מהן עיסה – בההיא כולם מצטרפים, דחשבינן כולם כאחד: ומי

רבינו חננאל

ונתן אלמא (עיקרן) [דעקורין] מן המעין הן ותלושי' נינהו והדר קרי להו מים חיים אל כלי אלמא מחוברים נינהו אלא מעלה עשו בהן דאע"ג דהן בכלי והן בתוך המעין (נקראים) [ונקראים] חיים וכי האי גונא בחולין (דלא) [לא] מטמאי' דכתיב (ויקרא יא) אך מעין ובור מקוה מים יהא טהור והכא במי חטאת כיון שהן בכלי מיטמאין ואין חבורן במעין *) מטהרן הנה מעלה: **רב** שימי אמר מהא טבל ועלה אוכל במעשר העריב שמשו אוכל בתרומה **) אמאי בעי הערב שמש והא טהור הוא אלא מעלה. רב אשי אמר מהא והבשר לרבות עצים ולבונה עצים ולבונה בני קבולי טומאה נינהו אלא מעלה עשו הכא נמי מעלה עשו: **מתני'** אלו דברים שאדם יוצא בהן ידי חובתו בפסח בחטים ובשעורים כו' הני אין אבל אורז ודוחן אם יעשה מהן מצה אינו יוצא בהן ידי מצה מדאוריי' מנא לן ופשטינן [ליה] מהאי קרא לא תאכל עליו חמץ שבעת ימים תאכל עליו מצות לחם עוני וגו' דברים שיתכן לבוא לידי חימוץ אותם הזהירה תורה שלא תניחם להחמיץ אלא תאכלם מצה אבל אלו שאין באים לידי חימוץ לעולם אלא לידי סרחון גם אם תאכלם מצה אינה חשובה מצה. ואוקימנא למתני' דלא כרבי יוחנן בן נורי דאמר כי האורז קרוב להחמיץ. פשטנא שמחמיץ הוא כלומר במהרה מדקתני וחייבין על חימוצו כרת: **קרמית** עשב כדאמרינן קורמי דאגמא: **אמר** ריש לקיש עיסה שנילושה ביין ושמן ודבש אין חייבין על חימוצה כרת קס"ד משום דהוה מצה עשירה ואותבי' עליה המחהו פי' המחהו לככר במשקה וגמעו אם חמץ הוא ענוש כרת ואם מצה היא אין אדם יוצא בה ידי חובתו בפסח דכיון שפתתו כמין שתיתא יצא מתורת לחם והא הכא הפת המחוי אין יוצא בה ידי חובתו בפסח וחייבין על חימוצו כרת ושני' לא תימא משום דהויא מצה עשירה אלא משום דנילושה במי

*) פירש רבינו בכאן הוא כפי' התוס' לעיל לד ע"ב ד"ה ונתן ודו"ק. **) מלשון רבינו נראה דגי' אחרת היה לו בד' הגמ' כאן דהראיה היא מתרומה עצמה דעשה בה התורה מעלה.

עין משפט נר מצוה

קיב א מיי' פ"ג מהל' מעשר שני הל' ז סמג לאוין רסד:

קיג ב מיי' פ"ז מהל' תרומות הלכה ב סמג לאוין רנז:

קיד ג מיי' פ"ו מהל' איסורי מזבח הלכה ח:

[ועי' תוס' לעיל יט. ד"ה אלמא ויותר מבואר בתו' חגיגה כג: ד"ה והא]

קטו ד מיי' פ"ה מהל' חו"מ הל' א ופ"ו הלכה ד סמג לאוין עט טוש"ע א"ח סי' תנג סעיף א:

קטז ה מיי' שם ופ"ו מהל' ביכורים הלכה ב טוש"ע שם וטוש"ע י"ד סי' שכד סעיף א:

קיז ו ז מיי' פ"ה מהל' חו"מ הל' ב ופ"ו הלכה ה סמג לאוין עט טוש"ע א"ח סימן תסב סעיף א:

[מנחות ע:]

מסורת הש"ס

נדה עא: יבמות עד: [נגעים פי"ד מ"ג]

חולין לו: [לעיל כד: ע"ש זבחי' לד. מו:]

[ע"ע תוספות זבחים לד. ד"ה ואפ"ה ותוס' מנחות כא. ד"ה ילאו]

מנחות ע.

[עי' בפירש"י דהכא ד"ה מין חיטין וכו' וע' בפרש"י מנחות דף ע. ד"ה כוסמין]

[ברכות לז. לקמן קיד:]

גס זה שם

[תוספת' דחלה פרק א']

חולין קכ.

[עיין פרש"י שבת קמה:]

תורה אור: ויקרא ז | דברים טז

גליון הש"ס

גמרא אלא מעלה. עיין משנה למלך פ"ג הלכה יז מהלכות פסולי המוקדשין:

הגהות מהר"ב רנשבורג [א] רש"י ד"ה חייבת בחלה וכו' אורז נמי לחם הוא. נ"ל קרמית נמי לחם הוא:

תורה אור

*ומי פירות אין מחמיצין.§ "יוצא בדמאי ובמעשר וכו'".§ דמאי?! *הא לא חזי ליה! כיון דאי בעי מפקר לנכסיה הוי עני ואוכל דמאי — השתא נמי חזי ליה. *דתנן: מאכילין את העניים דמאי ואת אכסניא דמאי. ואמר רב הונא: תנא, בית שמאי אומרים: אין מאכילין את העניים דמאי ואת האכסניא דמאי, ובית הלל אומרים: מאכילין.§ "מעשר ראשון שנטלה תרומתו וכו'".§ פשיטא, דכיון שנטלה תרומתו חולין הוי! לא צריכא, שהקדימו בשיבלים, ונטלה הימנו תרומת מעשר, ולא נטלה הימנו תרומה גדולה, וכדרבי אבהו. דאמר ר' אבהו אמר רבי שמעון בן לקיש: *מעשר ראשון שהקדימו בשיבלים — פטור מתרומה גדולה, שנאמר: °"והרמתם ממנו תרומת ה' מעשר מן המעשר". מעשר מן המעשר אמרתי לך, ולא תרומה גדולה ותרומת מעשר מן המעשר. אמר ליה רב פפא לאביי: אלא מעתה, אפילו *הקדימו בכרי נמי ליפטר! א"ל: עליך אמר קרא °"מכל מתנתיכם תרימו את כל תרומת ה'". ומה ראית?! האי — אידגן, והאי — לא אידגן.§ "מעשר שני והקדש שנפדו וכו'".§ פשיטא! הכא במאי עסקינן — שנתן את הקרן ולא נתן את החומש, וקא משמע לן דאין חומש מעכב.§ "והכהנים בחלה ובתרומה וכו'".§ פשיטא! מהו דתימא: מצה השוה לכל אדם בעינן, קמ"ל: *"מצות" "מצות" ריבה.§ "אבל לא בטבל וכו'".§ פשיטא! לא צריכא, בטבל טבול מדרבנן, שזרעו בעציץ שאינו נקוב.§ "ולא במעשר ראשון שלא נטלה תרומתו".§ פשיטא! לא צריכא, שהקדימו בכרי. מהו דתימא כדאמר ליה רב פפא לאביי, קא משמע לן כדשני ליה.§ "ולא במעשר שני והקדש שלא נפדו וכו'".§ פשיטא! לעולם דנפדו, ומאי "לא נפדו" — שלא נפדו כהלכתן. מעשר שני שפדאו על גב אסימון, דרחמנא אמר °"וצרת הכסף" — *דבר שיש לו צורה. והקדש — שחיללו על גבי קרקע, דרחמנא אמר: *°"ונתן הכסף וקם לו". תנו רבנן: יכול *יוצא אדם ידי חובתו בטבל שלא נתקן. כל טבל נמי, הא לא נתקן! אלא: בטבל שלא נתקן כל צורכו, שנטלה ממנו תרומה גדולה ולא נטלה ממנו תרומת מעשר, [מעשר] ראשון ולא מעשר שני, ואפילו מעשר עני, מנין — תלמוד לומר: °"לא תאכל עליו חמץ", מי שאיסורו משום בל תאכל עליו חמץ, יצא זה שאין איסורו משום בל תאכל חמץ, אלא משום בל תאכל טבל. ואיסורא דחמץ להיכן אזלא? אמר רב ששת: הא מני — ר' שמעון היא, דאמר: "אין איסור חל על איסור. דתניא, ר' שמעון אומר: האוכל

(במדבר יח; שם; דברים יד; ויקרא כז; דברים טז)

רש"י

דמאי הא לא חזי ליה. ואמרינן לקמן: מי שאיסורו משום בל תאכל חמץ לבדו, אתה יוצא בה לשום מצה — יצא מי שיש לו איסור אחר. א"נ: הויא לה מצוה הבאה בעבירה: השתא נמי חזי ליה. דחומרא דרבנן בעלמא הוא, דרוב עמי הארץ מעשרין הן: אכסניא. חיילות מלכי ישראל המוטלין על בני העיירות לזונן, להגין עליהם מאויביהן, וישראלים הן. והרי הן כעניים, הואיל ואינן במקומן: שהקדימו בשיבלים. את המעשר הקדים לתרומה גדולה קודם מירוח. דמן התורה תרומה קודמת למעשר, ד"ראשית" קריי' רחמנא, ומן הנותר הוא נותן מעשר ראשון ללוי. ועכשיו הערים הלוי וקידמו, כדי שלא יחסרנו הכהן אחד מחמשים. ונטלה הימנו תרומת מעשר כדינו. אבל תרומה גדולה הראשונה — לא נטלה הימנו. ואשמעינן מתני' דמותר, כרבי אבהו: מכל מתנותיכם. בלוים כתיב: את כל תרומת ה'. אפילו תרומה גדולה: ומה ראית. דאוקמת קרא דחיובא כשהקדימו בכרי, וקרא דפטורא כשהקדימו בשיבלין: האי. דנתמרח בכרי אידגן, וכיון דנקרא דגן — נעשה טבל לתרומה, כדכתיב: "ראשית דגנך": האי לא אידגן. וכי שקליה לוי עדיין לא הוה טבול לתרומה: טבול מדרבנן. ואפ"ה, מצוה הבאה בעבירה היא חשיב לה. ולא דמי לדמאי, וכדאמרן. דהתם אשכחן ביה היתירא לכתחילה — הלכך הכא בדיעבד נפיק: ולא במעשר ראשון שלא נטלה תרומתו. קא ס"ד בתרומת מעשר קאמר, וקא פריך: פשיטא! לא צריכא שהקדימו בכרי. והאי "תרומתו" דקתני — תרומה גדולה, דהוי חזי לאפרושי מיניה מעיקרא קאמר: כדאמר ליה רב פפא לאביי. לעיל בשמעתין: אסימון. מעה בלא צורה, פלאט"ה בלע"ז: ונתן הכסף וקם לו. במקדיש שדה כתיב: "ויסף חמישית כסף ערכך" וגו': כל טבל נמי לא איתקן. קושיא היא: או אפילו (אבילת) מעשר עני. שאין בו שום קדושה. דאילו מעשר ראשון — אית ביה תרומת מעשר שהיא קדושה, ומעשר שני כולו קדוש: מי שאיסורו משום בל תאכל חמץ. אתה יוצא בו ידי מצה בפסח, אם עשאו מצה:
האוכל

תוספות

ומי פירות אין מחמיצין. היינו להתחייב כרת, כדאמרינן בהדיא: אין חייבין על חימוצו כרת, אבל לאו אית ביה. ובסמוך נמי אמרינן*: אין לשין ביין ושמן ודבש, ואם לש — תשרף מיד. וחכמים נמי דאמרי תאכל — היינו משום שיכולין לשומרה מן החמץ כשאר עיסה, אבל לכולי עלמא מחמיצין. וקשה, דלקמן (דף מ.) מסקינן גבי *קימחא דאבישונא: אבל מי פירות שרי, דמי פירות אין מחמיצין. משמע דשרינן לגמרי. וכן פי' ר"ת: דאין מחמיצין כל עיקר. והא דאמר תשרף מיד — כשעירב עמהן מים, דאז ממהרות יותר להחמיץ. ועל הא אמר דאין בהן כרת, אבל לאו אית ביה. אבל היכא דלית ביה תערובת מים, כגון יין ושמן ושאר מי פירות — שרו לגמרי. וכן מוכח בסוף "כל המנחות באות מצה" (מנחות דף נז: ושם) דאמר: "אשר תקריבו" — לרבות מנחת נסכים לחימוץ, דברי רבי יוסי הגלילי. ופריך: מנחת נסכים מי פירות הן, ואין מחמיצין! אמר ריש לקיש, אומר היה רבי יוסי: מנחת נסכים מגבלה במים והיא כשירה. והשתא, אי סלקא דעתיך דריש לקיש ורבי *יוחנן איירי הכא בלא מים כלל, ואפילו הכי כרת ליכא אבל מלקות איכא, דחמץ נוקשה הוי — אמאי איצטריך למימר התם מגבלה במים? בלא גיבול מים נמי איצטריך קרא שלא תאפה חמץ, דהוי חמץ נוקשה, וחמץ נוקשה פסול למנחה. כדמשמע התם במנחות (דף נג.), דקאמר התם: שיאור דר' יהודה לרבי יהודה, דפסול למנחות. אלא ודאי היכא דליכא מים — אינו מחמיץ כלל. וקשה לרשב"א: דחומץ האדומי חשיב ליה בפרק "אלו עוברין" (לקמן דף מב.) חמץ דגן גמור ע"י תערובת. ואמאי? והא חומץ האדומי מפרש התם* דרמו ביה שעורים, פי': משימין השעורים ביין כדי שיתמיץ היטב, והא מי פירות אין מחמיצין! ואפילו אם משימין מים עמהן — אכתי לא הוי אלא חמץ נוקשה! ואומר ר"י: שהשעורים שורין במים קודם שמשימין ביין. ובמי ביצים נסתפק רש"י אי חשיב מי פירות או לא, לפי שאנו רואים שהעיסה נעשה עבה בהן יותר מבמים. אבל ר"ת נהג היתר בדבר, והיה נוהג לאכול בערב הפסח אחר ארבע שעות עוגה שנילושה בביצים. והא דקאמרינן *בירושלמי: האוכל מצה בערב פסח קודם זמנה כאילו בועל ארוסתו בבית חמיו — היינו מצה הראויה לצאת בה ידי חובה, וזו מצה עשירה היא:

יוצאין בדמאי. מסופק ר"י אי בעי למימר יוצא דוקא דיעבד, כדאמרינן: הואיל ומפקיר לנכסיה וחזי ליה — מכל מקום עדיין לא מפקיר להו. אי נמי: יוצאים אף לכתחלה, הואיל ושרי לעניים, ואכילת מצה נמי נקרא אכילת עניות: אכסניא מפרש בירושלמי: גוים: שחילל על גב קרקע דרחמנא אמר ונתן הכסף. תימה: אי כסף משמע ליה דווקא — נימעוט שוה כסף. ואי יליף מ"ישיב" דשוה כסף ככסף — אפילו קרקע נמי! ונראה לר"י, דילפינן בכלל ופרט וכלל: "ויסף חמישיתו" — כלל, "כסף" — פרט, "והיה לו" — חזר וכלל. מה הפרט מפורש — דבר המטלטל וגופו ממון וכו' יצאו קרקעות ועבדים ושטרות. וכן מוכח בפרק "יש בכור" (בכורות דף נא.), דתנן: אין פודין לא בעבדים ולא בשטרות ולא בקרקעות ולא בהקדשות. ומפרש התם בגמרא: ולא הקדשות בכל אלו. ובכור יליף התם בכלל ופרט וכלל. *וכן נמי יש לפרש הקדשות. ומיהו, תימה: מאי מיבעי ליה בפ' "הזהב" (ב"מ דף נד.): חומש מהו שיתחלל ע"ג קרקע? והא עיקר המיעוט בחומש כתיב, "ויסף חמישית כסף ערכך" (ויקרא כז):
האוכל

רבינו חננאל

במי פירות ומי פירות אין מחמיצין. ירושל' אין לשין עיסה במשקין אבל מקטפין אותה במשקין אמר רבי עקיבא מעשה שהייתי עם רבי אליעזר ורבי יהושע בספינה ולשתי מצתם במשקין. אין לשין בחמין מפני שחולטין ולא בפושרין מפני שהן מחמיצין: דמאי כב"ה דאמר מאכילין את העניים דמאי וכיון דחזו לעניים יוצא אדם בו בפסח וכבר פרשנוהו בכמה מקומות דדמאי הוא הלוקח פירות מעם הארץ ואינו יודע אם הן מעושרין אם לאו נותן מהם חלק אחד ממאה לכהן והן תרומת מעשר שחייב הלוי ליתן לכהן מעשר מן המעשר אבל תרומה גדולה שהיא אחד מחמישים ודאי הן מפרישים ואפילו עמי הארץ וכן מי שהפריש עמיר אחד מעשרה ונתנו לכהן קודם שיעשהו גורן וקודם שיוציאו ממנו תרומה גדולה לכהן ונתן הלוי ממנו תרומת מעשר והוא מעשר מן המעשר ואע"פ שתרומה גדולה לא נתן לכהן מותר ללוי אותו מעשר שלא נתחייב הלוי בתרומה גדולה אלא אם קבל הלוי מעשר מן הגורן אחר שהעמיד ישראל כרי אם הפריש ממנו מעשר ונתנו ללוי מקודם התרומה חייב בתרומה וחייב בתרומת מעשר הלוי ופשוטא היא והיא מפורשת בסוטה פרק אחרון: ובמעשר שני והקדש שנפדו אם נתן הקרן אע"פ שלא נתן עדיין החומש כבר שלו הוא וכן החלה והתרומה לכהנים הן ואע"פ שלישראל אסורה מצות מצות ריבה. טבל הוא שלא הורמה ממנו התרומה והמעשר ואע"פ שהיא תבואה שנזרעה בעציץ שאינו נקוב ואינה תרומת הארץ אלא תבואה זרועה בכלי מדאוריי' פטור מדרבנן חייב להפריש ממנו תרומה ומעשר לפיכך אינו מותר ואינו ראוי לאכילה וכ"ש טבל דאוריי': ולא במעשר ראשון שלא נטלה תרומתו כגון שהקדים בכרי ונתן אחד מעשרה בו ללוי ונמצא במעשר שלקח הלוי אחד מחמישים והיא תרומה גדולה וחייב עוד אחרי כן לתת לכהן מן הנשאר בידו חלק אחד מעשרה והיא תרומת מעשר ואפילו אם נתן תרומת מעשר ולא נתן התרומה גדולה אין יוצא בו ידי חובתו בפסח וכן במעשר הקדש שנפדו על אסימון והן מעות שאין בהן צורה כלומר לא נטבעו במטבע אלא הוחלק בלא צורה כאלו לא נפדו דפדיה כי האי גונא לא שמה פדיה משום דאין מתחלל אלא על כסף שיש עליו צורה שנאמר וצרת הכסף בידך ודייקינן וצרת דבר שיש עליו צורה למעוטי אסימון שאין עליו צורה: ת"ר יכול יוצא אדם בטבל שלא תקנו כהלכתו כגון שהפריש כל מה שחייב להפריש חוץ מדבר אחד ואפי' מעשר עני שמוציא בשנה השלישית ת"ל לא תאכל עליו חמץ מי שאיסורו משום לא תאכל חמץ יצא זה שאיסורו משום לא תאכל טבל פי' כל תבואה שלא נתקנה כהלכתה נקראת טבל ואקשי' עליה ואיסורא דחמץ היכא אזיל ודחי' הא מתניתא ר' שמעון היא דסבר אין איסור חמץ חל על איסור טבל

עין משפט נר מצוה

קיח א מיי' פ"ה מהל' חמץ הלכה ב סמג לאוין עו טוש"ע שם:
קיט ב מיי' פ"ו מהל' חמץ הלכה ז:
קכ ג מיי' פי"ו מהלכות מעשר הלכה יא:
קכא ד מיי' פ"ג מהל' תרומות הל' יג טור ש"ע י"ד סי' שלא:
קכב ה מיי' פ"ו מהל' מצה הלכה ח:
קכג ו ז שם הלכה ז:
קכד ח מיי' פ"ו מהל' איסורי ביאה הל' ח ופי"ד מהל' מאכלות אסורות הלכה יח:

מסורת הש"ס

[לקמן לו.] [תא"ג דלאבישונא כצ"ל] שבת קכז: ברכות מז. סוכה לה: עירובין לא. [ולפנינו בסוגי' לא נמצא רבי יוחנן רק ר"ל] [דף מב:] [נתן הכסף לא כתיב עי' תוס' שבת קכח. ד"ה ונתן ועי"ע תוס' מנחות נג: ד"ה אין מחמיצין כו']
[לקמן מ. מנחות נז:] דמאי פ"ג [מ"א] עירובין יז: [ברכות מז.] שבת קכז: עירובין לא: ביצה יג: תמורה ה. [לקמן לו.] [ב"מ מז.] [עי' תוס' סוכה ל. ד"ה משום] [ועיין תוספות בכורו' נא. ד"ה אימא וכו']

גליון הש"ס

גמרא ל"ל בטבל טבול מדרבנן. עיין לקמן קיד ע"ב תוד"ה אכלן דמאי:

קדושין עז: שבועות כד. נזיר ד. [כריתות כג.]

[לקמן לח:] [שם. לט:] [לעיל לה:] [נ"ל ולריש לקיש] לקמן קטו:

לעיל ל. כ"מ לא. זבחים לה: מנחות נה. [לקמן מ. ע"ש] [והביאה אל בני אהרן הכהנים וקמץ כנ"ל]

קכה א מיי' פ"ו מהל' מצה הלכה ח:

קכו ב ג מיי' שם הל' ה סמג לאוין עט טוש"ע או"ח סי' תסב סעיף א:

קכז ד מיי' שם פ"ה הלכה כ טו"ע שם סעיף ד בהג"ה:

קכח ה מיי' פי"ב מהל' מעשה הקרבנות הלכה כא:

קכט ו מיי' שם הל"כ:

קל ז מיי' שם הל' כג ופי"א מהל' פסולי המוקדשים הלכה ז:

קלא ח מיי' שם הל' ו:

קלב ט מיי' פי"ב מהל' מעשה הקרבנות הלכה כ:

קלג י מיי' פ"ו מהל' מצה הלכה ח:

תורה אור

*האוכל נבלה ביום הכפורים פטור. רבינא אמר: אפילו תימא רבנן; מי שאיסורו משום בל תאכל חמץ בלבד, יצא זה שאין איסורו משום בל תאכל חמץ בלבד, אלא אף משום בל תאכל טבל. מידי "בלבד" כתיב?! אלא מחוורתא כדרב ששת. ת"ר: יכול יוצא אדם ידי חובתו (דברים טז) במעשר שני בירושלים – ת"ל: °"לחם עוני" – (א) *מה שנאכל באנינות, יצא זה שאינו נאכל באנינות אלא בשמחה, דברי *ר' יוסי הגלילי. ר' עקיבא אומר: *"מצות", "מצות" ריבה, אם כן מה ת"ל: "לחם עוני" – פרט לעיסה שנילושה ביין ושמן ודבש. מאי טעמא דר' עקיבא? מי כתיב "לחם עוני" "עני" כתיב. ור' יוסי הגלילי: מי קרינן "עני"? עוני קרינן(ב). ור' עקיבא: האי דקרינן ביה עוני – כדשמואל, *דאמר שמואל: "לחם עוני" – לחם שעונין עליו דברים הרבה. וסבר ר"ע עיסה שנילושה ביין ושמן ודבש לא? והתניא: אין לשין עיסה בפסח ביין ושמן ודבש. ואם לש, רבן גמליאל אומר: תשרף מיד, וחכמים אומרים: יאכל. ואמר רבי עקיבא: שבתי היתה אצל רבי אליעזר ורבי יהושע, ולשתי להם עיסה ביין ושמן ודבש, ולא אמרו לי דבר. ואף על פי שאין לשין – מקטפין בו. אתאן לתנא קמא. וחכמים אומרים: את שלשין בו – מקטפין בו, ואת שאין לשין בו – אין מקטפין בו. ושוין שאין לשין את העיסה בפושרין. לא קשיא, הא – ביום טוב ראשון, הא – ביום טוב שני. כדאמר להו ר' יהושע(ג) לבניה: יומא קמא לא תלושו לי בחלבא, מכאן ואילך – לושו לי בחלבא. *והתניא: אין לשין את העיסה בחלב, ואם לש – כל הפת אסורה, מפני הרגל עבירה! אלא הכי קאמר: יומא קמא לא תלושו לי בדובשא, מכאן ואילך – לושו לי בדובשא. ואיבעית אימא: לעולם בחלבא, כדאמר רבינא: כעין תורא שרי, הכא נמי: כעין תורא.§ "ושוין שאין לשין את העיסה בפושרין".§ מאי שנא ממנחות? *דתנן: כל המנחות נילושות בפושרין, *(ומשתמרין) [נ"ל ומשמרין] שלא יחמצו! אם אמרו בזריזין – יאמרו בשאין זריזין? אי הכי מילתת נמי לתית! אלמה *אמר רבי זירא אמר רבה בר ירמיה אמר שמואל: חיטין של מנחות – אין לותתין אותה! לישה – בזריזין איתא, לתיתה – ליתא בזריזין. ולישה מי איתא בזריזין? והכתיב: °"ויצק עליה שמן וגו' והביאה *אל הכהן" (ויקרא ב) – *מקמיצה ואילך מצות כהונה, לימד על יציקה ובלילה שכשירה בכל אדם! לישה, נהי דבזריזין ליתא – במקום זריזין איתא. דאמר מר: בלילה כשירה בזר, חוץ לחומת עזרה – פסולה. לאפוקי לתיתה, דאינה בזריזין, ולא במקום זריזין. ומאי שנא ממנחת העומר? דתניא: מנחת העומר לותתין אותה, וצוברין אותה! ציבור שאני. תנו רבנן: יכול יוצא אדם ידי חובתו בבכורים – תלמוד לומר: °"בכל מושבותיכם תאכלו מצות" (שמות יב) – מצה הנאכלת בכל מושבותיכם, יצאו בכורים שאין נאכלין בכל מושבותיכם אלא בירושלים, דברי רבי יוסי הגלילי. רבי עקיבא אומר: מצה ומרור, מה מרור שאינו בכורים – אף מצה שאינה בכורים. אי מה מרור שאין במינו בכורים – אף מצה שאין במינה בכורים, אוציא

מנחות ע. יח.

האוכל נבילה ביום הכפורים. שוגג: פטור. מחטאת, דאין איסור יום הכפורים חל על איסור נבילה. ואם בו ביום נתנבלה – אפילו הכי היתה אסורה קודם יום הכפורים, משום אבר מן החי: מידי בלבד כתיב. קרא משמע, דכל מי שאיסור חמץ נוהג בו, אתה יוצא בו משום מצה: מי שנאכל באנינות. שמותר לאוכלו כשהוא אונן. דרוש ביה "לחם אוני", ומעשר שני אינו נאכל באנינות, דכתיב (דברים כו): "לא אכלתי באוני ממנו": מי כתיב עוני. בוי"ו, דתשמע מיניה אוני: שעונין עליו דברים. שגומרים עליו את ההלל, ואומרים עליו הגדה: אין לשין את העיסה. של מצות ביין ושמן ודבש – מפני שקרובה וממהרת להחמיץ, ואין אדם יכול לשומרה. לפיכך, אם לש – תשרף מיד. ובמועד קאמר, ולא ביום טוב. דהבערה שלא לצורך היא. *(ולר' יוחנן) דאמר לעיל: מי פירות אין מחמיצין – לא קשיא הך, דאיהו "אין חייבין על חימוצו כרת" קאמר, ולא הוי חמץ גמור, אלא חמץ נוקשה הוי – כלומר רע, ואותו חימוץ הן ממהרין להחמיץ, ואי אפשר לשומרן: וחכמים אומרים תאכל. דקסברי: אפשר לשומרה. והכא לא גרסינן מיד – דמשנאפה לא תחמיץ: שבתי היתה. שביתתי היתה, רגל פסח אחד אצל ר' אליעזר ור' יהושע: מקטפין. טחין פניה לאחר עריכתה: פושרין. ממהרין להחמיץ: יום ראשון. לילה הראשון, שהמצה חובה, בעינן "לחם עוני": אין לשין עיסה בחלב. כל ימות השנה, שלא יאכל בשר עמה: כעין תורא. מעט כעין של שור מותר ללוש בחלב, דאכיל ליה מיד בבת אחת, ולא משהי ליה דליגעי שנילוש בחלב: ומאי שנא ממנחות. דתנן בהו דאות מצות, ואפילו הכי נלושות בפושרין, ומשמרן שלא יחמיצו: הכי גרסינן: כהנים זריזין הם: לתיתה. לשורן במים מעט, ולכותשן במכתשת להסיר מורסנן, כדי שתהא סולתן נקיה: לתיתה ליתא בזריזין. כשמביאה הזר כבר היא סולת: לישה. כגון מנחת מחבת ומרחשת ומנחת מאפה תנור, שאופין אותה תחילה עשר חלות, ואחר כך פותתין אותן עד שמחזירן לסלתן, כדכתיב (ויקרא ב): "פתות אותה פתים", ואחר כך נותן שמן ובוללה, ויוצק וקומץ. וכשאופה תחילה נילושה בפושרין: לימד על יציקה ובלילה כו'. והני במנחת מאפה תנור לאחר לישה ואפייה ופתיתה ניהו: במקום זריזים איתא. בעזרה, שהמחבת והמרחשת כלי שרת הן, וכן תנור של מקדש. וכיון דבעזרה איתא – חזו לה כהנים, ומלמדין אותו להיזהר בה: ומאי שנא. שאר מנחות, דקאמר שמואל אין לותתין אותם, ממנחת העומר דתנן בה: לותתין אותה, וצוברין אותה, שיזובו מימיה: ציבור שאני. מנחת העומר קרבן ציבור היא, וכל עסקין שלה נעשין על פי בית דין; קצירתה, והיבהוב שלה, ולתיתה – הכל בבית דין, ובזריזין הוא. ואיכא דאמרי: צבור שאני, דהואיל וצוברין אותה – מימיה זבין ואין מחמיצין. ולאו מילתא היא. חדא, דבתוספתא קתני לה, ולא קתני וצוברין אלא ובוררין. ועוד, אי איכא תקנתא בצבור – (של) חיטים של מנחות נמי לילתתינהו ונילצברינהו: בבכורים. כגון כהן שהביאו לו חיטין בכורים בירושלים: בכורים אין נאכלין אלא בירושלים. שנאמר: "לא תוכל לאכול בשעריך" וגו', ואמר מר (מכות דף יז.): "ותרומת ידך" – אלו בכורים: מצה ומרור. הקישן הכתוב – "על מצות ומרורים": מרור אינו בבכורים. דתנן (בכורים פ"א מ"ג): אין מביאין בכורים אלא מז' מינין, דכתיב "מארצך" – משבח ארצך, במנחות בפ' "כל קרבנות" (דף פד.) ולקמן ב"מקום שנהגו" (דף נג.):

האוכל נבילה ביום הכפורים. פ"ה: אפילו נתנבלה ביום הכפורים – לא חיילא עלה איסור יוה"כ, דהרי הוה עלה איסור אבר מן החי. וקשה לר"י: דהא כי פקע איסור אבר מן החי – יחול עלה איסור יום הכפורים ונבילה בבת אחת, דמודה רבי שמעון באיסור בבת אחת! ומיהו י"ל: אפילו נתנבלה ביום הכפורים לא חייל עלה איסור יום הכפורים, דאיסור שאין זבות הוה ביה נמי מעיקרא, ואכתי לא פקע מיניה*:

[וע"ע תוס' חולין לז. ד"ה השתא ותוס' שבועות כד. ד"ה האוכל ע"ש]

עוני קרינן ביה. והא דגבי לולב (סוכה דף לב.) כ"ע מודו ד"כפת" כתיב, ולא אמר "כפות" קרינן, וילטרך שני לולבים ליטול! אור"י: משום דהתם סמכינן אקרא "פרי עץ הדר" – דלא משמע אלא חד, לכך מודו התם כ"ע דדרשינן מסורת*:

[וע"ע תוס' סוכה ו: ד"ה ור"ש ועוד שם לב. ד"ה כפת שכתבו דלריך טעמא וע"ע תוס' סנהדרין ד. ד"ה כולהו ותוס' זבחים מ. ד"ה לא נלרכה ותוס' נדה טו. ד"ה לא]

במקום זריזים איתא. וא"ת: והא הכא במנחת מאפה תנור מיירי, שהיתה נילושה בפושרים, ואותה מנלן שנבללת בעזרה? ושאר מנחה שנבללת בעזרה – לפי שהבלילה היתה בכלי שרת! וי"ל: דגם מאפה תנור היו לשין בעזרה סמוך לתנור של קודש, שלא תחמיץ. ורבינו אפרים בר אפרים הגבור מפרש: דע"כ היו לשין אותה בעזרה, לפי שהיו מודדין אותה בעשרון של קודש, כדתנן בפרק "שתי מדות" (מנחות פז.): עשרון מה היה משמש – בו מודד לכל המנחות*:

[ועי' תוס' סוכה ג. ד"ה ואי ותוס' מנחות ע. ד"ה ריש לקיש]

מה מרור שאין ביכורים. וליכא למימר: מרור היינו זית שהוא מר, כדדרשינן (*סנהדרין דף קח:): "והנה עלה זית טרף בפיה" אמרה יונה: יהא מזונותי מרורים כזית וכו'. דלקמן (דף לט.) אמר: מרור דומיא דמצה, מה מצה מין זרעים – אף מרור כן. ועוד: שזית – האילן מר ולא הפרי, כדמשמע "עלה זית". ואמרינן נמי (מכילתא פ' בשלח): "ויורהו ה' עץ" – זהו זית, שאין מר באילנות כזית*:

[עירובין יח:]

[וע"ע תוס' עירובין יח: ד"ה מרורין]

הדר

הגהות הב"ח

(א) גמ' לחם עוני מי שנאכל: (ב) שם קרינן ביה ור' עקיבא: (ג) שם ר' יהושע בן לוי לבניה:

גליון הש"ס

גמ' מידי בלבד כתיב. עיין בהר"ש פ"א מ"ג דטהרות וצ"ע:

רבינו חננאל

טבל דתניא האוכל נבלה ביום הכפורים פטור ולא אתי איסור יום הכפורים חייל אאיסור נבלה: **ת"ר** יכול יוצא אדם ידי מצה בפסח במעשר שני בירושלים ת"ל לחם עוני כי בעינן לחם הנאכל באוני יצא זה שאינו נאכל באוני אלא בשמחה דברי ר' יוסי הגלילי כדתנן בס"פ מעשר שני במנחה ביום טוב היו מתודים כיצד היה וידוי בערתי הקדש מן הבית זה מעשר שני וכו' עד לא אכלתי באוני ממנו אם אכלו באנינה לא היה יכול להתודות: **ר' עקיבא** אומר מצות

מצות ריבה אם כן מה ת"ל לחם עוני פרט למצה עשירה ואסיקנא לר' עקיבא כתיב עני למעוטי מצה עשירה וקרינן עוני כשמואל דאמר לחם שעונין אחריו דברים ואקשי' איני דר' עקיבא אוסר לאכול בפסח מצה עשירה והתניא אין לשין את העיסה ביין ושמן ודבש ואם לש ר"ג אומר תשרף מיד וחכמים אומרים תאכל מיד פי' אם אפאה אמר ר' עקיבא שבתי היתה אצל ר' אליעזר ור' יהושע ולשתי להם עיסה ביין ושמן ודבש ולא אמרו לי דבר ושנינן הא דאסור מצה עשירה ביום טוב ראשון בלבד בזמן שעונין אחריו דברין והן ההגדה שאמר מצה זו שאנו אוכלין על שום מה וכו' אסור אותו זמן לאכול מצה עשירה דבעינן עוני וזה שאמר לשתי להם עיסה ביין ושמן ודבש בשאר הימים ויש לומר כי דבר מועט לש להם כגון בני ר' יהושע שלשו בחלב כעין תורא שהוא דבר מועט וביום הראשון [אסור] ובשאר הימים מותר. ונתברר למביני מדע דסוגיא דברייתא הכי הוא אין לשין את העיסה ביין ושמן ודבש ואע"פ שאין לשין מקטפין בהן וחכמים אומרים אין לשין ואף לא מקטפין ואם לש או קיטף ר"ג אומר תשרף מיד ואפי' אפאה וחכמים אומרים תאכל מיד אם אפאה ודברי הכל זו הברייתא בשאר ימות הפסח היא שנויה זולתי יו"ט ראשון ומראין הדברים שהת"ק שאמר אע"פ שאין לשין בו מקטפין בו כך פי' דבריו אע"פ שאין לשין במים ושמן ואם לשו במים ושמן מקטפין בשמן מכלל שהלישה שאסר שמן על ידי מים הוא שאסר ומה שאסר בלישה שמן על ידי מים התיר בקיטוף וחכמים אסרו זה וזה הלישה והקיטוף ע"י מים הכל אסור וקיי"ל כחכמים שאפי' אם לש במים לבדו אסור לו לקטף בשמן כלל וכל שכן שאין לשין במים ושמן כלל: **ושוין** שאין לשין את עיסה בפושרין. ואמרי' אמאי לא והא כל המנחות נילושות [בפושרין] ומשמרן שלא יחמיצו ודחי' אם התירו לכהנים שהן זריזין ומשמרין העיסה שלא תחמיץ ומשום זריזותן התירו להן יתירו לכל אדם ודחי' לתיתה פעמים שתהיה שלא על ידי כהן והא לישה נמי יתכן שתהיה שלא על ידי כהן דהא מקמיצה ואילך מצות כהונה ולישה קמי הכי הוא ואפילו [הכי] לישה כי ליתא בכהנים אינה אלא בעזרה מקום שהכהנים רואים אותה אבל חוץ לחומת העזרה פסולה לתיתה אינה לא בכהנים ולא בעזרה לפיכך לא התירוה: **ת"ר** יכול יוצא אדם ידי חובתו בבכורים כו' בא ר"ע למעט הבכורים ממצה וממרור ואמר בעינן מצה כמרור מה מרור אין מביאים ממנו בכורים כי ירק הוא ולא פירי כך מצה אין מביאים מן הבכורים ואקשי'

אוציא חיטין ושעורין שיש במינן ביכורים! ת"ל: "מצות מצות" – ריבה. אי מצות מצות ריבה אפילו ביכורים נמי! הדר ביה רע"ק. דתניא: יכול יצא אדם ידי חובתו בביכורים – ת"ל: "בכל מושבתיכם תאכלו מצות" (שמות יב) – מצה הנאכלת בכל מושבות, יצאו ביכורים שאינן נאכלין בכל מושבות, אלא בירושלים. יכול שאני מוציא אף מעשר שני – תלמוד לומר: "מצות מצות" ריבה. ומה ראית לרבות מעשר שני ולהוציא ביכורים – מרבה אני מעשר שני שיש לו היתר בכל מושבות כדר' (אליעזר), ומוציא אני ביכורים שאין להן היתר בכל מושבות. *דא"ר (אליעזר): [א]מנין למעשר שני שנטמא שפודין אותו אפי' בירושלים – ת"ל: "כי לא תוכל שאתו" (דברים יד), ואין שאת אלא אכילה – שנאמר: "וישא משאת מאת פניו" (בראשית מג). מאן שמעת ליה דאמר: במעשר שני נפיק ביה – רבי עקיבא, וקממעיט להו לביכורים מ"בכל מושבתיכם". שמע מינה: הדר ביה. ור' יוסי הגלילי, תיפוק לי' מ"לחם עוני" – מי שנאכל באוני, יצא זה שאין נאכל אלא בשמחה! סבר ליה כרבי שמעון, *דתניא: [ב]ביכורים אסורין לאונן, ור' שמעון מתיר. מאי טעמא דרבנן – דכתיב: "לא תוכל לאכל בשעריך" (דברים יב) ואמר מר: *"תרומת ידך" – אלו ביכורים, דאיתקש ביכורים למעשר, מה [ג]מעשר אסור לאונן – אף ביכורים אסור לאונן. ורבי שמעון: תרומה קרינהו רחמנא, כתרומה; מה תרומה מותרת לאונן – אף ביכורים מותר לאונן. ורבי שמעון, נהי דהיקיש לית ליה שמחה מיהא מיכתב כתיבא בהו, דכתי' "ושמחת בכל הטוב" (שם כו)! ההוא לזמן שמחה הוא דאתא, *דתנן: [ד]מעצרת ועד החג – מביא וקורא, מהחג ועד חנוכה – מביא ואינו קורא. תנו רבנן: "לחם עני" – [ה]פרט לחלוט ולאשישה. יכול לא יצא אדם ידי חובתו אלא בפת הדראה – ת"ל: "מצות מצות" – [ו]ריבה, ואפילו כמצות של שלמה. א"כ מה ת"ל: "לחם עוני" – פרט לחלוט ולאשישה. ומאי משמע דהאי אשישה לישנא דחשיבותא – דכתיב: "ויחלק לכל העם לכל המון ישראל למאיש ועד אשה לאיש חלת לחם אחת ואשפר אחד ואשישה אחת וגו'" (ש"ב ו). ואמר רב חנן בר אבא: "אשפר" – אחד מששה בפר, "אשישה" – אחד מששה באיפה. ופליגא דשמואל, דאמר שמואל: אשישה – גרבא דחמרא, דכתיב: "ואהבי אשישי ענבים" (הושע ג). ת"ר: *אין אופין פת עבה *(ביום טוב) בפסח, דברי בית שמאי, ובית

רש"י

הדר ביה ר' עקיבא. מהך היקשא דמצה ומרור, ויליף ביכורים מ"בכל מושבותיכם": אף מעשר שני. בירושלים, הואיל ואינו נאכל בכל מושבות. מעתה, משהביאו לירושלים – שוב אינו יכול לחלל לאכול בחוץ, כדאמרינן במסכת מכות (דף כ.): מחיצה לקלוט מדרבנן, דמשקלטוהו מחיצות – שוב אינו נפדה: כר' אליעזר. דאם נטמא פודין אותו ואוכלין אותו בכל מקום. הלכך, כי לא ניטמא נמי, ולא נפדה – נפיק ביה: שאתו. כשלא תוכל לאוכלו, כגון זה שניטמא – "ונתת בכסף": מאן שמעת ליה כו' ר' עקיבא. לעיל, בברייתא קמייתא, וקממעט להו לביכורים מ"בכל מושבותיכם", ולא מהקיש מצה ומרור: ור' יוסי. למה ליה למילף ביכורים מ"בכל מושבותיכם"? תיפוק ליה מ"לחם עוני", מהיכא דנפקא ליה מעשר שני. בשלמא ר' עקיבא – לא פירש אוני: ואמר מר. במסכת מכות (דף יז.): אלו ביכורים. דכתיב בהו יד, "ולקח הכהן הטנא מידך" (דברים כו): תרומה מותרת לאונן. ביבמות ב"הערל" נפקא לן מ"וכל זר" יתירא, זרות אמרתי לך ולא אנינות: ה"ג: שמחה כתיב בהו "ושמחת בכל הטוב": זמן שמחה. בזמן קצירה ולקיטה, שאדם לוקט תבואתו ולבו שמח, הצריכו הכתוב קרייה ד"ארמי אובד אבי": מעצרת. דתנן במנחות (דף סח:): אין מביאין ביכורים קודם לעצרת, ששתי הלחם של עצרת מתירין הבאת ביכורין, דביכורים איקרו, דכתיב: "וביום הביכורים בהקריבכם מנחה חדשה" וגו': ועד החג. שבתוך הזמן הזה זמן לקיטה, ושמח במעשיו: מהחג ועד חנוכה אינו זמן שמחה, ואינו קורא. ומחנוכה ואילך אינו זמן הבאה, דתניא בספרי: "אשר תביא מארצך" – כל זמן שמצויין על פני ארצך, שלא כלו לחיה מן השדה: חלוט. אישקלדי"ר, ואחשיבות הוא: אשישה. גלוסקה גדולה: הדראה. שניטל כל הדרה, דהיינו פת קיבר: של שלמה. שהיה מעונג, כלומר: סלת נקייה: גרבא דחמרא. איפה של יין: וכמה

תוספות

אוציא חטין ושעורין שיש במינן ביכורים. (א) *א"ל: אם כן נוציא כל חמשת המינין שיש במינן ביכורים. דאנו לאו בעינן, דממעטינן לעיל אורז ודוחן:

אי מצות מצות ריבה אפי' ביכורים נמי. תימה לר"י: דנימא אהני ריבוי לרבות יש במינו ביכורים ואהני מיעוט למעט ביכורי'! ויש לומר: דסברא הוא, אי מרבינן הא – מרבינן נמי הא:

דאמר ר' אליעזר. נראה לר"י: דהא דאיצטריך למימר כר' אליעזר – היינו אי מחיצה לקלוט דאורייתא. אבל אי מחיצה לקלוט דרבנן – לא צריך דר' אליעזר, דהא נאכל בכל מושבות, שיכול להוציאו חוץ לירושלים ולפדותו. ומיהו רבי אליעזר מאי סבר: מחיצה לקלוט דרבנן, ואיצטריך קרא לנטמא, שיכול לפדותו אפי' בירושלים, ואם תאמר: והא מעשר שני נאכל בכל ערי ישראל, בנוב ובגבעון, כדתנן בפרק בתרא דזבחים (דף קיט:): באו לנוב וגבעון – הותרו הבמות, קדשי קדשים נאכלים לפנים מן הקלעים, קדשים קלים ומעשר שני נאכלין בכל ערי ישראל. ולקמן *חשבינן הא "נאכלין בכל מושבות" גבי חלות תודה ורקיקי נזיר, דקאמר ריש לקיש: חלות תודה ורקיקי נזיר נאכלין בנוב וגבעון, ולכך מפיק להו מקרא אחרינא מ"ושמרתם" ולא מצי מפיק להו מ"בכל מושבותיכם". וביכורים נמי נאכלין בנוב וגבעון ובכל ערי ישראל, דמאי שנא? והיכי ממעטינן להו מ"בכל מושבותיכם"? ויש לומר: דהכא לא ממעטינן להו מ"בכל מושבותיכם" אלא לזמן בית עולמים, ולא לזמן נוב וגבעון. ולקמן, גבי חלות תודה ורקיקי נזיר – איצטריך למידרש מ"ושמרתם" לזמן נוב וגבעון, ולא לזמן בית עולמים*:

מאן שמעת ליה דאמר מעשר שני נפיק ביה ר' עקיבא. אע"ג דכמה תנאי דרשי מסורת ולא מקרא, ולדידהו נפיק במעשר שני, דלא דרשינן אוני – מ"מ, אע"ג דס"ל דמסורת עיקר – ה"א דלא דרשי המקרא לסוף דרשה:

ורבי יוסי הגלילי תיפוק לי' שאינן נאכלין לאונן. ואם תאמר: לר' יוסי הגלילי, מעשר שני תיפוק ליה מ"בכל מושבותיכם" כמו ביכורים! וי"ל: דאי לאו עוני – ה"א דמושבותיכם אתא דוקא לביכורים. אבל מעשר שני שיכול להיות לו היתר בכל מושבות, אם נטמא כר"א – ה"א מצות מצות ריבה:

מה תרומה מותרת לאונן אף ביכורים. תימה לר"י, דבפרק בתרא דמכות (דף יז.) קתני: "ותרומת ידך" – אלו הביכורים. אמר ר' שמעון: וכי מה בא זה ללמדך? אם לאכלן חוץ לחומה, פירוש: דכתיב ברישא דקרא "לא תוכל לאכול בשעריך" – קל וחומר ממעשר הקל, וכו' והשתא נימא דאיצטריך קרא, דאי לאו קרא – הוה אמינא דלא נילף ממעשר הקל, דתרומה קרינהו רחמנא כדאמרינן הכא! ונראה לרשב"א: דלענין חוץ לחומה איכא למילף ממעשר טפי, לפי ששניהן ענין אחד הן, ששניהן טעונין קריאה והבאת מקום:

פרט לחלוט. משמע דחלוט הוי לחם, אלא דלא הוי לחם עוני. והא דאמרינן בסמוך: מאי חלות המסרת – חלוט של בעלי בתים, משמע דלא הוי לחם, מדפטר מן החלה. לקמן מיירי בבלילתו רכה כמו שאפרש לפנים. אי נמי: הכא בדהדר אפייה בתנור. אך קשה, דאמרי' ב"החולץ" (יבמות מ.): אע"ג דחלטיה מעיקרא, כיון דהדר ואפייה בתנור או באילפס – לחם קרי' ביה, ואדם יוצא ידי חובתו בפסח! ואומר רבינו תם: דהתם נמי מיירי בבלילתו רכה, דקודם אפייה לאו לחם הוא כלל, ואחר אפייתו הוא דחשיב לחם. וחשיב נמי לחם עוני, כיון שבלילתו רכה:

ובית

רבינו חננאל

ואקשי' אי הכי דמי שהוכשר למרור הוא שהוכשר למצה יש לומר [אי מה מרור] אין במינו בכורים כי ירק הוא ואין בכל מיני ירק בכורים ואף מצה בעינן דבר שאין במינו בכורים אוציא חטים ושעורים שיש במינן בכורים דתנן אין מביאי' בכורים חוץ משבעת המינים. ופרשי' בגמ' דהני שבעת המינים הן חטה ושעורה גפן ותאנה ורמון זית ותמרים ת"ל מצות מצות ריבה אפי' בכורים יוצא אדם בהן והדר ביה ר' עקיבא והודה לר' יוסי הגלילי דקא ממעט לבכורים מבכל מושבותיכ' דתניא יכול יהא אדם יוצא בבכורים ת"ל בכל מושבותיכם תאכלו מצות מצה הנאכלת בכל מושבות יצאו בכורים שאין נאכלים בכל מושבות וכו' ואוקימנא לר' עקיבא מדקא ממעט לבכורים ממושבות ש"מ הדר ביה מההיא דתניא מצות מצות ריבה חטים ושעורים אע"פ שיש במינן בכורים: **מאי** טעמא דרבנן דפליגי על ר' שמעון דאמרי בכורים אסורים לאונן ואמרי' דכתיב לא תוכל לאכול בשעריך מעשר דגנך וגו' ואמר מר ותרומת ידך אלו הבכורים הקישן הכתוב למעשר ובמעשר כתיב (דברים כו יד) לא אכלתי באוני מה מעשר אסור לאונן אף בכורים אסורים לאונן. ור' שמעון אמר לך התורה קרנהו תרומה מה תרומה מותרת לאונן דתניא בהדיא בגמרא יבמות פ' הערל אונן אסור במעשר ומותר בתרומה ובפרה טבול יום אסור בתרומה ומותר בפרה ובמעשר כו' אף בכורים מותרין לאונן [והא] דכתיב בבכורים ושמחת בכל הטוב וגו' לאו למעוטי אונן הוא דאתא אלא ללמדך שאין מביאין בכורים [וקורין] אלא עד זמן שמחה והן ימי החג: **ת"ר** לחם עוני פרט לחלוט ואשישה יכול לא יצא אלא בפת הדראה בלבד כלומר פת סובין שאוכל העני ת"ל מצות מצות ריבה אפי' כמצת שלמה שהיתה סלת יוצא בה לא מיעטה התורה אלא מצה עשירה כגון חלוט ואשישה והני מילי בלילה הראשון דגרסי' בירושלמי אר"י בן לוי אותו כזית שאדם יוצא בו ידי חובתו בפסח צריך שלא יהא בו משקין. ר' ירמיה אומר למצוה ר' יהודה בן פזי אומר לעיכוב היתיב [ר' בון בר חייא] והתנן חלות תודה ורקיקי נזיר יוצאין בהן והא אית בהו משקין אמר ר' יוסי תמן רביעית היא ומתחלקת לכמה מינין: **יוצאין** בפסח במצה עבה עד טפח כלחם הפנים ובמצה נא עד כדי שתפרס ולא תעשה גידין גידין:

עין משפט נר מצוה

[מהרש"א גורס וא"ת אם כן כו' ואנו לחם בעינן כו' ועי' רש"ל]

קלד א מיי' פ"ג מהל' מעשר שני הל"ג:

קלה ב מיי' פ"ג מהל' בכורים הלכה ו:

קלו ג מיי' פ"ג מהל' מעשר שני הל' ה:

קלז ד מיי' פ"ד מהל' בכורים הלכה יג:

קלח ה מיי' פ"ה מהל' מצה הל' ג טוש"ע או"ח סי' תנד סעיף ג:

קלט ו מיי' פ"ו מהל' מצה הל' ה טוש"ע או"ח סי' תנד סעיף א:

[נ"ל אלעזר]

[דף לח:]

[ועי' תוס' זבחים קיט. ד"ה באו]

מסורת הש"ס

[נ"ל אלעזר]

ב"מ נג: מכות יט: סנהדרין קיב.

[בכורים פ"ב מ"ב יבמות עג.]

[יבמות שם: מכות יז. חולין קכ: מעיל' טז.]

[בכורים פ"א מ"ו]

ביצה כב: וגם ליתא תיבת ביו"ט

הגהות הב"ח

(א) תוס' ד"ה אוציא וכו' בכורים ואינו לומר א"ל וכו' דלאו לחם בעינן:

וכמה פת עבה טפח. ואפי' הכי שרו בית הלל, אבל טפי מטפח – לא: שכן מצינו בלחם הפנים. שהוא אסור לבא חמץ, כדאמרינן במנחות (דף נז.): "כל המנחה אשר תקריבו" וגו' – לרבות לחם הפנים לחימוץ, לאזהרה שלא יחמילו. ואפילו הכי עובי דפנותיו טפח, דהיינו לחם שהיו לו פנים, ואין פנים פחותין *מטפח: אם אמרו. והתירו עובי טפח: לזריזין. כהנים שבקיאין בשימורו שלא יחמיץ, יתירו לכל אדם שאינן זריזין? בפת עמילה. שאינה ממהרת להחמיץ, שעמילתה מעכבתה. עמילה = ברייר"א, כדתנן (מנחות דף עו.): כל המנחות טעונין שלש מאות שיפה וחמש מאות בעיטה: בתנור חם. בכל יום תמיד היו מסיקין תנור של מקדש לאפיית מנחות ולחמי תודה. ושל מתכת היה, כדאמר בזבחים בפ' "דם חטאת" (דף צה.): בעצים יבשים. שהיו מביאים אותן מימות החמה, כדאמרינן בתענית (דף לא.): מחמשה עשר באב ואילך תשש כחה של חמה, ולא היו כורתין עצים למערכה: פת מרובה. הרבה חררין ביחד. ולאו משום חימוץ נקט לה. ובחררין דקים קאמר, ומשום דקא טרח טירחא דלא צריך הוא: ביחוד. בינו לביני. רביה דר' ירמיה – רב, רביה דרב – רבינו הקדוש. לישנא אחרינא: ביחוד – בבירור, כמו "וידעו ביחוד ששם ארון נגנז" (יומא דף נד.): בלישה. כשלשין אותה עבה היא העיסה, כשהיא כולה ביחד: הכי גרסינן: תניא נמי הכי ב"ש אומרים אין אופין פת עבה בי"ט. ולא גרסינן בפסח: תניא נמי הכי. דלאו משום חמץ נקט, אלא משום טירחא, דהא הכא לא תנא פסח: ובסריקין המצויירים. מצות המצויירות, ואע"פ שאמרו לכתחלה אסור – דיעבד שפיר דמי: שוהה עליהן. לציירן, ואין נותנין מהר לתנור, ומחמילין: אפשר יעשה. הצורה בדפוס, ויקבענה בסריק: כיון. כלומר: מהר, כדחיפה אחת: יאמרו כל הסריקין אסורין ושל בייתוס מותרין. שהרי רוב נחתומין אין להם אותו דפוס: לא של כל אדם אמרו. לאסור, דבעל הבית העושה אותן לעצמו אינו חושש לייפותן כל כך, ואינו שוהה עליהן: אלא של נחתומין. העושין למכור, ומקפידין על נויין, ושוהין על ציורן: איכא דאמרי לא של נחתומין אמרו. לאסור, שרגילין ובקיאין בדבר, ויש להן דפוסין: עושין סריקין. מצויירין כמין רקיקין, ובלבד שיהו דקין וקלושין דאין ממהרין להחמיץ. אבל לא מציירין את העבים כגלוסקאות, דמתוך עוביין מחמילין בשהייה מועטת: הסופגנין. עשויין כספוג: והדובשנין. מטוגנין בדבש, וכולן מין לחם: והאיסקריטין. עשויין כלפיחית, דמתרגמינן: איסקריטון (שמות טז), שלשין עיסתן רכה מאד: המסרת. תרגום של מחבת: ופטורין מן החלה. דכתיב (במדבר טו): "באכלכם מלחם הארץ" – והני לאו לחם נינהו. ולקמיה מפרש טעמא: והמדומע. חולין שנפלה תרומה לתוכן – פטור, ד"תרימו תרומה" כתיב, ולא שכבר היה תרומה: חלות של בעלי בתים. אינו נעשה כתקון לחם: ריש לקיש אכולהו קאי, ולאו לאפלוגי אדר' יהושע בן לוי אתא: מעשה אילפס הן. לפיכך לאו לחם הוא, דקא סבר: אין לחם אלא האפוי בתנור, כדכתיב: "לחמכם בתנור אחד" (ויקרא כו): והללו. להכי פטורין, לפי שעשאן בחמה ולא באור: שהרתיחה. האילפס ואחר כך הדביק בה הלחם, דהוה ליה כעין מעשה תנור – הלכך חייבין: הינא. אינה אפויה כל צרכה. לשון "אל תאכלו ממנו נא" (שמות יב): העשויה באילפס. ואע"ג דלחם בעינן, כדכתיב: "לחם עוני" (דברים טז): מאי מצה הינא. כלומר: כמה תאפה ויהא יוצא בה? שפורסה. שמשברה, לשון פרוסה: וכן לענין לחמי תודה. אם שחט הזבח עליהן, מאחר שנאפת כענין הזה – קידש הלחם, והתודה כשירה. דהואיל וקרמו פניה דתנן במנחות – כי האי גוונא בעינן:

תורה אור

ובית הלל מתירין. וכמה פת עבה? א"ר הונא: טפח, שכן מצינו בלחם הפנים טפח. מתקיף לה רב יוסף: [א]אם אמרו בזריזין – יאמרו בשאינן זריזין? אם אמרו בפת עמילה – יאמרו בפת שאינו עמילה? אם אמרו בעצים יבשין – יאמרו בעצים לחים? אם אמרו בתנור חם – יאמרו בתנור צונן? אם אמרו בתנור של מתכת – יאמרו בתנור של חרס? אמר ר' ירמיה בר אבא: שאילית את רבי ביחוד, ומנו – רב. איכא דאמרי: *רב ירמיה בר אבא אמר רב: שאילית את רבי ביחוד, ומנו – רבינו הקדוש. מאי פת עבה? [ב]פת מרובה. ואמאי קרו ליה פת עבה? משום דנפישא בלישה. ואי בעית אימא: באתריה דהאי תנא לפת מרובה פת עבה קרו ליה. מאי טעמא? אי משום דקא טרח טירחא דלא צריך – מאי איריא בפסח? אפילו בי"ט נמי! אין הכי נמי, והאי תנא ביום טוב של פסח קאי. תניא נמי הכי, בית שמאי אומרים: אין אופין פת *עבה ביום טוב, [ג]ובית הלל מתירין. *ת"ר: [ד]יוצאין בפת נקיה *ובהדראה, ובסריקין המצויירין בפסח, אע"פ שאמרו: אין עושין סריקין המצויירין בפסח. אמר רב יהודה: דבר זה שאל בייתוס בן זונין לחכמים: מפני מה אמרו אין עושין סריקין המצויירין בפסח? אמרו לו: מפני שהאשה שוהה עליה, ומחמצתה. אמר להם: אפשר יעשנה בדפוס, °ויקבענה כיון! *אמרו לו: יאמרו כל הסריקין – אסורין, וסריקי בייתוס – מותרין. אמר רבי אלעזר בר צדוק: פעם אחת נכנסתי אחר אבא לבית רבן גמליאל, והביאו לפניו סריקין המצויירין בפסח. אמרתי: אבא, לא כך אמרו חכמים [ה]"אין עושין סריקין המצויירין בפסח"? אמר לי: בני, לא של כל אדם אמרו, אלא של נחתומין אמרו. איכא דאמרי, הכי קאמר ליה: לא של נחתומין אמרו, אלא של כל אדם. א"ר יוסי: עושין סריקין *כמין רקיקין, ואין עושין סריקין *כמין גלוסקאות.(א) *ת"ר: הסופגנין, והדובשנין, ואיסקריטין, וחלת המסרת, והמדומע – פטורים מן החלה. מאי חלת המסרת? אמר רבי יהושע בן לוי: זה חלוט של בעלי בתים. אמר ריש לקיש: הללו מעשה אילפס הן. ורבי יוחנן [ו]אמר: מעשה אילפס חייבין, והללו שעשאן בחמה. מיתיבי: הסופגנין והדובשנין והאיסקריטין, עשאן באילפס – חייבין, בחמה – פטורין. תיובתיה דרבי שמעון בן לקיש! אמר עולא, אמר לך רבי שמעון בן לקיש: הכא במאי עסקינן – שהרתיחה ולבסוף הדביק – אבל הדביק ולבסוף הרתיחה מאי – הכי נמי דפטורין, אדתני סיפא "עשאן בחמה פטורין" ליפלוג וליתני בדידה: בד"א – כגון שהרתיחה ולבסוף הדביק, אבל הדביק ולבסוף הרתיחה – פטורין! חסורי מחסרא והכי קתני: בד"א – שהרתיחה ולבסוף הדביק, אבל הדביק ולבסוף הרתיחה – נעשה כמי שעשאן בחמה ופטורין. ת"ש: *[ז]יוצאין במצה הינא ובמצה העשויה [ח]באילפס! הכא נמי: שהרתיחה ולבסוף הדביק. מאי מצה הינא? אמר רב יהודה אמר שמואל: כל שפורסה ואין חוטין נמשכין הימנה. אמר רבא: *[ט]וכן לחמי תודה. פשיטא, ויקרא הכא "לחם" כתיב, והכא "לחם" כתיב! מהו דתימא: הואיל וכתיב: °"והקריב ממנו אחד

ובית הלל מתירין. טעמא דבית הלל כדאמרינן (ביצה דף יז.): מערמת אשה ואופה תנור מלא ככרות, אע"פ שאין צריכה רק לככר אחד. אבל למלאות התנור פעם אחרת – ליכא מאן דשרי*:

תנא בפסח קאי. תימה: דלא משני הכי בריש "ערבי פסחים" (לקמן צט:), דפריך: מאי איריא ערבי פסחים וכו'! וי"ל: דהתם פריך משבת, דהוי בכל שבוע, ולא שייך לשנויי דנקט ערבי פסחים משום דתנא בפסח קאי*:

ותנא

קמ א ש"ע או"ח סי' תס סעיף ה:
קמא ב ג מיי' פ"ג מהל' י"ט הל' ח טוש"ע או"ח סי' תקז סעיף ו:
קמב ד מיי' פ"ו מהל' מלה הל' ה סמג לאוין עט טוש"ע או"ח סי' תנד סעיף א:
קמג ה מיי' פ"ה מהל' מלה הל' טו סמג שם טוש"ע או"ח סי' תס סעיף ד:
[ועי' תוס' ביצה כב. ד"ה דנפיקי]
קמד ו מיי' פ"ו מהל' בכורים הלכה יב סמג עשין קמא טוש"ע י"ד סי' שכט סעיף ח:
קמה ז מיי' פ"ו מהל' מלה הלכה ו טוש"ע או"ח סי' תסא סעיף ג:
[וע"ע תוס' לקמן לט: ד"ה מאי]
קמו ח מיי' שם טוש"ע שם סעיף ב:
קמז ט מיי' פי"ב מהל' פסולי המוקדשין הלכה יז:

לקמן מ.
[גי' הערוך בע' רד הרדאה פי' לחם עב ובלשון לע"ז הוא אדר"ו]

[סוכה ה.]
מלת אמר חסר עי' ביצה כב:
[בביצה אי' מרובה]
[מ"ק יד.] חולין קז:
[גי' הערוך מן חלה פ"א מ"ד]
מנחות עח: [ע"ש]
[שם]

הגהות הב"ח
(א) גמ' כמין גלוסקאות תנן התם הסופגנין והדובשנין וכן גי' הר"ן:

גליון הש"ס
גמ' ויקבענה כיון. וכן במתני' פ"ז דתמיד מ"א פותח כיון. וכן במס' כלה עמד ונפל על פניו וכיון אבל:

רבינו חננאל
ת"ר אין אופין פת עבה בפסח וב"ה מתירין. וטרחי' לאוקמה במצה בפסח וכמה עבה טפח כעובי לחם הפנים שהיה מצה והיה עביו טפח ודחי' ואסקי' האי פת עבה פת מרובה היא ומשום טירחא ובכל יום טוב הוא ואמאי תנא בפסח משום דבענינא דפסח הוה קאי: **תניא** נמי הכי ב"ש אומר אין אופין פת עבה ביום טוב וב"ה מתירין: **ת"ר** יוצאין בפת הדראה ובסריקין המצויירין ואף על פי שאמרו אין עושין סריקין המצויירין בפסח ואמרי' מאי טעמא מפני שהאשה שוהה עליהן ומחמצתן ויעשו בדפוס ודחו ואמרו אפי' בדפוס אין עושין וסריקי ר"ג אמר ר' (יצחק) [צדוק] לר' אלעזר בנו לא של כל אדם אמרו אין עושין אלא של נחתומין דבעו מסקי ליה טפי שהו עלייהו. איכא דאמרי הכי אמר ליה לא של נחתומין אמרו דפקיעי ועבדו לעגל אלא של כל אדם אמר ר' דלא פקיעי דבי ר"ג פקיעי ר' יוסי אומר עושין סריקין כמין רקיקין ואין עושין סריקין כמין גלוסקאות: **ת"ר** הסופגנין והדובשנין והאסקריטין וחלת המשרת והמדומע פטורין מן החלה מאי חלת המשרת זה חלוט של בעלי בתים שאמרנו למעלה והן חלות אפויות במסרת על ידי ומפני שאינן אפויות בתנור אלא במסרת נקראו חלת המסרת פי' מדומע פירות שנתקנו ונפלה בהן תרומה נקרא דמוע. מאי טעמא הללו פטורין מן החלה ריש לקיש אמר מפני שהן מעשה אלפס ואינו קרוי לחם אלא האפוי בתנור ור' יוחנן אמר אפי' מעשה אלפס חייב בחלה והללו לא עשאן באלפס על ידי אור אלא בחמה ומותבינן לריש לקיש הסופגנין והדובשנין והאסקריטין עשאן באלפס חייבין בחמה פטורין ומשני כגון שהרתיחה האלפס ובסוף הדביק הסופגנין הללו באלפס חייבין [והכין קתני בד"א בשהרתיחה האלפס ולבסוף הדביק] שנמצאת אפייתן [כמעשה תנור] אבל הדביק ולבסוף הרתיח נעשה [כמי שעשאן] בחמה ופטור והא נמי דתני יוצאים במצה נא ובמצה העשויה באלפס אוקמ' בשהרתיחה ולבסוף הדביק ומצה נא כל שפורסה ואין חוטין נמשכים הימנה ואילו נגדי מינה חוטי בצק הוא עדיין ואסירי דבעינן לחם וליכא וכן לענין לחמי תודה

קמח א מיי' פ"ט מהל' מעשה קרבנות הלכה כב:

קמט ב מיי' פ"ו מהל' בכורים הל' יב טוש"ע י"ד סי' שכט סעיף ח:

קנ ג מיי' שם הל' ד:

ותנא קמא מאי שנא החליטה. תימה לר"י: מאי קבעי מינה? נימא דמר סבר עילאה גבר, ומר סבר תתאה גבר! ותירץ ר"י: דקפסיק ותני, אע"ג דלית ביה אלא שיעור חלה מצומצם. ולהכי קבעי: מ"ש דבין עילאה גבר ובין תתאה גבר – אי אפשר שלא יתבשל מעט ממנו וחסר ליה משיעוריה:

אמר לך רבי יוחנן תנאי היא דתניא. לא איצטריך לאשכוחי תנאי אלא ללישנא דאמרי לה זה וזה לפטור, אבל ללישנא דזה וזה לחיוב – איכא תנאי בהך ברייתא גופא, דע"כ הא דמחייבא – היינו באילפס. דאי בתנור, אבל באילפס פטור – א"כ ר' ישמעאל ברבי יוסי היינו חכמים: **דכולי** עלמא מעשה אילפס פטורים. פסק ר"ח כר"ל, מדקאמר דכולי עלמא מעשה אילפס פטורין. ועוד: דיתיב רבה ורב יוסף אחוריה דר' זירא – אליבא דר"ל מיירי. ולר"י נראה דכר' יוחנן קיי"ל, מדלא חשיב לה ב"החולץ" (יבמות לו.) בהדי ג' דהלכה כריש לקיש לגבי רבי יוחנן. ואומר ר"י: דעל ידי משקה מודה ר' יוחנן דמעשה אילפס פטור', ואין מברך עליו "המוציא" כדמוכח בירושלמי דמסכת חלה בפרק קמא דחלה, אמר ר' יוחנן: כל שהאור מהלך תחתיו – חייב בחלה, ומברכין עליו "המוציא" ואדם יוצא בה ידי חובתו בפסח. ריש לקיש אמר: אינו חייב בחלה, ואין מברכין עליו המוציא ואין אדם יוצא בו ידי חובתו בפסח. ואמר ר' יוחנן: ובלבד שיהא על ידי משקין. ואומר רבינו תם: דדווקא בבלילתו רכה פליגי, דר' יוחנן סבר: אפייתו באילפס עושהו לחם, וחייב בחלה, ור"ל סבר: אין עושהו לחם, ופטור. אבל בלילתו עבה – כולי עלמא מודו דחייב בחלה, אפי' על ידי משקה. דהא חיוב חלה הוי משעת גלגול, כדמוכח בכמה דוכתי וכן משמע במס' חלה, (פ"א מ"ה) דתנן: עיסה שתחלתה וסופה סופגנין – פטורה מן החלה, תחלתה סופגנין וסופה עיסה, תחלתה עיסה וסופה סופגנין – חייבת בחלה. ונראה לרבינו תם דהכי נמי מברכין עליו "המוציא", ומביא ראיה ממנחות (דף עה:) ומ"כיצד מברכין" (ברכות לז:) דאמר: היה עומד ומקריב מנחה בירושלים אומר "שהחיינו", נטלו לאוכלו – אומר "המוציא". וקפסיק ותני כל המנחות, אפי' מנחת מחבת ומרחשת, אע"פ שמטוגנת בשמן. ואין סברא לחלק בין מים לשמן. א"כ, על לפנצו"י ופיטלט"י אומר "בורא מיני מזונות", ועל גלטונ"י וירבל"י מברך "המוציא". ועל אופלטק"י נראה שאין מברך "המוציא" אף על פי שעושין אותו בלא משקה – דאין עליהם תוריתא דנהמא. תדע, שהרי אין מפרישין ממנו חלה, אפילו יש הרבה בסל אחד כשיעור חלה, אע"פ שהסל מצרפן לחלה. ואע"ג דטריתא אמרינן ב"כיצד מברכין" (שם) דחייב בחלה, ומברכין עליו "בורא מיני מזונות" – ההוא כדמפרש התם דגובלא בעלמא הוא, ואינו סועד הלב. ורבינו תם היה אומר דאף על גרימזל"י אין מברך "המוציא", דלית בהו תוריתא דנהמא, אף על גב דמסתמא חייב בחלה: **לחם** שאין אפוי בתנור אחד. ואם תאמר: מנלן לחלק בין בלילה רכה ובין בלילה קשה? והלא אינו תלויה לר' יהודה אלא באפוי בתנור אחד! ואומר רבינו תם, דהכי פירושו: לר' יהודה לחם האפוי בתנור וכו' – לחם שרגילין לאפות בתנור, היינו בלילתו קשה: **הדביק** מבפנים והרתיח מבחוץ מהו. לפ"ה, דמפרש דמיירי באילפס – תימה: אם כן במאי סבר רבה דפליגי רבי יוחנן וריש לקיש – ע"כ בהדביק מבפנים והרתיח מבפנים, אם כן מאי מיבעיא ליה לרב יוסף בתר הכי: הדביקה מבפנים ואבוקה כנגדו מהו? ונראה לר"י: דהכא בהדביק בתנור מיירי, ומיבעיא ליה: כיון דתנור הוא – לא חשיב מעשה אילפס, או דילמא: לא שנא. ולרב יוסף מיבעיא כשהדביק בתנור ולא הסיקו, אלא מתבשל מהיסק שכנגדו. וכן פירש רבינו חננאל:

אתיא

תורה אור

אֶחָד מִכָּל קָרְבָּן", א"אֶחָד" – *שֶׁלֹּא יִטּוֹל פָּרוּס, וְהָכָא כְּמַאן דִּפְרִיסָא דָּמְיָא, קמ"ל. *מֵיתִיבִי: הַמְּעִיסָּה, בֵּית שַׁמַּאי פּוֹטְרִין, וּב"ה מְחַיְּיבִין. הַחֲלִיטָה, בֵּית שַׁמַּאי מְחַיְּיבִין, וּבֵית הִלֵּל פּוֹטְרִין. אֵיזֶהוּ הַמְּעִיסָּה וְאֵיזֶהוּ הַחֲלִיטָה? הַמְּעִיסָּה – קֶמַח שֶׁעַל גַּבֵּי מוּגְלָשִׁין, הַחֲלִיטָה – מוּגְלָשִׁין שֶׁעַל גַּבֵּי קֶמַח. ר' יִשְׁמָעֵאל ב"ר יוֹסֵי אוֹמֵר מִשּׁוּם אָבִיו: זֶה וָזֶה לִפְטוּר, וְאָמְרִי לָהּ: בזֶה וָזֶה לְחִיּוּב, וַחֲכָמִים אוֹמְרִים: אֶחָד זֶה וְאֶחָד זֶה, עֲשָׂאָן בְּאִילְפָּס – פָּטוּר, בַּתַּנּוּר – חַיָּיב. וְתַנָּא קַמָּא, מַאי שְׁנָא הַמְּעִיסָּה וּמַאי שְׁנָא חֲלִיטָה? אָמַר רַב יְהוּדָה אָמַר שְׁמוּאֵל, וְכֵן א"ר יְהוּדָה* וְאִיתֵימָא ר' יְהוֹשֻׁעַ בֶּן לֵוִי: כְּמַחֲלוֹקֶת בָּזוֹ כָּךְ מַחֲלוֹקֶת בָּזוֹ. *וְתַבְרָא, מִי שֶׁשָּׁנָה זוֹ לֹא שָׁנָה זוֹ. קָתָנֵי מִיהַת: וַחֲכָמִים אוֹמְרִים אֶחָד זֶה וְאֶחָד זֶה, שֶׁעֲשָׂאָן בְּאִילְפָּס – פָּטוּר, בַּתַּנּוּר – חַיָּיב. תְּיוּבְתָּא דְּר' יוֹחָנָן! אָמַר לָךְ ר' יוֹחָנָן: תַּנָּאֵי הִיא. דְּתַנְיָא: יָכוֹל יְהֵא מְעִיסָּה וַחֲלוּטָה חַיָּיבִין בַּחַלָּה – ת"ל: "לֶחֶם", ר' יְהוּדָה אוֹמֵר: אֵין לֶחֶם אֶלָּא הָאָפוּי בַּתַּנּוּר. ר' יְהוּדָה הַיְינוּ תַּנָּא קַמָּא! אֶלָּא לָאו – מַעֲשֵׂה אִילְפָּס אִיכָּא בֵּינַיְיהוּ. תַּנָּא קַמָּא סָבַר: מַעֲשֵׂה אִילְפָּס חַיָּיבִין, וְר' יְהוּדָה סָבַר: מַעֲשֵׂה אִילְפָּס פְּטוּרִין, לֹא, דְּכוּלֵּי עָלְמָא – מַעֲשֵׂה אִילְפָּס פְּטוּרִין, וְהָכָא – כְּגוֹן שֶׁחָזַר וַאֲפָאוֹ בַּתַּנּוּר קָא מִיפַּלְגֵי. דְּתַנָּא קַמָּא סָבַר: כֵּיוָן שֶׁחָזַר וַאֲפָאוֹ בַּתַּנּוּר – לֶחֶם קָרֵינַן בֵּיהּ, וְר' יְהוּדָה סָבַר: אֵין לֶחֶם אֶלָּא הָאָפוּי בַּתַּנּוּר מֵעִיקָּרָא, וְכֵיוָן דְּמֵעִיקָּרָא לָאו בַּתַּנּוּר אַפְיֵיהּ – לָאו לֶחֶם הוּא. אָמַר רָבָא: מַאי טַעְמָא דְּר' יְהוּדָה – דִּכְתִיב: °"וְאָפוּ עֶשֶׂר נָשִׁים לַחְמְכֶם בְּתַנּוּר אֶחָד" לֶחֶם הָאָפוּי בְּתַנּוּר אֶחָד – קָרוּי לֶחֶם, וְשֶׁאֵין אָפוּי בְּתַנּוּר אֶחָד – אֵין קָרוּי לֶחֶם, יָתֵיב רַבָּה וְרַב יוֹסֵף אַחוֹרֵיהּ דְּרַבִּי זֵירָא, וִיתֵיב ר' זֵירָא קַמֵּיהּ דְּעוּלָּא. אֲמַר לֵיהּ רַבָּה לְר' זֵירָא: בְּעֵי מִינֵּיהּ מֵעוּלָּא: הִדְבִּיק מִבִּפְנִים וְהִרְתִּיחַ מִבַּחוּץ מַהוּ? אֲמַר לֵיהּ: מַאי אֵימָא לֵיהּ? דְּאִי אָמֵינָא לֵיהּ, אֲמַר לִי: הֵי נִיהוּ מַעֲשֵׂה אִילְפָּס? א"ל רַב יוֹסֵף לְרַבִּי זֵירָא: בְּעוֹ מִינֵּיהּ מֵעוּלָּא, הִדְבִּיק מִבִּפְנִים וַאֲבוּקָה כְּנֶגְדּוֹ מַהוּ. אֲמַר לֵיהּ: מַאי אֵימָא לֵיהּ? דְּאִי אָמֵינָא לֵיהּ, אֲמַר לִי: רוֹב עֲנִיִּים עוֹשִׂין כֵּן. אָמַר רַב אַסִי: *עִיסָּה שֶׁל מַעֲשֵׂר שֵׁנִי, לְדִבְרֵי ר' מֵאִיר – פְּטוּרָה מִן הַחַלָּה, לְדִבְרֵי חֲכָמִים – גחַיֶּיבֶת בַּחַלָּה,

מַצּוֹת

ויקרא כו

אֶחָד מִכָּל קָרְבָּן. "תְּרוּמָה לַה' לַכֹּהֵן הַזּוֹרֵק" וגו', אַרְבַּעַת מִינִין הָיוּ בָּהּ שֶׁל עֶשֶׂר עֶשֶׂר חַלּוֹת, וּמִכָּל מִין וָמִין נוֹתֵן אֶחָד לַכֹּהֵן, וְהַשְּׁאָר לַבְּעָלִים. וּכְתִיב "אֶחָד" – שֶׁלֹּא יִתֵּן לוֹ פְּרוּסָה: הַמְּעִיסָּה. הַחֲלִיטָה: פּוֹטְרִין. מִן הַחַלָּה: מוּגְלָשִׁין. רוֹתְחִין: וְתַנָּא קַמָּא כו'. בְּרֵישָׁא מְהַדַּר גְּמָרָא לְפֵירוּשָׁא דְּבָרַיְיתָא, דְּלָא תֶּיהֱוֵי מְשַׁבַּשְׁתָּא, וַהֲדַר מְסַיֵּים מִילְּתֵיהּ וּמוֹתִיב תְּיוּבְתָּא מִינָּהּ לְרַבִּי יוֹחָנָן: כְּמַחֲלוֹקֶת בָּזוֹ. כְּלוֹמַר: הַמְחַיֵּיב בָּזוֹ – מְחַיֵּיב בָּזוֹ, וְהַפּוֹטֵר בָּזוֹ – פּוֹטֵר בָּזוֹ. וְרֵישָׁא דְּמַפִּיךְ פְּלוּגְתַּיְיהוּ – לָאו חֲדָא תַּנָּא אֲמָרִינְהוּ וְקַשְׁיָין אַהֲדָדֵי, וּמִי שֶׁשָּׁנָה זוֹ לֹא שָׁנָה זוֹ. הַאי תַּנָּא אִית לֵיהּ דִּמְחוּמְרֵי בֵּית שַׁמַּאי וּמִקּוּלֵּי בֵּית הִלֵּל הִיא, וְתָנָא חֲלִיטָה וְהוּא הַדִּין לִמְעִיסָּה. וְהַאי אִית לֵיהּ דְּמִקּוּלֵּי בֵּית שַׁמַּאי וְחוּמְרֵי בֵּית הִלֵּל הִיא, וְתָנָא הַמְּעִיסָּה וְהוּא הַדִּין לַחֲלִיטָה: תַּבְרָא. קַשְׁיָין אַהֲדָדֵי: תַּנָּא קַמָּא סָבַר מַעֲשֵׂה אִילְפָּס חַיָּיבִין. וְהָכִי קָאָמַר: יָכוֹל תְּהֵא הַמְּעִיסָּה וְהַחֲלִיטָה חַיָּיבִין בַּחַלָּה – ת"ל: "לֶחֶם", וְהָנֵי לָאו לֶחֶם נִינְהוּ, דְּקוֹדֶם לִישָׁתָן מְבוּשָּׁלִין בְּרוֹתְחִין הֵן. אֲבָל מַעֲשֵׂה אִילְפָּס, שֶׁלֹּא נֶאֱפוּ אֶלָּא עַל הָאוּר – קְרוֹבִין הֵן לְמַעֲשֵׂה תַּנּוּר, וְלֶחֶם נִינְהוּ, וְחַיָּיב, וַאֲפִי' הִדְבִּיק וּלְבַסּוֹף הִרְתִּיחַ. וַאֲמַר לֵיהּ ר' יְהוּדָה: מַעֲשֵׂה אִילְפָּס נַמִי פְּטוּרִין, דְּאֵין לֶחֶם אֶלָּא הֶאָפוּי בַּתַּנּוּר: שֶׁחָזַר וַאֲפָאָן בַּתַּנּוּר. לְמַעֲשֵׂה אִילְפָּס. וְהָכִי קָאָמַר תַּנָּא קַמָּא: ת"ל "לֶחֶם" – וְהָנֵי לָאו לֶחֶם נִינְהוּ, דִּמְבוּשָּׁלִים בְּמַיִם הֵן. וְהוּא הַדִּין לְמַעֲשֵׂה אִילְפָּס נַמִי, שֶׁהִדְבִּיק וּלְבַסּוֹף הִרְתִּיחַ, נַמִי לָאו לֶחֶם נִינְהוּ. אֲבָל חָזַר וַאֲפָאוֹ בַּתַּנּוּר – לֶחֶם קָרֵינָא בֵּיהּ: וְר' יְהוּדָה סָבַר. אָפוּי בְּתַנּוּר אֶחָד בָּעֵינַן, וְלֹא בִּשְׁנֵי תַנּוּרִים, כְּגוֹן אִילְפָּס וְתַנּוּר: הִדְבִּיק מִבִּפְנִים. הַלֶּחֶם בָּאִילְפָּס: וְהִרְתִּיחַ מִבַּחוּץ. שֶׁנְּתָנָהּ עַל הָאוּר, כְּמוֹ שֶׁאָנוּ עוֹשִׂים: מַהוּ. מִי הָוֵי לֶחֶם: הֵי נִיהוּ. אֵלּוּ הֵן מַעֲשֵׂה אִילְפָּס שֶׁנֶּחְלְקוּ בּוֹ חֲכָמִים ר' יוֹחָנָן וְרֵישׁ לָקִישׁ: וַאֲבוּקָה כְּנֶגְדּוֹ. מִלְמַעְלָה, וְחוֹם הָאֵשׁ לוֹהֵט בָּאִילְפָּס וּמְמַהֵר אֲפִיָּיתוֹ, מַהוּ? מִי הָוֵי כְּעֵין תַּנּוּר אוֹ לֹא: רוֹב עֲנִיִּים עוֹשִׂין. כָּל מַעֲשֵׂה אִילְפָּס כֵּן, שֶׁאֵין לָהֶם עֵצִים, וּבְכָךְ הוּא מְמַהֵר לֶאֱפוֹת: לְדִבְרֵי רַבִּי מֵאִיר. דְּאָמַר בְּפֶרֶק שֵׁנִי דְּקִדּוּשִׁין (דף נד:): מַעֲשֵׂר מָמוֹן גָּבוֹהַּ הוּא – פְּטוּרָה מִן הַחַלָּה, כִּדְמְפָרֵשׁ, דַּ"עֲרִיסוֹתֵיכֶם" כְּתִיב, וְלֹא שֶׁל גָּבוֹהַּ:

וּמַלָּה

[מנחות עז: נדרים יב:]

חלה פ"א [מ"ו] [עדיות פ"ה מ"ב]

[נ"ל ר' יוחנן]

[ועי' תוס' כתובות עה: ד"ה תברא]

סוכה לה.

רבינו חננאל

תודה: **ת"ש** המעיסה שהיא קמח על גבי מוגלשים [פי' מוגלשים] מים רותחים בית שמאי פוטרים וב"ה מחייבים החליטה שהיא מוגלשים על גבי הקמח ב"ש מחייבים ב"ה פוטרים ר' ישמעאל אומר משום אביו כו' קתני מיהת וחכמים אומרים בין עיסה בין החליטה עשאן באילפס פטורים בתנור חייבים קשיא לר' יוחנן אמר לך ר' יוחנן תנאי היא וכך סידורא במסקנא המעיסה ב"ש פוטרים וב"ה מחייבים והוא הדין לחליטה ותנא אחר שונה החליטה ב"ש מחייבים וב"ה פוטרים וזהו פי' תברא מי ששנה זו לא שנה זו אלא תרי תנאי וכל חד מינייהו רישא וסיפא חדא קתני זה ופשוטה היא ודחי' לא כולי עלמא מעשה אילפס פטורה והכא בשחזר ועשאן בתנור ת"ק סבר כיון שחזר ואפאו בתנור לחם קרינא ביה ור' יהודה סבר אין לחם אלא האפוי בתנור בלבד מעיקרא: **אמר** רבא מאי טעמיה דר' עקיבא כו' ואסיקנא הדביק מבפנים והרתיח מבחוץ היינו מעשה אילפס הדביק במפנים ואבוקה כנגדו רוב עניים עושין כן: **אמר** ר' אסי עיסה של מעשר שני לדברי ר' מאיר פטורה מן החלה לדברי ר' יהודה חייבת בחלה

גמרא

מצות של מעשר שני, לְדִבְרֵי ר' מֵאִיר — אֵין אָדָם יוֹצֵא בָּהּ יְדֵי חוֹבָתוֹ בַּפֶּסַח, לְדִבְרֵי חֲכָמִי' — [א]יוֹצֵא בָּהּ יְדֵי חוֹבָתוֹ בַּפֶּסַח. אֶתְרוֹג שֶׁל מַעֲשֵׂר שֵׁנִי, לְדִבְרֵי ר' מֵאִיר — אֵין יוֹצֵא בּוֹ יְדֵי חוֹבָתוֹ בְּיוֹם טוֹב, לְדִבְרֵי חֲכָמִים — [ב]אָדָם יוֹצֵא בּוֹ יְדֵי חוֹבָתוֹ בְּיוֹם טוֹב. מַתְקִיף לָהּ רַב פַּפָּא: בִּשְׁלָמָא עִיסָּה — דִּכְתִיב: °"עֲרִיסֹתֵיכֶם" — מִשֶּׁלָּכֶם. אֶתְרוֹג נַמִי — דִּכְתִיב: °"וּלְקַחְתֶּם לָכֶם", *"לָכֶם" — מִשֶּׁלָּכֶם יְהֵא. אֶלָּא מַצָּה, מִי כְּתִיב "מַצַּתְכֶם"? אָמַר רָבָא וְאִיתֵימָא רַב יֵימָר בַּר שְׁלַמְיָא: אָתְיָא [ג]לֶחֶם לֶחֶם, כְּתִיב הָכָא: °"לֶחֶם עֹנִי", וּכְתִיב הָתָם: °"וְהָיָה בַּאֲכָלְכֶם מִלֶּחֶם הָאָרֶץ". מַה לְהַלָּן מִשֶּׁלָּכֶם — אַף כָּאן מִשֶּׁלָּכֶם. לֵימָא מְסַיַּיע לֵיהּ: *עִיסָּה שֶׁל מַעֲשֵׂר שֵׁנִי פְּטוּרָה מִן הַחַלָּה, דִּבְרֵי ר"מ. וַחֲכָמִים אוֹמְרִים: חַיֶּיבֶת. לֵימָא מְסַיַּיע?! הַיְינוּ הַךְ! הָכִי קָאָמַר (לֵיהּ): לֵימָא מִדִּפְלִיגִי בְּעִיסָּה, בְּהָנָךְ נַמִי פְּלִיגִי, אוֹ דִּילְמָא: שָׁאנֵי הָתָם, דִּכְתִיב "עֲרִיסֹתֵיכֶם עֲרִיסֹתֵיכֶם" תְּרֵי זִימְנֵי. בָּעֵי ר' שִׁמְעוֹן בֶּן לָקִישׁ: מַהוּ שֶׁיֵּצֵא אָדָם יְדֵי חוֹבָתוֹ בְּחַלָּה שֶׁל מַעֲשֵׂר שֵׁנִי בִּירוּשָׁלַיִם? אַלִּיבָּא *דְּר' יוֹסֵי הַגְּלִילִי — לָא תִּיבָּעֵי לָךְ, הַשְׁתָּא בְּחוּלִּין לָא נָפֵיק, בְּחַלָּתוֹ מִיבָּעֲיָא? כִּי תִּיבָּעֵי לָךְ — אַלִּיבָּא *דְּר' עֲקִיבָא, בְּחוּלִּין הוּא דְּנָפֵיק — דְּאִי מִיטַמּוּ יֵשׁ לָהֶן הֶיתֵּר בַּמּוֹשָׁבוֹת, אֲבָל חַלָּה דְּאִי מִטַּמְיָא לֵית לָהּ הֶיתֵּר בַּמּוֹשָׁבוֹת, וְלִשְׂרֵיפָה אָזְלָא — לָא נָפֵיק. אוֹ דִּילְמָא, אָמְרִינַן: הוֹאִיל וְאִילּוּ לֹא קָרָא עָלֶיהָ שֵׁם וְאִיטַּמִּי — אִית לָהּ הֶיתֵּר בַּמּוֹשָׁבוֹת וְנָפֵיק בָּהּ, הַשְׁתָּא נַמִי נָפֵיק. אִיכָּא דְּאָמְרִי: הָא וַדַּאי לָא תִּיבָּעֵי לָךְ, דְּוַדַּאי אָמְרִינַן "הוֹאִיל". כִּי תִּיבָּעֵי לָךְ: חַלָּה הַלָּקוּחַ בְּכֶסֶף מַעֲשֵׂר שֵׁנִי. וְאַלִּיבָּא דְּרַבָּנַן לָא תִּיבָּעֵי לָךְ, כֵּיוָן דְּאָמְרִי יִפָּדֶה — הַיְינוּ מַעֲשֵׂר. כִּי תִּיבָּעֵי לָךְ — אַלִּיבָּא דְּר' יְהוּדָה, דְּאָמַר יִקָּבֵר. *דִּתְנַן: [ד]הַלָּקוּחַ בְּכֶסֶף מַעֲשֵׂר שֵׁנִי שֶׁנִּטְמָא — יִפָּדֶה, ר' יְהוּדָה אוֹמֵר: יִקָּבֵר. מִי אָמְרִינַן: הוֹאִיל וְאִי לֹא לָקוּחַ הֲוֵי, וְהוֹאִיל וְלֹא קָרָא עָלֶי' שֵׁם וְאִיטַּמִּי — יֵשׁ לוֹ הֶיתֵּר בַּמּוֹשָׁבוֹת וְנָפֵיק בֵּי' — הַשְׁתָּא נַמִי נָפֵיק בֵּיהּ. אוֹ דִּילְמָא: חַד הוֹאִיל — אָמְרִינַן, תְּרֵי הוֹאִיל — לָא אָמְרִינַן? אָמַר רָבָא: מִסְתַּבְּרָא, שֵׁם מַעֲשֵׂר חַד הוּא. § [ה]"חַלַּת תּוֹדָה וּרְקִיקֵי נָזִיר וכו'". § מנה"מ? [ו]אָמַר רַבָּה: דְּאָמַר קְרָא וּשְׁמַרְתֶּם

תורה אור: במדבר טו; ויקרא כג; דברים טז; במדבר טו

רש"י

ומצה של מעשר כו' לדברי ר"מ אין אדם יוצא בה. ואפילו לא דריש עוני לשון עניות – בעינן מצה שלו, ולא של גבוה. ולקמן פריך: מי כתיב "מצתכם"? הכי קאמר. לימא מסייעא הא לכל מילתיה דרב אסי, דמדבהא פליגי – באתרוג נמי פליגי: תרי זימני. אבל התם "לכם" למעוטי שאול וגזול. אבל אתרוג של מעשר שני, האי דאתיהיב ליה לאכילה – נפיק ביה, ואפילו לר"מ: דר' יוסי הגלילי. דאמר לעיל: יצא זה שאינו נאכל באנינות: בחולין. לאחר שניטלה חלתו, לא נפיק בחולין דידיה: כי תיבעי לך לר"ע. דלא דריש אוני. ומיהו, היתר במושבות בעי, כדמיעט לעיל בכורים מהאי טעמא. ומעשר שני ריבה משום דאית ביה היתר מושבות אפי' לאחר שנכנס לירושלים אם נטמא, כרבי אלעזר: לשריפה אזלה. דתרומה טמאה אסורה באכילה, ובעודה טהורה אין לה היתר במושבות משום דמעשר שני הוא. ובתר דקלטוה מחיצות – לית ליה פדייה: או דילמא הואיל ואילו לא קרא עליה שם חלה אית לה היתר במושבות. אם נטמא ונפיק – השתא נמי לא פקע תורת מצה מינה משום קריאת שם חלה, דהא חלה בעלמא לא נפקא מכלל מצה, כדתנן מתניתין: והכהנים בחלה. אלא הא לחודה – משום דאסורה ליה במושבות, ואמרינן הואיל ונפיק: הלקוח בכסף מעשר שני. בירושלים, כדכתי' "ונתתה הכסף בכל אשר תאוה נפשך" וגו': ואליבא דרבנן. דפליגי עליה דרבי יהודה, ואמרי: לקוח בכסף מעשר שנטמא – יפדה, דאלימא למיתפס פדיונו. לא תיבעי לך, דאף על גב דהך חלה לית לה היתר במושבות, דכל זמן שלא נטמא אין לה פדייה בירושלים, ומשנטמאה שוב אין לה היתר אכילה – דהא חלה היא – אפילו הכי אמרינן: הואיל ואילו לא קרא עליה שם הוה לה היתר במושבות על ידי טומאה, דנפיק בה אף בירושלים – השתא נמי נפיק, כדאמרן במעשר גופיה: יקבר. כל לקוח בכסף מעשר שני שנטמא, משום דקלישא קדושתיה ולא אלים למיתפס פדיוניה. ואי נמי לא קרא עליה שם חלה – לא הוה ליה היתר במושבות: מאי מי אמרינן הואיל ואי לאו לקוח הוא. כלומר: הואיל ומעשר שני גופיה דאתי האי מחמתיה, וקיל האי מיניה – נפקינן במצה דידיה, דאית ליה היתר במושבות על ידי טומאה. והא דלית ליה היתר להאי – לאו חומרא הוא לגביה אלא קולא הוא, משום דלא אלים למיתפס פדיונו, הלכך לא חמיר כדמעיקרא. ואי משום דחלה הוא, ובלאו לקוח נמי לית ליה היתר – הכא נמי נימא "הואיל" אחרינא: הואיל ואילו לא קרא עליה שם, ולא לקוח הוא: או דילמא חד הואיל אמרינן. כגון חלת מעשר גופיה, דלא נפקי בה אלא ע"י הואיל ואי לא קרא עליה שם. אי נמי, חולין של לקוח לא נפקי בה אלא ע"י הואיל ואי לאו לקוח הוא – התם אמרינן הואיל ושרי. אבל חלת לקוח, דבעי תרי הואיל – לא אמרי'. וא"ת: בחלת מעשר גופיה נמי תרי הואיל איכא, הואיל ואי לא קרא עליה שם, והואיל ואי מיטמא פריק לה ואית ליה היתר במושבות – הכא לא קרינא הואיל דבר שיש בידו לעשות – לגרום לה טומאה מיד, ופריק: מסתברא שם מעשר חד הוא. וכי היכי דנפיק במעשר גופיה – נפיק בחלתו, הואיל ושם חלה לא נפיק בעלמא מכלל מצה. ונפיק נמי בחלת הלקוח, דהא מכח מעשר קאתה, ולא מחמרינן ליה מיניה: ושמרתם

תוספות

אתיא לחם לחם. הקשה הר"י דאורלינ"ש: כיון דילפינן לחם לחם, דבעינן מצה שלכם, אמאי איצטריך לעיל* למעוטי שלא יצא בטבל מי שאיסורו משום "בל תאכל חמץ" כו'? תיפוק ליה דבעי' שלכם, וטבל אינו שלכם! דהא אתרוג של דמאי דמכשרי ב"ה ב"לולב הגזול" (סוכה דף לה:), מפרש התם: משום דאי בעי מפקר לנכסיה והוי עני, וחזי ליה – השתא נמי שלכם קרינן ביה. משמע דטבל גמור לא חשיב שלכם! ותי' ר"י: אתרוג של טבל לא חשיב שלו – כיון שצריך ליתן ממנו לכהן וללוי, ובעינן שיהא כל האתרוג שלו. אבל מצה, שאם אכל כל כך שאם היה נותן ממנו תרומה או מעשר ממה שאכל אכתי אכל שיעור מצה – חשיב שפיר שלו. ורשב"א תירץ: דאיצטריך לעיל קרא להיכא שמה שיפרים יהיה שלו[א], כגון אם הוא כהן או לוי או ישראל עני. ונטל ממנו *ככר תרומה ומעשר ראשון, דשלכם קרינן ביה*: אבל חלתו דאי מטמיא. זו הסוגיא כמ"ד (מכות דף כ.) מחילה לקלוט דאורייתא, דאי מדרבנן – יש לה היתר מושבות, דאי יצאה חוץ למחילה נפדית אפילו טהורה. אי נמי: כיון דמדרבנן אין להם פדייה – לא חשיב נאכל בכל מושבות: או דילמא הואיל ואילו לא קרי לה שם. תימה לר"י: אי אמרת "הואיל", א"כ בכורים נמי נאכלים בכל מושבותיכם, הואיל ולא קרי ליה שם! וי"ל: דלא דמי, דשם בכורים אינו נאכל בכל מושבותיכם. אבל הכא – שם חלה נאכל בכל מושבותיכם, וכן שם מעשר לחודיה נאכל בכל מושבותיכם. הלכך, בחלת מעשר אמר שפיר "הואיל ולא קרי לה שם". ועוד הקשה: אי אמרת "הואיל" – מעשר שני נמי נאכל בכל מושבותיכם הואיל ולא העלהו לירושלים, ואמאי איצטריך לאוקמא לעיל (דף לו:) כרבי אלעזר? וי"ל: דאי לאו משום דר' אלעזר – לא חשיב שם מעשר שני נאכל בכל מושבותיכם משום דהואיל ולא העלהו לירושלים – כמו שאין לומר הואיל ולא קרא לו שם מעשר: רבי יהודה אומר יקבר. טעמיה דר' יהודה משום דדריש כסף ראשון ולא כסף שני, ולכך אינו נפדה לקוח טהור ברחוק מקום. וה"ה שאין נפדה טמא בקרוב מקום. דתרווייהו מחד קרא נפקי, מ"לא תוכל שאתו". ורבנן לא דרשי כסף ראשון ולא כסף שני, וסברי דלקוח טהור נפדה ברחוק מקום, וה"ה טמא בקרוב מקום. וקשה לרשב"א, דבריש "איזהו מקומן" (זבחים דף מט.) פריך: ולא מצינו שטפל חמור מן העיקר? והרי מעשר הוא נפדה, ולקוח אינו נפדה. דתנן: הלקוח שנטמא – יפדה, נטמא – אין, לא נטמא – לא. והיינו ברחוק מקום, דכה"ג מעשר עצמו נפדה. ובע"א לא הוי טפל חמור מן העיקר, *אלמא: לקוח לרבנן נמי אינו נפדה טהור ברחוק מקום! ותירץ ר"י: דהתם מיירי מדרבנן:

חלות תודה ורקיקי נזיר. נראה לר"י כפ"ה, דמיירי שלא נשחט עליהם הזבח, ולא הוקדשו. דאי הוקדשו – תיפוק ליה דבעינן "מצתכם" דגמרינן לעיל לחם לחם. ועוד, דקאמר: למכור בשוק יוצאין בהן, משמע דבלא הוקדשו מיירי. וה"פ: מצה המשתמרת לשם מצה – יצאה זו שמשתמרת לשם זבח, כשיקדישנה. וכן שאין נאכלין אלא ליום אחד – אקרא *דמשתמרת סמיך, דבעינן שתהא נשמרת לשם שבעה. והא דפריך: ותיפוק ליה שאין נאכלין באנינות, ושאין נאכלין בכל מושבות – ה"פ: שאין נעשה לאכול בכל מושבותיכם ולאכול באנינות. והא דלא פריך: שאין נעשה להיות מצתכם, אלא לגבוה – כיון דלא כתב בהדיא פסול דמצתכם – לא שייך למיפרך הכי: זאת

נ"ל ככר. [ועי' תוס' סוכה לה. ד"ה דאי בעין]

רבינו חננאל

וכן מצה של מעשר שני וכן אתרוג של מעשר שני אין יוצאין בהן ידי חובה ודייק מהא עיסה של מעשר שני פטורה מן החלה דברי ר' מאיר וחכמים אומרים חייבת נימא מדבהא פליגי בהני נמי פליגי ודחי' דלמא לעולם לא פליגי ושאני הכא דכתיב עריסותיכם תרי זימני ואמרי' מדכתיב תרי זימני בעינן עיסה שלכם שתהיה שלכם ממש של חולין ולא של מעשר שני דהא אינו שלכם אלא חשוב הוא כשלמים שהן קדשים והותרו לבעלים לאכלן בירושלים אבל אתרוג אע"ג דכתיב ולקחתם לכם למעוטי שאול וגזול הוא דאתא ולא למעוטי אתרוג של מעשר שני מצה נמי לא כתיב מצתכם ולחם לחם מחלה לא יליף: בעי ריש לקיש מהו שיוצא אדם בחלה של מעשר שני בירושלים אליבא דר' עקיבא דאמר אדם יוצא ידי חובתו במעשר שני בירושלים מי אמרינן בחולין דמעשר שני נפיק דאי מטמאי פריק להו לרבי אלעזר דאמר מנין למעשר שני שנטמא שפודין אותו ואפילו בירושלים שנאמר כי לא תוכל שאתו ואין שאת אלא אכילה שנאמר וישא משאת מאת פניו אלי' אבל חלה דאי מטמאי נשרפה לא נפיק בה או דלמא הואיל ואלו הוה מטמאי מקמי דנקרי עלה שם חלה הוה נפיק בה השתא (הוה) [נמי] נפיק בה: איכא דאמרי הא נמי לא תבעי לך דבודאי אמרי' נפיק בה דאמרי' הואיל וכי לא נטמא נפיק בה כי תיבעי לך בחלת לקוח כלומר קנה חטים מכסף מעשר שני ועשה מהן עיסה והוציא חלה ואליבא דרבנן דאמרי לקוח שנטמא יפדה לא תיבעי לך דבודאי נפיק דהיינו מעשר כי תיבעי לך אליבא דר' יהודה דאמר יקבר דתנן במעשר שני פ' שלישי לקוח במעות מעשר שני שנטמא יפדה ר' יהודה אומר יקבר מאי מי אמרי' הואיל ואלו [לא] היה לקוח והואיל ולא היה קורא עליהן שם חלה הוה נפיק בחולין דמעשר שני השתא נמי נפיק או דלמא חד הואיל אמרי' תרי הואיל לא אמרינן אמר רבא מסתברא שם מעשר כלומר כיון שאומר הואיל במעשר לא שנא חד ולא שנא תרי: וסוגיא דשמעתין סלקא דאין קרוי לחם אלא האפוי בתנור אבל מעשה אילפס פטור מן החלה ואין מברכין עליו המוציא ואין אדם יוצא בהן ידי חובתו בפסח ואשכחן בתלמוד ארץ ישראל בחלה אמר ר' יוחנן ובלבד במעשה אילפס על ידי משקה והא דתאני יוצאין בסופגנין שנעשו על ידי האור מוקים לה ריש לקיש בשהאור מהלך עליהם מן הצד ובהאור מהלך על תחתיהן הרתיח ובסוף הדביק שלא על ידי משקה לחם קרי ליה. ירושלמי בתחלת חלה ר' שמואל בר נחמן שמע להון כלהון מן הדין קרא ושם חטה שורה ושעורה נסמן וגו' חטה כמשמעה שורה שהיא עשויה כשורה ושעורה כמשמעה נסמן זה השיפון וכוסמת אלו כוסמין גבולתו עד כאן גבולתו של לחם וכי למדין מדברי קבלה אמר ר' סימון מדכתיב (ישעיה כח כו) ויסרו למשפט אלהיו יורנו כמי שהוא דבר תורה: חלות תודה ורקיקי נזיר עשאן לעצמו אין יוצא בהן מנא לן אמר רבא ושמרתם

עין משפט נר מצוה

קנא א מיי' פ"ו מהל' חמץ ומצה הלכה ח:
קנב ב מיי' פ"ח מהל' לולב הלכה ב:
קנג ג מיי' פ"ו מהל' חמץ ומצה הל' ז טוש"ע א"ח סי' תנד סעיף ד:
קנד ד מיי' פ"ב מהל' מעשר שני הל' א ב:
קנה ה ו מיי' פ"ו מהל' חמץ ומצה הלכה ט:

מסורת הש"ס

[סוכ' כז: וש"נ]
סנהדרין קיב: [סוכה לה:]
[לעיל לו.]
[שם]
ב"מ דף נג: סנהדרין קיג. מ"ש פ"ג [מ"י] זבחים מט.

גליון הש"ס

תוס' ד"ה ר"י כו' אמאי לקוח לרבנן ג"כ אינו נפדה. תמוה לי דלמאי לריך לזה הוכחה. הא מפורש כן בהך מתני' עצמה דקתני בסיפא א"ל לא אם אמרת במעשר שני עצמו שכן נפדה בריחוק מקום תאמר בלקוח שאינו נפדה בריחוק מקום ומדהשיב כן לרבנן מוכחא דרבנן מודו לו בזה:

הגהות מהר"ב רנשבורג

[א] בתוס' ד"ה אתי' לחם וכו' ורשב"א תירץ דאיצטריך לעיל קרא להיכא שמה שיפרים יהיה שלו. נ"ב עיין שו"ת שאגת ארי' דף פ"ה עמוד דלי"ת שזהו נגד ש"ס דחולין דף קל"א ע"א שאפילו מעני שבישראל מוציאין את המעשר עני ול"ע:

תורה אור

°"וּשְׁמַרְתֶּם אֶת הַמַּצּוֹת" — מַצָּה הַמִּשְׁתַּמֶּרֶת לְשֵׁם (שמות יב) מַצָּה, יָצְתָה זוֹ שֶׁאֵין מִשְׁתַּמֶּרֶת לְשֵׁם מַצָּה אֶלָּא לְשׁוּם זֶבַח. רַב יוֹסֵף אָמַר, אָמַר קְרָא: °"שִׁבְעַת (שם) יָמִים מַצּוֹת תֹּאכֵלוּ" — מַצָּה הַנֶּאֱכֶלֶת לְשִׁבְעַת יָמִים, יָצְתָה זוֹ שֶׁאֵינָהּ נֶאֱכֶלֶת לְשִׁבְעַת יָמִים אֶלָּא לְיוֹם וָלַיְלָה. תַּנְיָא כְּוָותֵיהּ דְּרַבָּה, וְתַנְיָא כְּוָותֵיהּ דְּרַב יוֹסֵף. תַּנְיָא כְּוָותֵיהּ דְּרַבָּה: יָכוֹל יֵצֵא יְדֵי חוֹבָתוֹ בְּחַלּוֹת תּוֹדָה וּרְקִיקֵי נָזִיר — תַּלְמוּד לוֹמַר: "וּשְׁמַרְתֶּם אֶת הַמַּצּוֹת" — מַצָּה הַמִּשְׁתַּמֶּרֶת לְשֵׁם מַצָּה, יָצְתָה זוֹ שֶׁאֵינָהּ מִשְׁתַּמֶּרֶת לְשֵׁם מַצָּה אֶלָּא לְשׁוּם זֶבַח. תַּנְיָא כְּוָותֵיהּ דְּרַב יוֹסֵף: יָכוֹל יֵצֵא אָדָם יְדֵי חוֹבָתוֹ בְּחַלּוֹת תּוֹדָה וּרְקִיקֵי נָזִיר, תַּלְמוּד לוֹמַר: "שִׁבְעַת יָמִים מַצּוֹת תֹּאכֵלוּ" — מַצָּה הַנֶּאֱכֶלֶת לְשִׁבְעָה, יָצְתָה זוֹ שֶׁאֵינָהּ נֶאֱכֶלֶת לְשִׁבְעָה אֶלָּא לְיוֹם וָלַיְלָה. וְתֵיפּוֹק לֵיהּ מִ"לֶּחֶם עֹנִי" — *מִי שֶׁנֶּאֱכָל בַּאֲנִינוּת, יָצָא זֶה שֶׁאֵינוֹ נֶאֱכָל בַּאֲנִינוּת אֶלָּא בְּשִׂמְחָה! סָבַר לָהּ כְּר' עֲקִיבָא, דְּאָמַר "עֹנִי" כְּתִיב. וְתֵיפּוֹק לֵיהּ דַּהֲוָה לֵיהּ מַצָּה עֲשִׁירָה! אָמַר שְׁמוּאֵל בַּר רַב יִצְחָק: רְבִיעִית הִיא, וּמִתְחַלֶּקֶת הִיא לְכַמָּה חַלּוֹת. וְתֵיפּוֹק לֵיהּ דְּאֵינָן נֶאֱכָלוֹת בְּכָל מוֹשָׁבוֹת! אָמַר רֵישׁ לָקִישׁ: זֹאת אוֹמֶרֶת חַלּוֹת תּוֹדָה וּרְקִיקֵי נָזִיר נֶאֱכָלִין בְּנוֹב וְגִבְעוֹן. *תַּנְיָא: אָמַר ר' אִילְעַאי, שָׁאַלְתִּי אֶת ר' אֱלִיעֶזֶר: מַהוּ שֶׁיֵּצֵא אָדָם בְּחַלּוֹת תּוֹדָה וּרְקִיקֵי נָזִיר? אָמַר לִי: לֹא שָׁמַעְתִּי. בָּאתִי וְשָׁאַלְתִּי לִפְנֵי ר' יְהוֹשֻׁעַ, אָמַר לִי: הֲרֵי אָמְרוּ חַלּוֹת תּוֹדָה וּרְקִיקֵי נָזִיר שֶׁעֲשָׂאָן לְעַצְמוֹ — אֵין אָדָם יוֹצֵא בָּהֶן, לִמְכּוֹר בַּשּׁוּק — יוֹצֵא בָּהֶן. כְּשֶׁבָּאתִי וְהִרְצֵיתִי דְּבָרִים לִפְנֵי ר' אֱלִיעֶזֶר, אָמַר לִי: בְּרִית, הֵן הֵן הַדְּבָרִים שֶׁנֶּאֶמְרוּ לוֹ לְמֹשֶׁה בְּסִינַי. אִיכָּא דְּאָמְרִי: בְּרִית, הֵן הֵן הַדְּבָרִים שֶׁנֶּאֶמְרוּ לוֹ לְמֹשֶׁה בְּסִינַי?! וְלָא טַעְמָא בָּעֲיָא? וְטַעְמָא מַאי? אָמַר רַבָּה: כֹּל לַשּׁוּק אִימְּלוֹכֵי מִימְלַךְ, אָמַר: אִי מִזְדַּבֵּן — מִזְדַּבֵּן, אִי לָא מִזְדַּבֵּן — אֵיפּוֹק בְּהוּ אֲנָא.§

מתני'

ושמרתם את המצות עביד לה שמירה לשם מצה. כל שימור שאתה משמרה שלא תחמיץ התכוון לשם מצה של מצוה: **יצאת כו'.** דלאו לשם מצה של מצות פסח עביד לה, אלא לשם מצה של זבח: **שאינה נאכלת לשבעה.** דלאחר יום ולילה הויא נותר, כדכתיב (ויקרא ז): "ובשר זבח תודת שלמיו ביום קרבנו" וגו'. והיכא דלא נשחט עליהן הזבח, אע"ג דעכשיו יש לה היתר לשבעה, מיהו כי עבדה — לאו לשם מצה הראויה למצוה איתכוון, דכי עבדה אדעתא לאיפסולי ביום ובלילה עבדה, ואית ליה לרב יוסף הא דרשה (דרבא*) דבעינן שימור לשם מצוה, ואההוא קרא סמיך, ובהא פליג: דאי נמי איכוין לה נמי לשימור מצת מצוה, למיפק בה משום תודה ומשום מצה — לא נפיק, דבעי' שימור לשום מצה כל שבעה: **ותיפוק ליה דאינה נאכלת לאונן.** ולמה לי קרא אחרינא? דכל קדשים אסורין לאונן, ביבמות (דף עג:) אתיא לן בק"ו: מה מעשר הקל אמרה תורה "לא אכלתי באוני", בשר קודש חמור — לא כל שכן? **סבר לה כרבי עקיבא דאמר.** לעיל (דף לו.): במצה של מעשר שני נפיק. ואע"ג דאסור לאונן, דלא דריש עוני לשון אוני, אלא עני כמסורת: **ותיפוק ליה.** כיון דדריש עני — הא לאו מצה ענייה היא, דהא נילושה בשמן: **רביעית היא.** חצי לוג שמן מביא לתודה, וחולקהו, חציו לעשר חלות ועשר רקיקין, וחציו לרבוכה. במסכת מנחות בפרק "שתי מדות" (דף פט.). ובנזירות לא היתה רבוכה אלא חלות ורקיקין, ולא היה מביא אלא רביעית, כדאמרינן נמי התם. הלכך, רביעית שמן לעשרים חלות גדולות שנעשות משבע עשרונות פחות שליש עשרון, שזה הוא שיעורן כדאמרינן התם ב"התודה"* — אין כאן עושר: **ותיפוק ליה דאינן נאכלות בכל מושבות.** אלא בירושלים, דמחיצת קדשים קלים לפנים מן החומה, כדכתיב (דברים יב): "ואכלת לפני ה' וגו' וכל נדריך אשר תדור", ואם יצאו נפסלין, דכתיב (שמות כב): "ובשר בשדה טרפה" וגו', כיון שיצא בשר חוץ למחיצתו — נאסר: **זאת אומרת.** מדלא נפקא ליה מ"בכל מושבותיכם" — קסבר: חלות תודה ורקיקי נזיר נאכלות בנוב וגבעון, ודלא כר"ש דאמר בפ"ק דמגילה (דף ט:) דלא קרב בנוב וגבעון, דהיינו במה גדולה, אלא פסחים וחובות הקבוע להן זמן. אבל חובות שאין להן זמן קבוע — לא. ודלא כמ"ד בפרק בתרא דזבחים (דף קיז.): כאן וכאן — במה גדולה דנוב וגבעון, ובמה קטנה שהיה עושה בראש גגו — לא קרבו ליחיד אלא עולה ושלמים. ועל אותן שקרבו בנוב וגבעון הוצרך להביא ראיה מ"ושמרתם את המצות" ומ"מצות תאכלו" וגו', דלא נפקי מ"בכל מושבותיכם" — דאית להו היתר בכל מושבות, שהיו יכולין להוליכן בכל מקום שירצו בתוך זמן אכילתן. דתנן בפרק בתרא דזבחים (דף קיב:): באו לנוב וגבעון — הותרו הבמות, קדשי קדשים נאכלין לפנים מן הקלעים, קדשים קלים ומעשר שני בכל ערי ישראל. עד שלא הוקם המשכן היו במות מותרות ועבודה בבכורות, משהוקם המשכן עבודה בכהנים ונאסרו הבמות. עברו את הירדן והוקבעו בגלגל ז' שכיבשו וז' שחילקו — היו הבמות מותרות. באו לשילה לאחר שחילקו, והוקבע משכן שם — נאסרו הבמות. וכולהו מפרש מקראי בפרק בתרא דזבחים. חרבה שילה בימי עלי, כשנשבה הארון בארץ פלשתים — באו להן לנוב, ולא היה שם משכן, אלא בית של אבנים היה, והוקבע שם מזבח הנחשת. אבל ארון לא היה שם, שכשהחזירוהו פלשתים עמד בקרית יערים עשרים שנה עד שמלך דוד והביאו לציון, ובציון עמד עד שבנה שלמה בית המקדש, כדכתיב (מ"א ח): "ויביאו הכהנים את ארון ברית ה'" וגו'. ומזבח הנחשת היה בנוב כל ימי שאול ושמואל, כדכתיב (ש"א כא): "ויאמר אין לחם חול אל תחת ידי כי אם לחם קודש [וגו'] המוסרים מלפני ה'". חרבה נוב על דבר זה, שהרגם שאול מפני שנתנו לחם לדוד, ובאו להם לגבעון, ויתן שם מזבח הנחשת עד שבנה שלמה הבית, כדכתיב בדברי הימים (א כא): **ברית.** שבועה: **ואיכא דאמרי.** בתמיה אמר ליה: וכי הן הדברים כו', דלא בעי טעמא כהלכה למשה מסיני? **וטעמא מאי.** גמרא בעי לה: וטעמא מאי שעשאן למכור בשוק לצורכי תודה יוצא בהן אם לא מכרן? הרי לא נשתמרה לשם מצה, אלא לשם זבח! **איפוק בהו אנא.** ידי חובת מצה:

מתני'

זאת אומרת חלות תודה ורקיקי נזיר. פ"ה: דלא אתי כר"ש, דאמר בפ"ק דמגילה (דף ט:) לא קרבו אלא פסחים וחובות הקבוע להם זמן, אבל שאין קבוע להם זמן – לא. וכפירושו משמע בפרק בתרא דזבחים (דף קיז.), דתניא התם: כל הנידר ונידב – קרב בבמה, ושאין נידר וכו' דברי ר' מאיר. וחכמים אומרים: לא קרבו אלא עולות ושלמים בלבד. רבי שמעון אומר: אף ליבור לא הקריבו אלא חובות הקבוע להן זמן. משמע דמודה ר' שמעון לחכמים דלא קרבו מנחה ונזירות בבמה. וקשה, דבפ"ק דמגילה (דף ט:) תנן: אין בין במה גדולה לבמה קטנה אלא פסח. זה הכלל: כל שנידר ונידב – קרב בבמה, שאין נידר וכו'. ואמר בגמרא: מני – ר"ש היא. א"כ לר' שמעון קרבה מנחה בבמה, דנידר ונידב הוא. ונזירות נמי קרב לדידיה בבמה, דהא ר"מ דקתני בהאי לישנא: כל שנידר ונידב קרב בבמה, וסבר רקיקי נזיר איכא בבמה, דאמר התם: מאי טעמא דר"מ – אמר קרא "לא תעשון ככל אשר אנחנו עושים וגו'". אמר להו משה: כי עליתון לארץ – ישרות אקריבו, חובות לא אקריבו. ומנחה ונזירות ישרות נינהו, דנזירות גופייהו נידר ונידב הוא, אע"ג דהקרבנות חובה. ורבנן מפרש התם דסברי אין מנחה בבמה, ונזירות אע"ג דנידר הוא – מ"מ הקרבן חובה, ונראה לר"י, דה"פ דמתניתין דמגילה: דאין חילוק בין במה גדולה לבמה קטנה אלא פסחים. זה הכלל: כל הנידר ונידב, הקרב בבמה גדולה – קרב בבמה קטנה, וכל שאין נידר וכו'. ולא נחית אלא לפרש מה שוה הגדולה לקטנה, אבל יש נידר ונידב כמו מנחה ונזירות שאין קריבין לא בזו ולא בזו:

נאכלים בנוב וגבעון. הקשה רבינו נסים: א"כ היכי ממעט ביכורים מ"בכל מושבות", והא ביכורים הוו חובה הקבוע להן זמן בזמן שמחה, דמעצרת עד החג מביא וקורא – א"כ קריבים בנוב וגבעון כמו פסחים, שהיו קריבים לכ"ע! ויש לומר: דביכורים, הואיל ויש להם זמן גדול כל כך – לא חשיב זמן קבוע. ורשב"א מפרש: דמשום הכי הוו ביכורים חובה שאין להן זמן קבוע, כיון שאם אין לו פירות – לא יביא ביכורים:

אלוותא

ושמרתם את המצות מצה המשתמרת לשם מצה יצתה זו כו' דברי רבה ורב יוסף פשוטין הן התורה כתבה (ויקרא ז' ט"ו) ביום זבחכם יאכל וכן כל הלחם הקרב עמה ואמרי' פשיטא דהא אין נאכלות באנינות ודחי' מתני' ר' עקיבא היא דאמר עני כתיב למעוטי מצה עשירה ותיפוק לי' דחלות תודה על ידי משקה עשויות ושנינן רביעית שמן היא ומתחלק לכמה חלות: **ברית** הן הן הדברים שנאמרו למשה בסיני. כלומר ודאי ברית פי' נשבע לו בשבועה הן הן הדברים למשה בסיני אע"פ כן לאו טעמא בעיא: **אמר** רבא כל לשוק אימלוכי מימלך אי מזדבני מזדבני ואי לא אפיק בהו אנא ש"מ שכל הדברים המפורשים משנה הלכה למשה מסיני הן ואע"פ שהן שנויין סתמא. ללישנא קמא ר' אליעזר אמר לר' אילעאי [ברית] הן הן הדברים וללישנא בתרא ר' יהושע עצמו הוא שאמר ברית הן הן הדברים:

ל"ל דרבה

[לעיל לו.]

תוספתא דחלה פ"א

[דף עז.]

קנו א ב מיי' פ"ז מהל' מצה הלכה יג סמג עשין מא טוש"ע א"ח סי' תעג סעיף ה:

קנז ג מיי' פ"ג מהל' כלאים הלכה ג סמג לאוין רעט טוש"ע י"ד סי' רצז סעיף יד:

[וע"ע תוס' סוכה לו: ד"ה בסיב ועוד שם תוס' יג. ד"ה אפקותא]

ס"ל חד הוא ומר הוא וזהו מר ירואר כצ"ל

מתני' [א]וְאֵלּוּ יְרָקוֹת שֶׁאָדָם יוֹצֵא בָּהֶן יְדֵי חוֹבָתוֹ בַּפֶּסַח: בַּחֲזֶרֶת, בַּתַּמְכָא, וּבַחַרְחֲבִינָא, וּבְעוּלָשִׁין, וּבַמָּרוֹר. *יוֹצְאִין בָּהֶן בֵּין לַחִין בֵּין יְבֵשִׁין. אֲבָל לֹא כְּבוּשִׁין וְלֹא שְׁלוּקִין וְלֹא מְבוּשָּׁלִין. וּמִצְטָרְפִין לִכְזַיִת, וְיוֹצְאִין בְּקֶלַח שֶׁלָּהֶן. וּבַדְּמַאי, וּבְמַעֲשֵׂר רִאשׁוֹן שֶׁנִּטְּלָה תְּרוּמָתוֹ, וּמַעֲשֵׂר שֵׁנִי וְהֶקְדֵּשׁ שֶׁנִּפְדּוּ.§ **גמ'** חֲזֶרֶת – חַסָּא. עוּלָשִׁין – הִינְדְּבִי. תַּמְכָא, אָמַר רַבָּה בַּר בַּר חָנָה: תַּמַכְתָּא שְׁמָהּ. חַרְחֲבִינָא, אָמַר רשב"ל: אַצְוָותָא דְּדִיקְלָא. וּבַמָּרוֹר – מְרִירָתָא. תָּנֵי בַּר קַפָּרָא; אֵלּוּ יְרָקוֹת שֶׁאָדָם יוֹצֵא בָּהֶן יְדֵי חוֹבָתוֹ בַּפֶּסַח: בְּעוּלָשִׁין, וּבַתַּמְכָא, בַּחַרְחֲלִין, בַּחַרְחֲבִינִין, וּבַחֲזָרִין. רַב יְהוּדָה אוֹמֵר: אַף עוּלְשֵׁי שָׂדֶה, וְעוּלְשֵׁי גִינָּה, וַחֲזֶרֶת. עוּלְשֵׁי גִינָּה וַחֲזֶרֶת?! הָא תָּנָא לַהּ רֵישָׁא! הָכִי קָאָמַר: אַף עוּלְשֵׁי שָׂדֶה כְּעוּלְשֵׁי גִינָּה וַחֲזֶרֶת. רַבִּי מֵאִיר אוֹמֵר: אַף עַסְוָוס, וְטוּרָא, וּמַר יְרוֹאָר. א"ל ר' יוֹסֵי: עַסְוָוס וְטוּרָא – *אֶחָד הוּא, וּמַר – זֶה הוּא יְרוֹאָר. תָּנֵי דְּבֵי (ר') שְׁמוּאֵל, אֵלּוּ יְרָקוֹת שֶׁאָדָם יוֹצֵא בָּהֶן יְדֵי חוֹבָתוֹ בַּפֶּסַח: בַּחֲזֶרֶת, בְּעוּלָשִׁין, וּבַתַּמְכָא, וּבַחַרְבִינִין, וּבַחַרְגִינִין, וּבַהַרְדּוּפְנִין. ר' יְהוּדָה אוֹמֵר: אַף חֲזֶרֶת יוֹלִין וַחֲזֶרֶת גַּלִּין כַּיּוֹצֵא בָּהֶן. *ר' אִילְעָא אוֹמֵר מִשּׁוּם ר"א: אַף עַרְקַבְלִים. וְחָזַרְתִּי עַל כָּל תַּלְמִידָיו וּבִקַּשְׁתִּי לִי חָבֵר, וְלֹא מָצָאתִי. וּכְשֶׁבָּאתִי לִפְנֵי ר"א בֶּן יַעֲקֹב הוֹדָה לִדְבָרַי. *ר' יְהוּדָה אוֹמֵר: כָּל שֶׁיֵּשׁ לוֹ שְׂרָף. ר' יוֹחָנָן בֶּן בְּרוֹקָה אוֹמֵר: כָּל שֶׁפָּנָיו מַכְסִיפִין. אֲחֵרִים אוֹמְרִים: [כָּל] יָרָק מַר יֵשׁ לוֹ שְׂרָף וּפָנָיו מַכְסִיפִין. א"ר יוֹחָנָן: מִדִּבְרֵי כּוּלָּן נִלְמַד: יָרָק מַר יֵשׁ לוֹ שְׂרָף וּפָנָיו מַכְסִיפִין. אָמַר רַב הוּנָא: הֲלָכָה כַּאֲחֵרִים. רָבִינָא אַשְׁכְּחֵיהּ לְרַב אַחָא בְּרֵיהּ דְּרָבָא דַּהֲוָה מְהַדֵּר *אַמְּרִירָתָא. א"ל: מַאי דַּעְתִּיךְ – דִּמְרִירָן טְפֵי, וְהָא חֲזֶרֶת תְּנַן, וְתָנָא דְּבֵי שְׁמוּאֵל חֲזֶרֶת, וְא"ר אוֹשַׁעְיָא: [ב]מִצְוָה בַּחֲזֶרֶת, וְאָמַר רָבָא: מַאי חֲזֶרֶת – חַסָּא. מַאי חַסָּא – דְּחָס רַחֲמָנָא עִילָּוָון. וְאָמַר ר' שְׁמוּאֵל בַּר נַחְמָנִי א"ר יוֹנָתָן: לָמָּה נִמְשְׁלוּ מִצְרִיִּים כְּמָרוֹר – לוֹמַר לָךְ: מַה מָּרוֹר זֶה שֶׁתְּחִילָּתוֹ רַךְ וְסוֹפוֹ קָשֶׁה, אַף מִצְרִיִּים – תְּחִילָּתָן רַכָּה וְסוֹפָן קָשֶׁה. א"ל: הָדְרִי בִּי. א"ל רַב רְחוּמִי לְאַבָּיֵי: מִמַּאי דְּהַאי מָרוֹר מִין יָרָק הוּא? אֵימָא מְרִירָתָא דִּכְוֹפְיָא! דּוּמְיָא דְּמַצָּה, מַה מַּצָּה גִּידּוּלֵי קַרְקַע – אַף מָרוֹר גִּידּוּלֵי קַרְקַע. וְאֵימָא הִירְדּוּף! דּוּמְיָא דְּמַצָּה, מַה מַּצָּה מִין זְרָעִים – אַף מָרוֹר מִין זְרָעִים, וְאֵימָא הַרְזִיפוּ! דּוּמְיָא דְּמַצָּה, מַה מַּצָּה שֶׁנִּיקַּחַת בְּכֶסֶף מַעֲשֵׂר – אַף מָרוֹר שֶׁנִּיקָּח בְּכֶסֶף מַעֲשֵׂר. א"ל רַבָּה בַּר רַב חָנִין לְאַבָּיֵי: אֵימָא מָרוֹר חַד! מְרוֹרִים כְּתִיב – וְאֵימָא מְרוֹרִים תְּרֵי! דּוּמְיָא דְּמַצָּה, מַה מַּצָּה מִינִין הַרְבֵּה – אַף מָרוֹר מִינִין הַרְבֵּה. אָמַר רַבָּה בַּר רַב הוּנָא אָמַר רַב: יְרָקוֹת שֶׁאָמְרוּ חֲכָמִים שֶׁאָדָם יוֹצֵא בָּהֶן יְדֵי חוֹבָתוֹ בַּפֶּסַח – כּוּלָּן נִזְרָעִין בַּעֲרוּגָה אַחַת. לְמֵימְרָא דְּלֵית בְּהוּ מִשּׁוּם כִּלְאַיִם. מְתִיב רָבָא: *[ג]חֲזֶרֶת וַחֲזֶרֶת גַּלִּין, עוּלָשִׁין וְעוּלְשֵׁי שָׂדֶה, כְּרֵישִׁין וּכְרֵישֵׁי שָׂדֶה, כּוּסְבָּר וְכוּסְבַּר שָׂדֶה, חַרְדָּל וְחַרְדָּל מִצְרִי, וּדְלַעַת הַמִּצְרִי וְהָרְמוּצָה – אֵינָם כִּלְאַיִם זֶה בָּזֶה. חֲזֶרֶת וַחֲזֶרֶת גַּלִּין – אִין, חֲזֶרֶת וְעוּלָשִׁין – לָא! וְכִי תֵּימָא כּוּלְּהוּ בַּהֲדָדֵי קָתָנֵי לְהוּ – וְהָא אָמַר רַב: זוּגוֹת זוּגוֹת קָתָנֵי! מַאי נִזְרָעִין דְּאָמַר רַב – נִזְרָעִין כְּהִלְכָתָן – כְּהִלְכָתָן תְּנֵינָא! עֲרוּגָה

רש"י

מתני' אֵלּוּ יְרָקוֹת שֶׁאָדָם יוֹצֵא בָּהֶן יְדֵי חוֹבָתוֹ בַּחֲזֶרֶת וּבַתַּמְכָא וּבְעוּלָשִׁי' וּבַחַרְחֲבִינָא וּבַמָּרוֹר. כּוּלְּהוּ מְפָרֵשׁ בַּגְּמָ': כְּבוּשִׁין. בְּחוֹמֶץ: שְׁלוּקִין. מְבוּשָּׁלִין הַרְבֵּה מְאֹד עַד שֶׁנִּימּוֹחִין: מְבוּשָּׁלִין. כְּדֶרֶךְ בִּישּׁוּל: וּמִצְטָרְפִין לִכְזַיִת. אִם אֵין לוֹ מֵאֶחָד מֵהֶן כַּזַּיִת, אֲבָל יֵשׁ לוֹ מִזֶּה חֲצִי זַיִת וּמִזֶּה חֲצִי זַיִת – מִצְטָרְפִין זֶה עִם זֶה כְּדֵי לָצֵאת יְדֵי חוֹבָתוֹ: וּבַדְּמַאי וּבְמַעֲשֵׂר רִאשׁוֹן כו'. אֲבָל בְּטֶבֶל לֹא. וְאַף עַל גַּב דְּמַעֲשַׂר יָרָק דְּרַבָּנַן – הָוְיָא לָהּ מִצְוָה הַבָּאָה בַּעֲבֵירָה, דּוּמְיָא דְּעָלִין שֶׁאֵינוֹ נָקוּב דַּאֲמַרַן בְּפִירְקִין*: **גמ'** חַסָּא. לִיטוּג"א: הִינְדְּבִי. עֵשֶׂב שֶׁקּוֹרִין קרישפל"א: תַּמַכְתָּא. מרוביי"א: **אַצְוָותָא** דְּדִיקְלָא. סִיב הַגָּדֵל וְנִכְרָךְ סָבִיב לַדֶּקֶל שֶׁקּוֹרִין ווידיל"א: מְרִירְתָא. אמירפויי"ל וְיֵשׁ אוֹמְרִים פופר"ץ: חַרְחֲלִין. לֹא אִיתְפָּרַשׁ שְׁמוֹ: וּבַחֲזָרִין. חֲזֶרֶת: עוּלְשֵׁי שָׂדֶה. אַע"ג דְּיֵשׁ לָהֶן שֵׁם לְוַאי, הֲרֵי הֵן כְּעוּלְשֵׁי גִינָּה: עַסְוָוס וְטוּרָא וּמַר יְרוֹאָה. מִינֵי יְרָקוֹת: הִירְדּוּפְנִין. יֵשׁ מְפָרְשִׁין אלויש"א: חֲזֶרֶת גַּלִּים. שֵׁם לְוַאי הוּא: עַרְקַבְלִין. מְפָרֵשׁ בְּסוֹף פ' שֵׁנִי דְּעֵירוּבִין: *אַצְוָותָא חַרְזַיְיתָא, הוּא סִיב גָּדוֹל וְעָב וּמִין לְעַצְמוֹ הוּא: וְחָזַרְתִּי עַל כָּל תַּלְמִידָיו. שֶׁל ר' אֱלִיעֶזֶר, וּבִקַּשְׁתִּי לִי חָבֵר לְסַיְּיעֵנִי, שֶׁשָּׁמַע דָּבָר זֶה מִפִּיו, וְלֹא מְצָאתִי: שְׂרָף. *כְּשֶׁחוֹתְכִין אוֹתוֹ בִּמְקוֹם חִיתּוּכוֹ יוֹצֵא מִמֶּנּוּ שְׂרָף לָבָן כֶּחָלָב, וְקוֹרִין לייטו"ן: מַכְסִיפִין. אֵינוֹ יָרֹק מְאֹד כְּכַרְתִּי, אֶלָּא פלדש: כָּל יָרָק מַר. תַּרְוַיְיהוּ אִית לֵיהּ, יֵשׁ לוֹ שְׂרָף וּפָנָיו מַכְסִיפִין, וְהֵן הֵן סִימָנֵי מָרוֹר: מִדִּבְרֵי כּוּלָּן. כָּל הַמְפָרְשִׁין שְׁמוֹת הַיְּרָקוֹת, כְּגוֹן מַתְנִי', וְתַנָּא דְּבַר קַפָּרָא, וְרַבִּי יְהוּדָה, וְר' מֵאִיר, וְתַנָּא דְּבֵי שְׁמוּאֵל – מִכּוּלָּן לָמַדְנוּ שֶׁהַמָּרוֹר יֵשׁ לוֹ שְׂרָף וּפָנָיו מַכְסִיפִין. שֶׁבְּכָל הַיְּרָקוֹת הַלָּלוּ רוֹאִין אָנוּ בָּהֶן הַסִּימָנִין הָאֵלּוּ: **אַמְּרִירְתָא**. פופר"ץ: וְהָא. אֲנַן רֵישָׁא דְּכוּלְּהוּ חֲזֶרֶת תְּנַן: וְתַנָּא דְּבֵי שְׁמוּאֵל. נַמִי חֲזֶרֶת תָּנָא בְּרֵישָׁא, אַלְמָא: הִיא קַדְמִי לְכוּלְּהוּ: מִצְוָה בַּחֲזֶרֶת. כִּדְמְפָרֵשׁ טַעְמָא כִּדְרָבָא וְר' יוֹנָתָן: מַאי חַסָּא. מַאי טַעְמָא קָרֵינַן לֵיהּ חַסָּא – מִשּׁוּם דְּזֵכֶר הוּא, דְּחַס רַחֲמָנָא עֲלַן, אַלְמָא לְהָכִי קַיְימָא: לָמָּה נִמְשְׁלוּ בַּמָּרוֹר. דִּכְתִיב (שמות א): "וַיְמָרְרוּ אֶת חַיֵּיהֶם": תְּחִילָּה רַכָּה. בַּתְּחִילָּה נִשְׁתַּעְבְּדוּ לָהֶן ע"י שָׂכָר שֶׁהָיוּ שׂוֹכְרִין אוֹתָן: מָרוֹר סוֹפוֹ קָשֶׁה. הַקֶּלַח שֶׁלּוֹ מִתְקַשֶּׁה כְּעֵץ: הָדְרִי בִּי. לֹא אוֹסִיף עוֹד: **מְרִירָתָא** דִּכְוֹפְיָא. מָרָה שֶׁל דָּג שֶׁשְּׁמוֹ כֵּן: כִּי מַצָּה. שֶׁהֲרֵי הוּקְשׁוּ: הִירְדּוּף. עֵץ שֶׁהִמְתִּיק בּוֹ מֹשֶׁה אֶת מֵי מָרָה, וְאָמְרִינַן (בסוטה) (מכילתא פרשת בשלח): נֵס בְּתוֹךְ נֵס, שֶׁהוּא הָיָה מַר, וְהוּא הִירְדּוּף: הַרְזִיפוּ. מִין זֶרַע, וְסַם הַמָּוֶת לִבְהֵמָה הוּא: הַרְזִיפוּ אֵינוֹ נִיקָּח בְּכֶסֶף מַעֲשֵׂר – דְּאֵינוֹ פְּרִי מַאֲכָל, וַאֲנַן אוּכְלָא בָּעֵינַן, דּוּמְיָא דְּיַיִן וְשֵׁכָר וּבָקָר וָצֹאן, כִּדְכְתִיב (דברים יד): "וְנָתַתָּה הַכֶּסֶף בְּכֹל אֲשֶׁר תְּאַוֶּה נַפְשְׁךָ" וגו': **וְאֵימָא** מָרוֹר חַד. מִינָא הוּא מֵהָנָךְ יְרָקוֹת, וְלָאו כָּל הָנֵי, אֶלָּא מַר שֶׁבְּכוּלָּן: כְּרֵישִׁין. כַּרְתִּי, כְּרֵישִׁין שֶׁל גִּינָּה: כְּרֵישֵׁי שָׂדֶה. שלוויי"ש: וְהָרְמוּצָה. מִין דְּלַעַת הוּא, וּבְמַסֶּכֶת נְדָרִים (דף נא.) מְפָרֵשׁ: קָרָא קַרְקוּזָאי: **אֵינָן כִּלְאַיִם זֶה בָּזֶה**. אַע"ג שֶׁיֵּשׁ שֵׁם לְוַאי לְאֶחָד – אֵינוֹ כִּלְאַיִם בַּחֲבֵירוֹ: חֲזֶרֶת בַּחֲזֶרֶת גַּלִּין. וְכֵן עוּלָשִׁין בְּעוּלְשֵׁי הַשָּׂדֶה, (זוגות זוגות כמו שהן שנויין): וְכִי **תֵּימָא** כּוּלְּהוּ בַּהֲדָדֵי קָתָנֵי. דִּבְכָל הָנֵי קָאָמַר דְּאֵינָן כִּלְאַיִם זֶה בָּזֶה, חֲזֶרֶת עוּלָשִׁין וּכְרֵישִׁין: זוּגוֹת זוּגוֹת. חֲזֶרֶת וַחֲזֶרֶת גַּלִּין, אוֹ עוּלָשִׁין וְעוּלְשֵׁי שָׂדֶה, וְכֵן כּוּלָּן, שָׁנִינוּ דְּאֵין כִּלְאַיִם זֶה בָּזֶה. אֲבָל חֲזֶרֶת בְּעוּלָשִׁין – לֹא: מַאי. כּוּלָּן נִזְרָעִין בַּעֲרוּגָה אַחַת, דַּאֲמַר רַב לְעֵיל? נִזְרָעִין כְּהִלְכָתָן קָא אָמַר, כְּדֵי שֶׁלֹּא יִינְקוּ זֶה מִזֶּה. כְּגוֹן חֲמִשָּׁה זֵרְעוֹנִין בַּעֲרוּגָה שֶׁל שִׁשָּׁה עַל שִׁשָּׁה טְפָחִים, כִּדְתְנַן בְּמַסֶּכֶת שַׁבָּת (דף פד:): אֲבָל

תוספות

אצוותא דדיקלא. נ"ל דהוי מין זרעים, דהא לקמן אמרינן: מה מצה מין זרעים – אף מרור מין זרעים*:

ואימא הירדוף כי מצה וכו'. בפ' "לולב הגזול" (סוכה דף לג:) פריך גבי הדס: ואימא הירדוף, אמר אביי: "דרכי' דרכי נועם". ופ"ה: דלא הוי נועם, כיון דהוי סם המות לבהמה. הכא נמי ה"מ לשנויי הכי, אלא דמשני שפיר טפי. אבל קשה לרשב"א, דלעיל אמר דהירדופני כשר למרור, ובפרק "אלו טרפות" (חולין דף נח:) משמע דהוי סם המות לבהמה, דאמר: בהמה שאכלה הירדופני – כשירה. ופריך: היינו הירדפוני היינו סם המות, ומשני: תרי גווני סם המות:

רבינו חננאל

מתני' אלו ירקות שאדם יוצא בהן ידי חובתו וכו' חזרת חסא עולשין הנדבי תמכה כך שמה חרחבינא אסוא דדיקלא ומרור מרריאתא: **אמר** רבי יוחנן מדברי כולן נלמוד ירק מר יש לו שרף ופניו מכסיפין אמר רב הונא הלכה כאחרים דאמרי ירק מר ופניו מכסיפין ויש לו שרף זהו מרור רב אחא בריה דרבא הוה מהדר אמררייתא דדברא אמר ליה רבינא מאי דעתיך דמרירן טפי והא אנן חזרת תנן וכן תאני בר קפרא ור' שמואל חזרת ואמר ר' אושעיא מצוה בחזרת וכו' אמר ליה (אמרי בי) [הדרי בי] ש"מ דכולי עלמא מצוה בחזרת דהיא חסא: **אימא** מררתא דכופיא יש מי שאומר המרה של בהמה ויש מי שאומר מרה של דג ששמו כופיא והיא שיבוטא והוא קולים האספנין ודחי' בעינן מרור גידולי קרקע כמצה דהא הקישו הכתוב (במדבר ט י"א) על מצות ומרורים פי' הרדוף הרדופא ואסיקנא מרורים כתיב מינין הרבה: **אמר** רבה בר רב הונא אמר רב ירקות ששנינו כגון חזרת ועולשין ותמכה וחרחבינה וכיוצא בהן שאדם יוצא בהן ידי חובתו בפסח משום מרור כולן נזרען בערוגה אחת דוקינן מינה כי אלו כולן מין אחד הן ואין בהן משום כלאים ומותיב רבא עליה חזרת וחזרת גלין עולשין ועולשין שדה כרישין כו' ואמרינן בסופה כולן נזרען בערוגה אחת ודייקי' דוקא חזרת וחזרת גלין דתרוייהו מין חזרת נינהו הני הוא דליתנהו כלאים בהדי הדדי הא חזרת ועולשין אע"ג דתרווייהו מין מרור אינון כלאים הוו וכי תימא הכי קתני כל מין חזרת וכל מין עולשין וכל מין כרישין וכל מין כוסבר וכל מין חרדל וכל מין דלעת אלו כולן ביחד נזרעין בערוגה והא רב הונא דאמר זוגות זוגות שנינו כלומר חזרת וחזרת גלין הנה זוג עולשין ועולשי שדה זוג אחד כרישין וכרישי שדה זוג אחד כי האי גונא זוגות זוגות בפני עצמן אינן כלאים הא כולהו בהדדי כלאים נינהו ושני' מאי נזרעין דקאמר רבה בר רב הונא כהילכתן כלומר אם בא לזרען בערוגה אחת נותן לכל אחד כדי עבודתו שלא יהא זרע אחד יונק מגבול חברו ואמרינן הא פשיטא מתני' היא

[לעיל דף לה:]
[ברכות לח:]
[דף כו: וע"ש בפרש"י ול"ע קצת]
נ"ל כשחותכין
עירובין כג.
[תוספתא פ"ב ע"ש]
[עי' תוס' סוכה יג. ד"ה מרריא' ותוס' חולין נט. ד"ה עיקרא]
כלאים פרק א. [מ"ב]
מראה אש מ"ז

עין משפט
נר מצוה

קנח א מיי' פ"ד מהל' כלאים הלכה ט טוש"ע י"ד סי' רלז סעיף לד:
קנט ב מיי' שם הלכה יג טוש"ע שם סעיף לז:
קס ג מיי' פ"ז מהלכות מצה הלכה יג סמג עשין מא טוש"ע א"ח סי' תעג סעיף ה:
קסא ד מיי' פ"ה מהל' חמץ הלכה יז סמג לאוין עט טוש"ע א"ח סי' תנד סעיף ג וסי' תסה סעיף א:
קסב ה מיי' שם הל' יט טוש"ע שם סעי' ב:
קסג ו מיי' וסמג שם טוש"ע א"ח סי' תסו סעיף א:
קסד ז ח מיי' שם הל' י טוש"ע שם סעיף ו:
קסה ט מיי' שם הלכה ד טוש"ע א"ח סי' תסג סעיף ב:
קסו י מיי' שם הל' ה טוש"ע שם סעי' ג:

ערוגה בת ו' טפחים זורעין לתוכה ה' זרעים. וא"ת: הואיל ורחוק ג' טפחים – לא ינקי מהדדי, דהא אמצעית אינה רחוקה מן האחרות אלא ג' טפחים, דבפרק "ר' עקיבא" (שבת דף פה.) משמע דד' מארבע רוחות הערוגה לא בקרנות, אלא באמצע הרוחות. א"כ יזרע לתוכה ט' זרעים, ג' שורות של ג' ג', ויהא רחוקים זה מזה ג' טפחים! ואומר ר"י: דהכא אינה משום יניקה, אלא משום עירבוב, לאחר שיהיו גדולים. ולא רצו חכמים להתיר יותר. ותדע, דאפי' חמשה לא היו מתירים אי לאו דנפקא לן בשבת בפרק "ר' עקיבא" (ג"ז שם) בהדיא מקרא. אע"ג דקים להו לרבנן דחמשה בשיתא לא ינקי – והיינו משום דאיכא למיחש לערבוביא. ואם תאמר: ואיך זורעים בתוכה חמשה זרעונים? והא אין רחוק זה מזה שלשה טפחים, דהא איכא מקום זריעה! ותירץ ר"ת: דטפחים של כלאים שוחקות, כדמוכח בריש עירובין (דף ד.). ור"י אומר: דגמירי דבהכי לא ינקי, אע"פ שיש מקום זרעים:

לא שלוקין ולא מבושלין. משמע דשליקה הוי טפי מבישול, דאי לאו הכי – הוי זו ואין צריך לומר זו. וכן משמע בכמה דוכתין. והא דתנן בפרק "ג' מינים" (נזיר דף מה:): היה מבשל השלמים או שולקן – אע"ג דשליקה הוי טפי מבישול לא הוי התם זו ואין צ"ל זו, דקמ"ל דבשליקה אינו יוצא מתורת בישול*:

ה"ג

*[א]ערוגה שהיא ששה על ששה טפחים – זורעין בתוכה חמשה זרעונין, ארבע על ארבע רוחות הערוגה ואחת באמצע. מהו דתימא: הני מילי – בזרעין, אבל בירקות לא, קמ"ל. למימרא דירקות אלימא מזרעים? *והתנן: [ב]כל מיני זרעים אין זורעין בערוגה אחת, כל מיני ירקות זורעין בערוגה אחת! מהו דתימא: הני מרור מין זרעים נינהו, קמ"ל. זרעים סלקא דעתך?! והא תנן "ירקות" ותני בר קפרא ירקות, ותני דבי שמואל ירקות! חזרת איצטריכא ליה, ס"ד אמינא: הואיל וסופה להקשות – ניתיב לה רווחא טפי. לאו א"ר יוסי בר' חנינא: קלח של כרוב שהוקשה – מרחיבין לו בית רובע. אלמא: כיון דסופו להקשות – יהבינן ליה רווחא טפי. ה"נ – ניתיב לה רווחא טפי, קמ"ל.§ "יוצאין בהן בין לחין בין יבשין כו'".§ א"ר חסדא: [ג]לא שנו אלא בקלח, אבל בעלין, לחין – אין, יבשין – לא. והא מדקתני סיפא "בקלח שלהן" מכלל דרישא עלין! פרושי קא מפרש, כי קתני "בין לחין בין יבשין" – אקלח. מיתיבי: *יוצאין בהן ובקלח שלהן, בין לחין בין יבשין, דברי ר' מאיר. וחכ"א: לחין – יוצאין בהן, יבשין – אין יוצאין בהן. ושוין שיוצאין בהן כמושין, אבל לא כבושין ולא שלוקין ולא מבושלין. כללו של דבר: כל שיש בו טעם מרור – יוצאין בו, וכל שאין בו טעם מרור – אין יוצאין בו. תרגומא אקלח. ת"ר: אין יוצאין בהן כמושין, משום ר"א בר' צדוק אמרו: יוצאין בהן כמושין. בעי רמי בר חמא: מהו שיצא אדם ידי חובתו במרור של מעשר שני בירושלים? אליבא דר' עקיבא *לא תיבעי לך – השתא במצה דאורייתא נפיק – במרור דרבנן מיבעי'?! כי תיבעי לך – אליבא דר' יוסי הגלילי *מאי? במצה דאורייתא הוא דלא נפיק – אבל מרור דרבנן נפיק או דילמא *כל דתקינו רבנן – כעין דאורייתא תקון. אמר רבא: מסתברא, מצה ומרור.§

מתני' [ד]אין שורין את המורסן לתרנגולים, אבל חולטין. [ה]האשה לא תשרה את המורסן שתוליך בידה למרחץ, אבל שפה היא בבשרה יבש. *[ו]לא ילעוס אדם חיטין ויניח על מכתו*, מפני שהן מחמיצות.§ **גמ'** תנו רבנן, אלו דברים שאין באין לידי חימוץ: האפוי, והמבושל, וחלוט שחלטו ברותחין. מבושל?! אדמבשל ליה מחמע! אמר רב פפא[א]: האפוי שבישלו קאמר. תניא, רבי יוסי ברבי יהודה אומר: [ז]קמח שנפל לתוכו דלף – אפילו כל היום כולו – אינו בא לידי חימוץ. אמר רב פפא: [ח]והוא *דעביד טיף להדי טיף. אמרי דבי ר' שילא: ותיקא שרי. והתניא: ותיקא אסור! לא קשיא: [ט]הא – דעבדיה במישחא ומילחא, הא – דעבדיה במיא ומילחא. אמר מר זוטרא: [י]לא לימחי איניש קדרא בקמחא דאבישנא, דילמא לא בשיל שפיר, ואתי לידי חימוץ. אמר רב יוסף: לא ליחלוט איניש

תרי

אבל בירקות לא. דירקות ינקי טפי: למימרא דירקות אלימא. לינק טפי מזרעים, דאיצטריך ליה למימר דאף ירקות נזרעין חמשה מינין בערוגה של ששה: כל מיני זרעים אין נזרעין בערוגה אחת. אפילו בשיעור הזה, משום דינקי טפי. והא דתנן: זורעין בתוכה חמשה זרעונין – בירקות קאמר, דנזרעים כהלכתן: מהו דתימא הני דמרור מין זרעים נינהו. ולא יזרעו בערוגה אחת, קמשמע לן רב דמין ירקות נינהו, ונזרעים: זרעים סלקא דעתך. היכי תיסק אדעתין דזרעים נינהו? והא כולהו תנאי ירקות קרי להו: חזרת איצטריכא ליה. לאשמועינן דנזרעת כשאר ירקות בערוגה עם ארבעה זרעונין: להקשות. קלח שלה נעשה עב: מרחיבין לו. מקום עד בית רובע, שלא יזרעו אצלו מין אחר: בית רובע. מקום זריעת רובע הקב. חצר המשכן היה שיעור לבית סאתים, וכל בית כור ובית סאה ובית רובע שבגמרא – לפי אותו חשבון: לא שנו. דיבש יש לו טעם מרור, אלא קלח, דמתוך שהוא עב אינו מתייבש, שיפסיד טעמו. אבל עלין יבשין – הרי הן כעפר בעלמא: מכלל דרישא בעלין. קא פסיק ותנא בהו בין לחים בין יבשים: כמושין. פלצד"ו: כללו של דבר כו'. קתני מיה' בדר' מאיר: יוצאין בהן ובקלחין שלהן, בין לחין בין יבשין. ומתני' נמי, מדמכשר ביבשים – רבי מאיר היא, ושמע מינה בעלין נמי אכשר: תרגומא. להא דקתני בדר' מאיר יבשין – אקלח קאמר: השתא מצה. דמעשר דידה דאורייתא, ואיכא למיפסלה משום דאין לה היתר במושבות – קאמר ר"ע דנפיק, הואיל ואי מטמיא פריק לה, ואית לה היתר: מרור. דמעשר ירק מדרבנן הוא, ומדאורייתא אית ליה היתר במושבות, מיבעיא?! כעין דאורייתא תקון. ואין לו היתר במושבות, ומרור איתקש למצה, מה מצה בעינן נאכלת בכל מושבות – אף מרור נמי בעינן יש לו היתר. לישנא אחרינא: מצה בזמן הזה דאורייתא, ומרור מדרבנן, בפרק בתרא (דף קטו.). וזה שמעתי. וקשיא לי: בזמן הזה מי מסקי מעשר שני לירושלים? ואי למאן דאמר קדושה ראשונה קידשה לשעתה וקידשה לעתיד לבוא – בהדיא איבעי ליה לפרושי בזמן הזה: מצה ומרור. הוקשו יחד, וכי היכי דמצה יש עליה שם מעשר שני, ולא נפיק ביה – אף מרור נמי שיש עליה שם מעשר שני, לא נפיק ביה: **מתני'** חולטין. ברותחין, שאין מניחין אותו להחמיץ: לא תשרה המורסן. לשוף בה בשרה, מפני שמחמיץ בשרייתו: אבל שפה היא. מורסן יבש בבשרה. ואע"פ שמים טופחין על בשרה: לא ילעום. לא יכוס: **גמ'** האפוי. לחם משנאפה, כל מה ששורים במים אינו מחמיץ: אדמבשל ליה מחמע. בעוד שהמים פושרים קודם שירתיחו הוא מחמיץ! ובדשדי ליה לתוך רותחין ליכא לאוקומה, דהא בהדיא תני לה: וחלוט שחלטו ברותחין: אפוי שבשלו. כלומר: אפוי, אפילו הוא מבשלו לאחר אפייה – אינו מחמיץ: דלף. מן הגג: אינו בא לידי חימוץ. שטירוד הדלף הנופל תמיד אינו מניחו להחמיץ: טיף להדי טיף. שנופלין טיפה אחר טיפה, סמוך ותכף, ואין שהות בינתים: ותיקא. מאכל קמח: מישחא ומילחא. בקימחא שרי, דמי פירות אין מחמיצין: לא לימחי איניש קדרא. שמעבין תבשיל הקדירה על ידי שממחין קמח לתוכו, ואפילו בקמחא דאבישונא שמתייבשה וניקלית בתנור. כשהיא לחה עושין אותה קלי בתנור, והרי היא כאפויה – אפילו הכי לא ליעביד: דילמא לא בשיל שפיר. לא נעשית קלי כל צרכה בתנור, ומחמצת בתבשיל. וכשהוא טורפה בקערה היא מחמצת, (ועוד) שאין דרך נתינתה לתוך תבשיל רותח: לא ליחלוט. ברותחין:

תרתי

כלאים פ"ג [מ"א] שבת דף פד: [קידושין לט:]
כלאים שם [מ"ב]
[ברכו' ד' לח:]
[לעיל לו.]
[שם]
[לעיל ל: וש"נ]
כתובות דף קג.
ס"א בפסח
[ע"ז ל:]

[ועי' תוס' זבחים ל: ד"ה לגוין ועי' ברש"י ור"ן ורא"ש נדרים מט. ד"ה הגודל]:

רבינו חננאל

היא מנין לערוגה שהיא ששה על ששה טפחים שזורעין בתוכה חמשה זרעונים כו' ודחי' מהו דתימא הני מילי זרעים אבל ירקות בעו טפי ואקשי' וכי ירקות אלימי מזרעים והא איפכא תנן כל מיני זרעים אין זורעין בערוגה וזורעין כל מיני ירקות בערוגה מהו דתימא הני מרורים כולן ששנינו מיני זרעים נינהו ואין זורעין אותן בערוגה בא רב להודיענו כי ירקות הן ונזרעין בערוגה אחת. **ואקשי'** והא מתני' ירקות קתני כל תנא תנא נמי ירקות קתני וליכא תנא דתני זרעים חזרת שסופה להקשות איצטריכא ליה סד"א ניתיב ליה רווחא טפי משאר ירקות כמו קלה של כרוב שהוקשה כלומר שגדל ונעשה קשה שמרחיבין לו בית רובע מכל צדדין פי' אין מניחין סביבותיו זרע כדי שישלח שרשיו לכל צד מפני שגדול הוא נעשה גם כך לחזרת קמ"ל דלא: **יוצאין** בהן באלו הירקות בין לחין בין יבשין. אמר רבא לא שנו יבשין אלא קלח אבל עלין לחין אין יבשין לא. ואתיבנא אין יוצאין בהן כמושין אבל לא כבושין ולא מבושלין וכו' ודברים פשוטין הן ורב חסדא פרק תרגומה אקלח אבל עלין אין יוצאין בהן אלא לחין ושוין שיוצאין בהן כמושין אבל לא כבושין ולא מבושלין זה הכלל כל שיש בו טעם מרור יוצאין בו: **בעי** רמי מהו שיצא אדם במרור של מעשר שני אליבא דר' עקיבא ופשטה רבה כשם שיוצאין במצה שהיא מדאורייתא כך יוצאין במרור שהוא מדרבנן: **מתני'** אין שורין את המורסן לתרנגולין אבל חולטין: **ת"ר** דברים שאין באין לידי חימוץ אסיקנא כגון אפוי שבשלו וחלוט שחלטו ברותחין תניא רבי יוסי ברבי יהודה אומר קמח שנפל לתוכו דלף דעביד טיף כנגד טיף אפילו כל היום כולו אינו בא לידי חימוץ ותיקא דהוא כגון שתיתא דעביד במשחא ובמלחא בקמחא שרי פירוש כי השמן מי פירות הוא ומי פירות אין מחמיצין אבל במיא ומלחא וקמחא אסור לא לימחי איניש קדירה בקמחא דאבשינא דלא בשיל שפיר ואתי לידי חימועא. הא דאמר רב יוסף לא נחלוט איניש

תרתי

הגהות מהר"י לנדא

א] אמר רב פפא האפוי שבישלו וכו'. חסר בליוני עין משפט מיי' פ"ה מהלכות חמץ הלכה ג:

תורה אור

תְּרֵי חִיטֵּי בַּהֲדֵי הֲדָדֵי — דִּילְמָא אָזְלָא חֲדָא וְיָתְבָה בְּצִירְיָא דַּחֲבֶרְתָּהּ, וְלָא סָלֵיק לְהוּ דִּיקוּלָא דְּמַיָּא מֵאַרְבַּע רוּחָתָא, וְאָתֵי לִידֵי חִימּוּץ. וַאֲמַר אַבַּיֵי: לָא לִיחְרוֹךְ אִינִישׁ תְּרֵי שִׁבּוּלֵי בַּהֲדֵי הֲדָדֵי, דִּילְמָא נָפְקֵי מַיָּא מֵהַאי וּבָלַע אִידָךְ, וְאָתְיָא לִידֵי חִימּוּץ. אֲמַר לֵי' רָבָא: א"ה — אֲפִילּוּ חֲדָא נַמִי, דִּילְמָא נָפֵיק מֵהַאי רֵישָׁא וּבָלַע אִידָךְ רֵישָׁא! אאֶלָּא אָמַר רָבָא: מֵי פֵּירוֹת נִינְהוּ, *וּמֵי פֵּירוֹת אֵינָן מַחְמִיצִין. וַהֲדַר בֵּיהּ אַבַּיֵי מֵהַהִיא, דְּכֹל אַגַּב מִדְלַיְיהוּ לָא מַחְמְצִי. דַּאֲמַר אַבַּיֵי: הַאי חַצְבָא דַּאֲבִישְׁנָא, סְחִיפָא — שָׁרֵי, זְקִיפָא — אָסוּר. רָבָא אָמַר: אֲפִילּוּ זְקִיפָא נַמִי שָׁרֵי, מֵי פֵּירוֹת נִינְהוּ, וּמֵי פֵּירוֹת אֵינָן מַחְמִיצִין. ת"ר: באֵין לוֹתְתִין *שְׂעוֹרִין בַּפֶּסַח, וְאִם לָתַת, נִתְבַּקְּעוּ — אֲסוּרוֹת, לֹא נִתְבַּקְּעוּ — מוּתָּרוֹת, ר' יוֹסֵי אוֹמֵר: שׁוֹרָן בַּחוֹמֶץ וְחוֹמֶץ צוֹמְתָן. *אָמַר שְׁמוּאֵל: אֵין הֲלָכָה כְּר' יוֹסֵי. א"ר חִסְדָּא אָמַר מָר עוּקְבָא: גלֹא נִתְבַּקְּעוּ מַמָּשׁ, אֶלָּא כֹּל שֶׁאִילּוּ מַנִּיחָן עַל פִּי חָבִית וְהֵן נִתְבַּקְּעוֹת מֵאֵילֵיהֶן. וּשְׁמוּאֵל אָמַר: נִתְבַּקְּעוּ מַמָּשׁ. עֲבַד שְׁמוּאֵל עוּבְדָא בְּדוֹרָא דְּבֵי בַּר חָשׁוּ נִתְבַּקְּעוּ מַמָּשׁ. אָמַר רַבָּה: בַּעַל נֶפֶשׁ לֹא יִלְתּוֹת. מַאי אִירְיָא בַּעַל נֶפֶשׁ? אֲפִילּוּ כּוּלֵּי עָלְמָא נַמִי, דְּהָא תַּנְיָא: אֵין לוֹתְתִין שְׂעוֹרִין בַּפֶּסַח! הָכִי קָאָמַר: דבַּעַל נֶפֶשׁ — אֲפִילּוּ חִיטִּין דִּשְׁרִירִי לֹא יִלְתּוֹת. א"ל ר"נ: מַאן דְּצָיֵית לֵיהּ לְאַבָּא אָכֵיל נַהֲמָא דְּעִיפּוּשָׁא. דְּהָא בֵּי רַב הוּנָא לָתְתִי, וּבֵי רָבָא בַּר אָבִין לָתְתִי. וְרָבָא אָמַר: אָסוּר לִלְתּוֹת. אֶלָּא הָא דְּתַנְיָא "אֵין לוֹתְתִין שְׂעוֹרִין בַּפֶּסַח" שְׂעוֹרִין הוּא — דְּלָא, הָא חִיטֵּי — שָׁרֵי?! לָא מִיבַּעְיָא קָאָמַר, לָא מִיבַּעְיָ' חִיטִּין, כֵּיוָן דְּאִית בֵּיהּ צִירְיָא — עָיְילֵי בְּהוּ מַיָּא, אֲבָל שַׂעֲרֵי דְּשִׁיעֵי — אֵימָא שַׁפִּיר דָּמֵי, קמ"ל. הֲדַר אֲמַר רָבָא: *מוּתָּר לִלְתּוֹת, *דְּתַנְיָא: יוֹצְאִין בְּפַת נְקִיָּה וְהַדְרָאָה, וְאִי אֶפְשָׁר נְקִיָּה בְּלֹא לְתִיתָה. אֵיתִיבֵיהּ רַב פַּפָּא לְרָבָא: הַקְּמָחִין וְהַסְּלָתוֹת שֶׁל גּוֹיִם, שֶׁל כְּפָרִים — טְהוֹרִים, וְשֶׁל כְּרַכִּין — טְמֵאִין. דִּכְפָרִים מ"ט? לָאו מִשּׁוּם דְּלָא לָתְתִי, וְקָא קָרֵי לֵיהּ סוֹלֶת! — תַּרְגּוּמָא אַקִּמְחָא. בָּתַר דִּנְפֵיק אֲמַר: מ"ט לָא אֵימָא לֵיהּ מֵהָא; *דְּאָמַר רַבִּי זֵירָא אָמַר רַב יִרְמְיָה אָמַר שְׁמוּאֵל: חִיטִּין שֶׁל מְנָחוֹת — אֵין לוֹתְתִין אוֹתָם, וְקָא קָרֵי לְהוּ סוֹלֶת! הֲדַר אֲמַר רָבָא: מִצְוָה לִלְתּוֹת, שֶׁנֶּאֱמַר °"וּשְׁמַרְתֶּם אֶת הַמַּצּוֹת" (שמות יב) אִי לָא דְּבָעֵי לְתִיתָה — שִׁימּוּר לְמַאי? אִי שִׁימּוּר דְּלִישָׁה — לָאו שִׁימּוּר הוּא, דְּאָמַר רַב הוּנָא: בְּצֵקוֹת שֶׁל גּוֹיִם אָדָם מְמַלֵּא כְּרֵיסוֹ מֵהֶן, וּבִלְבַד שֶׁיֹּאכַל כַּזַּיִת מַצָּה בָּאַחֲרוֹנָה. בָּאַחֲרוֹנָה — אִין, בָּרִאשׁוֹנָה — לָא. מ"ט — מִשּׁוּם דְּלָא עֲבַד בְּהוּ שִׁימּוּר. וְלַעֲבֵיד לֵיהּ שִׁימּוּר מֵאֲפִיָּה וְאֵילָךְ! אֶלָּא לָאו שְׁמַע מִינַּהּ — שִׁימּוּר מֵעִיקָּרָא בָּעֵינַן. וּמִמַּאי? דִּילְמָא שָׁאנֵי הָתָם, דִּבְעִידָּנָא דְּנָחֵית לְשִׁימּוּר — לָא עֲבַד לָהּ שִׁימּוּר. אֲבָל הֵיכָא דִּבְעִידָּנָא דְּנָחֵית לְשִׁימּוּר עָבֵיד לָהּ שִׁימּוּר — הָכִי נַמִי דְּשִׁימּוּר דְּלִישָׁה הָוֵי שִׁימּוּר. וַאפ"ה לָא הֲדַר בֵּיהּ רָבָא, דַּאֲמַר לְהוּ לְהָנְהוּ דִּמְהַפְּכִי כִּיפֵי: כִּי מְהַפְּכִיתוּ — הֲפִיכוּ לְשׁוּם מִצְוָה. האַלְמָא קָסָבַר: שִׁימּוּר מֵעִיקָּרָא — מִתְּחִלָּתוֹ וְעַד סוֹפוֹ בָּעֵינַן. מָר בְּרֵיהּ דְּרָבִינָא מַנְקַטָּא

תַּרְתֵּי חִיטֵּי. גַּרְעִינֵי חִיטִּין, אֶלָּא חֲדָא חֲדָא חִיטְּתָא: דִּילְמָא אָתְיָא חֲדָא וְיָתְבָה בְּצִירְיָא דַּחֲבֶרְתָּהּ. בְּסֶדֶק שֶׁל חֲבֶרְתָּהּ: דִּיקוּלָא דְּמַיָּא. רְתִיחַת הַמַּיִם: צִירְיָא. סֶדֶק, כְּמוֹ (א) טַיְילָא"ה חֲרִיפָא דְּמַלְרֵי זִיקֵי, דְּמַסֶּכֶת ע"ז (דף ל.): אִי הָכָא אֲפִילּוּ חֲדָא. שִׁבּוּלְתָּא נַמִי לָא לִיחֲרוֹךְ: דִּילְמָא נָפְקֵי מַיָּא. מֵחִיטֵּי דִּבְרֵישָׁא חֲדָא, וּבָלְעֵי חִטִּים דְּאִידָךְ רֵישָׁא: ה"ג: וַהֲדַר בֵּיהּ אַבַּיֵי דְּכֹל אַגַּב מִדְלַיְיהוּ לָא מַחְמְעֵי. כָּל דֶּרֶךְ נְפִילָתָם לָא מַחְמְעֵי: חַצְבָּא דַּאֲבִישׁוּנָא. כַּד שֶׁמְּיַיבְּשִׁין בְּתוֹכוֹ קְלָיוֹת בַּתַּנּוּר: סְחִיפָא שָׁרֵי. אִם פִּיו כָּפוּי לְמַטָּה, שֶׁיְּהוּ הַמַּיִם הַנִּפְלָטִין מִן הַקָּלִי עַל יְדֵי חוֹם הָאוּר זָבִין וְיוֹצְאִין לַחוּץ – שָׁרֵי: זְקִיפָא. שֶׁיְּהֵא זוֹקֵף כְּדַרְכּוֹ – אָסוּר, שֶׁהַמַּיִם נִפְלָטִין וְחוֹזְרִין וְנִבְלָעִין. וּמִדַּאֲמַר אַבַּיֵי סְחִיפָא שָׁרֵי מִשּׁוּם דְּדָיְיבִי אַבְּרָאֵי – שְׁמַע מִינָּהּ הֲדַר בֵּיהּ מִמַּאי דַּאֲמַר לְעֵיל לָא לִיחֲרוֹךְ אִינִישׁ תַּרְתֵּי שִׁיבָּלֵי, דְּהָנֵי נַמִי דָּיְיבִי מַיָּא וְשָׁרְקֵי וְנָפְלֵי, וְלָא מִיבַּלְּעִי בְּאִידָךְ: נִתְבַּקְּעוּ. מֵחֲמַת הַנִּיפּוּחַ, שֶׁמֵּחֲמַת הַמַּיִם אֲסוּרוֹת, דְּוַדַּאי מְמַהֲרוֹת לְהַחְמִיץ: שׁוֹרָן בַּחוֹמֶץ. אִם רוֹאֶה שֶׁנּוֹפְחוֹת – שׁוֹרָן בַּחוֹמֶץ: וְחוֹמֶץ צוֹמְתָן. אשטריינ"ב בְּלַעַ"ז, וְאֵינוֹ מַנִּיחָן לְהַחְמִיץ: וְהֵן מִתְבַּקְּעוֹת מֵאֵילֵיהֶן. שֶׁאֵינָן יְכוֹלוֹת לַעֲמוֹד מִפְּנֵי רֵיחַ הַיַּיִן: בְּדוֹרָא דְּבֵי בַּר חָשׁוּ. בַּכְּפָר שֶׁל אוֹתוֹ הָאִישׁ: נִתְבַּקְּעוּ מַמָּשׁ. כְּלוֹמַר: דְּאֵין אֲסוּרוֹת אֶלָּא נִתְבַּקְּעוּ מַמָּשׁ, וְאוֹתָן לֹא מְבוּקָּעוֹת מַמָּשׁ הָיוּ, וְהִתִּירָן: אָמַר רַבָּה גָּרְסִינַן: בַּעַל נֶפֶשׁ. *חָסִיד: הָכִי קָאָמַר אֲפִילּוּ חִיטֵּי. שֶׁהֵן קָשִׁין מִשְּׂעוֹרִין, וְאֵין מְמַהֲרִין לְהַחְמִיץ, בַּעַל נֶפֶשׁ לֹא יִלְתּוֹת. אֲבָל דְּלָאו (ב) בַּעַל נֶפֶשׁ, דְּלָא מַחֲמִיר עַל נַפְשֵׁיהּ כּוּלֵּי הַאי: דִּשְׁרִירָן. קָשִׁים: לְאַבָּא (ג). רַבָּה. הָכִי קָרֵי לֵיהּ לְשׁוֹן רַבָּנוּת: מַאן דְּצָאֵית לֵיהּ לְאַבָּא יֹאכַל לֶחֶם עִיפּוּשָׁא. כְּלוֹמַר: לֹא תְּהֵא סוֹלְתָּן נְקִיָּה: דְּהָא בֵּי רַב הוּנָא לָתְתִי. כּוּלָּהּ רַב נַחְמָן אֲמַר לָהּ: וְרָבָא אָמַר אָסוּר לִלְתּוֹת. לְכוּלֵּי עָלְמָא: דְּשִׁיעָן. שֶׁחֲלָקִין הֵן: וְהַדְרָאָה. קִיבָּר: שֶׁל כְּפָרִים טְהוֹרִים. לְפִי שֶׁאֵין מַקְפִּידִין עַל סוֹלְתָּן לַעֲשׂוֹתָן נְקִיָּה כָּל כָּךְ, וְלָא לָתְתִי לְחִיטֵּי דִּידְהוּ, וְנִמְצָא שֶׁלֹּא הוּכְשְׁרוּ. וְקָא קָרֵי לְהוּ סוֹלֶת, אַלְמָא: אֶפְשָׁר לִנְקִיָּה בְּלֹא לְתִיתָה: בָּתַר דִּנְפַק. רָבָא מִבֵּי מִדְרְשָׁא: אֲמַר. רַב פַּפָּא נִצְטַעֵר בְּעַצְמוֹ: מַדּוּעַ לֹא נִזְכַּרְתִּי לְהָשִׁיב לוֹ מֵהָא דְּאָמַר ר' יִרְמְיָה כו': וְאִי לָאו. לְתִיתָה דְּעַכְשָׁיו בָּעֵי שִׁימּוּר שֶׁלֹּא יַחֲמִיצוּ, שִׁימּוּר לָמָּה לִי? לָאו שִׁימּוּר הוּא. אִי לָא עֲבַד לֵיהּ שִׁימּוּר מִקַּמֵּי הָכִי: דְּאָמַר רַב הוּנָא גָּרְסִינַן: בְּצֵקוֹת שֶׁל גּוֹיִם. שֶׁמַּכִּיר בָּהֶן שֶׁלֹּא הֶחְמִיצוּ, שֶׁאֵין שָׁם לֹא קַרְנֵי חֲגָבִים וְלֹא הִכְסִיפוּ פָּנָיו, דְּהוּא הָוֵי סִימַן סִידּוּק וְסִימַן שִׂיאוּר, כִּדְלְקַמָּן: שֶׁיֹּאכַל כַּזַּיִת מַצָּה בָּאַחֲרוֹנָה. דִּבְהָא לָא נָפֵיק יְדֵי חוֹבַת מַצָּה, מִשּׁוּם דְּלָא הָוֵי לָהּ שִׁימּוּר לְשֵׁם מַצָּה, וְאַף עַל פִּי שֶׁאָנוּ רוֹאִין שֶׁאֵין כָּאן חִימּוּץ. וּמִיהוּ, לְמַצָּה שֶׁל מִצְוָה – שִׁימּוּר לִשְׁמָהּ בָּעֵינַן: בָּאַחֲרוֹנָה. (ד) הִיא מִצְוַת אֲכִילָתָהּ, שֶׁעִם הַפֶּסַח הִיא חוֹבַת אֲכִילָתָהּ, דִּכְתִיב קְרָא (שמות יב): "עַל מַצּוֹת וּמְרוֹרִים יֹאכְלוּהוּ", וּפֶסַח נֶאֱכָל עַל הַשּׂוֹבַע, כִּדְתְנַן (לקמן דף קיט:): אֵין מַפְטִירִין אַחַר הַפֶּסַח אֲפִיקוֹמָן: בָּרִאשׁוֹנָה לָא. כְּלוֹמַר: בַּאֲכִילָה רִאשׁוֹנָה שֶׁאָכַל מִבְּצֵקוֹת שֶׁל גּוֹיִם – לָא נָפֵיק: הָכִי גָּרְסִינַן: מַאי טַעְמָא דְּלָא עֲבַד לָהּ שִׁימּוּר. וְלָא גָּרְסִינַן: אִי נֵימָא דְּהָא וַדַּאי טַעְמָא מִשּׁוּם הָכִי הוּא: מֵאֲפִיָּיה וְאֵילָךְ. מַשְׁמַע מִשֶּׁמִּתְקַנָּהּ לַאֲפִיָּיה, כְּגוֹן עֲרִיכָתָהּ וְקִיטּוּפָהּ שֶׁלָּהּ וּנְתִינָתָהּ לַתַּנּוּר: וּמִמַּאי דִּילְמָא. לְעוֹלָם שִׁימּוּר דְּלִישָׁה שִׁימּוּר הוּא, וְאַע"ג דְּלָא אִיצְטְרִיךְ שִׁימּוּר מִקַּמֵּי הָכִי. וְהָכָא מַאי טַעְמָא לָא נָפֵיק – מִשּׁוּם דְּמִשְּׁעַת נְתִינַת מַיִם לְקֶמַח, שֶׁזֶּה דָּבָר הַמַּחְמֶצֶת – הָוְיָא צְרִיכָה שִׁימּוּר, וְזוֹ לֹא נַעֲשָׂה לָהּ שִׁימּוּר מֵהַהִיא עִידָּנָא דְּנָחֵית לְתוֹרַת שִׁימּוּר, דְּהַיְינוּ מִנְּתִינַת הַמַּיִם: וַאֲפִילּוּ הָכִי. דְּלָא אַשְׁכַּח רָבָא סִיַּיעְתָּא לְמִילְּתֵיהּ – לָא הֲדַר בֵּיהּ מִמַּאי דַּאֲמַר בָּעֵינַן שִׁימּוּר קוֹדֶם לִישָׁה: מְהַפְּכִי כִּיפֵי. הָעֳמָרִין, וְקוֹשְׁרִין אֶת הָעֳמָרִים בִּימוֹת הַקָּצִיר: מַנְקַטָּא

ה"ג ר"ח: **כל** שאילו מניחן על פי אבוב של קלאים והם מתבקעות. פירוש: כלי שבעלי קליות עושין בו קליות והוא מנוקב, כדאמרינן בפרק "ר' ישמעאל" (מנחות דף סו.): מניחין בתוך אבוב של קלאים, כדי *שתגמור האור בכולו. והם מתבקעות מכח האור, וכן מצא ר"י בספר ישן בשם רבינו תם:

תרגומא אקמחים. תימה: השתא אמאי תני סלתות? ויש לומר: דלגלדין קתני:

כי מהפכיתו כיפי הפכיתו לשם מצה. וא"ת: כיון דסבירא ליה דבעי שימור בשעת היפוך, אם כן היכי מוכח דמצוה ללתות? דילמא לאו מצוה היא, אלא דצריך שימור מתחלתו ועד סופו! ויש לומר: דעיקר שימור כדי שלא תחמיץ, וסבר רבא: אי לאו שיש שימור מחמץ בשעה שהוא עדיין דגן, כגון לתיתה – לא היה מצריך שימור בשעת בי דרי, מתחלת הדגון:

רבינו חננאל

תרתי חיטי בהדי הדדי כו' אלו הן כגון קליות והא דאמר אביי לא נחריך איניש תרתי שבלי בהדי הדדי לית הלכתא כוותיה אלא כרבא דאמר מי פירות אין מחמיצין וכן חצבא דאבישנא שהן שיבולי דשערי רטיבתא אמר אביי כשנותנין זה החצבא בתנור בימות הפסח ופיה למטה כל זיעה שיוצא מאותן השעורים נשפכין בתנור (ואם לאו) אסורין אלא אם ישארו אותן המים היוצאין מהן בחיצבא מחמיץ ולית הלכתא כאביי וקיימא לן כל מי פירות אין מחמיצין: **ת"ר** אין לותתין את השעורין בפסח ואם לתתן נתבקעו אסורות לא נתבקעו מותרות ואמר' לא נתבקעו ממש אלא כל שמניחין על פי הביב של קלאים והן כלים מאיליהם וכן הלכתא ור' יוסי דאמר שורן בחומץ מפני שהחומץ צומתתן לית הלכתא כוותיה דהא בהדיא אמר שמואל אין הלכה כר' יוסי והא דעביד שמואל עובדא נתבקעו ממש לא סמכינן עליה. אמר רבה בעל נפש כלומר המתרחק מריח עבירה ומדקדק הרבה על עצמו לא ילתות אפילו חטין דשריין פי' שהן חזקים מן השעורים ולא אתי לידי חימוץ הא לא ילתות כל שכן שעורים: **אמר** רב נחמן מאן דצאית לרבה אוכל פת מעופשת. פי' כגון פת קיבר שאין בה סלת דהא (בר) [בי] רב הונא ובי רבה בר אבוה לתתי ורבה אמר אסור ללתות. ומותבינן עליה אין לותתין את השעורים בפסח הא חטין שרי כו'. פי' צריא כגון סדק באמצעה של חטה אבל השעורים שיעו אין בהן סדק: **איכא** דאמרי אמר רבא מותר ללתות דתנן יוצאין בפת נקיה והדראה ואי אפשר לפת נקיה בלא לתיתה כלומר אם אין שורין את החטים לא יצא מהם סלת ומותיב רב פפא מהא דתאני הקמחין והסלתות של נכרים של כרכים טמאים ושל כפרים טהורים ש"מ מדקתני טהורין מכלל דלא הוכשרו וקרי להו סלתות הנה סלת בלא לתיתה ודחי רבא האי דקתני של כפרים טהורין אקמחים בלבד ולא אסלתות והא דאמר רבא אי אפשר לפת נקיה בלא לתיתה דחויה היא דהא משמע דשמואל אמרו חטים של מנחות אין לותתין וקרי להו התורה סלת הנה נמצאת בלא לתיתה. הדר אמר רבא מצוה ללתות דכתיב ושמרתם את המצות ואין שמור אלא שמור דחטים בלתיתה [דשימור דלישה לאו] שימור מדרב הונא דאמר הבצקות של נכרים אדם ממלא כריסו מהם ובלבד שיאכל כזית מצה באחרונה ואי הוה שמור דלישה שמור היה עושה שימור לבצק של נכרי ואינו צריך כזית אחר ודחי' הני בצקות של נכרים משום דלא אתחיל בהו ישראל בשמור דנכרי לאו בר שימור הוא אבל ישראל דבר שימור הוא אם התחיל מתחלה להשמר אפילו שימור דלישה הוי שימור אפילו הכי לא הדר ביה רבא דאמר רבא להנהו דהוו מהפכי לגורן והן העומרין הפכו לשם מצה כלומר הזהרו מהכשרת המים והפיכו להו למקום שאין בו הכשרת המים שיהיה שימור לשמו לשם מצה: **מר** בריה דרבינא מנקטא ליה בארבי. פי' בעיקריתם היתה

קנז א מיי' פ"ה מהל' חו"מ הלכה ד טוש"ע או"ח סי' תסג סעיף א:

קנח ב ג ד מיי' פ"ה מהלכות מצה הל' ו ז טוש"ע או"ח סימן תנג סעיף ה:

קנט ה מיי' שם הלכה ח ט טוש"ע או"ח סימן תנג סעיף ז:

[לעיל לה: מנחות נז:] [לקמן מב.] [לקמן מח.] ס"א ירא שמים החרד על נפשו [סנהדרין ה:] לעיל לז. לעיל לו. שמות יב

הגהות הב"ח

(א) רש"י ד"ה צירייא סדק כמו טיילא"ה. נ"ב לשון יון: (ב) ד"ה הכי קאמר וכו' דלאו בעל נפש לא מחמיר: (ג) ד"ה לאבא וד"ה מאן הס"ד: (ד) ד"ה באחרונה מצות כו' ותיבת היא נמחק:

גמרא

מַנְקַטָא לֵיהּ אִימֵּיהּ בְּאַרְבֵּי.§ הַהוּא אַרְבָּא דְּחִיטֵּי דְּטָבְעָא בְּחִישְׁתָּא, שָׁרְיָא רָבָא לְזַבּוֹנֵי לַגּוֹיִם. אֵיתִיבֵיהּ רַבָּה בַּר לֵיוָאִי לְרָבָא: *[א]בֶּגֶד שֶׁאָבַד בּוֹ כִּלְאַיִם — הֲרֵי זֶה *לֹא יִמְכְּרֶנּוּ לַגּוֹי, וְלֹא יַעֲשֶׂה (א) בּוֹ מַרְדַּעַת לַחֲמוֹר, אֲבָל עוֹשִׂין אוֹתוֹ תַּכְרִיכִין לַמֵּת. לַגּוֹי מַאי טַעְמָא לָא — לָאו מִשּׁוּם דַּהֲדַר מְזַבֵּין לְיִשְׂרָאֵל? הֲדַר אֲמַר רָבָא: [ב]לְזַבְּנִינְהוּ קַבָּא קַבָּא לְיִשְׂרָאֵל, כִּי הֵיכִי דְּכַלְיָא קַמֵּי פִּיסְחָא. תָּנוּ רַבָּנַן: אֵין מוֹלְלִין אֶת הַקְּדֵירָה בַּפֶּסַח, וְהָרוֹצֶה שֶׁיִּמְלוֹל — נוֹתֵן אֶת הַקֶּמַח וְאח"כ נוֹתֵן אֶת הַחוֹמֶץ. וְיֵשׁ אוֹמְרִים: אַף נוֹתֵן אֶת הַחוֹמֶץ וְאח"כ נוֹתֵן אֶת הַקֶּמַח. *מַאן י"א? א"ר חִסְדָּא: רַבִּי יְהוּדָה הִיא, *דִּתְנַן: [ג]הָאִילְפָּס וְהַקְּדֵירָה שֶׁהֶעֱבִירָן מְרוּתָּחִין — לֹא יִתֵּן לְתוֹכָן תַּבְלִין, אֲבָל נוֹתֵן לְתוֹךְ הַקְּעָרָה אוֹ לְתוֹךְ הַתַּמְחוּי. רַבִּי יְהוּדָה אוֹמֵר: לַכֹּל הוּא נוֹתֵן, חוּץ מִדָּבָר שֶׁיֵּשׁ בּוֹ חוֹמֶץ וָצִיר. וְנוּקְמַהּ כְּר' יוֹסֵי, *(דִּתְנַן), ר' יוֹסֵי אוֹמֵר: שׁוֹרָן בַּחוֹמֶץ, וְחוֹמֶץ צוֹמְתָן! כִּי אַשְׁמְעִינַן לֵיהּ לְרַבִּי יוֹסֵי — הָנֵי מִילֵּי דְּאִיתֵיהּ בְּעֵינֵיהּ, אֲבָל עַל יְדֵי תַּעֲרוֹבֶת — לָא. עוּלָּא אָמַר: [ד]אֶחָד זֶה וְאֶחָד זֶה אָסוּר, מִשּׁוּם *"לֵךְ לֵךְ אָמְרִינַן נְזִירָא, סְחוֹר סְחוֹר, לְכַרְמָא לָא תִּקְרַב". רַב פַּפִּי שָׁרֵי לֵיהּ *לְבוּרְדִּיקֵי דְּבֵי רֵישׁ גָּלוּתָא [ה]לְמִמְחָה קְדֵירָה בַּחֲסִיסֵי. אֲמַר רָבָא: אִיכָּא דְּשָׁרֵי כִּי הַאי מִילְּתָא בְּדוּכְתָּא דִּשְׁכִיחִי עַבְדֵי?! אִיכָּא דְּאָמְרִי: רָבָא גּוּפָא מָחֵי לָהּ קִידְרָא בַּחֲסִיסֵי.§

מתני' אֵין נוֹתְנִין קֶמַח לְתוֹךְ חֲרוֹסֶת אוֹ לְתוֹךְ הַחַרְדָּל, וְאִם נָתַן — יֵאָכֵל מִיָּד, וְרַבִּי מֵאִיר אוֹסֵר. *[ו]אֵין מְבַשְּׁלִין אֶת הַפֶּסַח לֹא בְּמַשְׁקִין וְלֹא בְּמֵי פֵירוֹת, [ז]אֲבָל סָכִין וּמַטְבִּילִין אוֹתוֹ בָּהֶן. מֵי תַשְׁמִישׁוֹ שֶׁל נַחְתּוֹם יִשָּׁפְכוּ, מִפְּנֵי שֶׁהֵן מַחְמִיצִין.§ **גמ'** אָמַר רַב כָּהֲנָא: מַחֲלוֹקֶת — לְתוֹךְ הַחַרְדָּל, אֲבָל לְתוֹךְ חֲרוֹסֶת — דִּבְרֵי הַכֹּל יִשָּׂרֵף מִיָּד. וְתַנְיָא נַמִּי הָכִי: [ח]אֵין נוֹתְנִין קֶמַח לְתוֹךְ הַחֲרוֹסֶת, וְאִם נָתַן — יִשָּׂרֵף מִיָּד. לְתוֹךְ הַחַרְדָּל, ר' מֵאִיר אוֹמֵר: יִשָּׂרֵף מִיָּד, [ט]וַחֲכָמִים אוֹמְרִים: יֵאָכֵל מִיָּד. אָמַר רַב הוּנָא בְּרֵיהּ דְּרַב יְהוּדָה אָמַר רַב נַחְמָן אָמַר שְׁמוּאֵל: הֲלָכָה כְּדִבְרֵי חֲכָמִים. א"ל רַב נַחְמָן בַּר יִצְחָק לְרַב הוּנָא בְּרֵיהּ דְּרַב יְהוּדָה: אַחֲרוֹסֶת

רש"י

מַנְקַטָא לֵיהּ אִימֵּיהּ. חִיטִּין מִתְּחִלַּת קָצִיר לְצוֹרֶךְ הַפֶּסַח, וְעַבְדָא לְהוּ שִׁימּוּר מֵעִיקָּרָא: בְּאַרְבֵּי. מְלֹא עֲרֵיבָה אוֹ עֲרֵיבוֹת הַרְבֵּה, וּמַצְנִיעָתָן לְבַדָּם לְצוֹרֶךְ הַפֶּסַח: חִישְׁתָּא. שֵׁם הַנָּהָר. טָבְעָה קוֹדֶם הַפֶּסַח, וְהָיוּ בָּהּ חִיטִּין: שֶׁאָבַד בּוֹ כִּלְאַיִם. שֶׁנֶּאֱרַג בּוֹ חוּט שֶׁל כִּלְאַיִם, וְאֵינוֹ נִיכָּר: הֲרֵי זֶה לֹא יִמְכְּרֶנּוּ לְגוֹי. דְּהוֹאִיל וְאֵין כִּלְאַיִם שֶׁבּוֹ נִיכָּרִים, אָתֵי לְזַבּוּנֵיהּ הַאי גּוֹי לְיִשְׂרָאֵל, וְלָבֵישׁ לְהוּ יִשְׂרָאֵל וְלָאו אַדַּעְתֵּיהּ: וְלֹא יַעֲשֶׂנּוּ מַרְדַּעַת לַחֲמוֹר. דִּילְמָא הָדַר שָׁקֵיל לֵיהּ מֵהָתָם, וְתוֹפְרוֹ בְּאֶחָד מִבְּגָדָיו: אֲבָל עוֹשֶׂה אוֹתוֹ תַּכְרִיכִין לַמֵּת. דְּמֵהָתָם תּוּ לָא שָׁקֵיל לֵיהּ, דְּבִגְדֵי הַמֵּת אֲסוּרִין בַּהֲנָאָה. וּמֵת אֵין מִצְוֹת נוֹהֲגוֹת בּוֹ, דִּכְתִי': "בַּמֵּתִים חָפְשִׁי" — כֵּיוָן שֶׁמֵּת אָדָם נַעֲשֶׂה חָפְשִׁי מִן הַמִּצְוֹת (שבת ל.). וְהָנֵי חִיטֵּי, כֵּיוָן דְּלָא מִינְכַּר חִימּוּץ דִּידְהוּ — אָתֵי הַאי גּוֹי וְהָדַר מְזַבֵּין לְהוּ לְיִשְׂרָאֵל: קַבָּא קַבָּא. קַב לָזֶה וְקַב לָזֶה, וְלֹא הַרְבֵּה לְאִישׁ א': מוֹלְלָן. בְּקֶמַח קָרֵי מְלִילָה כְּשֶׁנּוֹתְנִין קֶמַח לַתַּבְשִׁיל: וְאַחַר כָּךְ נוֹתֵן אֶת הַחוֹמֶץ. דְּאֵין הַחוֹמֶץ מַנִּיחוֹ לְהַחְמִיץ, לְפִי שֶׁמְּבַשְּׁלוֹ: וְיֵשׁ אוֹמְרִים אַף נוֹתֵן חוֹמֶץ תְּחִלָּה. דְּאַף עַל גַּב דְּחוֹמֶץ כְּבָר מְעוֹרָב בַּתַּבְשִׁיל — הוּא מְבַשֵּׁל אֶת הַנִּיתָּן בְּתוֹכוֹ: שֶׁהֶעֱבִירָן מֵעַל הָאוּר. מְרוּתָּחִין, עֶרֶב שַׁבָּת עִם חֲשֵׁיכָה: לֹא יִתֵּן לְתוֹכָן תַּבְלִין. דִּכְלִי רִאשׁוֹן מְבַשֵּׁל, וְנִמְצָא מְבַשֵּׁל תַּבְלִין בַּשַּׁבָּת: לְתוֹךְ הַקְּעָרָה. דִּכְלִי שֵׁנִי אֵינוֹ מְבַשֵּׁל: לַכֹּל הוּא נוֹתֵן. לְכָל מִינֵי מַאֲכָל הוּא נוֹתֵן תַּבְלִין בִּכְלִי שֵׁנִי, חוּץ מִדָּבָר שֶׁיֵּשׁ בּוֹ חוֹמֶץ וָצִיר, שֶׁהַחוֹמֶץ מְבַשְּׁלָן, וְאַף עַל גַּב שֶׁקָּדַם: הָנֵי מִילֵּי בְּעֵינֵיהּ. כְּשֶׁהַחוֹמֶץ בָּעַיִן, אֲבָל כְּשֶׁהוּא מְעוֹרָב בַּתַּבְשִׁיל — אֵין כֹּחוֹ חָזָק: אֶחָד זֶה וְאֶחָד זֶה. בֵּין חוֹמֶץ תְּחִלָּה בֵּין חוֹמֶץ בַּסּוֹף — אָסוּר: לְבוּרְדְקָאֵי. נַחְתּוֹמִין: בַּחֲסִיסֵי. קִמְחָא דְּאַבְשׁוּנָא: בְּדוּכְתָּא דִּשְׁכִיחִי עַבְדֵי. כְּגוֹן בֵּי רֵישׁ גָּלוּתָא, שֶׁהָעֲבָדִים מְזַלְזְלִין בִּדְבַר אִיסּוּר יוֹתֵר וְיוֹתֵר: **מתני'** חֲרוֹסֶת. אייגרו"ס, וְיֵשׁ בּוֹ חוֹמֶץ, וְעָשׂוּי לְטַבֵּל בּוֹ בָּשָׂר, וּרְגִילִים לָתֵת בּוֹ קֶמַח וְכָל דָּבָר שֶׁמַּקְהֶה אֶת טַעְמוֹ. וְקֶמַח לְאַחַר זְמַן מַחֲמִיץ וּמַקְהֶה אֶת הַטַּעַם: אֵין מְבַשְּׁלִין. דִּכְתִיב (שמות יב): "אַל תֹּאכְלוּ מִמֶּנּוּ נָא וּבָשֵׁל מְבוּשָּׁל" וגו': לֹא בְּמַשְׁקִין. אע"ג דִּכְתִיב "בַּמָּיִם". וְטַעְמָא מְפָרֵשׁ בַּגְּמָרָא: סָכִין. בִּשְׁעַת צְלִיָּיתוֹ: וּמַטְבִּילִין. בִּשְׁעַת אֲכִילָתוֹ: מֵי תַשְׁמִישׁוֹ שֶׁל נַחְתּוֹם. שֶׁמְּצַנֵּן בּוֹ יָדָיו בְּשָׁעָה שֶׁהוּא עוֹרֵךְ וּמְקַטֵּף אֶת הַמַּצָּה — יִשָּׁפְכוּ: **גמ'** מַחֲלוֹקֶת. דְּשָׁרֵי לֵיהּ תַּנָּא קַמָּא לְאוֹכְלוֹ מִיָּד — בְּנוֹתֵן לְתוֹךְ הַחַרְדָּל, לְפִי שֶׁהוּא חָזָק, וְאֵין מַנִּיחָהּ מַהֵר לְהַחְמִיץ: אַחֲרוֹסֶת

תוספות

לא יעשנו מרדעת לחמור. אומר ר"י: דדוקא בכלאים אבודים אסור לעשות מהן מרדעת, שמא יעשנו טלאי על בגדו, ולא יזהר נמי שלא יגע בבשרו. אבל בכלאים ידועים — שרי. כדאמרי' במסכת כלאים (פ"ט מ"ד): מרדעת החמור — אין בה משום כלאים, ומותר לעשות מהן כר וכסת, ובלבד שלא יגע בבשר. אע"ג דאמרינן בפ"ק דביצה (דף יד:*): אפי' עשר מצעות זו על גב זו אסור שמא תכרך לו נימא על בשרו — שמא כר וכסת ומרדעת אין רגילין ליכרך כל כך:

אבל עושהו תכריכין למת. וא"ת: והא איכא "לועג לרש" וגו' ובפרק "התכלת" (מנחות דף מא.) אמר רב טובי בר קיסנא אמר שמואל: כלי קופסא חייבין בציצית (אמר רב) ומודה שמואל בזקן שעשאה לכבודו שפטורה, והיא שעתא ודאי רמינן ליה משום "לועג לרש", ומהאי טעמא נמי לא יעשה כלאים למת! ואומר ר"ת: דציצית שקולה כנגד כל המצות, לכך איכא "לועג לרש" טפי, כדאמרינן ב"התכלת" (שם דף מג:): "וזכרתם את כל מצות ה'" — מלמד ששקולה ציצית כנגד כל המצות. והא דאמר בפ' "מי שמתו" (ברכות דף יח.): רבי חייא ורבי יונתן הוו שקלי ואזלי בבית הקברות, הוי שדיא תכלת דרבי יונתן, אמר ליה ר' חייא דלייה שלא יאמרו למחר באים אצלנו והיום מלעיגים אותנו, ואף על גב דמתים נמי יש להם ציצית! אומר ר"ת: דמכל מקום שייך בהן ליעוג, לפי שמראין עצמן כמצווין במצות והן אינן מצווין, ואינו דומה מצווה ועושה למי שאין מצווה ועושה. ומה שמסירים בזמן הזה מטליתות של מתים — סומכין אהא דתניא במסכת שמחות (פי"ב), אבא שאול בן בטנית צוה לבניו: *קברוהו תחת מרגלותיו של אבא, והתירו תכלת מפליוני, ובכמה דברים אנו סומכין על ספרים חיצונים ומניחין גמרא שלנו, דבפרק בתרא דמגילה (דף לא:) אמרי': ראש חודש אב שחל להיות בשבת — מפטירין "חדשיכם ומועדיכם" דהיינו חזון ישעיה*, ואנו מפטירין "השמים כסאי", וכן הוא בפסיקתא. ובפר' "ויחל" אנו קורין בתענית שלנו, אע"ג דתנן במגילה (גם זה שם) שקורין בתענית בקללות וברכות, ואנו סומכין על מס' סופרים (פי"ז ה"ז)*:

האילפס והקדירה שהעבירן מרותחין לא יתן לתוכן תבלין. מכאן אין להוכיח דעירוי ככלי שני, מדלא אשמעינן רבותא שלא יערה(ב) על הקערה שהתבלין בתוכה. דאדרבה: דוק מסיפא איפכא, דקתני: אבל נותן הוא לתוך הקערה, ולא קתני: אבל מערה על הקערה שיש בה תבלין. ונראה דאפילו שמואל דאית ליה "תתאה גבר", ותניא ב"כיצד צולין" (לקמן דף עו.) כוותיה — אפ"ה מבשל העירוי כדי קליפה, דאמר התם, תניא כוותיה דשמואל: חם לתוך צונן — קולף, צונן לתוך צונן — מדיח. ואם עירו רותחין על התרנגולת — צריך קליפה. וכלי שנשתמשו בכלי ראשון לא יוכל להגעילו ע"י עירוי — דאין מבשל אלא כדי קליפה, והוא בלע יותר מכדי קליפה. והא דאמרינן בפרק "כירה" (שבת דף מב.) דשרי חם לתוך צונן — יש לומר: כיון שאינו מבשל אלא כדי קליפה, הואיל והצונן של מטה מים שהוא דבר המתערב — אינו יכול להתבשל מחמת צוננות המים. אבל דבר שאינו מתערב — לא. ובשילהי ע"ז (דף עו.) אמר: *מר עוקבא זבן יורה מגוי ואהדר ליה גדנפא וכו'. ומסיק: כבולעו כך פולטו. מה בולעו בניצוצות — אף פולטו בניצוצות ואי עירוי ככלי ראשון הוא, מאי איריא משום דבלע בניצוצות? אפילו בלע בליעה גמורה פליט בניצוצות, דהיינו עירוי! אלא ודאי לא בשיל אלא כדי קליפה. והא דתנן בפרק "חבית" (שבת דף קמה:): כל שלא בא בחמין לפני השבת, מדיחין אותו בחמין בשבת וכו' — צריך לאוקמא בכלי שני, דבכלי ראשון אפילו הדחה אסורה. וקשה: דקתני דוקא מדיחין, אבל שורין — לא. והכא גבי תבלין קתני: אבל נותן לתוך הקערה או לתוך התמחוי — דהיינו אפילו שורין! ואומר ר"י: דהתם מיירי במידי דבר בישול, וכששורין אותו אפילו בכלי שני — מיחזי כמבשל. אבל תבלין עשויין למתק הקדירה, ולא מיחזי כמבשל. ובירושלמי בפרק "כירה" בעי: מהו ליתן תבלין מלמטה ולערות עליהן מלמעלה? ר' יונה אומר: אסור, דעירוי ככלי ראשון הוא. חיליה דר' יונה מן הדא: "וכלי חרש אשר תבושל בו ישבר" — א' שבישל בו וא' שעירה לתוכו רותח. ודחי ר' אסי תמן: כלי חרש בולע — תבלין אינו מבשל. התיב ר' אסי בר בון: והתניא אף בכלי נחשת כך. אית לך למימר כלי נחשת בלע?! בתמיה: **רבא** מחו ליה קידרא בחסיסי. פ"ה: קימחא דאבישונא. וקשה: דהא לעיל (דף לט:) אסרינן, וליכא מאן דפליג! ונראה לר"י: כדפירש בערוך בחסיסי — קמח של עדשים, דאין דרכם לבא לידי חימוץ כל כך: לא

עין משפט נר מצוה

קע א מיי' פ"י מהלכות כלאים הלכה כז טור שו"ע יו"ד סימן שא סעיף ח:

קעא ב מיי' פ"ה מהל' חמץ הלכה ט טוש"ע או"ח סימן תסז סעיף ח:

קעב ג מיי' פכ"ב מהל' שבת הלכה ו טור שו"ע או"ח סימן שיח סעיף ט:

קעג ד ה מיי' פרק ה מהלכות מצה הלכה ה טוש"ע או"ח סימן תסג סעיף ג:

קעד ו מיי' פ"ח מהל' ק"פ הלכה ז סמג לאוין שנ:

קעה ז שם הלכה ח:

קעו ח ט מיי' פ"ה מהלכות מצה הל' יט טוש"ע או"ח סימן תסד:

מסורת הש"ס

[וביומא סט.]

ע"ז סה: נדה סח:

שבת מב:

[נ"ל קברו אותי]

[עי' תוס' מגילה לא: ד"ה ר"ח אב וכו' וקל"ע ועי' תרומת הדשן סי' יט]

[וע"ע תוס' ברכות יח. ד"ה למחר וכב"ב עד. ד"ה פסקי ובע"ז סה: ד"ה אבל ובנדה סח: ד"ה אבל]

[עי' תוספות חולין לב. סד"ה וכנגדה]

[עמ"ש תוס' ב"ב נג: ד"ה מתן]

[נ"ל דתניא]

[שבת יג. כ"מ לב. ע"ז יח. נח: נט.]

[גי' הערוך למרדקין]

[עי' תוספות לקמן מא. ד"ה אין מבשלין]

נ"ל רב עקביה

הגהות הב"ח

(א) גמ' בר ליואי לרבא בגד שאבד וכו' לא יעשנו מרדעת לחמור כצ"ל: (ב) תוס' ד"ה אילפס וכו' שלא יערה הקערה כצ"ל ותיבת על נמחק:

רבינו חננאל

היתה משמרת אותם לשם מצה מתחלה: **ההיא** ארבא דטבעא בחישתא. כלומר טבעא ספינה בנהר התיר רבא למכור החטים שבספינה לנכרים ומותבינן ליה [מהא דתניא] הבגד שאבד בו כלאים הרי זה לא ימכרנו לנכרי חיישי' שמא יחזור הנכרי וימכרם לישראל אחר ולא יעשנו מרדעת לחמור אבל עושין אותו תכריכין למת הדר ביה רבא ושרנהו לזבונינהו קבא קבא לישראל כי היכי דניכלו קמי פסחא: **ת"ר** אין מוללין את הקדרה בפסח. פי' מלילות הקמח בקדרה והרוצה שימלול נותן הקמח ואח"כ החומץ ויש אומרים נותן החומץ ואח"כ נותן הקמח ואוקימ' יש אומרים ר' יהודה הוא דתאני בענין נתינת תבלין בשבת ר' יהודה אומר לכל הוא נותן חוץ מדבר שיש בו חומץ וציר כלומר החומץ והציר מבשל ומדלענין שבת לענין חמץ בפסח שרי דקדים ומבשיל ליה ולא אתי לידי חימוצא ונוקמה מאן יש אומרים ר' יוסי דאמר שורן בחומץ וחומץ צומתן ודחי' אימור דאמר ר' יוסי בחומץ לבדו שצומת אבל על ידי והחומץ מי קאמר עולא אמר בין החומץ מקודם בין אחרי כן הכל אסור למלול משום הרחק איסור כמו שאמר לנזיר התרחק מן הכרם שלא תאכל מן הענבים ר' אבא מיחי ליה בחסיסי כעין ות על רב פפי דשרי לדבי ריש גלותא אלא משום דעבדי דלא מעלי ועבדי איסורא: **אין** נותנין קמח לתוך החרוסת ולא לתוך החרדל ואם נתן לתוך החרדל יאכל מיד ור"מ אוסר אבל לתוך חרוסת ד מיד. תניא נמי הכי אין נותנין קמח לתוך חרוסת ואם נתן ישרף מיד לתוך החרדל ר' מאיר אומר ישרף מיד וחכמים אומרים יאכל מיד ואמר רב נחמן אמר שמואל הלכה כחכמים: **אין** מבשלין הפסח במשקין

אחרוסת קאמר. מי אית לך דרבנן נמי אחרוסת פליגי: לא סבירא לי. אלא בחרוסת נמי שרו, והלכה כמותן: כוותיה דרב כהנא מסתברא. דאמר: רבנן אחרוסת לא פליגי, וכי אמר שמואל הלכה כחכמים – אחרדל קאמר: אין הלכה כרבי יוסי. דאמר לעיל חומץ נותן: מאי לאו. מדלא צמית חטין שהתחילו ליפסח כבר, אלמא (ב) כשאר משקין הוא – אחמועי נמי מחמע את הניתן מתחלה לתוכו, כדרב כהנא. אלמא: שמואל כרב כהנא סבירא ליה. וכי קאמר שמואל הלכה כחכמים – אחרדל קאמר, ולא אחרוסת: לא מיצמת צמית. את שהתחיל להחמיץ, ולא מחמע נמי את הניתן לתוכו, דלא הוי כמים: במים. "ובשל מבושל במים": שמפיגין טעמן. שנותנין בו טעם שלהן: ובשל מבושל. רבויא הוא, דהוה ליה למיכתב "נא ומבושל": צלי קדר. שמבשלין אותו בקדירה בלא מים ובלא שום משקה, אלא מים הנפלטין משמנו. למאן דיליף לה מק"ו – הכא שרי, לרבי דיליף מרבויא – האי נמי "בשל מבושל" הוא: חייב. מלקות על אכילתו: ר' יוסי היא. דאמר: בישול לאחר אפיה – בישול הוא: יוצאין. ידי חובת מצה ברקיק השרוי בתבשיל לאחר אפייתו, ואף על פי שמתמסמס – לחם הוא, כל זמן שהוא קיים, שלא נימוח לגמרי. וכן במבושל: אבל לא במבושל. דלאו לחם קרינא ביה, ואע"פ שכבר נאפה בתנור – הואיל וחזר ובישלו – ביטלו מתורת לחם: שאני הכא דרבייה קרא. "ובשל מבושל". דהוי ליה למכתב ומבושל, וגזירת הכתוב הוא בפסח: יכול צלאו כל צורכו. ואח"כ בשלו יהא חייב? והאי תנא הוא דאמר לעיל: צלאו ואח"כ בישלו – חייב. לישנא אחרינא" יכול צלאו כל צרכו, דשויא חרוכא, כדמפרש, יהא חייב? דלאו צלי אש הוא, אלא קלי אש, ושרוף. וזה עיקר, וראשון אינו כלום; דההוא תנא, כיון דרבי קרא צלאו ואחר כך בישלו, מה לי שוייה חרוכא מה לי לא שוייה? חרוכא. שרוף: חי. לגמרי, שלא נצלה כלל: נא. צלי ואינו צלי: יכול יהא מותר. לאכול ממנו חי לכתחלה, דאפי' איסורא נמי ליכא, תלמוד לומר: "אל תאכלו ממנו נא, כי אם צלי אש", ולא זה שאינו צלי. והויא לאו שבכללות, והאי תנא סבר: אין לוקין על לאו שבכללות: כדאמרי פרסאי אברנים. אותה צלייה שבלשון פרסי קרויה אברנים, בלשון הקודש קרי נא: חמי טבריא. מעינות רותחין: פסח שבישלו בחמי טבריא חייב. על אכילתו. וקא סלקא דעתך משום דלא תאכל מבושל: דלאו תולדות אש היא. הלכך לאו בישול הוא, דליהוי חייב משום אב מלאכה: משום צלי אש. לאו דלא תאכל כי אם צלי אש איכא, ולא לאו דבישול. וסבר לוקין על לאו שבכללות: בהדיא. דחייב רב חסדא משום צלי אש, ולאו משום בישול:

תורה אור

אחרוסת קאמר מר, או אחרדל קאמר מר? א"ל: למאי נפקא מינה? לדרב כהנא, דאמר רב כהנא: מחלוקת – לתוך החרדל, אבל לתוך החרוסת – דברי הכל ישרף מיד, א"ל: *לא שמיע לי, כלומר לא סבירא לי. א"ר אשי: כוותיה דרב כהנא מסתברא, מדאמר שמואל: *אין הלכה כרבי יוסי. מאי לאו (א) – צמותי הוא דלא צמית הא חמועי – מחמעא. לא, דילמא לא מצמת צמית ולא חמוע מחמע. § "אין מבשלין וכו'". § ת"ר: °"במים" – אין לי אלא במים, שאר משקין מניין? אמרת: קל וחומר, ומה מים שאין מפיגין טעמן – אסורין, שאר משקין שמפיגין טעמן – לא כ"ש?! רבי אומר: במים – אין לי אלא מים, שאר משקין מניין – א ת"ל: °"ובשל מבשל" – מ"מ. מאי בינייהו? איכא בינייהו: צלי קדר. ורבנן האי "בשל מבשל" מאי עבדי להו? מבעי ליה לכדתניא: *ב בשלו ואח"כ צלאו, או שצלאו ואח"כ בשלו – חייב. בשלמא בשלו ואח"כ צלאו חייב – דהא בשליה, אלא צלאו ואח"כ בשלו הא צלי אש הוא, אמאי? אמר רב כהנא: הא מני – רבי יוסי היא, *דתניא: יוצאין ברקיק השרוי, ובמבושל שלא נימוח, דברי ר"מ. רבי יוסי אומר: ג יוצאין ברקיק השרוי, אבל לא במבושל, אע"פ שלא נימוח. עולא אמר: אפילו תימא ר"מ, שאני הכא דאמר קרא: *"ובשל מבשל" – מ"מ. ת"ר: ד יכול צלאו כל צורכו יהא חייב – ת"ל: °"אל תאכלו ממנו נא ובשל מבשל במים" נא ובשל מבשל אמרתי לך, ולא שצלאו כל צורכו. היכי דמי? אמר רב אשי: ה דשויא חרוכא. תנו רבנן: ו יכול אכל כזית חי יהא חייב – תלמוד לומר: "אל תאכלו ממנו נא ובשל מבשל" נא ובשל אמרתי לך, ולא חי. יכול יהא מותר – תלמוד לומר: °"כי אם צלי אש". היכי דמי נא? אמר רב: כדאמרי פרסאי אברנים. *אמר רב חסדא: ז המבשל בחמי טבריא בשבת – פטור. פסח שבשלו בחמי טבריא – חייב. מאי שנא בשבת דלא – דתולדות אש בעינן, וליכא. פסח נמי – לאו תולדות אש הוא. אמר רבא: ח מאי חייב *דקתני – דקא עבר משום "צלי אש". רב חייא בריה דרב נתן מתני לה להא דרב חסדא בהדיא, א"ר חסדא: המבשל בחמי טבריא בשבת – פטור, ופסח שבשלו בחמי טבריא – חייב, שעבר משום "צלי אש". אמר *רבא: *אכלו נא – לוקה

שמות יב | שם | שם | שם

לא שמיע לי כלומר לא סבירא לי. אף על גב דתניא כוותיה, קסבר: מתניתין פליגא:

מדאמר שמואל אין הלכה כרבי יוסי. השתא מדמי חומץ לחרוסת. וע"כ נראה לר"י דעולא דאמר לעיל בין כך ובין כך אסור – משום לך לך אמרינן נזירא סחור סחור לכרמא לא תקרב – פליג אדרב כהנא. דהא רב כהנא דאמר אבל לתוך חרוסת לדברי הכל ישרף, ולעולא לא אסר אלא משום לך לך אמרינן: **מאי** לאו מדלא מצמת מחמע. קשה לר"י, דלעיל קאמר: י"א אף נותן את החומץ, ואח"כ וכו'. ופריך: ולוקמא כר' יוסי, דאמר שורן בחומץ וחומץ צומתן. משמע דתנא קמא דיש אומרים – היינו ת"ק דר' יוסי, דלית ליה דחומץ צמית. ואפילו הכי קאמר נותן הקמח ואח"כ נותן את החומץ. אלמא קסבר: אע"ג דלא צמית – חמועי נמי לא מחמע! ואור"י: דלעיל איירי לפי המסקנא דהכא:

*__אין__ מבשלים את הפסח לא במשקין וכו'. תימה: למה שנאו כאן? אי משום דתנא ירקות שלוקות ומבושלות – א"כ מיד היה לו לשנות בסמוך אחריה: **איכא** בינייהו צלי קדר. פי': אי לוקה עליו אי לא. אבל לכולי עלמא פסול הוי, ועשה נמי אית ביה דצלי מחמת ד"א הוא, כדאמרינן בריש "כיצד צולין" (לקמן עה:): נטף מרוטבו על החרס וחזר עליו – יטול את מקומו, נגע בחרסו של תנור – יקלוף את מקומו. וכן שאר משקין לא איצטריך למילף אלא לענין מלקות, אבל פשיטא דלכל הפחות איכא עשה ד"כי אם צלי אש". וא"ת: והיכי יליף שאר משקין מק"ו? והא אין מזהירין מן הדין! ויש לומר: דהאי קל וחומר אינו אלא מגלה דבישול דקרא איירי אף בשאר משקין: **אמר** רב כהנא הא מני ר' יוסי היא. תימה: דרב כהנא דמוקי לה כרבי יוסי, לרבנן האי "בשל מבושל" מאי עבדי להו? דצלאו ואחר כך בישלו – לא צריך קרא, דמסברא ידעינן דבישול מבטל הצליה, כדאמר רבי יוסי גבי מצה. ויש לומר: דרב כהנא סבר דרבי יוסי יליף מ"בשל מבושל" דבישול מבטל אפייה: **אבל** לא במבושל. פ"ה: דבישול מבטל ליה מתורת לחם. ולפי' מיירי בבלילתו רכה, דבלילתו עבה לא נפיק מתורת לחם, כדפירש לעיל. ור"י מפרש: דמיירי בבלילתו עבה, ופסולה משום מצה עשירה. ומייתי דכי היכי דסבר רבי יוסי דבישול מפיק ליה מתורת אפייה לשוויה מצה עשירה, כאילו לא נאפה – ה"נ גבי פסח עקר מיניה בישול שם צליה: **עולא** אמר אפי' תימא ר' מאיר וכו'. הכא מדמי פסח לבישול מצה, והיינו דלא כמסקנא ד"כיצד מברכין" (ברכות דף לח:) דקאמר התם עולא משמיה דר' יוחנן: שלקות מברכין עליהם שהכל. ודחי: ע"כ לא קאמר רבי יוסי אלא דבעינן טעם לרבי יוסי דאית ליה הכא גבי מצה דבישול מבטל האפיה – ה"נ בישול מבטל מהם שם ירק. מצה. ועולא לטעמיה, דלא בעי לדחויא הכא טעמא דרבי יוסי דבעינן טעם מצה. והתם נמי קאמר דלרבי יוסי מברך שהכל: אכל

עין משפט נר מצוה

קעז א ב מיי' פ"ח מהל' ק"פ הלכה ז ח סמג לאוין שנ:

קעח ג מיי' פ"ו מהל' חמץ הלכה ו טור שו"ע או"ח סימן תסא סעיף ד:

קעט ד ה ו מיי' פ"ח מהלכות ק"פ הל' ו סמג לאוין שנ:

קפ ז מיי' פ"ט מהלכות שבת הלכה ג:

קפא ח מיי' פ"ח מהל' ק"פ הלכה י:

רבינו חננאל

במשקין ולא במי פירות אבל סכין אותו ומטבילין אותו בהם: **ת"ר** ובשל מבושל במים אין לי אלא במים שאר משקים מנין אמרת קל וחומר ומה מים שאין מפיגין טעם הבשר אסור שאר משקין שמפיגין טעמו של בשר אינו דין שאסור. ר' אומר במים אין לי אלא במים שאר משקין כמים מי פירות מנין ת"ל ובשל מבושל במים מכל מקום לר' דמפיק ליה מלשון בשול אפי' צלי קדר כיון שהוא עשוי כמין בשול אסור הוא ות"ק דממעט מכח הפגת הטעם צלי קדר מותר שאינו מפיג טעמו ות"ק דמייתי ליה לשאר משקין בק"ו ובשל מבושל מאי עביד ליה מבעי ליה דאפילו אם בשלו אחר שצלאו או צלאו אחר שבשלו חייב וכר' יוסי דתאני יוצא ברקיק השרוי אבל לא במבושל ואע"פ שלא נימוח הרי לר' יוסי אע"פ כי רקיק זה אפוי הוא כיון שבשלו יצא מתורת אפוי והרי הוא כמבושל כך זה הבשר אע"פ שצלאו כיון שבשלו יצא מתורת צלי והרי הוא כמבושל. צלאו כל צרכו כגון דשויא חרוכא פטור כי אינו חייב אלא על נא ועל מבושל פי' נא אברנים כגון שנצלה מעט אבל בשר חי לגמרי דלא עבר באש כלל אינו חייב: **אמר** רב חסדא המבשל בשבת בחמי טבריה פטור דלאו תולדות אור הן פסח שבשלו בחמי טבריא פטור אמר רבא ועובר משום דבעינן צלי אש וליכא: **אמר** רבא

[וגי' הכ"מ בפרק ח' מהלכות ק"פ דין ד' אמר אביי אבל נא לוקה וכו' רבא אמר אין לוקין על לאו שבכללות וכ"כ הכ"מ עוד בפרק י"ח מהלכות סנהדרין דין ג' וע"ע מ"ש הכ"מ פ"ה מהלכות נזירות דין ח' וראיה לגירסתם ממ"ש תוס' שבת קף כג: ד"ה גזירה ועוד שם ע: ד"ה נודע וכו' דאין מהדרך להקדים רבא לאביי וכ"כ בשאר דוכתי וכ"כ הרא"ש פ"ד דב"מ סימן י"ע שלא מגיע בכל הש"ס שקבע דברי רבא קודם וכו' ע"ש.]

מסורת הש"ס

(עירובין קב: וש"נ)

[לעיל מ.]

[תוספתא פ"ה]

ברכות לח:

[עי' תוס' חולין קטו. ד"ה שאין]

שבת מ:

[יותר נכון לגרוס מאי חייב דקאמר]

ב"מ קטו:

הגהות הב"ח

(א) גמ' אין הלכה כרבי יוסי מאי לאו מדלא צמית חמועי נמי מחמעא כצ"ל ותיבות צמותי הוא ותיבת הא נמחק: (ב) רש"י ד"ה מאי לאו וכו' אלמא בשאר משקין אחמועי כצ"ל ותיבת הוא נמחק:

לוקה שתים, מבושל — לוקה שתים, נא ומבושל — לוקה שלש. *אביי אמר: אין לוקין על לאו שבכללות. איכא דאמרי: *[א] תרתי הוא דלא לקי — חדא מיהת לקי. איכא דאמרי: חדא נמי לא לקי, דלא מייחד לאויה *כלאו דחסימה. *רבא *אמר: [ב] אכל זג — לוקה שתים, חרצן — לוקה שתים, זג וחרצן — לוקה שלש. אביי אמר: אין לוקין על לאו שבכללות. איכא דאמרי: תרתי הוא דלא לקי — חדא מיהת לקי. איכא דאמרי: חדא נמי לא לקי, דלא מייחד לאויה כלאו דחסימה. ת"ר: אכל כזית נא מבעוד יום — פטור, כזית נא משחשיכה — חייב. אכל כזית צלי מבעוד יום — לא פסל עצמו מבני חבורה, כזית צלי משחשיכה — פסל עצמו מבני החבורה. תניא אידך: יכול אכל כזית נא מבעוד יום יהא חייב, ודין הוא: ומה בשעה שישנו בקום אכול צלי — ישנו בבל תאכל נא, בשעה שאינו בקום אכול צלי — אינו דין שישנו בבל תאכל נא? או לא: בשעה שאינו בקום אכול צלי — ישנו בבל תאכל נא, בשעה שישנו בקום אכול צלי — אינו בבל תאכל נא. ואל תתמה, שהרי הותר מכללו אצל צלי — תלמוד לומר: °"אל תאכלו ממנו נא ובשל מבשל במים כי אם צלי אש", שאין תלמוד לומר "כי אם צלי אש" ומה תלמוד לומר "כי אם צלי אש" — לומר לך: *[ג] בשעה שישנו בקום אכול צלי — ישנו בבל תאכל נא, בשעה שאינו בקום אכול צלי — אינו בבל תאכל נא. *רבי אומר: אקרא אני "בשל" מה ת"ל "מבשל" — שיכול אין לי אלא שבישלו משחשיכה, בשלו מבעוד יום מנין — תלמוד לומר: "בשל מבשל" — מכל מקום. והאי "בשל מבשל" אפקיה רבי לצלי קדר ולשאר משקין! אם כן לימא קרא או "בשל בשל" או "מבשל מבשל", מאי בשל מבשל — שמעת מינה תרתי. תנו רבנן: [ד] אכל צלי מבעוד יום — חייב, וכזית נא משחשיכה — חייב. קתני צלי דומיא דנא, מה נא בלאו — אף צלי בלאו. בשלמא נא — כתיב: "אל תאכלו ממנו נא" אלא צלי מנלן? דכתיב: °"ואכלו את הבשר בלילה הזה" *בלילה — אין, ביום — לא. [ה] האי לאו הבא מכלל עשה הוא, וכל לאו *הבא מכלל עשה — עשה! אמר רב חסדא: הא מני — רבי

רש"י

לוקה שתים. משום "לא תאכל נא", ומשום "לא תאכלו כי אם צלי אש", ד"כי אם צלי אש" נמי אלאו ד"לא תאכלו" קאי: מבושל לוקה שתים. משום מבושל, ומשום "לא תאכלו כי אם צלי אש": לאו שבכללות הוא. דכולל בו כל מיני בשולים שאינן צליה לאסור: איכא דאמרי תרתי הוא דלא לקי. כיון שהוא לוקה משום נא [או] משום מבושל — תו לא לקי משום כלל ד"כי אם צלי אש": אבל חדא מיהא לקי. כגון המבשל בחמי טבריא ואכלו, דאין כאן מלקות דבישול, ולא מלקות של נא — לוקה משום "כי אם צלי אש": ואיכא דאמרי חדא נמי לא לקי. משום "כי אם צלי אש", דלא מיוחד לאויה דידיה כלאו דחסימה, שהוא מפרש איסורו, וסמיכא ליה פרשת מלקות לעיל מיניה: אכל זג לוקה שתים. נזיר שאכלו, משום "זג לא יאכל", ומשום "מכל אשר יעשה מגפן היין מחרצנים" וגו', ד"לא יאכל" קאי נמי א"מכל אשר יעשה": לאו שבכללות. אין לוקין על "מכל אשר יעשה" — דלאו שבכללות הוא, שכולל חרצנים וזגים וענבים לחים ויבשים ועלים ולולבין: תרתי לא לקי. היכא דאכל זג או חרצן ולקי עלייהו — לא לקי תו משום "מכל אשר יעשה". ומודה אביי דאם אכל זג וחרצן — לוקה שתים, דכיון דמפורש כל אחד לעצמו — קאי נמי אלאו דלא יאכל, והוי כמאן דכתב לאו אכל חד וחד. והכי מוכח במסכת נזיר, דלא פליג אביי אלא אמלקות ד"מכל אשר יעשה": חדא מיהא לקי. אם אכל עלין ולולבין, דאין כאן מלקות דזג וחרצן — לקי משום לאו ד"מכל אשר יעשה": אכל כזית נא מבעוד יום פטור. טעמא מפרש לקמיה מקראי: לא פסל את עצמו מבני חבורה. דאמרי' לקמן (דף פו.): אין הפסח נאכל לא בשתי חבורות כאחד, ואין האוכל אוכל בשני מקומות. ונפקא לן מ"בבית אחד יאכל", ומתרגמינן: בחבורא חדא יתאכל. ואכילה דמבעוד יום לאו אכילה היא, ומותר לאכול משתחשך עם בני חבורה שנמנה עמהן: כזית צלי משחשיכה. מפסח שנמנה עליו: פסל עצמו מבני חבורה. כדפרישית, שאין האוכל מותר לאכול הימנו בשני מקומות: בשעה שאינו בקום אכול צלי. דאין לו היתר אכילת צלי, אינו דין שישנו בלאו דלא תאכל נא: או לא. או לא נאמר כן, אלא בענין אחר: בשעה שישנו בקום אכול צלי, דהיינו בלילה, דכתיב: "ואכלו את הבשר בלילה הזה" — אינו בבל תאכל נא: ואל תתמה שהרי הותר מכללו אצל צלי. דהא אפילו צלי היה אסור לאכול ביום, כדכתיב: "ואכלו את הבשר בלילה הזה" — ולא ביום. וכשחשכה הותר מכלל איסור עשה דצלי, ונימא נמי: נהי דלא הותר לכתחלה אצל נא — מיהו לא לחייב עליה אם אכלו: שאין תלמוד לומר כי אם צלי אש. דהא כתיב לעיל מיניה "צלי אש ומצות" וגו': אקרא אני בשל. דייך הוה ליה בקריאת בשל: אין לי. שיתחייב על אכילת בשר אלא אם כן בישלו משחשיכה, שהוא עיקר זמנו: בישלו מבעוד יום. ואכלו משתחשך, מנין? והא אפקיה. רבי גופיה דרשיה לעיל לשאר משקין ולצלי קדר: בשל מבושל. מדשני בדבוריה דריש ביה דרשה אחריתי נמי: כזית צלי מבעוד יום חייב. מפרש ליה לקמיה: קתני. חיובא דצלי דמבעוד יום, דומיא דחיובא דנא משחשיכה: רבי

תוספות

אכל כזית נא לוקה שתים – משום נא ומשום כי אם צלי אש דהוי כאילו כתיב אל תאכלו כי אם צלי אש. הקשה הרר"י דאורלינ"ש: אמאי חשבי' בריש "אלו נערות" (כתובות דף ל.) בעולה לכהן גדול בעשה גרידא ד"כי אם בתולה מעמיו" כתיב. הא כי היכי דחשבינן הכא כי אם צלי אש בלאו – ה"נ ה"ל לאיחשובי בעולה לכהן גדול בלאו, דהוי כאילו כתיב "לא יקח כי אם בתולה"! וי"ל: דכי אם בתולה לא חשיב לאו – משום דסיפא דקרא מוכח עליו דהוי עשה, דכתיב: "כי אם בתולה מעמיו יקח אשה":

איכא דאמרי חדא מיהא לקי. פ"ה: בחי וחמי טבריא – חייב משום כי אם צלי אש. וקשה לר"ת: א"כ בין לאביי בין לרבא תיקשי להו ברייתא דלעיל, דתניא: נא ומבושל אמרתי לך, ולא חי. אלמא לא לקי על חי! ועוד: דאמר בפ' "המקבל" (ב"מ דף קטו:) אפלוגתא דרב הונא ורב יהודה בחובל ריחים ורכב, דרב יהודה אמר: לוקה שתים, ורב הונא אמר: לוקה שלש. ומסיק רבא: אנא דאמרי אפילו כרב יהודה, עד כאן לא קאמר רב יהודה התם – אלא ד"כי נפש הוא חובל" – לדברים אחרים הוא דאתא. אבל הכא "כי אם צלי אש" למאי אתא? ולפ"ה – הא איצטריך לחי ולחמי טבריא! לכ"נ לר"ת דאחי לא לקי לכו"ע, ד"כי אם צלי אש" לא משמע דאתא למלקות אלא לעשה, ד"כי אם צלי אש תאכלו", ולא דמי ל"כי נפש הוא חובל" דבההוא מודו כו"ע דלוקה אשאר דברים, כדקתני התם בהדיא בברייתא: חבל זוג של ספרים וצמד של פרות – לוקה שתים, ד"כי נפש הוא חובל" משמע שפיר בלשון לאו, שהוא נתינת טעם: כל שהוא דבר נפש – לא תחבול. ואתא שפיר הא דקאמר רבא התם דכי נפש הוא חובל – אתא לשאר דברים. אבל "כי אם צלי אש" – לא אתא אלא לעשה. ובנא ומבושל דווקא פליגי, דרבא סבר: להכי סמכיה לאלו – ללקות עליו על נא ומבושל שהם בני מילקא. ואביי אמר: אין לוקין על לאו שבכללות. והא דקאמר: חדא מיהת מילקא לקי – הכי פי': אם התרו בו משום "כי אם צלי אש" לבדו, אבל על מלקות נא ומבושל – לא ילקה, דלהכי מהני מה שכתוב בלשון כלל. ומיהו, לבדו מיהא לקי, שסמכו לאלו שהם בני מלקות: **אמר** רבא אכל זג לוקה שתים. הא פלוגתא דאביי ורבא איתמר איפכא בפ' "שלשה מינין" (נזיר דף לח:) וכהנה רבות בגמרא*:

שאין ת"ל כי אם צלי אש. אע"ג דאיצטריך להלקות עליו משום כי אם צלי אש – היינו נמי משום דסמכיה לנא ומבושל: **אם** כן לימא קרא בשל בשל או מבושל מבושל. הכא משמע דאורחיה דקרא לכפול תיבה אחת בענין אחד טפי מבשני עניינים, וכן ב"מרובה" (ב"ק דף סה.) גבי "המצא תמצא", וב"החובל" (שם דף פה:) גבי "ורפא ירפא". וקשה: דדריש "היו בודקין" (סנהדרין ד"מ:) קאמר: מדהוי ליה למיכתב "דרוש תדרוש" או "חקור תחקור", וכתב "היטב" – שמע מינה לאפנויי. משמע דאי הוה כתב הכי – לא הוה מופנה! ושמא התם לא חש לדקדק בלשון, רק להוכיח דמופנה*: לאמר

עין משפט נר מצוה

קפב א מיי' פ"ח מהל' ק"פ הלכה ד ופ' י"ח מהלכות סנהדרין הלכה ג:

קפג ב מיי' פ"ה מהל' נזיר הלכה ח:

קפד ג מיי' פ"ח מהל' ק"פ הלכה ד:

קפה ד ה שם הלכה ה:

רבינו חננאל

אכל נא לוקה שתים אחת משום נא ואחת משום צלי אש אכלו מבושל לוקה שתים נא ומבושל לוקה שלש ואביי אמר אין לוקין על לאו שבכללות כלומר לאו אחד כולל האוכל נא והאוכל מבושל שנא' אל תאכלו ממנו נא ובשל מבושל במים וגו': **איכא** דאמרי לאביי אכל נא ומבושל חדא מיהא לקי איכא דאמרי לא לקי כלל עד דמיחד לאויה כלאו דחסימה: **אמר** רבא נזיר שאכל זג לוקה שתים אחת משום שנאמר (במדבר ו' ד') מחרצנים ועד זג וגו' ואחת משום שנא' (שם) מכל אשר יעשה מגפן היין חרצן לוקה שתים זג וחרצן לוקה שלש אביי אמר אין לוקין וכו': **ת"ר** אכל כזית נא מבעוד יום פטור מאי טעמא אל תאכלו ממנו נא ובשל מבושל במים כי אם צלי אש בשעה שישנו בקום אכול צלי שהוא בלילה דכתיב ואכלו את הבשר בלילה הזה ישנו בבל תאכל נא מבעוד יום שאינו בבל תאכל צלי אינו חייב אם אכל נא אכל כזית נא משחשכה חייב שהרי ישנו בקום אכול צלי אכל כזית צלי מבעוד יום לא פסל עצמו מבני חבורה שאינה אכילת כזית צלי משחשכה פסל עצמו מבני חבורה וסוגיא דשמעתא כולה בענין הזה ואקשי' אהא דתניא אכל כזית צלי מבעוד יום חייב אמאי לאו הבא מכלל עשה עשה הוא האיך שנא' (שמות יב ח) ואכלו את הבשר בלילה הזה צלי אש בלילה אכול אותו ולא ביום זהו לאו הבא מכלל עשה

מסורת הש"ס

מנחות נח:

[שם]

[מכות יג: טו.]

[נ"ל אמר רבא עי' תוס' להכא ד"ה אמר רבה אמנם גי' הכ"מ בפ"ה מהלכות נזירות אמר אביי אכל זג וכו' רבא אמר אין לוקין על לאו שבכללות]

ב"מ קטו.

מכילתא פ' בא

[לקמן קכ:]

יבמות נד: נו: סח: עג: זבחים לד. חולין פא.

[הביאו תוס' מנחות נח: בפרוטרוט בד"ה ואיכא]

[וע"ע תוס' כתובות לט: ד"ה אין ותוס' ב"ק סה. ד"ה לכתוב ותוס' מנחות יז: ד"ה לכתוב]

תורה אור: שמות יב; שם

רבי יהודה היא, *דתניא: °שור ושה שרוע וקלוט נדבה תעשה אתו" – אאותו אתה מתפיס לבדק הבית, ואי אתה מתפיס תמימים לבדק הבית. מכאן אמרו: כל המתפיס תמימים לבדק הבית – עובר בעשה. אין לי אלא בעשה, בלא תעשה מנין – ת"ל: °"וידבר ה' אל משה לאמר" – לימד על כל הפרשה כולה שיהא בלא תעשה, דברי רבי יהודה. *אמר לו רבי לבר קפרא: מאי משמע? אמר לו: דכתיב "לאמר" – "לא" נאמר בדברים. בי רב אמרי: לאמר – לאו אמור.§ ב"מי תשמישו של נחתום וכו'".§ תני חדא: שופכין במקום מדרון, ואין שופכין במקום האשבורן. ותניא אידך: שופכין במקום האשבורן! לא קשיא; הא – דנפישי, דקוו. הא – דלא נפישי, דלא קוו. אמר רב יהודה: אשה לא תלוש אלא במים שלנו. דרשה רב מתנה בפפוניא. למחר אייתו כולי עלמא חצבייהו ואתו לגביה, ואמרו ליה: הב לן מיא! אמר להו: אנא גבמיא דביתו אמרי. *דרש רבא: דאשה לא תלוש בחמה, ולא בחמי חמה, ולא במים הגרופין מן המולייר, הולא תגביה ידה מן התנור עד שתגמור את כל הפת. (ווצריך* שני כלים, אחד שמקטפת בו ואחד שמצננת בו את ידיה. איבעיא להו: עברה ולשה מהו? זמר זוטרא אמר: מותר, רב אשי אמר: אסור. אמר מר זוטרא: מנא אמינא לה – דתניא: *אין לותתין השעורין בפסח. ואם לתת, נתבקעו – אסורים, לא נתבקעו – מותרין. ורב אשי אמר: *אטו כולהו חדא *מחיתא מחיתינהו? היכא דאיתמר – איתמר, והיכא דלא איתמר – לא איתמר.§

הדרן עלך כל שעה

ואלו חעוברין בפסח: כותח הבבלי, ושכר המדי, וחומץ האדומי, וזיתום המצרי, וזומן של צבעים, ועמילן של טבחים, וקולן של סופרים. ר"א אומר: אף תכשיטי נשים. זה הכלל: כל שהוא ממין דגן – הרי זה עובר בפסח. טהרי אלו באזהרה, ואין בהן משום כרת.§ **גמ'** ת"ר, שלשה דברים נאמרים בכותח הבבלי: מטמטם את הלב, ומסמא את העינים, ומכחיש את הגוף. מטמטם את הלב – משום נסיובי דחלבא, ומסמא את העינים – משום מילחא, ומכחיש את הגוף – משום קומניתא דאומא. *ת"ר: ג' דברים מרבין הזבל, וכופפין את הקומה ונוטלין *אחד מחמש מאות ממאור עיניו של אדם. אלו הן: *פת קיבר, ושכר חדש, וירק *חי. ת"ר: שלשה דברים ממעטין את הזבל, וזוקפין את הקומה, ומאירין את העינים. אלו הן: פת נקייה בשר שמן, ויין ישן. פת נקייה – דסמידא

רש"י

רבי יהודה היא. דאמר: לאו הבא מכלל "לאמור" – לאו הוא: שרוע. הוא שאחת מעיניו גדולה ואחת קטנה, וכן שאר אברים: קלוט. שפרסותיו קלוטות: נדבה תעשה אותו. לדמיו, הקדישהו לבדק הבית. ולנדר – להעלות קרבן – לא ירצה. וכתב "אותו" – אותו בעל מום אתה מתפיס לקדושת בדק הבית, ואין אתה מתפיס תמימים הראויין למזבח לבדק הבית: וידבר ה' וגו'. בתחלת הפרשה כתיב: לא נאמר בדברים. נוטריקון "לאמר": לאו אמור. אמור להן שיש איסור לאו בדברים. והכא גבי פסח נמי כתיב בתחלת הפרשה: "ויאמר ה' אל משה ואל אהרן לאמר": האשבורן. לשון תורה אור שבירה, שמשתבר הקרקע, ויש בקעים שהמים נאספים ושוהין בתוכן, ואין נבלעין, ומחמיצין: הכי גרסינן: הא דנפישי דקוו הא דלא נפישי דלא קוו. כשהן מרובות הן נקוות אל מקום אחד ואין נבלעות מהר ומחמיצות, וכשהן מועטות לא קוו: שלנו. בלילה. מפני שבימי ניסן המעיינות חמין, שעדיין ימות הגשמים הן, כדאמרינן ב"מי שהיה" (לקמן צד:): בימות הגשמים חמה מהלכת בשיפולו של רקיע, לפיכך כל העולם צונן ומעיינות חמין. הלכך מלינן בלילה ומצטננין: דרשה רב מתנה. ובלשון הקודש היו דורשין, וכסבורין השומעין שמים שלו הוא אומר: דביתו. תרגום של "לנו" (דביתו): לא בחמה. לפי שחום השמש מחממת: ולא בחמי חמה. במים שהוחמו בחמה, וכ"ש בחמי האור: הגרופים מן המולייר. דוד גדול של נחשת, ותלוי על האור כל שעה, ונחשתו עבה, ואפי' כשאין שם אור – מים שבשוליו חמים או פושרין: גרופים. לשון שיריים, שמגרפין מנחשתו של שוליו: ואל תגביה ידה מן התנור. כלומר: תהא עוסקת בבצק כל שעה: שמקטפת בו. טחה פני החררה במים: שמצננת בו ידיה. דאותן שמקטפת בהן מתחממות מחום ידיה והעיסה: עברה ולשה. בחמין: לא נתבקעו מותרות. ואע"ג דתנא אין לותתין – הכא נמי ל"ש, הואיל וחנו רואין שלא החמיץ, שאין שם לא סימני שיאור ולא סימני סידוק: מחיתא מחיתינהו. כולם אריגה אחת אריגת'?! משום דבחדא איסורא דרבנן תנא אם עבר מותר באכילה – בעית למימר נמי בכולהו? היכא דאתמר. בהדיא דלא קנסינן ליה – אתמר, והיכא דלא אתמר – לא אתמר. והלכך: עברה ולשה בחמין – קרובה למזיד היתה, ואסור. ולא דמי לבליקות של גוים דאמרינן (לעיל דף מ.): (א) ממלא אדם כריסו מהן – דהכא בעינן למיקנסיה דעברה אדרבנן. "מעשה אורג" מתרגמינן "עובד מחי" (שמות כח):

הדרן עלך כל שעה

ואלו עוברין. עליהן בבל יראה ובבל ימצא. וכולהו מפרש להו בגמרא, זיתום וזומן וקולן ועמילן: תכשיטי נשים. בגמרא מפרש: מין דגן. חמשה מינין: חיטין ושעורין וכוסמין ושבולת שועל ושיפון: ואין בהן כרת. אם אכלן, אבל לאו יש באכילתן. ובגמרא יליף לה כולה: **גמ'** מטמטם. לשון סתימה: מסמא את העינים משום מילחא. מלח סדומית יש, שמסמא את העינים, כשנוגע במלח וחוזר ונוגע בעין: נסיובי דחלבא. מישג"א: קומניתא דאומא. עיפושא. פת שמתעפש לאחר זמן בתוך הכותח: וכופפין את הקומה. כלומר: מתישין כחו: ירק חי. כגון כרישין ובצלים וחזרין, כשאוכל מהן הרבה תמיד: דסמידא

תוספות

לאמר לימד על כל הפרשה שהיא בלאו [א]. נראה לר"י: דהיינו דוקא בהנך דברים דאית בהו לאו הבא מכלל עשה, אבל שאר דברים לא:

הדרן עלך כל שעה

ואלו עוברין בפסח. פ"ה: לעבור עליהן בבל יראה ובבל ימצא. וגם ריב"א מדקדק מלשון "עוברים" דמשמע (ב) עוברין מן העולם. ואין נראה לר"ת, דמשמע דכל הנך מרבינן מ"כל מחמצת לא תאכלו" ואפילו באכילה לא הוה מיחייב אי לאו דרבייא קרא, ומהיכי תיתי בל יראה ובל ימצא? ונראה לר"ת: דאלו עוברין (ג) – פי': האוכלין ועוברין – היינו מעל השולחן, דלאו בני מיכל נינהו, אבל בל יראה ליכא: **רבי** אליעזר אומר אף תכשיטי נשים. היינו (ד) חמץ נוקשה. ואפילו הוי חמץ דגן גמור על ידי תערובות, מ"מ מדקאמר אף – משמע דמודה לת"ק. ובגמרא אמרי': דרבי אליעזר סבר נוקשה בעינייה בלא כלום. לכך נראה דגרס רבי אליעזר בחד מינייהו, או במתני' או בגמרא: הא

עין משפט נר מצוה

קפו א מיי' פ"ה מהל' ערכין הלכה ו:
קפז ב מיי' פ"ה מהל' חמץ הלכה טז סמג לאוין עט טור שו"ע או"ח סימן תנט סעיף ד:
קפח ג מיי' שם הלכה יא טור שו"ע או"ח סימן תנה סעיף א:
קפט ד מיי' שם הלכה יב טוש"ע או"ח סימן תנט סעיף א:
קצ ה מיי' שם טוש"ע שם סעיף ב:
קצא ו מיי' שם טוש"ע שם סעיף ג:
קצב ז מיי' שם טוש"ע שם סעיף ה:
א ח מיי' פ"ד מהלכות חמץ הלכה ח סמג לאוין עט טוש"ע או"ח סימן תמב סעיף א:
ב ט מיי' פ"א מהלכות חמץ הלכה ו:

מסורת הש"ס (שוליים)

תמורה ז: | ויקרא כב | שם | [שם] | [נ"ל ביתו] | יומא כח: | [נ"ל וצריכה] | [לעיל מ.] | [ברכות כד. וש"נ] | [וחולין נח: פרש"י בביאור נכון] | [פי' פסול' הסולת. ערוך] | [בעירובין ליתא מלת חי] | עירובין נה: | ברכות מג: שבת קיג: תענית י:

הגהות מהר"ב רנשבורג

[א] תוס' ד"ה לאמר לימד על כל הפרשה שהיא בלאו. נ"ב עיין מנחות דף נ"א בתוס' ד"ה אף כאן וכו' ודוק:

הגהות הב"ח

(א) רש"י ד"ה היכא איתמר וכו' דאמרן אדם מלא כריסו מהן:

(ב) תוס' ד"ה ואלו וכו' מלשון עוברים דמשמע. נ"ב פירוש מדלא קאמר עוברין עליהם: (ג) בא"ד ונראה לר"ת דאלו עוברין פי' האוכלין תז"מ ונ"ב ס"א האוכלן: (ד) ד"ה ר' אליעזר וכו' היינו חמץ נוקשה. נ"ב ולפי זה מוסיף ר"א דלת"ק [דוקא נוקשה] בעיניה ולר"א אף נוקשה [ע"י תערובת] ואי הוי חמץ דגן גמור ע"י תערובות [מוסיף] ר"א דאפילו תכשיטי נשים [דלא] הוי ראויים לאכילה:

רבינו חננאל

דמאכילתו בלילה שהוא עשה הבאתה לא תאכל ביום שהוא לאו וכל כי האי גונא עשה הוא ואין לוקין על עשה. אמר רב חסדא זו הברייתא לר' יהודה היא דתניא ושור ושה שרוע וקלוט נדבה תעשה אותו פי' אותו שהוא בעל מום אתה מתפיסו נדבה לבדק הבית ואי אתה מתפיס תמימים לבדק הבית אלא לנדר מתפיס תמימין מכאן אמרו כל המתפים תמימים לבדק הבית עובר בעשה דלאו הבא מכלל עשה הוא ואין לי אלא בעשה בלא תעשה מנין ת"ל וידבר ה' אל משה לאמר לימד על הפרשה כולה שהיא בלאו דברי ר' יהודה א"ל ר' לבר קפרא והיכן אתה מוצא בזה הפסוק לאו אמר ליה דכתיב לאמר לא יומרו דברים מכאן למדנו כל המימר ממה שכתוב ואפילו עשה עובר בלאו שהרי המיר דבי רב אמרי כן פרשו לאמר לא אמר כלומר על כל מצוה שבתורה גזר עליהן בלאו: **מי** תשמיש של נחתום ישפכו מפני שהן נקוין ומחמיצין פירורי העיסה הנגררים מן המים שנשתמש בהן כמו שרוחץ אותם נקוין ומחמי ואוקימ' אי נפישי דקוו וקיימו נשפכין במקום מדרון ואי לא נפישי אלא נבלעין ממקומן שופכין אפילו במקום האשבורן. אמר רב יהודה אין לשין אלא במים שאובין מאתמול ולנו בלילה דאינון מיא ביתו ונצטננו הרבה: **דרש** רבא אין לשין בחמה ולא במים חמין ולא במים הגרופין ולא אפילו במים שהוחמו בחמה פי' גרופין מושכין דכתיב (שופטים ה' כ"א) נחל קישון גרפם כלומר משכם ולא תגביה היד מן התנור כלומר לא תניח הפת מוטל ותתעסק בדבר אחר עד שתגמור את הפת ויש אומרים לא תגביה ידה מן הפת עד שתדבקהו בתנור וצריכה שני כלים במים אח' שמקטפת בו הפת בתוך התנור ואח' שמצננת ידיה עברה ולשה בחמין או במים גרופין או באלו כלן מאי ופשט רב אשי עברה ולשה אסור וקיימא לן כותיה: **הדרן עלך כל שעה**

פ"ג ואלו עוברין בפסח כותח הבבלי ושכר המדי וחומץ האדומי וזיתום המצרי וכו' כותח הבבלי אסור בפסח משום קומניתא דאומא דהיא חמץ פת ניקודים ואסור לאכלו בבשר משום נסיובי דחלבא פי' נסיובא פי' ריפתא

עין משפט
נר מצוה

ג א מיי' פ"ב מהלכות מעשר הלכה ז:

הא בדרווקא והא בדפורצני. והא דאמרינן שחזקתו מן התמד – היינו מתמד דפורצני, אבל דרווקי – טוב מאד, ואינם נעשים לעולם חומץ: **וסימניך** סיסני. ב"במה אשה יוצאה" (שבת סו.) גבי הקיטע יוצא בקב שלו – רבי יוסי אוסר, גרסינן: וסימניך סמ"ך סמ"ך – הוא סימן טוב יותר. והכא לא מצי למימר הכי – משום דשערי בשי"ן כתיב:

טיפולן של בנו' עשירי'. וא"ת: א"כ היינו (ג) תכשיטי נשים! ותירץ הר"י דאורלינ"ש: דהכא מיירי בפנים של מעלה(ד), דלא מאיס כל כך כשטופלים על פניהם. ותכשיטי נשים – היינו בפנים של מטה, שטופלי להסיר השער דמאיס טפי: למה

תורה אור

דסמידא, בשר שמן – דצפירתא דלא אפתח, יין ישן – עתיק עתיקי. כל מילי דמעלי להאי – קשה להאי, ודקשה להאי – מעלי להאי, בר מזנגבילא רטיבא, ופילפלי אריכתא, ופת נקייה, ובשר שמן, ויין ישן – דמעלי לכולי גופיה.§ "שכר המדי" – °דרמו ביה מי שערי.§ "וחומץ האדומי".§ דשדו ביה שערי. אמר רב נחמן *(בר יצחק): בתחלה, כשהיו מביאין נסכים מיהודה – לא היה יינם של יהודה מחמיץ עד שנותנין לתוכן שעורין, והיו קורין אותו חומץ סתם. ועכשיו אין יינם של אדומיים מחמיץ עד שנותנין לתוכן שעורין, וקורין אותו חומץ האדומי, לקיים מה שנאמר: °"אמלאה החרבה" יחזקאל כו *אם מלאה זו – חרבה זו, ואם מלאה זו – חרבה זו. רב נחמן בר יצחק אמר, מהכא: °"ולאם מלאם יאמץ". בראשית כה תניא, אמר רבי יהודה: ביהודה, בראשונה *הלוקח חומץ מעם הארץ – אינו צריך לעשר, מפני שחזקה אינו בא אלא מן התמד. ועכשיו, הלוקח חומץ מעם הארץ – צריך לעשר, שחזקתו אינו בא אלא מן היין. וסבר רבי יהודה תמד לאו בר עשורי הוא? והא (*תניא): **א המתמד ונתן מים במדה, ומצא כדי מדתו – פטור, ורבי יהודה מחייב! הכי קאמר: לא נחשדו עמי הארץ על °התמד. אי בעית אימא: נחשדו. ולא קשיא: הא – *בדרווקא, הא – בדפורצני.§ "וזיתום המצרי וכו'".§ מאי זיתום המצרי? *תנא רב יוסף: תלתא שערי, תלתא קורטמי, ותלתא מלחא. רב פפא מפיק שערי ומעייל חיטי, וסימניך סיסני. תרו להו, וקלו להו, וטחני להו, ושתו להו *מדיבחא ועד עצרתא. דקמיט – מרפי ליה, ודרפי – °מקמיט ליה. לחולה ולאשה עוברה – סכנתא.§ "וזומן של צבעים וכו'".§ הכא °תרגימו מיא דחיורי דצבעי בהו לבא*.§ "ועמילן של טבחים וכו'" – § פת תבואה °שלא הביאה שליש, שמניחה על פי קדירה ושואבת הזוהמא.§ "וקולן של סופרים וכו'"§ הכא תרגומא: פרורא דאושכפי. רב שימי מחוזנאה אמר: זה טיפולן של בנות עשירים שמשיירות אותו לבנות עניים. איני?! והא תנא רבי חייא: ארבעה מיני מדינה, ושלשה מיני אומנות. ואי אמרת טיפולן של בנות עשירים – מאי מיני אומנות איכא? ואלא מאי – פרורא דאושכפי, אמאי קרי ליה האי קולן של סופרים? קולן של רצענין מיבעיא ליה! אמר רב אושעיא: לעולם פרורא דאושכפי (א), ומאי קרי ליה קולן של סופרים – דסופרים נמי מדבקין בהו °ניירותיהן.§ "רבי אליעזר אומר אף תכשיטי נשים וכו'".§ תכשיטי נשים סלקא דעתך?! אלא אימא: אף טיפולי נשים, דאמר רב יהודה אמר רב: בנות ישראל שהגיעו

דסמידא. סולת: דצפירתא דלא אפתח. עז שלא ילדה: עתיק עתיקי. ישן של שלש שנים: כל דמעלי. לחולי זה – קשה לזה. המועיל ללב קשה לעינים, או לאחד מתחלואי שאר האברים: זנגבילא. זינזיבר"א: דרמו ביה שערי. שמטילין לתוכו מי שעורין, כגון שכר שלנו. ועושין אותו במדי: שכר המדי. לפי שבאותן הימים אין נוהגין לעשות שכר אלא מתמרים, ובמדי עושין שכר ממי שעורין כעין אותן שלנו, קרי ליה שכר המדי: דשדו ביה שערי. *ביין נותנין שעורין שלמים כדי להחמיצו. לפי שיינם טוב, ואינו בא לידי חימוץ עד שנותנין לתוכו שעורין: בתחילה. כשבית המקדש קיים, היו מביאין נסכים מיהודה, ובזכות הנסכים היה טעם ביינם ולא היה מחמיץ כו': אמלאה החרבה. רישא דקרא "יען אמרה צור לירושלים האח" וגו' – אתמלא מן חורבנה של ירושלים. וצור מאדום היא: ולאם מלאם יאמץ. כשעשו גבור – יעקב חלש. אין מלכות שניהם מתקיים יחד: תמד. בופי"ט. לפי שהיין היה טוב ואינו מחמיץ. וסתם חומץ שלהם מן תמד היה בא: ועכשיו. בטל טעם היין, וממהר להחמיץ: פטור. מלעשר, שהרי אין כאן אלא מים, שלא מצא אלא כדי מדתו. ואע"ג דחזותיה וטעמא חמרא – קיוהא דפירא בעלמא הוא דעייל ביה: ורבי יהודה מחייב. דאזיל בתר חזותא וטעמא: הכי קאמר. מתניתא קמייתא: לא נחשדו עמי הארץ מלעשר את התמד – לפי שאינו חשוב בעיניהם, לפיכך הלוקחו ממנו – פטור מן הדמאי: ואי בעית אימא נחשדו. ורבי יהודה במתניתא קמייתא – טעמיה משום דפטור אפי' ממעשר ודאי. ובתמד דפורצני קאמר, שנותנין מים בחרצנין והוא מחמיץ ומרתיח לאחר זמן כיין התוסס. והיינו תמד, ולית ביה אלא קיוהא דפירא. והא דקתני ר' יהודה מחייב – בדרווקא, שנותנין בשמרים מים, והוא נמי תמד. בההוא מחייב ר' יהודה אע"ג דלא מצא אלא כדי מדתו, לפי שהיין של שמרים מעורב בו, ומן המים נשאר בשמרים: קורטמי. מוריק"א, קרו"ג: וסימניך. שלא תטעה מאן אמר חיטי ומאן אמר שערי: סמ"ך סמ"ך. רב יוסף שיש סמ"ך בשמו אמר שערי. לישנא אחרינא: וסימניך סיסני – כלי ששמו כן, כדאמרינן (בכתובות) (ב"מ דף סו.): ואי אגביניהו בסיסני – קנה. ושם כלי זה יהא סימן לגירסא זו, דרב יוסף אמר שערי – שני סמכי"ן יחד: תרו להו. שורין אותן יחד: מדבחא ועד עצרתא. מפסח ועד עצרת: דקמיט. עצור מנקביו: מרפי ליה. משלשלו: ודרפי קמיט ליה. למי שיש לו שילשול מעצרו: סכנתא. שמשלשל יותר מדאי: מי סובין: דצבעו בהו לבא. מיא דחיורא. סרכ"א: פירורא דאושכפי. גלו"ד, והרצענים מדבקין בו את העור כשמתחלק לשתים, או מדבקין שתי עורות יחד לעשותן עבה. ודרכן לתת בה קמח של שיפון. ולקמיה מפרש מאי של סופרים: טיפולן של בנות עשירים. שהיא של סולת, משיירות משיוריהן לבנות סופרים – מלמדי תינוקות, שהן עניים. ומטיפולן של בנות עניים לא מצי למימר – דעניות אין להן סולת אלא סיד. טיפול – לשון מטפל ומדביק אותו דבר, או סיד או סולת על בשרן להשיר השער: והא תני ר' חייא. ויהיב סימנא בהני דמתני', ואמר: ארבע מיני מדינה שניטו בהם, הצריכין לכל אדם, בין אומן בין לא אומן. שהרי למאכל או לרפואה עשויין: כותח, שכר, וחומץ, וזיתום. אבל זומן אינו ראוי אלא לצבעים, וקולן של סופרים, ועמילן של נחתומין (ג) = נייר עשוי מעשבים ע"י דבק שקורין גלו"ד: תכשיטי נשים. הוא כחל ושרק, ובשמים שתולות בצואריהן להריח, ומאי חמץ איכא? שהגיעו

רבינו חננאל

ספסקא פסולת הסלת פת קיבר צפירתי דלא אפתח יש מי שאומר שעירה שעדיין לא ילדה כלומר לא נפתחה רחמה ויש אומר עופות צפרים שמנות שלא ילדו: **שכר** המדי רמי ביה שערי חומץ האדומי אין יינם של אדום מחמיץ עד שנותנים בו שעורים. פי' תמד דפורצני אחר שסוחטין הענבים נותני' שם על החרצנים שנים שלש' ימים ואחר כן סוחטין אותן היוצאת מהן נקראת תמד דפורצני והנותן מים בשמרי יין ומסננן היוצא מהן נקרא תמד דדוחקא: **זיתום** המצרי' משום שערי דאית בהו: **זומא** של צבעין. משום מיא דחיורא: **עמילן** של טבחים. הפת שעושין לשאוב הזוהמא של בשר נקרא עמילן של טבחים: **קולן** של סופרים. ויש מי ששונה קולה והדבר אחד הוא והוא אל נשי שמדבקין בו הסופרים ניירותיהם. אלו כולן השנוי' במשנתנו במקום שיש בתוכן מים אבל אין בהן מים הא קיי"ל מי פירות אין מחמיצין וכולהו על ידי מוי: **כותח** הבבלי הוא דיהיב בגויה קמחא דשערי. תאני ר' חייא שלשה מיני מדינה הן הכותח והשכר והחומץ וארבעה מיני אומנות זיתום מעשה אומנות הרופאים וזומא של צבעים ועמילן של טבחים וקולן של סופרים. ר' אליעזר אומר אף תכשיטי נשים תריצנא טיפולי נשים: ומצאנוהו מפורש בתלמוד ארץ ישראל אלו עוברין בפסח וכו' אמר ר' מונא תניא

[בילקוט פרשת תולדות וכן ביחזקאל כז רמז שסה לא נזכר בר יצחק וכזה א"ש בסמוך]

[נ"ל תנן]

[עי' תוס' ע"ז לד. ד"ה דורדיא ותוס' ב"ב נו: ד"ה אין הלכה]

מסורת הש"ס

[עי' תוספות לעיל לה: ד"ה מי פירות]

מגילה ו.

[תוספתא דמאי רפ"א ע"ש]

ב"ב צו. חולין כה: מעשרות פ"ה [מ"ו]

שבת קי. [ע"ש ברש"י]

[שבת קמו:]

[לבא כ"ה בפי' המשניות להרמב"ם ופי' רש"י פ"ב דחולין כח. לכא לבע עו אדום ע"ש]

הגהות הב"ח

(א) גמ' לעולם פרור דאושכפי ואמאי קרי: (ב) רש"י ד"ה והא תני רבי חייא וכו' ועמילן של טבחין נייר: (ג) תוס' ד"ה טיפולן וכו' א"כ היינו כ' [אין לומר] דהקושיא ר"א היינו ת"ק דהא פליג עלי דמוסיף אפילו נוקשה [ע"י תערובות] אי נמי חמץ דגן גמור על ידי תערובות [מוסיף דהוי] ראוי לאכיל אלא קשיא להו דאי טיפול כו' היינו תכשיטי נשים א כן מאי קאמר ר"א א תכשיטי נשים הא ת"ק נמ קאמר תכשיטי נשי ועיקר קושית התוס' הו דה"ל לפרש במאי דפליג ותירץ הר"י כו' דהכ מיירי בפנים של מעל ובלבע שעל פניה וכדתניא בפרק המגני אשה לא תעביר סרק פניה מפני שצובעת דל מאיס הפנים גם אם ל היתה טופלת ולכך [לא קר לה] תכשיטי נשים אבל מה שטופלת בפנים של מטה להסיר השיער דמאוס טפי אם לא היתה טופלת קרי לה תכשיטי נשים דכי דבזה מעביר המיאוס א"כ [תכשיט הוא] לה והשתא שפיר קמפרש [מאי דפליגי] דאותו טיפול דקרי לה תכשיטי נשים ידוע הו דהוי [נוקשה ע"י] תערובות א"כ חמץ דגן גמור [על ידי תערובות] וכל הלומדים פירשו דמאיס ולא מאיס על הטיפול ויש תימ לפרש כן דהא מתניתין לא קמיירי בטיפול שכבר טפלו הנשים בהן אלא מיירי במה שעושין לטפל בהן אע"פ שלא טפלו בה (ד) בא"ד ותירץ הר"י דאורליינש דהכא מיירי בפנים של מעלה כשטופלין על פניהם דלא מאיס כל כך ותכשיטי נשים כל"

*שהגיעו לפרקן ולא הגיעו(א) לשנים, בנות עניים טופלות אותן בסיד, בנות עשירים טופלות אותן בסולת, בנות מלכים בשמן המור, שנא': "ששה חדשים בשמן המור". (אסתר ב) *מאי שמן המור? רב הונא בר ירמיה אומר: סטכת, רב ירמיה בר אבא אמר: שמן זית שלא הביא שליש. תניא, ר' יהודה אומר: אנפיקנין – שמן זית שלא הביא שליש. ולמה סכין אותו – מפני שמשיר את השיער ומעדן את הבשר. § "זה הכלל כל שהוא ממין דגן". § תניא, א"ר יהושע: וכי מאחר ששנינו כל שהוא מין דגן הרי זה עובר בפסח – למה מנו חכמים את אלו – כדי שיהא רגיל בהן ובשמותיהן. כי הא, דההוא בר מערבא איקלע לבבל, הוה בישרא בהדיה. אמר להו: קריבו לי מתכילתא. שמע דקאמרי: קריבו ליה כותח. כיון דשמע כותח – פירש. § "הרי אלו באזהרה". מאן תנא דחמץ דגן גמור ע"י תערובות, ונוקשה בעיניה בלאו? אמר רב יהודה אמר רב: ר"מ היא. דתניא: שיאור ישרף, ונותנו לכלבו. והאוכלו – בארבעים. הא גופא קשיא! אמרת "שיאור ישרף" – אלמא: אסור בהנאה. והדר תני: ונותנו לפני כלבו – אלמא מותר בהנאה! הכי קאמר: שיאור ישרף – *דר"מ לר' מאיר, דר' יהודה לר' יהודה. ונותנו לפני כלבו – דר' מאיר לר' יהודה. והאוכלו בארבעים – אתאן לר' מאיר. שמעינן ליה לרבי מאיר: נוקשה בעיניה – בלאו, וכל שכן חמץ דגן גמור על ידי תערובת. רב נחמן אמר: ר"א היא, דתניא: אעל חמץ דגן גמור – ענוש כרת, על עירובו – בלאו, דברי ר' אליעזר. וחכמים אומרים: על חמץ דגן גמור – ענוש כרת, על עירובו – בלא כלום. ושמעינן ליה לר' אליעזר דאמר חמץ דגן גמור על ידי תערובת בלאו – וכל שכן נוקשה בעיניה. ורב נחמן, מ"ט לא אמר כרב יהודה? אמר לך: דילמא עד כאן לא קאמר ר"מ התם – אלא נוקשה בעיניה, אבל חמץ דגן גמור על ידי תערובת – לא. ורב יהודה מ"ט לא אמר כרב נחמן? אמר לך: עד כאן לא קאמר ר"א התם – אלא חמץ דגן גמור ע"י תערובת, אבל נוקשה בעיניה – לא אמר. תניא כוותיה דרב יהודה: "כל מחמצת לא תאכלו" (שמות יב) – לרבות כותח הבבלי, ושכר המדי, וחומץ האדומי, וזיתום המצרי. יכול יהא ענוש כרת – ת"ל: "כי כל אכל חמץ ונכרתה" (שם) על חמץ דגן גמור – ענוש כרת, ועל עירובו – בלאו. מאן שמעת ליה דאמר על עירובו בלאו – ר"א היא, ואילו נוקשה בעיניה – לא קאמר. ש"מ: נוקשה לר"א לית ליה. ור"א, עירובו בלאו מנא ליה? דכתיב: "כל מחמצת לא תאכלו" – אי הכי – כרת נמי לחייב, דהא כתיב "כי כל אכל מחמצת ונכרתה"! ההוא מיבעי ליה *לכדתניא: (*מחמצת) – אין לי אלא שנתחמץ מאליו, מחמת ד"א מניין – ת"ל: "כל(ב) מחמצת ונכרתה". אי הכי – דלאו נמי להכי הוא דאתא! אלא טעמא דר"א מ"כל" התם נמי, הכתיב "כל"! ההוא מיבעי ליה לרבות את הנשים. נשים, מדרב יהודה אמר רב נפקא. *דאמר רב יהודה אמר רב, וכן תנא דבי ר' ישמעאל, אמר קרא: "איש או אשה כי יעשו מכל חטאת האדם" (במדבר ה) – השוה הכתוב *איש לאשה לכל עונשין שבתורה! איצטריך,

סלקא

רש"י

שהגיעו לפרקן ולא הגיעו לשנים. שיש להן שערות כאילו הגיעו לפרקן, והן לא הגיעו לכלל שנים, ובושות על כך: עשירות טופלות אותן בסולת. ומשיר את השער: אנפיקינון. במנחות תנן: אנפקינון לא יביא. ומפרש ר' יהודה: אנפקינין הוא שמן זית כו': סטכת. לא איתפרש*: ומעדן את הבשר. אשקלייר"א: שיהא בקי בהן. שידע מה הן עושין אותו, שיהא נזהר בהן. כשיביאו לו כותח ידע שיש חלב, ויש שם חמץ אם פסח הוא: מתכילתא. שום לפתן לאכול בו את הפת: כיון דשמע. שקראו שמו כותח: פירש. שבקי היה, וידע שיש שם חלב: מאן תנא. דמתני', דאית ליה חמץ דגן גמור שנתערב במין אחר, ואינו בעין, שנימוח. אי נמי: חמץ נוקשה רע, ואיתיה בעיניה – מוזהרין על אכילתו בלאו. דקתני מתניתין כותח הבבלי ושכר המדי חמץ דגן גמור, אלא שנתערב בדבר אחר. ותכשיטי נשים – בעיניה הוא, אבל נוקשה הוא, דאינו ראוי לאכילה. וקתני: באזהרה, דעובר עליהן בלאו: שיאור. שלא נתחמץ כל צרכו. "שיאור" פליגי במתני', *ר"מ קרי שיאור את שהכסיפו פניו, וזהו תחלת חימוצו. ולר' יהודה הוי שיאור שהתחיל ליסדק כבר סדקין דקין כקרני חגבים, אחד לכאן ואחד לכאן. אבל שהכסיפו פניו לרבי יהודה – מצה היא. ולר"מ קרני חגבים חמץ גמור הוא. והכא הכי קאמר: שיאור ישרף – דאסור בהנאה. שיאור דר"מ, הכסיפו פניו – ישרף לר"מ. ושיאור דרבי יהודה – ישרף לרבי יהודה. וסיפא דקתני: ונותנו לפני כלבו – אליבא דרבי יהודה קאמר ליה, ואשיאור דר"מ קאי. והאוכלו בארבעים – אתאן לר"מ. כלומר: לר"מ, האוכלו לשיאור זה שרבי יהודה מתיר בהנאה – סופג את הארבעים. אלמא שמעינן ליה לר"מ דאית ליה חדא מהני תרתי דמתני', דקאמר: נוקשה בעיני' בלאו – כגון שיאור, דנוקשה הוא, דאינו ראוי לאכילה הואיל והחמיץ קצת ולא גמר. ולהחמיץ עיסות אחרות כשאור נמי לא חזי, וקאמר בלאו. וכ"ש חמץ גמור ע"י תערובת. דקסבר רב יהודה: ע"י תערובת חמיר מנוקשה בעין. והאי לאו דנוקשה נפקא ליה מ"כל מחמצת לא תאכלו" – "כל" רבויא הוא, כדלקמן: ועל עירובו בלאו. מ"כל מחמצת" כדלקמן: מ"ט לא אמר כדרב יהודה. דמוקי מתניתין כר"מ: רב נחמן ס"ל נוקשה בעיניה חמור מחמץ גמור ע"י תערובת: תניא כוותיה דרב יהודה. דאמר חמץ גמור בתערובת חמור: לענין כרת לא כתיב "כל מחמצת", אלא "כל אוכל חמץ". ולקמן מפרש ליה: כותח ושכר וחומץ וזיתום כולן חמץ גמור מעורב בהן. כותח איכא פת, ובהנך תלתא איכא שערי. וכולהו בני אכילה ושתיה נינהו. אבל זומן ועמילן וקולן, דנוקשה הוא ובעיניה, הואיל ולאו בני אכילה נינהו – לא תנינהו. והיינו כדרב יהודה, דאמר: מודה היה ר"א בנוקשה בעיניה דפטור: ור"א עירובו בלאו מנא ליה. פשיטא מדאפקיה בלשון מחמצת, וגבי כרת נמי מחמצת כתיב: ההוא. מחמצת דגבי כרת – לאו לעירובו אתא, אלא לנתחמץ מחמת דבר אחר: אי הכי. האי דגבי לאו נמי, אימא: לאזהורי שנתחמץ מחמת דבר אחר אתא, ואזהרה דתערובת מנא ליה? התם נמי. גבי כרת, הא כתיב: "כל אוכל מחמצת ונכרתה": לכל עונשין. מכאן שהנשים חייבות על כל לא תעשה שבתורה, שהרי עונשן מלקות:

מלות

תוספות

למה מנו חכמים את אלו. תימה לרשב"א: הא איצטריך למנותם לאשמועינן שהן בלאו ולא בכרת! ותירץ ר"י: דלא הוה ליה לאשמועינן אלא תרי מינייהו, חד לנוקשה בעיניה וחד ע"י תערובת. ועוד הקשה: דת"ק שמנאם לית ליה האי כללא, דהא איכא תכשיטי נשים שהן מין דגן ואין עובר בפסח, אלא רבי אליעזר הוא דקאמר לה:

מאן תנא חמץ גמור ע"י תערובת ונוקשה בעיניה בלאו. משמע בשמעתין דאי לאו דאיתרבי חמץ נוקשה למלקות – אפילו איסור לא היה בו. ותימה לר"י: דבפ"ק דחולין (דף כג.) בעי רבי זירא: הרי עלי לחמי תודה מן החמץ או מן המצה והביא שיאור מהו? שיאור דמאן, אי דר"מ לר"מ מלקי עליה – חמץ הוא. והשתא מנא ליה דהוי חמץ לענין תודה? דילמא שאני חמץ בפסח דרבייה קרא למלקות! (גרידא) ואור"י: דהתם נמי איכא שום קרא דמרבינן מיניה חמץ נוקשה. והא דתניא בפרק "כל המנחות באות מצה" (מנחות דף נג.): אין מחמילין בתפוחים, דהוי חמץ נוקשה כדמשמע התם – היינו לכתחילה, אבל בדיעבד – כשר:

ואילו נוקשה בעיניה לא קתני. וא"ת: ונימא דמשום הכי לא חשיב ליה, משום דכ"ש הוא, כדאמר רב נחמן! וי"ל: דאי כ"ש הוא – הוה ליה למיתני, לאשמועינן דלית ביה כרת:

ונותנו לפני כלבו דר"מ לרבי יהודה. מדאורייתא אפי' באכילה שרי, כדאמרינן בפ"ק דחולין (דף כג:*) דמצה מעלייתא היא, אלא מדרבנן אסור:

ההוא כל לאתויי נשים. תימה לר"י: הא תרי "כי כל" כתיבי גבי כרת, "כי כל אוכל חמץ ונכרתה" ו"כי כל אוכל מחמצת" ונרבינן עירובו לכרת! ואפילו לרבנן דלא דרשי "כל", "כי כל" דרשי! ואור"י: דפשיטא ליה לגמרא דאתא לשום דרשא:

סלקא

רבינו חננאל

תניא אמר ר' יהושע וכי מאחר ששנינו כל שהוא מין דגן הרי זה עובר בפסח למה מנו חכמים את אלו כותח הבבלי ושכר המדי ושאר המנויין במשנה והלא בכלן יש בהן מין דגן אלא כדי שיהא בקי בהן ובשמותיהן כי ההוא דאמר להו הבו לי מידי למכלא ביה רפתא שמע דקאמרי הבו ליה כותחא הוה בהדיה בשרא כיון דשמע כותח פירש דידע דאית ביה נסיובה דחלבא: **הרי** אלו באזהרה ואין בהן משום כרת. אמרינן מאן האי תנא דאית ליה חמץ דגן גמור על ידי תערובות כגון כותח הבבלי וכיוצא בו ונוקשא בעיניה כגון עמילן של טבחים וזומן של צבעין וקולן של סופרים בלאו אמר רב יהודה אמר רב ר"מ הוא דתניא שיאור ישרף וכו' ואוקימנא [דשיאור] דקרי ליה ר"מ שיאור והוא הכספת פנים תני ישרף וכן שיאור דקרי ליה ר' יהודה שיאור והוא כקרני חגבים תני ישרף ושיאור דר' מאיר דהוא הכספת פנים כגון נוקשא בעלמא הוא אומר ר' יהודה נותנו לפני כלבו כלומר מותר בהנאה. ור' מאיר אומר האוכלו בארבעים מיהא שמעינן לר' מאיר דאמר נוקשה בעיניה בלאו פי' נוקשה שאינו חמץ גמור וכל שכן חמץ על ידי תערובות. רב נחמן אמר מתני' ר' אליעזר היא דתניא על חמץ דגן גמור ענוש כרת ועל עירובו בלאו דברי ר' אליעזר וחכמים אומרים על עירובו בולא כלום שמעי' ליה לר' אליעזר דאמר חמץ דגן גמור על ידי תערובת בלאו וכש"כ נוקשא בעיניה רב יהודה לא אמר כרב נחמן אמר לך רב יהודה ר' אליעזר לא אמר אלא ע"י תערובות שהוא בלאו אבל נוקשא בעיניה לא: **תניא** כרב יהודה כל מחמצת לא תאכלו לרבות כותח הבבלי ושכר המדי וחומץ האדומי יכול יהא ענוש כרת ת"ל כי כל אוכל מחמצת לא תאכלו על חמץ דגן גמור ענוש כרת ועל עירובו בלאו מאן שמעת ליה בהדיא על עירובו בלאו ר' אליעזר ואלו הני דפשיטנא דאינון נוקשא בעיניה זומא של צבעין ועמילן של טבחים וקולן וזיתום שיירינהו ש"מ דלית ליה לר' אליעזר נוקשה בעיניה בלאו ואיתוקמא דמתני' ר"מ היא. ואפי' הכי דרשינן טעמא דר' אליעזר עירובו בלאו מנא ליה ופשטי' מדוקיא דקרא מדהוה ליה למכתב מחמצת לא תאכלו וכתב כל מחמצת לא תאכלו ואפי' ע"י תערובות בלאו ואם תאמר אי הכי אפי' כרת נמי ליחייב דהא כתיב מחמצת ונכרתה ודחי' ההוא (מחמץ) [מחמצת] דכרת מיבעי ליה להכין אין לי חמץ שנתחייב עליו [כרת] אלא חמץ שנתחמץ מאיליו נתחמץ ע"י ד"א כגון ע"י שאור וכיוצא בו מנין ת"ל כי כל אוכל מחמצת ונכרתה לרבות את שנתחמץ מחמת ד"א אי הכי מחמצת דלאו נמי להכי הוא דאתא ושנינן טעמא דר' אליעזר הדריש מכל מחמצת ואפילו עירובו אי הכי כרת נמי הכתיב ביה כל ההוא כל לרבות הנשים שחייבות בחמץ ודייקי' דוקיא דהני קראי בלאו דחמץ כתיב כל מחמצת לא תאכלו כתב כל מחמצת לרבות כל המחמיצין ואפי' ע"י תערובת לא תאכלו לאוקמיה בלאו. וכרת דחמץ כתיב ביה (לא תאכל) [כי כל אוכל] מחמצת בא ללמד לכל בני אדם שהן האוכלין שנאמר כי כל מחמצת ונכרתה (ולא) [ועוד] כתיב כי כל אוכל מחמצת ונכרתה חד כתיבא לרבות כי כל מי שיאכל ואפי' נשים

וראיה

עין משפט נר מצוה

ד א מיי' פ"א מהלכות חמץ הלכה ו סמג לאוין עט:

שבת פ. מו"ק ט: [ע"ש]

[וע"ש]

[לעיל כח: וכן בילקוט ליתא לתיבת מחמצת ועי' רש"י לעיל כח: כתב ה"ג חמץ אין לי אלא שנתחמץ מאליו]

[אשה לאיש]

מסורת הש"ס

[ובמנחות פי' רש"י שקורין בלישמא]

שם מנחות פו. מגילה יג:

[לקמן מח:]

[לקמן מח: מנחות נג. חולין כג:]

לעיל כח:

סוכה כח. יבמות פד. ב"ק טו. תמורה ב: נדה מח: [קדושין לה.]

הגהות הב"ח

(א) גמ' שהגיעו לפירקן ולא הגיעו בנות כל"ל ותיבת לשנים נמחק וכ"ב עי' פ' המוציא יין דף פ' ע"ב: (ב) שם דבר אחר מנין ת"ל כל אוכל מחמצת:

עין משפט נר מצוה

ה א מיי' פ"ו מהלכות מלה הלכה י סמג עשין מ טוש"ע או"ח סי' תעב סעיף יד:

ו ב מיי' פ"ה מהלכות איסורי מזבח הלכה א סמג לאוין שיח:

גמרא

סָלְקָא דַּעֲתָךְ אָמִינָא: הוֹאִיל וּכְתִיב °"לֹא תֹאכַל עָלָיו חָמֵץ שִׁבְעַת יָמִים תֹּאכַל עָלָיו מַצּוֹת" [דברים טז] כֹּל שֶׁיֶּשְׁנוֹ בְּקוּם אֱכוֹל מַצָּה — יֶשְׁנוֹ בְּבַל תֹּאכַל חָמֵץ, וְהָנֵי נָשֵׁי הוֹאִיל וְלֵיתְנְהוּ בְּקוּם אֱכוֹל מַצָּה, דַּהֲוָיא לֵיהּ מִצְוַת עֲשֵׂה שֶׁהַזְּמַן גְּרָמָא (הִיא) — אֵימָא בְּבַל תֹּאכַל חָמֵץ נַמִּי לֵיתְנְהוּ, קמ"ל. וְהַשְׁתָּא דְּאִתְרַבּוּ לְהוּ בְּבַל תֹּאכַל חָמֵץ — אִיתְרַבִּי נַמִּי לַאֲכִילַת מַצָּה, כְּרַבִּי (*אֱלִיעֶזֶר). דְּאָמַר ר"א*: [א]נָשִׁים חַיָּיבוֹת בַּאֲכִילַת מַצָּה דְּבַר תּוֹרָה, שֶׁנֶּאֱ': "לֹא תֹאכַל עָלָיו חָמֵץ וגו'" כֹּל שֶׁיֶּשְׁנוֹ בְּבַל תֹּאכַל חָמֵץ — יֶשְׁנוֹ בַּאֲכִילַת מַצָּה. וְהָנֵי נָשֵׁי נַמִּי, הוֹאִיל וְיֶשְׁנָן בְּבַל תֹּאכַל חָמֵץ — יֶשְׁנָן בְּקוּם אֱכוֹל מַצָּה. וּמַאי חָזֵית דְּהַאי "כָּל" לְרַבּוּיֵי נָשִׁים וּמַפְּקַתְּ עֵירוּבוֹ, אֵימָא לְרַבּוּיֵי עֵירוּבוֹ! מִסְתַּבְּרָא, קָאֵי בְּאוֹכְלִין — מַרְבֶּה אוֹכְלִין, קָאֵי בְּאוֹכְלִין מַרְבֶּה נֶאֱכָלִין?! מַתְקִיף לַהּ רַב נָתָן אֲבוּהּ דְּרַב הוּנָא (*בְּרֵיהּ דְּרַב נָתָן): וְכָל הֵיכָא דְּקָאֵי בְּאוֹכְלִין לָא מַרְבֶּה נֶאֱכָלִין? וְהָא תַּנְיָא: °"כִּי כָּל אֹכֵל חֵלֶב מִן הַבְּהֵמָה אֲשֶׁר יַקְרִיב" [ויקרא ז], אֵין לִי אֶלָּא חֵלֶב תְּמִימִין שֶׁרְאוּיִי לִיקָּרֵב, חֵלֶב בַּעֲלֵי מוּמִין מִנַּיִן — ת"ל: "מִן הַבְּהֵמָה". חֵלֶב חוּלִּין מִנַּיִן — ת"ל: "כִּי כָּל". וְהָא הָכָא, דְּקָאֵי בְּאוֹכְלִין וְקָא מַרְבֶּה נֶאֱכָלִין! הָתָם דְּלֵיכָּא אוֹכְלִין — מַרְבֶּה נֶאֱכָלִין, הָכָא דְּאִיכָּא אוֹכְלִין — לָא שָׁבֵיק לְהוּ לְאוֹכְלִין וּמַרְבֶּה נֶאֱכָלִין. וְרַבָּנַן דְּלֵית לְהוּ עֵירוּב — "כָּל" לָא דָּרְשִׁי. אֶלָּא, נָשִׁים מְנָא לְהוּ? "כָּל" — לָא דָּרְשִׁי, "כִּי כָּל" דָּרְשִׁי. וְר"א, אֵימָא: "כָּל" — לְרַבּוֹת אֶת הַנָּשִׁים, "כִּי כָּל" — לְרַבּוֹת אֶת עֵירוּבוֹ! וְכִי תֵּימָא: "כִּי כָּל" — ר"א לָא דָּרֵישׁ — וְהָתַנְיָא*: °"שְׂאֹר בַּל תַּקְטִירוּ" [שם ב] אֵין לִי אֶלָּא כּוּלּוֹ, מִקְצָתוֹ מִנַּיִן — ת"ל: ב"כָּל". עֵירוּבוֹ מִנַּיִן — ת"ל: "כִּי כָּל". מַאן שָׁמְעַתְּ לֵיהּ דְּדָרֵישׁ "כָּל" — רַבִּי אֱלִיעֶזֶר, וְקָא דָּרֵישׁ "כִּי כָּל"! קַשְׁיָא. *א"ר רַבִּי אַבָּהוּ אָמַר רַבִּי יוֹחָנָן: כָּל אִיסּוּרִין שֶׁבַּתּוֹרָה אֵין הֶיתֵּר מִצְטָרֵף לְאִיסּוּר, חוּץ מֵאִיסּוּרֵי נָזִיר, שֶׁהֲרֵי אָמְרָה תוֹרָה °"מִשְׁרַת" [במדבר ו]. וּזְעֵירִי אָמַר: אַף שְׂאוֹר בַּל תַּקְטִירוּ. כְּמַאן — כְּר"א, דְּדָרֵישׁ "כָּל". אִי הָכִי — לְעִנְיַן

רש"י

מִצְוַת עֲשֵׂה שֶׁהַזְּמַן גְּרָמָא. נָפְקָא לָן בְּפ"ק דְּקִידּוּשִׁין (דף כט.) דְּנָשִׁים פְּטוּרוֹת: קמ"ל. הַאי "כָּל" – דְּמוּזְהָרוֹת עַל הֶחָמֵץ, וְכֵיוָן דְּמוּזְהָרוֹת עַל לָאו דְּחָמֵץ – חַיָּיבוֹת בַּעֲשֵׂה דַּאֲכִילַת מַצָּה לַיְלָה הָרִאשׁוֹן, וְאע"ג דִּזְמַן גְּרָמָא. כְּר' אֱלִיעֶזֶר, הוֹאִיל וְיֶשְׁנָן בְּבַל תֹּאכַל חָמֵץ, דְּנָפְקָא לָן מִ"כָּל אוֹכֵל חָמֵץ" – יֶשְׁנָן בְּקוּם אֱכוֹל מַצָּה: קָאֵי בְּאוֹכְלִין. "כָּל" דְּגַבֵּי כָּרֵת בְּאוֹכְלֵי חָמֵץ כְּתִיב, אֲבָל "כָּל" דְּאַזְהָרָה – בְּנֶאֱכָל כְּתִיב, "כָּל מַחְמֶצֶת": קָאֵי בְּאוֹכְלִין מַרְבֶּה נֶאֱכָלִין. בִּתְמִיָּה: אֲשֶׁר יַקְרִיב. מַשְׁמַע: קֳדָשִׁים, וְשֶׁיִּהְיוּ תְּמִימִים: הָתָם דְּלֵיכָּא לְרַבּוּיֵי אוֹכְלִין. דְּהָא נָשִׁים מִדְּרַב יְהוּדָה נָפְקִי: (א) הִשְׁוָה הַכָּתוּב אִשָּׁה לְאִישׁ לְכָל עוֹנָשִׁין שֶׁבַּתּוֹרָה: הָכָא דְּאִיכָּא לְרַבּוּיֵי אוֹכְלִין. דְּנָשִׁים בְּאִיסּוּר חָמֵץ, דְּלָא נָפְקִי לָן מִדְּרַב יְהוּדָה, כְּדַאֲמַרַן לְעֵיל: לָא שָׁבֵיק אוֹכְלִין וּמַרְבֶּה נֶאֱכָלִין: וּפָרְכִינַן: וְרַבָּנַן. דִּפְלִיגִי אַדְּר"א בְּעֵירוּב דְּחָמֵץ, כֵּיוָן דְּלֵית לְהוּ לָאו בְּעֵירוּב. פְּשִׁיטָא "כָּל" דִּכְתִיב גַּבֵּי אַזְהָרָה דְּ"כָל מַחְמֶצֶת" לָא דָּרְשִׁי, וְהַשְׁתָּא עַל כָּרְחָךְ "כָּל" דְּגַבֵּי כָּרֵת לְרַבּוּיֵי נָשִׁים נַמִּי לָא דָּרְשִׁי, וְאֶלָּא נָשִׁים מְנָא לְהוּ? כָּל. דְּגַבֵּי אַזְהָרָה, דְּלָא כְּתִיב "כִּי" בַּהֲדֵיהּ – לָא דָּרְשִׁינַן לְרַבּוּיֵי נֶאֱכָלִין, דְּעֵירוּבוֹ. אֲבָל גַּבֵּי כָּרֵת דְּאוֹכְלִין כְּתִיב "כִּי כָּל אוֹכֵל" – דָּרְשִׁינַן לֵיהּ: וּמַקְשִׁינַן וְר"א אֵימָא כָּל. דְּכָרֵת לְרַבּוּיֵי נָשִׁים, "כִּי כָּל" דְּכָרֵת – לְרַבּוּיֵי עֵירוּבוֹ נַמִּי לְכָרֵת. דְּכֵיוָן דְּלֵיכָּא תּוּ אוֹכְלִין לְרַבּוּיֵי – מְרַבִּינַן בֵּיהּ נֶאֱכָלִין, כְּדַאֲמַרַן גַּבֵּי חֵלֶב. וְאֵימָא: עַל עֵירוּבוֹ בְּכָרֵת: אֵין לִי אֶלָּא כּוּלּוֹ. בִּזְמַן שֶׁכָּל הַהֶקְטֵר מִן הַשְּׂאוֹר: מִקְצָתוֹ. חֲצִי זַיִת, שֶׁאֵינוֹ הֶקְטֵר שָׁלֵם, דְּאֵין הַקְטָרָה פְּחוּתָה מִכַּזַּיִת: עֵירוּבוֹ מִנַּיִן. (ב) כְּשֶׁאֵינוֹ בָּעַיִן, אֶלָּא מְעוֹרָב וְנִבְלָל עִם מִנְחָה הוֹגֶנֶת שֶׁל מַצּוֹת לְאַחַר שֶׁאֲפָאָן, דְּאֵינָן בָּעַיִן: אֵין הֶיתֵּר מִצְטָרֵף לְאִיסּוּר. אָכַל חֲצִי זַיִת חֵלֶב וַחֲצִי זַיִת בָּשָׂר בְּבַת אַחַת – אֵין הֶיתֵּר מַשְׁלִים אֶת שִׁיעוּר הָאִיסּוּר לְחַיְּיבוֹ, חוּץ מֵאִיסּוּרֵי נָזִיר, שֶׁאִם אָכַל חֲצִי זַיִת עֲנָבִים וַחֲצִי זַיִת לֶחֶם בְּבַת אַחַת – חַיָּיב, שֶׁהֲרֵי אָמְרָה תּוֹרָה: "מִשְׁרַת עֲנָבִים לֹא יִשְׁתֶּה" – חַיָּיב עַל שְׁרִיַּית פִּתּוֹ בְּיַיִן. וְאִי אִיכָּא מַיִין לְחוּדֵיהּ כַּזַּיִת – לָמָּה לִי קְרָא? "וְכָל מִשְׁרַת" לָא גָּרְסִינַן. וְאִית דְּגָרְסִי לֵיהּ, וּמְפָרְשִׁי דַּאֲפִילּוּ לְרַבָּנַן דְּלָא דָּרְשִׁי "כָּל" – "וְכָל" דָּרְשִׁי. וְלָא הִיא, דְּהָא פָּרְכִינַן לְקַמָּן: הַאי מִיבַּעְיָא לֵיהּ לְכִדְתַנְיָא: מִשְׁרַת – לִיתֵּן טַעַם כְּעִיקָּר. וְאִם אִיתָא, נֵימָא לֵיהּ: אֲנָא טַעְמָא דִּידִי מִ"וְכָל". אֶלָּא מִמַּשְׁמָעוּתָא דְּמִשְׁרַת נָפְקָא לֵיהּ, "וְכָל" לָא דָּרֵישׁ: אַף שְׂאוֹר בַּל תַּקְטִירוּ. נַמִּי הֶיתֵּר מִצְטָרֵף לְאִיסּוּר, חֲצִי זַיִת קוֹמֶץ דִּשְׂאוֹר וַחֲצִי זַיִת דְּמַצָּה, וְאֵינָן מְעוֹרָבִין אֶלָּא כָּל אֶחָד נִיכָּר: כְּר"א דְּדָרֵישׁ כָּל. לְעֵיל. וּמֵהָתָם נָפְקָא לֵיהּ, כְּדַאֲמַרַן לְעֵיל: מִקְצָתוֹ מִנַּיִן – ת"ל: "כָּל". וְדָרֵישׁ לֵיהּ הָכִי: מִקְצָתוֹ מִנַּיִן חֲצִי זַיִת שְׂאוֹר וַחֲצִי זַיִת מַצָּה עִמּוֹ: אֲפִילּוּ

תוספות

סלקא דעתך אמינא כל שישנו בקום אכול מצה. תימה לר"י: היכי סלקא דעתך למידרש הכי? אדרבה, איפכא יש לדרוש, לאחומרא מקשינן! ואור"י: דס"ד דאורחיה דקרא דסיפא מפרש לרישיה, משום הכי אמר דבאכילת מצה תלוי, דכתיבא בסוף. ועוד יש לומר: דהכא יש לדרוש יותר היתר לנשים משום ג"ש דט"ו מחג הסוכות, והוו מיפטרי ממצה כמו מסוכה, דפטר להו בהדיא בפ' "הישן" (סוכה כח.) מהלכה למשה מסיני. יש מקשים: למה נשים אין חייבות בכלאי' משום דכל שישנו בלבישת שעטנז – ישנו בגדילים, כדדרשינן בערכין (דף ג:) גבי כהנים! ולפירוש ר"י, דפי' דמסיפא לרישא סברא לדרוש – קשה להפך שלא יהו נשים חייבות בכלאים. וכי תימא ה"נ – והא בפ"ק דבילה (דף יד:) משמע דכלאים לא חזו למידי*:

אין לי אלא כולו מקצתו מנין. בפרק "כל המנחות באות מצה" (מנחות נח.) מפרש אביי: אין לי אלא כולו – דהיינו כזית, מקצתו – חצי זית מניין. ורבא אמר התם, דה"ק: אין לי אלא קומץ כולו, מקצת קומץ מניין. ומסיק התם דאיכא בינייהו, דאביי סבר: דיש קומץ בפחות מב' זיתים, דהיינו כזית – לכך מפרש כולו כזית, וסבר נמי דיש הקטרה בפחות מזית. ואע"ג דבפ' "כיצד צולין" (לקמן עט.) א"ר יהושע: כל הזבחים שבתורה שנשתייר מהן כזית בשר וכזית חלב – זורק את הדם. משמע דאין הקטרה בפחות מכזית – הכא היינו טעמא משום דסבר דיש קומץ בפחות מב' זיתים, א"כ כשריבה הכתוב חצי קומץ – ע"כ ריבה חצי זית. ורבא סבר: אין קומץ בפחות מב' זיתים, ואין הקטרה בפחות מזית:

מאן שמעת ליה דדריש כל ר' אליעזר. אף על גב דר"ע נמי דריש "כל" בפ' "התערובות" (זבחים פב.) גבי כל חטאת – *לא קשה, דאפילו יהא כר"ע – מ"מ לא מישתמיט תנא למימר (שיסבור) שיהא תערובת חמץ בכרת. ועוד נראה לר"י: דאפילו לרבנן דלא דרשי הכא "כל" – דרשי בעלמא, בריש "מרובה" (ב"ק סג.) דאמר: "כל" רבויא הוא. ובפ' שני דסוכה (דף כח.), גבי "כל האזרח". ודווקא הכא לא דרשי – בדבר שאין סברא לרבות, כגון עירובו, וכגון נשים משום היקשא, וכגון מקצת דבל תקטירו. וה"פ: כמאן – כר"א, דדריש "כל" אפילו לדבר שאין סברא לרבות, כגון עירובו וכגון נשים. והא קאמר נמי דרבנן לא דרשי "כל":

חוץ מאיסורי נזיר. אע"ג דחטאת נמי קאמר לקמן לרבי יוחנן היתר מצטרף לאיסור – הכא לא חשיב חטאת, דבקדשים לא קמיירי:

כמאן כר"א דדריש כל. נראה לר"י: דזעירי משמע ליה דשאור היתר מצטרף לאיסור, מדקתני: עירובו מניין, ת"ל "כי כל". ומדרבי עירובו – א"כ היתר מצטרף לאיסור, והיינו כדרבא. דלדידיה ה"פ: מקצתו מניין – היינו זית שלם. אבל לאביי, דמפרש "מקצתו" מניין חצי זית – לא שייך היתר מצטרף לאיסור, דאמשהו דאיסור לחודיה מיחייב. והא דמרבה עירובו – היינו כשמתערב לגמרי, ולא אמר שיתבטל האיסור אגב ההיתר. והא דקאמר כמאן – כר"א, דדריש "כל" – משום דלרבנן, אף על גב דדרשי "כי כל" – לא מוקמא ליה לרבות עירובו, אלא לרבות מקצתו. ורש"י פירש: דזעירי משמע ליה "מקצת" היינו חצי זית קומץ דשאור, וחצי זית דמצה. ואין מעורבין אלא כל אחד ניכר. וק"ל לפירושו טובא. חדא: דלא הוי זעירי לא כאביי ולא כרבא. ועוד, מאי קאמר: כמאן כר"א הא כרבנן נמי אתיא, דהא "כי כל" דרשי, ומוקמינן ליה אמקצתו – דהיינו היתר מצטרף לאיסור לפ"ה. ועוד: בחמץ מנ"ל תערובת, כיון דלריך קרא להיתר מצטרף לאיסור? ועוד, דלפ"ה נ"ל: מקצתו מניין – פי' חצי זית איסור וחצי זית היתר שאינם מעורבים יחד, דאי לאו הכי – היינו עירוב. ולקמן גבי חטאת משמע דאין היתר מצטרף לאיסור אם לא שיתערב האיסור וההיתר יחד, דהא אמר: עד שיבלע בבשרה:

רבינו חננאל

וראיה מדלא כתיב אוכל כל מחמצת ונכרתה אלא כתיב כי כל אוכל מחמצת ונכרתה ש"מ לאוכלין קא מזהיר ואפילו נשים חייבות באכילת חמץ ומוזהרות באכילת מצה בפסח: **ואמרי'** מאי חזית דהאי כל דכרת מרבית לנשים בכרת וממעט עירוביו בכרת ואמרי' מסתברא קאי באוכלין מרבה אוכלין כלומ' כתב כל אוכל לרבות כל אדם האוכל ואפילו נשים וכתיב כל מחמצת לרבות כל המתחמץ ואפילו ע"י תערובת בלאו אבל לית ליה אורחא דקרא כדקאי באוכלין למשבק אוכלין לרבויי נאכלין ואמרינן איני דכל היכא דקאי באוכלין לא מרבה נאכלין והתניא כי כל אוכל חלב מן הבהמה אשר יקריבו ממנה קרבן לה' אין לי אלא חלב תמימים הראויה ליקרב חלב בעלי מומין מנין ת"ל מן הבהמה חלב חולין מנין ת"ל כי כל והא הכא כי כל אוכל חלב כתיב דמשמע אוכלין וקאי באוכלין וקא מרבי חלב חולין הנאכלין ושני' היכא דליכא אוכלין מרבה נאכלין אבל היכא דאית ליה לרבות אוכלין כגון הנשים לא שבק אוכלין ומרבה נאכלין ורבנן דלית להו לא בעירוביו משום דלא דרשו כל אם כן נשים שחייבות בכרת מנא להו ושני' כל לא דרשי כי כל דרשי ובכרת כתיב כי כל אוכל מחמצת ונכרתה: **ואקשי'** לר' אליעזר נימא כל לרבות נשים כי כל לרבות עירוב בכרת דתניא שאור לא תקטירו אין לי אלא כולו מקצתו מנין ת"ל כל שאור פי' כלום משאור. אפי' מקצתו. עירובו מנין ת"ל כי כל לרבות עירובו מאן שמעת ליה דדריש כל ר' אליעזר ודרש כי כל לרבות עירוביו ועלתה בקשיא: **אמר** ר' אבהו א"ר יוחנן אין היתר מצטרף לאיסור חוץ מאיסורי נזיר שהרי אלו אמרה תורה משרת ענבים הייתי למד שמשרת ענבים אסור למה כתב כל לאסור עירוביו: **זעירי** אמר אף שאור בבל תקטירו היתר מצטרף לאיסור ואם יש מקצת שאור ומצה משלים לכזית חייב כמאן כר' אליעזר דמרבה עירוביו מבל [יראה] אקשי' אם כן הוא כי זעירי אליבא דר' אליעזר [קאמר] אמאי אמר שאור ותו לא אפיל כותח

הגהות הב"ח

(א) רש"י ד"ה התם וכו' נפקי להשווה: (ב) ד"ה עירובו וכו' דאינו בעין:

מסורת הש"ס

לקמן לח:

[ויש למחוק כמו שמוחק הרש"ק בכריתות כה: גבי רב תחליפא אבוה דרב הונא בר תחליפא ועי' לקמן קיז: וזבחים ע:]

מנחות נח.

נזיר לה:

[נ"ל אלעזר]

[וע"ע תוס' יבמות ד. ד"ה דכתיב ותוס' שבועות כ: ד"ה כל ותוס' מנחות מג. ד"ה ור"ש ותוספות ערכין ג: ד"ה הכי]

[וע"ע תוס' זבחים פב. ד"ה ת"ל ותוס' מנחות יח: ד"ה קומץ עוד שם סד: ד"ה אמר]

לענין חמץ בפסח נמי. אין הכי נמי, ולאפוקי *מדאביי, דאמר: יש הקטרה לפחות מכזית, קמשמע לן: [א]דהקטרה לאו לפחות מכזית. יתיב רב דימי וקאמר לה להא שמעתא. אמר ליה אביי לרב דימי: וכל איסורין שבתורה אין היתר מצטרף לאיסור? והתנן: *[ב]המקפה של תרומה, והשום והשמן של חולין, ונגע טבול יום במקצתן — פסל את כולן. [ג]המקפה של חולין והשום והשמן של תרומה ונגע טבול יום במקצתן — לא פסל אלא מקום מגעו בלבד. והוינן בה: מקום מגעו אמאי פסולה? הא בטלי להו תבלין ברוב! ואמר רבה בר בר חנה: *מה טעם — הואיל וזר לוקה עליהן בכזית. היכי דמי — לאו משום דהיתר מצטרף לאיסור? לא, מאי כזית — דאיכא כזית בכדי אכילת פרס. וכזית בכדי אכילת פרס דאורייתא היא? [ד]א"ל: אין. אי הכי, אמאי פליגי רבנן עליה דר"א בכותח הבבלי? אלא מאי — משום דהיתר מצטרף לאיסור, סוף סוף אמאי פליגי רבנן עליה דר"א בכותח הבבלי? אלא: הנח לכותח הבבלי, דלית ביה כזית בכדי אכילת פרס. אי בעיניה *דקשריף וקאכיל ליה — *בטלה דעתיה אצל כל אדם, ואי משטר קשטר ואכיל — לית ביה כזית בכדי אכילת פרס. איתיביה: שתי קדירות, אחת של חולין ואחת של תרומה, ולפניהן שתי מדוכות, אחת של חולין ואחת של תרומה, ונפלו אלו לתוך אלו — מותרין. שאני אומר: תרומה לתוך התרומה נפלה, וחולין לתוך חולין נפלו. ואי אמרת כזית בכדי אכילת פרס דאורייתא — אמאי אמרינן "שאני אומר תרומה לתוך כו'"? א"ל: הנח לתרומת תבלין דרבנן. איתיביה: *שתי קופות, אחת של חולין ואחת של תרומה, ולפניהם ב' סאין אחת של חולין ואחת של תרומה, ונפלו אלו לתוך אלו — מותרין, שאני אומר: חולין לתוך חולין נפלו, תרומה לתוך תרומה נפלה. ואי אמרת כזית בכדי אכילת פרס דאורייתא — אמאי אמרינן "שאני אומר"? אמר ליה: [ה]הנח לתרומה בזמן הזה, דרבנן. והאי "משרת" להכי הוא דאתא? [ו]האי מיבעי ליה לכדתניא: "משרת" — ליתן

[ברכות לה: וש"נ] [illegible]

רש"י

אפילו חמץ נמי. דהא אמרינן על עירובו בלאו, והיינו נמי היתר מצטרף לאיסור: ומשני אין הכי נמי. דחמץ בפסח היתר מצטרף לאיסור, והאי דנקיט שאור — לאפוקי מדאביי, דאמר במנחות בפ' "כל המנחות באות": יש הקטרה בפחות מכזית, וחייב בהקטרת שאור כל דהו, ולא בעי צירוף. ומתרץ לברייתא דלעיל הכי: אין לי אלא כזית, חצי זית מנין — ת"ל: "כל", ויליף מינה דיש הקטרה לפחות מכזית, קא משמע לן דאין הקטרה, ואי איכא צירוף — אין, ואי לא — לא: להא שמעתא. דר' יוחנן: המקפה. תבשיל קפוי ועב של תרומה, כגון דייסא. והשום והשמן הנתונין בו לתבלין, היו של חולין: פסל. את כל הקדירה, דמקפה עיקר וטבול יום פוסל את התרומה: מקום מגעו אמאי פסל הא בטלו להו תבלין ברובא. דקא ס"ד דימוע מדרבנן הוא דאסור: ואמר רבה בר בר חנה. דימוע מדאורייתא הוא, וזר לוקה עליו בכזית, משום דיש שם תרומה עליה. הלכך, לגבי טומאה נמי שם תרומה עליה. ומיהו, לא חמירא כתרומה עצמה ליפסול את כולן. ומ"ט זר לוקה עליו בכזית — משום זרות, הא לא אכל כזית תרומה — לאו משום דהיתר מצטרף לאיסור? ומשני: מאי לוקה בכזית דקאמר — כזית בכדי אכילת פרס, שאם אכל פרס ממנו שיעור ארבעה ביצים — יש בו כזית תרומה. וקי"ל דכל שיעורי אכילת איסור, בין כזית של חלב ודם ובין כותבת דיום הכפורים, מצטרפין אכילת השיעור בכדי שהייה זו. שאם אכל כחרדל חלב, וחזר ואכל כחרדל עד שהשלים לכזית, אם אין מתחילת האכילה ועד סופה יותר משהיית כדי אכילת פרס באכילה בינונית — מצטרף, והוי כמו שאכלו בבת אחת וחייב. והכא נמי יש כאן תרומה כדי להצטרף כזית באכילת פרס ממנו: וכזית בכדי אכילת פרס דאורייתא. בתמיה, הא דאמור רבנן כזית מצטרף כשיעור שהיית אכילת פרס — מי הוי מדאורייתא, הלכה למשה מסיני כשאר שיעורין, דקא אמרת לוקה, ומתרצת משום דאכיל כזית מאיסור בר מהיתר: אמאי פליגי רבנן עליה דר' אליעזר בכותח. נהי נמי דלא דרשי "כל" לרבות עירובו, הא אכיל מיהא מאיסור כזית בכדי אכילת פרס: ואלא מאי. סבירא לך, האי לוקה דרבה משום דהיתר מצטרף לאיסור, ובחד כזית קאמר דלקי: סוף סוף אמאי פליגי רבנן עליה. יצטרף היתר לאיסור, וליחייב: אלא גרס: הנח לכותח הבבלי. דלא אכיל כזית מן החמץ כשיעור שהיית אכילת פרס. דהא כותח אינו עשוי לאכול אלא לטבל, ואי מתרמי ואכיל ליה ממש, דהשתא איכא כזית, ממהר להצטרף כשיעור אכילת פרס ממנו: בטלה דעתו. ולאו אכילה היא לחיובי עלה: ואי מישטר קא שטר. מטבל בתוכו כדרכו — ליכא כזית מן החמץ בכדי שהיית אכילת פרס. שכשאכל כדי אכילת פרס ממה שטיבל בתוכו — לא אכל מן הכותח אלא מעט, או שני זיתים או ארבעה, ובההוא פורתא ליכא מן החמץ כזית. ושכר המדי נמי, אף על גב דשתי ליה בעיניה — מיהו אין לך שותה ד' וג' כוסות שלא יפסיק וישהה בינתיים. הלכך, בכדי שהיית אכילת פרס לא שתי כזית מן החמץ לבד מן המים ושאר התערובת. שמתם שכר עיקרו מן התמרים או מתאנים, אלא שבמדי מערב עמהם מי שעורין קצת: פרס. הוא חצי ככר שמשערו בו עירובי תחומים, שהוא מזון שתי סעודות. ואליו לבית המנוגע, לטמא בגדים אם ישהה בו כדי אכילתו, שנתנה תורה שיעור שהייתו כדי סעודה, דכתיב (ויקרא יד): "והאוכל בבית יכבס את בגדיו", והלכה למשה מסיני דחצי ככר של שמונה ביצים הוא סעודה: שתי מדוכות. שהתבלין נידוכין בתוכן, פלפלין וזנגביל: אלו לתוך אלו. ממדוכות לתוך הקדירות: מותרין. קדירות חולין לזר: היכי אמרינן שאני אומר. ותלינן לקולא בעון מיתה, ודילמא תרומה לתוך חולין נפל, וכי אכיל לה — איכא כזית תרומה באכילת פרס. אלא שמע מינה: אי נמי ודאי נפל — לא מיחייב משום כזית בכדי אכילת פרס אלא מדרבנן, וכי מספקא לן — תלינן לקולא: במסכת נזיר גרסינן: ואלא מאי — היתר מצטרף לאיסור, היכי אמר "שאני אומר". אלא הנח לתרומת תבלין דמדרבנן, ד"ראשית דגנך תירושך ויצהרך" כתיב: קופות. גדולות, ובתוכן דגן, דהויא תרומה דאורייתא:

תוספות

לענין חמץ בפסח נמי. לר' יוחנן לא מצי פריך, דאיהו לא דריש "כל". ואם תאמר: והא בפרק בתרא דיומא (דף עד.) דריש רבי יוחנן מ"כל חלב" דחצי שיעור אסור מן התורה! ואור"י: דלא דריש אלא לאיסורא, אבל להתחייב מלקות כמו בכשיעור — לא, וכן גבי חמץ*:

ה"ג רש"י מקום מגעו אמאי פסל הא בטיל ברובא. ופירש: דס"ד השתא דדימוע דרבנן. וקשה לריב"א: דמשמע שהשום והשמן בעין, מדקתני: נגע במקצתן, ולא קתני במקצתה. ועוד, דתני סיפא: אימתי — בזמן שהן גוש בקערה. אבל אם היה מפוזר — טהור. ואי פסיל מקום מגעו משום מדומע — אדרבה, כי הוי מפוזר יש לו להיות מדומע יותר! ועוד: אמאי פסיל מקום מגעו ותו לא? כיון דחשיב כמו כולה תרומה על ידי דימוע — יפסל הכל, או לא יפסל אפילו מקום מגעו. דבהדיא איתא הא פלוגתא במסכת טבול יום בעיסה מדומעת, ומי שפוסלה — פוסלה לגמרי, ומי שמכשיר — מכשיר לגמרי! ונראה לר"י כפירוש ר"ת, דפירש: דמתניתין מיירי שהשום והשמן בעין, וכדגרס בכל הספרים: מקום מגעו אמאי פסל, והא לא הוי כבילה — והואיל דלא מקבל טומאה אלא מדרבנן אית לן למימר דבטלי אגב מקפה, כדפריש בפרק "כל שעה" (לעיל דף לג:):

לאו משום דהיתר מצטרף לאיסור. ומטעם הואיל אם היה מלקט מן השום או מן השמן כזית וילקה עליו — לית לן למימר שלא תבטל אגב מקפה, כיון שאין דרך אכילה בכך:

דאיכא כזית בכדי אכילת פרס. מקשין דב"השוחט" (חולין דף לד:*) אמרינן: הנח לנזיד הדמע דלית ביה כזית בכדי אכילת פרס. משמע דבסתמא לא הוי כזית בכדי אכילת פרס! ויש לומר: דהכא קים ליה דעסקינן בדאית ביה כזית בכדי אכילת פרס. ולפירוש ר"ת, דמוקי שהשום והשמן בעין — אתי שפיר, דאי הוי מעורב — לא הוי כזית בכדי אכילת פרס:

אלא מאי היתר וכו'. נראה דלא גרס ליה, דאי גרס ליה — א"כ מאי ס"ד דאביי לאקשויי? כיון דלדידיה נמי קשה. אלא לאביי א"ש, דפליגי עליה רבנן, דלר"ע דווקא אית ליה היתר מצטרף לאיסור בכל התורה, דגמר מנזיר. אבל לרבנן, דמוקמי משרת לטעם כעיקר — לית להו היתר מצטרף לאיסור בשום מקום. ועוד: דבנזיר בפ' "ג' מינים" (דף לז:) גרסינן גבי שתי קופות דבסמוך: בשלמא לדידי דאמינא היתר מצטרף לאיסור — דנפישי חולין. פי': לאביי, הא דהיתר מצטרף לאיסור — היינו כשיש מן האיסור יותר מן ההיתר, או שניהם בשוה. אבל כשהיתר רבה על האיסור — אין מצטרף. ולרב דימי — אין היתר מצטרף לאיסור בשום מקום, כדמסיק לקמן, דהוי חטאת ונזיר שני כתובים הבאים כאחד ואין מלמדין. וה"פ: א"ה, אמאי פליגי רבנן כו'. בשלמא לדידי — פליגי רבנן משום דר' אליעזר דריש 'כל', ואתא 'כל' לרבות אפילו כשהאיסור מועט. ורבנן לא דרשי 'כל', דכשהאיסור מועט — אין מצטרף, כמו בעלמא. אלא לדידך, אמאי פליגי? וכן גבי קופה ומדוכות, אתי שפיר לאביי:

הנח לתרומת תבלין דרבנן. קשה לרשב"א: כיון דתרומת תבלין דרבנן, גבי שום אמאי פסל מקום מגעו? ויש לחלק:

איתיביה שתי קופות. ואם תאמר, מאי פריך: אמאי אמרינן שאני אומר — והא פשיטא דבכל מקום מדאורייתא מין במינו בטל ברוב, והכא מיירי שרבו חולין על התרומה, כיון דסבר השתא דמיירי בתרומה דאורייתא, דבדאורייתא בעי רבייה אפילו לר' יוחנן ב"הערל" (יבמות דף פב.)! ואור"י: דבעי למימר בכל ענין, אפילו מין בשאינו מינו, כגון קמח חיטין בקמח שעורין, שאינו ניכר: והוא

ז א מיי' פ"ה מהל' איסורי מזבח הלכה ב:

[וע"ע תוספות שבועות כא: ד"ה כרבי שמעון]

ח ב מיי' פ"ח מהל' טומאת אוכלין הי"ב:

ט ג שם הל' יג:

י ד מיי' פי"ד מהל' מאכלו' אסורו' הל' ח:

יא ה מיי' פ"א מהל' תרומות הל' כו סמג עשין קלג טוש"ע י"ד סימן שלא סעיף ב:

יב ו מיי' פ"ה מהלכות נזיר הלכה ד:*

מנחות כו: [נזיר לו.]

טבול יום פ"ב [מ"ג נזיר לו.]

[ע"ש]

[פי' שגומע ואוכל כמו שורפה חיה בע"ז כט: עי' תוס' נזיר לו:]

לעיל ע: יבמות פב. נזיר לו: [תוספתא דתרומות פ"ו והא דלא מקשי ממשנה דתרומות פ"ו מ"ה עי' בר"ש שם]

רבינו חננאל

כותח הבבלי לרבי אליעזר היתר מצטרף לאיסור והוה ליה לזעירי למימנינהו לכלהו ושנינן אין הני כלהו היתר מצטרף לאיסור נינהו מיהו לא הזכיר זעירי השאור לבדו אלא לאפוקי מדאביי דאמר יש הקטרה בפחות מכזית אתא זעירי לאשמועינן דאין הקטרה בפחות מכזית ובעי צירוף להשלימו: אקשי' לר' אבהו ולר' יוחנן ליכא מידי אחריני דהיתר מצטרף לאיסור והתניא מקפה של חולין והשום והשמן של תרומה ונגע טבול יום במקצתו לא פסל אלא מקום מגעו והוינן בה מקום מגעו במקפה אמאי פסול ואמר משמי' דר' יוחנן הואיל וזר לוקה על המקפה בכזית מאי לאו משום דמקפה שהיא היתר מצטרף לאיסור לשום ולשמן שהן איסור ונעשית המקפה כלה איסור לפיכך זר האוכל ממנה לוקה אלמא לרבי יוחנן איכא דברים דהיתר מצטרף לאיסור מדאורייתא ושנינן לעולם לית ליה והכא כגון דאיכא במקפה שאכל הזר יש באותה אכילה כזית מן השום והשמן של תרומה ונצטרף השום והשמן ונעשו כזית ולפיכך לוקה שאינו לוקה אלא על התרומה ולא על המקפה ושיעור אכילה שמצטרפת מעט מעט עד שמצטרפין לכזית בכדי אכילת פרס דתני' אכל וחזר ואכל אם יש מתחלת אכילה ראשונה עד סוף אכילה אחרונה שיעור כדי אכילת פרס מצטרפי' וכמה היא כדי אכילת פרס מצאנו ששיער ר' חצי פרס שתי ביצים ואחד מעשרים בביצה נמצא הפרס ארבעה ביצים ואחד מעשרה בביצה ומפורש בעירובין פרק כיצד משתתפין בתחומין ואקשי' אי הכי בכותח הבבלי נמי נימא איכא כזית אוכל מקומניתא דאומא בכדי אכילת פרס ואמאי פליגי רבנן ואמרי בולא כלום ואמרינן שאני כותח הבבלי דלא משכחת בי' כזית בכדי אכילת פרס אי דקא גריף ואכיל כותח כגון אכילת הביצה בטלה דעתו כלומר אין זה דרך ארץ ואי דקא שטר ואכיל שהוא כעין טבילת פת במרק ליכא כזית מקומניתא דאומא כשיעור שעה כדי שיאכל אדם פרס ואם הוא יותר מזה השיעור אין מצטרפין וראשון ראשון בטל: ומותבינן מיהא שתי קדירות אחת של חולין ואחת של תרומה ולפניהם שתי מדוכות באחת תבלין של תרומה כו' ושנינן הנח לתרומת תבלין דאינה מן התורה לפי שאינם מיני תבואות ומותבי' תוב שתי קופות של חולין ושל תרומה ולפניהם שתי סאין אחת של חולין ואחת של תרומה ונפלו אלו לתוך אלו מותרין שאני אומר חולין לתוך חולין נפלו ואי כזית בכדי אכילת פרס מדאורייתא מצטרף כל ספק דאורייתא לחומרא אמאי תאני שאני אומר חולין לתוך חולין נפלו נמצא מיקל ומשני' כי תניא ההיא בתרומה בזמן הזה שהיא מדרבנן ואקשינן מדרך אחרת ומשרת להיתר מצטרף לאיסור הוא דאתא ההוא מיבעי ליה לכדתניא

אלִיתֵּן טַעַם כְּעִיקָּר שֶׁאִם שָׁרָה עֲנָבִים בְּמַיִם וְיֵשׁ בָּהֶן טַעַם יַיִן — חַיָּיב. מִכָּאן אַתָּה דָּן לְכָל הַתּוֹרָה כּוּלָּהּ: וּמָה נָזִיר שֶׁאֵין אִיסּוּרוֹ אִיסּוּר עוֹלָם, וְאֵין אִיסּוּרוֹ אִיסּוּר הֲנָאָה, וְיֵשׁ הֶיתֵּר לְאִיסּוּרוֹ — עָשָׂה בּוֹ טַעַם כְּעִיקָּר. כִּלְאַיִם, שֶׁאִיסּוּרוֹ אִיסּוּר עוֹלָם, וְאִיסּוּרוֹ אִיסּוּר הֲנָאָה, וְאֵין הֶיתֵּר לְאִיסּוּרוֹ — אֵינוֹ דִּין שֶׁיַּעֲשֶׂה טַעַם כְּעִיקָּר. וְהוּא הַדִּין לְעׇרְלָה בִּשְׁתַּיִם. הָא מַנִּי — רַבָּנַן הִיא, וְרַבִּי יוֹחָנָן דְּאָמַר כְּרַבִּי עֲקִיבָא. הֵי ר"ע? אִילֵּימָא ר"ע דְּמַתְנִי', דִּתְנַן: *רַבִּי עֲקִיבָא אוֹמֵר, בנָזִיר שֶׁשָּׁרָה פִּתּוֹ בְּיַיִן, וְיֵשׁ בּוֹ לְצָרֵף כְּדֵי כַּזַּיִת — חַיָּיב. וּמִמַּאי דְּמִפַּת וּמִיַּיִן? דִּילְמָא מִיַּיִן לְחוּדֵיהּ. וְכִי תֵּימָא: מִיַּיִן לְחוּדֵיהּ מַאי לְמֵימְרָא — הָא קמ"ל: דְּאע"ג דְּתַעֲרוֹבֶת. אֶלָּא ר"ע דְּבָרַיְיתָא. דְּתַנְיָא, ר"ע אוֹמֵר: נָזִיר שֶׁשָּׁרָה פִּתּוֹ בְּיַיִן, וְאָכַל כַּזַּיִת מִפַּת וּמִיַּיִן — חַיָּיב. וְר"ע, טַעַם כְּעִיקָּר מְנָא לֵיהּ? יָלֵיף מִבָּשָׂר בְּחָלָב. לָאו טַעְמָא בְּעָלְמָא הוּא וְאָסוּר — הָכָא נַמִּי, לָא שְׁנָא. *וְרַבָּנַן: מִבָּשָׂר בְּחָלָב לָא גָּמְרִינַן, דְּחִידּוּשׁ הוּא. וּמַאי חִידּוּשׁ? אִילֵּימָא דְּהַאי לְחוּדֵיהּ וְהַאי לְחוּדֵיהּ שָׁרֵי, וּבַהֲדֵי הֲדָדֵי אָסוּר — כִּלְאַיִם נַמִּי, הַאי לְחוּדֵיהּ וְהַאי לְחוּדֵיהּ שָׁרֵי, וּבַהֲדָדֵי אָסוּר! אֶלָּא: דְּאִי תָּרוּ לֵיהּ כּוּלֵּי יוֹמָא בְּחַלְבָא — שָׁרֵי, בַּשֵּׁיל לֵיהּ בִּשּׁוּלֵי — אָסוּר. וְר"ע נַמִּי, בָּשָׂר בְּחָלָב וַדַּאי חִידּוּשׁ הוּא! אֶלָּא: יָלֵיף מִגִּיעוּלֵי גוֹיִם, גִּיעוּלֵי גוֹיִם לָאו טַעְמָא בְּעָלְמָא הוּא — וְאָסוּר, הָכָא נַמִּי — ל"ש. וְרַבָּנַן: גִּיעוּלֵי גוֹיִם נַמִּי חִידּוּשׁ הוּא, דְּהָא כׇּל נוֹתֵן טַעַם לִפְגָם מוּתָּר, דְּגָמְרִינַן מִנְּבֵילָה — וְהָכָא אָסוּר. וְרַבִּי עֲקִיבָא — כִּדְרַב *חִיָּיא בְּרֵיהּ דְּרַב הוּנָא, דְּאָמַר: לֹא אָסְרָה תוֹרָה אֶלָּא *בִּקְדֵירָה בַּת יוֹמָא, הִלְכָּךְ לָאו נוֹתֵן טַעַם לִפְגָם הוּא. וְרַבָּנַן: קְדֵירָה בַּת יוֹמָא נַמִּי לֹא אֶפְשָׁר דְּלָא פָּגְמָה פּוֹרְתָּא. א"ל רַב אַחָא בְּרֵיהּ דְּרַב אָוְיָא לְרַב אַשִׁי: מִדְּרַבָּנַן נִשְׁמַע לְרַבִּי עֲקִיבָא, מִי לָא אָמְרִי רַבָּנַן "מִשְׁרַת" לִיתֵּן טַעַם כְּעִיקָּר — מִכָּאן אַתָּה דָּן לְכׇל אִיסּוּרִין שֶׁבַּתּוֹרָה. לְרַבִּי עֲקִיבָא נַמִּי: מִשְׁרַת — לְהֶיתֵּר מִצְטָרֵף לְאִיסּוּר, מִכָּאן אַתָּה דָּן לְכׇל אִיסּוּרִין שֶׁבַּתּוֹרָה כּוּלָּהּ! א"ל:
מִשּׁוּם

לִיתֵּן טַעַם כְּעִיקָּר. לַעֲשׂוֹת טַעְמוֹ שֶׁל אִיסּוּר כְּעִיקָּרוֹ וּמַמָּשׁוֹ: וְיֵשׁ בָּהֶן. בַּמַּיִם טַעַם יַיִן: חַיָּיב. בִּכְזַיִת מֵהֶן. וְהָא לָאו מִשּׁוּם הֶיתֵּר מִצְטָרֵף לְאִיסּוּר הוּא, אֶלָּא מִשּׁוּם דְּאִיתְעֲבֵיד לֵיהּ כּוּלֵּיהּ אִיסּוּר. אֲבָל הֶיתֵּר מִצְטָרֵף לְאִיסּוּר – לָא יָלְפִינַן מִינֵּיהּ: לְכׇל הַתּוֹרָה כּוּלָּהּ. שֶׁיְּהֵא טַעְמוֹ שֶׁל אִיסּוּרִין כְּמַמָּשׁוֹ: שֶׁאֵין אִיסּוּרָן אִיסּוּר עוֹלָם. אֶלָּא כַּמָּה שֶׁפֵּירֵשׁ. וְאִם סָתַם – שְׁלֹשִׁים יוֹם. וַעֲנָבִים וְיַיִן מוּתָּרִין לוֹ בַּהֲנָאָה: וְיֵשׁ לוֹ הֶיתֵּר לְאִיסּוּרוֹ. אַף תּוֹךְ זְמַן, עַל יְדֵי (הֲפָרַת) חָכָם [נ"ל התרת]: כִּלְאַיִם. כִּלְאֵי הַכֶּרֶם: אִיסּוּר עוֹלָם. זֶרַע חִטָּה וְחַרְצָן – הַכֹּל אָסוּר לְעוֹלָם: וְהוּא הַדִּין לְעׇרְלָה בִּשְׁתַּיִם. ק"ו זֶה אַתָּה דָּן לְעׇרְלָה בִּשְׁתֵּי דְּרָכִים, דְּאִיסּוּרוֹ אִיסּוּר הֲנָאָה, וְאֵין הֶיתֵּר לְאִיסּוּרוֹ בְּתוֹךְ שָׁלֹשׁ. מַה שֶּׁאֵין כֵּן בְּנָזִיר. וְאִיסּוּר עוֹלָם לֵיכָּא לְמֵימַר בֵּיהּ, דִּלְאַחַר שָׁלֹשׁ מוּתָּרוֹת: הָא מַנִּי. דְּאַפִּיקְתֵּיהּ לְהַאי קְרָא לְטַעַם כְּעִיקָּר, רַבָּנַן דִּפְלִיגִי אַדְּר"ע בְּהֶיתֵּר מִצְטָרֵף לְאִיסּוּר. וּלְקַמֵּיהּ מְפָרֵשׁ מַאי הִיא: הֵי ר"ע. מֵהֵי מִילְּתָא דְּר"ע שָׁמְעִינַן דְּהֶיתֵּר מִצְטָרֵף לְאִיסּוּר: דִּילְמָא מִיַּיִן לְחוּדֵיהּ. וְצֵירוּף שַׁיָּיךְ לְמִיתְנֵי בֵּיהּ, מִשּׁוּם דְּנִבְלַע בְּתוֹךְ הַפַּת. וְהֵיאָךְ מְשַׁעֲרִין כַּזַּיִת יַיִן? מְמַלֵּא כְּלִי מְפֶה לְפֶה, וּמֵבִיא זַיִת וְנוֹתֵן לְתוֹכוֹ, וְהַיַּיִן הַיּוֹצֵא הוּא כַּזַּיִת יַיִן. וְכֵן הוּא בְּתוֹסֶפְתָּא דְּנָזִיר: תַּעֲרוֹבֶת. שֶׁאֵינוֹ בָּעַיִן, שֶׁנִּבְלַע בַּפַּת: מִפַּת וּמִיַּיִן חַיָּיב. וּפְלִיגִי רַבָּנַן עֲלֵיהּ, דְּלֵית לְהוּ הֶיתֵּר מִצְטָרֵף לְאִיסּוּר. וְאִילּוּ פָּשַׁט הַיַּיִן בְּכׇל הַפַּת – לָא הֲווּ פְּלִיגִי רַבָּנַן עֲלֵיהּ, דְּהָא אִית לְהוּ טַעַם כְּעִיקָּר, וְאִיתְעֲבֵיד לֵיהּ פַּת גּוּפֵיהּ אִיסּוּר. וְהָכָא מִיהָא פְּלִיגִי עֲלֵיהּ, דְּטַעְמָא דְּר"ע מִשּׁוּם צֵירוּף הוּא. וְא"נ לָא נִשְׁרֵית כׇּל הַפַּת בַּיַּיִן – מִצְטָרֵף נַמִּי הֶיתֵּר לְאִיסּוּר לְחִיּוּבָא: וְר"ע. כֵּיוָן דְּמַפֵּיק לֵיהּ לְהַאי "מִשְׁרַת" לְהֶיתֵּר מִצְטָרֵף לְאִיסּוּר: טַעַם כְּעִיקָּר. הֵיכָא דְּלֵיכָּא מִידֵּי עִיקָּר, אֶלָּא טַעַם, כְּגוֹן שָׁרָה עֲנָבִים בְּמַיִם, מְנָא לֵיהּ? בָּשָׂר בְּחָלָב. בָּשָׂר שֶׁנִּתְבַּשֵּׁל בְּחָלָב, וְהַבָּשָׂר בְּעֵינֵיהּ, אֶלָּא שֶׁטַּעַם הֶחָלָב נִבְלַע בּוֹ: חִידּוּשׁ הוּא. כׇּל אִיסּוּרוֹ תֵּימַהּ הוּא, וּדְבַר חִידּוּשׁ שֶׁאֵינוֹ מָצוּי (א) בֵּינֵינוּ בִּשְׁאָר אִיסּוּרִין – לָא גָּמְרִינַן חוּמְרָא דִּידֵיהּ אַשְּׁאָר אִיסּוּרִין. דְּכִי הֵיכִי דִּשְׁאָר חִידּוּשִׁין דִּידֵיהּ לָא הָווּ בִּשְׁאָר אִיסּוּרִין – הַאי דְּטַעַם כְּעִיקָּר נַמִּי לָא תִּיגְמַר מִינֵּיהּ: וּמַאי חִידּוּשֵׁיהּ. מִשְּׁאָר מִילֵּי: אִילֵּימָא הַיְינוּ חִידּוּשֵׁיהּ. דִּשְׁנֵי דְּבָרִים הַמּוּתָּרִים הֵם, וּכְשֶׁנִּתְעָרְבוּ נֶאֱסָרִין, מַה שֶּׁאֵין כֵּן בִּשְׁאָר דְּבָרִים: הָא כִּלְאַיִם נַמִּי. דּוּגְמָתָן: תָּרֵי לֵיהּ. שׁוֹרֵהוּ בְּחָלָב כׇּל הַיּוֹם – שָׁרֵי. כְּלוֹמַר: מוּתָּר לְשׇׁרוֹתוֹ בְּתוֹכוֹ, וְאֵינוֹ עוֹבֵר עָלָיו אֲפִילּוּ עַל אֲכִילָתוֹ, דְּלָא אָסְרָה תוֹרָה אֶלָּא דֶּרֶךְ בִּישּׁוּל, וַאֲפִילּוּ יָהֵיב בֵּיהּ טַעְמָא. וּמִיהוּ, מִדְּרַבָּנַן אָסוּר: בַּשֵּׁיל לֵיהּ בִּשּׁוּלֵי אָסוּר. עוֹבֵר עַל בִּישּׁוּלוֹ, וְעוֹבֵר עַל אֲכִילָתוֹ: גִּיעוּלֵי גוֹיִם. קְדֵירָה שֶׁבִּישֵּׁל בָּהּ הַגּוֹי, וּכְשֶׁחוֹזֵר יִשְׂרָאֵל וּמְבַשֵּׁל בָּהּ – הִיא מַגְעֶלֶת בְּלִיעָתָהּ לְתוֹךְ שֶׁל יִשְׂרָאֵל. גִּיעוּל לְשׁוֹן מֵקִיא וּפוֹלֵט. וְהַתּוֹרָה אֲסָרַתּוּ בְּמַעֲשֵׂה מִדְיָן, "כׇּל דָּבָר אֲשֶׁר יָבֹא בָאֵשׁ" (במדבר לא) – דְּהַיְינוּ יוֹרוֹת וְקוּמְקְמוּסִין וְהַיּוֹצֵא בָּהֶן, שֶׁמַּרְתִּיחִין אוֹתָן עַל הָאוּר: דְּגָמְרִינַן מִנְּבֵילָה. דִּכְתִיב: "לֹא תֹאכְלוּ כׇל נְבֵלָה, לַגֵּר" וגו' (דברים יד), הָרְאוּיָה לַגֵּר – קְרוּיָה נְבֵלָה, שֶׁאֵינָהּ רְאוּיָה לַגֵּר – אֵינָהּ קְרוּיָה נְבֵלָה: וְהָכָא אָסוּר. דְּהַאי נַמִּי לִפְגָם הוּא, דְּאוֹתָהּ בְּלִיעָה מִשֶּׁשָּׁהֲתָה בְּדוֹפְנוֹ שֶׁל כְּלִי לַיְלָה אַחַת – הוּפַג טַעְמוֹ וְנִתְקַלְקֵל, וְתוּ לָא מַשְׁבַּחַת לָאוֹכֶל שֶׁהִיא נִפְלֶטֶת לְתוֹכוֹ: בַּת יוֹמָא. שֶׁבִּישֵּׁל בָּהּ הַגּוֹי בּוֹ בַּיּוֹם: דְּלָא פָּגְמָה פּוֹרְתָּא. מִטַּעַם הַכְּלִי נִפְגְּמָה הַבְּלִיעָה: מִדְּרַבָּנַן נִשְׁמַע לְר"ע. לְר' יוֹחָנָן פָּרֵיךְ, דְּאָמַר לְעֵיל: כׇּל אִיסּוּרִים שֶׁבַּתּוֹרָה אֵין הֶיתֵּר מִצְטָרֵף לְאִיסּוּר, חוּץ מֵאִיסּוּרֵי נָזִיר, וְאוֹקִימְנָא כְּר"ע. מִכְּדִי לְר"ע שָׁמְעִינַן לֵיהּ דְּאָמַר בְּאִיסּוּרֵי נָזִיר הֶיתֵּר מִצְטָרֵף לְאִיסּוּר, וּבִשְׁאָר אִיסּוּרֵי לָא אַיְירֵי מִידֵּי. וְר' יוֹחָנָן אַמַּאי לָא אָמַר דְּכִי הֵיכִי דְּאִית לֵיהּ בְּאִיסּוּרֵי נָזִיר אִית לֵיהּ נַמִּי בִּשְׁאָר אִיסּוּרֵי, הָא מִמַּאי דְּשָׁמְעִינַן לְהוּ לְרַבָּנַן בְּטַעַם כְּעִיקָּר, מָצֵינַן לְמִשְׁמַע מִינָּהּ נַמִּי דַּעְתֵּיהּ דְּר"ע בְּהֶיתֵּר מִצְטָרֵף לְאִיסּוּר: לָאו אָמְרִי רַבָּנַן כּוּ'. וְקָא אָמְרֵי נַמִּי הָכִי בִּשְׁאָר אִיסּוּרֵי לְר"ע נַמִּי דְּמַפֵּיק לָהּ לְהֶיתֵּר מִצְטָרֵף לְאִיסּוּר, אִיכָּא לְמֵימַר נַמִּי דְּאִית לֵיהּ מִכָּאן אַתָּה דָּן לְכׇל הַתּוֹרָה כּוּלָּהּ: אֲמַר לֵיהּ. כֵּיוָן דְּמוֹקֵי לֵיהּ ר"ע לְהֶיתֵּר מִצְטָרֵף לְאִיסּוּר – לָא מָצֵינַן לְמֵימַר מִכָּאן אַתָּה דָּן:
מִשּׁוּם

והוא הדין לערלה בשתים. וכן אמרינן בפ"ק דקדושין (דף לח.) גבי חדש. ופ"ה: דערלה אין איסורו איסור עולם – דאחר שלש מותר. וקשה: מה שמותר אחר שלש – היינו האילן, והאילן לא נאסר מעולם רק הפרי, והפרי אין לו היתר! ור"ת פי': הוא הדין לערלה בשתים – היינו בשנת ארבע, דיש היתר לאיסורו על ידי פדייה, או להביא לירושלים. ור"י מפרש: דנזיר וחדש אין איסורן איסור עולם – שהגדל מן הגפן אחר השלמת נזרו לא חל עליו איסור, וכן חדש היוצא מקנה השיבולת אחר הבאת העומר – לא חל עליו איסור, כיון שהשרים קודם העומר. וכן ערלה אחר ג' שנים, היוצא ממנו אין איסור חל עליו, ויש היתר לאיסורו יש לפרש כפ"ה: שנזיר תוך זמנו יש לו היתר על ידי שאלה. וחדש נמי, לר' יהודה דאמר: *יום הנף כולו אסור [מנחות סח.] – יש לו היתר תוך זמנו על ידי עומר. וערלה אין לה היתר תוך זמנה. וילדה בזקינה דבטלה – אין זה אילן דערלה, דפנים חדשות באו לכאן. ועוד מפר"י: שהפרי של חדש שנאסר כבר, וכן היוצא מן הגפן קודם השלמת נזירות – יש להן היתר בהשלמת זמן האיסור. אבל ערלה וכלאים, הפרי שנאסר – אין לו היתר. ופירוש זה נראה עיקר, דאין צריך להעמיד כר' יהודה. ואין להקשות לפי' זה: אמאי לא חשיב יש היתר לאיסור בשאלה ובעומר ויהא ג' בערלה? דיש לומר: דלא סבר כר' יהודה אלא האיר המזרח מתיר. ונזיר נמי, אי מתשיל – אין זה היתר לדבר שנאסר, שהחכם עוקר הנדר מעיקרו, ונמצא שלא נאסר מעולם. אבל לפי' קמא ה"מ לאתשובי מה שהפרי עצמו נאסר לעולם, והיה מולא בערלה שלש:

ודילמא מיין לחודיה. ולשון לצרף אתי שפיר, כלומר: לצרף היין הבלוע בתוכו:

ורבנן מבשר בחלב לא גמרינן דחידוש הוא. תימה לרשב"א: התינח לרבא, אלא לאביי דאית ליה בפרק "כל הבשר" (חולין דף קח.) דבשר בחלב לאו חידוש הוא, אמאי איצטריך למילף מנזיר לטעם כעיקר*):

אלא יליף מגיעולי גוים. הקשה ה"ר יוסף: היכי יליף רבי עקיבא טעם כעיקר בנזיר מגיעולי גוים? הא נזיר קל מכל איסור שבתורה, שאין איסורו איסור עולם ויש היתר לאיסורו! ותי': דבמדין נמי היו כליהן בלועות מיין, ואסורים לנזיר: **ורבנן** קדירה בת יומא נמי אי אפשר דלא פגמה פורתא. ואפ"ה אסר הכתוב, אם כן ליכא לאיפלוגי בין בת יומא לשאין בת יומא, וכולהו אסורים. ור"ע סבר: קדירה בת יומא לא פגמה כלל, אבל שאין בת יומא, דפגמא – שרי. דנ"ט לפגם מותר, דגמר מנבילה. וה"נ סבר ר"ש בפרק בתרא דמסכת ע"ז (דף סז:). ור"מ פליג עליה התם, וסבר נ"ט לפגם אסור, דגמר מגיעולי גוים דאסר הכתוב אע"ג דנ"ט לפגם הוא, דאפילו קדירה בת יומא אי אפשר דלא פגמה פורתא. וגיעולי גוים לאו חידוש הוא, ומה שהתיר הכתוב נבילה – מוקי לה בסרוחה מעיקרא. ולרבי מאיר מצי למילף נמי מגיעולי גוים לטעם כעיקר, כיון דלאו חידוש הוא, ואיכא השתא שלש מחלוקות בדבר:

*) [ועי' תוס' חולין קח. ד"ה מבשר וכו' כתבו לאביי חזר בו]

משום

רבינו חננאל

לכדתניא משרת ליתן טעם כעיקר שאם שרה ענבים במים ויש בהן טעם יין אסור ומכאן אתה דן לכל התורה כולה ומה נזיר שאין איסורו איסור עולם אלא עד מלאת ימי נזרו בלבד ואין הנאת היין עליו אסורה אלא שתייתו בלבד [ויש היתר לאיסורו] ואפי' זה היין בעצמו שנאסר לו אחר מלאת ימי נזרו הוא מותר בו שנא' (במדבר ו' כ') ואחר ישתה הנזיר יין עושה משרת ענבים שאין בו אלא טעם יין כענבים עצמן כלאים שאיסורן איסור עולם שנא' (ויקרא י"ט י"ט) את חקותי תשמרו חקים שחקקתי לך כבר כי באיסורן הן לעולם ואיסורן איסור הנאה דכתיב (דברים כ"ב ט) פן תקדש המלאה הזרע ודרשי' לה תוקדש תוקד אש ואין היתר לאיסורו דלשריפה אזיל אינו דין שיהיה בו טעם כעיקר והוא הדין [לערלה] בשתים שאיסורן איסור הנאה שנא' (ויקרא י"ט כ"ג) ערלים לא יאכל ודרשי' ביה אחד איסור הנאה ואחד איסור אכילה ואין היתר לזה האילן באלו שני ערלה כלל לא בו ולא בפירותיו אבל אחר כן מותר הפירות והאילן והרי משרת להכי הוא דאתא ומשני רבי יוחנן זו הברייתא לרבנן היא ואני לא אמרתי אלא אליבא דרבי עקיבא דתניא רבי עקיבא אומר אפילו שרה פתו ביין ואכל כזית מפת ומיין חייב אבל הא דתנן ר' עקיבא אומר אפי' שרה פתו ביין ויש בו כדי לצרף כזית אסור דחויה היא ודחי' ממאי דחצי זית פת וחצי זית יין עלייהו דמצטרפי ואסור דלמא כזית מיין לחודיה קאמר וקמ"ל אע"ג דליתיה היין לחודיה במקום אחד כיון דאית ביה שיעור לאיצטרופי כזית אסור: **ואמרי'** ורבי עקיבא דמפיק כל משרת להיתר מצטרף לאיסור ליתן טעם כעיקר שאסור מנא ליה ואמר מבשר וחלב שאין בחלב אלא טעם בשר וכן בבשר טעם חלב ואסירי כך כל התורה טעם כעיקר אסור ורבנן האי חדוש הוא דאי תרו לבשר כולי יומא בחלב שרי ואי מבשל להו בהדי הדדי אסירי ומאי שנא בישול משריה אלא חידוש הוא ור' עקיבא מחידוש היכי גמר ואמרי' אלא רבי עקיבא מגיעולי נכרים גמר לכל התורה כולה דהא גיעולי נכרים טעמא בעלמא הוא וכתיב (במדבר ל"א כ"ג) כל דבר אשר יבא באש תעבירו באש ותניא דברים שנשתמש בהן על ידי חמין כגון יורות וקומקמוסין ומחמי חמין מגעילן ומטבילן כו' וקתני בסיפא וכלן שנשתמש בהן עד שלא הטביל ולא הגעיל ולא ליבן אסור ואוקימנא למאן דתאני נותן טעם לפגם אסור. ורבנן בכל התורה כולה נותן טעם לפגם שרי דילפינן מנבלה דכתיב בה (דברים י"ד כ"א) תתננה ואכלה וכתיב בטריפה (שמות כ"ב ל') לכלב תשליכון אותו ודייקי' מינה אם נפגמה ונפסלה מלאכל הכלב פרחה ממנה תורת טומאת נבלה וגיעולי נכרים כיון דנותן טעם לפגם מותר והכא כתיב אסור חידוש הוא ומחידוש לא גמרי' ורבי עקיבא אומר אינו חידוש כדרב חייא בריה דרב הונא דאמר לא אסרה תורה אלא קדרה בת יומה דנותן טעם לשבח הוא ורבנן אפילו קדרה בת יומה אי אפשר דלא פגמה פורתא ומפורש בע"ז: **ותוב** אקשי' ורבי עקיבא למה לא למד לתורה כולה מיהא נמי הכי משרת להיתר
מצטרף

עין משפט נר מצוה: יג א ב מיי' פ"ה מהל' נזיר הל' ה:

מסורת הש"ס: נזיר [לד:] לז. שבועות כב. | חולין קח. | ע"ז סז: ע"ש איפכא ר"ה ברי' דרב חייא | [ע"ז עה: נזיר לז: ע"ש]

הגהות הב"ח

(א) רש"י ד"ה חידוש הוא וכו' שאינו מצוי כה"ג בשאר:

משום דהוה נזיר וחטאת *שני כתובין הבאין כאחד, ואין מלמדין. נזיר – הא דאמרן, חטאת מאי היא? *דתניא: °"כל אשר יגע בבשרה יקדש וגו'" – יכול אפילו לא בלעה, ת"ל: "בבשרה" – א עד שיבלע בבשר. ב "יקדש" – *להיות כמוה, שאם פסולה היא – תיפסל, ואם כשירה היא – תאכל כחמור שבה. ורבנן נמי, ניהוי נזיר וחטאת שני כתובין הבאין כאחד, ואין מלמדין! אמרי: הנהו מיצרך צריכי. ור"ע: מאי צריכי? בשלמא אי כתב רחמנא בחטאת – לא גמר נזיר מינה, *דחולין מקדשים לא גמרינן. אלא לכתוב רחמנא בנזיר, ותיתי חטאת ותגמור מיניה, דהא כל איסורין שבתורה קא גמר מנזיר. ורבנן אמרי לך*: מיצרך צריכי; חטאת – להיתר מצטרף לאיסור, וחולין מקדשים לא גמר. ומשרת – ליתן טעם כעיקר, ומכאן אתה דן לכל התורה כולה. ור' עקיבא – תרווייהו להיתר מצטרף לאיסור, והוו להו שני כתובין הבאין כאחד, וכל שני כתובין הבאין כאחד אין מלמדין. א"ל רב אשי לרב כהנא: אלא הא דתניא: °"מכל אשר יעשה מגפן היין מחרצנים ועד זג" – ג לימד על איסורי נזיר שמצטרפים זה עם זה. השתא לר"ע איסור והיתר מצטרפין, איסור ואיסור מיבעיא?! אמר ליה: איסור והיתר – בבת אחת, ד איסור ואיסור – בזה אחר זה.§

מתני' ה בצק שבסידקי עריבה, אם יש כזית במקום אחד – חייב לבער, ואם (*לא) – בטל במיעוטו. וכן לענין הטומאה, אם מקפיד עליו – חוצץ, ואם רוצה בקיומו – הרי הוא כעריבה.§

גמ' אמר רב יהודה אמר שמואל: לא שנו אלא במקום שאין עשויין לחזק, אבל במקום שעשויין לחזק – אינו חייב לבער. מכלל דפחות מכזית, אפי' במקום שאין עשוי לחזק – אינו חייב לבער. איכא ו דמתני לה אסיפא: "ואם לאו בטל במיעוטו". אמר רב יהודה אמר שמואל: לא שנו אלא במקום העשוי לחזק, אבל במקום שאין עשוי לחזק – חייב לבער. מכלל דכזית, אפילו במקום העשוי לחזק – חייב לבער. תניא כלישנא קמא, תניא כלישנא בתרא. תניא כלישנא קמא: בצק שבסידקי עריבה, במקום העשוי לחזק – אינו חוצץ, ואינו עובר. ובמקום שאין עשוי לחזק – חוצץ ועובר. במה דברים אמורים – בכזית, אבל בפחות מכזית, אפילו במקום שאין עשוי לחזק – אינו חוצץ ואינו עובר. ותניא כלישנא בתרא: *בצק שבסידקי עריבה, במקום העשוי לחזק – אינו

תורה אור: ויקרא ו; במדבר ו

רש"י

משום. דבדוכתא אחריתי נמי כתבה רחמנא, ושני כתובין הבאין כו'. אבל לרבנן, דמוקי ליה לטעם כעיקר – לא הוו שני כתובין הבאין כאחד, כדמפרש לקמיה: כל אשר יגע בבשרה. בשר חולין או שלמים, שזמן אכילתו מרובה מחטאת, ונגע בחטאת – יקדש. כדמפרש: להיות כמוה. שאם פסולה היתה החטאת, כגון פיגול או פסול אחר – תיפסל אף זו שבלעה ממנה. ואם כשירה היא החטאת – מהניא לבולעת הימנה לאסור באכילה אלא כחמור שבה, כחומר החטאת שנבלע בה: לפנים מן הקלעים, ולזכרי כהונה, וליום ולילה אחד: יכול אפילו לא בלעה. הנוגעת בה ממנה, קאמר רחמנא "יקדש" – ת"ל כו': תאכל. הבולעת כחמור שבה, שהרי יש בה ב' מינין, אחד חמור ואחד קל, וכלה הולכת אחר החמור. אלמא: היתר מצטרף לאיסור: מיצרך צריכי. תרוייהו, כדמפרש לקמיה, ולא הוו שני כתובין הבאין כאחד. דחד מחבריה לא מצי יליף, דנימא מדהדר כתביה לאידך ולא ילפא מחבריה ש"מ דווקא הכי*) קאמר: חולין. להחמיר, לא גמרי מדין קדשים. דדין קדשים להיות חמורין: ה"ג: ורבנן אמרי לך מיצרך צריכי. חטאת אשמועינן משום דהיתר מצטרף לאיסור, (א) ואי נמי לא איבלע בכולה, אי אכל חצי זית פיגול וחצי זית היתר בבת אחת – ניגמור מינה דבקדשי' ניחייב. ומיהו, בשאר איסורין לא אמרינן הכי, ואפילו בנזיר. דחולין מקדשים לא גמרינן. ומשרת – לאו לאגמורי היתר מצטרף לאיסור אתא בנזיר, אלא ליתן טעם כעיקר. דמגיעולי גוים לא יליף, דחידוש הוא, ואיצטריך למכתביה בנזיר. ומכאן אתה דן לכל התורה: ור' עקיבא. אית ליה גיעולי גוים לאו חידוש הוא, (ב) דלא מצריך קרא לטעם כעיקר. הלכך, לר"ע, כיון דשמעת ליה דמפיק משרת להיתר מצטרף לאיסור – על כרחיך תרוייהו הני להיתר מצטרף לאיסור אתו, והוה ליה חטאת קרא יתירא, דמצי למיגמר מנזיר, והוו להו שני כתובין הבאין כאחד. ומש"ה פשיטא ליה לרבי יוחנן דר"ע לא גמר שאר איסורין מנזיר – דהא לא מצי, דשני כתובין נינהו. והא ליכא למימר: משרת להיתר מצטרף לאיסור, וחטאת לטעם כעיקר – דגיעולי גוים חידוש הוא, ולא מצי גמר חטאת מינייהו, ואין כאן שני כתובין. דא"כ, טעם כעיקר בשאר איסורין מנא ליה? מגיעולי גוים – לא גמרינן, מקדשים – נמי לא גמרינן. ורבנן דפליגי עליה דר"א בכותח הבבלי, אלמא לית להו טעם כעיקר דאורייתא – מפקי להאי משרת להיתר מצטרף לאיסור כר"ע, ובגיעולי גוים סבירא להו דחידוש הוא כרבנן. והכי אמרינן נמי ב"כל הבשר", דאיכא למאן דאמר טעמו ולא ממשו דרבנן: לימד על איסורי נזיר כו'. מדכיילינהו לחרצנים וזגין בחדא אכילה, לימד שמצטרפין: השתא לרבי עקיבא. ל"ל דכתב רחמנא קרא להכי, השתא איסור והיתר מצטרפין כו': מתני' וכן לענין הטומאה. מפרש בגמ': גמ' ה"ג: ל"ש אלא במקום שאין עשוי לחזק, אבל במקום העשוי לחזק – אינו חייב לבער. מכלל דפחות מכזית, אפילו במקום שאין עשוי לחזק – אינו חייב לבער. ופירש: לא שנו דכזית במקום אחד חייב לבער – אלא שאין הסדקין בשולי עריבה, מקום הלקת מים, שיהא בצק זה מועיל לעריבה לחזק המים, אלא בדפנותיהן, מקום שאין עשוי לחזק. אבל אם במקום העשוי לחזק הן – בטלו לגבה, והוו כעץ, דמסתמא בטלינהו האי גברא להתם. ואפילו כזית אינו חייב לבער(ג): מכלל דפחות מכזית כו'. ותלמודא דייק ממילתא דשמואל, דאוקמה למתני' במקום שאין עשוי לחזק. וקתני מתני' בפחות מיכן בטל במיעוטו – שמע מינה דפחות מכזית לא חשיב. ואע"ג דאיכא בה פלגי זיתא טובא – הואיל ולאו במקום אחד נינהו, לא חשיבי: ה"ג: איכא דמתני לה אסיפא: פחות מיכן בטל במיעוטו, אמר רב יהודה אמר שמואל: לא שנו אלא במקום העשוי לחזק, אבל במקום שאין עשוי לחזק – חייב לבער. מכלל דכזית אפילו במקום העשוי לחזק חייב לבער. ואע"ג דודאי מבטיל ליה – אפילו הכי, כיון דחשיב – לא בטיל. ולישנא בתרא חמיר מקמא:

תוספות

משום דהוי נזיר וחטאת שני כתובין הבאין כאחד. תימה לרשב"א: אמאי לא קאמר נזיר וחמץ? דר"ע דריש "כל" בפ' "התערובת" (זבחים דף פב.): **ר"ח** גרס: כחומר שבהן. ומיירי בחטאת ושלמים, ואם נבלע החטאת בשלמים שנשחט אתמול – נאכל כחומר השלמים, ואינו נאכל בלילה. ואם נבלע החטאת בשלמים שנשחט היום – נאכל כחומר החטאת, ואינו נאכל למחר. ולשון הברייתא קשה, דאמר: עד שיבלע בבשרה. משמע דאיירי בהיתר שנבלע באיסור, והדר קאמר: יקדש להיות כמוה, משמע שהאיסור נבלע בהיתר:

ורבנן אמרי לך חטאת להיתר מצטרף לאיסור. אור"י: דבנזיר בפ' "ג' מינין" (דף לז:) משמע נזיר וחטאת לרבנן תרווייהו לטעם כעיקר. דקאמר התם: לריכ', דאי כתב רחמנא חטאת – חולין מקדשים לא גמרינן. ואי כתב רחמנא נזיר – חטאת מנזיר לא ילפינן, דחמיר איסוריה, דאפילו חרצן אסיר ליה:

בשמעתין משמע דטעם כעיקר דאורייתא, דילפינן מנזיר, דלאו אסמכתא היא. דמדר"ע דאמר לקי אהיתר מצטרף לאיסור בנזיר, נשמע לרבנן. וקשה מפ' "כל הבשר" (חולין דף קח.) וממסכת ע"ג (דף סז:), ושם מפורש:

*__כאן__ שלא במקום לישה. פ"ה: דשלא במקום לישה עובר בפחות מכזית. וקשה, דאמר לקמן: לא אמרן אלא בעריבה, אבל בבית – חייב לבער, משום דזימנין (ד) דמיכנף ונפלי אהדדי. ולפ"ה תיפוק ליה דפחות מכזית חייב לבער שלא במקום לישה! ונראה לר"י: דמקום העשוי לחזק – היינו את הכלי, בין במקום לישה ובין שלא במקום לישה עושין לחזק. אך במקום לישה יש להחמיר יותר, שיש לחוש שידבק מאותה עיסה לעיסה אחרת על ידי לישה, או תבלע מן הטעם. ולכך, כזית במקום לישה, אפילו עשוי לחזק – עובר, אף על גב דודאי מבטלו, כיון דאיכא תרתי לריעותא: כזית, ובמקום לישה. ופחות מכזית, אפילו במקום לישה, אי עשוי לחזק – לא גזרו ביה רבנן. דכיון שהוא דבר מועט – יכול לשמור שלא ילוש עליו. וכן כזית שלא במקום לישה, אי עשוי לחזק – אין עובר, אבל פחות מכזית ושלא במקום לישה – אפילו אין עשויה לחזק מותר:

כופת

שייך לע"ב

עין משפט נר מצוה

יד א מיי' פ"ח מהל' מעשה קרבנות הלכה טז:
טו ב שם הלכה טו:
טז ג ד מיי' פ"ה מהל' נזיר הלכה ג:
יז ה ו מיי' פ"ב מהל' חמץ הל' טו סמג עשין לט טוש"ע א"ח סי' תמב סעיף ז:

מסורת הש"ס

[לעיל כו. וש"נ]
נזיר לז: זבחים לז.
שם חולין נט.
[שבועות כו:]
[נזיר לז: ע"ש]
נ"ל הכי
[נ"ל לאו]
(תוספ' פ"ג)

רבינו חננאל

מצטרף לאיסור ומכאן אתה דן לכל התורה כלה ודחי' משום דהאי נזיר וחטאת שני כתובין הבאין כאחד ואין מלמדין נזיר הא דאמרן חטאת דתניא כל אשר יגע בבשרה יקדש יכול אע"פ שלא בלע ת"ל בבשרה עד שיבלע בבשרה יקדש להיות כמוה שאם פסולה היא תפסל ואם כשרה היא תאכל כחומר שבה פי' החטאת נאכלת ליום ולילה והשלמים לשני ימים ולילה אם ניתז*) (מדם) החטאת שנשחטה היום על חתיכת בשר שלמים שנשחטו מאתמול נאכל הבשר בתורת שלמים בו ביום בלבד אבל לא בלילה כבשר החטאת ואם נשחטו שניהם היום נאכל בתורת חטאת היום והלילה בלבד אבל לא למחר כשאר בשר שלמים הנה ההיתר נצטרף לאיסור וזהו פי' נאכל כחמור שבהן פעמים נאכל בתורת שלמים ופעמים נאכל בתורת חטאת כי השלמים שנשחטו מאתמול היום מותר ובלילה אסור באכילה והחטאת שנשחטה היום מותרת באכילה כל הלילה נמצאו השלמים בזה חמורין מן החטאת: **ורבנן** כי אמרי' שני כתובין הבאין כאחד היכא דתרוויהו חולין או תרוויהו קדשים נינהו אבל חד חולין והוא הנזיר וחד קדשים והוא חטאת מצטרך צריכי ולא קרינן בהו שני כתובין הבאין כאחד ונרחו הדברים וחזרו ואמרו חטאת להיתר מצטרף לאיסור ומשרת ליתן טעם כעיקר ומכאן אתה דן לכל התורה כלה איסור שבתורה**) בין בזה ובין בזה ור"ע תרגמה ליתן טעם כעיקר [גמרינן] מגיעולי נכרים חטאת ונזיר תרוויהו להיתר מצטרף לאיסור והוו להו שני כתובין הבאין כאחד ואין מלמדין ומקשי' רב אשי אליבא דרבי עקיבא הא דתניא מכל אשר יעשה מגפן היין מחרצנים ועד זג לימד על איסורי נזיר שמצטרפין זה עם זה השתא לרבי עקיבא חצי זית פת שהוא היתר וחצי זית יין מצטרפי חרצן [וזג] ששניהן אסורין לנזיר מיבעיא [illegible] איסור והיתר בבת אחת [illegible] **מתני'** בצק שבסדקי עריבה אם יש בו כזית במקום אחד חייב לבער ואם לאו בטל במיעוטו [illegible] במקום אחד***) [illegible] ובטל אע"פ שהוא כזית ש"מ דפחות מכזית אפילו במקום שאין עשוי לחזק אינו חייב לבער: **ואיכא** דמתני לה לרב יהודה אסיפא דקתני ואם לאו בטל במיעוטו ודייקינן לא שנו פחות מכזית בטל אלא במקום שעשוי

*) נראה דצ"ל מרוצע החטאת. **) נראה דצ"ל דאמר לכל התורה כולה כוונתו בין בקדשים בין בחולין אבל עדיין לשון צריך ביאור והבנה.
***) נראה דחסר כאן ואולי צ"ל כזית במקום אחד חייב לבער במקום שאינו עשוי לחזק אבל במקום וכו' [illegible] בטל אע"פ כו'.

הגהות הב"ח

(א) רש"י ד"ה ה"ג ורבנן וכו' לאיסור ואי נמי: (ב) ד"ה ורבי עקיבא וכו' ולא מלריך: (ג) ד"ה ה"ג לא וד"ה מכלל הד"א: (ד) תוספות ד"ה כאן וכו' דזימנין דמיכנף להו ונפלי:

אֵינוֹ חוֹצֵץ וְאֵינוֹ עוֹבֵר. בְּמָקוֹם שֶׁאֵין עָשׂוּי לְחַזֵּק – חוֹצֵץ וְעוֹבֵר. בַּמֶּה דְּבָרִים אֲמוּרִים – בְּפָחוֹת מִכַּזַּיִת, אֲבָל בְּכַזַּיִת – אֲפִילּוּ בְּמָקוֹם הֶעָשׂוּי לְחַזֵּק – חוֹצֵץ וְעוֹבֵר. קַשְׁיָין אַהֲדָדֵי! אָמַר רַב הוּנָא: סְמֵי קִילְּתָא מִקַּמֵּי חֲמִירְתָּא. *רַב יוֹסֵף אָמַר: תַּנָּאֵי שַׁקַּלְתְּ מֵעָלְמָא?! תַּנָּאֵי הִיא. דְּתַנְיָא: הַפַּת שֶׁעִיפְּשָׁה – חַיָּיב לְבָעֵר, מִפְּנֵי שֶׁרָאוּי לְשׁוֹחֲקָהּ וּלְחַמֵּעַ בָּהּ כַּמָּה עִיסּוֹת אֲחֵרוֹת. רַבִּי שִׁמְעוֹן בֶּן אֶלְעָזָר אוֹמֵר: בַּמֶּה דְּבָרִים אֲמוּרִים – בִּמְקוּיֶּימֶת לַאֲכִילָה, אֲבָל *כּוּפַת שְׂאוֹר שֶׁיִּחֲדָהּ לִישִׁיבָה – בָּטְלָה. מִדְּאָמַר ר' שִׁמְעוֹן בֶּן אֶלְעָזָר בָּטְלָה – מִכְּלָל דְּתַנָּא קַמָּא סָבַר לֹא בָּטְלָה, אַלְמָא קָסָבַר: כָּל כַּזַּיִת, אע"ג דִּמְבַטֵּל – לָא בָּטֵיל. אָמַר לֵיהּ אַבָּיֵי: תֵּרַצְתְּ בְּכַזַּיִת, פָּחוֹת מִכַּזַּיִת מִי תֵּרַצְתְּ? אֶלָּא: הָא וְהָא ר' שִׁמְעוֹן בֶּן אֶלְעָזָר הִיא, וְלָא קַשְׁיָא; הָא – בִּמְקוֹם לִישָׁה, הָא – שֶׁלֹּא בִּמְקוֹם לִישָׁה. אָמַר רַב אַשִׁי: לָא תֵּימָא שֶׁלֹּא בִּמְקוֹם לִישָׁה אַגַּבָּהּ דַּאֲגָנָא, אֶלָּא אַשִּׂיפְתָּא דַּאֲגָנָא. פְּשִׁיטָא! מַהוּ דְּתֵימָא: זִמְנָא דְּאָטֵיף וּמָטֵי לְהָתָם, קָא מַשְׁמַע לָן. א"ר נַחְמָן אָמַר רַב: הֲלָכָה כְּר' שִׁמְעוֹן בֶּן אֶלְעָזָר. אִינִי?! וְהָאָמַר רַב יִצְחָק בַּר אַשִׁי אָמַר רַב: [א]אִם טָח פָּנֶיהָ בְּטִיט – בְּטֵלָה. טָח – אִין, לֹא טָח – לָא! מַאן דְּמַתְנֵי הָא לָא מַתְנֵי הָא. אִיכָּא דְּאָמְרִי, אָמַר רַב נַחְמָן אָמַר רַב: אֵין הֲלָכָה כְּר' שִׁמְעוֹן בֶּן אֶלְעָזָר, דְּאָמַר רַב יִצְחָק בַּר אַשִׁי אָמַר רַב: אִם טָח פָּנֶיהָ בְּטִיט – בְּטֵלָה וכו'. אָמַר רַב נַחְמָן אָמַר שְׁמוּאֵל: *[ב]שְׁנֵי חֲצָאֵי זֵיתִים וְחוּט שֶׁל בָּצֵק בֵּינֵיהֶן, רוֹאִין: כֹּל שֶׁאִילּוּ יִנָּטֵל הַחוּט וְנִיטָּלִין עִמּוֹ – חַיָּיב לְבַעֵר, וְאִם לָאו – אֵינוֹ חַיָּיב לְבַעֵר. אָמַר עוּלָּא: [ג]לָא אֲמַרַן אֶלָּא בַּעֲרֵיבָה, אֲבָל בְּבַיִת – חַיָּיב לְבַעֵר. מַאי טַעְמָא – דְּזִימְנִין דְּכָנֵישׁ לְהוּ, וְנָפְלֵי גַּבֵּי הֲדָדֵי. אָמַר עוּלָּא, [ד]בָּעוּ בְּמַעַרְבָא: בַּיִת וַעֲלִיָּיה מַהוּ, בַּיִת וְאַכְסַדְרָא מַהוּ, שְׁנֵי בָתִּים זֶה לִפְנִים מִזֶּה מַהוּ? תֵּיקוּ. *ת"ר: [ה]הַפַּת שֶׁעִיפְּשָׁה וְנִפְסְלָה מִלֶּאֱכוֹל לָאָדָם, וְהַכֶּלֶב יָכוֹל לְאוֹכְלָהּ – מְטַמְּאָה טוּמְאַת אוֹכָלִין בִּכְבֵיצָה, וְנִשְׂרֶפֶת עִם הַטְּמֵאָה בַּפֶּסַח. מִשּׁוּם ר' נָתָן אָמְרוּ: אֵינָהּ מְטַמְּאָה. כְּמַאן אָזְלָא הָא דִּתְנַן, *[ו]כְּלָל אָמְרוּ בְּטָהֳרוֹת: כָּל הַמְיוּחָד לְאוֹכֶל אָדָם – טָמֵא עַד שֶׁיִּפָּסֵל מִלֶּאֱכוֹל לַכֶּלֶב. כְּמַאן – דְּלָא כְּר' נָתָן. תָּנוּ רַבָּנַן: *[ז]עֲרֵיבַת הָעַבְּדָנִין שֶׁנָּתַן לְתוֹכָהּ קֶמַח, תּוֹךְ שְׁלֹשָׁה יָמִים – חַיָּיב לְבַעֵר, קוֹדֶם שְׁלֹשָׁה – יָמִים אֵינוֹ חַיָּיב לְבַעֵר. אָמַר ר' נָתָן: בַּמֶּה דְּבָרִים אֲמוּרִים – שֶׁלֹּא נָתַן לְתוֹכָהּ עוֹרוֹת, אֲבָל נָתַן לְתוֹכָהּ עוֹרוֹת – אֲפִילּוּ תּוֹךְ שְׁלֹשָׁה אֵין חַיָּיב לְבַעֵר. אָמַר רָבָא: [ח]הֲלָכָה כְּר' נָתָן, אֲפִילּוּ יוֹם אֶחָד וַאֲפִילּוּ שָׁעָה אַחַת. § "וְכֵן [ט]לְעִנְיַן טוּמְאָה אִם מַקְפִּיד עָלָיו חוֹצֵץ וְאִם רוֹצֶה בְּקִיּוּמוֹ הֲרֵי הוּא כָּעֲרֵיבָה". § מִי דָּמֵי? הָתָם – בְּשִׁיעוּרָא תַּלְיָא מִילְּתָא, הָכָא – בִּקְפֵידָא תַּלְיָא מִילְּתָא. אָמַר רַב יְהוּדָה: אֵימָא וּלְעִנְיַן הַטּוּמְאָה אֵינוֹ כֵּן. א"ל אַבָּיֵי: הָא "וְכֵן לְעִנְיַן טוּמְאָה" קָתָנֵי! אֶלָּא אָמַר אַבָּיֵי: הָכִי קָאָמַר: וְכֵן

לְעִנְיַן

רש"י

אֵינוֹ חוֹצֵץ. אִם נִטְמֵאת וּבָא לְהַטְבִּילָהּ, דְּבָטֵיל לְגַבֵּי עֲרֵיבָה: וְאֵינוֹ עוֹבֵר. לְעִנְיַן חָמֵץ בַּפֶּסַח: בַּמֶּה דְּבָרִים אֲמוּרִים. דִּבְמָקוֹם שֶׁאֵין עָשׂוּי לְחַזֵּק עוֹבֵר בִּכְזַיִת. וְהַיְינוּ כְּלִישָּׁנָא קַמָּא, דְּאוֹקְמָהּ לְמַתְנִי' בְּשֶׁאֵין עָשׂוּי לְחַזֵּק, קָתָנֵי בָּהּ נַמִי הָכִי, דִּבְכַזַּיִת עוֹבֵר, וּבְפָחוֹת מִכַּזַּיִת בָּטֵל. אֲבָל אִי עָשׂוּי לְחַזֵּק – אֲפִילּוּ כַּזַּיִת בָּטֵל: קִילְּתָא מִקַּמֵּי חֲמִירְתָּא. קַמַּיְיתָא, דְּאֵינָהּ מִשְׁנָה: רַב יוֹסֵף אָמַר תַּרְוַיְיהוּ אִיתַּנְהוּ בֵּי מִדְרָשָׁא, וּמִשְׁנָה הֵן, וְתַנָּאֵי נִינְהוּ וּפְלִיגִי בְּהָכִי: תַּנָּאֵי שַׁקַּלְתְּ לָךְ מֵעָלְמָא. דְּלָא מַשְׁכַּחַתְּ תַּנָּאֵי דִּפְלִיגִי בְּהָכִי, דְּקָאָמְרַתְּ "סְמִי", דְּאֵינָהּ מִשְׁנָה: כּוּפַת. מטו"ן: שֶׁיִּחֲדָהּ לִישִׁיבָה גָּרְסִינַן. וְכוּפֶת שֵׁם דָּבָר הוּא. וּבְסֵדֶר טָהֳרוֹת טוּבָא אִיכָּא: כּוּפֶת שֶׁל עֵץ, וְכוּפֶת שֶׁל אֶבֶן: בְּטֵלָה. אַלְמָא: אִיכָּא דִּסְבִירָא לֵיהּ אֲפִי' כַּזַּיִת, מִכִּי מְבַטֵּיל לָהּ – בָּטֵל. וּמַתְנִי' קַמַּיְיתָא דְּקָתָנֵי נַמִי בְּמָקוֹם הֶעָשׂוּי לְחַזֵּק אֲפִילּוּ כַּזַּיִת בָּטֵל – רַבִּי שִׁמְעוֹן בֶּן אֶלְעָזָר הִיא, דְּכֵיוָן דְּאֵינָהּ מְקוּיֶּימֶת לַאֲכִילָה בָּטְלָה: תֵּרַצְתְּ כַּזַּיִת. שֶׁבְּמָקוֹם הֶעָשׂוּי לְחַזֵּק, דְּר"ש הִיא: פָּחוֹת מִכַּזַּיִת. בְּמָקוֹם שֶׁאֵין עָשׂוּי לְחַזֵּק. דְּקָשׁוּ נַמִי אַהֲדָדֵי. דְּקַמַּיְיתָא תָּנֵי אַף בְּמָקוֹם שֶׁאֵין עָשׂוּי לְחַזֵּק אֵין חַיָּיב לְבַעֵר, וּבַתְרַיְיתָא תָּנֵי חַיָּיב בְּמָקוֹם שֶׁאֵין עָשׂוּי לְחַזֵּק מִי קָא תָּרְצַתְּ? הָא לָא שָׁמְעִינַן לֵיהּ לְרַבִּי שִׁמְעוֹן דְּמֵיקֵל אֶלָּא בְּשֶׁאֵינָהּ מְקוּיֶּימֶת לַאֲכִילָה, אֲבָל בִּמְקוּיֶּימֶת לַאֲכִילָה – לָא שָׁמְעִינַן דְּשָׁנֵי לֵיהּ בֵּין כַּזַּיִת לְפָחוֹת מִכַּזַּיִת: אֶלָּא הָא וְהָא רַבִּי שִׁמְעוֹן בֶּן אֶלְעָזָר וְלָא קַשְׁיָא כָּאן בִּמְקוֹם לִישָׁה כָּאן שֶׁלֹּא בִּמְקוֹם לִישָׁה. מַתְנִיתִין בַּתְרַיְיתָא לָא קָרֵי מָקוֹם שֶׁאֵין עָשׂוּי לְחַזֵּק אֶלָּא מָקוֹם שֶׁאֵינוֹ מְקוֹם לִישָׁה כְּלָל, כְּגוֹן שָׂפָה הָעֶלְיוֹנָה. אֲבָל דְּפָנוֹת – קָרֵי מָקוֹם הֶעָשׂוּי לְחַזֵּק. וְקַמַּיְיתָא קָרֵי אַף דְּפָנוֹת מָקוֹם שֶׁאֵין עָשׂוּי לְחַזֵּק, וְאַף עַל גַּב דִּבְמָקוֹם לִישָׁה הוּא. וּמָקוֹם הֶעָשׂוּי לְחַזֵּק – קָרֵי שׁוּלַיִים. וְהָכִי קָאָמַר תַּנָּא קַמָּא: בְּמָקוֹם הֶעָשׂוּי לְחַזֵּק, כְּגוֹן שׁוּלַיִים שֶׁמְּקַבְּלִין אֶת הַמַּיִם – אֲפִילּוּ כַּזַּיִת אֵינוֹ עוֹבֵר. מָקוֹם שֶׁאֵינוֹ עָשׂוּי לְחַזֵּק מַיִם, כְּגוֹן דְּפָנוֹת, דִּמְקוֹם לִישָׁה הוּא וְלָאו מְקוֹם מַיִם – חוֹלֵץ וְעוֹבֵר. וּפָחוֹת מִכַּזַּיִת, אֲפִילּוּ בִּדְפָנוֹת נַמִי אֵינוֹ חוֹלֵץ, דְּכֵיוָן דְּמַהַנֵּי פּוּרְתָּא לְחַזֵּק עִיסָּה כְּשֶׁמְּשַׁפְשְׁפִין וְלָשִׁין שָׁם – בָּטֵיל. וּבְשֶׁלֹּא בִּמְקוֹם לִישָׁה, כְּגוֹן שָׂפָה עֶלְיוֹנָה – לָא אַיְירֵי הַאי תַּנָּא מִידֵּי, וּמוֹדֶה הוּא בָּהּ דַּאֲפִילּוּ פָּחוֹת מִכַּזַּיִת לָא בָּטֵיל בֵּיהּ. וְתַנָּא בַּתְרָא הָכִי קָאָמַר: מָקוֹם הֶעָשׂוּי לְחַזֵּק עִיסָּה, כְּגוֹן דְּפָנוֹת – אֵינוֹ חוֹלֵץ בְּפָחוֹת מִכַּזַּיִת. וְהָכִי נַמִי אָמְרַן בְּקַמַּיְיתָא: מָקוֹם שֶׁאֵין עָשׂוּי לְחַזֵּק, כְּגוֹן שָׂפָה הָעֶלְיוֹנָה חוֹלֵץ, וְאַף עַל גַּב דְּלֵיכָּא כַּזַּיִת, וְהָכִי נַמִי אָמְרַן בְּקַמַּיְיתָא. וְכַזַּיִת אֲפִילּוּ בִּדְפָנוֹת – חוֹלֵץ, וְהָכִי נַמִי תָּנְיָא בְּקַמַּיְיתָא: לָא תֵּימָא שֶׁלֹּא בִּמְקוֹם לִישָׁה. דְּאָמְרַן בֵּיהּ דַּאֲפִילּוּ בְּצִיר מִכַּזַּיִת חוֹלֵץ – הַיְינוּ גַּבָּהּ דַּאֲגָנָא מִבַּחוּץ, אֲבָל שִׂיפְתָּא דַּאֲגָנָא קָרֵי מְקוֹם לִישָׁה, וּבָטֵיל בֵּיהּ פָּחוֹת מִכַּזַּיִת: אֶלָּא שִׂיפְתָּא דַּאֲגָנָא. נַמִי קָרֵי שֶׁלֹּא מְקוֹם לִישָׁה, וְלָא בָּטֵיל בֵּיהּ בְּצִיר מִכַּזַּיִת: כְּלָלָא דְּתַרְוַיְיהוּ תַּנָּאֵי: שָׂפָה עֶלְיוֹנָה – אֲפִילּוּ פָּחוֹת מִכַּזַּיִת עוֹבֵר. שׁוּלַיִים – אֲפִילּוּ כַּזַּיִת אֵינוֹ עוֹבֵר. דְּפָנוֹת, כַּזַּיִת – עוֹבֵר, פָּחוֹת מִכַּזַּיִת – אֵינוֹ עוֹבֵר: זִימְנִין דְּאָטֵיף. פְּעָמִים שֶׁהִיא נָפָה עַל שָׂפָה עֶלְיוֹנָה, וַהֲוֵי מְקוֹם לִישָׁה: כְּרַבִּי שִׁמְעוֹן בֶּן אֶלְעָזָר. דְּכֵיוָן דְּבַטְלָהּ – בָּטְלָה, וַאֲפִילּוּ טוּבָא: טָח פָּנֶיהָ. שֶׁל כּוּפֶת שְׂאוֹר לְתַקְּנָהּ לִישִׁיבָה: מַאן דְּמַתְנֵי הָא. מִשְּׁמֵיהּ דְּרַב לָא מַתְנֵי הָא, וַאֲמוֹרָאֵי נִינְהוּ, וְאַלִּיבָּא דְּרַב: שְׁנֵי חֲצָאֵי זֵיתִים. בִּסְדָקֵי הָעֲרֵיבָה: חַיָּיב לְבַעֵר. דְּחוּט מְצָרְפָן, וַהֲוֵי כַּזַּיִת בְּמָקוֹם אֶחָד. וּבִדְפָנוֹת קָאֵי: לָא אֲמַרַן. דְּאִם אֵין נִיטָּלִין עִמּוֹ אֵינוֹ חַיָּיב לְבַעֵר – אֶלָּא בַּעֲרֵיבָה, דְּקָבִיעֵי בָּהּ: אֲבָל בְּבַיִת. אֲפִילּוּ שְׁנֵי חֲצָאֵי זֵיתִים שֶׁאֵין חוּט מְצָרְפָן חַיָּיב לְבַעֵר: זִימְנִין דְּכָנֵישׁ לְהוּ. מְכַבֵּד הַבַּיִת, וְנָפְלֵי אַהֲדָדֵי: בַּיִת וַעֲלִיָּיה. חֲצִי זַיִת בַּבַּיִת, וַחֲצִי זַיִת בָּעֲלִיָּיה. מִי חָיְישִׁינַן לְכִנּוּשֵׁי, דִּילְמָא כָּנֵישׁ לְהוּ וּמִתְחַבְּרָן, אוֹ לָא. אִם תִּמְצָא לוֹמַר בַּיִת וַעֲלִיָּיה לָא חָיְישִׁינַן, דְּהָא לָא מִקְרֵי דְּאָתֵי נְפוּל נָהֲוֵי מְכוּוָּן כְּנֶגֶד הַפֶּתַח – בַּיִת וְאַכְסַדְרָה מַהוּ? וְאִם תִּמְצָא לוֹמַר בַּיִת וְאַכְסַדְרָה, שֶׁדֶּרֶךְ הָאַכְסַדְרָה נִכְנָסִים וְיוֹצְאִין לַבַּיִת תָּמִיד, וְאֵין מְחִיצּוֹת שְׁלֵימוֹת חוֹלְקוֹת בֵּינֵיהֶם, שֶׁיֵּשׁ חַלּוֹנוֹת וּפְתָחִים לָאַכְסַדְרָה הַרְבֵּה מִכָּל צַד וַהֲוֵי כְּחַד בֵּיתָא, וְחָיְישִׁינַן דְּכָנֵישׁ כִּיבּוּדֵי בַּיִת וְאַכְסַדְרָה: שְׁנֵי בָתִּים זֶה לִפְנִים מִזֶּה. וְנִכְנָסִין לַפְּנִימִי דֶּרֶךְ הַחִיצוֹן, אֲבָל אֵין תַּשְׁמִישָׁן שָׁוֶה תָּדִיר מִזֶּה לָזֶה כְּבַיִת וְאַכְסַדְרָה, מַהוּ? מִי חָיְישִׁינַן דְּכָנֵישׁ כִּיבּוּדֵי בַּיִת זֶה בָּזֶה, אוֹ לָא: וְנִפְסְלָה מִלֶּאֱכוֹל לָאָדָם. וְנִתְקַלְקְלָה בְּעִיפּוּשָׁהּ מִמַּאֲכַל אָדָם: מְטַמְּאָה טוּמְאַת אוֹכָלִין. דְּכָל זְמַן שֶׁהִיא רְאוּיָה לַכֶּלֶב לֹא פָּקַע תּוֹרַת אוֹכֶל מִינָּהּ: וְנִשְׂרֶפֶת עִם הַטְּמֵאָה בַּפֶּסַח. אִם תְּרוּמָה טְהוֹרָה הִיא, דְּכֵיוָן דְּלָא חַזְיָא לְאָדָם מוּתָּר לְטַמְּאָהּ בְּיָדַיִם. וַאֲפִילּוּ לְר' יוֹסֵי, דְּאָמַר בְּפֶרֶק קַמָּא (דף יד.), זוֹ לְעַצְמָהּ וְזוֹ לְעַצְמָהּ: הַמְיוּחָד לְאוֹכֶל אָדָם, וְחָל עָלָיו שֵׁם אוֹכֶל – טָמֵא לְעוֹלָם, וַאֲפִילּוּ נִתְקַלְקֵל מֵאֲכִילַת אָדָם עַד שֶׁיִּפָּסֵל מֵאֲכִילַת כֶּלֶב: הָעַבְּדָנִין. שֶׁנּוֹתְנִין בָּהּ עוֹרוֹת לְעַבֵּד, וְנוֹתְנִין שָׁם קֶמַח: תּוֹךְ שְׁלֹשָׁה יָמִים. לַפֶּסַח. נָתַן קֶמַח לְתוֹכָהּ – עֲדַיִין שֵׁם חָמֵץ עָלֶיהָ, וּכְשֶׁבָּא הַפֶּסַח חַיָּיב לְבַעֵר, וַאֲפִילּוּ הָיוּ בָּהּ עוֹרוֹת: קוֹדֶם שְׁלֹשָׁה יָמִים. כְּבָר נִתְקַלְקְלָה ע"י רֵיחַ הַכְּלִי, וְאַף עַל פִּי שֶׁלֹּא נָתַן לְתוֹכָהּ עוֹרוֹת: רַבִּי נָתָן אוֹמֵר. לֹא נָתַן לְתוֹכָהּ עוֹרוֹת מוֹדֵינָא לָךְ דְּתוֹךְ שְׁלֹשָׁה יָמִים חַיָּיב לְבַעֵר, וְאַחַר שְׁלֹשָׁה יָמִים – לָא, שֶׁנִּתְקַלְקְלָה מֵרֵיחַ הַכְּלִי. אֲבָל נָתַן לְתוֹכָהּ עוֹרוֹת בַּקֶּמַח – בִּיטְּלָהּ מִתּוֹרַת חָמֵץ: אִם מַקְפִּיד עָלָיו. שֶׁעָתִיד לִיטְּלוֹ – חוֹלֵץ, וְאֵין טְבִילָה עוֹלָה לָהּ: בְּקִיּוּמוֹ. שֶׁיִּתְקַיֵּים בִּסְדָקָיו לִסְתּוֹם: מִי דָּמֵי. דְּקָתָנֵי "וְכֵן", הָתָם גַּבֵּי פֶּסַח – בְּשִׁיעוּרָא בְּכַזַּיִת וּבְפָחוֹת מִכַּזַּיִת תַּלְיָא מִילְּתָא. וְהָכָא תַּלְיָא מִילְּתָא בִּקְפֵידָא, לָא שְׁנָא פּוּרְתָּא וְלָא שְׁנָא טוּבָא:

לְעִנְיַן

תוספות

כופת שאור שיחדה לישיבה בטלה. אע"פ שראוי לאכילה, כיון שאין מקיימין אותו לאכילה – בטלה. כמו לענין טומאה, דאמרינן ב"העור והרוטב" (חולין דף קכט.) דבטלה, אע"פ שראוי לאכילה. כדאמרינן התם: בית שסיככו בזרעים – טהרו. וטומאתו לאו דאורייתא. דאי דאורייתא – א"כ מלינו אוכלים דמטמאי טומאה חמורה, ומשני: כשסיכם – מעשה עץ סיכם. משמע דמיירי בראוי לאכילה. ונראה לר"י, דכי היכי דפליגי לענין טומאה בפרק "במה בהמה" (שבת דף נג:) דרבנן סברי דכל הכלים עולין מטומאתם בשינוי מעשה, ורבי יהודה סבר דלא אמרינן שינוי מעשה לתקן אלא לקלקל – הכי נמי פליגי גבי *חמץ: לגבל

רבינו חננאל

שעשוי לחזק שנעשה כעץ אבל כזית אפילו במקום העשוי לחזק אסור וחייב לבער וכן במקום שאין עשוי לחזק אפי' כל שהוא אסור. תניא כלישנא קמא תניא כלישנא בתרא קשיין אהדדי אמר רב הונא סמי קמייתא דקילתא היא מקמי בתרייתא דהיא חמירתא ורב יוסף אמר תנאי היא דתניא פת שעפשה חייב לבער מפני שיכול לשוחקה ולחמץ בה כמה עיסות אחרות ר' שמעון בן אלעזר אומר בד"א במקויימת לאכילה אבל כופת שאור וייחדה לישיבה בטלה מכלל דת"ק סבר כל זית כזית אע"ג דמבטל ליה לא בטל*) דת"ק סבר כל כזית דתניא כלישנא קמא. אמר ליה אביי לרב יוסף שנית כזית פחות מכזית מאי אלא הא והא ר' שמעון הא דתניא כזית במקום העשוי לחזק חוצץ ועובר במקום לישה אבל פחות מכזית לא והתניא כזית במקום העשוי לחזק אינו חוצץ ואינו עובר שלא במקום לישה וכל שכן פחות מכזית שאפי' במקום שאין עשוי לחזק אינו עובר: **אמר** רב אשי לא תימא שלא במקום לישה אחורי אגנא כגון ספל שלשין בה אלא על שפת אגנא הוא שלא במקום לישה ומדחזי' רב אשי דפשיט שינויא דאביי ש"מ דהילכתא כותיה: **אמרי** משמיה דרב הלכה כר' שמעון בכופת שאור והוא דטח פניה בטיט: **שני** חצאי זיתים חמץ וחוט של בצק ביניהן רואין כל שאלו ינטל החוט ניטלין עמו כלומר חוט זה עב וחזק הוא חייב לבער מוקמינן לה [דמיירי] במקום העשוי לחזק (אפילו) ובמקום לישה דפחות מכזית אינו עובר אבל כזית עובר ואם החוט מצרפן נמצא כזית במקום אחד וחייב. אמר עולא לא אמרו אם ניטלין עם החוט אלא בעריבה אבל בבית אפי' אין ביניהם חוט חייב לבער מאי טעמא זמנין דכניש ונפלי אהדדי והוו להו כזית במקום אחד: **איבעי'** להו בית ועלייה בית ואכסדרה שני בתים זה לפנים מזה מהו ועלו בתיקו וכל תיקו דאיסורא לחומרא: **ת"ר** פת שעפשה ונפסלה מלאכל אדם והכלב יכול לאכלה מטמאה טמאת אוכלין בכביצה ונשרפת עם הטמאה בפסח. משום רבי נתן אמרו אין מטמאה וקיימא לן כת"ק דתנן כוותיה. כלל אמרו (בנותרות) [בטהרות] כל המיוחד לאכל אדם טמא עד שיפסל מלאכל הכלב: **ת"ר** עריבת העבדנין שנתן לתוכה קמח בשנים עשר או בשלשה עשר לניסן חייב לבער באחד עשר אין חייב לבער וכ"ש מקדם בד"א שלא נתן לתוכו עורות אבל נתן לתוכו עורות אפי' שעה אחת אינו חייב לבער וכן הלכה: **תוספתא** הקילור והאספלנית והרטיה שנתן לתוכן קמח אין צריך לבער מלוגמא שנסרחה אין צריך לבער: **וכן** לענין הטומאה אם בצק זה שבעריבה מקפיד עליו לקלפו חוצץ ולא עלתה לו טבילה ואם רוצה בקיומו כדי להיות הסדק סתום הרי הוא כעריבה ואינו חוצץ ואקשינן וכן לענין הטומאה מכלל שדין זה כדין זה והא בפסח בשיעור כזית חייב ובטומאה בקפידא תליא מילתא ואינו דומה זה לזה ואמר אביי וכן לענין

צירוף

*) נראה דל"ל דסב"ל כלישנא בתרא ות"ק דסבר דכל כזית לא בטיל היינו כלישנא קמא.

עין משפט נר מצוה

יח א מיי' שם הל' ט' טוש"ע שם סעיף יא:

יט ב ג ד מיי' שם הל' טז טוש"ע שם סעיף ח:

כ ה שם ס"ב וסעיף ט:

כא ו מיי' פ"ב מהל' טומאת אוכלין הלכה יט:

כב ז ח מיי' פ"ד מהל' חמץ הל' ט סמג עשין לט טוש"ע א"ח סי' תמב סעיף א:

כג ט מיי' פ"א מהל' מקוואות הלכה יב סמג עשין רמח:

[וע"ע תוספות סנהדרין סח. ד"ה נתנו]

מסורת הש"ס

[שבת נג: עירובין לז: כולה יט. סנהדרין סח.]

[חולין קכט.]

[תוספ' פ"ג]

לעיל טו:

טהרות פ"ח [מ"ו]

[כריתות כח.] [תוספ' פ"ג]

כד א מיי' פ"כ מהל' כלים הלכה ט:
כה ב מיי' פ"ה מהל' חמץ הלכה יג סמג לאוין עה טוש"ע או"ח סי' תנט סעיף ב:
כו ג מיי' פ"ח מהל' ביכורים הל' יא:
[נ"ל רב חסדא]
כז ד מיי' פ"א מהל' שאר אבות הטומאה הלכה ט:
כח ה מיי' פ"ד מהל' תפלה הלכה ב סמג עשין יט טוש"ע או"ח סי' צב סעיף ד וסימן קסג סעיף א:
כט ו מיי' פ"ג מהלכות י"ט הלכה ט סמג לאוין עה עט טוש"ע או"ח סי' תנז סעיף ב וסי' תקו סעיף ד:

לְעִנְיַן צֵירוּף טוּמְאָה בַּפֶּסַח. וּבִשְׁאָר יְמוֹת הַשָּׁנָה אִיכָּא פְּלוּגְתָּא. הֵיכִי דָמֵי? כְּגוֹן *דְּאִיכָּא פָּחוֹת מִכַּבֵּיצָה אוֹכָלִין, וְנָגְעוּ בְּהַאי בָּצֵק. בַּפֶּסַח דְּאִיסּוּרוֹ חָשׁוּב — מִצְטָרֵף, בִּשְׁאָר יְמוֹת הַשָּׁנָה, דִּבְקְפֵידָא תַּלְיָא מִילְּתָא, אִם מַקְפִּיד עָלָיו — מִצְטָרֵף, אִם רוֹצֶה בְּקִיּוּמוֹ — הֲרֵי הוּא כָּעֲרֵיבָה. מַתְקִיף לָהּ רָבָא: מִי קָתָנֵי מִצְטָרֵף? וְהָא חוֹצֵץ קָתָנֵי! אֶלָּא אָמַר רָבָא: וְכֵן לְהַעֲלוֹת טָהֳרָה לָעֲרֵיבָה. הֵיכִי דָמֵי — כְּגוֹן דְּאִיטְמִי הַךְ עֲרֵיבָה, וּבָעֵי לְאַטְבּוּלֵי. בַּפֶּסַח דְּאִיסּוּרוֹ חָשׁוּב — חוֹצֵץ, וְלָא סָלְקָא לָהּ טְבִילָה. בִּשְׁאָר יְמוֹת הַשָּׁנָה בִּקְפֵידָא תַּלְיָא מִילְּתָא, אִי מַקְפִּיד עָלָיו — חוֹצֵץ, וְאִם רוֹצֶה בְּקִיּוּמוֹ — הֲרֵי הוּא כָּעֲרֵיבָה. מַתְקִיף לָהּ רַב פָּפָּא: מִי קָתָנֵי "וְכֵן לְעִנְיַן טָהֳרָה"? הָא לְעִנְיַן טוּמְאָה קָתָנֵי! אֶלָּא אָמַר רַב פָּפָּא: וְכֵן לְעִנְיַן לְהוֹרִיד טוּמְאָה לָעֲרֵיבָה. הֵיכִי דָמֵי — א כְּגוֹן דְּנָגַע שֶׁרֶץ בְּהַאי בָּצֵק. בַּפֶּסַח, דְּאִיסּוּרוֹ חָשׁוּב — חוֹצֵץ, וְלֹא נָחֲתָה לָהּ טוּמְאָה. בִּשְׁאָר יְמוֹת הַשָּׁנָה, דִּבְקְפֵידָא תַּלְיָא, אִם מַקְפִּיד עָלָיו — חוֹצֵץ, אִם רוֹצֶה בְּקִיּוּמוֹ — הֲרֵי הוּא כָּעֲרֵיבָה.§

מתני' ב בְּצֵק הַחֵרֵשׁ, אִם יֵשׁ כַּיּוֹצֵא בּוֹ שֶׁהֶחְמִיץ — הֲרֵי זֶה אָסוּר.§ **גמ'** אִם אֵין שָׁם כַּיּוֹצֵא בּוֹ מַהוּ? א"ר אַבָּהוּ אָמַר ר' שִׁמְעוֹן בֶּן לָקִישׁ: כְּדֵי שֶׁיֵּלֵךְ אָדָם מִמִּגְדַּל נוּנַיָּא לִטְבֶרְיָא, מִיל. *וְנֵימָא מִיל! הָא קמ"ל דְּשִׁיעוּרָא דְּמִיל כְּמִמִּגְדַּל נוּנַיָּא וְעַד טְבֶרְיָא. *א"ר אַבָּהוּ אָמַר רַבִּי שִׁמְעוֹן בֶּן לָקִישׁ: ג לַגַּבָּל וְלַתְּפִלָּה וְלִנְטִילַת יָדַיִם — אַרְבָּעָה מִילִין. אָמַר רַב נַחְמָן בַּר יִצְחָק: אַיְיבוּ אֲמָרָהּ, וְאַרְבָּעָה אָמַר בָּהּ, וַחֲדָא מִינַּיְיהוּ עִבּוּד. דִּתְנַן: *ד וְכוּלָּן שֶׁעִיבְּדָן אוֹ שֶׁהִילֵּךְ בָּהֶן כְּדֵי עֲבוֹדָה — טְהוֹרִין, חוּץ מֵעוֹר הָאָדָם. וְכַמָּה כְּדֵי עֲבוֹדָה? א"ר (אִינְיָיא) א"ר יַנַּאי: כְּדֵי הִילּוּךְ אַרְבָּעָה מִילִין. א"ר יוֹסֵי בְּרַבִּי חֲנִינָא: *ה לֹא שָׁנוּ אֶלָּא לְפָנָיו, אֲבָל לְאַחֲרָיו — אֲפִילּוּ מִיל אֵינוֹ חוֹזֵר. אָמַר רַב אַחָא: וּמִינָּהּ, מִיל הוּא דְּאֵינוֹ חוֹזֵר, הָא פָּחוֹת מִמִּיל — חוֹזֵר.§

מתני' כֵּיצַד מַפְרִישִׁין חַלָּה בְּטוּמְאָה בְּיו"ט? ו ר"א אוֹמֵר: לֹא תִּקְרָא לָהּ שֵׁם עַד שֶׁתֵּאָפֶה. בֶּן בְּתֵירָא אוֹמֵר: תַּטִּיל בְּצוֹנֵן. א"ר יְהוֹשֻׁעַ:
לא

לְעִנְיַן צֵירוּף טוּמְאָה. כִּדְמְפָרֵשׁ וְאָזֵיל, דְּבַפֶּסַח תַּלְיָא מִילְּתָא בְּשִׁיעוּרֵיהּ: **וּבִשְׁאָר יְמוֹת הַשָּׁנָה אִיכָּא פְּלוּגְתָּא.** חִילּוּק בֵּין מַקְפִּיד לְשֶׁאֵינוֹ מַקְפִּיד, וְהַיְינוּ דְּתָנָא סֵיפָא: אִם מַקְפִּיד עָלָיו: **דְּאִיכָּא פָּחוֹת מִכַּבֵּיצָה אוֹכָלִין דְּנָגְעוּ בְּהַאי בָּצֵק.** הַדָּבוּק בָּעֲרֵיבָה, וְנָגְעָה בָּהֶן טוּמְאָה וְאִיטַּמּוּ, וַהֲדַר נָגְעוּ בָּהֶן אוֹכָלִים טְהוֹרִים: **בַּפֶּסַח.** דְּאִיסּוּר חָמֵץ מַחֲשִׁבוֹ, וְעוֹשֵׂהוּ חָשׁוּב. הוֹאִיל וְכַזַּיִת הוּזְכַּר לְהֵיחָשֵׁב לְעִנְיַן אִיסּוּר חָמֵץ, דְּלָא בָּטֵיל לְגַבֵּי עֲרֵיבָה כִּדְתַנְיָא רֵישָׁא — הַשְׁתָּא לְעִנְיַן טוּמְאָה נָמֵי לָא בָּטֵיל לְגַבֵּי עֲרֵיבָה, וּמִצְטָרֵף לְהַשְׁלִים לְכַבֵּיצָה, וְאַע"ג דְּאֵין מַקְפִּיד עָלָיו, וּמְטַמֵּא אֶת אֲחֵרִים: **בִּשְׁאָר יְמוֹת הַשָּׁנָה.** דְּלֵיכָּא לְמֵימַר אִיסּוּרוֹ אִישּׁוּבוֹ — בִּקְפֵידָא תַּלְיָא מִילְּתָא. אִם מַקְפִּיד עָלָיו — מִצְטָרֵף, דַּחֲשִׁיב אוֹכְלָא, הוֹאִיל וְסוֹפוֹ לִיטְּלוֹ: **וְכֵן לְהַעֲלוֹת לָהּ טָהֳרָה לָעֲרֵיבָה.** תַּלְיָא נָמֵי בְּשִׁיעוּרָא וְלָאו שִׁיעוּרָא בַּפֶּסַח. וְאִם מַקְפִּיד עָלָיו — קָאֵי אַשְּׁאָר יְמוֹת הַשָּׁנָה. כְּגוֹן דְּאִיטַּמִּי וְקָא מַטְבִּיל לָהּ, וְקָאָמַר דְּבַפֶּסַח, הוֹאִיל וּבְכַזַּיִת עוֹבֵר עֲלֵיהּ. וּבַדְּפָנוֹת אִיסּוּרוֹ אִישּׁוּבוֹ, דְּעַל כָּרְחוֹ צָרִיךְ לִיטְּלוֹ וְחָיֵיץ, דְּלָא הָוֵי כָּעֲרֵיבָה וַאֲפִי' אֵינוֹ מַקְפִּיד עָלָיו (א): **אֲבָל בִּשְׁאָר יְמוֹת הַשָּׁנָה.** בֵּין מְרוּבֶּה בֵּין מוּעָט, בִּקְפֵידָא תַּלְיָא מִילְּתָא: **וְכֵן לְהוֹרִיד טוּמְאָה לָעֲרֵיבָה.** עַל יְדֵי בָּצֵק זֶה תַּלְיָא נָמֵי בִּימוֹת הַפֶּסַח בְּשִׁיעוּרָא וְלָאו שִׁיעוּרָא, וְאִם מַקְפִּיד עָלָיו — אַשְּׁאָר יְמוֹת הַשָּׁנָה קָאֵי: ה"ג: וְהֵיכִי דָמֵי כְּגוֹן דְּנָגַע שֶׁרֶץ בְּהַאי בָּצֵק: **בַּפֶּסַח.** דְּכַזַּיִת אִיסּוּרוֹ אִישּׁוּבוֹ — חָיֵיץ, וְלָא הָוֵי כָּעֲרֵיבָה, וְלָא נָחֲתָא לָהּ שׁוּם טוּמְאָה לָעֲרֵיבָה וַאֲפִילּוּ אֵין מַקְפִּיד עָלָיו. וּבְפָחוֹת מִכַּזַּיִת, כִּי אֵינוֹ מַקְפִּיד עָלָיו — לָא (ב): **וּבִשְׁאָר יְמוֹת הַשָּׁנָה.** אִם מַקְפִּיד עָלָיו, אֲפִילּוּ בְּפָחוֹת מִכַּזַּיִת חוֹצֵץ: **וְאִם רוֹצֶה הוּא בְּקִיּוּמוֹ הֲרֵי הוּא כָּעֲרֵיבָה.** וְהָוֵי כְּאִילּוּ נָגַע שֶׁרֶץ בָּעֲרֵיבָה מַמָּשׁ: **מתני' בְּצֵק הַחֵרֵשׁ.** שֶׁאֵין נִיכָּר אִם הֶחְמִיץ אִם לָאו, שֶׁמְּשׁוּלֶּה הוּא כְּחֵרֵשׁ הַזֶּה שֶׁיֵּשׁ לוֹ אָזְנַיִם וְאֵינוֹ נִיכָּר אִם שׁוֹמֵעַ אִם לָאו, דְּאֵין אָדָם עוֹמֵד עַל בֵּירוּרוֹ וְעַל דַּעְתּוֹ. לִישָּׁנָא אַחֲרִינָא: בָּצֵק הַחֵרֵשׁ — קָשֶׁה כְּחֶרֶס, וְאֵינוֹ נִיכָּר שֶׁהֶחְמִיץ. ר"ל: הִכְסִיפוּ פָּנָיו, וְאֵין סִידּוּק לְסִימָן הַחִימּוּץ: **אִם יֵשׁ כַּיּוֹצֵא בוֹ שֶׁהֶחְמִיץ.** אִם יֵשׁ עִיסָּה אַחֶרֶת שֶׁנִּילּוֹשָׁה בְּשַׁעְתָּהּ וּכְבָר הֶחְמִיצָה: **גמ' מִמִּגְדַּל נוּנַיָּא לִטְבֶרְיָא.** דְּהַיְינוּ מִיל: **לַגַּבָּל וְלַתְּפִלָּה כו'.** מִשּׁוּם דְּרַבִּי אַבָּהוּ אֲמַר רֵישׁ לָקִישׁ נָקַט לָהּ: **לַגַּבָּל.** הַמְגַבֵּל עִיסַּת אֲחֵרִים בְּשָׂכָר, וּכְלֵי בַּעַל הַבַּיִת טְמֵאִים — עַד אַרְבַּע מִילִין הִטְרִיחוּהוּ חֲכָמִים לֵילֵךְ לַמִּקְוֶה לִטְבּוֹל כֵּלָיו. וְכֵן לַתְּפִלָּה, אִם מְהַלֵּךְ אָדָם בַּדֶּרֶךְ וּבָא עֵת לָלוּן וּלְהִתְפַּלֵּל, אִם יֵשׁ בֵּית הַכְּנֶסֶת לְפָנָיו בְּרִחוּק אַרְבַּע מִילִין — הוֹלֵךְ וּמִתְפַּלֵּל שָׁם, וְלָן שָׁם. וְכֵן לִנְטִילַת יָדַיִם לַאֲכִילָה, אִם עָתִיד לִמְצוֹא מַיִם לְפָנָיו בְּד' מִילִין — הוֹלֵךְ לְשָׁם וְנוֹטֵל אֶת יָדָיו: **ר' אַיְיבוּ אֲמָרָהּ.** לְהָא מִילְּתָא מִשְּׁמֵיהּ דְּרֵישׁ לָקִישׁ, וְלָא ר' אַבָּהוּ אֲמָרָהּ: **וְאַרְבָּעָה מִילֵּי אָמַר בָּהּ.** לְשִׁיעוּר אַרְבַּע מִילִין, הַיְינוּ תְּלָת וַחֲדָא מוֹסִיף (ג): **וּמַאי הִיא עִבּוּד.** שִׁיעוּר עִבּוּד שֶׁל עוֹר רַךְ הַמְטַמֵּא כְּבָשָׂר, כְּגוֹן הָנָךְ דְּחָשֵׁיב בְּ"הָעוֹר וְהָרוֹטֶב" — אַרְבַּע מִילִין הוּא, לְבַטְּלוֹ מִתּוֹרַת בָּשָׂר מֵחֲמַת עִיבּוּדוֹ: **כּוּלָּן.** כָּל אֵלּוּ שֶׁמָּנוּ חֲכָמִים בְּ"הָעוֹר וְהָרוֹטֶב" שֶׁעוֹרוֹתֵיהֶן מְטַמְּאִין כִּבְשָׂרָן, מִפְּנֵי שֶׁהוּא רַךְ וְדַרְכּוֹ לֶאֱכוֹל: **שֶׁהִילֵּךְ בָּהֶן.** דֶּרֶךְ עוֹרוֹת לְשׁוֹטְחָן לִפְנֵי דְּרִיסַת רַגְלֵי אָדָם, וְזֶהוּ תְּחִילַּת עִיבּוּדָן: **אֶלָּא לְפָנָיו.** הַנְּטִילַת יָדַיִם וְהַתְּפִלָּה דִּמְהַלֵּךְ בַּדֶּרֶךְ קָאֵי, דְּאִילּוּ גַּבָּל — יֵלֵךְ עַד ד' מִילִין, דְּמָה יֵשׁ לוֹ לְהַפְסִיד? וּמִינָּהּ. מֵהָא דְּר' יוֹסֵי בַּר חֲנִינָא, דְּאָמַר בְּהֶדְיָא: אֲפִי' מִיל אֵינוֹ חוֹזֵר — דַּוְקָא מִיל קָאָמַר, הָא פָּחוֹת מִמִּיל — חוֹזֵר: **מתני' כֵּיצַד מַפְרִישִׁין חַלָּה בְּטוּמְאָה.** שֶׁנִּטְמֵאת הָעִיסָּה, וְשׁוּב אֵין חַלָּה הַנִּיטֶּלֶת מִמֶּנָּה רְאוּיָה לַאֲכִילַת כֹּהֵן. כֵּיצַד מַפְרִישִׁין אוֹתָהּ בְּיוֹם טוֹב שֶׁל פֶּסַח? הֲרֵי אֵין יָכוֹל לְאֶפּוֹתָהּ — מֵאַחַר שֶׁאֵינָהּ רְאוּיָה לַאֲכִילָה. וּלְשֶׁהוֹתָהּ לְשׁוֹרְפָהּ לָעֶרֶב — אִי אֶפְשָׁר, שֶׁלֹּא תַּחְמִיץ. וּלְשׁוֹרְפָהּ אוֹ לְהַאֲכִילָהּ לִכְלָבִים — אִי אֶפְשָׁר, שֶׁאֵין שׂוֹרְפִין קָדָשִׁים בְּיוֹם טוֹב: **רַבִּי אֱלִיעֶזֶר אוֹמֵר לֹא תִקְרָא לָהּ שֵׁם.** חַלָּה: **עַד שֶׁתֵּאָפֶה.** תְּחִלָּה. דְּאַכַּתִּי כָּל חֲדָא וַחֲדָא חַזְיָא לֵיהּ, דְּמַפְרִישׁ מִכָּל חֲדָא פּוּרְתָּא. וּלְאַחַר אֲפִיָּיה אִם רָצָה — יַפְרִישׁ חַלָּה שְׁלֵימָה עַל כּוּלָּן, כִּדְתַנְיָא בַּגְּמָרָא, דְּקָסָבַר רַבִּי אֱלִיעֶזֶר: הַסַּל שֶׁהוּא רוֹדֶה מִן הַתַּנּוּר לְתוֹכוֹ, מְצָרְפוֹ לְחַלָּה:
לא

לגבל. פי' בערוך: דבאדם המהלך בדרך איירי, דומיא דתפלה, דאם יש גבל העושה עיסתו בטהרה ברחוק ד' מילין — ימתין עד שיגיע לאותו גבל. והשתא א"ש, דלא שנו אלא לפניו — קאי אכולהו: **ולתפלה.** נראה כפירוש הקונטרס, ולא כערוך דפירש: "לתפלה", היינו לרחוץ ידיו להתפלל. דהיכי דמי? אי בעידנא דצלותא — הא אמרינן בברכות (דף טו.): (*אביי) לייט אמאן דמהדר אמיא בעידן צלותא, דכתיב "ארחץ בנקיון כפי". ואי שלא בזמן תפלה — מאי איריא ד' מילין? אפי' טובא נמי! **לא** תקרא לה שם עד שתאפה. שאם היה (ד) קורא לה שם — לא היה יכול לאפותה ולא לשורפה, דאין שורפין קדשים ביו"ט, כדיליף ב"במה מדליקין" (שבת כד:) והיינו נמי טעמא הא דתנן התם: אין מדליקין בשמן שריפה ביו"ט. ותימה: בשלמא פסול קודש אין שורפין ביו"ט — שאין יכול להנות ממנה בשעת שריפה, אבל תרומה טמאה, שיכול להנות ממנה בשעת שריפה אמאי אין שורפים? כמו שמותר להדליק בשמן של חולין להנאתו — כך ישרוף תרומה טמאה להנאתו. וכי מפני שמצוה לשרוף מיגרע גרע? ותירץ ריב"א: דשמן של חולין מותר להדליק להנאתו, כמו שמותר לאכול. אבל תרומה טמאה, דאסורה בכל ההנאות — נמצא שהבערה אינה להנאה, אלא לשם מצות שריפה. אלא שהתורה לא הקפידה אם יהנה ממנה בשעת שריפה. לכך אין דוחה יו"ט, כשאר שריפת קדשים. מידי דהוי אנדרים ונדבות, למ"ד אין קרבים ביו"ט (ביצה דף יט.) אע"פ שיש בהן היתר לאכילת אדם, כיון דעיקרו לגבוה, וכהנים משולחן גבוה קזכו — אסור לשוחטן. ולמ"ד קרבים, קסבר: עיקר שחיטה לצורך אדם. אבל שריפת תרומה טמאה אינה לשם הנאה, מדאסר כל שאר הנאות, אלא ודאי לשם מצות ביעור הוא. ור"י פי': דודאי מותר לשרוף ביו"ט תרומה לצורך אוכל נפש, דלא שייך למימר משולחן גבוה קא זכו, אלא דגזרינן לצורך אטו שלא לצורך, דשלא לצורך אסור מן התורה, דגמרינן מקדשים שאין שורפין ביו"ט*: **עד** שתאפה. אומר ר"י: אנן שרינן לקרות לה שם קודם אפייה, אע"ג דפסקינן כר"א. דהא אי איכא כהן קטן — חזיא ליה, כדאמר בפרק "עד כמה" (בכורות כז.): אין תרומת ח"ל אסורה אלא למי שטומאה יוצאה עליו מגופו. וכן פסק בה"ג בסדר פסח בשם רב כהן לדק ריש מתיבתא. ואפי' ליכא כהן קטן, אי איכא כהן גדול — שרי, דחזיא ליה ע"י ביטול ברוב, כדאמר התם: רבה מבטל לה ברוב ואכיל לה בימי טומאה. וא"ת: ואמאי לא שרינן לאפות חלה טמאה מטעם דאמר (ר"א בר' שמעון) בפ"ב דביצה (דף יז.): אף ממלאה אשה תנור פת, אע"פ שאינה צריכה אלא לככר אחד מפני שהפת נאפה יפה כשהתנור מלא. ואמר (רבה) התם הלכה *כר"א ברבי שמעון. ואפילו נאמר דאסור לאפות מפני שאסור לטלטלה — מכל מקום כי לא קרא לה שם אמאי צריך לטעמא דהואיל? ואור"י: דטעמא [דאמרינן] בביצה לא שייך אלא בתנור, אבל כשאופה תחת גחלים — לא: **תטיל** בצונן. אור"י: דר"א ורבי יהושע לא פליגי אבן בתירא שלא תועיל הטלה לצונן, והיכא שאירע שקרא לה שם — אור"ת: תטיל בצונן:
הואיל

[עי' תוס' שבת לא. ד"ה אי לענין טומאה]
[מגילה כ:]
חולין קכב:
שם נדה נה.
[נ"ל איבו]
ברכות טו. חולין קכב.
[ועי' תוס' שבת כד: ד"ה לפי ותוס' ביצה כז: ד"ה ועל החלה]
[נ"ל שמעון בן אלעזר]
[נ"ל רבה]
נ"ל כר"ש בן אלעזר

הגהות הב"ח
(א) רש"י ד"ה וכן להעלות וד"ה אבל הד"א: (ב) ד"ה בפסח וד"ה ובשאר הד"א: (ג) ד"ה וארבעה וד"ה ומאי הד"א: (ד) תוס' ד"ה לא תקרא וכו' שאם היתה קורא לה שם לא היתה יכולה לאפותה וכו' ולכך אין דוחה:

גליון הש"ס
גמרא כגון דאיכא פחות מכביצה. עיין שבת לא ע"א תד"ה אי לענין: **שם** הא קמ"ל דשיעורא דמיל. עיין טורי אבן מגילה כ ע"ב ד"ה הא קמ"ל:

רבינו חננאל
צירוף טומאה וכי קתני לענין טומאה בפסח ובשאר ימות השנה איכא פלוגתא כיצד כגון דאיכא פחות מכביצה אוכלין בהאי עריכה ואית בה כזית בצק ונגעו בה בפסח דאיסורא חשוב להאי בצק ולמשקליה קאי מצטרף ואי נגעה בה טומאה איטמי אבל בשאר ימות השנה אם מקפיד עליו ובעי למשקליה מצטרף ואי לא לא אלא הרי הוא כעריבה דלא מצטרף ודחי רבא אי הכי מצטרף מיבעי ליה למתני במתני' אלא הכי קתני וכן להעלות טהרה לעריבה כגון שזו העריבה טמאה היא והטבילה ונמצא בה בצק בסדקיה בפסח דאיסורא חושבו וחייב לבערו חוצץ ולא עלתה לה טבילה בשאר ימות השנה אם רוצה בקיומו הרי בצק זה כעריבה ועלתה לו טבילה ואינו חוצץ ואוקמה רב פפא הכי וכן לענין טומאה להוריד טומאה לעריבה היכי דמי כגון דדביק בצק בהאי עריבה ונגע שרץ בבצק בפסח דחייב לבערו לאו כגופה דעריבה דמי ולא נטמאת העריבה בשאר ימות השנה אי מקפיד לקלפו ולא נחתה לה טומאה לעריבה ואם רוצה בקיומו הרי הוא כעריבה וכאלו נגע השרץ [בעריבה] ונטמאת: **בצק** החרש אם כיוצא בו שהחמיץ. כלומר אם יש מי שלש בבת אחת עמו והחמיץ אותו הבצק גם זה אסור שחמץ הוא ואע"פ שהוא חרש ואין אדם יכול להרגיש בו אין שם כיוצא בו אם שהה משעה שגמר הלישה כשעור הליכת מיל אסור שודאי החמיץ: **אמר** ר' אבהו אמר ריש לקיש לגבל כגון שיש לפניו המגבל בטהרה ולתפלה כגון שצריך להתפלל ויש לפניו מים ליטול ידיו ולנטילת ידים רוצה לאכל ואין לו מים ליטול ידיו ארבעת מילין פי' אם יש גבל העושה עיסתו בטהרה או אם יש מים ברחוק ארבעת מילין לפניו ימתין עד שיגיע לגבל ההוא שעושה בטהרה ויעשה לו עיסתו בטהר' וכן לא יתפלל ולא יאכל עד שיגיע למים ויטול ידיו: **והני** מילי דבעינן ד' מילין לפניו אבל לאחריו אפי' מיל אחד אין מטריחין אותו לחזור אלא עושה עיסתו במה שמזדמן לו ומקנה ידיו ומתפלל גם אוכל בבלאי חמתות בלא נטילה. וכן עבודת העור בהלוך ארבעת מילין נקרא עבודה ונטהר העבודת העור בהלוך מפורש בפרק העור והרוטב (דף קכב) **מתני'** כיצד מפרישין חלה בטומאה

לא זה הוא חמץ שמוזהרין עליו בבל יראה ובבל ימצא. אלא, מפרישתה ומניחתה עד הערב, ואם החמיצה – החמיצה.§ גמ' *לימא בטובת הנאה קמיפלגי, דר' אליעזר סבר: טובת הנאה ממון, ור' יהושע סבר: טובת הנאה אינה ממון. לא, דכולי עלמא סברי "טובת הנאה אינה ממון" והכא ב"הואיל" קמיפלגי. [א] דר' אליעזר סבר: אמרינן הואיל ואי בעי איתשיל עלה – ממוניה הוא. ור' יהושע סבר: לא אמרינן הואיל. *איתמר, האופה מיום טוב לחול, רב חסדא אמר: לוקה, רבה אמר: א אינו לוקה. רב חסדא אמר: לוקה, לא אמרינן "הואיל ומיקלעי ליה אורחים חזי ליה". רבה אמר: אינו לוקה, אמרינן הואיל. אמר ליה רבה לרב חסדא: לדידך, דאמרת לא אמרינן הואיל – היאך אופין מיום טוב לשבת? א"ל: משום עירובי תבשילין. ומשום עירובי תבשילין שרינן איסורא דאורייתא? אמר ליה: ב מדאורייתא צורכי שבת נעשין בי"ט, ורבנן הוא דגזרו ביה, גזירה שמא יאמרו אופין מי"ט אף לחול. וכיון דאצרכוה רבנן עירובי תבשילין – אית ליה היכירא. איתיביה: *ג בהמה המסוכנת לא ישחוט אלא כדי שיכול לאכול הימנה כזית צלי מבעוד יום. יכול לאכול – אע"ג דלא בעי למיכל. בשלמא לדידי, דאמרי "הואיל" – הואיל ואי בעי למיכל מצי אכיל – משום הכי ישחוט. אלא לדידך, דאמרת לא אמרינן "הואיל" – אמאי ישחוט? אמר ליה: משום הפסד ממונו. ומשום הפסד ממונו שרינן איסורא דאורייתא?! אמר ליה: אין, משום הפסד ממונו גמר בלבו לאכול כזית, ואי אפשר לכזית בשר בלא שחיטה. איתיביה: לחם הפנים נאכל

רש"י

לא זהו חמץ שמוזהרין עליו. כדמפרש בגמ', דלאו דידיה הוא לאחר שקרא עליה שם. וקרא כתיב, שלך אי אתה רואה, וזה אינו שלך ולא של חבירך, דאכתי לא מטא ליד כהן: גמ' טובת הנאה. דבר מועט, דתניא (בכורות דף כז.): רשאי ישראל לומר לחבירו הילך סלע ותן כל תרומותיך לבן בתי כהן. והיינו טובת הנאה שיש לו לישראל בחלה זו, שרשאי לתתה לכל כהן שירצה וליטול דבר מועט מאוהבו של כהן בשביל שיתנה לו. ר' אליעזר סבר: טובת הנאה ממון, והויא הך חלה כדידיה, ועבר עלה אי מחמיצה גביה. הלכך: אפי לה ברישא. ור' יהושע סבר: טובת הנאה אינה ממון, ולאו דידיה הוא, ואינו מוזהר עליה. ומשום פקדון נמי ליכא, דאכתי לא מטא לידא דכהן: לא דכולי עלמא טובת הנאה אינה ממון ובהואיל קא מיפלגי. ר' אליעזר סבר: עבר עליה משום הואיל ואי בעי מיתשיל עלה והדרה לטיבלא, ודידיה היא. דעל כל נדר והקדש ותרומה הקדוש באמירת פה – יכול לישאל לחכם ולעקור דבורו. הלכך ממוניה הוא, ועבר עליה. ומלאכת אפייתה נמי בי"ט כי לא קרא עליה שם. ואע"ג דאיכא חדא דלא חזיא – משתריא, דכל חדא וחדא איכא למימר הא לאו חלה היא. ואי נמי קרא עליה שם – מצי למיפא לה, הואיל ואי בעי מיתשיל עלה. מיהו, כיון דאית (א) לר"א הסל מצרפן לחלה – הכי שפיר טפי שתאפה תחלה משום רווחא דמילתא, וכל כמה דאפשר למיעבד שפיר בלא שום הואיל – ניחא למיעבד: לא אמרינן הואיל. הלכך על חימוצה אינו עובר, אבל על אפייתה עובר – דאיכא חדא דלא חזיא ליה: האופה מי"ט לחול. לאחר שאכל וגמר סעודתו, דפשיטא לן דלא חזיא ליה מידי האידנא עד אורתא שהוא חול: לוקה. משום "לא תעשה כל מלאכה": הואיל ואי מיקלעי ליה אורחין. שיהו צריכין לפת זה היום: היאך אופין מי"ט לשבת. אי לאו דאמרי' הואיל אי מיקלעי ליה אורחין – חזי ליה כוליה ליום טוב: מדאורייתא צורכי שבת נעשין ביו"ט. דכתיב (שמות יב): "אך אשר יאכל לכל נפש", ושבת ויו"ט חדא קדושה היא, דתרוייהו שבת איקרו, וכי היכי דמותר לבשל לבו ביום, מותר לבשל למחר: ורבנן הוא דגזור. כי לא אותיב עירוב תבשילין, כדי שלא יאמרו אופין אף לחול: בהמה מסוכנת. ורוצה לשוחטה ביום טוב, שלא תמות ויפסידנה: כזית צלי. זהו קל בבישולים: כדי שיכול לאכול. שיהא שהות ביום כדי להפשיט ולחתוך כזית ולצלות ולאכול, ואי איכא שהות כי האי שרי, ואע"ג דלא אכיל מינה: אמאי שחיט. הא לא צריך למיכל, שכבר אכל: משום הפסד ממונו. (ג) ויודע הוא שאינו מותר בלא אכילה, גמר בלבו לאנס את עצמו ולעבור על דעתו ולאכול כזית, והוה ליה כצריך לזית בי"ט. ומשום ההוא זית בעיא למישחטיה לכולה, דאי אפשר לכזית בשר בלא שחיטה. אבל הכא דליכא למימר גמר בלבו לאנס עצמו – משום הואיל לא שרינן איסורא דאורייתא, כיון דלא צריך למידי: לחם הפנים. כל שבת ושבת נאכל

תוספות

הואיל ואי בעי מיתשיל עליה. הקשה בקונטרס: א"כ יקרא לה שם, ואח"כ תאפה מטעם הואיל, ואי בעי – מיתשיל עלה. (ג) ואור"י: כיון שיכול לעשות בלא הואיל – אין לנו לעשות ע"י הואיל. וא"ת: א"כ אמאי שרי ר' אליעזר לאפות משום הואיל דכל חדא וחדא חזיא ליה כדלקמן, בלא הואיל יכול לעשות ע"י הטלה לצונן! ואור"י: דהכי עדיף טפי מהטלה לצונן, דאיכא למיחש שלא תזהר יפה, ויבא לידי חימוץ. ועוד י"ל: הואיל ואי בעי מיתשיל עלה – לא שכיח – לא אמר להתיר, כדמוכח לקמן גבי לחם הפנים ושתי הלחם דאין אפייתן דוחה יו"ט, אע"ג דאיכא למימר הואיל ואי בעי פריק ליה שאין התנור מקדש. שאם היה מקדש – א"כ יפסלו בלינה, כיון דאופין אותה קודם יו"ט. וכן מוכח במנחות (דף עב:), דמ"ד אין אפייתן דוחה י"ט קסבר דאין התנור מקדשן. ורשב"א פירש: כי נ"ל שדעת רש"י כיון שהסל מצרפן, וסופו ליטול אחת על כולן – נמצא שטרח בדבר שאין ראוי לאכילה – אלא מטעם הואיל שרי. דאי בעי לא מפריש חדא לחלה אלא בלע פורתא מכל חדא וחדא, וכל חדא וחדא חזיא ליה. וכיון דכי נמי לא תקרא לה שם עד שתאפה לא שרי אלא על ידי הואיל, ואם יקרא לה שם קודם שתאפה הוו תרי הואיל, ותרי הואיל לא אמרינן. וקשה לרשב"א לפירושו: כיון דאם יבלע מכל חדא וחדא יהא מותר בלא הואיל, היאך שרו רבנן למיעבד ע"י הואיל, כיון דאפשר בלא הואיל? ותירץ: שלא הטריחו חכמים לבלוע מכל אחת ואחת. ור"י מקשה: דהא כי נמי בלע מכל חדא וחדא אסור לאפות, כדמוכח בפ"ב דביצה (דף כא.) דאמר: עיסה של גוי ושל ישראל – אסור לאפות בי"ט. כיון דאפשר למיפלגה בלישה. ונראה לרשב"א לחלק: דדוקא בעיסת גוי אסרו מדרבנן, אבל גבי חלה – לא אסרו משום תיקון חלה. ואין נראה לריב"א מה שמשמע מתוך פ"ה, דאע"פ שהיה בהן כדי חיוב חלה מתחלה – בעינן צירוף סל להפריש אחת על כולן. וכן משמע בפסק שלו לקמן, דלא בעינן צירוף סל לר' אליעזר אלא כשלא היה בתחלה שיעור חלה. דאהכי מייתי לה לקמן *בשמעתין גבי הני נשי דאפיין קפיזי לפסחא. והכי תניא בהדיא במס' חלה (פ"ב משנה ד), דתנן: העושה עיסתו קבין קבין (ד) – פטור מן החלה עד שישוכו: ר' אליעזר אומר: אף הרודה ונותן לסל וכו'. משמע בהדיא דמיירי היכא דלא היה שיעור חלה, אבל היכא דיש שיעור חלה – לא בעינן צירוף סל להפריש מזה על זה, אלא הקפה בעלמא כדי לתרום מן המוקף, כמו בתרומה ומעשר דלא בעינן צירוף סל להפריש מזה על זה אלא הקפה. מיהו, נראה לר"י: דעם נתינה לסל בעינן נמי נגיעה בהדי הדדי, משום נטילת חלה מן המוקף. וכדאמר ר' אליעזר גופיה בפ' "כשם" (סוטה ל.): שתי עיסות, אחת טהורה ואחת טמאה – נותן פחות מכביצה באמצע, כדי ליטול מן המוקף. מדלא שרי על ידי צירוף סל – משמע דבעי נמי נגיעה:

הואיל אי בעי מיתשיל עלה. תימה לרשב"א: אמאי אמר בפרק "כל שעה" (לעיל דף לח.) דמצת מעשר שני אין יוצא בה בפסח. לר"מ דסבר מעשר שני ממון גבוה הוא, ולא חשיב מצתכם. הא הואיל אי בעי מיתשיל עלה – מחשבינן [ליה] כשלו! ועוד, דאמר לעיל (דף ה:): אבל אתה רואה של אחרים ושל גבוה – והא של גבוה נמי חשיב כשלו, הואיל אי בעי מיתשיל עליה! ותי' ר"י: דשאני הנהו, דכתיב בהו *"לה'", [ב] אע"ג דאי בעי מיתשיל עלה – חשבם הכתוב של גבוה. ועוד תי' ר"י: היכא דאתא הקדש ליד הגזבר – לא אמרי' הואיל אי בעי מיתשיל עלה, והואיל אי בעי פריק – נמי לא אמרינן, דאם כן היה קונה אותו. דאטו נחשוב חמץ של גוי כשלו, הואיל אי בעי קני ליה? ועוד תירץ: כיון שנתחמץ – שום אדם לא יפדנו. ול"ע בהנהו הואיל ד"כל שעה" (ג"ז שם): הואיל ולא קרא לה שם:

רבה אמר אינו לוקה. וא"ת: דאמר ב"המצניע" (שבת צה.) המכבד (ה) והרודה חלות דבש, שגג בשבת – חייב חטאת, הזיד ביום טוב – סופג את הארבעים, דברי רבי אליעזר. וחכמים אומרים: אין כאן אלא שבות. ואמאי לוקה לר' אליעזר? לימא: הואיל ומיקלעי ליה אורחים. ואפי' רבנן לא פטרי אלא משום דלא חשיבי דבש בכוורתו מחובר. ויש לומר: כגון שהדביש הדבש ואינה ראויה לאכול, ואפי' אי מיקלעי ליה אורחים לא חזי להו. אי נמי: ברודה סמוך לשקיעת החמה, שאפילו יבואו אורחים אין שהות ביום לאוכלו. ובהאי שינויא א"ש מה שהקשה ריב"א, דשמעינן ליה לרבה דאית ליה הכנה בריש מסכת ביצה (דף ב:) ובריש "בכל מערבין" (עירובין לח:), דאמר: אין יום טוב מכין לשבת. אי אמרת הואיל – היכא משכחת לה דאין יום טוב מכין לשבת? והשתא משכחת לה – סמוך לשקיעת החמה כדפרישית. ואם תאמר: אי אמרינן הואיל – א"כ בטלת כל מלאכת שבת – הואיל וראוי לחולה שיש בו סכנה! וי"ל: כיון דלא שכיח כלל – לא אמרינן הואיל: נאכל

עין משפט נר מצוה

ל א מיי' פ"א מהלכות י"ט הלכה טו סמג לאוין עה טוש"ע או"ח סי' תקג סעיף א:
לא ב מיי' פ"ו מהלכות י"ט הלכה א:
לב ג מיי' פ"א שם הלכה יב סמג שם טוש"ע או"ח סי' תלא סעיף ו:

רבינו חננאל

ביום טוב כו' נימא בטובת הנא' קא מיפלגי פי' אותה הנאה שיש לו לישראל לתת חלתו לאיזה כהן שירצה אע"פ שעיקר חלה חייב ליתנה לכהן אבל יש לו לבחור כהן לתתה לו שיחזיק לו טובת אותה הנאה ממון הוא ור' אליעזר אומר דממונו הוא וחייב עליה בבל יראה ובל ימצא ור' יהושע אומר אינו ממונו דאי מקדש בה אשה אינה מקודשת לפיכך אינו חייב עלי' כלל ודחי' לא כ"ע טובת הנאה אינה ממון ובהואיל פליגי ר' אליעזר סבר הואיל אי בעי מתשיל עליה ומפריש עליה כלומר הולך אצל חכם ואומר טעיתי וקריתי עליה שם חלה ומתירה לו החכם ויוצאת לחולין ונמצאת ממונו לפיכך עכשיו חייב עליה ור' יהושע סבר לא אמרי' הואיל השתא מיהא לא איתשל עלה מי יימר דמיתשיל עלה: איתמר האופה מיום טוב לחול רב חסדא אמר לוקה דהא לא חזי ליה האידנא רבה אומר אינו לוקה הואיל ואי מקלעי ליה אורחים חזי ליה השתא נמי לא לקי אמר ליה רבה לרב חסדא בשלמא לדידי דאית לי הואיל לפיכך אופין מיום טוב לשבת כיון דלא אפשר שרינן ליה אלא לדידך דלית לך הואיל איך אופין מיום טוב לשבת אמר ליה משום עירובי תבשילין אמר ליה משום עירובי תבשילין שרינן איסורא דאורייתא שלוקין עליה אמר ליה מדאורייתא יום טוב מכין לשבת ורבנן הוא דגזרו כדי שיאמרו מיום טוב לשבת אסור קל וחומר מיום טוב לחול וכיון דמנח עירובי תבשילין אית ליה הכירא ומותבי' עליה דרבה הא דתנן בהמה מסוכנת לא ישחוט וכו' ומשני משום הפסד ממונו גמר בלבו לאכול דאמר נשחט ונאכל

הגהות מהר"ב רנשבורג

[א] בגמ' דר"א סבר אמרינן הואיל ואי בעי מיתשל עלה ממוניה הוא. נ"ב ואע"ג דר"א כבי"ש ס"ל לטעות הקדש הקדש ואין נשאלין עליו עיין מ"ש בזה הרמ"ע מפאנו סי' ס"ב ול"ע בלשון רש"י כאן בד"ה לא דכ"ע וכו' שאין תירוצו דהרמ"ע מספיק לדבריו ועיין בתוי"ט במשנתנו בד"ה ר"א וכו' עי' תוס' חדשים סוף הסדר מועד: [ב] בתוס' ד"ה הואיל תימה לרשב"א וכו' ותירץ ר"י דשאני הנהו דכתיב בהו לה'. נ"ב ר"ל דכתיב בהו קודש לה' בסוף פ' בחקתי אבל חלה לאמר הש"ס הכא הואיל ואי בעי מיתשל עלה שאני דל"כ בה קודש כדמשני הש"ס בקדושין דף נ"ג ע"א יעוש"ה ודוק. אחרי שנים רבות שכתבתי זה יצא לאורה ס' מעין החכמה להגאון מוהרמ"ה וראיתי לו שם דף פ"ז ע"א בד"ה ומתורתו של הרמב"ן וכו' ישוב אחר בזה על התוס' והנלענ"ד כתבתי והוא אמת נכון יותר:

מסורת הש"ס

קדושין נח. נדרים פד: ב"מ יח: חולין קלא.
ביצה כח. לקמן סב:
ביצה כה. [ע"ש אבל נראה דהכא ברייתא היא דמייתי]
[קדש עיין קדושין נג.]

הגהות הב"ח

(א) רש"י ד"ה לא דכ"ע וכו' לאכול חדא וחדא כו' דאית ליה לר' אליעזר: (ב) ד"ה משום הפסד ממונו דיודע: (ג) תוס' ד"ה הואיל וכו' ואי בעי מיתשיל עלה ותירץ כיון שיכול כצ"ל ותיבת ואור"י נמחק: (ד) בא"ד במס' חלה כו' עיסתו קבין קבין נגעו זה בזה פטורין מן החלה: (ה) ד"ה רבה וכו' המכבד והמרבץ והרודה.

*נֶאֱכָל לְתִשְׁעָה, לַעֲשָׂרָה, וּלְאַחַד עָשָׂר – לֹא פָּחוֹת וְלֹא יוֹתֵר. כֵּיצַד? כְּדַרְכּוֹ – לְתִשְׁעָה, נֶאֱפָה בְּעֶרֶב שַׁבָּת – נֶאֱכָל בַּשַּׁבָּת לְתִשְׁעָה. חָל יוֹם טוֹב לִהְיוֹת בְּע"ש – נֶאֱכָל לַשַּׁבָּת לַעֲשָׂרָה. שְׁנֵי יָמִים טוֹבִים שֶׁל רֹאשׁ הַשָּׁנָה – נֶאֱכָל לַשַּׁבָּת לְאַחַד עָשָׂר, [א]לְפִי שֶׁאֵינוֹ דּוֹחֶה לֹא אֶת הַשַּׁבָּת וְלֹא אֶת הַי"ט. וְאִי אָמְרַתְּ צוֹרְכֵי שַׁבָּת נַעֲשִׂין בְּי"ט אַמַּאי לָא דָּחֵי י"ט? א"ל: *שְׁבוּת קְרוֹבָה – הִתִּירוּ, שְׁבוּת רְחוֹקָה – לֹא הִתִּירוּ. וּלְרשב"ג, דְּאָמַר *מִשּׁוּם רַבִּי שִׁמְעוֹן בֶּן הַסְּגָן: דּוֹחֶה אֶת י"ט, וְאֵינוֹ דּוֹחֶה אֶת יוֹם צוֹם, מַאי אִיכָּא לְמֵימַר? בְּהָא פְּלִיגִי; מָר סָבַר: שְׁבוּת קְרוֹבָה הִתִּירוּ, שְׁבוּת רְחוֹקָה לֹא הִתִּירוּ. וּמָר סָבַר: שְׁבוּת רְחוֹקָה נַמִי הִתִּירוּ. מְתִיב רַב מָרִי: *שְׁתֵּי הַלֶּחֶם אֵינָן נֶאֱכָלוֹת לֹא פָּחוֹת מִשְּׁנַיִם, וְלֹא יוֹתֵר עַל שְׁלֹשָׁה. כֵּיצַד? נֶאֱפוֹת עֶרֶב יוֹם טוֹב – נֶאֱכָלוֹת לְיוֹם טוֹב לִשְׁנַיִם, חָל י"ט לִהְיוֹת אַחַר הַשַּׁבָּת – נֶאֱכָלוֹת לְי"ט לִשְׁלֹשָׁה, [ב]לְפִי שֶׁאֵינָהּ דּוֹחָה לֹא אֶת הַשַּׁבָּת וְלֹא אֶת הַי"ט. וְאִי אָמְרַתְּ צוֹרְכֵי שַׁבָּת נַעֲשִׂין בְּי"ט, הַשְׁתָּא דְּשַׁבָּת בְּי"ט שָׁרֵי – דְּיוֹם טוֹב בְּיוֹם טוֹב מִיבַּעְיָא?! שָׁאנֵי הָתָם, דְּאָמַר קְרָא "לָכֶם" *"לָכֶם" וְלֹא לַגָּבוֹהַּ. וּלְרשב"ג, דְּאָמַר מִשּׁוּם ר"ש בֶּן הַסְּגָן: דּוֹחֶה אֶת יוֹם טוֹב, מַאי אִיכָּא לְמֵימַר? סָבַר לָהּ כְּאַבָּא שָׁאוּל, דְּאָמַר: *"לָכֶם" – לָכֶם וְלֹא לַגּוֹיִם. שְׁלַח לֵיהּ רַב חִסְדָּא לְרַבָּה בְּיַד רַב אַחָא בַּר רַב הוּנָא: מִי אָמְרִינַן "הוֹאִיל", וְהָא תְּנַן: *יֵשׁ חוֹרֵשׁ תֶּלֶם אֶחָד וְחַיָּיבִין עָלֶיהָ מִשּׁוּם שְׁמוֹנָה לָאוִין: הַחוֹרֵשׁ בְּשׁוֹר וַחֲמוֹר, וְהֵן מוּקְדָּשִׁים, וְכִלְאַיִם בַּכֶּרֶם, וּשְׁבִיעִית

רש"י

נֶאֱכָל לְתִשְׁעָה. לְיוֹם תְּשִׁיעִי לַאֲפִיָּיתוֹ: נֶאֱפֶה בְּעֶרֶב שַׁבָּת. זוֹ מְסַדְּרִין אוֹתָן לְמָחָר, וּלְשַׁבָּת הַבָּאָה מְסַלְּקִים אוֹתָן – הֲרֵי הוּא נֶאֱכָל לְשַׁבָּת הַבָּאָה לְיוֹם תְּשִׁיעִי לַאֲפִיָּיתוֹ: חָל י"ט בְּעֶרֶב שַׁבָּת. וְלֹא הָיוּ יְכוֹלִין לֶאֱפוֹת דָּבָר שֶׁלֹּא לְצוֹרֶךְ י"ט, וַאֲפָאוּהוּ מֵעֶרֶב י"ט שֶׁהוּא חֲמִישִׁי בְּשַׁבָּת – נֶאֱכָל לְשַׁבָּת שְׁנִיָּה דְּהַיְינוּ בַּעֲשָׂרָה: שְׁנֵי יָמִים שֶׁל ר"ה. חָלוּ בַּחֲמִישִׁי וְשִׁשִּׁי, כְּגוֹן שֶׁבָּאוּ עֵדִים מִן הַמִּנְחָה וּלְמַעְלָה, דִּתְנַן (ר"ה דף ל:): נוֹהֲגִים אוֹתוֹ הַיּוֹם קוֹדֶשׁ וּלְמָחָר קוֹדֶשׁ. נֶאֱפֶה בִּרְבִיעִי בְּשַׁבָּת, וְנֶאֱכָל בְּשַׁבָּת שְׁנִיָּה – לְאַחַד עָשָׂר. וְהַהוּא שַׁבָּת לָאו יוֹם צוֹם הוּא, דִּכְשֶׁהָיוּ בָּאִים עֵדִים לְאַחַר הַמִּנְחָה הָיוּ עוֹשִׂין אֱלוּל מְעוּבָּר, וּמוֹנִין מִיּוֹם שֵׁנִי, כִּדְאָמְרִינַן: שֶׁלֹּא הָיוּ מְקַבְּלִין אֶת הָעֵדִים לְקַדֵּשׁ בּוֹ בַּיּוֹם אא"כ בָּאִים קוֹדֶם הַמִּנְחָה. וְא"כ הָוֵי יוֹם צוֹם – מָאֵי אָכֵיל לֵיהּ לְאוֹרְתָא, דְּהָוֵי נֶאֱכָל לְיוֹם וְלַיְלָה, וּבַקֳּדָשִׁים לַיְלָה הוֹלֶכֶת אַחַר הַיּוֹם. וּשְׁנֵי יָמִים טוֹבִים שֶׁל ר"ה דַּוְקָא נָקַט, דִּבְזְמַן לֶחֶם הַפָּנִים לֹא הָיוּ שְׁנֵי יָמִים טוֹבִים שֶׁל גָּלִיּוֹת: שֶׁאֵינוֹ דּוֹחֶה. בַּאֲפִיָּיתוֹ: לֶחֶם הַפָּנִים. צָרְכֵי שַׁבָּת הוּא, שֶׁמְּסַלְּקִין וְאוֹכְלִין אוֹתוֹ בְּשַׁבָּת. וְאִי מִדְּאוֹרַיְיתָא נַעֲשִׂין בְּי"ט בַּגְּבוּלִין, וּמִדְּרַבָּנַן הוּא דְּאָסוּר – הָא בַּמִּקְדָּשׁ קַיְימָא לָן דְּלֹא גָּזְרוּ עַל הַשְּׁבוּת, וְאַמַּאי אֵינוֹ דּוֹחֶה? לְעוֹלָם צָרְכֵי שַׁבָּת. בְּי"ט אֵין בָּהֶן אֶלָּא מִשּׁוּם שְׁבוּת, וְדָקָא קַשְׁיָא לָךְ הָכָא לִישְׁתְּרֵי, דְּאֵין שְׁבוּת בַּמִּקְדָּשׁ: שְׁבוּת קְרוֹבָה. שֶׁל י"ט עַצְמוֹ, אוֹ שֶׁל אוֹתָהּ שַׁבָּת עַצְמָהּ, שֶׁצְּרִיכָה לְבוֹ בַּיּוֹם בַּמִּקְדָּשׁ – הִתִּירוּ: שְׁבוּת רְחוֹקָה. לִדְחוֹת שְׁבוּת י"ט זֶה בִּשְׁבִיל שַׁבָּת שְׁנִיָּה – לֹא הִתִּירוּ בַּמִּקְדָּשׁ: וְאֵינוֹ דּוֹחֶה אֶת יוֹם צוֹם הַכִּפּוּרִים. בַּאֲפִיָּיתוֹ, דְּאִיסּוּרָא דְּאוֹרַיְיתָא הוּא, דְּלֹא הוּתַּר בּוֹ אוֹכֶל נֶפֶשׁ. אֲבָל יו"ט – הוּתַּר בּוֹ אוֹכֶל נֶפֶשׁ, וְהַאי אוֹכֶל נֶפֶשׁ הוּא. וְאע"ג דְּאֵינוֹ צוֹרֶךְ לְי"ט – הֲרֵי צוֹרֶךְ לְשַׁבָּת, דְּהוּא נַמִי י"ט. הִלְכָּךְ, בְּעָלְמָא אִיסּוּר שְׁבוּת הוּא, וּבַמִּקְדָּשׁ לָא גְּזוּר, וְאע"ג דִּרְחוֹקָה הִיא: שְׁתֵּי הַלֶּחֶם. הַבָּאִין בָּעֲצֶרֶת: לִשְׁלֹשָׁה. לְפִי שֶׁאֲפָאוּם מֵעֶרֶב שַׁבָּת: בְּיוֹם טוֹב מִיבַּעְיָא. אִי נַמִי לָא חֲזוּ הַשְׁתָּא – הָא חֲזוּ לְבוֹ בַּיּוֹם, וּמִי גָּרְעֵי מִצָּרְכֵי שַׁבָּת שֶׁל מָחָר? דְּלְכֹל הַאי יוֹמָא לָא חֲזֵי לֵיהּ, דְּהָא סָעַד כְּבָר. אֶלָּא לָאו שְׁמַע מִינַּהּ: אֵין מוּתָּר בְּי"ט מִן הַתּוֹרָה אֶלָּא דָּבָר הָרָאוּי לוֹ אוֹתָהּ שָׁעָה. וְצָרְכֵי שַׁבָּת – טַעְמַיְיהוּ מִשּׁוּם הוֹאִיל דְּאוֹרְחִים, וּבְהָנֵי לֵיכָּא לְמֵימַר "הוֹאִיל", מִשּׁוּם דְּהַהִיא שַׁעְתָּא לָא חֲזֵי עַד שֶׁיִּשְׁחֲטוּ כְּבָשִׂים עֲלֵיהֶן וְיִזְרוֹק דָּמָן, וְכֵיוָן דַּהֲוָה אֶפְשָׁר לְמֶיעְבַּד מֵאֶתְמוֹל – לָא דָּחֵי לֵיהּ לְי"ט מִידֵּי דְּלָא חֲזֵי לֵיהּ: רַבָּן שִׁמְעוֹן כו'. לָא גָּרְסִי' בֵּיהּ: וְאֵינוֹ דּוֹחֶה יוֹם צוֹם – דְּמָה עִנְיַן יוֹם צוֹם סָמוּךְ לָעֲצֶרֶת? כְּאַבָּא שָׁאוּל. בְּמַסֶּ' בֵּיצָה (דף כ:): לָכֶם וְלֹא לַגּוֹיִם. אֲבָל לַגָּבוֹהַּ שָׁרֵי: בְּיַד רַב אַחָא. הִטְעִימוֹ תְּשׁוּבָה זוֹ, לְאוֹמְרָהּ לְרַבָּה מִשְּׁמוֹ: הַחוֹרֵשׁ בְּשׁוֹר וַחֲמוֹר. מִשּׁוּם "לֹא תַחֲרוֹשׁ" וגו': וְהֵן מוּקְדָּשִׁין. עוֹבֵר עַל הַשּׁוֹר שֶׁהוּא קָדְשֵׁי מִזְבֵּחַ מִשּׁוּם "לֹא תַעֲבוֹד בִּבְכוֹר שׁוֹרֶךָ", וְכָל הַקֳּדָשִׁים כִּבְכוֹר, וְעַל הַחֲמוֹר שֶׁהוּא קָדְשֵׁי בֶּדֶק הַבַּיִת – מִשּׁוּם לָאו דְּהֵזִיד בִּמְעִילָה, דְּאָמְרַן בְּפֶ' "כָּל שָׁעָה" (לעיל לג.): הֵזִיד בִּמְעִילָ' – בְּאַזְהָרָ'. וְגָמַר חֵטְא חֵטְא מִתְּרוּמָה – הֲרֵי שְׁלֹשָׁה לָאוִין חֲלוּקִין. וְלָא חָשֵׁיב אֶלָּא לָאוִין חֲלוּקִין:

תוספות

נאכל לאחד עשר יום. כגון שבאו עדים מן המנחה ולמעלה ביום חמישי, דנוהגין אותו היום קודש ולמחר קודש כי היכי דלא לזלזלו ביה לשנה הבאה, כשיבאו העדים קודם המנחה. כדמוכח בריש ביצה (דף ה:), ובתרא עיקר ומיניה מנינן יוה"כ. ויהא יוה"כ ביום א', ואז נאכל לי"א. אבל אם באו עדים קודם המנחה – א"כ למחר ביום ו' חול גמור הוא, ויכולין לאפות לחם אחר ביום ו', ולחם הראשון יפדה דאין התנור מקדש. כיון דקסבר דאינו דוחה לא שבת וי"ט. כדפרישית לעיל:

ואי אמרת צורכי שבת נעשים בי"ט. תימה לר"י: מאי פריך? והא רב חסדא לא פליג עליה דרבה אלא שמתיר לבשל בי"ט לשבת כמו שמותר לבשל לבו ביום, דקדושה אחת היא כדפ"ה. אבל בכה"ג דמייתי – אפי' לבו ביום אסורה, כדקתני סיפא גבי שתי הלחם, ובהא לא אמר רב חסדא שיעשו בי"ט יותר מרבה! ונראה לר"י, דה"פ לעיל: צרכי שבת נעשים בי"ט – לאו משום דקדושה אחת היא, אלא כלומר הואיל שהיא מצות שבת, אם לא יעשנה בי"ט – שוב לא יעשנה, חשיב כמו אוכל נפש די"ט. והשתא פריך שפיר: בשלמא לדידי דלא שריא בי"ט לשמחת י"ט, אלא בכה"ג שיהא עיקרו משום שמחת י"ט – והכא ליכא שמחת י"ט. וגבי שתי הלחם נמי, אין עיקרו לשמחת י"ט, אלא עיקרו משום זבח. אלא לדידך, דאמרת צורכי שבת נעשים בי"ט, וכל דבר שהוא מצוה וצריך לעשות בי"ט שאין לו זמן אחר – הכא אמאי לא דחי י"ט? וכן נראה לקמן גבי שתי הלחם. ורש"י פי' גבי שתי הלחם דלרבה א"ש, דלא שייכא הואיל – משום דההיא שעתא לא חזו עד שישחטו עליהם כבשים ויזרוק דמן. וקשה לר"י לפירושו: כיון דהגמרא אינה יודעת חילוק בין גבוה להדיוט, וכי בשביל שלא יהא עכשיו ראוי אע"פ שיהא ראוי לבו ביום יהא אסור? הלא כשאופה העיסה לאורחים אינה ראויה עד שתאפה, ושלמי חגיגה שמותר לשוחטן אע"פ שאסורים עד שיזרוק דמן, ושחט בהמתו נמי בשעת שחיטה אינה ראויה. אלא, כיון שמותר אחר זמן לבו ביום – לאו חסרון הוא. וא"כ תיקשי נמי לרבה! ומיהו: י"ל לפ"ה דשתי הלחם אין להם שום חסרון בגופו:

ולר"ש ב"ג דאמר דוחה י"ט. בשלמא לדידי דאמינא דסבירא ליה לת"ק דצורכי שבת אין נעשים בי"ט – איכא למימר דבהא פליגי ולא איירי אלא בדאורייתא. וקשה לך מת"ק. אי נמי אומר רשב"א: דאיכא למימר דפליגי, דמר סבר: אמרי' הואיל ויכול לפדותו. ומר סבר: לא אמרי' הואיל, דלא שכיח. כדפרי' לעיל. אלא לדידך, דאמרת דטעמא דת"ק משום שבות רחוקה – בהא ליפלוג עליה רשב"ג:

לכם ולא לגבוה. פי': אף ולא לגבוה, ודרשינן נמי ולא לגוי כדמוכח בביצה (דף כ:), דמאן דסבר: נדרים ונדבות אין קריבין בי"ט – דריש נמי "לכם" ולא לגוי, גבי אמרו להם בית שמאי לבית הלל: והלא כבר נאמר "לכם" ולא לגבוה:

ומוקדשין. פ"ה דבמוקדשין איכא תרתי: בשור עובר משום "לא תעבוד בבכור שורך" וחמור שהוא קדשי בדק הבית חייב משום מעילה. ובחנם דחק, דבשור גופיה מיחייב משום מעילה אם הוא עולה או חטאת. וקשה לר"י: דבפרק בתרא דמכות (דף כב.) אמר: מידי דאיתא בשאלה – לא קתני. ופריך: והרי הקדש! ומשני: בבכור. ופריך: והרי נזיר. והשתא מחמור הוה ליה לאקשויי לפ"ה, כיון דאיירי בחמור הקדש! וע"ק לפי': ליחשוב נמי כלאי זרעים, ולוקמא כגון שזרע הרבה מינין בכרם, דכי האי גוונא פריך במסכת מכות (דף כא.) לחשוב כמה לאוי! ונראה לר"י: דלא חשיב לאו דמעילה, דלא חשיב אלא הנך לאוי דלקי עלייהו אחרישה כל שהוא, אבל אלאו דמעילה לא לקי עד שיחרוש בשוה פרוטה. וכלאי הכרם מפרש ר"י דחשיב תרי לאוי – משום כלאי זרעים ומשום כלאי הכרם. וכן משמע כפי', מדלא קתני כלאי הכרם, אלא כלאים בכרם. והא דאמר רבי יאשיה: אינו חייב עד שיזרע חטה ושעורה וחרצן במפולת יד – לאו משום דלית ליה כלאי זרעים, אלא "אינו חייב" – משום כלאי הכרם קאמר. וכן משמע בירושלמי, דקאמר: על דעתיה דר' יאשיה כתיב "שדך לא תזרע כלאים" לאיזה דבר נאמר "לא תזרע כרמך כלאים", פי': כיון דבלא חרצן מיחייב משום שדך! ומשני: שאם התרו בו משום שדך – לוקה, ומשום כרמך – לוקה, וכן משמע בפ' "אותו ואת בנו" (חולין פב.) דקאמר: הזורע כלאים כלאים לוקה. ופריך: כלאים כלאים למה לי? ומסיק: מילתא אגב אורחיה קמשמע לן, דאיכא תרי גווני כלאים, לאפוקי מדרבי יאשיה דאמר עד שיזרע חטה וכו'. וקא משמע לן דכי זרע חטין וחרצן ושעורה וחרצן – נמי חייב. ומדלא נקט חטה ושעורה אלא חטה וחרצן – משמע דרבי יאשיה מודה בחטה ושעורה דלוקה משום כלאי זרעים. והא דאמרינן בפרק בתרא דבכורות (דף נד.) דתירוש ויצהר אין תורמין מזה על זה, מדכתיב: "כל חלב יצהר וכל חלב תירוש ודגן" תן חלב לזה וחלב לזה, אשכחן תירוש ויצהר, תירוש ודגן, דגן ודגן מנין? אמרת קל וחומר וכו'. ולרבי יאשיה מייתי לה הכי: מה תירוש ויצהר שאינם כלאים זה עם זה, אפילו

רבינו חננאל

קודם שתמות נבלה ואי אפשר לכזית בשר בלא שחיטה וכי קא שחיט לאכילה קא שחיט ואקשי' אהא דאמרי' מדאורייתא יום טוב מכין לשבת איני והתנן במנחות פי"א לחם הפנים נאכל לתשעה לעשרה לאחד עשר לא פחות ולא יותר כו' וקתני סיפא לפי שאינה דוחה לא את השבת ולא את יום טוב ושני' שבות קרובה התירו שבות רחוקה לא התירו כלומר יום טוב מכין לשבת שהוא אחריו אבל בלחם הפנים אינו מותר באכילה אלא לשבת הבאה שהיא שבת רחוקה לא התירה תורה ולרשב"ג דאמר משום ר' שמעון בן הסגן לחם הפנים דוחה יום טוב ואינו דוחה את יום צום כלומר אם חל יום הכפורים ערב שבת אינו דוחה אפיית לחם הפנים יום צום כמו שדוחה יום טוב קסבר אפי' שבת רחוקה התירו. ומותיב רב מרי משתי הלחם ואי אמרת יום טוב מכין לשבת יום טוב ליום טוב אמאי אינו מכין דתנן בשתי הלחם לפי שאינן דוחות לא שבת ולא יו"ט ומשני' שאני קדשים דאמר קרא יעשה לכם לכם ולא לגבוה ור"ש בן הסגן [סובר] לכם מותר ק"ו לגבוה ופשוטה היא: **שלח** רב חסדא לרבה (בר) [ביד] רב אחא בר הונא ומי אמרינן הואיל והתנן בפ' ואלו הן הלוקין יש חורש תלם אחד וחייב עליו שמונה לאוין ואלו הן החורש בשור וחמור [והן השור והחמור] מוקדשין חייב בשור אחת ובחמור אחר' כל אחת בפני עצמו

עין משפט נר מצוה

לג א מיי' פ"ה מהל' תמידין הלכה י סמג עשין קל:

לד ב מיי' פ"ה שם הל' ח סמג עשין קל:

מסורת הש"ס

מנחות ק: ערכין ח:

[שבת קיד:]

[מנחות ק:]

ג"ז שם ערכין ח:

[ביצה כ:]

[שם: כח. כח: מגילה ז:]

מכות כא:

גליון הש"ס

תוס' ד"ה ומוקדשין. ונראה לר"י עיין בטורי אבן ר"ה דף ד ד"ה לדקות:

לה א מיי' פט"ז מהל' מעשה קרבנות הלכה טו:
לו ב מיי' פ"א שם הלכה יד:

וּשְׁבִיעִית בְּיוֹם טוֹב, כֹּהֵן וְנָזִיר אַבֵּית הַטּוּמְאָה. וְאִי אָמְרִינַן הוֹאִיל – אַחֲרִישָׁה לָא לִיחַיֵּיב הוֹאִיל וַחֲזֵי לְכִיסּוּי דַּם צִיפּוֹר! א"ר פַּפָּא בַּר שְׁמוּאֵל: בַּאֲבָנִים מְקוּרְזָלוֹת, רְאוּיוֹת לְכוֹתְשָׁן! וּכְתִישָׁה בְּיוֹם טוֹב מִי שָׁרֵי? רְאוּיוֹת לְכוֹתְשָׁן כִּלְאַחַר יָד. בְּצוּנְמָא! צוּנְמָא בַּר זְרִיעָה?! צוּנְמָא מִלְּמַעְלָה, וְעָפָר תִּיחוּחַ מִלְּמַטָּה. וְתֵיפּוֹק לֵיהּ מִשּׁוּם עָפָר תִּיחוּחַ! אֶלָּא אָמַר מָר בַּר רַב אַשִׁי: בְּטִינָא. וְטִינָא בַּר זְרִיעָה הוּא? בְּמִתּוּנְתָּא. אֵיתִיבֵיהּ אַבַּיֵי: *הַמְבַשֵּׁל גִּיד הַנָּשֶׁה בְּחָלָב בְּיו"ט וְאוֹכְלוֹ, לוֹקֶה חָמֵשׁ: לוֹקֶה מִשּׁוּם מְבַשֵּׁל גִּיד בְּיוֹם טוֹב, וְלוֹקֶה מִשּׁוּם אוֹכֵל גִּיד, וְלוֹקֶה מִשּׁוּם מְבַשֵּׁל בָּשָׂר בְּחָלָב, וְלוֹקֶה מִשּׁוּם אוֹכֵל בָּשָׂר בְּחָלָב, וְלוֹקֶה מִשּׁוּם הַבְעָרָה. וְאִי אָמְרִינַן "הוֹאִיל" – אַהַבְעָרָה לָא לִיחַיֵּיב, הוֹאִיל דַּחֲזֵי לֵיהּ לְצָרְכּוֹ! אֲמַר לֵיהּ: אַפֵּיק הַבְעָרָה וְעַיֵּיל גִּיד הַנָּשֶׁה שֶׁל נְבֵילָה. וְהָתָנֵי רַבִּי חִיָּיא: לוֹקִין שְׁתַּיִם עַל אֲכִילָתוֹ וְשָׁלֹשׁ עַל בִּישּׁוּלוֹ, וְאִי אִיתָא: שָׁלֹשׁ עַל אֲכִילָתוֹ מִיבָּעֵי לֵיהּ! אֶלָּא: אַפֵּיק הַבְעָרָה וְעַיֵּיל עֲצֵי מוּקְצֶה. וּמוּקְצֶה דְּאוֹרַיְיתָא הוּא? א"ל: אִין, דִּכְתִיב: °"וְהָיָה בַּיּוֹם הַשִּׁשִּׁי וְהֵכִינוּ אֵת אֲשֶׁר יָבִיאוּ", וְאַזְהָרְתֵּהּ מֵהָכָא – °מִ"לֹּא תַעֲשֶׂה כָל מְלָאכָה". א"ל: וְהָא אַתְּ הוּא דְּאָמַרְתְּ; בְּעַאי מִינֵּיהּ מֵרַב חִסְדָּא, וְאָמְרִי לָהּ בְּעַאי מִינֵּיהּ מֵרַב הוּנָא: הֵבִיא שֶׂה מֵאֲפָר וּשְׁחָטוֹ תָּמִיד בְּיו"ט מַהוּ? *וְאַתְּ אָמַרְתְּ לָן, (אֲמַר לִי) עֲלָהּ: "שֶׂה" – וְלֹא הַבְּכוֹר, "אַחַת" – אוְלֹא מַעֲשֵׂר, "מִן הַצֹּאן" – בוְלֹא הַפַּלְגָּס, מִן

שמות טז | שם כ

תורה אור

רש"י

וּשְׁבִיעִית. דְּעוֹבֵר מִשּׁוּם "שָׂדְךָ לֹא תִזְרָע". וְחוֹרֵשׁ תּוֹלָדָה דְּזוֹרֵעַ, כְּגוֹן חוֹרֵשׁ לְכַסּוֹת אֶת הַזְּרִיעָה: וּבְכִלְאַיִם בַּכֶּרֶם. דְּבַהֲדֵי דְּקָא חָרֵשׁ מְחַפֶּה בְּכִלְאַיִם, וְהַמְחַפֶּה בְּכִלְאַיִם לוֹקֶה – הֲרֵי חֲמִשָּׁה. וְיו"ט – הֲרֵי שִׁשָּׁה. וְשַׁבָּת לָא תָּנָא, מִשּׁוּם דְּלָאו שֶׁנִּיתַּן לְאַזְהָרַת מִיתַת ב"ד הוּא, דְּאֵין לוֹקִין עָלָיו: וְכֹהֵן וְנָזִיר אַבֵּית הַטּוּמְאָה. שֶׁזֶּה בֵּית הַקְּבָרוֹת, וְהוּא כֹּהֵן וְנָזִיר, וְיֵשׁ כָּאן לָאו דְּכֹהֵן "לְנֶפֶשׁ לֹא יִטַּמָּא", וְלָאו דְּנָזִיר "עַל נֶפֶשׁ מֵת לֹא יָבֹא": אַחֲרִישָׁה. מִשּׁוּם לָאו דְּיו"ט לָא לִילְקֵי: דַּם צִפּוֹר. הוֹאִיל וְאִי מִזְדַּמְּנֵי לֵיהּ צִפֳּרִים וְחַיּוֹת טוֹבָא: בַּאֲבָנִים. דְּלָא חֲזוּ לְכִיסּוּי: רְאוּיוֹת לְכוֹתְשָׁן. קוּשְׁיָא הִיא: כִּלְאַחַר יָד. ע"י שִׁינּוּי, דִּשְׁבוּת בְּעָלְמָא הוּא, וְכֵיוָן דְּמִדְּאוֹרַיְיתָא שָׁרֵי – פָּקַע לֵיהּ מַלְקוֹת: טִינָא. טִיט לַח וְגָלוּל: מִתּוּנְתָּא. אֶרֶץ לַחָה, רְאוּיָה לִזְרִיעָה וְאֵינָהּ נַעֲשֵׂית עָפָר, אִם בָּא לְכוֹתְשָׁהּ הִיא מִדַּבֶּקֶת וְנִגְבֶּלֶת: לוֹקֶה מִשּׁוּם מְבַשֵּׁל גִּיד בְּי"ט. בִּישּׁוּל שֶׁאֵינוֹ רָאוּי, וְלוֹקֶה מִשּׁוּם מְבַשֵּׁל בָּשָׂר בְּחָלָב אֲפִילּוּ הוּא חוֹל, וְקָסָבַר: יֵשׁ בַּגִּידִים בְּנוֹתֵן טַעַם, וּבָשָׂר הֵם: מִשּׁוּם הַבְעָרָה. שֶׁלֹּא לְצוֹרֶךְ. דְּהַבְעָרָה מְלָאכָה לְעַצְמָהּ, וּבִישּׁוּל מְלָאכָה לְעַצְמוֹ: גִּיד הַנָּשֶׁה שֶׁל נְבֵלָה. דְּלוֹקֶה עַל אֲכִילָתוֹ מִשּׁוּם נְבֵילָה: שְׁתַּיִם עַל אֲכִילָתוֹ. אוֹכֵל גִּיד וְאוֹכֵל בָּשָׂר בְּחָלָב: שָׁלֹשׁ עַל בִּישּׁוּלוֹ. מִשּׁוּם הַבְעָרָה דְּי"ט, וּמִשּׁוּם בִּישּׁוּל דְּי"ט, וּמִשּׁוּם מְבַשֵּׁל בָּשָׂר בְּחָלָב אֲפִילּוּ בְּחוֹל: וְעַיֵּיל עֲצֵי מוּקְצֶה. דְּהָשְׁתָּא לֵיכָּא לְמֵימַר הוֹאִיל, דְּמִדְּאוֹרַיְיתָא אָסוּר לְהִשְׁתַּמֵּשׁ בְּאֵשׁ מוּקְצֶה בְּי"ט: מוּקְצֶה דְּאוֹרַיְיתָא. בִּתְמִיָּה: וְהֵכִינוּ. בִּמְזוּמָּן, שֶׁמְּזַמֵּן כָּל צוֹרְכּוֹ הַיּוֹם, וְיֹאמַר: דָּבָר זֶה לְצוֹרֶךְ הַיּוֹם, דְּמִשּׁוּם טוֹרַח מְלֶאכֶת שַׁבָּת לֹא צָרִיךְ, דִּכְתִיב: "אֵת אֲשֶׁר תֹּאפוּ אֵפוּ וְאֵת אֲשֶׁר תְּבַשְּׁלוּ בַּשֵּׁלוּ", וְכֵיוָן דְּלָאו מְזוּמָּן הוּא, וְהַכָּתוּב קְרָאוֹ הֲכָנָה – הָוְיָא לָהּ מְלָאכָה, וְעוֹבֵר עָלֶיהָ מִשּׁוּם "לֹא תַעֲשֶׂה כָל מְלָאכָה": בְּעַאי. שָׁאַלְתִּי: מֵאֲפָר. אָחוּ. וּמוּקְצֶה הוּא, שֶׁאֵינוֹ נִכְנָס לַיִּשּׁוּב יָמִים רַבִּים: תָּמִיד. עוֹלָה שֶׁל צִיבּוּר: מַהוּ. לִיקְרַב: שֶׂה וְלֹא אֶת הַבְּכוֹר. מַתְנִיתָא הִיא, וְדָרְשָׁה קְרָא דִּיחֶזְקֵאל (מה) גַּבֵּי קָרְבָּנוֹת: "וְשֶׂה אַחַת מִן הַצֹּאן מִן הַמָּאתַיִם מִמַּשְׁקֵה יִשְׂרָאֵל": שֶׂה וְלֹא אֶת הַבְּכוֹר. דְּשֶׂה מַשְׁמַע שֶׁיְּהֵא רָאוּי לִהְיוֹת בֵּין זָכָר בֵּין נְקֵבָה, דְּכוּלָּן בִּכְלַל שֶׂה, וּבְכוֹר אֵינוֹ אֶלָּא זָכָר: וְלֹא מַעֲשֵׂר. דְּמַעֲשַׂר בְּהֵמָה אֵינוֹ רָאוּי לְהַקְדִּישׁוֹ לְקָרְבָּן אַחֵר, וְהָכִי מַשְׁמַע: אֶחָד – שֶׁיְּהֵא לְבַד, וְלֹא זֶה שֶׁאֵינוֹ בָּא אֶלָּא מִכְּלַל עֲשָׂרָה: מִן הַצֹּאן. וְלֹא כָּל הַצֹּאן, מִיעוּטָא הוּא, לְהוֹצִיא. פַּלְגָּס יָצָא מִכְּלַל כֶּבֶשׂ, וְלִכְלַל אַיִל לֹא בָּא, וְהַיְינוּ כָּל חוֹדֶשׁ שְׁלֹשָׁה עָשָׂר. דְּכֶבֶשׂ בֶּן שָׁנָה הוּא, וְאַיִל מִשֶּׁנִּכְנַס לְשָׁנָה שְׁנִיָּה חוֹדֶשׁ שָׁלֵם, וְהָכִי מְפָרֵשׁ לָהּ בְּמַסֶּ' פָּרָה (פ"א משנה ג): מִן

תוספות

אפילו ע"י ד"א – אין מעשרין מזה על זה. תירוש ודגן, דגן ודגן, שהן כלאים ע"י דבר אחר וכו'. ע"י ד"א דקאמר – לא קאי אדגן ודגן, דבלאו דבר אחר מיחייב בחטים ושעורים לחוד. וטעמא דר' יאשיה דכלאים בכרם לא מיחייב אלא בשלשה מינין, ובכלאי זרעים מיחייב בב' מינין – מפר"י: דזריעת כלאים משמע בב' מיני זרעים, וחרצן לאו מין זריעה הוא. אבל אין לפרש משום דמשמע לא תזרע בהדי כרמך כלאים, אבל שדך בלא שום זרע קרוי שדה – דהא לא שייך לפרש כן גבי בהמתך. ולפירוש ר"י קשה: אמאי נקט שור וחמור? בשור לחודי' ה"מ לאשכוחי כלאים – בשור פסולי המוקדשים, כדאמר בפ' בתרא דמכות (דף כב.) דאמר רבי יצחק: המנהיג בשור פסולי המוקדשים – דלוקה, משום דעשאו הכתוב ב' גופים, דאיתקש לצבי ואיל. ולפ"ה ניחא, דליכא בפסולי המוקדשי' לאו דמעילה. ולפר"י י"ל: דמשום דעיקר כלאים בשור ובחמור כתיב – נקט שור וחמור: **ושביעית.** למ"ד בפ"ק דמועד קטן (דף ג.): חורש בשביעית אינו לוקה – מוקי הך דהכא בחורש ומחפה, דמחפה חייב משום זורע: **אחרישה** לא ליחייב הואיל וחזי לכיסוי דם צפור. אם היה דם צפור במקום חרישה. ובכה"ג, שאם היה מבקש עפר אחר יגנב הדם, או יטשטש ע"י מים, ולא יקיים מצות כיסוי. וגם מיירי שאין יכול לקפלו וליטלו – דאם לא כן לא שייך כאן דלידחי עשה לא תעשה, כדאמר ר"ל [בשבת] (דף קלג:): כל מקום שאתה מוצא עשה ולא תעשה, אם אתה יכול לקיים שניהם – מוטב, אם לאו – ידחה עשה לא תעשה: **באבנים** מקורזלות. פי': רכות, שהן ראויות לזריעה. מיהו, לא חזי לכיסוי עד שיכתוש, וגבי בית הכסא נמי, לפי שהן רכות ראויות יותר לקינוח מכשהן קשים. ולא כפ"ה דפי' התם בפ' "כירה" (שבת מג.): מקורזלות – חדות, דהכא לא א"ש. ורש"י מתקו כאן מן הספרים*: **כתישה** בי"ט מי שרי. הקשה ריב"א: מאי פריך? הא ודאי שרי כמו חרישה דשרי משום הואיל, הכא נמי כתישה! ועוד תימה: היכי פריך הכא דליתי עשה דכיסוי וידחה לאו די"ט? הא אין י"ט נדחה מפני עשה, דהא תנן ב"כילד צולין" (לקמן פג:): אין שריפת קדשים דוחה י"ט. ובפ' "במה מדליקין" (שבת כד:) יליף מקראי, או משום כדמסיק רב אשי התם די"ט עשה ולא תעשה הוא, ואין עשה דוחה לא תעשה ועשה! ומפרש רשב"ם: "הואיל וחזי לכיסוי דם ציפור" לא משום דחיה קאמר – אלא משום דאז לא צריך לחרישה אלא לעפרה, ופטור, *דהחופר גומא ואינו צריך אלא לעפרה פטור, משום דהוי מלאכה שאין צריכה לגופה. והשתא פריך שפיר: כתישה בי"ט מי שרי? דכתישה הוי כטחינה, וצריכה לגופה הוא, שמתכוון לעשות עפר לכסות, ולא משתרי לצורך כיסוי דאין עשה דוחה לא תעשה ועשה. וקשה לר"י: הא דחופר גומא פטור היינו דוקא בבית, דמקלקל הוא, כדמוכח בפ"ק דחגיגה (דף י.). והכא בשדה, דלזריעה קיימא, שמשביח את השדה בחרישה. ואפילו אי הוה התם דם ציפור – הוה חייב אי חריש בארעא דיליה. ואי אמרת הואיל ואי הוי מלאכה שאין צריכה לגופה פטור – השתא נמי פטור, א"כ ביטלת כל מלאכת שבת! ור"ת מפרש: דבחרישה דכלאים קאי, דליכא אלא לאו גרידא. אבל איום טוב לא קאי, וכגון שאם היה הולך לבקש עפר אחר היה הדם נבלע בקרקע. ומסיק: כתישה בי"ט מי שרי טפי, כיון דמשום י"ט אסור דמשום דאית ביה עשה ולא תעשה – גם משום כלאים לא שייך למיפטר בהואיל, דאפילו אם היה שם דם ציפור – אסור. ובתחלה נמי הוה מצי לשנויי חרישה בי"ט מי שרי, אלא דמשני ליה בע"א משום יגדיל תורה ויאדיר*: **ולוקה** משום הבערה. בפ"ק דביצה (דף יב:) אמר: הא מני – ב"ש היא, דלית להו מתוך. אבל לבית הלל – שרי אע"ג דלריך שיהא לורך היום – הא נמי חשיב לורך היום, אע"פ שאין ראוי לאוכלו אלא באיסור: **אהבערה** לא ליחייב. מכאן מוכיח ריב"א דרבה דאמר הואיל – היינו אפילו לבית שמאי אמר: **הואיל** וחזי לצורכו. בלא האי פירכא נמי קאמר במכות: אפיק הבערה, משום דקשיא ליה הא דקאמר רבה: חילוק מלאכות לשבת, ואין חילוק מלאכות לי"ט: **ועייל** עצי מוקצה. תימה לר"י: מ"מ ליתני גיד הנשה של נבילה, ולילקי נמי משום נבילה! **שה** ולא הבכור. פירש בקונט': דשה משמע בין זכר ובין נקיבה. ותימה: דהא בעולה איירי, דאין באה נקבה. וא"ת: אמאי איצטריך קרא שאין תמיד בא מבכור ומעשר? תיפוק ליה שאין מתנותיהן שוות! וי"ל, דהא אמר*: כל הניתני' במתן ד' שנתנו במתנה אחת – כיפר. וע"ק: היאך יעשה תמיד מבכור? הא קעבר משום כל שממנו לאשים – הרי הוא ב"בל תקטירו" (יבמות דף ק.)! וי"ל: כיון דמסיק ליה לשם עולה – דינו כדין עולה. ומהאי טעמא נמי ניחא לענין מתנה. ור"י פירש: דהאי קרא מישתעי בפסח, דכתיב ביה "שה תמים"(א) וקאמר שלא יביאנו לא דבכור ולא דמעשר. וא"ש השתא דמתנותיהן שוות, ולא תיקשי כל שממנו לאשים: **שה** ולא בכור. וא"ת: בפרק קמא דחגיגה (דף ח.) דנפקא לן מב"מסת ידך" דכל דבר שבא חובה אין בא אלא מן החולין! וי"ל: דהכא אסמכתא בעלמא היא, ומן המאתים שערלה בטילה במאתים – נמי אסמכתא היא. אך קשה ד"ממשקה ישראל" – מן המותר לישראל, דרשה גמורה היא, דמהאי קרא יליף בפ"ק דמנחות (דף ה:) דטריפה אסורה לגבוה: רבי

רבינו חננאל

וכלאים בכרם אחת והוא בשביעית ויו"ט שתים. כהן ונזיר אבות הטומאה שתים הרי ח' לאוין ואי ס"ד אמרי' הואיל אחרישה ביום טוב לא ליחייב הואיל וראוי לכסות באותה החפירה דם צפור ודחי' אותו מקום שחורש בו אבנים מקורזלות הם דלאו בני כסוי נינהו. אמרי' והא ראוי לכותשן כלאחר יד כו' ואוקמה רב אשי במתונא פי' קרקע שיש בו לחלוחית ואינו ראוי לכסות בו ויש מי שאומ' טיט יבש: **ומותיב** אביי המבשל גיד הנשה בחלב ביו"ט ואכלו לוקה חמש כו' ואי אמרינן הואיל אהבערה לא ניחייב הואיל וחזי ליה לצרכיה לבשל ולאכול ושני' אפיק הבערה ועייל גיד של נבלה. איני והתנן ר' חייא אומר לוקה שתים ושלשה על בישולו ואלו הן לוקה משום מבעיר אש שלא לצורך אכילה ולוקה משום מבשל גיד ביום טוב שאינו בר אכילה וכן משום בשר בחלב הרי שלשה בבישול ושתים באכילה משום אוכל גיד הנשה ומשום אוכל בשר בחלב ואם תוציא הבערה ותכניס גיד הנשה של נבלה ומשום אכילת נבלה יבואו שלשה על האכילה ושתים על הבישול והדר ומשני אפיק הבערה ועייל עצי מוקצה ואקשי' וכי מוקצה מדאורייתא הוא שלוקין עליו כו' והא את הוא דאמרת בעי מרב הונא ואמרי לה מרב חסדא הביא שה מן האפר פי' מן המדבר מקום המרעה ושחט תמיד ביום טוב מהו מי יש מוקצה לגבוה או לא ואמרת פשטה לן מהאי קרא ושה אחת מן הצאן [מן המאתים] ממשקה ישראל שה ולא בכור אחת ולא מעשר מן הצאן ולא מן הפלגם פסול שאינו לא כבש ולא איל ומפורש במס' פרה

ביצה יב. [ע"ש] מכו' כא. [ע"ש]

ס"א א"ל שה

[וע"ע תוס' סוכה לו: ד"ה מקורזלות]

[שבת עג:]

[עיין מ"ש תוס' חולין קמא. ד"ה לא צריכה וכו' בשם ריב"א]

[זבחים לו:]

הגהות הב"ח

(א) תוס' ד"ה שה ולא הבכור פי' ור"י וכו' פי' דהאי קרא משתעי בפסח דכתיב ביה שה תמים א"כ אתא קרא שיביאו פסח מדבר שיכול להיות אחת פי' נקבה דהיינו חולין ולא בכור ושה אחת כתיב וקאמר וכו':

גליון הש"ס

גמ' אחרישה לא ליחייב. עי' טורי אבן חגיג' באבני מלואים דף יח ד"א וכלל: שם ועייל עצי מוקצה. עי' מג"א סי' שכ"ה סק"ט:

"°מן המאתים" – ממותר שתי מאות שנשתיירו בבור. מכאן [א]לערלה שבטילה במאתים. "ממשקה ישראל" – *מן המותר לישראל. מכאן אמרו: [ב]אין מביאין נסכין מן הטבל. יכול לא יביא מן המוקצה, אמרת: מה טבל מיוחד שאיסור גופו גרם לו, אף כל שאיסור גופו גרם לו, [ג]יצא מוקצה שאין איסור גופו גרם לו אלא איסור דבר אחר גרם לו. ואי אמרת איסור מוקצה דאורייתא – מה לי איסור גופו מה לי איסור דבר אחר? ועוד: הא את הוא דאמרת: *[ד]חילוק מלאכות לשבת ואין חילוק מלאכות ליו"ט. אלא: אפיק הבערה ועייל עצי אשירה. ואזהרה מהכא: °"ולא ידבק בידך מאומה מן החרם". אמר ליה רב אחא בריה דרבא לאביי: ונלקי נמי משום °"ולא תביא תועבה אל ביתך"! אלא אפיק הבערה, ועייל עצי הקדש, ואזהרה מהכא: °"ואשריהם תשרפון באש לא תעשון כן לה' אלהיכם". אמר רמי בר חמא: הא דרב חסדא ורבה – מחלוקת דר"א ורבי יהושע היא. דר"א סבר: אמרינן "הואיל", ורבי יהושע סבר: לא אמרינן "הואיל". אמר רב פפא: ודילמא, עד כאן לא קאמר ר"א התם דאמרינן הואיל – אלא דבעידנא דקא עיילי לתנורא כל חדא וחדא חזיא ליה לדידיה, אבל הכא דלאורחין הוא דחזי, לדידיה לא חזי – אימא הכי נמי דלא אמרינן "הואיל". אמר רב שישא בריה דרב אידי: ודילמא לא היא. עד כאן לא קאמר רבי יהושע התם דלא אמרינן "הואיל" – אלא דאיכא חדא דלא חזיא, לא לדידיה ולא לאורחין. אבל הכא, דחזי מיהת לאורחין – אימא הכי נמי אמרינן "הואיל". אמרוה [רבנן] קמיה דרבי ירמיה ור' זירא. ר' ירמיה קיבלה, ר' זירא לא קיבלה. א"ל רבי ירמיה לרבי זירא: מילתא דקשיא לן ואתיא כמה שני, במאי פליגי ר"א ור' יהושע, השתא אמרוה משמיה דגברא רבה – ולא ניקבלה? אמר ליה: היכי אקבלה? דתניא, אמר ליה רבי יהושע: לדבריך, הרי הוא עובר משום* °"לא תעשה כל מלאכה" ושתיק ליה. ואי איתא – לימא ליה: טעמא דידי משום הואיל. א"ל: וליטעמיך, הא דתנינא בברייתא, אמר לו ר"א: לדבריך הרי הוא עובר משום "בל יראה ובל ימצא" ושתיק ליה. ה"נ דלא אהדר ליה? הא קא מהדר ליה במתני', דתנן: לא זהו חמץ שמוזהרין עליו משום בל יראה ובל ימצא. אלא: שתיק ליה בברייתא, ומהדר ליה במתני'. ה"נ אימור: שתיק ליה במתני', ואהדר ליה במכילתא אחריתי. תניא, רבי אומר: הלכה כר"א, ור' יצחק אמר: הלכה כבן בתירא. וכמה שיעור עיסה? רבי ישמעאל בנו של רבי יוחנן בן ברוקה אומר: בחיטין – קבין, ובשעורין – שלשת קבין. ר' נתן אומר משום ר"א: חילוף הדברים. והתניא, רבי ישמעאל בנו של ר' יוחנן בן ברוקה אומר: בחטין – שלשת קבין, ובשעורין – ארבעה קבין! לא קשיא; הא – בחסיכתא, הא – במעלייתא. אמר רב פפא: שמע מינה גריעין חיטי חסיכתא מחיטי מעלייתא, טפי מדגריעין שערי חסיכתא משערי מעלייתא. דאילו התם תילתא, והכא ריבעא. אמר רב: קבא מלוגנאה לפיסחא, וכן לחלה. (*והתניא)
חמשת

מן המאתים. על כרחיך אנסכים קאי, וקאמר: הביאו הנסכים עליו מן המאתים, שישתיירו מאתים בבור היין: מכאן לערלה שבטלה במאתים. דאי לאו בשאיסור מעורב בו קאי, אמאי מצריך מאתים? ובעלמא בסיפרי נפקא לן שפיר, דערלה וכלאי הכרם בטילין במאתים. והאי "מכאן" לאו דוקא, אלא אף כאן אתה יכול לסמוך קצת: איסור דבר אחר. שבת: הא את הוא דאמרת. ב"אלו הן הלוקין" (מכות דף כא:): חילוק מלאכות לשבת. שאם עשה שתים בהעלם אחד, או [אחת] בשתי העלמות – חייב שתים: ואין חילוק מלאכות ליום טוב. שאם עשה שתי מלאכות במזיד – אינו לוקה שתים. והכא ביום טוב קיימינן, ומחייבת ליה משום י"ט תרתי, משום מוקצה, ומשום מבשל גיד ביום טוב: אמר רמי בר חמא הא דרבה ורב חסדא. דאיפליגו גבי יום טוב, אי שרינן ליה משום הואיל או לא: מחלוקת רבי אליעזר ור' יהושע היא דרבי אליעזר סבר אמרינן הואיל. אע"ג דסופו להפריש אחת מהן לחלה, ונמצא שטרח בדבר שאינו ראוי לאכילה – אפי' הכי אמרינן: הואיל ואי בעי לא מפריש חדא לחלה, אלא בלע מכל חדא וחדא, ואיכא למימר בכל חדא חזיא ליה, ומותר לאפותה: ור' יהושע סבר לא אמרינן הואיל. כדי להתיר מלאכות יום טוב. ואהואיל ואי בעי מיתשיל עלה דלעיל – לא קאי רמי בר חמא, אלא אהואיל דאיסור מלאכת יום טוב: אלא דבעידנא דעיילי לה. איכא למימר בכל חדא וחדא חזיא ליה בלאו הואיל, דבכל חדא איכא למימר זו לא תהא לחלה: אבל הכא דלאורחין הוא דחזיא. והרי עדיין לא זימן לית ליה הואיל למישרייה לרבי אליעזר: דלא חזיא לא לדידיה ולא לאורחים. (א)והרי סופו ליטול אחת לחלה, שאין דרך לבלוע מכל אחת: אבל הכא. דכולהו חזו לאורחין, ואורחין שכיחי – אמרינן הואיל למישרייה. ואי קשיא: הא דאמר ר' יהושע לא זהו חמץ שמוזהרין כו' – אלמא לית ליה הואיל ואי בעי מיתשיל עלה אפילו לחומרא, וכל שכן הואיל דהכא לקולא – לא דמי, דהשתא מיהא לאו דידיה הוא. וכך שמעתי, ומגמגם לבי עלה. ונראה בעיני דאין הואיל בזה בדבר שאינו שלו, דנימא הואיל ואי בעי מייתי ליה ברשותיה – דאם כן הקדש דקיימא לן אבל אתה רואה של גבוה, ולא פליג ר"א – הא אי בעי פריק ליה והוי דידיה. ואף סוגיא דשמעתא לא מיתבא שפיר. וכמדומה דפירוש הכתוב ברישא דשמעתא: הואיל ואי בעי מיתשיל עליה – לא גר'. אלא הכי גר': ר' אליעזר סבר אמרי' הואיל, ור' יהושע סבר לא אמרינן הואיל. והכי פירושא: ר' אליעזר סבר שרי לאפותה, ואע"ג דסוף איכא חדא דלא חזיא ליה – אין כאן איסור מלאכה, הואיל וכל חדא וחדא חזיא ליה, דמצי למשקל מכל חדא פורתא. ור' יהושע סבר: לא אמרינן הואיל, דהא סופו ליטול אחת מהן לחלה. הלכך, כיון דטובת הנאה אינה ממון, ולא עבר עלה – מנחתה עד הערב ושורפה: אמרוה. להא דרמי בר חמא: מילתא דקשיא לן כו'. דטובת הנאה ממון ליכא לאוקמי פלוגתייהו לחוד. דנהי נמי דטובת הנאה ממון לר' אליעזר – אפילו הכי השתא נמי עובר משום "לא תעשה כל מלאכה", ומוטב לעבור על "בל יראה" מאליו ואינו עושה מעשה בידים, מלעבור על "לא תעשה כל מלאכה" ועושה מעשה בידים: טעמא דידי משום הואיל. ואין כאן חילול: אהדר ליה במכילתא אחריתא. ואיכא למימר דבתרווייהו פליגי, ר' אליעזר סבר: טובת הנאה ממון, הלכך אי מחמלה גביה – עבר עלה. ולאפותה קודם לכן אין כאן איסור, דאמרי' הואיל, ואיכא למימר בכל חדא חזיא ליה. ור' יהושע סבר: אינה ממון. הלכך, לא זהו חמץ שמוזהרין עליו. וכי אפי לה – עבר עלה, דלא אמרינן הואיל. והא דתריצנא לעיל דכולי עלמא טובת הנאה אינה ממון – הכתי לא שמיע לן הא דאהדר ליה ר' אליעזר לר' יהושע: הרי הוא עובר ב"בל יראה": הלכה כבן בתירא. תטיל לצונן: שיעור עיסה. לגוש בפסח, ולא יותר. שיכול לשומרה מידי חימוץ: חילוף הדברים. שהשעורין קרובין להחמיץ יותר מן החיטים: הא בחסיכתא הא במעלייתא. קמייתא במעלייתא, בתרייתא בחסיכתא. שש שלהן אינן אלא קביים טובות: שמע מינה. לענין מקח וממכר: גריען חיטי חסיכתא ממעלייתא טפי ממאי דגריען שערי חסיכתא ממעלייתא. דאילו בחיטי קתני בטובות קביים וברעות שלשת קבים, אלמא: גרעי תילתא. ואילו בשעורין, הטובות שלשת קבין והרעות ארבעה – ליכא גריעותא אלא ריבעא: קבא מלוגנאה. קב של אותו מקום: לפיסחא. שלא ללוש יותר כדי שיוכל לשומרו מן החימוץ: וכן לחלה. כהך שיעור עיסה נמי, כל ימות השנה להתחייב בחלה:
חמשת

רבי אומר הלכה כר' **אליעזר**. ה"ר יוסף פסק כרבי, משום דקיימא לן* כוותיה מחבירו, וכן מנהג. ור"י דוחה: דשמא לא קאמר הלכה כרבי מחבירו, דהא איפליגו רבה ורב חסדא בהכי. והא דהלכה כרבי מחבירו – היינו היכא דליכא פלוגתא דאמוראי:
חמשת

רבינו חננאל

מן המאה ממותר שתי מאות שנשתיירו בבור כלומר אפי' ערלה שהיא חמורה מן הכלאים עלתה (ונשתיירו) [ואם נשתיירו] מאתים מותרין הן מכאן לערלה שבטלה (במאה) [במאתים] ממשקה ישראל מן היין המותר לישראל מכאן אמרו אין מביאין נסכים מן הטבל יכול לא יביא מן המוקצה אמרת לא (יביא) ומה ראית להתירו גמרי' מטבל מה טבל מיוחד שאיסור גופו גרם לו יצא מוקצה שגופו תמים וכשר הוא ואיסור הכנה בא להרחיקו ואי ס"ד מוקצה אסור מן התורה איך מתירו ואיפריכא ומשני אפיק הבערה ועייל עצי אשרה ואזהרתיה ולא ידבק בידך מאומה מן החרם כו' ונדחת גם זו וכו' ואוקימנא אלא עייל עצי הקדש כו': **אמר** רמי בר חמא מחלוקת ר' אליעזר ור' יהושע במתני' בהואיל ופליגי בדרבה ורב חסדא ר' אליעזר סבר הואיל ואי בעי הא מפריש ואיבעי הא מפריש כל חדא וחדא חזיא ליה ושרי ליה למכליה לפיכך לא תקרא לה שם עד שתאפה ור' יהושע סבר לא אמרינן הואיל וכיון דאיכא חדא דלא חזיא ליה אסור ודחי רב פפא דלמא לא היא עד כאן לא קא שרי ר' אליעזר למפייה אלא הואיל ובעידנא דקא אפי לה כל חדא וחדא חזיא ליה אבל האופה מיום טוב לחול דבעידנא דקא אפי לא חזי ליה לבו ביום דהא אית ליה אחרים אימא לך אסור ר' אליעזר ודחי רב מיאשא נמי הא דרמי דלמא עד כאן לא אסר ר' יהושע באפיית הפת שלא הופרשה חלה ממנה אלא משום דאית ביה פת אחת שאינה ראויה לא לו ולא לאחרים מכחו מפני שהיא חלה (לכהן) [טמאה] אבל הכא לענין האופה מיום טוב לחול דאי מקלעי ליה אורחים חזי להאכיל להו שרי ר' יהושע: **אמרוה** הא דרמי קמי ר' זירא ולא קבלה אמר ליה ר' ירמיה אמאי לא קבלת אמר ליה ואמאי נקבלה דתניא בברייתא אמר (להם) [לו] ר' יהושע הרי (תנא) [הוא] עובר משום לא תעשה כל מלאכה כי אופה דבר שאינו ראוי לו ושתק ואי ס"ד בהואיל פליגי נימא ליה אינו עובר הואיל וכל חדא וחדא חזיא ליה אמאי שתיק ואלא מדאישתק לית ליה הואיל א"ל ר' ירמיה אי הכי הא דתנינא בברייתא אמר לו ר' אליעזר הרי הוא עובר משום לא יראה ולא ימצא ואשתיק ר' יהושע בברייתא הכי נמי (דהדר ביה) [דלא אהדר ליה] והא אהדר ליה במתני' לא זהו חמץ שמוזהרין עליו בבל יראה ובל ימצא אלא שתיק בברייתא ואהדר לי' במתני' ר' אליעזר נמי אימור אהדר ליה במכילתא אחריתא ואע"ג דמסתבר טעמא דר' יהושע*) ואמר אני אכריע כשאני אופה נמצאתי עובר על הוא לבדו יעשה לכם ועושה מעשה בידי וכשאני מניחה נמצאתי עובר ואיני עושה מעשה בידי. תניא אמר ר' הלכה כר' אליעזר דאמר לא תקרא לה שם עד שתאפה ואע"ג דאין למדין ממשנה דהיא תלמוד סמכינן אהא דאמר רב יהודה אמר שמואל הלכה כר' אליעזר שהרודה ונותן לסל הסל מצרפן דכלהו חדא טעמא היא: **ור'** יצחק אמר הלכה כבן בתירא דאמר תטיל לצונן: **ואע"ג** דפליגי ר' ישמעאל בנו של ר' יוחנן בן ברוקה ור' נתן בשיעור אפיית עיסה והוא אמר בחטין קביין דעבדי קביין חטין פת טפי מדעבדי תלתא קבי שערי וטירחא דהני טפי מהני ור' נתן אמר בחטין שלשת קבין דשרירן כלומר חזקין ויש בהן שמנונית ועיסתן לא מחמעא הייא פי' מהרה לפיכך אפילו שלשת קבין מותר אבל שעורים שאינן חזקים אלא כחושין מתחמצת עיסתן מהרה לפיכך אין אופין שעורים אלא קביין קביין ומקשי' ואמרינן ר' ישמעאל אומר קבין חטין והא תניא שלשת קבין חטין והוא דאמר שלשת קבין שעורין והא תניא ארבעת קבין שעורין ושני' הא דאמר קבין חטין חיטי מעלייתא והא דאמר שלשת קבין בחיטי חסיכתא רעים דקים כדמתרגמינן חסירתא ובישתא וכן בשעורים השעורים היפות שלשה קבין והרעות ארבעת קבין שנמצא עושות פת קבים חטים יפות כמו שלשת קבין רעות וכן בשעורים נמצא בין חטים יפות לחטים רעות שליש פחיתות ובשעורים רביע מכלל שהחטים הרעות כו' ודברים פשוטין הן: **אמר** רב קבא מלוגנאה לפסחא וכן לחלה וזה וזה שיעורן אחד הוא כי קבא מלוגנאה הוא
חמשת

*) נראה דיש טעות סופר בדבריו וכצ"ל טעמא דר"י ואני אכריע דכשאני אופה נמצאתי עובר על כל מלאכה לא יעשה בהם ועושה כו'.

עין משפט נר מצוה:
לז א מיי' פט"ו מהלכות מאכלות אסורות הלכה יז:
לח ב מיי' פ"ה מהל' איסורי מזבח הל"ט:
לט ג שם הלכה י:
מ ד מיי' פ"א מהל' יו"ט הלכה ג:

[לעיל כז.]

מסורת הש"ס: [מנחות ה. חולין ל: תמורה כט.] [מכות כא:] [צ"ל והתנן]

תורה אור: יחזקאל מה; דברים יג; שם ז; שם יב; שמות כ

הגהות הב"ח
(א) רש"י ד"ה דלא חזיא וכו' דהרי סופו:

[הך קרא בשבת כתיב ואולי צ"ל כל מלאכה לא יעשה בהם דכתיב גבי חג הפסח שמות יב טז]

מא א מיי' פ"ו מהל' ביכורים הלכה טו סמג עשין קמא טוש"ע י"ד סי' שכד סעיף א:
[וע"ע תוס' שבת טו. ד"ה רבי יוסי אומר ובעירובין פג: ד"ה שבעת]

מב ב מיי' פ"ה מהל' מלה הלכה יא סמג לאוין עט טור ש"ע א"ח סי' תנו ס"א:

מג ג ד טוש"ע א"ח סי' תנז ס"א:

מד ה ו מיי' פ"ו מהל' ביכורים הלכה טז יז סמג עשין קמא טוש"ע י"ד סי' שכה סעיף א:

מה ז מיי' פ"ה מהל' חמץ הלכה יג סמג לאוין עט טור ש"ע א"ח סי' תנט סעיף ב:

מו ח טור ש"ע שם:

רבינו חננאל

חמשת רבעים ועוד והן שיעור הקמח להוציא מהן חלה: **אמר** רב יוסף הני נשי דידן. כלומר בני בתאי נהגו למיפא קפיזא קפיזא בפסח שהוא מקבא מלוגנאה ואמר להו אביי נתרחקו מאיסור דחמץ ואפקעו תורת חלה. אמר ליה לא מפקעינן מחלה אלא עבדין כר' אליעזר דתנן ר' אליעזר אמר הרודה ונותן לסל הסל מצרפן לחלה ואמר רב יהודה אמר שמואל הלכה כרבי אליעזר בככרות שנושכות זו את זו ונראות כאלו נכנסות זו בתוך זו ואפי' בענין שאין נושכות הסל מצרפן: **בעי** ר' ירמיה טבלא שאין לה לבזביז. פירוש לבזביז מסגרת מהו מי מצרפן לחלה דאויר כלי מצרף והא איכא אויר או דלמא תוך כלי מצרף והא לית ליה תוך ועלתה בתיקו: **תניא** רבי אליעזר אומר הסל מצרפן לחלה וקיימ' לן כותיה ר' יהושע אומר תנור מצרפן רשב"ג אומר ככרות נושכות זו את זו מצטרפות: **מתני'** ר"ג אומר שלש נשים לשות כאחת ואופות בתנור אחד זו אחר זו וזו אחר זו אע"פ שכולן (לשו) [יאפו] בתנו' אחד אחת מסיקה התנור ואופה והשניה אחריה והשליש' אחריה וקמ"ל אע"פ שיהא הבצק שוהה כדי שלשה הסקות ושתי אפיות אינו בא לידי חמוץ וטוב לעשות כך אבל ארבע נשים ללוש כאחת לא נתברר כי התיר רשב"ג ללוש לקטף ולאפות אשה אחת והאחרת שלשה עמה ממתנת לה: **וחכמי'** אומרים שלש נשים עוסקות בבצק אחת לשה וכשתתחיל לערוך אחרת לשה וזה שעורכת מסיקה ואופה וזו שלשה אחריה עורכ' וכשתתחיל הראשונה לאפות והשני' לערוך מתחלת השלישית ללוש נמצאת בבת אחת הראשונה אופה והשניה עורכת והשלישית לשה ואין אחת מהן ממתנת לחברתה אלא כולן עוסקות וזו היא ששנינו בחיצונה לשה היא מקטפת וחברתה לשה תחתיה מקטפת היא אופה וחברתה מקטפת תחתיה [והשלישית לשה] אופה היא לשה וחברתה אופה תחתיה [והשלישית מקטפת] וחוזרות חלילה כל זמן שעסוקות בבצק אינו בא לידי חמוץ: **ר'** עקיבא אומר לא כל הנשים ולא כל העצים ולא כל התנורים שוין זה הכלל תפח תלטוש בצונן ויש אומרים תפח: **שיאור** ישרף והאוכלו פטור סדוק ישרף והאוכלו חייב כרת כו' במשנתנו שנה לנו דברי ר' מאיר בלשון חכמים ובברייתא שנה לנו דברי ר' מאיר בלשון חכמים לרבי יהודה השיאור כקרני חגבים והסדוק שנתערבו סדקיו זה בזה ולר' מאיר שיאור שהכסיפו פניו כאדם שעמדו שערותיו סידוק כקרני חגבים מ"ט שאין לך סדק מלמעלה שאין בו כמה סדקין מלמטה ובתרווייהו האוכלו שיאור דר' יהודה סידוק לר' מאיר: **ת"ר** אי זהו (סידוק) [שיאור] כקרני חגבים סידוק שנתערבו סדקיו זה בזה וזה וזה האוכלו חייב כרת ואקשי' מאן שמעת ליה דאית ליה האי סברא ר' יהודה וכי ר' יהודה מחייב אקרני חגבים כרת והתנן שיאור ישרף והאוכלו פטור דברי ר' יהודה ושני' אימא זה וזה כלומר בין סידוק כקרני חגבים בין סידוק שנתערבו סדקיו זה בזה לר' מאיר אחד הוא כל סדק זה וזה חייב כרת וקי"ל כר'

חמשת רבעים קמח. רש"י לא גרס "ועוד", משום דחמשה לוגין ליפוריס בנמוס הוי כעיסת מדבר. ור"ת מפרש: דהיינו כר' יוסי, דאמר בפ"ק דשבת (דף טו.): חמשה – פטורים. חמשה ועוד – חייבין. והיינו טעמא דר' יוסי, דלאחר הפרשת חלה בעינן שיעור עריסותיכם*:

לא שנו אלא ככרות שנושכות זו את זו. תימה: דלא משמע הכי במסכת חלה (פ"ב משנה ד), דתנן: העושה עיסתו קבין – פטור מן החלה, עד שיסוכו. רבי אליעזר אומר: אף הרודה וכו'. אלמא: לא בעי ר' אליעזר שישוכו. ואי לא גרס "אף" – אתי שפיר דמצי למימר דבעי תרתי: שישוכו, ויתנם לסל:

לשבות

---

*[א]חֲמֵשֶׁת רְבָעִים קֶמַח וְעוֹד חַיָּיבִין בְּחַלָּה! הָכִי קָאָמַר: קַבָּא מְלוֹגְנַאי נַמִי [ב]אַהַאי שִׁיעוּרָא קָאֵי. אֲמַר רַב יוֹסֵף: הָנֵי נָשֵׁי דִּידָן [ג]נְהוּג לְמֵיפָא קְפִיזָא קְפִיזָא לְפִיסְחָא. א"ל אַבַּיֵי: מַאי דַּעְתִּיךְ – לְחוּמְרָא, חוּמְרָא דְּאָתֵי לִידֵי קוּלָּא הוּא, דְּקָא מַפְקַע לַהּ מֵחַלָּה! א"ל: דְּעָבְדָן כְּר' אֱלִיעֶזֶר, (*דְּתַנְיָא), *רַבִּי אֱלִיעֶזֶר אוֹמֵר: [ד]הָרוֹדֶה וְנוֹתֵן לַסַּל – הַסַּל מְצָרְפָן לְחַלָּה. וְאָמַר רַב יְהוּדָה אָמַר שְׁמוּאֵל: [ה]הֲלָכָה כְּרַבִּי אֱלִיעֶזֶר. א"ל: וְהָא אִיתְּמַר עֲלָהּ, אָמַר רַבִּי יְהוֹשֻׁעַ בֶּן לֵוִי: לֹא שָׁנוּ אֶלָּא כִּכָּרוֹת שֶׁל בָּבֶל, שֶׁנּוֹשְׁכוֹת זוֹ מִזּוֹ, אֲבָל כְּעָכִין – לֹא! הָא אִיתְּמַר עֲלָהּ, א"ר חֲנִינָא: אֲפִי' כְּעָכִין. בָּעֵי ר' יִרְמְיָה: טַבְלָא שֶׁאֵין לָהּ לִבְזְבֵּזִין °מַהוּ? [ו]תּוֹךְ כְּלִי בָּעִינַן – וְהָא לֵיכָּא, אוֹ דִּילְמָא: אֲוִיר כְּלִי בָּעִינַן – וְהָא אִיכָּא? תֵּיקוּ.§ תַּנְיָא, ר' אֱלִיעֶזֶר אוֹמֵר: הַסַּל מְצָרְפָן, ר' יְהוֹשֻׁעַ אוֹמֵר: תַּנּוּר מְצָרְפָן. רַבָּן שִׁמְעוֹן בֶּן גַּמְלִיאֵל אוֹמֵר: כִּכָּרוֹת[א] שֶׁל בָּבֶל שֶׁנּוֹשְׁכוֹת זוֹ מִזּוֹ – מִצְטָרְפוֹת.§ **מתני'** רַבָּן גַּמְלִיאֵל אוֹמֵר: שָׁלֹשׁ נָשִׁים לָשׁוֹת כְּאַחַת, וְאוֹפוֹת בְּתַנּוּר אֶחָד, זוֹ אַחַר זוֹ. וַחֲכָמִים אוֹמְרִים: שָׁלֹשׁ נָשִׁים עוֹסְקוֹת בְּבָצֵק כְּאַחַת, אַחַת לָשָׁה, וְאַחַת עוֹרֶכֶת, וְאַחַת אוֹפָה. ר' עֲקִיבָא אוֹמֵר: °לֹא כָּל הַנָּשִׁים וְלֹא כָּל הָעֵצִים וְלֹא כָּל הַתַּנּוּרִים שָׁוִין. זֶה הַכְּלָל: תָּפַח – תִּלְטוֹשׁ בְּצוֹנֵן.§ **גמ'** ת"ר: לָשָׁה, הִיא מְקַטֶּפֶת וַחֲבֵירְתָּהּ לָשָׁה תַּחְתֶּיהָ. מְקַטֶּפֶת – הִיא אוֹפָה וַחֲבֵירְתָּהּ מְקַטֶּפֶת תַּחְתֶּיהָ, וְהַשְּׁלִישִׁית לָשָׁה. אוֹפָה – הִיא לָשָׁה, וַחֲבֵירְתָּהּ אוֹפָה תַּחְתֶּיהָ, וְהַשְּׁלִישִׁית מְקַטֶּפֶת, וְחוֹזֶרֶת חֲלִילָה. [ז]כָּל זְמַן שֶׁעוֹסְקוֹת בְּבָצֵק אֵינוֹ בָּא לִידֵי חִימּוּץ.§ "ר"ע אוֹמֵר לֹא כָּל הַנָּשִׁים וכו'".§ תַּנְיָא, אָמַר רַבִּי עֲקִיבָא: דַּנְתִּי לִפְנֵי רַבָּן גַּמְלִיאֵל, יְלַמְּדֵנוּ רַבֵּינוּ בְּנָשִׁים זְרִיזוֹת אוֹ בְּנָשִׁים שֶׁאֵין זְרִיזוֹת? בְּעֵצִים לַחִים אוֹ בְּעֵצִים יְבֵשִׁים? בְּתַנּוּר חַם אוֹ בְּתַנּוּר צוֹנֵן? אָמַר לִי: אֵין לְךָ אֶלָּא מַה שֶּׁשָּׁנוּ חֲכָמִים, זֶה הַכְּלָל: תָּפַח תִּלְטוֹשׁ בְּצוֹנֵן.§ **מתני'** שִׂיאוּר יִשָּׂרֵף, *וְהָאוֹכְלוֹ פָּטוּר, סִידּוּק – יִשָּׂרֵף, וְהָאוֹכְלוֹ חַיָּיב כָּרֵת. אֵיזֶהוּ שִׂיאוּר – כְּקַרְנֵי חֲגָבִים, סִידּוּק – שֶׁנִּתְעָרְבוּ סְדָקִין זֶה בָּזֶה, דִּבְרֵי רַבִּי יְהוּדָה. וַחֲכָמִים אוֹמְרִים: [ח]זֶה וָזֶה הָאוֹכְלוֹ חַיָּיב כָּרֵת. וְאֵיזֶהוּ שִׂיאוּר – כָּל שֶׁהִכְסִיפוּ פָּנָיו, כְּאָדָם שֶׁעָמְדוּ שַׂעֲרוֹתָיו.§ **גמ'** תָּנוּ רַבָּנַן: *אֵיזֶהוּ שִׂיאוּר – כָּל שֶׁהִכְסִיפוּ פָּנָיו כְּאָדָם שֶׁעָמְדוּ שַׂעֲרוֹתָיו. סִידּוּק – כְּקַרְנֵי חֲגָבִים, *דִּבְרֵי ר' מֵאִיר. וַחֲכָמִים אוֹמְרִים: אֵיזֶהוּ שִׂיאוּר – כְּקַרְנֵי חֲגָבִים, סִידּוּק – שֶׁנִּתְעָרְבוּ סְדָקִין זֶה בָּזֶה. וְזֶה וָזֶה הָאוֹכְלוֹ חַיָּיב כָּרֵת. וְהָאֲנַן תְּנַן: שִׂיאוּר יִשָּׂרֵף, וְהָאוֹכְלוֹ פָּטוּר, דִּבְרֵי רַבִּי יְהוּדָה! אֵימָא: לְרַבִּי מֵאִיר זֶה וָזֶה הָאוֹכְלוֹ חַיָּיב כָּרֵת. אָמַר רָבָא: מַאי טַעְמָא דְּר' מֵאִיר – אֵין לְךָ כָּל סֶדֶק וָסֶדֶק מִלְּמַעְלָה שֶׁאֵין לוֹ כַּמָּה סְדָקִים מִלְּמַטָּה.§

מתני'

חֲמֵשֶׁת רְבָעִים. לוּגִּין צִיפּוֹרִים, שֶׁהֵן שִׁבְעָה וָעוֹד מִדְבָּרִיִּים, שֶׁזֶּה הוּא שִׁיעוּר הָעוֹמֶר שֶׁהָיְתָה עִיסַּת מִדְבָּר, שֶׁנֶּאֱמַר גַּבֵּי חַלָּה (במדבר טו): "רֵאשִׁית עֲרִיסוֹתֵיכֶם" – כְּדֵי עֲרִיסוֹתֵיכֶם, דְּהַיְינוּ עִיסַּת מִדְבָּר, שֶׁהוּא עוֹמֶר לַגּוּלְגּוֹלֶת, וְהוּא עֲשִׂירִית הָאֵיפָה. וְהָאֵיפָה שָׁלֹשׁ סְאִין, וּסְאָה שִׁשָּׁה קַבִּין מִדְבָּרִיּוֹת. חֲשׁוֹב עִישּׂוּר שֶׁבָּהֶן, וְתִמְצָא שִׁבְעַת רִבְעֵי קַב וּבֵיצָה וְחוֹמֶשׁ בֵּיצָה. כֵּיצַד? חֲלֵק שָׁלֹשׁ סְאִין שֶׁהֵן שְׁמוֹנָה עָשָׂר קַבִּין וַעֲשֵׂה מֵהֶן רִבְעֵי קַב, הַיְינוּ לוּגִּין – וְתִמְצָא בָּהֶן שִׁבְעִים וּשְׁנַיִם לוֹג. טוֹל עִישּׂוּר שֶׁל שִׁבְעִים – הֲרֵי שִׁבְעָה. וְהַשְּׁנַיִם הַנִּשְׁאָרִים – שְׁתֵּים עֶשְׂרֵה בֵּיצִים הֵן, עִישּׂוּר שֶׁלָּהֶן – בֵּיצָה וְחוֹמֶשׁ בֵּיצָה. הֲרֵי שִׁבְעַת רְבָעִים וָעוֹד, דְּהוּא בֵּיצָה וְחוֹמֶשׁ בֵּיצָה. וִירוּשַׁלְמִים הוֹסִיפוּ עַל הַמִּדּוֹת שְׁתוּת מִלְּבַר, שֶׁהוּא חוֹמֶשׁ מִלְּגָו, שֶׁנָּתְנוּ שִׁשָּׁה מִן הָרִאשׁוֹנִים בְּתוֹךְ חֲמִשָּׁה הָאַחֲרוֹנִים – הֲרֵי שֵׁשֶׁת רְבָעִים הָרִאשׁוֹנִים נַעֲשׂוּ חֲמִשָּׁה, וְהָרוֹבַע וּבֵיצָה וְחוֹמֶשׁ הַנִּשְׁאָרִים נַעֲשׂוּ רוֹבַע, שֶׁהָרוֹבַע שֵׁשׁ בֵּיצִים. עֲשֵׂה מֵהֶן חָמֵשׁ בֵּיצִים גְּדוֹלוֹת, וְהַבֵּיצָה וְחוֹמֶשׁ בֵּיצָה נַעֲשֵׂית בֵּיצָה גְּדוֹלָה, שֶׁנִּיתּוֹסֵף עָלֶיהָ חוּמְשָׁא מִלְּגָו, דְּהוּא שְׁתוּת מִלְּבַר – הֲרֵי שֵׁשׁ בֵּיצִים גְּדוֹלוֹת, דְּהוּא רוֹבַע קַב גָּדוֹל. הֲרֵי עוֹמֶר הַמִּדְבָּר שִׁשָּׁה רְבָעִים יְרוּשַׁלְמִיִּים. וּסְאָה צִיפּוֹרִית עוֹדֶפֶת עַל יְרוּשַׁלְמִית שְׁתוּת מִלְּבַר, כִּדְאָמַר בְּעֵירוּבִין (דף פג.), הֲרֵי עוֹמֶר שֶׁהָיָה שִׁשָּׁה רְבָעִים יְרוּשַׁלְמִיִּים נִכְנָס בְּחָמֵשׁ צִיפּוֹרִיִּים: נָהוּג לְמֵיפָא. בְּפִיסְחָא קְפִיזָא קְפִיזָא, שְׁלֹשֶׁת לוּגִּין, לְחוּמְרָא – לְשׁוֹמְרוֹ מִן הַחִימּוּץ: **אָמַר לֵיהּ**. כְּר' אֱלִיעֶזֶר סְבִירָא לָן, דְּהַסַּל מְצָרְפָן לְחַלָּה לְאַחַר אֲפִיָּיתָן. וְהָאִידָּנָא קַיְימָא לָן כְּר' אֱלִיעֶזֶר בְּחַלָּה שֶׁל אוּר, דְּאֵין שׂוֹרְפִין קָדָשִׁים בְּיוֹם טוֹב, וּלְהַשְׁהוֹתָהּ אִי אֶפְשָׁר. וּמִשֶּׁנִּקְרָא עָלֶיהָ שֵׁם אָסוּר לַאֲפוֹתָהּ – דְּהָא לָאו לַאֲכִילָה הִיא, וְלָא קָרֵינַן עֲלָהּ שֵׁם, אֶלָּא עוֹשֶׂה חֲרָרָה קְטַנָּה אֵצֶל גְּדוֹלָה, וְאוֹפֶה שְׁתֵּיהֶן, וּכְשֶׁהוּא רוֹדֶה נוֹתְנָן לִכְלִי וְהוּא מְצָרְפָם. וְנוֹטֵל הַקְּטַנָּה וְקוֹרֵא שֵׁם, וּמְבָרֵךְ, וּמַצְנִיעָהּ וְשׂוֹרְפָהּ מִשֶּׁתֶּחְשַׁךְ, אוֹ לְמָחָר. וְכֵן הוֹרָה לָנוּ רַבֵּינוּ יַעֲקֹב בֶּן יָקָר: שֶׁנּוֹשְׁכוֹת זוֹ אֶת זוֹ. שֶׁהֵן רְחָבוֹת וַעֲגוּלּוֹת כְּעֵין שֶׁלָּנוּ, וּכְשֶׁמַּדְבִּיקִין זוֹ אֵצֶל זוֹ בַּתַּנּוּר נוֹשְׁכוֹת זוֹ מִזּוֹ, הִלְכָּךְ חֲדָא הִיא: **אֲבָל** כְּעָכִין. קוייליו"ש בְּלַעַ"ז, אֲרוּכִין וּקְלָרִין, וְאֵין נוֹשְׁכִין זֶה מִזֶּה: טַבְלָא שֶׁאֵין לָהּ לִבְזְבֵּז. מִסְגֶּרֶת וְשָׂפָה סָבִיב לָהּ, וְרָדָה פַּת לְתוֹכָהּ מִן הַתַּנּוּר: מַהוּ. שֶׁתִּצְטָרֵף לְר' אֱלִיעֶזֶר: תַּנּוּר מְצָרְפָן.[ב] אַף תַּנּוּר מְצָרְפָן, אַף עַל פִּי שֶׁלֹּא נְתָנָן לְסַל: כִּכָּרוֹת שֶׁל בָּבֶל כו'. אֲבָל כְּעָכִין לֹא: **מתני'** רַבָּן גַּמְלִיאֵל אוֹמֵר שָׁלֹשׁ נָשִׁים לָשׁוֹת כְּאַחַת. כָּל אַחַת מְלֹא הַתַּנּוּר, וְאֵין כָּאן חִימּוּץ. אַף עַל פִּי שֶׁהָאַחַת מַמְתֶּנֶת עַד שֶׁיֹּאפוּ הַשְּׁתַּיִם: וַחֲכָמִים אוֹמְרִים. אֵין לְהָקֵל כָּל כָּךְ שֶׁיְּהוּ לָשׁוֹת כְּאַחַת, אֶלָּא שָׁלֹשׁ נָשִׁים עוֹסְקוֹת כָּל אַחַת בַּבָּצֵק שֶׁלָּהּ: **אַחַת** לָשָׁה. הָאַחֲרוֹנָה לָשָׁה, כְּשֶׁחֲבֵירְתָּהּ הָאֶמְצָעִית מְקַטֶּפֶת, וְהַשְּׁלִישִׁית שֶׁלָּשָׁה תְּחִלָּה אוֹפָה. וְסִידְרָא מְפָרֵשׁ בַּגְּמָרָא: **לֹא** כָּל הַנָּשִׁים. יֵשׁ עַצְלָנִיּוֹת, וּמַחֲמִילוֹת אִם יִשְׁהוּ כָּל כָּךְ, וְיֵשׁ תַּנּוּר שֶׁאֵינוֹ חַם מַהֵר, וְיֵשׁ עֵצִים שֶׁאֵינָם נִבְעָרִים מַהֵר: זֶה הַכְּלָל תָּפַח. הַבָּצֵק בְּיָדָהּ שֶׁהִיא רוֹאָה שֶׁרוֹצֶה לִתְפּוֹחַ: תִּלְטוֹשׁ. יָדֶיהָ בְּמַיִם צוֹנֵן וּתְקַטְּפֶנָּה, וּתְצַנְּנֶנּוּ: **גמ'** **תָּנָא** לָשָׁה הִיא מְקַטֶּפֶת. אַדְּרַבָּנַן קָאֵי. הָרִאשׁוֹנָה שֶׁקָּדְמָה לָלוּשׁ מְלֹא הַתַּנּוּר קָטָן שֶׁלָּהֶן תְּחִלָּה, כְּשֶׁהִיא מְקַטֶּפֶת, דְּהַיְינוּ עֲרִיכָה שֶׁקּוֹרִין אנטוורטי"ר, וַחֲבֵירְתָּהּ מַתְחֶלֶת לָלוּשׁ עִיסָּה שֶׁלָּהּ: מְקַטֶּפֶת **הִיא אוֹפָה**. וְזוֹ הָרִאשׁוֹנָה שֶׁהָיְתָה מְקַטֶּפֶת עַכְשָׁיו, וְגָמְרָה קִיטּוּפָהּ – הִיא אוֹפָה וְנוֹתֶנֶת לַתַּנּוּר. וַחֲבֵירְתָּהּ שֶׁהָיְתָה לָשָׁה מְקַטֶּפֶת תַּחְתֶּיהָ, וְהַשְּׁלִישִׁית לָשָׁה. וּכְשֶׁגָּמְרָה רִאשׁוֹנָה לֶאֱפוֹת – גָּמְרָה אֶמְצָעִית לְקַטֵּף וְאַחֲרוֹנָה לָלוּשׁ – הֲרֵי הָאֶמְצָעִית הַמְקַטֶּפֶת אוֹפָה, וַחֲבֵירְתָּהּ הָאַחֲרוֹנָה מְקַטֶּפֶת תַּחְתֶּיהָ, וְהָרִאשׁוֹנָה חוֹזֶרֶת וְלָשָׁה. שֶׁהָיוּ תַּנּוּרִין קְטַנִּים, וְלֹא הָיְתָה מַסְפֶּקֶת [אֶלָּא] כִּמְלֹא תַּנּוּר: וְכֵן חוֹזְרוֹת חֲלִילָה. 'חֲלִילָה' לְשׁוֹן מָחוֹל סָבִיב סָבִיב: דַּנְתִּי לִפְנֵי רַבָּן גַּמְלִיאֵל. שֶׁהָיָה אוֹמֵר כְּלָל דָּבָר בְּכָל שָׁלֹשׁ נָשִׁים לָשׁוֹת כְּאַחַת, וּמַמְתֶּנֶת הָאַחַת עַד שֶׁיֹּאפוּ הַשְּׁתַּיִם: **מתני'** שִׂיאוּר. שֶׁלֹּא הֶחְמִיץ כָּל צָרְכּוֹ: סִידּוּק. כְּשֶׁהוּא מַחֲמִיץ נַעֲשִׂין בּוֹ סְדָקִין: קַרְנֵי חֲגָבִים. סֶדֶק לְכָאן וָסֶדֶק לְכָאן: זֶה וָזֶה הָאוֹכְלוֹ בְּכָרֵת. דְּקַרְנֵי חֲגָבִים נַמִי סִידּוּק הָוֵי: **וְאֵיזֶהוּ שִׂיאוּר**. שֶׁפָּטוּר – זֶה שֶׁאֵין בּוֹ סֶדֶק. אֲבָל הִכְסִיפוּ פָּנָיו, כְּאָדָם שֶׁעָמְדוּ שַׂעֲרוֹתָיו וּמִתּוֹךְ פַּחַד וְרֶתֶת פָּנָיו מַכְסִיפִין: **גמ'** חֲכָמִים. דְּבָרַיְיתָא הוּא ר' יְהוּדָה דְּמַתְנִי', וַחֲכָמִים דְּמַתְנִי' הוּא ר' מֵאִיר: ה"ג בְּבָרַיְיתָא: וַחֲכָמִים אוֹמְרִים אֵי זֶהוּ שִׂיאוּר – כְּקַרְנֵי חֲגָבִים, סִידּוּק שֶׁנִּתְעָרְבוּ סְדָקִין זֶה בָּזֶה, וְזֶה וָזֶה הָאוֹכְלוֹ בְּכָרֵת: וְהָא **אֲנַן** תְּנַן. דְּר' יְהוּדָה פָּטַר בְּשִׂיאוּר דִּידֵיהּ. דְּאַע"ג דְּאָמַר יִשָּׂרֵף, לָא מִיחַיֵּיב עֲלָהּ לֹא מַלְקוֹת וְלֹא כָּרֵת: **אֵימָא** לְרַבִּי מֵאִיר זֶה וָזֶה. בֵּין שִׂיאוּר דְּרַבִּי יְהוּדָה דְּקַרְנֵי חֲגָבִים, בֵּין סִידּוּק – חַיָּיבִין כָּרֵת, דְּתַרְוַיְיהוּ לְרַבִּי מֵאִיר סִידּוּק נִינְהוּ: כַּמָּה סְדָקִין מִלְּמַטָּה. בְּתוֹכוֹ. הִלְכָּךְ, כִּי הָוֵי לְמַעְלָה כְּקַרְנֵי חֲגָבִים – הָוֵי לְמַטָּה כְּנִתְעָרְבוּ סְדָקִין:

מתני'

שבת טו: [חלה פ"ב מ"ו] עדיות פ"א [מ"ב]

[נ"ל דתנן]

נדה ח. [חלה פ"ב מ"ד]

לעיל מג.

מכילתא פ' בא

[לעיל מג. מנחות נג. חולין כג:]

הגהות הגר"א

[א] גמ' רשב"ג אומר ככרות כו' נ"ב הוא תנור והוא דברי ת"ק דמתני' דחלה ועיין תוס': [ב] רש"י ד"ה תנור מצרפן אף תנור כו' נ"ב בירושלמי (פ"ב דחלה) איתא דוקא תנור ולא סל:

גליון הש"ס

גמ' מהו תוך כלי בעינן. עיין טורי אבן חגיגה כד ע"א ד"ה דאורייתא: **מתני'** לא כל הנשים. כעין זה יבמות קכ ע"ב:

מתני' *[א] ארבעה עשר שחל להיות בשבת – מבערין את הכל מלפני השבת, דברי ר"מ. וחכמים אומרים: בזמנו. ר"א בר צדוק אומר: תרומה – מלפני השבת, וחולין – בזמנן.§ גמ' *תניא, ר"א בר צדוק אומר: פעם אחת שבת אבא ביבנה, וחל ארבעה עשר להיות בשבת, ובא זונין ממונה של ר"ג, ואמר: הגיע עת לבער את החמץ. והלכתי אחר אבא, וביערנו את החמץ.§ מתני' [ב] ההולך לשחוט את פסחו ולמול את בנו, ולאכול סעודת אירוסין בבית חמיו, ונזכר שיש לו חמץ בתוך ביתו. אם יכול לחזור ולבער ולחזור למצותו – יחזור ויבער, ואם לאו – מבטלו בלבו. להציל מן *הגוים, ומן הנהר, *ומן הלסטים, ומן הדליקה, ומן המפולת – יבטל בלבו. ולשבות שביתת הרשות – יחזור מיד. *[ג] וכן מי שיצא מירושלים ונזכר שיש בידו בשר קדש, אם עבר צופים – שורפו במקומו, ואם לאו – חוזר ושורפו *לפני הבירה מעצי המערכה. ועד כמה הן חוזרין? ר"מ אומר: זה וזה בכביצה, ר' יהודה אומר: זה וזה בכזית. וחכמים אומרים: בשר קדש – בכזית, וחמץ – [ג] בכביצה.§ גמ' ורמינהו: ההולך לאכול סעודת אירוסין בבית חמיו ולשבות שביתת הרשות – יחזור מיד! א"ר יוחנן: לא קשיא; הא – ר' יהודה, הא – רבי יוסי, דתניא: סעודת אירוסין – רשות, דברי ר' יהודה. רבי יוסי אומר: מצוה. והשתא, דאמר רב חסדא: מחלוקת – בסעודה שניה, אבל בסעודה ראשונה – דברי הכל מצוה. אפילו תימא הא והא ר' יהודה, ולא קשיא; הא – בסעודה ראשונה, הא – בסעודה שניה. תניא, אמר רבי יהודה: אני לא שמעתי אלא סעודת אירוסין, אבל לא סבלונות. אמר לו ר' יוסי: אני שמעתי סעודת אירוסין וסבלונות. תניא, רבי שמעון אומר: [ד] כל סעודה שאינה של מצוה – אין תלמיד חכם רשאי להנות ממנה. כגון מאי? א"ר יוחנן: כגון בת כהן לישראל, ובת תלמיד חכם לעם הארץ. דא"ר יוחנן: בת כהן לישראל – אין זווגן עולה יפה. מאי היא? אמר רב חסדא: או אלמנה או גרושה או זרע אין לה. במתניתא תנא: קוברה או קוברתו, או מביאתו לידי עניות. איני? והא א"ר יוחנן: הרוצה שיתעשר – ידבק בזרעו של אהרן, כל שכן שתורה וכהונה מעשרתן – לא קשיא: [ה] הא – בת"ח, הא – בעם הארץ. ר' יהושע נסיב כהנתא, חלש. אמר: לא ניחא ליה לאהרן דאדבק בזרעיה, דהוי ליה חתנא כי אנא. רב אידי בר אבין נסיב כהנתא, נפקו מיניה תרי בני סמיכי, רב ששת בריה דרב אידי ור' יהושע בריה דרב אידי. אמר ר"פ: *אי לא נסיבנא °כהנתא לא איעתרי. אמר רב כהנא: אי לא נסיבנא כהנתא – לא גלאי. אמרו ליה: והא למקום תורה גלית! לא גלאי כדגלי אינשי. אמר רבי יצחק: כל הנהנה מסעודת הרשות לסוף גולה, שנא': °"ואכלים כרים מצאן ועגלים מתוך מרבק", וכתיב: "לכן עתה יגלו בראש גולים".§ ת"ר: כל ת"ח המרבה סעודתו בכל מקום – סוף מחריב את ביתו, ומאלמן את אשתו, ומייתם את גוזליו, ותלמודו משתכח ממנו, ומחלוקות רבות באות עליו, ודבריו אינם נשמעים ומחלל שם שמים ושם רבו ושם אביו, וגורם שם רע לו ולבניו ולבני בניו עד סוף כל הדורות. מאי היא? °אמר אביי: קרו ליה בר מחים תנורי. רבא אמר: בר מרקיד בי כובי. רב פפא אמר: בר מלחיך פינכי. רב שמעיה אמר: בר מך רבע.§ ת"ר: לעולם ימכור אדם כל מה שיש לו וישא בת ת"ח. שאם מת או גולה – מובטח לו שבניו ת"ח, ואל ישא בת ע"ה – שאם מת או גולה בניו ע"ה. ת"ר: לעולם ימכור אדם כל מה שיש לו וישא בת ת"ח, וישיא בתו לת"ח. משל לענבי הגפן בענבי הגפן, דבר נאה ומתקבל. ולא ישא בת עם הארץ – משל לענבי הגפן בענבי הסנה, דבר כעור ואינו

(בשוליים: תורה אור; עמוס ו)

רש"י

מתני' מבערין את הכל. בין חולין בין תרומה, חוץ מכדי אכילתו לשבת. אבל כל מה שעתיד לבער – יבער: תרומה מלפני השבת. שאינו יכול להאכילה לא לזרים ולא לבהמת זרים, ולהשהותה אי אפשר. אבל חולין אין צריך לבער אלא בזמנו, שיכול למצוא להן אוכלים הרבה: גמ' שבת. נשתהה שם שבת אחת: מתני' ההולך. בארבעה עשר: אם יכול. שיש שהות ביום: להציל מן הגוים. את ישראל הנרדפין: יבטל בלבו. ולא יחזור. ואפי' יש שהות, דמדאורייתא סגי ליה בביטול בעלמא: לשבות שביתת הרשות. שהיה הולך להחשיך על התחום לקנות שביתה שם כדי שיהא לו משם ולהלן אלפים, לילך למחר שם לדבר הרשות – יחזור מיד. אבל לקנות שביתת מצוה, כגון שילך מחר חוץ לתחום לבית האבל או לבית המשתה – היינו כהולך לשחוט את פסחו: שיש בידו בשר קודש. עמו בדרך, ונפסל ביוצא. שמחיצת קדשים קלים חומת ירושלים: אם עבר צופים. שם כפר שיכול לראות בית המקדש משם: שורפו במקומו. ולא הטריחוהו לחזור: ואם לאו חוזר ושורפו כו'. כדאמרן ד"כל שעה" (לעיל כד.): "בקודש באש תשרף" – דבמקום אכילתו שריפתו: זה וזה. חמץ דאמרן לעיל ונזכר שיש לו חמץ בביתו, ובשר קודש שעמו: בכביצה. אבל בפחות, גבי חמץ – יבטל בלבו, וגבי בשר קודש – שורפו במקומו: גמ' סעודה שניה. כך הוא דרך החתנים, לאחר סעודת אירוסין חוזר ומשגר סבלונות לארוסתו, וסועד שם: אני לא שמעתי. שתהא מצוה אלא סעודת אירוסין לבדה, אבל לא סעודת סבלונות: סבלונות. דורונות, כלים נאים: בת כהן. צריכה להינשא לכהנים, ולא לפגום משפחתה להינשא לישראל: אין זווגן עולה יפה. במזל טוב: מאי היא. מה עולה בידן: או אלמנה או גרושה או זרע אין לה. כדכתיב (ויקרא כב): "ובת כהן כי תהיה לאיש זר", וסמיך ליה: "ובת כהן כי תהיה אלמנה וגרושה וזרע אין לה" וגו': או קוברה. בלא זמן: תלמיד חכם. (א) הוא שבח לו. אבל עם הארץ ואינו כהן – גנאי הוא לו לאהרן, ונענשים: לא גלאי. רב כהנא גלה מבבל לא"י, כדאמר ב"הגוזל ומאכיל" (ב"ק קיז.): לא גלאי כדגלו אינשי. שאר תלמידים יוצאין מדעתן, ואני יצאתי על כרחי, מחמת מרדין ואימת מלכות: ומאלמן את אשתו. שמבקש לימודו ואי אפשר לו, וגולה למזונות, והרי אשתו באלמנות חיות: גוזליו. יתומין: ותלמודו משתכח. שאינו עסוק לחזור עליו: ומחלוקות רבות באות עליו. מחמת ששכח תלמודו, או הקפות שמקיף מחנונין לסעודותיו: קרו ליה. לבנו: מרקיד בי כובי. כדרך הליצנים, שמשחקין ומרקדין בחנויות להשקותן בשכרן: מלחיך פינכי. קערות: מך רבע. מקפל לבושו ורובץ וישן. כך דרך המשתכרין, אינו מספיק לילך לביתו ולשכב על מטתו, אלא מקפל לבושו תחתיו וישן: מך. כמו: בר חמרא, מוך שקיק וגו' (*תענית דף ו:): ואינו

תוספות

לשבות שביתת הרשות. פ"ה: שהיה הולך להחשיך על התחום לקנות שביתה שם, ולילך ד' אלפים לדבר הרשות. וקשה: א"כ תיקשי למ"ד בפ' "בכל מערבין" (ערובין לא.): אין מערבין אלא לדבר מצוה! ונר' לר"י דה"פ: לשבות שביתת הרשות – שהולך לשמוח בפסח בבית אוהבו או קרובו: אם עבר צופים. פי' בקונט': שם כפר. וקשה לר"י: א"כ ה"ל למימר וכמדתו לכל רוח, כדתניא בפ' "מי שהיה טמא" (לקמן צג:): איזהו דרך רחוקה – מן המודיעין ולחוץ, וכמדתה לכל רוח. ואור"י: דבתוספתא דמכילתין מפרש בהדיא: איזהו צופים – הרואה ואין מפסיק. פי': כל מקום סביב ירושלים שיכול לראותו משם: ושורפו לפני הבירה. פ"ה: כדאמר פ' "כל שעה" (דף כד.): בקודש באש ישרף – במקום אכילתו שריפתו. וקשה לר"י: אי דאורייתא הוא – מה לי עבר צופים ומ"ל לא עבר צופים! וי"ל: דמן התורה יכול לשורפה בכ"מ שירצה, דבפרק "כל שעה" (ג"ז שם) לא מרבינן אלא פסולי קדשי קדשים ואימורי קדשים קלים, אבל שאר קדשים שנאכלים לזרים – לא מרבינן. ומה שהצריכו חכמים לשרוף הני דהכא לפני הבירה – היינו גזירה אטו קדשי קדשים: לפני הבירה. בזבחים בפ' "טבול יום" (דף קד:) פליגי: אאי בירה? אמר רבה בר בר חנה א"ר יוחנן: מקום יש בהר הבית ובירה שמו, ר"ל אמר: כל הבית כולו הוי בירה, שנאמר: *"אל הבירה אשר הכינותי": וחכמים אומרים בשר קודש בכזית וחמץ בכביצה. אומר ריצ"א: דמפרש בירושלמי משום דבשר קודש לית ליה תקנה בביטול – החמירו בכזית, אבל חמץ אית ליה תקנה בביטול – לא החמירו עד כביצה: תניא א"ר יהודה. תימה: אמאי לא מייתי תניא נמי הכי מהך דהכא, לרב חסדא? אמר

עין משפט נר מצוה

מז א מיי' פ"ג מהל' חמץ הלכה ג סמג עשין לט טוש"ע א"ח סי' תמד סעיף א:

מח ב מיי' שם שם הל' ט טוש"ע שם סעיף ז:

מט ג מיי' פרק יט מהלכות פסולי המוקדשין הלכה ח:

מט [ג] [מיי' פ"ג מהל' חמץ הל' ט טוש"ע א"ח סי' תמד סעיף ז]:

נ ד מיי' פ"ה מהלכות דעות הלכה ב:

נא ה מיי' פכ"א מהל' אסורי ביאה הלכה לא סמג לאוין קכו טור ש"ע אה"ע סי' ב ס"ח:

מסורת הש"ס

[לעיל דף יג. וקף כ:]

[תוספתא פ"ג]

ס"א הגיים

ס"א ל"ג

לקמן דף פח: ברכות דף מט:

[עי' פירש"י לקמן פ"א: ד"ה נטמא וכו' לפני הבירה וכו']

[נ"ל ולבנות]

הגהות הב"ח

(א) רש"י ד"ה תלמיד חכם שבת הוא לו:

[עי' תוס' לקמן דף קיג. ד"ה אמר]

[ברכות נט.]

רבינו חננאל

כר' מאיר דשנה לן תנא בלשון החכמים מתני' ארבעה עשר שחל להיות בשבת מבערין הכל מלפני השבת דברי ר' מאיר ר' אליעזר אומר תרומה מלפני השבת וחולין בזמנן וקיי"ל כר' אלעזר בר' צדוק: תניא ר' אלעזר ברבי צדוק אומר פעם אחת שבת אבא ביבנה וחל ארבעה עשר להיות בשבת כו': מתני' ההולך לשחוט את פסחו ולמול את בנו ולאכול סעודת אירוסין בבית חמיו ונזכר כו' ורמינהי ההולך לאכול סעודת אירוסין בבית חמיו ולשבות שביתת הרשות יחזור מיד והכא קתני במתני' יבטל בלבו מכלל שאין מחייבין אותו לחזור ושניג' מתני' ר' יוסי היא דסבר סעודת אירוסין מצוה וביעור חמץ נמי מצוה מיהו ביעור חמץ אפשר לקיימה בביטול חמץ וישלים סעודת אירוסין שנמצא מקיים שתיהן. ובריי' ר' יהודה דסבר סעודת אירוסין רשות כגון שביתת הרשות ולדברי הכל חייב לחזור מיד דתניא סעודת אירוסין רשות דברי ר' יהודה ר' יוסי אומר מצוה והשתא דאמר רב חסדא מחלוקת בסעודה שניה אבל בסעודה ראשונה אפי' ר' יהודה מודה דמצוה אפי' תימא מתני' ר' יהודה ובסעודה ראשונה שהיא מצוה ברייתא בסעודה שניה שהיא רשות:

תניא אמר ר' יהודה אני לא שמעתי אלא סעודת אירוסין בלבד אמר ר' יוסי אני שמעתי סעודת אירוסין וסבלונות: ירושלמי לשבות שביתת הרשות לשבות אצל ר' או מי שהוא גדול ממנו אמר ר' יוסי בר בון גדול השלום שהותיר לשני דברים שהיתרו עליהן כרת מילה ושחיטת פסח: תניא א"ר אלעזר כל סעודה שאינה של מצוה אין תלמיד חכם רשאי להנות ממנה כגון מאי א"ר יוחנן כגון בת כהן [לישראל] או בת תלמיד חכם אצל עם הארץ לפי שאין זיווגן עולה יפה דכתיב ובת כהן כי תהיה אלמנה וגרושה וזרע. אמר רב כהנא אי לא נסיבנא כהנתא לא גלאי ומעשה דרב כהנא מפורש בתגלחת בתרא כי שמטיה לקועה להווא גברא וערק לארץ ישראל: אמר ר' יצחק כל הנהנה מסעודת הרשות לסוף גולה שנא' אוכלים כרים מצאן ועגלים מתוך מרבק וכתיב בתריה לכן עתה יגלו בראש גולים: ת"ר תלמיד חכם המרבה סעודתו בכ"מ לסוף מחריב את ביתו ומאלמן את אשתו ומייתם את גוזליו ותלמודו משתכח ומחלוקות רבות [באות] עליו ודבריו אין נשמעין ומחלל שם שמים ושם אביו ושם רבו וגורם שם רע לו ולבניו עד סוף כל הדורות וקרו לו בר מיחם תנורא ובר

וְאֵינוֹ מִתְקַבֵּל.§ תָּנוּ רַבָּנַן: אלְעוֹלָם יִמְכּוֹר אָדָם כָּל מַה שֶּׁיֵּשׁ לוֹ וְיִשָּׂא בַּת תַּלְמִיד חָכָם. לֹא מָצָא בַּת תַּלְמִיד חָכָם — יִשָּׂא בַּת גְּדוֹלֵי הַדּוֹר. לֹא מָצָא בַּת גְּדוֹלֵי הַדּוֹר — יִשָּׂא בַּת רָאשֵׁי כְּנֵסִיּוֹת. לֹא מָצָא בַּת רָאשֵׁי כְּנֵסִיּוֹת — יִשָּׂא בַּת גַּבָּאֵי צְדָקָה. לֹא מָצָא בַּת גַּבָּאֵי צְדָקָה — יִשָּׂא בַּת מְלַמְּדֵי תִינוֹקוֹת. וְלֹא יִשָּׂא בַּת עַמֵּי הָאָרֶץ, מִפְּנֵי שֶׁהֵן שֶׁקֶץ, וּנְשׁוֹתֵיהֶן שֶׁרֶץ, *וְעַל בְּנוֹתֵיהֶן הוּא אוֹמֵר: °"אָרוּר שׁוֹכֵב עִם כָּל בְּהֵמָה" (דברים כז). תַּנְיָא, ר' אוֹמֵר: עַם הָאָרֶץ אָסוּר לֶאֱכוֹל בְּשַׂר (בְּהֵמָה), שֶׁנֶּאֱמַר: °"זֹאת תּוֹרַת הַבְּהֵמָה וְהָעוֹף" (ויקרא יא) — כָּל הָעוֹסֵק בַּתּוֹרָה — מוּתָּר לֶאֱכוֹל בְּשַׂר בְּהֵמָה וָעוֹף, וְכָל שֶׁאֵינוֹ עוֹסֵק בַּתּוֹרָה — אָסוּר לֶאֱכוֹל בְּשַׂר בְּהֵמָה וָעוֹף.§ אָמַר רַבִּי אֶלְעָזָר: עַם הָאָרֶץ מוּתָּר לְנוֹחֲרוֹ בְּיוֹם הַכִּיפּוּרִים שֶׁחָל לִהְיוֹת בַּשַּׁבָּת. אָמְרוּ לוֹ תַּלְמִידָיו: ר', אֱמוֹר לְשׁוֹחֲטוֹ! אָמַר לָהֶן: זֶה — טָעוּן בְּרָכָה, וְזֶה — אֵינוֹ טָעוּן בְּרָכָה.§ אָמַר רַבִּי אֶלְעָזָר: עַם הָאָרֶץ אָסוּר לְהִתְלַוּוֹת עִמּוֹ בַּדֶּרֶךְ, שֶׁנֶּאֱמַר: °"כִּי הִיא חַיֶּיךָ וְאוֹרֶךְ יָמֶיךָ" (דברים ל) — עַל חַיָּיו לֹא חָס — עַל חַיֵּי חֲבֵירוֹ לֹא כָּל שֶׁכֵּן. אָמַר רַבִּי שְׁמוּאֵל בַּר נַחְמָנִי אָמַר רַבִּי יוֹחָנָן: עַם הָאָרֶץ מוּתָּר לְקוֹרְעוֹ כְּדָג. אָמַר רַבִּי שְׁמוּאֵל בַּר יִצְחָק: וּמִגַּבּוֹ.§ תַּנְיָא, אָמַר רַבִּי עֲקִיבָא: כְּשֶׁהָיִיתִי עַם הָאָרֶץ אָמַרְתִּי: מִי יִתֵּן לִי תַּלְמִיד חָכָם וַאֲנַשְּׁכֶנּוּ כַּחֲמוֹר. אָמְרוּ לוֹ תַּלְמִידָיו: רַבִּי, אֱמוֹר כַּכֶּלֶב! אָמַר לָהֶן: זֶה — נוֹשֵׁךְ וְשׁוֹבֵר עֶצֶם, וְזֶה — נוֹשֵׁךְ וְאֵינוֹ שׁוֹבֵר עֶצֶם.§ תַּנְיָא, הָיָה רַבִּי מֵאִיר אוֹמֵר: כָּל הַמַּשִּׂיא בִּתּוֹ לְעַם הָאָרֶץ — כְּאִילּוּ כּוֹפְתָהּ וּמַנִּיחָהּ לִפְנֵי אֲרִי. *מָה אֲרִי דּוֹרֵס וְאוֹכֵל וְאֵין לוֹ בּוֹשֶׁת פָּנִים — אַף עַם הָאָרֶץ מַכֶּה וּבוֹעֵל וְאֵין לוֹ בּוֹשֶׁת פָּנִים.§ תַּנְיָא, רַבִּי אֱלִיעֶזֶר אוֹמֵר: *אִילְמָלֵא אָנוּ צְרִיכִין לָהֶם לְמַשָּׂא וּמַתָּן — הָיוּ הוֹרְגִין אוֹתָנוּ. תָּנָא רַבִּי חִיָּיא: כָּל הָעוֹסֵק בַּתּוֹרָה לִפְנֵי עַם הָאָרֶץ — כְּאִילּוּ בּוֹעֵל אֲרוּסָתוֹ בְּפָנָיו, שֶׁנֶּאֱמַר: °"תּוֹרָה צִוָּה לָנוּ מֹשֶׁה מוֹרָשָׁה" (דברים לג) אַל תִּקְרֵי "מוֹרָשָׁה" אֶלָּא *"מְאוֹרָסָה". גְּדוֹלָה שִׂנְאָה שֶׁשּׂוֹנְאִין עַמֵּי הָאָרֶץ לְתַלְמִיד חָכָם, יוֹתֵר מִשִּׂנְאָה שֶׁשּׂוֹנְאִין אוּמּוֹת הָעוֹלָם אֶת יִשְׂרָאֵל, וּנְשׁוֹתֵיהֶן יוֹתֵר מֵהֶן.§ תָּנָא: שָׁנָה וּפֵירֵשׁ — יוֹתֵר מִכּוּלָּן. תָּנוּ רַבָּנַן: שִׁשָּׁה דְּבָרִים נֶאֶמְרוּ בְּעַמֵּי הָאָרֶץ: באֵין מוֹסְרִין לָהֶן עֵדוּת, וְאֵין מְקַבְּלִין מִמֶּנּוּ עֵדוּת, וְאֵין מְגַלִּין לָהֶן סוֹד, גוְאֵין מְמַנִּין אוֹתָן אַפּוֹטְרוֹפּוֹס עַל הַיְתוֹמִים, וְאֵין מְמַנִּין אוֹתָן אַפּוֹטְרוֹפּוֹס עַל קוּפָּה שֶׁל צְדָקָה, וְאֵין מִתְלַוִּין עִמָּהֶן בַּדֶּרֶךְ. וְיֵשׁ אוֹמְרִים: אַף אֵין מַכְרִיזִין עַל אֲבֵידָתוֹ — וְתַנָּא קַמָּא: *זִמְנִין דְּנָפֵיק מִינֵּיהּ זַרְעָא מַעַלְיָא וְאָכֵיל לֵיהּ, שֶׁנֶּאֱמַר: °"יָכִין וְצַדִּיק יִלְבָּשׁ" (איוב כז).§ "וְכֵן מִי שֶׁיָּצָא וכו'".§ *לְמֵימְרָא דְּרַבִּי מֵאִיר סָבַר כַּבֵּיצָה הוּא דַּחֲשִׁיב, וְרַבִּי יְהוּדָה סָבַר כַּזַּיִת נַמִי חֲשִׁיב? וּרְמִינְהִי: *עַד כַּמָּה הֵן מְזַמְּנִין — דעַד כַּזַּיִת, וְרַבִּי יְהוּדָה אוֹמֵר: עַד כַּבֵּיצָה! אָמַר רַבִּי יוֹחָנָן: מוּחְלֶפֶת הַשִּׁיטָה, אַבַּיֵי אָמַר: לְעוֹלָם לֹא תֵּיפוֹךְ; הָתָם בִּקְרָאֵי פְּלִיגֵי, הָכָא בִּסְבָרָא פְּלִיגֵי. הָתָם בִּקְרָאֵי פְּלִיגֵי; רַבִּי מֵאִיר סָבַר: °"וְאָכַלְתָּ" (דברים ח) — זוֹ אֲכִילָה, "וְשָׂבָעְתָּ" — זוֹ שְׁתִיָּה, *וַאֲכִילָה בְּכַזַּיִת. וְרַבִּי יְהוּדָה סָבַר: "וְאָכַלְתָּ וְשָׂבָעְתָּ" — אֲכִילָה שֶׁיֵּשׁ בָּהּ שְׂבִיעָה, וְאֵיזוֹ זוֹ — בְּכַבֵּיצָה. הָכָא בִּסְבָרָא פְּלִיגֵי. דְּרַבִּי מֵאִיר סָבַר: חֲזָרָתוֹ *כְּטוּמְאָתוֹ, מַה טּוּמְאָתוֹ בְּכַבֵּיצָה — אַף חֲזָרָתוֹ בְּכַבֵּיצָה, וְר' יְהוּדָה סָבַר: חֲזָרָתוֹ כְּאִיסּוּרוֹ

רש"י

וְאֵינוֹ מִתְקַבֵּל. לַשּׁוֹמְעִים: גְּדוֹלֵי הַדּוֹר. אַנְשֵׁי מַעֲשֶׂה וְצַדִּיקִים: בַּת גַּבָּאֵי צְדָקָה. שֶׁאֵין מְמַנִּין אֶלָּא אִם כֵּן טוֹבִים וְנֶאֱמָנִין: נְשׁוֹתֵיהֶן שֶׁרֶץ. שֶׁאֵינָן זְהִירוֹת בְּמִצְוֹת: עִם כָּל בְּהֵמָה. שֶׁדּוֹמוֹת לִבְהֵמָה, שֶׁאֵין לָהֶן לֵב לְהָבִין: כִּי הִיא חַיֶּיךָ וְאוֹרֶךְ יָמֶיךָ עַל חַיָּיו לֹא חָס. לִלְמוֹד תּוֹרָה וְלִחְיוֹת: עַל חַיֵּי חֲבֵירוֹ לֹא כָּל שֶׁכֵּן. וְיֵשׁ לִדְאוֹג שֶׁמָּא יַהַרְגֶנּוּ: וּמִגַּבּוֹ. דְּתוּ לָא חַיֵּי, כִּדְאָמְרִינַן בִּשְׁחִיטַת חוּלִּין (דף כא:): קְרָעוֹ כְּדָג — מְטַמֵּא בְּאֹהֶל מִיָּד, וְאַף עַל גַּב שֶׁמְּפַרְפֵּר. וְאָמַר רַבִּי שְׁמוּאֵל בַּר רַב יִצְחָק: וּמִגַּבּוֹ: אִילְמָלֵא צְרִיכִין אָנוּ לָהֶם. לִמְזוֹנוֹתֵיהֶן וּלְעֶזְרָתָם, הָיוּ הוֹרְגִין אוֹתָנוּ: כְּאִילּוּ בָּא עַל אֲרוּסָתוֹ בְּפָנָיו. שֶׁמְּבַיְּישׁוֹ: מְאוֹרָסָה. לְכָל קְהִילּוֹת יַעֲקֹב: שָׁנָה וּפֵירֵשׁ. תַּלְמִיד שֶׁשָּׁנָה וּפֵירֵשׁ מִן הַתּוֹרָה, וְיוֹדֵעַ כַּמָּה תַּלְמִידֵי חֲכָמִים מְגַנִּים אֶת עַמֵּי הָאָרֶץ, וְכַמָּה הֵם שְׁפָלִים בְּעֵינֵיהֶם — שׂוֹנֵא יוֹתֵר מִכּוּלָּם: אֵין מוֹסְרִין לוֹ עֵדוּת. אֵין מְזַמְּנִין אוֹתוֹ לִשְׁמוֹעַ דָּבָר לְהָעִיד עָלָיו: וְאֵין מְגַלִּין לוֹ סוֹד. שׁוּם דְּבַר סֵתֶר, לְפִי שֶׁהוֹלֵךְ רָכִיל וּמְגַלֶּה: עַל הַיְתוֹמִין. שֶׁחָשׁוּד עַל הַגָּזֵל: הַמּוֹצֵא אֲבֵידָה חַיָּיב לְהַכְרִיז. כִּדְאָמְרִי' בְּ"אֵלּוּ מְצִיאוֹת" (ב"מ כא.). וְעַם הָאָרֶץ לָאו אָחִיךָ הוּא, דְּאֵינוֹ עוֹשֶׂה מַעֲשֵׂה עַמְּךָ: מְזַמְּנִין. שְׁלֹשָׁה שֶׁאָכְלוּ כְּאַחַת. דִּתְנַן: חַיָּיבִין לְזַמֵּן, וְאֵין רַשָּׁאִין לֵיחָלֵק: וְאָכַלְתָּ וְשָׂבָעְתָּ. מֵהַאי קְרָא נָפְקָא לַן בִּרְכַּת (הַזִּימּוּן) [והמזון נ"ל] בִּבְרָכוֹת (דף מח:): חֲזָרָתוֹ. וּמִדְּרַבָּנַן הִיא. וְאַשִּׁיעוּר טוּמְאָתוֹ אַסְמְכוּהָ, וְטוּמְאַת אוֹכָלִין בְּכַבֵּיצָה: כְּאִיסּוּרוֹ

תוספות

אמר רב כהנא אי לאו דנסיבי כהנתא לא גלאי. משמע שלא היה כהן. והא דאמרינן בפ"ק דקדושין (דף ח.): רב כהנא שקל סודרא בפדיון הבן — בשביל אשתו היה לוקח, כדאמרינן בפ' "הזרוע" (חולין דף קלב.): רב כהנא הוה אכיל בשביל אשתו. והא דאמר בפרק "ערבי פסחים" (לקמן קיג.), א"ל רב לרב כהנא: פשוט נבילתא בשוקא ושקול אגרא, ולא תימא כהנא [וגברא] רבא אנא — לא בשביל שהיה כהן, אלא שכך היה שמו: **לא** מצא בת גבאי צדקה ישא בת מלמדי תינוקות. משמע דגבאי צדקה עדיפי ממלמדי תינוקות. והא דאמר בפרק "השותפין" (ב"ב ח:): "והמשכילים יזהירו כזוהר הרקיע" — אלו גבאי צדקה, "ומצדיקי הרבים ככוכבים" — אלו מלמדי תינוקות. צ"ל דזוהר הרקיע עדיף מזוהר כוכבים: **מה** ארי דורס ואוכל. פר"ת: דורס ואוכל ואין ממתין עד שתמות, אף עם הארץ אינו ממתין עד שתתפייס*: **ויש** אומרים אף אין מכריזין על אבידתו. וא"ת: מאין יודע שהיא של ע"ה? *ואור"י: כגון שיירא של ע"ה עוברת, וראינו שנפל מהם. והשתא משמע דדוקא אין מכריזין על אבידתו, אבל לגזול בידים — לא. אע"ג דלית ליה הא סברא דבסמוך, אפשר דנפיק מיניה ברא מעליא. ותימה לר"י: אמאי ממונו אסור. השתא גופו מותר, שמותר לקורעו כדג — ממונו לא כל שכן? דכה"ג אמר ב"הגוזל בתרא" (ב"ק קיט.) ובע"ז (דף כו.) גבי מוסר, למאן דלית ליה סברא דאפשר דנפיק מיניה ברא מעליא. ונר' לר"י: דלעיל איירי במכיר וכופר להכעיס, דה"ל הריגתו כמו פיקוח נפש, שהוא לסטין וחשוד על הדמים. דאי לאו הכי — היאך מותר להורגו ביום הכפורים שחל להיות בשבת? הלא אפילו גוי אסור! וכן משמע הלשון: על חייו אינו חס, דמכיר וכופר. דיש הרבה עניני ע"ה, כדמוכח בסוטה בפ' "היה נוטל" (דף כב.). ואור"י: דמה שאנו מקבלים עדות מע"ה — כדאמר בפרק "חומר בקדש" (חגיגה כב.): כמאן מקבלים האידנא סהדותא מע"ה — כרבי יוסי: **ואכלת** זו אכילה. נראה דהני שיעורי כזית וכביצה דלא הוי אלא אסמכתא, וכן פ"ה בפרק "מי שמתו" (ברכות כ:) גבי הא דאמר: בן מברך לאביו, ומוקי לה כגון דאכל האב שיעור דרבנן. ופ"ה שם: דהיינו כזית וכביצה, דמדאורייתא בעינן שביעה גמורה. וכן מוכח התם, דקאמר: לא אשא פנים לישראל, שכתבתי להם "ואכלת ושבעת וברכת" והן מדקדקים על עצמם בכזית וכביצה?! וקשה: דבפרק "ג' שאכלו" (שם מח.) אמר: ינאי מלכא ומלכתא כרכי ריפתא בהדי הדדי, אמר מאן יהיב לן גברא דמברך לן. אייתוהו לרבי שמעון בן שטח וכו' שתה ובריך להו. וקאמר: רבי שמעון בן שטח לגרמיה הוא דעבד, דלעולם אינו מוציא אחרים ידי חובה עד שיאכל כזית דגן. משמע דאם אכל כזית דגן — היה מוציא אחרים. ואי כזית דרבנן — היכי מפיק להו? הא אמר דלא אתי דרבנן ומפיק דאורייתא! ואור"י: דהיינו דוקא קטן אינו מוציא אותו שאכל שיעור דאורייתא, אבל גדול אפילו לא אכלי כלל — יכול להוציא אחרים מדאורייתא:

הדרן עלך אלו עוברין

עין משפט נר מצוה

נב א מיי' שם הל' לב טוש"ע שם ס"ו:

נג ב מיי' פי"א מהל' עדות הלכה ב סמג לאוין ריד טור ש"ע ח"מ סימן לד סעיף יז:

נד ג מיי' פ"י מהל' נחלות הלכה ו סמג עשין נו טוש"ע ח"מ סי' רל סעיף ב:

[וע"ע תוס' קדושין ח. ד"ה ר"כ וב"ב קי. ד"ה ולא ובחולין קלב. ד"ה ר"כ]

נה ד מיי' פ"ה מהלכות ברכות הל' ח סמג עשין כו טוש"ע א"ח סי' קפד סעי' ו וסי' קנו ס"ד:

[וע"ע תוס' חולין סא. ד"ה הדורס ותוס' ב"ק עז: ד"ה דרס]

[וע' תוס' ב"מ כב: ד"ה אי ליכא]

[אולי צ"ל אלמלי ביו"ד עי' תוס' מגילה כא. ד"ה אלמלא]

רבינו חננאל

ובר מרקיד בי כובא ובר מלחך פנכי ובר מך רבעי: **תניא** ר' אומר עם הארץ אסור לאכול בשר שנאמר זאת תורת הבהמה. אמר ר' אלעזר עם הארץ מותר לנוחרו ביום הכפורים שחל להיות בשבת אמרו לו תלמידיו כו' ואסור להתלוות עמו בדרך: **ת"ר** גדולה שנאה ששונאין עמי הארץ תלמידי חכמים כו' ונשותיהן כו' שנה ופירש יתר מכולן: **ת"ר** ששה דברים נאמרו בעמי הארץ אין מוסרין להם עדות ואין מקבלין מהן עדות ואין מגלין להם את הסוד ואין ממנין מהם אפוטרופין על היתומים ואין ממנין אותן אפוטרופין על קופה של צדקה ואין מתלוין עמהן בדרך ויש אומרים אף אין מכריזין על אבדתן ות"ק זימנין דנפיק מיניה זרעא מעליא יכין וצדיק ילבש:

מתני' וכן מי שיצא מירושלים ונזכר שיש בידו בשר קדש אם עבר צופים שורפו כו' פי' שם מקום שעומד שם וצופה בכל צד שורפו במקום שנזכר ואם לא עבר הצופים חוזר כו' עד כמה חוזרין ר"מ אומר בין חמץ בין בשר קדש כביצה ר' יהודה אומר זה וזה בכזית וחכמים אומרים בשר קדש כזית וחמץ (כבותבת) [כביצה] ואקשי' ורמינהי עד כמה מזמנין עד כזית ר' יהודה אומר עד כביצה מכלל דלר"מ כזית חשוב ולר' יהודה כביצה ומשני' ר' יוחנן מוחלפת השיטה כלומר חלף דברי ר' מאיר לר' יהודה ודברי ר' יהודה לר' מאיר כי תני מדבריהם על דבריהם. אביי אמר לעולם לא תפוך והתם בענין זימון בקראי פליגי ר"מ סבר ואכלת זו אכילה ושבעת זו שתיה ומצינו אכילה כזית ור' יהודה סבר לא בעינן אכילה שיש בה שביעה ולא תהיה פחות מכביצה והכא בסברא פליגי ר"מ מקיש ליה לטומאה מה טומאה בכביצה אף חזרתו בכביצה ר' יהודה אומר כנותר

גליון הש"ס

גמ' אמר ר"ע כשהייתי ע"ה. עי' כתובות סב. ע"ב תוס' ד"ה דהוא לנוע:

מסורת הש"ס

(עירובין נה:)

(סנהדרין נ: ע"ש)

[ברכות נז. סנהדרין נט.]

[ב"ק קיט.]

[ברכות מט:]

ברכות דף מה. יומא דף עט:

[יומא פ.]

[לקמן קכא.]

א א מיי' פ"ח מהל' י"ט הל' יח סמג לאוין עה טוש"ע או"ח סי' תסח סעיף ג ד:

*כְּאִיסּוּרוֹ, מָה אִיסּוּרוֹ בִּכְזַיִת — אַף חֲזָרָתוֹ בִּכְזַיִת. תַּנְיָא, ר' נָתָן אוֹמֵר: זֶה וָזֶה כִּשְׁתֵּי בֵיצִים, וְלֹא הוֹדוּ לוֹ חֲכָמִים. °"וְהָיָה בַּיּוֹם הַהוּא לֹא יִהְיֶה אוֹר יְקָרוֹת וְקִפָּאוֹן". מַאי "יְקָרוֹת וְקִפָּאוֹן"? א"ר אֶלְעָזָר: זֶה אוֹר, שֶׁיָּקָר בָּעוֹלָם הַזֶּה, וְקָפוּי לָעוֹלָם הַבָּא. ר' יוֹחָנָן אָמַר: אֵלּוּ נְגָעִים וְאֳהָלוֹת, שֶׁיְּקָרִין הֵן בָּעוה"ז וּקְפוּיִין הֵן לָעוֹלָם הַבָּא. וְר' יְהוֹשֻׁעַ בֶּן לֵוִי אָמַר: אֵלּוּ בְּנֵי אָדָם, שֶׁיְּקָרִין הֵן בָּעוֹלָם הַזֶּה וּקְפוּיִין הֵן לָעוה"ב. *כִּי הָא דְּרַב יוֹסֵף בְּרֵיהּ דְּר' יְהוֹשֻׁעַ בֶּן לֵוִי חֲלַשׁ וְאִיתְנְגִיד. כִּי הֲדַר, אֲמַר לֵיהּ אֲבוּהּ: מַאי חֲזֵית? אֲמַר לֵיהּ: עוֹלָם הָפוּךְ רָאִיתִי, עֶלְיוֹנִים לְמַטָּה וְתַחְתּוֹנִים לְמַעְלָה. אֲמַר לוֹ: בְּנִי, עוֹלָם בָּרוּר רָאִיתָ. וַאֲנַן הֵיכִי הָתָם? כִּי הֵיכִי דְּאִיתוּ אֲנַן הָכָא, הָכִי אִיתִינַן הָתָם. וְשָׁמַעְתִּי שֶׁהָיוּ אוֹמְרִים: *אַשְׁרֵי מִי שֶׁבָּא לְכָאן וְתַלְמוּדוֹ בְּיָדוֹ. וְשָׁמַעְתִּי שֶׁהָיוּ אוֹמְרִים: הֲרוּגֵי מַלְכוּת אֵין אָדָם יָכוֹל לַעֲמוֹד בִּמְחִיצָתָן. (וּמַאן) נִינְהוּ? אִילֵימָא ר"ע וַחֲבֵירָיו — מִשּׁוּם הֲרוּגֵי מַלְכוּת וְתוּ לָא? אֶלָּא: הֲרוּגֵי לוֹד. °"בַּיּוֹם הַהוּא יִהְיֶה עַל מְצִלּוֹת הַסּוּס קֹדֶשׁ לַה'" מַאי "מְצִלּוֹת הַסּוּס"? א"ר יְהוֹשֻׁעַ בֶּן לֵוִי: עָתִיד הַקָּבָּ"ה לְהוֹסִיף עַל יְרוּשָׁלַיִם, עַד שֶׁהַסּוּס רָץ וּמֵצִיל. ר' אֶלְעָזָר אָמַר: כָּל מְצִילּוֹת שֶׁתּוֹלִין לַסּוּס בֵּין עֵינָיו יִהְיֶה קֹדֶשׁ לַה'. וְר' יוֹחָנָן אָמַר: כָּל בִּיזָּה שֶׁבּוֹזְזִין יִשְׂרָאֵל עַד שָׁעָה שֶׁהַסּוּס רָץ וּמֵצִיל — יִהְיֶה קֹדֶשׁ לַה'. בִּשְׁלָמָא לְמַאן דְּאָמַר כָּל בִּיזָּה שֶׁבָּזְזוּ יִשְׂרָאֵל — הַיְינוּ דִּכְתִיב °"וְהָיָה הַסִּירוֹת בְּבֵית ה' כַּמִּזְרָקִים לִפְנֵי הַמִּזְבֵּחַ". אֶלָּא לְמ"ד בְּהָנָךְ תַּרְתֵּי — מַאי "וְהָיָה הַסִּירוֹת בְּבֵית ה'"? מִילְּתָא אַחֲרִיתִי קָאָמַר, דְּמִתְעַתְּרֵי יִשְׂרָאֵל וּמִתְנַדְּבֵי וּמַיְיתֵי. בִּשְׁלָמָא לְמ"ד בִּיזָּה — הַיְינוּ דִּכְתִיב °"וְלֹא יִהְיֶה כְנַעֲנִי עוֹד בְּבֵית ה' צְבָאוֹת". אֶלָּא לְמ"ד הָנָךְ תַּרְתֵּי — מַאי "וְלֹא יִהְיֶה כְנַעֲנִי"? א"ר יִרְמְיָה: °"אֵין כָּאן עָנִי". וּכְנַעֲנִי מְנָלַן *דְּאִיקְּרֵי תַּגָּר — דִּכְתִיב: °"וַיַּרְא שָׁם יְהוּדָה בַּת אִישׁ כְּנַעֲנִי". מַאי כְּנַעֲנִי? אִילֵימָא כְּנַעֲנִי מַמָּשׁ — אֶפְשָׁר בָּא אַבְרָהָם וְהִזְהִיר אֶת יִצְחָק, בָּא יִצְחָק וְהִזְהִיר אֶת יַעֲקֹב, וִיהוּדָה אָזֵיל וְנָסֵיב?! אֶלָּא אָמַר רַבִּי שִׁמְעוֹן בֶּן לָקִישׁ: בַּת גַּבְרָא תַּגָּרָא, דִּכְתִיב: °"כְּנַעַן בְּיָדוֹ מֹאזְנֵי מִרְמָה", וְאִיבָּעֵית אֵימָא, מֵהָכָא: °"אֲשֶׁר סוֹחֲרֶיהָ שָׂרִים כִּנְעָנֶיהָ נִכְבַּדֵּי אָרֶץ".§ °"וְהָיָה ה' לְמֶלֶךְ עַל כָּל הָאָרֶץ בַּיּוֹם הַהוּא יִהְיֶה ה' אֶחָד וּשְׁמוֹ אֶחָד" אַטּוּ הָאִידָּנָא לָאו אֶחָד הוּא?! אָמַר רַבִּי אַחָא בַּר חֲנִינָא: לֹא כָּעוֹלָם הַזֶּה הָעוֹלָם הַבָּא; הָעוֹלָם הַזֶּה, *עַל בְּשׂוֹרוֹת טוֹבוֹת אוֹמֵר "בָּרוּךְ הַטּוֹב וְהַמֵּטִיב", וְעַל בְּשׂוֹרוֹת רָעוֹת אוֹמֵר "בָּרוּךְ דַּיַּין הָאֱמֶת". לָעוֹלָם הַבָּא — כּוּלּוֹ "הַטּוֹב וְהַמֵּטִיב". "וּשְׁמוֹ אֶחָד", מַאי "אֶחָד", אַטּוּ הָאִידָּנָא לָאו שְׁמוֹ אֶחָד הוּא?! א"ר נַחְמָן בַּר יִצְחָק: "לֹא כָּעוֹלָם הַזֶּה הָעוֹלָם הַבָּא; הָעוֹלָם הַזֶּה — נִכְתָּב בְּיוּ"ד הֵ"י וְנִקְרָא בְּאָלֶ"ף דָּלֶ"ת, אֲבָל לָעוֹלָם הַבָּא כּוּלּוֹ אֶחָד — *נִקְרָא בְּיוּ"ד הֵ"י, וְנִכְתָּב בְּיוּ"ד הֵ"י. *סָבַר רָבָא לְמִדְרְשֵׁהּ בְּפִירְקָא. א"ל הַהוּא סָבָא: "לְעָלַם" כְּתִיב, ר' אֲבִינָא רָמֵי: כְּתִיב, °"זֶה שְּׁמִי לְעֹלָם *וְזֶה זִכְרִי לְדֹר דֹּר". אָמַר הַקָּבָּ"ה: לֹא כְּשֶׁאֲנִי נִכְתָּב אֲנִי נִקְרָא, נִכְתָּב אֲנִי בְּיוּ"ד הֵ"א, וְנִקְרָא אֲנִי בְּאָלֶ"ף דָּלֶ"ת.§

הדרן עלך אלו עוברין

*מָקוֹם אשֶׁנָּהֲגוּ לַעֲשׂוֹת מְלָאכָה בְּעַרְבֵי פְסָחִים עַד חֲצוֹת — עוֹשִׂין, מָקוֹם שֶׁנָּהֲגוּ שֶׁלֹּא לַעֲשׂוֹת — אֵין עוֹשִׂין. הַהוֹלֵךְ מִמָּקוֹם שֶׁעוֹשִׂין לְמָקוֹם שֶׁאֵין עוֹשִׂין, אוֹ מִמָּקוֹם שֶׁאֵין עוֹשִׂין לְמָקוֹם שֶׁעוֹשִׂין — *נוֹתְנִין עָלָיו חוּמְרֵי מָקוֹם שֶׁיָּצָא מִשָּׁם, וְחוּמְרֵי מָקוֹם שֶׁהָלַךְ לְשָׁם וְאַל

רש"י

כְּאִיסּוּרוֹ. שֶׁל חָמֵץ. וּבְשַׂר קוֹדֶשׁ נַמִּי, מִשֶּׁנִּפְסַל בְּיוֹצֵא אָסוּר בַּאֲכִילָה: יְקָרוֹת וְקִפָּאוֹן. הַיְינוּ דְּהַיְירֵי בִּירוּשָׁלַיִם, בְּגִילּוּת שְׁעָרֶיהָ, דְּקָתָנֵי "וְכֵן מִי שֶׁיָּצָא מִירוּשָׁלַיִם" כו' — פָּתַח בְּהָא פָּרָשָׁתָא, דְּבָעֵינַן לְמֵימַר קַמָּן שֶׁעָתִיד הקב"ה לְהוֹסִיף עַל יְרוּשָׁלַיִם: אוֹר שֶׁיָּקָר בָּעוֹלָם הַזֶּה. כְּשֶׁחַמָּה מְאִירָה בִּגְבוּרָתָהּ, וְאוֹרָהּ גָּדוֹל — אוֹתוֹ אוֹר חָשׁוּב וְיָקָר שֶׁלָּהּ — יְהֵא קָפוּי וְקַל לָעוֹלָם הַבָּא. כָּל דָּבָר קַל קָרֵי קָפוּי — צָף עַל הַמַּיִם. "וַיָּצֶף הַבַּרְזֶל" מְתַרְגְּמִינַן "וּקְפָא פַרְזְלָא" (מלכים ב ו): בְּנֵי אָדָם שֶׁיְּקָרִים. עֲשִׁירִים וַחֲשׁוּבִים, וְאֵינָן טוֹבִים לַמָּקוֹם: אִיתְנְגִיד. גָּוַע, וּפָרְחָה רוּחוֹ: עֶלְיוֹנִים לְמַטָּה. אוֹתָן שֶׁהָיוּ כָּאן חֲשׁוּבִים רָאִיתִי קַלִּים: וַאֲנַן. תַּלְמִידֵי חֲכָמִים הֵיכִי אִיתִינַן הָתָם? הֲרוּגֵי מַלְכוּת וְתוּ לָא. לֹא הָיְתָה בָּהֶן מַעֲלָה אַחֶרֶת שֶׁיֶּחְשְׁבוּ עָלֶיהָ אֶלָּא זוֹ בִּלְבָד? הֲרוּגֵי לוֹד. שְׁנֵי אַחִים הָיוּ שֶׁמָּסְרוּ עַצְמָן *עַל יִשְׂרָאֵל, שֶׁהוֹדוּ עַל עַצְמָן הֲרִיגַת בַּת מֶלֶךְ, שֶׁהָיוּ מַטִּילִין אוֹתָהּ עַל כָּל יִשְׂרָאֵל: עַד שָׁעָה שֶׁהַסּוּס רָץ וּמֵצִיל. כְּשִׁיעוּר מְרוּצַת הַסּוּס עַד חֲצִי הַיּוֹם. וּלְשׁוֹן מֵצִיל — שֶׁצִּילּוֹ תַּחְתָּיו. שֶׁכָּל שְׁעוֹת הַיּוֹם חַמָּה נוֹטָה לַצְּדָדִין, וְצֵל הָאָדָם וְצֵל הַבְּהֵמָה נוֹטֶה לְצִידּוֹ. כְּשֶׁחַמָּה בַּמִּזְרָח — צֵל הָאָדָם לַמַּעֲרָב. אֲבָל בַּחֲצִי הַיּוֹם חַמָּה עוֹמֶדֶת בְּאֶמְצַע הָרָקִיעַ, בְּרֹאשׁ כָּל הָאָדָם, וְצֵל הַסּוּס תַּחְתָּיו. בְּפֵי' ר' מָכִיר זצ"ל מְצָאתִי: כָּל מְצִילּוֹת. כְּלוֹמַר שֶׁתּוֹלִין לַסּוּס לְנוֹי וּלְקַשְׁקֵשׁ, לְשׁוֹן מְצִלְתַּיִם (ד"ה א יג): יִהְיֶה קוֹדֶשׁ לַה'. שֶׁיִּתְנַדְּבוּ יִשְׂרָאֵל נִדְבוֹתֵיהֶן לַמִּקְדָּשׁ: כָּל בִּיזָּה שֶׁיָּבוֹזּוּ יִשְׂרָאֵל. מִן הַגּוֹיִם בְּיוֹם אֶחָד עַד חֲצוֹת — יִהְיוּ קוֹדֶשׁ לַה', שֶׁיְּבִיאוּם נְדָבָה לַמִּקְדָּשׁ: הַסִּירוֹת כַּמִּזְרָקִים. אַף הַסִּירוֹת יִהְיוּ שֶׁל כֶּסֶף וְשֶׁל זָהָב, שֶׁתְּהֵא שָׁם בִּיזָּה רַבָּה לְהֶקְדֵּשׁ: מַאי וְהָיָה הַסִּירוֹת כַּמִּזְרָקִים. הָא בִּמְצִילּוֹת הַסּוּס לֵיכָּא הֶקְדֵּשׁ כּוּלֵּי הַאי: דְּמִיתְעַתְּרֵי יִשְׂרָאֵל. יִתְעַשְּׁרוּ יִשְׂרָאֵל. וּבְשׂוֹרָה אַחֶרֶת הִיא: כְּנַעֲנִי. לֹא יִהְיוּ צְרִיכִין גִּזְבָּרִין לַעֲשׂוֹת סְחוֹרָה בְּנִכְסֵי הֶקְדֵּשׁ, לְפִי שֶׁיְּהֵא שָׁם עוֹשֶׁר גָּדוֹל מִן הַבִּיזָּה: בָּא אַבְרָהָם וְהִזְהִיר אֶת יִצְחָק. שֶׁהִשְׁבִּיעַ לֶאֱלִיעֶזֶר "לֹא תִקַּח אִשָּׁה לִבְנִי מִבְּנוֹת הַכְּנַעֲנִי" (בראשית כד): וְיִצְחָק אֶת יַעֲקֹב. "לֹא תִקַּח אִשָּׁה מִבְּנוֹת כְּנָעַן" (שם כח): כּוּלּוֹ הַטּוֹב וְהַמֵּטִיב. שֶׁאֵין שָׁם בְּשׂוֹרָה רָעָה: לְמִידְרְשֵׁיהּ בְּפִירְקָא. קְרִיָּיה דְּיוּ"ד הֵ"י דְּאַרְבַּע אוֹתִיּוֹת, דְּרָשֶׁיהָ וְטַעֲמֶיהָ הַתְּלוּיִים בּוֹ: לְעָלַם כְּתִיב. "זֶה שְּׁמִי לְעֹלָם" חָסֵר וָי"ו, לְשׁוֹן הַעֲלָמָה: כְּתִיב זֶה שְּׁמִי לְעֹלָם. בְּהַעֲלָמָה. וּכְתִיב "זֶה זִכְרִי", דְּמַשְׁמַע קְרִיָּיה וְלֹא הַעֲלָמָה. לָשׁוֹן אַחֵר: כֵּיוָן דִּכְתַב "זֶה שְּׁמִי" — פְּשִׁיטָא דְּזֶה זִכְרִי, הֵיאַךְ יִקָּרֵא אֶלָּא בִּשְׁמוֹ? לֹא כְּשֶׁאֲנִי נִכְתָּב. שְׁנֵי שֵׁמוֹת לִימְּדוֹ, שֵׁם הַכְּתִיבָה וְשֵׁם הַקְּרִיָּיה:

הדרן עלך אלו עוברין

מָקוֹם שֶׁנָּהֲגוּ. עַד חֲצוֹת. חֲצִי הַיּוֹם: שֶׁלֹּא לַעֲשׂוֹת. כְּדֵי שֶׁלֹּא יְהֵא טָרוּד בִּמְלָאכָה וְיִשְׁכַּח בִּיעוּר חֲמֵצוֹ, וּשְׁחִיטַת הַפֶּסַח, וְתִקּוּן מַצָּה לְצוֹרֶךְ הַלַּיְלָה. דְּמִצְוָה לִטְרוֹחַ מִבְּעוֹד יוֹם כְּדֵי לְהָסֵב מַהֵר, כִּדְאָמַר בְּפֶרֶק בַּתְרָא (דף קט.): "חוֹטְפִין מַצָּה בְּלֵילֵי פְסָחִים בִּשְׁבִיל תִּינוֹקוֹת שֶׁלֹּא יִשְׁנוּ": וְאַל

[לקמן קכא.] [כ"כ י:] [תענית יח:] [כתובות עז: כ"כ י.] [כ"כ עה.] [ברכות נד.] [נכתב ביו"ד ה"י ונקרא ביו"ד ה"י כך הוא נכון וכ"ה בילקוט שמות רמז קע"א] יבמות יג: חולין יח: [קיז.]

תוספות

מקום שנהגו. אור"י בשם ריב"א: דמפרש בירושלמי מאי שנא ערבי פסחים משאר י"ט — משום דזמן הפסח מחצות ואילך. ואף יחיד קאמר התם, בשאר ימות השנה ביום שמביא קרבן — אסור במלאכה, ופריך: אם כן יהא כל היום אסור, כמו יחיד שמביא קרבן! ומפרש התם: משום דראוי להקריב משחרית, אבל פסח אינו יכול להקריבו אלא אחר חצות, כדנפקא לן מ"בין הערבים". ופריך: אם כן קרבן תמיד, שהוא לכל ישראל וקרב בכל יום, יהא בכל יום אסור במלאכה! ומשני: שאני תמיד שהתורה הוציאה מן הכלל, דכתיב: "ואספת דגנך", ואם כל ישראל יושבים ובטלים — מי יאסוף להן דגנן? ומשמע התם דמדאורייתא אסורה. ונראה דאף בזמן הזה דליכא הקרבה, כיון שנאסר אז — אסור לעולם: העושה

גליון הש"ס

גמ' א"ר אין כאן עני. עי' שבת סג ע"א רש"י ד"ה לא יהלך:

רבינו חננאל

כנותר מה נותר איסורו בכזית דאכילה כתיב ביה אף חזרתו: וכיון שהזכיר אם לא עבר הצופים חוזר רש"מ עד הצופים מירושלים הוא חשוב הוצרך מהאי קרא והיה ביום ההוא יהיה על מצלות הסוס קדש לה' ואמר ר' יהושע בן לוי עתיד הקב"ה להוסיף על ירושלים עד שעה שהסוס רץ ומציל פי' חצי היום שהצל של סוס תחתיו ומפני זה פתח והיה ביום ההוא לא יהיה אור יקרות וקפאון פי' ר' אלעזר אור שהוא יקר בעולם הזה כלו כדכתיב (משלי ו כג) כי נר מצוה ותורה אור וכתיב (שמואל א ג א) ודבר ה' היה יקר בימים ההם קפוי הוא מצוי לעולם הבא וכל דבר מצוי ביד הרבים בזול הוא דכתיב (יואל ג א) ביום ההוא אשפוך את רוחי על כל בשר ונבאו ריש לקיש דרשו בתלמוד נגעים ואהלות שהוא יקר עכשיו כו' ור' יוחנן אמר אלו בני אדם שנראין בעולם הזה יקרים ונכבדים קפויים הם לעולם הבא כי הא דיוסף בריה דר' יהושע בן לוי חלש כאלו פרחה נשמתו איתפח אמר ליה אבוה מאי חזית אמר ליה עולם הפוך ראיתי עליונים למטה כלומר היקרים החשובים בעולם הזה כדכתיב (ישעיה יג יב) אוקיר אנוש מפז ואדם מכתם אופיר ראיתי אותם תחתונים במדרגה התחתונה והיורדים בעולם הזה ראיתי בעליה למעלה מאלו אמר ליה בני עולם ברור ראית כלומר האמת שם הוא שהוא לשם עליון הוא העיקר אמר ליה ואנו אנה מקומנו אמר ליה אנו חשיבותינו התם כי הכא ושמעתי אשרי מי שבא לכאן ותלמודו בידו יש מי שאומר שגורס על פה כי הלך וגרסתו עמו ויש מי שמפרש מי שיבא בכאן ומעשיו מיסדים ותלמודו שקים כל מה שלמד נמצא כאלו הביא ראיותיו עמו והרוגי מלכות אין כל בריה ולשון יכולה במחיצתן ואסיקנא לאו ר"ע וחבריו דהללו מעלתן גדולה זולתי מצות הריגתם אלא שני אחים שהיו בלוד בשעה שנמצאת בת קיסר הרוגה ובקשו להרוג כל יהודי בשבילה ואמרו שני האחים אנו הרגנוה כדי להציל כל ישראל ונהרגו הן וכו': והיה ה' למלך [על כל הארץ] ביום ההוא יהיה ה' אחד ושמו אחד [יהיה] ה' אחד שאין שם בשורה רעה שצריך לומר ברוך דיין האמת אלא הטוב בכל שהכל טוב שאין שם רע ושמו אחד כר"נ בר יצחק דאמר בעולם הזה שמי נכתב ביוד הא ונקרא באלף דלת אבל בעולם הבא כולו אחד כשאני נכתב כך אני נקרא: רבה סבר למדרשה בפירקא ולגלותו א"ל ההוא סבא זה שמי לעלם חסר ו' כתיב כלומר עלמיה [וזה] זכרי כשאני נקרא עכשיו באלף דלת ובעולם [הבא] בשמי שנא' זה שמי לעולם:

הדרן עלך ואלו עוברין

מקום שנהגו לעשות מלאכה בערבי פסחים עד חצות עושין כו' ומתמה' מאי אר"א ערבי פסחים אפי' כל ערובה נמי דתניא העושה מלאכה בערבי שבתות ובערבי ימים טובים מן המנחה ולמעלה אינו רואה סימן ברכה

251–253; 259